United States Government Accountability Office

**GAO**

Report to Congressional Requesters

August 2010

# DEFENSE ACQUISITIONS

## Navy's Ability to Overcome Challenges Facing the Littoral Combat Ship Will Determine Eventual Capabilities

**GAO**

Accountability ★ Integrity ★ Reliability

GAO-10-523

# GAO

Accountability·Integrity·Reliability

# Highlights

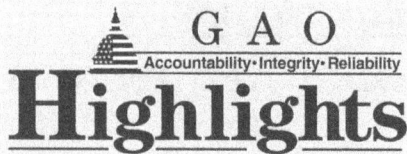

Highlights of GAO-10-523, a report to congressional requesters

# DEFENSE ACQUISITIONS

## Navy's Ability to Overcome Challenges Facing the Littoral Combat Ship Will Determine Eventual Capabilities

## Why GAO Did This Study

The Navy's Littoral Combat Ship (LCS) is envisioned as a reconfigurable vessel able to meet three missions: surface warfare, mine countermeasures, and anti-submarine warfare. It consists of the ship (seaframe) and the mission package it carries and deploys. The Navy plans to invest over $25 billion through fiscal year 2035 to acquire LCS. However, recurring cost growth and schedule delays have jeopardized the Navy's ability to deliver promised LCS capabilities.

Based on a congressional request, GAO (1) identified technical, design, and construction challenges to completing the first four ships within current cost and schedule estimates, (2) assessed the Navy's progress developing and fielding mission packages, and (3) evaluated the quality of recent Navy cost analyses for seaframes and their effect on program progress. GAO's findings are based on an analysis of government and contractor-generated documents, and discussions with defense officials and key contractors. This product is a public version of a For Official Use Only report, GAO-10-1006SU, also issued in August 2010.

## What GAO Recommends

GAO recommends the Secretary of Defense take actions to ensure more realistic cost estimates, timely incorporation of design changes, and coordination of seaframe and mission package acquisition. The Department of Defense concurred with each of these recommendations.

View GAO-10-523 or key components. For more information, contact Belva Martin at (202) 512-4841 or martinb@gao.gov.

## What GAO Found

The Navy faces technical, design, and construction challenges to completing the first four seaframes within current cost and schedule estimates. The Navy and its shipbuilders have learned lessons from construction of the first two seaframes that have positioned them to more effectively construct future vessels. However, technical issues with the first two seaframes have yet to be fully resolved. Addressing these technical issues has required the Navy to implement design changes at the same time LCS 3 and LCS 4 are being built. Incorporating changes during this phase will likely require additional labor hours beyond current forecasts. Together, these challenges may hinder the ability of shipbuilders to apply lessons learned to follow-on ships and could undermine anticipated benefits from recent capital investments in the LCS shipyards.

Challenges developing mission packages have delayed the timely fielding of promised capabilities, limiting the ships' utility to the fleet during initial deployments. Until these challenges are resolved, it will be difficult for the Navy to align seaframe purchases with mission package procurements and execute planned tests. Key mine countermeasures and surface warfare systems encountered problems in operational and other testing that delayed their fielding. For example, four of six Non-Line-of-Sight Launch System missiles did not hit their intended targets in recent testing, and the Department of Defense has since canceled the program. Further, Navy analysis of anti-submarine warfare systems has shown the planned systems do not contribute significantly to the anti-submarine warfare mission. These combined challenges have led to procurement delays for all three mission packages. Mission package delays have also disrupted program test schedules—a situation exacerbated by early deployments of initial ships—limiting their availability for operational testing. In addition, these delays could disrupt program plans for simultaneously acquiring seaframes and mission packages. Until mission packages are proven, the Navy risks investing in a fleet of ships that does not deliver promised capability.

The Navy entered contract negotiations in 2009 for fiscal year 2010 funded seaframes with an incomplete understanding of LCS program costs. These contract negotiations proved unsuccessful, prompting the Navy to revise its acquisition strategy for the program. The contractors' proposals for construction of the next three ships exceeded the approximate $1.4 billion in funds the Navy had allocated in its fiscal year 2010 budget. In response, the Navy revised its strategy to construct one seaframe design instead of two for fiscal year 2010 ships and beyond in an effort to improve affordability. Navy cost analyses completed prior to the failed negotiations in 2009 lack several characteristics essential to a high-quality cost estimate. These characteristics include the completion of sensitivity and uncertainty analyses and an independent review of the cost estimate. The Navy plans to complete a more comprehensive cost estimate before award of additional ship contracts in 2010.

# Contents

# Figures

**GAO**

Accountability * Integrity * Reliability

**United States Government Accountability Office**
**Washington, DC 20548**

August 31, 2010

The Honorable Solomon Ortiz
Chairman
The Honorable J. Randy Forbes
Ranking Member
Subcommittee on Readiness
Committee on Armed Services
House of Representatives

The Honorable Gene Taylor
Chairman
The Honorable W. Todd Akin
Ranking Member
Subcommittee on Seapower and Expeditionary Forces
Committee on Armed Services
House of Representatives

The Navy's Littoral Combat Ship (LCS) is envisioned as a vessel able to be reconfigured to meet three different mission areas: mine countermeasures, surface warfare, and anti-submarine warfare. Its design concept consists of two distinct parts—the ship itself (seaframe) and the mission package it carries and deploys. The Navy currently plans to invest over $25 billion to acquire LCS seaframes and mission packages through fiscal year 2035. However, recurring cost growth and schedule delays in the program have jeopardized the Navy's ability to deliver promised LCS capabilities.

In light of these developments, you asked us to evaluate LCS planning and implementation efforts. In response to this request, we (1) identified technical, design, and construction challenges to completing the first four seaframes within current cost and schedule estimates; (2) assessed the Navy's progress developing and fielding mission packages; and (3) evaluated the quality of recent Navy cost analyses for seaframes and their effect on program progress. This product is a public version of a For Official Use Only report, GAO-10-1006SU, also issued in August 2010.

To identify challenges to completing the first four seaframes, we analyzed Department of Defense and contractor-generated documents that addressed technical challenges and cost and schedule performance for LCS seaframes including sea trial reports for the first two ships, construction progress briefings, and monthly contract performance reports. We corroborated this information through discussions with

GAO-10-523  Littoral Combat Ship

officials responsible for managing LCS design and construction activities including Navy program officials, technical authorities, and requirements officers; LCS prime contractors and shipbuilders; and the Office of the Secretary of Defense. To assess the Navy's progress developing and fielding mission packages, we reviewed documents that outline LCS mission package plans and performance including program schedules and recent test reports. We also held discussions with Navy program offices and Department of Defense agencies responsible for acquiring and testing key LCS mission systems to gather additional information on remaining risks to mission package development and integration. To evaluate the quality of recent Navy cost analyses, we compared the Navy's total ownership cost baseline estimate for the LCS program against the characteristics inherent in high-quality cost estimates as outlined in our cost estimating and assessment guide.[1] In addition, we interviewed LCS cost analysts and program officials to supplement our analysis and gain additional visibility into the Navy's process for developing its cost estimate. A more detailed description of our scope and methodology is presented in appendix I.

We conducted this performance audit from July 2009 to August 2010 in accordance with generally accepted government auditing standards. Those standards require that we plan and perform the audit to obtain sufficient, appropriate evidence to provide a reasonable basis for our findings and conclusions based on our audit objectives. We believe that the evidence obtained provides a reasonable basis for our findings and conclusions based on our audit objectives.

## Background

LCS is designed to move fast and transport manned and unmanned mine countermeasures, surface warfare, and anti-submarine warfare systems into theater. For LCS, the seaframe consists of the hull; command and control systems; automated launch, handling, and recovery systems; and certain core combat systems like an air defense radar and 57-millimeter gun. The Navy is procuring the first four ships in two different designs from shipbuilding teams led by Lockheed Martin and General Dynamics. Lockheed Martin and General Dynamics currently build their designs at Marinette Marine and Austal USA shipyards, respectively. Figure 1 shows

---

[1]See GAO, *GAO Cost Estimating and Assessment Guide: Best Practices for Developing and Managing Capital Program Costs*, GAO-09-3SP (Washington, D.C.: Mar. 2009).

the first two LCS seaframes, USS Freedom (LCS 1) and USS Independence (LCS 2).

**Figure 1: LCS Seaframes**

USS Freedom (LCS 1)

USS Independence (LCS 2)

Sources: Lockheed Martin (left); General Dynamics (right).

Note: LCS 1 is a steel monohull while LCS 2 is an aluminum trimaran.

The Navy is embedding LCS's mine countermeasures, surface warfare, and anti-submarine warfare capabilities within mission packages. These packages are comprised of unmanned underwater vehicles, unmanned surface vehicles, towed systems, and hull- and helo-mounted weapons. Table 1 identifies the systems included in the LCS mission packages.

**Table 1: Systems Included in the Baseline LCS Mine Countermeasures, Surface Warfare, and Anti-Submarine Warfare Mission Packages**

| Mine Countermeasures Mission Package | Surface Warfare Mission Package | Anti-Submarine Warfare Mission Package[a] |
|---|---|---|
| Airborne Laser Mine Detection System | MK 46 30-Millimeter Gun System | Multi-Function Towed Array |
| Airborne Mine Neutralization System | Non-Line-Of-Sight Launch System and Missiles[b] | Remotely Towed Active Source |
| AN/AQS-20A Sonar | Maritime Security Module | Multi-Static Off-Board Source |
| Remote Minehunting System | | Remote Multi-Mission Vehicle |
| Coastal Battlefield Reconnaissance and Analysis System | | Unmanned Surface Vehicle |
| Organic Airborne and Surface Influence Sweep System | | Unmanned Surface Vehicle Dipping Sonar |
| Rapid Airborne Mine Clearance System | | Unmanned Surface Vehicle Towed Array System |
| Unmanned Surface Vehicle with Unmanned Surface Sweep System | | |

Source: Navy.

Note: Aviation assets and support equipment including the MH-60R helicopter, MH-60S helicopter, MQ-8B Vertical Take-off and Landing Tactical Unmanned Aerial Vehicle, mission package computing environment, and stowage containers are not included.

[a]The Navy is evaluating new configurations for future anti-submarine warfare mission packages.

[b]The Navy planned to employ the Army's Non-Line-of-Sight Launch System and Missiles to provide LCS with a small boat engagement capability, but the program was canceled in May 2010 because of performance and cost problems. The Navy is evaluating alternative weapon systems to replace the Non-Line-of-Sight Launch System and Missiles.

Fundamental to the capability of the LCS seaframe is its ability to move quickly ahead of other ships and deploy its offboard sensors to secure lanes of transit. To deploy LCS's mine countermeasures and anti-submarine warfare systems, the Navy will rely extensively on (1) automated launch, handling, and recovery systems embedded in each seaframe and (2) helicopters and unmanned aerial vehicles. The Navy's acquisition approach is to populate initial versions of mission packages with a mixture of developmental and production-representative systems, gradually moving to all production-representative systems that constitute the baseline configuration for each package. The Navy plans to procure 55 seaframes and 64 mission packages (24 mine countermeasures, 24 surface warfare, and 16 anti-submarine warfare) as part of the LCS program.

The Navy has required LCS seaframes to meet Level 1 survivability standards. Ships built to Level 1 are expected to operate in the least severe environment, away from the area where a carrier group is operating or the general war-at-sea region. These vessels should also maintain good handling in bad weather—including seas above 30 feet high (sea state 8)[2]—and have systems for fighting fires on board the ships, hardening against electromagnetic pulses, and protection against chemical, biological, or radiological contamination. Unlike surface warships like cruisers and destroyers, Level 1 ships (including LCS) are not designed to maintain their mission capabilities after incurring substantive damage. Current ships in the fleet built to the Level 1 standard include material support ships, mine-warfare vessels, and patrol combatants.

Two broad categories of contract types are available for government procurements, including ship procurement: fixed-price and cost-reimbursement. Fixed-price contracts provide for a firm price or, in appropriate cases, an adjustable price that may include a ceiling price, a target price, or both. This contract type places the risk on the contractor, who generally bears the responsibility of increased costs of performance. Cost-reimbursement contracts provide for payment of allowable incurred costs, to the extent prescribed in the contract. This contract type places most of the risk on the government, which may pay more than budgeted should incurred costs be more than expected when the contract was signed.

The Navy awarded cost-reimbursable contracts for detail design and construction of the first two seaframes—LCS 1 and LCS 2—in December 2004 and October 2005 for $188.2 million and $223.2 million, respectively. It later exercised options on each of these contracts in June and December 2006 for construction of the third and fourth ships (LCS 3 and LCS 4). However, changing technical requirements, evolving designs, and construction challenges increased the government's estimated prices at completion for the LCS 1 and LCS 2 seaframes to about $500 million each. This cost growth precipitated concern within the Navy that similar outcomes were possible for LCS 3 and LCS 4. In response, the Navy reassessed program costs and structure, revisited the acquisition strategy for future ships, and entered into negotiations with its shipbuilders to convert the LCS 3 and LCS 4 contracts into fixed-price contracts. The Navy was unable to reach agreement with its shipbuilders on fixed-price terms

---

[2]The Navy classifies sea states on a scale of 0 to 9 depending on the roughness of the water as caused by wind or other disturbances. Sea states 0 to 3 represent calm to slight seas of 4 feet or less. Sea state 4 is characterized by moderate seas of 4 to 8 feet. Sea states 5 to 6 range from rough to very rough seas between 8 to 20 feet. Sea states 7 to 9—the most challenging marine conditions—reflect high to extremely rough seas, including seas above 20 feet.

for these ships, subsequently leading the Navy to terminate, in part, the LCS 3 and LCS 4 contracts in April and November 2007 for the convenience of the government. In March and May 2009, the Navy awarded new fixed-price contracts for LCS 3 and LCS 4. According to the Navy, work completed and materials procured under the terminated original contract options for LCS 3 and LCS 4—totaling approximately $192 million—are not included in the current contract values for those ships.

In our work on shipbuilding best practices, we found that achieving design stability before start of fabrication is a key step that leading commercial shipbuilders and ship buyers follow to ensure their vessels deliver on-time, within planned costs, and with planned capabilities.[3] Leading commercial firms assess a ship design as stable once all basic and functional design activities have been completed. Basic and functional design refers to two-dimensional drawings and three-dimensional, computer-aided models (when employed) that fix the ship's hull structure; set the ship's hydrodynamics; route all major distributive systems including electricity, water, and other utilities; and identify the exact positioning of piping and other outfitting within each block of the ship. At the point of design stability, the shipbuilder has a clear understanding of both ship structure as well as ship electrical, piping, and other systems that traverse individual blocks of the ship. To achieve design stability, shipbuilders need suppliers (also called vendors) to provide complete, accurate system information prior to entering basic design. This vendor-furnished information describes the exact dimensions of a system or piece of equipment going into a ship, including space and weight requirements, and also requirements for power, water, and other utilities that will have to feed the system.

As is typical for all ships, the LCS construction phase includes several steps: block fabrication, assembly and outfitting of blocks, block erection, launch, and delivery. During block fabrication, metal plates are welded together into elements called blocks. Blocks are the basic building units for a ship, and when completed they will form completed or partial compartments, including accommodation space, engine rooms, and storage areas. Blocks are generally outfitted with pipes, brackets for

---

[3]See GAO, *Best Practices: High Levels of Knowledge at Key Points Differentiate Commercial Shipbuilding from Navy Shipbuilding*, GAO-09-322 (Washington, D.C.: May 13, 2009).

machinery or cabling, ladders, and any other equipment that may be available for installation at this early stage of construction. This allows a block to be installed as a completed unit when it is welded to the hull of the ship. Installing equipment at the block stage of construction is preferable because access to spaces is not limited by doors or machinery, unlike at later phases. Blocks are welded together to form grand blocks and then erected with other grand blocks in a drydock or, in the case of LCS, in a building hall. Finally, once the ship is watertight and the decision is made to launch—or float the ship in water—the ship is then towed into a quay or dock area where final outfitting and testing of machinery and equipment like main engines will occur. Afterwards, the ship embarks on sea trials where performance is evaluated against the contractually required specifications and overall quality is assessed. Following sea trials, the shipyard delivers the ship to the buyer.

LCS 1 was delivered to the Navy in September 2008, with LCS 2 following in December 2009. The Navy has also accepted delivery of five partial mission packages to date. Currently, LCS 1 is on deployment, LCS 2 is undergoing post-delivery work, and LCS 3 and LCS 4 remain in different stages of construction. In addition, development and testing activities for the mine countermeasures, anti-submarine warfare, and surface warfare mission packages continue. The Navy deployed LCS 1 two years ahead of its previous schedule and prior to the ship completing initial operational test and evaluation. The Navy also stated that early deployment is possible for LCS 2.

Initial operational test and evaluation is intended to assess a weapon system's capability in a realistic environment when maintained and operated by sailors, subjected to routine wear-and-tear, and employed in typical combat conditions against a simulated enemy who fights back. During this test phase, the weapon system is exposed to as many actual operational scenarios as possible—a process that reveals the weapon system's capabilities under stress. Once the fleet has attained the ability to effectively employ and operate the weapon system, initial operational capability is achieved.

Until September 2009, the Navy planned to continue buying both ship designs. In September 2009, the Navy announced it was revising the LCS program's acquisition strategy and would select one seaframe design before awarding contracts for any additional ships. In the National

Defense Authorization Act for Fiscal Year 2010, Congress mandated a $480 million cost cap for each LCS, starting with fiscal year 2011 funded seaframes.[4] In an effort to comply with this mandate, Navy officials have stated that a major program review (milestone B)—and completion of an independent cost estimate—will precede further contract awards in the program.

Cost estimates are necessary for government acquisition programs, like LCS, for many reasons: to support decisions about funding one program over another, to develop annual budget requests, to evaluate resource requirements at key decision points, and to develop performance measurement baselines. A cost estimate is a summation of individual cost elements, using established methods and valid data, to estimate the future costs of a program, based on what is known today. The management of a cost estimate involves continually updating the cost estimate with actual data as they become available, revising the estimate to reflect changes, and analyzing differences between estimated and actual costs—for example, using data from a reliable earned value management system.

# Ongoing Development of Key Seaframe Systems Could Impede Efficient Construction of Initial Follow-On Ships

The Navy faces technical, design, and construction challenges to completing the first four seaframes within current cost and schedule estimates. The Navy and its shipbuilders have learned lessons from construction of the first two seaframes that can be applied to construction of future vessels. However, technical issues with the first two seaframes have yet to be fully resolved, posing risk of design changes to follow on ships already under construction. Addressing these technical issues has required the Navy to implement design changes at the same time LCS 3 and LCS 4 are being built. Incorporating changes during this phase may disrupt the optimal construction sequence for these ships, requiring additional labor hours beyond current forecasts. Together, these challenges may hinder the ability of shipbuilders to apply lessons learned to follow on ships and could undermine anticipated benefits from recent capital investments in the LCS shipyards.

---

[4]Pub. L. No 111-84, § 121 (c). Section 121(d) also authorizes the Secretary of the Navy to waive and adjust provisions of the cost limitation upon making certain findings and other conditions.

## Cost Growth and Schedule Delays Have Hampered Construction of the First Four Ships

Initial LCS seaframes have required more funding and taken longer to construct than the Navy originally planned. The Navy has accepted delivery of the first two ships (LCS 1 and LCS 2), which, according to the Navy, reduces the likelihood of additional cost increases and schedule delays on those ships. Further, the Navy's decision to partially terminate, and later re-award, construction contracts for follow-on ships (LCS 3 and LCS 4) changed the planned delivery dates for those ships. Tables 2 and 3 highlight the cost growth and schedule delays associated with the first four ships of the class.

**Table 2: Cost Growth on Initial LCS Seaframes**

Dollars in millions

| Ship | Initial budget | Fiscal year 2011 budget | Total cost growth | Cost growth as a percent of initial budget |
|------|---------------|------------------------|-------------------|--------------------------------------------|
| LCS 1 | $215.5 | $537.0 | $321.5 | 149.2% |
| LCS 2 | $256.5 | $607.0[a] | $350.5 | 136.6% |
| LCS 3-4 | $1,260.7[b] | $1,357.7 | $97.0 | 7.7% |

Source: GAO analysis of President's budget data.

Note: Fiscal year 2011 budget figures identified for LCS 1 and LCS 2 exclude funding associated with certain design, planning, and program management activities for these ships. These funds total $170.0 million and $177.0 million for LCS 1 and LCS 2, respectively.

[a]Total excludes Department of Defense reprogramming actions in July 2010 that added $5.256 million in funding to complete post-delivery work on LCS 2.

[b]Initial budget figure for LCS 3 and LCS 4 reflects the total Shipbuilding and Conversion, Navy (SCN) funds the Navy requested in fiscal year 2009 to construct two LCS seaframes plus the value of funds and materials applied from the two canceled, fiscal year 2006 funded LCS seaframes. Congress originally appropriated $440 million in fiscal year 2006 to construct these two ships

**Table 3: Delays in Delivering Initial LCS Seaframes**

| Ship | Initial planned delivery date | Current estimated/actual delivery date | Total construction delays |
|------|------------------------------|----------------------------------------|---------------------------|
| LCS 1 | January 2007 | September 2008 | 20 months |
| LCS 2 | October 2007 | December 2009 | 26 months |
| LCS 3 | November 2012 | February 2012 | N/A |
| LCS 4 | January 2013 | April 2012 | N/A |

Source: GAO analysis of President's budget data.

Note: Initial planned delivery dates for LCS 3 and LCS 4 reflect the planned schedules for two fiscal year 2009 funded LCS seaframes. Previously, the Navy funded these two ships in fiscal year 2006 and expected deliveries in October 2008. The Navy's decision to partially terminate construction contracts for the two fiscal year 2006 ships, coupled with Congress's decision to rescind appropriations for one fiscal year 2008 funded seaframe, account for several months of schedule gains realized for LCS 3 and LCS 4.

## First Two Seaframes Delivered to the Fleet, but Technical Challenges Currently Limit Their Capabilities

The Navy accepted delivery of LCS 1 and LCS 2 with both seaframes in an incomplete state and with outstanding technical issues. After experiencing significant cost increases and schedule delays on these ships, the Navy judged it more cost efficient to accept the incomplete ships and resolve remaining issues post-delivery. According to Navy officials, this step afforded the Navy more control over remaining work and provided the ability to use repair yards that charge less than the builder in some instances. Although the ships are currently in service, the Navy continues to address technical issues on each seaframe. Addressing these issues has required the Navy to schedule extensive post-delivery work periods for each ship, which were not fully anticipated at the time of lead ship contract awards. For instance, to resolve the LCS 1 issues, the Navy allocated several months for two industrial post-delivery availability periods in 2009. A similar schedule is planned for LCS 2.

The Navy has made significant progress resolving LCS 1 deficiencies. While challenges with several systems were identified at delivery, the Navy deferred testing of other systems until after delivery. The shipbuilder had not completed installation of several LCS 1 systems prior to delivery, contributing to Navy decisions to defer key elements of the ship's acceptance trials until later.[5] Most notably, the Navy deferred testing of the ship's launch, handling, and recovery system—a system instrumental to deploying and recovering mission package elements that, if not performing adequately, will impair LCS capability. To date, a full demonstration of this system remains incomplete. Navy simulations to date have identified risks in safely launching and recovering mission systems that experience pendulous motion during handling—such as the remote multi-mission vehicle and unmanned surface vehicle systems. Navy officials stated, however, that the fleet successfully demonstrated operation and movement of an embarked 11-meter rigid-hull inflatable boat, having used one extensively for counterdrug operations in the Caribbean in March 2010.

Another challenge for LCS 1 launch, handling, and recovery is the potential for unacceptably high water levels during high sea states in the waterborne mission zone—the area at the stern end of the ship designed to launch watercraft through stern doors and down a ramp directly into the water. Further, LCS 1's launch, handling, and recovery system has also

---

[5]In addition, Navy officials stated that environmental and treaty constraints prohibited testing of several ship systems within the confines of the Great Lakes.

experienced difficulty safely moving payloads on the ship. Most notably, payload handling cranes will not be installed until a future maintenance period in fiscal year 2013.

Like LCS 1, the Navy identified several significant technical deficiencies on LCS 2 during that ship's acceptance trials. However, because LCS 2 was only recently delivered (December 2009), the Navy remains in the early stages of addressing the issues facing that ship. Similar to LCS 1, the Navy chose to accept delivery of LCS 2 prior to the shipbuilder completing installation of key systems. The incomplete condition of the ship contributed to Navy decisions to defer key elements of acceptance trials until after delivery. As was the case with LCS 1, these deferments included testing of the LCS 2 launch, handling, and recovery system for mission watercraft.

LCS 2 is designed to employ a twin boom extensible crane system to launch, handle, and recover mission watercraft. This system includes the crane, synthetic lift lines, and a straddle carrier. The synthetic lift lines attach to the crane to retrieve watercraft, but remain an unproven, new capability to the Navy. Another risk to the system is the ability of the straddle carrier to interface with, maneuver, and return to stowage the rigid-hull inflatable boat, remote multi-mission vehicle, and unmanned surface vehicle systems—three of the largest watercraft the Navy plans to embark on LCS 2. According to the Navy, the straddle carrier was used to successfully move the remote multi-mission vehicle and unmanned surface vehicle during onboard trials in March 2010.

## Continuing Design Changes Could Hinder Efficient Construction of LCS 3 and LCS 4

The Navy's efforts to resolve technical issues affecting LCS 1 and LCS 2, implement cost reduction measures, and increase mission capability have led to design changes for LCS 3 and LCS 4, several of which are not yet complete. These design changes have affected the configuration of several major ship systems for LCS 3 and LCS 4 including propulsion, communications, electrical, and navigation. The Navy is working to implement these design changes concurrent with LCS 3 and LCS 4 construction activities. Incorporating design changes on the lead seaframes while the follow-on ships are under construction may disrupt the optimal construction sequence for LCS 3 and LCS 4, requiring additional labor hours beyond current forecasts. As we have previously reported, by delaying construction start until basic and functional design is completed and a stable design is achieved, shipbuilders minimize the risk of design changes and the subsequent costly rework and out-of-sequence work these changes can drive.[6]

## Benefits Derived from Recent Process Improvements and Capital Investments in the LCS Shipyards May Not Be Fully Realized on Early Follow-On Ships

The Navy and its shipbuilders learned valuable lessons from the construction of the lead ships that can save time and money on the construction of follow-on ships. The shipbuilding teams have implemented process improvements based on these lessons and made capital investments in their yards in an effort to increase efficiency. Despite the various improvements to capacity and processes at the shipyards, capitalizing on these improvements might be challenging given the significant design changes still occurring in the program. As technical issues are resolved on the lead seaframes, this, in general, leads to redesign—and potentially costly rework—for initial follow-on ships. Thus, while efficiencies will be gained as a result of the shipyards' improvement, remaining technical issues on the seaframes will likely continue to jeopardize the Navy's ability to complete the first four seaframes within planned cost and schedule estimates.

## Mission Package Delays Limit Ship Capabilities in the Near Term and Pose Risk to Efficient Execution of Program Acquisition and Test Plans

Challenges developing and procuring mission packages have delayed the timely fielding of promised capabilities, limiting the ships' utility to the fleet during initial deployments. Until these challenges are resolved, it will be difficult for the Navy to align seaframe purchases with mission package procurements and execute planned tests. Key mine countermeasures and surface warfare systems have encountered technical issues that have delayed their development and fielding. Further, Navy analysis of LCS anti-submarine warfare systems found these capabilities did not contribute significantly to the anti-submarine warfare mission. These challenges have led to procurement delays for all three mission packages. For instance, key elements of the surface warfare package remain in development, requiring the Navy to deploy a less robust capability on LCS 1. Mission package delays have also disrupted program test schedules—a situation exacerbated by decisions to deploy initial ships early, which limit their availability for operational testing. In addition, these delays could disrupt program plans for simultaneously acquiring seaframes and mission

---

[6]See GAO, *Best Practices: High Levels of Knowledge at Key Points Differentiate Commercial Shipbuilding from Navy Shipbuilding*, GAO-09-322 (Washington, D.C.: May 13, 2009).

packages. Until mission package performance is proven, the Navy risks investing in a fleet of ships that does not deliver promised capability.

## Challenges Developing LCS Mission Package Systems Have Delayed Their Planned Fielding Dates

Development efforts for most of these systems predate the LCS program—in some cases by 10 years or more. Recent testing of mission package systems has yielded less than desirable results. To date, most LCS mission systems have not demonstrated the ability to provide required capabilities. Further, the Navy has determined that an additional capability will be incorporated into future anti-submarine warfare mission packages. The existing anti-submarine warfare mission package procurement is temporarily suspended, and performance will be assessed during at-sea testing in 2010. In addition to the sensors, vehicles, and weapons included in each mission package, each LCS will rely on aircraft and their support systems to complete missions.

## Mine Countermeasures

Mine countermeasures missions for LCS will involve detecting, classifying, localizing, identifying, and neutralizing enemy sea mines in areas ranging from deep water through beach zones.[7] We have previously reported on challenges the Navy faces in transitioning the mine countermeasures mission to LCS.[8] Figure 2 illustrates how the Navy plans to employ the LCS mine countermeasures systems against mine threats.

---

[7]While the Navy will use LCS systems to detect mines in the very shallow (40 feet to 30 feet water only), surf (less than 10 feet to 0 feet water), and beach zones, other military assets will neutralize these mines.

[8]See GAO, *Defense Acquisitions: Overcoming Challenges Key to Capitalizing on Mine Countermeasures Capabilities*, GAO-08-13 (Washington, D.C.: Oct. 12, 2007).

**Figure 2: Operational Concept for LCS Mine Countermeasures Systems**

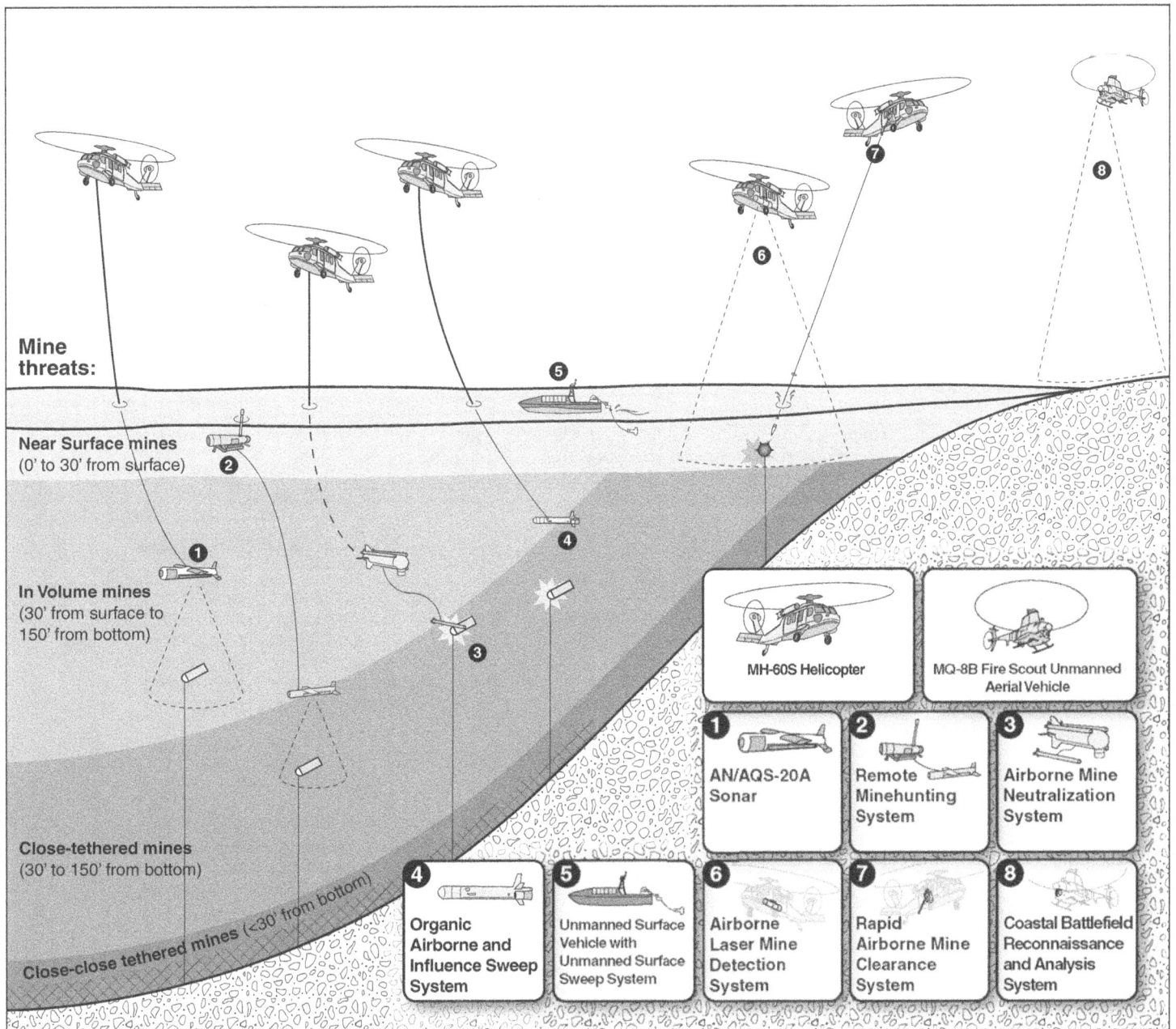

Mine threats:

Near Surface mines
(0' to 30' from surface)

In Volume mines
(30' from surface to
150' from bottom)

Close-tethered mines
(30' to 150' from bottom)

Close-close tethered mines (<30' from bottom)

MH-60S Helicopter

MQ-8B Fire Scout Unmanned
Aerial Vehicle

❶ AN/AQS-20A Sonar

❷ Remote Minehunting System

❸ Airborne Mine Neutralization System

❹ Organic Airborne and Influence Sweep System

❺ Unmanned Surface Vehicle with Unmanned Surface Sweep System

❻ Airborne Laser Mine Detection System

❼ Rapid Airborne Mine Clearance System

❽ Coastal Battlefield Reconnaissance and Analysis System

Source: GAO analysis of Navy data.

Table 4 shows the status of mine countermeasures mission package systems.

**Table 4: Navy's Progress Developing and Fielding Mine Countermeasures Mission Package Systems**

| Mission system | Capabilities description | Development status | Estimated fielding date |
|---|---|---|---|
| AN/AQS-20A Sonar | Provides identification of bottom mines in shallow water and detection, localization, and classification of bottom, close-tethered, and volume mines in deep water | System has met performance requirements in developmental testing. Operational testing has been delayed, however, due to decertification of the system following integration problems with the common tow cable that connects it to the MH-60S helicopter. | 2011 |
| Airborne Laser Mine Detection System | Detects, classifies, and localizes floating and near-surface moored mines in deep water | System has demonstrated partial capability during developmental testing. Current challenges include the ability to detect mines at the required maximum depth or classify mines at surface depths. | 2011 |
| Airborne Mine Neutralization System | Identifies and neutralizes unburied bottom and moored sea mines in shallow water that are impractical or unsafe to counter using existing minesweeping systems | System has successfully streamed and deployed an inert neutralizer in developmental testing. The mount that connects the system to the MH-60S carriage, stream, tow, and recovery system is being redesigned following loss of a test unit. | 2011 |
| Coastal Battlefield Reconnaissance and Analysis System | Provides intelligence preparation of the battlefield information, which accurately depicts tactical objectives, minefields, and obstacles in the surf zone, on the beach, and through the beach exit during amphibious and expeditionary operations; future increments planned will provide active (day/night), surf zone, buried minefield detection, and real-time processing capabilities | System has demonstrated capability to detect buried mines on the beach when flown from the MH-53 helicopter, but has yet to be integrated with its host platform, the MQ-8B Vertical Take-off and Landing Tactical Unmanned Aerial Vehicle. | 2012 |
| Organic Airborne and Surface Influence Sweep System | Provides organic, high-speed magnetic/acoustic influence minesweeping capability where mine hunting is not feasible (adverse environmental conditions) | Engineering development model experienced excessive corrosion at its interface point with the common tow cable during testing from an MH-53E helicopter. The Navy has implemented a design solution, and new models are in production. | 2012 |

| Mission system | Capabilities description | Development status | Estimated fielding date |
|---|---|---|---|
| Remote Minehunting System | Underwater vehicle towing the AN/AQS-20A sonar used to detect, classify, locate, and identify minelike objects | The Navy abandoned initial operational test and evaluation of this system in June 2007 following reliability issues—both software and hardware related—affecting the underwater vehicle. Subsequent plans for resuming this testing in September 2008 were deferred because of continuing concerns about the reliability of the underwater vehicle, and the scheduled test was downgraded to an operational assessment. Spurred by cost growth facing the system, the Office of the Secretary of Defense recently completed a review of the program, subsequently deciding to allow the system to continue development. The Navy is currently executing a reliability growth plan for the system. | 2015 |
| Unmanned Surface Vehicle with Unmanned Surface Sweep System | Micro-turbine-powered magnetic towed cable and acoustical signal generator towed from an unmanned surface craft | Prototypes of the unmanned surface vehicle have experienced connectivity and communication issues at distance, reliability issues with their electrical generators, and software malfunctions. Additionally, the Navy is redesigning the cable planned to tow the unmanned surface sweep system due to durability concerns. The unmanned surface sweep system remains in early development. | 2015 |
| Rapid Airborne Mine Clearance System | Mounted 30-millimeter gun firing supercavitating projectiles to neutralize near-surface and floating moored mines | Separate engineering development models of the gun and targeting pod have been tested with mixed results. Gun testing demonstrated the need to redesign the bushing (shock absorber). Targeting pod testing revealed problems reacquiring minelike objects and maintaining a gun lock on them. The Navy is rewriting software to address the targeting pod issues. | 2017 |

Source: GAO analysis of Navy data.

For two of the LCS mine countermeasures systems—the Remote Minehunting System and the Airborne Laser Mine Detection System—the Navy has delayed further production pending successful resolution of developmental challenges. These systems both entered production in 2005. According to Navy officials, relaxing the performance requirements for the Remote Minehunting System and the Airborne Laser Mine Detection System is one option under consideration.

- **Airborne Laser Mine Detection System:** Testing of this system has revealed problems detecting mines at the required maximum depth and classifying mines at surface depths. According to Navy officials, the system's required maximum detection depth could be reduced because the system can currently detect mine-like objects at depths that extend below the keels of all ships in the fleet. According to Director, Operational Test and Evaluation officials, however, the system is currently incapable of providing this capability with the required accuracy. Further, Navy officials report that the Remote Minehunting System could provide coverage in near-surface areas of the water that the Airborne Laser Mine Detection System currently cannot reach.

- **Remote Minehunting System:** Operational testing of this system in 2008 revealed significant reliability shortfalls associated with the underwater vehicle. Most notably, the system was only able to function for 7.9 hours before failing—far short of its minimum requirement. Director, Operational Test and Evaluation officials report that since the 2008 event, the Navy's estimated mean time between failures for the system has increased to 45 hours. According to Navy officials, testing and design changes are expected to last into 2011. While the Navy is actively exploring ways to improve Remote Minehunting System reliability, it is also considering reducing the reliability requirement by half.

Surface Warfare

Surface warfare for LCS involves detecting, tracking, and engaging small boat threats; escorting ships; and protecting joint operating areas. Figure 3 illustrates how the surface warfare mission package functions.

**Figure 3: Operational Concept for LCS Surface Warfare Systems**

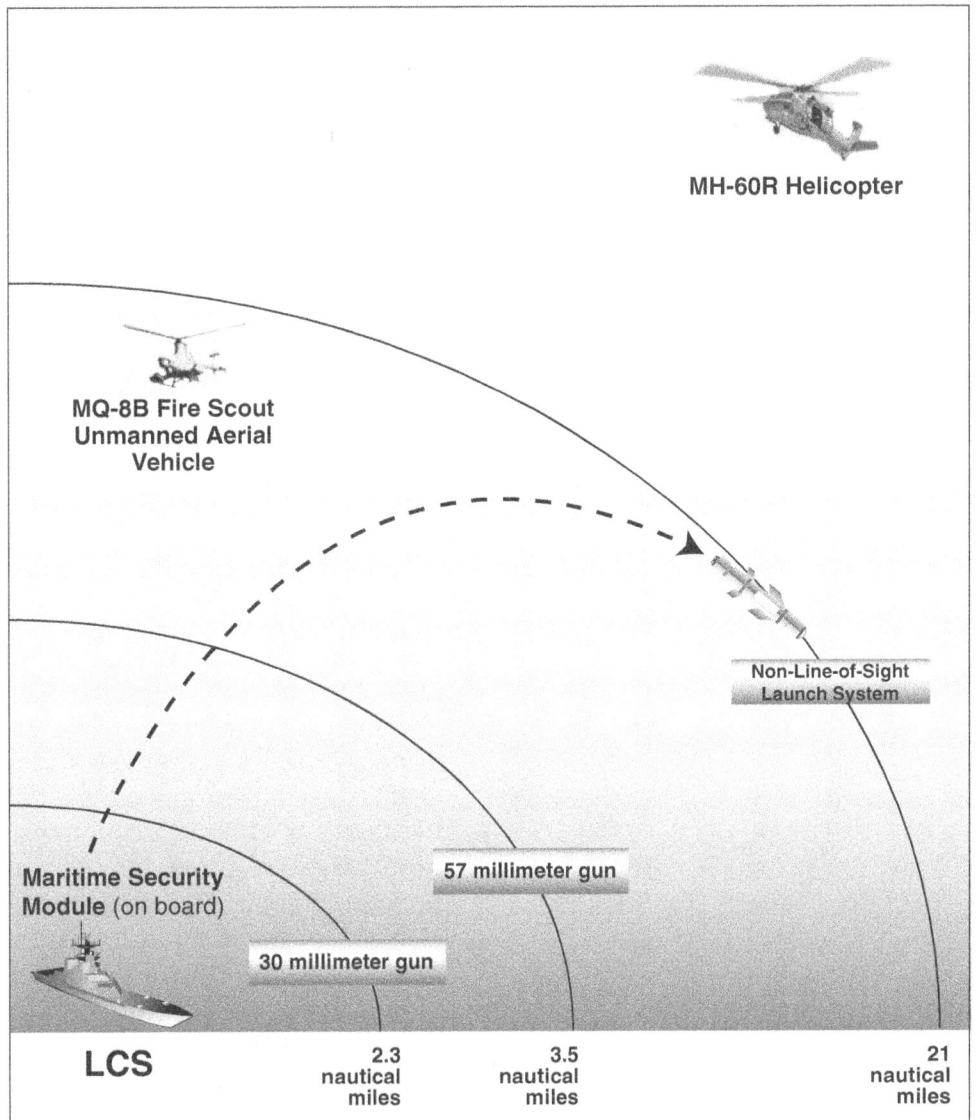

MH-60R Helicopter

MQ-8B Fire Scout
Unmanned Aerial
Vehicle

Non-Line-of-Sight
Launch System

Maritime Security
Module (on board)

57 millimeter gun

30 millimeter gun

LCS

2.3 nautical miles

3.5 nautical miles

21 nautical miles

Source: U.S. Navy.

Note: The 57-millimeter gun is a core seaframe system.

GAO-10-523 Littoral Combat Ship

Table 5 shows the status of surface warfare mission systems.

**Table 5: Navy's Progress Developing and Fielding Surface Warfare Mission Package Systems**

| Mission system | Capabilities description | Development status | Actual/estimated fielding date |
|---|---|---|---|
| MK 46 30-Millimeter Gun Module | Two-axis stabilized chain gun that can fire up to 250 rounds per minute employing a forward-looking infrared sensor, camera, and laser rangefinder | Structural test firing completed from LCS 1 in September 2009. Currently, the system has not been fully integrated with the combat systems for either of the lead seaframes. | 2010 |
| Maritime Security Module | Complement of 19 personnel operating in two teams on LCS that provide capability to conduct visit, board, search, and seizure operations against potential threat vessels | The Navy installed a prototype Maritime Security Module in LCS 1 for the ship's early deployment that included 2 11-meter rigid hull inflatable boats and two berthing/sanitation modules. | 2010 |
| Non-Line-of-Sight Launch System | Container launch unit and precision attack missile for use against moving and stationary targets | Testing in July 2009 intended to demonstrate the system's ability to neutralize a target while fired from a rolling platform (similar to a ship) proved unsuccessful due to a malfunctioning sensor and battery connector. During Army operational testing in January and February 2010, the precision attack missile failed to hit its intended target four out of six times. Recent cancellation of the Non-Line-of-Sight Launch System program has prompted the Navy to seek alternatives to include on LCS. | 2014 |

Source: GAO analysis of Navy data.

The surface warfare package remains unproven as a key system, the Non-Line-of-Sight Launch System, was recently canceled prior to completing development. The system—developed under the Army's Future Combat System program—progressed slower than anticipated due to technical challenges and associated test failures. These issues—along with Army fiscal year 2011 budget estimates showing missiles could cost up to $466,000 each—prompted the Army to revisit its commitment to the program. In May 2010, this process culminated with the Under Secretary of Defense for Acquisition, Technology and Logistics approving the Army's request to cancel the program. In response, Navy officials report they are now evaluating potential alternatives to the Non-Line-of-Sight Launch System—including modifications to existing missile systems—to substitute into the surface warfare mission package.

## Support Aircraft

In addition to systems outlined above, the Navy plans to employ aircraft in different configurations to execute LCS missions. Table 6 highlights the status of key mission package support aircraft.

**Table 6: Navy's Progress Developing and Fielding Key Mission Package Support Aircraft**

| Mission system | Capabilities description | Development status | Actual/estimated fielding date |
|---|---|---|---|
| MH-60R Helicopter[a] | Ship-based helicopter designed to operate from several types of Navy vessels. Key capabilities include dipping sonar and sonobuoy acoustic sensors, multi-mode radar, electronic warfare sensors, and a forward looking infrared sensor with laser designator. Employs torpedoes, Hellfire air-to-surface missiles, and crew-served mounted machine guns. | Initial operational capability achieved in 2005. September 2009 testing revealed deficiencies associated with the data link (Link 16) and with the automatic video tracking feature of the helicopter's targeting system. | 2005 |
| MQ-8B Vertical Take-off and Landing Tactical Unmanned Aerial Vehicle[b] | Unmanned rotary wing air vehicle designed to provide intelligence, surveillance, reconnaissance, and targeting data to tactical users. | Low-rate initial production units are scheduled to complete initial operational test and evaluation onboard a Navy frigate in 2010. The Navy plans to field the system exclusively onboard LCS, where it will connect with and deploy the Coastal Battlefield Reconnaissance and Analysis System. However, integration with the Coastal Battlefield Reconnaissance and Analysis System and LCS seaframes is not scheduled to occur until after the MQ-8B achieves initial operational capability. | 2010 |
| MH-60S Helicopter[c] | Helicopter modified into three variants (Fleet Logistics, Airborne Mine Countermeasures, and Armed Helicopter) and optimized for operation in the shipboard/marine environment. Installed systems differ by variant based on mission. The Navy is procuring the Airborne Mine Countermeasures variant in two increments of capability. | Operational testing of the Airborne Mine Countermeasures variant in 2008 was unsuccessful due to reliability issues with the Carriage, Stream, Tow, and Recovery System used to deploy, tow, and retrieve several of the LCS mine countermeasures systems. Further, the on-board command and control console used to monitor and communicate with deployed airborne mine countermeasures systems required a series of software updates to fix computer freezes and other glitches that were degrading performance. The Navy has rescheduled initial operational test and evaluation events for this variant to December 2010. | 2011[d] |

Source: GAO analysis of Navy data.

[a]MH-60R helicopter supports deployment of the surface warfare and anti-submarine warfare mission packages.

[b]MQ-8B Vertical Take-off and Landing Tactical Unmanned Aerial Vehicle supports deployment of all three LCS mission packages.

[c]MH-60S helicopter supports deployment of the mine countermeasures mission package.

[d]Denotes estimated fielding date for the initial increment of the MH-60S airborne mine countermeasures variant.

In addition to these technical challenges, other factors may constrain availability of the three LCS support aircraft.

- **MH-60R Helicopter:** According to Navy officials, while this system has completed its first deployment with a carrier strike group, the earliest possible date that it will deploy onboard an LCS is the end of fiscal year 2013. Navy officials reported that because of fleet demand for the helicopter, initial MH-60Rs will be assigned to the carrier strike group elements (e.g., destroyers, cruisers, and frigates) before deploying with an LCS. As of January 2010, the Navy had accepted delivery of 46 MH-60Rs of a planned quantity of 252.

- **MH-60S Helicopter:** The Navy has certified flight operations of the armed variant of this helicopter from LCS 1. Previous plans called for only the mine countermeasures variant of the MH-60S to fly from the LCS. As of December 2009, 159 of 275 MH-60S helicopters had been delivered.

- **MQ-8B Vertical Take-off and Landing Tactical Aerial Vehicle (known as Fire Scout):** The Navy is conducting operational testing of Fire Scout onboard a frigate, but intends to field the system with LCS exclusively. Reliability and availability issues uncovered during fiscal year 2010 testing have delayed the program's fielding schedule. Previously, the Navy expected to reach a full-rate production decision on Fire Scout in March 2010. The Navy has since deferred this decision to May 2011.

## Developmental Challenges with Individual Systems Have Contributed to Mission Package Procurement Delays

The Navy is buying mission packages through an incremental approach by incorporating systems into the respective mission packages when systems achieve minimum performance requirements. Figure 4 illustrates the effect that recent developmental challenges have had upon mission package procurement plans.

**Figure 4: Recent Changes to Navy Mission Package Procurement Plans**

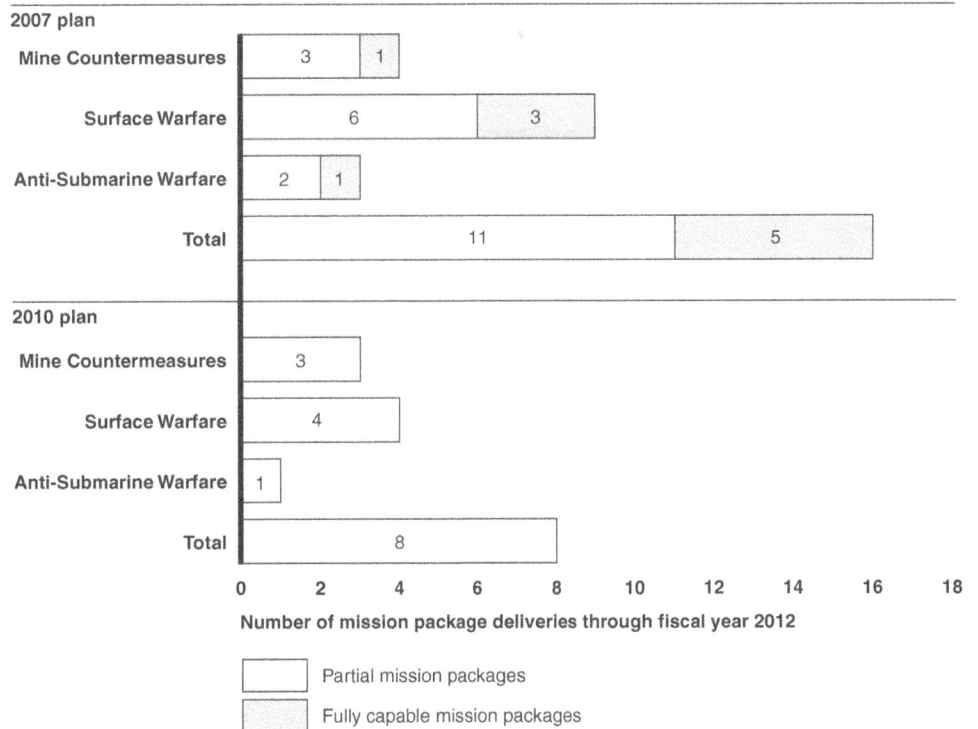

2007 plan

| | |
|---|---|
| Mine Countermeasures | 3 / 1 |
| Surface Warfare | 6 / 3 |
| Anti-Submarine Warfare | 2 / 1 |
| Total | 11 / 5 |

2010 plan

| | |
|---|---|
| Mine Countermeasures | 3 |
| Surface Warfare | 4 |
| Anti-Submarine Warfare | 1 |
| Total | 8 |

Number of mission package deliveries through fiscal year 2012

☐ Partial mission packages
☐ Fully capable mission packages

Source: GAO analysis of Navy data.

In 2007, the Navy anticipated that a total of 16 mission packages would be delivered by 2012 with all three types of mission packages reaching their full configuration by that date. In recent years, the Navy has deferred planned procurements of LCS mission packages due, in part, to developmental challenges facing mission systems. Under the Navy's 2010 plan, the Navy plans to acquire 8 mission packages by 2012 with no mission package having achieved its full configuration of capabilities.

To date, the Navy has taken delivery of five partial mission packages—two surface warfare, two mine countermeasures, and one anti-submarine warfare. The Navy delayed procurement of the fiscal year 2009 funded mine countermeasures package due to technical issues and resulting operational testing delays. Delivery of the two partial surface warfare mission packages occurred in July 2008 and March 2010, respectively. The first surface warfare package included two engineering development models for the 30-millimeter gun, but did not include the launcher or missiles for the Non-Line-of-Sight Launch System. The second surface warfare mission package included the 30-millimeter gun module and the launcher component—but no missiles—for the Non-Line-of-Sight Launch System.

Because of planned configuration changes to the anti-submarine warfare mission package, the Navy does not plan to buy additional quantities of this package until the new configuration is settled. According to Navy officials, recent warfighting analyses showed that the baseline anti-submarine warfare package did not contribute significantly to the anti-submarine warfare mission. The first package will undergo developmental testing, with results used to inform decisions on future configuration. The Navy conducted end-to-end testing on the first anti-submarine warfare mission package in April 2009 and plans to continue developmental testing in fiscal year 2010. During the 2009 end-to-end test, the Navy found that the unmanned surface vehicle and its associated sensors will require reliability and interface improvements to support sustained undersea warfare.

## Mission Package Procurement Delays Could Disrupt Program Plans for Simultaneously Acquiring Seaframes and Mission Packages and Will Limit the Ships' Utility During Initial Deployments

While the Navy now plans to purchase 17 ships and 13 mission packages between fiscal year 2011 and fiscal year 2015, developmental delays facing key mission package systems have positioned the Navy to acquire significant numbers of seaframes before mission packages are proven. This development represents a reversal for the LCS program. In prior years, the Navy deferred purchase of mission packages to account for delays in constructing seaframes. However, as key mission package systems entered operational testing—producing less than successful results—and seaframe design and construction progressed, planned alignment of seaframe and mission package purchases suffered further disruption.

Until mission package performance is proven, the Navy risks investing in a fleet of ships that does not deliver its promised capability. As the Navy stated, the underlying strength of the LCS lies in its innovative design—interchangeable mission equipment that allows the ship to be used for different missions. Fundamental to this approach is the capability to rapidly install interchangeable mission packages into the seaframe. Absent significant capability within its mission packages, seaframe functionality is largely constrained to self-defense as opposed to mission-related tasks.

In addition, the Navy has deployed LCS 1 earlier than originally scheduled and is evaluating a similar course for LCS 2. For these deployments, the Navy is employing hybrid—limited and incomplete—versions of mission packages. The package on LCS 1 includes one mission system (two 30-millimeter guns), the armed variant of the MH-60S helicopter, and the maritime security module. According to Navy officials, deploying LCS 1 two years ahead of schedule allows them to incorporate lessons that can only be learned in a deployment setting. LCS 1 will conduct operations where it will be able to take advantage of its speed and will be equipped with an incomplete version of the surface warfare package. Because the surface warfare mission package is incomplete, the range of missions LCS 1 is capable of executing will be constrained during its initial deployment.

Furthermore, the surface warfare mission package onboard LCS 1 has yet to be fully integrated with the seaframe and lacks key capabilities necessary to defeat surface threats. For example, the 30-millimeter guns have undergone testing with the LCS 1 seaframe, but have yet to be fully integrated with the ship's combat suite. Also, while the guns provide a close range self-defense capability, Navy officials report LCS 1 is currently unable to automatically transfer tracking data from the ship's radar to the 30-millimeter guns. In addition, because of excess MH-60R helicopter demands, the Navy has assigned the armed helo variant of the MH-60S helicopter to LCS 1 for its maiden deployment. Although this MH-60S variant carries air-to-surface missiles and crew-served side machine guns (among other offensive capabilities), it does not have the multi-mode radar found on the MH-60R—a shortfall that could constrain LCS 1's ability to execute surface warfare missions.

## Mission Package Delays Coupled with Early Deployment of LCS Seaframes Require Deferral of Key Test Events

Neither LCS seaframe design—nor any of the three LCS mission packages—has completed initial operational test and evaluation. Normally after a lead ship completes its post-delivery maintenance period, initial operational test and evaluation occurs—generally planned for within 1 year of ship delivery. In the case of LCS, initial operational test and evaluation will encompass both seaframes and mission packages. Under the program's 2008 Test and Evaluation Master Plan, LCS 1 was to begin operational testing with the initial systems in the mine countermeasures mission package in the second quarter of fiscal year 2010. The mission systems that were to be tested included the Remote Minehunting System, the MH-60S helicopter (mine countermeasures variant), AN/AQS-20A mine detecting sonar, Unmanned Surface Vehicle with Unmanned Surface Sweep System, Airborne Mine Neutralization System, and Airborne Laser Mine Detection System. However, as noted above, these mission systems have experienced developmental challenges and none are ready to be tested on the seaframe. The Navy has since postponed operational testing of the mine countermeasures mission package to the second quarter of fiscal year 2013, now planned to occur onboard LCS 2.

In addition, early deployments of seaframes postpone their availability to complete planned testing events. For example, although LCS 1 deployed 2 years earlier than scheduled, its first operational testing event with a mission package was delayed by 3 years.[9] The Navy faces several risks in deploying the LCS 1 before it has completed initial operational test and evaluation. For example, Department of Defense testing officials stated that because LCS 1 and LCS 2 are such revolutionary designs, the lead ships should be put through a rigorous testing and evaluation process—in a controlled environment—to best understand their capabilities and limitations. Additionally, the testing officials reported that the ship's maintenance and support strategy was of significant concern to them. According to the testing officials, LCS—more so than other ships—will have to rely heavily on shore-based support, which is an unproven concept.

## Incomplete Cost Analyses in the LCS Program Have Undermined Program Progress

The Navy entered contract negotiations in 2009 for fiscal year 2010 funded seaframes with an incomplete understanding of LCS program costs. These contract negotiations proved unsuccessful, prompting the Navy to revise its acquisition strategy for the program. The contractors' proposals for construction of the next three ships exceeded the approximate $1.4 billion in funds the Navy had allocated in its fiscal year 2010 budget. In response, the Navy revised its strategy to construct one seaframe design instead of two for fiscal year 2010 ships and beyond in an effort to improve affordability. Navy cost analyses completed prior to the failed negotiations in 2009 lack several characteristics essential to a high quality cost estimate. These characteristics include the completion of sensitivity and uncertainty analyses and an independent review of the cost estimate. The

---

[9]Under the LCS program's 2008 Test and Evaluation Master Plan, the Navy planned to conduct an operational assessment of LCS 1—employing elements of the first mine countermeasures mission package—beginning the second quarter of fiscal year 2010. The Navy's fiscal year 2011 budget estimates show LCS 1 will now begin operational testing in the third quarter of fiscal year 2013 using the surface warfare mission package.

Navy plans to complete a more comprehensive cost estimate before award of additional ship contracts in 2010.

## Unsuccessful Contract Negotiations in Late 2009 Prompted the Navy to Restructure Its Acquisition Strategy for the LCS Program

The Navy budgeted $1.38 billion in fiscal year 2010 for construction of three ships (LCS 5, LCS 6, and LCS 7) at a cost of $460 million each. The Navy planned to award construction contracts for these ships in November 2009, to include the purchase of at least one ship of each LCS seaframe design. Navy officials were confident they had gained sufficient knowledge from construction activities associated with the first four seaframes to support a cost efficient, dual design strategy going forward. As part of this strategy, the Navy solicited proposals from each of the LCS prime contractors for construction of up to three ships on a fixed-price basis. The industry teams returned their proposals in August 2009 and, according to Navy officials, included pricing significantly above the Navy's expectations. Lockheed Martin and General Dynamics officials stated that the fixed-price terms the Navy sought prompted a forthright assessment of remaining program risks—including technical, design, and funding uncertainties—and subsequent pricing of that risk in their proposals.

Due to the sharp differences between the Navy cost expectations and the contractor proposals with respect to LCS pricing, the Navy concluded the negotiations without awarding contracts for any new ships. Further, Navy leadership stated it had no reasonable basis to find that the LCS program would be executable going forward under the current acquisition strategy, which prompted the Navy to outline a new acquisition strategy in September 2009 aimed at improving program affordability by selecting one design for the fiscal year 2010 ships and beyond. Under the terms of the new strategy, the Navy will contract with a single source on a fixed-price basis for up to 10 ships (2 ships awarded per year) through fiscal year 2014. The strategy also outlines plans to issue a second solicitation for up to another 5 ships to be constructed at a separate yard with awards planned between fiscal years 2012 and 2014. The first source will provide the combat systems for the 5 additional ships constructed by the second shipyard. Navy officials stated that the new acquisition approach will produce cost benefits attributable to near-term competitive pricing pressures between the two current LCS shipbuilding teams, economic order quantity purchases of key materials, efficiencies associated with potentially moving to a single, common combat system, and significantly reduced total ownership costs for the Navy.

While the new acquisition strategy for the LCS program promises improved affordability, the Navy's failure to recognize the unexecutable nature of the previous strategy—before engaging in the costly, time consuming process of requesting proposals—has not come without penalty. Contract awards for LCS 5, LCS 6, and LCS 7 have been delayed by at least 9 months, subsequently disrupting planned workloads—and potentially increasing the overhead costs charged to existing Navy contracts—in the LCS shipyards. Most importantly, however, the unsuccessful negotiations and revised strategy represent the latest delay to delivery of promised capabilities to the fleet, which is depending heavily on LCS to take over several current and future missions. Figure 5 highlights the resequencing of key LCS program events following the revised acquisition strategy, which delayed contract awards for the fiscal year 2010 funded ships.

**Figure 5: Schedule of Key Near-term Events as Outlined in the LCS Program's 2009 and 2010 Acquisition Strategies**

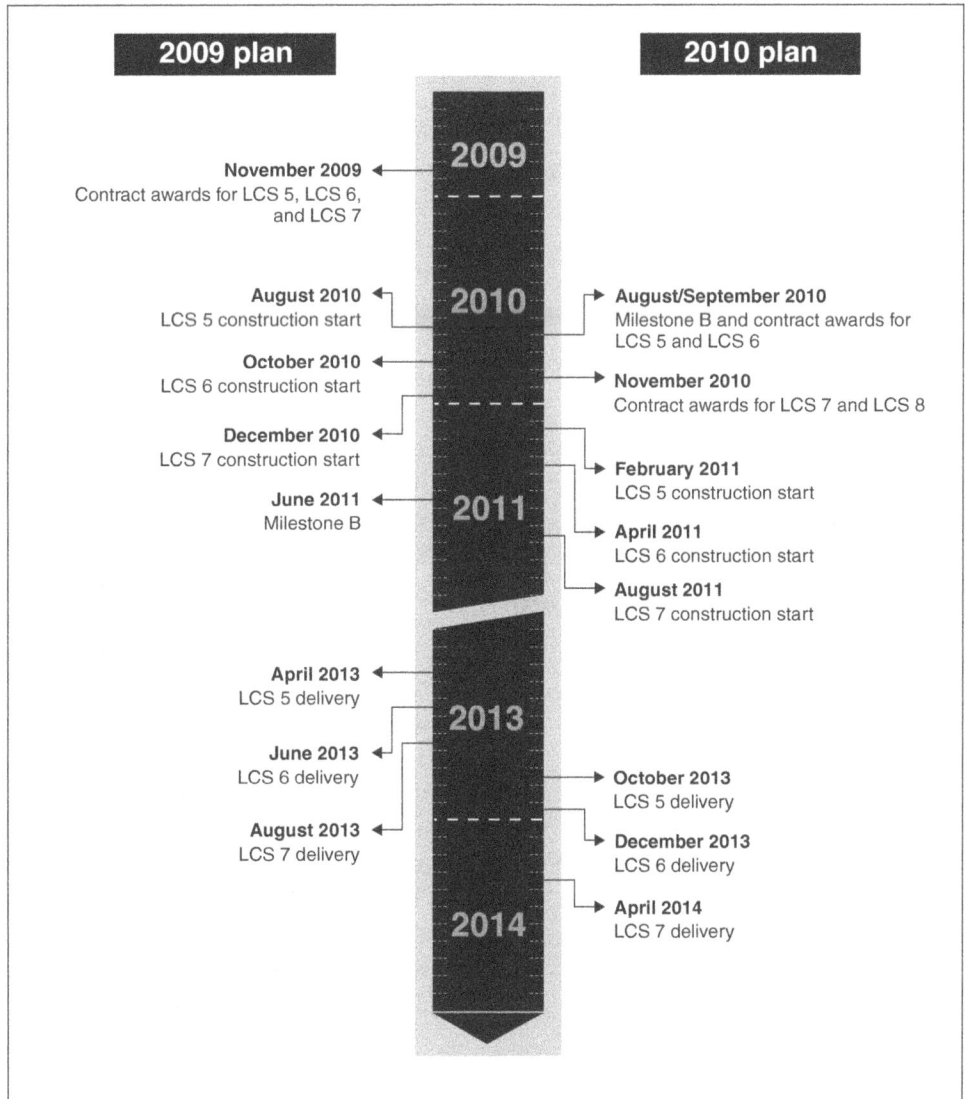

**2009 plan**

**November 2009**
Contract awards for LCS 5, LCS 6, and LCS 7

**August 2010**
LCS 5 construction start

**October 2010**
LCS 6 construction start

**December 2010**
LCS 7 construction start

**June 2011**
Milestone B

**April 2013**
LCS 5 delivery

**June 2013**
LCS 6 delivery

**August 2013**
LCS 7 delivery

**2010 plan**

**August/September 2010**
Milestone B and contract awards for LCS 5 and LCS 6

**November 2010**
Contract awards for LCS 7 and LCS 8

**February 2011**
LCS 5 construction start

**April 2011**
LCS 6 construction start

**August 2011**
LCS 7 construction start

**October 2013**
LCS 5 delivery

**December 2013**
LCS 6 delivery

**April 2014**
LCS 7 delivery

2009
2010
2011
2013
2014

Source: GAO analysis.

Under the new acquisition strategy, the LCS program must complete a major program review (milestone B) before award of fiscal year 2010 ship contracts. The previous acquisition strategy deferred this review until June 2011—after award of the three fiscal year 2010 ship contracts. While holding the milestone B decision earlier than planned is an improvement, most ship programs align milestone B with the decision to authorize the start of detail design—a decision that dates back to 2004 in the LCS program.

In support of the milestone B review, Department of Defense policy requires the Navy to provide its own cost estimate for the program.[10] In response, the Navy plans to submit a program life cycle cost estimate, which will be completed by Naval Sea Systems Command's Cost Engineering and Industrial Analysis division. In addition, federal statute requires that for major defense acquisition programs (including LCS), an independent estimate of life cycle costs be prepared and provided to the milestone decision authority before the approval is given to proceed with Engineering and Manufacturing Development.[11] The responsibility for the independent cost estimate is assigned to the Director, Cost Assessment and Program Evaluation within the Department of Defense.

## Navy Cost Analyses Completed Ahead of Contract Negotiations in 2009 Lacked Key Elements Needed to Ensure High Quality

Because the Department of Defense has not yet completed a milestone B review of the LCS program—to include development and evaluation of a comprehensive Navy cost estimate and independent cost estimate—the typical mechanisms and processes for assessing program affordability were not carried out ahead of the Navy's 2009 contract negotiations, which turned out to be unsuccessful. Instead, Navy officials reported their cost expectations for fiscal year 2010 funded seaframes were largely framed by the pricing agreements reached with Lockheed Martin and General Dynamics for LCS 3 and LCS 4 construction, respectively. Apart from this data, the Navy had few alternative sources available that forecast LCS program costs. Most prominent of these sources was analysis completed in June 2009 as part of the LCS total ownership cost baseline estimate.[12] The Navy chartered this estimate to investigate ways it could alter the LCS seaframe designs to reduce its total ownership cost in the program. The estimate reflected the life cycle costs of the proposed two-design, 55 ship LCS class—not including mission packages—and was divided into

---

[10]Department of Defense Instruction 5000.02, *Operation of the Defense Acquisition System* Enclosure 4 Table 3 (Dec. 8, 2008).

[11]Engineering and manufacturing development has the same meaning as system development and demonstration as referred to in 10 U.S.C. § 2434.

[12]In June 2009, Navy cost estimators completed their preliminary analysis of LCS total ownership costs and briefed key findings to senior Navy leaders. The Navy later recorded this analysis in the *LCS Total Ownership Cost Baseline Estimate Documentation* (Aug. 25, 2009).

sections covering (1) research, development, testing, and evaluation; (2) procurement; and (3) operations and support costs. The estimate also updated a set of previous Navy and Department of Defense estimates for LCS 3 and LCS 4 that were completed in November 2008 in support of the program's milestone A-Prime review[13] and March and May 2009 contract awards for those ships.

Our analysis of the procurement section of the LCS total ownership cost baseline found the estimate lacks several characteristics essential to a high-quality cost estimate.[14] To complete this analysis, we compared the Navy's estimate to best practices criteria, as outlined in GAO's Cost Estimating and Assessment Guide and presented in appendix II.[15] These criteria characterize high-quality cost estimates as those that are credible, comprehensive, well-documented, and accurate. Table 7 highlights the key findings of our analysis.

---

[13]On December 18, 2008, the Defense Acquisition Board conducted a Milestone A-Prime review of the LCS program to determine the readiness of the program to continue the Technology Development phase and to procure fiscal year 2009 ships and mission packages.

[14]We previously assessed the quality of the Navy's operating and support cost estimates for LCS. See GAO, *Littoral Combat Ship: Actions Needed to Improve Operating Cost Estimates and Mitigate Risks in Implementing New Concepts*, GAO-10-257 (Washington, D.C.: Feb. 2, 2010).

[15]See GAO, *GAO Cost Estimating and Assessment Guide: Best Practices for Developing and Managing Capital Program Costs*, GAO-09-3SP (Washington, D.C.: Mar. 2009).

**Table 7: Extent to Which the Navy's Total Ownership Cost Baseline Estimate for LCS Procurement Was Well-Documented, Comprehensive, Accurate, and Credible**

| Four characteristics of high-quality cost estimates and 12 key steps[a] | Not met | Minimally met | Partially met | Mostly met | Fully met |
|---|---|---|---|---|---|
| Well-documented | | | X | | |
| Define the estimate's purpose (Step 1) | | | | X | |
| Define the program characteristics (Step 3) | | | X | | |
| Identify ground rules and assumptions (Step 5) | | X | | | |
| Obtain the data (Step 6) | | | | X | |
| Document the estimate (Step 10) | | X | | | |
| Present the estimate to management for approval (Step 11) | | | X | | |
| Comprehensive | | | X | | |
| Develop the estimating plan (Step 2) | | | X | | |
| Determine the estimating approach (Step 4) | | | | X | |
| Identify ground rules and assumptions (Step 5) | | X | | | |
| Accurate | | | X | | |
| Develop the point estimate and compare to an independent cost estimate (Step 7) | | | X | | |
| Update the estimate to reflect actual costs and changes (Step 12) | | | | X | |
| Credible | | X | | | |
| Develop the point estimate and compare to an independent cost estimate (Step 7) | | | X | | |
| Conduct a sensitivity analysis (Step 8) | | X | | | |
| Conduct risk and uncertainty analysis (Step 9) | X | | | | |

Source: GAO analysis of Navy data.

[a]These 12 steps are outlined in additional detail in appendix II.

Note: The ratings used in this analysis are as follows: "Not met" means that the Navy did not provide evidence that satisfied the criterion; "Minimally met" means that the Navy provided evidence that satisfies a small portion of the criterion; "Partially met" means that the Navy provided evidence that satisfies about half of the criterion; "Mostly met" means that the Navy provided evidence that satisfies a large portion of the criterion; "Fully met" means that the Navy provided complete evidence that satisfies the entire criterion.

In developing the LCS total ownership cost baseline estimate, the Navy excluded certain key costs, used overly optimistic assumptions, inadequately documented its analyses, and did not perform analyses needed to identify levels of confidence and certainty in the cost estimate. As a result of these weaknesses, the LCS program total ownership cost baseline estimate is not reliable for decision making.

| Well-documented | Cost estimates are *well-documented* when they can be easily repeated or updated and can be traced to original sources through auditing. Rigorous documentation increases the credibility of an estimate and helps support an organization's decision making process. The documentation should explicitly identify the primary methods, calculations, results, rationales, assumptions, and sources of the data used to generate each cost element. All the steps involved in developing the estimate should be documented so that a cost analyst unfamiliar with the program can recreate the estimate with the same result. |

The level of documentation detailing the Navy's LCS procurement cost model is insufficient for someone unfamiliar with the program to easily recreate the estimate. The level of detail in the total ownership cost estimate does not reflect the full level of detail available for the LCS program, leaving managers with incomplete information on which to base program decisions. The Navy documented the LCS technical baseline in a July 2006 report—the Cost Analysis Requirements Description—describing program requirements, purpose, technical characteristics, development plan, acquisition strategy, operational plan, and risks. Navy estimators, however, did not rely upon this document in developing their estimate because the Cost Analysis Requirements Document is out of date and does not reflect current program approaches, seaframe configurations, and developmental challenges. Alternatively, Navy cost estimators relied on the current LCS build specification, ship weight reports, and known design changes to inform their understanding of the ships' technical characteristics. Since then, the Navy reports it has updated the LCS Cost Analysis Requirements Document in anticipation of the program's milestone B review.

In addition, the Navy divided the procurement content of its estimate into cost categories for plans, basic construction, change orders, government furnished equipment, other items, and outfitting and post-delivery. For most of these elements, Navy cost estimators relied on historical data and subject matter experts as sources of data. For the basic construction cost element, the Navy relied primarily on contractor cost proposals dating to May 2008 and November 2008. According to the Navy, the proposal data provided an accurate starting point for basic construction cost modeling because industry teams were instructed to base their proposals on their actual labor and material costs and/or estimates for lead ships. The Navy reports it traced the proposal data to November 2008 cost performance reports submitted by the contractors. The Navy then adjusted the proposals' estimates for labor hours and materials to reflect, for instance, known changes in pricing.

However, as we recently reported, earned value management systems in each of the LCS shipyards do not meet Defense Contract Management Agency requirements for validation.[16] Consequently, cost and schedule data reported by the prime contractors cannot be considered fully reliable.[17] The LCS cost estimate does not include any evidence that the Navy adjusted its basic construction cost estimates to account for this uncertainty.

Comprehensive

Estimates are *comprehensive* when they contain a level of detail that ensures that all pertinent costs are included and no costs are double-counted. It is important to ensure the completeness, consistency, and realism of the information contained in the cost estimate.

The Navy chartered a working group at the outset of the total ownership cost baseline estimate. Group members included representatives from the Naval Center for Cost Analysis; Naval Sea Systems Command's Ship Engineering and Logistics, Maintenance, and Industrial Operations directorates; Chief of Naval Operations' Surface Warfare directorate, Space and Naval Warfare Systems Command; Program Executive Office for Integrated Warfare Systems; and the RAND Corporation. This group developed a study plan for the LCS estimate that identified goals, set deadlines for completing key tasks, and outlined required resources. In addition, the group met biweekly and provided cross-checks and verification to the Navy cost team's estimating assumptions and results. Upon completion of the procurement cost analysis, Navy estimators briefed out results to the Commander, Naval Sea Systems Command, in June 2009.

Further, our analysis found that the Navy's LCS estimate identifies ground rules and assumptions from which the estimate is derived. However, it does not identify potential effects that changes to key assumptions—such as allocation of ships between contractors and changes to the technical baseline of the ship—could have upon the cost estimate. Also, the estimate does not identify how budget constraints could affect program plans or the potential effects that continued design refinements to the lead ships may have upon construction cost outcomes of follow-on ships.

---

[16]See GAO, *Defense Acquisitions: Assessments of Selected Weapons Programs*, GAO-10-388SP (Washington, D.C.: Mar. 30, 2010).

[17]Under the terms of the LCS 3 and LCS 4 contracts, the shipyards must achieve earned value management system certification within 28 months from the date of contract award.

In addition, the Navy did not complete evaluations of risk distributions for its cost estimating assumptions. Alternatively, cost estimators relied on discussions with ship designers, engineers, and technicians from the Navy and contractors to identify the scope of certain procurement cost elements. Navy cost analysts report they will complete evaluations of risk distributions for assumptions used in the LCS program life cycle cost estimate being developed for the milestone B review.

The Navy also relied upon industry-provided work breakdown structures for LCS 1, LCS 2, and LCS 3—that it then mapped to its own ship work breakdown structure—to identify the work tasks necessary to deliver LCS seaframes. Following completion of the total ownership cost estimate, the Navy received the LCS 4 work breakdown structure from industry, which it will use in developing the milestone B program life cycle cost estimate.

**Accurate**

Estimates are *accurate* when they are based on an assessment of the costs most likely to be incurred. Therefore, when costs change, best practices require that the estimate be updated to reflect changes in technical or program assumptions and new phases or milestones.

The total ownership cost baseline estimate discretely estimated LCS 3 and LCS 4 basic construction costs separate from the cost performance outcomes being realized on LCS 1 and LCS 2. This approach was used because, according to Navy cost estimators, distinguishing nonrecurring work on the first two ships from work that would recur on future ships—a necessary step for deriving follow-on ship costs—was too challenging an undertaking given the major design changes and construction rework that occurred on the lead ships. Further, LCS 3 and LCS 4 represented a slightly different technical baseline from LCS 1 and LCS 2, leading the Navy to judge it more appropriate to use the initial follow-on ships as the basis of estimates for future ships.

After developing their cost estimates for LCS 3 and LCS 4, the Navy estimators applied a 94 percent learning curve to the basic construction cost elements to arrive at construction estimates for future ships of each design. However, because Austal USA and Marinette Marine have only recently begun building complex Navy ships such as LCS, the historical data available to Navy cost analysts for deriving an accurate learning curve was constrained. As a result, the Navy developed its LCS learning curve based primarily on construction outcomes for alternative vessels and, in some cases, alternative shipyards including (1) 14 Coast Guard buoy tenders built at Marinette Marine, (2) 13 Cyclone-class coastal patrol ships built at Bollinger Shipyards, and (3) 10 patrol craft built at Austal facilities in Australia. According to the Navy, this data produced a widely varied range of potential LCS learning curves, which contributed to the Navy's decision to arrive at a curve for LCS that was toward the high end of the range (i.e., more conservative).

Navy cost estimators stated that their current work to develop a program life cycle cost estimate for LCS precludes future updates to the total ownership cost baseline. Additional cost estimates post-milestone B in the program will rely on the program life cycle cost estimate—and corresponding independent cost analysis—as starting points.

Credible

Estimates are *credible* when they have been cross-checked with an independent cost estimate and when a level of uncertainty associated with the estimate has been identified. An independent cost estimate provides the estimator with an unbiased test of the reasonableness of the estimate and reduces the cost risk associated with the project by demonstrating that alternative methods generate similar results.

Our analysis found that the total ownership cost baseline was not compared to an independent cost estimate. Comparing against an independent cost estimate provides an unbiased test of whether a program office or service-level cost estimate is reasonable. It is also used to identify risks related to budget shortfalls or excesses. According to Navy officials, the total ownership cost estimate was not tied to a major program milestone. As such, development of a corresponding independent cost estimate was not required. The Navy did, however, complete peer reviews, engage in discussions with program officials for classes of ships used as analogies in the estimate, and utilize expert opinion and work groups to cross-check for accuracy and omissions.

In addition, we found the Navy did not complete sensitivity or uncertainty analyses for LCS procurement cost elements. A sensitivity analysis provides a range of costs that span a best and worst case spread. In general, it is better for decision makers to know the range of potential costs that surround a point estimate and the reasons behind what drives that range than to just have a point estimate from which to make decisions. Sensitivity analysis can provide a clear picture of both the high and low costs that can be expected, with discrete reasons for what drives them. Uncertainty analysis provides the basis for adjusting estimates to reflect unknown facts and circumstances that could affect costs, and it identifies risk associated with the cost estimate. In order to inform decision makers about the likelihood of success, an uncertainty analysis should be performed for every cost estimate, as an organization varies the effects of multiple elements on costs, and as a result, can express a level of confidence in the point estimate. Further, because numerous risks can influence the estimate, they should be examined for their sources of uncertainty and potential effect, and they should be modeled to determine how they can affect the uncertainty of the cost estimate.

Navy cost estimators identified major procurement cost drivers in the program, but do not plan to complete sensitivity or uncertainty analyses for those drivers until shortly before milestone B. Navy officials cited the change to the program's acquisition strategy shortly following completion of the total ownership cost estimate as their rationale for deferring these analyses. Without sensitivity and uncertainty analyses, the Navy cannot fully account for the effect various risks can have on the overall total ownership cost estimate.

## Conclusions

The Navy is counting on LCS as its primary means to defeat sea mines, counter low-end surface threats, and prosecute enemy submarines in coastal waters. Further, LCS—with its planned 55 seaframes and 64 mission packages—represents a large component of the Navy's future surface fleet, making it key to the Navy's ability to maintain global presence.

However, the Navy's ability to deliver a capable, affordable LCS remains unproven. Staying within budget will require the Navy to achieve design stability before beginning construction of future ships. Moreover, LCS testing remains in its infancy, as the first operational testing event involving a seaframe and partial mission package has been deferred to fiscal year 2013. In addition, the Navy now expects individual mission package systems to remain in development through 2017. Until LCS capabilities are demonstrated through operational testing, the Navy cannot be certain that the seaframes and mission packages it is buying will be able to execute the missions that the fleet plans to assign to LCS vessels.

Further, decisions to deploy the lead ship early and complete previously unplanned maintenance periods have rendered current program test plans obsolete. Testing delays to key mission package elements—followed by prudent Navy decisions to defer new procurements of these systems—have created an imbalance between seaframe and mission package acquisition plans. For example, the Navy now plans to fund construction of 17 seaframes between fiscal years 2011 and 2015—whereas only 13 mission packages will be purchased during that time. This situation could be exacerbated should the Navy encounter additional difficulties resolving the substantial technical issues facing the mine countermeasures package.

In addition, although the Navy has emphasized the importance of affordability to successful outcomes in the LCS program, it continues to make key investment decisions without a clear understanding of program costs. For LCS, the Navy determined it appropriate to award contracts for four ships and conduct negotiations for three more without completing a detailed, programwide, independent cost estimate—a strategy that contributed to less than optimal results. High-quality cost estimates are well-documented, comprehensive, accurate, and credible—characteristics that are not fully embodied in the Navy's most recent cost estimate for LCS procurement. Shortfalls include the lack of sensitivity and uncertainty analyses and an independent review of the cost estimate. Continuing technical challenges and design changes on initial seaframes further complicate the Navy's efforts to identify future LCS costs. Until these issues are resolved, and a high-quality estimate of program costs is developed, the Navy cannot be confident that the LCS capabilities it promises can be attained at prices it is willing to pay.

## Recommendations for Executive Action

We recommend the Secretary of Defense take the following four actions:

To attain the level of knowledge needed to retire design risk and reduce construction disruptions, ensure changes identified in building and testing the first four ships are incorporated into the basic and functional design by the start of construction for future LCS seaframes.

To provide a meaningful framework for evaluating seaframe and mission package performance, update the LCS test and evaluation master plan to (1) account for any early deployments of seaframes and the significant developmental challenges faced by key mission package systems and (2) identify alternative approaches for completing seaframe and mission package initial operational test and evaluation.

To safeguard against excess quantities of ships and mission packages being purchased before their combined capabilities are demonstrated, update the LCS acquisition strategy to account for operational testing delays in the program and resequence planned purchases of ships and mission packages, as appropriate.

To provide a sound basis for future LCS investment decisions, ensure that future LCS cost estimates—including the program life cycle cost estimate currently planned for milestone B—are well-documented, comprehensive, accurate, and credible.

## Agency Comments and Our Evaluation

The Department of Defense agreed with all of our recommendations. However, in responding to our recommendation to ensure changes identified in building and testing the first four ships are incorporated into the basic and functional design by the start of construction for future LCS seaframes, the department stated that the program can use existing ship and class design services contracts to execute additional changes after contract award. As our prior work has shown, however, this practice has been tried before in Navy shipbuilding programs and has consistently contributed to ship deliveries that are over cost and behind schedule. As such, we would expect the Navy to set the bar extremely high for making design changes to ships that are already under construction.

The department's written comments can be found in appendix III of this report. The department also provided technical comments, which were incorporated into the report as appropriate.

We are sending copies of this report to interested congressional committees, the Secretary of Defense, and the Secretary of the Navy. The report is also available at no charge on the GAO Web site at http://www.gao.gov.

If you or your staff have any questions about this report, please contact me at (202) 512-4841 or martinb@gao.gov. Contact points for our Offices of Congressional Relations and Public Affairs may be found on the last page of this report. GAO staff who made major contributions to this report are listed in appendix IV.

Belva M. Martin
Acting Director
Acquisition and Sourcing Management

# Appendix I: Scope and Methodology

This report evaluates Littoral Combat Ship (LCS) planning and implementation efforts. Specifically, we (1) identified technical, design, and construction challenges to completing the first four seaframes within current cost and schedule estimates, (2) assessed the Navy's progress developing and fielding mission packages, and (3) evaluated the quality of recent Navy cost analyses for seaframes and their effect on program progress.

To identify challenges in completing the first four seaframes, we analyzed Department of Defense and contractor-generated documents that addressed technical challenges and cost and schedule performance for LCS seaframes including Navy test reports; Navy Supervisor of Shipbuilding reports; monthly contract performance reports; integrated baseline reviews; reports to Congress; sea trial reports for the first two ships; and construction progress briefings. To identify design changes and to understand the impact of these changes to the construction processes for seaframes, we reviewed LCS contracts and change orders; program schedules for LCS 3 and LCS 4; monthly contract performance reports; weekly Supervisor of Shipbuilding reports; and quarterly ship production progress conference briefings. We also reviewed information from contractors outlining process improvements and capital investments at each of the LCS shipyards aimed at increasing capability and capacity needed to support efficient construction of LCS seaframes. To further corroborate documentary evidence and gather additional information in support of our review, we conducted interviews with relevant Navy and industry officials responsible for managing the design and construction of LCS seaframes, such as the LCS Seaframe program office; Program Executive Office, Ships; Supervisor of Shipbuilding officials; Lockheed Martin and General Dynamics (LCS prime contractors); Marinette Marine and Austal USA (LCS shipbuilders); and MTU (LCS 2 and LCS 4 diesel engine vendor). We also held discussions with LCS technical authorities, testing agents, and requirements officers from Naval Sea Systems Command's Ship Engineering directorate; Director, Operational Test and Evaluation; American Bureau of Shipping; Commander, Navy Operational Test and Evaluation Force; Office of the Chief of Naval Operations' Surface Warfare directorate; and Naval Surface Warfare Center-Panama City division.

To assess the Navy's progress developing and fielding mission packages, we analyzed documents outlining LCS mission package development plans and performance including program schedules, test reports, and budget submissions. In order to evaluate the realism of mission package testing and procurement plans, we analyzed and compared mission package development schedules and test reports against LCS seaframe construction, delivery, and testing schedules. To further corroborate documentary evidence and gather additional information in support of our review, we held discussions with Navy program offices and Department of Defense agencies responsible for acquiring and testing key LCS mission systems including the Program Executive Office for Littoral and Mine Warfare; LCS Mission Modules program office; Unmanned Maritime Vehicles program office; and the Mine Warfare program office; Director, Operational Test and Evaluation; Commander, Operational Test and Evaluation Force, Navy. To gather additional information on remaining risks to mission package development and integration, we interviewed relevant Navy officials from the MH-60R Helicopter program office, MH-60S Helicopter program office, Navy and Marine Corps Tactical Multi-Mission Unmanned Aerial Systems program office, and Naval Surface Warfare Center-Panama City division.

To evaluate the quality of recent Navy cost analyses for LCS seaframes, we compared the Navy's total ownership cost baseline estimate for LCS procurement to best practices criteria as outlined in GAO's Cost Estimating and Assessment Guide. These criteria characterize high-quality cost estimates as those that are credible, comprehensive, well-documented, and accurate. To supplement our analysis and gain additional visibility into the Navy's process for developing its LCS estimate, we interviewed officials from Naval Sea Systems Command's Cost Engineering and Analysis directorate; LCS Seaframe program officials; and the Director, Cost Assessment and Program Evaluation.

We conducted this performance audit from July 2009 to August 2010 in accordance with generally accepted government auditing standards. Those standards require that we plan and perform the audit to obtain sufficient, appropriate evidence to provide a reasonable basis for our findings and conclusions based on our audit objectives. We believe that the evidence obtained provides a reasonable basis for our findings and conclusions based on our audit objectives.

# Appendix II: GAO Methodology Used to Perform Cost Estimating Analysis

To evaluate estimated Littoral Combat Ship (LCS) seaframe procurement costs as outlined in the Navy's total ownership cost baseline (August 2009), GAO employed criteria from our Cost Estimating and Assessment Guide.[1] In developing this guide, GAO cost experts identified 12 steps consistently applied by cost-estimating organizations throughout the federal government and industry and considered best practices for the development of reliable cost estimates. These 12 steps—and their related measures—are identified below.

Step One: Define the Estimate's Purpose
- Are the purpose and scope of the cost estimate defined and documented?
  a. Is the level of detail the estimate is conducted at consistent with the level of detail available for the program?
  b. Have all applicable costs been estimated, including life cycle costs?
  c. Is the scope of the estimate defined and documented?

Step Two: Develop the Estimating Plan
- Did the team develop a written study plan that:
  a. Determined the estimating team's composition and whether the team is from a centralized office;
  b. Identified which subject matter experts the team will rely on for information;
  c. Outlined the estimating approach (see Step four);
  d. Identified a master schedule for completing the estimate that provided adequate time to do the work.

Step Three: Define the Program Characteristics
- Is there a documented technical baseline description that is contained in a single document? If yes, does it include the following:
  a. What the program is supposed to do—requirements;
  b. How the program will fulfill its mission—purpose;
  c. What it will look like—technical characteristics;
  d. Where and how the program will be built—development plan;
  e. How the program will be acquired—acquisition strategy;
  f. How the program will operate—operational plan;
  g. Which characteristics affect cost the most—risk.

---

[1] See GAO, *GAO Cost Estimating and Assessment Guide: Best Practices for Developing and Managing Capital Program Costs*, GAO-09-3SP (Washington, D.C.: Mar. 2009).

Step Four: Determine the Estimating Structure
- Is there a defined work breakdown structure (WBS) and/or cost element structure?
  a. Is the WBS product-oriented, traceable to the statement of work, and at an appropriate level of detail to ensure that cost elements are neither omitted nor double-counted?
  b. Is the WBS standardized so that cost data can be collected and used for estimating future programs?
  c. Does the cost estimate WBS match the schedule and earned value management (EVM) WBS?
  d. Is the WBS updated as the program becomes better defined and to reflect changes as they occur?
  e. Is there a WBS dictionary that defines what is included in each element and how it relates to others in the hierarchy?

Step Five: Identify Ground Rules and Assumptions
- Are there defined ground rules and assumptions that document the rationale and any historical data to back up any claims?
  a. Have risks associated with any assumptions been identified and traced to specific WBS elements?
  b. Have budget constraints, as well as the effect of delaying program content, been defined?
  c. Have inflation indices and their source been identified?
  d. If the program depends on a participating agency or agency's equipment have the effects of these assumptions not holding been identified?
  e. Have items excluded from the estimate been documented and explained?
  f. If technology maturity has been assumed, does the estimate address the effect of the assumption's failure on cost and schedule?
  g. Did cost estimators meet with technical staff to determine risk distributions for all assumptions so they could use this information for sensitivity and uncertainty analysis?

Step Six: Obtain the Data
- Was the data gathered from valid historical actual cost, schedule, and program and technical sources?
  a. Do the data apply to the program being estimated and have they been analyzed for cost drivers?
  b. Have the data been collected from primary sources and adequately documented as to the source, content, time, units, an assessment of the accuracy of the data and reliability, and any circumstances affecting the data?

c. Are data continually collected and stored for future use?
d. Did analysts meet with the data sources to better understand the program and ask them about the data?
e. Were the data reviewed and benchmarked against historical data for reasonableness?
f. Were the data analyzed using scatterplots and descriptive statistics and were they normalized to account for cost, sizing units, etc. so they are consistent for comparisons?

Step Seven: Develop the Point Estimate and Compare It to an Independent Cost Estimate
- Did the cost estimator consider various cost estimating methods like analogy, engineering build up, parametric, extrapolating from actual costs, and expert opinion (if none of the other methods can be used)?
  a. If the parametric method was used as the estimating method, were the cost estimating relationships (CER) statistics examined to determine its quality?
  b. Were learning curves used if there was much manual labor associated with production and were production rate and breaks in production considered?
  c. Was the point estimate developed by aggregating the WBS cost estimates by one of the cost estimating methods?
  d. Were results checked for accuracy, double-counting, and omissions and were validated with cross checks and independent cost estimates?
  e. If software is a major component of the cost estimate were software estimating best practices from Chapter 12 of the Guide addressed?

Step Eight: Conduct a Sensitivity Analysis
- Did the cost estimate include a sensitivity analysis that, using a range of possible costs, identified the effects of changing key cost driver assumptions or factors? Were the following steps taken:
  a. Key cost drivers were identified;
  b. Cost elements representing the highest percentage of cost were determined and their parameters and assumptions were examined;
  c. The total cost was reestimated by varying each parameter between its minimum and maximum range;
  d. Results were documented and the reestimate repeated for each parameter that was a key cost driver;
  e. Outcomes were evaluated for parameters most sensitive to change.

Step Nine: Conduct Risk and Uncertainty Analysis
- Was a risk and uncertainty analysis conducted that quantified the imperfectly understood risks and identified the effects of changing key cost driver assumptions and factors? Were the following steps performed:
  a. A probability distribution was modeled for each cost element's uncertainty based on data availability, reliability, and variability;
  b. The correlation (i.e., relationship) between cost elements was accounted for to capture risk;
  c. A Monte Carlo simulation model was used to develop a distribution of total possible costs and an S curve showing alternative cost estimate probabilities;
  d. The probability associated with the point estimate was identified.
  e. Contingency reserves were recommended for achieving the desired confidence level;
  f. The risk-adjusted cost estimate was allocated, phased, and converted to then year dollars for budgeting, and high-risk elements were identified to mitigate risks;
  g. A risk management plan was implemented jointly with the contractor to identify and analyze risk, plan for risk mitigation, and continually track risk.

Step Ten: Document the Estimate
- Did the documentation describe the cost estimating process, data sources, and methods step by step so that a cost analyst unfamiliar with the program could understand what was done and replicate it?
  a. Are supporting data adequate for easily updating the estimate to reflect actual costs or program changes and using them for future estimates?
  b. Did the documentation describe the estimate with narrative and cost tables and did it contain an executive summary, introduction, and descriptions of methods, with data broken out by WBS cost elements, sensitivity analysis, risk and uncertainty analysis, management approval, and updates that reflect actual costs and changes?
  c. Did the detail address best practices and the 12 steps of high-quality estimates?
  d. Was the documentation mathematically sensible and logical?
  e. Did it discuss contingency reserves and how they were derived from risk and uncertainty analysis?
  f. Did the documentation include access to an electronic copy of the cost model and are both the documentation and the cost model stored so that authorized personnel can easily find and use them for other cost estimates?

Step Eleven: Present the Estimate to Management for Approval
- Was there a briefing to management that included a clear explanation of the cost estimate so as to convey its level of competence?
  a. Did the briefing illustrate the largest cost drivers by presenting them logically with backup charts for responding to more probing questions?
  b. Did the briefing include an overview of the program's technical foundation and objectives, the life cycle cost estimate in time-phased constant year dollars, a discussion of ground rules and assumptions, the method and process for each WBS cost element estimate including data sources, the results of sensitivity and risk/uncertainty analysis along with a confidence interval, the comparison of the point estimate to an independent cost estimate with a discussion of any differences and whether the point estimate is reasonable, an affordability analysis based on funding and contingency reserves, a discussion of any concerns or challenges, conclusions, and recommendations for approval?
  c. Was any feedback from the briefing including management's acceptance of the estimate acted on and recorded in the cost estimate documentation?

Step Twelve: Update the Estimate to Reflect Actual Costs and Changes
- Is there a process for the estimating team to update the estimate with actual costs as it becomes available?
  a. Was the estimate updated to reflect changes in technical or program assumptions and was there a discussion how these changes affected the cost estimate?
  b. Did the cost estimates get replaced with actual costs? Were the actual costs from an EVM system?
  c. Did the estimate discuss lessons learned for elements whose actual costs or schedules differed from the estimate?

# Appendix III: Comments from the Department of Defense

OFFICE OF THE UNDER SECRETARY OF DEFENSE
3000 DEFENSE PENTAGON
WASHINGTON, DC 20301-3000

ACQUISITION
TECHNOLOGY
AND LOGISTICS

AUG 24 2010

Ms. Belva M. Martin
Acting Director, Acquisition and Sourcing Management
U.S. Government Accountability Office
441 G Street NW
Washington, DC 20548

Dear Ms. Martin:

This is the Department of Defense (DoD) response to the GAO draft report 10-523 "DEFENSE ACQUISITIONS: Navy's Ability to Overcome Challenges Facing the Littoral Combat Ship Will Determine Eventual Capabilities" dated June 30, 2010, (GAO Code 120834). Detailed comments on the report recommendations are enclosed.

The Department appreciates the opportunity to comment on the draft report. For further questions concerning this report, please contact Darlene Costello, Deputy Director, Naval Warfare, 703-697-2205.

Sincerely,

David G. Ahern
Director
Portfolio Systems Acquisition

Enclosure:
As stated

GAO DRAFT REPORT DATED JUNE 30, 2010
GAO-10-523 (GAO CODE 120834)

"DEFENSE ACQUISITIONS: NAVY'S ABILITY TO OVERCOME
CHALLENGES FACING THE LITTORAL COMBAT SHIP WILL
DETERMINE EVENTUAL CAPABILITIES"

DEPARTMENT OF DEFENSE COMMENTS
TO THE GAO RECOMMENDATIONS

**RECOMMENDATION 1:** The GAO recommends that the Secretary of Defense
ensure changes identified in building and testing the first four ships are
incorporated into the basic and functional design by the start of construction for
future Littoral Combat Ship (LCS) seaframes. (See page 36/GAO Draft Report.)

**DoD RESPONSE:** Concur. The Navy has been operating both LCS designs and
collecting design performance data. The Navy will continue to actively test and
report on ship performance as the first two follow ships are delivered and operated
in the Fleet so that the design performance of future ships is enhanced using
empirical data. The Fiscal Year (FY) 2010 solicitation uses the technical baseline
of the FY 2009 ships, plus known government directed changes, to establish a
stable baseline for the near term awards. The program can use existing ship and
class design services contracts to execute additional changes through the program's
formal configuration management process after contract award. The Department
also will review post-delivery test sequencing to ensure testing results can inform
future purchases as early as practicable.

**RECOMMENDATION 2:** The GAO recommends that the Secretary of Defense
update the LCS test and evaluation master plan to (1) account for any early
deployments of seaframes and the significant developmental challenges faced by
key mission package systems and (2) identify alternative approaches for
completing seaframe and mission package initial operational test and evaluation.
(See page 36/GAO Draft Report.)

**DoD RESPONSE:** Concur. The Navy will update the LCS Test and Evaluation
Master Plan (TEMP) after the down-select and the Milestone B decision to reflect
the changes in the program. The updated TEMP will reflect the new LCS
acquisition strategy approved in January 2010. In addition, it will address the test
and evaluation strategy of Developmental Testing (DT) and Operational Testing
(OT) for one mission package on each of the lead ships. This will support
achievement of initial operational capability as defined in the Flight 0 Capability

2

Development Document. The remaining LCS mission packages are scheduled for
DT/OT on LCS 3, 4, and 5.

**RECOMMENDATION 3**: The GAO recommends that the Secretary of Defense
update the LCS acquisition strategy to account for operational testing delays in the
program and resequence planned purchases of ships and mission packages, as
appropriate. (See page 36/GAO Draft Report.)

**DoD RESPONSE**: Concur. The Navy understands that alignment of the seaframe
and mission modules production milestones must occur to meet requirements for
initial operational test and evaluation and further production decisions. An
updated schedule is under development. The Navy will continue to deliver LCS
seaframes as currently planned and to field mission module capability in a spiral
fashion as new systems are matured, tested, and accepted by the Fleet. In addition,
the Department will review post-delivery test sequencing to ensure testing results
can inform future purchases as early as practicable.

**RECOMMENDATION 4**: The GAO recommends that the Secretary of Defense
ensure that future LCS cost estimates-including the program life cycle cost
estimate currently planned for milestone B- are well-documented, comprehensive,
accurate, and credible. (See page 37/GAO Draft Report.)

**DoD RESPONSE**: Concur. However, the cost analyses referenced in the draft
GAO report were used to support investigatory trade studies and were not intended
as a budget quality estimate, nor intended to inform contract negotiations. The
estimate was developed to establish a cost baseline for the overall LCS program life
cycle to be used as a point of departure for conducting cost trade-off analyses. In
preparation for the program's Milestone B review, the Navy produced a complete
cost estimate for the entire system lifecycle. This estimate fully incorporated cost
estimating best practices, including cost risk, cost driver sensitivity analyses, and a
fully documented Independent Cost Estimate (ICE), in accordance with NAVSEA
05C's 12-Step Cost Estimating Process. Additionally, NAVSEA 05C held
discussions with OSD's Cost Assessment and Program Evaluation (CAPE) group.
CAPE also prepared an ICE for the LCS program to support the Milestone B
review.

# Appendix IV: GAO Contact and Staff Acknowledgments

| | |
|---|---|
| **GAO Contact** | Belva M. Martin, (202) 512-4841 or martinb@gao.gov |
| **Acknowledgments** | In addition to the contact named above, key contributors to this report were Karen Zuckerstein, Assistant Director; Greg Campbell; Christopher R. Durbin; Kristine Hassinger; Jeremy Hawk; Jasmin Jahanshahi; Julia P. Jebo; Jason Kelly; and Amber N. Keyser. |

| | |
|---|---|
| **GAO's Mission** | The Government Accountability Office, the audit, evaluation, and investigative arm of Congress, exists to support Congress in meeting its constitutional responsibilities and to help improve the performance and accountability of the federal government for the American people. GAO examines the use of public funds; evaluates federal programs and policies; and provides analyses, recommendations, and other assistance to help Congress make informed oversight, policy, and funding decisions. GAO's commitment to good government is reflected in its core values of accountability, integrity, and reliability. |
| **Obtaining Copies of GAO Reports and Testimony** | The fastest and easiest way to obtain copies of GAO documents at no cost is through GAO's Web site (www.gao.gov). Each weekday afternoon, GAO posts on its Web site newly released reports, testimony, and correspondence. To have GAO e-mail you a list of newly posted products, go to www.gao.gov and select "E-mail Updates." |
| **Order by Phone** | The price of each GAO publication reflects GAO's actual cost of production and distribution and depends on the number of pages in the publication and whether the publication is printed in color or black and white. Pricing and ordering information is posted on GAO's Web site, http://www.gao.gov/ordering.htm.<br><br>Place orders by calling (202) 512-6000, toll free (866) 801-7077, or TDD (202) 512-2537.<br><br>Orders may be paid for using American Express, Discover Card, MasterCard, Visa, check, or money order. Call for additional information. |
| **To Report Fraud, Waste, and Abuse in Federal Programs** | Contact:<br><br>Web site: www.gao.gov/fraudnet/fraudnet.htm<br>E-mail: fraudnet@gao.gov<br>Automated answering system: (800) 424-5454 or (202) 512-7470 |
| **Congressional Relations** | Ralph Dawn, Managing Director, dawnr@gao.gov, (202) 512-4400<br>U.S. Government Accountability Office, 441 G Street NW, Room 7125<br>Washington, DC 20548 |
| **Public Affairs** | Chuck Young, Managing Director, youngc1@gao.gov, (202) 512-4800<br>U.S. Government Accountability Office, 441 G Street NW, Room 7149<br>Washington, DC 20548 |

United States Government Accountability Office

# GAO

Report to the Subcommittee on Readiness and the Subcommittee on Seapower and Expeditionary Forces, Committee on Armed Services, House o Representatives

February 2010

# LITTORAL COMBAT SHIP

# Actions Needed to Improve Operating Cost Estimates and Mitigate Risks in Implementing New Concepts

GAO

Accountability ★ Integrity ★ Reliability

GAO-10-257

February 2010

# LITTORAL COMBAT SHIP

## Actions Needed to Improve Operating Cost Estimates and Mitigate Risks in Implementing New Concepts

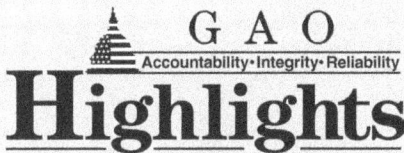

## GAO
Accountability · Integrity · Reliability

# Highlights

Highlights of GAO-10-257, a report to the Subcommittee on Readiness and the Subcommittee on Seapower and Expeditionary Forces, Committee on Armed Services, House of Representatives

## Why GAO Did This Study

The Navy plans to spend about $28 billion to buy 55 Littoral Combat Ships (LCS) and at least 64 interchangeable mission packages to perform one of three missions—mine countermeasures, antisubmarine warfare, and surface warfare—in waters close to shore. The Navy has been developing two different LCS seaframes and plans to select one for production in 2010. Due to the small 78-person crew size—40 core crew, 23 for aviation detachment, and typically 15 for mission packages—the Navy is developing new concepts for personnel, training, and maintenance. GAO was asked to assess the extent to which DOD has (1) estimated LCS long-term operating and support costs and (2) developed plans to operate and support LCS. To do so, GAO compared Navy cost estimates to DOD guidance and GAO best practices; and analyzed Navy plans to implement its concepts for personnel, training, and maintenance and the extent these plans included assessments of program risk.

## What GAO Recommends

GAO recommends, among other things, that DOD develop an estimate of the long-term operating and support costs which fully reflects best practices and use this estimate in making key program decisions, and conduct and consider the results of a risk assessment before committing to buy LCS ships in the future. DOD generally agreed with the recommendations.

View GAO-10-257 or key components. For more information, contact John Pendleton at (404) 679-1816 or pendletonj@gao.gov.

## What GAO Found

The Navy estimated operating and support costs for LCS seaframes and mission packages in 2009, but the estimates do not fully reflect DOD and GAO best practices for cost estimating and may change due to program uncertainties. GAO's analysis of the Navy's 2009 estimates showed that the operating and support costs for seaframes and mission packages could total $84 billion (in constant fiscal year 2009 dollars) through about 2050. However, the Navy did not follow some best practices for developing an estimate such as (1) analyzing the likelihood that the costs could be greater than estimated, (2) fully assessing how the estimate may change as key assumptions change, and (3) requesting an independent estimate and comparing it with the program estimate. The estimates may also be affected by program uncertainties, such as potential changes to force structure that could alter the number of ships and mission packages required. The costs to operate and support a weapon system can total 70 percent of a system's costs, and the lack of an estimate that fully reflects best practices could limit decision makers' ability to identify the resources that will be needed over the long term to support the planned investment in LCS force structure. With a decision pending in 2010 on which seaframe to buy for the remainder of the program, decision makers could lack critical information to assess the full costs of the alternatives.

The Navy has made progress in developing operational concepts for LCS, but faces risks in implementing its new concepts for personnel, training, and maintenance that are necessitated by the small crew size. Specifically, the Navy faces risks in its ability to identify and assign personnel given the time needed to achieve the extensive training required. GAO's analysis of a sample of LCS positions showed an average of 484 days of training is required before reporting to a crew, significantly more than for comparable positions on other surface ships. Moreover, the Navy's maintenance concept relies heavily on distance support, with little maintenance performed on ship. The Navy acknowledges that there are risks in implementing its new concepts and has established groups to address how to implement them. However, these groups have not performed a risk assessment as described in the 2008 National Defense Strategy. The Strategy describes the need to assess and mitigate risks to executing future missions and managing personnel, training, and maintenance. If the Navy cannot implement its concepts as envisioned, it may face operational limitations, have to reengineer its operational concepts, or have to alter the ship design. Many of the concepts will remain unproven until 2013 or later, when the Navy will have committed to building almost half the class. Having a thorough risk assessment of the new operational concepts would provide decision makers with information to link the effectiveness of these new concepts with decisions on program investment, including the pace of procurement.

_____ United States Government Accountability Office

# Contents

**GAO**

Accountability * Integrity * Reliability

United States Government Accountability Office
Washington, DC 20548

February 2, 2010

The Honorable Solomon Ortiz
Chairman
The Honorable J. Randy Forbes
Ranking Member
Subcommittee on Readiness
Committee on Armed Services
House of Representatives

The Honorable Gene Taylor
Chairman
The Honorable W. Todd Akin
Ranking Member
Subcommittee on Seapower
   and Expeditionary Forces
Committee on Armed Services
House of Representatives

With the ability to maneuver in shallow waters inaccessible to other surface combatants, the Littoral Combat Ship (LCS) is a new class of warship meant to facilitate U.S. Navy access to and operations in the littorals, which are waters close to shore. The Navy plans a major investment in the LCS program, which could cost $28 billion to buy 55 ships and related, interchangeable combat capability. The planned 55 ships would comprise about 38 percent of the Navy's surface combatants [1] in a 313-ship Navy. The Navy is using two contractors to build differently designed ships, called seaframes. As of October 2009, the Navy had procured two ships (one of each design) and contracted for two more (one of each design). The Navy plans to select one design in fiscal year 2010. To increase flexibility, the LCS's combat capability will be contained in removable, interchangeable mission packages [2] to perform one of three primary missions—mine countermeasures, antisubmarine warfare, and

---

[1] Surface combatant is a collective term including destroyers, cruisers, frigates, and the Littoral Combat Ship.

[2] Each mission package consists of mission systems (such as weapons and sensors), support equipment, crewmembers, and an aviation detachment of manned helicopters and unmanned aerial vehicles.

GAO-10-257 Littoral Combat Ship

surface warfare[3] concentrating on countering small surface boat attacks. Each LCS ship will carry only one package at any given time. Further, since the cost to operate and support a weapon system traditionally accounts for over 70 percent of the total cost over a system's lifetime, the resources needed to operate and support the LCS seaframes and mission packages could be significant over time.

In 2005, the Navy began developing an LCS concept of operations which broadly describes these unique approaches to personnel, training, and maintenance and outlines the responsibilities of shore organizations to support LCS operations. LCS differs from other Navy ships in three key areas—personnel, training, and maintenance. First, a deployed LCS will have a total of 78 personnel on board comprised of 40 core crewmembers to operate the ship, 15 to operate the mission packages, and 23 for the aviation detachment. A crew of this size is significantly less than on other surface combatants—about 172 for a frigate and about 254 for a destroyer. In order to increase operational availability, the Navy intends to rotate crews about every 4 months to enable each LCS to deploy continuously for up to 18 months. Second, due to the decision to operate the ship with 40 sailors, training will be tailored to each position and include training in skills outside the crewmember's specialty. For example, a fire fighter specialist is also required to be trained in an engineering skill area. Third, the crew will perform minimal maintenance on board the ship and will rely extensively on support from organizations ashore to perform maintenance and administrative functions such as maintaining supply and pay records.

Considering the Navy's unique LCS concept of operations, you asked us to review the Navy's efforts to estimate the program's operating and support costs and to plan for how the ship will be operated and supported considering the small crew size. For this review, we assessed the extent to which the Navy has (1) estimated the long-term operating and support costs for LCS seaframes and mission packages; and (2) developed and implemented plans to operate and support the LCS particularly in the areas of personnel, training, and maintenance.

To assess the extent to which the Navy estimated the long-term operating and support costs for LCS seaframes and mission packages, we reviewed documentation of seaframe and mission package cost estimates prepared

---

[3] The surface warfare package includes a maritime security module which could be employed by itself without the other components of the surface warfare package.

by the Naval Sea Systems Command. We compared the estimates to cost estimating best practices identified by the Office of the Secretary of Defense's Office of the Director of Cost Assessment and Program Evaluation (CAPE)[4] as well as in our *GAO Cost Estimating and Assessment Guide.*[5] To assess the extent to which the Navy analyzed the force structure requirements underlying the planned purchase quantities of LCS seaframes and mission packages, we reviewed force structure analysis documents and met with officials of the Assessments and Surface Warfare divisions of the Office of the Chief of Naval Operations. Although, as discussed later in this report, the Navy's estimates did not fully reflect best practices, they were based on a cost estimating process we deemed sufficient for reporting the results of our analysis of the Navy's operating and support cost estimates.

To assess the extent to which the Navy has developed and implemented plans to operate and support LCS, particularly in the areas of personnel, training, and maintenance, we reviewed and analyzed the Department of Defense (DOD) and Navy guidance and reviewed key studies and planning documents including the *LCS Wholeness Concept of Operations.*[6] We also reviewed prior GAO products and DOD guidance on risk management to assess the extent that Navy plans included assessments of program risk. To estimate long term LCS personnel requirements, we analyzed Navy documentation and validated the results with appropriate Navy officials. To compare LCS training days to training days for other surface ships, we first identified a non-probability sample of LCS positions from both seaframes based on criteria for which positions required a wide variety of training or, based on Navy information, might be hard to fill. Then we compared the required training days for these LCS positions with comparable positions on two other surface ships. We validated the data

---

[4] This office was formerly known as the Cost Analysis Improvement Group. The functions of that office were transferred to the Office of the Director of Cost Assessment and Program Evaluation by the Weapon Systems Acquisition Reform Act of 2009, Pub. L. No. 111-23 § 101 (2009). See the note at 10 U.S.C. § 139c. Office of the Secretary of Defense, Cost Analysis Improvement Group, *Operating and Support Cost Estimating Guide* (Arlington, Va., October 2007), Office of the Secretary of Defense, Cost Analysis Improvement Group, *Operating and Support Cost Estimating Guide* (Arlington, Va., May 1, 1992).

[5] GAO, *GAO Cost Estimating and Assessment Guide*, GAO-09-3SP (Washington, D.C.: March 2009).

[6] U.S. Fleet Forces Command, *Littoral Combat Ship Platform Wholeness Concept of Operations (Revision C)* (Sept. 24, 2009).

and results with appropriate Navy officials. On the basis of the work described above, we concluded that the data had no limitations and were sufficiently reliable for our purposes.

We conducted this performance audit from October 2008 to February 2010 in accordance with generally accepted government auditing standards. Those standards require that we plan and perform the audit to obtain sufficient, appropriate evidence to provide a reasonable basis for our findings and conclusions based on our audit objectives. We believe that the evidence obtained provides a reasonable basis for our findings and conclusions based on our audit objectives.

## Results in Brief

The Navy has estimated operating and support costs for LCS seaframes and mission packages, but the estimates do not fully reflect DOD and GAO best practices for cost estimating and may change due to program uncertainties. Our analysis of the Navy's 2009 estimates showed that the operating and support costs for the planned seaframes and mission packages could total $84.8 billion through about 2050.[7] However, although the Navy demonstrated some aspects of a high-quality cost-estimating process, we found that it did not follow some key cost-estimating best practices, including analyzing the likelihood that the costs could be greater than estimated, fully assessing how the estimate may change as key assumptions change, and requesting an independent estimate and comparing it to the program estimate. Typically, an independent estimate is prepared for a program's second milestone decision point, referred to as Milestone B,[8] when lead and initial follow-on ships are normally approved. However, the Navy has not yet passed this milestone decision point or included operating and support costs in its annual reports to Congress on LCS. In addition, the Navy's LCS operating and support cost estimates may change due to program uncertainties such as changes to the operational concepts, or completing and updating analyses of the required quantities of seaframes and mission packages. Specifically, Navy officials said that they had not analyzed the quantities required for one of the mission

---

[7] All dollar figures in this report are in constant fiscal year 2009 dollars. The Navy assumes that each LCS seaframe will have a service life of about 25 years. The Navy can expect to pay operating and support costs until the last LCS is retired—the timing of which could vary depending on when the last seaframe enters service.

[8] Department of Defense Instruction 5000.02. *Operation of the Defense Acquisition System*, Enclosure 2, Figure 1 (Dec. 8, 2008).

packages or updated the quantities required for another package after the contents changed. Also, any changes in key assumptions, such as homeporting or crewing, could change the seaframe quantities required, which in turn could affect estimates of the program's total operating and support costs. Considering that operating and support costs are typically about 70 percent of a program's total costs, the information available to decision makers is limited without an estimate of the long-term operating and support costs that fully reflects best practices and without reporting these costs to DOD and Congress. However, such a complete cost estimate could enhance decision makers' ability to make fully informed trade-off and investment decisions. For example, decision makers could benefit from an analysis of the long-term operating and support costs of each seaframe before deciding which one to buy for the remainder of the program. Also, decision makers could benefit from an analysis of the costs of options for what to do with the two ships of the design that is not selected. In addition, the absence of an independent cost estimate and analyses of how operating and support costs could increase over time limits the ability of decision makers to assess the affordability of LCS within the broader portfolio of Navy and DOD programs and to identify the resources that will be needed over the long term to support the planned investment in the LCS force structure. Further, information available to decision makers could be enhanced by basing estimates of the program's total operating and support costs on complete and current analyses of seaframe and mission package quantities. To enhance decision making, we are recommending that DOD develop, and annually update, an estimate of the LCS program's long-term operating and support costs that fully reflects best practices and use this estimate to make key program decisions such as which seaframe to buy, to annually report the estimated costs to Congress, and to update force structure analyses. DOD agreed to annually report the estimated costs to Congress and to update force structure analyses. Although DOD stated that the Navy will prepare updated costs estimates, one for each seaframe, DOD stated that, since the Navy has not released the solicitation for the fiscal year 2010-2014 purchase of LCS, it is premature to discuss the criteria for selecting one seaframe design. Since operating and support costs constitute over 70 percent of a system's life-cycle costs, we continue to believe that decision makers should consider long-term operating and support costs when deciding which of the two seaframes to buy for the remainder of the program.

The Navy has made progress, but faces risks in planning to operate and support LCS, particularly in implementing its new concepts for personnel, training, and maintenance. Although the Navy is conducting studies to determine personnel requirements for LCS, it has not fully identified these requirements for the ship and shore support and faces risks in its ability to identify and assign personnel over the long term. The Navy also faces risks in implementing its concept to achieve the extensive LCS training required as well as implementing its maintenance concept. The Navy acknowledges that there are risks in implementing its new LCS operational concepts and has established some groups that focus on the details of how to implement the concepts. However, these groups have not performed a risk assessment as outlined in the 2008 *National Defense Strategy*.[9] The Strategy describes the need to assess and mitigate risk including risks relating to the department's capacity to execute future missions and manage personnel, training, and maintenance. If the Navy cannot implement its concepts as envisioned, the Navy may face operational limitations, may have to reengineer its operational concepts, or may have to alter the ship design after committing to building almost half the class. In contrast, having a thorough risk assessment of the new operational approaches to personnel, training, and maintenance would provide decision makers with information to link the effectiveness of these new operational concepts with decisions on program investment, specifically the pace of procurement. To improve decision making, we are recommending that the Navy conduct a risk assessment and consider the results before committing to buy LCS ships in order to link procurement with evidence that the Navy is progressing in its ability to implement its new operational concepts. DOD partially agreed with our recommendation stating that it agrees such risk assessments are appropriate and should be conducted. However, DOD also stated that the acquisition strategy has changed from annual procurements to buying LCS ships in fiscal years 2010, 2012, and 2015 and proposed reviewing the risk assessments at these intervals. We believe that DOD's proposal meets the intent of our recommendation but emphasize that, given the new acquisition approach, it is even more important to conduct the risk assessment and consider the results before making procurement decisions since the department will be committing to several ships in each of the years cited and there will be a gap of several years between each procurement decision. A more detailed discussion of DOD's comments and our responses to these comments follow the Recommendations for Executive Action section of this report.

---

[9] Department of Defense, *National Defense Strategy* (June 2008).

# Background

## Program Description

The LCS is being developed to assure access to the littorals that are threatened from mines, submarines, and surface forces. The LCS program consists of two distinct parts, the ship itself—called a seaframe—and the mission package it carries and deploys to provide combat capability. In addition to the capabilities associated with the mission packages, the LCS may be expected to perform inherent capabilities such as homeland defense, search and rescue, or humanitarian assistance. The Navy is using two contractors to build differently designed seaframes. As of December 2009, the Navy had bought two ships of each design, of which the first ship of each design has been delivered. The Navy plans to select one design in fiscal year 2010 for the remainder of the class. Figure 1 shows each of the seaframes.

**Figure 1: Two Littoral Combat Ship Seaframes**

USS Freedom (LCS 1)

USS Independence (LCS 2)

Source: The Navy.

By the end of fiscal year 2015, the Navy plans to have bought up to 23 of the planned 55 ships. These ships represent a significant investment in the LCS program not only for procurement but also for long-term operating and support costs. A weapon system's life-cycle costs include research and development, procurement, military construction, operations and support,[10] and disposal. Since operating and support costs are historically the largest portion (over 70 percent) of a weapon system's lifetime costs, these costs were the focus of our analysis of the Navy's LCS cost estimates.

The LCS seaframe's combat capability will be provided by one of three interchangeable mission packages. Each mission package will also include an aviation detachment of manned helicopters and unmanned aerial vehicles. Currently the Navy plans to buy 64 mission packages for three mission areas—24 for mine countermeasures, 16 for antisubmarine warfare, and 24 for surface warfare. The surface warfare mission package also includes a module for maritime security, primarily to provide capability for boarding other ships. The Navy has not yet decided how many maritime security modules it will buy.[11] Table 1 below describes the basic mission of each mission package.

**Table 1: Description and Quantity of LCS Mission Packages**

| Mission package | Planned quantity | Package mission |
| --- | --- | --- |
| Mine Countermeasures | 24 | Detect and neutralize mines |
| Anti-submarine Warfare | 16 | Detect submarines and protect forces in transit |
| Surface Warfare | 24 | Detect, track and engage small boat threats |

Source: GAO analysis of Navy information.

The Navy plans to incrementally add capability to these packages over time, and, according to Navy officials, may develop additional mission packages as needed.

---

[10] Operating and support costs are the resources required to operate and support a weapon system and include maintenance of equipment/infrastructure, operations of forces, training and readiness, base operations, personnel, and logistics.

[11] Although the Navy reported to congress that its objective is to buy 55 maritime security modules, Navy officials stated that future analysis could result in the Navy actually buying fewer of these modules. Naval Sea Systems Command, Program Executive Officer for Littoral and Mine Warfare, *Report to Congress: Littoral Combat Ship Mission Packages*, (Washington, D.C.: May 2009).

GAO-10-257 Littoral Combat Ship

## Rotational Crewing for LCS

The Navy intends to rotationally crew LCS to enable each seaframe to remain deployed for up to 18 months. The Navy plans to have four crews for every three ships with one of the three ships being deployed at any one time. Since the LCS crew is smaller than the crews on many other surface ships, the Navy plans to rotate the core crews after about 4 months (117 days) to help reduce crew fatigue. During the 2-week turnover period, the crews and contractors will perform preventive and corrective maintenance and resupply the ship. Navy officials stated that one benefit to having more crews than ships is that the Navy is able to quickly replace a deployed crew member who becomes sick or injured with a comparably trained sailor. The primary benefit of rotational crewing will be the ability to maintain a deployed seaframe for up to 18 months continuously while allowing the crews to relieve one another and return to their homeport without undue hardship. The seaframes would be rotated every 18 months with a 30-day overlap period.

## Navy Organizations Are Intended to Monitor Development of and Resolve Implementation Issues with the LCS Concept of Operations

Given the challenges in implementing new concepts for personnel, training, and maintenance, the Navy established several groups to identify and resolve challenges it faces. These groups include an Oversight Board, a Council of Captains, and two cross-functional teams. These groups are comprised of members from across the Navy and, collectively, these groups identify and review issues and barriers to implementing the LCS concepts articulated in the *Wholeness Concept of Operations* and work together to jointly develop solutions.

- Oversight Board: The board is chaired by the Commander Naval Surface Forces and the membership includes executive-level representatives from program executive offices, program sponsors, and other major stakeholders from across the Navy. The board is supported by a senior executive-level working group called the Council of Captains. The board meets quarterly to consider key issues that require high-level decisions. For example, issues discussed this past year included the need to support development of distance support capabilities, and the need to fund aviation crews for the detachments that will support LCS operations.
- Cross functional teams: Two cross functional teams support the Oversight Board—one focused on manning and training issues and the other focused on maintenance and logistics issues. For example, the manning and training team is working on issues such as upgrading the shore-based trainers and the need to determine the appropriate level of shore support personnel. Also, the maintenance and logistics team has raised issues, such as remotely monitoring the condition of ship systems and funding for distance support development.

In addition, the LCS Program Office, an office within the Naval Sea Systems Command, chairs the Risk Management Board. The board's work is predominately contained within the LCS Program Office and focuses on identifying, measuring, and mitigating technical, schedule, and cost risks. Navy officials stated that the board differs from the other groups in that the risks it manages are almost exclusively focused on development and production—issues within the program office's control. The few operationally related risks that the board has identified to date include: personnel operating the launch and recovery equipment, personnel transporting supplies on board, potential for increased crew fatigue caused by the ship's motion, and crew training. According to Navy officials, the mitigation for the training issues is the ongoing study to develop a long-term LCS training plan and the mitigation for the personnel issues is to observe and learn from the ongoing test and trials period and initial deployments and then make adjustments, if needed.

# The Navy's Operating and Support Cost Estimates Do Not Fully Reflect Best Practices and May Change Due to Program Uncertainties

## The Navy Estimated Operating and Support Costs for the LCS Program

The Navy has estimated operating and support costs that include most elements of the LCS program.[12] Our analysis of the Navy's 2009 estimates showed that the operating and support costs for the planned seaframes and mission packages could total $84.8 billion which amounts to about

---

[12] Due to the upcoming decision to select one of the two seaframes that the Navy will buy for the remainder of the program, the details of the Navy's estimates are considered business sensitive.

$61.7 million per seaframe annually to operate and support both the seaframes and mission packages.[13]

For the seaframes, the Navy's 2009 estimate of operating and support costs projected a total of $64.1 billion based on a 25-year service life.[14] According to Navy officials, this estimate assumed a nearly even split of the two seaframe types as the seaframes have different operating and support cost profiles. However, the Navy has announced that it will choose one of the two seaframe designs in 2010 so the associated operating and support costs will likely change depending on the design selected.

For the mission packages, operating and support costs could total $20.8 billion. The Navy provided us with its estimate of the average annual operating and support costs of each mission package. Therefore, to calculate the total operating and support costs, we multiplied the average annual estimates by the number of packages of each type with an expected 30-year service life. The Navy's most recent estimates were prepared to support the fiscal year 2010 budget but did not include the antisubmarine package since its contents are under development; therefore, we used the prior year's estimate to calculate the operating and support costs for this mission package.

---

[13] Since significant LCS operational capabilities are derived from the mission packages—the ability to counter mines, submarines, and small surface boats, and to conduct maritime security operations—and since the mission packages are part of the LCS program, we calculated the average annual operating and support cost by dividing the $84.8 billion by the number of seaframes and the expected seaframe service life.

[14] The Navy can expect to pay operating and support costs until the last LCS is retired. Therefore, if the last LCS is purchased in 2025, then, based on the 25-year expected service life of each seaframe, the Navy could expect to pay operating and support costs through about 2050.

## Operating and Support Cost Estimates Do Not Fully Reflect Best Practices

Although the Navy has estimated operating and support costs, we found that the Navy had not fully implemented cost estimating best practices. According to DOD and GAO best practices for cost estimating,[15] a credible cost estimate should include the following three steps:

- analyze the likelihood that the costs could be greater than estimated,
- assess how the cost estimate may change in response to changes in key program assumptions, and
- compare the estimate to an independently developed estimate.

The Navy's estimates showed some aspects of a high-quality cost estimating process. For example, the estimates included most cost categories recommended by DOD's cost estimating best practices—such as personnel, maintenance, and sustaining support—and documented ground rules and assumptions, methodologies, and data sources. However, our assessment of the Navy's operating and support cost estimates showed that the Navy did not take two of the three steps listed above to ensure the estimates' credibility, and only partially completed the other step.

First, the Navy did not perform an analysis to assess the likelihood that the operating and support costs for either the seaframe or mission packages could be greater than estimated. This analysis, known as a risk analysis, estimates the likelihood that operating and support costs could rise beyond what was projected and the degree of the possible increase. We reported in 2009 that out of 10 of DOD's largest acquisition programs, 5 had increased overall acquisition costs from their first full cost estimate.[16] Of those that didn't, three programs sharply reduced procurement quantities, and unit costs increased for all but one of the systems. According to best practices, a credible cost estimate should include a risk analysis that shows the range of possible costs and the likelihood that costs could increase to particular levels. The results of a risk analysis are usually shown in a cumulative probability distribution or "S-curve." Figure 2 below shows a notional example of an S-curve.

---

[15] Office of the Secretary of Defense, Cost Analysis Improvement Group, *Operating and Support Cost Estimating Guide*, (Arlington, Va., October 2007), Office of the Secretary of Defense, Cost Analysis Improvement Group, *Operating and Support Cost Estimating Guide* (Arlington, Va., May 1, 1992), and GAO, *GAO Cost Estimating and Assessment Guide*, GAO-09-3SP (Washington, D.C.: March 2009).

[16] GAO, *Defense Acquisitions: Assessments of Selected Weapon Programs*, GAO-09-326SP (Washington, D.C.: Mar. 30, 2009).

**Figure 2: Notional Example of Risk Analysis Results Displayed in an S-curve Showing the Range and Likelihood of Possible Cost Increases**

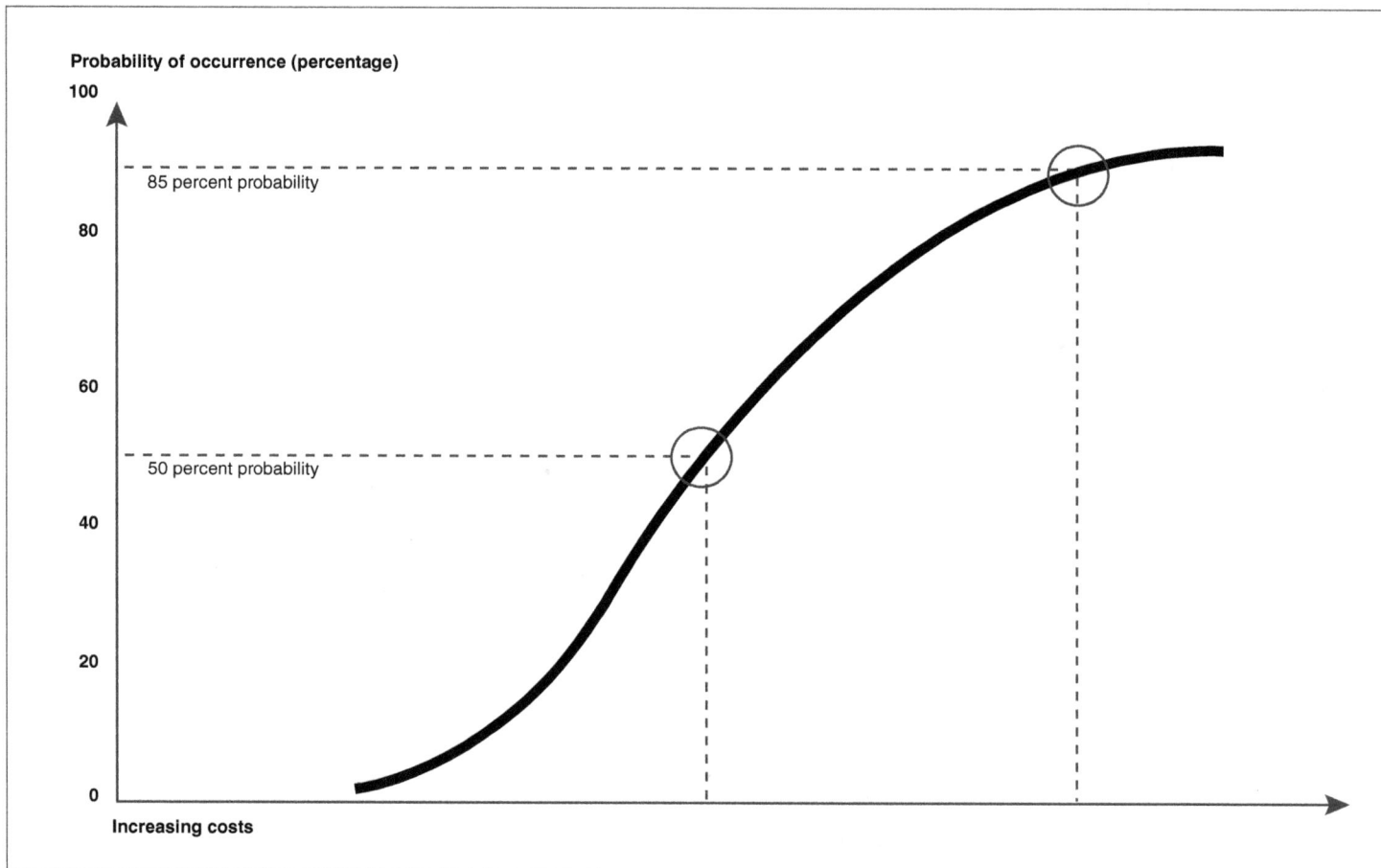

Source: GAO analysis.

This notional example shows that the higher the cost estimate, the greater the probability that actual costs will not exceed the estimate. Navy guidance indicates that the confidence level of a program's cost estimate should be above 85 percent to merit a "green" or low-risk designation and that a confidence level of less than 60 percent merits a "red" or high-risk designation.[17] The Weapon Systems Acquisition Reform Act of 2009

---

[17] Naval PoPS Criteria Handbook, *A Program Health Assessment Methodology for Navy and Marine Corps Acquisition Programs* (September 2008), issued by the Assistant Secretary of the Navy for Research Development and Acquisition.

requires that the confidence level—usually developed based on an analysis of the likelihood that costs will be greater than estimated—for cost estimates be disclosed and, if less than 80 percent, justified.[18] Navy cost estimating officials told us that they have not yet decided what confidence level they will use for the operating and support cost estimate prepared for the next milestone decision point. Since the Navy has not performed this risk analysis, neither the Navy nor DOD decision makers have a full picture of the range of possible operating and support costs and the likelihood of costs increasing beyond the estimates discussed above.

Second, according to DOD and GAO best practices, a credible cost estimate should include an assessment of how the cost estimate may change in response to changes in key program assumptions. This is known as a sensitivity analysis of cost drivers. Such an analysis helps decision makers identify areas that could significantly affect a program's cost, choose between program alternatives, and mitigate risks. Cost drivers could include operational plans and assumptions such as crew size, maintenance plans, or the system's expected useful life. The Navy has identified several cost drivers for the LCS program, including fuel, manning, maintenance, and infrastructure. However, to date the Navy has only completed analysis of one of these cost drivers—fuel—and, officials said, is conducting analyses of other areas such as manning and maintenance. Without a more complete identification and analysis of key cost drivers, the Navy may not have a complete picture of how changes in program operations or assumptions could affect operating and support costs.

Third, according to DOD and GAO best practices, a credible cost estimate should be developed and compared to an independently developed cost estimate. DOD and Navy guidance require that an independent life-cycle cost estimate, including an estimate of operating and support costs, be completed for a shipbuilding program at the program's Milestone B decision point, when lead and initial follow-on ships are normally

---

[18] Pub. L. No. 111-23, §101(2009), codified at 10 U.S.C. §2334 (d). Specifically, the law requires the Director of Cost Assessment and Program Evaluation, as well as the Secretary of the military department concerned to each disclose the confidence level used in establishing a cost estimate for a major defense acquisition program, the rationale for selecting such confidence level, and, if such confidence level is less than 80 percent, the justification for selecting a confidence level of less than 80 percent in certain documentation specified in the statute.

approved, and at the Navy's internal review, referred to as Gate 4,[19] which occurs just before Milestone B. As the LCS program has not gone through Milestone B, no independent life-cycle cost estimate has been performed for the LCS program. Specifically, neither the Naval Center for Cost Analysis nor the Office of the Secretary of Defense's Office of the Director of Cost Assessment and Program Evaluation (CAPE) has developed an independent estimate of LCS operating and support costs according to Navy and CAPE officials. Independent cost estimates are one of the best and most reliable methods of validating a cost estimate. Past experience has shown that an independent estimate, prepared by an entity separate from those connected to the program, tends to be higher and more accurate than estimates developed by a system's program office. In a previous review of DOD acquisition programs, we found that 19 of 20 independent estimates developed by CAPE were higher than the service estimate. Even so, some of the CAPE's estimates understated actual program costs.[20]

In addition, two other important elements of a cost estimate were omitted from the documentation the Navy provided to us on the mission package operating and support costs prepared in July 2009. First, Navy officials told us that they had not updated and therefore did not include the estimate for the antisubmarine package because the contents are under development.[21] However, the Navy plans to buy 16 of these packages. According to DOD and GAO best practices, cost estimates should be complete and account for all possible costs. Further, the Navy did not show total lifetime operating and support costs or costs expected in each year of the program—instead, the Navy only showed average annual mission package operating and support costs. Showing cost estimates for each year of the program, known as time phasing, is also a best practice and necessary for use in the formulation of and comparison with actual program budgets.

---

[19] The internal Navy review that occurs just prior to the second DOD milestone decision point is known as the Gate 4 review. Secretary of the Navy Instruction 5000.2D, *Implementation and Operation of the Defense Acquisition System and the Joint Capabilities Integration and Development System*, paragraph 2.5.5.5 and Annex 20A (Oct 16, 2008).

[20] GAO, *Defense Acquisitions: A Knowledge-Based Funding Approach Could Improve Major Weapon System Program Outcomes*, GAO-08-619 (Washington, D.C.: July 2, 2008).

[21] Our analysis of the mission package operating and support costs used the Navy's 2008 estimate of the annual operating and support costs for the antisubmarine package.

## Operating and Support Cost Estimates Are Likely to Change Due to Program Uncertainties

The Navy has not yet decided which one of the two LCS seaframes it will buy for the remainder of the program, leading to uncertainty about the effects of this program decision on the operating and support cost estimates developed to date. Also, the Navy has not yet decided what it will do over the long term with the two ships of the design that is not chosen. The Navy currently plans to deploy these two ships as they become available, according to Navy officials. Since the two designs will require separate training facilities and core crew, and since each design has unique equipment and therefore different maintenance requirements, continuing to support both designs may carry a cost premium. Likewise, deciding which one of the two LCS seaframes to buy is likely to, in turn, affect decisions on issues such as infrastructure and training requirements, with accompanying cost implications.

The Navy's force structure analyses supporting the planned purchase quantities of mission packages are incomplete, adding to uncertainty about costs in future budget years. Our prior work has shown that a knowledge-based decision-making process can help provide a comprehensive analytic basis for an acquisition program, including determining the optimum quantities of LCS seaframes and mission packages.[22] This information in turn can help decision makers evaluate the affordability of the LCS program and establish funding priorities. Navy officials from two divisions within the Office of the Chief of Naval Operations—the Surface Warfare Division and the Assessments Division—said they were unaware of any analysis supporting the total planned quantities for either the surface warfare package or its maritime security module. Also, Navy officials said that the Navy has not performed a force structure analysis on the antisubmarine package because the contents are under development. The Navy has not performed a complete analysis of LCS seaframe and mission package quantities because certain information needed for the analyses was not yet available, including decisions on potential changes to program operating assumptions and requirements. Further, an analysis of LCS seaframe and mission package quantities is not included in the Assessments Division's fiscal year 2010 agenda.

---

[22] GAO, *Missile Defense: DOD Needs to More Fully Assess Requirements and Establish Operational Units before Fielding New Capabilities*, GAO-09-856 (Washington, D.C.: Sept 16, 2009). GAO, *Defense Acquisitions: A Knowledge-Based Funding Approach Could Improve Major Weapon System Program Outcomes*, GAO-08-619 (Washington, D.C.: July 2, 2008), and GAO, *Defense Acquisitions: Assessments of Selected Weapon Programs*, GAO-08-467SP (Washington, D.C.: Mar. 31, 2008).

The planned force structure of 55 LCS seaframes is based on a 2005 analysis of requirements for responding to possible overseas conflicts and meeting overseas presence requirements, which officials said they revalidated in 2007 and 2008. However, this analysis is based, in part, on certain assumptions that are not yet verified. For example, one assumption is that rotational crewing plans will work as expected, allowing a greater presence per ship than the traditional one crew per ship. However, rotational crewing has never been routinely conducted by the Navy for an entire class of surface combatants. If the Navy switches to a different crewing model, a different number of ships could be required to sustain the same presence, or alternatively, a different number of crews could be required. The expected purchase of 55 seaframes is also based on an assumption that some ships would be homeported overseas, according to Navy officials. If the assumed number homeported overseas changes, then the number of LCS needed to maintain the same presence requirements could also change. If these assumptions change due to program decisions or operating experience, the total number of LCS seaframes needed to meet requirements may change. It may be important for Navy and DOD decision makers to have updated and complete force structure analyses for the LCS program since any changes to the planned purchase quantities as a result of updated force structure analyses would affect the program's total operating and support costs. Without such analyses, decision-makers may not be able to effectively evaluate the affordability of the program.

Finally, the LCS cost estimates could change as actual operating data become available and operational concepts are refined. Since little actual LCS operating and support data are available to date, the estimates are currently based on data from other systems, and the estimates could change as actual cost data become available. The cost estimates are also based on new operational concepts for personnel, training, and maintenance. These new concepts are not fully developed, tested, and implemented, and, if these concepts change, the estimates could change. For example, the Navy has not yet fully developed or implemented a comprehensive training plan, and it is possible that the plan could cost more or less than the training costs accounted for in the current estimates.

## Upcoming Program Decisions Would Benefit from Further Analysis of Long-Term Operating and Support Costs

Decision makers could benefit from further analysis of the program's long-term operating and support costs before making key program and investment decisions. Since operating and support costs constitute a major portion of system life-cycle costs—over 70 percent—they are critical to the evaluation of acquisition alternatives. Navy officials told us that they are developing criteria for selecting one seaframe for the remainder of the program; however, at this time it is not clear that the criteria will include a comparison of the operating and support costs of each seaframe or whether the estimates will be developed according to all three steps for ensuring credibility and the results presented to decision makers in the Navy and DOD.

According to DOD and GAO best practices for cost estimating, decision makers should consider affordability at major decision points, and a comparative analysis should be done to identify costs and benefits of competing alternatives, including an operating and support estimate of each alternative.[23] The lack of cost estimates that fully meet best practices, such as including an analysis to assess the likelihood that costs will be greater than estimated, raises questions about the credibility of the estimates that have been produced to date and limits the ability of decision makers to make fully informed program and investment decisions, such as:

- accurately assessing the affordability of LCS within the broader portfolio of Navy and DOD programs,
- identifying the resources needed over the long term to support the planned investment in the LCS force structure,
- assessing the long-term cost implications of alternative acquisition strategies such as which seaframe the Navy will buy for the remainder of the 55-ship class, and
- analyzing the costs of options for what to do with the two seaframes of the design that is not selected.

According to DOD acquisition guidance, at the Milestone B decision point lead and initial follow-on ships are normally approved and an independent life-cycle cost estimate for the program, including operating and support costs, is required.[24] The Milestone B decision point for the LCS program has been delayed several times. Originally scheduled for January 2007, Navy officials now say they plan to hold the milestone in May or June 2010.

---

[23] Office of the Secretary of Defense, Cost Analysis Improvement Group, *Operating and Support Cost Estimating Guide*, (Arlington, Va., October 2007), and GAO, *GAO Cost Estimating and Assessment Guide*, GAO-09-3SP (Washington, D.C.: March 2009).

[24] Department of Defense Instruction 5000.02, *Operation of the Defense Acquisition System* (Dec. 8, 2008).

According to Naval Sea Systems Command officials, the Navy plans to develop a life-cycle cost estimate including operating and support costs and have an independent cost estimate prepared by CAPE to support the program's Milestone B decision in May or June 2010. Navy officials told us they plan to complete the other two steps for a credible estimate—analyzing the likelihood that costs will increase over time, and fully assessing the effects of changing key program assumptions—at Milestone B. However, Navy officials said that this information may not be presented to top decision makers in the Navy and DOD, and therefore may not inform key program decisions such as the decision of which seaframe to buy for the remainder of the program. Further, congressional decision makers may not be fully aware of the LCS program's operating and support costs since, to date, the LCS Selected Acquisition Reports submitted to Congress have not included operating and support cost estimates.[25] Operating and support costs are required to be included in such reports for programs that have passed Milestone B[26] and, as previously noted, the LCS program has not yet passed that point. Without the benefit of current, credible estimates of the long-term operating and support costs, congressional decision makers may not be fully aware of the resources that will be needed over time to support the ships for which DOD requests funds to buy each year.

---

[25] Section 2432 of Title 10 of the U.S. Code requires the Secretary of Defense to submit selected acquisition reports to Congress on current major defense acquisition programs.

[26] Section 2436 of Title 10 of the U.S. Code requires that selected acquisition reports for the first quarter of a fiscal year, called comprehensive selected acquisition reports, include a full life-cycle cost analysis for each major defense acquisition program. A full life-cycle cost analysis is required in the second, third, and fourth quarters of a fiscal year if a major defense acquisition program was not included in the most recent comprehensive selected acquisition report.

# The Navy Has Made Progress but Faces Risks in Implementing Its Plans to Operate and Support LCS

## The Navy Faces Risks in Implementing Its Personnel Plans over the Long Term

Although the Navy is conducting studies to determine personnel requirements for LCS, it has not fully identified the number of ship and shore support personnel required to support LCS over the long term and faces risks in its ability to identify and assign personnel over the long term. Additionally, the Navy has not routinely rotationally crewed an entire class of surface combatants; therefore, the concept being planned for the LCS class is unproven. Although the Navy rotationally crews some small ships, such as the mine countermeasure ships, the Navy has only experimented with rotationally crewing surface combatants such as destroyers and only did so for a short time.[27]

The current Navy plan for a 40-person core crew has not yet been validated by an analysis of the crew's expected workload. Early Navy estimates indicated that the core crew might need to be more than 40 to mitigate a concern that a crew this small could experience fatigue. For example, one study raised the issue that crew fatigue could affect missions which could be mitigated by temporarily augmenting the crew or modifying how missions are conducted. The 40-person core crew size was based upon the results of a 2005 conference to explore options for reducing the size of the core crew, which was not the typical workload analysis. The Navy's Manpower Analysis Center typically conducts analyses of a ship's workload to determine the number and type of personnel required to complete all operational and maintenance tasks. However, this analysis for the LCS core crew and the three mission packages is not scheduled to be complete until after the first full deployment, around fiscal year 2014.[28]

---

[27] GAO, *Force Structure: Ship Rotational Crewing Initiatives Would Benefit from Top-Level Leadership, Navy-wide Guidance, Comprehensive Analysis, and Improved Lessons-Learned Sharing*, GAO-08-418 (Washington, D.C.: Mar. 29, 2008).

[28] Navy officials stated that they had not yet been directed to include an analysis of the maritime security module of the surface warfare package.

The Navy's initial analysis to identify shore personnel requirements is due by the end of 2009; however, the full requirements for shore personnel may not be known for several years. Due to the limited crew size, many administrative and maintenance duties will have to be performed ashore rather than on board as on other surface ships and will be managed by LCS squadrons. [29] Navy officials estimated that the number of people needed in a squadron organization to manage and support 12 to 15 LCSs might be about 170. The LCS squadrons are likely to be larger than squadrons for other surface ships since their responsibilities for the level of shore-based support required for the small core crew will be greater. However, Navy officials said that they will not know how large the LCS squadrons should be until they have experience with supporting deployed ships. In addition, the shore support personnel required will be affected by outstanding decisions, such as where to homeport the ships and the long-term maintenance strategy. Since the Navy has not yet completed its studies to identify the LCS personnel requirement, we compiled Navy estimates of the personnel that may be required to support LCS over the long term. Specifically, we added Navy estimates of the personnel that may be required for the ship crews, mission package crews, and the LCS squadrons to derive a total number of personnel that may be required for the program. Table 2 below shows that the total personnel required for the LCS program over the long term might be approximately 4,600 people.

**Table 2: Estimate of the Total Navy Personnel Required for a Fleet of 55 LCS Ships**

| | Estimate of Navy personnel required[a] |
|---|---|
| Ship crews | 2,880 |
| Mission package crews[b] | 888[c] |
| LCS squadrons (ashore) | 680 to 850 |
| **Total personnel required** | **4,448 to 4,618** |

Source: GAO compilation of Navy data.

[a]The personnel estimate is for Navy personnel only and does not include contractor personnel who are currently performing most maintenance.

---

[29] The LCS Class Squadron coordinates all shore support and is responsible for the overarching management of seaframes, mission packages, and personnel. The Navy plans to establish several numbered squadrons to manage the day-to-day details of administrative, personnel, operational, maintenance, distance support, logistics, and training functions for a specific number of LCSs.

ᵇThe total number of personnel for mission package crews includes personnel for three types of mission packages—mine countermeasures, antisubmarine warfare, and surface warfare. Currently, additional personnel are required to support maritime security operations. The Navy is reviewing options for providing personnel using existing personnel. However if additional personnel are required for each maritime security module, the additional personnel could total up to 432.

ᶜNavy officials stated that there is a proposal to reduce the number of mission package crews for antisubmarine warfare, mine countermeasures, and surface warfare. If approved, the total number of personnel for mission package crews could decrease to 465. Also, if the Navy decides to use personnel from the other warfare packages, the total number of personnel for mission packages could also decrease.

The above estimate of the total personnel required does not include aviation crews, which could total an additional 1,656 people. We did not include aviation crew personnel in the table because these crews are not totally dedicated to LCS and may be tasked to support other ship types, according to Navy officials. The Navy has the core and mission package crews in its personnel plans, but to date has not funded all the aviation crews. According to Navy officials, if the aviation crews are not funded in the Navy's fiscal year 2012 budget, then the Navy may begin to experience shortfalls in aviation crews beginning in fiscal year 2014.

The Navy also faces risks in its ability to identify and assign personnel to LCS over the long term due to the requirement for relatively senior, highly trained personnel. Specifically:

- LCS sailors must be experienced sailors and positions must be filled by a person of the exact pay grade required, which could limit the pool of personnel available. Sailors must also commit to serving on an LCS crew for 36 months after completing their LCS training. Considering the concept for rotational crewing, a sailor might serve two or three 4-month deployments during their 36-month LCS tour for a total of 8 to 12 months of LCS deployment time.
- The number of requirements that potential sailors must meet in order to qualify for an LCS assignment is rigorous. For example, potential LCS sailors must meet current physical fitness standards as well as have passed the previous 18 months of physical fitness assessments. In contrast, sailors are considered qualified for assignment on other surface ships if they passed the most recent physical fitness test. Also, sailors will not be considered for assignment to LCS if they are color blind or have a pending application for the officer commissioning program.
- Due to the longer training time required to prepare LCS sailors, the Navy's Personnel Command must identify personnel 18 to 24 months prior to when they need them to report to the LCS crew. For other surface ships, the Personnel Command needs to identify personnel only 5 to 9 months ahead of time. Personnel Command officials stated that they must manually identify the personnel for LCS since the computer system

normally used to identify personnel can only identify personnel up to12 months in advance. Due to the increased workload resulting from the manual process, the Navy Personnel Command has set up a separate office specifically to handle LCS personnel assignments and added eight positions. Officials stated that they will likely need more personnel as more ships and mission packages enter service. Since the average annual turnover rate is about one-third, according to Navy officials, the Personnel Command will have to manually identify a significant number of replacement sailors each year to support the LCS program.

## The Navy Faces Risks in Achieving the Extensive LCS Training Requirements

The Navy has made progress in identifying LCS-unique training requirements, but faces risks in implementing its training concept. According to the Navy's concept for LCS,[30] sailors must be ready to perform their duties when they arrive on board without additional supervised, on-the-job training that is typical of other surface ships. The Navy calls this the "train to qualify" standard. In contrast, it is typical on other ships for a sailor to complete his or her training on board via supervised, on-the-job training. According to Navy officials, it may take about 6 months of onboard on-the-job training for a sailor on other surface ships to reach the same level of proficiency as that described in the concept for LCS sailors. The Navy's approach to LCS training is different than for other surface ships since the small LCS crew size means that there is little capacity on board for supervised training and no training group on board the ship as is typical of other surface ships. LCS sailors will also be required to be trained in several skill areas outside their primary specialty. For example, an LCS Damage Control Assistant will also have to train in an engineering skill area and an Electronics Technician will also have to train in a Fire Controlman skill area. In addition, LCS sailors will be expected to perform various collateral duties, such as serving as the crew's barber and running the ship's store.

The Navy expects to complete a study of LCS training by the end of 2009 but may not fully implement the results for several years. The Navy began this study to fully identify LCS training requirements and to recommend alternatives for providing training over the life of the LCS program. This is a complex process since training requirements for the core crew are unique for each position on the two seaframes. Although the Navy has identified LCS-specific training requirements for both seaframes and the

---

[30] U.S. Fleet Forces Command, *Littoral Combat Ship Platform Wholeness Concept of Operations* (Revision C) (Sept. 24, 2009).

three mission packages, the Navy has not yet completed plans for how to provide this training over the long term. Further, the training plan resulting from the Navy's LCS training study may not be fully implemented until about 2013 or after, largely due to the need to develop and buy simulators and virtual training facilities. Depending on homeporting decisions, the Navy may need to build comparable simulators on the east coast as well as the west coast. Although the Navy has built one shore-based trainer for each seaframe, the trainers will need to be upgraded in accordance with the training study results and to meet the train-to-qualify standard. Until the results of the training analysis are implemented, the Navy has developed an interim solution, called the LCS Academy, to provide LCS-specific training and fill training gaps.

Another reason the training required prior to the sailor coming on board the LCS is longer and more extensive than for other surface ships is that the training requirements include courses outside of the sailor's primary specialty. To assess the training requirements for LCS versus other surface ships, we compared the training days required before a sailor reports to an LCS crew to the training days required before a sailor reports to other types of surface ships.[31] Our analysis of a sample of LCS positions showed that the number of training days required before an LCS sailor reports to the crew is significantly longer than for sailors in comparable positions on other ships—an average of 484 days versus 126 days for an amphibious transport docking ship and 103 days for a destroyer.[32] The lowest number of training days required for an LCS position in our sample was 264 and the highest was 832. Figure 3 below shows the average number of training days for the positions in our sample on a typical destroyer, amphibious transport docking ship, and the LCS.

---

[31] To do the analysis, we identified a non-probability sample of 15 enlisted positions from the 40-person LCS core crews of both seaframes. The sample was based on identifying LCS positions that were critical or required cross-training. Next, we compared the training days required before reporting on board for comparable positions on other surface ships. See appendix I for a complete description of the analysis methodology including a discussion of the sample selection criteria.

[32] Navy officials noted that some positions on an Aegis ship also have lengthy training requirements, such as training for sailors who work on the Aegis radar. Since this type of equipment is not on LCS, the related positions were not part of our sample.

**Figure 3: Comparison of Average Training Days Required before Reporting on Board for LCS with Two Other Surface Ships for a Sample of Positions**

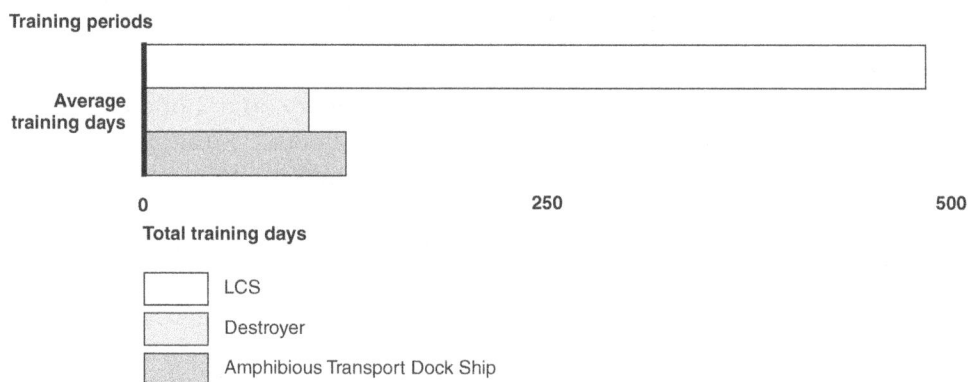

Training periods

Average training days

Total training days

0    250    500

☐ LCS
▨ Destroyer
▨ Amphibious Transport Dock Ship

Source: GAO analysis of Navy data.

As noted above, a sailor on ships other than LCS may spend an additional 6 months completing training on board via supervised, on-the-job training. Therefore, even accounting for this time, the LCS training time required is significantly higher. Implementing the LCS concept of train-to-qualify has two important effects. First, the costs to train sailors before they report to an LCS crew are likely to be significantly higher than for other surface ships due to the longer training time required before the sailors report to a crew and due to the costs to build and sustain the shore-based training facilities. Second, the longer training time before reporting to a crew is the major reason that the Personnel Command has to identify people 18 to 24 months before they report to an LCS crew, which Navy documents have indicated may be unsustainable using the current personnel distribution system.

## The Navy Faces Risks in Implementing Its Maintenance Concept

The Navy also faces risks in implementing the maintenance concept being developed to allow for a small assigned crew. Performing preventive maintenance is an important factor in maintaining the material condition of the ship. According to the Navy's Board of Inspection and Survey, deferred maintenance was a key factor in some surface ships having significant material problems identified during recent inspections.[33] The risks for LCS are in preventive maintenance—periodic tasks to keep equipment in good condition—and distance support—moving work from

---

[33] Navy Board of Inspection and Survey, *2008 INSURV Annual Report* (undated).

the ship to the shore. Regarding preventive maintenance, the Navy is still assessing how much preventive maintenance the core crew can accomplish. Due to the small core crew size, a significant amount of maintenance has to be moved off ship. The initial analysis was that 20 to 30 man-years of preventive maintenance would have to be moved off of the ship. According to the Navy's LCS concept, the core crew is expected to do little or no corrective maintenance and minimal preventive and facilities maintenance.[34] The rest would be done during in-port periods—by the crew or contractors—or by teams that fly out to the ship to perform maintenance during crew turnover periods. As of October 2009, Navy officials stated that well over 50 percent of the preventive maintenance had been transferred from the ship to the shore and is being accomplished by contractors under the interim support plan agreement. In contrast, on other surface ships, the crew performs all preventive maintenance and much corrective maintenance that involves diagnosing problems and completing somewhat complex repairs. During fiscal year 2009, the Navy spent $6.0 million on the interim support plan for seaframe preventive and facilities maintenance. The Navy is also still working to resolve issues in the system developed for LCS to schedule and track accomplishment of preventive maintenance.

The Navy also faces risks in implementing its plans for distance support. Distance support is a key enabler for supporting LCS and requires the capability to move information to and from the ship. Although other ships in the Navy rely to some extent on distance support, Navy officials stated that distance support is critical to enabling LCS to operate as envisioned in the operational concept due to the small crew size. According to the concept, many administrative functions are also planned to be moved ashore such as postal, administrative records, logistic support, and maintenance and fuel records. Commander, Naval Surface Forces established LCS distance support requirements in April 2009, which included developing the capability to move the workload for 120 processes from the ship to the shore. Navy officials stated that they are still evaluating what work to move ashore and how to do so. The processes identified to date include identifying corrective maintenance, monitoring crew qualifications, fuel reporting, and remote monitoring of the condition of some ship systems. However, the Navy has not yet provided funding for

---

[34] Preventive maintenance refers to periodic tasks to keep equipment in good condition such as inspections, lubrication, or calibration. Facilities maintenance includes deep cleaning and preservation.

the development, implementation, and long-term sustainment of these distance support capabilities. If these capabilities are not fully developed and maintained, then the crew's workload could increase or the crew size might need to be increased.

In addition, the Navy does not yet have a long-term maintenance strategy for the LCS seaframes and mission packages. Currently, the Navy has interim support plans for both the seaframes and mission packages that include contractor-provided maintenance. The Navy intends to develop and implement a long-term maintenance strategy by about 2015 for the mission packages and by the end of 2011 for the seaframes. The long-term strategy may continue to employ mostly contractor-provided maintenance or could consist of a combination of contractor- and service-provided maintenance in a Navy shipyard. According to Navy officials, the Navy has not yet analyzed core logistics capabilities for the LCS program but plans to do so as part of its analysis to identify a long-term maintenance strategy. Under section 2464 of Title 10 U.S. Code, DOD is required to maintain a "core logistics capability" that is government owned, government operated, and that uses government personnel, equipment, and facilities. However, we reported in May 2009 that DOD has neither identified nor established core capabilities in a timely manner for certain new systems that were included in the May 2009 report.[35] Consequently, among other things, we recommended that DOD require an initial core assessment early in the acquisition process, preferably before Milestone B, and that acquisition strategies for new or modified systems include either a plan for establishing core capability within 4 years of initial operational capability, or a statement that no core capability requirements were identified.

## A Risk Assessment Could Inform Key Procurement Decisions

Despite risks in implementing its new LCS operational concepts, the Navy has not specified the potential operational effects or identified alternative approaches if its concepts cannot be implemented as envisioned. The 2008 *National Defense Strategy* describes the need to assess and mitigate risk in the execution of defense programs critical to national security, including risks relating to the department's capacity to execute future

---

[35] GAO, *Depot Maintenance: Actions Needed to Identify and Establish Core Capability at Military Depots*, GAO-09-83 (Washington, D.C.: May 14, 2009).

missions and manage personnel, training, and maintenance.[36] Our prior work also showed that a risk assessment is a best practice that informs an organization's decision making and includes identifying potential risks and identifying countermeasures to reduce the risks.[37]

The Navy acknowledges that there are risks in implementing its new LCS operational concepts for personnel, training, and maintenance, and has established some groups to manage the details of how to implement the concepts, such as the cross-functional teams and the Oversight Board. These groups identify and review issues and barriers to implementing the LCS concepts and work together to jointly develop solutions. In addition, the LCS program office has established a Risk Management Board, which monitors issues primarily related to development and production of the seaframe and mission packages and focuses on technical, schedule, and cost risks. In general, this board does not focus on personnel, training, and maintenance risks. Although the work these groups perform is important, their scope does not include a thorough risk assessment as described in DOD's Strategy and GAO best practices. These groups are focused on how to make the operational concepts work and, as yet, have not fully identified operational risks and assessed alternatives to mitigate the risks if these new concepts for personnel, training, and maintenance cannot be implemented as intended. In the case of LCS, a thorough risk assessment could be used, for example, to: identify the operational limitations if a 40-person core crew experiences undue fatigue and assess alternatives to the 40-person core crew or to identify the operational limitations if the distance support does not work as intended and assess alternatives for supporting a small crew. Without such a risk assessment to inform decision makers, the Navy faces unspecified operational and program risks at the same time that it plans to buy a total of 23 ships by the end of fiscal year 2015. Although the LCS operational testing is expected to provide some insights into the effectiveness of the new operational concepts, according to Navy officials, the tests are not scheduled to be

---

[36] Department of Defense, *National Defense Strategy* (June 2008). The *National Defense Strategy* defined risk in terms of the potential for damage to national security combined with the probability of occurrence and the measurement of the consequences should the risk remain unaddressed.

[37] GAO, *Homeland Defense: Actions Needed to Improve Management of Air Sovereignty Alert Operations to Protect U.S. Airspace*, GAO-09-184 (Washington,D.C.: Jan. 27, 2009). GAO, *Force Structure: Joint Seabasing Would Benefit from a Comprehensive Management Approach and Rigorous Experimentation Before Services Spend Billions on New Capabilities*, GAO-07-211 (Washington, D.C.: Jan. 26, 2007).

completed until about fiscal year 2014. As shown in figure 4 below, the Navy plans to make a significant investment in LCS force structure before it has information indicating whether the operational concepts are likely to be successful.

**Figure 4: Timeline Comparing the Navy's LCS Procurement Plans with Key Events Affecting Implementation of the Operational Concepts**

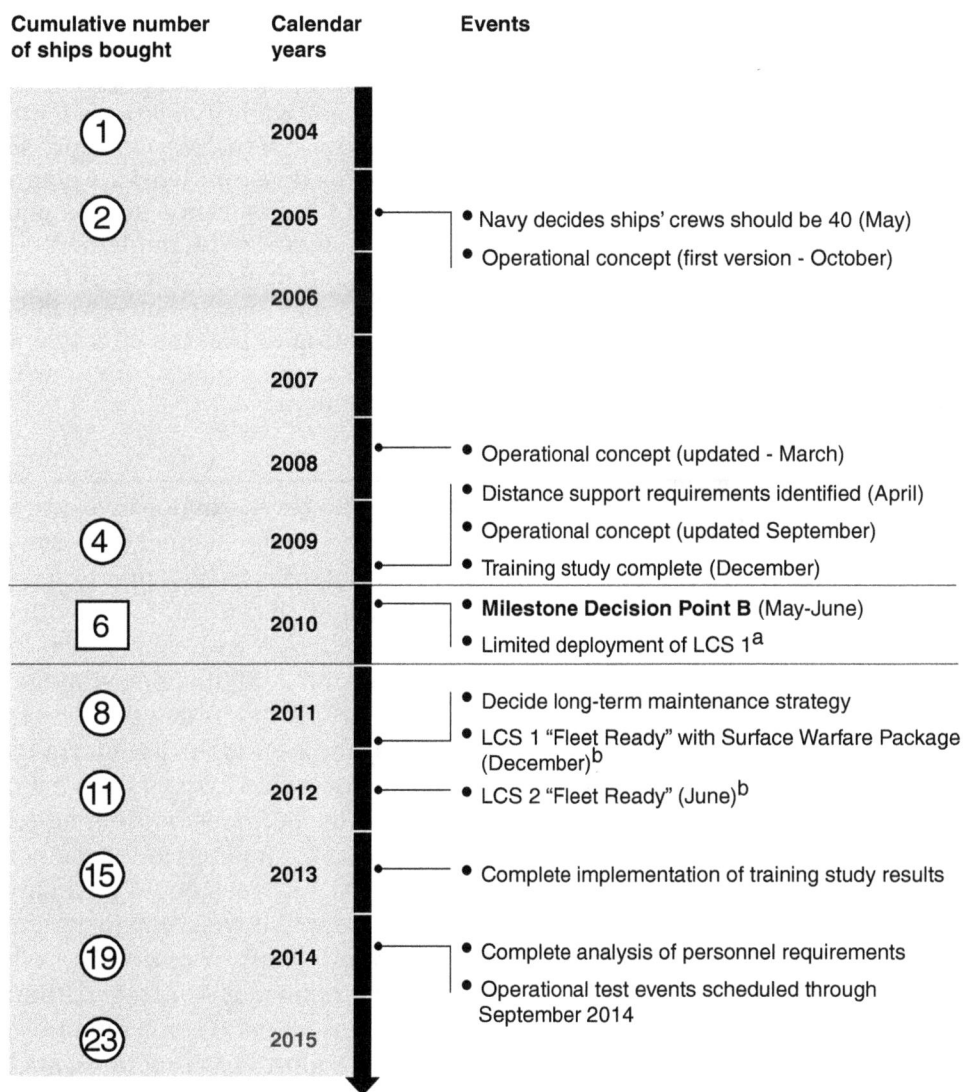

| Cumulative number of ships bought | Calendar years | Events |
|---|---|---|
| (1) | 2004 | |
| (2) | 2005 | • Navy decides ships' crews should be 40 (May) <br> • Operational concept (first version - October) |
| | 2006 | |
| | 2007 | |
| | 2008 | • Operational concept (updated - March) <br> • Distance support requirements identified (April) |
| (4) | 2009 | • Operational concept (updated September) <br> • Training study complete (December) |
| [6] | 2010 | • **Milestone Decision Point B** (May-June) <br> • Limited deployment of LCS 1[a] |
| (8) | 2011 | • Decide long-term maintenance strategy <br> • LCS 1 "Fleet Ready" with Surface Warfare Package (December)[b] |
| (11) | 2012 | • LCS 2 "Fleet Ready" (June)[b] |
| (15) | 2013 | • Complete implementation of training study results |
| (19) | 2014 | • Complete analysis of personnel requirements <br> • Operational test events scheduled through September 2014 |
| (23) | 2015 | |

Source: GAO analysis of Navy data.

[a]Although Navy officials expect to gather useful information about how to operate and support LCS during this limited deployment, the deployment will not fully reflect how the Navy intends to deploy LCS as described in the *Wholeness Concept of Operations*, according to Navy officials. For example, the ship will not be deployed for 18 months, may not rotate crews, and will have more than 78 people on board such as contractors to provide additional support and assistance.

[b]"Fleet Ready" means that a specific LCS and mission package combination has completed some testing and certification and is ready for a deployment tasking, according to a Navy official.

If the operational concepts for personnel, training, and maintenance cannot be implemented as desired, then, according to Navy officials, the Navy may face operational limitations, may have to reengineer its operational concept, or may have to make significant design changes to the ship after committing to building 23 ships which represents a significant portion (42 percent) of the class. Further, without an assessment identifying the operational effects and without exploring alternatives, if the Navy's approach to personnel, training, and maintaining LCS ships does not work as planned the Navy risks continuing to buy ships without the assurance that its plans for personnel, training, and maintenance can be implemented as envisioned. In contrast, having a thorough risk assessment of the new operational approaches to personnel, training, and maintenance would provide decision makers with information to link the effectiveness of these new operational concepts with decisions on program investment, specifically the pace of procurement.

## Conclusions

Given the Navy's major investment in the LCS program, it is critical that DOD and congressional decision makers have a complete cost estimate that fully reflects best practices—including analyses of how costs may increase with time and vary with changing program assumptions, as well as comparison with an independently developed estimate. Such estimates are needed to enable decision makers to assess the program's affordability, including the long-term, recurring operating and support costs, and assess the long-term operating and support costs of all the acquisition alternatives before a decision is made. Specifically, having complete estimates of the long-term operating and support costs that are periodically updated and based on results of complete and current force structure analyses could be an important factor for decision makers to consider when weighing program investment alternatives such as which seaframe to buy or options for what to do with the two seaframes of the design that is not selected. Although the Navy's operating and support cost estimates showed some qualities of a sound estimating process, the Navy did not follow best practices, such as requesting an independent estimate and comparing it to the program estimate, analyzing the likelihood that costs will increase, and analyzing the effects on the estimate of key cost drivers. Further, the Navy's force structure analyses of the quantities of required seaframes and mission packages are incomplete and based on assumptions, such as how many ships may be homeported overseas, which, if changed, could change the quantities required. Changes in the quantities of required seaframes and mission packages could affect estimates of the program's total operating and support costs. Cost estimates that fully reflect best practices and are based on complete and current force structure analyses of required quantities could enhance the ability of decision makers to identify the resources needed over the long term to support the seaframes and mission packages and assess the affordability of the LCS program. Further, decision makers in both DOD and Congress lack a complete picture of the likely long-term operating and support costs that will be incurred when buying an increasing number of LCS ships, hampering their ability to make sound program and investment decisions.

At the beginning of the LCS program, the Navy stated that reducing the number of ship personnel would be a major factor in lowering operating and support costs. As a result, the Navy's decision to operate the LCS with a core crew of only 40 sailors drove the need to develop new operational concepts. Currently, these concepts are broadly stated and the Navy has not fully developed the details to implement its vision for identifying personnel, providing LCS-unique training over the long term, or shifting maintenance from the ship to shore. Although the Navy acknowledges its approach entails risk, the Navy has not specified what the potential operational effects might be if its concept cannot be fully implemented as envisioned. For example, the Navy has not specified potential negative consequences to LCS missions or identified mitigating strategies if there are not enough or insufficiently trained personnel on board or if the distance support concepts cannot be fully implemented. The Navy's LCS plans represent a significant investment to achieve its force structure goals at a time when there are competing demands for limited resources. However, without a thorough risk analysis including an assessment of alternatives, the Navy faces undefined and, potentially significant operational and program risks. If the operational concepts for personnel, training, and maintenance cannot be implemented as desired, the Navy may face operational limitations, may have to reengineer its operational concept, or may have to make significant design changes to the ship after committing to building almost half of the class. For example, a thorough risk assessment could help the Navy identify the operational risks of a 40-person core crew, such as whether the crew can operate continuously for a 30-day mission without undue fatigue. A risk assessment could assess the alternatives such as the pros and cons of conducting shorter missions or increasing the size of the crew. Having such a risk assessment would enable decision makers to identify and assess: the operational effects if these concepts cannot be implemented as envisioned; alternatives to mitigate these risks; and information to link the effectiveness of these new operational concepts with decisions on program investment, specifically how many ships the Navy should buy each year. Moreover, doing so could help the Navy avoid costly retrofits if ship design changes are needed in order to implement its new concepts.

## Recommendations for Executive Action

We recommend that the Secretary of Defense take the following six actions:

In order to assess the long-term affordability of the LCS program and enhance decision making ability for the LCS program, we recommend that the Secretary of Defense direct the Secretary of the Navy to take the following actions:

- before deciding which seaframe to buy, produce a complete estimate of the long-term operating and support costs which fully reflects cost estimating best practices for each seaframe and use these updated estimates in deciding which seaframe to buy for the remainder of the program;
- use an updated estimate as a basis for analyzing the costs and benefits of options regarding the two seaframes built but not selected for long-term production, and use the results of this analysis in making the decision of how to use, or whether to retire, these seaframes;
- annually update the cost estimate for the long-term operating and support costs of the seaframe and each mission package using cost estimating best practices and submit the results to DOD as well as to Congress as part of the LCS Selected Acquisition Report;
- perform complete and updated force structure analyses on the LCS mission packages to help determine the appropriate purchase quantities over the life of the program, and use these updated quantities for the mission package cost estimate; and
- perform an updated seaframe force structure analysis when key underlying assumptions affecting seaframe quantities change, such as crewing policy, overseas homeports, or presence requirements, and use this updated analysis to adjust quantities and to update the seaframe cost estimate.

To improve the Navy's ability to make better informed LCS program and investment decisions, we recommend that the Secretary of Defense direct the Secretary of the Navy to perform a risk assessment and consider the results before committing to buy LCS ships each year in order to link procurement with evidence that the Navy is progressing in its ability to implement its new personnel, training, and maintenance concepts and has taken actions to mitigate the operational effects if these concepts cannot be implemented as intended. Specifically, this analysis should identify and assess the:

- operational limitations the Navy may face if the Navy's approach to personnel, training, and maintenance cannot be implemented as envisioned;
- possible alternatives, such as changes to the concepts or the ship design, and the related costs of those alternatives if the Navy's approach to LCS personnel, training, and maintenance cannot be implemented as envisioned in its concept of operations; and
- personnel policies and processes to reduce the risks to the LCS program. Such a holistic review could include the processes for identifying and assigning personnel, requirements LCS personnel must meet to qualify for assignment to an LCS crew, and identifying the total ship and shore LCS personnel required steady state to support the program over the long term.

## Agency Comments and Our Evaluation

In written comments on a draft of this report, DOD agreed with four recommendations and partially agreed with two of our six recommended actions. The department's comments are reprinted in their entirety in appendix II. DOD also provided technical comments, which we have incorporated as appropriate.

DOD partially agreed with our first recommendation that the Navy produce an estimate of the long-term operating and support costs and use these estimates in deciding which seaframe to buy. DOD stated that the Navy will prepare two cost estimates, one for each seaframe design, that will include estimates of the total operating and support costs for the entire class of LCS ships. However, DOD stated that, since the Navy has not released the solicitation for the fiscal year 2010-2014 buy, it is premature to discuss the down-select criteria included in the solicitation. While we appreciate the sensitivity of discussing criteria for the down-select prior to the release of the solicitation, we noted in the report that operating and support costs are critical to any evaluation of acquisition alternatives since these costs constitute over 70 percent of system life-cycle costs. We continue to believe that decision makers should consider long-term operating and support costs when deciding which of the two seaframes to buy for the remainder of the program. DOD also stated that the LCS seaframe estimate we reviewed for the report was developed solely to support trade study analysis and was not intended as a budget quality estimate. We understand this was the case, but the seaframe estimate we analyzed was the only estimate available even though the Navy has bought four LCS ships. The intent of our recommendation is to encourage DOD to develop a comprehensive cost estimate to assist decision makers as the program moves forward.

DOD agreed with our recommendation to use updated operating and support cost estimates to analyze the costs and benefits of options regarding the two seaframes built but not selected for long-term production. However, DOD stated that the Navy intends to operate and maintain the two non-selected LCS ships as part of the total LCS force structure but will continue to explore options to keep, sell, or retire the two non-selected ships during annual budget reviews. DOD's response implies that, for the present, the department has decided to keep the two non-selected LCS ships without considering the results of a complete analysis of the costs and benefits of keeping the ships compared to other alternatives. As we point out in the report, it is important that estimates of long-term operating and support costs are available to decision makers to assess alternatives before a decision is made. However, if the department's intent is to do such a cost analysis of alternatives and consider the results as part of the annual budget process, then their actions would meet the intent of our recommendation. DOD also agreed with our recommendations to include an annual update to the operating and support costs for the LCS program in the Selected Acquisition Report, and our recommendations to update both the seaframe and mission package force structure analyses and use these results in updating operating and support cost estimates.

DOD partially agreed with our sixth recommended action that DOD perform a risk assessment and consider the results before committing to buy LCS ships each year in order to link procurement with evidence that the Navy is progressing in its ability to implement its new personnel, training, and maintenance concepts. DOD stated that it agrees such risk assessments are appropriate and should be conducted. However, DOD disagreed that the risk assessment results should be linked to annual procurement decisions since the acquisition strategy is now to buy LCS in blocks—that is multiple ships—in fiscal years 2010, 2012, and 2015. DOD stated that, as an alternative, it will consider reviewing the risk assessments for personnel policies, training, and maintenance planning at the start of each new block buy. At the time of our review, the acquisition strategy involving the block buys was not yet approved by DOD. We believe that DOD's proposed alternative approach would meet the intent of our recommendation. However, we also believe that, given the new acquisition approach, it is even more important that DOD conduct the risk assessment and consider the results before making a procurement decision for each block buy since the department will be committing to several ships with each block and there will be a gap of several years between each block buy. As we point out in our report, without such a risk assessment to inform each procurement decision, the Navy risks buying ships without the assurance that its plans for personnel, training, and maintenance can be implemented as envisioned.

We are sending copies of this report to the Secretary of Defense; the Secretary of the Navy; Naval Sea Systems Command; and Fleet Forces Command. In addition, the report will be available at no charge on the GAO Web site at http://www.gao.gov.

If you or your staff have any questions, please call me at (404) 679-1816. Contact points for our Offices of Congressional Relations and Public Affairs may be found on the last page of this report. Staff members who made key contributions to this report are listed in appendix III.

John H. Pendleton
Director
Defense Capabilities and Management

# Appendix I: Scope and Methodology

To assess the extent to which the Navy estimated the long-term operating and support costs for the Littoral Combat Ship (LCS) seaframes and mission packages, we reviewed documentation of seaframes and mission package cost estimates prepared by the cost-estimating division of the Naval Sea Systems Command. We met with officials from Naval Sea System Command's cost-estimating division, as well as the program offices responsible for developing both seaframes and mission packages, to discuss and document the methodologies employed in the estimates. We also met with the Office of the Secretary of Defense's office of the Director of Cost Assessment and Program Evaluation (CAPE) to determine the extent to which CAPE had reviewed Navy cost estimates for LCS and produced an independent estimate. We compared the estimates to cost estimating best practices identified by the CAPE[1] and in the *GAO Cost Estimating and Assessment Guide*,[2] and reviewed Department of Defense (DOD) and Navy acquisition regulations. To assess the extent to which the Navy analyzed the force structure requirements underlying the planned purchase quantities of LCS seaframes and mission packages, we met with officials of the Assessments and Surface Warfare divisions of the Office of the Chief of Naval Operations. We also reviewed documents reflecting the force structure analyses the Navy performed on LCS seaframes and mission packages.

Although the Navy's estimates did not fully reflect best practices, they were based on a cost-estimating process that we deemed sufficient for reporting, with appropriate limitations. To calculate an average annual seaframe operating and support cost estimate, we divided the Navy's estimate of total operating and support costs of LCS seaframes by the planned purchase quantity of seaframes and by their expected service life. We multiplied the average annual estimated mission package operating and support cost for each mission package by the planned purchase quantity of that mission package and the assumed service life. We then added together the seaframe and mission package totals. To obtain an average annual seaframe cost that included the cost of mission packages, we divided this total program operating and support estimate by the

---

[1] Office of the Secretary of Defense, Cost Analysis Improvement Group, *Operating and Support Cost Estimating Guide* (Arlington, Va., October 2007), Office of the Secretary of Defense, Cost Analysis Improvement Group, *Operating and Support Cost Estimating Guide* (Arlington, Va., May 1, 1992).

[2] GAO, *GAO Cost Estimating and Assessment Guide*, GAO-09-3SP (Washington, D.C.: March 2009).

number of seaframe service years (seaframe quantity times assumed service life). We validated the methodology and results of our analysis with relevant officials from the Naval Sea Systems Command. However, our analysis of the Navy estimates is approximate and does not fully reflect cost estimating best practices as described in the report.

To assess the extent to which the Navy has developed and implemented plans to operate and support LCS, particularly in the areas of personnel, training, and maintenance, we reviewed and analyzed DOD and Navy guidance, the *LCS Wholeness Concept of Operations*, and instructions on personnel, training, and maintenance as well as key studies and planning documents. We also reviewed prior GAO products and DOD guidance on risk management to assess the extent that Navy plans included assessments of program risk. In addition, we interviewed officials at Headquarters, Department of the Navy and Navy Sea Systems Command for personnel, training, and maintenance as well as Fleet Forces Command, Commander, Naval Surface Forces, Navy Personnel Command, Bureau of Naval Personnel, and Navy Manpower Analysis Center.

To estimate long-term LCS personnel requirements, we analyzed Navy documentation, including personnel estimate documentation and the concept of operations, and validated the results with Navy officials at the offices listed above. To compare LCS training days to training days for other surface ships, we first identified a non-probability sample of LCS positions from both seaframes which were for critical positions such as the most senior enlisted personnel (E-8 or above), or those that generally met three of the following four criteria:

- a position that required training in several areas outside the sailor's primary specialty;
- a position for a specialty that was on a list of 14 specialties which the Commander, Naval Surface Forces determined to have "unique cross rate training";
- a position for a specialty which, at the time, was filled at less than 100 percent or a position for a specialty which, at the time, was filled at less than 100 percent at the lower levels, which might lead to less availability in the future; and
- a position in the unplanned loss pool.

To identify the training days required prior to reporting to an LCS crew, we obtained the training days required for the positions in our sample based on the Navy's study of training requirements for LCS. We reviewed the process of how the Navy study team developed the course time requirements by speaking with knowledgeable officials and found the process was reasonable. To identify the training days required before reporting to a destroyer and amphibious transport docking ship, we obtained the training days required for comparable positions in our sample. We validated these data in meetings with Naval Sea Systems Command and Bureau of Naval Personnel officials. Finally, we compared the training days for LCS with the training days for the destroyer and amphibious transport docking ship. We reviewed the results of this comparison with Bureau of Naval Personnel, Fleet Forces Command, Naval Sea Systems Command, and several offices within the Office of the Chief of Naval Operations who generally agreed with the data, methodology, and results. Based on the work described above we concluded that the data were sufficiently reliable for our purposes.

We conducted this performance audit from October 2008 through February 2010 in accordance with generally accepted government auditing standards. Those standards require that we plan and perform the audit to obtain sufficient, appropriate evidence to provide a reasonable basis for our findings and conclusions based on our audit objectives. We believe that the evidence obtained provides a reasonable basis for our findings and conclusions based on our audit objectives.

# Appendix II: Comments from the Department of Defense

OFFICE OF THE UNDER SECRETARY OF DEFENSE
3000 DEFENSE PENTAGON
WASHINGTON, DC 20301-3000

ACQUISITION
TECHNOLOGY
AND LOGISTICS

JAN 21 2010

Mr. John H. Pendleton
Director, Defense Capabilities and Management
U.S. Government Accountability Office
441 G Street, N.W.
Washington, DC 20548

Dear Mr. Pendleton:

This is the Department of Defense response to the GAO draft report, GAO-10-257, "LITTORAL COMBAT SHIP: Actions Needed to Improve Operating Cost Estimates and Mitigate Risks in Implementing New Concepts," dated December 14, 2009 (GAO Code 351278). The Department's comments on the six specific recommendations are enclosed.

The Department concurs with recommendations 2, 3, 4, and 5. The Department partially concurs with recommendations 1 and 6. In response to recommendation 1, the Department agrees that life cycle cost estimates should be completed for both LCS designs, but it is premature to discuss whether life cycle costs will be a factor in down-selecting to a single design because the solicitation for the FY 2010 block buy has not been released. The partial concur on recommendation 6 relates to Department concerns about using the recommended risk assessments as decision criteria at annual buy decisions. The Department proposes instead to consider the risk assessments prior to major procurement decisions in FY 2010, FY 2012, and FY 2015.

The Department appreciates the opportunity to comment on the draft report. Technical comments were provided separately. For further questions concerning this report, please contact Ms. Darlene Costello, Deputy Director, Naval Warfare, 703-697-2205.

Sincerely,

David G. Ahern
Director
Portfolio Systems Acquisition

Enclosure:
As stated

**GAO DRAFT REPORT – DATED DECEMBER 14, 2009**
**GAO CODE 351278/GAO-10-257**

**"LITTORAL COMBAT SHIP: Actions Needed to Improve Operating Cost
Estimates and Mitigate Risks in Implementing New Concepts"**

**DEPARTMENT OF DEFENSE COMMENTS
TO THE RECOMMENDATIONS**

**RECOMMENDATION 1:** The GAO recommends that the Secretary of Defense direct
the Secretary of the Navy to, before deciding which seaframe to buy, produce a complete
estimate of the long-term operating and support costs which fully reflects cost estimating
best practices for each seaframe and use these updated estimates in deciding which
seaframe to buy for the remainder of the program.

**DOD RESPONSE:** Partially concur. The Navy will prepare two Program Life Cycle
Cost Estimates (PLCCEs) in support of the Milestone B Defense Acquisition Board
review of the Littoral Combat Ship (LCS) program, one for each of the potential
outcomes of the down-select decision. The PLCCEs will be developed using best cost
estimating practices (including cost risk, cost driver sensitivity analyses, and an
Independent Cost Estimate, in accordance with the Naval Sea Systems Command cost
estimating group documented 12-step cost estimating process) and include estimates of
the total operating and support costs for the entire class of LCS ships, including costs to
operate and support the two ships of the non-selected design expected to remain as
operational units in the Navy's LCS force structure. GAO should note that the LCS
seaframe estimate reviewed by the GAO for this report was developed solely to support
trade study analysis and was not intended as a budget quality estimate.

The Navy has not released the solicitation for the FY2010-FY2014 block buy, therefore,
it is premature to discuss the down-select criteria included in the solicitation. For
reference purposes this recommendation will be identified as item GAO-10-257-01.

**RECOMMENDATION 2:** The GAO recommends that the Secretary of Defense direct
the Secretary of the Navy to use an updated estimate as a basis for analyzing the costs
and benefits of options regarding the two seaframes built but not selected for long-term
production, and use the results of this analysis in making the decision of how to use, or
whether to retire, these seaframes.

**DOD RESPONSE:** Concur. The costs for operating and supporting the two non-
selected Littoral Combat Ships (LCS) will be included in the life cycle cost estimates

Enclosure
Page 1 of 4

prepared for the Milestone B Defense Acquisition Board (DAB) review. These estimates will be used to inform the DAB on the cost of keeping the two non-selected seaframes compared to procuring two more seaframes of the selected design and selling-off or retiring the two non-selected seaframes. However, at this point, the Navy intends to operate and maintain the two non-selected LCS seaframes as part of the total LCS force structure. There is currently no plan to procure two additional seaframes of the selected design to make up any reduction in force structure caused by selling-off or retiring the two non-selected LCS seaframes. At this time, the Department accepts the risk of keeping the two non-selected seaframes, but will continue to explore options to keep, sell, or retire the two non-selected seaframes during annual budget reviews. For reference purposes this recommendation will be identified as item GAO-10-257-02.

**RECOMMENDATION 3:** The GAO recommends that the Secretary of Defense direct the Secretary of the Navy to annually update the cost estimate for the long-term operating and support costs of the seaframe and each mission package using cost estimating best practices and submit the results to the Department of Defense as well as to Congress as part of the Littoral Combat Ship (LCS) Selected Acquisition Report.

**DOD RESPONSE:** Concur. The Office of the Secretary of Defense will ensure that the Navy's Selected Acquisition Report for the Littoral Combat Ship program will reflect an annual update to the operating and support costs for the seaframe and mission packages using the Program Life Cycle Cost Estimates information prepared for the Milestone B Defense Acquisition Board review as the baseline. For reference purposes this recommendation will be identified as item GAO-10-257-03.

**RECOMMENDATION 4:** The GAO recommends that the Secretary of Defense direct the Secretary of the Navy to perform complete and updated force structure analyses on the Littoral Combat Ship mission packages to help determine the appropriate purchase quantities over the life of the program, and use these updated quantities for the mission package cost estimate.

**DOD RESPONSE:** Concur. The Navy will update the force structure analyses used to determine the number and types of mission packages to be procured over the life of the program as Littoral Combat Ship mission requirements evolve.

When adjustments to the mission package procurement objectives are deemed necessary, they will be rolled into the annual updates to the operating and support costs for the program. However, it should be noted that adjustments to the mission package procurement objectives may be deemed necessary on an annual basis.

These adjustments to the mission package procurement objectives will be rolled into the annual updates to the operating and support costs for the program as they evolve.

Enclosure
Page 2 of 4

However, it should be noted that these mission package adjustments might not occur annually. For reference purposes this recommendation will be identified as item GAO-10-257-04.

**RECOMMENDATION 5:** The GAO recommends that the Secretary of Defense direct the Secretary of the Navy to perform an updated seaframe force structure analysis when key underlying assumptions affecting seaframe quantities change, such as crewing policy, overseas homeports, or presence requirements, and use this updated analysis to adjust quantities and to update the seaframe cost estimate

**DOD RESPONSE:** Concur. The Navy will update its seaframe force structure analysis as required to reflect changes in key underlying assumptions that affect the force structure. If the procurement quantities for seaframes changes, then the Navy will update the seaframe cost estimate and report the resulting changes in program operating and support costs in the following Selected Acquisition Report for the Littoral Combat Ship program. For reference purposes this recommendation will be identified as item GAO-10-257-05.

**RECOMMENDATION 6:** The GAO recommends that the Secretary of Defense direct the Secretary of the Navy to perform a risk assessment and consider the results before committing to buy Littoral Combat Ship (LCS) ships each year in order to link procurement with evidence that the Navy is progressing in its ability to implement its new personnel, training, and maintenance concepts and has taken actions to mitigate the operational effects if these concepts cannot be implemented as intended. Specifically, this analysis should identify and assess the:

• operational limitations the Navy may face if the Navy's approach to personnel, training, and maintenance cannot be implemented as envisioned;

• possible alternatives, such as changes to the concepts or the ship design, and the related costs of those alternatives if the Navy's approach to LCS personnel, training, and maintenance cannot be implemented as envisioned in its concept of operations; and

• personnel policies and processes to reduce the risks to the LCS program. Such a holistic review could include the processes for identifying and assigning personnel, requirements LCS personnel must meet to qualify for assignment to a LCS crew, and identifying the total ship and shore LCS personnel required steady state to support the program over the long term.

Enclosure
Page 3 of 4

**DOD RESPONSE**: Partially concur. The Department agrees that risk assessments are appropriate and should be conducted. However, the Department disagrees that the results of these assessments should be linked to annual procurement decisions for Littoral Combat Ship (LCS) seaframes. The Acquisition Strategy for the LCS program lays out a plan for two block buys of LCS seaframes over the period from Fiscal Year (FY) 2010 through FY 2014. These block buys are specifically intended to promote acquisition cost reductions to make the program more affordable over the long term. To assure a stable program, the integrity of the block buys needs to be maintained. As an alternative, the Department will consider reviewing the risk assessments for personnel policies, training, and maintenance planning at the start of each new block buy. Those review points would occur at the Milestone B Defense Acquisition Board (DAB) review in FY 2010 and at the DAB reviews prior to the FY 2012 block buy and the FY 2015 procurement. While these review points do not occur annually, as recommended by the GAO, the Department accepts the risk in considering these performance assessments at procurement decision points spaced at two or three year intervals and will continue to monitor risk assessments for personnel policies, training, and maintenance planning during the intervening years. For reference purposes this recommendation will be identified as item GAO-10-257-06.

Enclosure
Page 4 of 4

# Appendix III: GAO Contact and Staff Acknowledgments

## GAO Contact

John H. Pendleton, (404) 679-1816, pendletonj@gao.gov

## Acknowledgments

In addition to the contact named above, Patricia W. Lentini, Assistant Director; Brenda M. Waterfield; James R. Bancroft; Simon J. Hirschfeld; Linda S. Keefer; and Grace Coleman made key contributions to this report.

# Navy Littoral Combat Ship (LCS) Program: Background, Issues, and Options for Congress

Ronald O'Rourke
Specialist in Naval Affairs

June 10, 2010

Congressional Research Service

7-5700

www.crs.gov

RL33741

CRS Report for Congress ———————————————————————————

*Prepared for Members and Committees of Congress*

# Summary

The Littoral Combat Ship (LCS) is a relatively inexpensive Navy surface combatant equipped with modular "plug-and-fight" mission packages. The basic version of the LCS, without any mission packages, is referred to as the LCS sea frame.

The Navy wants to field a force of 55 LCSs. The first two (LCS-1 and LCS-2) were procured in FY2005 and FY2006 and were commissioned into service on November 8, 2008, and January 16, 2010. Another two (LCS-3 and LCS-4) were procured in FY2009 and are under construction. Two more (LCS-5 and LCS-6) were procured in FY2010.

The Navy's FY2011-FY2015 shipbuilding plan calls for procuring 17 more LCSs in annual quantities of 2, 3, 4, 4, and 4. The Navy's proposed FY2011 budget requests $1,231.0 million in procurement funding for the two LCSs that the Navy wants to procure in FY2011, and $278.4 million in FY2011 advance procurement funding for the 11 LCSs that the Navy wants to procure in FY2012-FY2014. The Navy's proposed FY2011 budget also requests procurement funding to procure LCS mission packages, LCS module weapons, and research and development funding for the LCS program.

There are currently two very different LCS designs—one developed and produced by an industry team led by Lockheed, and another developed and produced by an industry team led by General Dynamics. LCS-1 and LCS-3 use the Lockheed design; LCS-2 and LCS-4 use the General Dynamics design.

On September 16, 2009, the Navy announced a proposed new LCS acquisition strategy. Under the strategy, the Navy would hold a competition to pick a single design to which all LCSs procured in FY2010 and subsequent years would be built. (The process of selecting the single design for all future production is called a down select.) The winner of the down select would be awarded a contract to build 10 LCSs over the five-year period FY2010-FY2014, at a rate of two ships per year. The Navy would then hold a second competition—open to all bidders other than the shipyard building the 10 LCSs in FY2010-FY2014—to select a second shipyard to build up to five additional LCSs to the same design in FY2012-FY2014 (one ship in FY2012, and two ships per year in FY2013-FY2014). These two shipyards would then compete for contracts to build LCSs procured in FY2015 and subsequent years.

Section 121(a) and (b) of the FY2010 defense authorization act (H.R. 2647/P.L. 111-84 of October 28, 2009) grant the Navy contracting and other authority needed to implement this new LCS acquisition strategy.

The Navy plans to make the down select decision and award the contract to build the 10 LCSs sometime this summer.

FY2011 issues for Congress include whether to approve, reject, or modify the Navy's request for FY2011 procurement and advance procurement funding for the LCS program, and whether to provide any additional direction to the Navy regarding LCS acquisition strategy.

# Contents

## Tables

## Appendixes

## Contacts

# Introduction

The Littoral Combat Ship (LCS) is a relatively inexpensive Navy surface combatant equipped with modular "plug-and-fight" mission packages. The basic version of the LCS, without any mission packages, is referred to as the LCS sea frame.

The Navy wants to field a force of 55 LCSs. The first two (LCS-1 and LCS-2) were procured in FY2005 and FY2006 and were commissioned into service on November 8, 2008, and January 16, 2010. Another two (LCS-3 and LCS-4) were procured in FY2009 and are under construction. Two more (LCS-5 and LCS-6) were procured in FY2010.

The Navy's FY2011-FY2015 shipbuilding plan calls for procuring 17 more LCSs in annual quantities of 2, 3, 4, 4, and 4. The Navy's proposed FY2011 budget requests $1,231.0 million in procurement funding for the two LCSs that the Navy wants to procure in FY2011, and $278.4 million in FY2011 advance procurement funding for the 11 LCSs that the Navy wants to procure in FY2012-FY2014. The Navy's proposed FY2011 budget also requests procurement funding to procure LCS mission packages, LCS module weapons, and research and development funding for the LCS program.

There are currently two very different LCS designs—one developed and produced by an industry team led by Lockheed, and another developed and produced by an industry team led by General Dynamics. LCS-1 and LCS-3 use the Lockheed design; LCS-2 and LCS-4 use the General Dynamics design.

On September 16, 2009, the Navy announced a proposed new LCS acquisition strategy. Under the strategy, the Navy would hold a competition to pick a single design to which all LCSs procured in FY2010 and subsequent years would be built. (The process of selecting the single design for all future production is called a down select.) The winner of the down select would be awarded a contract to build 10 LCSs over the five-year period FY2010-FY2014, at a rate of two ships per year. The Navy would then hold a second competition—open to all bidders other than the shipyard building the 10 LCSs in FY2010-FY2014—to select a second shipyard to build up to five additional LCSs to the same design in FY2012-FY2014 (one ship in FY2012, and two ships per year in FY2013-FY2014). These two shipyards would then compete for contracts to build LCSs procured in FY2015 and subsequent years.

Section 121(a) and (b) of the FY2010 defense authorization act (H.R. 2647/P.L. 111-84 of October 28, 2009) grant the Navy contracting and other authority needed to implement this new LCS acquisition strategy.

The Navy plans to make the down select decision and award the contract to build the 10 LCSs sometime this summer.

FY2011 issues for Congress include whether to approve, reject, or modify the Navy's request for FY2011 procurement and advance procurement funding for the LCS program, and whether to provide any additional direction to the Navy regarding LCS acquisition strategy. Decisions that Congress makes on this issue could affect future Navy capabilities and funding requirements, and the shipbuilding industrial base.

# Background

## The LCS in General

The LCS program was announced on November 1, 2001.[1] The LCS is a relatively inexpensive Navy surface combatant that is to be equipped with modular "plug-and-fight" mission packages, including unmanned vehicles (UVs). Rather than being a multimission ship like the Navy's larger surface combatants, the LCS is to be a focused-mission ship equipped to perform one primary mission at any one time. The ship's mission orientation can be changed by changing out its mission packages. The basic version of the LCS, without any mission packages, is referred to as the LCS sea frame.

The LCS's primary intended missions are antisubmarine warfare (ASW), mine countermeasures (MCM), and surface warfare (SUW) against small boats (including so-called "swarm boats"), particularly in littoral (i.e., near-shore) waters. The LCS program includes the development and procurement of ASW, MCM, and SUW mission packages for LCS sea frames. Additional missions for the LCS include peacetime engagement and partnership-building operations, intelligence, surveillance, and reconnaissance (ISR) operations, maritime intercept operations, operations to support special operations forces, and homeland defense operations.

The LCS displaces about 3,000 tons, making it about the size of a corvette (i.e., a light frigate) or a Coast Guard cutter. It has a maximum speed of more than 40 knots, compared to something more than 30 knots for the Navy cruisers and destroyers. The LCS has a shallower draft than Navy cruisers and destroyers, permitting it to operate in certain coastal waters and visit certain ports that are not accessible to Navy cruisers and destroyers. The LCS employs automation to achieve a reduced "core" crew of 40 sailors. Up to 35 or so additional sailors are to operate the ship's embarked aircraft and mission packages, making for a total crew of about 75, compared to more than 200 for the Navy's frigates and about 300 (or more) for the Navy's current cruisers and destroyers.

## Two Industry Teams, Each with Its Own Design

On May 27, 2004, the Navy awarded contracts to two industry teams—one led by Lockheed Martin, the other by General Dynamics (GD)—to design two versions of the LCS, with options for each team to build up to two LCSs each. The two teams' LCS designs are quite different— Lockheed's design is based on a steel semi-planing monohull, while GD's design in based on an aluminum trimaran hull. The two ships also use different combat systems (i.e., different collections of built-in sensors, computers, software, and tactical displays) that were designed by

[1] On November 1, 2001, the Navy announced that it was launching a Future Surface Combatant Program aimed at acquiring a family of next-generation surface combatants. This new family of surface combatants, the Navy stated, would include three new classes of ships: a destroyer called the DD(X)—later redesignated the DDG-1000—for the precision long-range strike and naval gunfire mission; a cruiser called the CG(X) for the air defense and ballistic missile mission, and a smaller combatant called the Littoral Combat Ship (LCS) to counter submarines, small surface attack craft, and mines in heavily contested littoral (near-shore) areas. For more on the DDG-1000 program, see CRS Report RL32109, *Navy DDG-51 and DDG-1000 Destroyer Programs: Background and Issues for Congress*, by Ronald O'Rourke. For more on the CG(X) program, see CRS Report RL34179, *Navy CG(X) Cruiser Program: Background for Congress*, by Ronald O'Rourke.

each industry team. The Navy states that both designs meet the Key Performance Parameters (KPPs) for the LCS program. The Lockheed team built LCS-1 and is building LCS-3 at Marinette Marine of Marinette, WI. The General Dynamics team built LCS-2 and is building LCS-4 at the Austal USA shipyard of Mobile, AL.[2]

## Planned Procurement Quantities

The Navy plans to field a force of 55 LCS sea frames and 64 LCS mission packages (16 ASW, 24 MCM, and 24 SUW). The Navy's planned force of 55 LCSs would account for about 18% of the Navy's planned force of 3131 ships of all types.[3]

The Navy's five-year (FY2011-FY2015) shipbuilding plan calls for procuring 17 LCSs in annual quantities of 2, 3, 4, 4, and 4. The Navy's 30-year (FY2011-FY2040) shipbuilding plan shows three LCSs per year for FY2016-FY2019, two per year for FY2020-FY2024, a 1-2-1-2 pattern for FY2025-FY2033, and two per year for FY2034-FY2040. LCSs scheduled for procurement in the final years of the 30-year plan would be replacements for LCSs that will have reached the end of their 25-year expected service lives by that time.

## Unit Procurement Cost Cap

LCS sea frames procured in FY2010 and subsequent years are subject to a unit procurement cost cap. The legislative history of the cost cap is as follows:

- The cost cap was originally established by **Section 124 of the FY2006 defense authorization act** (H.R. 1815/P.L. 109-163 of January 6, 2006). Under this provision, the fifth and sixth ships in the class were to cost no more than $220 million each, plus adjustments for inflation and other factors.

- The cost cap was amended by **Section 125 of the FY2008 defense authorization act** (H.R. 4986/P.L. 110-181 of January 28, 2008). This provision amended the cost cap to $460 million per ship, with no adjustments for inflation, and applied the cap to all LCSs procured in FY2008 and subsequent years.

- The cost cap was amended again by **Section 122 of the FY2009 defense authorization act** (S. 3001/P.L. 110-417 of October 14, 2008). This provision deferred the implementation of the cost cap by two years, applying it to all LCSs procured in FY2010 and subsequent years.

- The cost cap was amended again by **Section 121(c) and (d) of the FY2010 defense authorization act** (H.R. 2647/P.L. 111-84 of October 28, 2009). The provision adjusted the cost cap to $480 million per ship, excluded certain costs from being counted against the $480 million cap, included provisions for adjusting that figure over time to take inflation and other events into account, and

---

[2] Austal USA was created in 1999 as a joint venture between Austal Limited of Henderson, Western Australia and Bender Shipbuilding & Repair Company of Mobile, AL. The GD LCS team also includes GD/BIW as prime contractor to provide program management and planning, provide technical management, and to serve as "LCS system production lead."

[3] For more on the Navy's planned 313-ship fleet, see CRS Report RL32665, *Navy Force Structure and Shipbuilding Plans: Background and Issues for Congress*, by Ronald O'Rourke.

permitted the Secretary of the Navy to waive the cost cap under certain conditions.[4]

## Growth in LCS Sea Frame Procurement Costs

The Navy originally spoke of building LCS sea frames for about $220 million each in constant FY2005 dollars. Estimated LCS sea frame unit procurement costs have since more than doubled. The FY2011 budget estimates the procurement costs of LCS sea frames to be procured in FY2011-FY2015 at roughly $600 million each in then-year dollars. For a detailed discussion of cost growth on LCS sea frames from the FY2006 budget cycle through the FY2009 budget cycle, see **Appendix B**.

## 2007 Program Restructuring and Ship Cancellations

The Navy substantially restructured the LCS program in 2007 in response to significant cost growth and delays in constructing the first LCS sea frames. This restructuring led to the cancellation of four LCSs that were funded in FY2006 and FY2007. A fifth LCS, funded in FY2008, was cancelled in 2008. For details on the 2007 program restructuring and the cancellation of the five LCSs funded in FY2006-FY2008, see **Appendix C**.

---

[4] Section 121(d)(1) states that the Secretary of the Navy may waive the cost cap if:

  (A) the Secretary provides supporting data and certifies in writing to the congressional defense committees that—

    (i) the total amount obligated or expended for procurement of the vessel-

      (I) is in the best interest of the United States; and

      (II) is affordable, within the context of the annual naval vessel construction plan required by section 231 of title 10, United States Code; and

    (ii) the total amount obligated or expended for procurement of at least one other vessel authorized by subsection (a) has been or is expected to be less than $480,000,000; and

  (B) a period of not less than 30 days has expired following the date on which such certification and data are submitted to the congressional defense committees.

## New Acquisition Strategy Announced in September 2009

On September 16, 2009, the Navy announced a proposed new LCS acquisition strategy.[5] Under the strategy, the Navy would hold a competition to pick a single design to which all LCSs procured in FY2010 and subsequent years would be built. (The process of selecting the single design for all future production is called a down select.) The winner of the down select would be awarded a contract to build 10 LCSs over the five-year period FY2010-FY2014, at a rate of two ships per year. The Navy would then hold a second competition—open to all bidders other than the shipyard building the 10 LCSs in FY2010-FY2014—to select a second shipyard to build up to five additional LCSs to the same design in FY2012-FY2014 (one ship in FY2012, and two ships per year in FY2013-FY2014). These two shipyards would then compete for contracts to build LCSs procured in FY2015 and subsequent years.

Section 121(a) and (b) of the FY2010 defense authorization act (H.R. 2647/P.L. 111-84 of October 28, 2009) grant the Navy contracting and other authority needed to implement this new LCS acquisition strategy.

The Navy plans to make the down select decision and award the contract to build the 10 LCSs sometime this summer 2010.[6]

For additional background information on the Navy's new acquisition strategy, see **Appendix D**.

## FY2011 Funding Request

The Navy's proposed FY2011 budget requests $1,231.0 million in procurement funding for the two LCSs that the Navy wants to procure in FY2011, and $278.4 million in FY2011 advance procurement funding for the 11 LCSs that the Navy wants to procure in FY2012-FY2014. The Navy's proposed FY2011 budget estimates the procurement costs of LCS sea frames to be procured in FY2011-FY2015 at roughly $600 million each in then-year dollars. The Navy's

---

[5] Prior to the Navy's announcement of September 16, 2009, the Navy had announced an acquisition strategy for LCSs to be procured in FY2009 and FY2010. Under this acquisition strategy, the Navy bundled together the two LCSs funded in FY2009 (LCSs 3 and 4) with the three LCSs to be requested for FY2010 into a single, five-ship solicitation. The Navy announced that each LCS industry team would be awarded a contract for one of the FY2009 ships, and that the prices that the two teams bid for both the FY2009 ships and the FY2010 ships would determine the allocation of the three FY2010 ships, with the winning team getting two of the FY2010 ships and the other team getting one FY2010 ship. This strategy was intended to use the carrot of the third FY2010 ship to generate bidding pressure on the two industry teams for both the FY2009 ships and the FY2010 ships.

The Navy stated that the contracts for the two FY2009 ships would be awarded by the end of January 2009. The first contract (for Lockheed Martin, to build LCS-3) was awarded March 23, 2009; the second contract (for General Dynamics, to build LCS-4) was awarded May 1, 2009. The delay in the awarding of the contracts past the end-of-January target date may have been due in part to the challenge the Navy faced in coming to agreement with the industry teams on prices for the two FY2009 ships that would permit the three FY2010 ships to be built within the $460 million LCS unit procurement cost cap. See also Statement of RADM Victor Guillory, U.S. Navy Director of Surface Warfare, and RADM William E. Landay, III, Program Executive Officer Ships, and Ms. E. Anne Sandel, Program Executive Officer Littoral and Mine Warfare, before the Subcommittee on Seapower and Expeditionary Forces of the House Armed Services Committee [hearing] on the Current Status of the Littoral Combat Ship Program, March 10, 2009, pp. 7-8.

[6] Source: Spoken testimony of Sean Stackley, Assistant Secretary of the Navy (Research, Development and Acquisition), at a May 6, 2010, hearing on Navy shipbuilding programs before the Seapower subcommittee of the Senate Armed Services Committee, as reflected in the transcript for the hearing.

---

proposed FY2011 budget also requests procurement funding to procure LCS mission packages, and research and development funding for the LCS program.

# Issues for Congress

## New Acquisition Strategy Announced in September 2009

The new LCS acquisition strategy announced by the Navy on September 16, 2009, poses several potential oversight questions for Congress, including the following:

- Did the timing of the Navy's September 2009 announcement of the new strategy—very late in the congressional process for reviewing, marking up, and finalizing action on the FY2010 defense budget—provide Congress with sufficient time to adequately review the proposal prior to finalizing its action on the FY2010 defense budget?

- Does the Navy's proposed strategy allow the Navy enough time to adequately evaluate the operational characteristics of the two LCS designs before selecting one of those designs for all future production?

- Does the Navy's proposed method for conducting the LCS down select—the Request for Proposals (RFP)—appropriately balance procurement cost against other criteria, such as life-cycle operation and support (O&S) cost and ship capability?

- What risks would the Navy face if the shipyard that wins the competition to build the 10 LCSs in FY2010-FY2014 cannot build them within the contracted cost?

- How does the Navy plan to evolve the combat system on the winning LCS design to a configuration that has greater commonality with one or more existing Navy surface ship combat systems?

- What are the Navy's longer-term plans regarding the two "orphan" LCSs that are built to the design that is not chosen in the down select?

- What potential alternatives are there to the Navy's new acquisition strategy?

Each of these questions is discussed briefly below.

### Enough Time for Adequate Congressional Review of Navy Proposal?

One potential issue for Congress concerning the Navy's proposed acquisition strategy is whether the timing of the Navy's September 2009 announcement of the new LCS acquisition strategy—very late in the congressional process for reviewing, marking up, and finalizing action on the FY2010 defense budget—provided Congress with sufficient time to adequately review the proposal prior to finalizing its action on the FY2010 defense budget. The announcement of the Navy's proposed acquisition strategy on September 16, 2009, came

- after the defense committees of Congress had held their hearings to review the FY2010 budget submission;

- after the FY2010 defense authorization bill (H.R. 2647/S. 1390) and the Department of Defense (DOD) appropriations bill (H.R. 3326) had been reported in the House and Senate;

- after both the House and Senate had amended and passed their versions of the FY2010 defense authorization bill, setting the stage for the conference on that bill; and

- after the House had passed its version of the FY2010 DOD appropriations bill.

The timing of the Navy's announcement was a byproduct of the fact that the Navy was not able to see and evaluate the industry bids for the three LCSs that the navy had originally requested for FY2010 until August 2009. The September 16, 2009, announcement date may have been the earliest possible announcement date, given the time the Navy needed to consider the situation created by the bids, evaluate potential courses of action, and select the newly proposed acquisition strategy.

Although the Navy might not have been able to present the proposed strategy to Congress any sooner than September 16, the timing of the Navy's announcement nevertheless put Congress in the position of being asked to approve a major proposal for the LCS program—a proposal that would determine the basic shape of the acquisition strategy for the program for many years into the future—with little or no opportunity for formal congressional review and consideration through hearings and committee markup activities.

A shortage of time for formal congressional review and consideration would be a potential oversight issue for Congress for any large weapon acquisition program, but this might be especially the case for the LCS program, because it would not be the first time that the Navy has put Congress in the position of having to make a significant decision about the LCS program with little or no opportunity for formal congressional review and consideration. As discussed in previous CRS reporting on the LCS program, a roughly similar situation occurred in the summer of 2002, after Congress had completed its budget-review hearings on the proposed FY2003 budget, when the Navy submitted a late request for the research and development funding that effectively started the LCS program.[7]

---

[7] The issue of whether Congress was given sufficient time to review and consider the merits of the LCS program in its early stages was discussed through multiple editions of past CRS reports covering the LCS program. The discussion in those reports raised the question of whether "Navy officials adopted a rapid acquisition strategy for the LCS program in part to limit the amount of time available to Congress to assess the merits of the LCS program and thereby effectively rush Congress into approving the start of LCS procurement before Congress fully understands the details of the program." The discussion continued:

> With regard to the possibility of rushing Congress into a quick decision on LCS procurement, it can be noted that announcing the LCS program in November 2001 and subsequently proposing to start procurement in FY2005 resulted in a situation of Congress having only three annual budget-review seasons to learn about the new LCS program, assess its merits against other competing DOD priorities, and make a decision on whether to approve the start of procurement. These three annual budget-review seasons would occur in 2002, 2003, and 2004, when Congress would review the Navy's proposed FY2003, FY2004, and FY2005 budgets, respectively. Congress' opportunity to conduct a thorough review of the LCS program in the first two of these three years, moreover, may have been hampered:
>
> - **2002 budget-review season (for FY2003 budget).** The Navy's original FY2003 budget request, submitted to Congress in February 2002, contained no apparent funding for development of the LCS. In addition, the Navy in early 2002 had not yet announced that it intended to employ a rapid acquisition strategy for the LCS program. As a result, in the early

(continued...)

Supporters of the idea of approving the Navy's proposed acquisition strategy as part of Congress's work to finalize action on the FY2010 defense budget could argue one or more of the following:

- The timing of the Navy's proposal, though not convenient for Congress, nevertheless represented a good-faith effort by the Navy to present the proposal to Congress at the earliest possible date. The Navy conducted multiple briefings with congressional offices starting in September 2009 to explain the proposed strategy.

- The LCS program needed to be put on a more stable long-term path as soon as possible, and if Congress did not approve the proposal as part of its work in finalizing action on the FY2010 defense budget, another year would pass before the LCS program could be put on a stable path approved by Congress.

- Although cost growth and construction problems with the LCS program can be viewed as a consequence of past attempts to move ahead too quickly on the LCS program, the Navy's new acquisition strategy does not risk repeating this experience, because it does not represent another attempt to move ahead on the program at an imprudent speed. To the contrary, the strategy seeks to reduce execution risks by limiting LCS procurement to a maximum of four ships per year and providing a stable planning environment for LCS shipyards and suppliers.

---

(...continued)

> months of 2002, there may have been little reason within Congress to view the LCS program as a significant FY2003 budget-review issue. In the middle of 2002, the Navy submitted an amended request asking for $33 million in FY2003 development funding for the LCS program. Navy officials explained that they did not decide until the middle of 2002 that they wanted to pursue a rapid acquisition strategy for the LCS program, and consequently did not realize until then that there was a need to request $33 million in FY2003 funding for the program. By the middle of 2002, however, the House and Senate Armed Services committees had already held their spring FY2003 budget-review hearings and marked up their respective versions of the FY2003 defense authorization bill. These two committees thus did not have an opportunity to use the spring 2002 budget-review season to review in detail the Navy's accelerated acquisition plan for the LCS program or the supporting request for $33 million in funding.
>
> - **2003 budget-review season (for FY2004 budget).** To support a more informed review of the LCS program during the spring 2003 budget-review season, the conferees on the FY2003 defense authorization bill included a provision (Section 218) requiring the Navy to submit a detailed report on several aspects of the LCS program, including its acquisition strategy. In response to this legislation, the Navy in February 2003 submitted a report of eight pages in length, including a title page and a first page devoted mostly to a restatement of Section 218's requirement for the report. The House and Senate Armed Services committees, in their reports on the FY2004 defense authorization bill, have expressed dissatisfaction with the thoroughness of the report as a response to the requirements of Section 218. (For details, see the "Legislative Activity" section of this report.) It is thus not clear whether the defense authorization committees were able to conduct their spring 2003 budget-review hearings on the FY2004 budget with as much information about the LCS program as they might have preferred.

(See, for example, CRS Report RL 32109, *Navy DD(X), CG(X), and LCS Ship Acquisition Programs: Oversight Issues and Options for Congress*, by Ronald O'Rourke, updated July 29, 2005, pp. CRS-59 to CRS-60. This discussion was carried through multiple updates of CRS reports covering the LCS program.)

- If the proposed strategy were not approved by Congress as part of its action on the FY2010 budget, the LCSs procured in FY2010 would be more expensive to procure, since they would not benefit from economies of scale that would come from awarding the FY2010 ships as part of a contract that also includes LCSs to be procured in FY2011-FY2014.

Supporters of the idea of deferring a decision on the Navy's proposed acquisition strategy until the FY2011 budget cycle could argue one or more of the following:

- Navy briefings to Congress on the proposed strategy starting in September 2009, though helpful, were not sufficient for Congress to fully understand the features and potential implications of the Navy's proposed acquisition strategy—much less the relative merits of potential alternatives to that strategy.

- The risks of making a quick decision on the Navy's proposed acquisition strategy, with little time for formal congressional review and consideration, are underscored by the history of the LCS program, which includes substantial cost growth and construction problems that can be viewed as the consequence of past attempts to move ahead quickly on the program, without more-extensive congressional review and consideration.

- The desire to avoid a paying a relatively high cost for LCSs procured in FY2010, though real, should not have been a controlling factor in this situation (i.e., should not have been "the tail that wags the dog"). Paying a higher cost for LCSs procured in FY2010, though not optimal, would be an investment to buy time for Congress to more fully review and consider the merits of both the Navy's proposal and potential alternatives to it. Problems avoided through a full congressional review and consideration of the Navy's proposal and potential alternatives during the FY2011 budget cycle could eventually save the Navy a lot more money than the Navy hopes to save on the LCSs procured in FY2010 by procuring them as part of a contract that also includes LCSs to be procured in FY2011-FY2014.

- Approving the Navy's proposed acquisition strategy at a late juncture in the annual congressional process for reviewing and marking up the defense budget would set an undesirable precedent from Congress's standpoint regarding late submissions to Congress of significant proposals for large defense acquisition programs, and encourage DOD to do the same with other large weapon acquisition programs in the future in the hopes of stampeding Congress into making quick decisions on major proposals for those programs.

### Enough Time to Evaluate the Two Designs' Operational Characteristics?

Regarding the question of whether the Navy's proposed acquisition strategy allows the Navy enough time to adequately evaluate the operational characteristics of the two LCS designs before selecting one of those designs for all future production, potential questions for Congress include the following:

- Since LCS-1 as of September 2009 had been in commissioned service for less than a year, and LCS-2 as of that date had not yet been delivered to the Navy, how firm was the basis for the Navy's determination that both LCS designs meet the Navy's operational requirements for LCS?

- By late spring or early summer of 2010—when the Navy plans to award a contract to the winner of the down select—the Navy will have had only a limited time to evaluate the operational characteristics of LCS-1 and LCS-2 through fleet exercises and use in actual Navy deployments. Will the Navy at that point have a sufficient understanding of the two designs' operational characteristics to appropriately treat the operational characteristics of the two designs in the down select?

The Navy and its supporters could argue that the Navy has chosen a preferred design for other new Navy ships (such as the DDG-1000 destroyer) on the basis of paper designs only, and consequently that the Navy would have a firmer basis for performing the LCS down select than it has had on other shipbuilding programs. They can argue that the Navy has a good understanding of the basic differences between the ships—that the Lockheed design, for example, may have better features for supporting small boat operations (which are used for certain LCS missions), while the General Dynamics design may have better features for supporting helicopter and unmanned aerial vehicle (UAV) operations (which are used for certain LCS missions).

Skeptics could argue that the Navy in the past has talked about performing an extensive operational review of each design prior to settling on an acquisition strategy for follow-on ships in the program, and that the innovative nature of the LCS—a modular ship with plug-and-fight mission packages and a small crew—increases the risks associated with selecting a single LCS design before performing such an extensive operational review. Skeptics could argue that the Navy is depriving itself of the opportunity to better understand, through exercises and real-world deployments, the implications for overall fleet operations of building all LCSs to one design or the other before performing the down select.

## Weight Given to Procurement Cost vs. Other Factors in Request for Proposals (RFP)

Some observers, particularly supporters of the General Dynamics LCS design, argue that the Navy's proposed method for evaluating the two LCS designs in the LCS down select—set forth in the Request for Proposals (RFP) for the down select—focuses too much on procurement cost and not enough on other factors, particularly life-cycle fuel cost, other components of life-cycle operating and support (O&S) cost, and ship capability. Other observers, particularly supporters of the Lockheed LCS design, argue (as does the Navy) that the Navy's proposed method for conducting the LCS down select adequately takes into account factors other than procurement cost. The issue is viewed as having the potential for leading to a protest of the Navy's down select decision by the firm that is not selected.[8]

---

[8] For examples of articles discussing this issue, see Sean Reilly, "Loser To Fight In LCS Deal?" *Mobile (AL) Press-Register*, March 28, 2010: 1; Cid Standifer, "Austal USA, GD Officials Criticize Navy's RFP Criteria For LCS Award," *Inside the Navy*, March 29, 2010; Zachary M. Peterson, "Navy LCS Proposal Request Seeks 'Qualitative' Total Ownership Cost Figures," *Inside the Navy*, March 22, 2010; Emelie Rutherford, "Navy Stands By LCS Due Date As Hill Backers Of Each Bidder Swap Barbs," *Defense Daily*, March 18, 2010: 2-3; Geoff Fein, "General Dynamics' LCS Burns Less Fuel At Higher Speeds, Navy Documents Show," *Defense Daily*, March 2, 2010: 1-2; Geoff Fein, "Sessions Presses Navy Over Fairness of LCS RFP Evaluation," *Defense Daily*, March 1, 2010: 6-7; Geoff Fein, "USS Independence [LCS-2] Is The More Fuel Efficient of Two LCS Variants, Austal Official Says," *Defense Daily*, February 24, 2010: 2-3; Geoff Fein, "LCS RFP: Greater Emphasis Placed On Ship Price, Less On Life-Cycle Cost," *Defense Daily*, January 29, 2010: 5-7; Christopher P. Cavas, "RFP for LCS: Cost Main Factor in Winning Bid," *NavyTimes.com*, January 28, 2010.

---

Regarding the role of life-cycle operation and support (O&S) cost in the Navy's down select decision, a February 2010 Government Accountability Office (GAO) report stated:

> The Navy estimated operating and support costs for LCS seaframes and mission packages in 2009, but the estimates do not fully reflect DOD and GAO best practices for cost estimating and may change due to program uncertainties. GAO's analysis of the Navy's 2009 estimates showed that the operating and support costs for seaframes and mission packages could total $84 billion (in constant fiscal year 2009 dollars) through about 2050. However, the Navy did not follow some best practices for developing an estimate such as (1) analyzing the likelihood that the costs could be greater than estimated, (2) fully assessing how the estimate may change as key assumptions change, and (3) requesting an independent estimate and comparing it with the program estimate. The estimates may also be affected by program uncertainties, such as potential changes to force structure that could alter the number of ships and mission packages required. The costs to operate and support a weapon system can total 70 percent of a system's costs, and the lack of an estimate that fully reflects best practices could limit decision makers' ability to identify the resources that will be needed over the long term to support the planned investment in LCS force structure. With a decision pending in 2010 on which seaframe to buy for the remainder of the program, decision makers could lack critical information to assess the full costs of the alternatives.[9]

A February 8, 2010, press report stated that "the Navy will draw up total life-cycle cost estimates for both the Lockheed Martin and General Dynamics versions of the Littoral Combat Ship before the program goes before the Defense Acquisition Board this year for its Milestone B. review. The service included the announcement in a response to a Government Accountability Office report that criticized LCS life-cycle estimates."[10]

At the request of Senator Jeff Sessions, the Congressional Budget Office (CBO) analyzed the impact of O&S cost and other types of costs on the total life-cycle costs of the LCS and (for purposes of comparison) four other types of Navy ships. The results of CBO's analysis were released in the form of an April 28, 2010, letter to Senator Sessions. The letter states:

> CBO projected the life-cycle cost of the LCS-1 under three different assumptions about the average annual amount of fuel the ship will use over its 25-year life: low, moderate, and high. In all three scenarios, procurement costs dominate the life-cycle cost of the LCS-1, ranging from 58 percent to 66 percent of the total.... Personnel costs make up 14 percent to 16 percent of the LCS-1's total life-cycle cost in the various scenarios, and fuel costs account for 8 percent to 18 percent.
>
> The low-fuel case assumes that the LCS-1 generally operates at relatively low speeds—10 knots or less 90 percent of the time it is under way and 30 knots or more only about 3 percent of the time. That speed profile is based in part on how the Navy operated the LCS-1 between March 2009 and March 2010. In that scenario, operation and support costs total 33 percent of the ship's life-cycle cost: 16 percent for personnel costs, 8 percent for fuel costs (assuming that the ship consumes 25,000 barrels of fuel per year), and 9 percent for other O&S costs....
>
> The moderate-fuel case—which CBO considers the most likely of the three scenarios—assumes that the LCS-1 operates at 30 or more knots for about 5 percent of the time, at 14

---

[9] Government Accountability Office, *Littoral Combat Ship[:] Actions Needed to Improve Operating Cost Estimates and Mitigate Risks in Implementing New Concepts*, GAO-10-257, February 2010, summary page.

[10] Cid Standifer, "Navy Will Project Operation Costs Of Both LCS Models for DAB Review," *Inside the Navy*, February 8, 2010.

knots to 16 knots 42 percent of the time (a range that might be typical when the ship was traveling from its home port to a deployment location), and at less than 12 knots for the rest of its time under way. In that scenario, O&S costs total 34 percent of the ship's life-cycle cost: 15 percent for personnel, 11 percent for fuel, and 8 percent for other O&S costs. The moderate speed profile would result in fuel usage of about 35,000 barrels per year, slightly less than the 37,600 barrels that the Navy assumed in formulating its 2011 budget request. By comparison, the [Navy's] FFG-7 class frigates consumed about 31,000 barrels of fuel per ship in 2009.

The high-fuel case assumes that the LCS-1 operates at 30 or more knots for about 20 percent of its time under way, an assumption based partly on a speed profile developed by the Naval Sea Systems Command for the LCS program. In that scenario, O&S costs represent about 40 percent of the ship's life-cycle cost—more than in the other scenarios for the LCS-1 but less than for any of the other types of ships considered in this analysis. Personnel costs make up 14 percent of the life-cycle total; fuel costs, 18 percent; and other O&S costs, 8 percent. Projected fuel usage in this scenario is about 67,000 barrels per year. That estimate is unlikely to be exceeded in actual practice: It is twice the historical average for frigates and about 80 percent of the amount used by the Navy's destroyers (which do not have the capability to speed at 40 knots, as the littoral combat ship does, but are three times larger than the LCS-1).[11]

At a May 6, 2010, hearing on Navy shipbuilding programs before the Seapower subcommittee of the Senate Armed Services Committee, Senator Sessions questioned Sean Stackley, the Navy's acquisition executive (i.e., the Assistant Secretary of the Navy [Research, Development and Acquisition]), regarding the role of fuel costs in the Navy's evaluation of the two LCS designs. For the text of this exchange, see **Appendix E**.

## Potential Risks If First Shipyard Cannot Build Ships Within Cost

A third potential issue for Congress concerning the Navy's proposed acquisition strategy concerns the potential risks the Navy would face if the shipyard that wins the competition to build the 10 LCSs in FY2010-FY2014 cannot build them within the contracted cost. The competition between the two existing LCS industry teams to be the winner of the down select could be intense enough to encourage the teams to bid unrealistically low prices for the contract to build the 10 ships.

The Navy and its supporters could argue that the Navy's plan to award a fixed-price contract to the winner of the down select would shift the cost risk on the 10 ships from the government to the shipyard. They could also argue that the Navy plans to carefully evaluate the bid prices submitted by the two industry teams for the down select to ensure that they are realistic, and that the existence of the second LCS shipyard would provide the Navy with an ability to continue building LCSs if production at the first yard were disrupted due to financial issues.

Skeptics could argue that even with a fixed-price contract, the Navy's proposed strategy poses cost risks for the government, because a shipyard could submit an unrealistically low bid so as to win the down select, and then recover its losses on those 10 ships by rolling the losses into prices for downstream ships in the program. Alternatively, the shipyard could present the Navy with the prospect of going out of business and disrupting the LCS production effort unless the Navy were to provide a financial bailout to cover the yard's losses on the 10 ships. Skeptics could argue that

---

[11] Letter dated April 28, 2010, from Douglas W. Elmendorf, Director, CBO, to the Honorable Jeff Sessions, pp. 3-5. The letter is available online at http://www.cbo.gov/ftpdocs/114xx/doc11431/04-28-SessionsLetter.pdf.

Navy decisions dating back to the 1970s to award multi-ship construction contracts to shipyards that had not yet built many ships of the kind in question sometimes led to less-than-satisfactory program outcomes, including substantial financial bailouts.

## Increasing LCS Combat System Commonality with Other Combat Systems

A fourth potential issue for Congress regarding the Navy's proposed acquisition strategy concerns the Navy's plan to evolve the combat system on the winning LCS design to a configuration that has greater commonality with one or more existing Navy surface ship combat systems. The Navy in its September 16, 2009, announcement did not provide many details on this part of its proposed acquisition strategy, making it difficult to evaluate the potential costs and risks of this part of the strategy against potential alternatives, including an alternative (which Navy officials have discussed in the past) of designing a new LCS combat system that would, from the outset, be highly common with one or more existing Navy surface ship combat systems.

## Navy's Longer-Term Plans Regarding Two "Orphan" Ships

A fifth potential issue for Congress concerning the Navy's proposed acquisition strategy concerns the Navy's longer-term plans regarding the two "orphan" LCSs built to the design that was not selected in the down select. The Navy states that it plans to keep these two ships in the fleet because they will be capable ships and the Navy has an urgent need for LCSs. These two LCSs, however, will have unique logistic support needs, potentially making them relatively expensive to operate and support. At some point, as larger numbers of LCSs enter service, the costs of operating and supporting these two ships may begin to outweigh the increasingly marginal addition they make to total LCS fleet capabilities. Potential alternatives to keeping the ships in the active-duty fleet as deployable assets include selling them to foreign buyers, converting them into research and development platforms, shifting them to the Naval Reserve Force (where they would be operated by crews consisting partially of reservists), or decommissioning them and placing them into preservation (i.e., "mothball") status as potential mobilization assets. Potential questions for Congress include the following:

- Does the Navy intend to keep the two orphan LCSs in the active-duty fleet as deployable assets for a full 25-year service life?

- If so, how would be the life-cycle operation and support (O&S) costs of these two ships compare to those of the other LCSs? In light of these O&S costs, would it be cost effective to keep these two ships in the active-duty fleet as deployable assets for a full 25-year service life, particularly as large numbers of LCSs enter service?

- If the Navy does not intend to keep the two orphan LCSs in the active-duty fleet as deployable assets for a full 25-year service life, when does the Navy anticipate removing them from such service, and what does the Navy anticipate doing with them afterward?

## Potential Alternatives to Navy's New Strategy

A sixth potential issue for Congress concerns potential alternatives to the Navy's new acquisition strategy for acquiring LCSs procured in FY2010 and subsequent years. A variety of alternatives can be generated by changing one or more elements of the Navy's proposed strategy. One alternative would be a strategy that would keep both LCS designs in production, at least for the time being. Such a strategy might involve the following:

- the use of block-buy contracts with augmented EOQ authority, as under the Navy's proposed acquisition strategy, to continue producing both LCS designs, so as to provide stability to shipyards and suppliers involved in producing both LCS designs;

- the use of Profit Related to Offer (PRO) bidding between the builders of the two LCS designs, so as to generate competitive pressure between them and thereby restrain LCS production costs;[12] and

- designing a new LCS combat system that would have a high degree of commonality with one or more existing Navy surface ship combat systems and be provided as government-furnished equipment (GFE) for use on both LCS designs—an idea that was considered by the Navy at an earlier point in the program.

Supporters of an alternative like the one outlined above could argue that it would

- provide stability to LCS shipyards and suppliers;

- use competition to restrain LCS production costs;

- permit the Navy to receive a full return on the investment the Navy made in creating both LCS designs;

- reduce the life-cycle operation and support costs associated with building two LCS designs by equipping all LCSs with a common combat system;

- allow the Navy to design an LCS combat system that is, from the outset, highly common with one or more of the Navy's existing surface ship combat systems;

- achieve a maximum LCS procurement rate of four ships per year starting in FY2011 (two years earlier than under the Navy's proposal), thus permitting more LCSs to enter service with the Navy sooner;

- build both LCS designs in substantial numbers, thereby avoiding a situation of having a small number of orphan LCS ships that could have potentially high operation and support costs;

- preserve a potential to neck down to a single LCS design at some point in the future, while permitting the Navy in the meantime to more fully evaluate the operational characteristics of the two designs in real-world deployments; and

- increase the potential for achieving foreign sales of LCSs (which can reduce production costs for LCSs made for the U.S. Navy) by offering potential foreign buyers two LCS designs with active production lines.

---

[12] Under PRO bidding, the two shipyards would compete not for LCS quantities (because each shipyard would know that it was going to build a certain number of LCSs over the term of their block-buy contracts), but rather for profit, with the lowest bidder receiving the higher profit margin. PRO bidding has been used in other defense acquisition programs where bidders do not compete for quantity. The Navy, for example, began using PRO bidding in the DDG-51 destroyer program it in the 1990s.

Supporters of the Navy's proposed acquisition strategy could argue that an alternative like the one outlined above would, compared to the Navy's proposed strategy

- achieve lower economies of scale in LCS production costs by splitting production of LCS components between two designs;

- achieve, at the outset of series production of LCSs, less bidding pressure on shipyards, and thus higher LCS production costs, than would be achieved under the Navy's proposed strategy of using a price-based competition to select a single design for all future LCS production;

- miss out on the opportunity to restrain LCS costs by using the level of efficiency achieved in building an LCS design at one shipyard as a directly applicable benchmark for gauging the level of efficiency achieved by the other shipyard in building the same LCS design;

- increase Navy LCS program-management costs and the burden on Navy program-management capabilities by requiring the Navy to continue managing the construction of two very different LCS designs;

- achieve lower economies of scale in LCS operation and support costs because the two LCS designs would still differ in their basic hull, mechanical, and electrical (HM&E) systems, requiring the Navy to maintain two separate HM&E logistics support systems;

- receive only a limited return on the investment the Navy made in developing the two current LCS combat systems (since LCSs in the long run would not use either one), and require the Navy to incur the costs and the technical risks associated with designing a completely new LCS combat system;

- require the Navy to build some number of LCSs with their current combat systems—which are different from one another and from other Navy surface ship combat systems—while awaiting the development of the new LCS combat system, and then incur the costs associated with backfitting these earlier LCSs with the new system when it becomes available;

- send to industry a signal that is undesirable from the government's perspective that if the Navy or other parts or DOD begin producing two designs for a new kind of weapon system, the Navy or DOD would be reluctant to neck production down to a single design at some point, even if government believes that doing so would reduce program costs while still meeting operational objectives; and

- miss out on the opportunity that would be present under the Navy's proposed acquisition strategy to increase the potential for achieving foreign sales of LCSs by offering potential foreign buyers an LCS design that, through U.S. production, enjoys significant economies of scale for both production and operation and support.

## Unit Procurement Cost Cap

A second potential issue for Congress for FY2011 is where the estimated procurement costs of LCSs stand in relation to the unit procurement cost cap for the LCS program as amended by Section 121(c) and (d) of the FY2010 defense authorization act (H.R. 2647/P.L. 111-84 of October 28, 2009). As mentioned earlier, the Navy's proposed FY2011 budget estimates the procurement costs of LCS sea frames to be procured in FY2011-FY2015 at roughly $600 million each in then-year dollars. At first glance, this appears to be well above the $480 million unit procurement cost cap. As also mentioned earlier, however, the cost cap excludes certain costs from being counted against the $480 million cap, includes provisions for adjusting that figure over time to take inflation and other events into account, and permits the Secretary of the Navy to waive the cost cap under certain conditions.

## Cost Growth on LCS Sea Frames

A third potential issue for Congress concerns cost growth on LCS sea frames. Potential questions for Congress on this issue include the following:

- Has the Navy taken sufficient action to prevent further cost growth on LCS sea frames?

- Has the Navy financed cost growth on LCS sea frames by reducing funding for the procurement of LCS mission packages? For example, is cost growth on LCS sea frames linked in some way to the reduction in the planned number of LCS mission packages from an earlier figure of 90 to 110 to the current figure of 64? If the Navy has financed cost growth on LCS sea frames by reducing funding for the procurement of LCS mission packages, how might this have affected the capabilities of the planned 55-ship LCS fleet?

- In light of the cost growth, is the LCS program still cost-effective? What is the LCS sea frame unit procurement cost above which the Navy would no longer consider the LCS program cost-effective?

- If Congress had known in 2004, when it was acting on the FY2005 budget that contained funding to procure LCS-1, that LCS sea frame unit procurement costs would increase to the degree that they have, how might that have affected Congress's views on the question of approving the start of LCS procurement?

## Total Program Acquisition Cost

DOD has not reported a total estimated acquisition (i.e., research and development plus procurement) cost for the entire LCS program, including both 55 LCS sea frames and 64 LCS mission packages. Supporters of the LCS program could argue that substantial data is available in the FY2011 budget submission on annual LCS research and development and procurement costs for the period FY2011-FY2015. Skeptics could argue that a major acquisition program like the LCS program should not proceed to higher annual rates of production until the program's potential total acquisition costs is reported and assessed against other defense spending priorities.

## Operation and Support (O&S) Cost

At the request of Senator Jeff Sessions, the Congressional Budget Office (CBO) analyzed the impact of operation and support (O&S) cost and other types of costs on the total life-cycle costs of the LCS and (for purposes of comparison) four other types of Navy ships. The results of

CBO's analysis were released in the form of an April 28, 2010, letter to Senator Sessions.[13] CBO estimates in the letter that LCS-1 (the Lockheed Martin LCS design) would have an O&S cost, in constant FY2010 dollars, of $41 million to $47 million per year, depending on how often the ship travels at higher speeds and consequently how much fuel the ship uses each year.[14] For an excerpt from CBO's letter, see the earlier section entitled "Weight Given to Procurement Cost vs. Other Factors in Request for Proposals (RFP)."

A February 2010 Government Accountability Office (GAO) report stated:

> The Navy estimated operating and support costs for LCS seaframes and mission packages in 2009, but the estimates do not fully reflect DOD and GAO best practices for cost estimating and may change due to program uncertainties. GAO's analysis of the Navy's 2009 estimates showed that the operating and support costs for seaframes and mission packages could total $84 billion (in constant fiscal year 2009 dollars) through about 2050. However, the Navy did not follow some best practices for developing an estimate such as (1) analyzing the likelihood that the costs could be greater than estimated, (2) fully assessing how the estimate may change as key assumptions change, and (3) requesting an independent estimate and comparing it with the program estimate. The estimates may also be affected by program uncertainties, such as potential changes to force structure that could alter the number of ships and mission packages required. The costs to operate and support a weapon system can total 70 percent of a system's costs, and the lack of an estimate that fully reflects best practices could limit decision makers' ability to identify the resources that will be needed over the long term to support the planned investment in LCS force structure. With a decision pending in 2010 on which seaframe to buy for the remainder of the program, decision makers could lack critical information to assess the full costs of the alternatives.[15]

A February 8, 2010, press report stated:

> The Navy will draw up total life-cycle cost estimates for both the Lockheed Martin and General Dynamics versions of the Littoral Combat Ship before the program goes before the Defense Acquisition Board this year for its Milestone B. review.
>
> The service included the announcement in a response to a Government Accountability Office report that criticized LCS life-cycle estimates.[16]

## Operational Concepts

The same GAO report cited above also stated:

> The Navy has made progress in developing operational concepts for LCS, but faces risks in implementing its new concepts for personnel, training, and maintenance that are necessitated by the small crew size. Specifically, the Navy faces risks in its ability to identify and assign

---

[13] Letter dated April 28, 2010, from Douglas W. Elmendorf, Director, CBO, to the Honorable Jeff Sessions, 8 pp. The full text of the letter is available online at http://www.cbo.gov/ftpdocs/114xx/doc11431/04-28-SessionsLetter.pdf.

[14] Letter dated April 28, 2010, from Douglas W. Elmendorf, Director, CBO, to the Honorable Jeff Sessions, Table 1 on page 7.

[15] Government Accountability Office, *Littoral Combat Ship[:] Actions Needed to Improve Operating Cost Estimates and Mitigate Risks in Implementing New Concepts*, GAO-10-257, February 2010, summary page.

[16] Cid Standifer, "Navy Will Project Operation Costs Of Both LCS Models for DAB Review," Inside the Navy, February 8, 2010.

---

personnel given the time needed to achieve the extensive training required. GAO's analysis of a sample of LCS positions showed an average of 484 days of training is required before reporting to a crew, significantly more than for comparable positions on other surface ships. Moreover, the Navy's maintenance concept relies heavily on distance support, with little maintenance performed on ship. The Navy acknowledges that there are risks in implementing its new concepts and has established groups to address how to implement them. However, these groups have not performed a risk assessment as described in the 2008 National Defense Strategy. The Strategy describes the need to assess and mitigate risks to executing future missions and managing personnel, training, and maintenance. If the Navy cannot implement its concepts as envisioned, it may face operational limitations, have to reengineer its operational concepts, or have to alter the ship design. Many of the concepts will remain unproven until 2013 or later, when the Navy will have committed to building almost half the class. Having a thorough risk assessment of the new operational concepts would provide decision makers with information to link the effectiveness of these new concepts with decisions on program investment, including the pace of procurement.[17]

## Combat Survivability

A December 2009 report from DOD's Director of Operational Test and Evaluation stated:

> LCS was designated by the Navy as a Level I survivability combatant ship, but neither design is expected to achieve the degree of shock hardening as required by the CDD [Capabilities Development Document]. Shock hardening (ability to sustain a level of operations following an underwater explosive attack) is required for all mission critical systems, as required by a Level 1 survivability requirement. Only a few selected subsystems will be shock hardened, supporting only mobility to evacuate a threat area following a design-level shock event. Accordingly, the full, traditional rigor of Navy-mandated ship shock trials is not achievable, due to the damage that would be sustained by the ship and its many non-shock-hardened subsystems.
>
> The LCS LFT&E [Live Fire Test and Evaluation] program has been hampered by the Navy's lack of credible modeling and simulation tools for assessing the vulnerabilities of ships constructed to primarily commercial standards (American Bureau of Shipping Naval Vessel Rules and High Speed Naval Craft Code), particularly aluminum and non-traditional hull forms. Legacy LFT&E models were not developed for these non-traditional factors, nor have they been accredited for such use. These knowledge gaps undermine the credibility of the modeling and simulation, and increase the amount of surrogate testing required for an adequate LFT&E program.
>
> The LCS is not expected to be survivable in a hostile combat environment as evidenced by the limited shock hardened design and results of full scale testing of representative hull structures completed in December 2006.[18]

---

[17] Government Accountability Office, *Littoral Combat Ship[:] Actions Needed to Improve Operating Cost Estimates and Mitigate Risks in Implementing New Concepts*, GAO-10-257, February 2010, summary page.

[18] Department of Defense, Director, Operation Test and Evaluation, *FY 2009 Annual Report*, December 2009, p. 147.

## Technical Risk

### Seaframe

Regarding technical risk in developing the LCS seaframe, GAO reported the following in March 2010:

**Technology Maturity**

Seventeen of 19 critical technologies for both LCS designs are mature. For LCS 2, the trimaran hull and aluminum structure are nearing maturity. The Navy identified watercraft launch and recovery—essential to complete the LCS antisubmarine warfare and mine countermeasures missions—as a major risk to both seaframe designs. Watercraft launch and recovery systems have not been fully demonstrated for either seaframe. On the LCS 1, the Navy is conducting dynamic load testing, but integration with the Remote Multi-Mission Vehicle—a physically stressing system to launch and recover—is not scheduled to occur until after the ship's shakedown cruise. For LCS 2, factory testing of the twin boom extensible crane revealed performance and reliability concerns that were not fully addressed prior to installation. In addition, program officials report the LCS 2 main propulsion diesel engines have not completed a required endurance test, in part due to corrosion in each engine's intake valves. As an interim solution, the Navy has installed new intake valves, which enabled the ship to complete acceptance trials. LCS 2 has also experienced pitting and corrosion in its waterjet tunnels. The Navy has temporarily fixed the issue and plans to make weld repairs to pitted areas during a future dry dock availability.

**Design and Production Maturity**

The Navy could not provide data on completion of basic and functional drawings—a metric of design stability—at the start of LCS 1 and LCS 2 construction. The Navy used a concurrent design-build strategy for the two seaframes, which proved unsuccessful. Implementation of new design guidelines, delays in major equipment deliveries, and strong focus on achieving schedule and performance goals resulted in increased construction costs. LCS 1 and LCS 2 still require design changes as a result of maturing key systems. At the same time, shipbuilders are constructing modules for the next two ships, LCS 3 and LCS 4. At fabrication start for each ship, approximately 69 percent (LCS 3) and 57 percent (LCS 4) of basic and functional drawings were complete. Starting construction before drawings are complete could result in costly out-of- sequence work and rework to incorporate new design attributes. Incomplete designs at construction also led to weight increases for LCS 1 and LCS 2. According to the Navy, this weight growth contributed to a higher than desired center of gravity on LCS 1 that degraded the stability of that seaframe. Acceptance trials showed LCS 1 may not meet Navy stability requirements in a damaged condition. In response, the Navy added internal and external buoyancy tanks. For LCS 3, the contractor has incorporated a design change to extend the transom by four meters to improve stability.

**Other Program Issues**

In an effort to improve affordability in the LCS program, the Navy modified its acquisition strategy for future seaframes. The new strategy calls for selecting one seaframe design and awarding one prime contractor and shipyard a fixed-price incentive contract for construction of up to 10 ships between fiscal year 2010 and fiscal year 2014. Navy officials report that the earned value management systems (EVMS) in each of the LCS shipyards do not yet meet Defense Contract Management Agency requirements. Under the terms of the LCS 3 and LCS 4 contracts, the shipyards must achieve EVMS certification within 28 months from the date of the award. Until those requirements are met, cost and schedule data reported by the prime contractors cannot be considered fully reliable.

**Program Office Comments**

According to the Navy, the LCS program continues to deliver vital capability with the recent commissioning of LCS 2. The Navy stated that LCS 1 now meets the damage stability requirement with the addition of external tanks on the rear of the ship. The shipbuilder incorporated additional stability improvements to the design for LCS 3. In the continuing effort to ensure the delivery of affordable LCS capability, the Navy said it revised the acquisition strategy in 2009 to down select to a single design in fiscal year 2010 and procure up to 10 ships in a block buy. The winner of this competition will also be responsible for developing a technical data package to support competition for a second shipbuilder to build up to 5 ships in fiscal year 2012-2014. Construction continues on LCS 3 and LCS 4. To address corrosion of the waterjet tunnels, the Navy tated that electrical isolation of propulsion shafts from the waterjets is being incorporated and a plan is in place to renew the corroded metal in the waterjet intake tunnels.[19]

## Mission Packages

Regarding technical risk in developing the modular mission packages for the LCS, an April 26, 2010, news report stated:

The Littoral Combat Ship program lacks a 'timely' test program plan for the mission packages slated to deploy aboard the vessels, putting the effort at a 'medium' risk for cost increases ... according to a new study by the Pentagon's acquisition directorate....

'The program has major integration challenges between seaframes and MPs' [mission packages], the study states. 'To address this issue, the program established an Integrated Product Team ... the team has identified numerous deficiencies and verified corrections within each seaframe.'[20]

GAO reported the following in March 2010:

**Technology Maturity**

Operation of the MCM, SUW, and ASW packages on the LCS requires a total of 22 critical technologies, including 11 sensors, 6 vehicles, and 5 weapons. Of these technologies, 16 are mature and have been demonstrated in a realistic environment. In the past year, the Navy removed three critical technologies from LCS mission modules due to changes in future ASW packages.

The Navy has accepted delivery of two partially capable MCM mission packages; however, the program has delayed the procurement of the fiscal year 2009-funded package due to technical issues and the resulting operational test delays. Four MCM systems—the Unmanned Surface Vehicle (USV), Unmanned Sweep System (USS), Organic Airborne and Surface Influence Sweep (OASIS), and Rapid Airborne Mine Clearance System

[19] Government Accountability Office, *Defense Acquisitions[:] Assessments of Selected Weapon Programs*, GAO-10-388SP, March 2010, p. 96.

[20] Zachary M. Peterson, "DOD Report: LCS Program Faces 'Medium Risk,' Integration Challenges, *Inside the Navy*, April 26, 2010. Material in brackets as in original.

(RAMICS)—have not yet been demonstrated in a realistic environment, and two others—the Airborne Laser Mine Detection System (ALMDS) and Remote Minehunting System (RMS)—cannot meet system requirements. ALMDS has been unable to meet its mine detection requirements at its maximum depth or its mine detection and classification requirements at surface depths. RMS demonstrated poor system reliability, availability, and maintainability in a September 2008 operational assessment, and program officials report the system is currently undergoing a series of tests to try to improve its reliability. Program officials also reported that the cable used to tow certain airborne MCM systems had to be redesigned following test failures with two systems.

The Navy accepted delivery of one partially capable SUW mission package in July 2008. This package included two engineering development models for the 30 mm gun, but did not include the Non-Line-of-Sight Launch System (NLOS-LS) launcher or missiles. Integration of the gun with LCS 1 was completed in January 2009. The gun module design appears stable with 100 percent of its drawings released to manufacturing. According to program officials, NLOS-LS was tested in August 2009, but was unable to fire due to a malfunctioning sensor and battery connector. The program expects delivery of the second SUW mission package in March 2010. It will include the 30 mm gun module and the NLOS-LS launcher, but no missiles.

The Navy accepted delivery of one partially capable ASW mission package in September 2008, but plans to reconfigure the content of future packages before procuring additional quantities. According to Navy officials, recent warfighting analyses showed that the baseline ASW package did not provide sufficient capability to meet the range of threats. The current package will undergo developmental testing and the results will inform future configuration decisions. The first package underwent end-to-end testing in April 2009 and will undergo developmental testing in fiscal year 2010. During the 2009 end-to-end test, the Navy found that the USV and its associated sensors will require reliability and interface improvements to support sustained undersea warfare.

**Other Program Issues**

Recent changes to the LCS seaframe acquisition strategy may necessitate changes to the LCS mission module acquisition strategy and testing plans. For example, the new seaframe strategy calls for the program to select a single design in fiscal year 2010. According to program officials, the first mission modules will still be tested on both seaframe designs, but future mission modules could be tested on one or both seaframe designs.

**Program Office Comments**

The Navy stated that early packages will be delivered with partial capability, with systems added to the packages as they reach the level of maturity necessary for fielding. According to the Navy, the USV, USS, OASIS, and RAMICS have not entered production or been demonstrated in an operational environment. However, ALMDS and RMS have to date achieved a majority of their key performance requirements. The Navy stated these systems will be available in time to support planned retirement of legacy MCM forces. According to the Navy, it has initiated a program to address RMS reliability. The Navy noted that the program recently declared a critical Nunn-McCurdy cost breach and is under review by the Under Secretary of Defense (Acquisition, Technology & Logistics). Further, the Navy stated it has resolved technical issues related to the helicopter tow cable and the associated systems are ready to resume testing, while mission package acquisition and testing strategies have been updated to reflect seaframe acquisition strategy changes.[21]

## Impact of Army Recommendation to Cancel NLOS-LS

The Army reportedly decided on April 22, 2010, to recommend that DOD cancel an Army missile program known as the Non-Line of Sight Launch System (NLOS-LS).[22] DOD in early to mid-May 2010 reportedly authorized the Army to cancel the program.[23] Prior to these reports, the Navy planned to use NLOS-LS as part of the LCS surface warfare (SUW) mission package. Under Navy plans, an LCS equipped with the SUW package would nominally be armed with three NLOS missile launchers, each with 15 missiles, for a total of 45 missiles. The missiles could be used to counter swarm boats or other surface threats. In light of the proposed cancellation of NLOS-LS, the Navy reportedly is assessing options for fulfilling the NLOS role in the SUW mission package.[24]

A potential oversight issue for Congress is how the cancellation of NLOS-LS will affect LCS mission capabilities. At a May 6, 2010, hearing on Navy shipbuilding programs before the Seapower subcommittee of the Senate Armed Services Committee, Senator Jack Reed questioned Sean Stackley, the Navy's acquisition executive (i.e., the Assistant Secretary of the Navy [Research, Development and Acquisition]), and Lieutenant General George Flynn, Deputy Commandant, Combat Development and Integration, and Commanding General, Marine Corps Combat Development Command, regarding the impact the cancellation of the NLOS-LS program. For the text of this exchange, see **Appendix F**.

# Legislative Activity for FY2011

## FY2011 Funding Request

The Navy's proposed FY2011 budget requests $1,231.0 million in procurement funding for the two LCSs that the Navy wants to procure in FY2011, and $278.4 million in FY2011 advance procurement funding for the 11 LCSs that the Navy wants to procure in FY2012-FY2014. The Navy's proposed FY2011 budget also requests procurement funding to procure LCS mission packages, LCS module weapons, and research and development funding for the LCS program.

---

[21] Government Accountability Office, *Defense Acquisitions[:] Assessments of Selected Weapon Programs*, GAO-10-388SP, March 2010, p. 98.

[22] Kate Brannen, "U.S. Army Asks to Cancel NLOS-LS," *DefenseNews.com*, April 23, 2010; Jason Sherman, "Army Cancels NLOS-NS, Frees Up Billions For Other Procurement Needs," *Inside the Navy*, April 26, 2010; Sebastian Sprenger, "NLOS-LS Seen As Effective—But To Pricey—In Key Army Analysis," *Inside the Navy*, May 3, 2010.

[23] "Out of Sight," *Defense Daily*, May 17, 2010.

[24] Zachary M. Peterson, "Navy 'Assessing Options' In Lieu Of Army's Cancellation Of NLOS Missile," *Inside the Navy*, May 3, 2010.

# FY2011 Defense Authorization Bill (H.R. 5136/S. 3454)

## House

The House Armed Services Committee, in its report (H.Rept. 111-491 of May 21, 2010) on the FY2011 defense authorization bill (H.R. 5136), recommends approval of the Navy's FY2011 procurement and advance procurement funding requests for LCS sea frames (page 73) and LCS modules (page 81, line 029). The report recommends reducing by $8.9 million the Navy's FY2011 procurement funding request for LCS module weapons for "NLOS-LS program termination" (page 68, line 030). The report recommends increasing the Navy's FY2011 request for LCS research and development funding by $75.0 million for Navy NLOS-NS development, and by $4.25 million for axial-flow high-power-density waterjets (page 148).

The report states:

> Littoral Combat Ship
>
> The Littoral Combat Ship program has failed its initial intent to build inexpensive ships with modular capability and field them to the fleet at a high rate. None of those goals have been met. The ships are expensive; the modular capability has not been tested or verified; and in some cases is still undergoing development; and only two of the ships have been delivered to the Navy.
>
> Last year, the committee supported the request of the Secretary of the Navy and the Chief of Naval Operations to revamp the acquisition strategy for these vessels and to down-select to one variant of the ship with the award of the fiscal year 2010 two-ship authorization. The new acquisition strategy is aimed at reducing overall costs by procuring 10 ships in the Future Years Defense Plan using a fixed price incentive contract in fiscal year 2010 with priced options for 8 additional ships, 2 per year, in fiscal years 2011–15. In addition, the government would gain all rights to the technical data package required to compete the winning design to a second source shipyard which would build 5 additional ships, for a total of 15 ships, between fiscal years 2012 and 2015. The committee supported this plan as the best alternative to provide needed capability to the fleet in the shortest time possible, at the least cost. The plan was also proposed to the committee as the best way to divorce the prime contractors from the program and to transition the ship's installed combat systems to government furnished equipment that complimented equipment currently in use in the fleet.
>
> As of this report, the Navy has received the proposals from the two authorized competitors and is in the process of source selection leading to contract award. The committee is cautiously optimistic that, with a down-select to one variant and stability in the construction schedule, this troubled program can begin to fulfill its original purpose of providing capable ships, in quantity, at an affordable cost. (Pages 76-77)

The report also states:

> Littoral Combat Ship Module weapons
>
> The budget request contained $9.8 million for Littoral Combat Ship (LCS) Module Weapons, of which $8.9 million was requested for procurement of 45 non-line-of-sight launch system (NLOS–LS) missiles.
>
> The committee notes that the Army has terminated the NLOS-LS program, and even if it is continued by the Navy, an additional year of development work will be required. As a result,

the committee does not agree with Navy procurement funding for NLOS–LS in fiscal year 2011. In title II of this report, the committee recommends an increase in Navy research and development funding to support continued development work for the NLOS–LS program if the Navy determines that is in the best interest of the LCS program.

The committee recommends $0.9 million, a decrease of $8.9 million, for LCS Module weapons. (Page 69)

The report also states:

Navy non-line-of-sight launch system development

The budget request contained $226.3 million in PE 63581N[25] for Littoral Combat Ship mission module research and development but contained no funds for the non-line-of-sight launch system (NLOS–LS).

The committee notes that the Army's termination of the NLOS–LS could leave the Navy's Littoral Combat Ship (LCS) without sufficient capability to defeat small boat threats and unable to provide precision fire support to Marine Corps forces. The committee is informed that the NLOS–LS will likely require only one more year of research and development work to achieve threshold requirements. Therefore, in order to take advantage of the $1.5 billion in development funds spent to date, the committee encourages the Navy to complete development of the NLOS–LS system for use on the LCS. The committee also directs the Assistant Secretary of the Navy for Research, Development, and Acquisition to provide a report to the congressional defense committees by December 15, 2010, on the feasibility and utility of the Navy completing development of the NLOS–LS. The report should include an analysis of possible unit cost reduction options.

The committee recommends $301.3 million, an increase of $75.0 million, in PE 63581N for research and development of the NLOS–LS for use on the LCS. (Pages 159-160)

## Senate

The FY2011 defense authorization bill (S. 3454), as reported by the Senate Armed Services Committee (S.Rept. 111-201 of June 4, 2010), recommends approval of the Navy's requests for FY2011 procurement and advance procurement funding for LCS sea frames (see page 677 of the printed bill), LCS modules (page 680, line 29), and LCS module weapons (page 675, line 30). The committee's report states:

The Littoral Combat Ship (LCS) program has made progress during the past year and the recent decision to move to a single design should improve affordability. The LCS fleet is expected to comprise 55 vessels of the Navy's 313–ship fleet force structure. Even modest cost growth in this large component of the fleet magnifies the problem of achieving that objective. The committee notes that the Navy's acquisition strategy for the LCS program introduces competition for this class of ships and is therefore cautiously optimistic that this program is making progress. (Page 41)

The committee's report also states:

---

[25] Line items in DOD research and development accounts are called program elements (PEs).

**Littoral combat ship report**

The committee has concluded that the projected ship decommissioning and construction schedule presented in the Navy's program described in its "Report to Congress on Annual Long-Range Plan for Construction of Naval Vessels for FY 2011" could have a negative effect on some of the Nation's Navy bases. This would arise because of a gap that will occur as a result of small surface combatants being retired years before Littoral Combat Ship replacements will arrive.

The Navy's 2010 document ''Report on Strategic Plan for Homeporting the Littoral Combat Ship'' provided the committee with the Navy's notional strategic plan for stationing the Littoral Combat Ship through fiscal year 2020. In order to fully understand the effects of the Navy's current decommissioning and shipbuilding timeline, the committee directs the Secretary of the Navy to submit a report to the congressional defense committees that would provide the timeline and detailed homeport locations for the Littoral Combat Ships that will be delivered through 2020. The committee directs the Secretary of the Navy to submit the reports at the time the President submits his fiscal year 2012 budget proposal to Congress.

As the Navy finalizes its plans, the committee encourages the Navy to expedite delivery of the Littoral Combat Ship to those Navy bases that need replacement ships to mitigate capability gaps that will result from the retirement of smaller surface combatants. (Page 116)

# Appendix A. Summary of Congressional Action in FY2005-FY2010

This appendix presents a summary of congressional action on the LCS program in FY2005-FY2010.

## FY2005

In FY2005, Congress approved the Navy's plan to fund the construction of the first two LCS sea frames using research and development funds rather than shipbuilding funds, funded the first construction cost of the first LCS (LCS-1), required the second LCS (LCS-2) to be built (when funded in FY2006) to a different design from the first, prohibited the Navy from requesting funds in FY2006 to build a third LCS, and required all LCSs built after the lead ships of each design to be funded in the SCN account rather than the Navy's research and development account.

## FY2006

In FY2006, Congress funded the procurement of LCSs 2, 3, and 4. (The Navy requested one LCS for FY2006, consistent with Congress's FY2005 action. Congress funded that ship and provided funding for two additional ships.) Congress in FY2006 also established a unit procurement cost limit on the fifth and sixth LCS sea frames of $220 million per ship, plus adjustments for inflation and other factors (Section 124 of the FY2006 defense authorization bill [H.R. 1815/P.L. 109-163] of January 6, 2006), required an annual report on LCS mission packages and made procurement of more than four LCSs contingent on the Navy certifying that there exists a stable design for the LCS.

## FY2007

In FY2007, Congress funded the procurement of LCSs 5 and 6. (The Navy canceled these two ships in 2007 before they were placed under contract for construction.)

## FY2008

In FY2008, Congress accepted the Navy's cancellation of LCSs 3 through 6; funded the procurement one additional LCS in FY2008 (which the Navy called LCS-5);[26] significantly reduced the Navy's FY2008 funding request for the LCS program; amended the LCS sea frame unit procurement cost cap to $460 million per ship for LCSs procured in FY2008 and subsequent years (Section 125 of the conference report [H.Rept. 110-477 of December 6, 2007] on H.R. 1585, the FY2008 defense authorization bill, which was enacted as H.R. 4986/P.L. 110-181 of

---

[26] The Navy apparently called this ship LCS-5 because the original LCS-5 and LCS-6 were canceled by the Navy before they were replaced under contract, leaving LCS-4 as last LCS under contract to have been canceled. In spite of its designation, LCS-5 would have been the third LCS in the restructured LCS program, and was the seventh to have been funded by Congress.

January 28, 2008); and required the Navy to use fixed-price-type contracts for the construction of LCSs procured in FY2008 and subsequent years.

The Navy in 2007 requested that Congress amend the existing unit procurement cost cap for the fifth and sixth ships to $460 million, plus adjustments for inflation and other factors. Congress amended the cost cap to $460 million, but applied it not only to the fifth and sixth LCSs, but to all LCSs procured in FY2008 and subsequent years. The use of fixed-price contracts for future LCSs was something that the Navy had stated an intention to do as part of its plan for restructuring the LCS program.

## FY2009

In FY2009, Congress delayed the implementation of the LCS sea frame unit procurement cost cap by two years, to ships procured in FY2010 and subsequent years (Section 122 of the FY2009 defense authorization act [S. 3001/P.L. 110-417 of October 14, 2008]); rescinded $337 million in FY2008 shipbuilding funds for the LCS program, effectively canceling the funding for the LCS procured in FY2008 (Section 8042 of the FY2009 defense appropriations act [Division C of H.R. 2638/P.L. 110-329 of September 30, 2008]); and funded the procurement of two LCSs at a cost of $1,020 million.

## FY2010

In FY2010 Congress funded the procurement of two LCSs at a cost of $1,080 million and rescinded $66 million in FY2009 Other Procurement, Navy (OPN) funding for LCS mission modules. Section 121 of the FY2010 defense authorization act (H.R. 2647/P.L. 111-84 of October 28, 2009) granted the Navy contracting and other authority to implement the LCS acquisition strategy that the Navy announced on September 16, 2009, and amended the LCS unit procurement cost cap. Section 122 of the act requires the LCS program to be treated as a major defense acquisition program (MDAP) for purposes of program management and oversight. Section 123 of the act requires a report on the Navy's plan for homeporting LCSs.

# Appendix B. Cost Growth on LCS Sea Frames

This appendix presents details on cost growth on LCS sea frames from the FY2006 budget cycle through the FY2009 budget cycle.

## 2006

The proposed FY2007 Navy budget, submitted in February 2006, showed that:

- the estimate for the first LCS had increased from $215.5 million in the FY2005 budget and $212.5 million in the FY2006 budget to $274.5 million in the FY2007 budget—an increase of about 27% from the FY2005 figure and about 29% form the FY2006 figure;

- the estimate for the second LCS increased from $213.7 million in the FY2005 budget and $256.5 million in the FY2006 budget to $278.1 million—an increase of about 30% from the FY2005 figure and about 8% from the FY2006 figure; and

- the estimate for follow-on ships scheduled for FY2009-FY2011, when the LCS program was to have reached a planned maximum annual procurement rate of six ships per year, had increased from $223.3 million in the FY2006 budget to $298 million—an increase of about 33%.

The Navy stated in early 2006 that the cost increase from the FY2006 budget to the FY2007 budget was due mostly to the fact that LCS procurement costs in the FY2006 budget did not include items that are traditionally included in the so-called end cost—the total budgeted procurement cost—of a Navy shipbuilding program, such as Navy program-management costs, an allowance for changes, and escalation (inflation). The absence of these costs from the FY2006 LCS budget submission raised certain potential oversight issues for Congress.[27]

## 2007

On January 11, 2007, the Navy reported that LCS-1 was experiencing "considerable cost overruns." The Navy subsequently stated that the estimated shipyard construction cost of LCS-1 had grown to $350 million to $375 million. This suggested that the end cost of LCS-1—which

---

[27] These oversight issues included the following:

—Why were these costs excluded? Was this a budget-preparation oversight? If so, how could such an oversight occur, given the many people involved in Navy budget preparation and review, and why did it occur on the LCS program but not other programs? Was anyone held accountable for this oversight, and if so, how? If this was not an oversight, then what was the reason?

—Did the Navy believe there was no substantial risk of penalty for submitting to Congress a budget presentation for a shipbuilding program that, for whatever reason, significantly underestimated procurement costs?

—Do LCS procurement costs in the budget now include all costs that, under traditional budgeting practices, should be included? If not, what other costs are still unacknowledged?

—Have personnel or other resources from other Navy programs been used for the LCS program in any way? If so, have the costs of these personnel or other resources been fully charged to the LCS program and fully reflected in LCS program costs shown in the budget?

also includes costs for things such as Navy program-management costs and an allowance for changes—could be in excess of $400 million. The Navy did not publicly provide a precise cost overrun figure for LCS 2, but it stated that the cost overrun on LCSs 1 and 2 was somewhere between 50% and 75%, depending on the baseline that is used to measure the overrun.

The Government Accountability Office (GAO) testified in July 2007 that according to its own analysis of Navy data, the combined cost of LCSs 1 and 2 had increased from $472 million to $1,075—an increase of 128%.[28] CBO testified in July 2007 that:

> Several months ago, press reports indicated that the cost could well exceed $400 million each for the first two LCS sea frames. Recently, the Navy requested that the cost cap for the fifth and sixth sea frames be raised to $460 million, which suggests that the Navy's estimate of the acquisition cost for the first two LCSs would be around $600 million apiece....
>
> As of this writing, the Navy has not publicly released an estimate for the LCS program that incorporates the most recent cost growth, other than its request to raise the cost caps for the fifth and sixth ships. CBO estimates that with that growth included, the first two LCSs would cost about $630 million each, excluding mission modules but including outfitting, postdelivery, and various nonrecurring costs associated with the first ships of the class. As the program advances, with a settled design and higher annual rates of production, the average cost per ship is likely to decline. Excluding mission modules, the 55 LCSs in the Navy's plan would cost an average of $450 million each, CBO estimates.[29]

## 2008

The proposed FY2009 budget, submitted in February 2008, showed that the estimated end costs of LCS-1 and LCS-2 had increased to $531 million and $507 million, respectively (or to $631 million and $636 million, respectively, when OF/DP and FST MSSIT costs are included, or to $606 million and $582 million, respectively, when OF/DP costs are included, but FST MSSIT costs are not included).

## 2009

The proposed FY2010 budget, submitted in May 2009, showed that the estimated end costs of LCS-1 and LCS-2 had increased to $537 million and $575 million, respectively (or to $637 million and $704 million, respectively, when OF/DP and FST MSSIT costs are included, or to $612 million and $650 million, respectively, when OF/DP costs are included, but FST MSSIT costs are not included). CBO reported on June 9, 2008, that:

> Historical experience indicates that cost growth in the LCS program is likely. In particular, using the lead ship of the FFG-7 Oliver Hazard Perry class frigate as an analogy, historical cost-to-weight relationships indicate that the Navy's original cost target for the LCS of $260

---

[28] Defense Acquisitions[:] Realistic Business Cases Needed to Execute Navy Shipbuilding Programs, Statement of Paul L. Francis, Director, Acquisition and Sourcing Management Team, Testimony Before the Subcommittee on Seapower and Expeditionary Forces, Committee on Armed Services, House of Representatives, July 24, 2007 (GAO-07-943T), pp. 4 and 22.

[29] Statement of J. Michael Gilmore, Assistant Director for National Security, and Eric J. Labs, Senior Analyst, [on] The Navy's 2008 Shipbuilding Plan and Key Ship Programs, before the Subcommittee on Seapower and Expeditionary Forces Committee on Armed Services U.S. House of Representatives, July 24, 2007, p. 18.

million in 2009 dollars (or $220 million in 2005 dollars) was optimistic. The first FFG-7 cost about $670 million in 2009 dollars to build, or about $250 million per thousand tons, including combat systems. Applying that metric to the LCS program suggests that the lead ships would cost about $600 million apiece, including the cost of one mission module. Thus, in this case, the use of a historical cost-to-weight relationship produces an estimate that is less than the actual costs of the first LCSs to date but substantially more than the Navy's original estimate.

Based on actual costs the Navy has incurred for the LCS program, CBO estimates that the first two LCSs could cost about $700 million each, including outfitting and postdelivery and various nonrecurring costs associated with first ships of a class but excluding mission modules. However, as of May 1, 2008, LCS-1 was 83 percent complete and LCS-2 was 68 percent complete. Thus, additional cost growth is possible, and CBO's estimate reflects that cost risk.

Overall, CBO estimates that the LCSs in the Navy's plan would cost about $550 million each, on average, excluding mission modules. That estimate assumes that the Navy would select one of the two existing designs and make no changes. As the program advanced with a settled design and higher annual rates of production, average ship costs would probably decline. If the Navy decided to make changes to that design, however, the costs of building future ships could be higher than CBO now estimates.[30]

## Reasons for Cost Growth

Various reasons have been cited for cost growth in the LCS program, including the following:

- **Unrealistically low original estimate.** Some observers believe that the original cost estimate of $220 million for the LCS sea frame was unrealistically low. If so, a potential follow-on question would be whether the LCS represents a case of "low-balling"—using an unrealistically low cost estimate in the early stages of a proposed weapon program to help the program win approval and become an established procurement effort.

- **Impact of Naval Vessel Rules (NVR).** Navy and industry officials have attributed some of the cost growth to the impact of applying new Naval Vessel Rules (NVR)—essentially, new rules specifying the construction standards for the ship—to the LCS program. The NVR issued for the LCS program incorporated, among other things, an increase in the survivability standard (the ability to withstand damage) to which LCSs were to be built.[31] Building the ship to a higher survivability standard represented a change in requirements for the ship that led to many design changes, including changes that made ship more rugged and more complex in terms of its damage-control systems. In addition, Navy and industry officials have testified, the timing of the issuing of NVR

---

[30] Congressional Budget Office, *Resource Implications of the Navy's Fiscal Year 2009 Shipbuilding Plan*, June 8, 2008, pp. 26-27.

[31] The LCS was earlier conceived as a ship that would be built to a survivability standard that would be sufficient, in the event of significant battle damage, to save the ship's crew, but not necessarily the ship. The survivability standard for the LCS was increased as part of the issuing of NVR to one that would be sufficient to save not only the ship's crew, but the ship as well. (Other U.S. Navy combat ships are built to a still-higher survivability standard that is sufficient not only to save the crew and the ship, but to permit the ship to keep fighting even though it has sustained damage.)

created a situation of concurrency between design and construction in the LCS program, meaning that the ship was being designed at the same time that the shipyard was attempting to build it—a situation long known to be a potential cause of cost growth. This concurrency, Navy officials testified, was a consequence of the compressed construction schedule for the LCS program, which in turn reflected an urgency about getting LCSs into the fleet to meet critical mission demands.

- **Improperly manufactured reduction gear.** Navy and industry officials testified that cost growth on LCS-1 was partly due to a main reduction gear[32] that was incorrectly manufactured and had to be replaced, forcing a reordering of the construction sequence for the various major sections of the ship.

- **Increased costs for materials.** Some observers have attributed part of the cost growth in the program to higher-than-estimated costs for steel and other materials that are used in building the ships.

- **Emphasis on meeting schedule combined with cost-plus contract.** Some portion of cost growth on LCS-1 has been attributed to a combination of a Navy emphasis on meeting the ship's aggressive construction schedule and the Navy's use of a cost-plus contract to build the ship.[33]

- **Shipyard Performance.** Shipyard performance and supervision of the LCS shipyards by the LCS team leaders and the Navy has been cited as another cause of cost growth.[34]

## July 2007 GAO Testimony

GAO testified in July 2007 that:

> We have frequently reported on the wisdom of using a solid, executable business case before committing resources to a new product development effort....

---

[32] A ship's reduction gear is a large, heavy gear that reduces the high-speed revolutions of the ship's turbine engines to the lower-speed revolutions of its propellers.

[33] The Senate Armed Services Committee, as part of its discussion of the LCS program in its report (S.Rept. 110-77 of June 5, 2007) on the FY2008 defense authorization bill (S. 1547), stated:

> Reviewing this LCS situation will undoubtedly result in a new set of "lessons learned"' that the acquisition community will dutifully try to implement. However, the committee has previously expressed concerns about the LCS concept and the LCS acquisition strategy. The LCS situation may be more a case of "lessons lost." Long ago, we knew that we should not rush to sign a construction contract before we have solidified requirements. We also knew that the contractors will respond to incentives, and that if the incentives are focused on maintaining schedules and not on controlling cost, cost growth on a cost-plus contract should surprise no one. After the fact, everyone appears ready to agree that the original ship construction schedule for the lead ship was overly aggressive. (Page 98)

[34] See Katherine McIntire Peters, "Navy's Top Officer Sees Lessons In Shipbuilding Program Failures," *GovermentExecutive.com*, September 24, 2008; Christopher J. Castelli, "Audit Exposes Failed Management of Troubled Littoral Warship," *Inside the Navy*, February 4, 2008; Christopher J. Castelli, "Audit Reveals Both LCS and Industry Teams Violated Management Rules," *Inside the Pentagon*, July 10, 2008 (reprinted in essentially identical form, with the same headline, in the July 14, 2008, issue of sister publication *Inside the Navy*).

A sound business case would establish and resource a knowledge-based approach at the outset of a program. We would define such a business case as firm requirements, mature technologies, and an acquisition strategy that provides sufficient time and money for design activities before construction start. The business case is the essential first step in any acquisition program that sets the stage for the remaining stages of a program, namely the business or contracting arrangements and actual execution or performance. If the business case is not sound, the contract will not correct the problem and execution will be subpar. This does not mean that all potential problems can be eliminated and perfection achieved, but rather that sound business cases can get the Navy better shipbuilding outcomes and better return on investment. If any one element of the business case is weak, problems can be expected in construction. The need to meet schedule is one of the main reasons why programs cannot execute their business cases. This pattern was clearly evident in both the LPD 17 [amphibious ship] and LCS programs. In both cases, the program pushed ahead with production even when design problems arose or key equipment was not available when needed. Short cuts, such as doing technology development concurrently with design and construction, are taken to meet schedule. In the end, problems occur that cannot be resolved within compressed, optimistic schedules. Ultimately, when a schedule is set that cannot accommodate program scope, delivering an initial capability is delayed and higher costs are incurred....

What happens when the elements of a solid business case are not present? Unfortunately, the results have been all too visible in the LPD 17 and the LCS. Ship construction in these programs has been hampered throughout by design instability and program management challenges that can be traced back to flawed business cases. The Navy moved forward with ambitious schedules for constructing LPD 17 and LCS despite significant challenges in stabilizing the designs for these ships. As a result, construction work has been performed out of sequence and significant rework has been required, disrupting the optimal construction sequence and application of lessons learned for follow-on vessels in these programs....

In the LCS program, design instability resulted from a flawed business case as well as changes to Navy requirements. From the outset, the Navy sought to concurrently design and construct two lead ships in the LCS program in an effort to rapidly meet pressing needs in the mine countermeasures, antisubmarine warfare, and surface warfare mission areas. The Navy believed it could manage this approach, even with little margin for error, because it considered each LCS to be an adaptation of an existing high-speed ferry design. It has since been realized that transforming a high-speed ferry into a capable, networked, survivable warship was quite a complex venture. Implementation of new Naval Vessel Rules (design guidelines) further complicated the Navy's concurrent design-build strategy for LCS. These rules required program officials to redesign major elements of each LCS design to meet enhanced survivability requirements, even after construction had begun on the first ship. While these requirements changes improved the robustness of LCS designs, they contributed to out of sequence work and rework on the lead ships. The Navy failed to fully account for these changes when establishing its $220 million cost target and 2-year construction cycle for the lead ships.

Complicating LCS construction was a compressed and aggressive schedule. When design standards were clarified with the issuance of Naval Vessel Rules and major equipment deliveries were delayed (e.g., main reduction gears), adjustments to the schedule were not made. Instead, with the first LCS, the Navy and shipbuilder continued to focus on achieving the planned schedule, accepting the higher costs associated with out of sequence work and rework. This approach enabled the Navy to achieve its planned launch date for the first Littoral Combat Ship, but required it to sacrifice its desired level of outfitting. Program officials report that schedule pressures also drove low outfitting levels on the second Littoral Combat Ship design as well, although rework requirements have been less intensive to date. However, because remaining work on the first two ships will now have to be completed out-of-sequence, the initial schedule gains most likely will be offset by increased labor hours to finish these ships.

The difficulties and costs discussed above relate to the LCS seaframe only. This program is unique in that the ship's mission equipment is being developed and funded separately from the seaframe. The Navy faces additional challenges integrating mission packages with the ships, which could further increase costs and delay delivery of new antisubmarine warfare, mine countermeasures, and surface warfare capabilities to the fleet. These mission packages are required to meet a weight requirement of 180 metric tons or less and require 35 personnel or less to operate them. However, the Navy estimates that the mine countermeasures mission package may require an additional 13 metric tons of weight and seven more operator personnel in order to deploy the full level of promised capability. Because neither of the competing ship designs can accommodate these increases, the Navy may be forced to reevaluate its planned capabilities for LCS.[35]

---

[35] Defense Acquisitions[:] Realistic Business Cases Needed to Execute Navy Shipbuilding Programs, Statement of Paul L. Francis, Director, Acquisition and Sourcing Management Team, Testimony Before the Subcommittee on Seapower and Expeditionary Forces, Committee on Armed Services, House of Representatives, July 24, 2007 (GAO-07-943T), pp. 8-11.

# Appendix C. 2007 Program Restructuring and Ship Cancellations

The Navy substantially restructured the LCS program in 2007 in response to significant cost growth and delays in constructing the first LCS sea frames. This restructuring led to the cancellation of four LCSs that were funded in FY2006 and FY2007. A fifth LCS, funded in FY2008, was cancelled in 2008. This appendix presents the details of the program restructuring and ship cancellations.

## 2007 Program Restructuring

### March 2007 Navy Restructuring Plan

In response to significant cost growth and schedule delays in the building of the first LCSs that first came to light in January 2007 (see next section), the Navy in March 2007 announced a plan for restructuring the LCS program that:

- canceled the two LCSs funded in FY2007 and redirected the funding for those two ships to pay for cost overruns on earlier LCSs;

- announced an intention to lift a 90-day stop-work order that the Navy had placed on LCS-3 in January 2007—provided that the Navy reached an agreement with the Lockheed-led industry team by April 12, 2007, to restructure the contract for building LCSs 1 and 3 from a cost-plus type contract into a fixed price incentive (FPI)-type contract—or terminate construction of LCS-3 if an agreement on a restructured contract could not be reached with the Lockheed team by April 12, 2007;

- announced an intention to seek to restructure the contract with the General Dynamics-led industry team for building LCSs 2 and 4 into an FPI-type contract—if LCSs 2 and 4 experienced cost growth comparable to that of LCSs 1 and 3—and, if such a restructuring were sought, terminate construction of LCS-4 if an agreement on a restructured contract for LCS-2 and LCS-4 could not be reached;

- reduced the number of LCSs requested for FY2008 from three to two (for the same requested FY2008 procurement funding of $910.5 million), and the number to be requested for FY2009 from six to three; and

- announced an intention to conduct an operational evaluation to select a favored design for the LCS that would be procured in FY2010 and subsequent years, and to conduct a full and open follow-on competition among bidders for the right to build that design.[36]

---

[36] Source: Navy briefing to CRS and Congressional Budget Office (CBO) on Navy's proposed LCS program restructuring plan, March 21, 2007.

## April 2007 Termination of LCS-3

On April 12, 2007, the Navy announced that it had not reached an agreement with Lockheed on a restructured FPI-type contract for LCS-1 and LCS-3, and consequently was terminating construction of LCS-3.[37] (The Navy subsequently began referring to the ship as having been partially terminated—a reference to the fact that Lockheed was allowed to continue procuring certain components for LCS-3, so that a complete set of these components would be on hand to be incorporated into the next LCS built to the Lockheed design.) (The designation LCS-3 is now being reused to refer to one of the two LCSs procured in FY2009.)

## November 2007 Termination of LCS-4

In late September 2007, it was reported that the Navy on September 19 had sent a letter to General Dynamics to initiate negotiations on restructuring the contract for building LCSs 2 and 4 into an FPI-type contract. The negotiations reportedly were to be completed by October 19, 2007—30 days from September 19.[38] On November 1, 2007, the Navy announced that it had not reached an agreement with General Dynamics on a restructured FPI-type contract for LCS-2 and LCS-4, and consequently was terminating construction of LCS-4.[39] (The designation LCS-4 is now being reused to refer to one of the two LCSs procured in FY2009.)

# Cancellation of Prior-Year Ships

**Table C-1** below summarizes the status of the nine LCSs funded by Congress from FY2005 through FY2009. As shown in the table, of the nine ships, five were later canceled, leaving four ships in place through FY2009—LCSs 1 and 2, and the two LCSs funded in FY2009. Ship designations LCS-3 and LCS-4 are being reused as the designations for the two ships funded in FY2009.

---

[37] Department of Defense News Release No. 422-07, April 12, 2007, "Navy Terminates Littoral Combat Ship 3."

[38] Geoff Fein, "Navy Seeking To Negotiate FPI Contract With General Dynamics," *Defense Daily*, September 24, 2007; Geoff Fein, "Navy, General Dynamics Meet To Discuss New LCS Fixed Price Structure," *Defense Daily*, September 27, 2007; Tony Capaccio, "General Dynamics Urged To Take Fixed Price On Warship Contract," *Bloomberg News*, September 28, 2007; Jason Sherman, "Navy, General Dynamics Discuss Fixed-Price Contract For LCS," *Inside the Navy*, October 1, 2007.

[39] Department of Defense News Release No. 1269-07, November 1, 2007, "Navy Terminates Littoral Combat Ship (LCS 4) Contract."

### Table C-1. Status of LCSs Funded in FY2005-FY2009

| Ships funded | FY funded | Navy hull designation | Status |
|---|---|---|---|
| 1st | 2005 | LCS-1 | **Commissioned into service** on November 8, 2008. |
| 2nd | 2006 | LCS-2 | **Under construction**; ship launched April 26, 2008 and scheduled to be delivered to the Navy in late-2009. |
| 3rd | | LCS-3 (not the same ship as LCS-3 below) | **Canceled by Navy** in April 2007 after being placed under contract due to inability to come to agreement with contractor on revised (fixed-price) contract terms for LCSs 1 and 3. |
| 4th | | LCS-4 (not the same ship as LCS-4 below) | **Canceled by Navy** in November 2007 after being placed under contract due to inability to come to agreement with contractor on revised (fixed-price) contract terms for LCSs 2 and 4. |
| 5th | 2007 | none (ship canceled before being placed under contract) | **Canceled by Navy** in March 2007 before being placed under contract as part of Navy's LCS program restructuring; funds reapplied to cover other program costs. |
| 6th | | none (ship canceled before being placed under contract) | **Canceled by Navy** in March 2007 before being placed under contract as part of Navy's LCS program restructuring; funds reapplied to cover other program costs. |
| 7th | 2008 | LCS-5 (for a while, at least, although the ship was canceled before being placed under contract) | **Canceled by Navy following Congress's decision** in September 2008, as part of its action on the FY2009 defense appropriations bill, to rescind the funding for the ship. |
| 8th | 2009 | LCS-3 (not the same ship as LCS-3 above; the ship designation is being reused) | **Funded in FY2009 and Under Construction.** Contract to build the ship awarded to Lockheed Martin on March 23, 2009. Ship is currently under construction. |
| 9th | | LCS-4 (not the same ship as LCS-4 above; the ship designation is being reused) | **Funded in FY2009 and Under Construction.** Contract to build the ship awarded to General Dynamics on May 1, 2009. Ship is currently under construction. |

**Source:** Prepared by CRS.

# Appendix D. LCS Acquisition Strategy Announced in September 2009

This appendix presents additional background information on the LCS acquisition strategy announced by the Navy on September 16, 2009.

A September 16, 2009, Department of Defense (DOD) news release on the proposed new acquisition strategy stated:

> The Navy announced today it will down select between the two Littoral Combat Ship (LCS) designs in fiscal 2010. The current LCS seaframe construction solicitation [for the FY2010 LCSs] will be cancelled and a new solicitation will be issued. At down select, a single prime contractor and shipyard will be awarded a fixed price incentive contract for up to 10 ships with two ships in fiscal 2010 and options through fiscal 2014. This decision was reached after careful review of the fiscal 2010 industry bids, consideration of total program costs, and ongoing discussions with Congress.
>
> "This change to increase competition is required so we can build the LCS at an affordable price," said Ray Mabus, secretary of the Navy. "LCS is vital to our Navy's future. It must succeed."
>
> "Both ships meet our operational requirements and we need LCS now to meet the warfighters' needs," said Adm. Gary Roughead, chief of naval operations. "Down selecting now will improve affordability and will allow us to build LCS at a realistic cost and not compromise critical warfighting capabilities."
>
> The Navy cancelled the solicitation to procure up to three LCS Flight 0+ ships in fiscal 2010 due to affordability. Based on proposals received this summer, it was not possible to execute the LCS program under the current acquisition strategy and given the expectation of constrained budgets. The new LCS acquisition strategy improves affordability by competitively awarding a larger number of ships across several years to one source. The Navy will accomplish this goal by issuing a new fixed price incentive solicitation for a down select to one of the two designs beginning in fiscal 2010.
>
> Both industry teams will have the opportunity to submit proposals for the fiscal 2010 ships under the new solicitation. The selected industry team will deliver a quality technical data package, allowing the Navy to open competition for a second source for the selected design beginning in fiscal 2012. The winner of the down select will be awarded a contract for up to 10 ships from fiscal 2010 through fiscal 2014, and also provide combat systems for up to five additional ships provided by a second source. Delivery of LCS 2, along with construction of LCS 3 and LCS 4 will not be affected by the decision. This plan ensures the best value for the Navy, continues to fill critical warfighting gaps, reduces program ownership costs, and meets the spirit and intent of the Weapons System Acquisition Reform Act of 2009....
>
> The Navy remains committed to the LCS program and the requirement for 55 of these ships to provide combatant commanders with the capability to defeat anti-access threats in the littorals, including fast surface craft, quiet submarines and various types of mines. The

Navy's acquisition strategy will be guided by cost and performance of the respective designs as well as options for sustaining competition throughout the life of the program.[40]

A September 16, 2009, e-mail from the Navy to CRS provided additional information on the proposed new strategy, stating:

> The Navy remains committed to a 55 ship LCS program and intends to procure these ships through an acquisition strategy that leverages competition, fixed price contracting and stability in order to meet our overarching objectives of performance and affordability.
>
> In the best interest of the Government, the Navy cancelled the solicitation to procure up to three LCS Flight 0+ ships in FY10 due to affordability.
>
> Based on proposals received in August, the Navy had no reasonable basis to find that the LCS Program would be executable going forward under the current acquisition strategy, given the expectation of constrained budgets.
>
> In the near future, and working closely with Congress, the Navy will issue a new FY10 solicitation which downselects between the two existing designs and calls for building two ships in FY10 and provides options for two additional ships per year from FY11 to FY14 for a total of ten ships. The intent is for all of these ships to be built in one shipyard, which will benefit from a stable order quantity, training and production efficiencies to drive costs down. Both industry teams will have the opportunity to submit proposals for the FY10 ships under the new solicitation.
>
> To sustain competition throughout the life of the program and in conjunction with the downselect, the Navy will develop a complete Technical Data Package which will be used to open competition for a second source of the selected design in FY12, awarding one ship with options for up to four additional ships through FY14, to a new shipbuilder.
>
> Our FY10 solicitation will call for the prime to build an additional five combat systems to be delivered as government-furnished equipment for this second source shipyard. Separating the ship and combat systems procurement will enable bringing the LCS combat system into the broader Navy's open architecture plan.
>
> In short, this strategy calls for two shipbuilders in continuous competition for a single LCS seaframe design, and a government-provided combat system.
>
> The revised strategy meets the full spirit and intent of the Weapon Systems Acquisition Reform Act of 2009 by increasing Government oversight, employing fixed price contract types, maximizing competition, leveraging open architecture, using Economic Order Quantity and Block Buy strategies, and ensuring future competition for shipbuilding as enabled by development of a Technical Data Package to solicit ships from a second shipyard.
>
> We also continue to work closely with Congress on the Navy's LCS procurement intentions....
>
> The Navy intends to continue with construction and delivery of LCS 3 and LCS 4, ultimately for use as deployable assets. We will continue to explore all avenues to ensure this is an affordable program.[41]

---

[40] Department of Defense, "Littoral Combat Ship Down Select Announced," News Release 722-09, September 16, 2009, available online at http://www.defenselink.mil/releases/release.aspx?releaseid=12984.

The Navy briefed CRS and CBO about the proposed new acquisition strategy on September 22, 2009. Points made by the Navy in the briefing included the following:

- The bids from the two industry teams for the three LCSs requested in the FY2010 budget (which were submitted to the Navy in late July or early August 2009[42]) were above the LCS unit procurement cost cap in "all scenarios."

- Negotiations with the industry teams were deemed by the Navy to be not likely to result in award prices for the FY2010 ships that were acceptable to the Navy.

- The Navy judged that the current LCS teaming arrangements "considerably influenced costs" in the FY2010 bids.

- The Navy judged that it cannot afford more than a two-ship award in FY2010 within the amount of funding ($1,380 million) requested for LCS sea frame procurement in FY2010.

- In response to the above points, the Navy decided to seek a new acquisition strategy for LCSs procured in FY2010 and subsequent years that would make the LCS program affordable by leveraging competition, providing stability to LCS shipyards and suppliers, producing LCSs at efficient rates, giving industry incentives to make investments that would reduce LCS production costs, and increase commonality in the resulting LCS fleet.

- Under the Navy's proposed new strategy, the winner of the LCS down select would be awarded a contract to build two ships procured in FY2010, with options to build two more ships per year in FY2011-FY2014. The contract would be a block-buy contract augmented with Economic Order Quantity (EOQ) authority, so as to permit up-front batch purchases of long leadtime components, as would be the case under a multiyear procurement (MYP) contract. Unlike an MYP contract, however, the block buy contract would not include a termination liability.

- The winner of the down select would deliver to the Navy a technical data package that would permit another shipyard to build the winning LCS design.

- The Navy would hold a second competition to select a second LCS bidder. This competition would be open to all firms other than the shipyard that is building the 10 LCSs in FY2010-FY2014. The winner of this second competition would be awarded a contract to build up to five LCSs in FY2012-FY2014 (one ship in FY2012, and two ships per year in FY2013-FY2014).

- The Navy would maintain competition between the two shipyards for LCSs procured in FY2015 and subsequent years.

- The prime contactor on the team that wins the LCS down select (i.e., Lockheed or General Dynamics) would provide the combat systems for all the LCSs to be

---

(...continued)

[41] Email from Navy Office of Legislative Affairs to CRS, entitled "LCS Way Ahead," September 16, 2009.

[42] See, for example, Christopher P. Cavas, "LCS Bids Submitted to U.S. Navy," *DefenseNews.com*, August 3, 2009, which states: "Lockheed Martin announced its proposal was sent to the Navy on July 31, and rival General Dynamics confirmed its plans were sent in by the Aug. 3 deadline." See also Bettina H. Chavanne, "Lockheed Submits First LCS Proposal Under Cost Cap Regulations," *Aerospace Daily & Defense Report*, August 4, 2009: 5.

procured in FY2010-FY2014—the 10 that would be built by the first shipyard, and the others that would be built by the second shipyard.

- The structure of the industry team that wins the down select would be altered, with the prime contractor on the team being separated from the shipyard (i.e., the shipyard building the 10 LCSs in FY2010-FY2014). The separation, which would occur some time between FY2010 and FY2014, would be intended in part to prevent an organizational conflict of interest on the part of the prime contractor as it provides combat systems to the two shipyards building LCSs.

- The current combat system used on the selected LCS design will be modified over time to a configuration that increases its commonality with one or more of the Navy's existing surface ship combat systems.

- The Navy intends to complete the construction and delivery of LCS-3 and LCS-4.

- The Navy believes that the proposed acquisition strategy does the following: maximize the use of competition in awarding contracts for LCSs procured in FY2010-FY2014; provide an opportunity for achieving EOQ savings with vendors; provide stability and efficient production quantities to the shipyards and vendors; provide an opportunity to move to a common combat system for the LCS fleet; and provide the lowest-possible total ownership cost for the Navy for the resulting LCS fleet, in large part because the fleet would consist primarily of a single LCS design with a single logistics support system. The Navy also believes the proposed strategy is consistent with the spirit and intent of the Weapon Systems Acquisition Reform Act of 2009 (S. 454/P.L. 111-23 of May 22, 2009).

Regarding the Navy's ability to sustain a competition between two LCS builders for LCS construction contracts years from now, when the annual LCS procurement rate is projected to drop to 1.5 ships per year (i.e., a 1-2-1-2 pattern), Undersecretary of the Navy Robert Work stated:

> "We are going to be able to compete those. We will be able to compete three [ships] every two years and one of the yards will win two and one yard will win one. Sometimes, we'll do a five multi-year [procurement contract]. We have all sorts of flexibility in here," he said.[43]

---

[43] Geoff Fein, "Official: Navy OK With Either LCS, New Acquisition Plan Adds Flexibility In Out Years," *Defense Daily*, February 18, 2010: 3.

# Appendix E. May 2010 Navy Testimony Regarding Fuel Costs as Evaluation Factor

At a May 6, 2010, hearing on Navy shipbuilding programs before the Seapower subcommittee of the Senate Armed Services Committee, Senator Jeff Sessions questioned Sean Stackley, the Navy's acquisition executive (i.e., the Assistant Secretary of the Navy [Research, Development and Acquisition]), regarding the role of fuel costs in the Navy's evaluation of the two LCS designs. The following is text of the exchange:

SENATOR SESSIONS:

Secretary Stackley, yesterday, Defense News reported that Secretary Mabus, the Navy secretary, in his remarks to the Navy League on May 5th, stated that "energy efficiency, both in the manufacturing process and in the final product would increasingly be a factor in judging program"—reform—"performance, as well as in the contract awards."

Earlier, he said, in October of last year at an energy forum, "First, we're going to change the way the Navy and the Marine Corps awards contracts, that lifetime energy costs of a building or a system and the fully burdened costs of fuel in powering those will be a mandatory evaluation factor used when awarding contracts.

"We're going to hold industry contractually accountable for meeting energy targets and system efficiency requirements." And he goes on to emphasize that more.

And in September of '09, he said, "One of the drivers for me is the affordability of being able to operate the force. We no longer have the luxury to say it's a good deal on price, or let's buy it, we have to get our arms around the lifecycle costs."

Do you agree that that's the right way to purchase a ship or anything, but—any vehicle, but a ship, particularly, that you want to know not only how much it costs today, but how much fuel it will use and how much it will cost to operate that? Is that a factor that should given weight in the process?

STACKLEY:

Sir, we—the secretary has outlined his goals for energy, and we are putting a lot of effort into not just meeting his goals, but building the path to get there.

When we look at how we procure our ships, we bring total ownership cost into the equation, and we evaluate not just—we look at not just the procurement costs, but we look at, again, the ownership costs throughout the life of the program, which includes—that includes energy, it includes manpower, it includes maintenance and modernization considerations in addition to the upfront procurement cost.

SESSIONS:

Well, I think you said that you agree with the secretary. Is that right?

STACKLEY:

I would—I would always agree with the secretary, sir.

(LAUGHTER)

SESSIONS:

Well, especially when he's correct, as he is in that statement.

But I didn't hear you say precisely that you are at that level now. He said, we're going to—"the first thing we're going to do is fix this energy matter."

So I'm asking you today, when you look at Littoral Combat Ship competition, is that effectively being evaluated in the bid process? It certainly seems that it should be?

STACKLEY:

We took a look at, inside of the—of the larger category of ownership costs, we took a look at—we considered it as an evaluation factor, compared the two designs, and arrived at an evaluation inside the technical portion of the LCS award criteria that would address improvements to total ownership costs, which would include energy as well as maintenance and modernization.

SESSIONS:

Well, the fact that that is a very long and complex answer makes me nervous. Because my analysis of it is that it does not do just what the secretary said.

And I would offer, for the record, Mr. Chairman, a report from the Congressional Budget Office that's analyzed this particular question. The way I read the report, it's pretty clear to me that the Navy has not sufficiently calculated the fuel costs of this ship.

Has the—in calculating the comparative fuel costs of the two ships, and that's what you mean by those words you gave us, doesn't it? You compare the cost of one ship and its normal operating procedure and you compare the cost of the other. Correct? Is that what you mean?

STACKLEY:

We look at total ownership cost, which includes all the factors, including energy, yes, sir.

SESSIONS:

Well, let's focus on the energy part of cost. Do you consider how much it costs to run one ship and you consider the cost of the other one? That's what it means. Does it not?

STACKLEY:

Yes, sir.

SESSIONS:

And have you calculated and reduced to dollar amounts, the estimated fuel cost of operating these ships, each one, through the lifecycle?

STACKLEY:

We've looked at the different ways in which the Navy would operate the ship—because, clearly, fuel costs are dependent upon how you would operate the ship—and ran the respective analyses for the two different designs.

SESSIONS:

Well, I'm well aware of that, but that's—that would be part of how you would calculate it. So have you calculated it to a dollar- and-cent figure, so you can compare actual cost?

STACKLEY:

Yes, sir. In accordance with the different ways in which we would operate the ship, inside of the total...

SESSIONS:

How much do you calculate for the LCS 1 and the LCS 2? What are the figures for each?

STACKLEY:

I would not provide those in an open forum because the respective figures that were used— that we have used are proprietary. However, we have provided that information through other means to the CBO, in forming their report.

SESSIONS:

Well, as I would read the CBO report, it would conclude that Navy inadequately scored that.

But, do I hear you saying you have an actual dollar-and-cent figure that you've used in evaluating the life-cycle cost, that now—that the Navy has and is applying to this ship?

STACKLEY:

To be exact, we took a look at the total ownership cost for the two competing designs. We looked at maintenance, modernization, manpower and fuel consumption. When we look at fuel consumption, we have to consider the different ways in which the Navy would operate the ship.

And then we looked at the total ownership costs, side by side, for the two different designs, considering different categories for the way the Navy would...

(CROSSTALK)

SESSIONS:

Surely you would have to reduce this variable speed to some sort of a factor that you could evaluate in terms of dollars and cents. That's what CBO said.

(CROSSTALK)

SESSIONS:

It's been done before, hasn't it?

STACKLEY:

Yes, sir. So as you read through the CBO report, what they point out is, one, there's a range in terms of the percent of the total ownership cost that's made up by fuel, and also there's a range for how much of an impact the different mission type of operations have on that percent. And within that range, you could have one design being better than the other and vice versa.

So, in fact, the outcome of the analysis for total ownership cost is highly sensitive to the way that the Navy would operate the ships. And depending on which...

(CROSSTALK)

SESSIONS:

I couldn't agree more. But have you calculated that?

STACKLEY:

Yes, sir.

SESSIONS:

And you would agree, would you not, that if you didn't properly calculate that, then it could be unfair to one competitor or another?

STACKLEY:

What I would definitely agree to is that there is a degree of uncertainty around the estimates. And so within—when you say not properly calculating it, I would say that the Navy's estimate is not so much of a point estimate, as it is a number plus or minus a certain percentage of uncertainty.

And so, I would not—I would not suggest that we've been unfair to one or the other based on that calculation.

SESSIONS:

Mr. Stackley, I've not been able to follow those answers. It's awfully complex to me. It would seem to me that you would, if you were buying an automobile, and got better gas mileage than another one, you would calculate over the expected life of that car, how many dollars you spend on fuel on each one.

And are you saying that you have done that in this case, and—this competition—and that you are prepared at some point to make that public?

STACKLEY:

Two things. One, you say, within the competition. The analysis that you are referring to is not a part of the award criteria.

SESSIONS:

Oh. So—well, then are you going to make it a part of the award evaluation or not?

STACKLEY:

No, sir. What we do have as a part of the award criteria is how to improve upon total ownership cost. When we do the analysis of total ownership cost, which includes fuel, and we put side by side comparison between the two designs, then the outcome of that analysis is entirely dependent on the assumptions you make with regards to how the Navy would operate the ship, where the range of operations is entirely within what the LCS will be called to perform.

SESSIONS:

Well, the CBO, faced with those circumstances, came up with a range, did they not?

STACKLEY:

Yes, sir.

SESSIONS:

And the range was something like eight to 18.

STACKLEY:

It was eight percent to 11 percent for a frigate-type of combatant, which would include an LCS.

SESSIONS:

And they estimated the moderate range would be 11. That was their guesstimate of—that was their estimate of what the...

STACKLEY:

Yes, sir.

SESSIONS:

... fuel costs should be. Have you used—do you use that figure or a different one?

STACKLEY:

We used the baseline figures that we have for the two designs. The other information that the CBO pointed toward was the operating regime of the ships, where they would nominally spend 95 percent of their time at 16 knots or less, 5 percent of their time north of that speed.

So you have a range of variability of 5 percent inside of the CBO's numbers, driven by the way you operate the ships, for a cost factor that's 11 percent of the total ownership cost.

SESSIONS:

Well, I would—thank you, Mr. Chairman.

I would just say that this is a very serious matter. And I would expect—I'm not able to follow your answers, and my concern is that you're not adequately accounting for differences of fuel. And I intend to follow it.

I hope that you conduct this correctly, but if not, I think—I think we would not have had a fair competition.[44]

---

[44] Source: Transcript of hearing.

# Appendix F. May 2010 Navy Testimony Regarding Impact of NLOS-LS Cancellation

At a May 6, 2010, hearing on Navy shipbuilding programs before the Seapower subcommittee of the Senate Armed Services Committee, Senator Jack Reed questioned Sean Stackley, the Navy's acquisition executive (i.e., the Assistant Secretary of the Navy [Research, Development and Acquisition]), and Lieutenant General George Flynn, Deputy Commandant, Combat Development and Integration, and Commanding General, Marine Corps Combat Development Command, regarding the impact the cancellation of the NLOS-LS program. The following is text of the exchange:

SENATOR REED:

Let me ask a question, then yield to Senator Wicker. And I might have one more question, but going back to the decision about the DDG- 51 versus the DDG-1000. The DDG-1000 was developed with the principal mission of close fire support for forcible entry, principally the Marine Corps.

Then the Navy made the decision that they could do that by other means, and the more pressing need was missile defense, which the DDG- 51 seems more capable. Part of that decision, I understand, is the thought that essentially the Navy could adopt an Army system, the non- line of sight launch system, NLOS. But now it appears that the Army is getting ready to abandon the development of that system, forcing you to have no system or to adopt the cost of that system, rather than bootstrapping on the Army.

So, I'm just, Admiral Blake, if NLOS is canceled, which it appears close to be, what's your backup plan? But more importantly, I'd like everyone to comment on this general topic. What are we going to do to ensure close fire support for forcible entry of Marines?

BLAKE:

Well, sir, first of all, for the NLOS program, the NLOS was looked at from the Navy perspective to go on the LCS. It was going to be a part of the surface package, the surface modular package [for the LCS]. It was going to go on there.

And it was going to be used—one of the missions it was going to be used for was for the swarming boat issue. What we are doing right now is because of the Army's announcement that they are potentially looking at terminating the program, we have been—we are going back and evaluating for that particular module.

If, in fact that program is terminated and it is decided that the Navy would not go down that path, then what would we have to do in order to meet the key performance parameters for that particular module on the LCS.

REED:

Thank you. That helps to clarify.

Can I assume then, Secretary Stackley, to my comment, that the close fire support would be provided not by a destroyer, but by the LCS? Is that correct, the operational concept, Mr. Secretary?

STACKLEY:

No, sir. There's a naval surface first support capability. That requirement is met by what is called a triad. First, there's organic artillery, there is air, then there's naval surface fires. So that triad is intended to meet the overarching or capstone requirement.

And we look at—you started with the DDG-1000 with the advanced con [sic: gun] system [the DDG-1000's 155 mm Advanced Gun System] to [help meet] the overall requirement, and we look at other surface ships, basically [the] five-inch 54 [caliber gun], basically which is common to the DDG-51 and the [CG-47 class] cruiser. And with the NLOS, we looked at a capability that the LCS could further contribute to that [naval surface fire support] campaign problem.

REED:

General Flynn, since your Marines are going to have to make the forceful entry, you have the last word on the whole topic and NLOS, too.

FLYNN:

Sir, over a year ago we agreed that the solution, and this was at the same time we were examining the DDG-1000, we agreed to look for a joint analysis of alternatives [AOA] to determine the way ahead for naval surface fires. A key part of that had, as Secretary Stackley said, is our belief in the triad, that no single leg of the triad can meet all the demands of it. And we see naval surface fires as providing volume and accuracy as a key part of that triad.

As part of the joint AOA, we looked at 71 alternatives, and we came down to the six most promising. One of them was the NLOS system. If it proved promising, it would have to have an extended range, but that was one of the alternatives. And that was one of the areas that we were also looking to capitalize on the Navy's building of the LCS platform.

If NLOS proves not to be effective, then the only other option that's available right now is the development of the five-inch round, the extended range round for extended use off the DDG-81 and higher class [destroyer] hull forms. And that really needs to be upon 12-ish (ph) [sic: a POM-12 issue],[45] because right now there is no [new] naval surface fire [capability], with the exception of the DDG-1000 in the program of record. The next promising or viable thing seems to be the extended five-inch range [shell]. And that would meet the requirement.[46]

---

[45] The Program Objective Memorandum, or POM, is an internal DOD document used to develop DOD's proposed budget. POM-12 is the POM for the proposed FY2012 budget that DOD will submit to Congress in February 2011.

[46] Source: Transcript of hearing.

# Appendix G. Potential for Common Hulls

Some observers, including some Members of Congress, have expressed interest in the idea of using common hulls for Coast Guard cutters and smaller Navy combatants, so as to improve economies of scale in the construction of these ships and thereby reduce their procurement costs. In earlier years, this interest focused on using a common hull for the LCS and the Offshore Patrol Cutter (OPC), a cutter displacing roughly 3,000 tons that is to be procured under the Coast Guard's Deepwater acquisition program.[47] More recently, this interest has focused on using a common hull for the LCS and the National Security Cutter (NSC), a cutter displacing about 4,300 tons that is also being acquired under the Deepwater program. This appendix presents information regarding the idea of using common hulls for Coast Guard cutters and smaller Navy combatants.

## July 2009 CBO Report

A July 2009 CBO report examines options for the Navy and Coast Guard to use common hulls for some of their ships. The report states that:

> some members of Congress and independent analysts have questioned whether the Navy and the Coast Guard need to purchase four different types of small combatants and whether—in spite of the services' well-documented reservations about using similar hull designs—the same type of hull could be employed for certain missions. To explore that possibility, the Congressional Budget Office (CBO) examined three alternatives to the Navy's and the Coast Guard's current plans for acquiring littoral combat ships and deepwater cutters.
>
> - Option 1 explores the feasibility of having the Coast Guard buy a variant of the Navy's LCS—specifically, the semiplaning monohull—to use as its offshore patrol cutter.
>
> - Option 2 examines the effects of reducing the number of LCSs the Navy would buy and substituting instead a naval version of the Coast Guard's national security cutter. (The rationale for this option is that, according to some analysts, the NSC's longer mission range and higher endurance might make it better suited than the LCS to act as a "patrol frigate," which would allow the Navy to carry out certain activities—maritime security, engagement, and humanitarian operations—outlined in the sea services' new maritime strategy.)
>
> - Option 3 examines the advantages and disadvantages of having the Coast Guard buy more national security cutters rather than incur the costs of designing and building a new ship to perform the missions of an offshore patrol cutter.
>
> According to CBO's estimates, all three alternatives and the services' plans would have similar costs, regardless of whether they are calculated in terms of acquisition costs or total life-cycle costs (see Table 1).6 CBO's analysis also indicates that the three alternative plans would not necessarily be more cost-effective or provide more capability than the services' existing plans. Specifically, even if the options addressed individual problems that the Navy and Coast Guard might confront with their small combatants, it would be at the cost of creating new challenges. For instance, Option 1—which calls for using the LCS monohull for the Coast Guard's OPC—would provide less capability for the Coast Guard from that

---

[47] For more on the Deepwater program, see CRS Report RL33753, *Coast Guard Deepwater Acquisition Programs: Background, Oversight Issues, and Options for Congress*, by Ronald O'Rourke.

service's perspective and at a potentially higher cost. Option 2 could provide the Navy with capability that, in some respects, would be superior for executing the peacetime elements of its maritime strategy; but that enhanced peacetime capability would sacrifice wartime capability and survivability. Option 3 would allow the Coast Guard to replace its aging cutters more quickly at a slightly higher cost but without the technical risk that is associated with designing and constructing a new class of ships, which the service's existing plan entails. It would, however, provide fewer mission days at sea and require the Coast Guard to find new home ports for its much larger force of national security cutters.[48]

# Reported Proposal to Build Variant of NSC for Navy

In January 2008, it was reported that Northrop Grumman, the builder of the NSC, had submitted an unsolicited proposal to the Navy to build a version of the NSC for the Navy as a complement to, rather than a replacement for, the LCS.

## January 14, 2008, Press Report

A press report dated January 14, 2008, stated:

> The U.S. Navy is stumbling to build the ship it wants—the Littoral Combat Ship (LCS)—so shipbuilder Northrop Grumman is urging the service to turn to a ship it can get sooner and cheaper: a patrol frigate version of the Coast Guard's National Security Cutter (NSC).
>
> "We have listened to what the Navy has said—to be more efficient, be innovative and produce affordable and capable ships," said Phil Teel, president of Northrop's Ship Systems sector. "The patrol frigate is a response to that, and to the Navy's new National Maritime Strategy."
>
> Northrop's analysts have studied remarks and themes oft repeated by senior Navy leaders and concluded a de facto requirement exists for a frigate-size ship capable of handling a range of low- and mid-intensity missions. Those missions, said Eric Womble, head of Ship Systems' Advanced Capabilities Group, are detailed in the Navy's new Maritime Strategy and include forward presence, deterrence, sea control, maritime security, humanitarian assistance and disaster response.
>
> "You don't want a high-end Aegis ship to handle those missions," Womble said, "you want something cheaper and smaller."
>
> The National Security Cutter (NSC) as configured for the Coast Guard could easily handle those roles, Womble said.
>
> The first NSC, the Bertholf, successfully carried out its initial trials in early December and will be commissioned this year by the Coast Guard. Womble said a Navy version would avoid the first-of-class issues that have plagued numerous Navy programs, including both designs being built for the LCS competition.
>
> Northrop in late December began briefing select Navy leaders on its unsolicited proposal. The company is taking pains to avoid presenting the ship as an LCS alternative, instead

---

[48] Congressional Budget Office, *Options for Combining the Navy's and the Coast Guard's Small Combatant Programs*, July 2009, p. 2.

calling it an LCS "complement," which is being built under a competition between Lockheed Martin and General Dynamics.

Key features of Northrop's concept are:

—The ship is based on a proven design already under construction.

—The NSC's weapons, sensors and systems already have a high degree of commonality with Navy systems, increasing affordability.

—While the NSC is 15 knots slower than the 45-knot LCS, the cutter can stay at sea up to two months, much longer than the LCS.

The report also stated:

Northrop is claiming it can deliver the first ship at the end of 2012 at an average cost of less than $400 million per ship, exclusive of government-furnished equipment, in fiscal 2007 dollars. That's close to the $403 million contract cost of the third NSC, which incorporates all current design upgrades.

A major element of Northrop's proposal, Womble said, is that the Navy should make no changes to the current Block 0 design. "That's the only way we can deliver the ship at this price."

The design, however, has plenty of room for upgrades, Womble claimed, and Northrop is proposing future upgrades be handled in groups, or blocks, of ships, rather than modifying individual ones. Those upgrades could include non-line-of-sight missiles, SeaRAM missile launchers and more capabilities to handle unmanned systems. The design even has room for an LCS-like reconfigurable mission area under the flight deck, he claimed.

Northrop admits the ships are deficient in one significant Navy requirement: full compatibility with the Naval Vessel Rules (NVR), essentially building codes developed by the Naval Sea Systems Command and the American Bureau of Shipping. The belated application of the NVR to both LCS designs was a major factor in the cost growth on those ships.

Most of the NSC design already is NVR-compatible, Womble said, but upgrading the entire design to NVR standards would involve a fundamental redesign and eliminate the proposal's cost and construction time attributes.

"We'd need a waiver [from the NVR rules] to make this proposal work," he said.

The report also stated:

Navy Response: 'No Requirement'

The official response from the Navy to Northrop's proposal so far is unenthusiastic.

"There is currently no requirement for such a combatant," said Lt. Clay Doss, a Navy spokesman at the Pentagon. The Navy's other surface ship programs, he said, "address specific requirements."

Doss did note that "the Navy and Coast Guard have considered a common platform for the LCS and the Coast Guard's National Security Cutter. However, due to the unique mission requirements of each service, a common hull is not a likely course of action."

Problems with the LCS have caused some observers to predict the program's demise, but the Navy "is completely committed to the LCS program," Doss said. "We need 55 Littoral Combat Ships sooner rather than later, and we need them now to fulfill critical, urgent war-fighting gaps."

Northrop however, is not alone in proposing the NSC as an LCS alternative. Coast Guard Capt. James Howe, writing in the current issue of the U.S. Naval Institute's Proceedings magazine, is urging Navy leaders to consider the NSC.

"I think the Navy should look at it," he said Jan. 10. "Northrop is building a naval combatant here. It has standard U.S. Navy weapon systems as part of its packages. Its communications are interoperable. It can handle underway replenishment. If there's a possibility it could be a cost saver or a good deal for the Navy, it needs to be explored."

Howe, who said he was unaware of Northrop's patrol frigate proposal, agreed the NSC is capable of further enhancements. "There's a lot of space on that ship," he said.

'Potential Game-changer'

Northrop likely is facing an uphill battle with its patrol frigate, as the Navy culturally prefers to dictate requirements based on its own analysis.

But the Navy is having trouble defending the affordability of its shipbuilding plan to Congress and bringing programs in on budget. One congressional source noted the service "can't admit their plan won't work." An unsolicited proposal, the source said, "opens the way for someone else to come up with a potential game-changer."

Northrop's plan, the source said, may be an unexpected opportunity.

"Northrop is listening to the people who have been criticizing the Navy's shipbuilding plan," the source said. "They've gotten a sense that maybe the Navy is looking for a solution, and the Navy can't produce a solution because it might be too embarrassing."

One more aspect that could be at work in the Northrop proposal: "I think there's something coy going on here," the source said. "They may be promoting this as an LCS complement, but their idea might be part of a strategic plan to replace the LCS."[49]

## January 17, 2008, Press Report

A press report dated January 17, 2008, stated:

Northrop Grumman Corp said on Wednesday [January 16, 2008, that] a proposal to turn its 418-foot Coast Guard cutter into a new class of Navy frigates is sparking some interest among U.S. Navy officials and lawmakers.

---

[49] Christopher P. Cavas, "Northrop Offers NSC-Based Vessel To Fill LCS Delays," *Defense News*, January 14, 2008.

Northrop is offering the Navy a fixed price for the new ship of under $400 million and could deliver the first one as early as 2012 to help out with maritime security, humanitarian aid and disaster response, among other things, said Eric Womble, vice president of Northrop Grumman Ship Systems.

So far, the officials briefed have found Northrop's offer "intriguing," Womble told Reuters in an interview. "They like the fact that we're putting an option on the table. No one has told us, 'Go away, don't come back, we don't want to hear this'," Womble said.

At the same time, the Navy says it remains committed to another class of smaller, more agile ships—the Littoral Combat Ships (LCS) being built by Lockheed Martin Corp (LMT.N: Quote, Profile, Research) and General Dynamics Corp (GD.N: Quote, Profile, Research)— amid huge cost overruns.

"There currently is no requirement for a frigate," Navy spokesman Lt. Clay Doss said. He said the Navy and Coast Guard had discussed a common hull during the initial stage of the LCS competition, but agreed that was "not a likely course of action due to the unique mission capabilities."

For now, he said the Navy was proceeding as quickly as it could with the 55-ship LCS program as well as design work on a new DDG-1000 destroyer, and a planned cruiser, CG-X....

The report also stated:

Virginia-based defense consultant Jim McAleese said the fixed-price offer could be good news for the Navy, which has typically borne the risk of cost-based shipbuilding contracts.

"That is a potential catalyst that could have a huge impact on the way the Navy buys small- and mid-sized surface combatants," McAleese said.

Northrop says its new Coast Guard cutter also experienced some cost growth, but says that was mainly due to requirements added after the Sept. 11, 2001, hijacking attacks. The first of the new ships is due to be delivered to the Coast Guard in March, followed by one ship annually over the next few years.

Northrop said it could offer the Navy a fixed price on the frigate because design work on the ships is already largely completed. Its price excludes government-furnished equipment that would still have to be put on board.

"We're not advocating an LCS replacement," said spokesman Randy Belote. "But after listening to the Navy leadership and studying the new maritime strategy, we think we can get hulls and capabilities into the water at a much faster pace."

Womble said Northrop analysts and an outside consultant studied the Navy's needs and concluded the Navy could use another ship that can operate in shallow water, be forward deployed, has the range and endurance to operate independently, and can work with U.S. allies, if needed.

The press report also stated:

The proposed ship can be deployed for 60 days without new supplies, has a range of 12,000 nautical miles, and can travel at 29 knots, fast enough to keep up with other warships. That compares to 20 days and a range of 3,500 miles for LCS.

Northrop began sharing a PowerPoint presentation about the proposal with Navy officials and lawmakers at the end of December, and has already met with several senior officials, including Chief of Naval Operations Adm. Gary Roughead.

It could deliver the first frigate by 2012, if the Navy was able to add $75 million for long lead procurement items into the fiscal 2009 budget proposal to be sent to Congress next month, Northrop said.

The frigate is about 75 percent compliant with special requirements that apply only to U.S. Navy ships. Northrop said it believed it could qualify for waivers on the remaining 25 percent because similar waivers were granted in the past.[50]

# Author Contact Information

Ronald O'Rourke
Specialist in Naval Affairs
rorourke@crs.loc.gov, 7-7610

---

[50] Andrea Shalal-Esa, "Northrop Offers US Navy New Ship For Fixed Price," *Reuters*, January 17, 2008.

---

[H.A.S.C. No. 111–18]

# THE NAVY LITTORAL COMBAT SHIP PROGRAM

HEARING

BEFORE THE

## SEAPOWER AND EXPEDITIONARY FORCES SUBCOMMITTEE

OF THE

## COMMITTEE ON ARMED SERVICES HOUSE OF REPRESENTATIVES

ONE HUNDRED ELEVENTH CONGRESS

FIRST SESSION

HEARING HELD
MARCH 10, 2009

U.S. GOVERNMENT PRINTING OFFICE

54–408                    WASHINGTON : 2010

For sale by the Superintendent of Documents, U.S. Government Printing Office
Internet: bookstore.gpo.gov  Phone: toll free (866) 512–1800; DC area (202) 512–1800
Fax: (202) 512–2104  Mail: Stop IDCC, Washington, DC 20402–0001

# CONTENTS

## CHRONOLOGICAL LIST OF HEARINGS

### 2009

## TUESDAY, MARCH 10, 2009

## THE NAVY LITTORAL COMBAT SHIP PROGRAM

### STATEMENTS PRESENTED BY MEMBERS OF CONGRESS

### WITNESSES

### APPENDIX

# THE NAVY LITTORAL COMBAT SHIP PROGRAM

---

House of Representatives,
Committee on Armed Services,
Seapower and Expeditionary Forces Subcommittee,
*Washington, DC, Tuesday, March 10, 2009.*

The subcommittee met, pursuant to call, at 10:04 a.m., in room 2118, Rayburn House Office Building, Hon. Gene Taylor (chairman of the subcommittee) presiding.

## OPENING STATEMENT OF HON. GENE TAYLOR, A REPRESENTATIVE FROM MISSISSIPPI, CHAIRMAN, SEAPOWER AND EXPEDITIONARY FORCES SUBCOMMITTEE

Mr. TAYLOR. The hearing will come to order. Good morning and welcome.

Today the subcommittee meets in open session to receive testimony on the Littoral Combat Ship (LCS) program.

Our witnesses today are Rear Admiral Vic Guillory, director of surface ship programs for the chief of naval operations; Rear Admiral Bill Landay, the program executive officer for the surface ship structure; and Ms. Anne Sandel, program executive officer for Littoral and mine warfare.

I want to thank our witnesses for being with us.

To call the LCS program troubled would be an understatement. The fact of the matter is that this program has so far delivered one ship—one ship.

But a look at the plan from just two years ago, we should by now have at least four ships delivered, three more nearing completion from a fiscal year 2008 authorization, six more under contract from a fiscal year 2009 authorization, and today we should be discussing the authorization of six more ships for fiscal year 2010. That would be a total of 19 ships.

So instead of having 13 delivered or under contract, with another 6 in this year's budget, we have 1 ship delivered that will likely tip the scales well above two-and-a-half times the original estimate, and 1 ship that might finish this summer with similar, if not higher, cost growth.

The Navy canceled two previously authorized ships. No ships were placed under contract for fiscal year 2008, and no contract award has been made for the two ships authorized for fiscal year 2009—all of this from the program that was hailed as a poster child for its transformational and affordable acquisition strategy.

It seems all the program has accomplished is transforming a realistic goal of achieving a 313-ship fleet into a very real disappointment in which neither competitor shows remorse for being a year late and hundreds of millions of dollars over budget.

And from what I can see, neither competitor has a plan or even a desire to do any better, because they can count on the Navy throwing more money at their problems.

This program is not just a lesson of over optimism, poor management and lack of poor oversight, even though all those things occurred in spades.

The fundamental lesson is flawed strategic planning, flawed in the belief that the government can pass on to industry decisions that are inherently governmental, flawed in the belief that untested, unproven concepts, such as reconfigurable mission modules, can be incorporated into an acquisition program without testing and verifying the concept of surrogate platforms, and finally flawed to the absence of a Plan B for needed capability in the fleet.

I believe it is a lack of Plan B which has tethered the Navy so completely to this program. Particularly in the area of mine warfare, the LCS is the only future they see. Dropping the LCS program to develop another mine warfare platform is viewed as unacceptable on the schedule. And they might be correct.

However, because the Navy is at this moment stuck with continuing the LCS program, it does not mean its current strategy for buying these ships has to continue.

I have nothing against either of the lead contractors, but I know this. They both contracted to build a ship for $220 million, and they did not even come close.

I understand the Navy was guilty of changing the design specifications with the implementation of the Naval Vessel Rules, but I fail to see how that resulted in more than doubling the price and slipping 18 months of schedule.

I am also concerned that the Navy has not been able to come to terms with the contractors for the ships authorized last year. It appears to me the solution is simple. We need to bring true competition to this program, not the pseudo competition we currently have between the two poor performers, but true competition based on price, schedule and quality.

I have been asking for over two years if our nation owns the rights to the design drawings of the ships so they can bid them out directly to any shipyard with the capability of constructing the vessels. The answer seems to be yes and no.

I have got to believe at this point we should know every inch of bar, angle iron and plate in those ships, every piece of pipe. And every inch of weld ought to be on someone's CAD. And if it isn't by now, I would like to hear why.

I understand the prepared witness testimony will address this question. However, I would like the witnesses today, on the record, to explain that position and answer in layman's terms, not in the language of professional acquisition executive, the exact claim the government has on the technical design rights to both the sea frame and the combat system.

Then I would like our witnesses to explain how long it would take, what organization would be responsible—in particular who would be responsible—and how much it would cost to develop the technical data package described in the prepared statement that is required to bid ships directly to other shipyards or to current shipyards divorced of their lead contractors.

Ranges of cost and time are acceptable. What is not acceptable is taking this question for the record.

So far I have discussed just one ship, just what the Navy refers to as the sea frame. Today's hearing for the first time brings in an official responsible for the mission packages that are purported to give this vessel a multi-mission capability.

Although at least one of each type of mission modules has been developed, I am very concerned that major components of the overall mission package are still under development and have not been thoroughly tested. Therefore, I would request that Ms. Sandel update the subcommittee on the remaining development and testing for all the mission packages.

I would also like to know if anything in existing Navy platforms can operate with an LCS mission module as a stopgap capability filler until sufficient LCS ships are constructed.

Everyone should understand that the current situation of these vessels, costing in excess of a half a billion dollars, cannot continue. There are too many other needs and too little resources to pour money into a program that was designed to be affordable.

I would also like to remind all of the parties involved, particularly right now, that you do not want to be the program that is breaking the bank. From what I read in the newspapers, there are no protected programs in the ongoing debate on affordability.

Of course, none of the witnesses sitting in front of us today was responsible for the program when it began. They inherited a mess, and they are doing their best to fix it. I appreciate that.

Now is the time for frank talk on what needs to be done. We need the best price and the best quality we can get for these vessels, whether with the current lead contractors, after they finally get the message, or changing course and bidding directly with other shipyards.

Before I ask the ranking member for his remarks, I would like to remind the subcommittee that competition sensitive information, such as current estimates of prices, are protected by statute.

However, the Navy has agreed to answer these types of questions directly to individual members in an appropriate forum and under the conditions agreed to by the Navy, general counsel at our committee.

I now call my friend from Missouri for any remarks he may wish to make.

[The prepared statement of Mr. Taylor can be found in the Appendix on page 47.]

## STATEMENT OF HON. W. TODD AKIN, A REPRESENTATIVE FROM MISSOURI, RANKING MEMBER, SEAPOWER AND EXPEDITIONARY FORCES SUBCOMMITTEE

Mr. AKIN. Thank you, Mr. Chairman.

And welcome to the hearing. Thank you all for visiting us on what is a rather substantial topic.

Today is my first opportunity to join the subcommittee in overseeing the Navy's shipbuilding program. I have already begun to grasp the many complexities unique to the acquisition of battle force ships.

4

I recently had the opportunity to join Congressman Taylor at Austal USA in Mobile, Alabama, where the LCS–2 is under construction, and it is certainly an innovative ship. But even a newcomer to shipbuilding can see that much remains to be done.

I understand this program has faced many challenges, but a simple principle seems to have gotten lost. The principle isn't exclusive to shipbuilding: in sum, the importance of transparency and accountability in acquisitions programs grounded in sound strategy. And that cannot be overstated.

Sadly, in its early days the LCS program appears to have lacked accountability. Many important steps have been taken to rectify the situation, but the program still lacks a well-conceived strategy.

At various times in the last two years, the Navy has proposed a fly-off and down-select between these two flight zero ships, to be followed by a redesign for a flight one ship, investing in a class design services effort to convert the selected design to build to print and recompeting the class, redesigning the ships to include a common combat system in both, and last, an apparent desire to procure both ships from the existing teams with minimal changes.

We cannot reasonably expect the industry teams to make the investments in facilities and designs for affordability we demand, if we cannot articulate what we want to buy.

Further, we cannot reasonably expect the taxpayers to continue to fund ships that we cannot definitively say what we want. Even Obama's sweeping comments about cutting defense spending and weapons programs, do any of us believe we can defend a program for which we have no acquisition strategy and for which we have long since surpassed the acquisition cost target identified in the programs key requirements document?

Just last week, the president stated far too often that spending is plagued by massive cost overruns and an absence of oversight and accountability. We need more competition for contracts, more oversight when they are carried out.

His goal is to save $40 billion a year, and many observers have cautioned that this won't be possible unless he starts to kill major Pentagon weapons systems.

Now, I am in no way advocating that the LCS program fall victim to such a cut. I have every reason to believe that this program represents a critical capability for our warfighters. Despite the cost overruns, it can still become the most affordable ship in the Navy's fleet.

But there remain many questions which have not been answered to my satisfaction. I am going to list five of those.

First, is the LCS program still affordable within the context of the overall shipbuilding program? That is, what would we have to give up in order to afford 55 of these ships at a cost of approximately half a billion dollars?

Second, although the Navy has pushed for buying the LCS in substantial numbers prior to an operation evaluation of the first ships, given that the operational valuation of these ships will now be conducted within the next 18 months, would it be prudent to wait to procure additional vessels until the evaluation is complete?

Third, the high cost of shipbuilding frequently has its roots in decisions we make to protect the industrial base. These decisions have merit.

We want to ensure that this nation has surge capability and doesn't lose the national treasure that is the shipyard worker, but we need to be very cautious about increasing capacity for which the Navy lacks the volume to support.

And the fourth question: When the Navy has canceled two ships, failed to award the fiscal year 2008 ship before the appropriations rescinded the funds, and has yet to reach agreement on the 2009 ships, it has elected to incrementally fund construction on follow-on vessels.

Again, these decisions may be expedient in the near term to avoid layoffs, but will we lack here in two years discussing root causes of cost growth for the follow-on vessels and citing incremental funding?

Fifth, I want to applaud Secretary Stackley's determination to control costs. He has wisely chosen not to award follow-on contracts if the industry teams can't demonstrate they are on the glide slope to $460 million.

He has also forced behavior changes on LCS–2 to prioritize completion of construction. Yet if we accept delivery of ships or award ships that do not have all systems fully integrated, what bill are we leaving for a future Congress?

Lastly, the mission packages are really what make LCS a valuable tool for the warfighter. The Navy has not taken aggressive steps to integrate and test these mission systems or train crews on the systems on other platforms.

I echo the chairman's strong concern that we cannot continue to wait for LCS to be available in sufficient numbers to develop and deploy these capabilities.

Mr. Chairman, thank you for holding the hearing today.

Admiral Guillory, Admiral Leahy and Ms. Sandel, I look forward to your testimony and thank you for being with us.

Mr. TAYLOR. I thank the ranking member. We have been joined by Mr. Stupak, who represents the Marinette area, so with unanimous consent I would ask that he be allowed to join the subcommittee for the day.

The chair now recognizes the gentleman from Michigan for five minutes.

Mr. STUPAK. Well, thank you, Mr. Chairman. And it has been 15 years since I sat on this committee. It is good to be back on this side of the dais. And thank you for your interest in the LCS program.

You know when you take a look at this program here from concept to design to a functional ship—we built one up in Marinette Marine, the first one, Freedom, which was actually commissioned in Milwaukee, Wisconsin, on November 8, 2008, and will be stationed at San Diego naval base—this is a whole new ship, like I said, a new design, new concept.

Since 9/11 we have new adversaries. We have different types of missions. So the Navy needed a new ship, and your target started from scratch on a concept to a full ship that was built and presented to the Navy, built up in Marinette Marine.

Lockheed Martin had to partner with Marinette Marine to build the first LCS because of the strong advantage of constructing a ship in a mid-tier shipyard. Mid-tier shipyard shipbuilders facilitate competitiveness and establish affordable approach to a program.

The chairman is right. We should have 19 more ships, and we are happy to build the next 18 up in Marinette Marine.

But there has been some—because it was a new design, a new concept, constantly changing it, there were delays, but in the meantime as we built the first ship, since then we have had to lay off 150 employees at Marinette Marine.

This week they were going to lay off another 200, but because of a partial award of the LCS contract to Lockheed Martin on February 27th, those layoffs have been—they are not going to do the layoffs.

The full award of the contract and successful continuation of the program would stabilize the employment in this region.

But the LCS is not only vital to the economy of northern Michigan, it is also immensely—production prospects for the U.S. and abroad—all of our allies are very excited about this new ship, this new class of warfare ship.

We could bring in many, many more ships, more than just what the Navy needs and being built and cruised here in the United States. You know with the Navy there is also—besides warfare, we see anti-piracy operations. We see humanitarian aid operations, what this ship is suited for.

The recent award of the LCS contract, the one I just spoke about that was partially awarded here on February 27th, has taken some time to get these complex negotiations done between the Navy and the shipbuilders.

There were many production standards that are shifting to try to get these contract details without changing so we can get the ship that can be built at the cost of chairman spoke of, but not the first few.

The lead ships are always—a lead program on anything is always more expensive than originally thought of, but as you put more ships out, that price will go down.

As the Navy continues to fix the contract awards for ships authorized and funded in fiscal year 2009, I encourage the Navy, Lockheed Martin and General Dynamics to expediently address the contract details so that construction can proceed without further delays.

We are willing, ready and able and can produce the type of ship that the Navy needs.

So with an experienced team in place and production facilities on line, the program is ready for an early transition to full rate production. Doing so will reduce the costs and minimize the learning curves.

The LCS program is not only important to my Menominee Marinette area, but also the future capabilities of the Navy and to the defense of this nation.

So I urge the committee to consider not only the local impact of the award and the shipbuilding technology that we brought with this brand-new type of ship, but also to continue its discussions regarding the future of the current contracts and of the LCS program with the Navy, because this ship, which is needed with our new adversaries and the new demands on our country, the LCS is a ship that is appropriate to meet the needs of the Navy.

And we are proud to be playing a part in building such a ship for the Navy and for this nation.

Thank you, Mr. Chairman. With that, I yield back.

Mr. TAYLOR. The chair thanks the gentleman from Michigan.

Our witnesses today are Rear Admiral Victor Guillory, Director of Surface Warfare Division, United States Navy; Rear Admiral William Landay, Program Executive Officer for Ships, the United States Navy; and Ms. Anne Sandel, Program Executive Officer of Littoral and Mine Warfare.

The chair recognizes Admiral Guillory.

### STATEMENT OF REAR ADM. VICTOR G. GUILLORY, USN, DIRECTOR, SURFACE WARFARE DIVISION, N86, U.S. NAVY

Admiral GUILLORY. Excuse me. Chairman Taylor, Ranking Member Akin, distinguished members of the subcommittee, thank you for the opportunity to appear before you today to address the Navy's Littoral Combat Ship program.

Along with Rear Admiral Bill Landay and Ms. Anne Sandel, we thank the committee for its continued support and active interest in the Navy shipbuilding programs.

We have prepared a written statement and asked that it be entered into the record.

Mr. TAYLOR. Without objection.

Admiral GUILLORY. I would like to begin my remarks, Mr. Chairman, by stating the Navy remains committed to the LCS program. LCS fills warfighting gaps in support of maritime dominance in the Littorals in its strategic chokepoints around the world.

The LCS expands the battle space by complementing our inherent blue water capability. The LCS program will deliver capabilities to close validated warfighting gaps in mine countermeasures, surface warfare and anti-submarine warfare.

In addition to LCS' inherent speed, agility, shallow draft, payload capacity and reconfigurable mission spaces, the ship is an ideal platform for conducting additional missions in support of the maritime strategy to include irregular warfare and maritime security operations, such as counterpiracy operations.

The strength of LCS lies in its innovative design approach, applying modularity for operational flexibility. LCS has over 40 percent internal volume, giving reconfiguration capabilities for up to 200 tons of equipment.

This ability to modify the LCS' physical configuration with different mission packages give the operational commander credible options for responding to changing warfighting requirements.

The Navy also remains committed to procuring 55 LCSs. We are systematically pursuing cost reduction measures to ensure delivery of future ships on a schedule that affordably paces evolving threats.

Affordability will be realized through a regular review of warfighting requirements and applying lessons learned from the construction and that test and evaluation of sea frames admission packages.

The Navy, as part of its annual review of its shipbuilding program, expect there will be sufficient force structure with our existing frigates and mine warfare ships until LCS delivers in quantity to meet deployment requirements.

Legacy mine warfare ships and frigates are planned to be phased out gradually. These decommissioning to be balanced with LCS mission package and sea frame deliveries to mitigate warfare risk.

In summary, Mr. Chairman, the Navy remains committed to the LCS program. A 55-ship LCS class will give our Navy the advantage it needs to maintain dominance in the Littorals.

In the near term, the Navy continues to work diligently to find efficiencies in construction and test and evaluation phases so that the Littoral Combat Ships are delivered as deployable assets in as timely a manner as practical.

We appreciate your strong support and the opportunity today to testify before the subcommittee regarding the LCS program. I will be pleased to answer your questions following the opening remarks by Admiral Landay and Ms. Sandel.

Thank you, Mr. Chairman.

[The joint prepared statement of Admiral Guillory, Admiral Landay, and Ms. E. Anne Sandel can be found in the Appendix on page 54.]

Mr. TAYLOR. Thank you, sir.

Admiral Landay.

### STATEMENT OF REAR ADM. WILLIAM E. LANDAY, USN, PROGRAM EXECUTIVE OFFICER, SHIPS, U.S. NAVY

Admiral LANDAY. Chairman Taylor, Congressman Akin, distinguished members of the committee, I would also like to thank you for the opportunity to appear here today and discuss the Navy's Littoral Combat Ship program.

I appreciate your personal attention to LCS, including recent visits by members of the committee to some of our shipbuilders.

When the LCS program was initiated, it had two overarching goals: to address, identify and validate the warfighter in requirements in the Littoral battle space and to challenge many of the existing processes, procedures and conventions in naval shipbuilding that many believed had become too slow, risk adverse, and focused on a narrow set of solutions sets.

There was a belief held by some in both the Department of Defense (DOD) and the shipbuilding industry that we needed a different approach, one that allowed less conventional designs, greater use of commercial standards, and be focused on adapting existing systems available from throughout the world instead of along the R&D development effort.

LCS was seen as a class of ship that would benefit greatly from such an approach. Today we are 6 years into this effort, and as we look back, the results are mixed.

In some areas we have been successful. We have the first ship delivered 6 years after the program started, and based on initial inspections and evaluation, it is performing as required.

And we are close to delivering our second ship of a significantly different design later this year, two ships delivered in the time we traditionally would be completing initial design studies.

These are ships with unique capabilities to support mission packages, unmanned vehicle launch and recovery, open architectures, and a number of proven Hull, Mechanical and Electrical (HM&E) and combat systems from outside our traditional sources.

The reduced crew size of this vessel and its reliance on many practices from the commercial maritime industry drove us to more aggressive use of electronic navigation, unmanned and automated engineering spaces, improved focus on human interface to reduce workload, and automated damage control systems practices, which will have a great applicability to other ships throughout the fleet.

These parts of the program we have executed well.

Unfortunately, there are other aspects of the program where we have not had similar success. While we wanted to challenge our practices and processes, in a number of cases we overlooked hard learned, fundamental lessons of shipbuilding.

You must have a solid, mature design before you start construction. You cannot be negotiating standards and adding new technical requirements while you are building a ship. And if you have to make major changes, you need to stop and get them right, because rework kills productivity.

And you must have sufficient experience to management dedicated to the program to be able to identify and deal with rapidly emerging issues.

We have addressed these issues and LCS today in the following ways.

The design for both ships is mature, and we are incorporating revisions to specific areas based on lessons learned from the construction of the initial ship, proposed production improvements, acceptance inspections and early stages of the post-delivery testing period.

These revisions will be in place by the start of construction on the 2009 ships.

The Navy has increased the staff assigned to the program office and at the shipyards to monitor performance. The program staff has grown from eight to 20 personnel, with additional 12 billets assigned as the two lead ships complete delivery and post-delivery milestones this year, and more ships are placed under contract.

Similar increases have been made in the waterfront oversight area.

The fiscal year 2009 and fiscal year 2010 options will be fixed price contracts to ensure that costs and schedule adherence remain a primary focus both to industry and the government program teams.

There are no new technical or warfighting requirements added to the fiscal year 2009 ships.

We have two shipbuilding teams, who have the experience of building their initial ship, and we have worked to incorporate the lessons learned from the first ship into their follow-on production. Learning curve benefits should be evident on the fiscal year 2009 and 2010 ships.

In closing, LCS brings a critical capability to our nation. The Navy is committed to controlling costs and has taken actions to correct issues in the program. These corrections are in place, and we continue to work on improving our performance and that of our industry teams.

There are challenges that still remain in this program as we work to get to steady-state production, but we believe that we are prepared to handle them as they emerge.

Again, thank you for this opportunity to appear before the committee, and I look forward to your questions.

Mr. TAYLOR. Thank you, Admiral.

The chair now recognizes Ms. Sandel.

## STATEMENT OF E. ANNE SANDEL, PROGRAM EXECUTIVE OFFICER, LITTORAL AND MINE WARFARE, U.S. NAVY

Ms. SANDEL. Chairman Taylor, Ranking Member Akin, distinguished members of the subcommittee, good morning. My name is Anne Sandel.

Mr. TAYLOR. Ms. Sandel, you going to either have to turn on your mic or get closer to it.

Ms. SANDEL. Good morning. Chairman Taylor, Ranking Member Akin, distinguished members, I am Anne Sandel, the program executive officer for Littoral mine warfare.

I welcomed the opportunity to be here today to testify before the committee and to talk about the Littoral and Mine Warfare (LMW) programs, which have made significant contributions in developing and acquiring and maintaining operationally superior and affordable systems, providing assured access for U.S. and coalition forces to Littoral.

Our efforts are sharply focused to meet the joint warfighting forces requirements for dominance and for system access.

Today I am here specifically to discuss the LCS mission modules program and share with you the progress we have made in designing, developing, procuring, integrating and testing the mission modules for the Littoral Combat Ship.

The Navy has completed the rollout for the first of each type of mission package, has installed the mission package computing environment within LCS-1, and has initiated American Customer Satisfaction Index (ACSI) integration testing for the anti-submarine warfare mission package.

Each package provides warfighting capabilities for the one of three focused mission areas: mine countermeasures, which are detection and neutralization of mine threats; surface warfare for maritime security missions and defeating small boat attacks; and anti-submarine warfare, countering the shallow water diesel submarine threat.

These mission packages can be changed out over a 96-hour in port period so the ship is reconfigured and optimized for a different mission.

Mission package reconfiguration in LCS affords the combatant commander of flexible response to changing warfighting environments and is one of the signature design elements of the LCS class.

The quantity of each mission package type differs, based on analysis of projected operational requirements. Therefore, mission packages are developed and procured separately from the sea frame, a revolutionary concept to shipbuilding.

Employing an open business model facilitates upgrades to the LCS to warfighting capabilities as the threats evolve, and the open concept also helps us to reduce the total ownership cost of LCS over the years to come.

Again, we appreciate the sport of the House Armed Services Subcommittee, and I personally thank you for the opportunity to talk to today, and I look forward to answering your questions.

Mr. TAYLOR. The chair thanks all of our witnesses.

Admirals, again, I very much appreciate your many, many years of service to our nation and the hardships of your time you spent away from your families, and the hardships you have endured.

My frustration is not with your service records. My frustration is with your program.

If 60 Minutes were to walk through your door, put a microphone in front of you and say, "Admiral, you got something that was supposed to be a simple ship, mass-produced for about $220 million apiece. They are 18 months behind schedule, $300 million over schedule. Apparently every inch of the second vessel was welded by hand rather than by machine, and I don't see any plans that any future vessels are going to be produced any cheaper or any faster. And by the way, the competition that was supposed to be winner take all is now you have basically said, 'No, we are going to build some of each,' so you got two D-minus students, who are being graded on a curve, and so they have automatically got a C now, because they are only competing against each other."

Tell me how you would answer that question.

Admiral GUILLORY. Well, sir, I would like to start.

If, as you laid out, they walk through the door with a microphone and asked me about LCS, I think I would start out by reassuring them that the requirements for the ship was based upon a lot of study and a lot of analysis.

It clearly focused on the capability gaps in three major areas, as Ms. Sandel has laid out.

Mr. TAYLOR. Admiral, it is not about the need for the vessel. It is about the delivery and the cost of the vessel. No one is doubting the need. What we are doubting is whether or not these vessels at the present time are affordable, whether the next series is going to be any more affordable, that they will be built on time, because these weren't built on time.

So what has changed between vessels one and two that gives you, or more importantly, this Congress, which has to look the American taxpayer in the eye, any confidence that any follow-on vessels are going to be any closer to being on time and anywhere near the original projected cost?

I ought to also remind you that the price of aluminum is one-half of what it was two years ago, the price of copper is down just as dramatically, that there are machine shops and shipyards all over this country that are desperate for work.

And so the question would be, what makes you feel you owe these two shipyards anything, as far as the future, and what steps are you taking to broaden your base of suppliers and turn some of these opportunities into savings for the taxpayer and a fleet in the Navy saying sooner rather than later?

Admiral LANDAY. Mr. Chairman, let me take that part of the question, since it is directed more at the acquisitions side.

I would tell you today we have far more confidence in our ability to understand and have in fact mitigated the risk of these ships, because we have in fact built one and are about 85 percent complete on the other second one.

Initially, as we have discussed before, we started a design, and we started construction before our design was complete. Our designs now are very complete.

We have learned a lot of lessons in the course of the construction of the first two ships, from the imposition of Naval Vessel Rules to changes to rework that. In some cases the government required of them and in some cases the contractors had themselves.

We have learned those lessons, and we have incorporated those into the follow-on ships starting with the fiscal year 2009 ships.

We have implemented or seen the yards implement infrastructure improvement, going to the modular manufacturing facilities. We have seen infrastructure improvements being put in place that will start to come online this year that will continue to improve their processes.

We have spent a fair amount of time over the last year with both of the companies, going back and looking at specifications that we put in place that may have driven costs and having a discussion with them on whether we would still leave those in place or whether we could remove those.

We worked very hard with both companies to ensure that the design package that will be in place for the second ship is far more complete and incorporates many of the lessons learned that we made during the course of the first ship.

So we have done a lot to ensure that what happened on the first ship is not in place to happen on the second ship. And we also know that across our history, shipbuilders, good shipbuilders—and we believe both of these are good shipbuilders—get better as they get to go to the second and third ships in the series.

And so we do believe that the learning curve that we would expect to see from any good shipbuilders we are going to see in these two ships as they go down to the next set of ships.

Having said that, there is a very strong focus with us with those shipbuilders to ensure they are focused on costs and they are focused on price.

And one of the reasons why we have not yet awarded our fiscal year 2009 ships is because we continue to have very strong discussions with both shipbuilders in areas where we believe there can be some cost savings or where they believe we are driving costs into their program.

So I would tell you today we believe we are much more confident that we understand these ships. The shipbuilder you know, will get better over the next set of ships.

Mr. TAYLOR. Well, Admiral, since you said that, this subcommittee has about $14 billion a year to build 10 or 12 ships, and that is what we have to do, assuming that those ships are going to last for 30 years in order to get to a 300-ship Navy.

We have to deal in hard numbers. So having said, you did not mention the price of aluminum being down. You did mention that you think the shipyards would do better next time.

So what do you anticipate the cost of LCS–3 and LCS–4 to be? What should this subcommittee budget?

Admiral LANDAY. Well, sir, again, I am reluctant to talk costs to you in this——

Mr. TAYLOR. Sir, we have to talk costs.

Admiral LANDAY. But I am in the middle of the contract negotiations.

Mr. TAYLOR. You may be reluctant all day long, because at the moment I have got to tell you, Admiral, I don't think this ship is a bargain. I think these suppliers are taking advantage of our nation, and I am very reluctant to allocate a dime.

Now, we are going to work with the will of the subcommittee, but I think we need some reassurances that you have prices under control, and that translates into hard and fast numbers.

Admiral LANDAY. Well, yes, sir, and again, I would be happy in a closed session to tell you what we think those numbers are, based on the ongoing contract discussions.

What I can tell you is we understand that there is a cost cap. And as Secretary Stackley talked to you, we are working to ensure that we are driving both of these ships toward that cost cap for fiscal year 2010.

Now, what we are going to—the cost of the ship is going to be in fiscal year 2009 will be a function of what the end results of the contract discussions are. But I will tell you they are on a path to get toward the cost cap.

Mr. TAYLOR. The chair recognizes Mr. Akin.

Mr. AKIN. Thank you, Mr. Chairman.

I have a couple of bites and quick questions, and then maybe some little longer. The first thing is in terms of this program, is it really clear that there is one person in charge of this program?

Admiral LANDAY. Yes, the program manager and then the Program Executive Officer (PEO), the job that I have, are responsible for executing the acquisition part of it.

The Chief of Naval Operations (CNO), Admiral Guillory, as part of N86 (Surface Warfare Division), is responsible for setting the requirements consistent with the way that we do most ship classes.

And then Ms. Sandel has the mission packages under the broad auspice of my responsibility as PEO ships and the program manager.

Mr. AKIN. One of the things that I learned early on—I used to work for IBM—is if you have something that is really an important project, you need to have one person, who has got the responsibility for it, held accountable for it.

And so when I am looking at something, which is more than 100 percent over budget and 18 months late, it says to me somewhere along the line something went wrong.

I guess maybe backing up a little bit, was the $250 million ship—was that something that was just a pipedream to begin with?

Were these things low bid by both builders, knowing that the thing would go up, and they just basically said, "Hey, the way the game is played, quote a low number, get the contract, and then jack it up."

Is that the way we do it? Or is there anything that we have to prevent bidders from doing that?

Admiral GUILLORY. Sir, I will start with that question. The 220 number that was initially estimated for the cost of the Littoral Combat Ship, the sea frame, the ship itself, was based upon a number of factors.

Those factors included the fact that it was being built on commercial standards. The strategy was to look at what would be commercially available, propulsion, hull mechanical and electrical systems, and take advantage of the attributes that have been demonstrated in the commercial sector and deliver to the ship the high-speed, shallow draft warship that we——

Mr. AKIN. So stop just a minute. So what you are saying is that 220 was based on a commercial hull design, not the Navy higher requirements type of hull design. Is that right?

Admiral GUILLORY. Yes, sir. That is correct.

Mr. AKIN. Okay. Then we made the decision to go from a commercial type hull to a hull that had all kinds of additional capabilities, take shock and everything like that, so it is much different and heavier than a commercial hull would be. Is that correct?

Admiral GUILLORY. Yes, sir. Naval Vessel Rules——

Mr. AKIN. And who made—so as soon as you do that, you make the hull much more expensive, right?

Admiral GUILLORY. There is cost associated with strengthening the ship.

Mr. AKIN. So who made that decision to go from the commercial to a Navy standard hull, then?

Admiral GUILLORY. Well, that was a Navy decision, and it was a decision made based upon the recommendations from the technical community. It was based upon the survivability needs for a warship that is going to go in harm's way and survivability requirements for a ship to do that, which commercial standards could not meet.

Mr. AKIN. Okay. Okay. So what you have already—what you are telling me is is we started with one idea, which was a commercial type hull. Then we threw that strategy aside and went to a more robust kind of hull.

I am not questioning whether which one is better or not. I don't know. But I know one thing, and that is you are changing your mind as you are going along, right? You start with a commercial hull. Now you say we are going to go to a more robust kind of hull that will cost more money.

Were there other major kinds of changes in the design, which also resulted in this more than doubling of its cost? Well, if you had to pick the three things that kept us from the $200 million to the $400-something million, what are the three biggest contributors to those costs increasing?

Admiral LANDAY. Well, I would say the change to Naval Vessel Rules——

Mr. AKIN. The hull design, basically?

Admiral LANDAY. The hull design. Yes, sir.

Mr. AKIN. Okay. The second thing would be what?

Admiral LANDAY. We did that while we were getting ready, or had already awarded the contract and were in fact in the early stages of construction, so it required us to do a lot of concurrent design change as we were going, which ends up driving you into a lot of rework into the program.

Mr. AKIN. Which is still the same point, which is we changed the hull design.

Admiral LANDAY. Yes, sir.

Mr. AKIN. Okay. So that is the biggest single one. What is the second biggest single one?

Admiral LANDAY. Again, the rework, as I mentioned, kind of related to that.

I would say that the third key piece of this is in any new program, the cost growth, the unknown unknowns were more significant than we expected. We always expect that there are going to be some. I think we found there to be more than we had expected in both of these yards—again, not unique to those yards——

Mr. AKIN. What were those unknown unknowns connected with? What were the main ones?

Admiral LANDAY. I would say that, again, the design, the use of American Bureau of Shipping standards, which is a new process that we had in place, and some confusion initially as we build our business rules on how we would look with American Bureau of Standards, which drove a fair amount of re-look and multiple looks at the design, which then slowed the design down.

On LCS–1 we had a problem with the reduction gear initially. It turned out to be much longer than we thought, which again caused us to do some concurrent redesign. You know so that I would say would be the second key piece that we found in it. And then——

Mr. AKIN. That was LCS–1. You had something in the reduction gear.

Admiral LANDAY. Yes, sir. In the initial design——

Mr. AKIN. How big is that compared to just this completely redesigning the hull?

Admiral LANDAY. It ended up being about a 26-week implication and a fair amount of rework.

Mr. AKIN. So timewise, it hurt us.

Admiral LANDAY. Yes, sir. And then——

Mr. AKIN. Cost?

Admiral LANDAY. And then as a result of that, what we did at the time—again, not understanding how long I think that total delay was going to be—we tried to continue concurrent construction around that and then got ourselves in a situation where we had to come back and do a fair amount of rework as that period stretched out.

Mr. AKIN. It seems to me that what I am seeing, and I don't want to overdo my time here, Mr. Chairman, but what it seems like to me, there is a pattern from the start, and that was that we have been changing our mind as we go along. And that, as you know, is deadly to a project.

Admiral LANDAY. Yes, sir.

Mr. AKIN. You start with the concept we are going to go with a more commercial, cheaper hull, and then just when you get that started building, then you go and change it to a more robust warfighting kind of, which is a different design, and it is going to raise the cost of whole lot.

And now we have gotten to the point where we have built two different trial ships, and we are talking about building some more of them. And the Navy is even saying now, "Oh, we kind of like both of them." You know we are going to have every single ship. The Navy is going to be a custom ship, if we don't have discipline to say, "You have got to make a decision. You are going to have to stick with it."

If we keep changing the requirements, we haven't even had a chance to test either one of them. We are going to start to buy more of them. It seems like from just a couple of weeks since I took the trip, it seems like it is a little hazy as to exactly what is our acquisition strategy.

We are going to get—you know we have got this one started, the other one partly started. We have got to buy some of it. We are going to buy four, and then we are going to test them. We are going to partly test them. And we are going to get both of them. Do the Marines like—what—one better than the other?

It seems like there are a lot of questions, where there is not a clear-cut this is where we are starting, this is what it is going to look like, and it is clearly defined. It doesn't seem like we are nailing things down.

And the indecisiveness seems like it is costing us a whole lot of money. Do you want to respond?

Admiral LANDAY. Yes, sir. Well, I would certainly tell you in the 2009 and the fiscal year 2010 ships, what we have told both of the shipbuilders, and what we have put in our request for proposal, is we are going to build exactly the same ship we built for LCS–1 and LCS–2, that we are not changing requirements in that either—technical requirements or warfighting requirements—and that there are some, you know, things we learned in shipbuilding that would tweak the design.

So to your question of a lot of change which drove it, we clearly recognize that. That is not going to be the case in fiscal year 2009, 2010——

Mr. AKIN. But we are not getting much of a bargain on the third and fourth ships, are we? They are about the same cost as the first two, aren't they?

Admiral LANDAY. Well, again, there is, we believe—I mean we are working with the companies to drive that cost again toward the goal of $460 million in the cost cap——

Mr. AKIN. Are they going to——

Admiral LANDAY. I think we are going to——

Mr. AKIN. Before they are going to give you a real good price, they are going to want to know how many they are going to build of these.

Admiral LANDAY. Absolutely. Yes, sir.

Mr. AKIN. And it seems like to me I am not quite sure why we are going to build the third and the fourth till we know which one of the two we are going to choose.

And I am a little reluctant to say you know when you say, "Well, we want to buy both of them." Now again, you—what you are doing, you are making decisions, which just drives the cost of ships up.

And somewhere along the line, we got to—I don't want to overdo the questions, but you can see why we have some concerns about what is going on, I think.

Admiral LANDAY. Yes, sir.

Mr. AKIN. Thank you, Mr. Chairman.

Mr. TAYLOR. The gentlewoman from Maine is recognized now for five minutes.

The gentleman from Maryland, Mr. Bartlett, for five minutes.

Mr. BARTLETT. Thank you very much.

Clearly, these ships were very much over cost and behind schedule. And the reasons for that are both the industry and us here in Congress. We have already talked about the Naval Vessel Rules increasing the cost and probably stretching out the schedule.

But a second thing that we in this committee were really complicit in was agreeing to the original schedule on how soon we put the ship in the water that enormously increased cost and stretched out the schedule, because a lot of things that that should have been upside down were now done in the water, which is very much more expensive and stretches the thing out.

So mistakes are made on both sides, and it is a little unfair to lay all of this increase in costs and stretch out of the schedule to the industry, because we were complicit in some of that.

Well, we now have the first Freedom class Littoral Combat Ship delivered, and I am told that the crew is pretty happy with its performance.

But clearly, affordability, as our chairman so aptly pointed out, remains a critical objective for this program. No matter how desirable it is, there comes the cost at which it is too expensive to afford, and we are going to put the money somewhere else.

I understand you have continued to work with the industry teams to refine the design and drive down the cost. Other successful surface combatant programs, such as the Arleigh Burke-class, achieved a significant savings by streamlining the production process.

Understand that the acquisition of specific long lead-time items could reduce the ship construction schedule by as much as 20 percent, which would be about 10 months.

What are your thoughts regarding an advance procurement that would acquire long lead materials to expedite this much-needed ship?

Admiral LANDAY. Yes, sir. We believe advance procurement is a vital tool to continue to drive the cost of this program and any program down, the ability to buy long lead material or specialty material certainly an example.

Had we used a long lead or an advance procurement (AP) strategy on the reduction gear on LCS–1, we would have run into the same problem, but we would have seen it much earlier in the process, or even before we started. So we certainly agree that an AP strategy is one that will help us as we go forward.

Mr. BARTLETT. Multi-year procurements have proven to be a sound investment strategy. They permit industry to accomplish long-term planning and result in significant savings to the government and the taxpayers. Most importantly, they introduce the stability that many of our acquisition programs need.

Have you evaluated the savings that could be achieved on the Littoral Combat Ship program by implementing multi-year procurement? What would the Navy want—when would the Navy want to begin implementing such an approach?

Admiral LANDAY. Well, yes, sir. We definitely have looked at multi-year procurements, block buy procurements, the economic order quantity (EOQ) savings that you potentially get out of such a strategy. And one of our goals is to get to those kinds of strategies as quickly as possible.

One of the key things we want to make sure we do in our fiscal year 2009 ships is ensure that we do in fact have the design issues resolved as we had proposed.

And so our current strategy right now is to tie our fiscal year 2009 and fiscal year 2010 ships together in a common buy to start getting some pressure and quantity savings through those ships.

And so it would be in the fiscal year 2011 time period that I think we would be looking to go to a block, multi-year, or somewhere in that timeframe is where we would see that from an acquisition strategy perspective.

Still having some of the discussions within the Navy on exactly where you want to go, but that would be the timeframe that I would see us looking at it.

Mr. BARTLETT. Thank you. When the Littoral Combat Ship was first pitched to the Congress, it was a revolutionary idea, where you would have a ship that was capable of multi missions and that its mission could be changed during the fight. You wouldn't have to leave the fight and steam to port somewhere to put on the new mission packages.

Now that is an impossibility, because we do not have a medium lift helicopter that is large enough to change these mission packages during the fight.

And so the utility, the capabilities of the Littoral Combat Ship I think have been enormously diminished, because we now have to leave the fight, steam to port to change the mission packages, and then come back to the fight.

I know the argument is made that, gee, a larger medium lift helicopter wouldn't fit on the deck, and it is just because we designed it. We could easily change that. It now fits the 60. We could easily change that so that it would fit a medium lift helicopter.

Don't you think that the absence of this ability to change the packages during the fight seriously degrades the overall capabilities of the Littoral Combat Ship?

Admiral GUILLORY. Yes, sir. I would like to answer that question. The requirements for the LCS to change mission packages in response to an operational commander's tasking is to do it in a 96-hour period, and then the Concept of Operations (CONOPS) is designed to do it in port.

That includes changing out the mission packages and also doing the required testing in that period, to then return the ship to sea and to the fight.

The 60 Romeo and 60 Sierra series aircraft are designed to support that mission area, and those aircraft meet the requirements for the ships, sir.

Mr. BARTLETT. That maybe your program now, sir, but that is not what was pitched to the Congress when the Littoral Combat Ship was first sold to us. They were going to change the mission packages during the fight. You now cannot do that, and so you have to steam away and come back.

It wasn't 96 hours before. It was just a few hours, very few hours, when this thing was pitched to us.

Thank you very much, Mr. Chairman.

Mr. TAYLOR. The chair thanks the gentleman.

The chair now recognizes the gentleman from Washington, Mr. Larsen.

Mr. LARSEN. Thank you, Mr. Chairman.

First, for Ms. Sandel. On page eight of the testimony, it is noted that contract options for mission modules to be exercised annually.

My understanding one of the themes of the LCS, one of the themes of this hearing, as well as themes of the several previous hearings on LCS, has been the whole idea of controlling the requirements or understanding the requirements.

So what can you tell us about the mission module acquisition strategy that gives us some comfort that there will be some control on the requirements, especially as—if we are going to be going on a year-to-year annual contract, that the next contract after year one won't add, you know, the next five things to the contract that things will be really neat and really cool to have as part of the mission module package, and then year two to year three, and year three to year four?

Ms. SANDEL. That is an excellent insight, and I am going to——

Mr. LARSEN. Can you like just get right into that microphone?

Ms. SANDEL. Yes, sir.

Two pieces to that I believe that we have identified in the way that this acquisition is structured for the procurement of the mission systems and then for the mission packages.

The mission systems, which comprise the mission packages, each have their own independent industry partner or warfare center procuring agent that we have identified, so there are at least about 22 different mission systems comprising the three separate mission areas that ultimately end up being a package.

So that is one level of indenture that we have the ability to drive down and to cost and schedule and award these on separate contracts for each mission system. And that is another level of detail we could certainly be due either to walk you through.

So that is one particular area of control with regard to requirements creep and scope growth that those particular mission systems, without the—often have sponsors you know—or the fleet encouragement and direction, we would not drive cost or schedule or scope increase.

The second piece to that is the annual award or the re-award with the addressing the mission package integration production and award of the integrator that produces the package itself.

So you have the system that comprises it with the support equipment, all the infrastructure, all the things that happen that have to become a mission package.

That is the production and assembly contract that has been awarded in 2006. And that then becomes an annual event that we re-look and determine have they met the cost and schedule.

Mr. LARSEN. Is there a cost cap on that contract?

Ms. SANDEL. Yes, sir. Currently, it is a $159 million value, and that 10-year period of performance is predicated on past performance. So if they don't meet their warranty requirements and term requirements for that year, they will not be continuing into the future.

Mr. LARSEN. $159 million per year? $159 million per year?

Ms. SANDEL. A $159 million ceiling complete.

Mr. LARSEN. Per year.

Ms. SANDEL. No, sir.

Mr. LARSEN. Okay. Overall?

Ms. SANDEL. Yes.

Mr. LARSEN. Okay. Okay. Over 10 years.

Ms. SANDEL. Yes.

Mr. LARSEN. All right.

And just remind me. Is that then going to be run much like the— so is a contract awardee a system integrator?

Ms. SANDEL. He is not a system integrator in the sense that we have typically grown up with. It is a package production and assembly, so it is a greater role, taking multiple disparate mission systems, putting them together within the container, the computing environment, all the handling equipment.

So it is a level of detail and experience required that we are working closely together with the individual and the organization.

Mr. LARSEN. Okay.

Mr. Chairman, the reason I asked those questions, and I know that in the grand scope of a $460 million, $500 million ship, this might not be the greatest cost driver, or potentially greatest cost driver, but it would remind us that we are going to use the ship without mission packages that are—you know, that were and are affordable. So I think we are going to have to watch that aspect of it as well.

Admiral Landay, are you responsible for the assessment of the frigate and minesweeper availability and capabilities to fill in the gap left from the lack of LCS deployment?

Admiral LANDAY. No, sir, not me. That is really an Office of the Chief of Naval Operations (OPNAV) function.

Mr. LARSEN. Then could you talk to that plan?

Admiral GUILLORY. Yes, sir. The frigates will—of which we have 30 in inventory right now, active ships—begin leaving the inventory in our 30-year shipbuilding plan beginning in 2010, and throughout the next decade, they are decommissioned.

The mine countermeasures ships reach their service lives near the end of the decade, approximately 2016, 2017 timeframe, and then they begin to exit the inventory or are decommissioned.

LCS, as it comes aboard, is not a replacement for the frigates, but will do many of the missions that frigates do today. It will execute those missions with a 40-man crew, as opposed to a nearly

200-man crew that the Oliver Hazard Perry-class guided missile frigates (FFGs) currently have when they go to sea.

Of course, the mine countermeasure ships that we have today responding to combatant command (COCOM) combatant commander demand signals around the world, the Littoral Combat Ship with the mine countermeasure mission packages would essentially take up the watch in those areas.

And so we are closely examining the 30-year shipbuilding plan and the decommissioning plan to ensure that it's balanced and that we ramp up the capacity of LCS mission packages sure as the decommissioning of frigates and mine countermeasure ships occur.

Mr. LARSEN. And I understand that. We are not talking about a one-to-one replacement, but we are certainly talking about capabilities replacing capabilities.

And so what are you thinking in terms of frigate decommissioning and the capabilities that frigates have compared to the LCS capability that would, let us call it, supplement or complement it?

Are we going to be delaying frigate decommissioning in order to accommodate the delays in the LCS capabilities?

Admiral GUILLORY. I believe that we will continue to examine the decommissioning plan and the ramp-up plan of LCS. I mean, as we have all recognized, we have had delivery challenges with Littoral Combat Ship.

And we will have to continue to monitor that as we go forward to ensure as LCS is delivered and are deployable ready, that is matched up with what the frigates—as frigates are leaving the inventory, because many of the missions that the frigates do today, LCS will also do.

And so at this point we believe we have it right, that the decommissioning plan is balanced with the Littoral Combat Ship delivery and the mission package delivery. But that is under constant review, continual review.

Mr. LARSEN. Oh, it is still under review.

Admiral GUILLORY. Yes, sir.

Mr. LARSEN. Yes. Okay. Thank you. Yes, sure.

Admiral Landay, in your testimony you kept talking about the package of ships over 2009 and 2010 is the exact term you used, but over 2009 and 2010 we will do this, or over 2009 and 2010 we will do this, but then when you talk about warfighting capability, you actually didn't mention 2010 ships.

You said there would be no new warfighting capabilities on the 2009 ships, but then you neglected to talk about ships in 2010. Are you telling us that you are going to be adding different, new capabilities on the 2010 ships?

Admiral LANDAY. No, sir. Right now our strategy about, again, the 2009 ships or the key contract ones, but our strategy is basically to get the shipbuilders into serial production, where we can drive the efficiencies in production and cost, the recurring cost out of those programs as fast as we can.

There is right now and nothing on the horizon that would cause us, that we see, to put either warfighting or additional technical requirements into those packages.

And in our request for proposal that is out on the street, we ask them to bid us the fiscal year 2009 baseline and the same baseline

as options for the fiscal year 2010 ships. So right now we do not
see any additional requirements that will come into either of those
two ships.

Mr. LARSEN. Okay. A broader question is we noted in our separation memo for the securing, and I haven't heard it being interesting questions were being addressed in testimony, the vessels currently are too expensive to build at a rate necessary to fulfill the goal of 55 vessels without forcing other trade-offs.

There is an interesting headline in one of the dailies here on Capitol Hill about the Air Force budget, the debate about tankers and long-range bombers, which I have a direct somewhat of an interest in.

But the question, though, remains is what kind of trade-offs are you making? I mean if we are going to get to 55 LCS by a certain date to get to a 313, 319-ship Navy, what are the trade-offs that are being made? And the most obvious one within the Navy shipbuilding is the Arleigh Burke-class guided missile destroyer (DDG–51) versus the Zumwalt-class guided missile destroyer (DDG–1000).

I just would be interested to understand what the Navy's position is today on that trade-off.

Admiral GUILLORY. Sir, I think I would say it is not a trade-off as more as it is a all hands effort to continuing to look at the requirements, to look at the cost versus capabilities, and to review that in a transparent way to take every opportunity to weigh those requirements and perhaps reduce requirements, if it makes a ship more affordable and still not compromise the warfighting requirements for the ship.

That process, just in my domain as director of surface warfare, is one that I spend a lot of my time involved with, preparing assessments, preparing recommendations to review the requirements, the individual key performance parameters and key attributes for the ship, to ensure that we have it right to meet the warfighting requirements, but perhaps if it is reducing those requirements are changing those requirements would make the ship more affordable in the near term or lifecycle costs, to also make sure the leadership has that to make a determination and try to continue to drive down the cost.

You know it is not a destination so much as it is a something that it is part of will we do now all the time with LCS. And again, it is a commitment I think for the long-term, sir.

Mr. LARSEN. Well, I will just end here. I think that we are going to continue to provide guidance to help the Navy with some decisions, and I will also note that we don't sometimes do a very good job of providing that guidance on what I would yet call trade-offs.

If we are going to have a $14 billion shipbuilding budget, then in our world I think there are—we do look at it as trade-offs, because it is a limited amount of dollars, and what the Navy builds over a certain period of time to get to a certain number of ships is going to require some tough decisions not just by you, but by us on this side of the microphone as well.

Thank you.

Admiral LANDAY. Sir, and if I could just add in to what Admiral Guillory said, you know the other piece of it from the acquisition side is, as we have talked about, for us to continue to drive the cost of those ships down.

Now, as Mr. Bartlett mentioned, certainly when they get to multi-year procurements, Economic Order Quantity purchases (EOQs), there are acquisition opportunities that drive some of those costs now. We, equally and very closely with the N86 folks, are looking at cost trade-offs, the cost of requirements, what we may be doing to impact those.

So I would tell you there is a very ongoing and rigorous and vigorous affordability initiative that is in place that I think will continue to key up as we go.

And we have been successful on many programs when we start doing that—Virginia, DDG–51 is a good example of as you get into serial production, there are more opportunities to continue to go after some of those affordabilities, and we are doing that as well.

Mr. LARSEN. Thank you.

Thank you, Mr. Chairman.

Mr. TAYLOR. The chair recognizes the gentleman from Virginia, Mr. Wittman, for five minutes.

Mr. WITTMAN. Thank you, Mr. Chairman.

Admiral Landay, in looking at the specifications on the second Littoral Combat Ship, I see that it is outfitted with a foreign manufactured main propulsion diesel engine, and I was wondering have these engines been certified by the American Bureau of Shipping, and do they meet the Navy's specifications as outlined in the contract.

And if not, can you tell us when these engines would be brought into compliance with the Navy's specifications and when they would be certified by the American Bureau of Shipping.

Admiral LANDAY. Yes, sir. They are required under Naval Vessel Rules in our contract with the prime General Dynamics to Meet American Bureau of Shipping Naval Vessel Rule requirements.

So the engines will in fact be classed and certified under that. The engines have been through just about all of those certifications. There is one additional test that is ongoing right now, but the company is required to meet that test, and the prime contractor will ensure that they do meet that test.

So they will comply with Naval Vessel Rules as outlined by American Bureau of Shipping and concurred with by the Navy technical authorities.

Mr. WITTMAN. So that is going to be taking place. He said they are in the process of doing that. Do you have a hard stop time when that is to be achieved?

Admiral LANDAY. Well, sir, the remaining test is what they call a 1,500-hour run test. You know basically it is about a 60-day test by the time you do it.

Obviously, as sometimes happens in those tests, something will come up. They will have to stop the test, kick something, look at it, and then start the test up again.

But we anticipate that they should have that test completed at or close to delivery of the ship. They have already passed through 500-hour tests, a number of other tests on there. This is the long-term endurance test, but they are required to meet that.

And if they don't meet that, it will be under—you know by the time we take delivery, it would be a warranty item to the manufacturer and the prime contractor.

Mr. WITTMAN. Thank you.

I am also concerned about the suggestions for moving this LCS program to other shipyards. And this process in the past has cost more than $100 million when executed on previous surface combatant programs. And as you know, it has resulted in significant schedule delays.

And I was wondering what is your estimate of the additional cost and further delays that would result on the program, if the acquisition strategy were significantly changed?

Admiral LANDAY. Obviously, any time, as we have talked before, that you change your acquisition strategy or your process in midstream, there are some implications to that.

We, as we have looked at bringing a second source in as a possibility, we have looked at what we did back in previous days with you know some of our other destroyers.

I would tell you a very broad, raw estimate of this would be on the order of about $60 million per ship, and probably about 18 months to 2 years per sea frame in order to have in place a package that we think we could compete very effectively.

Then obviously, the next issue is it becomes another the yard in a—or lead ship in a new yard. It will be a function of how well that yard is able to ramp up.

The advantages at this point we wouldn't anticipate bringing new design, new package to that yard. It would be a pretty solid design.

But obviously, as with anybody, there is a ramp up when you start the first shipping go to the second one.

Mr. WITTMAN. I want to go back and talk a little bit more about acquisition strategy. In looking at the acquisition strategy, it appears that there is not a clear or approved acquisitions strategy for LCS.

And I know that the Navy has proposed several different strategies over the last three years from a fly-off between two ships followed by a down-select, to a fly-off and possible down-select, to converting the selected design, to build a print and recompeting the class, to buying both vessels from the existing teams.

And I was wondering with the increasing emphasis on acquisition reform, and we just had a meeting this morning talking about how we perform that process, why should the Navy continue to procure vessels for which there is no acquisition strategy?

And again, we have been back and forth on this. I know there is a lot of consternation about those portions of the program where we have had some problems.

But it seems like to me if we are ever going to get to a point to clearly move forward this program, there has to be a clearly defined acquisition strategy.

And I am just wondering where are we going with that, and when will that acquisition strategy be defined?

Admiral LANDAY. Well, obviously, as I mentioned, we have a strategy for the fiscal year 2009 and 2010 ships, as I talk to you.

One of the discussions that we will have as we go forward in our acquisition strategy is are we in fact going to go and down-select to a single ship, or are we going to stay with the two-ship design?

Each design brings—because of the way that we did that—brings capabilities that we think have real value to us. When you talk a 55-ship class, and you potentially talk 25, 27, depending on how split that up, potentially of each one of those, there is still a pretty sizable class and enough opportunity in there to get learning and to get benefit out of that.

So I would tell you right now it is not a specific time where we would look at a down-select or going to a single one. It is really getting the ships out to the fleet and to getting input from the fleet, from the operators, balanced always, of course, to the cost of the ships.

You know if we find out one ship turns out to be significantly more expensive than another, then that becomes part of the discussion in our acquisition strategy.

But as we have always said before, one of the key inputs we want to make sure we get is get both designs out there operating so that we can get a good assessment of the pros and cons of each one of the designs.

Admiral GUILLORY. Sir, if I may just add one additional factor, that while the first two ships do give us a learning opportunity, and not only for the sea frames themselves, but for the mission package development and the launch and recovery systems, we appreciate the committee's support for the 2009 and 2010 ships, because those ships address the capacity issue, the fact that we need the ships today for missions that we have today.

And if those ships were here today and deployable ready today, I would have little doubt that they would not find themselves perhaps off the coast of Somalia or other places in the world where econo-piracy threatens our ships and our commercial traffic.

So there is prudence in learning from the two ships, and there is a plan to do that. However, there is also a compelling need I believe, certainly from my perspective, to address the capacity and capability gap that we have today.

And the ships in 2009 and 2010 will go a long way to addressing that, sir.

Mr. WITTMAN. Thank you, Mr. Chairman.

Mr. TAYLOR. The gentleman from Michigan, Mr. Stupak, for five minutes.

Mr. STUPAK. Thank you, Mr. Chairman. And thank you again for your courtesy in allowing me to do this, sitting in on this hearing today.

Admiral Landay, you spoke in your testimony about solid and mature design. Do you believe you have that solid and mature design now for the LCS?

Admiral LANDAY. Yes, sir, we do, certainly for LCS–1, which we are taken through the initial acceptance testing. We believe we have a solid design there. Now, there are pieces of the design package that we are continuing to work through.

We believe we have a solid design for LCS–2, and we will assess that when we get that ship delivered and go through testing as well.

Mr. STUPAK. LCS–1 Freedom was just built up in my neck of the woods there—Menominee Marinette area.

When you look back at that design, now that you have been through the first one, is it realistic to expect that the ship can be purchased at $220 million or $250 million?

Or now that you have a design down, when you have gone from commercial to your Navy standards for the hull and propulsion issue, is it realistic with hindsight not to say that the ships are going to cost only $220 million or $250 million?

Admiral LANDAY. Well, no, sir. I think as we look at the ship as we currently have it designed today, we would not be able to build that ship for $220 million. That is a true statement.

We believe we can build it for less than the first ship cost, as we get in those production efficiencies and affordability. But yes, sir, I do not think we would be able to build that for $220 million.

Mr. STUPAK. When you talk about your production efficiencies and long leads, so ship number 20 should be significantly less than ship number one. Ship number 40 should be less than ship number 20, on down the line, correct?

Admiral LANDAY. Yes, sir.

Mr. STUPAK. Freedom LCS–1, which is already—it is in San Diego right now—any problem with the workmanship, the quality of that ship?

Admiral LANDAY. No, sir. Actually, she is in Norfolk right now doing a post-delivery. She will be going to San Diego later on. We still have additional testing to do with her here on the East Coast before we send her over—and testing, I mean things we were unable to do in the Great Lakes do because of requirements and restrictions of there.

You know all the ships have issues that pop up. That is why we do a pretty thorough shakedown and testing, but we have not heard anything from the crew or our process with it.

Mr. STUPAK. So as far as the craftsmanship, there is no problem there. The problem with the first one was design changes, different standards that the Navy had put in on the ship, then. This is not a problem with the yard.

Admiral LANDAY. Well, yes, sir. I mean obviously then there is also production efficiencies, and you know I think in some cases both yards assumed they could build the ship more efficiently than it turned out that they could in a lead ship.

I think they have learned from that, and we certainly expect that the next ship—they would produce it more efficiently.

Mr. STUPAK. Okay.

Let me ask you this question. Both shipyards have planned to improve their production capabilities. And hopefully, this will lower the cost of the ships.

What other benefits does the Navy realized by using the same yards to build the ships? Could you just in layman's terms? What other benefits are there besides repeat in production? Do we see a taxpayer savings?

Admiral LANDAY. Well, obviously, as you mentioned, the repeat and the learning curve, as we call it, as the yards get more efficient, as the production process is improved, as the workforce see opportunities to streamline the process is one of the key issues, obviously, as you get more production in a yard, there is a tendency in that yard to put more infrastructure in place themselves to support the continued moving down the production line.

Obviously, if there is additional Navy work that goes into a yard as they perform well in one program and maybe have an opportunity to compete for other, there is a sharing of overheads and other things across those yards.

Mr. STUPAK. In your testimony or answer to a question, you indicated—or maybe it was the other admiral—with the frigate, you have 200 people on, and LCS you are going to 40 people.

Is that cost savings figured in over 30 years, the life of the ship, as to the value to the Navy? And is that part of what cost factor you look at?

Admiral GUILLORY. Yes, sir. That was part of our calculus, considering the lifecycle cost of the ship. From my experience, manpower continues to be the most expensive single element of a program over the life of that program.

And it is just amazing to think that the missions and the capability this ship will be able to deliver with essentially a 40-person crew—and many of the missions we have today are done by frigates—is a huge step forward, and I think it will be reflected in the overall lifecycle cost of that ship.

Mr. STUPAK. Do you have any estimation what is the cost of going from 200 to 400 sailors on a ship?

Admiral GUILLORY. No, sir, but we can provide that information to you, sir.

Mr. STUPAK. Then may I ask one more question, if I may, Mr. Chairman?

You indicate there is much interest in the LCS by other countries, our allies. Have any of the allies placed an order for any of the ships, or appear to be working with you to place such an order?

Admiral LANDAY. No, sir. There are no orders currently placed by any other country. There has been significant interest from a number of countries.

So there have been discussions, answering questions with them, you know through the typical process, but so far there has not necessarily been an order. I think they are waiting to you know see the performance of the ship as we go through our post-delivery test and trials.

But I can tell you there is significant interest. We have had riders on the ship, and there continues to be great interest in it.

Mr. STUPAK. Thank you. I have no further questions.

Mr. Chairman, again, thank you for your courtesies.

Mr. TAYLOR. The chair thanks the gentleman from Michigan.

Admiral, on my visits to the yards, I have seen Captain Murdock there, and I would presume Captain Murdock's job is to make sure that the ribs, the frames, the scantlings are all there, that he has got some sort of a set of specs that he is checking, that he has an original set of plans that he is checking against what is being done to make sure that what the shipyard is doing is matching what you have on paper. Is that correct?

Admiral LANDAY. Yes, sir. And the design is actually the shipyard's design. The design is endorsed by the American Bureau of Ships (ABS) under the Naval Vessel Rules, and then both ABS and the Navy supervisor shipbuilding ensure that the ship is built to the design that we certified.

Mr. TAYLOR. Does he use computer-assisted drafting in order to generate those specs that he uses to ensure that the shipyard is following?

Admiral LANDAY. Yes, sir. They use commercial computer-aided design (CAD) programs that are available.

Mr. TAYLOR. Okay. So I would think using that, he ought to know every pound of aluminum that goes into one and every pound of steel that goes into the other. Is that correct?

Admiral LANDAY. Yes, sir.

Mr. TAYLOR. So what percentage of the cost of those vessels is materials—raw materials—not engines, just steel and aluminum to get the hulls?

Admiral LANDAY. I don't know that off the top of my head, sir. I could get that for you. I just——

Mr. TAYLOR. Well, Admiral, the point that I hopefully am making is anyone who can read the commodities section of the paper knows what the price was and the price of aluminum is one-half of what it was two years ago.

We have a nation that is $11 trillion in debt mostly because we are not doing a good enough job in trying to find some bargains for the taxpayers. So who in your organization is responsible for putting a pencil to how much actually goes into those vessels and how much we ought to be saving now over 2 years ago?

Admiral LANDAY. Well, part of that is the ongoing contract discussions with both——

Mr. TAYLOR. No, sir. Who in your organization? I would like a name, Admiral.

Admiral LANDAY. Well, the program manager and then myself as the final source selection authority for the next contracts. That is one of the things that we have in there.

One of the discussions we have had with both companies in the original bids that they gave us for the fiscal year 2009 ships, you know they were based on a certain timeframe in which we would have got the prices.

We asked both companies to go back and see what they could get, reductions in those prices based on new prices of the material.

At the same time, there are affordability initiatives that we work with both of the companies to try to drive the neighbor, manpower and even material out of it.

Mr. TAYLOR. One thing at a time.

Admiral LANDAY. Sir?

Mr. TAYLOR. So if I called your program manager and said, "What did you pay for this deal a couple of years ago, and if you had to buy it again today," he could give me an answer this afternoon?

Admiral LANDAY. Sir, he should be able to.

Mr. TAYLOR. Okay.

What percentage of LCS–1 was welded by hand, as opposed to on a panel line?

Admiral LANDAY. I could get that for you. I don't know.

Mr. TAYLOR. Who in your organization would know that?

Admiral LANDAY. The program manager and his team would know that.

Mr. TAYLOR. Could Captain Murdock give you an off-the-top-of-his-head estimate?

Admiral LANDAY. We could get it for you, sir. We can get it. We can get it for you. He doesn't necessarily——

Mr. TAYLOR. Well, would you say 100 percent was done by hand?

Admiral LANDAY. No.

Mr. TAYLOR. Okay. Would you say 90 percent was done by hand?

Admiral LANDAY. I think about half.

Mr. TAYLOR. Okay.

On the Austal ship, which is LCS–2, what percentage of that ship was welded by hand?

Admiral LANDAY. Certainly higher than that. I think it is closer to about 70 percent.

Mr. TAYLOR. Okay. You are now speaking with the shipyards about building 3 and 4. Marinette would get 3. Austal would get 4.

What percentage of LCS–3 do you expect to be welded by hand, and what percentage on a panel line?

Admiral LANDAY. Certainly, we would expect LCS–3 to be less. Again, I would have to go back into the contract discussions in your bids.

Mr. TAYLOR. Well, how much? Admiral, what is your goal?

Admiral LANDAY. Pardon?

Mr. TAYLOR. If we can see things like panel lines save money over hand welding——

Admiral LANDAY. Right.

Mr. TAYLOR [continuing]. Speed the process——

Admiral LANDAY. Right.

Mr. TAYLOR [continuing]. Wouldn't it be reasonable that the Navy is telling the contractor this is how much I expect to be done by machine next time?

Admiral LANDAY. No, sir. What we tend to tell the contractor is that we want to see the ship built at the cheapest cost consistent with your processes and infrastructure at the time.

Mr. TAYLOR. Admiral, with all due respect, we have opposite challenges. Their goal is to make as much money as they can for the shareholders. Our goal should be to deliver a first-class ship to the Navy at a reasonable cost to the taxpayers. Those are different goals.

Admiral LANDAY. But both of us have the same goals, because they will deliver a good cost to their shareholders, and be able to deliver a good product to our ships, if in fact they continue to drive the cost of their ships down, we get ourselves into serial production.

In fiscal year 2010, they have an opportunity competitively to potentially win some more ships, so it is definitely in their interest to drive the target price of their ships down consistent with——

Mr. TAYLOR. Admiral, with all due respect for your many years of service, I respectfully disagree. I really have seen no effort on the part of either contractor to try to improve their process, because right now all they got to do is compete with that other guy, who is also not doing much to improve his process.

And if the Navy isn't going to step in and say you have to do a better job, who is?

Admiral LANDAY. Well, we have told them that they have to do a better job. We have not stepped in and told them specifically how to build their ship and their process. In Austal, as an example——

Mr. TAYLOR. But, well, Admiral, wait. Admiral, if I may, because the subcommittee also funds the David Taylor Research Center. And we spent a lot of money out there, and there are a lot of very smart people out there.

Admiral LANDAY. Right.

Mr. TAYLOR. And I thought the purpose of their research center, one of the many purposes, was to find more affordable ways to build more ships.

Admiral LANDAY. Right.

Mr. TAYLOR. So why isn't the expertise of David Taylor being turned loose to find a more affordable way to build what was supposed to be an affordable warship that is now 18 months late and 100 percent over budget?

Admiral LANDAY. Specifically on David Taylor, again I think there are processes as we develop them through our ManTech program or our research and development (R&D) program through the National Shipbuilding Research Program (NSRP) and those organizations that moved those R&D concepts out into their shipbuilders, now there is an avenue to do that.

Mr. TAYLOR. When I walked through Austal shipyard a couple of weeks ago, I saw absolutely no effort being made to save the taxpayers a dime.

Admiral LANDAY. Well, I——

Mr. TAYLOR. Like Orange County choppers when we ought to be kicking out Hondas.

Admiral LANDAY. You are talking about down in Austal, sir?

Mr. TAYLOR. Yes, sir.

Admiral LANDAY. I can tell you in Austal there is over a $100 million investment going on in there to get them to a modular manufacturing facility. That facility will be online in the May timeframe. It is about halfway done.

If you remember coming into the yard, off to the left you saw a big building that was being built. Many of the processes that we expect them to be able to do in that modular manufacturing facility, which we think will have a significant improvement in their productivity, we are testing out right now, and some of that work that you saw in the back part of that shop.

There is a major investment going on in that yard, and there is a significant investment planned for the other yard to work many of those specific areas.

Mr. TAYLOR. And Admiral, did Austal make that investment, or did the taxpayers make that investment?

Admiral LANDAY. I believe it was the state made the investment.

Mr. TAYLOR. State taxpayers.

Admiral LANDAY. Yes, sir.

Mr. TAYLOR. And if I am not mistaken, some of that was also Katrina money.

Admiral LANDAY. Yes, sir.

Mr. TAYLOR. Okay.

Admiral, I asked in my opening statement how long would it take and what organization would be responsible and how much would it cost to develop the technical data package that is required to build the ships directly in a free and open competition.

Admiral LANDAY. Yes, sir. And our estimate at this point, as we have looked through that, is on the order of about $60 million per ship, probably 18 months in order to have that package ready to go, from when we snap the baseline.

And one of the key issues, when you want to get to a build to print concept, where basically we are going to contract with a shipyard, and we are going to evaluate the shipyard not on the performance of the ship, but on the performance of the specific work package that I gave him under the contract, is to ensure that we have incorporated all of that change.

So under a build to print concept, for example, we would not want to go into build to print contract until we had been through our post-shakedown availability through all of our testing, all of our evaluation, to ensure that the ship that we would put under that contract has got a very solid baseline, and we understand what it is.

Now, having said that, there are a lot of things that you got to do in preparation for that.

One is to clean up the drawing. So in a new ship—you know first of a class, you have a drawing. The shipyard came up with the drawing. We start to build that ship. We find issues, interferences, changes, whatever it is. We annotate. The shipyard does those drawings.

When you get done, what you want to go back in is clean up all those drawings, make sure all those changes, revisions, modifications are fully incorporated into the drawing.

We are doing that right now with the fiscal year 2009 in both of the shipyards, so we are taking those first steps. But what we would really want to do before we would get to a build to print concept is to define what that baseline is, because any change I make after that baseline is all going to be change on me, and it is going to be change to the target, not change on the share lines.

Mr. TAYLOR. Okay. So just for clarification, if this committee wanted to reserve all of our options as far as a free and open competition on follow-on ships, we would have to allocate approximately $60 million per design.

Admiral LANDAY. Yes, sir. That would be our estimate at this point.

Mr. TAYLOR. To be expended at David Taylor, or where?

Admiral LANDAY. We haven't necessarily decided where it would be. Well, there are a couple of ways that we could do it. One of them would be to go out. Some of that is this. Some of that would be to the individual shipyards to clean up, as I said, the work packages they have in place.

And then we would have either a subsequent design agent that could be Naval Sea Systems Command (NAVSEA) or that could be a contractor like Gibbs & Cox or somebody like that, who builds then that design package for us out of the designs that we get.

So when you think build to print, you have got to remember that it is going to be more than just the hull of the ship and the distrib-

uted systems. It is really the entire integrated ship that you want
to look at, so it is the combat systems implications, the cables, the
testing.

You know how do you test that ship? How are you going to put
all that in? That all becomes part of an integrated data package,
if we are going to go to build to print for the entire ship.

But it would be a third-party source in our mind, who would—
you would take that design responsibility, and whether that would
be the Navy under NAVSEA or whether that would be you know
one of the other design houses, we haven't decided that yet.

Mr. TAYLOR. Admiral, given that, what are the chances that the
mission modules will be ready prior to LCS–2 going to sea?

Admiral LANDAY. The mission modules? Well, there are some
mission modules that are currently ready right now.

Ms. SANDEL. Yes, sir. If you would allow me, we delivered, as you
are aware, initial mission modules in each system with Anti-Submarine Warfare (ASW) and mine countermeasures and the Surface
Warfare (SUW).

We are in varying levels of technical maturity and testing in
every one of those areas, so we have timed ourselves to be in sequence to the sea frame.

We have intentionally slowed down in some areas of design and
development and testing in order to pay this sea frames so that we
are not delivering ahead of need, but having them available for the
testing required to be able to support the requirements.

We have intentionally taken the same steps back to go ahead
and pace ourselves to not buy things in advance and having them
sitting on the dock awaiting a sea frame. So we are in lockstep as
far as alignment of schedules.

Mr. TAYLOR. Has any thought been given to putting those modules on other platforms?

Ms. SANDEL. Sir, we have been asked by your organization to
take a look at alternative platform studies, and that is in process
right now, and Admiral Guillory may want to speak to that little
bit more.

But we have analysis ongoing, as well as experimentation to design the desire. How will we do this, and if it is feasible, and how
would you go about it.

Mr. TAYLOR. And when should we expect an answer on that?

Ms. SANDEL. The language requested it be submitted with the
submission of the fiscal year 2010 budget.

Mr. TAYLOR. So we should already have it?

Ms. SANDEL. It is in process to be submitted. Yes, sir.

Mr. TAYLOR. The chair recognizes the gentleman from Pennsyl-
vania, Admiral Sestak.

Mr. SESTAK. Thank you, Mr. Chairman. I apologize. I was at another committee on healthcare, which is kind of why I initially got
into this line of work.

I wanted to ask—and if these have been asked, I would apologize. I jotted down a few notes while I was in the other hearing—
at the end of January, you had said you were going to award a contract for the two fiscal year 2009 ships, and they were going to be
bundled into the three that will be the fiscal year 2010.

Does a delay on that have to do it all with that they are having problems meeting that cap, the $460 million cap, for the fiscal year 2010 ships?

Admiral LANDAY. Well, I will say that the real focus on the fiscal year 2009 ships and the way we had proposed that was we wanted the fiscal year 2010 ships to be options when they provided us their bids for the fiscal year 2009 ships.

And the intent is to try to get both more pricing pressure and more economic or the quantity opportunities for the shipbuilders buy them potentially being able to look at four—you know, four, three, two or one, depending on how that worked.

So right now the delay—and again, our goal had been in the January timeframe. It was really going to be function of when both sides could come to agreement. The delay has been as much in trying to continue to work through affordability and cost reduction efforts on both sides on the 2009 ship——

Mr. SESTAK. Does the delay have anything to do with their having problems meeting that cost cap fiscal year 2010 ships?

Admiral LANDAY. Well, we will see when we get their final work. But, yes, sir, that is one of the key drivers that we are working very hard, is that we are on a path to do that, and everybody understands that is one of the requirements.

Mr. SESTAK. I guess is LCS–2—has the price—have you had any budget growth on that since what was in the fiscal year 2009, what was presented in the fiscal year 2009 budget?

Admiral LANDAY. We will be able to deliver the ship for the money that we had in the budget. Yes, sir. I mean there have certainly been some cost growth that eating into the program manager's reserves into the program.

Mr. SESTAK. About how much?

Admiral LANDAY. I can get it to you, sir, separately.

Mr. SESTAK. Do you think it would—in a GAO study that was done and other times, they have talked about the aircraft carrier being funded at a confidence level of less than 40 percent and ships being funded—and I understand perhaps the LCS initially—at less than 50 percent confidence factors for the prices that you provide Congress in the budget.

Do you think at this stage of the game with the issues that have been attendant to the LCS in costing, confidence, as you come forward again, that we should cost it now to at least 80 percent costing factor?

What is the downside of telling us we have got an 80 percent confidence factors, that that is what the real price is?

Admiral LANDAY. Yes, sir. I think at an individual program level—you know if you just looked at LCS stand-alone, certainly you would like to do that. When you look across all of the shipbuilding programs and the balance, obviously, that the department needs to do in terms of risk versus capability, I think that is really the trade that we have to make.

Mr. SESTAK. So is the $460 million—is that at 80 percent confidence factor in your pricing right now?

Admiral LANDAY. No.

Mr. SESTAK. What is it?

Admiral LANDAY. I would say it is probably 50 percent.

Mr. SESTAK. So there is a 50 percent chance at best that we might hit the $460 million.

Admiral LANDAY. As we currently, yes, sir, as we currently have the ship designed, absent any affordability—now, again, you get into multi-years and EOQs, and that helps to drive that cost down.

Mr. SESTAK. I will ask you a question. I guess that my overarching question is the Navy has been able to afford $12 billion to $14 billion per year for Navy shipbuilding, but you came forward last year and said we now need $20 billion, which is I guess about an 80 percent or so increase.

With 50 percent confidence factors coming forward and less on other types of vessels, what kind of confidence do you have that if we almost double your procurement budget, that is going to get us—I mean how are you going to afford all this?

I mean what is the confidence of having come forward last year and told us that your procurement budget has to leap from $12 billion, $20 billion or $22 billion, and yet we are kind of getting confidence factors of 50 percent or less when you come forward?

How comfortable are you with that $22 billion?

Admiral GUILLORY. Sir, the question you ask certainly goes beyond the information I am prepared to provide a response to. And I think we will take that for the record and get back to you on that.

But if I may say that, the confidence factor also reflects the maturity of the program, too.

And if you look at the Arleigh Burke-class and the—you know as we are still in building 1/08 it is coming down. The building wait is now—the confidence factor in funding that ship is certainly different than the confidence factor of funding an LCS, and that is pretty understandable.

So it is a combination of statistics and numbers, but it is also a confidence factor based upon the maturity, and also the priorities of across the shipbuilding portfolio.

And ideally, certainly as a resource sponsor, I would be very grateful if all my ships were funded to the 80 percent level or some higher percentage. However, I do recognize that that is——

Mr. SESTAK. Excuse me. I wasn't talking about funding at that level. I was just asking should you come to Congress and let us know that when we buy the new aircraft carrier, it is only at a 35 percent confidence factor. That was my only question, not to what funding.

Let me then bring it back to LCS, one final question. What is the status of the Navy's stated intentions in the July 2007 testimony to move to a common combat system for LCS? I may have missed that in the——

Admiral LANDAY. No, sir. We continue to look across the board at opportunities to go common across the two sea frames. We did in fiscal year 2007 do an initial study on a common combat system. The look at the time, based on the assumptions that we used in that study, was about a wash.

The savings that you would get lifecycle from a training infrastructure perspective were offset by the impacts from a non-recurring engineering of making changes to the ships.

We currently have a second study that we have just started, as the Navy has gone to its objective architecture, which should give us more flexibility. We are going back and taking another look at that.

So we are continuing to look at those opportunities, but unless we see there to be a significant trade-off, we right now don't have anything in place on the fiscal year 2009 or 2010 ships to go to that.

However, I would say in our fiscal year 2010 contract, one of the things we have asked shipyards to give us, in addition to the price for a ship, is also to break that price down and give us options to buy essentially a core sea frame without a combat system, the cost of buying a combat system, and then the cost of buying a combat systems equipment in there as a——

Mr. SESTAK. So you may or may not go to a common combat system. Is that what I should take up?

Admiral LANDAY. Well, in fiscal year 2009 or 2010, I do not expect——

Mr. SESTAK. But then perhaps maybe later.

Admiral LANDAY. We are looking at it. And it all depends on what the business case will play out.

Mr. SESTAK. Thank you.

My question—I didn't mean to ask the question that you really weren't here for testimony. I guess the reason I asked it is that I have been quite struck by the demands of the Nation for accountability and clarity of the mortgage security issues on Wall Street.

I wonder if we ourselves in the Defense Department here in Congress might want to have more of that transparency upfront on how confident are we about this mortgage we are actually taking out on our future for our children. How good is that price you know in a sense, that you come forward with all the time?

And I was quite struck by the GAO study, although I was cognizant of it in a prior life, of how good these confidence factors are, because we tend to sometimes berate people for coming forward and telling us it is going to cost more, but maybe for you upfront that LCS would come in for less than 50 percent confidence factor, we might approach it differently.

But thanks for your comments.

Admiral LANDAY. Yes, sir.

Mr. TAYLOR. The chair thanks the gentleman.

The chair now recognizes the gentleman, the ranking member from Missouri, Mr. Akin.

Mr. AKIN. Thank you, Mr. Chairman.

I just have a couple of quick questions. First of all, is this ship mostly viewed as a Navy ship in terms of its use, or does the Marine Corps have a sense that this is something that they would be using as well?

Admiral GUILLORY. This is a Navy ship, and with its payload capacity, it is certainly—there are opportunities perhaps to bring Marines aboard and execute missions, but right now it is essentially a Navy ship. Yes, sir.

Mr. AKIN. I understand that all the ships are Navy ships, but I just got to think that there has got to be a difference. Some of them are specifically designed for the Marine Corps. This is not specifically designed for Marine Corps use. Is that right?

Admiral GUILLORY. No sir.

Mr. AKIN. Okay. So there may be some cross applicability. You might be able to put some Marines on board, but it is being used as a Navy platform for naval use, as opposed to Marine use. Is that correct?

Admiral GUILLORY. Yes, sir. That is correct.

Mr. AKIN. Okay.

Second thing. I think I heard in terms of these different missions packages, I thought what I heard you saying was that these things will be ready to plug in, and they will be fully integrated when we take acceptance of the ship. Is that correct, or did I misunderstand?

Ms. SANDEL. If I may, yes, sir, it is at varying levels of technical maturity. As the program was originally envisioned and laid out, there was a spiraled development of the mission packages themselves.

So the systems that comprise those mission packages many times were developmental items or engineering design models or a low rate initial production, so we have always understood that we took the design as it was in progress, and it was being tested and developed, and then ultimately going to be fielded.

So when we get to the point that we have the mission package for the mine countermeasure system, for instance, it will have the systems embedded in it that have been designed to interface standard. It will have the supporting equipment, and it will be ready for testing on the sea frame and in accordance with the sea frame schedule.

However, the interesting part is, like we have talked about controlling costs on the contract, this is also one aspect, that this is unusual. We have the ability to test the very detailed level of testing on these mission systems, which are individual programs of record, prior to their being incorporated into the mission package.

So each program is walking through its testing regime as it comes to the sea frame. So we have gotten a delivery of an asset that has been fully tested, understood to perform, then is integrated into the package and delivered for the end-to-end testing to make sure the interfaces are all available and forming.

Mr. AKIN. I thought I heard sort of a yes and a kind of yes and a kind of no answer, I think.

What I am hearing you say is, yes, the mission packages will be available and integrated, and they can be plugged into the ship, but they are in a state of spiral development, which means that they may or may not work or may be changed significantly over a period of time. Is that correct?

Ms. SANDEL. I would state that slightly differently. Yes to your first part. Second, they will work, because we will not deliver a component or mission system to the package for end-to-end testing that wasn't performing.

Mr. AKIN. How many different separate mission packages are there total?

Ms. SANDEL. In individuals, we have the mine countermeasure mission package, the surface warfare mission package, and the anti-submarine mission package. They are comprised of individual numbers and quantities, depending on the requirements and the sponsor.

Those are comprised of 8 to 10 systems in each area, so you have a complexity level where you are delivering systems to be integrated to be tested in a mission package.

So you are going to have technical development as you move forward and——

Mr. AKIN. So there are three missions packages at this point, totally?

Ms. SANDEL. Yes, sir.

Mr. AKIN. Okay.

I come back to the first question I asked the beginning of the hearing, and I felt like I got a kind of maybe, sort of answer.

My question is, is there one person who is being measured and held accountable for the delivery or, from the Navy point of view, who is in charge of this program, makes all the decisions and can say, "Yes, I understand you want to do this, this and this. We have looked at it all, and this is my decision. This is what we are going to do, and this is how we are going to move forward."

Is there any one person in charge? I understand the idea of the team concept of leadership. I understand it is good to get a lot of input from different people. I understand breaking a project into component parts.

But ultimately somebody has got to be held accountable, and somebody has to make the decisions. Is there one person who this is their baby, and they are held accountable for it in the Navy?

Admiral LANDAY. Yes, sir. The acquisition——

Mr. AKIN. What is his name, and what position is it?

Admiral LANDAY. Captain Jim Murdock, sitting behind me, who is the acquisition program manager at this point, is the person responsible for delivering the LCS program.

Now, Captain Murdock does not have the authority, for example, to change requirements of the program. Captain Murdock does not have the authority, nor do I, to change the missions of the program.

His job is, as we build the ship as it has currently been laid out by OPNAV folks to those requirements, and if we cannot do that, then we will go back to the OPNAV folks and explain to them what the issues are, and then that will be keyed up.

But in terms of do their bring the ship to the capabilities that have been given to us by the CNO, the program manager is the one person responsible for the ship.

Mr. AKIN. So can the mission requirements or parameters or specifications on the ship be changed?

Admiral LANDAY. Yes, but not by Captain Murdock. Captain Murdock would go back to Admiral Guillory, and collectively we would go to the senior Navy leadership and say, "The cost of this requirement to get there is far more than we expected. There is an impact." And we would have that discussion with them.

This is part of the process that has changed as a result of early LCS lessons learned.

Mr. AKIN. Who is it who is—so there is no one further up the line, then, that basically is in charge, that could basically make that decision. It is all a group decision whether or not you are going to change a requirement of this or that. Is that right?

Admiral GUILLORY. No, sir. For general requirements generation, I am responsible for staffing back and taking it forward to the chief of Naval operations——

Mr. AKIN. Right.

Admiral GUILLORY [continuing]. Admiral Roughead.

Admiral Roughead is authorized to approve key attributes for the ship. Key performance parameters are approved by the Joint Requirements Oversight Council (JROC), the Joint Staff, the chairman of Joint Chiefs of Staff, and of which the ship has 10 key performance parameters.

It has 37 key attributes. Attributes include launch and recovery of aircraft, what type of sea state that the ship ought to be able to do that in. Those are the authority of the chief of naval operations to approve or to change.

Mr. AKIN. I guess what I am getting at is I don't understand your organizational structure that well. Maybe it is all just crystal clear to you who is responsible for what, but from my point of view, when I look at the big picture, this thing looks like the rudder has been shot out of it, and it is just drifting all over the place as a program.

And it seems like, because of the fact that you start with one number and one set of parameters and you change it, and it doubles the cost of the ship.

And then now we have got these two different ships, and it is not quite clear which one you are going to buy, and yet you still want to build more both of them. It just seems to me like the whole thing is wandering some.

And it seems to me that there should be one person, who ultimately has got to have to make those decisions and have a game plan and start moving forward with it.

And what you are telling me is well, it is sort of yes and sort of no. And I understand there needs to be input, but somebody's got to be in charge of it. And it seems to me like it is drifting.

Maybe I am mistaken, but at least the data seems to suggest there is a lot of changes that have been moving through this program, which have been very expensive.

I will let you respond.

Admiral LANDAY. Well, I would say on the acquisition side, clearly—and we have identified that up front—there have been some changes to this program, which drove costs.

One of the outcomes of that is, as we went back and looked at our process and we said as these changes were coming into the program, how did senior Navy leadership understand and were informed and had the ability to influence and make decisions on those changes?

Before, our process was probably not as clean, so the secretary has put in a what I call six-gate two-bat pass process to where now we periodically on the acquisition side will go back to the larger organization, which includes the Assistant Secretary of the Navy for Research, Development and Acquisition (ASN (RD&A)), the U.S. Secretary of the Navy (SECNAV) acquisition representative and the CNO staff, or the commandant if it affects the Marine Corps, and we walk them through that.

So you know Mr. Sestak's comment about confidence. We would have those discussions with them. If we come in and sat now and say, "The cost of this ship is growing, because we can't figure out how to get through a certain requirement," instead of just continuing to grow the cost, we now have a mechanism, a better mechanism to go back and have that discussion with Admiral Guillory and the OPNAV.

But in the end there is two pieces of it. There is a requirements levied by the operational side, the CNO. The acquisition community under ASN (RD&A) is responsible for executing that. And together at that point, CNO, SecNav, ASN (RD&A) as a staff is where those two pieces come together.

So if there is a requirements trade, the CNO has to be part of that. If there is an acquisition implication of that, then the acquisition side of it. So it is the way that the process is set up to work.

Mr. AKIN. Thank you very much.

Mr. TAYLOR. I guess I will open this up to the panel. Will the second LCS be delivered with a functional combat system?

Admiral LANDAY. Yes, sir. It is our goal right now that we would deliver that ship to meet with all the capabilities that it needs. As you know, we——

Mr. TAYLOR. Do you have the time set for that, Admiral?

Admiral LANDAY. We are looking for delivery in the September timeframe.

Mr. TAYLOR. So by September it is going to have a functional combat system.

Admiral LANDAY. Yes, sir.

Mr. TAYLOR. Admiral, several of us have touched on it, but I am going to give you an analogy that I continue to be troubled with.

I guess all of us at one time or another have hired someone to paint our house. Sometimes you do it by the job, or if you trust the person, you do by the hour.

I am getting the impression we hired someone to paint our house on a fairly trust—you know I trust you, he trusts me. But I come to my house, and he is using a one-inch brush, and I am paying him by the hour.

I think it is every bit my right to say, "You know what? You are not trying to save me any money. You are trying to drag this out." That is the impression I get with both of these builders.

And I have seen—again, I want to give you this opportunity while we still have time, to tell me what they are doing—not building additional buildings to get people out of the weather, but what are they doing to automate their processes, because we know a huge portion of the cost of this vessel is the welds—in addition to the metal, the welds. And there are a heck of a lot of welds on that Trimaran.

So what steps, concrete steps, are being taken to automate that process, because I will use the analogy. The subcommittee visited the Hyundai yard about two years ago. It was fortunate to spend about four hours in that yard.

In the four hours I was there, I saw them doing everything from making propellers on-site, shafts on-site, bearings on-site, making the engine on-site. And every Saturday, another hull was launched.

The four hours I was there, I never heard a grinder, which meant that every well was being cut perfectly, so someone didn't have to go back and fix it. Every cut of the metal was being done perfectly, so someone didn't have to go back and fix it.

When I visit Austal, when I visit Marinette, I hear a lot of grinders. I hear a lot of mistakes getting fixed by somebody doing manual labor to undo it.

So what is being done, and particularly who in your organization is walking through there, knowing that we are basically their only customer and saying, "You know what? There is a better way to do this, and we expect you to do that."

Who is doing that?

Admiral LANDAY. I would tell you that the key—the overall program team is doing that combination of our supervisor of shipbuilding, who is our lead waterfront technical representative in the program office.

So we have lots of discussions with the companies. We, for example, just recently put together a team about 2 months ago that was program folks, shipyard folks, and outside shipbuilding experts to walk stem to stern both of those ships with the companies and look for opportunities where we would propose back to them and say, "There should be a better way to do this. You are welding too much pipe. You need to start bending pipe. You are doing too much effort in here."

And so there is a very aggressive effort to—with them—I mean they are a part of this—to look for those opportunities.

We have seen in what has been proposed to us in the fiscal year 2009 program. We have seen where they have also proposed production efficiencies.

We have seen where the companies have told us under some of their company award or in capital expenditure (CAPEX), if we go down that path, additional equipment that they would buy, be it pipe bending machines or other things to improve their process.

The Austal facility that I mentioned to you, that modular manufacturing facility, is not just a building. It is to take that facility and walk down similar lines that you saw before in the Hyundai plant that you talked about, about getting us into a more logical, leaned out manufacturing process.

There are always going to be additional things we can do, but the first step of this that we thought was particularly critical, and we see both companies doing, is looking to improve the lean processes they have in place to make this more modular, to get the production inefficiencies out of their process.

And then from there, if there are additional investments that they need to make in terms of infrastructure machines, the companies have both indicated plans where they would go forward and do that.

But from the Austal, you know what you saw in that one shed it is exactly those processes that we see the company working very hard to improve and the result of why they went to this modular manufacturing facility.

Mr. TAYLOR. Okay, for the record it is my understanding that the materials for LCS–3 and LCS–4 have already been purchased, so we are not really going to get any savings as a result of the price of commodities going down.

But for the record, should we want to continue with these programs, I would like to know the difference between what we paid for the first two ships—that is for each—and what it would cost if we bought those materials today.

For the record, I would like to know what percentage of each of those vessels was welded by hand, what percentage was done by machine, and what is your target for vessels 3 and 4 and vessels 5 and 6.

Admiral LANDAY. Yes, sir.

Mr. TAYLOR. Okay. When should I expect those answers, Admiral?

Admiral LANDAY. We should be able to get you percentages of ships of 1 and 2, I would say by today; 3 and 4 and 5 and 6 I just need to go back and you know take a look through the contract. I would say by the end of the week I should be able to tell you what those are.

[The information referred to was communicated verbally and is not available for print.]

Mr. TAYLOR. Okay. Thank you, sir.

Mr. Akin.

Again, we want to thank our witnesses. In fairness to the workers at Marinette, I do want to say that I had the opportunity to visit LCS–1 in Norfolk. The commanding officer of the ship was ecstatic with its performance. And I think in fairness to those workers, they should know that.

In fairness to the taxpayers, it was 18 months late and over twice over budget. It is the latter that we need to improve, and it is the latter that I hope the Navy is focused on improving.

But I want to thank our witnesses for being with us.

This hearing is adjourned.

[Whereupon, at 12:05 p.m., the subcommittee was adjourned.]

# APPENDIX

MARCH 10, 2009

# PREPARED STATEMENTS SUBMITTED FOR THE RECORD

MARCH 10, 2009

The hearing will come to order.

Good morning and welcome. Today the subcommittee meets in open session to receive testimony on the Littoral Combat Ship Program. Our witnesses today are RADM Vic Guillory, Director of Surface Ship Programs for the Chief of Naval Operations, RADM Bill Landay, the Program Executive Officer for Surface Ship Construction, and Ms. Anne Sandel, the Program Executive Officer for Littoral and Mine Warfare. I thank the witnesses for taking the time to be with us today.

To call this program troubled would be an understatement. The fact of the matter is this program has so far delivered one ship. Just one ship. When I look at the plan from just two years ago, we should by now have at least four ships delivered, three more nearing completion from a fiscal year 2008 authorization, six under contract from a fiscal year 2009 authorization, and today we should be discussing the authorization of six more ships for fiscal year 2010. That would be a total of 19 ships. So instead of having 13 delivered or under contract with another 6 in this year's budget we have one ship delivered that will likely tip the scales north of two and a half times the original estimate and one ship that might finish this summer, with similar if not higher cost growth. The Navy cancelled two previously authorized ships, no ships were placed under contract for fiscal year 2008 and no contract award has been made for the two ships authorized for fiscal year 2009. And all this is from the program that was hailed as a poster child for its "transformational" and "affordable" acquisition strategy. It seems all the program has accomplished is "transforming" a realistic goal of achieving a 313 ship fleet to an unrealistic goal.

This program is not just a lesson of over-optimism, poor management, and a lack of proper oversight. Even though all those things occurred in spades, the fundamental lesson is flawed strategic planning. Flawed in the belief that the government can pass on to industry decisions that are inherently governmental; flawed in the belief that untested and unproven concepts, such as reconfigurable mission modules, can be incorporated into an acquisition program without testing and verifying the concept on surrogate platforms; and finally flawed due to the absence of a "plan B" for needed capability in the Fleet.

I believe it is the lack of "plan B" which has wedded the Navy so completely to this program. Particularly in the area of mine warfare, the LCS is the only future they see. Dropping the LCS program to develop another mine warfare platform is viewed as unacceptable in schedule. And they might just be correct.

But because the Navy is stuck with continuing the LCS program does not mean that the current strategy for buying these ships has to continue. I have nothing against either of the lead contractors, but I know this; they both contracted to build a ship for $220 million dollars and they did not even come close. I understand the Navy was guilty of changing the design specifications with the implementation of Naval Vessel Rules but I fail to see how that resulted in more than doubling the price and slipping 18 months of schedule. I am also concerned that the Navy has not been able to come to terms with the contractors for the ships authorized last year.

It appears to me the solution is simple. Bring true competition into this program, not the pseudo competition we currently have between the two variants of ships but true competition based on price, schedule, and quality. I have been asking for over two years if the government owns the rights to the design drawings of the ships so they can bid them out directly to any shipyard with the capability of constructing the vessels. The answer seems to be yes and no. I understand that the prepared witness testimony address this question, however I would like the witnesses today, on the record, to explain that position and answer in layman's terms, not the language of the professional acquisition executive, the exact claim the government has on the technical design rights to both the seaframe and the combat system. I would then like the witnesses to explain how long it would take, what organization would be responsible, and how much it would cost to develop the "technical data package" described in the prepared statement that is required to bid the ships directly to other shipyards, or the current shipyards divorced of the lead contractors. Ranges of cost and time are acceptable, what is not acceptable is taking the question for the record.

But so far I have discussed just the ship, just what the Navy refers to as the "seaframe". Today's hearing for the first time brings in the official responsible for the mission packages that are purported to give this vessel multi-mission capability. And although at least one of each type of mission modules has been developed I am very concerned that major components of the overall "mission package" are still under development or have not been thoroughly tested. Therefore I would request that Ms. Sandel update the subcommittee on the remaining development and testing for all of the mission packages. I would also like to know if any existing Navy platforms can operate with an LCS mission module as a stop-gap capability filler until sufficient LCS ships are constructed.

Everyone should understand that the current situation of these vessels costing in excess of a half billion dollars cannot continue. There are too many other needs and too little resources to pour money into the program that was designed to be affordable. I would also caution that, particularly right now, you don't want to be the program that is breaking the bank. From what I read in the newspapers there are no "protected programs" in the ongoing debate on affordability.

Of course, none of the witnesses sitting in front of us today was responsible for the program when it began. They have inherited a mess and are doing their best to fix what they can. I appreciate that. But now is the time for frank talk on what needs to be done. We need the best price and the best quality we can get for these vessels whether with the current lead contractors after they finally get the message or changing course and bidding directly to shipyards.

Before I ask the Ranking Member for his remarks I would like to remind the subcommittee that competition sensitive information such as current estimates of prices are protected by statute. However, the Navy has agreed to answer these types of questions directly to individual Members in the appropriate forum and under the conditions agreed to by the Navy

General Counsel and the Committee.

I now call on my friend from Missouri for any remarks he may wish to

make.

STATEMENT OF

RADM VICTOR GUILLORY, U.S. NAVY
DIRECTOR OF SURFACE WARFARE

AND

RADM WILLIAM E. LANDAY, III
PROGRAM EXECUTIVE OFFICER SHIPS

AND

MS. E. ANNE SANDEL
PROGRAM EXECUTIVE OFFICER LITTORAL AND MINE WARFARE

BEFORE THE

SUBCOMMITTEE ON SEAPOWER AND EXPEDITIONARY FORCES

OF THE

HOUSE ARMED SERVICES COMMITTEE ON

THE CURRENT STATUS OF THE LITTORAL COMBAT SHIP PROGRAM

MARCH 10, 2009

## INTRODUCTION / REQUIREMENT

Mr. Chairman, distinguished members of the Subcommittee, thank you for the opportunity to appear before you today to address the Navy's Littoral Combat Ship (LCS) program. We thank the Committee for its continued support and active interest in Navy shipbuilding programs.

The Navy remains committed to the LCS program. LCS fills warfighting gaps in support of maintaining dominance in the littorals and strategic choke points around the world. The Navy remains committed to procuring 55 LCSs, and is aggressively pursuing cost reduction measures to ensure delivery of future ships on a schedule that affordably paces evolving threats. This will be accomplished by matching required capabilities, to a recurring review of warfighting requirements through applying lessons learned from the construction and test and evaluation periods of seaframes and mission packages.

The LCS program is structured in flights of seaframes and spirals of mission packages. This allows the relatively rapid change in technologies and threats associated with the modular mission packages to be continuously improved through incremental upgrades without major design impacts to seaframes. The result is a program that minimizes the risks of a highly interdependent system of systems by decoupling seaframe procurement from mission package procurement. This allows continuous cost efficient delivery of state-of-the-art capability to the warfighter via new mission package upgrades.

The LCS program capabilities address specific and validated capability gaps in Mine Countermeasures (MCM), Surface Warfare (SUW) and Anti-Submarine Warfare (ASW). The Concept of Operations and design specifications for LCS were developed to meet these gaps with focused mission packages that deploy manned and unmanned vehicles to execute a variety of missions. LCS's inherent characteristics (speed, agility, shallow draft, payload capacity, reconfigurable mission spaces, air/water craft capabilities) combined with its core Command, Control, Communications, Computers and Intelligence (C4I), sensors, and weapons systems, make it an ideal platform for hosting additional Maritime Strategy mission areas, such as Irregular Warfare and Maritime Security Operations.

The Navy, as part of its annual review of its shipbuilding program, expects there will be sufficient force structure with our existing frigates and mine warfare ships until LCS delivers in quantity to meet overarching deployment requirements.

Legacy mine warfare ships and frigates are planned to be phased out gradually. These decommissionings will be balanced with LCS mission package and seaframe deliveries to mitigate warfare risks.

LCS 1, USS FREEDOM, was delivered to the Fleet on September 18, 2008 — six years and one day after the program was established. LCS 2, the future USS INDEPENDENCE, was christened in Mobile, AL, on October 4, 2008. Later this year the program will have delivered a second ship of a completely different design.

While the initial cost and schedule objectives for the program were overaggressive, they did provide the tension and urgency for these achievements. Although the concurrent design and construction of LCS revealed challenges for meeting the original cost and schedule objectives, the Navy will apply lessons learned to this program as well as other shipbuilding programs.

At the Subcommittee's request, the Navy is pleased today to discuss an overview of the history of the LCS program, the current status of LCS 1 and LCS 2, and the future acquisition strategy for the LCS program.

## BACKGROUND

The LCS acquisition strategy, approved in May 2004, was based on the tenets of modular and open system architecture, Cost-As-an-Independent-Variable design process, a rapid construction cycle and continuous competition at all levels of the program. The Navy awarded contracts for construction of the first four LCS seaframes, with Lockheed Martin (LM) and General Dynamics (GD) awarded two ships each. Fabrication of LCS 1, the first LM ship, began in February 2005 and the ships delivered in September 2008. Fabrication on LCS 2 , the first GD ship, began in November 2005 and this ship will deliver this year. LCS 3 and 4 options were exercised in June and December 2006, respectively.

Cost growth on both variants resulted in a detailed assessment of program cost and structure. The Navy sought to restructure the contracts for LCS 3 and 4 to fixed-price incentive terms to more equitably balance cost and risk, but could not come to terms and conditions that were acceptable to both parties. On April 12, 2007, the Navy terminated construction of LCS 3 for convenience under the Termination clause of the contract. On November 1, 2007, the Navy terminated construction of LCS 4 for convenience under the Termination clause of the contract. Based on program restructuring, the Navy requested and received congressional approval to reprogram FY 2007 shipbuilding appropriations to fund cost increases on LCS 1 and 2.

At the direction of Assistant Secretary of the Navy for Research, Development, and Acquisition (ASN(RDA)), the LCS program underwent a thorough independent assessment to review the cause of the cost growth and evaluate the way forward.

The results of that assessment identified a number of factors key to the program's poor performance. The Navy has actively addressed those key findings in the program as it operates today:

- The design for both ships is mature and we are incorporating revisions to specific areas based on the lessons learned from the construction of the initial ships, proposed production improvements, acceptance inspections and the early stages of the post delivery testing period. Those revisions will be in place for the start of construction of the FY 2009 ships.

- The Navy has increased the staff assigned in the program office and at the shipyards to monitor performance. The program office staff has grown from eight to 20 civilian personnel, focusing on critical production, acquisition, and financial management specialties. An additional 12 billets have been assigned as the two lead ships complete delivery and post delivery milestones this year and more ships are placed under contract.

57

Military staff has increased from three to five assigned. Officers with new ship construction experience were assigned to the program manager and production manager positions.

- The Supervisors of Shipbuilding doubled the staff at each LCS shipbuilder. Focusing resources to the waterfront, the program office works closely with the Supervisors to sustain a daily drumbeat in monitoring production progress on these lead ships, identifying and monitoring key metrics that maintain progress to key events.

- To improve technical decision making and reduce the time to resolve technical issues, especially as related to the application of Naval Vessel Rules, the program office and the Naval Sea Systems Command Chief Engineer have placed senior managers and technical authorities on the waterfront.

- New performance baselines were implemented for each contract to help monitor and control cost, with contracting incentive structures to support improved progress. We continue to work closely with the industry teams to improve their performance and Earned Value Management System measurement and reporting capabilities.

- The FY 2009 and FY 2010 contracts will be fixed-price contracts to ensure cost and schedule adherence remain a primary focus of both the industry and the government program teams.

**AFFORDABILITY**

The Navy has implemented a comprehensive cost-reduction program for LCS. Taking advantage of lessons from other shipbuilding programs' affordability initiatives such as the DDG 51 value engineering program, the T-AKE "take cost" program and the Virginia-class cost-reduction initiative, this ongoing effort seeks to reduce acquisition cost and total ownership cost through continuous assessment of operational and technical requirements, improvement of production processes, and implementation of acquisition strategies that will lead to stable production and improved purchasing leverage. Examples of areas under review by this program include:

- A joint team of industry, government and independent experts have conducted a "stem-to-stern" inspection of each ship to identify areas of inefficiency or where alternative production methods can improve production efficiencies.

- The Navy implemented a Total Ownership Cost (TOC) reduction review jointly overseen by the ASN(RDA) and Vice Chief Naval Operations to look for improvements in total lifecycle costs.

- The Navy has initiated a second study to look at the Total Ownership Cost return on investment of a common combat system. The initial study conducted in 2007 did not support a payback sufficient to support the upfront integration and additional

4

procurement costs. The Navy's development of its objective architecture for combat systems provided a different set of assumptions to be considered for this new study.

- Finally, infrastructure improvements are either under review or in progress at both yards that will improve production efficiencies and reduce costs.

## CURRENT STATUS OF LCS 1 AND LCS 2

### USS FREEDOM (LCS 1)

USS FREEDOM was built by the Lockheed Martin-led team at the Marinette Marine shipyard in Marinette, WI, and was commissioned on November 8, 2008. Due to restrictions on some testing in the Great Lakes, acceptance testing was broken into two phases. Acceptance Trial 1 (AT) evaluated the ship, propulsion, navigation and some communications. Acceptance Trial 2 will evaluate the remaining communications and most of the combat systems. In August 2008, the Navy's Board of Inspection and Survey (INSURV) conducted Acceptance Trial 1 on LCS 1 and found the ship to be "capable, well-built, and inspection-ready," and recommended that the Chief of Naval Operations authorize delivery of the ship following the correction or waiver of cited material deficiencies, a standard practice in Navy shipbuilding.

During inspection, INSURV identified 21 "starred" deficiencies onboard LCS 1. This is a relatively low number and compares favorably to other first-of-class ships. The Navy developed a plan to address these deficiencies in a timely, prioritized sequence – 12 were closed prior to delivery, five more will be closed during the ship's current Industrial Post Delivery Availability, and the final four will be closed during Post Shakedown Availability (PSA) in FY 2010.

After acceptance, the crew conducted a vigorous shakedown of the ship during her transit from the building yard to Norfolk, VA. Encountering adverse weather and numerous instances of challenging ship handling evolutions, the crew reported the ship performed superbly during the 2,400 mile journey. LCS 1 will undergo AT 2 and additional test and trials period intended to complete certifications and mission package integration testing.

### INDEPENDENCE (LCS 2)

INDEPENDENCE is being built by the General Dynamics team at the Austal USA shipyard in Mobile, AL. She was christened on October 4, 2008, and is expected to deliver in 2009, with Initial Builder's Trials and Acceptance Trials to complete prior to ship delivery. Following delivery and commissioning, LCS 2 will transit to Norfolk, VA, and conduct a post delivery test and trials period similar to FREEDOM.

Facing similar lead ship challenges on INDEPENDENCE, Navy leadership directed General Dynamics to take a phased approach to completing the ship. The initial phase prioritized efforts on that scope of work required to safely take INDEPENDENCE to sea, demonstrating propulsion and additional systems and components necessary for communications and safe navigation. Based on performance to this goal, a second phase of work would be authorized focusing on only those core combat systems necessary to demonstrate a basic detect-to-engage capability required during an acceptance trial. The third phase is the remaining systems and components required to demonstrate complete combat systems and communications capabilities of the complete sea frame. At this time, the program manager has authorized phase 1 and 2 work. Phase 3 remains contingent on performance of the first two phases. It is still the program manager's intention to present a complete ship to INSURV at acceptance trial.

The Navy monitors progress through daily assessments, weekly analysis of key metrics on production and test progress, and conducts monthly progress and cost reviews with the contractor to ensure that corrective actions are implemented and effective. As of February 2009, all four of the ship's generators have been started and vital shipboard electrical systems have completed initial testing, aligning with current schedule projections for ship delivery. The program expects to achieve main propulsion engines light-off in April and May, with a goal of Builder's Trials in late June. The program is prudently managing resources to be able to address any potential challenges.

Status of Mission Package Procurement

The modular open system architecture used for the LCS design allows independent development of seaframes and mission packages that integrate across a controlled interface specification to ensure complete interoperability. This allows the relatively rapid change in technologies associated with the modular mission packages (MPs) to be continuously improved through incremental upgrades without major design impacts to seaframes. The result is a program that minimizes the risks of a highly interdependent system of systems by decoupling seaframe procurement from mission package procurement, and allows continous cost efficient delivery of state-of-the-art capability to the warfighter via new misison package upgrades.

The underlying strength of the LCS lies in its innovative design approach, applying modularity for operational flexibility. Fundamental to this approach is the capability to rapidly install interchangeable mission packages into the seaframe. The ability to modify the LCS physical configuration with different MPs in less than a 96-hour period gives the operational commander a uniquely flexible response to changing theater warfighting requirements. This also allows the LCS warfighting capability to quickly adapt to evolving threats, using improved technology. To achieve this flexibility, the Navy is developing and procuring specific numbers of MPs to meet the Fleet's warfighting requirements. A mission package consists of mission systems which are integrated to form mission modules, Sailors organized into mission module and aviation crew detachments and supporting aircraft. Each mission package provides warfighting capability for one of three focused mission areas:

- Mine Countermeasures (MCM)
- Surface Warfare (SUW)
- Anti-Submarine Warfare (ASW)

The first SUW and ASW mission packages were rolled out in FY 2008 and joined the first MCM mission package, which was delivered in FY 2007. Land-based and at-sea testing of mission package components began in FY 2008 and continues in FY 2009. Through an Integrated Test and Evaluation framework, the LCS Mission Modules program office is working very closely with the responsible mission systems program offices in Naval Sea Systems Command, Naval Air Systems Command and the Army to ensure that all Mission System Program of Record, as well as LCS shipboard testing events, demonstrates required warfighting effectiveness and suitability. Formal LCS sea frame testing of mission packages commences in FY 2009 and continues through FY 2012.

The LCS Mission Modules program office has adopted an open business model that leverages Participating Acquisition Resource Managers' (PARMs) developmental efforts for both program-of-record and non-program-of-record systems and components. This process minimizes LCS Mission Modules program investments of research and development dollars required to mature unique technologies. In addition, the process allows for package procurement flexibility by limiting integration of immature technologies/systems. This is done by continuous evaluation of system maturity through a disciplined system engineering framework. Through this open business model, the LCS Mission Modules program procures mature mission systems from PARMs and then engages an industry partner for Package Production and Assembly (PP&A) of mission packages.

## FUTURE ACQUISITION STRATEGY FOR THE LCS PROGRAM

### LCS Acquisition Strategy

In October 2008, the Undersecretary of Defense for Acquisition, Technology and Logistics (USD(AT&L)) approved a revised acquisition strategy for LCS to cover procurement of the FY 2009 and FY 2010 ships. The updated acquisition strategy combines the FY 2009 procurement and FY 2010 options in order to maximize competitive pressure on pricing as a key element of cost control. Increasing the quantity solicited by adding the FY 2010 ships to the FY 2009 solicitation as options will also enable industry to better establish longer term supplier relationships and offer the potential for discounting to the prime contractors and subcontractors. FY 2010 ship options will be a competition for quantity.

Acquisition strategies for FY 2011 and outyear ships are under development. The Navy's strategy will be guided by cost and performance of the respective designs, as well as options for sustaining competition throughout the life of the program. Evaluations of combat systems and hull, mechanical and electrical (HM&E) performance will be conducted throughout those tests and trial periods and, as was mentioned earlier, we are already looking for opportunities to reduce total ownership costs through commonality, reductions or consolidations based on return-on-investment analysis.

### FY 2009 and FY 2010 Contract Awards

As a result of congressional direction contained in the FY 2009 Defense Appropriations Act, the Navy amended the LCS seaframe construction solicitation to delete the FY 2008 ship. This amended solicitation continues the competition between the two incumbent industry teams. The Navy may award one ship to each industry team in FY 2009 and intends to hold a competition for the FY 2010 option ships soon after award of the FY 2009 contracts. Affordability remains a key tenet of the LCS program as the Navy works with industry to provide this capability for the lowest cost.

The FY 2009 and FY 2010 awards will be fixed-price incentive contracts, with the Navy anticipating that each LCS prime contractor receives one ship in FY 2009. The Navy remains committed to effective cost control and has modified contracting strategies and management practices to provide program stability. The FY 2009 and FY 2010 ships will be designated as Flight 0+ and will include only existing approved engineering changes along with improvements to construction or fabrication procedures. The Navy will incorporate further lessons learned from LCS 1 and 2 sea trials into the FY 2009 and FY 2010 ships prior to production. Any such changes will be limited to those essential for safety, operability or affordability. Furthermore, the RFP requests that the proposals for the FY 2010 option ships include alternative prices for both a full-up ship and separately priced contract line item numbers (CLINs) for a core seaframe (only systems for safe operation at sea), core combat system and individual combat systems and equipments (such as the gun or radar). This allows us the opportunity to manage the integration of the combat systems separately if that proved to be more affordable.

In the interim prior to FY 2009 contract awards, both industry teams were authorized and funded to pursue limited design and construction efforts while source selection proceeded. The scope of these efforts was carefully coordinated with prime contractors with an eye on preserving critical shipbuilding skills or to improve production process engineering. Once the FY 2009 ships are awarded, these sustaining efforts will be subsumed in the shipbuilding contracts.

Mission Modules Acquisition Strategy

At the time of its inception in FY 2004, the Mission Modules program office decided to utilize government labs to build the first two of each type of mission package. The Navy Labs (Naval Surface Warfare Center Panama City (NSWC PC), Naval Undersea Warfare Center Newport (NUWC NPT), SPAWAR Systems Center San Diego (SSC SD) and Naval Surface Warfare Center Dahlgren (NSWC DD)) are developing, integrating, testing and delivering the first six mission packages. This approach was implemented to ensure responsiveness to refined requirements and reduce the financial risk to the Navy associated with cost-type contracts for this unique concept. This strategy has been very advantageous to the Mission Modules program. Once these initial mission packages are completed by the warfare centers, the package production and assembly will transition to Northrop Grumman.

Following a competitive solicitation, Northrop Grumman was awarded a contract in January 2006 to provide a range of package production and assembly functions specified by the Navy. The contract contains Award Fee/Award Term provisions covering a term of up to ten years, with contract options exercised annually. Awarding the options is contingent on continued excellent contractor performance in preceding years, and is assessed annually.

As Northrop Grumman steps into a production and assembly role, the Navy labs will transition into the Technical Direction Agent and In-Service Engineering Agent role. This transition began in 2008 with the transfer of the Technical Data Packages from the Navy labs to Northrop Grumman in 2008 and continues in 2009.

Rights in Technical Data and Computer Software

It is the Navy's legal and contractual position that the Navy has Government Purpose Rights (GPR) to the seaframe designs of both LCS variants and, as such, can solicit full and open competition for either seaframe design after an adequate design package for such a competition is developed.

For clarity, those rights are as follows:

- Seaframe – The government has GPR to the design of both seaframes. We did not seek the rights to the individual equipments in the seaframe (for example we do not have GPR to the Rolls Royce engine that we could provide to another engine manufacturer to produce for the government). Another shipbuilder or the government would have to contract with the individual equipment manufacturers for fabrication and delivery of the equipment for shipboard installation or, alternatively, negotiate a license with the individual equipment manufacturers based on the equipment, specifications and interfaces detailed in the seaframe design.

- Combat Systems – We have GPR to the technical data pertaining to the LM combat systems, architecture and interfaces. It currently resides in our shared repository. The GD Integrated Combat Management Systems (ICMS) is based on the Thales TACTICOS system for which Northrop Grumman is the sole U.S. licensee. Another shipbuilder or the government would have to either enter into a contract with Northrop Grumman for production and delivery of the ICMS or, alternatively, obtain a license for that system from Northrop Grumman. As with the seaframe, we do not possess GPR to the specific equipments for either system such as the gun, electronic warfare system or radar.

Any third parties seeking to compete on LCS would need to either contract directly with the equipment manufacturers for fabrication and delivery of the required equipment and associated software or, alternatively, negotiate licensing agreements for the equipment and software with the respective vendors. This is similar to the current approach in place with the LM and GD teams. An alternative approach would be for the government to contract directly with the equipment manufacturers and provide the equipment and software to the shipbuilder as Government Furnished Equipment/Government Furnished Information.

LCS "Build-to-Print" Design Concept

To implement a competitive "build-to-print" seaframe acquisition, there remains a significant effort to finalize those revisions to the design that have resulted during construction, as well as lessons learned from LCS Flight 0 production improvement initiatives, developmental/ operational testing and at-sea testing. There is a considerable amount of work necessary to convert a design package developed by a specific shipyard based on its own particular production capabilities and processes to one that can be provided to another qualified shipbuilder as a government furnished design.

The amount of effort necessary to prepare the LCS data packages to support a full and open competition derives from the structure of the initial LCS acquisition strategy. The foundation of the LCS procurement is not a traditional detailed drawing package but the Navy-established requirements detailed in the Capabilities Development Document (CDD). Each industry team developed from the CDD a Specified Performance Document (SPD) that describes the required performance to meet the CDD requirements, then a build specification detailing how to build a ship to meet that performance. From these three documents, drawings and specifications detailing exactly what to construct were then developed. The contractual technical baseline is defined by the CDD, SPD and the build specifications, not the drawings. Configuration management is accomplished at the build specification level.

At present in the LCS acquisition, industry has developed drawing packages for LCS 1 and LCS 2. These include digital product models, extracted drawings and drawing liens, representing multiple changes accomplished to the drawings during production. Thus, while appropriate for use in construction by the existing industry teams, these packages were not envisioned to be used as the foundation documents for a build to print solicitation. It would not be prudent to pursue a build-to-print contract for the current design package until it fully reflects those changes.

The Navy's FY 2009 budget request did request funds to begin refinement of the Flight 0+ baseline design drawings and associated documentation into detailed production drawings and documents. These drawings will also incorporate production, assembly and fabrication lessons learned from the previous seaframes as well as operator feedback from the seaframe and mission package crews obtained during the testing and trials period. Additional time and resources will be necessary to complete a build-to-print package.

The build to print package requires the development of a neutral-format computer-aided design model (both 2-D and 3-D and STEP compliant) for the total ship, clearing all interferences for the model, and review and update of all additional required documentation to ensure that requirements are sufficiently detailed and "generic" to enable providers other than the incumbent to bid (e.g., the design can't reflect six-inch bent pipe if only the incumbent has facilities sufficient to accomplish this). The timing for completion of such a drawing package is dependent on completion of testing for the LCS lead ships. LCS 1 must complete Acceptance Trials 2 in Spring 2009 as well as seaframe developmental testing/operational testing or integration testing with mission packages. LCS 2 has not been delivered and must complete a similar test and trials period. The Navy is developing an estimate for LCS class design services needed to support this maturation.

Furthermore, to implement a full-and-open acquisition targeted at gaining increased access to additional shipyards, an approach must also be developed for the acquisition of the combat systems/networks/control systems/C4I equipment. To mitigate this risk for combat systems efforts under a build-to-print acquisition, the Navy would either need to direct the shipyards to contract with the current primes as subcontractors, or assume the role of providing the combat systems/networks/control systems/C4I equipment as GFE and develop the infrastructure necessary to serve as the integrator for the program.

**LESSONS LEARNED**

The Navy has incorporated many of the lessons learned from the initial LCS ships into overall acquisition policy and in specific shipbuilding programs.

64

On February 26, 2008, the Navy issued SECNAVNOTE 5000, which instituted an Acquisition Governance Improvement Six-Gate reporting, reviewing and oversight process that provides specific criteria for areas such as requirements, funding, and technical performance including a Probability of Program Success (PoPS) tool. This new process ensures that the various stakeholders from the resources, requirements and acquisition communities address and revisit at defined intervals, issues associated with technical maturity, affordability and program health.

Guidance emphasizing the use of independent engineering technical review boards and responsibility for Configuration Steering Boards to monitor requirements changes has been promulgated.

Initiatives to expand the size of the acquisition workforce and to evaluate the composition and experience of program offices are underway. Similar initiatives are underway in the technical and SUPSHIPS areas.

A rigorous production readiness review (PRR) prior to the start of fabrication is in place for shipbuilding programs. It was utilized for the start of fabrication for the DDG 1000, and will be used in the Joint High Speed Vessel (JHSV) program as well as the FY 2009 LCS ships.

A critical aspect of the PRR is design maturity. DDG 1000 requirements were that the design was at least 85% complete prior to start fabrication, including all units scheduled to start construction in the first six months. Similar criteria will govern the start of fabrication for JHSV and subsequent new ship designs.


## SUMMARY

In summary, the Navy remains committed to the LCS program. LCS remains a critical warfighting requirement for our Navy to maintain dominance in the littorals and strategic choke points around the world.

The Navy continues to address the problems encountered in the early stages of the program and to implement improvements across the entire shipbuilding portfolio. We appreciate your strong support and the opportunity to testify before the Subcommittee. We will be pleased to answer any questions you may have.

Remarks by Donald C. Winter
Secretary of the Navy
USS FREEDOM (LCS 1)
Commissioning Ceremony
Milwaukee, Wisconsin
Saturday, November 8, 2008

Distinguished guests, ladies and gentlemen, I am delighted to be with you today as we welcome into the Fleet a new ship, the first in its class—USS FREEDOM.

Today's day of triumph was achieved through perseverance and a determination to overcome many obstacles.

The challenge of building a totally new class of ship was formidable, and today's achievement represents a number of firsts.

The first Littoral Combat Ship.

The first warship built in Wisconsin since World War II.

The first time we have worked with the American Bureau of Ships to class a combatant.

The first U.S. warship designed to accommodate mission modules.

We have learned a lot along the way.

We have forged new relationships and established new partnerships.

It was not easy.

But I am convinced that we now have a very capable warship that fills a critical need.

Furthermore, LCS is a cost-effective warship, and I am looking forward to the day when we have all 55 LCS's in the Fleet.

I would like to thank the entire Navy-industry team for your efforts in bringing us to this critical point in the program.

Your long hours in making this warship sea-worthy and combat-ready have paid off.

Treasure this day, and walk proudly in the future as you read about the great achievements of USS FREEDOM in the years ahead.

It can now be said that while Wisconsin is famous for the Green Bay Packers, and Michigan famous for its Wolverines . . .

Well, OK, in most years, but let us not talk about that right now . . .

Anyway, with USS FREEDOM, you have now given the entire world an opportunity to see what Wisconsin and Michigan talent can do in building one of the world's most advanced and innovative warships!

Our Nation needs this ship.

We face challenges and threats in the littorals around the world.

From terrorists in small boats to mine warfare in vital waterways to diesel submarines deployed by hostile powers to pirates interdicting maritime commerce, the U.S. Navy faces a wide array of threats that must be countered.

USS FREEDOM—the first of many Littoral Combat Ships to come—will help us do so.

The global economy is highly vulnerable to maritime threats.

We saw that in April 2004, when terrorists attempted to attack an oil platform in the Northern Arabian Gulf.

The terrorists failed—but the attack sent oil prices and insurance rates soaring, even though no damage was done to the platform.

Today, we also see this vulnerability in the Nigerian Delta, where instability and threats are adding to the cost of critical energy resources.

And we have seen this vulnerability time and time again off the Somali coast, were ever more brazen pirates threaten, plunder, and terrorize merchant ships in innocent passage across international waters.

These developments threaten the Suez Canal trade route, and they represent a challenge to every nation that depends on maritime security for their prosperity and their survival.

With USS FREEDOM, we are responding to these threats.

In this platform, we are making the right investments in our future security and prosperity.

For those of you who will have the privilege of serving in FREEDOM, you will play a leading role protecting our Nation's interests, and in ensuring the stability of the global economy.

You will also be called upon to serve in a ship whose namesake defines the very aspirations of the American people, and of people the world over.

Freedom is a powerful word.

Our Founding Fathers fought a war to achieve it; generations of Americans overcame many challenges to defend it; and tens of millions of immigrants have come to our shores to experience it.

We take our freedoms as our national birthright—the freedom of religion, freedom of the press, freedom of assembly, the freedom to petition our government for a redress of grievances.

We understand freedom to mean that we have the right to chart our own course in life, to pursue our dreams, and to voice our opinions freely, without fear of reprisal.

Our freedom is a precious gift—and we must defend it.

As President Dwight D. Eisenhower stated, "History does not long entrust the care of freedom to the weak or the timid."

Our Nation now entrusts the care of freedom to those who serve in this great ship.

USS FREEDOM will be called upon to go in harm's way, and to defend the freedom that previous generations have passed on to us.

From every corner of the globe, and from every port of call, let freedom ring.

May God bless this ship, the Sailors who serve in her, and may God continue to bless America.

Remarks by Donald C. Winter
Secretary of the Navy
USS INDEPENDENCE (LCS 2)
Christening Ceremony
Austal Shipyard
Mobile, Alabama
Saturday, October 4, 2008

Senator Sessions, Congressman Bonner, distinguished guests, ladies and gentlemen, I am delighted to be with you today as we christen USS INDEPENDENCE.

Littoral Combat Ship is a timely response to one of the evolving challenges we face—the need to provide presence in the littorals around the world.

The threats to our interests in the littorals come in many forms and they are global, ranging from terrorist attacks using small boats; to mine warfare in strategically sensitive areas; to diesel submarines emanating from rogue nations; to pirates off the coast of Somalia and elsewhere around the globe.

In this context, we would do well to fully recognize how potentially vulnerable the global economy is to maritime threats.

The world's system of trade—90 percent of which is transported by sea—is so tightly integrated that minor shocks and interruptions can have dramatic, instantaneous effects that reverberate worldwide.

For example, an unsuccessful terrorist attack on an oil platform in the North Arabian Gulf in April 2004 sent world oil prices and insurance rates soaring—within days—costing the world's economy billions of dollars, even though no damage was done to the platform.

More recently, unrest and instability in the Nigerian Delta have added to the rising cost of oil.

The lesson is clear—the security of critical resources is prey to a variety of threats, from piracy to the frequently voiced threats made by terrorists and rogue nations.

Indeed, just over a week ago Somali pirates seized a Ukrainian vessel laden with military weaponry.

This seizure follows a growing trend of pirate attacks that are disrupting critical sea lines of communication.

These developments are a source of concern that extends far beyond East Africa, for such attacks are taking place close to major choke points of maritime commerce such as the Suez Canal.

Pirates are becoming more aggressive, better armed, and ever more audacious in their depredations against commercial shipping.

This incident with the Ukrainian ship FAINA—given the possible role of its cargo in arming rebel groups in Africa—underscores the point that maritime threats can have a worldwide impact not only on the global economy, but on the political and security domains as well.

With a multi-mission platform such as LCS, we are making investments in capabilities to meet these challenges.

USS INDEPENDENCE will play a pioneering role in our Nation's effort to protect our interests, and to ensure the stability of the global economy.

For those of you who will have the privilege to serve in her, your ship's name carries special significance in carrying on a distinguished legacy as the sixth U.S. Navy warship to be called USS INDEPENDENCE.

The first Independence was a 10-gun sloop that served during the War of Independence.

The second USS INDEPENDENCE  was called upon in 1815 to deter Barbary pirates from preying upon American merchant commerce.

Three more Navy ships named Independence followed, with distinguished service in defense of the Nation from 1919 through Operation Desert Storm.

The future USS INDEPENDENCE will build on her illustrious past, and honor American communities from coast to coast that bear the name "Independence."

In so doing, this ship acknowledges the enduring foundation of our Nation.

Indeed, the word "independence" embodies what the Founding Fathers came to regard as "the glorious cause."

Declaring our independence was not enough.

We had to fight for it.

One of our Nation's greatest orators—Daniel Webster—upon the deaths of John Adams and Thomas Jefferson—captured eloquently the spirit of independence that has guided this country since its birth:

"It is my living sentiment, and by the blessing of God it shall be my dying sentiment—Independence now and Independence forever."

With this ship, you now have the opportunity to help preserve the hard-won independence of our Founding generation, and the generations which have followed in their footsteps.

May God bless this ship, the Sailors who serve in her, and may God continue to bless America.

# Littoral Combat Ship (LCS)

## Executive Summary

- The Defense Acquisition Executive authorized procurement of two FY09 ships, one of each design. Affordability and impending budget constraints have driven the Navy to cancel the FY10 solicitation and pursue a down select to one design for FY10 ships and beyond with a fixed price incentive contract.
- The Navy revised the T&E strategy to provide the lead ships to the fleet earlier, but with only one partial mission package capability rather than all three.
- The Navy intends to employ the two ships of the design not selected through their operational service life so the current T&E strategy reflecting comprehensive testing for both designs is still applicable.
- The Navy has directed their Operational Test Agency (OTA) to conduct a Quick Reaction Assessment (QRA) on Littoral Combat Ship (LCS) 1's operational capability to support a rapid early deployment.
- Early developmental test results revealed that LCS 1 is unable to meet the Navy's stability requirements and has exhibited inherent weaknesses in combat system component performance.
- LCS 2 experienced delays in completing Builder's Trials and planned delivery due to emergent propulsion related deficiencies.
- LCS was designated by the Navy as a Level I survivability combatant ship, but is not expected to achieve the degree of shock hardening required by the Capabilities Development Document (CDD).

## System

- The LCS is designed to operate in the shallow waters of the littorals where larger ships cannot maneuver as well. It can accommodate a variety of individual warfare systems (mission modules) assembled and integrated into interchangeable mission packages.
- There are two competing basic ship (seaframe) designs:
  - LCS 1 is a semi-planing monohull constructed of steel and aluminum.
  - LCS 2 is an aluminum trimaran or stabilized monohull design.
- Common characteristics:
  - Combined (2) diesel and (2) gas turbine engines with (4) waterjet propulsors
  - Sprint speed in excess of 40 knots, draft of less than 20 feet, and range in excess of 3,500 nautical miles
  - Accommodate up to 76 (air detachment, mission module personnel, and core crew of no more than 50)
  - Identical Mission Package Computing Environment for mission module component transparency

LCS 1

LCS 2

  - Large hangar to embark MH-60R/S with multiple Vertical Take-off Unmanned Aerial Vehicles (VTUAVs)
  - 57 mm BOFORS Mk 3 gun with dissimilar gun fire control systems
- The designs have different combat systems for self-defense against anti-ship cruise missiles
  - LCS 1: COMBATSS-21, an Aegis-based integrated combat weapons system with a TRS-3D (German) Air/Surface search radar, Ship Self-Defense System Rolling Airframe Missile (RAM) interface (one 16 cell launcher), and a DORNA (Spanish) Electro-Optical/Infrared (EO/IR) for 57 mm gun fire control.
  - LCS 2: Integrated combat management system (derived from Dutch TACTICOS system) with a Swedish 3D Air/Surface search radar (Sea Giraffe), one RAM launcher integrated into Close-In Weapons System (Mk15 CIWS) search and fire control radars (called SeaRAM), and Sea Star SAFIRE EO/IR for 57 mm gun fire control.
- More than a dozen individual programs of record, involving sensor and weapon systems and other off-board vehicles, make up the individual mission modules. Some of which include:

- Remote Multi-Mission Vehicle, an unmanned semi-submersible that tows a special sonar to detect mines
- Organic Airborne Mine Countermeasures, a family of systems employed from an MH-60S designed to detect, localize, and neutralize all types of sea mines
- Unmanned Surface Vehicles, used in both mine and anti-submarine warfare applications
- VTUAV, specifically the Fire Scout
- The Navy plans to acquire a total of 55 LCS, the first four being a mix of the two competing designs and the remaining seaframes a single design.

## Mission

- The Maritime Component Commander can employ LCS to conduct Mine Warfare, Anti-Submarine Warfare, or Surface Warfare (SUW), based on the mission package fitted into the seaframe. With the Maritime Security Module installed, the ship can conduct sustained Level 2 Visit Board Search and Seizure Maritime Interception Operations. Mission packages are designed to be interchangeable, allowing the Maritime Component Commander flexibility to reassign missions.
- Commanders can employ LCS in a maritime presence role regardless of the installed mission package based on capabilities inherent to the seaframe.
- The Navy can deploy LCS alone or in conjunction with other ships.

## Prime Contractors

- LCS 1 Prime: Lockheed Martin Maritime Systems and Sensors, Washington, District of Columbia; Shipbuilder: Marinette Marine, Marinette, Wisconsin
- LCS 2 Prime: General Dynamics Corporation Marine Systems, Bath Iron Works, Bath, Maine Shipbuilder: Austal USA, Mobile, Alabama

## Activity

- DOT&E approved the Test and Evaluation Master Plan (TEMP) in December 2008.
- The Defense Acquisition Board held a Milestone A-Prime review on December 18, 2008, to proceed with procurement of two (one of each design) FY09 ships (LCS 3 and 4) and mission packages.
- On June 11, 2009, the Navy revised the T&E strategy to provide the lead ships to the fleet sooner albeit with only one (vice three) partial mission package capability.
- On September 22, 2009, the Navy unveiled a revised acquisition strategy to down select to one design for the FY10 ships and beyond. The Navy intends to employ the two ships of the unselected design through their operational life expectancy.
- LCS 1:
  - The Navy commissioned LCS 1 on November 8, 2008.
  - The Navy's Board of Inspection and Survey completed a second Acceptance Trial (AT-2) in May 2009 to examine aspects of the ship's performance that could not be evaluated during the initial trial.
  - The ship conducted structural test firings of core weapon systems and basic air defense performance characterization events in June 2009.
  - In July 2009, the Navy directed their OTA to conduct a QRA on the operational capability of USS *Freedom* (LCS 1) for maritime security operations in support of a rapid early deployment. A deployment nearly two years early will delay developmental testing and the initial phase of IOT&E until after the ship returns.
  - In September 2009, developmental test events were conducted in surface warfare and air defense. The Navy installed the initial increment of the Surface Warfare (SUW Mission Package, including two 30 mm gun mission modules and mission package application software, conducted structural test firings of both 30 mm guns, and completed several basic surface gunnery events.
- LCS 2:
  - Builder's Trials commenced in July 2009. Main propulsion engine material problems have delayed completion until October 2009.
  - Acceptance trials are scheduled for late November 2009.
  - Delivery is now scheduled for December 18, 2009.
- In July and August 2009, the Navy conducted end-to-end developmental testing of selected Mine Countermeasures (MCM) Mission Package components, including the Remote Multi-Mission Vehicle with the AN/AQS-20A towed sonar and the Unmanned Surface Vessel with the Unmanned Surface Sweep System using a containerized Mission Package Portable Control System embarked in Research Vessel Athena.
- Funding constraints have delayed the Navy from completing the survivability assessments for LCS 1 and LCS 2 LFT&E until 2010.

## Assessment

- The proposed changes to acquisition will not alter the test and evaluation strategy. Ships of the unselected design will be fleet operational units and will undergo the same testing as those of the winning design.
- LCS 1:
  - Acceptance trial results assessed Deck and Weapons as unsatisfactory. Specific deficiencies include a non-standard anchor chain configuration, and combat system (COMBATSS-21) performance problems associated with the WBR-2000 passive Electronic Support Measure system, the TRS-3D radar, and the DORNA EO/IR gun fire control system.

- Analysis of the results of stability testing conducted in FY08 revealed that the ship will exceed limiting draft in the full load condition. This reduces the reserve buoyancy provided by compartments above the waterline and the ship's capability to withstand damage and heavy weather. This condition also renders the ship incapable of meeting the Navy's stability standard of withstanding flooding to 15 percent of the length along the waterline and could sink sooner than expected. The Navy intends to install external tanks to effectively lengthen the stern to increase buoyancy prior to early deployment and to modify the future hull design with a lengthened transom.
- Early fielding of lead ships in test remains consistent with recent Navy practice; e.g., USS *Virginia* (SSN 774) and USS *San Antonio* (LPD-17). As stipulated in Section 231 of the National Defense Authorization Act of 2007, an Early Fielding Report will be submitted.
- Although equipment performance issues delayed completion of the 30 mm gun structural test firings, results of those events and the core weapons structural test firings were satisfactory.
- Early air target tracking tests identified combat system performance deficiencies that will seriously degrade the ship's air defense capability unless corrected. Plans to repeat the tests with software upgrades were delayed by multiple TRS-3D radar power supply failures, the cause of which has not yet been identified.
- Completion of basic air defense performance characterization events has been delayed due to repeated TRS-3D radar power supply failures.
- LCS 2:
  - Builders trials were initially delayed due to reported leaks at the gas turbine shaft seals. More testing identified additional deficiencies related to the main propulsion diesel engines, thus further delaying completion of the trials until October 2009.
- MCM mission package end-to-end test objectives were met, but communication problems associated with the unmanned remotely controlled vehicles indicates more development of component systems is needed prior to fleet integration.
- LCS was designated by the Navy as a Level I survivability combatant ship, but neither design is expected to achieve the degree of shock hardening as required by the CDD. Shock hardening (ability to sustain a level of operations following an underwater explosive attack) is required for all mission critical systems, as required by a Level 1 survivability requirement. Only a few selected subsystems will be shock hardened, supporting only mobility to evacuate a threat area following a design-level shock event. Accordingly, the full, traditional rigor of Navy-mandated ship shock trials is not achievable,

due to the damage that would be sustained by the ship and its many non-shock-hardened subsystems.
- The LCS LFT&E program has been hampered by the Navy's lack of credible modeling and simulation tools for assessing the vulnerabilities of ships constructed to primarily commercial standards (American Bureau of Shipping Naval Vessel Rules and High Speed Naval Craft Code), particularly aluminum and non-traditional hull forms. Legacy LFT&E models were not developed for these non-traditional factors, nor have they been accredited for such use. These knowledge gaps undermine the credibility of the modeling and simulation, and increase the amount of surrogate testing required for an adequate LFT&E program.
- The LCS is not expected to be survivable in a hostile combat environment as evidenced by the limited shock hardened design and results of full scale testing of representative hull structures completed in December 2006.

**Recommendations**
- Status of Previous Recommendations. The Navy satisfactorily addressed all but three of the previous nine recommendations. Recommendations concerning a risk assessment on the adequacy of Level I survivability, detailed manning analyses to include mission package support, and solidifying the acquisition strategy for long-range planning still remain.
- FY09 Recommendations. The Navy should:
  1. Continue to address LCS deficiencies identified in Acceptance Trials and early developmental testing and incorporate appropriate modifications, especially in stability and the TRS-3D radar performance and integration with other combat system components.
  2. Codify another revised T&E strategy in a TEMP revision that provides for completion of IOT&E in LCS 1 following early fielding deployment and supports completion of IOT&E in LCS 2 and subsequent ships prior to operational deployment.
  3. Enlist the support of the T&E community to evaluate the performance of LCS 1 and the Navy's shore support organization during the ship's first operational deployment and compile appropriate lessons learned.
  4. Assess the testable shock severity achievable during ship shock trials for both LCS variants in order to predict the degree of shock hardness and survivability expected of these ships in a combat shock environment.
  5. Develop a robust LFT&E program to address knowledge gaps in assessing the vulnerabilities of ships constructed primarily to commercial standards including aluminum structures and non-traditional hull-forms, to include 57 mm gun system and Non-Line-of-Sight missile lethality.

# Littoral Combat Ship (LCS)

## Executive Summary
- The Navy restructured the Littoral Combat Ship (LCS) program to include two "Flight 0" ships (one of each seaframe design) and five "Flight 0+" ships (mix of seaframes under negotiation). The Navy's long-term strategy is to acquire 55 LCS; however, no final decision has been made beyond these first seven platforms.
- The Navy accepted delivery of LCS 1 in September 2008. Delivery of LCS 2 has slipped to the second half of FY09.
- The Integrated Product Team completed the Test and Evaluation Master Plan (TEMP) and it is in the review process.

**LCS 1**

**LCS 2**

## System
- The LCS is a new class of ship designed to operate in the shallow waters of the littorals where larger ships cannot maneuver as well. It can accommodate a variety of individual warfare systems (mission modules) assembled and integrated into interchangeable mission packages.
- There are two competing basic ship (seaframe) designs:
  - The Lockheed Martin design (LCS 1) is a steel monohull.
  - The General Dynamics design (LCS 2) is an aluminum tri-maran style hull.
- The designs propose different combat systems for self-defense against anti-ship cruise missiles.
- Both designs use combined diesel and gas turbine engines with waterjet propulsors.
- More than a dozen individual programs of record, involving sensor and weapon systems and other off-board vehicles, have been chosen to make up the individual mission modules. All but three are Acquisition Category (ACAT) II and ACAT III programs.
- The Navy plans to acquire a total of 55 LCS, but the mix of platforms is undecided.

## Mission
- The Maritime Component Commander can employ LCS to conduct Mine Warfare (MIW), Anti-Submarine Warfare (ASW), or Surface Warfare (SUW), based on the mission package fitted into the seaframe. Mission packages are designed to be interchangeable, allowing the Maritime Component Commander flexibility to reassign missions.

- Commanders can employ LCS in a maritime presence role regardless of the installed mission package based on capabilities inherent to the seaframe.
- The Navy can deploy LCS alone or in conjunction with other ships.

## Prime Contractors
- LCS 1: Lockheed Martin
- LCS 2: Bath Iron Works
        General Dynamics

## Activity
- LCS 1 completed acceptance trials on August 22, 2008. The Navy's Board of Inspection and Survey recommended that the Chief of Naval Operations accept delivery, provided that designated deficiencies were either corrected or waived.

- The Navy restructured the LCS program to include two Flight 0 ships (one of each seaframe design) and five Flight 0+ ships (mix of seaframes under negotiation). A Milestone

A-prime decision is expected to approve procurement and determine the mix of the five Flight 0+ ships.

- Although the Navy accepted delivery of LCS 1 in September 2008, LCS 2 has slipped to 3QFY09. Shipyard work will continue for several months after delivery.
- The Navy began IOT&E of the Organic Airborne Mine Countermeasures (OAMCM) variant of the MH-60S, which will deploy and operate Airborne Mine Countermeasure (AMCM) mission modules from LCS. These systems are part of the LCS Mine Countermeasures Mission Package. During the first operational test of the OAMCM MH-60S and the AN/AQS-20A towed sonar sensor, multiple problems associated with the deployment and retrieval of the AN/AQS-20A sensor caused the Program Office to de-certify the system, suspending the IOT&E pending investigation and remedial action.
- The Remote Mine-hunting System (RMS), another key element of the Mine Warfare Mission Package, conducted an operational assessment (OA) in September 2008 aboard USS *Bainbridge* (DDG 96). RMS IOT&E, originally scheduled for June 2007, has been postponed because of performance and reliability issues and may now occur in conjunction with LCS operational testing.
- Other mission systems in support of ASW and SUW modules are in various stages of developmental testing.
- The IOT&E strategy for the first of each of the two seaframes received concurrence from the Integrated Product Team and a final version of the TEMP is in coordination for approval. However, test planning beyond Flight 0+ is unfeasible until the Navy solidifies a future acquisition strategy.

## Assessment

- The LCS program endures a great deal of uncertainty due to the unknown mix of future ships and organizational complexity related to monitoring mission module test and development in addition to component integration with both seaframes.
- The IOT&E strategy is constructed to allow operational testing of both LCS seaframes with each mission package. Under the strategy, all three mission packages will be tested as spiral developments on both seaframes, and ship self-defense testing is integrated into the Navy's Ship Self-Defense Test and Evaluation Enterprise effort.
- LCS is designed to have a small crew, and the operational concept relies heavily on shore-based support. Navy plans for this support are still maturing. Shore-based support will be assessed during IOT&E.

## Recommendations

- Status of Previous Recommendations. The Navy satisfactorily addressed all but two of the previous eight recommendations. The remaining two recommendations merit additional emphasis.
- FY08 Recommendation.
  1. The Navy needs to solidify the LCS Acquisition Strategy to allow for realistic long-range planning. Program uncertainty has cascading effects on production and testing management.

# Littoral Combat Ship (LCS)

## Executive Summary
- The Navy is pursuing purchase of at least 15 baseline configuration or "Flight 0" ships through FY09, up from 13 reported in FY05.
- The Navy's Test and Evaluation Strategy is inappropriate for the proposed acquisition strategy.
- Early Operational Assessment reports indicate high-level risks in systems integration, manning, and survivability.

## System
- The Littoral Combat Ship (LCS) is a new class of ship designed to operate in the shallow waters of the littorals where larger ships cannot maneuver as well. It can accommodate a variety of individual warfare systems (mission modules) assembled and integrated into interchangeable mission packages.
- There are two competing basic ship (seaframe) designs:
  - The Lockheed Martin design is a steel monohull.
  - The General Dynamics design is an aluminum tri-maran style hull.
- The designs propose different combat systems for self-defense against anti-ship cruise missiles.
- Both designs use combined diesel and gas turbine engines with waterjet propulsors.
- More than a dozen individual programs of record, involving sensor and weapon systems and other off-board vehicles, have been chosen to make up the individual mission modules. All but three are Acquisition Category (ACAT) II and ACAT III programs.

## Mission
- The Maritime Component Commander can employ LCS to conduct Mine Warfare (MIW), Anti-Submarine Warfare,

or Surface Warfare, based on the mission package fitted into the seaframe. Mission packages are designed to be interchangeable, allowing the Maritime Component Commander flexibility to reassign missions.
- Commanders can employ LCS in a maritime presence role regardless of the installed mission package based on capabilities inherent to the seaframe.
- The Navy can deploy LCS alone or in conjunction with other ships.

## Activity
- No developmental or operational testing was conducted in 2007.
- In March 2007, the Navy announced that it was restructuring the LCS program because of significant cost growth. The revised acquisition plan reduced the number of Flight 0 ships to be acquired, included a "Fly-Off" between the two seaframe designs in 2009, and called for the start of Flight 1 ship acquisition in 2010. Flight 1 was to be based on the seaframe design selected during the Fly-Off, but would include a Common Combat System and Common Command, Control, Communications, Computers, and Intelligence Systems provided by the government. The revised acquisition plan also called for renegotiation of the contract for LCS 3.

Those negotiations were ultimately unsuccessful and the LCS 3 contract was terminated.
- In July 2007, the Navy announced its intention to amend the new acquisition strategy to retain the option of acquiring Flight 1 ships based on both seaframe designs.
- The first LCS Mission Package, a partial MIW Mission Package, was delivered at Naval Surface Warfare Center, Panama City, Florida, in September 2007.
- The Integrated Test Team continued to develop plans for LCS 1 and LCS 2 Post-Delivery Tests and Trials, developmental testing, and operational testing, which are now expected to commence in the fall of 2008.

- Commencement of the System Development and Demonstration Phase (Milestone B) has been postponed to 2008.

## Assessment
- The LCS program does not have an approved acquisition strategy that reflects the acquisition decisions announced during 2007. The multitude of program changes has delayed development of an appropriate test and evaluation strategy, and pending congressional action, appears likely to cause further program revisions.
- The Navy's citation of urgent operational need and stated intention to deploy LCS 1 and LCS 2 as early as possible threatens to compress the post delivery schedules for LCS 1 and LCS 2 and reduce the time available for critical tests and trials normally conducted on lead ships. These tests and trials include developmental testing, deficiency correction, signature measurements, sensor accuracy determination, and determination of operational effectiveness and suitability of the sea frames.
- Pending an approved acquisition strategy, DOT&E's intention is that IOT&E be conducted on LCS 1 and LCS 2 seaframes prior to fleet introduction even though only MIW Mission Packages will be available and those packages will be incomplete. This will provide the warfighters a system for which sea frame mission capability has been determined.
- Several phases of follow-on operational test and evaluation will be required to assess the operational effectiveness and operational suitability of the baseline (fully-capable) MIW, Anti-Submarine Warfare, and Surface Warfare mission packages.
- The lead Flight 1 ship should also undergo IOT&E before it is introduced into the fleet. If the Navy opts to acquire Flight 1 ships based on both seaframe designs, then IOT&E of both lead ships will be required.

## Recommendations
- Status of Previous Recommendations. The Navy fully addressed two of eight prior recommendations and is making progress on two others. The Navy still needs to complete the risk assessment to confirm that Level I survivability is sufficient for a class of small combatants (FY05). It also must continue its analysis to determine the minimum number of MIW mission module programs of record that will be sufficient to provide genuine MIW capability (FY05). Additionally, the Navy must revise the test and evaluation strategy to conduct IOT&E on the lead ships (seaframes) of each design (FY06). It must also revise LCS lead ship post delivery schedules to include test events such as signature measurement, analysis of performance characteristics, and sensor accuracy to determine basic performance baselines before deployment (FY06). Finally, the Navy must continue detailed manning analyses to determine the appropriate number of personnel necessary to man LCS, with mission packages, given its level of automation and systems integration (FY06).
- FY07 Recommendations. None.

# Littoral Combat Ship (LCS)

## Executive Summary
- The Navy is pursuing purchase of 13 Flight 0 ships instead of the original four.
- The Navy should pay particular attention to the crew size and manning policies to ensure they meet Littoral Combat Ship (LCS) needs.
- The LCS is designed to meet only Level 1 (minimal) survivability standards. This is the standard for logistics ships. Other combatant ships meet Level II standards.

## System
- The LCS is a new class of ship designed to accommodate a variety of individual warfare systems (mission modules) assembled and integrated into interchangeable Mission Packages (MPs).
- There are two different basic ship (seaframe) designs, one each from the Lockheed-Martin and General Dynamics teams.
  - Lockheed-Martin design is a steel monohull.
  - General Dynamics design is an aluminum tri-maran.
- Both designs use combined diesel and gas turbine engines with waterjet propulsors.
- More than a dozen individual program of record sensor and weapon systems along with other off-board vehicles have been chosen to be LCS mission modules.

- The designs propose different combat systems for self-defense against anti-ship cruise missiles.

## Mission
- The Maritime Component Commander can employ LCS to conduct focused missions of either Mine Warfare, Anti-Submarine Warfare, or Surface Warfare, based on the MP fitted into the seaframe. MPs are designed to be interchangeable allowing the Maritime Component Commander flexibility to reassign missions.
- LCS can be employed in a maritime presence role regardless of the MP based on capabilities inherent to the seaframe.
- LCS can be deployed alone or in company of other ships.

## Activity
- The Navy conducted an Early Operational Assessment (EOA) of the Lockheed-Martin Flight 0 LCS ship design and the Mine Warfare MP from March 2005 to June 2005 under a DOT&E-approved test plan. The EOA report was issued on September 6, 2005.
- The LCS program conducted technology risk reduction activities using Engineering Development Models of systems planned for inclusion into the Mine Warfare MP. Use of surrogate platforms such as High-Speed Vessel 2 and Sea Fighter (formerly called X Craft) to assist in mission module development continues.
- The Lockheed-Martin and General Dynamics teams have both conducted underwater explosion testing of sample materials as part of the Live Fire testing program.

## Assessment
The EOA testing was adequate for this stage of development. It highlighted several high-risk areas for the Lockheed-Martin design with the Mine Warfare MP, including:
- Inadequate integration of several combat system elements with the COMBATTS-21 combat management system. This is an issue due to the small number of personnel that

will be assigned. Automation will be necessary to prevent watchstander overload.
- Unknown performance capability of the chosen surface and air search radar in a littoral environment.
- Execution of the Mine Warfare mission will depend on several Acquisition Category II and lower programs, the schedules of which do not appear well synchronized with the first seaframes. This may preclude testing a viable Mine Warfare capability until the later hulls.
- Integrated Logistic Support planning is inadequate for both the seaframe and Mine Warfare MP.
- Personnel safety concerns were identified in analysis of equipment designed for launch/recovery and control of off-board vehicles.
- The EOA report also raised concerns that planned LCS crew size may be inadequate to support maintenance and operation of the seaframe, aviation assets, and the Mine Warfare MP. Projected manning is 40 personnel for the seaframe, 20 for the aviation detachment, and 15 for the MP (75 total). There will be very little extra capacity for personnel beyond the 75 projected. No specific analysis was presented to confirm that

75 is the right number of personnel rather than the desired number.

The Navy is considering design trade-off studies to assess options that preserve or increase survivability while remaining at or below the planned unit cost of $220 Million. LCS is currently designed to have only Level 1 (minimal) survivability. This is the standard for logistics ships. Other combatant ships meet Level II standards.

DOT&E approved a Test and Evaluation Strategy document for LCS based on a planned procurement of four (two Lockheed-Martin and two General Dynamics) Flight 0 ships. The Navy is now planning to buy as many as 13 Flight 0 ships. This change in acquisition strategy requires reevaluation of OT&E and LFT&E plans.

The Navy has not identified all of the necessary instrumented shallow water testing ranges and facilities needed to evaluate LCS and support training.

### Recommendations
The Navy should:
1. Reassess the level of combat system integration to be sure missions can be accomplished with a small number of watchstanders. Closely evaluate personnel training and assignment policies to be sure they will support keeping appropriately trained people available for LCS. Conduct appropriate analysis to ensure 75 is in fact the appropriate number of personnel necessary to accomplish LCS missions.
2. Examine ashore support infrastructure to ensure its consonance with LCS manning policies; of particular concern is proper maintenance support.
3. Assess the risks to be sure Level 1 survivability is sufficient for a 13-ship class of small combatants.
4. Perform analysis to determine the minimum number of the various Mine Warfare mission module program of records that will be sufficient to provide genuine Mine Warfare capability.
5. Identify and resource all necessary instrumented shallow water testing ranges and facilities.

# Littoral Combat Ship (LCS) Characteristics Task Force
## Final Report
## 31 July 2002

CDR Carl Carlson
Bradd C. Hayes
Hank Kamradt
with
Gregg Hoffman

# Report Documentation Page

*Form Approved*
*OMB No. 0704-0188*

| 1. REPORT DATE **31 JUL 2002** | 2. REPORT TYPE | 3. DATES COVERED **-** |
|---|---|---|
| 4. TITLE AND SUBTITLE **Littoral Combat Ship (LCS) Characteristics Task Force** | | 5a. CONTRACT NUMBER |
| | | 5b. GRANT NUMBER |
| | | 5c. PROGRAM ELEMENT NUMBER |
| 6. AUTHOR(S) | | 5d. PROJECT NUMBER |
| | | 5e. TASK NUMBER |
| | | 5f. WORK UNIT NUMBER |
| 7. PERFORMING ORGANIZATION NAME(S) AND ADDRESS(ES) **Naval War College,Newport ,RI,02841** | | 8. PERFORMING ORGANIZATION REPORT NUMBER |
| 9. SPONSORING/MONITORING AGENCY NAME(S) AND ADDRESS(ES) | | 10. SPONSOR/MONITOR'S ACRONYM(S) |
| | | 11. SPONSOR/MONITOR'S REPORT NUMBER(S) |

**12. DISTRIBUTION/AVAILABILITY STATEMENT**
**Approved for public release; distribution unlimited**

**13. SUPPLEMENTARY NOTES**
**The original document contains color images.**

**14. ABSTRACT**
**see report**

**15. SUBJECT TERMS**

| 16. SECURITY CLASSIFICATION OF: | | | 17. LIMITATION OF ABSTRACT | 18. NUMBER OF PAGES **71** | 19a. NAME OF RESPONSIBLE PERSON |
|---|---|---|---|---|---|
| a. REPORT **unclassified** | b. ABSTRACT **unclassified** | c. THIS PAGE **unclassified** | | | |

**Littoral Combat Ship (LCS)**
**Characteristics Task Force**
**Final Report**
**31 July 2002**

CDR Carl Carlson
Bradd C. Hayes
Hank Kamradt

with

Gregory Hoffman

## INTRODUCTION

### Tasking

In December 2001, the Navy Staff's Director, Surface Warfare (N76), requested the Naval War College's assistance in defining the characteristics that should be used and the technology opportunities available when constructing a littoral combat ship (LCS) — the smallest member of a new family of ships being developed by the Navy. The tasking was driven by an ambitious schedule that precluded a zero-based study; therefore, the Naval War College assembled a multi-disciplinary team of subject matter experts to examine current and proposed programs from which they gleaned the most promising ideas. The process began with a core group that met in Newport, RI, in March 2002. This group approved characteristic guidelines and constraints (detailed below) and selected primary and secondary missions that littoral combat ship variants should perform. The initial workshop was followed by a series of workshops that drilled more deeply into the characteristics that the LCS should possess for each mission area. An integration effort took the data gleaned from these workshops and merged them into options presented in a draft report. A final LCS characteristics integration workshop was held 26-27 June 2002 during which the draft report was reviewed and options refined. Results of that workshop are incorporated into this report.

Task force members were asked to take an "open and honest" look at all options. They found, however, that the proverbial "clean sheet of paper" they were given was not entirely free of fingerprints and more were added as the process advanced. Although we were aware of all the opinions and options on LCS that were being discussed, including at the time of the integration workshop a list of characteristics purportedly for the Flight 0/Baseline 0 LCS (see Appendix A), we continued to operate in as honest and independent a manner as we could. Even before receiving the Baseline/Flight 0 characteristics list, participants

> **LCS is:**
> a practical, significantly smaller surface combatant. (N76)
> ... fast, stealthy, low-cost ... little punch individually (*Norfolk Virginian-Pilot*)
> ... a practical warship with evolutionary features. (*Inside the Navy*)
> ... according to senior Navy officials, many agree that LCS should be a 2,000-ton to 2,500 ton corvette-sized ship. (*Jane's Defence Weekly*)
> ... LCS will have three primary missions – mine countermeasures, antisubmarine warfare, and countering swarms of small combatants. (VCNO)

1

understood that some options were unavailable to them. Nevertheless, they pressed forward and examined a broad array of options. One constraint participants knew would not change was affordability.

Prior to the initial workshop the Commander, Naval Surface Forces Pacific, released a message providing his thoughts about the littoral combat ship. His representative was provided an opportunity to discuss the message early in the March 2002 workshop and it served as a straw man concept during discussions. The message can be found at Appendix B.

The mission areas selected during this initial conference were then explored more deeply in follow-on workshops. The tasks proposed and prioritized by mission area workshop participants are found in Appendix C. The principal take-aways from these workshops are found in Appendix. D.

**Multiple options examined**

It became abundantly clear as the workshops progressed that no single LCS concept was going to satisfy everyone who had a dog in the fight. Three distinct camps emerged during the workshops with each camp supporting a different, but highly credible vision of what the LCS should be. Supporting the first variant are those who continue to see the LCS as a multipurpose ship that can be used to carry unmanned (often autonomous) warfighting equipment into the theater and then rely its speed to move out of harm's way. Under this concept, the LCS is the sea base for deployed (that is, offboard) sensors and weapon systems. Proponents of this concept envision few, if any, organic weapons systems and sensors carried on the ship. They point to the experimental High Speed Vessel (HSV) as a good first step approximation of the ship. We call this "Type A" LCS.

Others see the LCS as a stealthy, fast, maneuverable, but smaller than the other variants, vessel that can go toe-to-toe with littoral challenges. Proponents of this option favor a ship that carries a very small crew (30 to 40 personnel), no helicopter detachment, and fly-in modules which are accompanied by the crew to man them. We call this "Type B" LCS.

Finally, there are those favoring a larger-sized ship that possesses some of the characteristics of both Types A and B, but with more robust indigenous capabilities than either of those concepts envision. This group favors the LCS carrying an organic helicopter, a small multipurpose modular launcher, a medium/small caliber gun, an active/passive sonar (probably towed), a multi-function type radar, and unmanned systems as they become available. We call this "Type C" LCS.

Support for each of these types remained firm, even during the final integration workshop. As shown in the attached data, participants at the final workshop confirmed what we found during the mission area workshops; namely, the "Type C" LCS is the preferred choice if only a single variant is going to be pursued. This is because Type C has more capability and fewer endurance, payload, and sustainability challenges than the other two types. In addition, Type A and, to a lesser extent, Type B are primarily conceived to support systems that are currently unavailable. Type C would provide acceptable near-term (transitional) capabilities as well as a platform designed with transformation and future growth in mind. Participants referred to it as "the 80 percent solution."

The following data was gathered when participants were asked to rank order LCS variants if one, two, or all three were pursued. Nearly 60 percent of the participants would first pursue a Type C variant, while Types A and B were favored by approximately 20 percent of participants as their first choice. Type A might have been shortchanged in the vote since we had labeled it a "truck" and some participants argued as such it should not even be considered an LCS variant, but a logistics ship. Arguments to the contrary were made, but labels are powerful. We explained that the term "truck" was descriptive and not meant to be pejorative.

**Rank Sum**

| | |
|-----|-----------|
| **88** | 1. Type C |
| **68** | 2. Type B |
| **60** | 3. Type A |

**Number of Votes in Each Rating**

| | 1st Choice | 2nd Choice | 3rd Choice | Mean | STD |
|------------|-----------|-----------|-----------|------|------|
| 1. Type C -- | 21 | 10 | 5 | 1.56 | 0.73 |
| 2. Type B -- | 7 | 18 | 11 | 2.11 | 0.71 |
| 3. Type A -- | 8 | 8 | 20 | 2.33 | 0.83 |

If designing a small capable ship were not difficult enough, the missions that workshop participants assigned to the LCS (as discussed below) involve tasks that have historically proven immensely challenging to the Navy. These challenges remain immense and trying to tackle all of them with a single type of ship, especially a very small ship, stretches credulity — even with new technologies. Based on LCS mission characteristics, we believe there is considerable merit in continuing to consider all three types of LCS for the following reasons: Type A can be fielded quickly and operating it can help answer a lot of questions about the value of speed in mission performance and the benefits or drawbacks of alternative hull forms. Type B would primarily be used to support special operations, near-shore surface warfare, and maritime intercept operations — missions where stealth, small size, and speed pay particularly high dividends. Type C gives the Navy a ship that can bolster fleet end strength (one of the CNO's goals) and work with or independent of battle groups. We believe that LCS Type C will become a real workhorse of the future Navy and the focal point of coalition littoral operations.

Even though we continued to see three separate variants described during the integration workshop, we were not supported by participants in our conclusion that all three variants should be pursued. They voted (as shown below) to recommend pursuing two variants vice three (dropping Type A for the reasons noted above). Participants also believed the Navy would find it politically infeasible to pursue all three variants. We asked participants to rank order their preferred course of action: one ship, two ships, or three ships. As can be seen, all participants made pursuing two variants either their first or second choice.

| Number of variants to pursue | 1st Choice | 2nd Choice | 3rd Choice |
|---|---|---|---|
| Two ships | 17 | 19 | 0 |
| Single ship | 14 | 12 | 10 |
| Three ships | 5 | 5 | 26 |

The remainder of this study reports the findings of the initial, mission area, and integration workshops.

## INITIAL WORKSHOP

In order to stimulate thinking, participants at the March 2002 workshop were asked four questions that examined the reasons the littoral combat ship program sprang to life.

*Question 1. Is the littoral combat ship a mission/capabilities focused frigate or corvette-sized ship optimized for littoral environments?*

The simple answer to this question is yes. The task force was formed to help the Navy design a ship. The question is why? The Chief of Naval operations has established the goal of a 375-ship fleet — approximately 100 more than current ship plans support. Without a small, affordable ship that 375 figure is unreachable. As we understood the tasking, the CNO does not want 375 ships that are so small they are incapable of contributing to the Navy's forward presence mission, nor so lacking in capability that they must be kept from harm's way. The bottom line is that the littoral combat ship must help the Navy increase its force structure and be capable of satisfying some forward presence requirements.

*Question 2. Is the littoral combat ship a very small displacement, advanced technology vessel?*

If the answer to question one is yes, then the answer to this question must be no. Unfortunately, the matter is not that simple. The littoral combat ship became the darling of Congressional and military reformers because they were swayed by Vice Admiral (ret.) Arthur Cebrowski's arguments in favor of the *Streetfighter* concept, which envisioned a small, fast, networked vessel that could operate effectively in the littorals. They believe that a ship, in order to be transformational, must look, move, and act very differently than ships of the past — and, most importantly, it must be fast. The CNO is on record favoring a minimum 50-knot ship. Regardless of the size of the LCS, it must satisfy those who will only believe the Navy is transforming when they see it sail something radically new. That notion segues into the next question.

4

*Question 3. Is the littoral combat ship an answer looking for a question?*

Since the littoral combat ship was being discussed before a mission for it was determined, some would answer this question in the affirmative. LCS may be a way to scratch the itch of military reformers in order to silence critics who insist the Navy has failed to develop a transformational road map, but that begs the question of why the Navy must transform. Surely the expeditionary nature of the naval service shouldn't change; after all, the Army and Air Force are being lauded for becoming more expeditionary. On the other hand, real operational shortfalls associated with littoral warfare exist in the current force, and one compelling alternative to deal with those gaps is to explore the potential of a new ship designed for littoral conditions.

*Question 4. Is the littoral combat ship a set of access capabilities that can be addressed by several types of surface ships/vessels, or by platforms other than ships?*

There is a growing consensus that operational shortfalls do exist. That does not mean, however, that answering this question affirmatively requires one to answer question one negatively — they are not mutually exclusive. In fact, one of the keys to keeping LCS costs down will be to leverage its capabilities by exploiting weapons and sensors carried by other ships or platforms (including unmanned systems carried on the LCS).

Following the philosophical discussion engendered by these questions, participants were exposed to an array of program options and operational alternatives to help them understand what missions might prove practical for such a ship. Although several participants wanted to jump directly to mission area discussions, workshop facilitators felt that exposing them to operational alternatives would make the mission discussion richer and broader.

HOW MANY PROGRAMS SHOULD THE NAVY PURSUE?

Participants were asked to considered the possibility that more than a single variant should be pursued. We asked this question because there were three prominent concepts of operation being pushed by various factions in the Navy. Although three options remained prominent throughout the process, the options changed significantly as the various workshop discussions proceeded. *The options presented at the initial workshop were not the same options presented at the integration workshop.*

*Option 1. Single ship.*

A single ship option suits the N76 tasking, but if operational shortfalls are a real driver for the program, a single ship might not provide the Navy with the flexibility and capability that it needs. This can be somewhat mitigated by ensuring the ship is not a single-mission ship. The more missions a ship can sequentially perform, however, the larger its size. Size, in turn, affects speed, and the larger the ship the more difficult it becomes to generate a high top end velocity. Size also affects cost. The pressure was obviously to keep the ship small.

*Option 2. Two ships.*

There are honest differences of opinion about how the LCS should operate. Some people expect it to enter the littoral and remain there to fight. Others believe it should only dash in to perform a quick mission — such as dropping sensors or offloading special forces — and then dashing quickly back to a safe distance. One group favoring this concept of operations sees the LCS operating much as an aircraft operates off of a carrier; even changing crews after each mission if required. The "stay and fight" and "dash in/dash out" visions of LCS are probably mutually exclusive and satisfying both requires the development two different ships.

*Option 3. Family of ships.*

Critics of a small craft approach trumpet the past challenges the Navy has confronted when trying to keep ships like PHMs and MCHs forward deployed (or even homeported overseas). Some believe that a scheme involving a large LHA-type ship that carries a number of different platforms is the best way to overcome current operational shortfalls, avoid past challenges that confront small vessels, and still demonstrate a commitment to transformation. A scheme based on a so-called "mother ship" fails, because of cost, to satisfy the CNO's desire to increase force structure significantly. As a result, this concept was quickly replaced by a concept favoring a ship based on the experimental High Speed Vessel.

As the initial workshop proceeded, there was a growing sense that a single ship-type would have a difficult time satisfying all operational requirements. This question, therefore, remains an open issue. Many of the questions surrounding a single ship-type, especially if it is a small ship, involve the special logistics support it would require and/or the need for overseas ports and all that entails. These issues will be discussed later in the report.

WHAT GUIDELINES SHOULD DIRECT MISSION AREA WORKSHOPS?

Participants were presented with a series of macro guidelines that could be used to start the narrowing process. Some participants bristled that these guidelines were considered before the question of what missions the LCS should perform. The guidelines were designed to provoke discussion as opposed to representing a *fait accompli* decision about ship design. As a result some were changed during the course of the discussion before being approved. In order to determine a sense of agreement, participants were asked to rate their feelings on a five-point scale from strongly agree to strongly disagree (with strongly agree rating a 5 and strongly disagree rating a 1). Results are shown below. The approved guidelines were used during all subsequent workshops and, as will be evident from the results of the integration workshop discussed later, were followed.

*Guideline 1. The ship must be capable of networking with other platforms and sensors.*

The Navy has declared that network-centric warfare is the transformational touchstone that guides all new system acquisitions. Although there was strong agreement that networking was the *sine qua non* of the littoral combat ship, there was a sharp division between those who believed it must be fully networked to all systems and those who believed it only needs to be connected in areas directly affecting its mission performance. There was agreement that the LCS must be both a user and a provider of sensor data.

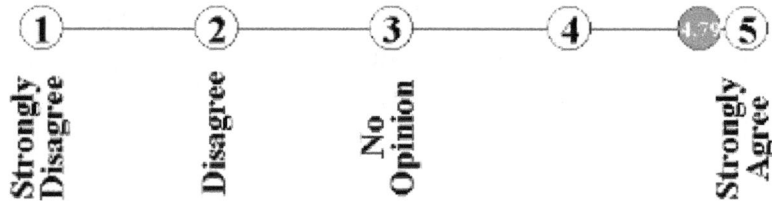

As the vote demonstrates, there was unanimity that mission area workshops needed to consider how networking could be used to conduct LCS missions.

*Guideline 2. The ship must be useful across the spectrum of conflict.*

The rationale behind this guideline is the belief that the ship must play an integrated role in both the Navy's combat and peacetime operational concepts in order to maximize its value to the service and nation. Although the ship is being designed to address operational combat shortfalls, most of its service life will be spent supporting peacetime operations. Even though participants agreed with this statement, they didn't want this statement to imply that the ship should be a jack-of-all-trades. They believed it should be able to conduct peacetime exercises, maritime intercept operations and similar missions in times of tension, as well as carry out its wartime roles.

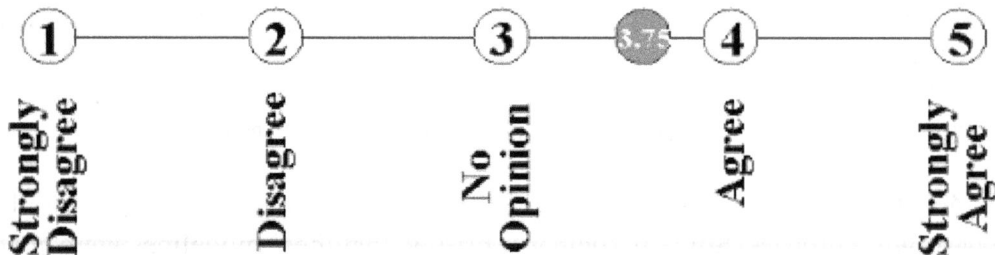

The vote shows approval, but greater disagreement, than with the first guideline. Most of those who disagreed with the statement were concerned with the term "spectrum of conflict" — believing it implied the LCS would be a general rather than a specialized combatant, thus dramatically increasing its size and cost. Mission area workshop participants were advised of this concern and were admonished to concentrate on combat requirements.

*Guideline 3. The ship must be able to contribute to sustained forward naval presence.*

Most participants agreed that unless the LCS can take its place in the deployment rotation, it becomes a burden to the rest of the fleet rather than a force multiplier. It also fails to achieve the real purpose behind the CNO's objective of having a 375-ship fleet. Those who didn't believe that the LCS must be capable of deploying with the battle group argued that it could be stationed forward. Appendix A indicates that the Navy staff believes the ship should be able to remain forward for up to three years.

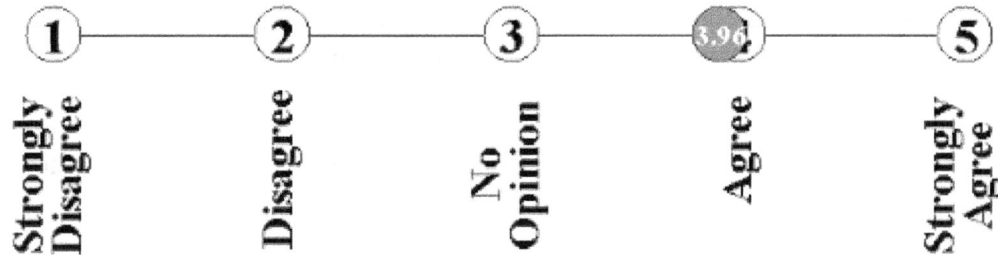

| (1) | (2) | (3) | (3.96) | (5) |
|---|---|---|---|---|
| Strongly Disagree | Disagree | No Opinion | Agree | Strongly Agree |

The vote shows that there was good agreement that the LCS must contribute to the Navy's forward presence mission.

*Guideline 4. The littoral combat ship logistics support, especially unique requirements, must be included in each mission area discussion.*

Many small ship concepts on the table advertise they are self-deployable. Physics, however, undermines the rhetoric. Very small ships can deploy, but require frequent refueling and carry few if any weapons. A ship reporting on station with neither fuel nor weapons, and that requires frequent servicing (and maybe even a dedicated support ship), is more of a burden than an asset on already stretched support forces. Nevertheless, if the information in Appendix A is accurate, the Flight 0 ships are expected to deploy without a payload, making logistics support a serious question. Most participants believed a smaller LCS would require special handling (including special support ships or overseas bases) in order make it as flexible and sustainable as it will need to be.

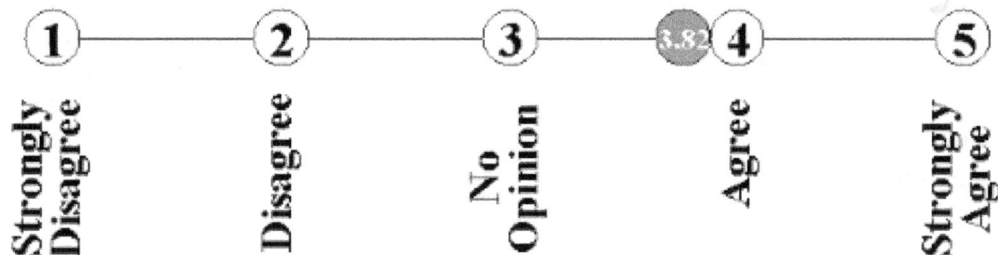

| (1) | (2) | (3) | (3.82)(4) | (5) |
|---|---|---|---|---|
| Strongly Disagree | Disagree | No Opinion | Agree | Strongly Agree |

Participants eventually fell into two camps, each supporting a different size of ship. Hence, it was not surprising that those supporting a smaller ship would argue against factors that undermine their favored position. They insisted that if a small LCS was the right answer, then investing in an appropriate logistics train to support it was also the right answer. Since the N76 representative had indicated in his opening remarks that a separate class of support ship was not in the offing, participants agreed eventually that logistics were an important challenge for further discussion.

*Guideline 5. The ship should be capable of operating manned vertical lift aircraft.*

Both mission requirements and common sense underpin this principle. Vertical lift aircraft can extend surface ship sensor and weapons reach as well as facilitate at-sea support. Originally, this guideline was limited to helicopters, but participants didn't want to begin with any restrictions on later discussions. As the workshop progressed, it became clear that most participants believed the LCS should handle aircraft up to the size of H-60 helicopters (both Army and Navy). There was divergence, however, about whether it should be a lily pad or capable of supporting a detachment. Those who favored the former capability did so with the understanding that being a lily pad meant more than simply landing helicopters for refueling.

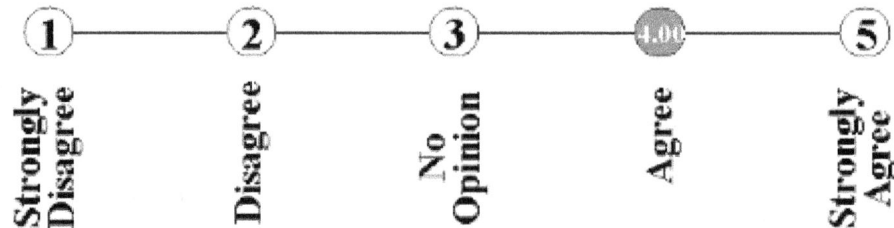

1 —— 2 —— 3 —— 4.00 —— 5

Strongly Disagree | Disagree | No Opinion | Agree | Strongly Agree

Participants, although agreeing on this guideline, didn't vote on the issue of whether the ship should have a hangar. Most felt there were many good reasons for having a hangar — from facilitating reduced radar signatures to protecting aircraft from salt spray and corrosion during transits. Some felt that restricting the discussion to a topside hangar was inappropriate, believing the ship might be better using an elevator and mission deck to achieve the same ends.

*Guideline 6. The ship should operate with optimized or reduced manning.*

This guideline provoked sharp debate about the benefits and risks of reduced manning. Manpower costs are generally the largest lifecycle costs associated with ships. Thus, reducing manpower makes great sense. Nevertheless, reduced manpower generates new challenges, only some of which can be solved by automation. Again and again issues of peripheral duties (such as launching and recovering unmanned vehicles, hotel services, damage control, and boarding parties) as well as crew rest, mission fatigue, and endurance were raised. Those favoring reduced manning believed LCS must be highly automated, and that the core crew must be augmented by appropriate "mission crews," a concept we discuss later in this report. Those favoring an optimized/larger crew appreciated the flexibility and sustainability a larger crew brings.

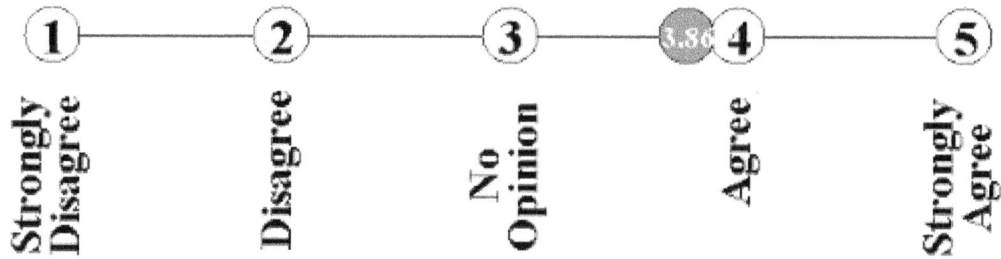

Although reduced manning is one of the imperatives for the littoral combat ship, the vote reflects that participants remain sensitive to the risks associated with smaller crews.

*Guideline 7. The ship should use open architecture and modularity.*

Ships (such as aircraft carriers) and aircraft (such as the B-52) that have demonstrated extremely long, yet useful, service lives have taken advantage of open architecture (that is, they have remained useful because they have, with modest modification, remained capable of carrying modernized weapons systems). Service life (and perhaps) flexibility can also be improved using modular techniques. Participants agreed that open architecture is a goal worth pursuing. There was much more debate about the benefits of modularity. Strong support was expressed for modular ideas involving vertical launch systems, manned and unmanned vehicles, but much less support was offered for conex box (containerized) modular concepts because of cost, storage, maintenance, forward logistics and training challenges.

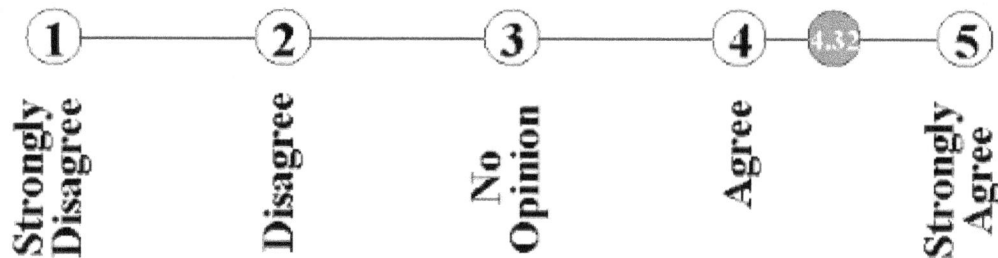

Because most participants agreed that open architecture was worth pursuing and that modularity could be achieved through manned and unmanned systems as well as weapons systems that can perform more than one mission (such as the vertical launch system), they showed strong approval for this guideline.

*Guideline 8. The ship should be capable of launching, recovering, and operating manned, unmanned, and autonomous vehicles.*

ASW, mine detection & clearance, and intelligence collection will increasingly depend on unmanned vehicles and offboard sensors. Both modularity and flexibility, as noted above, are enhanced with this capability. Originally this guideline addressed only unmanned systems. Special forces representatives reminded participants that they use some small manned vehicles (like jet skis and rigid hull inflatable boats) to support their

10

missions. A lot of participants believed unmanned vehicles would be the heart of the LCS system. Nevertheless, there was a big concern about when such vehicles would be ready for the fleet, leading to a discussion of a phased or evolutionary LCS design approach. They were also concerned how a drastically reduced crew would be able to launch and recover some of the unmanned vehicles that people are envisioning.

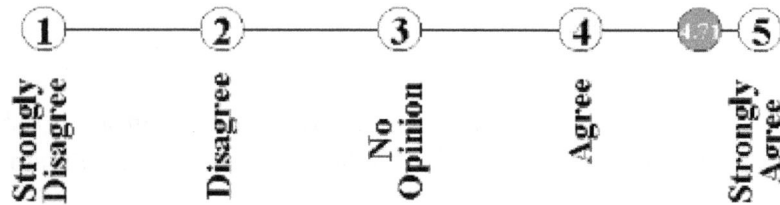

The vote shows the high degree of consensus achieved by participants on this subject. This was a strong endorsement for the Navy to move ahead as quickly as possible with unmanned vehicle programs that could be candidates for LCS.

*Guideline 9. The ship should have core, organic self-defense capabilities.*

This guideline was added during the first workshop. Participants agreed that you couldn't send a ship and its crew in harm's way and not provide them with some capability for self-defense. The level of this capability, however, was an issue. Most agreed that kinetic self-defense weapons are required while a few argued that stealth and speed should be its primary self-defense capabilities.

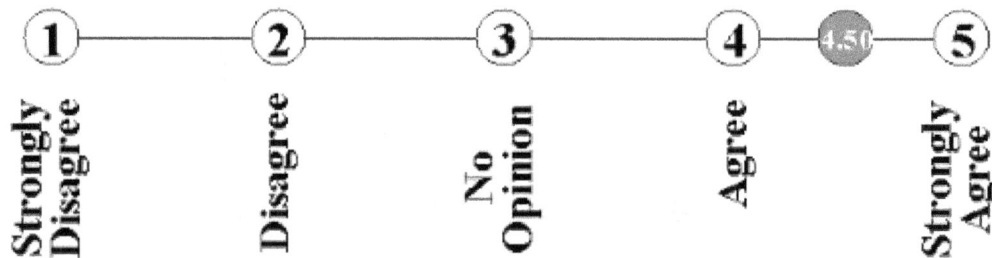

Strong support for this guideline was unsurprising, even though the value of speed and stealth as primary self-defense systems was debated. Those who favored kinetic systems pointed out that the LCS was being designed to operate in areas of high coastal traffic and anyone with good eyesight and a cell phone could counter the most expensive stealth designs available, while speed alone is of little help against a cruise missile. Mission area workshop participants were asked to consider weapons systems that could perform both mission and self-defense roles, thus achieving a synergism and affordability in line with the design philosophy.

FOR WHICH MISSION AREAS SHOULD THE LCS BE DESIGNED?

By the time participants were provided the opportunity to discuss mission areas, they had taken part in rich give-and-take discussions about the ship and the philosophy behind it.

To stimulate mission area discussions, they were given a list of missions that had been proposed in news articles and concept briefings.

- Assured Access to the Littoral
  - Mine Warfare
  - Prosecution of Small Boats
  - Prosecution of Diesel Submarines
  - Prosecution of Air and Cruise Missiles
  - Deployment of Expeditionary Sensor Grid
- Support of Special Warfare
  - Local Fire Support/ASUW
  - Insertion/Extraction/Resupply of SOF
  - Information Operations
- Presence Operations
  - MIO, NEO, Exercises, Force Protection
- Homeland Defense
  - Dominant maritime awareness
  - Air and Sea interdiction

An in-depth discussion about each area (and others proposed by participants) resulted in the selection of four primary missions and two secondary missions.

*Primary missions*

As the following vote demonstrates, there was overwhelming agreement that prosecution of small boats, mine countermeasure warfare, littoral anti-submarine warfare, and intelligence, surveillance, & reconnaissance should be primary missions for the LCS.

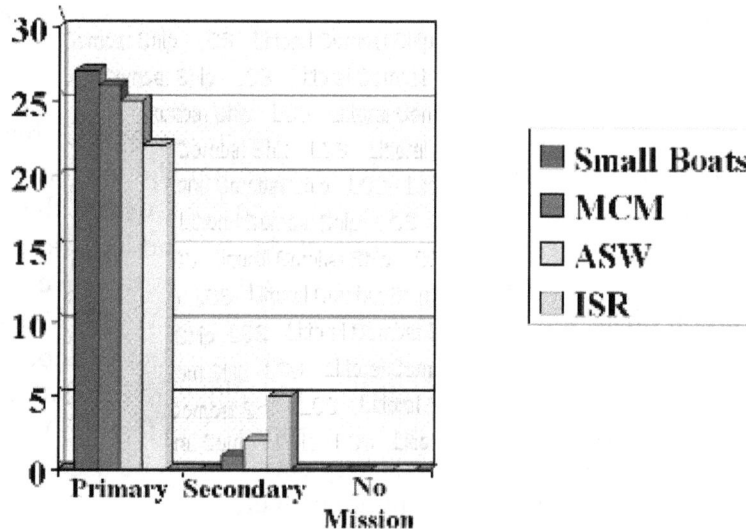

There was strong consensus (90% agreement) that homeland defense (primarily the ability to conduct maritime interception operations) and special operations support should be secondary missions for the LCS. Nine other missions were considered, but garnered too little support for further consideration. Those missions included: environmental data collection, logistics lily pad, anti-air and anti-cruise missile prosecution, unconventional warfare (working with indigenous special forces), counter-drug & law enforcement, area force protection, non-combatant evacuation operations, humanitarian assistance, and offensive mining. Some of these missions were rejected as too ambitious for the LCS (such as strike and naval surface fire support). Others were rejected because the LCS could assist in their execution (such as humanitarian assistance and NEO), but needn't have its design altered specifically to conduct them.

PRELIMINARY NARROWING OF LCS CHARACTERISTICS

As a result of the discussions surrounding approval of the guidelines and selection of mission areas, a preliminary narrowing of LCS characteristics was possible. These results were briefed to N76 following the initial workshop. The ship should be designed to support:

- Four primary missions identified (see above)
- Two secondary missions identified (see above)
- Maximum networking
- Open architecture
- Some modularity

- Optimized manning
- Battle group deployments
- Helicopter operations
- Some organic self-defense
- Unmanned and manned vehicles

These categories narrowed follow-on discussions, but much detail was left to be worked out during the mission area and integration workshops. For example, the decision that the LCS will be air capable doesn't answer the question about whether the ship will support lily pad or organic detachment operations. As noted earlier, three groups emerged during these discussions — one supporting a concept that relied almost entirely on offboard sensors and weapons we call "Type A," one supporting a much smaller ship we call "Type B," and the last supporting a larger ship we call "Type C." The following table shows the differences between the three concepts.

As the mission area workshops progressed, support for the Type C ship increased, but support for the other concepts never completely evaporated. One reason Type C gained increasing support was that it became more and more obvious that the size limitations of Type B would adversely affect mission accomplishment and logistics support, and that Type A was dependent on systems still unavailable if it was to move beyond logistics missions and accomplish war fighting missions such as ASW and MCM. Having said that, there was growing support for the idea that, to the extent possible, the LCS's capabilities should be contained in the vehicles it deploys, rather than in hardwired, organic systems. A concomitant benefit of this approach is that the vehicles developed for use by the LCS, and the mission payloads they carry, could be used from almost any platform — helping create, in effect, a modular fleet.

| | Type A | Type B | Type C |
|---|---|---|---|
| Deployability | Deployable in support of the battle group | Deployable when accompanied by battle group | Deployable independent of battle group |
| Endurance | Range more important than endurance | Capable of short (<week) independent operations | Capable of lengthy (>month) independent operations |
| Helicopter ops | Supports lily pad/detachment ops | Supports lily pad operations | Supports helicopter detachment |
| Mission capability | Lift, support OOV mission | Single-mission | Multi-mission (sequentially) |
| UV operations | Complete reliance on unmanned vehicles | Controls unmanned vehicles | Supports & Operates unmanned vehicles |
| Logistics | Could be part of new logistics framework | New logistics framework required | Normal logistics support |
| Manning | Minimum manning | Reduced manning | Optimal manning |
| Concept of ops | Dashes in/out of littoral | Dashes in/out of littoral | Operates in littoral |
| Connectivity | Fully netted | Mission netted | Fully netted |
| Modularity | RO/RO modular | Mostly modular (single mission or module) | Highly modular (open architecture) |
| Stealth | Reduced signatures | Stealthy | Low signatures |
| Speed | High speed | Very high speed | High speed |

**Roles and missions.**

As noted at the beginning of this report, March 2002 workshop participants decided that the Littoral Combat Ship should be designed for four primary missions (littoral ASW, intelligence preparation of the battlefield (ISR), MCM, and small boat prosecution) and two secondary missions (homeland defense/maritime intercept operations and special operations support). These missions coincided fairly well with SURFPAC's straw man proposal (Appendix B). The next portion of this report parses the SURFPAC message in order to compare and contrast it with our findings.

*Littoral ASW.*

> *"USV/UUV's emphasizing acoustic modular payloads such as side-scan and high-frequency active sonars to detect ... low doppler, near bottom subs in shallow, high ambient noise environment. UAV's emphasizing non-acoustic modular payloads such as multi-spectral/hyper-spectral camera, tactical synthetic aperture radar (TSAR), advanced radar periscope detection device (ARPDD), and EO/IR. On board weapons/self-defense systems might include a vertically-launched 'hedgehog' type of ASW rocket for quick reaction and mobile, acoustic decoys."* CNSP 010200Z MAR 02

14

Littoral ASW presents enormous challenges — beginning with trying to detect, locate, and track quiet, submerged diesel submarines in a high ambient noise environment. Shallow water challenges also face ASW weapons. No single system is envisioned for overcoming these challenges. ASW workshop participants identified and prioritized 23 tasks (see Appendix C) they believed the LCS should have the capability to conduct. They stressed the ability to deploy a variety of helicopter systems, hull-mounted or towed systems, and unmanned systems, and being able to exchange data with other battle group assets. They were split about whether the LCS should support an organic helicopter or simply serve as a lily pad for helicopter operations. Just over half indicated the LCS should have either one or two aircraft on board and just under half indicated it should serve as a lily pad.

Since one purpose of the LCS during conflict will be to punch a hole in adversary defenses permitting the introduction of follow-on forces, it will be a prime target during the initial stages of fighting. Participants therefore insisted the ship needs a surface ship torpedo defense (SSTD). Speed (40 to 50 knots) was also often mentioned as desirable for torpedo evasion and prosecution repositioning. Participants recognized that speedy operations might pump a lot of sound into the water, but didn't see this as inconsistent with the requirement for acoustic signature reduction because the times that speed would be needed are when the submarine is already aware of the ship's presence. Speed could also prove useful in positioning the ship far enough ahead of the force to conduct ASW prosecution effectively before remaining battle group assets arrive. They also asserted that the ship requires an onboard, standoff offensive ASW weapon.

Some participants argued that the LCS should be used to lay a broad area sensor grid that is exploited by others to prosecute submarines. Speed might prove useful in laying such a grid. As in other areas, however, many of the sensors and unmanned systems envisioned are currently unavailable requiring at least the first flight of ships to use currently available systems. A real ship needs real capabilities. If unmanned off-board sensor systems eventually become the centerpieces of LCS capabilities, connectivity and bandwidth become very important issues.

Participants believed that ASW will remain an art form that will require more attention and training than an "optimally" manned crew can provide. For that reason, they believed that the crew would have to be augmented with approximately ten ASW experts when that mission was anticipated. They recommended that the core crew be trained in the launch and recovery of manned and unmanned systems supporting this mission, but the actual systems would be operated by the ASW detachment. Ideally, these systems will use the same handling equipment and techniques as systems used in other mission areas.

### *Intelligence preparation of the battlefield.*

> *"In order to enhance the capability to collect, process, and disseminate information and conduct OTH ISRT missions, LCS concept development should consider the CNO strategic studies group (SSG) ForceNet concept. ForceNet is defined as 'the architecture and building blocks of sensors,*

*networks, decision aids, weapons, warriors, and supporting systems integrated into a highly adaptive, human-centric, comprehensive system that operates from seabed to space, from sea to land.' It envisions a seabed-to-space, multi-tiered sensor grid, integrated information systems, information converted to actionable knowledge, and distributed combat capability (both manned and unmanned) to enable a fully prepared and informed warrior. The naval fires network (NFN) and other potential systems should be explored for ability to provide time critical targeting and info superiority. Data fusion technologies that enhance decision making and combat action in a reduced manning environment are essential to making LCS a viable platform in a future of reduced financial resources. LCS must be able to leverage all available information without requiring an inordinate number of organic sensors and with minimal/optimum manning.* " CNSP 010200Z MAR 02

Calling the LCS a "node" has become fashionable in the network centric warfare era. Many participants pointed out, however, that ideas like FORCEnet are concepts not capabilities. Participants in this ISR workshop and other mission area workshops provided a number of *real* connections they believed the LCS should have. As one participant wrote, this means "bandwidth, bandwidth, bandwidth." SURFPAC was wise in pointing out that data fusion technologies are the glue that makes network centric warfare work, especially when crews are small. They will be physically unable to monitor all the circuits with which people envision the LCS being connected. When the mission requires the collection of compartmentalized data, the LCS may have to support cryptology detachments. Because the littoral is a crowded and noisy environment, a good operational picture is the bedrock requirement for successfully operating there. Some participants believed that this awareness would come through the deployment and monitoring of an extensive sensor grid (which doesn't currently exist). Others believed awareness would be generated as the result of onboard sensors, sensors employed by organic manned and unmanned systems, and from sensors deployed by others.

ISR workshop participants identified and prioritized 29 tasks (see Appendix C) they believed the LCS could be called on to conduct. Like participants in other mission area workshops, they bet on future development, and gave their highest priority to launching, recovering and supporting unmanned systems that do not yet exist. They also stressed automated data fusion along the lines suggested by SURFPAC along with the use of artificial intelligence systems. They also stressed connectivity.

The problem is larger, of course, than simply connecting to US military systems. It is anticipated that the LCS will serve as one of the principal assets involved when conducting coalition operations, which means it must be interoperable with friends and allies. It will also conduct maritime interception operations, which means it much be able to communicate with merchant shipping. When it conducts MIO operations in defense of the homeland, it must be able to coordinate with the Coast Guard and other government agencies and departments. Emission control is likely to be an issue for the LCS since even with all of this connectivity, the ship must be able to operate as clandestinely as possible. Participants believed that open architecture and digital electronics were key to meeting all these challenges.

Participants went beyond technology sensors and stressed the importance of supporting human intelligence in the form of special operating forces. Like participants at other workshops, participants of this workshop were split concerning the need for a helicopter detachment vice providing the LCS with only lily pad capabilities. Since participants believed that a ship involved in data collection and dissemination must be in the environment for long periods, they put much less stress on speed than other mission areas and stressed instead the endurance required by the ship.

### Mine countermeasures.

> *"USV/UUV's emphasizing acoustic modular payloads such as side-scan and high-frequency active sonars to detect mines ... in shallow, high ambient noise environment."* CNSP 010200Z MAR 02

Participants at the MCM workshop did not envision the LCS itself as a mine hunting or mine sweeping vessel per se. High among the 28 tasks they identified in this mission area (see Appendix C) were launching, recovering, and supporting a variety of manned and unmanned systems that would perform the actual mission. More work has been done on unmanned and autonomous systems in the MCM area than in any other. The Remote Minehunting System (RMS) offers an excellent example of the type of unmanned system that should be incorporated on the LCS. If the sonars used by RMS can be adapted for use in shallow water ASW, the Navy will make a big leap towards its goal of relying more on unmanned systems for future missions. Participants believed that unmanned systems should go beyond current systems by incorporating identification and destruction systems in unmanned systems. Until that capability exists, the LCS will need to be capable of hosting a 10-person EOD/SOF detachment along with its equipment. Much like ASW, MCM is an art form and the ship would probably also require a crew enhancement when this mission was contemplated. The primary responsibility of the core LCS crew would be supporting these teams and their equipment.

The manned systems most often mentioned were helicopters. Unfortunately, the size of the sleds pulled by MH-53 helicopters are too large for H-60s and no one believed the LCS should be capable of landing the MH-53 on board. As a result, participants were split between those who believed the LCS should be a lily pad and those who believed it needed to support up to two organic helicopters.

MCM remains a time intensive endeavor, which means that MCM assets have to be in the risk area well ahead of the main force in order to locate mines so they can be avoided or, if necessary, destroyed. The requirement is not to clear all mines, but to punch a hole big enough in adversary defenses to permit access by follow-on forces. Although participants indicated that the LCS must have sufficient speed to arrive ahead of the force, the fact of the matter is that MCM assets must deploy so far in advance of the main force that speed is only a secondary consideration. In order for the LCS to operate in as many potentially mined areas of interest as possible, ship draft is an important consideration as is magnetic signature reduction.

### Small boat prosecution

> *"UAV/USV's with various modular payloads such as electro-optical/ infrared (EO/IR) to provide real-time or near real-time imagery; laser target designator/range finder capable of supporting weapons launch; and a tactical weapon (e.g., Hellfire-like weapon). These payloads will enable detection, ID, tracking, and engagement of surface threats prior to their weapons release range. On board weapons might include next-generation stabilized chain guns, small arms, and future directed or pulsed energy weapons."* CNSP 010200Z MAR 02

This mission requires many of the same capabilities as maritime interception operations with the major differences being that small boat prosecution requires even better sensing and much more capable offensive weapons. Threat detection is a critical challenge. Small boats are hard to detect beyond their effective weapons range and, even if detected, distinguishing between hostiles and non-hostiles can be difficult. For this reason, participants stressed the importance of a multi-function radar and electro-optical and infrared systems as well as off-board sensors. While there is a tendency to view small craft as very short-range threats, some patrol boats are capable of launching attacks beyond the horizon. Relying on short-range guns will not be sufficient for dealing with this issue. In addition to small and medium caliber guns, it is essential that LCS be equipped with weapons capable of providing significant punch at over the horizon ranges. Another challenge when prosecuting small boats is the sheer size of the attack that can be launched. A single ship can be overwhelmed and the chances of disabling or destroying all incoming threats beyond their weapons range rapidly diminishes as the size of the attack increases. Participants' organic weapons of choice were a rapid firing, small and medium caliber gun and anti-ship missiles. Because participants had a healthy skepticism that onboard systems were the total answer, they strongly advocated having an armed, organic helicopter or UAV on board to complement onboard weapons systems and provide "defense in depth" when operating in a high risk environment.

This is one mission area where speed and maneuverability play important offensive and defensive roles. In fact, participants made speed and maneuverability their highest priority along with long-range detection of small boats and the ability to prosecute them with unmanned vehicles. Participants believed that prosecuting small boats was one mission area that the ship must be able to conduct all the time. Although prosecuting small boats could be "the" assigned mission of the LCS, a more likely possibility is that it would have to prosecute them while conducting other missions. When appropriate unmanned vehicles are developed for this mission area, detecting, localizing and destroying threats at appropriate distances should become easier.

### *Special operations*

Special operations personnel would like the Navy to provide them with hulls that they can outfit themselves as dedicated special operations vessels. Barring that possibility, they made their highest priority a robust, secure C4ISR capability (including SOF dedicated spaces and communications when special forces are on board). That was closely followed by the requirement to launch and recover SOF craft in 4 to 6 foot seas and 18-20 knots of wind. Finally, they would like to have berthing and hotel support for 32- to 45-man detachments, with the ability to support up to 100 personnel for short periods. This implies the ship must be capable of handling all of their equipment as well. At a minimum, the LCS should be capable of handling two RHIBs.

As expected, SOF workshop participants also stressed the importance of speed and stealth (especially reduced RCS, IR, and visual profile) for their missions. They would also like the ship to have a draft as shallow as 9 feet, so that it could take them as close to shore as possible for insertion (although in the integration workshop they backed off somewhat from the 9-foot draft requirement). This mission area was the only one where participants expressed a desire to have long-range weapons in order to provide cover (overwatch) for insertion and extraction. Since they believed the ship must fight toe-to-toe with adversaries, they recommended the ship be both heavily armed and armored (even though it was pointed out that armor and speed isn't a cheap combination). Part of the firepower could be provided by armed helicopters (2 preferred), which could be provided either by the Navy or Army.

### *Homeland defense/maritime intercept operations*

One of the recurring arguments for small ships is that the Navy has been required to use expensive, large ships to conduct intercept operations that are better conducted by smaller vessels. Because intercept operations are generally conducted by single ships, participants insisted that the LCS must have organic weapon systems so that it can conduct this mission "alone and unafraid." As noted earlier, intercept operations pose a stressing communications environment, and participants made "secure, interoperable communications" with all necessary MIO elements their highest priority. Closely behind was the ability to maintain a single, integrated common operating picture. Even though vessels of interest are generally commercial vessels, finding the target vessel among a myriad of other vessels is a difficult challenge. When vessels of interest are smaller, high speed boats, the LCS must have the sprint capability necessary to reposition for intercept. On the other hand, MIO is often a waiting game and the ship must be able to loiter in areas of interest for extended periods.

Participants also noted that any ship engaged in intercept operations must be ready to operate without (or provide for the absence of) crew members tasked as steaming or prize teams. Since some boardings are non-cooperative, the ship must also be ready provide berthing and hotel services for boarding teams and be able to support their equipment (RHIBs and helicopters). Plans for berthing and providing hotel services for up to 32 people is a reasonable requirement and in line with SOF requirements mentioned above.

Since MIO seldom involves the use of deadly force, participants recommended fielding non-lethal technologies for disabling or holding a non-cooperative vessel at risk. They also stressed investment in sensors that can assist in standoff searches and real-time television monitoring of boarding parties. Participants also recommended investing in unmanned systems that could be used for search and support.

*Integration workshop*

In June 2002, a final integration workshop was conducted at the Naval War College in Newport, RI. A briefing drawn from the interim report was used as the straw man for discussion. Since most of the participants at the integration workshop had attended one or more of the other workshops, we wanted them to validate, or modify our portrayal of the findings from those workshops. We began by having them comment on the "bullets" we created for each workshop with an eye towards telling us what we missed. For the most part, participants indicated that we had captured the most important issues. A copy of unedited comments was provided to the sponsor following the workshop. Participants were then asked to comment on the "maneuvering board" characteristics described below. They were given the opportunity to indicate a "threshold" and an "objective" level for each characteristic. Since all characteristics are not of equal value, participants were asked to compare characteristics head-to-head in a pairwise comparison exercise as well as weight the characteristics using an allocation exercise. Our desire was to ensure internal consistency and to provide a prioritized list of characteristics for ship designers. We also wanted to compare their preferences against the guidelines the working group had established at the beginning of the process to determine how true they were to the process.

The second day of the workshop examined the three LCS variants that emerged from the mission area workshops. Participants were asked for their preferred variant and their preferred course of action (pursuing one, two, or all three variants). As noted in the introduction, nearly 60 percent of the participants would first pursue a Type C variant, while Types A and B were favored by approximately 20 percent of participants as their first choice. In addition, they voted to recommend pursuing two variants vice three (dropping Type A for the reasons noted in the introduction). The results of the integration workshop voting will be interspersed in the following discussion of consolidated characteristics.

CONSOLIDATED LCS CHARACTERISTICS

One of the reasons we included the COMNAVSURFPAC (CNSP) message in Appendix B is that the straw man ship it proposes, although not shared with participants at any but the first workshop, turned out to capture much of what was proposed during the six mission area workshops. In the following section we examine the consolidated characteristics of the LCS, and we will once again parse the SURFPAC message and compare it to workshop results. (For more detail on workshop results, see Appendices C and D.)

**Broad concept.**

> *"LCS is envisioned to be a fast, agile, stealthy, relatively small and affordable surface combatant. Its warfighting capabilities should be optimized for versatility in the littorals for anti-access and 'gapfiller' missions against asymmetric threats. A defining characteristic should be extensive reliance on a variety of organic unmanned vehicles. The ship should leverage transformational weapons, sensors, data fusion, C4ISR, materials, hull design, propulsion, 'smart' control systems, optimal manning concepts, and self-defense systems to enable it to survive and thrive in an adverse littoral environment."* CNSP 010200Z MAR 02

This general description remains fairly accurate of either a Type B or C LCS variant. The big difference is in how participants and SURFPAC define "relatively small." We agree with the SURFPAC message that the ship's capabilities should determine its size, and we would add that externally imposed size "restrictions" should be avoided. The accelerated schedule on which the LCS has been placed may limit incorporation of some transformational systems because many, like most unmanned vehicles, are not ready for operational use. One undeniable fact is that the ship must be able to utilize current systems as surrogates for those not yet available if it is going to be useful as a warship (vice a logistics ship) in the near term. We are also struck by the fact that the LCS has been given missions (like mine countermeasures and littoral antisubmarine warfare) that the Navy has historically had difficulty performing. These missions have not become easier. Mine hunting and sweeping remains a slow, tedious process whether conducted by autonomous systems or manned mine hunters and sweepers. There are some synergies, however. Systems used for locating mines might also be used for finding quiet submarines in the same littoral waters. This was a course strongly recommended during the integration workshop.

There are still differences of opinion concerning the operational concept that should be used by the LCS. Some contend that the LCS should be a fast, maneuverable delivery vehicle whose primary function is to employ off-board sensors and autonomous unmanned vehicles in the littoral, withdraw to a safe distance, and then rush in to recover them when their mission is complete (i.e., the Type A LCS). NWDC has published a "business plan" casting its experimental High Speed Vessel as a model that LCS could build upon, one that would rely on overseas bases from which an LCS squadron would operate and where LCS would retire to change out modular mission packages. Others see the LCS as a ship that may have to engage in small skirmishes while in the littoral, such as when extracting special forces personnel. They would like to see a ship that is relatively more heavily armed, faster and more stealthy than proponents of Type A. They also believe the ship must be relatively small and highly maneuverable (i.e., the Type B LCS). Finally, some see the LCS as a ship that must freely operate in the littoral, and from the beginning be as capable as possible of punching a hole in adversary defenses in order to enable the introduction of other forces into the area (i.e., Type C LCS).

Beyond these general ideas, we did not dwell on operational concepts. The LCS characteristics discussed in the remainder of this paper, if adopted, should make the ship adaptable to many current and future (yet to be defined) employment concepts. We begin by discussing individual characteristics and will close with more focused mission area characteristics.

Manning deserves a special mention. Much of the press that has been generated concerning the LCS has focused on the fact that it will have a small crew. As noted earlier, workshop participants expressed concerns about sailing a ship tasked with important and difficult military missions that need to be conducted in areas of high risk using dramatically reduced crews. In fact, every mission area workshop, by a wide margin, insisted that the ship requires crew augmentation in order to carry out specific missions. When participants at the integration workshop were asked if they agreed with this assessment, they unanimously agreed or strongly agreed. This fact has enormous consequences, not only for designing berthing and hotel services aboard the ship but for personnel policies, training curricula, and logistic support as well.

**Speed and agility.**

> *"In order to survive and accomplish its missions, LCS must be considerably faster and more agile than current surface combatants. The speed and agility of LCS will be critical for efficient and effective conduct of the littoral missions envisioned. ... Further, the survivability of LCS will depend in part on its speed, maneuverability, and stealthy design. However, LCS does not necessarily have to be capable of sustaining its top speed for extended periods. It may be sufficient that it be able to cruise at 30 knots and sprint at 50 knots — possibly to avoid a small boat or sub threat, intercept a potential terrorist smuggling vessel over the horizon, or retire from a SOF extraction mission. The requirement for speed may necessitate tradeoffs in size and weight of permanently installed weapons systems."* CNSP 010200Z MAR 02

Fifty knots sprint seems to have become a line in the sand for the LCS — one that may prove so costly that it will adversely affect other LCS characteristics. SURFPAC points out that the desire for speed must be weighed against other tradeoffs. We strongly agree. Nobody expressed a requirement for LCS to run around at high speed all the time. The comment that "it may be sufficient that [the LCS] be able to cruise at 30 knots and sprint at 50 knots" falls very much in line with participants at our workshops. Our sense of the workshops is that the LCS must be able to deploy with battle groups and have a sprint capability of between 40-50 knots in order to carry out specific missions. In fact, nearly two-thirds of all comments concerning speed indicated this was the proper top-end range. When we asked participants at the integration workshop if they agreed with this assessment, nearly 60 percent agreed.

We asked in two different ways about the importance of speed compared to other LCS characteristics. When asked to allocate a fixed amount among the characteristics, participants rated LCS connectivity twice as important as speed. They also rated the operation of offboard sensors nearly twice as important as speed. Organic sensors and weapons were also rated higher than speed. In head-to-head comparisons between characteristics, speed only ranked higher than endurance and range.

The two mission areas during which participants indicated top end speed was not important were the Mine Countermeasures and Intelligence Preparation of the Battlefield (ISR) workshops. They believed the LCS only needed sufficient speed to reach the operating area ahead of the battle group. Once on station, speed didn't matter. SURFPAC talks about the possibility of using "electric drive," but preliminary indications are that state-of-the-art electric systems that could fit in the LCS are not capable of generating the required speeds. Most participants favored a dual propulsion system — one for cruise (a diesel) and the other for sprint (a gas turbine).

We also asked mission area participants about range and endurance. The majority of participants believed the LCS needed to be capable of deploying with a battle or surface action group and steam unrefueled between the East Coast and the Mediterranean (or the West Coast and Hawaii). We set that distance at a nominal 4000 nautical miles. Endurance responses reverted back to the differences noted in the initial workshop. Those favoring a small, Type B ship believed LCS needed to be able to operate independently for a week or less. The vast majority of participants, however, believed it needed to be able to operate independently for a month or longer. During the integration workshop, range and endurance were clearly the areas where participants believed trade-offs should be made. When asked to weight characteristics, range and endurance fell out on the bottom. In head-to-head comparisons, range beat endurance and endurance was never selected as being more important than any other characteristic. This finding is consistent with Baseline/Flight 0 guidelines found in Appendix A.

**Unmanned vehicles.**

> *"Because size, speed, topside weight, fuel, and affordability considerations will limit ship-launched weapons and sensors, LCS is envisioned to make extensive use of a variety of organic unmanned aerial vehicles (UAV's), unmanned surface vehicles (USV's), and unmanned underwater vehicles (UUV's). An organic system of UV's, fully netted to the ship, brings many advantages to the table. UV's would serve as battlespace extenders, allowing LCS to conduct missions over the horizon*

*and support the war ashore. They are force multipliers that will allow a single ship to conduct a variety of missions with limited outside support. LCS should provide inherent modular-mission capability through easily interchangeable UV payloads. The missions a system of organic UV's will enable or enhance include intel, recon, surveillance, and targeting (ISRT), OTH SUW, MCM, sigint, comm relay, chem/bio recon, EW, and combat SAR, to name only a few."* CNSP 010200Z MAR 02

Participants at all workshops agreed that, when available, unmanned vehicles should be extensively used by the LCS. They also agreed that LCS modularity should primarily be contained in "interchangeable UV payloads." Since few of these systems are available, we asked participants at the integration workshop to consider RHIBs and helicopters as surrogates for offboard organic vehicles (OOVs) in their votes. Only networking was ranked as more important than operating OOVs when asked to weight the characteristics. In head-to-head competition, operating RHIBs/USVs and helicopters/UAVs each won 8 of the 9 comparisons in which they were matched. In the comparison against each other, helicopters/UAVs beat RHIBs/USVs 56 to 44 percent. Clearly the Navy must make the development of OOVs a priority if this vision for the LCS is to be realized.

This begs the question of how these systems should be launched and recovered. There is good news and bad news in this area. The bad news is that there are not very many unmanned systems ready for service on the LCS. That's also the good news, since it means that the Navy can insist that developed systems use common, automated launch and recovery systems (one for sea and another for air vehicles) and common command and control systems. Many participants believed that a stern ramp was an affordable, efficient method for launch and recovery of USVs (as well as manned RHIBs). The fewer personnel required to perform the operations the better, with full automation the goal. Since much of LCS's mission capability will eventually be contained in unmanned systems, they must also be extremely reliable and day/night all weather systems. If speed really is an important survivability factor for the LCS, then speed of launch and recovery is also critical. Ideally, systems would be able to be launched quickly while the ship is operating at high speeds. Since unmanned systems are unlikely to form the initial combat capability of the LCS, if real war fighting capability is to be achieved in the near term, current manned systems must be accommodated at least for initial LCS flights.

**Air capability.**

> *"A flight deck for operating, fueling, and supporting UAV's is essential. LCS is not envisioned to maintain a full air detachment (i.e., SH-60 det) with the space/material impact and maintenance support manning that entails, but must retain the ability to support helicopter operations such as refueling, lillypad, and vertrep."* CNSP 010200Z MAR 02

Mission area workshop participants clearly departed from this "no det" vision of LCS. Helicopters proved important for almost every mission area. In head-to-head characteristic comparisons, operating helicopters/UAVs lost out only to being networked as the most important characteristic for the LCS to have. A large majority of participants believed that the LCS should operate and support at least one helicopter (meaning an organic assset). Seventy percent of participants at the integration workshop either agreed or strongly agreed that the LCS should have an organic helicopter, at least until UAVs become available. That means that the LCS must have a hangar. Participants recommended that the LCS be capable of operating Army as well as Navy helicopters (their size is the same but their wheel bases are different). If (when?) helicopters are replaced by UAVs, the facilities used by helicopters should be readily adaptable for unmanned vehicles. A hangar was also considered important in order to maintain a low radar cross section when aircraft are aboard.

**RHIB and USV capability.**

> *"Ship configuration should allow for smooth launching and recovery of a variety of UUV's, USV's, rescue boats, and SOF craft without the need for davits that are cumbersome, add topside weight, and increase radar cross-section. The most likely solution is through a stern ramp or gate but may also include a variable depth capability for LCS."* CNSP 010200Z MAR 02

Participants at all workshops agreed that smooth launching and recovery of unmanned and manned systems was critical. As noted above, connectivity was the only characteristic deemed more important for the LCS than the ability to launch and recover offboard organic vehicles. None of our workshops discussed "variable depth capability" for launch and recovery, favoring the "stern ramp" approach for as many seaborne systems as possible. Many of the mission areas could use either manned RHIBs or unmanned USVs (like Spartan) to help them execute their tasks.

Participants at the integration workshop were asked to consider RHIBs as surrogates for USVs. They were also briefed on mission area workshop results that indicated two 11-meter RHIBs were the minimum required for several mission areas. When asked if they agreed, 73 percent voted in the affirmative. This means that the LCS must be capable of adequately supporting their associated personnel as well. Augment teams of up to 15 individuals per boat should be planned for.

**Self-defense systems.**

> *"On board hard kill/active systems might include fixed vertically-launched air defense weapons as well as man portable missiles (e.g., stinger-like) for air and small boat defense. On board soft kill/passive systems could include both active and passive decoys, ECM with potential for dynamic signature control, and towed acoustic decoys (e.g., nixie-like device)."* CNSP 010200Z MAR 02

Workshop participants agreed that the ship should come equipped with missiles, but more often expressed a preference for something like the Rolling Airframe Missile (RAM) than they did for man portable missiles. We agree with SURFPAC that a vertically launched system provides more flexibility for both offense and defense than does a purely defensive missile. Even more often than missiles, however, participants mentioned small and medium caliber rapid-fire guns. However, these weapons alone do not have the range and punch required to deal with much of the threat encountered in the littoral. Participants also agreed that a full range of decoys and torpedo defense systems are important for the ship's survivability. When integration workshop participants were asked about the range of self-defense weapons, 84 percent of them agreed that it should possess local area weapons (i.e., weapons with more than a point defense capability).

Although the data clearly demonstrates that participants from the workshops were strongly committed to organic offboard vehicles, they also felt that the LCS would be asked to fight in one of the most complex and dangerous environments in the world and a total reliance on OOVs for self-defense was unwise. As a result, organic weapons were rated fourth among characteristics the LCS should have and organic sensors close behind at sixth. In the head-to-comparisons, the order of sensors and weapons reversed, but they remained fourth and fifth in the voting. This is an area they clearly do not want shortchanged.

**On board sensors.**

> *"On board systems would likely include ESM, surface search radar, periscope detection, CBR detection (e.g., CAPDS, AN/KAS-1, M31E1 biological integrated detection system (BIDS)), mast mounted sights (e.g., FLIR, night vision, electro-optical, laser range finder), and 2-D air search radar. Other possibilities: small scale 3-D air search radar, towed array, towed active sonar."* CNSP 010200Z MAR 02

As noted in the paragraph above, integration workshop participants believed that the LCS must have some onboard sensors in order to defend itself. In the mission area workshops, radars were the most oft mentioned required on board sensor. Because of the number of missions assigned to the LCS, a small, multifunction radar would seem ideal. Next to radars, electro-optical/infrared systems were the most often mentioned, followed by sonar and ESM. Seventy-three percent of integration workshop participants agreed that sensor range needed to match weapons range, namely, local area sensors (which they interpreted to mean sensors with ranges beyond point defense range).

Participants proposed some unique employment schemes for some sensors, such as positioning UUVs within the hull so that its sensors could be deployed even when stowed.

**Hull configuration.**

Identifying preferred hull forms was beyond the charter we were given. A discussion of the benefits and drawbacks of various hull forms can be found in the companion to this study entitled, *Littoral Combat Ship (LCS) Technology Opportunities*. In this section we discuss some of the proposed ship characteristics that did emerge during workshop discussions.

### Stealth.

> "Stealth will complicate the enemy's ISR and targeting solutions, enhance survivability, and facilitate certain missions such as SOF insertion and extraction. Topside design should provide a small radar cross-section through use of composite materials and a multi-spectral stealthy configuration. In addition, design should allow for mission stealth capability such as an enclosed 'moon pool' capability for SOF insertion operations." CNSP 010200Z MAR 02

There were a lot of discussions about the value of stealth when operating in a high traffic, littoral environment. If LCS is primarily a night fighter (the preferred mode for SOF), then topside stealth probably makes a lot of sense. If, however, we don't cede the day to the adversary, then participants questioned the benefit of stealth versus its cost. Nevertheless, participants believed that reducing the ship's radar cross section should be a design objective. Since any fisherman in a dhow with a cell telephone can easily counter sophisticated signature reduction efforts, lowering the visual signature of the LCS is also important and the second most often mentioned signature concern. Magnetic, acoustic, infrared, and radio frequency signature reductions were also mentioned often. As expected, which signature was stressed depended upon which workshop was concerned. The MCM workshop stressed magnetic and acoustic signature reduction, while the ASW workshop overwhelmingly stressed acoustic signature reduction. Recognizing this, we divided signatures concerns into above water and below for the integration workshop. Added together, signature concerns would have placed fourth, behind connectivity and operating airborne and seaborne OOVs. Above water signature concerns placed slightly higher than below water signature concerns. For head-to-head comparisons, signatures were lumped together and were selected in two out of every three comparisons they were in. That said, we would agree with the Appendix A list that this is one area where trade-offs should be made.

### Draft.
> "The draft must be relatively shallow (20 feet or less) in order to facilitate shallow-water and near-land excursions." CNSP 010200Z MAR 02

Participants agreed that a draft of 20 or less is desired for LCS. This will permit the ship to conduct mine countermeasure and maritime intercept operations in waters currently denied to deeper draft vessels. SOF workshop participants desired a 9-foot draft, although their representatives backed off of this requirement during the integration workshop.

### At sea replenishment.

> "In addition to vertrep capability inherent in the inclusion of a flight deck, LCS will require an at-sea fueling capability. This would provide for

*interoperability with legacy platforms as well as enable operations with allied navies. Also, since all future combatants will operate with reduced manning, LCS should capitalize on automated and modular unrep technologies for all at-sea and inport commodity handling."* CNSP 010200Z MAR 02

We disagreed with the Appendix A recommendation that the Baseline 0 LCS "transit without payload, at most economical speed, not in company with battle group." Workshop participants believed that the LCS must be capable of steaming with the fleet — which means it must be able to resupply in the same way as other battle group assets.

Because it will be smaller than other ships, its magazines risk being emptied more quickly; hence, the LCS requires an at-sea reload capability. Again, workshop participants didn't agree with the Appendix A recommendation that the Baseline 0 LCS should transit without payload, believing that such a sustainment paradigm would place an extra burden on the logistics force during peacetime and become unworkable during conflict.

Participants agreed with SURFPAC that automation in this and every other possible area is essential for helping keep down the size of the LCS crew.

**Propulsion and engineering systems.**

> *"Propulsion systems must provide a high speed capability. However, in recognition of fuel, size, endurance, and engineering tradeoffs, speed does not necessarily have to be sustained for long periods. It may be sufficient for LCS to only have a high-speed dash capability. Transformational propulsion and engineering systems, such as electric drive, should be explored not only to produce high speeds but to take into account optimal manning concepts such as propulsion, electric plant, and damage control automation and monitoring systems to support a minimum maintenance requirement."* CNSP 010200Z MAR 02

As mentioned earlier, it doesn't appear that electric drives of sufficient power densities will develop in time for inclusion in initial flights of the LCS; hence, the preference for a dual propulsion system (one for cruise and one for sprint). Automated engineering systems are essential in order to reduce crew size and workload. As little at sea maintenance as possible should have to be conducted on the LCS. This is particularly important if the Navy adopts innovative crew strategies, such as Sea Swap, which requires ships to remain on station for significant periods.[1]

CONCLUSIONS

---

[1] Sea Swap was developed as part of the VCNO's Task Force Sierra work. Experiments being conducted under that name by COMNAVSURFPAC should not be confused with Task Force Sierra recommendations.

The Naval War College was tasked to provide N76 with "characteristics" for the Littoral Combat Ship. We took this to mean that we were to provide the broad outlines within which those tasked to come up with requirements and ship designs were to operate. In pursuing this objective we attempted to obtain the views of subject matter experts from both the fleet and technical fields. The data collected (mostly in the form of written opinions) filled over 500 unedited pages that were provided to the sponsor and program manager. This overview draws on the highlights of that data. Despite the myriad of opinions about the LCS (some of them strongly held), we tried to get an honest assessment of the desires and requirements of the fleet in putting our recommendations together. We understand there are tradeoffs to be made as the process goes forward. We hope this report helps those who must make these tradeoffs understand some of the consequences involved.

The following "maneuvering board" chart encapsulates our effort to integrate the data we collected. We like the maneuvering board analogy because it shows where the maneuvering room is located as requirements are firmed and cost/benefit analyses are completed. As the chart shows, we tried to avoid specific systems in favor of increasing "levels" of complexity and cost. This chart was presented to the integration workshop to see if we had accurately captured the inputs from the other workshops. Even though we changed it to satisfy some of their concerns, individual characteristic sectors were approved with an average 71 percent approval rating (the range was from 51 to 94 percent).

In order to ensure we filled in the maneuvering board correctly (that is, that we captured inputs from each of the mission area workshops), we had integration workshop participants provide us with threshold (minimum) and objective (desired) targets in each of the characteristic areas. That data is reported below.

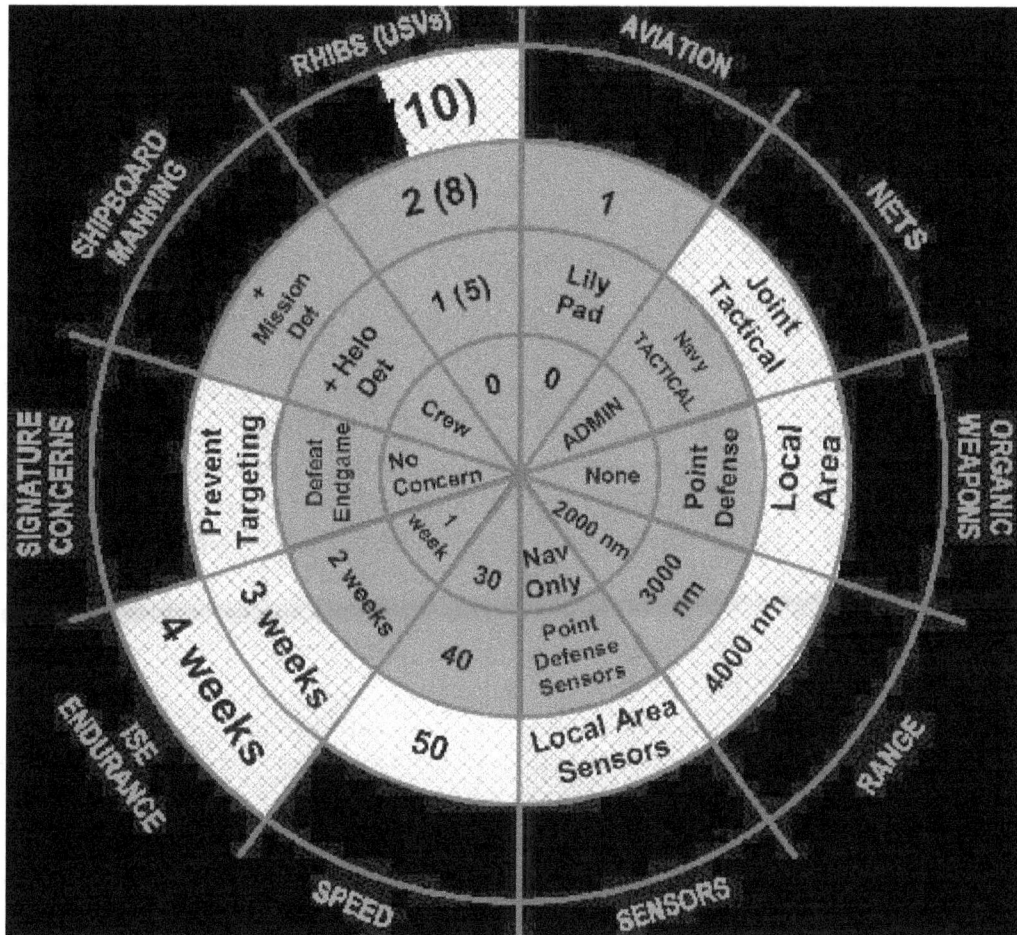

In explaining the above maneuvering board chart, we will start at shipboard manning and move counter-clockwise. We explained to participants at the integration workshop that they should consider the rings cumulative as they proceed outward. This is indicated by the solid red coloring of the maneuvering board "cells." The cross-hatched, lighter red coloring of some outer cells indicates that the results fall some where in between the adjacent cells. Details are provided in the following sections. For example, we assumed that if they voted for mission detachment crewing for the ship, that they were also voting for the core crew and the helicopter detachment crew (based on the fact that they had also recommended the LCS have an organic helicopter).

## Shipboard manning

Every mission area workshop concluded that the "optimized" core crew of the LCS would be insufficient to carry out the mission and nearly two-thirds of all participants believed the ship should support a helicopter detachment. Hence, the colored red portion of the chart shows that the ship should be designed to provide berthing and hotel services for the core crew, the helo detachment crew, and the augment or mission detachment crews of up to 32 people. There was a 94 percent agreement that the LCS would have to have its crew augmented depending on the mission with which it was tasked. Hence, designs should take this threshold requirement into account. Their objective target was more bifurcated, with 47 percent recommending mission detachments as the objective and 44 percent recommending a fully capable completely manned crew (i.e., no helicopter or mission detachments needed) as the objective. This vote reflected a belief that for many tasks an optimized crew would find itself undermanned, even with augmentation.

### Signature concerns

The range of signature concerns put forward in the mission area workshops ranged from "no concern" by some participants in the MIO workshop to "preventing detection" in the special operations workshop. Stealth, however, is expensive and considering how easily some efforts at stealth could be countered, most participants fell somewhere between defeating the endgame (i.e., preventing weapons homing or detonation) and preventing targeting by stressing affordable signature reduction, hence the cross-hatched lighter red coloring over the "Prevent Targeting" cell and the dark red coloring over the lesser included portions of this pie-shaped section of the chart. If all three types of LCS mentioned in the report are pursued, then Type B LCS should place more stress on stealth than either Types A or C. As noted earlier, for the integration workshop we divided signature concerns into two areas: above and below water signature concerns.

Participants indicated that the threshold target for *below water signatures* should be defeating the endgame, with 68 percent indicating that as their choice. When asked about their objective target, 55 percent indicated that they would like to see sufficient signature reduction to prevent targeting. When they were asked these same questions for *above water signatures*, 69 percent indicated their threshold target would be defeating the endgame and 58 percent indicated their objective target would be preventing targeting.

### Endurance

We were surprised when participants at every workshop favored the LCS having an on station or independent steaming endurance of at least four weeks. As noted earlier, this desire for long endurance was not as strongly held in the integration workshop as desires for other capabilities. In fact, it finished last in the voting. In order to achieve the best possible endurance, it appears that the LCS must have a dual propulsion system that permits efficient, low speed steaming and loiter as well as a high top end sprint speed. It also means the ship must have enough stores for extended operations. Participants at the integration workshop indicated their threshold target would be two weeks (with 62 percent selecting that number), while their objective target would be 4 weeks (with 76 percent selecting that number).

### Speed

During the initial workshop, the value of speed was openly questioned. As the mission area workshops proceeded, participants provided numerous justifications for a fairly high speed vessel, but few participants believed that 50 knots should be a hard target. Most participants favored speeds between 40 and 50 knots for short periods of time (hours, not days). Even though speed fell near the bottom of the votes at the integration workshop, those favoring high speeds are a vocal and unwavering minority. It may be a political reality that the ship has to achieve 50 knots, but for our working groups it was certainly not a highly valued operational requirement. When asked for their speed targets, integration workshop participants indicated that 40 knots was their threshold target (with 64 percent selecting that number). Consistent with the relatively low value placed on speed, the majority of those not voting for a 40 knots threshold voted for a slower, not faster speed, with 24 percent voting for 30 knots and only 12 percent voting for 50 knots. When asked what their objective (desired) target for speed was, they indicated 50 knots (64 percent), with 18 percent selecting 60 knots and the same percentage selecting 40 knots.

### *Sensors*

We tried to get a sense from participants about how far out organic sensors needed to be effective. This was important because most participants believed that the ship must have a reduced visual signature (meaning a low profile), which could greatly reduce sensor range. Although some participants did believe the ship should possess the ability to conduct broad area surveillance, most were convinced that access to such information was more important than having an organic ability to sense at long-range. On the other hand, all participants believed that the ship needed to have coverage sufficient for self-defense. Some missions (especially, small boat prosecution, MIO, and special operations) required more than point defense sensors. These sensors, however, need not be on the ship to the extent they can be carried by manned or unmanned vehicles carried by the ship. We specifically asked integration workshop participants for their sensor target ranges. When asked about threshold sensor ranges, they were evenly split between point defense and local area sensors (48 percent each). When queried about their objective (desired) sensor ranges, 70 percent of them indicated they preferred local area sensors, with 24 percent indicating they preferred broad area sensors.

### *Range*

Across every workshop there was a consistent belief that the LCS should be capable of crossing the Atlantic Ocean or reaching Hawaii from the West Coast unrefueled. It was clear at the integration workshop, however, that range, endurance, and speed were the three areas in which participants felt there was a great deal of tradespace. When asked for their threshold range target, 39 percent indicated that the ship should have a 3000 nautical mile range, with 27 percent indicating a 2000 nautical mile range, and another 24 percent indicating a preference for a 4000 nautical mile range. When asked for their desired (objective) range, 70 percent indicated they preferred 4000 nautical miles. The other votes were spread from 1000 to 6000 nautical miles.

### *Organic weapons*

Although some participants believed that weapons carried by manned or unmanned systems on the ship should be considered "organic," we interpreted organic weapons to mean onboard systems, especially since few unmanned systems exist and some people (though less than half our participants) believe the LCS should not support an organic helicopter. Few participants believed the ship should be unarmed, and only a few more believed that it should be capable of conducting over-the-horizon attacks, including land attack. Although there was a consensus during the mission area workshops that point defense systems were a must, participants also accepted the reality that point defenses were insufficient to defeat all littoral risks. For that reason, a medium caliber gun, a defensive missile, and a vertical launch system capable of carrying a variety of defensive and offensive weapons were favorite candidates of most participants. At the integration workshop, participants were consistent in matching weapons to sensors. They split their threshold target vote for organic weapons between point defense (55 percent) and local area (45 percent) weapons. When asked about their objective (desired) target for organic weapons, 64 percent indicated they preferred local area weapons, while another 33 percent indicated they preferred broad area (over-the-horizon) weapons.

### Connectivity

The range of connectivity we offered participants started with administrative connectivity (messages and emails) up to a robust node capable of real-time connectivity with others despite the scenario. Most mission area participants indicated that as a minimum they needed tactical connectivity with other US Navy assets, but many believed that the promise of network centric warfare would not be realized if the LCS fell short of full joint tactical connectivity. Although integration workshop participants had great difficulty defining exactly what particular levels of connectivity really meant, they established as their threshold target something between Navy tactical connectivity (39 percent) and Joint tactical connectivity (55 percent). They established Joint tactical connectivity (67 percent) as their objective target, with the other 33 percent of participants preferring the more robust coalition tactical connectivity.

We had more difficulty deciding how to describe the levels of connectivity than the levels of any other characteristic. We settled on this breakdown based on discussions with command and control experts and a study by Paul Davis in which he concluded that "not all interoperability is equally important."[2] Davis was looking primarily at coalition operations, but his general observations are more widely applicable. He drew the following figure to underscore his point.

---

[2] Paul K. Davis, "Transforming the Armed Forces," in The Global Century: Globalization and National Security, volume 1, edited by Richard L. Kugler and Ellen L. Frost (Washington, DC: National Defense University Press, 2001), p. 437.

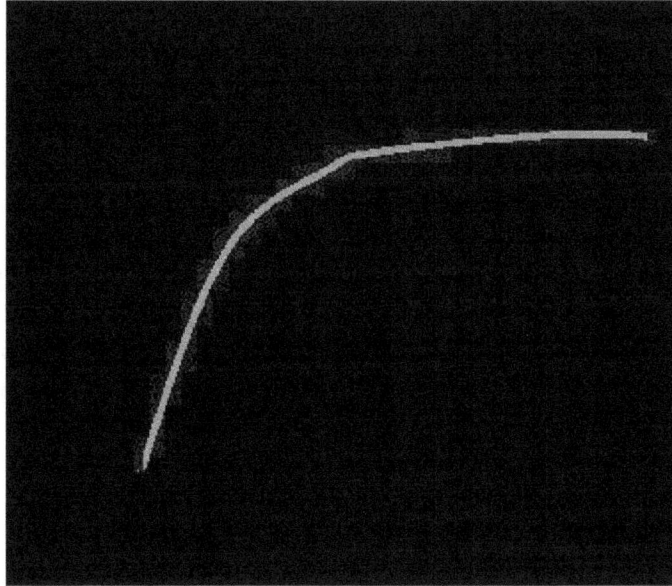

The bottom line is that participants believed strongly in connectivity, but demonstrated a healthy skepticism that LCS would be a full-up network centric vessel when it first becomes operational. Their desire is for a ship that can be connected to networks as they become available. Since connectivity means bandwidth, the ship should be designed with plenty of it — this will permit the ship to transform as new capabilities emerge. They also recommended that most of the analysis be done on the offboard sensors (increasing their cost), which then broadcast back only essential information, thereby greatly reducing bandwidth demand.

### Aviation

Aviation capabilities, more than any other area except perhaps speed, sparked impassioned debate. Operators who had deployed on ships that didn't support helicopter detachments warned that this was a mistake. On the other hand, proponents of Type B LCS argued that planning for a ship with other than lily pad capability would make the ship too large and expensive to be transformational. In the end, nearly two-thirds of mission area workshop participants believed the ship should be designed to support an organic helicopter. Virtually no one believed it should have no helicopter capability. This sentiment was mirrored during the integration workshop, where participants were asked to consider helicopters as surrogates for UAVs. When asked for their threshold capability, 58 percent indicated the LCS should support an organic helicopter, while 40 percent indicated it should only host lily pad operations. This changed significantly when asked for their desired air capability. Fifty-eight percent indicated they preferred the LCS to support two organic helicopters, with another 40 percent indicating it should host a single organic helicopter.

### Rigid-hull inflatable boats

We selected rigid hull inflatable boats as an important characteristic since they currently support numerous missions and can serve as surrogates for unmanned surface vessels

34

currently under development. Since both MIO and special operations workshop participants indicated that two RHIBs were the minimum required to conduct these missions, two was accepted as the standard. Integration workshop participants took our suggestion to consider RHIBs as USV surrogates seriously, and surprised us by indicating the LCS should support many more than two we suggested. For example, when asked to establish a threshold level of support, 36 percent indicated the threshold should be 3, 45 percent indicated it should be 5, and 15 percent indicated it should host as many as 8 RHIBs/USVs. When asked about their desired level of support, 39 percent indicated they preferred 5, 18 percent indicated they preferred 8, and 36 percent indicated they preferred 10 RHIBs/USVs. Participants did not simply ignore the 11-meter RHIB footprint, they indicated they were supporting the development of smaller UAVs so that the ship could support more of them in the same space initially utilized by two or three 11-meter RHIBs.

### Final thoughts

This report was prepared in response to the N76 tasking to develop the characteristics of a single LCS. That is how we interpreted our tasking, and so that is how we proceeded. That is also how participants at the integration workshop viewed the tasking and they called the Type C LCS the 80 percent solution. Like us, however, they were neither deaf nor blind to the arguments and proposals being raised elsewhere. In fact, we tried to expose them to as many of those arguments and proposals as we could. This was to ensure that promising alternatives were included and that workshop participants who were proponents of these other concepts felt their views were heard. As noted in the introduction, after sorting out the discussion, we believed we heard three distinct variants of LCS being discussed. A summation of the arguments in support of each of the three alternatives is found below.

We also wanted to give participants at the integration workshop the opportunity to weight various characteristics against one another, believing that real direction is only provided when people are forced to make impossible choices (like what is more important to you, weapons or sensors?). The following pie chart indicates the cumulative investment participants made when asked to allocate $100 among the 11 characteristics presented during the workshop. The actual percentages are of less significance than the relative values. For example, participants believe that the real trade space for the LCS is found in the ship's endurance, range, and speed — certainly not a conclusion one would reach from what one reads in the press -- with connectivity deemed almost twice as important as speed.

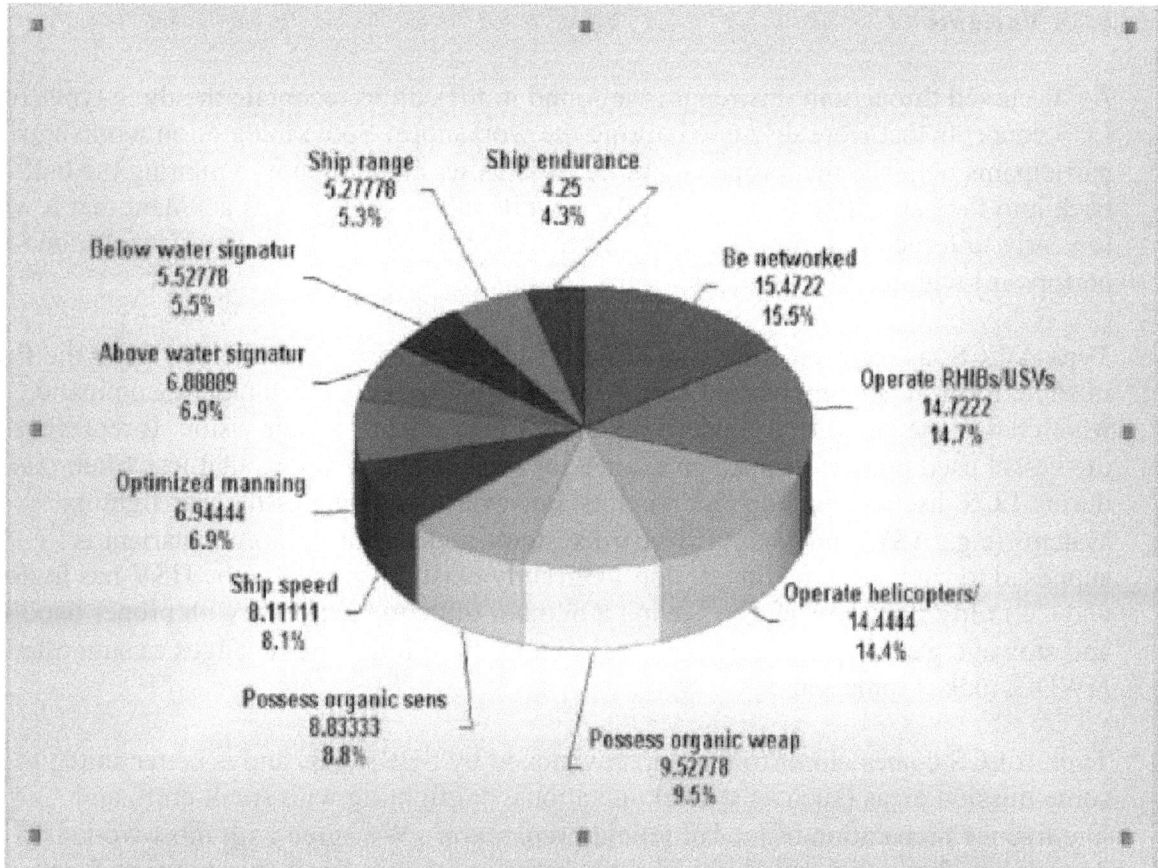

We conducted the head-to-head (pairwise) comparisons in order to verify that the group was being internally consistent in how it rated the various characteristics. This is how the rankings turned out under the two rating methods:

**Allocation Exercise**
1. Connectivity (15.5%)
2. Operate RHIBs/USVs (14.7%)
3. Operate helos/UAVs (14.4%)
4. Signature reduction (combined 12.4%)
5. Possess organic weapons (9.5%)
6. Possess organic sensors (8.8%)
7. Ship speed (8.1%)
8. Optimized manning (6.9%)
9. Ship range (5.3%)
10. Ship endurance (4.3%)

**Pairwise Comparisons**
1. Connectivity (won 8 of 9 pairings)
2. Operate RHIBs/USVs (won 8 of 9)
3. Operate helos/UAVs (won 8 of 9)
4. Possess organic sensors (won 6 of 9)
5. Possess organic weapons (won 5 of 6)
6. Signature reduction (won 4 of 9)
7. Ship speed (won 2 of 9)
8. Optimized manning (won 2 of 9)
9. Ship range (won 1 of 9)
10. Ship endurance (won 0 of 9)

Overall one would have to conclude that integration workshop participants were highly consistent in their votes.

**LCS Variants**

As discussed throughout this report, we found it difficult to reconcile the three types of LCS concepts that were discussed during the workshops. Some integration workshop participants believed that proposing three variants was tantamount to punting the ball back into the Navy Staff's end of the field, while others were just as adamant that it was too early to foreclose promising alternatives. After all was said and done, we decided to go forward with the three options for the reasons described below.

Type A LCS, as represented by a modified High Speed Vessel, is likely to enter the fleet in some form. It is being pushed hard by the Navy Warfare Development Command, which has come out with a "business plan" for implementing their vision. It represents the vessel used primarily as a conveyance for sensors and weapons that was often raised during LCS discussions. The fact remains, however, that many of the war fighting systems (e.g., ASW and MCM off-board systems and sensor grids) this variant is supposed to carry into the littoral don't currently exist. Fortunately, the HSV has logistics and C2 utility right now and so buying a number of them, equipped with proper handling and stowage gear for small craft and helicopters, as well as other changes as suggested by NWDC, makes some sense.

Type B LCS comes closer to the ship envisioned by SURFPAC and is better suited to some mission areas (such as special operations, dogfighting with small craft, and intelligence preparation of the battlefield preparation). We agree with most workshop participants, however, that sustainability challenges with a small ship are significant and the bulk of littoral combat ships might not be of this type. Because of its size limitations, Type B probably should deploy in conjunction with a support vessel, perhaps a Type A LCS, which could help it overcome some of the challenges associated with its smaller size. We do not believe these ships should be built with the concept of supporting them at shore bases in or near the conflict. We feel that such a concept gives up (at least in part) one of the Navy's great strengths, namely the ability to operate independently of near-by friendly and secure bases. Type B could be similar to Sweden's *Visby* or an up-scaled version of Norway's *Skjold*, with focus on stealthy technology and high speed and short-range onboard weapons. The *Visby* is long on stealth and shorter on speed (40 knots), while the *Skjold* is long on speed and shorter on payload.

Type C LCS satisfies the majority of requirements established at the outset of this process. It is a ship with real capability, fills a very real force structure requirement, and is transformational. Current systems that participants recommended be used on this type LCS to ensure near-term war fighting capability from the outset can also act as surrogates for future systems. For example, helicopters serve as a substitute for unmanned aerial vehicles. Spaces (like hangars) provided for organic helicopters will prove useful for housing newer systems when they come on line. RHIBs are an excellent substitute for unmanned surface vehicles under development, and the Remote Minehunting System is a good substitute for learning to operate the next generation of unmanned underwater vehicles. As envisioned, nothing about the ship makes it obsolete as new systems become available. In fact, we think the transition from current to new systems would be smooth, and more importantly deliver a ship capable of immediately carrying out the critical war fighting missions it has been assigned.

The Navy is already exploring vessels that could fill each niche (i.e., HSV, *Skjold*, and *Triton*) and Sweden is moving ahead with the *Visby* class. In general, continuing to consider all three types of LCS could simultaneously increase force structure, satisfy transformation advocates, and help fill operational gaps — the three purposes for which we believe the littoral combat ship process was begun.

As reported in the introduction, integration workshop participants did not support our recommendation to move ahead with all three variants. Forty-seven percent of integration workshop participants recommended that the Navy move forward with only two of the variants. Most of those who voted for two variants believed that Type A was not an LCS but a logistics ship, and they favored pursuing Types B and C. Others believed that Type C was a step too far and preferred to see Types A and/or B evolved into a Type C as technologies mature. Thirty-eight percent recommended pursuing a single ship type, believing that the Navy will not commit sufficient resources to pursuing more than one variant. Approximately 15 percent of participants agreed with our recommendation to pursue all three options.

If the Navy Staff follows the recommendation to pursue two types, integration workshop participants voted Types C (86%) and Type B (69%) as their two favorites. By contrast, only 44 percent voted Type A into the two top spots. If the Navy staff pursues a single type, participants recommend Type C (58%), with 22 percent recommending Type A and 19 percent recommending Type B, as noted in the chart contained in the introduction.

We recognize that LCS is a fast moving train and that some decisions may already have been made on some of the issues considered in this report. However, given the high stakes involved for those who will serve on LCS ships and for the Navy's effectiveness in future conflicts, we hope the careful analysis of the broad and diverse expertise of the study participants who informed these findings and recommendations will receive due consideration in deciding the future direction of LCS development.

**Appendix A
Navy Staff
Littoral Combat Ship, Flight 0
Guidance**

"The CNO and others have also provided some early decisions on the definition of those first two test ships. ... These decisions include the following"

- ? lily pad for H-60
- ? full support to embarked OH-58Us
- ? transit without payload, at most economical speed, not in company with battle group
- ? 220M$ for construction of ship, not to include payload
- ? stay in theater for 2-3 years
- ? give up endurance for capability
- ? may accompany [battle group] in theater
- ? 1000 to 2000 tons displacement
- ? focus on crew, survivability, as in a fighter aircraft
- ? damage control – focus on aviation firefighting
- ? signature control – some
- ? 2 [Close-in Weapon Sytem] 1Bs
- ? Nulka
- ? no onboard ASW weapons or sensors, except NIXIE
- ? nav[igation] radar
- ? [Cooperative Engagement Capability], receive only
- ? [Electro-optical] sight
- ? minor caliber gun, fairly cheap
- ? radar – not ready to specify just yet
- ? air control [capable]
- ? no steel, aluminum ship (first two)
- ? sprint speed of 50 kts
- ? no basing assumptions provided
- ? want study to define UAVs, offboard vehicles
- ? NetCentric connectivity (whatever that means)
- ? R[H]IBs
- ? goal – get as much mission capability into first two ships as possible, within above guidelines
- ? plug and play – pursue the concept

**Appendix B
Commander, Naval Surface Forces Pacific
message concerning the Littoral Combat Ship**

```
ROUTINE
R 010200Z MAR 02 ZYB PSN 236646L27
FM COMNAVSURFOR SAN DIEGO CA//N00//
TO NAVWARCOL NEWPORT RI//00//
NAVWARCOL NEWPORT RI//00//
INFO COMFLTFORCOM NORFOLK VA//N00/N01/N8//
CINCPACFLT PEARL HARBOR HI//N00/N01/N83//
CINCPACFLT PEARL HARBOR HI//N00/N01/N83//
COMNAVSURFLANT NORFOLK VA//N00/N01/N8//
CNO WASHINGTON DC//N76/N763//
CNO WASHINGTON DC//N76/N763//
COMNAVSEASYSCOM WASHINGTON DC//N00/N53C/N05//
CNR ARLINGTON VA//N00/N33//
CNR ARLINGTON VA//N00/N33//
CNA ALEXANDRIA VA//JJJ///
PEO THEATER SURFACE COMBATANTS WASHINGTON DC//PMS400B//
PEO SURFACE STRIKE WASHINGTON DC//PMS500//
COMNAVWARDEVCOM NEWPORT RI//N3/N8/N9//
NAVPGSCOL MONTEREY CA//03//
NAVPGSCOL MONTEREY CA//03//


BT
UNCLAS //N08000//
***THIS IS A 2 SECTION MESSAGE COLLATED BY DMDS***

MSGID/GENADMIN/COMNAVSURFOR//
SUBJ/LITTORAL COMBAT SHIP (LCS) CONCEPT DEVELOPMENT//
POC/FORD, M/CDR/CNSP N8A/TEL: 619-437-3142/DSN: 577-3142/
EMAIL: FORD.MICHAEL@CNSP.NAVY.(SMIL).MIL//
```

RMKS/1. THE PURPOSE OF THIS MESSAGE IS TO PROVIDE INITIAL INPUT ON LCS ROLES AND MISSIONS, WARFIGHTING CHARACTERISTICS, AND OPERATIONAL CONCEPTS. THESE PRELIMINARY IDEAS ARE INTENDED TO PROVIDE FOOD FOR THOUGHT AND DISCUSSION DURING THE UPCOMING LCS CHARACTERISTICS WORKING GROUP TO BE HELD AT THE NAVAL WAR COLLEGE 4-5 MAR.

2.    BROAD CONCEPT. LCS IS ENVISIONED TO BE A FAST, AGILE, STEALTHY, RELATIVELY SMALL AND AFFORDABLE SURFACE COMBATANT. ITS WARFIGHTING CAPABILITIES SHOULD BE OPTIMIZED FOR VERSATILITY IN THE LITTORALS FOR ANTI-ACCESS AND "GAPFILLER" MISSIONS AGAINST ASYMMETRIC THREATS. A DEFINING CHARACTERISTIC SHOULD BE EXTENSIVE RELIANCE ON A VARIETY OF ORGANIC UNMANNED VEHICLES. THE SHIP SHOULD LEVERAGE TRANSFORMATIONAL WEAPONS, SENSORS, DATA FUSION, C4ISR, MATERIALS, HULL DESIGN, PROPULSION, "SMART" CONTROL SYSTEMS, OPTIMAL MANNING CONCEPTS, AND SELF-DEFENSE SYSTEMS TO ENABLE IT TO SURVIVE AND THRIVE IN AN ADVERSE LITTORAL ENVIRONMENT.

3.    ROLES AND MISSIONS. THE LITTORAL ENVIRONMENT IS ENEMY-FRIENDLY. IT IS CONGESTED, WITH POTENTIAL THREATS DISPERSED AMONG BACKGROUND SHIPPING, AIR TRAFFIC, AND DIVERSE MARINE LIFE. IT IS, BY DEFINITION, AN AREA OF SHALLOW WATER AND POOR ACOUSTIC CONDITIONS. IT IS LIKELY CLOSE TO ENEMY AIRFIELDS AND PORTS. THREATS ARE CHALLENGING: MINES, DIESEL SUBMARINES, SMALL BOATS, PATROL CRAFT, LOW-SLOW FLYERS, SHORE FIRES, AND ANTI-SHIP CRUISE MISSILES. PRIMARY MISSIONS FOR THE LCS SHOULD BE THOSE THAT ENSURE AND ENHANCE FRIENDLY FORCE ACCESS TO LITTORAL AREAS. ACCESS-FOCUSED MISSIONS INCLUDE MCM, SHALLOW-WATER ASW, AND COUNTER SMALL BOAT ATTACK. THESE ARE ENABLING MISSIONS THAT WILL ALLOW LCS TO LEAD THE WAY INTO OR THROUGH A CHOKE POINT, SLOC, OR AOA FOR FOLLOW-ON NAVAL FORCES. LCS CHARACTERISTICS AND CAPABILITIES SHOULD ALSO MAKE IT WELL-SUITED TO "GAPFILLER" MISSIONS, ALLOWING COMMANDERS

TO SAVE CG'S AND DDG'S FOR HIGH END MISSIONS SUCH AS TMD AND LAND ATTACK. GAPFILLER MISSIONS MIGHT INCLUDE MIO, SLOC PATROL AND INTERDICTION, NEO AND AMPHIB RAID SUPPORT, SOF INSERTION AND EXTRACTION, LEO, OPDEC, COMBAT SAR, AND RADAR PICKET. ADDITIONALLY, LCS SHOULD UTILIZE A "PLUG AND PLAY" CAPABILITY WHICH WOULD READILY ALLOW THE WARFARE COMMANDER TO CUSTOMIZE LCS FOR A PARTICULAR MISSION, ENHANCING OR REDUCING SENSORS AND CAPABILITIES AS REQUIRED.

4.      SPEED AND AGILITY. IN ORDER TO SURVIVE AND ACCOMPLISH ITS MISSIONS, LCS MUST BE CONSIDERABLY FASTER AND MORE AGILE THAN CURRENT SURFACE COMBATANTS. THE SPEED AND AGILITY OF LCS WILL BE CRITICAL FOR EFFICIENT AND EFFECTIVE CONDUCT OF THE LITTORAL MISSIONS ENVISIONED ABOVE. FURTHER, THE SURVIVABILITY OF LCS WILL DEPEND IN PART ON ITS SPEED, MANEUVERABILITY, AND STEALTHY DESIGN. HOWEVER, LCS DOES NOT NECESSARILY HAVE TO BE CAPABLE OF SUSTAINING ITS TOP SPEED FOR EXTENDED PERIODS. IT MAY BE SUFFICIENT THAT IT BE ABLE TO CRUISE AT 30 KNOTS AND SPRINT AT 50 KNOTS - POSSIBLY TO AVOID A SMALL BOAT OR SUB THREAT, INTERCEPT A POTENTIAL TERRORIST SMUGGLING VESSEL OVER THE HORIZON, OR RETIRE FROM A SOF EXTRACTION MISSION. THE REQUIREMENT FOR SPEED MAY NECESSITATE TRADEOFFS IN SIZE AND WEIGHT OF PERMANENTLY INSTALLED WEAPONS SYSTEMS.

5.      UNMANNED VEHICLES (UV'S). BECAUSE SIZE, SPEED, TOPSIDE WEIGHT, FUEL, AND AFFORDABILITY CONSIDERATIONS WILL LIMIT SHIP-LAUNCHED WEAPONS AND SENSORS, LCS IS ENVISIONED TO MAKE EXTENSIVE USE OF A VARIETY OF ORGANIC UNMANNED AERIAL VEHICLES (UAV'S), UNMANNED SURFACE VEHICLES (USV'S), AND UNMANNED UNDERWATER VEHICLES (UUV'S). AN ORGANIC SYSTEM OF UV'S, FULLY NETTED TO THE SHIP, BRINGS MANY ADVANTAGES TO THE TABLE. UV'S WOULD SERVE AS BATTLESPACE EXTENDERS, ALLOWING LCS TO CONDUCT MISSIONS OVER THE HORIZON AND SUPPORT THE WAR ASHORE. THEY ARE FORCE MULTIPLIERS THAT WILL ALLOW A SINGLE SHIP TO CONDUCT A VARIETY OF MISSIONS WITH LIMITED OUTSIDE SUPPORT. LCS SHOULD PROVIDE INHERENT MODULAR-MISSION CAPABILITY THROUGH EASILY INTERCHANGEABLE UV PAYLOADS. THE MISSIONS A SYSTEM OF ORGANIC UV'S WILL ENABLE OR ENHANCE INCLUDE INTEL, RECON, SURVEILLANCE, AND TARGETING (ISRT), OTH SUW, MCM, SIGINT, COMM RELAY, CHEM/BIO RECON, EW, AND COMBAT SAR, TO NAME ONLY A FEW.

6.      WARFIGHTING CAPABILITIES. BECAUSE OF REQUIREMENTS FOR SPEED AND STEALTH, NUMBER AND WEIGHT OF PERMANENTLY INSTALLED WEAPONS SYSTEMS MAY NEED TO BE MINIMIZED, WITH UV'S AND OTHER MODULAR MISSION PACKAGES PROVIDING MOST OF THE WARFIGHTING CAPABILITIES.

A.      SUW

(1)      UAV/USV'S WITH VARIOUS MODULAR PAYLOADS SUCH AS ELECTRO-OPTICAL/ INFRARED (EO/IR) TO PROVIDE REAL-TIME OR NEAR REAL-TIME IMAGERY; LASER TARGET DESIGNATOR/RANGE FINDER CAPABLE OF SUPPORTING WEAPONS LAUNCH; AND A TACTICAL WEAPON (E.G., HELLFIRE-LIKE WEAPON). THESE PAYLOADS WILL ENABLE DETECTION, ID, TRACKING, AND ENGAGEMENT OF SURFACE THREATS PRIOR TO THEIR WEAPONS RELEASE RANGE.

(2)      ON BOARD WEAPONS MIGHT INCLUDE NEXT-GENERATION STABILIZED CHAIN GUNS, SMALL ARMS, AND FUTURE DIRECTED OR PULSED ENERGY WEAPONS.

B.      USW

(1)      USV/UUV'S EMPHASIZING ACOUSTIC MODULAR PAYLOADS SUCH AS SIDE-SCAN AND HIGH-FREQUENCY ACTIVE SONARS TO DETECT MINES AND LOW DOPPLER, NEAR BOTTOM SUBS IN SHALLOW, HIGH AMBIENT NOISE ENVIRONMENT.

(2)      UAV'S EMPHASIZING NON-ACOUSTIC MODULAR PAYLOADS SUCH AS MULTI-SPECTRAL/HYPER-SPECTRAL CAMERA, TACTICAL SYNTHETIC APERTURE RADAR (TSAR), ADVANCED RADAR PERISCOPE DETECTION DEVICE (ARPDD), AND EO/IR.

(3)      ON BOARD WEAPONS/SELF-DEFENSE SYSTEMS MIGHT INCLUDE A VERTICALLY-LAUNCHED "HEDGEHOG" TYPE OF ASW ROCKET FOR QUICK REACTION AND MOBILE, ACOUSTIC DECOYS.

C.    OTHER SELF-DEFENSE SYSTEMS.
(1)    ON BOARD HARD KILL/ACTIVE SYSTEMS MIGHT INCLUDE FIXED VERTICALLY-LAUNCHED AIR DEFENSE WEAPONS AS WELL AS MAN PORTABLE MISSILES (E.G., STINGER-LIKE) FOR AIR AND SMALL BOAT DEFENSE.
(2)    ON BOARD SOFT KILL/PASSIVE SYSTEMS COULD INCLUDE BOTH ACTIVE AND PASSIVE DECOYS, ECM WITH POTENTIAL FOR DYNAMIC SIGNATURE CONTROL, AND TOWED ACOUSTIC DECOYS (E.G., NIXIE-LIKE DEVICE).
D.    ON BOARD SENSORS. ON BOARD SYSTEMS WOULD LIKELY INCLUDE ESM, SURFACE SEARCH RADAR, PERISCOPE DETECTION, CBR DETECTION (E.G., CAPDS, AN/KAS-1, M31E1 BIOLOGICAL INTEGRATED DETECTION SYSTEM (BIDS)), MAST MOUNTED SIGHTS (E.G., FLIR, NIGHT VISION, ELECTRO-OPTICAL, LASER RANGE FINDER), AND 2D AIR SEARCH RADAR. OTHER POSSIBILITIES: SMALL SCALE 3-D AIR SEARCH RADAR, TOWED ARRAY, TOWED ACTIVE SONAR.
E.    C4ISR/INFORMATION WARFARE. IN ORDER TO ENHANCE THE CAPABILITY TO COLLECT, PROCESS, AND DISSEMINATE INFORMATION AND CONDUCT OTH ISRT MISSIONS, LCS CONCEPT DEVELOPMENT SHOULD CONSIDER THE CNO STRATEGIC STUDIES GROUP (SSG) FORCENET CONCEPT. FORCENET IS DEFINED AS "THE ARCHITECTURE AND BUILDING BLOCKS OF SENSORS, NETWORKS, DECISION AIDS, WEAPONS, WARRIORS, AND SUPPORTING SYSTEMS INTEGRATED INTO A HIGHLY ADAPTIVE, HUMAN-CENTRIC, COMPREHENSIVE SYSTEM THAT OPERATES FROM SEABED TO SPACE, FROM SEA TO LAND." IT ENVISIONS A SEABED-TO-SPACE, MULTI-TIERED SENSOR GRID, INTEGRATED INFORMATION SYSTEMS, INFORMATION CONVERTED TO ACTIONABLE KNOWLEDGE, AND DISTRIBUTED COMBAT CAPABILITY (BOTH MANNED AND UNMANNED) TO ENABLE A FULLY PREPARED AND INFORMED WARRIOR. THE NAVAL FIRES NETWORK (NFN) AND OTHER POTENTIAL SYSTEMS SHOULD BE EXPLORED FOR ABILITY TO PROVIDE TIME CRITICAL TARGETING AND INFO SUPERIORITY. DATA FUSION TECHNOLOGIES THAT ENHANCE DECISION MAKING AND COMBAT ACTION IN A REDUCED MANNING ENVIRONMENT ARE ESSENTIAL TO MAKING LCS A VIABLE PLATFORM IN A FUTURE OF REDUCED FINANCIAL RESOURCES. LCS MUST BE ABLE TO LEVERAGE ALL AVAILABLE INFORMATION WITHOUT REQUIRING AN INORDINATE NUMBER OF ORGANIC SENSORS AND WITH MINIMAL/OPTIMUM MANNING.
7.    HULL CONFIGURATION. HULL DESIGN TRADE-OFF CONSIDERATIONS SHOULD BALANCE NEEDS FOR HIGH-SPEED DASH CAPABILITY, ENDURANCE, SIZE, SEAKEEPING, AND STEALTH. SPECIFIC REQUIREMENTS:
A.    STEALTH. STEALTH WILL COMPLICATE THE ENEMY'S ISR AND TARGETING SOLUTIONS, ENHANCE SURVIVABILITY, AND FACILITATE CERTAIN MISSIONS SUCH AS SOF INSERTION AND EXTRACTION. TOPSIDE DESIGN SHOULD PROVIDE A SMALL RADAR CROSS-SECTION THROUGH USE OF COMPOSITE MATERIALS AND A MULTI-SPECTRAL STEALTHY CONFIGURATION. IN ADDITION, DESIGN SHOULD ALLOW FOR MISSION STEALTH CAPABILITY SUCH AS AN ENCLOSED "MOON POOL" CAPABILITY FOR SOF INSERTION OPERATIONS.
B.    DRAFT. THE DRAFT MUST BE RELATIVELY SHALLOW (20 FEET OR LESS) IN ORDER TO FACILITATE SHALLOW-WATER AND NEAR-LAND EXCURSIONS.
C.    AIR CAPABILITY. A FLIGHT DECK FOR OPERATING, FUELING, AND SUPPORTING UAV'S IS ESSENTIAL. LCS IS NOT ENVISIONED TO MAINTAIN A FULL AIR DETACHMENT (I.E., SH-60 DET) WITH THE SPACE/MATERIAL IMPACT AND MAINTENANCE SUPPORT MANNING THAT ENTAILS, BUT MUST RETAIN THE ABILITY TO SUPPORT HELICOPTER OPERATIONS SUCH AS REFUELING, LILLYPAD, AND VERTREP.
D.    BOAT AND UV WATER-LAUNCH CAPABILITY. SHIP CONFIGURATION SHOULD ALLOW FOR SMOOTH LAUNCHING AND RECOVERY OF A VARIETY OF UUV'S, USV'S, RESCUE BOATS, AND SOF CRAFT WITHOUT THE NEED FOR DAVITS THAT ARE CUMBERSOME, ADD TOPSIDE WEIGHT, AND INCREASE RADAR CROSS-SECTION. THE MOST LIKELY SOLUTION IS THROUGH A STERN RAMP OR GATE BUT MAY ALSO INCLUDE A VARIABLE DEPTH CAPABILITY FOR LCS.

E.     SHIP QUIETING. BECAUSE OF THE PREVALENCE OF MINE AND SUB THREATS IN THE LITTORALS, LCS SHOULD BE DESIGNED WITH SHIP QUIETING, NOISE MONITORING, AND EQUIPMENT SHOCK MOUNTING IN MIND.

F.     AT SEA REPLENISHMENT. IN ADDITION TO VERTREP CAPABILITY INHERENT IN THE INCLUSION OF A FLIGHT DECK, LCS WILL REQUIRE AN AT-SEA FUELING CAPABILITY. THIS WOULD PROVIDE FOR INTEROPERABILITY WITH LEGACY PLATFORMS AS WELL AS ENABLE OPERATIONS WITH ALLIED NAVIES. ALSO, SINCE ALL FUTURE COMBATANTS WILL OPERATE WITH REDUCED MANNING, LCS SHOULD CAPITALIZE ON AUTOMATED AND MODULAR UNREP TECHNOLOGIES FOR ALL AT-SEA AND INPORT COMMODITY HANDLING.

8.     PROPULSION AND ENGINEERING SYSTEMS. PROPULSION SYSTEMS MUST PROVIDE A HIGH SPEED CAPABILITY.  HOWEVER, IN RECOGNITION OF FUEL, SIZE, ENDURANCE, AND ENGINEERING TRADEOFFS, SPEED DOES NOT NECESSARILY HAVE TO BE SUSTAINED FOR LONG PERIODS. IT MAY BE SUFFICIENT FOR LCS TO ONLY HAVE A HIGH-SPEED DASH CAPABILITY. TRANSFORMATIONAL PROPULSION AND ENGINEERING SYSTEMS, SUCH AS ELECTRIC DRIVE, SHOULD BE EXPLORED NOT ONLY TO PRODUCE HIGH SPEEDS BUT TO TAKE INTO ACCOUNT OPTIMAL MANNING CONCEPTS SUCH AS PROPULSION, ELECTRIC PLANT, AND DAMAGE CONTROL AUTOMATION AND MONITORING SYSTEMS TO SUPPORT A MINIMUM MAINTENANCE REQUIREMENT.

9.     SMART SYSTEMS. TO ENHANCE MISSION ACCOMPLISHMENT AND SURVIVABILITY WITH OPTIMAL MANNING, LCS SHOULD LEVERAGE THE LATEST IN SMART SHIP SYSTEMS, INTEGRATED THROUGH A ROBUST LOCAL AREA NETWORK.

A.     INTEGRATED BRIDGE SYSTEM. SYSTEMS TO CONSIDER INCLUDE AUTOMATED PILOTING, SHIP'S COURSE TRACK ANALYSIS, RADAR AND DIGITAL NAUTICAL CHART OVERLAY, ELECTRONIC NAV, AND COLLISION AVOIDANCE SYSTEMS.

B.     DAMAGE CONTROL. AN AUTOMATED, REAL-TIME DC MANAGEMENT SYSTEM WILL BE ESSENTIAL.

C.     WIRELESS INTERNAL COMMUNICATIONS SYSTEM. PORTABLE/HAND HELD INTRA-SHIP COMMS.

D.     FUEL CONTROL SYSTEM. DIGITAL CONTROL SYSTEM FOR FUEL FILL AND TRANSFER.

E.     MACHINERY CONTROL SYSTEM. AUTOMATED PROPULSION AND ELECTRICAL PLANT CONTROLS.

F.     INTEGRATED CONDITION ASSESSMENT SYSTEM. AUTOMATED CONDITION BASED MAINTENANCE RECORDER FOR ENGINEERING AND COMBAT SYSTEMS EQUIPMENT.

G.     INTEGRATED COMBAT SYSTEMS CONTROLS USING DATA FUSION TECHNOLOGIES.

H.     ENHANCED AUTOMATED COMMUNICATIONS, INCLUDING COLLABORATIVE/CHAT NETWORKS TO AID IN DECISION MAKING.

10.     ADDITIONAL POTENTIAL TRANSFORMATIONAL SYSTEM: PERSONNEL TRACKING AND MONITORING SYSTEM (PTMS). AUTOMATED SYSTEM INTEGRATED INTO SHIP'S LAN TO COMBINE MAN OVERBOARD, TRACKING, AND PHYSIOLOGICAL MONITORING TO LOCATE AND MONITOR PERSONNEL.

11.     KEY POINTS. GIVEN THAT DESIGN TRADEOFFS MUST BE MADE, IT IS IMPORTANT TO REMEMBER TWO KEY POINTS DURING CONCEPT DEVELOPMENT:

A.     LET CAPABILITIES DRIVE SIZE. LCS SHOULD BE A RELATIVELY SMALL WARSHIP TO SUPPORT REQUIREMENTS FOR SPEED, AGILITY, STEALTH, AND AFFORDABILITY. HOWEVER, IT MUST BE LARGE ENOUGH TO OPERATE A WIDE VARIETY OF UNMANNED VEHICLES AND HELICOPTERS AND HAVE ENOUGH OFFENSIVE AND DEFENSIVE WEAPONS TO ENABLE THE SHIP TO CARRY OUT ITS ANTI-ACCESS MISSIONS. PRE-CONCEIVED NOTIONS OF THE SHIP'S SIZE SHOULD NOT DRIVE DESIGN TRADEOFFS THAT MIGHT ULTIMATELY LEAVE LCS UNPREPARED TO ACCOMPLISH ITS MISSIONS OR DEFEND ITSELF. WHILE SIZE IS IMPORTANT, WARFIGHTING CAPABILITIES ARE CRITICAL.

B.     LCS WILL NOT BE ABLE TO DO EVERYTHING. IT IS IMPORTANT NOT TO LET LCS TURN INTO A GOLD PLATED CADILLAC, EXPECTING IT TO BE ABLE TO DO

EVERYTHING A DD(X) OR CG(X) WILL BE ABLE TO DO. IT SHOULD BE VERSATILE
FOR A VARIETY OF LITTORAL MISSIONS AS DESCRIBED ABOVE, BUT ITS
CAPABILITIES, COST, AND SIZE SHOULD BE FOCUSED ON MEETING THE KEY
MISSIONS WHILE REMAINING AFFORDABLE.// BT #1030 NNNN

**Appendix C**
**Mission Area Workshop Results**
**Prioritized Task Lists**

# Proposed Small Boat Ops. Capabilities
## (Dahlgren Splinter Group - 02 May 2002)

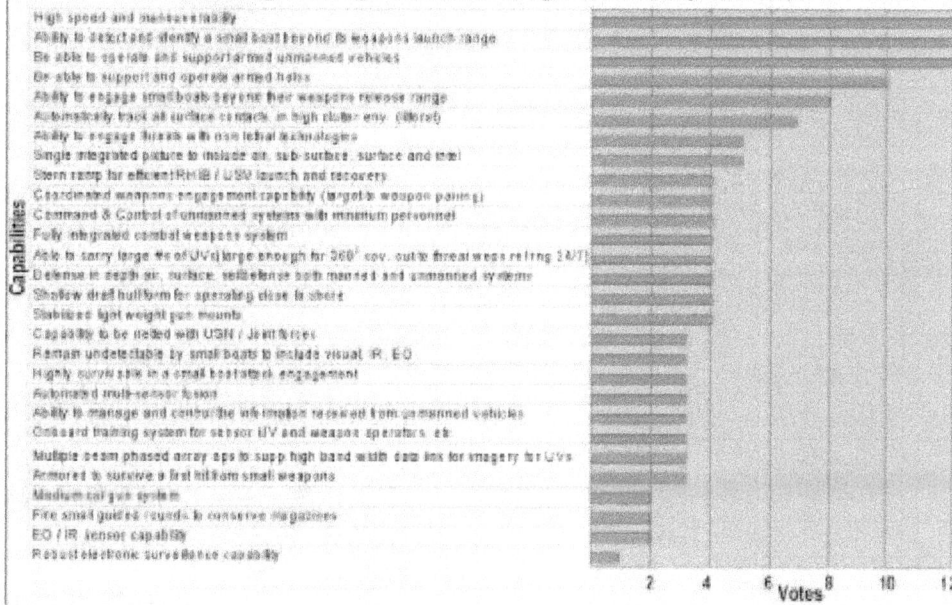

# Proposed Littoral ASW Capabilities
## (COMNAVSPECWARCOM Splinter Group – 24 May 2002)

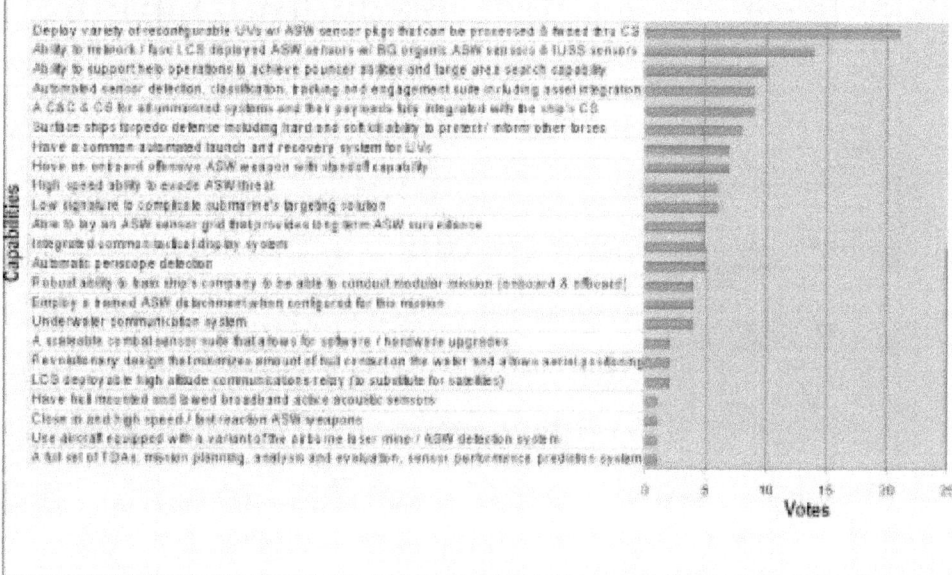

Proposed ISR Capabilities
(COMNAVSPECWARCOM Splinter Group – 22 May 2002)

Proposed MCM Capabilities
(Panama City Splinter Group - 09 May 2002)

## Proposed Special Operations
### (COMNAVSPECWARCOM Splinter Group – 21 May 2002)

Robust secure C4ISR capacity that connects & processes info to/from deployed NSW
Launch / recover SOF craft in 4-6 foot seas and 18-20 knot winds
Capable of berthing / hotel support for 32 men and short term support for 160 personnel
Provide JSOTF fwd [command element] w/ ded. C&C sps. & SOF ded. mission ping spaces
Lily pad for helos
Heavily armored and aimed for off. and def. fight w/ small craft and / or extraction support
Act as a mothership for SOF operations (air, surface & sub surface)
Greater than 45 knots speed
Provide overwatch w/in range of the ship's organic wpns sys (over the last protection of SOF)
Support armed/unarmed UAV / UUV / USV
Operate / control armed / unarmed URV / UUV / USV
Support two SOF RHIBs per embarked seal platoon
Reduced signatures
Ability to support two MH-60
Stern launch / recovery ramp for RHIB / AUV / SDV
Modular weapon capability to include guns, surface to surface, surface to air
Realtime 3D rendering of area of projection / engagement (sub surface, surface, air)
Survive / escape a CBR environment
4000nm range
Low signatures
Support NSW (Naval Special Warfare) task unit
Onboard maintenance capability for NSW systems, vehicles
Maximize ability to sustain & repair battle damage
Max. draft 9 feet
Redundant method of recovering SOF craft
Support FSB (forward staging base)
Operate in a CBR environment

Capabilities

0   5   10   15   20
Votes

## Proposed HLS / D – MIO Capabilities
### (NWC Splinter Group - 24 April 2002)

Secure interoperable comms with all elements
Ability to go into shallow water (20 ft draft)
Organic weapons on LCS (not alone and afraid)
Single integrated COP
Ability to support and operate multiple manned and unmanned offboard systems
Integrated RHIB / helo capability over the horizon
Capable of ISE for MIO defense
Propulsion system compatible with shallow water OPS
Non-lethal capability to stop non-cooperating ship
Ability to search containers without opening them
Multiple all weather boarding team delivery vehicles
Surge capability for personnel and weapons
Rehersal system to show target ship characteristics / layout
Remote CBRNE sensing of target ship
Modular mission packages for unmanned vehicles plug and play
Biometric analysis by the boarding party of target ship personnel
Use of Army attack helos
Automated two way language translation for boarding parties
Automated DC
Mission well deck
Ability to take Command & Control of any communicate w/ any unmanned system
CODAG propulsion system
Parametric sonar system (BG ATFP)
Ability to use UAV for logistics support

Capabilities

0   1   2   3   4   5
Mean

12

**Appendix D**
**Mission Area Workshops**
**Principal Take-aways**

# LCS Required Characteristics
## ASW Workshop

- Desire is to exploit unattended sensors and sensors on OOVs.
- At least one organic manned helicopter needed.
- Weapons: UVs and helos, a QR standoff ASW weapon, a close in ASW weapon, and torpedo defense weapons
- Onboard sensors include radar, hull sonar (HF/MF), towed sensor, and periscope detection system
- Requires crew augmentation/specialization: (ASW is a highly perishable "art form")
- Speed principally for torpedo evasion.
- Acoustic signature control most important.

# LCS Required Characteristics
## ISR Workshop

- **Need open C4ISR architecture**
  - Sensors/processors/radios need to be tied in to apertures, power, and cooling
- **Robust networking/bandwidth/spectrum requirements**
  - Need at least T1
  - Real time data exchange with UVs, offboard systems, and other platforms
  - Full connectivity with Joint/Allied/National/Law Enforcement
- **Numbers of sensors and platforms important**
  - Maximize use of offboard systems
  - Control of theater level UV assets desired
- **Automated data fusion and analysis critical**
- **Persistent dwell important**
- **Equip with dedicated intel/cryptologic space with dedicated nets**
- **Practical stealth important to ISR mission**

# LCS Required Characteristics
## MCM Workshop

- LCS focus: area MCM search, map & avoid, and limited neutralization (punch through)
- Ability to carry, support and operate manned, remote, and autonomous unmanned vehicles mandatory
- Requires crew augmentation (MCM is still an art form) for identification and destruction (improved AUVs may eventually be good enough)
- Speed only required to get ahead of BG or SAG
- Organic MCM places equipment where it is needed sooner, but doesn't speed actual MCM process
- Embed organic MIW intel capability onboard LCS


# LCS Required Characteristics
## Anti-Small Boat Workshop

- Must be able to engage targets from close aboard to ranges beyond threat weapons launch range
- Fast reaction small craft, aircraft (manned and unmanned), and armed helos preferred method to counter threat
- Area and point defenses and high engagement rates against near-simultaneous multiple targets required
- Agility and burst speed of 40 to 50 knots useful for improving engagement geometry
- Must be able to receive and exploit offboard cueing, tracking and identification resources as well as organic capability
- Consider non-lethal options to temporarily neutralize potential threat

# LCS Required Characteristics
## SOF Workshop

- Support/launch/recover SOF insertion/extraction vehicles
  - NSW RHIB (Minimum 2-boat 11m), SDV, Mk5
- Full C4I suite including SOF unique collaboration/ planning systems and radios
- Responsive close-in NSFS
- At least 1 armed helo (prefer 2)
- Visual/IR/Radar signature control important.
- Support for up to 50 SOF personnel
- Rehearsal and training space
- 45+ knots
- 2000+ NM Range/2 Weeks+ endurance
  - Need to work ahead of the main force arrival

# LCS Required Characteristics
## MIO/HLD Workshop

- Deploy two or more boarding teams simultaneously
- Embark at least one, preferably two, helicopters
- Embark at least two RHIBs/team delivery vehicles
- Reposition at high (40+ knot) speed
- Unrefueled range of 4000 nm/30 days endurance
- Approximately 20 foot maximum draft
- Improved connectivity with relevant joint/interagency/coalition partners and boarding parties
- People intensive mission
- Shipboard weapons capable of stopping/ holding at risk noncompliant vessels (including nonlethal options)

**Appendix E**
**Final LCS Characteristics Briefing**

# Littoral Combat Ship
# LCS

Defining Operational
Characteristics
Integration Briefing

# NWC LCS Effort

- Tasked by N-76 in December 2001
- Two Tasks:
  - Define operational characteristics of LCS
  - Identify promising technologies for LCS
- NWC effort is pre–AOA/ORD
- Final Report Submitted 31 July 2002

# Characteristics Tasking Memo Schedule (Accelerated)

| Event | NLT |
|---|---|
| • Detailed Plan | 30 Jan 02 |
| • Scope Defined | 28 Feb 02 |
| • Interim Report | 14 Jun 02 |
| • Final Report | 31 Jul 02 |

# Operational Characteristics Process

1. Workshop with fleet operators to develop preliminary LCS mission areas and overarching guidelines.

2. Follow on workshops combining fleet operators and technical experts to develop tasks for each of the mission areas.

3. Final integration workshop

# Why Are We Doing This?

Is LCS:

1. A 'mission/capabilities focused Frigate/Corvette-sized follow-on optimized for littoral environments?

2. A very small displacement, advanced technology vessel?

3. An answer looking for a question?

4. A set of littoral access capabilities that could be addressed by several types of surface ships/vessels, or by platforms other than ships?

*To Increase Force Structure*

*To Satisfy Transformation Critics*

*To Address Operational Shortfalls*

# Workshops

- Initial workshop (guidelines and missions)

- Homeland Defense/Maritime Intercept Operations

- Small Boat Prosecution

- Mine Countermeasures

- Special Operations

- ISR Battlefield Preparation

- Antisubmarine Warfare

- Integration Workshop

*Involved over 200 fleet operators & subject matter experts*

# Candidate Missions & Follow-on Workshops

- Participants selected four primary missions:

  Prosecution of Small Boats

  Mine Counter-Measures

  Shallow water Anti-Submarine Warfare

  Intelligence, Surveillance, & Reconnaissance

- And two secondary missions:

  Homeland Defense/Maritime Intercept Operations

  Special Operations:

    Direct Action

    Strategic Reconnaissance

    Information Operations

# Guidelines

1. The ship must be capable of networking with other platforms and sensors.

2. The ship must be useful across the spectrum of conflict.

3. The ship must be able to sustain or support forward naval presence.

4. LCS System logistics, especially special requirements, must be included in each mission area discussion.

5. The ship should be capable of operating manned vertical lift aircraft.

6. The ship should operate with optimized/reduced manning.

7. The ship should use open architecture and modularity.

8. The ship should be capable of launching, recovering and operating manned, unmanned, and autonomous vehicles.

9. The ship should have core, organic self-defense capabilities.

# Overarching Guidelines

The ship must be capable of networking with other platforms and sensors. 4.79

The ship should be capable of launching, recovering and operating manned, unmanned, and autonomous vehicles. 4.71

The ship should have core, organic self-defense capabilities. 4.50

The ship should use open architecture and modularity. 4.32

The ship should be capable of operating manned vertical lift aircraft. 4.00

The ship must be able to sustain or support forward naval presence. 3.96

The ship should operate with optimized/reduced manning. 3.86

LCS System logistics, especially special requirements, must be included in each mission area discussion. 3.82

The ship must be useful across the spectrum of conflict. 3.75

Score is a scale of 1 (no) to 5 (yes)

# Guideline 1

## The ship must be capable of networking with other platforms and sensors.

There was a sharp division between those who believed the LCS must be fully networked to all systems (FORCENET) and those who believed it only needs to be connected in areas directly affecting its mission performance. There was agreement that LCS will be both a user & a provider of data.

22

# Guideline 2

## The ship must be useful across the spectrum of conflict

Although participants agreed with this statement, they didn't want this statement to imply that the ship should be a jack-of-all-trades. They believed it should be able to conduct peacetime exercises, maritime intercept operations and similar missions in times of tension, as well as carry out its wartime role.

# Guideline 3

## The ship must be able to sustain forward naval presence.

While there was general consensus favoring the statement, there were differences about how it should be interpreted. Some believed it means that ships must be capable of deploying with the battle group while others argued that it could be stationed forward. The former was much more strongly supported than the latter.

# Guideline 4

## LCS System logistics, especially special requirements, must be included in each mission area discussion.

There were heated discussions about logistics. Most believed a smaller LCS would require special handling (including special support ships) in order make it as flexible and sustainable as it will need to be.

# Guideline 5

## The ship should be capable of operating manned vertical lift aircraft.

Originally, this guideline was limited to helicopters, but participants didn't want to begin with any restrictions on later discussions. As the workshop progressed, it became clear that most participants believed the LCS should handle aircraft up to the size of SH-60 helicopters. There was divergence, however, about whether it should be a lily pad, or capable of supporting a detachment with most favoring the former.

# Guideline 6

## The ship should operate with optimized or reduced manning.

This guideline provoked sharp debate about the benefits and risks of reduced manning. Again and again issues of peripheral duties (such as launching & recovering unmanned vehicles, hotel services, damage control, and boarding parties) were raised. Those favoring reduced manning believed LCS must be highly automated. Those favoring an optimized crew appreciated the flexibility and sustainability a larger crew brings.

# Guideline 7

## The ship should use open architecture and modularity.

Everyone agreed open architecture, although difficult to achieve, is a goal worth pursuing. There was much more debate about the benefits of modularity. Strong support was expressed for modular ideas involving vertical launch systems and unmanned vehicles, but much less support was offered for conex box-like modular concepts because of cost, storage, maintenance, forward logistics and training.

# Guideline 8

## The ship should be capable of launching, recovering and operating manned, unmanned, and autonomous vehicles.

This guideline at first addressed only unmanned and autonomous systems. Special Operations representatives reminded us, however, that the LCS might be a candidate platform for launching manned vehicles they use. A lot of participants believed unmanned vehicles would be the heart of the LCS system. Big concern about when such vehicles would be ready for the fleet, leading to a discussion of a phased or evolutionary LCS design approach .

# Guideline 9

## The ship should have core, organic self-defense capabilities.

Participants agreed that you couldn't send a ship and its crew in harm's way and not provide some capability for self-defense. The level of this capability, however, was an issue. Most agreed that kinetic self-defense weapons are required while a few argued that stealth and speed should be its primary self-defense capabilities.

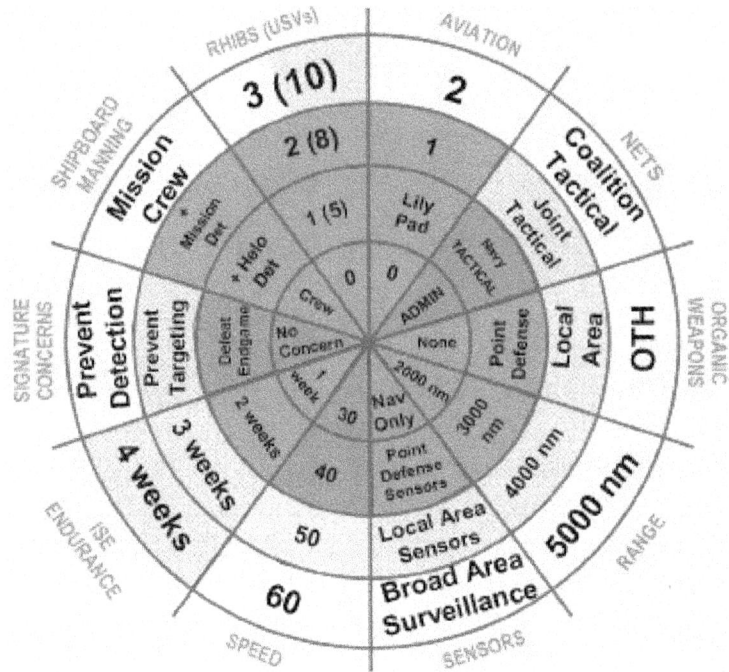

# Characteristics Prioritization

Participants were asked to prioritize characteristics in two different ways:

• First, they were asked to "weight" the characteristics. They were given $100 to spend on all of the characteristics. They were told that a characteristic on which they spent $20 should be considered twice as important as a characteristic on which they spent $10.

• Second, they were asked to compare characteristics head-to-head. From each pair of characteristics they were asked to select the characteristic they felt was more important – no ties and no abstentions.

The objective was to test participant consistency in prioritizations.

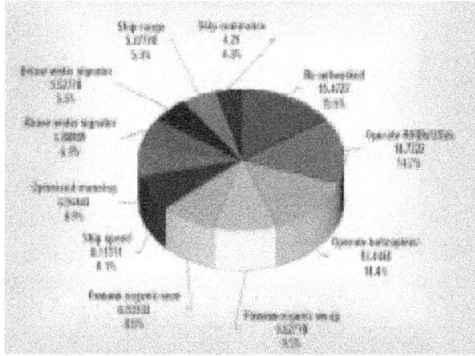

1. Be networked (15.5%)
2. Operate USVs/RHIBs (14.7%)
3. Operate UAVs/Helos (14.4%)
4. Organic weapons (9.5%)
5. Organic sensors (8.8%)
6. Ship Speed (8.1%)
7. Optimized manning (6.9%)
8. Above water signatures (6.5%)
9. Below water signatures (5.5%)
10. Ship range (5.3%)
11. Ship endurance (4.3%)

*Top 3 characteristics considered almost three times as important as bottom three*

# Pairwise Comparisons

CHARACTERISTICS (WON – LOST Record)

1. Be networked (Won 8 – Lost 1 to Operate USVs/RHIBs)
2. Operate USVs/RHIBs (Won 8 – Lost 1 to Operate UAVs/Helos)
3. Operate UAVs/Helos (Won 8 – Lost 1 to Be networked)
4. Organic sensors (Won 6 – Lost 3)
5. Organic weapons (Won 5 – Lost 4)
6. Signatures (Won 4 – Lost 5)
7. Ship Speed (Won 2 – Lost 7)
8. Optimized manning (Won 2 – Lost 7)
9. Ship range (Won 1 – Lost 8)
10. Ship endurance (Won 0 – Lost 9)

*Signatures were not separated into above and below water*

28

# Dual Method Comparison

| WEIGHTED PRIORITIES | PAIRWISE COMPARISONS | |
|---|---|---|
| 1. Be networked | 1. Be networked | Top 5 the same |
| 2. Operate USVs/RHIBs | 2. Operate USVs/RHIBs | |
| 3. Operate UAVs/Helos | 3. Operate UAVs/Helos | |
| 4. Organic weapons | 4. Organic sensors | |
| 5. Organic sensors | 5. Organic weapons | |
| 6. Ship Speed | 6. Above water signatures | Middle the same |
| 7. Optimized manning | 7. Ship Speed | |
| 8. Above water signatures | 8. Optimized manning | |
| 9. Below water signatures | | |
| 10. Ship range | 9. Ship range | Bottom 2 the same |
| 11. Ship endurance | 10. Ship endurance | |

| | Type A | Type B | Type C |
|---|---|---|---|
| Deployability | Deployable in support of the battle group | Deployable when accompanied by battle group | Deployable independent of battle group |
| Endurance | Range more important than endurance | Capable of short (<week) independent operations | Capable of lengthy (>month) independent operations |
| Helicopter ops | Supports lily pad/detachment ops | Supports lily pad operations | Supports helicopter detachment |
| Mission capability | Lift, support OOV mission | Single-mission | Multi-mission (sequentially) |
| UV operations | Complete reliance on unmanned vehicles | Controls unmanned vehicles | Supports & Operates unmanned vehicles |
| Logistics | Could be part of new logistics framework | New logistics framework required | Normal logistics support |
| Manning | Minimum manning | Reduced manning | Optimal manning |
| Concept of ops | Dashes in/out of littoral | Dashes in/out of littoral | Operates in littoral |
| Connectivity | Fully netted | Mission netted | Fully netted |
| Modularity | RO/RO modular | Mostly modular (single mission or module) | Highly modular (open architecture) |
| Stealth | Reduced signatures | Stealthy | Low signatures |
| Speed | High speed | Very high speed | High speed |

# How Many Options Should We Consider?

Workshop participants made it clear that no single
ship would completely satisfy all LCS proponents

Every participant made
two variants their
first or second choice

| FIRST CHOICE | | |
|---|---|---|
| 1 | 2 | 3 |
| 38.8% | 47.2% | 13.8% |

| SECOND CHOICE | | |
|---|---|---|
| 1 | 2 | 3 |
| 33.3% | 52.7% | 13.8% |

| THIRD CHOICE | | |
|---|---|---|
| 1 | 2 | 3 |
| 28.7% | 00.0% | 72.2% |

Participants were asked to rank order their preferences
concerning **how many** variants that should be pursued

# How Many Options Should We Consider?

Workshop participants made it clear that no single
ship would completely satisfy all LCS proponents

Participants saw Type C
as 80% solution

| FIRST CHOICE | | |
|---|---|---|
| A | B | C |
| 22.2% | 19.4% | 58.3% |

| SECOND CHOICE | | |
|---|---|---|
| A | B | C |
| 22.2% | 50.0% | 27.7% |

| THIRD CHOICE | | |
|---|---|---|
| A | B | C |
| 55.5% | 30.5% | 13.8% |

Participants were asked to rank order their preference for
**which variant** should be pursued

## How Many Options Should We Consider?

Workshop participants made it clear that no single ship would completely satisfy all LCS proponents

Question still open about how many and which variants to pursue

However, work furthest along on Type A

Project leaders recommend pursuing 3 variants of LCS which together should satisfy all requirements. Integration workshop participants recommend pursuing two variants (B & C).

IF SINGLE SHIP PURSUED, PARTICIPANTS RECOMMEND TYPE C

# Final Thoughts

- Report prepared with single ship type in mind (Type C – Frigate).

- Single ship type unlikely to satisfy all proponents or critics.

- Recommend pursuing two or three types, with emphasis on Type C, in order to meet greatest number of objectives and build on investments already being made by the Navy.

- Here's why we recommend that approach:

# Final Thoughts

• Type A LCS, the "capability conveyor" represented by the High Speed Vessel, is focused on the lift/deployment/recovery of OOVs mission. The ship should be properly equipped to handle and deploy unmanned vehicles, deployable sensors, and to support Type B LCS operations.

• Type B LCS, the "pouncer" represented by the Visby or Skjold, comes closer to SURFPAC's LCS concept and is a better fit for some missions (like dogfighting with small craft and delivering special forces) than either Type A or C. It's smaller size requires the support of a support vessel.

• Type C LCS, the "80% solution" represented by an upscaled Triton, is the best force structure fit for the Navy and the most useful ship in both the short- and long-term. Current systems act as surrogates for future transformational systems not yet available.

THE LITTORAL COMBAT SHIP:
IS THE US NAVY ASSUMING TOO MUCH RISK?

A thesis presented to the Faculty of the U.S. Army
Command and General Staff College in partial
fulfillment of the requirements for the
degree

MASTER OF MILITARY ART AND SCIENCE
General Studies

by

JONATHAN C. RUSSELL, LCDR, USN
B.S., United States Naval Academy, Annapolis, Maryland, 1993

Fort Leavenworth, Kansas
2006

| | Report Documentation Page | | Form Approved OMB No. 0704-0188 |
|---|---|---|---|

| 1. REPORT DATE **16 JUN 2006** | 2. REPORT TYPE | 3. DATES COVERED |
|---|---|---|

| 4. TITLE AND SUBTITLE **Littoral combat ship: is the US Navy assuming too much risk?** | 5a. CONTRACT NUMBER |
|---|---|
| | 5b. GRANT NUMBER |
| | 5c. PROGRAM ELEMENT NUMBER |
| 6. AUTHOR(S) **Jonathan Russell** | 5d. PROJECT NUMBER |
| | 5e. TASK NUMBER |
| | 5f. WORK UNIT NUMBER |

| 7. PERFORMING ORGANIZATION NAME(S) AND ADDRESS(ES) **US Army Command and General Staff College,1 Reynolds Ave.,Fort Leavenworth,KS,66027-1352** | 8. PERFORMING ORGANIZATION REPORT NUMBER **ATZL-SWD-GD** |
|---|---|

| 9. SPONSORING/MONITORING AGENCY NAME(S) AND ADDRESS(ES) | 10. SPONSOR/MONITOR'S ACRONYM(S) |
|---|---|
| | 11. SPONSOR/MONITOR'S REPORT NUMBER(S) |

12. DISTRIBUTION/AVAILABILITY STATEMENT
**Approved for public release; distribution unlimited.**

13. SUPPLEMENTARY NOTES
**The original document contains color images.**

14. ABSTRACT

**The purpose of this research is to explore the current risks associated with the Littoral Combat Ship (LCS). There are several compelling reasons for the radical changes incorporated in the LCS design. A better understanding of the risks that the ship and crew will assume is vital to the proper use of this new platform and will help ensure the safety of both. This study does not advocate complete risk mitigation aboard the LCS, but strives to increase the overall risk awareness. The risk of combining so many new and untested elements on a single ship must be understood by all of those who are involved in its implementation. The arrival of the first LCS, projected to be operational in 2007, will represent a reduced manning concept designed from the ground up and the first of a new family of US naval combatants built to face the future maritime threats. With the proposed ship class of up to fifty-five ships, the US Navy needs to make sure that LCS is not assuming too much risk.**

15. SUBJECT TERMS

| 16. SECURITY CLASSIFICATION OF: | | | 17. LIMITATION OF ABSTRACT | 18. NUMBER OF PAGES | 19a. NAME OF RESPONSIBLE PERSON |
|---|---|---|---|---|---|
| a. REPORT **unclassified** | b. ABSTRACT **unclassified** | c. THIS PAGE **unclassified** | **1** | **79** | |

MASTER OF MILITARY ART AND SCIENCE

THESIS APPROVAL PAGE

Name of Candidate: Lieutenant Commander Jonathan C. Russell

Thesis Title: The Littoral Combat Ship: Is the US Navy Assuming Too Much Risk?

Approved by:

_____, Thesis Committee Chair
Robert M. Brown, M.M.A.S.

_____, Member
Phillip G. Pattee, M.M.A.S.

_____, Member, Consulting Faculty
Ronald E. Cuny, Ph.D.

Accepted this 16th day of June 2006 by:

_____, Director, Graduate Degree Programs
Robert F. Baumann, Ph.D.

# ABSTRACT

THE LITTORAL COMBAT SHIP: IS THE US NAVY ASSUMING TOO MUCH RISK?, by LCDR Jonathan C. Russell, 79 pages.

The purpose of this research is to explore the current risks associated with the Littoral Combat Ship (LCS). There are several compelling reasons for the radical changes incorporated in the LCS design. A better understanding of the risks that the ship and crew will assume is vital to the proper use of this new platform and will help ensure the safety of both. This study does not advocate complete risk mitigation aboard the LCS, but strives to increase the overall risk awareness. The risk of combining so many new and untested elements on a single ship must be understood by all of those who are involved in its implementation. The arrival of the first LCS, projected to be operational in 2007, will represent a reduced manning concept designed from the ground up and the first of a new family of US naval combatants built to face the future maritime threats. With the proposed ship class of up to fifty-five ships, the US Navy needs to make sure that LCS is not assuming too much risk.

# ACKNOWLEDGMENTS

I would like to thank my committee chair Mr. Robert Brown, committee member Mr. Phillip Pattee, and consulting faculty Dr. Ronald Cuny for their help and expert advice throughout this project.

I would also like to thank the staff at the Combined Arms Research Library (CARL) for their excellent assistance with my research. Whether keeping me informed on the latest subject information or processing thesis permissions, CARL proved to be a valuable asset.

Finally, to my family, thank you for your continual support. Once again, I could not have done it without you.

# TABLE OF CONTENTS

# ACRONYMS

| | |
|---|---|
| CO | Commanding Officer |
| CSG | Carrier Strike Group |
| DC | Damage Control |
| ESF | Expeditionary Strike Force |
| ESG | Expeditionary Strike Group |
| FRP | Fleet Response Plan |
| HCO | Human Capital Object |
| ISO | International Standards Organization |
| ISR | Intelligence, Surveillance and, Reconnaissance |
| KSA | Knowledge, Skills, and Abilities |
| LCS | Littoral Combat Ship |
| MEU | Marine Expeditionary Unit |
| MIO | Maritime Interception Operations |
| NPDC | Naval Personnel Development Command |
| POE | Projected Operational Environment |
| ROC | Required Operational Capability |
| SAG | Surface Action Group |
| SMD | Ship Manning Document |

# ILLUSTRATIONS

# TABLES

# CHAPTER 1

## INTRODUCTION AND BACKGROUND

> Have we not ourselves much to blame for it in this
> exclusive devotion to the mechanical matters? Do we not hear,
> within and without, the scornful cry of disparagement that
> everything is done by machinery in these days, and that we are
> waxing old and decaying, ready to vanish away? Everything done
> by machinery! As if the subtlest and most comprehensive mind
> that ever wrought on this planet could devise a machine to meet the
> innumerable incidents of sea and naval war.
>
> Alfred T. Mahan, 1888

### Introduction

On 2 June 2005 the US Navy began building the first Littoral Combat Ship

(LCS), the USS *Freedom*. The LCS represents the first of a new family of surface

combatants designed to face the challenges of the twenty-first century. The USS *Freedom*

is the first ship of a class which the Navy envisions may grow to as many as fifty-five in

number. This ship is designed to operate and fight in the congested littorals and carry out

a wide range of mission tasks against a very unpredictable enemy. In addition, the LCS is

designed with reduced manning from the ground up. As Navy planners make decisions

today that will affect tomorrow's fleet, how the LCS is manned and the risks the ship will

assume due to several other new design features are critical issues.

The USS *Freedom* is part of the US Navy's transformation plan. Transformation

is a defense-wide initiative that describes the military's need to be adequately prepared

for the challenges of the twenty-first century. The US Navy's framework for

transformation is "Sea Power 21" with its three components: Sea Strike, Sea Shield, and

Sea Basing. These components provide the vision of how the US Navy will project offensive power, ensure global defense, and maintain the ability to operate at sea as a sovereign entity. Important elements to both naval transformation and the Sea Power 21 vision are the need to operate in the littorals, conduct network-centric operations, and utilize unmanned vehicles while operating with reduced personnel (Clark 2002, 34). The LCS is designed to support these elements with a reduced crew of highly trained sailors able to perform multiple tasks in several different mission areas. The success of the LCS will help determine how reduced manning as well as other design features will be implemented in future fleet designs like the next generation destroyer DD(X) and cruiser CG(X).

One of the key tenets of Sea Power 21 is the focus on the design of systems that will enable war-fighters to be more efficient decision-makers with fewer personnel. The need to lower the cost of operating a ship by reducing the overall crew size has become a top priority for the US Navy. Challenged by a decreasing defense budget, the US Navy realizes the importance of smart spending and the need to preserve its greatest asset-- people. Operations and support costs, which include the cost of personnel, maintenance, consumables, and sustaining support, have remained relatively constant while the Navy's total operational budget has decreased. The cost of personnel alone comprises over 50 percent of the operations and support costs for a navy ship (Hinkle 2004, 4). The ability to reduce the operational cost of the fleet by lowering the number of sailors required aboard its ships has the potential to save these vital funds.

Along with budget constraints, the US Navy is getting smaller. Since the 1980s and the Reagan administration's goal of the 600-ship navy, a lot has changed. The United States is no longer racing to keep up with a large Soviet naval threat. The US Navy is building a smaller and more capable fleet, one that will face a less defined threat. However, with the current battle force of just over 280 ships, every ship will count. Of these 280 ships in the current force, barely a hundred are surface combatants to include cruisers, destroyers and frigates as well as various other war fighting ships. This number is the lowest since the late 1930s. However, the current vision is to build the fleet back to approximately 313 ships (Cavas 2005, 1). The LCS will play a large role in this expansion. Today's naval leadership suggests that the Navy should not fixate on the large numbers of the 1980s but focus on a smaller and more capable fleet. Those in support of the reduced manning concept believe that smaller and more capable crews, enabled with new technology and training, will be able to achieve mission success. However, decreasing the overall manning requirements to the lowest levels must be balanced with ship survivability and overall risk.

As the Navy builds a more efficient fleet, it finds itself with a wide range of missions and an increased operational tempo. The Fleet Response Plan (FRP) instituted in December 2003 gives the US Navy the ability to surge multiple ship formations in response to emergencies. Under the current FRP, Carrier Strike Groups (CSGs) and Expeditionary Strike Groups (ESGs) that have just returned from deployments will be on alert for a certain period for short-notice deployment. In addition, CSGs and ESGs approaching deployments will also be in surge windows prior to deploying. This increased operational tempo has put even greater strain on today's Navy. The ability to reduce the crew size required to man these strike groups has the potential to reduce the strain on the individual sailor and could also give the Navy more flexibility. Any added flexibility will depend on how the personnel removed from the ships are utilized. If the

Navy does not maintain end strength and reduces its overall numbers as a result of reduced manning, the individual sailor tempo (in the US Navy commonly referred to as personnel tempo or PERSTEMPO) will remain the same.

Along with the challenges of reduced budgets, fewer ships, and increased operational tempo, the US Navy faces a new and deadly threat. The bombing of the USS *Cole* (DDG-67) on 12 October 2000 was a clear reminder of how unpredictable the current threat is. As the Navy builds a new fleet it needs to make sure that its crews have the ability to properly protect their ships. The results of the USS *Cole* investigation produced several lessons learned. One of these lessons was that damage control efforts of the crew were instrumental in the survival of the ship.

Damage control (DC), the ability for the ship's crew to protect itself from fire and flooding, is a manpower intensive activity. A major conflagration is damage control at its worst. The Office of the Chief of Naval Operations through its Navy tactics, techniques, and procedures (NTTP) publications defines a major conflagration as:

> Damage of magnitude that cannot be readily handled by conventional DC organization; therefore, all-hands participation is required to save the ship. A major conflagration may also involve mass personnel casualties. It is imperative that command, control, and communications be established and maintained to effectively coordinate DC actions over a prolonged period of time. The inflicted damage must be brought under control immediately and simultaneously; combat systems must be kept in or returned to a state of battle readiness. (US DoN 2004b, 10-1)

As the Navy determines the reduced numbers required to man the LCS, the crew's ability to combat fire and flooding must be addressed. In the past, technology has been a major factor in helping reduce the demands on manpower; however, there are some functions that cannot be easily replaced by machine. For example, when electricity is not available during a casualty and automatic sensors, valves, and pumps are not functioning properly, manpower may be the only option available to save the ship.

## Research Questions

The objective of this study is to evaluate the risks associated with the reduced manning design on the LCS. The primary question that the study addresses is: Is the US Navy assuming too much risk with reduced manning aboard the LCS?

Secondary questions include the following:

1. What level of risk is the US Navy assuming with the LCS reduced manning design?

2. Will the LCS be able to conduct damage control and repair in a mass conflagration environment and save the ship?

3. Will the multiple tasked "hybrid sailor" have sufficient skills and training to compensate for the reduced crew size aboard the LCS?

4. Will the LCS be able to maintain mission capability and accomplish the mission in the littorals while operating independently?

5. Will the rapid acquisition timeline of the LCS allow follow-on designs to benefit from the initial Flight 0 prototypes?

## Significance of the Study

This thesis examines the potential risks associated with the reduced manning design aboard the new LCS. As the US Navy plans to build as many as fifty-five of these ships, it is very important that the risks associated with the LCS design be fully understood and minimized. Furthermore, other future Navy ship designs may also benefit from this research.

The study is organized into four subsequent chapters: chapter 2 presents the literature used in this study to research the primary and secondary questions; chapter 3 presents the research methodology used to analyze the data; chapter 4 contains the study's analysis; and chapter 5 summarizes the results of the study, provides a conclusion, and closes with recommendations for further study.

## Background

Leveraging technology to reduce the crew size is not a new concept. Commercial maritime industry has been using reduced manning to cut cost for years. A 100,000-ton merchant ship going to sea with a crew of only thirty is not uncommon. The US Navy has also seen crew reduction in its recent past. An 8000-ton World War II cruiser typically had a crew of 800 to 1,500 sailors compared to a modern-day Arleigh Burke-class destroyer of comparable size with only 326 sailors (Klain 1999, 66). Most of these gains occurred due to the advances in the engineering plant. The rise of gas turbine technology and the ability to monitor ship spaces remotely greatly reduced the crew required to operate the plant. The gas turbine engine was incorporated into the design of the Spruance (DD-963) class destroyer and Oliver Hazard Perry (FFG-7) class frigate. Several critics insisted that the design changes, resulting in such large crew reduction, would never work. However, history has proven the gas turbine to be more reliable than the steam plant ships of the 1950s and 1960s (Klain 1999, 66).

The US Navy conducted its first "Smart Ship" experiment aboard the guided-missile cruiser USS *Yorktown* (CG-48) in 1997. The goal of Smart Ship was to see how minor crew reductions aboard an operational ship would affect its ability to accomplish all required tasks. The experiment successfully reduced the workload and manpower requirements while enhancing combat readiness and improving the crew's quality of life. The results further indicated that the use of cost-effective commercial technology as well as policy and procedural changes allowed crewmembers to focus more on their war fighting and professional skills, instead of repetitive tasks. The Smart Ship experiment allowed USS *Yorktown* to achieve incremental manning reductions. The ship's crew further realized that greater changes in reduced manning would require complete platform and systems integrated design (Schank 2005, 109).

In a further effort to reduce required crew size without affecting performance, the US Navy began two experiments in 2002, one on east coast, which included six surface ships, a submarine, and a strike fighter squadron. The West Coast experiment was called the "Optimal Manning Experiment" and included the USS *Mobile Bay* (CG-53) and USS *Milius* (DDG-69). The USS *Mobile Bay* crew shrank to 308 sailors after 34 billets were cut and the USS *Milius*, after cutting 53 billets, reduced the enlisted crew to 237 (Wise 2003, 16). Again through the use of new technologies, procedures, and policies, the ships' crews were able to reduce manning by 34 and 53 enlisted sailors, respectively. Their success centered on the innovative use of personnel to accomplish shipboard tasks. Remote monitoring through the use of additional video cameras, increased use of distance support, which is the ability to contact technicians ashore when troubleshooting equipment at sea, and the use of specialized ashore-based teams to conduct preventative maintenance, played an important role in manning reductions.

The East Coast experiment, called the "The Fleet Manning Experiment" included the destroyer USS *Mahan* (DDG-72), the cruiser USS *Monterey* (CG-61), the aircraft carrier USS *George Washington* (CVN-73), the amphibious assault ship USS *Nassau* (LHA-4), the submarine USS *Oklahoma City* (SSN-723), and Strike Fighter Squadron 34. The commanding officers were asked to identify warfare requirements, to match people to the requirements, and then to deploy with their results. Results from the units involved were mixed:

- *Mahan*-cut 18 sailors, enlisted crew 286
- *Monterey*-detached 30 sailors, enlisted crew 295
- *George Washington*-added 48 sailors, enlisted crew 3,045
- *Nassau*-cut 26 sailors, enlisted crew 1,016
- *Oklahoma City*-added 1 sailor, enlisted crew 130
- *VFA-34*-added 16, total squadron 218. (Wise 2003, 18, emphasis mine)

These experiments illustrate the path that the US Navy has taken to help determine the minimal number of sailors needed to accomplish unit tasking and the ability to integrate these tasks with the assigned personnel. As a result, several new and innovative approaches to better utilize personnel were discovered. Finally, by reducing the menial jobs required of the crew such as preservation and maintenance through aggressive outsourcing to the private sector, there were fewer requirements on the crew, further allowing its reduction.

The LCS concept began in 1998 when the US Navy started looking at designs for a small and fast surface combatant. The study, named "Streetfighter," was conducted at the Naval War College. Vice Admiral Arthur Cebrowski, who became the president of the college that same year, led the study in an effort to find new naval concepts for fighting in the heavily defended littorals. Admiral Cebrowski is also known for his help in developing the concept of network-centric warfare and as a leader in naval transformation (O'Rourke 2005, 21).

The LCS not only represents a new class of ships but also a completely different approach to war fighting. The LCS will have a modular mission capability that will allow the ship to reconfigure its mission focus on short notice. Fleet or operational commanders will be able to select from mission areas which include mine countermeasures, antisurface warfare, and shallow-water antisubmarine warfare allowing increased flexibility in a dynamic threat environment. These "plug-and-fight" mission capabilities will complement inherent ship capabilities which support maritime interception operations (MIO), intelligence, surveillance, and reconnaissance (ISR), homeland defense, special operations, and logistics support. Appendix A provides a complete list of the LCS's focused and inherent mission capabilities.

In May 2004, the Department of the Navy awarded Lockheed Martin and General Dynamics--Bath Iron Works individual contracts to build two LCSs each. The USS *Freedom* represents the Lockheed Martin design which is currently being built at Marinette Marine, Marinette, Wisconsin, with an expected delivery to the US Navy in early 2007. The General Dynamics design (LCS-2), in production at Austal USA shipyards in Mobile, Alabama, will be delivered to the Navy in the fall of 2007. Each design will be dramatically different in an effort to give the Navy the best possible options for the design of the remaining fleet. Lockheed Martin's design will center around a steel monohull while the General Dynamics design will focus on an all-aluminum trimaran. Both of the proposed design drawings are shown in figure 1.

Figure 1.    Lockheed Martin and General Dynamics LCS Designs
*Source:* Lockheed Martin and General Dynamics LCS Designs, Peoships Littoral Combat Ship [database on-line]; available from http://peoships.crane.navy.mil; Internet; accessed on 14 March 2006.

Both LCS designs will be relatively small with a displacement between 1,000-4,000 tons compared to current ship designs--Arleigh Burke-class destroyer, approximately 9,000 tons, and the Oliver Hazard Perry Class Frigate, approximately 4,000 tons. The reduced displacement and new hull design will give the LCS a maximum draft of only twenty feet allowing for greater shallow-water operations capability. The LCS will also be fast, capable of speeds of between 40 to 50 knots. With a focus on the littoral environment, the LCS will be deployed as part of a large group (CSG or ESG) or tasked to conduct independent operations.

In addition to new war-fighting capabilities, the LCS will change the way the Navy thinks about development and acquisition timelines. The LCS program will support the rapid delivery of two development phases called "Flights." The first four ships will be Flight 0, followed quickly by the Flight 1 design. Development phases are not new to the Navy, but the short period of time between development and acquisition is unique. The development of the Arleigh Burke-class destroyer took over a decade before the first ship was delivered. In contrast, the LCS will have its first Flight 0, the USS *Freedom* (LCS-1), only five years after the official start of the LCS program.

As the US Navy continues to pursue the design features of the new LCS, incorporating individual tasks and finding innovative ways to reduce crew manning, recognizing the risk that will be assumed with these reductions will be essential to the success of its future fleet.

## Assumptions

An initial assumption made during this study is that the US Navy will continue to pursue reduced manning. In addition, the US Navy will continue to pursue advanced technology systems that will support current and future ship designs.

## Definitions of Terms

The following is a list of terms and phrases that are used throughout this thesis:

Carrier Strike Group (CSG). A CSG is an independent deployable group of US Navy ships which typically include one aircraft carrier and approximately six surface combatants made up of cruisers, destroyers and frigates, one or two attack submarines, and one or two supply ships.

Expeditionary Strike Group (ESG). An ESG is an independent deployable group of US Navy ships which typically include three amphibious ships capable of embarking a Marine Expeditionary Unit (MEU), and one to three surface combatants and one to two attack submarines. The main difference between the CSG and the ESG is the fact that the latter is centered on amphibious capability and Marine support vice the aircraft carrier.

Future US Navy Cruiser (CG(X)). CG(X) is the third member of the future "family of ships." This multi-mission capable cruiser will focus on air dominance.

Future US Navy Destroyer (DD(X)). DD(X) is the centerpiece of the US Navy's future family of ships. This destroyer is designed with multiple warfare capabilities with a focus on land attack, robust self-defense, and stealth technologies, as well as a reduced crew design.

LCS Seaframe. The core platform of the LCS; the naval equivalent of an airframe.

Major Conflagration. A major conflagration at sea is a large shipboard fire which often results in personnel causalities. This fire can be caused by several different events to include internal fires and explosions from weapons handling mishaps or large fuel spills which result in fire, as well as external attack from missiles, torpedoes, and mines.

Reduced Manning. Reduced manning can be referred to as minimum manning or optimal manning. Optimal manning is the fewest number of crew members required to man a ship while taking into consideration the use of technology and human factors. Minimal manning is calculated based on associated ship workload and may not include additional factors. For this reason, minimal manning often refers to the lowest possible crew limit.

Ship's Manning Document (SMD). The SMD is a document that identifies the manpower requirements for a US Navy ship. Manpower requirements are based on several criteria which include the Required Operational Capabilities (ROC), the Ship's characteristics, as well as other inputs.

Five Vector Model (5VM). The 5VM is a career-planning tool for sailors that focuses on five separate areas: professional development, personal development, leadership, certifications and qualifications, and performance.

## Limitations

The study does not discuss reduced manning on all US Navy platforms and will limit its focus to the current Arleigh Burke-class destroyer and the LCS. There are many factors aboard ship that have a direct effect on reduced manning; however, due to the limited time available to conduct this research, the areas mentioned in this thesis' primary and secondary questions are this study's primary focus. Furthermore, specific discussion of technologies to be utilized aboard the LCS is limited in scope due to the available information and sensitivities involved in the ongoing design competition between Lockheed Martin and General Dynamics.

CHAPTER 2

LITERATURE REVIEW

This chapter reviews the literature as it relates to this study's primary research question: Is the US Navy assuming too much risk with reduced manning aboard the LCS? The literature review is organized around each the following secondary questions: (1) What level of risk is the Navy assuming with the LCS reduced manning design? (2) Will the LCS be able to conduct damage control and repair in a mass conflagration environment and save the ship? (3) Will the multiple tasked "hybrid sailor" have sufficient skills and training to compensate for the reduced crew size aboard the LCS? (4) Will the LCS be able to maintain mission capability and accomplish the mission in the littorals while operating independently? and (5) Will the rapid acquisition timeline of the LCS allow follow-on designs to benefit from the initial Flight 0 prototypes?

In order to fully understand the current issues of reduced manning in the US Navy and the potential effects and risks associated with the reduced manning design aboard the LCS, several types of documents were reviewed. Numerous magazine and journal articles have been written on the subject of reduced manning and they can be divided into two basic groups of thought--those who fully welcome and support the new design and those who question a naval combatant's ability to accomplish its mission with such a design. In addition, there are several studies and reports concerning the feasibility of reduced manning aboard the LCS.

Studies on reduced manning for the future destroyer DD(X) program and the current Arleigh Burke-class destroyer were also reviewed. Even though the LCS is a very different platform in both physical design and mission, the challenges of reduced

manning facing the DD(X) and the testing already conducted aboard Arleigh Burke-class

destroyers provide insight into potential challenges for the LCS program. Government

documents also illustrate the current strategy and concept of operations for LCS, as well

as many of the current issues and concerns of US Congress on the performance and

acquisition of the LCS program. In addition, a review of shipboard firefighting doctrine

helped establish the current requirements and tasks that the Navy uses to combat

shipboard fires. Documents supporting two naval ship incidents were also reviewed to

support the vignettes used in this study.

## Level of Risk

It is important to understand the Navy's current doctrine to fully appreciate the

significance of the LCS. The role the LCS will play as well as the risks it will assume is

defined through doctrine. "Sea Power 21" was introduced by the Chief of Naval

Operations in 2001 and establishes the guiding principles for the Navy's future:

> To realize the opportunities and navigate the challenges ahead, we must have a clear vision of how our Navy will organize, integrate, and transform. "Sea Power 21" is that vision. It will align our efforts, accelerate our progress, and realize the potential of our people. "Sea Power 21" will guide our Navy as we defend our nation and defeat our enemies in the uncertain century before us. (Clark 2002, 33)

Sea Power 21 is a change from the US Navy's blue-water doctrine, which focused on the

deep water battle, to an increased focus on the littoral environment. The LCS is designed

to support all three of the Sea Power 21 pillars: Sea Strike, Sea Shield, and Sea Basing.

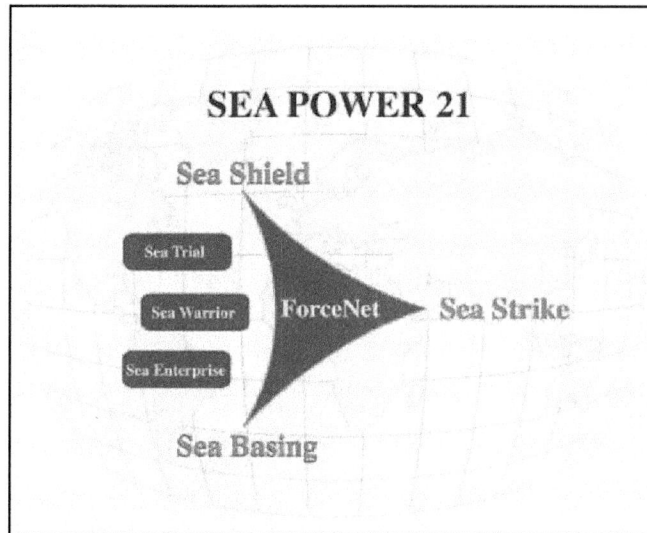

Figure 2.  Sea Power 21
*Source:* Vern Clark, "Sea Power 21: Projecting Decisive Joint Capabilities," *United States Naval Institute Proceedings* 128, no. 10:33, reprinted with permission; Copyright © (2002) U.S. Naval Institute/www.usni.org.

The LCS will directly support Sea Strike which is the ability to project offensive power through the direct support of the Marine Corps and Special Operations Forces units. Sea Shield will also be supported through the employment of focused and inherent mission capabilities and limited self-defense. In addition, the LCS will protect US allies and friends and will be able to support sea-based theater and strategic defense against ballistic missiles. Finally, Sea Basing, which refers to the Navy's ability to operate at sea as a sovereign entity without concerns of access and political constraints, will be part of the LCS's list of capabilities. These three pillars will be molded together by what the Navy calls ForceNet which will integrate warriors, sensors, command and control, platforms, and weapons into a networked, distributed combat force (Clark 2002, 34).

In addition, the LCS will be completely involved in the three supporting organizational processes called Sea Trial, Sea Warrior, and Sea Enterprise which are defined as follows:

- Sea Trial    Delivering innovation and rapid technology development to the fleet

- Sea Warrior    Investing in Sailors and ensuring they are properly trained and utilized

- Sea Enterprise    Substituting technology for manpower to achieve war-fighting effectiveness at the best cost  (Clark 2002, 39-40)

The LCS is designed to support these initiatives and increase the development of enhanced war-fighting capabilities for the fleet. Providing rapid technology, training US Navy sailors to achieve reduced manning and replacing sailors with technology to reduce cost are all part of the new vision. How the LCS adjusts to these dramatic changes will determine its success as well as the success of other future ship designs.

In line with Sea Power 21, the US Navy released the *Littoral Combat Ship Concept of Operations* in December 2004. This document provides insight into how the US Navy plans to use the LCS in future operations. Understanding how the LCS will be employed and the operational environment it will face will help determine the potential risks. As mentioned in chapter 1, the LCS will have inherent capabilities that will complement mission-focused capabilities. This design is intended to reduce the overall cost of the LCS as well as allow a smaller crew to operate the ship's core systems and capabilities (US DoN 2004a, ii).  The actual manning numbers will be dependant upon what mission package an LCS has installed. Individual mission packages will be sized to fit into a twenty-foot International Standards Organization (ISO) container and can be pre-positioned or shipped to any location in the world (US DoN 2004a, v). This will allow the LCS to reconfigure in homeport or in theater and may cause a short-notice change in required manning. Manning numbers, which are closely tied to mission assignments, will present challenges for the LCS crew.

The LCS may deploy as part of a Carrier Strike Group, Expeditionary Strike Group, Surface Action Group, or independently. Regardless of who it deploys with, the LCS is by design dependant on ships in company to provide the defensive capability it lacks. The US Navy's intent is for the future destroyer (DD(X)) or future cruiser (CG(X)) to provide this capability when in company with the LCS. The future DD(X) with its proposed advanced gun system and land attack capability and the CG(X) with its air dominance capability provide the perfect complement to the LCS. The LCS may also operate with other ships of its class, ideally with each ship configured for a different mission in order to provide greater collective capabilities. However, when assigned to operate independently, the LCS will assume additional risks due to its lack of offensive capability against a large missile-armed surface ship (US GAO 2005, 3). Regardless, the LCS will be required to operate in the littorals where there is sufficient threat from mines, submarines, and small boat swarm attack.

The Navy Warfare Development Command, who was instrumental in the development of the LCS Concept of Operations, summarized how the LCS will increase its survivability through several factors:

> The LCS force and individual platforms become less susceptible to detection and less vulnerable to attack through the employment of:

- Agility (high speed in a variety of sea conditions and missions)

- Speed: In ASW [antisubmarine warfare], speed would allow LCS to cut off an enemy submarine's avenues of approach, and would help in evading sub-fired torpedoes. Against airborne threats, it would allow LCS to more rapidly skirt an aircraft's search window and improve the effectiveness of anti-ship cruise missile countermeasures. Tactical speed benefits also would include faster wide-baselining for ESM [electronic support measures] and quicker combat search and rescue response.
- Off board combat systems and on board sensors and weapons
- Area maneuver by the large numbers of both the LCS force and its off board sensors and weapons
- Powerful networking to power projection assets for increased awareness
- Signature management
- Force dispersal (decreases risk averseness in high threat regions)

In addition to an LCS division's dispersion and maneuver, their operations in the complex and cluttered littoral environment will further serve to mitigate risk. (DoN 2003a, 8, emphasis mine)

Based on these factors the LCS will rely heavily on its speed, agility, reduced signature (the ability for the ship to decrease radar detection through structural design and the use of radar absorbing material), and sensors to maintain situational awareness. The LCS is built to avoid conflict by evading a threat at high speed. The littoral environment, even without increased surface vessel traffic, will pose additional navigational challenges which may prevent the LCS from having the ability to fully utilize its speed advantage.

Several Congressional Research Service (CRS) reports have addressed the LCS and reduced manning. Ronald O'Rourke, a specialist in National Defense, is the leading voice to Congress on the LCS and other US Navy ship programs. In these reports, O'Rourke expresses concern that the US Navy did not conduct enough research on the LCS prior to building its first prototype:

> Absent a formal study, they [LCS critics] could argue, the Navy has not, for example, shown why it would be necessary or preferable to send a small and potentially vulnerable manned ship into heavily defended littoral waters to deploy helicopters or UVs [unmanned vehicles] when helicopters or UVs could be launched from larger ships operating further offshore. . . . The Administration, LCS critics could argue, is being proposed on the basis of "analysis by assertion."

19

They can argue that while it may be acceptable to build one or a few ship as operational prototypes without first having analytically validated the cost-effectiveness of the effort, it is quite another thing to propose a potentially 55-ship program costing billions of dollars without first examining through rigorous analysis whether this would be the most cost-effective approach. (O'Rourke 2006, 4, emphasis mine)

It can be argued that the "Streetfighter" project of 1999-2001 was part of that research due to the similarities of its littoral focus. The Streetfighter, which was first revealed to the public in 1999, came under heavy debate due to questions about overseas sustainability and payload constraints. Also, due to the small size of the LCS, ship survivability and ability to survive a substantial weapon hit are also a concern (O'Rourke 2005, 21).

The United States Government Accountability Office (GAO) also expressed similar concerns for the LCS program in a report that it released in March 2005. The GAO's primary concern was that the US Navy has not fully analyzed the larger surface combat threat to LCS operations. The fact that the LCS, in accordance with its concept of operations, will operate independently will require a thorough understanding of the threats that it will face. The potential threat of a large combatant, armed with medium caliber guns, torpedoes, and anti-ship missiles needs to be fully addressed (GAO 2005, 16). Taking this threat into consideration is critical in determining the ship's survivability and the risks that it will assume in the littorals.

Key to the LCS's reduced manning plan is the ability to limit the necessary work required from the sailors. The LCS maintenance strategy builds on the Surface Force maintenance initiative called "Shipmain" which focuses on process improvement of the fleet maintenance system. In addition, the Fleet Response Plan (FRP) and the increased demand on fleet readiness have required the Navy to look for a smarter way to maintain its ships. As a result, the LCS core crew and mission package personnel will only perform routine maintenance to include visual inspections and basic servicing actions (US DoN 2004a, ix). Private contractors will provide maximum support in order to minimize the workload of the crew. This will be a cultural change for the US Navy since commanding officers are accustomed to having more control over their ships. Relying heavily on several private contractors to ensure the readiness and ability of their ship to meet mission tasking will be a challenge. Commanding officers, who have overall responsibility for their ship, will have to work with multiple contractors in order to prepare their ships for sea.

## Damage Control and Mass Conflagration

There is no greater danger to a ship's survivability than fires and flooding. How a ship fights fires and flooding will become even more important on a ship with reduced manning. Proper utilization of every person aboard is important in order to prevent the worst form of damage--a mass conflagration. Navy technical manuals and warfare publications provide valuable information on techniques and procedures used to combat fires at sea.

Existing naval doctrine for fighting shipboard fires is located in naval ships' technical manuals (NSTM) and naval warfare publications (NWP). NSTM 555, Volume 1, *Surface Ship Firefighting*, provides the basic procedures for fighting fires on naval vessels. Even though NSTM 555 does not specifically address reduced manning it provides the organizational approach to fighting fires and the positions required. This provides a basis for comparison when looking at the LCS approach to fighting fires with reduced manning. NSTM 555 also provides the appropriate background on basic classification of fires and the recommended equipment and procedures to use when combating each type.

NWP 3-20.31, *Surface Ship Survivability,* clearly relates damage control to ship survivability. This publication provides procedures and guidance on how to prevent, combat and restore from shipboard damage. It is important to understand the complexities of combat at sea and the effect of a mass conflagration on a reduced manning crew. NWP 3-20.31 helps to identify many of the hazards that sailors will face to include the need for rapid power restoration, the effects of shock hazards due to weapon impacts, and personnel protection against chemical, biological and radiological (CBR) attack. A mass conflagration environment will require all hands to be highly trained in multiple areas in order to accommodate any loss in crew caused by internal or external damage to the ship.

Crew training has always played a very important role in a crew's ability to protect a ship during a fire at sea. How the crew reacts to the emergency often is a result of extensive training and preparation. The US Navy understands the importance of training and is developing a new sailor training program to support the reduced manning concept aboard the LCS.

Hybrid Sailor

The sailors of the USS *Freedom* are already training even though their ship is still being built; this is typical for a US Navy ship during its construction phase prior to commissioning. The sailors that will man the first LCS will be cross-trained in order to support the reduced manning requirements of the ship. Sailors will attend schools that were previously considered to be outside of their designated fields. These new cross-trained sailors are being called the Navy's first "hybrid sailors." This new training plan directly supports "Sea Power 21" and is part of the Sea Warrior initiative.

The Navy has been making significant changes to the way it trains its sailors since July 2001 when Chief of Naval Operations Admiral Vern Clark launched Task Force EXCEL – Excellence Through Commitment to Education (Harris 2005, 46). Several tools were created in an effort to balance the training requirement of the fleet with the career training needs of the individual sailor. Today sailors utilize a career planning tool called the Five Vector Model (5VM) which focuses on five areas of sailor development: professional development, personal development, leadership, certifications and qualifications, and performance. This tool allows sailors to see what they have accomplished, similar to a résumé, and what they should focus on for future personal and professional growth.

The Naval Personnel Development Command (NPDC), which was established in 2003 to carry out the CNO's Task Force EXCEL vision, is in charge of the Navy's education and training program. In 2004, NPDC tasked four of its learning centers with the development of the LCS's Learning Center of Excellence program. The Center for Surface Combat Systems, Naval Engineering, Service Support and Information Dominance are all working to define the skills necessary for the LCS sailor (Henson 2005, 1). The Navy is using Human Capital Objects (HCOs) to help determine the required skills for the LCS sailors using a process that aligns work requirements with job positions. Furthermore, the Navy has determined that SkillsNET's technology, developed by a skills assessment firm, will be the tool to develop these HCOs. SkillsNET will be used to drive all training, education and proficiency requirements for all officers and enlisted sailors in the Navy community (SkillsNET Corporation 2006). This new

technology uses the five concentration areas of the Five Vector Model to develop what

the company calls "skill objects."

> The company collects workforce data, including individual skills gap information, to define the workforce and its parameters, not just in an occupational sense but in the broader application of knowledge skills, resources, and other items that encompass the performance of an occupational skill. The information is all put together in a "skill object." (Henson 2005, 47)

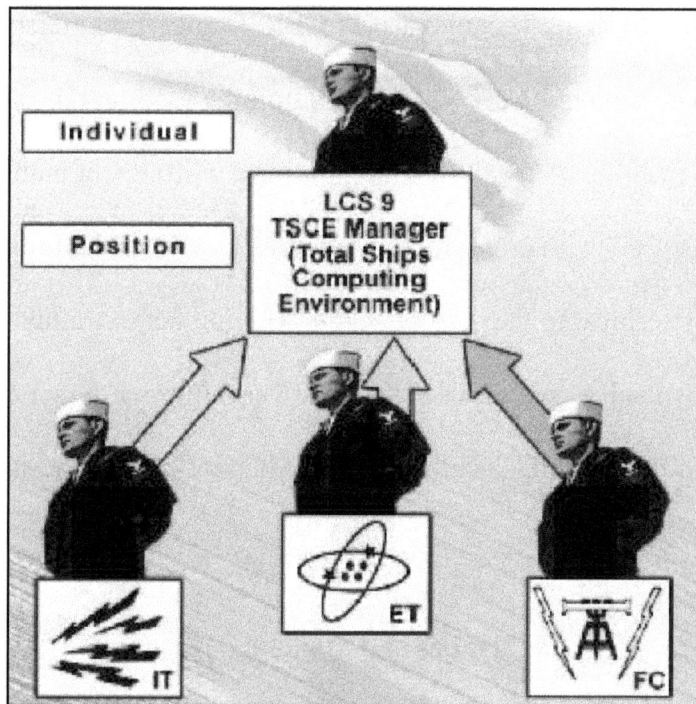

Figure 3.   LCS Hybrid Sailor Skill Objects
*Source:* "Sea Warrior: A True Revolution in Training," *CHIPS Magazine,* October-December 2005, 10.

Knowing what skills will be required on the LCS by using skill objects is the first

step but the next step is determining who receives the training. Vice Admiral J. Kevin

Moran, Commander, Naval Education and Training Command, explains the challenges of training the new LCS sailor:

> Under the old way, we would deliver all IT [Information Systems Technicians] SkillObjects to ITs; we would deliver all jet mechanic SkillObjects to jet mechanics. In the future, we will be delivering IT SkillObjects not only to ITs, but to other ratings in order to better fit an individual for a position. Since we are more effectively utilizing our manpower, we can then optimally man our units. This is the concept we are using right now to prepare the crew for the Littoral Combat Ship (CHIPS 2005, 9, emphasis mine).

Figure 3 provides an example of three different sailors with different specialties or ratings, (Information Systems Technicians (IT), Electronics Technician (ET), and a Fire Controlman (FC)) obtaining the necessary cross training to obtain the skills required to man the new LCS position of Total Ship Computing Environment manager. As the US Navy mans the first LCS with cross trained sailors the value of the individual sailor becomes even more critical to the ship's success. Having better trained sailors with multiple skills is by itself a smarter use of manpower; however, when crew size is reduced as a result, the individual sailor becomes more critical to the ship's mission capability.

## Watch Stations and Manning Documents

The Navy's Ship Manning Document (SMD) presents the manpower requirements for the LCS. SMD's often rely heavily on the ships Required Operational Capability (ROC) and Projected Operational Environment (POE) to help determine the required manning. The ROC provides a detailed definition of a particular unit's mission statement and the POE describes the specific operating environment in which the unit is expected to operate. Presently, the LCS does not have a ROC and POE and the LCS concept of operations is the only document available that describes the mission and anticipated operating environment for the LCS.

Furthermore, the USS *Freedom* is still in the process of finalizing their Ship Manning Document. I obtained and reviewed its draft copy. The current proposed crew size for LCS-1 is forty personnel. A detailed billet analysis by Naval Sea Systems Command (NAVSEA) is still in progress which consists of reviewing each individual billet assigned to the LCS focusing on the following areas: tasks identified for each individual, workload required by each individual, knowledge, skills, and abilities (KSAs) of each individual, and training required.

## Rapid Acquisition Timeline

Based on the rapid acquisition timeline of the Flight 0 ships, there may not be sufficient time to incorporate new design features learned from the Flight 0 models prior to Flight 1 model delivery. In a 2005 report to congress, the United States Government Accountability Office expressed concern about the immature technologies present in the LCS design and their effect on the acquisition timeline:

> Immature technologies increase risk that some systems will not perform as expected and may require additional time and funding to develop. The impact of delaying technology is less capability for the Flight 0 ships and less information for the Flight 1 ship design. (GAO 2005, 4)

Similar to immature technology concerns, having enough time between Flight designs is critical to LCS manning. The LCS has two different manning requirements--a core crew which mans the ship without the mission package, referred to as the "seaframe" on the LCS, and the crew required to man the individual mission packages. Core seaframe manning should remain relatively constant; however, total crew numbers will fluctuate

26

based on installed mission packages. If it is determined that additional manning is required based on Flight 0 operational testing, there may not be sufficient time to incorporate this design change in follow-on Flights. The LCS program presents rapid employment of technology and basic manning methods which are new to the Navy. Many of the risks associated with the LCS program are discussed in greater detail in chapter 4.

Finally, several articles and reports on the incidents involving the USS *Stark* and the USS *Cole* were reviewed. Both ships were involved in major damage control efforts: USS *Stark* was struck by two Exocet missiles and the USS *Cole* attacked by shipborne suicide bombers.

Very little has been written about the USS *Stark* incident with the exception of Levinson and Edward's book, *Missile Inbound: The Attack on the Stark in the Persian Gulf*. This book provided a detailed account of the events leading up to and during the attack. As a result of numerous interviews conducted by the authors, this book provides a great deal of information about the crew's reaction to a mass conflagration. In addition, the investigation report submitted to US Congress in 1987 was also reviewed.

Concerning the USS *Cole* attack, the US Department of Defense Commission Report published in 2001, was reviewed which provided several lessons learned from the incident. However, other articles describing the details of the attack proved more valuable in understanding the crew's reaction to the incident and how their innovative actions played a large role in saving the ship.

This chapter provides an overview of the available literature on the US Navy's reduced manning program and presents many of the issues and concerns that directly affect the LCS. Chapter 3 provides the methodology that this study uses to help determine the potential risks associated with the LCS design and presents the framework

for the analysis in chapter 4.

# CHAPTER 3

## RESEARCH METHODOLOGY

The methodology used to answer the primary research question is a risk management process known as the *Australian and New Zealand STandard 4360*. This model, which has been accepted and is being used globally to measure risk, provides the following five-step process: establish the context, identify risks, analyze risks, evaluate risks, and treat risks. This model has become a standard primarily in the business community; however, it provides a generic risk management process that can be used to help determine the associated risk with the LCS and its reduced manning design. Figure 4 provides a visual representation of this process.

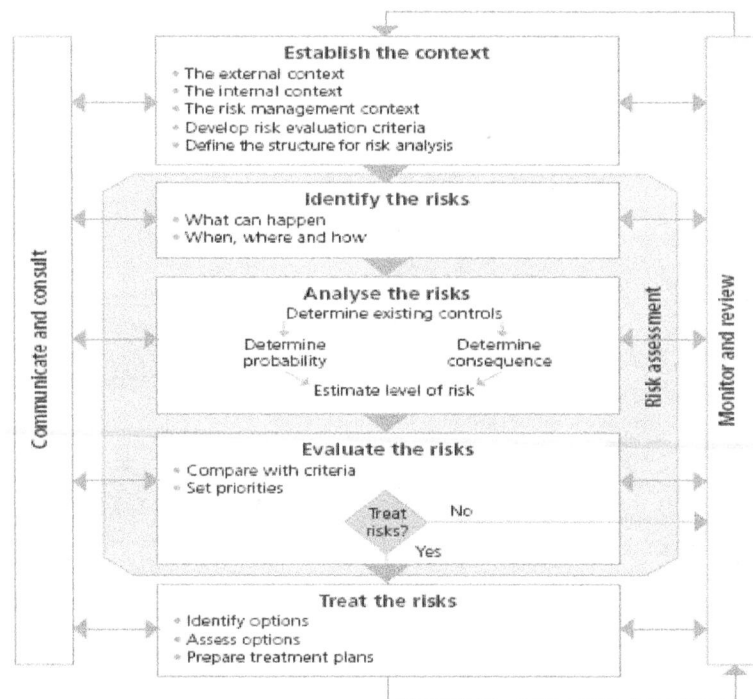

Figure 4.    The Risk Management Process
*Source:* "Chapter 3: The Risk Management Process," *Standards Association of Australia,* 2004, 39; [database on-line]; available from http://www.standards.com.au; Internet; accessed on 15 December 2005.

29

This chapter introduces each of the five steps and explains how they will be applied in answering the primary and secondary research questions of this study.

In Step 1 (Establish the Context), risk evaluation criteria are developed based on the secondary research questions. First, this study will review each of these criteria using the *"STandard 4360"* model and discuss them in detail in chapter 4. Then, the study will analyze internal and external context for each of the criteria. In the case of the LCS, internal context will focus on the things over which the US Navy has control, such as required capabilities or mission requirements. US Navy cultural considerations and resistance to change also provide internal context and will be included in the study. External context will deal with the factors over which the US Navy has little or no control, that is, the operational environment and threat. Establishing the risk management context is also an important part of this step. Chapter 1 provides the limitations and delimitations as well as the significance of this research. This study will focus on the following risk evaluation criteria.

Table 1.   Risk Evaluation Criteria

| Risk Criterion | Objective |
| --- | --- |
| Survivability | Ship's crew will be able to conduct damage control / repair in mass conflagration environment and save the ship |
| Reduced manning w/ Hybrid Sailors | Fewer sailors with better training will replace larger / traditional crews |
| Mission Accomplishment | Ship will maintain mission capability and accomplish the mission in the littorals while operating independently |
| Acquisition timeline | Rapid delivery to the Fleet will provide the necessary littoral capability |

Finally, the study will use the *Australian and New Zealand STandard 4360* model for the structure of the risk analysis.

In Step 2 (Identify the Risks), the study will look at each of the risk criteria from Step 1 in greater detail. The terms "retrospective" and "prospective risks" will be useful in this analysis of the LCS. Retrospective risks are those risks that have previously occurred such as accidents or incidents. The USS *Cole* bombing provides a good example of retrospective risks, a risk that the LCS will certainly face during its lifetime. The term prospective risk deals with risks that have not happened yet but might happen in the future.

It is also important to understand that not all risk is bad. The SWOT analysis, which looks at the strengths, weaknesses, opportunities, and threats associated with risk, helps to illustrate both the positive and negative risks associated with the LCS. The following SWOT analysis for the LCS is conducted in chapter 4:

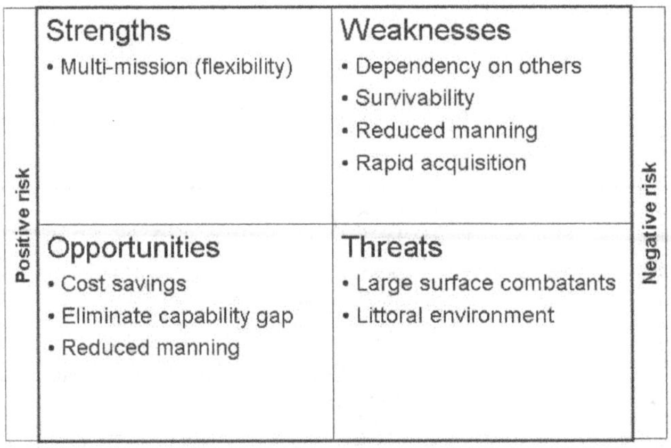

| | Strengths | Weaknesses | |
|---|---|---|---|
| **Positive risk** | • Multi-mission (flexibility) | • Dependency on others<br>• Survivability<br>• Reduced manning<br>• Rapid acquisition | **Negative risk** |
| | **Opportunities**<br>• Cost savings<br>• Eliminate capability gap<br>• Reduced manning | **Threats**<br>• Large surface combatants<br>• Littoral environment | |

Figure 5.   Strengths, Weaknesses, Opportunities, and Threats (SWOT) Analysis
*Modified from Source*: "Chapter 3: The Risk Management Process," *Standards Association of Australia,* 2004, 29; [database on-line]; available from http://www.standards.com.au; Internet; accessed on 15 December 2005.

In Step 3 (Analyze the Risks), the study will analyze the risks using the following simple equation (Risk = Consequence x Likelihood) (Standards Association of Australia 2004, 31). This equation will help determine the different levels of risk that the LCS may face. As likelihood increases from rare to frequent and the consequence increases from minor to significant, so will the risk. Understanding this relationship will help assess and evaluate the different risks found during the literature review and frame conclusions and possible recommendations. In addition, a qualitative approach provides the best analysis of the literature available on the LCS and will be used throughout this study. However, there are some disadvantages to the qualitative approach since it is subjective in nature. Therefore, I will keep my personal opinion to a minimum and limited to areas where my personal experience warrants it.

In Step 4 (Evaluate the Risks), this study will answer the primary research question: Is the US Navy assuming too much risk with reduced manning aboard the LCS? Using the analysis and comparing it to the risk criteria listed in figure 5, will help provide recommendations for mitigating potential risks.

In Step 5 (Treat the Risks), this study will identify and assess the options to reduce risk. The *Australian and New Zealand STandard 4360* provides several options when dealing with risk: accept it, avoid it, change the likelihood of occurrence, change the consequences and/or share the risk. These options will be helpful when making recommendations in regards to the LCS and reduced manning.

In summary, the *Australian and New Zealand STandard 4360* provides a model for analyzing the risk criteria associated with the LCS reduced manning design and will

32

help answer the primary and secondary research questions of this study. Chapter 4 applies this methodology and provides the resulting analysis.

# CHAPTER 4

## ANALYSIS

The LCS, a proposed class of fifty-five ships, will soon become a significant portion of the US Navy's future surface combatant fleet. With its reduced crew design, this ship will operate in the congested littorals and be asked to go into harms way. Even though there are several attractive reasons to reduce crew size, this modification increases the overall risk of operating the LCS. The US Navy must ensure that the LCS has the capability to operate safely in peacetime as well as combat without assuming an unacceptable level of risk. It is important, therefore, that decision makers as well as ship designers are aware of other risks that are present in the current LCS design.

This chapter analyzes the literature presented in chapter 2 using the risk management model known as the *Australian and New Zealand STandard 4360.* This model is used to answer the secondary questions which are listed as risk criteria. As a result of answering the secondary questions, this study's primary research question: Is the US Navy assuming too much risk with reduced manning aboard the LCS, is answered. This chapter begins with a general analysis of the issues surrounding the LCS and establishes the context of the analysis. Risk criteria are then analyzed further to include two vignettes which illustrate the risks that US Naval ships have faced in recent history and the role that their crews' actions have played in the survival of both.

### Establishing the Context

In accordance with the *Australian and New Zealand STandard* model, risk identification is at the source of risk management. In order to identify what is "at risk" this study will define the context of the risk assessment by establishing the internal and external context associated with the LCS. Internal context of the LCS program deals mainly with those factors over which the US Navy has control. By the development and approval of the concept of operations for the LCS, the Navy has the ability to control the environment in which the LCS is tasked to operate. The LCS concept of operations clearly states that the LCS will most likely operate with other strike group assets such as ESGs or CSGs but may also operate independently (US DoN 2004a, vii). This is an important factor to consider when looking at how much risk the LCS will assume. The US Navy has the ability to assign or not assign the LCS to conduct a particular mission. A better understanding of the potential threats to the LCS and the risks it will assume will help determine the proper tasking for the LCS.

Additional internal context includes the perceived need for the US Navy to fill a littoral mission gap. This presents risk either way. If the US Navy decides to delay or even cancel production of the LCS, there would be a mission capabilities gap related to the Navy's reduced capability in the littorals. A study conducted by the United States Government Accountability Office in March of 2005 indicated concerns that the current acquisition timeline would not allow the Flight 1 designs time to benefit from the initial prototype testing (GAO 2005, 31). The US Navy responded to the study by stating that it is attempting to balance acquisition risk with the risk of delaying the closure of the littoral mission gap. The Navy also stated that it is willing to accept additional risks in the initial Flight 0 design in order to field the needed mission capability, "The Navy intends for LCS Flight 0 to deliver an immediate capability to the fleet to address critical littoral anti-access capability gaps and to provide risk reduction for follow-on flights." (GAO 2005, 42)

External context deals with the factors over which the US Navy has limited control. The bombing of the USS *Cole* is a reminder that the US Navy operates in a very volatile and unpredictable threat environment. Even though the Navy has the opportunity to learn lessons from past experiences, it will not be able to predict future threats with any level of certainty. Without the ability to control the future threat environment, these factors and their associated risks will have to be assumed. In addition, budget constraints and the need to accomplish more with less, provide additional external pressures which have led to the interest and investment in reduced manning designs. Even though the US Navy could pursue other options to solve the problem of budget constraints, there is significant interest, both internally and externally, to have the Navy reduce its crew numbers.

### Identify the Risk

Part of determining the acceptable level of risk involves reviewing all forms of risk. Risk itself is not always bad. A strengths, weaknesses, opportunities and threats (SWOT) analysis (figure 6) is a useful tool that can represent both the negative and positive risks associated with the LCS. This study used the SWOT analysis to divide risks into positive (strengths and opportunities) and negative risks (weaknesses and threats). Potential positive risks associated with the LCS were found to be the multi-mission capability and the flexibility that it provides the US Navy. Additionally, the modular capability promises the ability to quickly change the ship's primary mission in theater as mission requirements dictate. For example, if the current operational environment demands more mine warfare assets, any LCS in theater will have the capability (assuming the modules are also in theater and a secure port is available to support the conversion) to be reconfigured and assigned the task to support the new mission area (US DoN 2004a, v). The exact amount of time to reconfigure a ship has yet to be determined since the individual mission modules have not been delivered to the Navy and will not be tested until the first LCS is in operation in 2007. However, preliminary design documents for the Flight 0 LCS indicate that mission package change-out (including operational testing or OPTEST) should not exceed four days (DoN 2003b, 4).

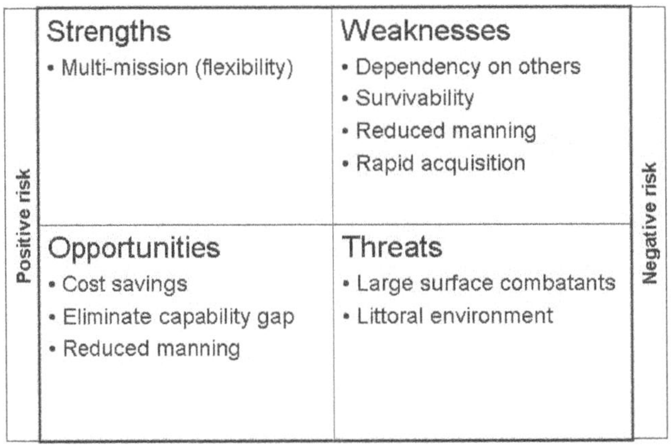

| | Strengths<br>• Multi-mission (flexibility) | Weaknesses<br>• Dependency on others<br>• Survivability<br>• Reduced manning<br>• Rapid acquisition | |
|---|---|---|---|
| Positive risk | Opportunities<br>• Cost savings<br>• Eliminate capability gap<br>• Reduced manning | Threats<br>• Large surface combatants<br>• Littoral environment | Negative risk |

Figure 6.   Strengths, Weaknesses, Opportunities, and Threats (SWOT) Analysis
*Modified from Source*: "Chapter 3: The Risk Management Process," *Standards Association of Australia,* 2004, 29; [database on-line]; available from http://www.standards.com.au; Internet; accessed on 15 December 2005.

Additional positive risk of the LCS is its low cost relative to other surface combatants. The current price tag on an Arleigh Burke-class destroyer is approximately $1.7 billion, making the cost of the LCS, projected at less than $300 million without mission modules, very attractive (Cavas 2005, 2). In a highly competitive military budget environment, each service is doing its best to accomplish more with less. The LCS presents the US Navy an opportunity, through reduced unit cost, to increase fleet numbers at a discount.

Finally, the LCS provides the US Navy with a platform that will implement reduced manning from the ground up. The LCS, leading a family of reduced manning ship designs, will be the first naval combatant designed to operate with a crew that is drastically smaller than that of the traditional warship. As illustrated in chapter 1, the current Arleigh Burke-class destroyer enjoyed limited success in crew reductions. Ship crews involved in the manning reduction experiments recognized that further reductions would require more drastic design changes. Crew reductions based on changes in policies and procedures helped spark interest in reduced crew designs but could not provide the reductions that are projected for the LCS and other future ship designs. Since manning accounts for up to 50 percent of the total life cycle cost of a ship, a reduction in crew size has significant potential to save the US Navy vital funds (Riche 1997, 74). This study found that reduced manning was both an opportunity and a potential weakness. The LCS's reduced crew, even though it presents significant savings, may be the ship's limiting factor. Assessing the risk that the LCS will assume with reduced manning, as well as other risks, is the focus of this study.

Negative risks associated with the LCS include its dependency on others whether it is other surface combatants offsetting its limited combat system suite capabilities when facing a larger enemy combatant (O'Rourke 2005, 44) or shore facilities providing support such as maintenance and administration to offset its reduced crew and organic capability. This dependency will require the LCS to operate in company with better armed surface combatants and remain closely coordinated with shore support. An LCS operating independently in the littoral or deep water environment will be highly dependant on others for support and assume additional risk as a result.

One of the major concerns which became apparent during this study was a question of the ability of the LCS to save itself during a major conflagration. Recent naval incidents involving fire and flooding have proven to be crew-intensive events. With the optimal crew design of the LCS, where every sailor is assigned a specific role or multiple roles that support mission accomplishment, can this ship design sustain combat damage and still be able to save itself? The objective of this study is not to determine the necessary crew numbers required to maintain such a capability, but to look at the risks that are associated with such a design.

Two vignettes presented later in this chapter provide examples of actual ship casualties caused by external attacks and illustrate the important role that individual ship crews played in saving their ship. These incidents of fire, flooding and a major conflagration are retrospective risks and helpful in this study's final analysis.

Finally, the littorals present a complicated environment for any surface combatant to operate in. Increased ship density, reduced maneuverability and stand-off distance, are just a few of the many challenges that ships face in this congested operating area. This coupled with the fact that terrorists are heavily reliant on asymmetrical attack, often their only means against a much stronger conventional force, further complicates the problem in the littorals. Not knowing how and when the next attack on a US Naval combatant will occur presents prospective risks.

Based on the SWOT analysis, this study has developed four risk evaluation criteria associated with the LCS: ship survivability, reduced manning with "Hybrid Sailors", the ability to accomplish the mission, and the rapid acquisition timeline. Table 2 below lists these risk criteria with their associated objectives. In accordance with the *Australian and New Zealand STandard* model, the inability to accomplish the objectives of any of the listed criteria presents unacceptable risks.

Table 2.    Risk Evaluation Criteria

| Risk Criterion | Objective |
|---|---|
| Survivability | Ship's crew will be able to conduct damage control / repair in mass conflagration environment and save the ship |
| Reduced manning w/ Hybrid Sailors | Fewer sailors with better training will replace larger / traditional crews |
| Mission Accomplishment | Ship will maintain mission capability and accomplish the mission in the littorals while operating independently |
| Acquisition timeline | Rapid delivery to the Fleet will provide the necessary littoral capability |

The first risk that this study reviews is the LCS's ability or inability to survive during a mass conflagration. Next, the use of highly trained "Hybrid Sailors" presents additional risks for the LCS. Managing the crew of a future LCS where every single sailor plays a critical role in mission success presents several challenges. The third risk criterion that this study addresses is the LCS's ability or inability to accomplish its mission. This criterion is directly related to the first because if the LCS does not have the proper survivability then it is at risk and may not be able to accomplish the mission.

Finally, the rapid acquisition timeline of the LCS promises to provide the US Navy with the needed littoral warfare capabilities, although not without assuming additional risks.

## Analyze the Risk

This study approaches the risk analysis by first reviewing two individual ship casualties. The following vignettes provide two real world examples of US Navy surface combatants that were attacked and significantly damaged, and the challenges that the crews faced during the damage control efforts.

## Vignettes: Practical Examples from the Past

History provides many examples of how ships have faired during casualties at sea. Whether the casualty has been caused by enemy attack or occurred during normal ship operations, the damage and challenges to the crew have been similar. The following vignettes provide examples of two ships: the USS *Stark* and the USS *Cole*. Both ships were involved in major damage control efforts: USS *Stark* was struck by two Exocet missiles and the USS *Cole* was attacked by suicide bombers. Both examples illustrate the important role that the individual crews played in saving their ships and provide insight into the challenges that tomorrow's ships may face in future operations. In addition, these examples further depict the inherent risks that US naval ships assume in an ever-changing environment and provide potential lessons for the LCS. Even though they depict different ship types and crew manning than those of the LCS, these vignettes still furnish a potential glimpse of how the LCS would fair in a similar situation given its current assumed risks.

## Vignette Number One: USS *Stark*, 17 May 1987

### Background

USS *Stark* (FFG-31), an Oliver Hazard Perry class frigate, deployed as part of the Middle East Force (MEF) and was assigned to protect Kuwaiti and Saudi oil tankers as well as vital shipping lanes in the straits of Hormuz. Leading up to the incident, hostilities between Iran and Iraq were increasing as both countries began attacking unarmed tankers, the development which later became known as the "Tanker War."

On 17 May 1987, the USS *Stark* was operating off the coast of Bahrain in international waters when it was struck by two Exocet missiles launched from an Iraqi F-1 Mirage fighter. Even though the fighter was detected and queried as part of standard procedure, there was no detection of the missile launch. Both missiles hit without warning. The first missile impacted the port side hull creating a nine-foot-by-twelve-foot hole in the bulkhead. The missile failed to detonate on impact; however, its propellant burst into flames aiding in the spread of fire throughout the ship. Twenty-five seconds later the second missile hit nearby and immediately exploded (Grosick, 1988, 14). The double missile hit resulted in the death of thirty-seven crew members and the injury of twenty-one.

Following the attack, the remaining crew members struggled to save the ship. Firefighting and damage control efforts presented several challenges as the crew rapidly realized that they were dealing with a major conflagration. As a result of the missile impacts, the primary fire main piping (which provides pressurized firefighting water throughout the ship) was ruptured and required the crew to use hoses to re-route the water around several damaged areas. The fire became so hot in some places that the ship's aluminum superstructure began to melt. The intense heat further led to the spread of the fire due to radiant heat causing adjacent spaces to catch fire. Crew estimates following the incident are that temperatures reached 1,800 degrees in some spaces (US Congress 1987, 26). Adding to the challenges facing the crew, the ship began to develop a seventeen-degree list as a result of flooding caused by accumulating firefighting water (US Congress 1987, 26).

The brave and resourceful crew of the USS *Stark* managed to gain control of the fire and damage control efforts twenty hours following the attack and eventually returned the ship unassisted to Bahrain. The USS *Stark* was repaired and later returned to service.

## USS *Stark* Analysis

Many of the lessons learned from the USS *Stark* incident can be applied to the new LCS. First, the USS *Stark* incident provides a real world example of what challenges a ship may face during a major conflagration. Immediately following the attack, fire main pressure was not adequate and had to be re-routed, all communications were disabled with the exception of emergency hand-held radios, the ship began developing a severe list and extreme temperatures caused the ship superstructure to melt in some spaces. In addition to the chaos, the officers and crew, with an initial strength of 201 personnel, were dealing with the loss of almost 20 percent of their ship's company (Levinson and Edwards 1997, 8). Based on the investigation report following the incident, there is little doubt that the actions of USS *Stark's* crew saved the ship. Several reports support this conclusion and describe the actions of the crew as the primary reason for her survival following the attack:

Based on the interviews with *Stark* crew members and MEF officers, it became apparent that the crew's success in containing the fire, controlling the damage, and reducing the list considerably reduced the scale of damage that might otherwise have devastated *Stark*. The crew's actions may well have saved the ship. (US Congress 1987, 26)

Levinson and Edwards in their book titled "*Missile Inbound – The attack of the Stark in the Persian Gulf,*" noted that damage control efforts were directly affected by this missile attack:

Repair Two, isolated in the forecastle area, was critically hampered by the loss of men, including the death of EMCS (Senior Chief Electrician's Mate) Stephen Kiser, one of its two repair party leaders, and the locker quickly fell victim to smoke and fire damage. Communication with Repair Two was lost shortly after the fire started. The death of several experienced damage-control CPOs - the "loss of khaki"- made the job of saving the *Stark* that much more difficult. (Levinson and Edwards 1997, 23)

In addition, following the major firefighting, the USS *Stark* did not have enough crew members to support the vital "reflash watches" used to monitor spaces throughout the ship to ensure the fires remained out. Not until two other destroyers in the area provided assistance was the USS *Stark* able to support this task (Levinson and Edwards 1997, 31). By reducing crew numbers on the new LCS to as low as forty personnel the loss of 20 percent of the crew during an initial attack could be devastating to the ship's ability to deal with the resulting damage. For example, if the LCS received a similar hit in the vicinity of its Mission Control Center, a space designed to have up to nine personnel on watch during normal operations, according to draft watch station manning documents of USS *Freedom*, the potential loss of more than 20 percent of the core crew could rapidly be achieved.

Another reason for the USS *Stark's* damage control success was a result of the Commanding Officer's insistence that the ship's crew conduct cross-training. Repair lockers trained their sailors to conduct multiple tasks that were normally conducted by other positions, in case of personnel losses within their respective lockers. This training requirement implemented on the USS *Stark* is similar to the US Navy's "hybrid sailor" training concept which implies that a sailor that can do the job of two or three sailors is better. However, the LCS emphasis on cross-training is more focused on better economy rather than increased redundancy as in the case of the USS *Stark*. The much smaller crew of the LCS will, without a doubt, be populated by more versatile sailors, but due to its small size, will not have the redundancy of the USS *Stark's* crew. LCS sailors appear to already be over-leveraged, having to perform multiple tasks on a daily basis in order to accommodate the crew reduction. The loss of only a few "hybrid sailors" could have a large effect on the LCS's performance and survival, especially during a major conflagration.

Finally, this incident further illustrates that even a high technology ship, with an advanced combat system suite, is vulnerable to attack. The Exocet missile, which typically maneuvers to within a few meters above the ocean surface in its terminal phase and travels just under the speed of sound, provides little time to react (Grosick, 1988, 14). The Exocet missile is still a threat to the US Navy surface fleet along with a long list of other more capable missiles. In addition, the LCS will be most likely employed in the littoral waters which present further challenges as a ship faces increased ship density, reduced maneuverability, and reduced stand-off distance, making it even harder to identify the threat and react in time to prevent attack.

## Vignette Number Two: USS *Cole*, 12 October 2000

### Background

On 12 October 2000, the USS *Cole* (DDG-67) was conducting a routine fuel stop in the harbor of Aden, Yemen, at a water-borne refueling platform known as a dolphin. During the refueling operation a small craft was allowed to approach along the USS *Cole's* port side. The small craft, loaded with explosives, detonated and tore a forty-by-forty-foot hole in the port side of the ship. The resulting hole caused major flooding in the *Cole's* engineering spaces and provided an immediate challenge for the startled crew.

Aggressive actions by the crew to isolate damaged electrical systems and contain fuel ruptures were critical to the prevention of deadly fires which could have resulted in a major conflagration and loss of the ship. The crew continued their damage control efforts in extreme heat and stress for more than ninety-six hours (Global Security Database 2006). On the third day, the ship's portable pumps could no longer stay ahead of the flooding that was rapidly filling the engine rooms. The static head pressure was too great for the small pumps to push the water out of the spaces almost three stories below. The ship was sinking. The ship's crew quickly reacted and began using buckets to remove the water that was flooding the ship: "Technology on the billion-dollar, state-of-the-art warship had failed. The enlisted men began forming a bucket brigade" (Thomas 2001, 2). In an effort to overcome the pump problem, the *Cole's* Executive Officer suggested cutting a hole in the side of the ship just above the waterline in an effort to reduce the work load on the pumps (Thomas 2001, 2). The plan worked. The USS *Cole* successfully dewatered the engineering spaces, an outcome that was critical to the ship's stability.

46

This would later prove to be one of many examples of how the crew's fast reaction and ingenuity kept the USS *Cole* afloat.

The attack resulted in the death of seventeen sailors and injury of almost twice that number. Due to the extensive damage, the USS *Cole* returned to the United States with the aid of a semi-submersible heavy-lift ship. The ship was repaired, and like the USS *Stark,* eventually returned to service.

## USS *Cole* Analysis

The USS *Cole* is a recent reminder that US Navy surface combatants are vulnerable and will remain vulnerable as the United States faces a new and unpredictable enemy. Terrorists will continue to seek out single vulnerabilities and have the advantage of determining when and how they will strike (US Army TRADOC 2005, 4-1). This has certainly made the US Navy's job of mitigating these risks even more complicated.

Several lessons learned that relate to this study are found in the investigation of the USS *Cole* bombing. The investigation found that ships transiting into theater, often traveling thousands of miles between refueling, lacked the time and resources to properly determine the safety of potential locations for port stops. As a result, ships relied heavily on outside support to help detect, disrupt and mitigate terrorist attacks (US DoD 2001, 2). In the case of the LCS, with a reduced crew, this outside support will also be important. With a crew that is already heavily tasked there will be little room for additional crew workload.

Not directly reflected as a lesson learned following the investigation but derived from the crew's actions, is the need to avoid the over-reliance on technology. Following the bombing, with unreliable power, the ship found itself sinking. If not for the ingenuity of the crew and the decision to deviate from standard procedures, the ship may have been lost. Similar to the USS *Stark* example, this study questions the impact this event would have had on a reduced manning ship. Following the loss of over 15 percent of the total crew along with almost no automated damage control capability, could the LCS have survived this attack?

## LCS Risk Analysis

Applying the lessons from the USS *Stark* and USS *Cole* this study analyzes the risk of the LCS using the following equation (Risk = Consequence x Likelihood). Each of the risk criteria were placed in a risk evaluation matrix based on both the consequence and the likelihood of each risk criterion occurring. The risk analysis equation indicates that as the likelihood increases from rare to frequent and the consequence of the risk increases from minor to significant, so will the level of risk.

The circle on the matrix in figure 7 identifies where the majority of medium and high risks occur and therefore will be the focus of this study. In addition, assumptions were made to determine what would be the likelihood that each of the risk criteria would not be met. These assumptions are discussed in detail as each risk is analyzed.

The first risk analyzed was reduced manning and the use of "hybrid sailors." This study found that this manning concept assumes a high level of risk. The likelihood of this risk is high since it will be continuously employed throughout the life cycle of the ship and the impact or consequence will be significant if ship manning does not support mission accomplishment and ship survival. Even though the addition of an aviation detachment, which could add up to twenty personnel to the crew, and the additional personnel associated with individual mission packages called "mission specialist," could

48

add up to fifteen more, these numbers are deceiving. Since these personnel are not part of the "core crew," and their presence will fluctuate as the aviation detachments or mission packages embark and disembark, these numbers cannot be relied upon without assuming additional risks. To assume that a crew of seventy-five (core crew plus aviation detachment and mission specialists) will always be present, train together and be able to respond as a well-trained team is unrealistic based on the fluidity associated with the current manning plan.

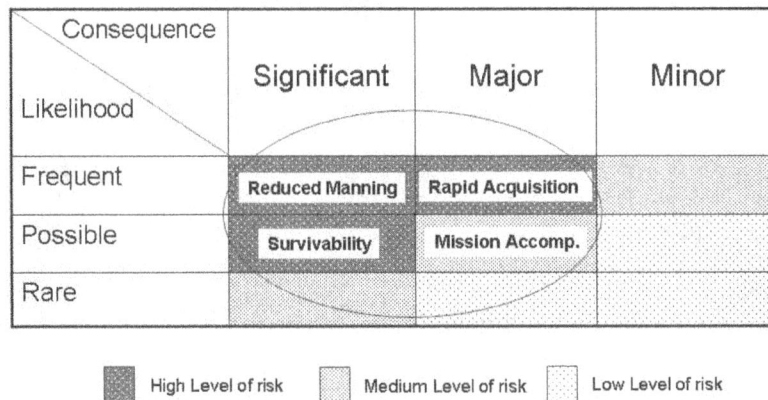

| Consequence / Likelihood | Significant | Major | Minor |
|---|---|---|---|
| Frequent | Reduced Manning | Rapid Acquisition | |
| Possible | Survivability | Mission Accomp. | |
| Rare | | | |

High Level of risk    Medium Level of risk    Low Level of risk

Figure 7.   Analysis Matrix for Determining Level of Risk
Modified from Source: "Chapter 3: The Risk Management Process," *Standards Association of Australia,* 2004, 31; [database on-line]; available from http://www.standards.com.au; Internet; accessed on 15 December 2005.

Therefore, in order to determine the risk that the LCS would have to assume during normal operations due to manning, this study focused on the "core crew" number of forty personnel. It is worth noting that this core crew will consist of blue and gold teams. This two-crew policy will allow for a "shore-based" and "at-sea" rotation where the shore-based crew will be available to rapidly support any manning deficiencies identified by the at-sea crew. The logic behind that design is that a "back-up crew" will help prevent any vital crew manning shortfalls. The two-crew policy will surely help prevent potential personnel gaps due to disciplinary action, emergency leave, or other short-fused loss of personnel; however, when the ship is at sea conducting operations, the forty sailors assigned will be required to complete all assigned tasks on their own without rapid support and crew replacement.

In order to facilitate crew reductions on the LCS, shore facilities will have to assume several functions normally accomplished by a traditionally manned naval combatant. LCS crew will still have to accomplish basic preventative maintenance; however, shore facilities, including the ship's Immediate Superior in the Chain of Command (ISIC), will have to support the ship much more than in the past (Lundquist 2005, 8). Risks are associated with this model as seen in recent history with the Oliver Hazard Perry-class frigate. When the new frigate, with its reduced manning design, was promised increased shore infrastructure support to help relieve the stress on the crew in the late 1970s, shore facilities were not ready or organized by the time the frigates became operational. As a result, the crews had to assume the additional work load that was originally assigned ashore. The promise that the LCS will have all the necessary shore support to properly offset its reduced crew size has not yet been tested and adds additional risk to the program.

The next risk analyzed was ship survivability. Damage control is a crew-intensive activity and therefore a capability that is closely tied to crew numbers. Recent advances in damage control technology such as remotely operated firefighting systems and "smart" sensors, which can detect and take initial steps in the damage control efforts, will no doubt provide the ability to use sailors in a more efficient manner. However, damage control systems must be extremely reliable and able to survive the rigors of a combat environment in order to be effective. As the previous vignettes illustrate, the high-technology solution to damage control is not always available when a ship suffers extensive damage. Both the USS *Stark* and USS *Cole* survived as a result of their crews' actions. Furthermore, the USS *Cole*, a modern and highly advanced ship, provides an example of a ship's crew who used low technology and innovative methods as the available means to conduct damage control which saved the ship. The inherent risk in reducing the manning on a ship, down to the bare essentials, results in less redundancy and fewer sailors to fight the damage and lend a hand in the ship saving effort. The consequence of a LCS not being capable of recovering from damage resulting from an attack is significant.

The likelihood of future attacks on US naval combatants is without argument high, especially in the congested littoral environment where the ships are exposed to multiple hazards to include mines, small boat attack, shoal water and decreased stand-off distance. Again, the attack on the USS *Cole* reminds the US Navy that the current threat is complex and the enemy will use any means available to strike on a timeline of his choosing; the LCS must be ready.

Next, mission accomplishment was analyzed. In essence, if the ship cannot "stay in the fight" for any reason and fails to complete its assigned mission, it not only fails to complete the mission but also becomes a liability to the other surface combatants operating in company. An inability to accomplish the mission would have major consequences. If the LCS is tasked to operate independently and cannot accomplish the mission, it not only fails the mission, but may present the inability to provide the appropriate level of organic ship survivability.

The mission package that the LCS has installed could make the difference in the ship's ability to properly defend itself against a credible threat. The LCS concept of operations provides insight into this design limitation:

> While the seaframe will include inherent self-defense capabilities, other combat systems will not be permanently installed. Rather, the major elements of the ship's combat system will be embedded in the LCS mission packages and modules. (US DoN 2004a, iii)

For example if an LCS is assigned to conduct antisubmarine warfare in the littorals and has the associated mission module installed, it may be vulnerable to other threats and will have to assume additional risks. Since US Navy commanders have control of where they send the LCS, this will help prevent assigning the ship to a task or environment where it may not be successful. However, due to the dynamic littoral environment the US Navy cannot expect to anticipate all potential threats and required missions. Therefore, how the LCS is configured based on the assessed threat environment will be very important to the ship's success.

Finally, the rapid acquisition timeline of the LCS was analyzed. The LCS design incorporates drastic changes to the way the US Navy has done business in the past such as new technology, reduced manning and new training methods. There will undoubtedly be several changes to the design as the Flight 0 ships become operational. Sufficient time may not be available to incorporate these modifications in follow-on flights (Flight 1 and up) based on the projected six-month acquisition timeline. Future flights are at risk if they cannot benefit from the lessons learned from the initial prototypes. The USS *Freedom* (Flight 0 prototype) is scheduled for delivery from Marinette Marine in 2007; however, follow-on Flight 1 models will be in production only six-months later. Furthermore, the fact that several of the mission modules will not arrive until after ship delivery to the Navy and will therefore be unavailable for testing, presents compelling reasons to slow the acquisition process down (GAO 2005, 21).

The early procurement of the Arleigh Burke-class destroyer, the only US Navy surface combatant in production since FY1989 (O'Rourke 2005, 10), provides a good example of ship design changes that occur during acquisition. The Flight I and II designs of the Arleigh Burke-class destroyer did not have the capability to embark helicopters. After the ships were placed in operation, the US Navy found that the need for this shipboard capability was greatly underestimated and follow-on Flight IIA designs added the facilities to support two SH-60 helicopters. As a result, the first twenty-eight ships in the Arleigh Burke-class do not have this highly valued capability (Polmar 2001, 143). With the radical design changes of LCS there are sure to be modifications that will need to be made. Allowing sufficient time for these modifications to be identified and incorporated will be essential to the improvement of the ship's design.

Using the *Australian and New Zealand STandard 4360* methodology this chapter has established the context and identified and analyzed the risks associated with the LCS. Chapter 5 evaluates the risks, summarizes the study's findings, and provides recommendations for reducing the risks that are present in the LCS design. The next chapter also offers recommendations for further study on this topic.

# CHAPTER 5

## CONCLUSIONS AND RECOMMENDATIONS

The arrival of the first LCS, the USS *Freedom*, will present a new chapter in US naval history. When USS *Freedom* becomes operational in 2007, it will represent the first ship designed from the ground up for reduced manning and the first of a new family of surface combatants built to face the future maritime threat. With the proposed ship class of up to fifty-five total ships, the US Navy needs to make sure that the LCS is successful. The purpose of this research was to explore the current risks associated with the LCS and to continue the discussion and debate on the utility of this ship. As mentioned in chapter 4, there are several compelling reasons for the radical changes incorporated in the LCS design; however, a better understanding of the risks that the ship and crew will assume is vital to the proper use of this new platform and will help ensure the safety of both. This study does not advocate the complete mitigation of the risks associated with the LCS, but strives to increase the overall awareness of these risks. The risk of combining so many new and untested elements on a single ship must be understood by all of those who are involved in its implementation. Finally, as the first reduced manning ship in a family of future ship construction (DD(X) and CG(X)), the spotlight is on the LCS. Lessons learned from the LCS will directly affect follow-on ship designs and the decision to continue the use of reduced manning.

In chapter 4, the *Australian and New Zealand STandard* model was used to identify the risks associated with the LCS. After several risks were reviewed using a strengths, weaknesses, opportunities and threats (SWOT) analysis, four risk evaluation criteria were identified with their associated objectives: survivability, reduced manning with "hybrid sailors", mission accomplishment, and acquisition timeline. Next, these individual risk criteria were analyzed and ranked. In addition, two vignettes were used to provide historical examples of the risks that were similar to those that the LCS will face. These examples are a reminder that warships should be designed for war and should have the ability to survive a hit, continue fighting, and return home safely. This chapter evaluates the identified risks, provides suggestions for risk treatment or mitigation, and concludes with recommendations for further research.

## Evaluate the Risk

As mentioned in chapter 4, not all risks are considered negative. As the SWOT analysis illustrates, positive risks resulting in strengths and opportunities have some very attractive features. This being said, the US Navy is assuming a high level of risk with the LCS reduced manning design. The following paragraphs summarize the study's findings following the comparison of the original risk criteria with the risks found during the analysis. This evaluation also answers the secondary questions of this study. Table 3 represents a summary of the LCS risk evaluation.

In the case of reduced manning and the use of "hybrid sailors" this study found that there are several variables that will affect the overall risk. Many of these variables are still in their early stages of development. The training of the new hybrid sailor has just begun and the sailors that will report to the USS *Freedom* are only now beginning to pool their skills for a ship that is still being built.

Table 3.    Risk Evaluation Summary

## Risk Evaluation Summary

| Risk Criterion (in order of priority) | | Research Questions | Findings (Accept or Treat?) |
|---|---|---|---|
| Reduced Manning and Hybrid Sailors | | What level of risk is the Navy assuming with the Littoral Combat Ship reduced manning design? | • High level of risk assumed |
| | | Will the multi-tasked "hybrid sailor" have sufficient skills and support to compensate for the reduced manning onboard the LCS without assuming too much risk? | • TBD – Monitor crew morale closely to ensure we are not overburdening our ship crews and that they are sufficiently supported from shore |
| Survivability | INCREASED RISK | In the hostile environment of the littorals, is the LCS assuming too much risk with its ability to conduct damage control and recover from a mass conflagration? | • Yes – (Treat) Train crews extensively on damage control while avoiding excessive reliance on high-technology solutions |
| Mission Accomplishment | | Will the LCS have the necessary capability to allow it to accomplish its mission in the littorals while operating independently without assuming excessive risk? | • No – (Treat) Avoid mission creep by educating Navy planners/leaders on the proper use of the LCS to limit excessive exposure to risks |
| Acquisition Timeline | | Will the rapid acquisition timeline of the LCS assume too much risk by not allowing follow-on designs to benefit from the initial Flight 0 prototype? | • Yes - (Treat) Slow down acquisition process in order to fully benefit from Flight 0 production |

Furthermore, the shore infrastructure that promises to support and relieve a significant burden from the LCS sailors is still waiting for the first ship to come off the production line. However, this does not remove the risks that will be present as these two pieces of the puzzle come together. This study recommends that this process be closely monitored as the first Flight 0 ships become operational. It is extremely important that these newly designed crews are fully supported. If they are not, the loss of crew morale will surely degrade the ships' mission capability.

With regards to ship survivability, the study found that the LCS is assuming a high level of risk. Attempting to provide sufficient ship survivability with a reduced crew size while operating in the high-threat environment of the littorals, involves risk. The two vignettes used in this study further illustrate the complexity of this problem. The USS

*Cole* and the USS *Stark* were saved due to an aggressive crew who fought for the ship's life when computers and automation failed. Focused damage control training with an emphasis on innovative solutions, while reducing the over-reliance on modern technology to solve the problem, is the way to treat this risk. In addition, closely monitoring the lessons learned from initial Flight 0 prototypes will help to facilitate the improvement and survivability of follow-on designs. Increasing the number of "core crew" if necessary to make the ship safer may be the long range solution as the US Navy begins to truly understand the rigors this ship and reduced crew will face. In today's volatile world, the US Navy will never be able to mitigate all the risks with any ship design; however, this ship will eventually find itself in a major conflagration situation and it must be ready. With a future LCS fleet consisting of up to fifty-five ships, there is a lot at stake.

Closely related to ship survivability is the ship's ability to accomplish its mission. For a ship that is highly dependant on outside support, proper mission assignment is critical to reduce risk. Furthermore, if the LCS is tasked to operate independently, where outside support is even more limited, the ship will assume the greatest risk. Here again, the US Navy is in the position to mitigate some of this risk. Operational commanders as well as planners should be ultimately familiar with the capabilities and limitations of the LCS in order to prevent the ship from being over-tasked. Ship limitations based on crew size and mission package configurations are not in the current Navy culture. This culture change will have to occur in order to protect the LCS from operating outside of its capabilities and limitations and assuming too much mission risk.

Finally, the rapid acquisition timeline of the LCS will limit the proper integration of lessons learned from initial Flights 0 prototypes and therefore assumes too much risk. This process should be slowed down in order to sufficiently allow design changes to be incorporated in follow-on Flight 1 designs. The LCS platform represents a large combination of new changes in ship design. There are likely to be several improvements required as the US Navy tests the initial prototype. The chapter 4 example of the Arleigh Burke-class destroyer is a reminder that sometimes these initial prototypes result in major design changes. Delaying the initial LCS designs for additional testing, and not immediately filling the littoral mission gap capability, may be a better choice that results in a better Flight 1 ship design. Furthermore, if the initial prototypes determine that the manning is not sufficient on the LCS and needs to be increased, berthing design changes may be necessary. These changes will most likely require large modifications in the ship design, changes that would present significant challenges under the current timeline.

## Conclusions

The four risk evaluation criteria present a considerable amount of risk for the LCS. However, a majority of these risks can be treated by education, close monitoring and prudent use of the LCS. To treat the LCS as simply another new weapon system without due regard for the significant changes that it presents would, without a doubt, present unacceptable risks for the LCS. These changes are not only in the area of technology and procedure, but also include the cultural changes and the mental shift in how the US Navy has been doing business for the past several decades. Previous surface combatants have been multi-mission capable whereas the LCS uses modular "plug and fight" technology that will require greater planning timelines as ships are required to reconfigure for different missions. Also, the potential loss of the "traditional control" associated with a ship's commanding officer (CO) will present a new challenge. As a result of the LCS's heavy dependence on the shore facilities to not only relieve the work load on its reduced crew but also to provide an increased number of required services necessary in order to keep the ship operational, the CO will be even further removed from the driver's seat. CO's have traditionally held full responsibility for their ships and their job will become more difficult as they find themselves in less control.

This study found definite value in the reduced manning design and its ability to better utilize personnel along with the use of "hybrid sailors." However, the results indicated a high level of risk that should be recognized by all of those who are involved in the application of the LCS. Based on the results of this study, the US Navy should proceed with the LCS cautiously. As the US Navy moves aggressively towards the future, it would be unwise to rush ship acquisition considering many of the elements that comprise the ship are new and untested both physically and culturally.

It is impossible to mitigate all risks present with any ship design, especially a naval combatant in a navy with a finite budget; however, understanding the risks and developing an awareness of their combined effects will help to mitigate the risks that this study identified. Those involved with the LCS in the future would be well served to understand these risks, especially during the early years of development when combining so many new and different elements. It is this study's recommendation that the LCS be given considerable time for testing and training. There is little doubt that the LCS, even with the longest timeline, will require some changes; however, the goal should be to avoid large-scale design changes. A rush to full-mission status without the benefits of a full utilization of the prototypes could present exceptional risks, risks that are not worth taking. The success of the LCS may very well rely on training and ship design; this ship needs sufficient time to develop and refine both.

Risk assessment and management is an on-going process and requires continual review. Following the USS *Cole* bombing, Secretary of the Navy Richard Danzig recognized the need to understand risk and make sure that it was in balance. "Secretary Danzig asked the CNO to work with the joint staff and within the Navy to strengthen procedures assuring that risk is repeatedly recognized, reassessed and balanced." (Cole 2001, 11) The need to recognize, and constantly reassess the risks that are present with the LCS cannot be over-emphasized. As the operation environment and threats change, the risk that the LCS will assume will also change. Only by careful monitoring and reassessing can the US Navy provide the protection that the LCS deserves.

<u>Recommendations for Further Research</u>

Based on the limitations of this study, mentioned in chapter 1, there were several other risk-producing areas on the LCS that were not covered. For example, there are risks associated with the materials used in ship design. The Lockheed Martin LCS design will center on a steel monohull whereas the General Dynamics design will focus on an all-aluminum trimaran hull. Additional study of the pros and cons based on these two designs and their selected materials would be helpful in determining additional LCS risk exposure. Moreover, based on the challenges that the USS *Stark* faced following her attack as several areas of the aluminum superstructure reached melting point, the use of different materials will be important when determining risk.

Additional research could also focus on specific ship features and new technologies as part of the General Dynamics and Lockheed Martin designs. During the writing of this study many of the design specifics were either unavailable or not releasable to the public due to the design competition between the two shipbuilders. As more information becomes available and decisions are made as to which design is awarded contract for follow-on flights, more detailed research into the risks associated with specific design features and technologies could be conducted. In addition, as LCS sister ships get closer to production, research similar to this study needs to be conducted on the future destroyer and cruiser (DD(X) and CG(X)) designs.

Another recommendation for additional research involves revisiting this study's questions again after the initial Flight 0 prototypes become operational. The availability of actual test results would be beneficial in answering this study's question about the long-term effect of reduced manning and the use of the "hybrid sailor." This study's recommendation in reference to this question was to monitor their progress closely; future research could accomplish this and continue a productive dialogue on this topic.

The US Navy needs to continue to take heed of Secretary Danzig's words following the USS *Cole* bombing. The US Navy needs to continue the effort of recognizing and reassessing the risks associated with its ships and especially the new LCS design. Only by continually revisiting this topic will the US Navy be certain to recognize and rebalance these risks as necessary.

# APPENDIX A

## EXAMPLES OF LITTORAL COMBAT SHIP MISSIONS

| Focused missions | Examples of tasks |
|---|---|
| Littoral mine warfare | • Detect, avoid, and/or neutralize mines<br>• Clear transit lanes<br>• Establish and maintain mine cleared areas |
| Littoral antisubmarine warfare | • Detect all threat submarines in a given littoral area<br>• Protect forces in transit<br>• Establish antisubmarine barriers |
| Littoral surface warfare | • Detect, track, and engage small boat threats in a given littoral area<br>• Escort ships through choke points<br>• Protect joint operating areas |
| **Inherent Missions** | |
| Battle space awareness | • Intelligence, surveillance, and reconnaissance |
| Joint littoral mobility | • Provide transport for personnel, supplies and equipment within the littoral operating area |
| Special operations forces support | • Provide rapid movement of small groups of special operations forces personnel<br>• Support hostage rescue operations<br>• Support noncombatant evacuation operations<br>• Support and conduct combat search and rescue |
| Maritime interdiction/interception | • Provide staging area for boarding teams<br>• Employ and support MH-60 helicopters for maritime interdiction operations<br>• Conduct maritime law enforcement operations, including counternarcotic operations, with law enforcement detachment |
| Homeland defense | • Perform maritime interdiction/interception operations in support of homeland defense<br>• Provide emergency, humanitarian and disaster assistance<br>• Conduct marine environmental protection<br>• Perform naval diplomatic presence |
| Antiterrorism/force protection | • Perform maritime interdiction/interception operations in support of force protection operations<br>• Provide port protection for U.S. and friendly forces and protection against attack in areas of restricted maneuverability |

*Source:* GAO Report 05.255.2005. *See* U.S. Government Accountability Office (GAO). 2005.

WORKS CITED

Cavas, Christopher. 2005. U.S. Ship Plan to Cost 20% More: Price Control will be Key to Finding 313-Vessel Fleet. Article on-line. Available from http://defensenews.com. Internet. Accessed on 14 March 2006.

Clark, Vern. 2002. Sea Power 21: Projecting Decisive Joint Capabilities. *United States Naval Institute Proceedings* 128, no. 10:31-41.

Cole, Dick, and Joseph Gunder. 2001. USS Cole: Where Do We Go From Here? *Surface Warfare* 26, no. 1:11.

Global Security Database. DDG 67 Cole: Determined Warrior. Article on-line. Available from http://www.globalsecurity.org/military/agency/navy/ddg-67.htm. Internet. Accessed on 9 February 2006.

GAO Report 05.255.2005. *See* U.S. Government Accountability Office (GAO). 2005.

Grosick, Frederick, Patrick Massey, and Mark Peterson. 1988. *Harpoon Employment in Naval Antisurface Warfare (ASUW)*. Alabama: Air University, United States Air Force. Accession Number: AD-A202-045.

Harris, Paul. 2005. Training's New Wave: The U.S. Navy aims to ensure that a fully trained sailor is always in the right place at the right time. *Training and Development Magazine,* August, 45-48.

Henson, Susan. 2005. LCS Crew to be Hybrid Sailors. *All Hands Magazine*, 12 July, 1.

Hinkle, James, and Terry Glover. 2004. *Reduced Manning in DDG 51 Class Warship: Challenges, Opportunities and the Way Ahead for Reduced Manning on all United States Navy Ships*. Arlington: Anteon Corporation. OMB No 074-0188.

Klain, David. 1999. How Can we Save Ships with Small Crews? *United States Naval Institute Proceedings* 125, no. 9:66-69.

Levinson, Jeffery, and Randy Edwards. 1997. *Missile Inbound: The Attack on the Stark in the Persian Gulf.* Maryland: Naval Institute Press.

Lindquist, Edward. 2005. First Littoral Combatant Taking Shape in Midwest. *Surface Warfare* 30, no. 4:6-11.

Moran, Kevin. 2005. Sea Warrior: A True Revolution in Training, interview with Vice Admiral J. Kevin Moran, Commander, Naval Education and Training Command. *CHIPS Magazine,* October-December, 10.

NTTP 3-20.31. 2004. *See* U.S. Department of the Navy, Officer of the Chief of Naval Operations. 2004.

O'Rourke, Ronald. 2005. *Navy DD(X), CG(X), and LCS ship Acquisition Programs: Oversight Issues and Options for Congress.* The Library of Congress, Congressional Research Service. Order Code-RL32109.

_____. 2006. *Navy Littoral Combat Ship (LCS): Background and Issues for Congress.* The Library of Congress, Congressional Research Service. Order Code-RS21305.

Peoships Littoral Combat Ship. 2006. Lockheed Martin and General Dynamics LCS Designs, Database on-line. Available from http://peoships.crane.navy.mil. Internet. Accessed on 14 March 2006.

Polmar, Norman. 2001. *The Naval Institute Guide to the Ships and Aircraft of the U.S. Fleet.* Maryland: Naval Institute Press.

Schank, John, Roland Yardley, Jessie Riposo, Harry Thie, Edward Keating, Mark Arena, Hans Pung, John Birkler, and James Chiesa. 2005. Options for Reducing Costs in theUnited Kingdom's Future Aircraft Carrier (CVF). Article on-line. Available from http://www.rand.org. Internet. Accessed on 14 March 2006.

SkillsNET Corporation. 2006. Database on-line. Available from http://www.skillsnet.com. Internet. Accessed on 14 March 2006.

Standards Association of Australia. 2004. Chapter 3: The Risk Management Process (AS/NZS 4360). Available from http://www.standards.com.au. Internet. Accessed on 15 December 2005.

Thomas, Evan, and Sharon Squassoni. 2001. Desperate Hours: The Blast Claimed 17 Lives and Crippled a Destroyer. The Inside Story of the Heroic Bid to Save the USS Cole. *Shipmate*, June, 9-13.

U.S. Army Training and Doctrine Command. 2005. *Terror Operations: Case Studies in Terrorism*, DCSINT Handbook No 1.01, 4-1 to 4-13.

U.S. Congress. House. Committee on Armed Services House of Representatives. 1987. *Report on the Staff Investigation into the Iraqi Attack on the USS Stark.* 100th Cong., 1st sess., Committee Print 8.

U.S. Department of Defense. 2001. *USS Cole Commission Report Executive Summary.* January.

U.S. Department of the Navy. 2003a. Navy Warfare Development Command. Littoral Combat Ship Concept of Operations, V3.1. Article on-line. Available from http://www.nwdc.navy.mil. Internet. Accessed on 14 March 2006.

_____. 2003b. *Preliminary Design Interim Requirements Document for Littoral Combat Ship (LCS) Flight 0*. February, Serial no. N763F-S03-026.

_____. 2004a. *Littoral Combat Ship Concept of Operations*, December.

_____. 2004b. Officer of the Chief of Naval Operations. NTTP 3-20.31, *Navy Tactics, Techniques, and Procedures (NTTP), Surface Ship Survivability* Newport, RI: DCNO, October.

U.S. Government Accountability Office. 2005. *Defense Acquisitions: Plans Need to Allow Enough Time to Demonstrate Capability of First Littoral Combat Ships*. March. GAO-05-255.

Wise, Alexis. 2003. Militarizing Commercial Automation for Integrated Power System Warship Command and Control, 5 December 2003. Article on-line. Available from, http://nerc.aticorp.org/papers/warships.pdf.

# SOURCES CONSULTED

Bennis, P.M. 1994. Aftermath of a Tragedy. *Fathom*, July-August, 24.

Bost, Robert, and George Galdorisi. n.d. Transforming Coalition Naval Operations by Using Human Systems Integration to Reduce Warship Manning: Lessons Learned from the United States Navy DDG 51 Warship Reduced Manning Study. California: The Ninth International Command and Control Research and Technology Symposium. Available from http://whitepapers.silicon.com. Internet. Accessed on 14 March 2006.

Bost, Robert, James Mellis, and Philip Dent. n.d. Is the Navy Serious about Reducing Manning on Its Ships? Available from http://www.manningaffordability.com. Internet. Accessed on 14 March 2006.

Cloud, David. 2005. Navy to Expand Fleet with New Enemies in Mind. *New York Times*, 5 December.

Cordle, John. 2001. Manning DD-21. *United States Naval Institute Proceedings* 127, no. 2:59-61.

Enockson, Elizabeth. 2005. PCU Freedom, Hybrid Sailors Experience New Way of Training. Navy Newsstand. Available from http://www.news.navy.mil. Internet. Accessed on 14 March 2006.

Garza, Michael A. 2001. DD21 Land Attack Destroyer: Effect of Reduced Crew on Damage Control. Master of Military Art and Science thesis, U.S. Army Command and General Staff College, Ft. Leavenworth, KS.

Kaufman, A. I., J. T. Buontempo, J. F. Nance, S. M. Ouellette, and E. Zdankiewicz. 2004. *How Many Sailors to Man a Surface Combatant?* Alexandria, VA: Institute for Defense Analyses. IDA Paper P-3782.

Lavell, Kit. 2003. New Technology Transforming Naval Power. Available from http://www.signonsandiego.com. Internet. Accessed on 14 March 2006.

Lehmann, John. 2004. Will the Littoral Combat Ship Pass Muster? *United States Naval Institute Proceedings* 130, no. 6:71.

Stubbs, Bruce. 2005. Smarter Security for Small Budgets. *United States Naval Institute Proceedings* 131, no. 8:37-41.

Sweetman, Bill. 2005. Small, Speedy, Shallow LCS Signals Major Shift. *International Defense Review,* November.

U.S. Congressional Budget Office. 2003. *Transforming the Navy's Surface Combatant Force*. The Congress of the United States, March.

Vining, Pierre. 1999. Can a Minimum-Manned Ship Survive Combat? *United States Naval Institute Proceedings* 125, no. 4:80-83.

# INITIAL DISTRIBUTION LIST

Combined Arms Research Library
U.S. Army Command and General Staff College
250 Gibbon Ave.
Fort Leavenworth, KS 66027-2314

Defense Technical Information Center/OCA
825 John J. Kingman Rd., Suite 944
Fort Belvoir, VA 22060-6218

Mr. Robert M. Brown
DJMO
USACGSC
1 Reynolds Ave.
Fort Leavenworth, KS 66027-1352

Mr. Phillip G. Pattee
DJMO
USACGSC
1 Reynolds Ave.
Fort Leavenworth, KS 66027-1352

Dr. Ronald E. Cuny
DGDP
USACGSC
1 Reynolds Ave.
Fort Leavenworth, KS 66027-1352

# CERTIFICATION FOR MMAS DISTRIBUTION STATEMENT

1. Certification Date: 16 June 2006

2. Thesis Author: LCDR Jonathan C. Russell, USN

3. Thesis Title: The Littoral Combat Ship: Is the US Navy Assuming Too Much Risk?

4. Thesis Committee Members:        Robert M. Brown, M.M.A.S. _____

  Signatures:                          Phillip G. Pattee, M.M.A.S.  _____

                                      Ronald E. Cuny, Ph.D.      _____

5. Distribution Statement: See distribution statements A-X on reverse, then circle appropriate distribution statement letter code below:

(A)  B  C  D  E  F  X      SEE EXPLANATION OF CODES ON REVERSE

If your thesis does not fit into any of the above categories or is classified, you must coordinate with the classified section at CARL.

6. Justification: Justification is required for any distribution other than described in Distribution Statement A. All or part of a thesis may justify distribution limitation. See limitation justification statements 1-10 on reverse, then list, below, the statement(s) that applies (apply) to your thesis and corresponding chapters/sections and pages. Follow sample format shown below:

EXAMPLE

| Limitation Justification Statement | / | Chapter/Section | / | Page(s) |
|---|---|---|---|---|
| Direct Military Support (10) | / | Chapter 3 | / | 12 |
| Critical Technology (3) | / | Section 4 | / | 31 |
| Administrative Operational Use (7) | / | Chapter 2 | / | 13-32 |

Fill in limitation justification for your thesis below:

| Limitation Justification Statement | / | Chapter/Section | / | Page(s) |
|---|---|---|---|---|
| _____ | / | _____ | / | _____ |
| _____ | / | _____ | / | _____ |
| _____ | / | _____ | / | _____ |
| _____ | / | _____ | / | _____ |
| _____ | / | _____ | / | _____ |

7. MMAS Thesis Author's Signature: _____

STATEMENT A: Approved for public release; distribution is unlimited. (Documents with this statement may be made available or sold to the general public and foreign nationals).

STATEMENT B: Distribution authorized to U.S. Government agencies only (insert reason and date ON REVERSE OF THIS FORM). Currently used reasons for imposing this statement include the following:

    1. Foreign Government Information. Protection of foreign information.

    2. Proprietary Information. Protection of proprietary information not owned by the U.S. Government.

    3. Critical Technology. Protection and control of critical technology including technical data with potential military application.

    4. Test and Evaluation. Protection of test and evaluation of commercial production or military hardware.

    5. Contractor Performance Evaluation. Protection of information involving contractor performance evaluation.

    6. Premature Dissemination. Protection of information involving systems or hardware from premature dissemination.

    7. Administrative/Operational Use. Protection of information restricted to official use or for administrative or operational purposes.

    8. Software Documentation. Protection of software documentation - release only in accordance with the provisions of DoD Instruction 7930.2.

    9. Specific Authority. Protection of information required by a specific authority.

    10. Direct Military Support. To protect export-controlled technical data of such military significance that release for purposes other than direct support of DoD-approved activities may jeopardize a U.S. military advantage.

STATEMENT C: Distribution authorized to U.S. Government agencies and their contractors: (REASON AND DATE). Currently most used reasons are 1, 3, 7, 8, and 9 above.

STATEMENT D: Distribution authorized to DoD and U.S. DoD contractors only; (REASON AND DATE). Currently most reasons are 1, 3, 7, 8, and 9 above.

STATEMENT E: Distribution authorized to DoD only; (REASON AND DATE). Currently most used reasons are 1, 2, 3, 4, 5, 6, 7, 8, 9, and 10.

STATEMENT F: Further dissemination only as directed by (controlling DoD office and date), or higher DoD authority. Used when the DoD originator determines that information is subject to special dissemination limitation specified by paragraph 4-505, DoD 5200.1-R.

STATEMENT X: Distribution authorized to U.S. Government agencies and private individuals of enterprises eligible to obtain export-controlled technical data in accordance with DoD Directive 5230.25; (date). Controlling DoD office is (insert).

# Littoral Combat Ship - Support Tender (LCS-ST)

LCDR Ethan Proper, USN, LT Richard Jones, USN, LT Colin Dunlop, USN

LT Kyriakos Avgouleas, HN

The LCS Support Tender (*LCS-ST*) conversion study provides an alternative to new ship acquisition where an inactive *Newport Class Tank Landing Ship* (specifically the LST-1190 hull) is modified to provide three primary functions for the LCS fleet; the ability to (1) conduct underway replenishment (UNREP) and resupply operations of the LCS and Riverine boats; (2) conduct repairs to mission modules without the need of homeport IMA facilities and (3) the ability to repair, retest, reload, configure, and swap mission modules without returning to a homeport. The requirements of the *LCS-ST* were derived from the NAVSEA 05D Light Logistics Link (L3) project, where a commercial off-shore vessel is converted to provide LCS tender functions and mission module support.

The *LCS-ST* conversion is accomplished through modifications to internal arrangement, topside structure, and insertion of significant crane and rigging services. The focal point of the converted design is the rearranged vehicle stowage well (VSW) which provides new functionality to hold ten operational mission modules, two module maintenance areas, and two RHIB maintenance areas. The VSW is fitted with a full access bridge crane and clam shell deck access to a 4th deck hold. Service galleries, mounted on the port and starboard bulkheads, provide required module services such as air, fuel, LAN, and freshwater cooling. The propulsion and electric plant are unchanged during the design. Additionally, the conversion requires minimal modifications to LST structure or watertight boundaries.

A detailed analysis indicates the study is feasible from a hydrodynamic, stability and structural standpoint. The cost analysis, based on a NAVSEA 017 cost model, estimates a total conversion cost (including reactivation) of $165M (FY2007$).

| Dimension | Value |
|---|---|
| LBP | 500 feet |
| Length Overall | 517.85 feet |
| Beam | 68.12 feet |
| Draft | 15.1 ft (Min Op) / 19.3 ft (Full load) |
| Max Section Coefficient (Cx) | 0.886 |
| Prismatic Coefficient (Cp) | 0.569 |
| Block Coefficient (Cb) | 0.504 |
| Waterplane Coefficient (Cwp) | 0.711 |
| Lightship Displacement | 6493 LT |
| Full Load Displacement | 9117 LT |

| Cost | Value |
|---|---|
| Reactivation Cost | $ 42M |
| Conversion Cost | $ 123M |
| Annual Operating Cost over 10 years | $ 497M |
| Total Life Cycle Cost (2007$) | $ 662M |

# The Littoral Combat Ship

## From Concept to Program

Case Studies in Defense Transformation
Number 7
Duncan Long and Stuart Johnson

Sponsored by the Office of the Deputy Assistant Secretary of Defense
Forces Transformation and Resources

Prepared by the Center for Technology and National Security Policy

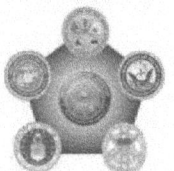

# Report Documentation Page

*Form Approved*
*OMB No. 0704-0188*

Public reporting burden for the collection of information is estimated to average 1 hour per response, including the time for reviewing instructions, searching existing data sources, gathering and maintaining the data needed, and completing and reviewing the collection of information. Send comments regarding this burden estimate or any other aspect of this collection of information, including suggestions for reducing this burden, to Washington Headquarters Services, Directorate for Information Operations and Reports, 1215 Jefferson Davis Highway, Suite 1204, Arlington VA 22202-4302. Respondents should be aware that notwithstanding any other provision of law, no person shall be subject to a penalty for failing to comply with a collection of information if it does not display a currently valid OMB control number.

| 1. REPORT DATE **2007** | 2. REPORT TYPE | 3. DATES COVERED **00-00-2007 to 00-00-2007** |
|---|---|---|

| 4. TITLE AND SUBTITLE | 5a. CONTRACT NUMBER |
|---|---|
| **The Littoral Combat Ship. From Concept to Program** | 5b. GRANT NUMBER |
| | 5c. PROGRAM ELEMENT NUMBER |
| 6. AUTHOR(S) | 5d. PROJECT NUMBER |
| | 5e. TASK NUMBER |
| | 5f. WORK UNIT NUMBER |

| 7. PERFORMING ORGANIZATION NAME(S) AND ADDRESS(ES) **Center for Technology and National Security Policy,National Defense University,BG 20 Ft. Lesley J. McNair,Washington,DC,20319** | 8. PERFORMING ORGANIZATION REPORT NUMBER |
|---|---|

| 9. SPONSORING/MONITORING AGENCY NAME(S) AND ADDRESS(ES) | 10. SPONSOR/MONITOR'S ACRONYM(S) |
|---|---|
| | 11. SPONSOR/MONITOR'S REPORT NUMBER(S) |

12. DISTRIBUTION/AVAILABILITY STATEMENT
**Approved for public release; distribution unlimited**

13. SUPPLEMENTARY NOTES
**The original document contains color images.**

14. ABSTRACT

15. SUBJECT TERMS

| 16. SECURITY CLASSIFICATION OF: | | | 17. LIMITATION OF ABSTRACT | 18. NUMBER OF PAGES | 19a. NAME OF RESPONSIBLE PERSON |
|---|---|---|---|---|---|
| a. REPORT **unclassified** | b. ABSTRACT **unclassified** | c. THIS PAGE **unclassified** | | **16** | |

Standard Form 298 (Rev. 8-98)
Prescribed by ANSI Std Z39-18

**Duncan Long** is a Research Associate at the Center for Technology and National Security Policy (CTNSP). He holds a Master of International Affairs degree from the School of International and Public Affairs, Columbia University, and a BA from Stanford University.

**Stuart Johnson** is a Senior Analyst with the RAND Corportation. Prior to that, he served as the Chair for Force Transformation Studies in the Center for Technology and National Security Policy at National Defense University. He has been Director of International Security and Defense Policy programs at the RAND Corporation, Senior Scientist at the Naval War College, and Director of Systems Analysis at NATO Headquarters. Dr. Johnson is a graduate of Amherst College and has a PhD in Physics from the Massachusetts Institute of Technology.

## Introduction

After the end of the Cold War, the United States faced a sharply diminished threat in the ocean commons. The Soviet Union broke up and its navy was taken over by the Russian Federation, which scaled back sharply on its shipbuilding and operational deployment. The U.S. Navy soon found itself without a global competitor.

The Navy moved to refocus itself to meet the post-Cold War environment in September 1992, when the Secretary of the Navy, the Chief of Naval Operations, and the Commandant of the Marine Corps signed ...*From the Sea*. This white paper outlined a "fundamental shift away from open-ocean warfighting on the sea toward joint operations conducted *from the sea*."[1] It was followed in November 1994 by *Forward...From the Sea*, another Navy-Marine Corps paper that refined ...*From the Sea* and elaborated on the importance of peacetime forward presence operations. While retaining its ability to maintain strategic dominance in the ocean commons, the Navy was adopting a new, interventionist outlook that focused strongly on what was taking place on shore.

This focus on influencing operations ashore drew the Navy into the littoral.[2] Naval strategists noted that the littoral is where the great bulk of the world's population lives, where much of its wealth is generated, and where lines of communication for ocean-borne cargo begin and end. Moreover, it is the area through which an expeditionary military force must pass and in which supporting Naval forces must operate.

Operating in the littoral presents a complex collection of challenges. As ...*From the Sea* put it, the "mastery of the littoral should not be presumed." ...*From the Sea* recognized that "Some littoral threats–specifically mines, sea-skimming cruise missiles, and tactical ballistic missiles–tax the capabilities of our current systems and force structure." In the past decade, swarming small boats (armed with short range missiles or a payload of explosives) and diesel submarines have also been cited by the Navy as obstructing U.S. access to the littoral. These systems enable even relatively unsophisticated adversaries to adopt a strategy of anti-access and area denial (A2/AD), whereby the defender seeks to prevent the attacker from bringing strike power to bear with a layered, but not symmetric force-on-force, defense of the approaches.

## New, Small Ships for a New Era

Faced with A2/AD challenges, Navy strategy initially focused on avoiding operating in the littoral and, instead, on projecting power *over* the littorals using air power, missiles, and gunfire, delivered by aircraft, surface combatants, and missile-launching submarines already in the fleet. Exposure to mines and anti-ship cruise missiles would be minimized

---

[1] "From the Sea: Preparing the Naval Service for the 21st Century," 1992. Available online at <http://www.chinfo.navy.mil/navpalib/policy/fromsea/fromsea.txt>. Accessed on August 9, 2006. Emphasis added through italics.

[2] The littoral can be demarcated in several ways, but a useful way to think about it is as that stretch of shore from which events on the water can be influenced and that swath of ocean from which events on shore can be influenced.

by using long-range weapons and standing off from the shore as far as possible. This operational focus was embodied in the DD-21 Land Attack Destroyer program, which, in the late 1990s, was the centerpiece of the Navy's surface combatant procurement plans. The proposed ship, of which Navy initially was to build 32, was tailored for projecting power on land. Its primary mission would be to support ground forces. Gradually, however, elements within the Navy began to conceive of the need to operate *in* the littorals, and operate there persistently, rather than relying on standoff munitions and occasional sorties through the littoral to support the land battle. These elements saw the shortcomings of the current systems and force structure alluded to by ...*From the Sea* and proposed a way to fill the gap with new, small surface combatants.

The evolution towards a new class of ships for littoral operations began gradually. Though the Navy had had small ships in the fleet for many years (including such platforms as the *Asheville* class of patrol gunboats, the *Pegasus* class of hydrofoil missile boats, and the *Cyclone* class of coastal patrol craft), they had never been well integrated into the fleet and had seldom been used effectively. There were advocates for an expanded small ship role in the battle force, notably then-CAPT Wayne Hughes, a professor at the Naval Postgraduate School, who wrote an influential book on fleet tactics in 1986.[3] Hughes argued that fleet combat would favor whichever side could preserve its combat power for the longest period during an exchange of missile salvos, and that the survivability of combat power could be achieved through distributing it from several large missile-carrying ships to a dispersed fleet of smaller missile-armed ships. These small missile ships could sortie out from a mothership, much as aircraft do from an aircraft carrier. The arguments of Hughes and others who favored this approach did not readily find traction, however.

Another impetus to small ships was programmatic. As a 1997 GAO report indicated, the Navy's shipbuilding program faced a significant fiscal challenge. The unit cost of the ships the Navy had designed to replace its aging fleet was up sharply. If it were to meet its stated force structure goal of 346 ships (later increased to 375), the Navy would have to either spend more or buy less expensive ships. The GAO did not explicitly suggest a small ship, and it did not focus on the A2/AD and the littoral, but it did point out that adding increased capability (such as the Aegis radar system) to multimission ships was the main driver of increased unit costs. To meet its force structure goals, the GAO suggested that the Navy might consider cheaper (if not necessarily smaller), "tailored capability" ships that would perform only one or two missions, like anti-submarine warfare (ASW) or anti-aircraft defense (AAD).

The strategic need to gain access and operate in and around the littorals was taken up by the Chief of Naval Operations' Strategic Studies Group (SSG) housed at the Naval War College. The SSG is a group of naval officers that undertakes special studies for the CNO on innovative naval warfare concepts. From 1998 to 2000, the SSG focused on how the Navy should operate in and dominate the littoral. Though the SSG did not make a specific proposal for a new type of small combatant, it argued for two attributes for the

---

[3] Wayne P. Hughes, Jr., *Fleet Tactics: Theory and Practice* (Annapolis, MD: Naval Institute Press, 1986). This book was updated for coastal operations in 2000.

future fleet and its platforms that became central to the small ship debate: distributed combat power, to include a greater number of networked combat ships, the use of unmanned vehicles (UVs) and offboard sensors, and modularity to provide mission flexibility.

The SSG concluded that combat power in the current Navy was tied to particular hulls. The battle force ships were capable of carrying out a variety of missions. For example, the Navy's main destroyer type, the DDG-51 *Arleigh Burke* class had the capacity to conduct ASW, fleet air defense, land attack, mine warfare (MIW), and other missions. All this combat power would be lost if the fleet lost that one ship. The SSG argued that distributing this combat power on UVs, such as unmanned aerial vehicles (UAVs) to deliver strikes ashore and unmanned undersea vehicles (UUVs) to hunt for mines and submarines, would make the fleet's combat power more survivable. In this, the SSG echoed Hughes's analysis. Further, distributed, unmanned sensors would allow the fleet to develop more robust battlespace knowledge than would sensors limited to the area around a single hull. Battlespace knowledge and the network needed to exploit this knowledge were seen by the SSG to be essential to dominating the complex littoral environment.

Modularity was also important to the SSG's thinking on littoral challenges. Modularity— the ability to tailor a platform's capabilities on a mission-by-mission basis—provided valuable and affordable flexibility. A fleet that distributed its combat power using UVs was inherently modular; ships could embark the necessary UVs for the mission at hand.[4] A further level of modularity was also available: the UVs themselves could be configured to carry different sensor and weapons packages. Modularity also made it easier to upgrade platforms when new technologies became available.

As the SSG developed analyses on littoral challenges, a parallel effort to address the Navy's role in the littorals was underway at the Naval War College, led by its President, VADM Arthur Cebrowski. VADM Cebrowski was concerned that the Navy was not keeping itself relevant to the emerging threat environment. If the Naval services were going to project power "forward from the sea," they would have to be capable of maintaining a persistent presence in the littoral, not just sortieing into or overflying it to launch missiles or deliver troops. This was something that neither the existing nor the programmed fleet was well suited to do.

Cebrowski and Hughes co-authored a widely discussed article in the fall of 1999 in the U.S. Naval Institute journal *Proceedings*[5] that further developed the concept of distributed power and linked it specifically to a new class of ship. The principal problem, as the authors saw it, was that the fleet was "tactically unstable." An increasing portion of the Navy's combat power was vested in a diminishing number of hulls, and the combat power of these ships was growing out of proportion to their survivability. The Navy had cause to be concerned about its ability to operate in high-risk littoral environments.

---

[4] *Naval Power Forward*, Report of the Chief of Naval Operations Strategic Studies Group XIX, September 2000, 4-1.
[5] Arthur K. Cebrowski and Wayne P. Hughes, Jr., "Rebalancing the Fleet," *Proceedings*, November 1999.

Adversaries could employ relatively affordable measures—submarines and mines, of course—but Cebrowski and Hughes were especially concerned about small boats armed with anti-ship missiles that could attack U.S. surface combatants in coastal areas. U.S. surface combatants, meanwhile, were increasing in expense and capability and decreasing in number. As the loss of a ship became an ever-costlier prospect, both in dollars and in combat power, Cebrowski and Hughes warned, the Navy was in danger of becoming risk averse, or self-deterring, and putting itself at a significant operational disadvantage in littoral operations.

The solution to this emerging problem, Cebrowski and Hughes proposed, was a two-tiered fleet made of an Economy A force and an Economy B force. The Economy A force, composed of CVNs, DDG-51s, CG-47s, and later DD-21s, would provide the power projection capability and dominate the broad ocean commons. The Economy B force, composed of a family of smaller, less expensive ships, would counter access denial threats in the littorals. Distributing combat power among more platforms would make the fleet more tactically stable and lessen the need to expose Economy A ships, and the large amount of combat power they contain, to littoral dangers. More hulls would also provide a greater ability to sense in a cluttered littoral environment thereby developing greater battlespace awareness.

The Economy B force proposed in the article was based on a concept called *Streetfighter*.[6] *Streetfighter*, developed and espoused by Cebrowski, assumed a central position in the debate on the Navy's need for a new class of small ships. The *Streetfighter* concept called for a family of small ships that would be fast, networked, and modular and would make extensive use of unmanned vehicles. They would also be austerely manned and cheap enough to afford in large numbers. Cebrowski and others pointed to technological advances in the commercial sector, especially in ship speed, sea-keeping, and payload fraction, as enabling factors for a new class of small warships.

Expendability was one of the foundations of the *Streetfighter* concept: the Navy could put these ships at risk since, if one were lost, the Navy lost only a small fraction of the aggregate combat power inherent in the distributed Economy B fleet. In their article on rebalancing the fleet, Cebrowski and Hughes called for the *Streetfighter*/Economy B force to "cost less than 10% as much as Economy A, comprise more than 25% of total numbers, and be expected to suffer most of the combat losses in littoral warfare."[7] This line of thinking was controversial. Many in the Navy were unhappy with the idea of a "ship designed to lose."

Besides restoring tactical stability to the fleet and improving the Navy's ability to assure access, advocates attributed various other benefits to a new class of small ships. Among them:

---

[6] The term *Streetfighter* was coined by ADM Don Pilling, then VCNO, in a speech to the American Shipbuilding Association in 1999.
[7] Cebrowski and Hughes, 32.

- Small ships would relieve highly capable multimission ships of the need to perform such tasks as maritime interdiction operations (MIO) that made poor use of their considerable potential combat power and stretched the current fleet thin.

- Small ships would rejuvenate the maritime industrial base by allowing shipyards that could not produce large surface combatants to compete for contracts. Only a few naval shipbuilding yards were capable of building large surface combatants, creating mutual dependency between the industry and the Navy—the yards needed consistent work to maintain their infrastructure, and the Navy needed the yards to survive to guarantee a future source of ships. More, smaller ships, it was hoped, would create a more competitive industry, stimulating innovation and lowering costs.

- A fleet composed in part of smaller, less expensive ships, would scale better than the then-programmed fleet. With the then-programmed fleet, if the Navy needed to cut money from the procurement budget it had few options but to cut one of the very few multi-billion dollar ships it funded each year, and thus had to chose between cutting a big chunk of combat power or cutting nothing at all. By the same token, it took a large amount of additional funding to scale up procurement by even one ship. Smaller, less expensive ships could be added or subtracted without causing such turbulence in the shipbuilding program.

Variations on the *Streetfighter* concept emerged between 1999 and 2000, all firmly rooted in a class of ships that were numerous, small, fast, networked, and modular. The three main variations can be broadly described as follows: distributed offense, distributed defense, and delivery of off-board weapons and sensors.[8]

The distributed defense model had small, fast ships acting as screens for the main battle force in the littoral. This was the model that was tested when the *Streetfighter* concept received its first major exposure, in the Naval War College Global 1999 wargame. The annual Global game has typically been a key vehicle for the Naval leadership to explore and assess innovations in force structure and operational concepts. Cebrowski directed that two different types of small combatants be inserted into the game. These were a ship with a 160-ton payload capacity that carried either an ASW or MIW module, and a ship with a 400-ton modular payload that served primarily as a missile magazine.[9] Participants made effective use of the small ships as front-line combatants. A key finding was that the Red force submarines and surface combatants were reluctant to expose themselves for the sake of firing on a small ship, and so the small ships were able to operate with a surprising degree of survivability.

The distributed offense model was conceived of as a flotilla of very small ships supported by a mothership. Such a concept was described by Hughes, both in his early writings and

---

[8] This typology is described in Robert Work's thorough examination of the LCS program and its antecedents, *Naval Transformation and the Littoral Combat Ship* (Washington, DC: Center for Strategic and Budgetary Analysis, 2004) 61.
[9] Ibid., 61.

in an article in the February 2000 issue of *Proceedings*.[10] Hughes's notional ships were modular, displaced ~300 tons, and could be outfitted both to deal with littoral threats like mines and to launch land attack missiles. The mothership was one possible solution to the challenges that the so-called "iron triangle" of naval architecture imposed—the trade-offs between speed, payload, and endurance inevitable in any ship design. By using a mothership, small ships could be fast and have a useful payload because they would not need to self-deploy across large distances or sustain themselves for long periods of time on station.

The most fully developed *Streetfighter*-type design focused on the delivery of off-board weapons and sensors. It came from a design exercise called Sea Lance. Sea Lance arose out of a 2000 Naval Warfare Development Center (NWDC) and Defense Advanced Research Projects Agency (DARPA) study called Capabilities for the Navy After Next (CNAN). CNAN addressed the importance of achieving access in the littorals. Part of the CNAN solution to the problem was an Expeditionary Warfare Grid. This grid is a net of unattended sensors (like radar buoys and sonar buoys) and unattended weapons (like floating torpedoes and cruise missiles) laid in coastal waters. In mid-2000, Cebrowski challenged students at the Naval Postgraduate School to design a system that would be able to implement the CNAN grid concept. The NPG team proposed a team of two ships: a small combatant and a mule, a ship towed behind the combatant that would carry the elements of the Expeditionary Warfare Grid. While the grid and the mule were unique among *Streetfighter*-type proposals, the Sea Lance combatant (as designed) stuck closely to important *Streetfighter* principles. It was small: less than 500 tons full load displacement. It was designed to implement network centric warfare. It made significant use of off-board systems, and so had inherently modular capability. It was also expendable: its low cost (less than $100M for the first ship), austere manning (a crew of 13), and numbers (there would be squadrons of 10 ships with their mules) meant that it could be risked in the hazardous littoral environment.

These three *Streetfighter*-type concepts were employed in the Global 2000 wargame.[11] Here, the concepts began to blend together.[12] The core elements were the same to start with: the ships were small, fast, networked, and modular. Developers added to this the most attractive attributes of the three ships and dropped out others. The Sea Lance's emphasis on offboard capability (a feature also emphasized earlier by the SSG) became a signal feature of the *Streetfighter* concept, which included both manned and unmanned offboard systems. The very smallest of the *Streetfighter*-type designs dropped off the table, as did the idea of using a mothership; developers focused on ships capable of self-deploying.

This conceptual work was supplemented by some naval architectural design and experimentation. NWDC experimented with a borrowed Australian fast catamaran in

---

[10] Wayne P. Hughes, Jr., "22 Questions for *Streetfighter*," *Proceedings*, February 2000.
[11] The Global 2000 wargame also included two other small ship designs: a modular, fast transport and a small aviation ship.
[12] Work, 62.

2000,[13] and later partnered with ONR, Navy Special Warfare Command, the Army, and the Marine Corps to lease such a ship in 2001. The ship, dubbed the High Speed Vessel (HSV), was used in part to experiment with small ship concepts. Though it was not a combatant, it was fast, shallow draft, and spacious, and thus could act as a stand-in for a *Streetfighter*-type vessel as well as demonstrate the value of having a fast connector for a future sea base. In addition, the Office of Naval Research developed a Littoral Support Craft-Experimental (LSC-X). Its keel was laid in 2003 and it was delivered in 2005. The ship, an aluminum catamaran that displaces 950 tons, is designed to accommodate modular payloads, can travel at speeds of up to 50 knots, and can deploy 2 helicopters. The program was designed to demonstrate the benefits of having a small craft for littoral operations. The Navy took delivery of the LSC-X (renamed FSF-1 *Sea Fighter*) in 2005.

While the design characteristics of a specific *Streetfighter* ship remained relatively indistinct, this did not prevent criticism of its attributes. With trade-offs necessary between speed, payload, and endurance, some questioned the premium *Streetfighter* placed on speed. Was a top speed of 50+ knots worth the reduced payload and endurance? If so, what analysis supported that conclusion? Others questioned whether current technology permitted the high payload fractions that Cebrowski suggested were possible.

## Accepting a Small Ship

While NWDC and others continued to develop the *Streetfighter* concept, the Navy began to pay serious attention to the idea of developing a new small ship. Though by no means all in the Navy welcomed a new small combatant, there was broad agreement that assuring access to the littorals was important, that the Navy was not well prepared to deal with some important littoral threats (like submarines, mines, and small boats), and that the projected force structure was not adequate to meet the Navy's global demands.[14] Among other inputs, classified campaign analyses done in 1999-2001 showed that the programmed fleet lacked the capability to cope with enemy littoral activity in some projected combat scenarios.[15] This insight led the Navy staff to generate a report in early 2002 calling for small ships to provide the sorts of capabilities called for by *Streetfighter* advocates: anti-submarine warfare, mine warfare, and surface warfare against small boat threats.[16]

Two important developments in Washington steered the Navy towards developing a new class of small ship with such capabilities: in 2000 ADM Vern Clark became the CNO and in 2001 Donald Rumsfeld became the Secretary of Defense. When ADM Clark became

---

[13] Work, 63.

[14] The Navy had already restructured its science and technology (S&T) program to refocus on 12 technologies that it saw as important to the new era, littoral mine warfare and anti-submarine warfare among them.

[15] Interview with Charles Werchado and Web Ewell, OSD/PA&E, 8 November 2006.

[16] It is important to note, however, that while adherents to the idea of new investment in small ships grew in numbers within the Navy, they did not always identify their position with *Streetfighter*. The *Streetfighter* concept was popularly identified with some negative attributes— including a lack of endurance—that were not characteristics of all *Streetfighter*-type designs. Work, 67-68.

the CNO in July 2000, he ordered his staff to study the advantages and disadvantages of the *Streetfighter* concept.[17] This represented the first significant assessment of the merits of a new class of small ships by the surface Navy community. This interest in new ship types was coupled with a close examination of ships already programmed. Soon after Clark became CNO, Secretary of Defense Donald Rumsfeld made transforming the military an important priority. The 2001 Quadrennial Defense Review (QDR) entailed a review of every defense program. The DD-21 was foremost among the Navy programs whose transformation credentials were questioned. The DD-21 incorporated a broad array of advanced technologies, but it was large and expensive. Moreover, the main source of its firepower—the big guns on its deck—was reminiscent of the battleships that had only recently been retired from the fleet.

On November 1, 2001, one month after the QDR report was officially released, small combatants in the Navy made an important breakthrough. The DD-21 was to be replaced by a family of ships: the DD(X) (today called DDG-1000), the CG(X), and a small combatant, the LCS. A confluence of factors led to this action. The DD-21 was targeted by OSD for elimination due in part to its high cost and in part to a judgment that it was not sufficiently transformational to cope with the emerging security environment. Separately, the Navy, with CNO Clark's strong advocacy, wanted to add a small ship. A new class of small ship would meet identified capabilities gaps and enable the Navy to meet its numerical force structure goals. As mentioned earlier in the context of the 1997 GAO report, it was widely recognized that the Navy could not afford a 375-ship composed of existing platform designs. The comparatively low-cost LCS was the only way to reach the desired end strength; it could be bought in large numbers and could perform the sorts of low-intensity peacetime missions that were taxing the existing fleet.[18]

## The LCS Program

The LCS program quickly gathered steam. Analysis from OSD, a task force at the Naval War College, and the LCS Program Office (established in February 2002) contributed to developing the ship's basic attributes. Key points of debate included whether the ship should embark a helicopter, whether it needed to reach speeds of 50 knots, and whether it needed to be capable of self-deploying across the Pacific. A ship that had no helicopter and had no need of self-deploying could be quite small and reach speeds of over 50 knots. This description most closely matches early *Streetfighter* designs, although some *Streetfighter*-type proposals had included a helicopter and left questions of endurance to future designers. A self-deploying, helicopter-carrying ship would have to be larger and slower.

Analysis in N-81 and in OSD's Office of Program Analysis and Evaluation (PA&E) strongly supported a self-deploying ship that, primarily for ASW and MIW purposes,

---

[17] Work, 64.

[18] The Navy was later criticized for not doing enough analysis on the need for a new class of ship for littoral operations. The Navy reexamined this question in 2004 and found that in fact the LCS, rather than new operating concepts for existing platforms, was best suited for the required littoral missions.

embarked a helicopter.[19] This was later echoed by a study team at the Naval War College. The Navy's Surface Warfare (Requirements) Directorate (N76) tasked the Naval War College to study what the LCS should be able to do and what technologies it should incorporate. An LCS Task Force used a series of workshops to analyze these questions. The Task Force identified three primary missions and three secondary missions for LCS.[20] The primary missions matched the capability gaps identified by earlier Navy analysis:

1. Anti-submarine warfare
2. Mine warfare
3. Surface warfare (SUW) against small boats

The secondary missions were:

1. Maritime interdiction
2. Special operations forces (SOF) insertion and support
3. Tasks related to command, control, communications, computer, intelligence, surveillance, and reconnaissance (C4ISR)

The Task Force also recommended that the LCS mission be accomplished by three separate types of ships: a ship to speed into the littoral, deploy off-board (largely autonomous) sensors and weapons, and depart; a small combatant designed primarily to fight other small ships; and a larger, corvette-type ship that would have some of the capabilities of each of the other two. If only one type of LCS could be built, however, the Task Force recommended that it be the corvette. Through modularity, organic combat power, and use of unmanned systems, this corvette could cover the range of missions identified.

The Task Force also concluded that the LCS should carry a helicopter, particularly to enable ASW and MIW. The helicopter would also have to be organic, with a hanger to shelter it and diminish the ship's radar signature. This increased the required size of the ship.

The LCS Program Office and Naval Sea Systems Command (NAVSEA) also did their own analysis, dubbed "Analysis of Multiple Concepts" (AMC).[21] They considered five

---

[19] Interview with Charles Werchado and Web Ewell, OSD/PA&E, November 8, 2006.

[20] CDR Carl Carlson, Bradd C. Hayes, Hank Kamradt with Gregg Hoffman. "Littoral Combat Ship (LCS) Characteristics Task Force Final Report," July 31, 2002.

[21] This AMC was done in place of the Analysis of Alternatives (AoA) typically required of weapons procurement programs. Though OSD determined that the analysis done for the LCS was adequate, the program was faulted for not rigorously considering non-ship alternatives to the LCS missions and for completing the AMC well after the Navy released the initial request for proposals to industry. This approach created the sense that LCS analysis (or at least the formal AMC) was being done after the answer had been determined.

basic LCS alternatives, which were examined by the Naval Surface Warfare Center at Dahlgren from 2002 to 2004.[22] The five alternatives were:

- a small combatant with high speed but low endurance;
- a Coast Guard cutter;
- a larger combatant analogous to a frigate;
- a slightly smaller, self-deploying, modular advanced combatant; and
- a multi-purpose lift ship.

The AMC determined that the best alternative was the advanced combatant. In concurrence with OSD and NWDC analysis, the AMC concluded that this combatant would have some inherent self-defense capability but get the majority of its combat power from modules; embark a helicopter; have trans-oceanic endurance; and have an optimal speed of between 40 and 50 knots.

The LCS faced few programmatic hurdles. CNO Clark was a strong advocate of the ship, both within the Navy and with Congress, terming it his "number one budget priority."[23] His vision statement for the Navy, *Sea Power 21*, featured discussion of the littoral threat and of the LCS's role in defeating it.[24] In August 2002, less than a month after the NWC Task Force produced its final report, the Navy issued an initial request for proposals to industry to present LCS concepts. Six contracts were awarded for this concept work in November 2002. These proposals were downselected to three companies in July 2003 when Lockheed Martin, General Dynamics, and Raytheon were given contracts to develop detailed designs for the first LCS Flight. The Navy made the decision to initially procure more than one sea frame design and experiment with them before downselecting to a single prime contractor. In May 2004, both Lockheed and GD were awarded LCS contracts. They are building the LCS in shipyards (GD at Austal USA in Alabama; Lockheed at Marinette Marine in Wisconsin and Bollinger Shipyards in Texas and Louisiana) that have not recently built major Navy warships.

The Navy plans to procure 55 LCSs in flights. Flight 0 is being developed now, using ready or low-risk technology. The Navy decided in 2006 to extend Flight 0 from 4 ships to at least 15 ships, and also retain both Lockheed and GD as prime contractors through the 15th ship, which is due in FY2009.[25] Flight 1 is in development.

The LCS's three major missions will be those identified by the NWC Task Force: ASW, MIW, and SUW. LCS will also have the ability to perform what the requirements

---

[22] *Analysis of Multiple Concepts – Littoral Combat Ship Study Phase III Report*, Naval Surface Warfare Center, Theater Warfare Systems Department, January 30, 2004.

[23] Scott C. Truver, "The Navy Plans to Develop the LCS with 'Lightening Speed," *Sea Power*, May 2003. Available online at <http://www.navyleague.org/sea_power/may_03_15.php>.

[24] Vern Clark, "Sea Power 21: Projecting Decisive Joint Capabilities," *Proceedings*, October 2002. Available online at <http://www.chinfo.navy.mil/navpalib/cno/proceedings.html>.

[25] Congress, however, has voiced concerns about the added cost of procuring two dissimilar designs. See Senate Report 109-254 – National Defense Authorization Act for Fiscal Year 2007. Available online at <http://thomas.loc.gov/cgi-bin/cpquery/?&dbname=cp109&sid=cp109njDpq&refer=&r_n= sr254.109&item=&sel=TOC_253717&>.

document terms "inherent missions": joint logistics, SOF insertion and support, and ISR. It will further have the flexibility to carry out maritime interdiction operations (MIO). A forward deployed LCS will operate independently in limited scenarios (such as MIO or SOF support), with a squadron of other forward deployed LCSs to maintain a presence in important theaters in advance of hostilities, and with a carrier or expeditionary strike group in high threat environments. The ships will have a crew of around 75 personnel: 40 core crew and 35 to man the mission modules and helicopters.

The capabilities for accomplishing the three major missions will be largely modular. Lockheed and GD are building the LCS sea frames, which will be capable of a top speed of roughly 45 knots, displace roughly 3000 tons (one third the displacement of an *Arleigh Burke* class destroyer), have a range of around 3,500 miles (giving them trans-Pacific capability), and have a payload capacity of between 180 and 210 tons. The sea frames will use this payload capacity to accommodate a modular mission package, which will be built separately from the sea frame and installed on the ship in accordance with operational needs. There will be three types of mission packages for the Flight 0 LCSs, one each for ASW, MIW, and SUW. They will be swappable in 1–4 days. These mission modules make substantial use of both manned and unmanned off-board systems. The Navy plans to procure around 90 total modules, which Northrop Grumman was given a contract to integrate. Both GD's and Lockheed's designs can accommodate two MH-60 helicopters, which provide critical capability for MIW and ASW.

Though the LCS has progressed quickly from plans to ship (the first vessel, from Lockheed, should be complete in February 2007, less than six years after the program was first announced), issues remain to be resolved. The program is more expensive than anticipated. The Navy initially planned to spend $220M on each sea frame. The cost is now estimated to be $270M. The mission modules will cost an average of $150M per ship. Total system acquisition costs could come to more than $470M per ship.[26] Critics also point to possible operational shortcomings. The LCS will not, for instance, have substantial self-defense capability against other warships or aircraft, limiting its ability to operate alone in high-threat areas. Its small crew will have difficulty performing manpower-intensive MIO, and it will be difficult to accommodate the large number of men needed to support a helicopter detachment. Its reliance on slower offboard systems to perform its major missions will limit the utility of its high speed in some scenarios, like escort duty. Even if all works as planned, the Navy still faces the task of learning to operate a new class of ship, one whose small size, modularity, and minimal manning bring new challenges along with new capabilities.

---

[26] Ronald O'Rourke, "Navy Littoral Combat Ship (LCS): Background and Issues for Congress," Congressional Research Service, April 19, 2006.

# Instructor's Guide to LCS Case Study

*Question 1: How would the LCS be different if different decisions had been made on these five key points?*

*Helicopter.* Making the LCS capable of supporting helicopters was an important driver of several ship characteristics. First and foremost, it made the ship bigger. A flight deck required both surface area and structural reinforcement, adding to size, weight, and cost. Further, the decision was made that a "lilypad" CONOPs (that is, the LCS would be configured to operate a helicopter only for brief stretches) was not sufficient for the LCS's mission needs: it would have to be able to embark and support a helicopter indefinitely. This meant that a hanger needed to be designed for the ship. This sheltered the helicopter from the elements and provided a lower radar signature than would a helicopter on the deck, but also took up more space.

The helicopter for the LCS also added to the ship's manning requirement. Of the 35 personnel not part of the core crew, 15 are supposed to man the embarked mission module while 20 are to support the helicopters and UAVs. That is fewer personnel than support helicopters on surface combatants today, and both the lower numbers and the concept of tasking these personnel to handle both the helicopters and the UAVs is resisted by the naval aviation community.

Without a helicopter, however, the LCS would have had to look for different options to perform its core missions, particularly ASW and MIW.

*Mothership.* One innovative idea for a new class of small ships was to make use of a mothership, from which small combatants would sortie, just as aircraft sortie from aircraft carriers. By adopting such a concept, which was proposed by Hughes and others, the Navy would have been able to build smaller, individually less expensive ships for use in the littoral. Because these ships did not have to self-deploy or sustain themselves for long periods, naval architects could have designed increased speed and payload fraction in place of the endurance needed for transoceanic deployment but *not* needed for tactical mission execution. Their low cost, low manning, and higher numbers would have made such combatants less costly to lose in combat.

The LCS was instead designed to self-deploy and, in some cases, operate independently of other ships. This meant it had to be large enough to carry the fuel and supplies necessary to transit the Pacific while still having a useful payload. Its size is one factor in its higher cost and lower planned numbers compared to the sort of hypothetical littoral ships that would operate from a mothership.

*Modularity.* The LCS derives the capability it needs to perform its major missions from modular mission packages. While modularity was a long-standing feature of the notional small ships featured in the debates preceding the LCS program, a small ship could have been built without it. Indeed, in keeping with the initial *Streetfighter* concept of a family of small ships, the fleet could have been provided with a range of littoral capabilities by making different members of that family tailored to different missions. Tailored ships would present fewer logistical challenges. Tailored ships would also have a lower up-front unit cost, with no need to invest in multifunctional interfaces and no need to buy more than one tailored combat suite per ship. Though the Navy must find a way to make the LCS's modules and the specialized crews to man them readily accessible to the theater of operations, the ship offers the promise of being able to change the fleet's capabilities mix to meet the Navy's immediate needs. In the long term, the Navy can hope that the LCS will realize cost savings compared to a tailored littoral alternative, as the ship's modularity makes it comparatively easy to upgrade existing systems or add entirely new ones, thus providing an inherent hedge against obsolescence.

*One LCS or Several?* The initial *Streetfighter* concept called for a family of small ships, and as late as the NWC LCS Task Force workshops in 2002, there were advocates for building more than one kind of littoral craft. These advocates saw littoral missions that were best performed by several *types* of craft (as distinct from the Lockheed and GD *designs*, which, while different, are built to identical mission requirements) rather than one jack-of-all-trades LCS. Alternative small ship designs included both those intended to employ land attack and anti-ship missiles, a ship to fight other small surface craft, a small aviation ship, a ship designed primarily to deploy unattended, off-board systems, and a corvette-size ship like the LCS. Though the LCS's modularity gives it the flexibility to attend to a range of missions, any of these ships would arguably be better optimized for a specific littoral mission than the LCS. A sensor-deploying ship, for instance, could contribute more battlespace awareness than the LCS. It would also be less able to perform other missions, like countering small ships. Ships designed to perform one mission well (including those with some modular capabilities but fewer inherent capabilities than the LCS) could also be more austere and could be procured for a lower unit cost than a ship designed to perform several missions. Such low-cost,[27] single-mission ships could be acquired in greater numbers and would fit more neatly with the initial *Streetfighter* concept, which called for ships that could be treated as expendable. Such ships would also likely be less capable of operating independently than the LCS, and might have less range, limiting their usefulness in some scenarios.

*Strike, Air Defense, and Anti-Ship Capability.* To keep the LCS relatively low cost, the Navy could not give it the full spectrum of capabilities of other multimission surface combatants. Most notably, the LCS does not have significant strike capability, air defense capability, or capability to counter large surface ships. In omitting robust capability in these areas, the Navy made important decisions on the cost of these capabilities versus their value. The perceived value was based on the environment in which the Navy envisioned the LCS operating, the degree to which the current fleet could provide the capabilities in question, and the concept of operations intended for the ship. Consequently, the LCS concept of operations calls for the ship to operate with the rest of the battle fleet in many scenarios, particularly in high threat environments, rather than independently.

---

[27] Note that the over-all cost to the Navy of several distinct procurement programs could be higher than the LCS alternative.

*Question 2. Is the LCS a Transformational Platform? Does it Transform the Fleet Structure?*

The LCS as a platform has least one potentially transformational attribute: its modularity. Modular mission packages give the ship an operational flexibility not found in previous surface combatants. Modularity also means new technologies can be added to the LCS faster and at lower cost than if its capabilities were fully integrated.

The LCS could also have a transformative impact on the fleet across the spectrum of naval operations. In combat and pre-hostility scenarios, the LCS plays an important role in distributing the fleet's combat power and sensors. Through the larger numbers of ships and the unmanned vehicles they employ, LCSs will make the fleet's combat power more survivable and the fleet as a whole more tactically stable, enabling it to defeat A2/AD threats with reduced risk. Greater numbers of smaller platforms will present enemies with a more complex ISR and targeting challenge. More ships spread over a greater area, each distributing sensors through the use of unmanned vehicles, will provide enhanced battlespace knowledge.

The LCS could also have a transformative effect in operations short of combat. By adding greater numbers of ships to the fleet that are capable of self-deploying and operating independently, the Navy can improve its operational efficiency. The LCS will free high-end, multimission combatants from performing such tasks as MIO (to guard sea lines of communication or support sanctions), humanitarian assistance, and non-combatant evacuations.

*Question 3. How is the LCS Similar to the Streetfighter Concept? How is it Different?*

The LCS has most of the same key attributes as the *Streetfighter* concept: it is a small, fast, networked, and modular surface combatant that will make significant use of unmanned vehicles. There are significant differences in the degree to which it possess these attributes. The LCS is larger and slower than the speed posited by some *Streetfighter* concepts. This was driven in part by a decision to prioritize self-deployment and an organic helicopter for LCS, capabilities not found in most mooted *Streetfighter*-type designs.

The one of the primary differences between LCS and *Streetfighter* is a contentious one: its expendability. The initial *Streetfighter* concept, as outlined by Cebrowski and Hughes in 1999, called for a ship that was small enough and present in large enough numbers that the Navy could readily risk them in hazardous littoral waters without fear of losing a significant amount of combat power. Many took issue both with the idea that any ship should be considered expendable and the idea that the Navy was unwilling to risk the ships it already had. Regardless, the LCS was certainly not built with the explicit aim that it be expendable. Its cost (estimated at over $450 million) and numbers (planned procurement of 55 ships) suggest that the Navy does not plan on losing large numbers of them. Further, its CONOPS call for it to operate under the protection of the rest of the fleet in most threatening situations.

# Littoral Combat Ship - Support Tender (LCS-ST)

LCDR Ethan Proper, USN, LT Richard Jones, USN, LT Colin Dunlop, USN

LT Kyriakos Avgouleas, HN

The LCS Support Tender (*LCS-ST*) conversion study provides an alternative to new ship acquisition where an inactive *Newport Class Tank Landing Ship* (specifically the LST-1190 hull) is modified to provide three primary functions for the LCS fleet; the ability to (1) conduct underway replenishment (UNREP) and resupply operations of the LCS and Riverine boats; (2) conduct repairs to mission modules without the need of homeport IMA facilities and (3) the ability to repair, retest, reload, configure, and swap mission modules without returning to a homeport. The requirements of the *LCS-ST* were derived from the NAVSEA 05D Light Logistics Link (L3) project, where a commercial off-shore vessel is converted to provide LCS tender functions and mission module support.

The *LCS-ST* conversion is accomplished through modifications to internal arrangement, topside structure, and insertion of significant crane and rigging services. The focal point of the converted design is the rearranged vehicle stowage well (VSW) which provides new functionality to hold ten operational mission modules, two module maintenance areas, and two RHIB maintenance areas. The VSW is fitted with a full access bridge crane and clam shell deck access to a 4$^{th}$ deck hold. Service galleries, mounted on the port and starboard bulkheads, provide required module services such as air, fuel, LAN, and freshwater cooling. The propulsion and electric plant are unchanged during the design. Additionally, the conversion requires minimal modifications to LST structure or watertight boundaries.

A detailed analysis indicates the study is feasible from a hydrodynamic, stability and structural standpoint. The cost analysis, based on a NAVSEA 017 cost model, estimates a total conversion cost (including reactivation) of $165M (FY2007$).

| Dimension | Value |
|---|---|
| LBP | 500 feet |
| Length Overall | 517.85 feet |
| Beam | 68.12 feet |
| Draft | 15.1 ft (Min Op) / 19.3 ft (Full load) |
| Max Section Coefficient (Cx) | 0.886 |
| Prismatic Coefficient (Cp) | 0.569 |
| Block Coefficient (Cb) | 0.504 |
| Waterplane Coefficient (Cwp) | 0.711 |
| Lightship Displacement | 6493 LT |
| Full Load Displacement | 9117 LT |

| Cost | Value |
|---|---|
| Reactivation Cost | $ 42M |
| Conversion Cost | $ 123M |
| Annual Operating Cost over 10 years | $ 497M |
| Total Life Cycle Cost (2007$) | $ 662M |

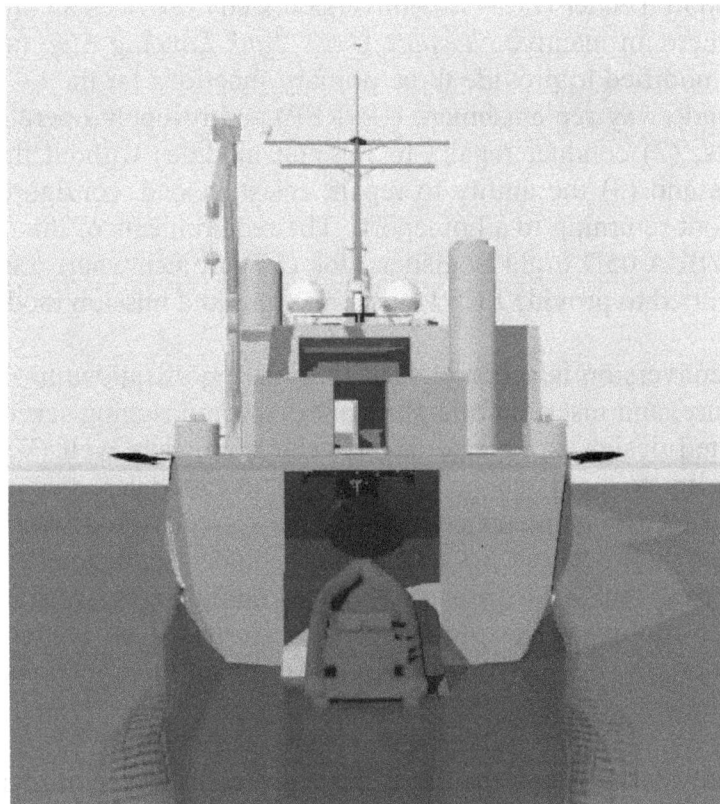

# NAVAL POSTGRADUATE SCHOOL

## MONTEREY, CALIFORNIA

# THESIS

**AN EXPLORATORY ANALYSIS OF LITTORAL COMBAT SHIPS' ABILITY TO PROTECT EXPEDITIONARY STRIKE GROUPS**

by

Motale E. Efimba

September 2003

Thesis Advisor:                Thomas Lucas
Second Reader:              Russell Gottfried

THIS PAGE INTENTIONALLY LEFT BLANK

| REPORT DOCUMENTATION PAGE | | *Form Approved OMB No. 0704-0188* |
|---|---|---|

Public reporting burden for this collection of information is estimated to average 1 hour per response, including the time for reviewing instruction, searching existing data sources, gathering and maintaining the data needed, and completing and reviewing the collection of information. Send comments regarding this burden estimate or any other aspect of this collection of information, including suggestions for reducing this burden, to Washington headquarters Services, Directorate for Information Operations and Reports, 1215 Jefferson Davis Highway, Suite 1204, Arlington, VA 22202-4302, and to the Office of Management and Budget, Paperwork Reduction Project (0704-0188) Washington DC 20503.

| 1. AGENCY USE ONLY *(Leave blank)* | 2. REPORT DATE<br>September 2003 | 3. REPORT TYPE AND DATES COVERED<br>Master's Thesis | |
|---|---|---|---|
| 4. TITLE AND SUBTITLE: An Exploratory Analysis of Littoral Combat Ships' Ability to Protect Expeditionary Strike Groups | | 5. FUNDING NUMBERS | |
| 6. AUTHOR(S) Motale E. Efimba | | | |
| 7. PERFORMING ORGANIZATION NAME(S) AND ADDRESS(ES)<br>Naval Postgraduate School<br>Monterey, CA 93943-5000 | | 8. PERFORMING ORGANIZATION REPORT NUMBER | |
| 9. SPONSORING /MONITORING AGENCY NAME(S) AND ADDRESS(ES)<br>N/A | | 10. SPONSORING/MONITORING AGENCY REPORT NUMBER | |

**11. SUPPLEMENTARY NOTES** The views expressed in this thesis are those of the author and do not reflect the official policy or position of the Department of Defense or the U.S. Government.

| 12a. DISTRIBUTION / AVAILABILITY STATEMENT<br>Approved for public release; distribution is unlimited | 12b. DISTRIBUTION CODE |
|---|---|

**13. ABSTRACT** *(maximum 200 words)*

This thesis uses an agent-based simulation model named EINSTein to perform an exploratory study on the feasibility of using Littoral Combat Ships (LCSs) to augment or replace the current defenses of Expeditionary Strike Groups (ESG). Specifically, LCS's ability to help defend an ESGs in an anti-access scenario against a high-density small boat attack is simulated. Numbers of CRUDES (CRUiser, DEStroyer, Frigate) ships are removed and LCSs are added to the ESG force structure in varying amounts to identify force mixes that minimize ship losses. In addition, this thesis explores various conceptual capabilities that might be given to LCS. For example, helicopter/Unmanned Combat Aerial Vehicles (helo/UCAVs), Stealth technology, close-in high volume firepower, and 50+ knot sprint capability. Using graphical analysis, analysis of variance, and large-sample comparison tests we find that being able to control aircraft is the most influential factor for minimizing ship losses. Stealth technology is another significant factor, and the combination of the two is highly effective in reducing ship losses. Close-in high volume firepower is effective only when interacting with helo/UCAVs or stealth. 50+ knot sprint capability is potentially detrimental in this scenario. An effective total sum of CRUDES ships and LCS is between five and seven platforms.

| 14. SUBJECT TERMS Einstein, LCS, Littoral Combat Ship, ESG, Expeditionary Strike Group, Assured Access, Agent-Based Simulation | | | 15. NUMBER OF PAGES<br>386 |
|---|---|---|---|
| | | | 16. PRICE CODE |

| 17. SECURITY CLASSIFICATION OF REPORT<br>Unclassified | 18. SECURITY CLASSIFICATION OF THIS PAGE<br>Unclassified | 19. SECURITY CLASSIFICATION OF ABSTRACT<br>Unclassified | 20. LIMITATION OF ABSTRACT<br>UL |
|---|---|---|---|

NSN 7540-01-280-5500

Standard Form 298 (Rev. 2-89)
Prescribed by ANSI Std. 239-18

THIS PAGE INTENTIONALLY LEFT BLANK

# AN EXPLORATORY ANALYSIS OF LITTORAL COMBAT SHIPS' ABILITY TO PROTECT EXPEDITIONARY STRIKE GROUPS

Motale E. Efimba
Lieutenant, United States Navy
B.S., United States Naval Academy, 1997

Submitted in partial fulfillment of the
requirements for the degree of

## MASTER OF SCIENCE IN OPERATIONS RESEARCH

from the

## NAVAL POSTGRADUATE SCHOOL
### September 2003

Author:          Motale E. Efimba


Approved by:     Thomas Lucas
                 Thesis Advisor


                 Russell Gottfried
                 Second Reader


                 James N. Eagle
                 Chairman, Department of Operations Research

THIS PAGE INTENTIONALLY LEFT BLANK

# ABSTRACT

This thesis uses an agent-based simulation model named EINSTein to perform an exploratory study on the feasibility of using Littoral Combat Ships (LCSs) to augment or replace the current defenses of Expeditionary Strike Groups (ESG). Specifically, LCS's ability to help defend an ESGs in an anti-access scenario against a high-density small boat attack is simulated. Numbers of CRUDES (CRUiser, DEStroyer, Frigate) ships are removed and LCSs are added to the ESG force structure in varying amounts to identify force mixes that minimize ship losses. In addition, this thesis explores various conceptual capabilities that might be given to LCS. For example, helicopter/Unmanned Combat Aerial Vehicles (helo/UCAVs), Stealth technology, close-in high volume firepower, and 50+ knot sprint capability. Using graphical analysis, analysis of variance, and large-sample comparison tests we find that being able to control aircraft is the most influential factor for minimizing ship losses. Stealth technology is another significant factor, and the combination of the two is highly effective in reducing ship losses. Close-in high volume firepower is effective only when interacting with helo/UCAVs or stealth. 50+ knot sprint capability is potentially detrimental in this scenario. An effective total sum of CRUDES ships and LCS is between five and seven platforms.

THIS PAGE INTENTIONALLY LEFT BLANK

# TABLE OF CONTENTS

# LIST OF FIGURES

# LIST OF TABLES

THIS PAGE INTENTIONALLY LEFT BLANK

# LIST OF KEY WORDS SYMBOLS, ACRONYMS AND ABBREVIATIONS

| | |
|---|---|
| Agent | Most primitive entity in EINSTein |
| ANOVA | ANalysis Of VAriance |
| ARG | Amphibious Readiness Group |
| | |
| Baseline | An ESG consisting of three CRUDES ships and three amphibious ships |
| | |
| Choke Point | A narrow body of water flanked by land that connects two large bodies of water |
| CIC | Combat Information Center, a radar display room |
| CIWS | Close In Weapon System |
| CNA | Center for Naval Analyses |
| CO | A unit's Commanding Officer (usually in the context of a ship's captain) |
| CRUDES | Cruiser, Destroyer and Frigate ships |
| CSG | Aircraft Carrier Strike Group |
| | |
| EDATF | Emergency Defense Air Task Force |
| EINSTein | Enhanced ISAAC (see below) Neural Simulation Toolkit |
| Enemy | Different colored (in reference to agents) |
| ESG | Expeditionary Strike Group |
| | |
| Firepower | High volume close-in firepower |
| Friendly | Like colored (in reference to agents) |
| | |
| GOO | Gulf Of Oman |
| | |
| Harpoon | BGM-84, a cruise missile to attack surface vessels |
| Helo | Helicopter(s) |
| | |
| ISAAC | Irreducible Semi-Autonomous Adaptive Combat |

| | |
|---|---|
| "Knee" | "Knee of the curve" i.e. point of optimization where additional spending adds low proportion of benefit (decreased margin of return) |
| LCAC | Landing Craft Air Cushion |
| LCS | Littoral Combat Ship |
| LCU | Utility Landing Craft |
| MOE | Measure Of Effectiveness |
| MSE | Mean Square Error |
| MSS | Mean Sum of Squares |
| NAG | Northern Arabian Gulf |
| OTH-T | Over-The-Horizon Targeting |
| RAM | Rolling Airframe Missile |
| RPG | Rocket Propelled Grenade |
| Run-Set | A group of discrete simulation runs using a uniform set of inputs |
| SAG | Surface Action Group |
| SOP | Standard Operating Procedures |
| Speed | 50-60 knot sprint capability. |
| Stealth | Stealth Technology |
| TTP | Tactics Techniques and Procedures |
| UCAV | Unmanned Combat Aerial Vehicle |

# ACKNOWLEDGMENTS

I'd like to thank my father Robert for giving be a shining example for academic excellence. Andrew Ilachinski and Greg Cox for developing EINSTein and providing a foundation for my study. Jeff Kline for introducing me to this wonderful and potentially impacting thesis topic. Vince Roske and the members of the Joint Staff's J8-Warfighting Analysis Division for funding my experience tour and introducing me to contacts. Richard Snead for continued guidance. Paul and Susan Sanchez for design techniques. Russ Gottfried for being the "darned XO." Finally, Tom Lucas for being my advisor.

THIS PAGE INTENTIONALLY LEFT BLANK

# EXECUTIVE SUMMARY

The United States' naval expeditionary forces' capabilities allow for quick reaction to hostilities, providing humanitarian aid, power projection, providing logistical support to forces ashore, as well as other operations. Oceangoing amphibious landing ships in Expeditionary Strike Groups (ESGs) transport troops, vehicles, and supplies all over the world wherever they are needed and provide military commanders greater flexibility in planning operations. However, if the amphibious ships encounter resistance while moving into position to perform operations, they need to fight their way into position for expeditionary operations.

Due to amphibious ship design for maximizing the support of various amphibious waterborne and airborne operations, they have limited combat capabilities. These ships are armed only with Close In Weapon Systems (CIWS) and small arms (25mm machineguns and smaller) for own ship's defense and have no major fire control system. However, amphibious aircraft carriers have, in addition to the above weapons, short-range NATO Sea Sparrow missiles and Rolling Airframe Missiles (RAM) for air defense. In order to counter littoral threats, where amphibious operations are performed, the Navy has transformed Amphibious Readiness Groups to ESGs by assigning dedicated combatant ships: cruisers, destroyers, and frigates (CRUDES), to protect the three amphibious ships. The CRUDES ships have tremendous firepower provided by extensive fire control systems, a wide array of anti-surface and anti-air missiles, and main gun(s). However, they require large crews and are expensive to build, and operate. Insufficient numbers of CRUDES ships in an ESG is a potential liability against high-density small boat attacks or coordinated surface action. This study investigates such a scenario.

Looking to the future, areas in which we may perform amphibious operations do not tend to have large navies with large combatant ships—like destroyers or greater. Many costal nations defend their coasts at affordable cost with patrol boats and possibly missile corvettes, meeting a "green water" (littoral) navy requirement. Corvettes, coastal patrol boats, and smaller vessels equipped with small arms and possibly four Exocet or Styx missiles are considerably less expensive than CRUDES ships and require a fraction of the crew. Also, the attack by a small, suicidal boat laden with explosives, rendering USS COLE out of action for nineteen months, showed that small boat attacks are a viable threat against the U.S. Navy. One question this study explores is: **"How can the U. S. Navy effectively counter the high-density small boat threat?"**

Recently, the Navy has announced that it is creating a new type of ship, the Littoral Combat Ship (LCS), to augment carrier strike groups' (CSG) and ESGs' protection in coastal environments. These ships will be approximately the size of a corvette, possibly with options such as: the capability to control a helicopter or Unmanned Combat Aerial Vehicle (UCAV), an organic helicopter or UCAV, the latest stealth technology, the ability to shoot surface-to-surface missiles for high volume close-in firepower, and 50-plus knot sprint capability. Although they are oceangoing, they are envisioned to fight in the littoral area, where our ESGs operate, with greater flexibility, greater numbers, and at a lower cost than CRUDES ships. Other questions this study explores are: **"Is the LCS a better option than the U.S. Navy's current arsenal to defend ESGs? What capabilities enhance LCS's performance?"**

This thesis uses an agent-based simulation model named EINSTein (Enhanced ISAAC (Irreducible Semi-Autonomous Adaptive Combat) Neural Simulation Toolkit), developed by the Center for Naval Analyses (CNA), to explore these questions. EINSTein allows for investigation on how various LCS candidates might perform in a range of scenarios. In war, each unit has a Commanding Officer (CO) who has an overall mission and specific tasks pertaining to the unit or sub-group of units. However, each CO is different, with a different personality and perspective, and a characteristic way of fighting in the war. This is a major reason why EINSTein was chosen for this study; agent-based models allow for these personality differences. Two other reasons why EINSTein was chosen for this study are agent-based models are fast and tend to be stochastic, allowing for an analyst to explore many scenarios, capabilities and assumptions in a relatively short amount of time. Since agent-based models are stochastic, no two discrete runs are the same. Moreover, we get a distribution of possible outcomes from any given input combination, simulating chance and Clausewitz's "fog of war."

This thesis explores varying ESG ship force structures and LCS capabilities in an anti-access scenario where the ESG is traveling through a choke point to reach its amphibious operations area. Employing the same threat, a high-density small boat attack, observations are taken on ship survivability by platform type. Alternatives compared include the current CRUDES supported ESG, with and without organic armed aircraft, and LCS replacement of CRUDES platforms. Additionally, this study reviews different LCS design factors and their interaction, to determine which are most effective. Effectiveness is measured by the number of platforms lost by the force.

By analyzing the data with Analysis of Variance (ANOVA) and large-sample comparison tests, aircraft are found to be the most influential factor in minimizing ship losses, with or without LCS. Furthermore, this particular finding is consistent with the U.S. Navy's decision to design the initial block of LCS with the capability to employ and support an organic helicopter. For LCS, stealth technology is another significant factor, and the combination of stealth and air capability are effective in reducing ship losses. However, designing a hangar on a ship could reduce a ship's stealthiness. Therefore, if stealth and aircraft are considered for LCS design, planners may opt for LCS to possess aircraft control capability while a larger ship (amphibious aircraft carrier or CRUDES ship) provides aircraft with logistical support.

Close-in high volume firepower on board LCS is effective only when interacting with helo/UCAVs or stealth. This capability is a good choice if aircraft or stealth (not both) can be combined with another capability. However, all three capabilities employed can effectively eliminate ship losses. A 50-plus-knot sprint capability is potentially detrimental in this scenario when LCS platforms depart from the mutual force defense. When LCS operates within the strike group, defending against attackers, enhanced speed is no factor due to stationing requirements of remaining in a smaller area and staying with slower ships. An effective total sum of CRUDES ships and LCS is between five and seven platforms. It is recommended that at least one of these platforms be a CRUDES ship for air defense capability, added command and control, and fire support for amphibious operations.

EINSTein is an abstraction of fleet tactical warfare. The thesis spends a fair amount of discussion time to draw the connection between agent activity and shipboard operations. Nevertheless, its depiction of the effects of design considerations rings plausible for this scenario. A properly designed experimental study accounted for individual factors and interactions. It yielded results that enable analytical approaches, warfare designs and alternatives to be compared. This research provides a quantitative basis for further, higher resolution studies that should consider the measurable benefits of air capability and stealth and the relative ineffectiveness of tactical speed for this new littoral combatant ship.

# I. INTRODUCTION AND PROBLEM

## A. INTRODUCTION

### 1. Amphibious Operations

The United States' naval expeditionary forces' capabilities allow for quick reaction to hostilities, providing humanitarian aid, power projection, providing logistical support to forces ashore, as well as other operations. Oceangoing amphibious landing ships in Expeditionary Strike Groups (ESGs) transport troops, vehicles, and supplies all over the world wherever they are needed and provide military commanders greater flexibility in planning operations. However, if the amphibious ships encounter resistance while moving into position to perform operations, they need to fight their way into position for expeditionary operations.

According to the Joint Doctrine for Amphibious Operations, amphibious operations "can be generally broken down into five major types: assaults, withdrawals, demonstrations, raids and other amphibious operations."[1] Amphibious assaults involve moving landing forces from ships to a hostile or potentially hostile shore. An amphibious withdrawal is the extraction of friendly forces from a hostile or potentially hostile shore to a ship. Amphibious demonstrations are shows of force "to deceive with the expectation of deluding the enemy to a course of action unfavorable to it."[2] On the other hand, amphibious raids are swift incursions to or temporary occupations of an objective, followed by a planned withdrawal. Other amphibious operations consist of noncombatant evacuation operations, foreign humanitarian assistance and logistic support of forces ashore.[3]

Amphibious ships have been designed to support these missions. They have built-in stern wells that are wide enough to allow Landing Craft Air Cushion (LCAC) and utility landing craft (LCU) to enter and transport Marines, Marine equipment, other passengers or amphibious operation equipment. Also, all amphibious ships have flight

---

[1] S. A. Fry, *Joint Publication 3-02: Joint Doctrine for Amphibious Operations* (Washington, DC: Joint Staff, 2001), I-2.

[2] Ibid., I-2.

[3] Ibid., I-3.

decks to support air amphibious operations. Amphibious ships are armed only with Close In Weapon Systems (CIWS) and small arms (25mm machineguns and smaller) for self-defense and have no major fire control system. The exceptions are amphibious aircraft carriers which have, in addition to the above weapons, short-range NATO Sea Sparrow missiles and Rolling Airframe Missiles (RAM) for air self-defense.[4]

## 2. Amphibious Asset Protection, from ARGs to ESGs

Amphibious ships are not designed for fighting hostile naval forces, especially highly maneuverable patrol craft.[5] Increasing this mission capability would decrease available shipboard space for supplies and Marine forces, the focus of the ships' mission. The design of amphibious ships left Amphibious Readiness Groups (ARGs) (composed of three amphibious ships) vulnerable to attacks by littoral countries, in particular, surface navy and land-based air action. ARGs' primary organic offensive weapons against surface navy action were small arms. The amphibious aircraft carriers have short range NATO Sea Sparrow and RAM for own ship's defense if attackers use surface-to-surface missiles. The Emergency Defense of the Amphibious Task Force (EDATF) is another available defensive entity in an ARG. The EDATF is made up of Marine AV-8 Harrier jump jets, AH-1 Cobra helicopters and UH-1 Iroquois helicopters, which can swiftly defeat enemy forces in the air or on the water.[6] However, the drawback of the EDATF is that all the aircraft need to be in the air or quickly have safe wind direction and speed for launching from the carriers. Also, employing the EDATF takes away air assets, fuel, and ammunition originally apportioned to the Marine Air-Ground Task Force (MAGTF) for ground operations. ARGs required better offensive capabilities and layered defense against surface threats.

---

[4] Norman Polmar, *The Naval Institute Guide to the Ships and Aircraft of the U.S. Fleet* (Annapolis, MD: Naval Institute Press, 1993) 160-181.

[5] Norman Polmar, *The Naval Institute Guide to the Ships and Aircraft of the U.S. Fleet* (Annapolis, MD: Naval Institute Press, 1993) 160-181.

[6] John Jamison, "Marines and Sailors Recreate History with Emergency Defense Bent on Protecting the Amphibious Task Force, " *Marines Online*, March 1997. Available from the World Wide Web @ http://www.hqmc.usmc.mil/marines.nsf/0/5a6b7811d5841c9f8525645d00750a32?OpenDocument. Accessed 30 August 2003.

In order to counter littoral threats, the Navy has transformed ARGs to Expeditionary Strike Groups (ESGs) by assigning dedicated combatant ships: cruisers, destroyers, and frigates (CRUDES), to protect the amphibious ships.[7] These ships have tremendous firepower provided by extensive fire control systems, a wide array of anti-surface and anti-air missiles, and main gun(s) with barrel sizes of 76mm or greater. However, they require large crews and are expensive to build and operate. For example, AEGIS Destroyers have a crew of 325 sailors and cost approximately $930 million per ship ($CY93).[8] Crew requirements and costs of the CRUDES ships restrict their numbers in the fleet, and so only three are assigned to ESGs. An insufficient number of CRUDES ships in an ESG is a potential liability against high-density small boat attacks or coordinated surface action.[9] This study investigates such a scenario.

### 3. Sea Base Protection

Once forces are ashore, the vessels providing the sea base for such ground forces remain on station to support operations at the objective. The sea base, composed of the amphibious ships from the ESG and potentially maritime preposition supply ships, is vulnerable to surface threats. The maritime preposition supply ships are logistical ships that, with no weapons listed, have less defensive fighting power than any of the ships in an ESG.[10] The sea base relies on the protection of the CRUDES ships assigned to the participating ESG and the sea base is set up well after the Navy establishes sea control for the particular littoral area. However, high-density small boat attacks remain a hazard for the duration of an operation.

## B. PROBLEM

### 1. Probable Threat

Looking to the future, areas in which we may perform amphibious operations do not tend to have large navies with large combatant ships—like destroyers or greater.

---

[7] Deep Blue, *Expeditionary Strike Force Concept: Far ... From the Sea the Power of Teamwork.* (Sherman Oaks, CA: Aretè Associates, 2003) 2-6.

[8] Norman Polmar, *The Naval Institute Guide to the Ships and Aircraft of the U.S. Fleet* (Annapolis, MD: Naval Institute Press, 1993) 105, 125, 136, 147.

[9] Jessica Davis, "New Expeditionary Strike group to Enhance Navy-Marine Corps Team," *Navy Newsstand*, December 2002. Available from the World Wide Web @ http://www.news.navy.mil/search/display.asp?story_id=9403. Accessed 25 July 2003.

[10] Norman Polmar, *The Naval Institute Guide to the Ships and Aircraft of the U.S. Fleet* (Annapolis, MD: Naval Institute Press, 1993) 289-292.

Many costal nations will have patrol boats and possibly missile corvettes because of costs and the need for only a "green water" (littoral) navy. These nations defend their coasts well at an affordable cost. Corvettes, coastal patrol boats and smaller vessels equipped with small arms and possibly four Exocet or Styx missiles are considerably less expensive than CRUDES ships and require a fraction of the crew.[11] [12] Consequently, these countries can field a more abundant fleet of smaller ships for the price of one or two CRUDES ships. The attack by a small, suicidal boat laden with explosives, on USS COLE showed that small boat attacks are a viable threat against the US Navy. The attack rendered USS COLE out of action for nineteen months.[13] One question this study intends to explore is: **"How can the U. S. Navy effectively counter the high-density small boat threat?"**

## 2. LCS Option

Recently, the Navy has announced that it is creating a new type of ship, the Littoral Combat Ship (LCS), to augment carrier strike groups' (CSG) and ESGs' protection in coastal environments.[14] These ships will be approximately the size of a corvette, possibly with options such as: the capability to control a helicopter or Unmanned Combat Aerial Vehicle (UCAV), an organic helicopter or UCAV, the latest stealth technology, the ability to shoot surface-to-surface missiles for high volume close-in firepower, and 50-plus knot sprint capability.[15] Although they are oceangoing, they are envisioned to fight in the littoral area, where our ESGs operate, with greater flexibility and numbers than other combatant CRUDES ships. In addition, the LCS is

---

[11] Norman Polmar, *The Naval Institute Guide to the Ships and Aircraft of the U.S. Fleet* (Annapolis, MD: Naval Institute Press, 1993) 103-145, 206.

[12] John Pike, "Pohang (PCC Patrol Combat Corvette)," *Global Security.org*, July 2002. Available on the World Wide Web @ http://www.globalsecurity.org/military/world/rok/pohang.htm. Accessed 16 September 2003.

[13] David Icenhour, "Keys to the County Presented Aboard USS COLE," *Alexander County News Release*, July 2002. Available from the World Wide Web @ http://www.co.alexander.nc.us/news/2002%20News%20Releases/Key%20to%20the%20County%20USS%20Cole.htm. Accessed 25 July 2003.

[14] Sandra I Erwin, "Littoral Combat Ship Moving Closer to Reality," *National Defense Magazine*, April 2003. Available from the World Wide Web @ http://www.nationaldefensemagazine.org/article.cfm?Id=1079. Accessed 20 August 2003.

[15] Naval Warfare Development Command. *Littoral Combat Ship Concept of Operations Development SITREP* (Newport, RI: Naval Warfare Development Command, November 2002).

envisioned to have a lower cost and a smaller crew per ship than current escort ships.[16] [17] However, the addition of a new combat system may not necessarily yield the desired results or efficiencies. Other questions this study intends to explore are: **"Is the LCS a better option than the U.S. Navy's current arsenal to defend ESGs? What capabilities enhance LCS's performance?"** These questions are answered in the Data and Analysis chapter.

## C.    WHY AGENT BASED SIMULATION?

There are no easy answers to the questions posed above. In particular, there are tremendous uncertainties about what situation, where and whom ESGs might have to fight when LCSs are proposed to deploy in the fleet. Furthermore, we do not know what equipment and accompanying tactics potential threats might use. Simulation is a way to explore such questions. Running simulations allows for investigation on how various LCS candidates might perform in a range of scenarios.

Agent-based models are types of simulations that have recently been used to help explore questions like those above. Agent-based simulations create entities that perform various actions. Each agent simulates a unit (a soldier, aircraft, tank, ship, armored vehicle, artillery, etc.) that acts (move, sense, shoot, communicate, etc.) autonomously or cooperatively. The overriding missions for each unit in the simulation are to fight, survive, make sure the agent's teammates survive and destroy the enemy. Real war is similar. In war, each unit has a Commanding Officer (CO) that has an overall mission and specific tasks pertaining to the unit or sub-group of units. However, each CO is different, with a different personality and perspective, and a characteristic way of fighting in the war. This is a major reason why an agent-based model was chosen for this study; agent-based models allow for these personality differences.

Two other reasons why an agent-based model was chosen for this study are agent-based models are fast and tend to be stochastic. A discrete run in an agent-based model will usually take no longer than a minute. This speed allows an analyst to explore many

---

[16] U.S. Navy, *Department of Defense Information Paper: Background Assumptions on 30 Year Shipbuilding Plan*, September 2003.

[17] Sandra I Erwin, "Littoral Combat Ship Moving Closer to Reality," *National Defense Magazine*, April 2003. Available from the World Wide Web @ http://www.nationaldefensemagazine.org/article.cfm?Id=1079. Accessed 20 August 2003.

scenarios, capabilities and assumptions in a relatively short amount of time. Since agent-based models are stochastic, no two discrete runs are the same. Moreover, we get a distribution of possible outcomes from any given input combination. The variability simulates chance and Clausewitz's "fog of war." For these reasons this thesis utilizes the agent based simulation, EINSTein, developed by the Center for Naval Analyses (CNA).

# II. MODEL AND SIMULATION

## A. INTRODUCTION

This chapter explains the EINSTein model, discusses the testing scenario, and goes over the assumptions and factors used in this study. The EINSTein section talks about the model, its strengths and its limitations. The anti-access scenario and baseline personalities and capabilities are explained in the scenario section. The assumptions and factors section discusses key assumptions made in this study and starts to describe the factors that are explored.

## B. EINSTEIN

### 1. Model

Enhanced ISAAC (Irreducible Semi-Autonomous Adaptive Combat) Neural Simulation Toolkit (EINSTein) will be used to gain insights to answer the questions of and possible trade offs between force composition and options. Andrew Ilachinski created EINSTein to be an artificial-life laboratory (Agent-based simulation) for exploring self-organized emergence in land combat.[18] Greg Cox of the Center for Naval Analysis modified it for use in naval warfare, which will be discussed later in this chapter.

EINSTein is a model that is a stochastic time-step simulation. Time-step simulations break time into equal periodic increments. For example, if an agent moves three squares per time-step, then an agent will move to a new square three squares away from its current position at the next time-step. This is similar to what a knight can do in chess. The knight, and agent, never is located in any of the squares between its current position and future position but moves (like teleportation) from the current position to the future position. Unlike chess, all the agents in EINSTein may move simultaneously at

---

[18] Andrew Ilachinski, *ISSAC/EINSTein: An Artificial-Life Approach to Land Combat* (Alexandria, VA: Center For Naval Analyses, February 2003). Available from the World Wide Web @ http://www.cna.org/isaac/. Accessed 28 February 2003.

every time step.  EINSTein uses ISAAC agents that can represent individual combat units from troops, to aircraft, to capital ships.[19]  ISAAC agents contain four main characteristics:

Doctrine: a default local-rule set specifying how to act in a generic environment

Mission: goals directed behavior

Situation Awareness: sensors generating an internal map of the environment

Adaptability: an internal mechanism to alter behavior and/or rules[20]

These characteristics are appropriate for naval warfare.  The doctrine characteristic is in keeping with the U.S. Navy's doctrinal approach of every ship having a set of standard operating procedures (SOP) and battle orders, which give ship COs (Commanding Officers) and their crews guidance on what actions to take for various situations.  Naval Strike Group Commander's intentions, which contain the battle group goals, are simulated in this model by the mission characteristic.  The situational awareness characteristic is appropriate in simulating the bridge and Combat Information Center (CIC, tactical display room) working in concert using radars, chart position fixes, visual observations and tactical data link information to maintain the battle space picture for the ship.  EINSTein's adaptability characteristic models a CO and the crew's ability to take calculated risks is combat, given the battle space picture.

The EINSTein battlefield is a two dimensional area where no two agents occupy the same position.  The agents, only red or blue, are initially positioned in either a formation that the user specifies or at random.  Both sides (red and blue) have a single "flag" that symbolizes a tactical objective to gain or defend.  Agents exist in one of three states: alive (undamaged), injured (damaged), or killed (dead).  A set of distinctive personalities and abilities can be defined for squad members existing in each state.  Each agent has a set of operating characteristics (sensor range, firing range, communications

---

19 Andrew Ilachinski, *ISSAC/EINSTein: An Artificial-Life Approach to Land Combat* (Alexandria, VA: Center For Naval Analyses, February 2003). Available from the World Wide Web @ http://www.cna.org/isaac/. Accessed 28 February 2003.

20 Andrew Ilachinski, *Towards a Science of Experimental Complexity: An Artificial-Life Approach to Modeling Warfare* (Alexandria, VA: Center For Naval Analyses, February 2000). Available from the World Wide Web @ http://www.cna.org/isaac/. Accessed 28 February 2003.

range, and communications weight, i.e. level of information) within which it senses and assimilates simple forms of local information, and a personality, which determines the general manner in which the agent responds to its environment.[21]

The agents are grouped into squads. Each side (red and blue) can have up to ten squads. Agents in a particular squad have the same set of personalities, abilities and operating characteristics. This is similar to COs of ships in the same class using the same doctrine when operating in a battle group. Also, ships in a class will have virtually the same operating and fighting capabilities. In a fleet there is little difference in the tactics, techniques and procedures (TTP) from one cruiser to another cruiser. On the other hand, there is a major difference between the SOPs of a cruiser and an Amphibious ship because of the different radar systems, weapon systems, maneuverability and size, to mention just a few reasons.

### a.    *Personality and Movement*

The personalities of agents are defined by a six-component (personality weight) vector, $\mathbf{w} = [w_1, w_2, \ldots, w_6]$. The weights can be any real number. A positive personality weight represents an attraction. On the other hand, negative weights represent repulsion. Weights of zero represent indifference. The six components that an agent has the propensity to be attracted to move toward or a desire to move away from are:

$w_1$ = desire to move to or from alive friendly agents (like-colored agents)

$w_2$ = desire to move to or from alive enemy agents (different colored agents)

$w_3$ = desire to move to or from injured friendly agents

$w_4$ = desire to move to or from injured enemy agents

$w_5$ = desire to move to or from friendly flag

$w_6$ = desire to move to or from enemy flag

---

[21] Andrew Ilachinski, *ISSAC/EINSTein: An Artificial-Life Approach to Land Combat* (Alexandria, VA: Center For Naval Analyses, February 2003). Available from the World Wide Web @ http://www.cna.org/isaac/. Accessed 28 February 2003.

EINSTein takes each weight ($w_i$) and divides it by the total personality weight (the sum of the absolute value of the individual weights=$\Sigma_i |w_i|$) to calculate the percentage of the total personality weight that $w_i$ merits. EINSTein uses this percentage against other weights' percentages, along with what the agent senses, to generate movement that maximizes the agent's utility during a particular time-step. If there are multiple most enticing moves for an agent at a particular time-step, the agent will randomly choose one of them. See Ilachinski, ISSAC/EINSTein: An Artificial-Life Approach to Land Combat, http://www.cna.org/isaac/ for the details on how the value of potential moves are calculated.

The CRUDES ships' (agents') alive personality vector in the anti-access scenario is 10, 40, 0, 40, 0, 10, for weights $w_1$ through $w_6$, respectively. If a CRUDES ship had an alive friendly ship to starboard and an alive enemy ship to port, it will desire to move toward the alive enemy ship. However, if a CRUDES ship is flanked in the same way by an alive enemy ship and an injured enemy ship, the agent will randomly choose between the two options. This choice simulates a CO's judgment. Some CO's might think that the injured enemy ship is less of a threat, therefore approaching and engaging the alive enemy ship would be the best decision. Other COs would think that the injured enemy ship is an easier threat to eliminate and would reduce the combined enemy fighting capability. So, approaching the injured enemy ship would be the better of the two decisions. EINSTein's advancements allow for agents moving in a formation, as well.

An agent's personality may also be augmented by a set of meta-rules that take into account its environmental conditions. The class-1 meta-rule prevents an agent from moving toward an enemy flag unless it is surrounded locally by a minimum number of friendly agents. The class-2 meta-rule prevents an agent from moving toward friendly agents once a threshold number of friendly agents surround the agent. Other rules deal with engaging in combat, retreat, pursuit, support, and holding position. These personalities and meta-rules serve as battle orders from a strike group commander to subordinate unit commanders. In the test runs of the anti-access scenario, the amphibious ships often maneuvered into combat with the CRUDES ships rather than following behind the CRUDES ships. To improve fidelity, amphibious ships have a cluster meta-

10

rule set established so they have a greater desire to cluster than approach the enemy flag. The clustering meta-rule is set so that the amphibious ships desire to cluster with at least four friendly ships. Considering that there are only three amphibious ships in an Expeditionary Strike Group (ESG), the amphibious ships follow CRUDES ships and LCSs to the objective, following the meta-rule to cluster with a minimum of four friendly ships.

### b. *Combat*

EINSTein's combat uses an agent's maximum number of targets to engage to determine how many targets to randomly choose for targeting that are within the agent's firing range. Then, EINSTein uses uniform random variables against an agent's single shot probability of hitting to determine if the agent hits the targeted agents. If an agent is hit its state is degraded. The degradation progresses from alive to injured, then injured to dead. Once an agent degrades to the injured state, it uses the set of injured personality traits and ability traits defined for its squad's injured state. If an agent is degraded to the state of dead, the agent ceases to exist. Fratricide is a possibility that can be enabled in EINSTein's combat simulation, adding to the realism. Harpoon (BGM-84) is a great example of a weapon used by the U.S. Navy that has fratricide as a possible result. Although navy crews are trained to employ Harpoon to minimize fratricide, Harpoon's seeker looks for and locks onto the first ship it can see while it is in terminal phase. It does not differentiate between friendly, enemy or neutral shipping. There are other weapons that navies employ that do not differentiate between targets. Human error and the "fog of war" coupled with these weapons bring about the possibility of fratricide.

### c. *EINSTein for Naval Combat*

A snapshot of EINSTein being used for naval combat analysis is shown below in Figure 1. The picture is taken from Dr. Greg Cox's, from the Center for Naval Analyses, simulation "Gamelet," held at the Naval Postgraduate School. In this scenario, blue enemy ships are poised to defend the Northern Arabian Gulf (NAG) from red U.S. ships in a CSG starting in the Gulf Of Oman (GOO) trying to reach their objective in the NAG. The four blue dots in Iran are shore missile batteries. The single red dot to the left of the "10" is an AWACS plane providing enemy position information to the red ships in the CSG.[22]

# Act 1, Scene 1: The baseline

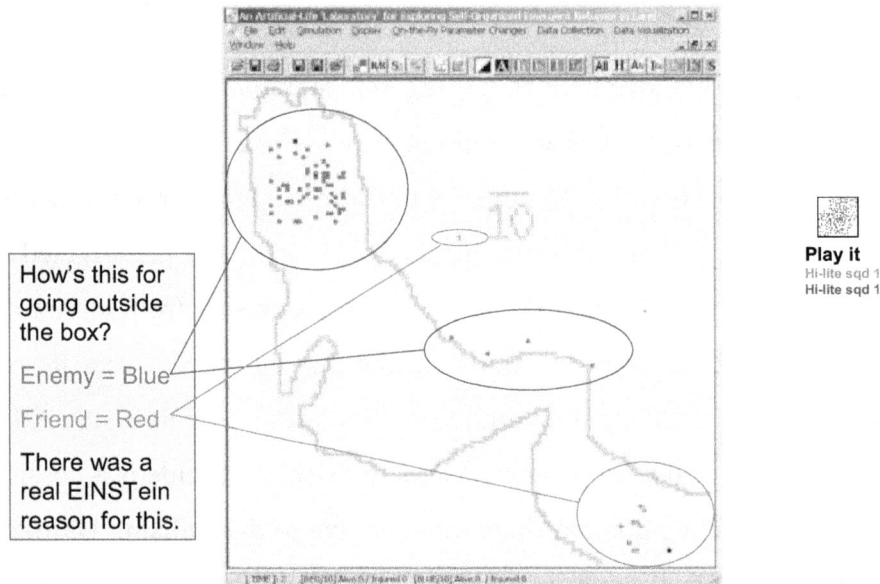

Figure 1    Example of EINSTein Window

To modify EINSTein for naval combat, Dr. Cox removed all the terrain aspects unless he wanted to create impassable land surrounding the water. He modeled capabilities and personalities to (abstractly) emulate real platforms. He used these platforms in a naval scenario where he and students explored the utility of LCS and possible LCS capabilities for augmenting CSG defense. The study of the "Gamelet" exposed insights on influential LCS factors and influential tactics that would be beneficial to defending a CSG from an enemy Surface Action Group (SAG).

Dr. Cox's "Gamelet" serves as a blueprint for this thesis. The battlefield, enemy small boats, and CRUDES ships were borrowed from the "Gamelet," with slight modifications. The baseline LCS, firepower factor, stealth factor and speed factor are

---

[22] Greg E. Cox, *EINSTein Visits the Persian Gulf (via Monterey, California): A Naval Requirements War 'Gamelet' Held at the Naval Postgraduate School 11-15 FEBRUARY 2002*, (Alexandria, VA: Center for Naval Analyses, March 2002).

also borrowed from Dr. Cox's "Gamelet." This study took note of the strengths and weaknesses of using EINSTein to explore naval combat, and decided that EINSTein's strengths greatly outweigh its weaknesses for exploratory purposes.

## 2. Strengths

EINSTein has proven to be a way to gain insights on combat and combat performance. Over the past two winter quarters at the Naval Postgraduate School, Dr. Cox has involved students in Joint Campaign Analysis in his exploratory study of LCS. He and students used EINSTein to simulate LCS's participation in protecting a CSG in an anti-access scenario.[23] The study demonstrated that agent-based models could effectively simulate naval warfare. The study encompassed in this thesis utilizes some of the techniques learned from Dr. Cox's study.

In terms of their personalities, agents act like COs in charge of their ships. All the COs know the operational objective, but each has slightly different methods for accomplishing the mission. Specific benefits include that the model is stochastic. A set of inputs will produce different outputs for each discrete simulation run, thus providing a range of outcomes. EINSTein, like many agent based models, is a quick model in which many runs can be performed in a short time (approximately ten seconds to perform one 500 step run). This enables us to look at many scenarios and variables in a reasonable amount of time. Finally, additional naval studies were performed with EINSTein in the Naval Postgraduate School's Joint Campaign Analysis class.

Picking up where previous naval studies left off and making adjustments for this scenario was not difficult. EINSTein's allowance for fratricide adds to the model's ability to simulate combat. Weapon systems like harpoon missiles and small arms are fire-and-forget weapons that do not differentiate between friend and foe. Once those missiles reach a designated area they begin searching and then attack the first contact they acquire. Small arms fire travels in a fairly straight line, so rounds hit whatever is in their path. The fog of war and motion of the ocean limits a small arms operator's ability to properly aim at opposing

---

[23] Greg E. Cox, *EINSTein Visits the Persian Gulf (via Monterey, California): A Naval Requirements War 'Gamelet' Held at the Naval Postgraduate School 11-15 FEBRUARY 2002*, (Alexandria, VA: Center for Naval Analyses, March 2002).

forces and adds to the possibility to fratricide. Fratricide is set in the model to a range of ten squares from a platform's position with a one percent probability of hitting friendly forces.

### 3.    Limitations and Required Abstractions

In general, EINSTein is a low-resolution model that is best at gleaning broad insights as opposed to detailed predictions. For this study, EINSTein's notable limitations are its treatment of speed, time, ship performance capabilities, and aircraft. There are only five levels for speed (0, 1-4). The scale is fixed so EINSTein has relative size and speed limitations. For this study one level of speed will equate to 25 knots. An agent that simulates most ships will have a speed of 1, i.e. simulating 25 knots. Agents that simulate the fastest ships, those that can achieve approximately 50 knots, will have a speed of 2. Helicopters and UCAVs will have a speed of 4 to represent their ability to fly approximately 100 knots.[24][25] Speed and ranges are relative to how one considers a time-step. This study uses one square on the EINSTein battlefield to equal one nautical mile (NM). Considering that it takes a CRUDES ship 25 time-steps to move 25 squares, 25 time-steps will be considered an hour in the model.

Although the time step aspect makes simulating real life easier, the simulation loses some of the fluidity of real life. Certain events, like an agent entering a sensor arc of another agent, could be missed if the event would have occurred in the period between time-steps. A ship or aircraft's performance in the model depends on its abilities and personality, so inputs must be adjusted and tested to ensure proper reactions. Sometimes a personality vector does not take full advantage of the platform's abilities. This study will use one set of personality vectors to a level that seemed reasonable for all capabilities. Using one set of personality vectors was done as a control mechanism in order to focus on the ship configurations and capabilities.

---

[24] Dennis Sorensen, *Naval Unmanned Aerial Vehicles*, (Patuxent River, MD: Navy Unmanned Aerial Vehicles- PMA263, September 2003). Available on the World Wide Web @ http://uav.navair.navy.mil/vtuav/default.htm. Accessed 5 September 2003.

[25] Norman Polmar, *The Naval Institute Guide to the Ships and Aircraft of the U.S. Fleet* (Annapolis, MD: Naval Institute Press, 1993) 441.

For the aircraft, there is more than one way to simulate a helicopter or UCAV in EINSTein. One approach is to create a squad of aircraft agents. The other is to increase the weapon range and sensor range of the ship that in real life would be controlling the aircraft. Both methods do not properly emulate an aircraft's need to return to its base ship to replenish expended munitions. The first method's aircraft never return to the ship to reload and the second sets both the ships' and aircrafts' weapons at the same capability in range and probability of hit. In method one, a squad of aircraft in the model will become fairly autonomous, sometimes allowing aircraft to fly outside of the safe aircraft flying distance from its controlling ship. The second method doesn't take into account that the aircraft can be shot down, losing their benefits, and that the opposing forces have to target aircraft and ships separately. This is the most significant shortcoming in the model due to limited control of aircraft agents and a degree of abstraction. This study uses method 1 to simulate aircraft, taking advantage of their contribution, but capturing their vulnerability to enemy fire.

Another drawback of EINSTein is that there is no way to add neutral shipping. The only agents that exist in this model are opposing red and blue agents. Neutral shipping complicates combat situations by adding more ships that need to be examined for neutrality or hostility and adding ships to avoid from shooting. Platforms on both sides have perfect battlespace knowledge of contact position, battle damage assessment on each contact, and IFF (Identification Friend or Foe, whether the platform a friend or a foe) inside of their sensor range,

## C. SCENARIO

This study required plausible scenarios to properly examine the capabilities of LCS. The scenarios have to examine operations in littoral areas and properly flex the probable threats. This study focuses on surface threats. Considering how much damage a small boat with explosives inflicted to USS COLE (DDG 67) and the likelihood that most countries near potential ESG operating areas will only have small boats, this study uses the high-density small boat attack as the primary threat to the ESG. Another reason the high-density small boat attack was used in this study was because some of these small

15

boats, like Boghammer Patrol Boats, carry RPG (Rocket Propelled Grenades) and cruise missiles. Like the Exocet that took USS STARK (FFG 31) out of action, cruise missiles can deliver crippling damage to larger combat ships.

The enemy force consists of one squad of thirty high-speed small boat agents. Their personalities and capabilities are the exact same as the high-speed small boat agents used in Dr Greg Cox's previous studies. The enemy high-speed boats are envisioned to be a midpoint boat between the common motorboat with a machine gun and a Fast Patrol Boat (FPB 354).[26] The model's enemy high-speed boats' key capabilities are shown below in Table 1.

| | Movement per time step | | Staying Power | | Sensor/Fire range | | S S Phit (no. engage) | |
|---|---|---|---|---|---|---|---|---|
| Squad | Alv | Inj | Alv | Inj | Alv | Inj | Alv | Inj |
| HS Boats | 2 | 1 | 1 | 1 | 15/8 | 8/4 | 0.05 (1) | 0.025 (1) |

Table 1    Red Force High-Speed Boat Capabilities

### 1.    Red Force

#### a.    *Enemy High-Speed Small Boat Capabilities*

When undamaged, a high-speed boat's movement in this model is up to two squares per time step (approximately fifty knots). After receiving one direct hit, the high-speed boats transition from the undamaged to the damaged state. Undamaged high-speed boat's sensors can detect up to fifteen NM, simulating low quality surface search radar and low quality CIC (tactical display room) with limited manning. The high-speed boat can shoot up to eight NM from its position. The shooting range models small arms and the occasional possibility of using an RPG or an Exocet missile. Also, the high-speed boats can engage one target per time-step with a five percent probability of hitting the target, which simulates the ability to only bring one weapon system to bear because of small crew size and the inaccuracy of using a human as the fire control system. The probability of hit may seem low for modern weapon systems. However, in EINSTein, each ship will fire weapons at all targets within its sensor and weapon ranges each time-

---

[26] Peene- Werft GmbH, *Naval Shipbuilding: Fast Patrol Boat FPB 354*, (Stralsund, Germany: Peene-Werft GmbH, September 2003). Available on the World Wide Web @ http://www.peene-werft.de/en/schiffe/d_fpb354.html#top. Accessed 16 September 2003.

step. The low values account for the probability that the target is actually engaged and hit—which includes the probabilities that the target is identified, tracked, attacked and hit.

When damaged, the high-speed small boat agents' movement is slowed to one square per time step, simulating degraded propulsion performance (approximately twenty-five knots). A damaged high-speed boat's transition to a dead state occurs after receiving one direct hit. Damaged high-speed boat's sensors can detect up to eight NM, simulating that the surface search radar is destroyed and the boat is using visual sensors. To simulate only having small arms and RPGs as weapons and injured operators the high-speed small boat agents can shoot up to four NM from the agent's position, and can engage one target per time-step with a two and a half percent probability of hitting.

**b.**      ***Red Force Enemy High-Speed Small Boat Personalities***

The enemy high-speed small boat personalities are shown below in Table 2. An undamaged high-speed small boat most desires to approach undamaged (alive) and damaged (injured) enemy (blue in this case) forces equally and desires to approach the enemy objective (enemy flag) half as much. The desire to approach the enemy objective helps to initiate an engagement between blue and red forces. These personalities fit in with an aggressive attack style expected from a high-density small boat attack. The boats seek out the enemy and then aggressively stay with the enemy until the enemy is destroyed. This personality also takes advantage of the high-density small boat attack's numbers. The aggressiveness drives more small boats to flood the enemy combatant's radar picture, making it harder for enemy combatants to target individual small boats—like a shark with a school of fish. A damaged high-speed small boat also seeks to engage undamaged and damaged enemy ships equally. These injured personalities are set as such because high-speed small boats will likely be already near blue forces when they are damaged. Red force boats focus only on destroying blue ships.

| Squad | When Alive | | | | | | When Injured | | | | | |
| --- | --- | --- | --- | --- | --- | --- | --- | --- | --- | --- | --- | --- |
| | To alv friend | To alive enemy | To inj friend | To inj enemy | To friend flag | To enemy flag | To alv friend | To alive enemy | To inj friend | To inj enemy | To friend flag | To enemy flag |
| HS Boats | | 40 | | 40 | | 20 | | 50 | | 50 | | |

Table 2      Red Force High-Speed Boat Personalities

17

## 2.    Blue Force Capabilities

The scenario this study examines is an ESG in an anti-access setting. ESG agents' capabilities are listed below in Table 3. When undamaged, all the ESG agents move one square per time-step, simulating their ability to transit at approximately twenty-five knots. Taking into account the large size of amphibious ships and their defensive weapons, in this model, these platforms can take two direct hits before transitioning from the undamaged state to the damaged state. CRUDES ships tend to have a more capable defensive weapons suite so they have the capacity to take three direct hits before becoming damaged in this model. Note: this does not mean CRUDES ships can absorb three hits without damage, rather it is used to account for the CRUDES ship's defensive weapons—i.e., many incoming missiles will be successfully countered by hard kill and soft kill measures.

| Squad | Movement per time step | | Staying Power | | Sensor/Fire range | | S S Phit (no. engage) | |
|---|---|---|---|---|---|---|---|---|
| | Alv | Inj | Alv | Inj | Alv | Inj | Alv | Inj |
| Amphibs | 1 | 1 | 2 | 2 | 20/10 | 10/7 | 0.10 (2) | 0.05 (1) |
| CRUDES | 1 | 1 | 3 | 2 | 30/20 | 20/15 | 0.15 (2) | 0.075 (1) |
| LCS | 1 | 1 | 1 | 1 | 20/10 | 10/7 | 0.10 (1) | 0.05 (1) |

Table 3    Baseline Blue ESG Force Capabilities

The baseline LCS is envisioned to have similar defensive capabilities as the enemy high-speed boats so it can only take one direct hit before transitioning from the undamaged state to the damaged state.[27] In the model, amphibious ships and LCSs can detect contacts twenty NM away emulating higher quality surface search radars, tactical data links, and a CIC manned with a trained crew. CRUDES ships detect platforms within thirty NM of their position due to their ability to use quality radars (like the SPY-1 and Combined Antenna System), use tactical data links, and having their CIC manned with a highly trained crew.

---

[27] Sandra I Erwin, "Littoral Combat Ship Moving Closer to Reality," *National Defense Magazine*, April 2003. Available from the World Wide Web @ http://www.nationaldefensemagazine.org/article.cfm?Id=1079. Accessed 20 August 2003.

To simulate an amphibious ship and LCS being armed with small arms, as well as systems like CIWS and NATO Sea Sparrow (in surface mode), in the model amphibious ships and LCSs can shoot up to a distance of ten NM from their position. CRUDES ships, with their better weapon systems, like SM-2 (in surface mode) or Harpoon missiles, can shoot up to twenty NM from their position. Amphibious ships can engage two targets (thanks to greater manning) with a ten percent probability of hit (decent fire control). On the other hand, LCSs can only shoot one target (lower manning) with the same ten percent probability of hit. CRUDES ships, with their better combat and fire control suites, can shoot two targets with a fifteen percent probability of hitting them.

Upon being damaged there is no change to the ship's speed. Damaged amphibious and CRUDES ships can take two more direct hits before destruction, simulating their ability to take substantial amounts of damage before being sunk or completely knocked out of combat. Damaged LCSs, like the enemy high-speed boats, can only take one direct hit before being destroyed. In the model, amphibious ships and LCSs simulate having decreased radar ranges and a degraded tactical data link by limiting their detection range to ten NM from their position. CRUDES ships do the same by limiting their sensor detection range to twenty NM when damaged. Amphibious ships and LCSs have a firing range of seven NM to simulate the loss of some primary weapons with a better ability for fire control than the high-speed boats. CRUDES ships are expected to have one of their primary surface weapons when damaged, so their firing range is fifteen NM. All damaged ships can only engage one target. Amphibious ships and LCSs shoot with a five percent probability of hitting while CRUDES ships shoot and hit with a probability of seven-and-a-half percent. This lower probability simulates degraded fire control capability. ESG unit personalities will be discussed in the following section. Alternative LCS capabilities will be discussed in the next chapter.

### 3.    Anti-Access Situation and Blue Force Personalities

The anti-access scenario simulates an ESG transiting through a choke point. A choke point is a narrow body flanked by land that connects two large bodies of water. There is little room for ships to maneuver in a choke point. The Straits of Gibraltar, the Formosa Straits and waterways in between the North Sea and the Baltic Sea are examples. ESGs will have to pass through one to reach some littoral areas so its ships can perform amphibious operations. A group of ships transiting a choke point usually can only pass in a line or at the most two abreast. The exit of a choke point is an excellent place to deploy forces to resist transiting ships. Resisting forces can virtually cross the "T" by positioning their forces at the exit so that many of the resisting ships can shoot their weapons while the transiting force will only have a portion of their ships that can shoot weapons without risk of fratricide.

This thesis analyzes an ESG transiting from its starting point in the GOO to its destination up in the NAG in an anti-access scenario. The ESG attempts to pass through the Straits of Hormuz while fending off a high-density small boat attack. The ESG (blue) agents' personalities are shown below in Table 4. The individual weights add up to one hundred ($\Sigma_i\ |w_i|=100$) to ease recognition of the percentage of the total personality weight devoted to a component of the personality vector. When undamaged, amphibious ships in the model desire to move toward friendly undamaged friendly platforms with forty percent of the total personality weight, damaged (injured) friendly platforms with forty percent of the total personality weight, and the objective (enemy flag) with twenty percent of the total personality weight. The undamaged personality vector emulates amphibious ship COs' desire to say with the protection of other ships while also desiring to approach the objective to perform amphibious operations. Damaged amphibious ships desire to be near undamaged platforms for safety is shown by increasing that weight to forty five percent of the total weight and lowering the desire to approach the objective to fifteen percent of the total weight. However, the meta-rule for the amphibious ship, explained in Chapter II, section A-1-a, paragraph 3, makes the amphibious ships most desire to cluster with at least four platforms.

| Anti-Access Personalities | | | | | | | | | | | | |
|---|---|---|---|---|---|---|---|---|---|---|---|
| Squad | When Alive | | | | | | When Injured | | | | | |
| | To alv friend | To alv enemy | To inj friend | To inj enemy | To friend flag | To enemy flag | To alv friend | To alv enemy | To inj friend | To inj enemy | To friend flag | To enemy flag |
| Amphibs | 40 | | 40 | | | 20 | 45 | | 40 | | | 15 |
| CRUDES | 10 | 40 | | 40 | | 10 | 20 | 20 | 20 | 30 | | 10 |
| LCS | 10 | 25 | 10 | 40 | | 15 | 20 | 15 | 20 | 30 | | 15 |
| Helo/UCAV | 10 | 25 | 10 | 40 | | 15 | 30 | 10 | 20 | 30 | | 10 |

Table 4    Blue ESG Force Anti-Access Personalities

Undamaged CRUDES ships' desire to engage enemy ships undamaged and damaged cover forty percent of the total personality weight each. Their tendencies to move toward fellow alive ships and approach the objective encompass ten percent each. This study uses an aggressive CRUDES CO personality to better protect the amphibious ships. Their mission is to seek out and eliminate the threat so that the amphibious ships can perform their mission out of harms way. The undamaged CRUDES ships try to engage enemy ships before the amphibious ships are inside the enemy ships weapons range. When damaged, CRUDES ships become less aggressive and try to take advantage of numbers while still trying to engage the enemy. Now, thirty percent of their personality weight is devoted to trying to finish off damaged enemies.

CRUDES COs' desires to join with undamaged friendly forces, to join with injured friendly forces, and to engage undamaged enemy ships, are twenty percent each, balancing desires to protect the ESG and join with friendly forces for added protection. CRUDES ships also have a meta-rule enabled to not proceed to the objective in the NAG unless they are near three other friendly platforms. This meta-rule was enabled so that the CRUDES ships would not leave the amphibious ships behind on their way to the objective. The meta-rule was not enabled on the LCSs because it would be futile when the LCSs have the speed factor enabled and can move twice the speed of the amphibious ships that try to follow. This has implications for the simulated LCS activity, as discussed in Chapter IV. Amphibious ships make it to the objective in most runs when they and another platform survive.

LCS COs, when commanding an undamaged ship, also have an aggressive personality. They desire finishing off damaged enemies most, with forty percent of the total personality weight given to this task. Next is their desire to engage undamaged enemy ships, covering twenty five percent of the weight. The strike group commander's intent that LCSs scout ahead is forced on LCSs by giving their COs' desire to approach the objective fifteen percent of the total weight. Finally, the LCS COs desire to join with friendly forces, undamaged and damaged, with ten percent of the total weight each. Undamaged helo/UCAVs (helicopter/Unmanned Combat Aerial Vehicles) are given the same personality vector as an undamaged LCS.

Damaged LCSs have less aggressive COs. Their COs most desire to finish off damaged enemy ships, but this comprises only thirty percent of the total personality weight. The COs desire to join the protection of friendly forces, damaged and undamaged, with twenty percent apiece. They desire to approach the objective and undamaged enemy ships with fifteen percent of the total weight each. Damaged helo/UCAVs also aggressively desire to engage damaged enemy ships with thirty percent of their total personality weight, however they desire to seek the protection of undamaged friendly forces with the same percentage of the total weight. The balance between aggressive and conservative allows for the possibility of an aggressive pilot protecting the ESG at all costs or a conservative pilot attempting to maximize the number of friendly forces engaging enemy forces. Like damaged CRUDES ship COs and damaged LCS COs, damaged helo/UCAV pilots desire to join damaged friendly forces with twenty percent of the weight, and desire to both approach the objective and engage undamaged enemy ships with fifteen percent.

The battlefield is shown in Figure 2. The initial blue center of gravity, referred to in EINSTein as the blue flag, is positioned in the GOO and the red flag is positioned in the NAG. Blue platforms and red platforms are randomly positioned near their respective flag for each run. Initially, personalities drive the ESG forces (blue) toward the NAG and the enemy high-speed small boats (red) toward the GOO. They meet at the northbound exit of the Strait of Hormuz and engage in a fight-to-the-finish. At the end of the run cycle (500 time steps), data is collected and the battlefield is randomly reset for the next run until a run set is completed. The line above the "10" to the left of the red forces shows the length of 10 NM (squares) in the model.

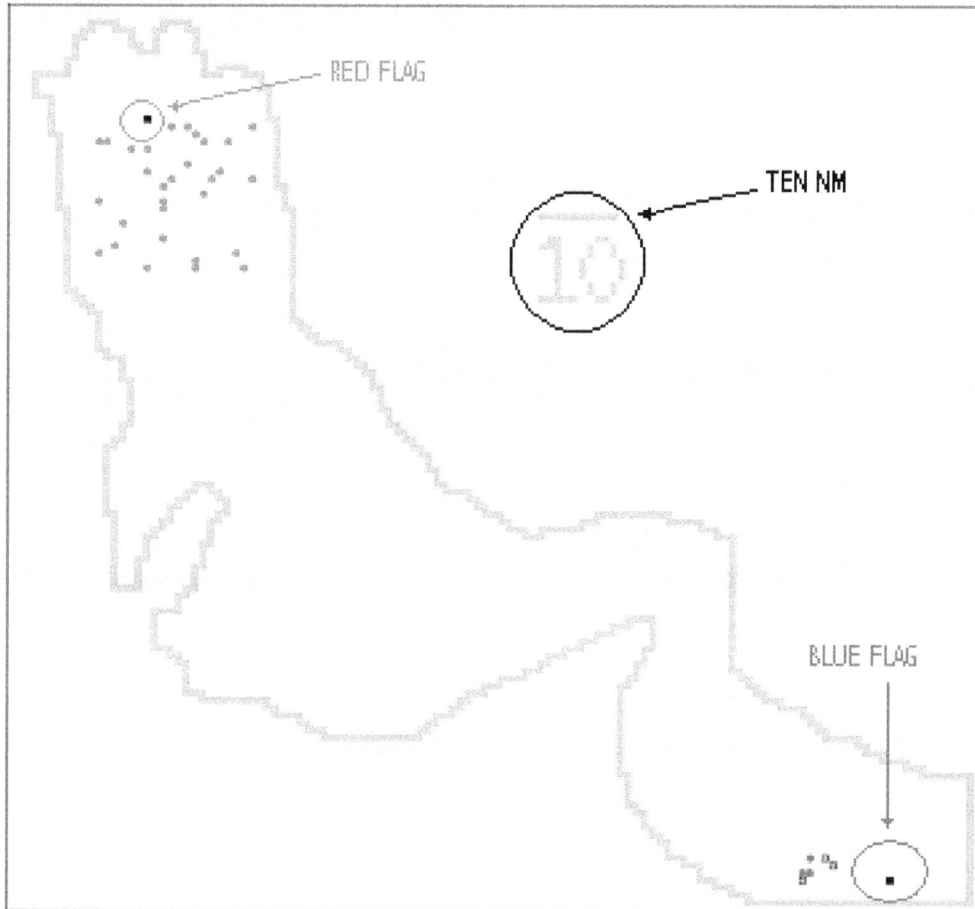

Figure 2    Anti-Access Battlefield

## D.    ASSUMPTIONS AND FACTORS

### 1.    Assumptions

As with all models, there are by-products of the simulation and assumptions made with this study. Some by-products, like how many EINSTein time-steps represent an hour of real time, have been mentioned above. That there is no change in personality, even though a ship might have different capabilities, isolates the effects of changing the capabilities even though the personality vectors do not optimize specific capabilities. This experiment assumes that the LCS will be armed with weapons limited to line of sight ranges. LCS is not expected to be armed with Over-The-Horizon Targeting (OTH-T) weapons like the PEGASUS class PHM.[28] [29]  OTH-T weapons require larger ships

---

[28] Sandra I Erwin, "Littoral Combat Ship Moving Closer to Reality," *National Defense Magazine*, April 2003. Available from the World Wide Web @ http://www.nationaldefensemagazine.org/article.cfm?Id=1079. Accessed 20 August 2003.

[29] Norman Polmar, *The Naval Institute Guide to the Ships and Aircraft of the U.S. Fleet* (Annapolis, MD: Naval Institute Press, 1993) 197.

and will raise the cost of LCS for the weapon system, and also the requirement of capabilities to effectively use the weapons. Another assumption made in this thesis is that sea-based UCAV capabilities will be available shortly after the LCS enters the fleet.[30]

This study assumes that the LCS will have some sort of tactical data link. The tactical data link might not allow LCS to target and shoot beyond the horizon, but it allows the LCS to know the battlespace situation for quick and appropriate response. Although some newer tactical data links allow ships to cooperatively engage the enemy with other ships' fire control data as their own, most of the ships in the fleet do not have tactical data links with that capability. CRUDES are modeled in EINSTein to operate the same. Of course, DDGs, FFGs and CGs differ from each other. Each class of ships has specific weapon systems (and numbers of weapon systems), radar systems, fire control systems, and operating speeds. In fact, even CGs within the same class differ from each other. TICONDEROGA class CGs built before USS BUNKER HILL (CG 52) are equipped with the MK 26 guided missile launcher system, while BUNKER HILL and later TICONDEROGA class CGs have the MK 41 vertical launch system increasing missile capacity and missile launching speed.[31] For our purposes, we assume that these ships are qualitatively similar with respect to the capabilities of LCS, amphibious ships and enemy high-speed boats.

### 2. Factors

Along with the baseline LCS, the Navy is looking at four options to improve LCS combat performance. Those options are helo/UCAVs, stealth technology, high volume close-in firepower, and 50+ knot sprint capability. This study will model these capability factors in the anti-access scenario and explore possible interactions between the factors. Also, this study will examine these factors' effects in a diverse set of ESG ship combinations.

---

[30] Cynthia Curiel, "Northrop Grumman Given Approval to Design, Build X-47B Navy UCAV Demonstrators; Award Strengthens UAV Partnership with Defense Department," *Northrop Grumman Press Release*, May 2003. Available from the World Wide Web @ http://www.capitol.northgrum.com/contracts/ngcontr050103b.html. Accessed 27 August 2003.

[31] Norman Polmar, *The Naval Institute Guide to the Ships and Aircraft of the U.S. Fleet* (Annapolis, MD: Naval Institute Press, 1993) 105-6, 125-6, 143.

# III. EXPERIMENTAL DESIGN

## A. INTRODUCTION

This chapter covers the Littoral Combat Ship (LCS) design factors, the experimental design, and data farming. The LCS design factors section discusses the four options (potential LCS capabilities) explored in this study and how they are modeled in EINSTein. The experimental design section explains the mathematical process used to ensure all combinations of the factors are simulated, as well as all of the possible Expeditionary Strike Group (ESG) ship configurations incorporating LCS. Data farming techniques and some Measures of Effectiveness (MOEs) are discussed in the data farming section.

## B. FACTORS

To obtain insights about what features may improve LCS's performance, this study explores four Littoral Combat Ship design factors: helicopters/Unmanned Combat Aerial Vehicles (helo/UCAVs), stealth technology (stealth), high volume close-in firepower (firepower), and 50+ knot sprint capability (speed). The baseline LCS (for reference), modified LCS, and Helicopter/UCAV capabilities, as modeled in EINSTein, are listed below in Table 5. The changes to the LCS capabilities are in bold.

| | Movement per time step | | Staying Power | | Sensor/Fire range | | S S Phit (no. engage) | |
|---|---|---|---|---|---|---|---|---|
| LCS | 1 | 1 | 1 | 1 | 20/10 | 10/7 | 0.10 (1) | 0.05 (1) |
| LCS stealth | 1 | 1 | **3** | **2** | 20/10 | 10/7 | 0.10 (1) | 0.05 (1) |
| LCS firepower | 1 | 1 | 1 | 1 | **20/7** | **10/5** | **0.20 (4)** | **0.10 (2)** |
| LCS speed | **2** | 1 | 1 | 1 | 20/10 | 10/7 | 0.10 (1) | 0.05 (1) |
| Helo/UCAV | 4 | 2 | 3 | 1 | 30/10 | 10/7 | 0.10 (1) | 0.05 (1) |

Table 5     LCS, Modified LCS, and Helo/UCAV Capabilities

### 1. Helicopters and Unmanned Combat Aerial Vehicles

This study considers helicopters and UCAVs to be the same type of entity in the model, similar to our grouping of CGs, DDGs, and FFGs as CRUDES ships. Helos and

UCAVs fly at approximately the same speed and carry similar weapons, such as hellfire missiles.[32] [33] Helos and UCAVs do differ in flight characteristics and operation; however, these differences are relatively small (like the differences between CRUDES ships), justifying the abstraction of placing helos and UCAVs in the same category.

As explained above in Chapter II, section A-3, paragraph 3, Helo/UCAVs exist as a squad of agents in this model. They emulate the variability of a pilots' decision-making process and the possibility that a helo/UCAV can be shot down. When the helo/UCAV factor is enabled for a run-set, all controlling ships (CRUDES and LCS) have helo/UCAVs. The number of helo/UCAVs for that run-set equals the sum of CRUDES ships and LCSs. This does disregard scenarios in which CRUDES ships have helos and LCSs do not, but these situations can be considered as times when the CRUDES ships' helos are in a no-fly status.

When undamaged, helo/UCAVs fly up to four squares per time-step (approximately 100 knots).[34] [35] When damaged, their speed drops to up to two squares per time-step (approximately fifty knots) to simulate degraded engines, hydraulics problems, or an injured pilot. Because the helo/UCAVs are fighting high-speed small boats with negligible anti-air capability, undamaged helo/UCAVs can absorb three direct hits before becoming damaged. The high-speed small boats are limited to visual air searches and would only have small arms weapons and RPGs (Rocket Propelled Grenades) available to shoot down aircraft. Damaged helo/UCAVs' lack of maneuverability and smoke make them easier to target, thus only one direct hit is required to destroy a damaged helo/UCAV.[36] Thanks to their altitude and radar systems,

---

[32] Public Affairs Office, *U.S. Air Force Fact Sheet: RQ-1 Predator Unmanned Aerial Vehicle* (Langley AFB, VA: Air Combat Command, May 2002). Available on the World Wide Web @ http://www.af.mil/news/factsheets/RQ_1_Predator_Unmanned_Aerial.html. Accessed 29 July 2003.

[33] Norman Polmar, *The Naval Institute Guide to the Ships and Aircraft of the U.S. Fleet* (Annapolis, MD: Naval Institute Press, 1993) 441.

[34] Dennis Sorensen, *Naval Unmanned Aerial Vehicles*, (Patuxent River, MD: Navy Unmanned Aerial Vehicles- PMA263, September 2003). Available on the World Wide Web @ http://uav.navair.navy.mil/vtuav/default.htm. Accessed 5 September 2003.

[35] Norman Polmar, *The Naval Institute Guide to the Ships and Aircraft of the U.S. Fleet* (Annapolis, MD: Naval Institute Press, 1993) 441.

[36] Peene- Werft GmbH, *Naval Shipbuilding: Fast Patrol Boat FPB 354*, (Stralsund, Germany: Peene-Werft GmbH, September 2003). Available on the World Wide Web @ http://www.peene-werft.de/en/schiffe/d_fpb354.html#top. Accessed 16 September 2003.

undamaged helo/UCAVs have a sensor range of thirty NM (squares). However, damaged helo/UCAVs are reduced to using the crew's vision or degraded sensors at altitude, which limits their sensor range to ten NM. Undamaged helo/UCAVs have access to weapons, such as Penguin missiles, Hellfire missiles, and small arms, allowing them to shoot one target at up to ten NM away with a ten percent probability of hit. Damaged helo/UCAVs have damaged fire control systems and an injured crew, so they can shoot one target seven NM away with only a five percent probability of hitting.

### 2. Stealth Technology

Stealth technology makes LCS more difficult to target. From this difficulty, stealth also makes LCS harder to hit, damage and destroy. To account for stealth in EINSTein, a stealthy LCS has better staying power than a baseline LCS. The staying power of an undamaged stealthy LCS is set at three hits, compared to one hit for an undamaged baseline LCS, before it becomes damaged. A damaged, stealthy LCS's staying power improves to two hits before it is destroyed. Damaged baseline LCSs are destroyed after only receiving one hit. The change to staying power was made because it directly affects LCS's survivability. EINSTein does not allow for changing a platform's probability to hit a specific platform. Altering the probability of hit for the enemy high-speed boats would affect their ability to also hit CRUDES and amphibious ships, which is not the intention of the LCS stealth improvement. LCS's staying power was adjusted because it isolates the enemy high-speed boats' ability to damage and destroy a stealthier LCS.

### 3. Close-In High Volume Firepower

Close-in high volume firepower (firepower) gives LCS the capability to develop fire control solutions on multiple targets at shorter ranges with greater lethality. Firepower's benefits are that it increases the number of contacts LCS can target and engage, and it increases the LCS's probability to hit the targets. Firepower shortens the range LCS can shoot. The shorter range might require LCS to enter an enemy platform's weapons range before LCS is able to shoot the platform, creating a situation where LCS can be damaged before it ever takes a shot. However, the expectation is that because of the enemy's low probability of hit, LCS will engage and destroy more enemies with the firepower factor.

In EINSTein, the firepower factor shortens the undamaged and damaged shooting ranges to seven NM and five NM, respectively. However, the firepower factor increases an undamaged LCS's maximum number of targets that it can engage to four, with a twenty percent probability of hitting. Firepower allows a damaged LCS to engage two targets with a ten percent probability of hitting.

### 4. Speed, the 50+ Knot Sprint Capability

The speed factor increases LCS's undamaged speed to two squares per time-step (approximately fifty knots), simulating the 50+ knot capability. A damaged LCS, like a damaged baseline LCS, transits at twenty-five knots (one square per time-step). Speed is not modeled to affect a platform's survivability (direct hits required to degrade the platform from one state to another). The cruise missile's speed justifies this assumption. The harpoon missile, which travels at a speed of .85 mach (approximately 562 knots), would fly over twenty two NM (squares) in the period of one time-step.[37] Given its speed, a harpoon missile would not have significantly more difficulty attacking a ship that travels one more NM per time-step than its normal target that transits at twenty five knots. The speed factor is expected to give LCS the ability to engage enemy forces further away from the ESG's amphibious ships.

### C. EXPERIMENTAL DESIGN

Each factor can have its own effects, beneficial and detrimental, on LCS's ability to defend ESGs. Factors that are enabled simultaneously give LCSs the effects of all the enabled factors and the enabled factors' interactions. The interactions provide effects that could not be explored unless the factors that bring it out are enabled both separately and simultaneously. For example, stealth coupled with firepower could give LCS the survivability to consistently close the enemy to take advantage of the increased firepower, therefore improving ESG defense.

This study took an organized approach to design the experiment so that all factors and their interactions could be examined. Table 6 displays the design of experiment. Using binary addition, four factors create sixteen different combinations to examine in this study, from r0, which has no factors enabled, to r15 which has all the factors enabled.

---

[37] Norman Polmar, *The Naval Institute Guide to the Ships and Aircraft of the U.S. Fleet* (Annapolis, MD: Naval Institute Press, 1993) 484-5.

The left most column lists the factors being used (helo's stands for helo/UCAV). A factor is used in a particular run-set if there is a "1" in its row below the run-set name. A "0" in the factor's row below a run-set's name signifies that the factor will not be enabled for the run-set.

| factors | run-sets | | | | | | | | | | | | | | | |
|---|---|---|---|---|---|---|---|---|---|---|---|---|---|---|---|---|
| | r0 | r1 | r2 | r3 | r4 | r5 | r6 | r7 | r8 | r9 | r10 | r11 | r12 | r13 | r14 | r15 |
| helo's | 0 | 1 | 0 | 1 | 0 | 1 | 0 | 1 | 0 | 1 | 0 | 1 | 0 | 1 | 0 | 1 |
| stealth | 0 | 0 | 1 | 1 | 0 | 0 | 1 | 1 | 0 | 0 | 1 | 1 | 0 | 0 | 1 | 1 |
| firepower | 0 | 0 | 0 | 0 | 1 | 1 | 1 | 1 | 0 | 0 | 0 | 0 | 1 | 1 | 1 | 1 |
| speed | 0 | 0 | 0 | 0 | 0 | 0 | 0 | 0 | 1 | 1 | 1 | 1 | 1 | 1 | 1 | 1 |

Table 6    Design of Experiment

The sixteen run sets (r0-r15) allow us to methodically explore how the factors and interactions affect a disposition of ships. Run-set r0 has no additional capabilities, thus using the baseline LCS. Run-set r1 includes helo/UCAVs in ESG defense. The r2 run-set uses stealthier LCSs. Helo/UCAVs combine with stealthy LCSs to defend the ESG in r3. Run-set r4 uses the firepower factor. Run-set r5 uses helo/UCAVs and close-in high volume firepower. Stealthy LCSs with firepower are used in the r6 run-set. Run-set r7 enables the helo/UCAV, stealth and firepower factors. The high-speed LCS is used for ESG defense in run-set r8. Speed and helo/UCAV factors are enabled in r9. Run-set r10 uses stealthy, speedy LCSs in ESG defense. R11 employs helo/UCAV, stealth and speed factors. Speedy LCSs with firepower are utilized in r12. Run-set r13 incorporates speed, firepower and helo/UCAVs. R14 utilizes stealthy, speedy LCSs with increased firepower. All four factors are enabled in run-set r15.

## 1.    Ship Dispositions

The normal force structure mixture of an ESG is three amphibious ships and three CRUDES ships. This was the baseline ship disposition for this study. From the baseline, CRUDES ships were removed and LCSs added to the ESG for additional force structure mixtures to examine. The top two rows of Table 7 display the various alternative ship combinations that were added to the three amphibious ships to create an ESG for this study. No CRUDES ships were added to the baseline ESG because an extra CRUDES ship would add cost and manpower requirements greater than the baseline, not following the goal of reducing the manpower and dollar costs of an ESG. No LCSs were added to the three CRUDES disposition because manpower and dollar costs would also be greater than what the baseline requires.

| run | 3crudes 0lcs | 2crudes 1lcs | 2lcs | 3lcs | 4lcs | 5lcs | 1crudes 1lcs | 2lcs | 3lcs | 4lcs | 5lcs | 6lcs | 7lcs | 0crudes 1lcs | 2lcs | 3lcs | 4lcs | 5lcs | 6lcs | 7lcs |
|---|---|---|---|---|---|---|---|---|---|---|---|---|---|---|---|---|---|---|---|---|
| r0 | x | x | x | x | x | x | x | x | x | x | x | x | x | x | x | x | x | x | x | x |
| r1 | x | x | x | x | x | x | x | x | x | x | x | x | x | x | x | x | x | x | x | x |
| r2 | | x | x | x | x | x | x | x | x | x | x | x | x | x | x | x | x | x | x | x |
| r3 | | x | x | x | x | x | x | x | x | x | x | x | x | x | x | x | x | x | x | x |
| r4 | | x | x | x | x | x | x | x | x | x | x | x | x | x | x | x | x | x | x | x |
| r5 | | x | x | x | x | x | x | x | x | x | x | x | x | x | x | x | x | x | x | x |
| r6 | | x | x | x | x | x | x | x | x | x | x | x | x | x | x | x | x | x | x | x |
| r7 | | x | x | x | x | x | x | x | x | x | x | x | x | x | x | x | x | x | x | x |
| r8 | | x | x | x | x | x | x | x | x | x | x | x | x | x | x | x | x | x | x | x |
| r9 | | x | x | x | x | x | x | x | x | x | x | x | x | x | x | x | x | x | x | x |
| r10 | | x | x | x | x | x | x | x | x | x | x | x | x | x | x | x | x | x | x | x |
| r11 | | x | x | x | x | x | x | x | x | x | x | x | x | x | x | x | x | x | x | x |
| r12 | | x | x | x | x | x | x | x | x | x | x | x | x | x | x | x | x | x | x | x |
| r13 | | x | x | x | x | x | x | x | x | x | x | x | x | x | x | x | x | x | x | x |
| r14 | | x | x | x | x | x | x | x | x | x | x | x | x | x | x | x | x | x | x | x |
| r15 | | x | x | x | x | x | x | x | x | x | x | x | x | x | x | x | x | x | x | x |

Table 7    Ship Disposition and Run-Set Plan

This thesis makes some hypotheses about possible force structure mixtures. Specifically, they are that with two CRUDES ships, one CRUDES ship and zero CRUDES ships, the optimal amount of LCSs to add to minimize ESG losses will be somewhere between one and five, one and seven, and one and seven, respectively. This study assumes that the "knee in the curve" (the place where additional forces do not add reduced benefit per force unit) for ship losses will be found in these ship dispositions.

The sixteen run sets for each disposition of ships are shown in Table 7. An "x" indicates that factors for the row's run-set are examined with the column's ship combination. The ship disposition of one CRUDES ship and four LCSs protecting three amphibious ships requires examination of all sixteen run-sets. However, the ship disposition with three CRUDES and zero LCS protecting the ESG only requires run sets r0 and r1 because the ship disposition includes no LCSs. Therefore, performing the other run sets that include LCS factors would not aid this analysis. Run-sets with the helo/UCAV factor enabled use an additional squad of helo/UCAVs. The amount of helo/UCAVs for a particular ship combination equals the sum of CRUDES ships and LCSs. So, for example, an ESG with two CRUDES and three LCSs will have a squad of five helo/UCAVs flying in run-set r1.

## D.     DATA FARMING

Data farming is a concern for simulation studies. EINSTein allows users to retrieve survival data and statistics for the agents in individual runs. In addition, visually undamaged platforms maintain the original red or blue, and damaged platforms can be switched to change to a light red or light blue to show their change in status. Destroyed platforms are not shown unless the user toggles the "Display where red/blue agents were killed" setting. However, this study did not require showing destroyed platforms for measurements. Also, users can highlight specific squads, but there is no coloration difference in the members of a highlighted squad.

Unfortunately, finding damaged units by squad requires manual data collection. Specifically, at the end of a discrete run, an EINSTein user has to highlight a specific squad and take note of how many damaged (lighter colored) platforms are left in the blue force (not in the highlighted squad). Then, that number is subtracted from the total damaged for the blue forces (which is listed at the bottom of the simulation window) to calculate the number of damaged platforms in the highlighted squad. Finally, the number of damaged platforms in the highlighted squad is subtracted from the number of highlighted squad members to calculate the number of undamaged squad members. From that information a user knows how many undamaged and damaged platforms are in the highlighted squad and can enter that information into the database. This thesis used Microsoft Excel spreadsheets for storing the data. The total number of surviving platforms in a squad equals the sum of the number of undamaged platforms in the squad plus the number of damaged platforms in the same squad.

### 1.     Measures of Effectiveness

Measures of Effectiveness (MOEs) are ways to quantify the goals of this study. This study's goal is to find a force structure mix in concert with LCS capabilities that protect an ESG in an anti-access scenario so that the amphibious ships can perform amphibious operations at the objective. To quantify this goal, we create MOEs of amphibious ship survivors and amphibious ships damaged. Other MOEs relate to CRUDES survival, LCS survival, and helo/UCAV survival. The reasons for developing other MOEs include that the amphibious ships will need some protection once they arrive at the objective and establish the sea base for forces ashore and the navy does not want to spend money on a platform and place it in a position to be destroyed.

## 2. Initial Data Farming Issues

Now that the potential MOEs have been established, this study looks at what data output can be recovered (farmed) from EINSTein. EINSTein has a quick "Multiple Time-Series (Averages/Distributions)" run mode that can perform 100 runs of our scenario in less than two minutes. However, the mode does not break down the survivability data into specific squads and combines injured and killed into one casualty category. EINSTein was originally created for ground combat, and it is understood that injured and killed soldiers would be grouped as causalities for a ground commander. A damaged ship can still operate to some degree and effectively draw fire away from high value units, making it different from an injured soldier. EINSTein's "Interactive Time-Series (Default)" run mode allows users to perform discrete runs. Damaged platforms and specific squads can be highlighted, enabling a user to farm run data in the process mentioned in the first paragraph of the Data Farming section. However, this is a slow and tedious process, with a 50 run run-set taking between 10 and 30 minutes, depending on the number of squads and the variability of the data. One advantage of this approach is that the analyst visually assesses each run—thus gaining insights on the dynamics behind the numbers.

This study uses four input measures: starting number of amphibious ships, starting number of CRUDES ships, starting number of LCSs, and starting number of helo/UCAVs. At the end of the runs, output data is placed in up to eight categories on a Microsoft Excel spreadsheet:

Number of undamaged amphibious ships at the end of a run

Number of damaged amphibious ships

Number of undamaged CRUDES ships

Number of damaged CRUDES ships

Number of undamaged LCSs

Number of damaged LCSs

Number of undamaged helo/UCAVs

Number of damaged helo/UCAVs

Averages, minimums, maximums, and standard deviations can be created from and for these measures.

### 3.  Number of Required Runs

This study used "Multiple Time-Series (Averages/Distributions)" run mode with the baseline inputs (3 amphibious ships, 3 CRUDES ships, run-set r0) to try to find the minimum required number of runs to perform to have data that encompasses most of the possibilities. Run-sets of 50, 100, 150 and 200 runs were performed. The standard deviations of the attrition data, shown in Table 8, show that there is little change in the estimate of the standard deviation of the casualty data (injured + killed) gained from doing more than 50 runs. Therefore, each run-set consists of 50 discrete runs. The 50 replications results in an estimated standard deviation on the mean number of blue ships attrited, our primary MOE, of $1.8455/\sqrt{(50)}=0.26$. 50 replications of 16 run-sets examining 19 ship combinations equates to 15,200 runs with LCS. An additional 100 runs are required to get the baseline and 3 CRUDES ship r1 run-sets.

|  | Number of Baseline Runs | | | |
| --- | --- | --- | --- | --- |
|  | 50 | 100 | 150 | 200 |
| Blue attrition stdev | 1.8455 | 1.7511 | 1.7616 | 1.7651 |
| Red attrition stdev | 4.457 | 4.3531 | 3.9715 | 3.6374 |

Table 8    Baseline Runs' Attrition Estimated Standard Deviations as a Function of the Number of Replications

THIS PAGE INTENTIONALLY LEFT BLANK

# IV.  DATA AND ANALYSIS

## A.  INTRODUCTION

This chapter discusses the output data and the analysis.  The data section talks about the observations, and discusses a slight personality adjustment to LCSs (Littoral Combat ships) and helo/UCAVs (Helicopters/Unmanned Combat Aerial Vehicles).  The analysis section reviews the MOEs (Measures Of Effectiveness), and the three data groups.  The analysis section also discusses analysis techniques, results, and graphical methods.  Finally, the key findings section focuses on the results that are significant across the board and identifies the ship force mixtures and capabilities that perform the best.

## B.  DATA

### 1.  Spreadsheet

This thesis uses a Microsoft Excel spreadsheet to store data and perform computations.  Each spreadsheet is formatted like Table 9, which is the spreadsheet displaying the baseline (three CRUDES ships defending three amphibious ships, no factors enabled) run-set data.  The initial numbers of amphibious ships, CRUDES ships, LCSs and helo (helo/UCAVs) are shown at the top.  The spreadsheet is then divided into (from left to right) a reference column explaining what information is displayed in the row of the reference; alive (undamaged) amphibious ships' column; injured (damaged) amphibious ships' column; total surviving (undamaged + damaged) amphibious ships' column; alive (undamaged) CRUDES ships' column; injured (damaged) CRUDES ships' column; total surviving (undamaged + damaged) CRUDES ships' column; alive (undamaged) LCSs' column; injured (damaged) LCSs' column; total surviving (undamaged + damaged) LCSs' column; alive (undamaged) helo/UCAVs' column; injured (damaged) helo/UCAVs' column; and total surviving (undamaged + damaged) helo/UCAVs' column.  The exception to this is the sample mean (xbar), calculated for the number of injured platforms associated with that column, and the average, calculated for the total number of lost (destroyed) platforms associated with the particular column.

| | Starting Values for the Run-set | | | | |
|---|---|---|---|---|---|
| | amphibs | crudes | lcs | helo | |
| | 3 | 3 | 0 | 0 | |

| | amphib alive | amphib inj | total amphib | crudes alive | crudes inj | total crudes |
|---|---|---|---|---|---|---|
| min | 0 | 0 | 0 | 0 | 0 | 0 |
| xbar | 1.28 | 0.56 | 1.84 | 0.1 | 0.3 | 0.4 |
| max | 3 | 3 | 3 | 3 | 3 | 3 |
| sig | 1.1959114 | 0.786623 | 1.33033677 | 0.46291005 | 0.646813 | 0.7824608 |
| sigxb | 0.16912741 | 0.111245 | 0.18813803 | 0.06546537 | 0.091473 | 0.11065667 |

| | | amphib inj | amphibs lost | | crudes inj | crudes lost |
|---|---|---|---|---|---|---|
| xbar | | 0.56 | 1.16 | | 0.3 | 2.6 |

| run | amphib alive | amphib inj | total amphib | crudes alive | crudes inj | total crudes |
|---|---|---|---|---|---|---|
| 1 | 2 | 1 | 3 | 1 | 0 | 1 |
| 2 | 0 | 0 | 0 | 0 | 0 | 0 |
| 3 | 1 | 2 | 3 | 0 | 0 | 0 |
| 4 | 3 | 0 | 3 | 0 | 2 | 2 |
| 5 | 0 | 3 | 3 | 0 | 0 | 0 |
| 6 | 0 | 0 | 0 | 0 | 0 | 0 |
| 7 | 0 | 1 | 1 | 0 | 0 | 0 |
| 8 | 1 | 2 | 3 | 0 | 1 | 1 |
| 9 | 0 | 0 | 0 | 0 | 0 | 0 |
| 10 | 3 | 0 | 3 | 3 | 0 | 3 |
| 11 | 0 | 0 | 0 | 0 | 0 | 0 |
| 12 | 0 | 0 | 0 | 0 | 0 | 0 |
| 13 | 1 | 1 | 2 | 0 | 0 | 0 |
| 14 | 3 | 0 | 3 | 0 | 0 | 0 |
| 15 | 1 | 1 | 2 | 0 | 0 | 0 |
| 16 | 0 | 1 | 1 | 0 | 0 | 0 |
| 17 | 0 | 0 | 0 | 0 | 0 | 0 |
| 18 | 3 | 0 | 3 | 0 | 1 | 1 |
| 19 | 3 | 0 | 3 | 0 | 0 | 0 |
| 20 | 1 | 2 | 3 | 0 | 0 | 0 |
| 21 | 2 | 1 | 3 | 0 | 0 | 0 |
| 22 | 2 | 0 | 2 | 0 | 0 | 0 |
| 23 | 0 | 0 | 0 | 0 | 0 | 0 |
| 24 | 3 | 0 | 3 | 0 | 1 | 1 |
| 25 | 3 | 0 | 3 | 0 | 1 | 1 |
| 26 | 0 | 0 | 0 | 0 | 0 | 0 |
| 27 | 2 | 0 | 2 | 0 | 0 | 0 |
| 28 | 0 | 0 | 0 | 0 | 0 | 0 |
| 29 | 0 | 0 | 0 | 0 | 0 | 0 |
| 30 | 2 | 1 | 3 | 0 | 0 | 0 |
| 31 | 2 | 1 | 3 | 0 | 0 | 0 |
| 32 | 0 | 0 | 0 | 0 | 0 | 0 |
| 33 | 0 | 0 | 0 | 0 | 0 | 0 |
| 34 | 1 | 2 | 3 | 0 | 0 | 0 |
| 35 | 2 | 1 | 3 | 0 | 0 | 0 |
| 36 | 1 | 0 | 1 | 0 | 0 | 0 |
| 37 | 1 | 2 | 3 | 0 | 3 | 3 |
| 38 | 1 | 1 | 2 | 0 | 1 | 1 |
| 39 | 3 | 0 | 3 | 0 | 2 | 2 |
| 40 | 0 | 0 | 0 | 0 | 0 | 0 |
| 41 | 0 | 2 | 2 | 0 | 1 | 1 |
| 42 | 0 | 0 | 0 | 0 | 0 | 0 |
| 43 | 0 | 0 | 0 | 0 | 0 | 0 |
| 44 | 3 | 0 | 3 | 0 | 1 | 1 |
| 45 | 2 | 1 | 3 | 1 | 1 | 2 |
| 46 | 3 | 0 | 3 | 0 | 0 | 0 |
| 47 | 2 | 1 | 3 | 0 | 0 | 0 |
| 48 | 2 | 1 | 3 | 0 | 0 | 0 |
| 49 | 3 | 0 | 3 | 0 | 0 | 0 |
| 50 | 2 | 0 | 2 | 0 | 0 | 0 |

Table 9     Baseline Data Spreadsheet

Below the starting values are the initial statistics, these where calculated from the data below (in the same column). From top to bottom, the minimum value, average, maximum value, sample standard deviation (sig), and estimated standard deviation of the population average (sigxb) are calculated and displayed. Next is the losses section, where the average number of injured platforms and lost platforms are calculated and displayed. The average number of platforms injured, in the particular column, is taken from above value in average number of injured platforms. The average number of platforms lost, in the particular column, is calculated by subtracting the average number of total surviving platforms from the starting number of the platform for the run-set.

The final section is the data collection section. A run-set consists of 50 discrete runs of the simulation with the particular input values, ship disposition and factors (rX). At the end of each discrete run the number of undamaged and damaged platforms are entered in the row of the run's sequential number. For example, after the thirteenth run, data is entered in the same row as the "13" under the "run" column. The total number of surviving platforms is calculated by taking the sum of the number of undamaged platforms and the damaged platforms—i.e. summing the two cells to the left. The rest of these spreadsheets are displayed in Appendix A (Data).

### 2.    Mini Analysis

Looking at the raw data and statistical calculations, one can take note of outliers and trends. Also, rough comparisons can be gleaned from the data. Helo/UCAVs seem to have a significant impact on ship survival, often improving average ship survival by two ships or more. However, helo/UCAVs also take massive losses. In the best cases helo/UCAV losses drop below 50%. This is because they perform very aggressively, rushing headlong into battle with enemy ships. The aim of this thesis is improving the survivability of ESG (Expeditionary Strike Group) ships, however. Helo/UCAVs are supporting elements in this endeavor, meant to help increase ship survivability. LCS speed appears to be detrimental to ship survival, yet speed slightly benefits helo/UCAV survival. Also, LCSs with stealth and firepower appears formidable.

### 3.    Slight Change in Personality

It was noticed during initial runs that helo/UCAVs did not completely act as desired. LCS and helo/UCAV personalities were originally set as shown in Table 10, and were used for the ship configurations of two CRUDES ships and one through three LCSs. In approximately one-fifth of the trials with helo/UCAV factors set, it was noticed that when undamaged helo/UCAVs engage enemy ships, they would leave combat to pursue the objective (enemy flag), placing the rest of the ESG in a vulnerable position. This characteristic of the helo/UCAV reduced their contributions to providing locating information on and attriting the threat. The platforms' desire to engage undamaged (alive) enemies had equal weight with their desire to approach the objective. To counter this, LCS and helo/UCAV personality vectors were altered, as shown in Table 4, to increase the motivation to engage enemy ships over pursuing the objective. These new vectors were used for the rest of the simulation runs.

| Anti-Access Personalities | | | | | | | | | | | |
|---|---|---|---|---|---|---|---|---|---|---|---|
| | When Alive | | | | | | When Injured | | | | |
| Squad | To alv friend | To alv enemy | To inj friend | To inj enemy | To friend flag | To enemy flag | To alv friend | To alv enemy | To inj friend | To inj enemy | To friend flag | To enemy flag |
| Amphibs | 40 | | 40 | | | 20 | 45 | | 40 | | | 15 |
| CRUDES | 10 | 40 | | 40 | | 10 | 20 | 20 | 20 | 30 | | 10 |
| LCS | 10 | 20 | 10 | 40 | | 20 | 20 | 10 | 20 | 30 | | 20 |
| Helo/UCAV | 10 | 20 | 10 | 40 | | 20 | 30 | | 20 | 30 | | 20 |

Table 10    Blue ESG Force Anti-Access Personalities (2 CRUDES, 1-3 LCS)

## C.    ANALYSIS

Initially, for this study the primary MOE was the average total number of ships that survive. However, if more ships are added, the number of ships that survive could conceivably also increase and the "knee" of the curve (the point where the benefits of additional ships lessens) with reference to numbers would not be visible. Conceivably, 2 CRUDES + 2 LCS-r0 (for a total of 7 ships, including the amphibious ships) could have an average of 4 ships surviving while 2 CRUDES + 3 LCS-r0 (for a total of 8 ships) could have an average of 5 ships surviving. The 2 CRUDES + 3 LCS-r0 looks better than the 2 CRUDES + 2 LCS-r0 based on this MOE, however they both lose 3 ships. Therefore, adding one LCS to 2 CRUDES + 2 LCS-r0 adds no benefit to ship survivability, yet it is not easily visible using average total surviving ships as the MOE.

In order to deal with attrition properly, this thesis uses **the average number of ships lost as the primary MOE**. This MOE does not give undue advantage to the ESGs with greater numbers of ships. Looking at the example in the previous paragraph, the average number of ships lost MOE would show that adding one LCS to 2 CRUDES + 2 LCS-r0 does not reduce the number of ships lost. Therefore, adding a LCS to 2 CRUDES + 2 LCS-r0 would waste an asset and its cost, and the "knee" of the curve in this scenario may lie at the 2 CRUDES + 2 LCS-r0 level, or less, for any 2 CRUDES-r0 case. If the average number of ships that survive is the same for 2 CRUDES + 2 LCS-r0 and 2 CRUDES + 3 LCS-r0, then the average number of ships lost will be greater for 2 CRUDES + 3 LCS-r0. Again, signifying no added benefit of adding 1 LCS. However, if the total number of ships lost for 2 CRUDES + 3 LCS-r0 is less than the total number of ships to 2 CRUDES + 2 LCS-r0, then the added LCS does improve survivability. The added LCS survives and helps some of the ships that are destroyed in the 2 CRUDES + 2 LCS-r0 run-set survive. The total number of ships lost is calculated by taking the sum of average number of amphibious ships lost, average number of CRUDES ships lost, and average number of LCSs lost.

## 1. Data Organization

This study organizes the data into four distinct groups based on the number of CRUDES ships involved. The groups are 3 CRUDES, 2 CRUDES, 1 CRUDES and 0 CRUDES. Each is distinct from the others, and has enough similarities within the group to enable analysis and establishing the number of LCSs as a design factor. Each group would utilize different tactics due to the number of CRUDES ships in the ESG. Also, "knees" in curves comparing average total ships lost against number of LCSs are visible in graphical comparisons. Conceivably, the "knee" of the curves could exist at approximately the same number of LCS added to the CRUDES. Therefore, there is a possibility to find a sufficient amount of LCSs to add to the CRUDES ships in the set that reaches the point that minimizes ship losses per LCS added. Another benefit of organizing the data into these groups is that force planners have options on the number of CRUDES ships to assign to an ESG.

### a.    *3 CRUDES*

The 3 CRUDES set of data has no LCSs and consists of 2 run-sets: the baseline and r1 (three CRUDES ships controlling three helo/UCAVs). The data is summarized in Table 11. The CRUDES column shows the number of CRUDES examined, and the LCS column displays the number of LCS examined. The Run-Set column displays the particular run-set examined, and the Helo, Stealth, Firepower and Speed columns show if the factor is enabled in the run-set. The Total Ship Loss column displays the average total ship loss for the ship disposition shown on the row coupled with the run-set factors over 50 runs. The 3 CRUDES set makes no change from what is currently out in the fleet. Analysis shows that employing helo/UCAVs for ship defense is highly beneficial in this scenario—at least as modeled in this thesis.

| CRUDES | LCS | Run-Set | Helo | Stealth | Firepower | Speed | Total Ship Loss |
|--------|-----|---------|------|---------|-----------|-------|-----------------|
| 3 | 0 | r0 | 0 | 0 | 0 | 0 | 3.76 |
| 3 | 0 | r1 | 1 | 0 | 0 | 0 | 0.58 |

Table 11    3 CRUDES Data Prepared for Analysis

There are many comparison methods that can be used to analyze the 3 CRUDES set's data. However, because both run-sets comprise large sample populations (50 observations), both run-sets are independent of each other, and each run-set has its own population mean and variance (standard deviation squared), this thesis uses a large-sample comparison test to analyze the 3 CRUDES set's data.[38] The Central Limit Theorem states that if there is a set of independent identically distributed random samples from a population and the sample set is sufficiently large, the sample mean will be approximately distributed as a normal distribution with a mean of the true mean and standard deviation equal to the true standard deviation divided by the square root of the number of samples in the set. Except in rare circumstances, if a sample set contains more than thirty observations the Central Limit Theorem can be used.[39] Therefore, the Central Limit Theorem is applied to all the data in this thesis, and analysis techniques that require data with a normal distribution, like the large-sample comparison test, are utilized.

---

[38] Jay L. Devore, *Probability and Statistics for Engineering and the Sciences: Fifth Edition* (Pacific Grove, CA: Duxbury, 2000) 360.

[39] Jay L. Devore, *Probability and Statistics for Engineering and the Sciences: Fifth Edition* (Pacific Grove, CA: Duxbury, 2000) 235-6.

The average ship loss for the baseline is 3.76 and the average ship loss for the 3 CRUDES-r1 run-set is 0.58. Using the large-sample comparison test, the null hypothesis, $H_0$, is that the baseline's average ship loss is statistically equal to the 3 CRUDES-r1 run-set's average ship loss. The alternate, $H_a$, is that the baseline's average ship loss is statistically greater than the 3 CRUDES-r1 run-set's average ship loss. Table 12 shows the comparison test and results. The comparison test uses the average ship losses, the sample standard deviations of ship loss, over the two samples, each of 50 runs, to calculate z in Equation 1.

| Large-Sample Comparison Test | | |
|---|---|---|
| | r0 | r1 |
| Avg Ship Loss | 3.76 | 0.58 |
| Standard Deviation | 1.80204 | 1.011969 |
| Sample Size | 50 | 50 |
| | | |
| z = | 10.87991614 | |
| P-value | 0 | |

Table 12     Large-Sample Comparison Test on the 3 CRUDES Data

$$z = \frac{r0\_avg\_ship\_loss - r1\_avg\_ship\_loss}{\sqrt{\dfrac{r0\_stdev^2}{50} + \dfrac{r1\_stdev^2}{50}}}$$

Equation 1     Large-Sample Comparison Test Formula to Calculate z

The P-Value is the probability that we would observe data as extreme, or more extreme, than what occurred if the two population means are identical. The P-value is calculate by $1-\Phi(z)$, where $\Phi(z)$ is the cumulative distribution function of a standard normal distribution evaluated at z. The P-value is essentially 0 for this case. Therefore, because the probability of achieving these observations, if the null hypothesis is true, is so close to zero, this result cannot be considered to be merely the result of chance. Consequently, we conclude that air assets matter. However, no helo/UCAVs survived any of the 3 CRUDES-r1 runs. Therefore, at risk to themselves, they engaged and attrited the threat sufficiently so that the CRUDES ships successfully engaged the remainder. In addition, by being out front, the air assets served as scouting platforms, providing situational awareness to the ships of the ESG.[40]

### b.   2 CRUDES

The 2 CRUDES set has fewer organic land attack missiles and organic naval fire support systems than the baseline for amphibious operations. However, its command and control capabilities are greater than those of an ESG with zero or one CRUDES ship. The 2 CRUDES ESGs also have LCS. The 2 CRUDES data group is displayed in Appendix B (Data Groups for Analysis). A graph of average total ship loss vs. number of LCS, for each run-set, is shown in Figure 3. With the exception of the baseline, r4 (firepower), r8 (speed), and r12 (firepower and speed) LCS configurations, adding LCSs to the 2 CRUDES ESGs yields fewer losses. Note, the points in the graph are estimates. The standard deviation of each is estimated as the run-set's sample standard deviation divided by the square root of the sample size. The sample standard deviation is usually around 1.5 and the sample size is always 50. Thus, the random points have associated standard deviations of about $1.5/\sqrt{50}$, which equals .21. For cases with fewer losses, the sample standard deviations are usually much smaller than 1.5.

---

[40] Wayne P. Hughes, *Fleet Tactics and Coastal Combat* (Annapolis, MD: U.S. Naval Institute, 2000) 92-3.

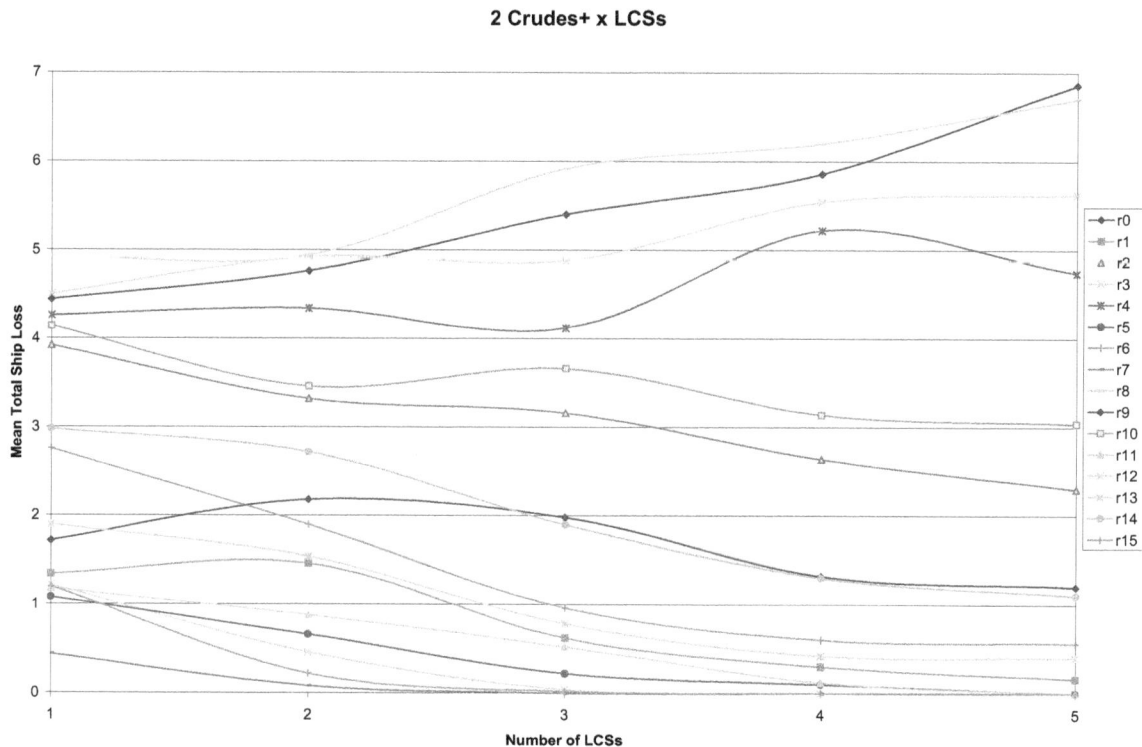

Figure 3    2 CRUDES + X LCS, Ship Loss vs. Number of LCS

Taking a look at the main factors (baseline, helo/UCAV, stealth, firepower, and speed) by themselves, in Figure 4, helo/UCAV (r1) and stealth (r2) ship losses diminish as LCSs are added. However, when LCSs are added to the baseline (r0), and speed (r8) cases, they merely add to ship losses. The firepower (r4) case does not appear to change force performance, seemingly almost flat and indicating that 1 LCS might be the "knee" of that particular line. The total ship loss for 2 CRUDES + 2 LCS is higher than 2 CRUDES + 1 LCS. This is consistent with the 1 and 0 CRUDES sets of data using that run-set. These graphs provide good preliminary analysis and ANOVA (ANalysis Of VAriance) will provide further detailed review. The body of this study displays graphs of note, but all may be found in Appendix D (Graphs).

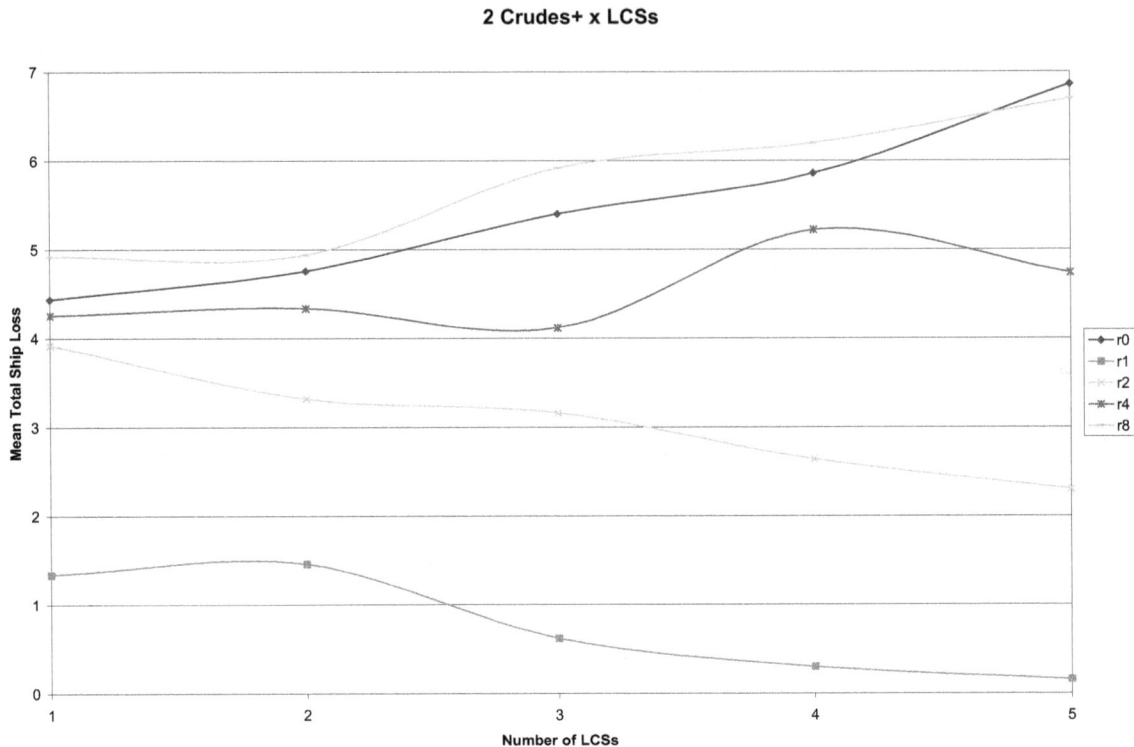

Figure 4    2 CRUDES + X LCS, Ship Loss vs. Number of LCS, Main Factors Only

ANOVA was performed, individually, on the 2-, 1-, and 0- CRUDES sets. ANOVA is a collection of statistical procedures for the analysis of quantitative responses from experimental units.[41]  It is the approach this study is taking in order to discern which factors account for significant differences in force performance.  The null hypothesis is that there is no difference in the average number of ships lost if a factor is changed (whether a LCS capability is enabled or not, the number of LCSs assigned to the ESG, and combinations of the aforementioned factors).  The alternate is that force survival does change as a particular factor changes.  This approach is taken for each main factor and each multiple factor interaction of interest.

The number of LCSs, whether or not air assets are present, whether or not stealth is employed, whether firepower is augmented, and whether high-speed is used, are all characteristics that may contribute to differences in ESG effectiveness.  The number of LCSs characteristic takes the number of LCS assigned to an ESG so the factor could

[41] Jay L. Devore, *Probability and Statistics for Engineering and the Sciences: Fifth Edition* (Pacific Grove, CA: Duxbury, 2000) 402.

44

be one of five or six numbers. The other factors are binary, meaning that they are 1 if they are enabled and 0 if not. In zero, one or two CRUDES force dispositions, ANOVA will examine average total ship loss as a function of number of LCSs, the helo/UCAV factor, stealth, firepower, and/or speed. Interactions among these design considerations are also examined.

The ANOVA of the 2 CRUDES force total ship losses as a function of the factors (numbers of LCSs, Helo/UCAV, stealth, firepower, and speed), including up to three-way interactions (e.g., number of LCSs * if the stealth factor is enabled * if the speed factor is enabled), is shown in Table 13. An interaction occurs when the effect of one factor depends on the values of other factors. There are a sufficient amount of residuals to use to check the model. Residuals are the sample counterparts of error terms and equal the differences between observed and predicted average ship losses. The residual mean square error (MSE, which is under the Mean Sq and in line with residuals, in the table) measures the variation of estimates around a parameter. A good residual MSE should be as low as possible to show that the sample estimates are near the observed simulation outputs. However, if there are too few residuals the model will be over-fit.[42]

An over-fit model may not have much variability in its evaluation, but its predictive accuracy will be quite poor. The residual mean square error of this model, 0.0559, is significantly better (smaller) than the ANOVA model using the same function with only two-way interactions (e.g., number of LCSs * if the stealth factor is enabled), which has a residual MSE 0.2737. Also, the ANOVA model with three-way interactions has a better residual MSE than the ANOVA model using the same function with up to four-way interactions, which has a residual MSE of 0.0560. Another test for the ANOVA model with three-way interactions is the residual plot. The residual plot in Figure 5 shows that the residuals have a normal looking, homoscedastic pattern. This means the data fits the model, but not perfectly, as there is randomness. In addition, the expectation is that hypothesis tests in the ANOVA are unbiased.

---

[42] Lawrence C. Hamilton, *Regression with Graphics: A Second Course in Applied Statistics* (Pacific Belmont, CA: Duxbury, 1992) 32, 73.

|  | Df | Sum of Sq | Mean Sq | F Value | Pr(F) |
|---|---|---|---|---|---|
| LCS.f | 4 | 4.0100 | 1.0025 | 17.941 | 0.0000015 |
| HELO | 1 | 204.6080 | 204.6080 | 3661.733 | 0.0000000 |
| STEALTH | 1 | 57.0882 | 57.0882 | 1021.669 | 0.0000000 |
| FIREPOWER | 1 | 12.4031 | 12.4031 | 221.970 | 0.0000000 |
| SPEED | 1 | 4.4462 | 4.4462 | 79.571 | 0.0000000 |
| LCS.f:HELO | 4 | 2.5767 | 0.6442 | 11.528 | 0.0000413 |
| LCS.f:STEALTH | 4 | 5.9270 | 1.4818 | 26.518 | 0.0000001 |
| LCS.f:FIREPOWER | 4 | 0.9260 | 0.2315 | 4.143 | 0.0125266 |
| LCS.f:SPEED | 4 | 0.1673 | 0.0418 | 0.748 | 0.5700467 |
| HELO:STEALTH | 1 | 21.6112 | 21.6112 | 386.761 | 0.0000000 |
| HELO:FIREPOWER | 1 | 3.2886 | 3.2886 | 58.854 | 0.0000002 |
| HELO:SPEED | 1 | 0.0000 | 0.0000 | 0.001 | 0.9776283 |
| STEALTH:FIREPOWER | 1 | 0.3672 | 0.3672 | 6.572 | 0.0181029 |
| STEALTH:SPEED | 1 | 0.2442 | 0.2442 | 4.370 | 0.0489123 |
| FIREPOWER:SPEED | 1 | 0.0110 | 0.0110 | 0.198 | 0.6611606 |
| LCS.f:HELO:STEALTH | 4 | 8.1823 | 2.0456 | 36.608 | 0.0000000 |
| LCS.f:HELO:FIREPOWER | 4 | 1.2244 | 0.3061 | 5.478 | 0.0035053 |
| LCS.f:HELO:SPEED | 4 | 0.0834 | 0.0208 | 0.373 | 0.8251777 |
| LCS.f:STEALTH:FIREPOWER | 4 | 0.2971 | 0.0743 | 1.329 | 0.2918246 |
| LCS.f:STEALTH:SPEED | 4 | 0.0125 | 0.0031 | 0.056 | 0.9937063 |
| LCS.f:FIREPOWER:SPEED | 4 | 0.1582 | 0.0395 | 0.708 | 0.5956583 |
| HELO:STEALTH:FIREPOWER | 1 | 1.4742 | 1.4742 | 26.384 | 0.0000435 |
| HELO:STEALTH:SPEED | 1 | 0.5746 | 0.5746 | 10.283 | 0.0042365 |
| HELO:FIREPOWER:SPEED | 1 | 0.2142 | 0.2142 | 3.834 | 0.0636347 |
| STEALTH:FIREPOWER:SPEED | 1 | 0.0174 | 0.0174 | 0.311 | 0.5826719 |
| Residuals | 21 | 1.1734 | 0.0559 |  |  |

Table 13    ANOVA of the 2 CRUDES Set's Total Ship Losses, Including Up to 3-Way Interactions

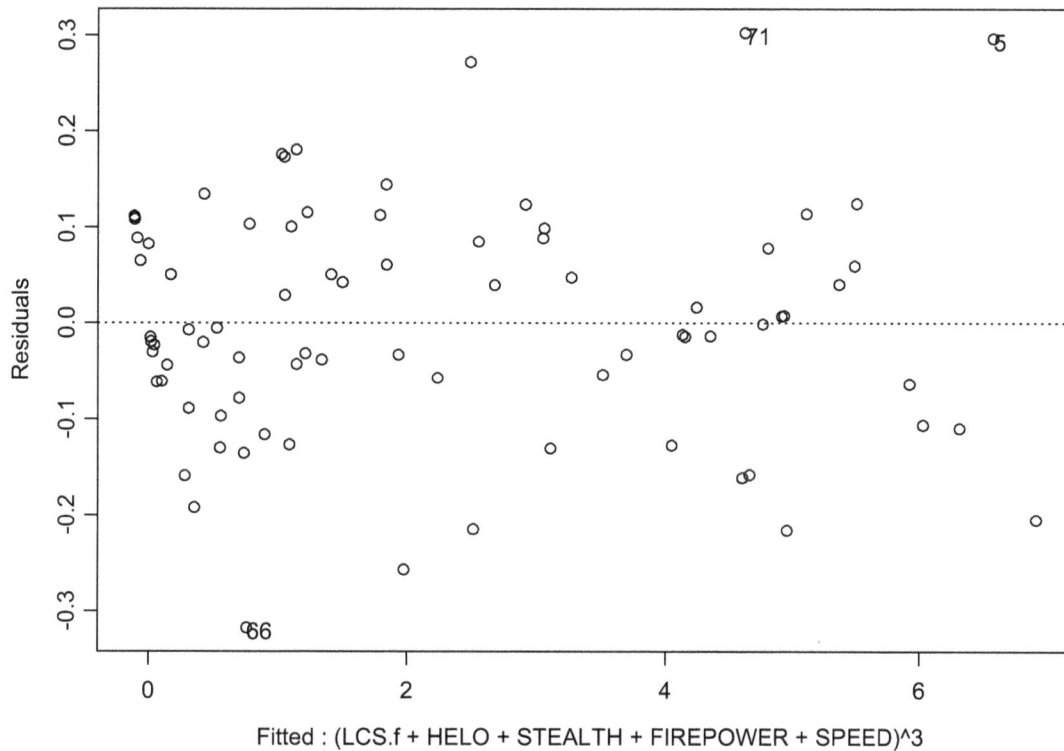

Figure 5    Residual Plot for the 2 CRUDES ANOVA

Looking at the ANOVA in Table 13, the Pr(F) column gives the P-value for each model term. When it is sufficiently small—on the order of less than 1-in-20 chance—the factor or interaction is statistically significant. The factors and interactions with a significant P-value are in bold print. All the factors (helo/UCAV, stealth, firepower, speed and numbers of LCSs) influence ship loss by themselves. The SS (Sum of Squares) under the "Sum of Sq" header measures how much variability is explained by that factor. The larger the SS, the more influential the factor or interaction is.

The influence of helo/UCAVs is almost four times greater than the next largest, stealth. Presence of aircraft is the single most influential factor when it comes to force effectiveness. This study looks at graphical comparisons later to discover if the helo/UCAV factor's influence has a beneficial or detrimental effect on average ship loss. Figure 6, comparing r2 (stealth) to r3 (stealth + helo/UCAV), shows that aircraft have a beneficial effect on preventing ship loss. Ship loss for r3 bottoms out at 0 at

47

approximately three LCSs or more, and r2 performs consistently worse by two ship losses. Other graphs that display similar comparisons isolating the helo/UCAV factor are in Appendix D.

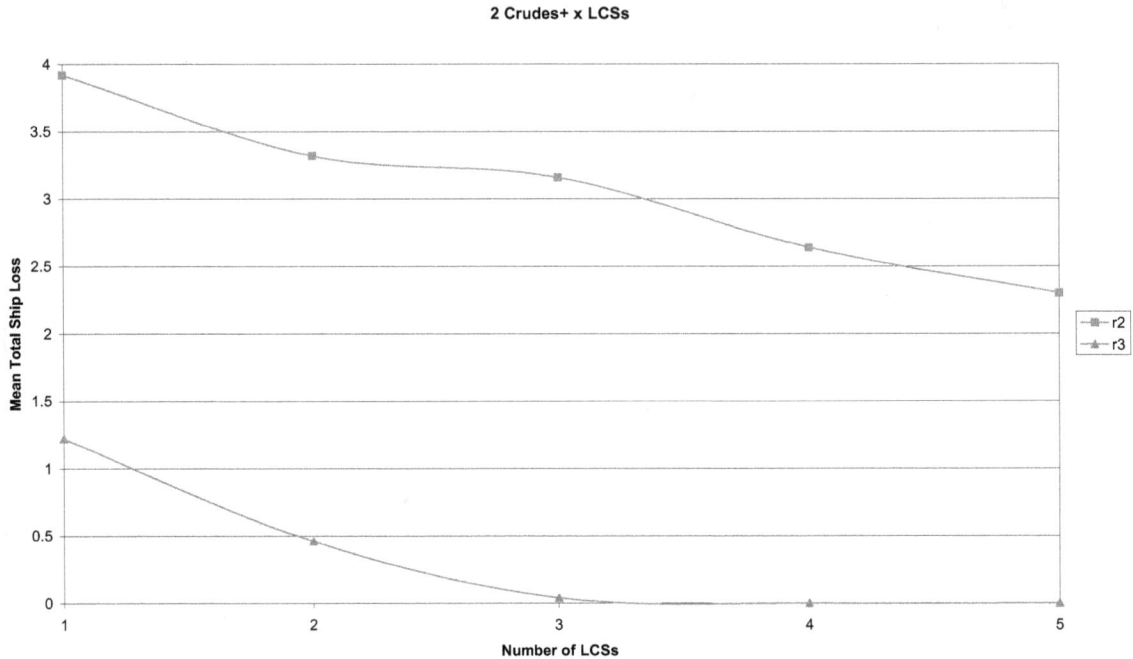

Figure 6    2 CRUDES + X LCS, Ship Loss vs. Number of LCS, r2 and r3

The next most influential factor is stealth. Its ability to explain variability in the MOE, under SS, is more that two times greater than the next largest contributor, the interaction between air assets and stealth. Stealth is also significant, with a very beneficial effect on reducing ship losses [Appendix D]. Because the helo/UCAV interaction with stealth is the next most influential term, having both aircraft and stealth makes an ESG well protected. If all factors cost the same and only two could be chosen, then helo/UCAVs and stealth would be the best choices in this scenario.

Firepower comes in fourth for influence and it has a positive influence. The interaction of numbers of LCS, the helo/UCAV factor and the stealth factor is next, further highlighting how the helo/UCAV-stealth combination is advantageous to have for an ESG in this situation. The results for speed, an influential factor, are mixed. Figure 7, the graph comparing r1 (helo) and r9 (helo and speed), as well as others, shows speed has a potentially detrimental effect. The speed effect shows that not all influential factors

48

have a beneficial effect on average total ship loss. LCSs with the speed factor acted too aggressively. They would tend to charge ahead of the CRUDES ships, thus allowing the threat to engage the ESG piecemeal. A smart CO (Commanding Officer) would not do this. More importantly, if using speed is detrimental to force effectiveness, then this tactical capability would be worthless. The other factors in bold are significant, but the aforementioned factors provide the most significant influence on average ship loss.

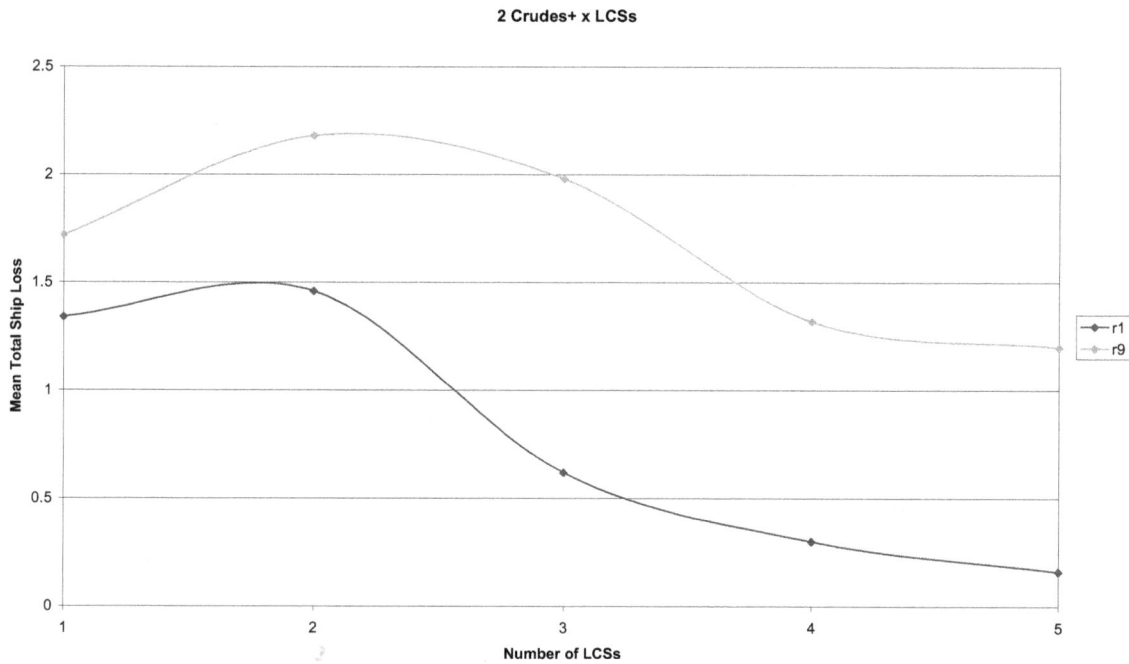

Figure 7    2 CRUDES + X LCS, Ship Loss vs. Number of LCS, r1 and r9

### c.    1 CRUDES

The 1 CRUDES set only has a single organic land attack missile shooter and naval fire support system, for amphibious operations, but has the flexibility to have the amphibious aircraft carrier or the CRUDES ship as the strike group command and control platform. The 1 CRUDES set also has the benefits of LCS. The summary of the 1 CRUDES data is displayed in Appendix B (Data Groups for Analysis). A graph of the average total ship loss vs. number of LCS, separated by run-set, is shown in Figure 8. Like the 2 CRUDES display, the 1 CRUDES display shows, with the exception of r0, r4, r8, and r12, that the run-sets improve with additional LCSs. For the main effects in Figure 9, helo/UCAV (r1) and stealth (r2) losses shrink with each additional LCS. On

49

the other hand, the baseline (r0), and speed (r8) cases get worse with more LCS ships. The average ship loss for the firepower (r4) case does not seem to change as LCSs are added.

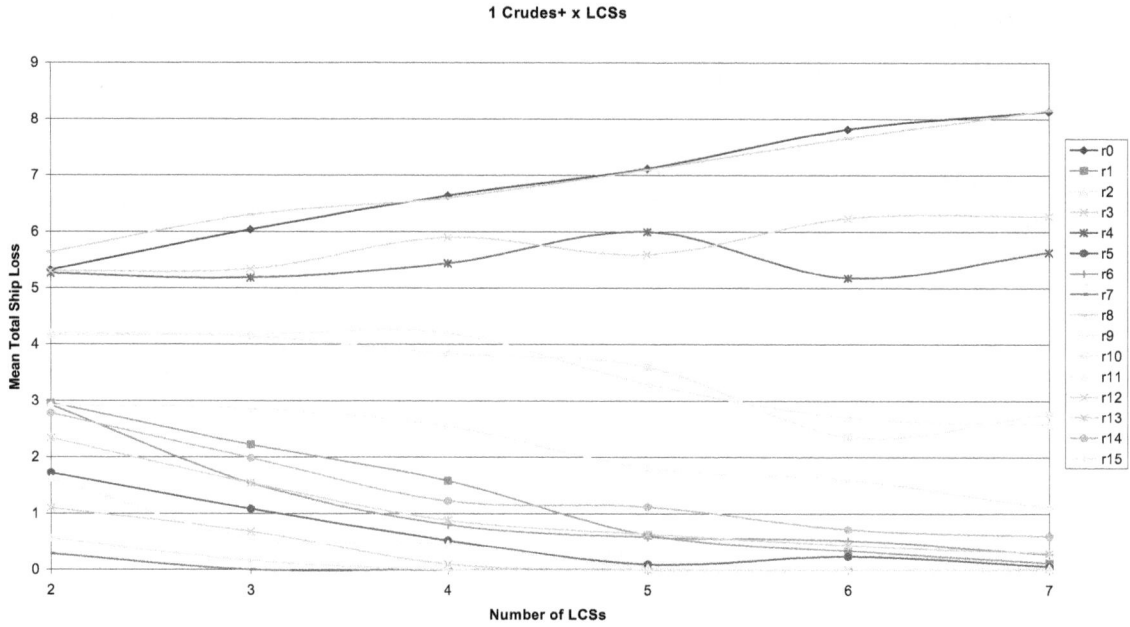

Figure 8    1 CRUDES + X LCS, Ship Loss vs. Number of LCS

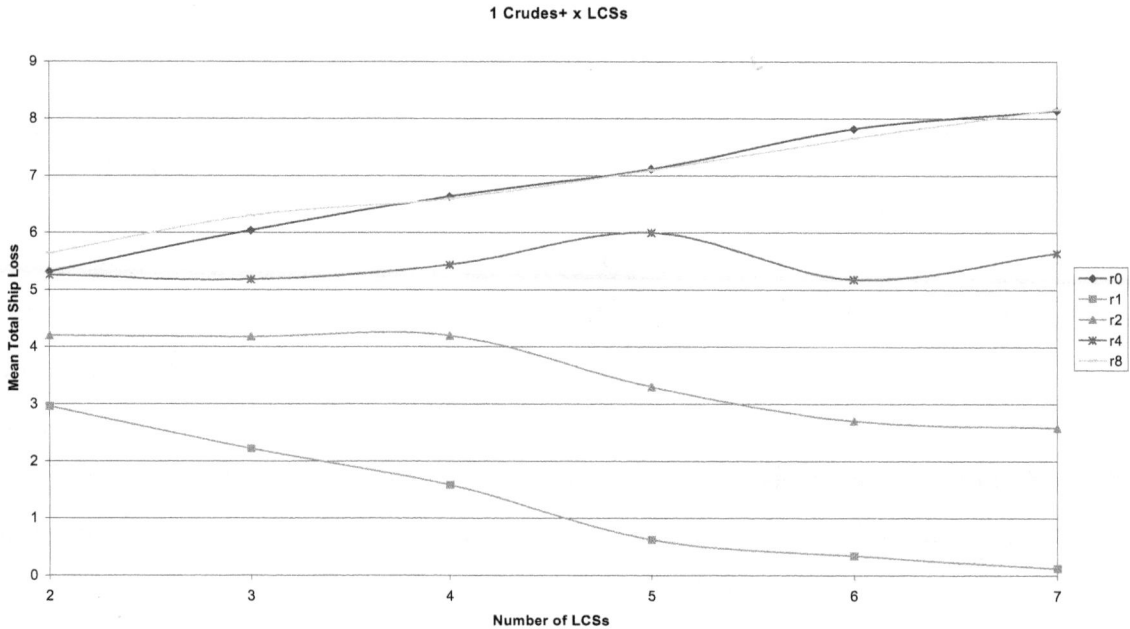

Figure 9    1 CRUDES + X LCS, Ship Loss vs. Number of LCS, Main Factors Only

The ANOVA of the performance for the 1 CRUDES ESG is summarized in 0. Like with the ANOVA model chosen for the 2 CRUDES set, there are sufficient residuals to use to check this chosen model. The residual MSE for this model, 0.0724, is better (smaller) than the ANOVA model using the same function with only three-way interactions, which has a residual MSE 0.1137. The chosen model has only a slightly worse residual MSE than the ANOVA model using the same function with up to four-way interactions, which has a residual MSE of 0.0648. However, the chosen model is better when it comes to allowing for variability (number of residuals). The chosen ANOVA model has 21 residuals for comparison to the function while the ANOVA model with up to four-way interactions only has 5 residuals. In a step-wise approach, analysis shows that the interaction of number of LCSs, the helo/UCAV factor, stealth, and firepower yields a P-value of 0.0108198, showing a significant effect on average ship loss. Additionally, the model passes the residual plot check. The residual plot, which is displayed in Appendix D, shows a homoscedastic and normal distribution about zero.

| | Df | Sum of Sq | Mean Sq | F Value | Pr(F) |
|---|---|---|---|---|---|
| **LCS.f** | 5 | 8.3928 | 1.6786 | 23.192 | 0.0000001 |
| **HELO** | 1 | 304.0240 | 304.0240 | 4200.516 | 0.0000000 |
| **STEALTH** | 1 | 144.3542 | 144.3542 | 1994.454 | 0.0000000 |
| **FIREPOWER** | 1 | 33.3233 | 33.3233 | 460.407 | 0.0000000 |
| **SPEED** | 1 | 1.6224 | 1.6224 | 22.416 | 0.0001124 |
| **LCS.f:HELO** | 5 | 4.9900 | 0.9980 | 13.789 | 0.0000049 |
| **LCS.f:STEALTH** | 5 | 4.2129 | 0.8426 | 11.641 | 0.0000177 |
| LCS.f:FIREPOWER | 5 | 0.6875 | 0.1375 | 1.900 | 0.1372766 |
| LCS.f:SPEED | 5 | 0.0265 | 0.0053 | 0.073 | 0.9956677 |
| **HELO:STEALTH** | 1 | 48.0534 | 48.0534 | 663.925 | 0.0000000 |
| **HELO:FIREPOWER** | 1 | 8.0042 | 8.0042 | 110.589 | 0.0000000 |
| HELO:SPEED | 1 | 0.2440 | 0.2440 | 3.371 | 0.0805358 |
| STEALTH:FIREPOWER | 1 | 0.2204 | 0.2204 | 3.045 | 0.0955858 |
| **STEALTH:SPEED** | 1 | 0.5104 | 0.5104 | 7.052 | 0.0147939 |
| FIREPOWER:SPEED | 1 | 0.0054 | 0.0054 | 0.075 | 0.7874095 |
| **LCS.f:HELO:STEALTH** | 5 | 17.9690 | 3.5938 | 49.654 | 0.0000000 |
| **LCS.f:HELO:FIREPOWER** | 5 | 2.9450 | 0.5890 | 8.138 | 0.0002114 |
| LCS.f:HELO:SPEED | 5 | 0.0856 | 0.0171 | 0.237 | 0.9418963 |
| LCS.f:STEALTH:FIREPOWER | 5 | 0.7443 | 0.1489 | 2.057 | 0.1117734 |
| LCS.f:STEALTH:SPEED | 5 | 0.1950 | 0.0390 | 0.539 | 0.7446132 |
| LCS.f:FIREPOWER:SPEED | 5 | 0.0881 | 0.0176 | 0.244 | 0.9384032 |
| **HELO:STEALTH:FIREPOWER** | 1 | 3.7446 | 3.7446 | 51.737 | 0.0000004 |
| **HELO:STEALTH:SPEED** | 1 | 0.2904 | 0.2904 | 4.012 | 0.0582456 |
| **HELO:FIREPOWER:SPEED** | 1 | 0.4538 | 0.4538 | 6.269 | 0.0206068 |
| STEALTH:FIREPOWER:SPEED | 1 | 0.0748 | 0.0748 | 1.034 | 0.3208633 |
| **LCS.f:HELO:STEALTH:FIREPOWER** | 5 | 1.4373 | 0.2875 | 3.972 | 0.0108198 |
| Residuals | 21 | 1.5199 | 0.0724 | | |

Table 14    ANOVA of the 1 CRUDES Set's Total Ship Losses, Including Up to 3-Way Interactions + # LCSs*helo/UCAV*stealth*firepower

Again, the null hypothesis is that a design factor or interaction makes no difference on average ship loss. The probability of observing the results in this study, were the null hypothesis true, Pr(F), is almost zero for all the main effects and several interactions highlighted in bold in Table 14. Next, the explained variance, "Sum of Sq" column, provides insight into which factors are more influential (cause variation in the response) on force performance. Preasence of helo/UCAVs is more than twice as influential than the next largest, which is stealth. Helo/UCAVs remain the most influential factor when it comes minimizing ship losses. The plots in Appendix D show that the presence of helo/UCAVs leads to lower average ship loss, including displays that isolate the helo/UCAV factor.

As in the 2 CRUDES group, the next most influential single factor is again stealth. Stealth's SS is more than three times greater than the next largest term, helo/UCAV's interaction with stealth. Not only is stealth significant, it has a beneficial effect on minimizing ship loss. The fact that helo/UCAVs interaction with stealth is the next most influential term shows that having both helo/UCAVs and stealth makes an ESG well defended. Again, firepower comes in fourth for influence and it has a positive influence. The interaction of number of LCSs, helo/UCAVs, and stealth makes a decent showing for influence. These factors provide the most significant influence on force performance.

### d. 0 CRUDES

The 0 CRUDES set has no organic Tomahawk missiles or organic naval gunfire systems for amphibious operations. However, a fleet commander has greater flexibility in employing CRUDES ships, which includes assigning them on demand to launch land attack missiles or provide naval fire support for amphibious operations. The amphibious aircraft carrier is the only major strike group command and control platform in the ESG. The 0 CRUDES data is displayed in Appendix B (Data Groups for Analysis).

A graph of the average total ship loss vs. number of LCS, separated by run-set, is shown in Figure 10. Like the 2 and 1 CRUDES displays, the 0 CRUDES display shows, with the exception of r0, r4, r8, and r12, that the run-sets get better with each added LCS. Speed and firepower are not good options by themselves. Also,

52

looking at the main effects in Figure 11, helo/UCAV (r1) and stealth (r2) diminish losses with each additional LCS. On the other hand, the baseline (r0), speed (r8), and now firepower (4) cases get worse as LCSs are added. Simply stated, more ships with these capabilities are more targets that can be lost.

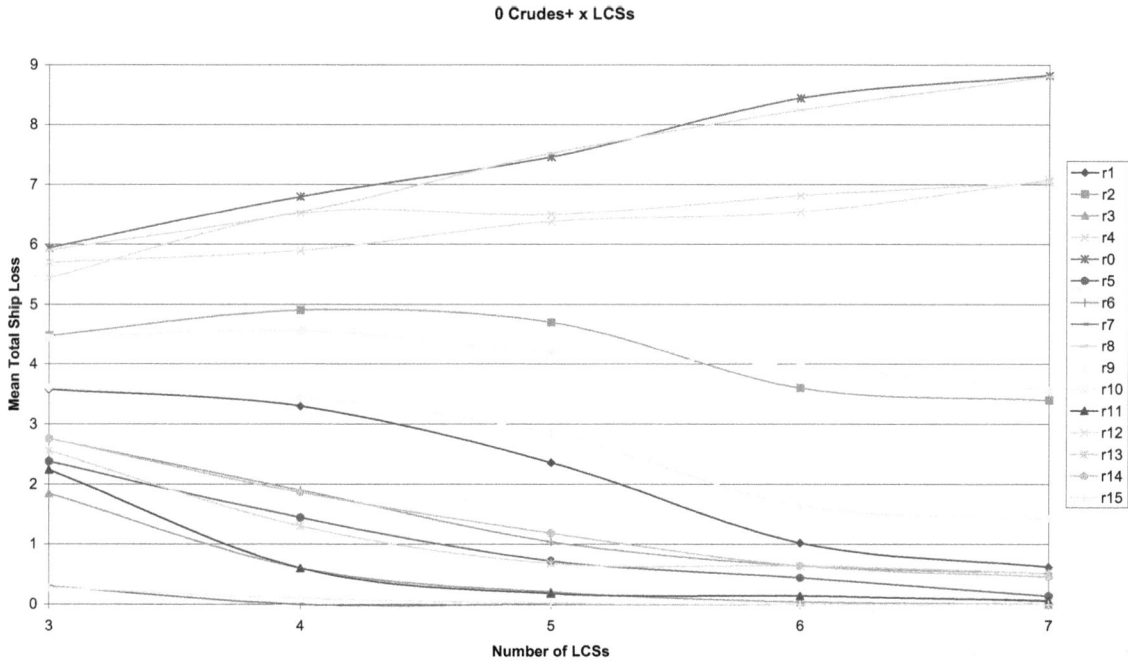

Figure 10    0 CRUDES + X LCS, Ship Loss vs. Number of LCS

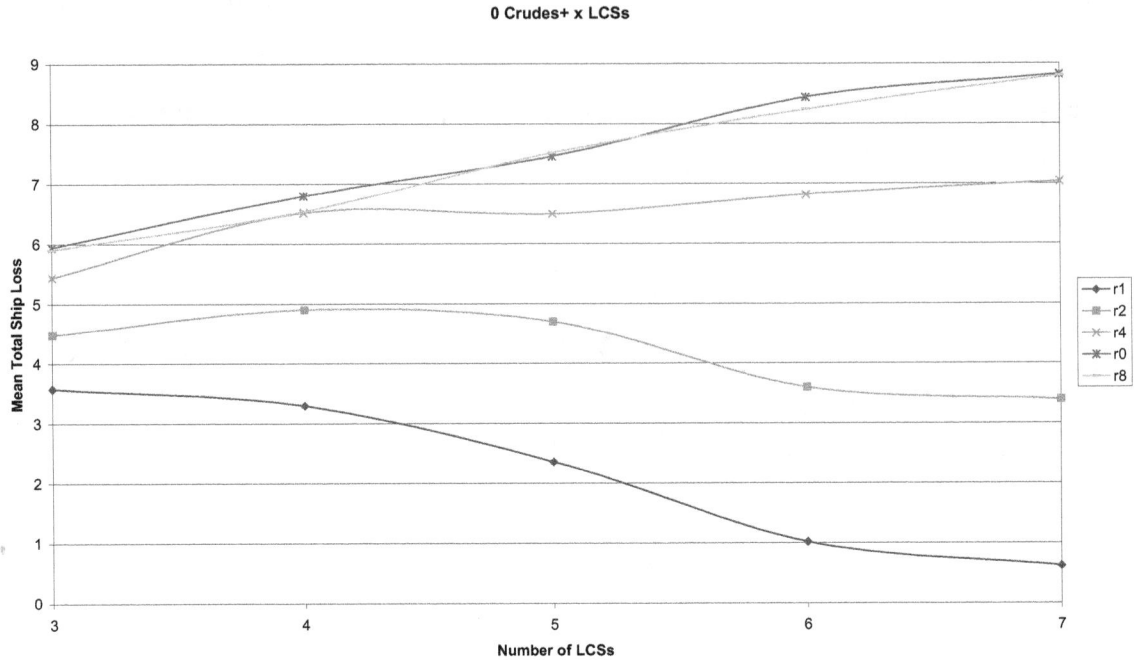

Figure 11    0 CRUDES + X LCS, Ship Loss vs. Number of LCS, Main Factors Only

Like the 1 CRUDES set's ANOVA model, the 0 CRUDES set's ANOVA model of force performance is a function of number of LCSs and the four LCS factors, with interactions, in 0. This model has sufficient residuals to check model adequacy. By including the four-way interaction, the unexplained variance in this model is 20% of that for the model with only three-way interactions. The chosen ANOVA model has a slightly worse residual MSE than the ANOVA model using the same function with up to four-way interactions, but it has seventeen residuals for comparison, as opposed to the model with up to four-way interactions which has only has four residuals. The interaction of number of LCSs, the helo/UCAV factor, stealth, and firepower has a P-value, Pr(F), close to zero. Again, the residuals comply with the normality and homoscedasticity assumptions, as shown in Appendix D.

| | Df | Sum of Sq | Mean Sq | F Value | Pr(F) |
|---|---|---|---|---|---|
| **LCS.f** | **4** | **6.1828** | **1.5457** | **57.84** | **0.0000000** |
| **HELO** | **1** | **291.4661** | **291.4661** | **10907.08** | **0.0000000** |
| **STEALTH** | **1** | **153.6242** | **153.6242** | **5748.84** | **0.0000000** |
| **FIREPOWER** | **1** | **40.2996** | **40.2996** | **1508.07** | **0.0000000** |
| SPEED | 1 | 0.0396 | 0.0396 | 1.48 | 0.2400798 |
| **LCS.f:HELO** | **4** | **10.3625** | **2.5906** | **96.94** | **0.0000000** |
| **LCS.f:STEALTH** | **4** | **4.1066** | **1.0266** | **38.42** | **0.0000000** |
| **LCS.f:FIREPOWER** | **4** | **0.3206** | **0.0802** | **3.00** | **0.0482526** |
| LCS.f:SPEED | 4 | 0.2362 | 0.0591 | 2.21 | 0.1112523 |
| **HELO:STEALTH** | **1** | **37.5106** | **37.5106** | **1403.70** | **0.0000000** |
| **HELO:FIREPOWER** | **1** | **5.1918** | **5.1918** | **194.28** | **0.0000000** |
| **HELO:SPEED** | **1** | **0.2856** | **0.2856** | **10.69** | **0.0045207** |
| **STEALTH:FIREPOWER** | **1** | **1.1761** | **1.1761** | **44.01** | **0.0000042** |
| STEALTH:SPEED | 1 | 0.0162 | 0.0162 | 0.61 | 0.4462951 |
| FIREPOWER:SPEED | 1 | 0.0396 | 0.0396 | 1.48 | 0.2400798 |
| **LCS.f:HELO:STEALTH** | **4** | **18.1258** | **4.5315** | **169.57** | **0.0000000** |
| **LCS.f:HELO:FIREPOWER** | **4** | **4.3364** | **1.0841** | **40.57** | **0.0000000** |
| LCS.f:HELO:SPEED | 4 | 0.0322 | 0.0081 | 0.30 | 0.8729508 |
| **LCS.f:STEALTH:FIREPOWER** | **4** | **0.3423** | **0.0856** | **3.20** | **0.0393104** |
| LCS.f:STEALTH:SPEED | 4 | 0.1094 | 0.0273 | 1.02 | 0.4234147 |
| LCS.f:FIREPOWER:SPEED | 4 | 0.0476 | 0.0119 | 0.45 | 0.7741740 |
| **HELO:STEALTH:FIREPOWER** | **1** | **8.0011** | **8.0011** | **299.41** | **0.0000000** |
| HELO:STEALTH:SPEED | 1 | 0.1022 | 0.1022 | 3.83 | 0.0670954 |
| HELO:FIREPOWER:SPEED | 1 | 0.0530 | 0.0530 | 1.99 | 0.1768911 |
| STEALTH:FIREPOWER:SPEED | 1 | 0.0361 | 0.0361 | 1.35 | 0.2610174 |
| **LCS.f:HELO:STEALTH:FIREPOWER** | **4** | **1.9255** | **0.4814** | **18.01** | **0.0000061** |
| Residuals | 17 | 0.4543 | 0.0267 | | |

Table 15     ANOVA of the 0 CRUDES Set's Total Ship Losses, Including up to 3-Way Interactions + # LCSs*helo/UCAV*stealth*firepower

All significant factors are in bold in the ANOVA summary table. All main effects (with the exception of speed), without any interactions, influence ship loss. Helo/UCAV capability is almost two times more influential than the next factor, stealth. So again, Helo/UCAV is the most influential factor when it comes to ship losses. Figure 12 compares r4 (firepower) to r5 (helo/UCAV + firepower) and the other graphical comparisons in Appendix D show that helo/UCAVs lower the average number of ships lost. Graphs that display similar comparisons isolating the helo/UCAV factor are in Appendix D.

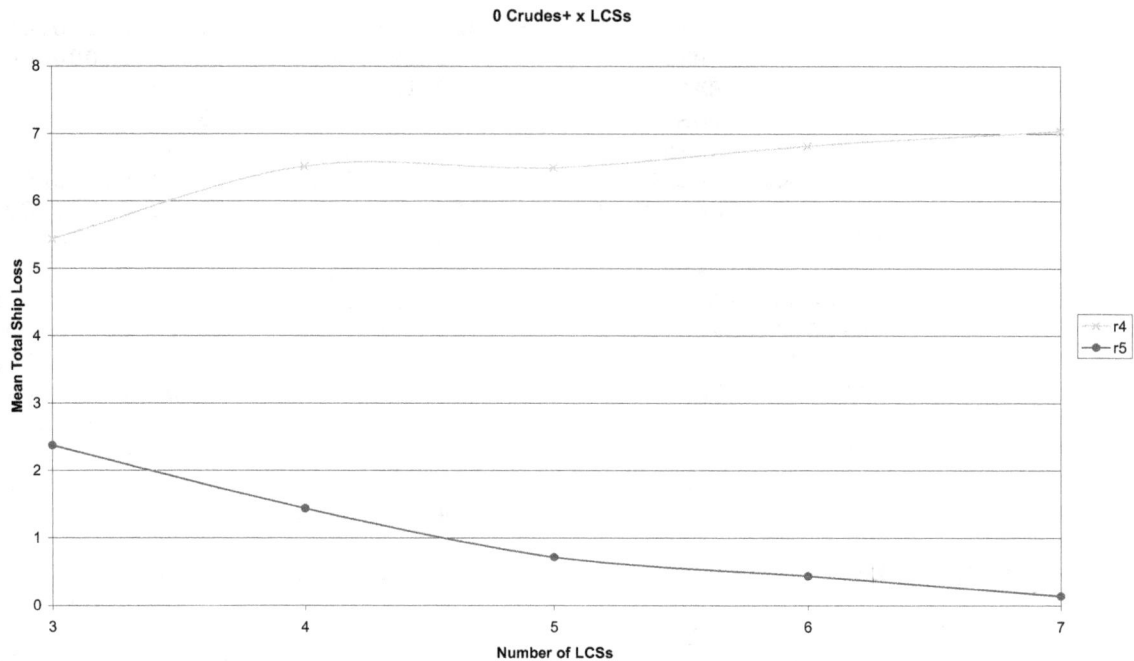

0 Crudes+ x LCSs

Figure 12    0 CRUDES + X LCS, Ship Loss vs. Number of LCS, r4 and r5

Again, the next most influential factor is stealth. Stealth is more than three times greater than the third largest factor, firepower. Stealth is also very significant, and looking at graphical comparisons in Appendix D we see that stealth has a beneficial effect on ship loss. Firepower is the third most influential factor on average ship loss and it has a positive influence. The helo/UCAV interaction with stealth comes in a close fourth and is almost two times greater than the next most influential term, the interaction of numbers of LCSs, helo/UCAV, and stealth. These factors provide the most significant influence on average ship loss.

## D.    KEY FINDINGS

Across the board helo/UCAV is the most significant factor in reducing ship losses, and the baseline, firepower alone, speed alone, and firepower with speed are not good options to choose. When LCSs are involved, stealth is also very significant in reducing ship losses. Having both air assets and stealth design prove beneficial in reducing ship losses. Firepower is influential when designed with helo/UCAVs or stealth. Figure 13 shows that r6 (stealth + firepower) performs substantially better than r2 (stealth).

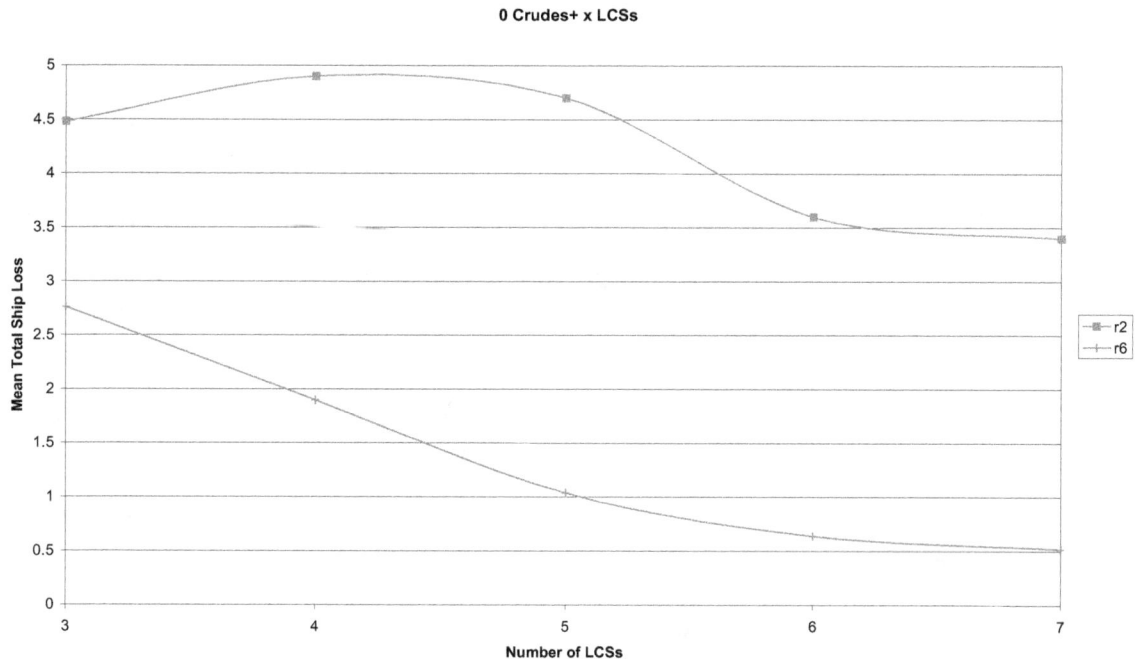

Figure 13    0 CRUDES + X LCS, Ship Loss vs. Number of LCS, r2 and r6

## 1.    Best Performers of Each Set

This thesis set a threshold number that a run-set's average ship loss needs to achieve for the particular run-set can be considered as acceptable. Keeping with the Chief of Naval Operations statement that LCSs were not going to be expendable, the threshold is set so that average losses has to be less than or equal to one ship.[43] The only run-set that met that requirement in the 3 CRUDES set is 3 CRUDES-r1—i.e., with helo/UCAVs. The run-sets of the 2 CRUDES set that met this requirement are displayed in Figure 14. Figure 15 displays the run-sets in the 1 CRUDES set that met the requirement. The run-sets from the 0 CRUDES set that reduced losses to less than one ship are shown in Figure 16. Run-sets r1 (helo/UCAV), r3 (helo/UCAV + stealth), r5 (helo/UCAV + firepower), r6 (stealth + firepower), r7 (helo/UCAV, stealth and firepower), r11 (helo/UCAV, stealth and speed), r13 (helo/UCAV, firepower and speed), and r15 (helo/UCAV, stealth, firepower and speed) beat the threshold at some point (i.e., with enough LCSs) for the 2-0 CRUDES sets. Run-set r14 (stealth, firepower and speed)

---

43 Marty Kauchak, "Navigating Changing Seas: Navy Chief Harbors No Illusions About the Challenges that Lie Ahead," *Armed Forces Journal International* (August 2002): 4. Available on the World Wide Web @ http://www.afji.com/AFJI/Mags/2002/August/navigating_4.html. Accessed 24 September 2003.

was one of the best for the 1 and 0 CRUDES sets.  Additionally, looking at the graphs, it seems no matter the number of CRUDES ships the "knee" of the curve seems to exist somewhere between five and seven total platforms protecting the three amphibious ships. This means if the ESG has 2 CRUDES ships, a commander should probably add three to five LCSs, with the capabilities that make it one of the best, for a well-protected ESG— i.e. the sum of CRUDES ships and LCSs should equal between five and seven.

Using the best performing run-set r7, this study examined force structures of 1 CRUDES + 1 LCS and 2 LCSs defending ESG and the data is displayed in Appendix A (Data).  The average ship loss is 1.54 and 0.94, respectively; meaning one of fewer protecting platforms could be available after such an engagement.  Considering the ESG requires defense once it has reached its objective, 1 CRUDES + 1 LCS, 2 LCSs and 1 LCS would not be an effective defense for ESG in this scenario.  This section's key findings lead to other interesting conclusions, discussed in Chapter V.

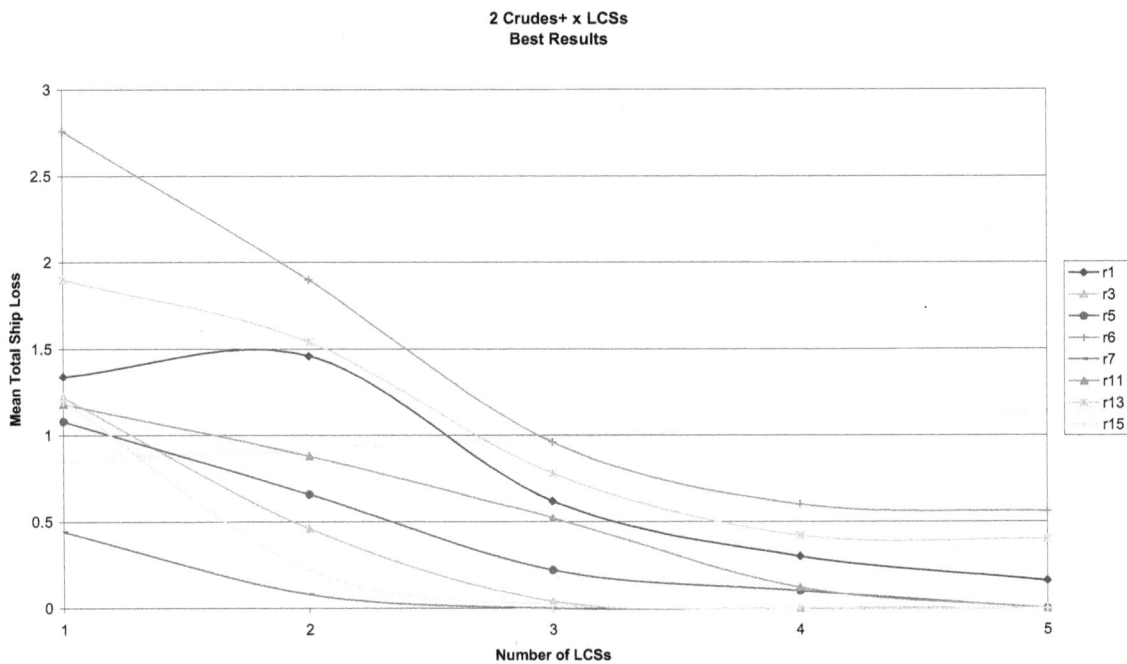

Figure 14    Best of 2 CRUDES + X LCSs

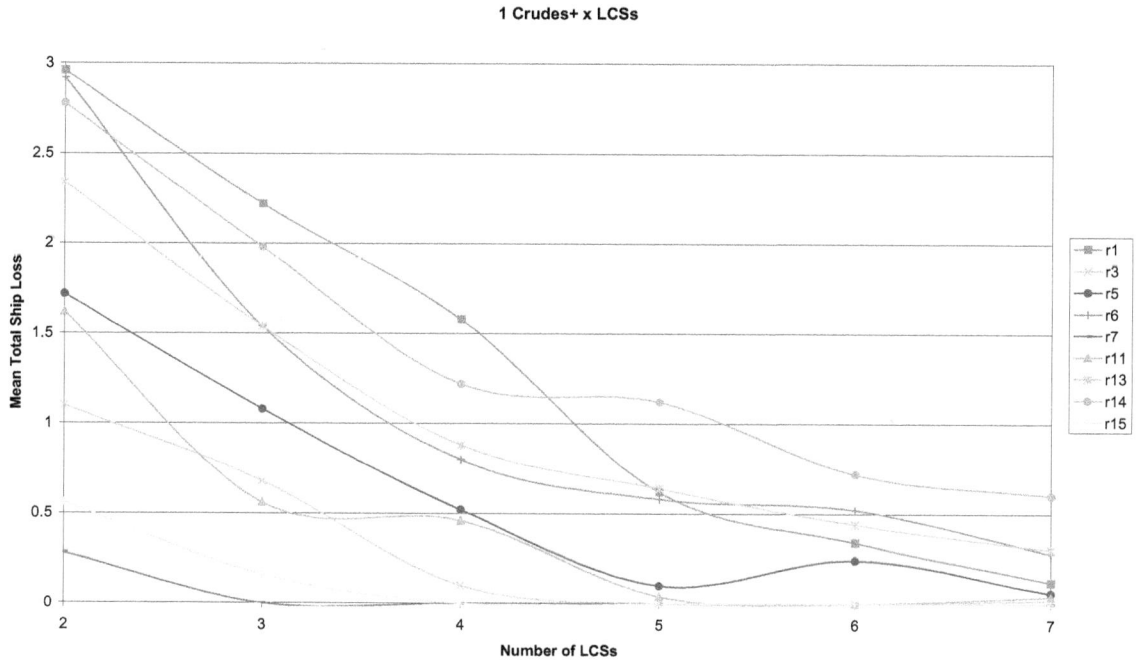

Figure 15    Best of 1 CRUDES + X LCSs

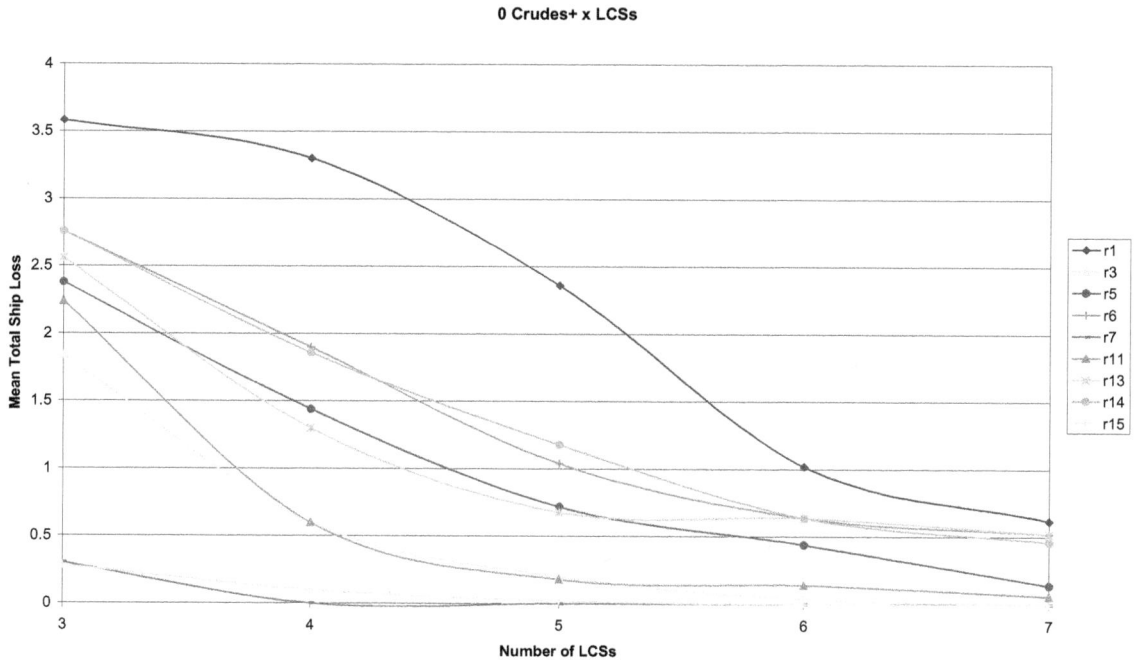

Figure 16    Best of 0 CRUDES + X LCS

THIS PAGE INTENTIONALLY LEFT BLANK

# V. CONCLUSIONS AND FUTURE STUDIES

## A. INTRODUCTION

This chapter discusses conclusions, makes recommendations, and talks about potential future studies. The conclusions and recommendations section discusses conclusions made from the analysis and comes up with recommendations on LCS (Littoral Combat Ship) numbers and capabilities to successfully protect ESGs (Expeditionary Strike Groups) against a high-density small boat attack. The future studies section discusses possible additional studies examining LCS possibilities.

## B. CONCLUSIONS AND RECOMMENDATIONS

When designing a new class of ship, such as the Littoral Combat Ship, many options must be considered. Before metal is bent, decisions must be made about what capabilities are required. This study uses the EINSTein simulation to explore the potential effectiveness of various force mixes and LCS capabilities to protect an ESG. Before summarizing our conclusions and recommendations it is important to emphasize that these findings are based on an exploratory analysis with a relatively simple and highly abstract model. The numbers, characteristics and tactics of the enemy were fixed. Therefore, the results should be viewed as tentative working hypotheses that should be tested with other means—perhaps more detailed models.

This study's primary finding is that a helo/UCAV (helicopters/Unmanned Combat Aerial Vehicle) capability is consistently the most significant factor in reducing ship losses in this scenario. All run-sets with the helo/UCAV factor enabled, except for r9 (helo/UCAV and speed), decreased the average number of ships lost to less than one. These findings are consistent with the U.S. Navy's decision to design the initial block of LCS with the capability to employ and support an organic helicopter.

The combination of both helo/UCAV and stealth factors achieved average ship losses for ESG ships below 1.0, given at least four protecting platforms (CRUDES + LCS), below 0.5, given at least five protecting platforms, and almost no losses, given seven protecting platforms. These outcomes merit strong consideration that LCS should probably have both the capability to control a helo/UCAV and a stealthy hull. Designing

LCS with a helicopter hangar or UCAV maintenance facilities might offset the effects of building a stealthy hull. Equipping LCS with only control capabilities would allow for a more compact and stealthier LCS hull form, while reaping the benefits of armed air support for maritime missions, if a larger platform, like the amphibious carrier or a CRUDES ship, could be charged with the duties of providing logistic support for the helo/UCAVs. Such an approach would enable LCS's weight, space and crew to be used for other purposes.

Close-in high volume firepower does not appear to add as much capability as the helo/UCAV and stealth factors. However, combining it with helo/UCAVs or stealth lowers average ship losses to below 1. If program officers are forced to choose either helo/UCAV or stealth (no combination of the two) designs, this study recommends purchasing the helo/UCAV and firepower for LCSs.

As modeled in this study, and if not used wisely, tactical speed is a potential liability to LCS protection of the ESG. In all the cases with a high-speed design, force effectiveness is worse than when it is not enabled. Smart Commanding Officers would not tend to leave the mutual defense of the ESG, and this study could have used a meta-rule to model this behavior. Why introduce speed when it is unwise to use it? When LCS operates within the strike group, defending against attackers, enhanced speed is no factor due to stationing requirements of remaining in a smaller area and staying with slower ships. Also, the other factors would most likely add weight to LCS, increasing the cost to have the high-speed ability, so speed is not a recommended capability.

Although the 0 CRUDES set has good results for ESG defense in this study, tactical experience dictates that ship force mixtures should have at least one CRUDES ship to defend the force. At least one CRUDES platform enhances ESG air defense capabilities, enables greater flexibility in support of amphibious operations, improves command and control, contributes land attack capability, and provides naval surface fire support. Only in the most permissive tactical scenario does a 0 CRUDES alternative make sense, and force planners cannot assume this to be the case.

## C. FUTURE STUDIES

### 1. Defending an ESG Sea-Base

When ESGs arrive in a theater, they may perform amphibious operations without establishing an "iron mountain" ashore. During this sea-to-objective maneuver (STOM), the force establishes a sea-base to provide logistical support for forces ashore. To maintain a reliable tether and preserve the flow of supplies and support, the force maintains station in a limited maneuvering area. This presents a vulnerability in need of defense. The same threat used in this thesis is a viable scenario for an ESG providing a sea-base, making it a reasonable focus of analysis in EINSTein. A tentative set of personalities for such a study is listed in Table 1, see also the scenario described by Figure 1. Ship force structures and LCS capabilities can be explored in a similar fashion to this study to find beneficial alternatives.

| | In Theater Personalities | | | | | | | | | | | |
|---|---|---|---|---|---|---|---|---|---|---|---|---|
| | When Alive | | | | | | When Injured | | | | | |
| Squad | To alv friend | To alv enemy | To inj friend | To inj enemy | To friend flag | To enemy flag | To alv friend | To alv enemy | To inj friend | To inj enemy | To friend flag | To enemy flag |
| Amphibs | 33 | | 33 | | 33 | | 33 | | 33 | | 33 | |
| CRUDES | 30 | 30 | | 40 | | | 30 | 20 | 20 | 30 | | |
| LCS | 15 | 25 | 20 | 40 | | | 25 | 15 | 25 | 35 | | |
| Helo/UCAV | 15 | 20 | 15 | 40 | | | 25 | 20 | 25 | 30 | | |

Table 16    Blue Agent In Theater Personalities

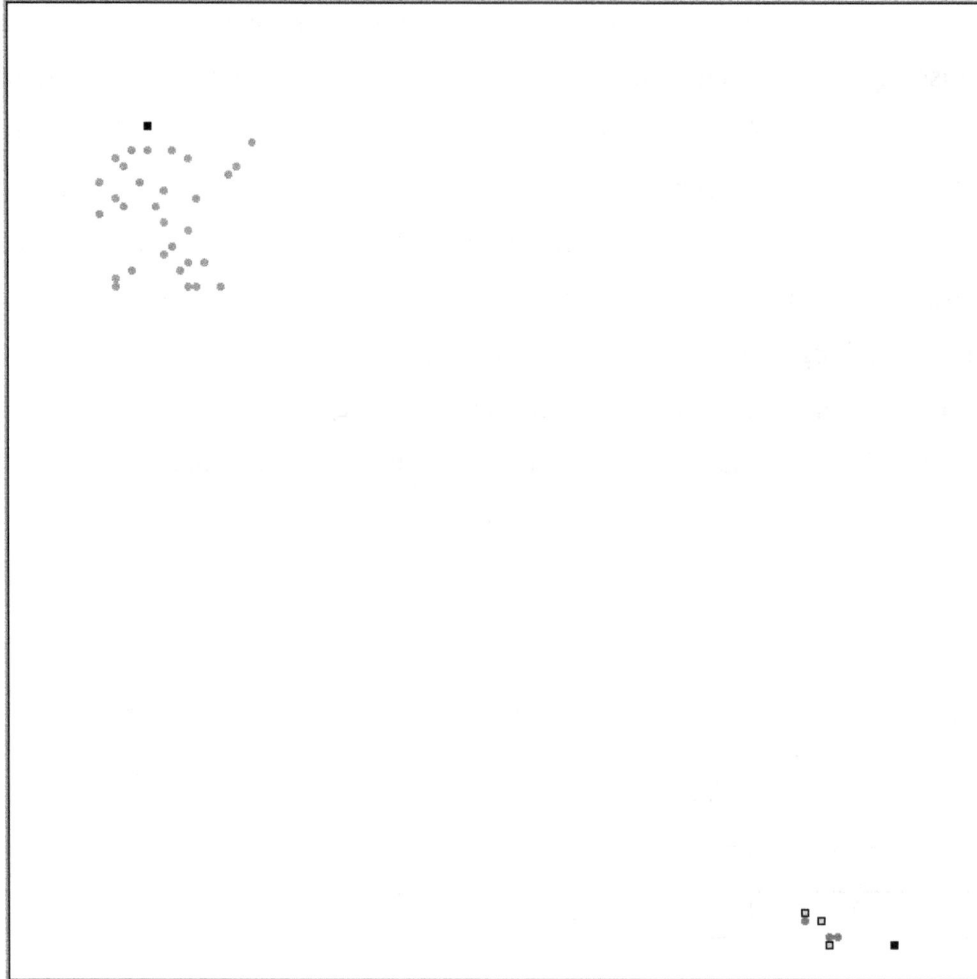

Figure 17    In Theater Battlefield

## 2.    LCS Modularity

LCS modularity is another issue that needs to be explored.  LCSs are perceived to have modularity, meaning that part of the vessel will be able to be switched when different missions are required.  One module can best suit LCS for defense against a surface threat like that explored here.  Other modules outfit LCS with ASW (Anti-Submarine Warfare), MIW (Mine Warfare), or possibly AW (Air Warfare) capabilities.  All of these capabilities should be explored in viable scenarios to find what specific capabilities would help LCS defend an ESG or CSG (Carrier Strike Group) against submarine, mine or air threats.

## 3.    LCS Acquisition and Deployment in the Fleet

As with all new combat systems, the acquisition process can be quite lengthy—with many milestones.  Networks, linear programming and non-linear programming models can help the U.S. Navy acquire LCS in an efficient manner. CPM (Critical Path Management) models show tasks that can delay acquisition if these tasks are not completed on time. Also, CPM helps create a well-organized schedule. Networks, linear programming and non-linear programming models can also help the U.S. Navy deploy newly acquired LCSs to where they are needed and arrange deployment schedules so that fleet requirements are met while minimizing crew deployment time.

### 4.    Logistics

Many agent-based models like EINSTein and its predecessor, ISAAC, focus purely on combat. Other agent-based models include logistical aspects that can be explored in future studies. Some of these studies could explore the viability of using LCSs to protect landing craft providing logistical support for troops ashore. Other studies could examine the logistical limits of operating LCS.

## D.    CONCLUDING REMARKS

As discussed, EINSTein is an abstraction of fleet tactical warfare and requires a fair amount of discussion to draw the connection between agent activity and shipboard operations. Nevertheless, its depiction of the effects of design considerations rings plausible for this scenario. A properly designed experimental study accounted for individual factors and interactions. It yielded results that enable analytical approaches, warfare designs and alternatives to be compared. This research provides a quantitative basis for further, higher resolution studies that should consider the measurable benefits of air capability and stealth and the relative ineffectiveness of tactical speed for this new littoral combatant ship.

THIS PAGE INTENTIONALLY LEFT BLANK

# APPENDIX A.  DATA

## A.  INTRODUCTION

This appendix displays all the raw data observations from the EINSTein simulation runs.  The data is categorized by the ESG's ship disposition and particular run-set (group of factors) used.  The initial numbers of amphibious ships, CRUDES ships, LCSs and helo (helo/UCAVs) are shown at the top.  The table is then divided into (from left to right) a reference column explaining what information is displayed in the row of the reference; alive (undamaged) amphibious ships' column; injured (damaged) amphibious ships' column; total surviving (undamaged + damaged) amphibious ships' column; alive (undamaged) CRUDES ships' column; injured (damaged) CRUDES ships' column; total surviving (undamaged + damaged) CRUDES ships' column; alive (undamaged) LCSs' column; injured (damaged) LCSs' column; total surviving (undamaged + damaged) LCSs' column; alive (undamaged) helo/UCAVs' column; injured (damaged) helo/UCAVs' column; and total surviving (undamaged + damaged) helo/UCAVs' column. The exception to this is the sample mean (xbar), calculated for the number of injured platforms associated with that column, and the average, calculated for the total number of lost (destroyed) platforms associated with the particular column.

## B.  DATA

# NAVAL
# POSTGRADUATE
# SCHOOL

## MONTEREY, CALIFORNIA

# THESIS

**SECURITY ENHANCEMENT OF LITTORAL COMBAT
SHIP CLASS UTILIZING AN AUTONOMOUS
MUSTERING AND PIER MONITORING SYSTEM**

by

Philip Stubblefield

March 2010

| | |
|---|---|
| Thesis Advisors: | Rachel Goshorn |
| | Deborah Goshorn |
| Second Reader: | Mark Stevens |

**Approved for public release; distribution is unlimited**

THIS PAGE INTENTIONALLY LEFT BLANK

| REPORT DOCUMENTATION PAGE | | *Form Approved OMB No. 0704-0188* |
|---|---|---|

Public reporting burden for this collection of information is estimated to average 1 hour per response, including the time for reviewing instruction, searching existing data sources, gathering and maintaining the data needed, and completing and reviewing the collection of information. Send comments regarding this burden estimate or any other aspect of this collection of information, including suggestions for reducing this burden, to Washington headquarters Services, Directorate for Information Operations and Reports, 1215 Jefferson Davis Highway, Suite 1204, Arlington, VA 22202-4302, and to the Office of Management and Budget, Paperwork Reduction Project (0704-0188) Washington DC 20503.

| 1. AGENCY USE ONLY *(Leave blank)* | 2. REPORT DATE March 2010 | 3. REPORT TYPE AND DATES COVERED Master's Thesis | |
|---|---|---|---|
| 4. TITLE AND SUBTITLE Security Enhancement of Littoral Combat Ship Class Utilizing an Autonomous Mustering and Pier Monitoring System | | 5. FUNDING NUMBERS | |
| 6. AUTHOR(S) Stubblefield, Philip N | | | |
| 7. PERFORMING ORGANIZATION NAME(S) AND ADDRESS(ES) Naval Postgraduate School Monterey, CA 93943-5000 | | 8. PERFORMING ORGANIZATION REPORT NUMBER | |
| 9. SPONSORING /MONITORING AGENCY NAME(S) AND ADDRESS(ES) N/A | | 10. SPONSORING/MONITORING AGENCY REPORT NUMBER | |

| 11. SUPPLEMENTARY NOTES The views expressed in this thesis are those of the author and do not reflect the official policy or position of the Department of Defense or the U.S. Government. . IRB Protocol number . |
|---|

| 12a. DISTRIBUTION / AVAILABILITY STATEMENT Approved for public release; distribution is unlimited | 12b. DISTRIBUTION CODE |
|---|---|

**13. ABSTRACT (maximum 200 words)**

Littoral Combat Ships (LCS) are designed and built to have minimum crew sizes thus, while the ship is in port, there are fewer crewmembers to facilitate pier monitoring, security, and conducting mustering of personnel. The crew of LCS ships presently have too many responsibilities to ensure 100% coverage of the Pier area 100% of the time, and cannot manually maintain a real time muster of all ships personnel. This lack of coverage and situational awareness could make LCS ships vulnerable to terrorist attacks or terrorist monitoring.

This thesis addresses the capability gap for complete and automated personnel mustering and situational awareness in the pier area for LCS class ships. Through applying the Systems Engineering process, the concept, external systems diagram, requirements, and functional architectures for a generic solution are proposed. The proposed solution is an autonomous system utilizing facial recognition software to maintain a muster of the ship's crew, while in parallel monitoring the pier area, looking for any known person of interest (e.g., terrorists) and providing appropriate alerts.

Additionally, this thesis provides a demonstrable proof-of-concept prototype system solution, named Pier Watchman. Its instantiated physical architecture of a specific autonomous solution to pier monitoring and personnel mustering is provided.

| 14. SUBJECT TERMS Systems Engineering, Facial Recognition, Force Protection, Pier Security, Mustering | 15. NUMBER OF PAGES 115 |
|---|---|
| | 16. PRICE CODE |

| 17. SECURITY CLASSIFICATION OF REPORT Unclassified | 18. SECURITY CLASSIFICATION OF THIS PAGE Unclassified | 19. SECURITY CLASSIFICATION OF ABSTRACT Unclassified | 20. LIMITATION OF ABSTRACT UU |
|---|---|---|---|

NSN 7540-01-280-5500

Standard Form 298 (Rev. 2-89)
Prescribed by ANSI Std. 239-18

i

THIS PAGE INTENTIONALLY LEFT BLANK

# SECURITY ENHANCEMENT OF LITTORAL COMBAT SHIP CLASS UTILIZING AN AUTONOMOUS MUSTERING AND PIER MONITORING SYSTEM

Philip N. Stubblefield
Lieutenant, United States Navy
B.S., Jacksonville University, 2003

Submitted in partial fulfillment of the
requirements for the degree of

**MASTER OF SCIENCE IN SYSTEMS ENGINEERING**

from the

**NAVAL POSTGRADUATE SCHOOL
March 2010**

Author:           Philip Stubblefield

Approved by:      Rachel Goshorn
                      Co-Advisor

                      Deborah Goshorn
                      Co-Advisor

                      Mark Stevens
                      Second Reader

                      Clifford Whitcomb
                      Chairman, Department of Systems Engineering

THIS PAGE INTENTIONALLY LEFT BLANK

# ABSTRACT

Littoral Combat Ships (LCS) are designed and built to have minimum crew sizes thus, while the ship is in port, there are fewer crewmembers to facilitate pier monitoring, security, and conducting mustering of personnel. The crew of LCS ships presently have too many responsibilities to ensure 100% coverage of the Pier area 100% of the time, and cannot manually maintain a real time muster of all ships personnel. This lack of coverage and situational awareness could make LCS ships vulnerable to terrorist attacks or terrorist monitoring.

This thesis addresses the capability gap for complete and automated personnel mustering and situational awareness in the pier area for LCS class ships. Through applying the Systems Engineering process, the concept, external systems diagram, requirements, and functional architectures for a generic solution are proposed. The proposed solution is an autonomous system utilizing facial recognition software to maintain a muster of the ship's crew, while in parallel monitoring the pier area, looking for any known person of interest (e.g., terrorists) and providing appropriate alerts.

Additionally, this thesis provides a demonstrable proof-of-concept prototype system solution, named Pier Watchman. Its instantiated physical architecture of a specific autonomous solution to pier monitoring and personnel mustering is provided.

THIS PAGE INTENTIONALLY LEFT BLANK

# TABLE OF CONTENTS

# LIST OF FIGURES

# LIST OF TABLES

THIS PAGE INTENTIONALLY LEFT BLANK

# LIST OF ACRONYMS AND ABBREVIATIONS

AOA            Analysis of Alternatives

CAT5           Category Five

COAL          Common Operational Activities List

COTS          Commercial Off-the-Shelf

DOD           Department of Defense

DRM           Design Reference Mission

ESD            External Systems Diagram

FOV            Field of View

FTP             File Transfer Protocol

IDEF0         Integrated Definition for Function Modeling

IEEE           Institute of Electrical and Electronics Engineers

JCA            Joint Capability Area

KFP            Known Friendly Person

LAN           Local Area Network

LCS            Littoral Combat Ship

MIT            Massachusetts Institute of Technology

NCSE          Net-Centric Systems Engineering

NTA           Naval Tasks

NTTL          Navy Tactical Task List

OOD           Officer of the Deck

OPSIT         Operational Situation

OV             Operational View

PCA    Principal Component Analysis

PDL    Program Design Language

POE    Projected Operating Environment

POI    Person of Interest

PTZ    Pan Tilt Zoom

SOF    Special Operations Force

UKP    Unknown Person

UJTL    Universal Joint Task List

UMD    University of Maryland

USCG    United States Coast Guard

WMA    Warfighting Mission Area

# EXECUTIVE SUMMARY

The USS Freedom class of Littoral Combat Ships (LCS) are designed and built to have minimum crew sizes. LCS was designed with maximum automation to facilitate this minimum manning concept. The core crew is a compliment of 40 sailors with an additional 35 personnel for the mission package crew (Globalsecurity, 2009). This minimum crew concept means that, while the ship is in port, there are fewer crewmembers to facilitate pier monitoring and maintaining pier security. Additionally, there are fewer sailors to conduct basic duties such as the mustering of personnel. However, the watch standers and personnel for LCS presently have too many responsibilities to ensure 100% coverage of the pier area, 100% of the time, and, thus, they cannot manually maintain a 100% muster of all ship's personnel 100% of the time. This lack of coverage and situational awareness could make LCS ships vulnerable to terrorist attacks or terrorist monitoring.

Using a Systems Engineering approach, this thesis designs and recommends a generalized solution for the problems associated with having a reduced crew size on LCS ships. Initially, this thesis provides a concept, external systems diagram (ESD), requirements, and functional architecture of a generic solution, and then instantiating a real-world physical architecture of an autonomous system that provides real-time, automatic mustering and pier monitoring capability for enhanced situational awareness. The viability of the generic solution is then verified through construction and testing of a proof-of-concept system.

The generic functional architecture designates that the mustering of personnel must be performed while in parallel monitoring the pier area. Additionally, this generic functional architecture requires that the solution maintain a database local to the LCS ship that stores the identity of all personnel in the pier area and onboard the ship. The database will have three sets: known friendly persons (e.g., crewmembers), persons of interest (e.g., wanted terrorists), and unknown persons. Figure 1 provides a representation of the way in which this database will function. The database will be utilized to maintain the mustering status of the LCS's crew, any detected persons of interest, and all unknown persons.

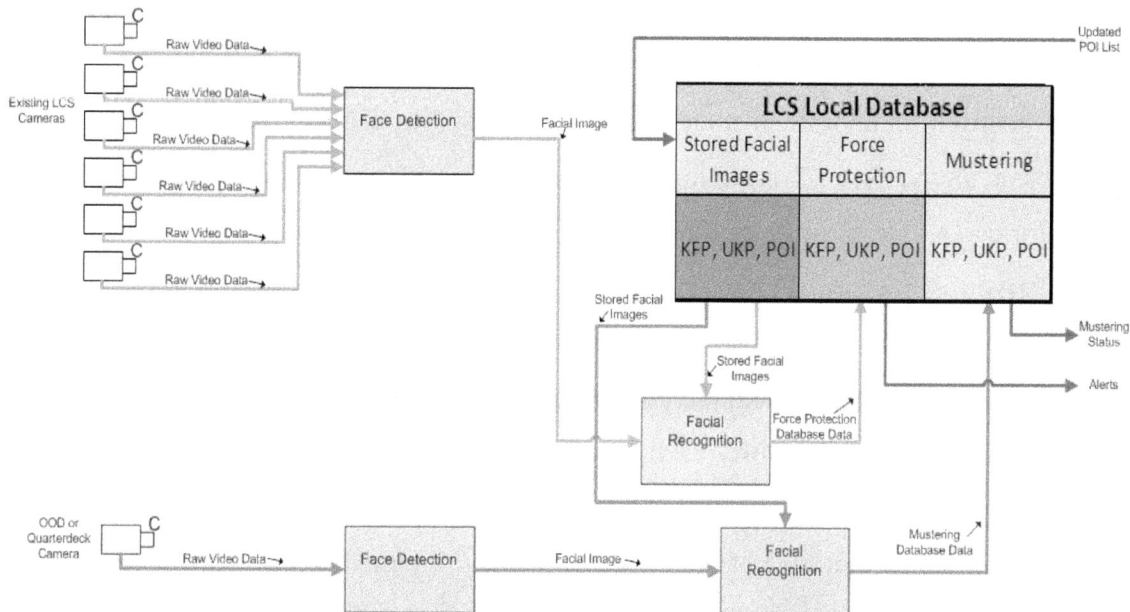

Figure 1.    Generic Database Diagram

In order to meet the requirements provided in the generic functional architecture and conform to the present LCS crew size an automated solution was chosen. Additionally, the automated option would leverage existing LCS capabilities (e.g., external cameras), be cost effective, feasible, economical, and reduce the workload on the present crew. One such enabling technology is automatic facial recognition, where a computer is "trained" to detect faces from video data and then correlate detected faces with stored faces in a database to automatically "recognize" a face. In Figure 1, all of the functions to do with facial recognition and facial detection, and updating the respective databases would be done automatically.

First, the proposed automated system will utilize LCS's existing external cameras to provide automated situational awareness of the pier area. These cameras will constantly monitor the pier area around the ship. As an LCS ship is already designed with six external cameras that provide 360 degrees of video coverage around the ship

(Hurley, 2010), facial recognition technology applied to video data from these cameras will attempt to automate 100% surveillance awareness. The proposed system will process the live video feeds identifying persons by attempting facial recognition on any individuals within the system's line of sight. Upon detection of a face in the pier area, all facial images will be matched against the known database, which will be updated based on a positive or undefined match. Figure 1 displays the interaction of the LCS local database to the rest of the automated system. This figure also designates the three categories for facial images: Known Friendly Person (KFP), Unknown Person (UKP), and Person of Interest (POI). Updates to the stored facial images database for the POIs and KFPs will be performed as needed to facilitate both an accurate muster and POI status. Upon significant positive correlation between a detected face and a face of a POI (e.g., terrorist) that was stored in the database, the system will automatically provide an alert to the watch standers for determination of any need for further action. Additionally, all facial images that do not match a previously obtained image will be categorized as UKP and given a unique identifier. The system will then autonomously monitor the unknown person's movements for behavior that matches a predetermined set of suspicious activities. If the unknown person's activities are considered suspicious, an alert will be provided to the watch standers to determine whether further action is necessary.

Second, the proposed system will perform mustering of all ship's personnel as they board and exit the ship. In addition to the existing external cameras on the LCS platform, the proposed autonomous system for mustering includes the addition of one camera located at the entrance and exit location from the ship (normally termed "quarterdeck"), which is moveable depending upon where the brow of the ship is located. The field of view of the camera will capture the face of all persons that enter/exit the ship. The system will capture the face of all personnel as the ship's personnel follow the standard procedure of facing the Officer of the Deck (OOD) and requesting permission to come aboard/go ashore. The additional camera will be incorporated into the OOD's podium so that the ships personnel will face both the OOD and the mustering camera at the same time as they come and go from the ship. Upon significant positive correlation between a detected face of a crewmember crossing the ship's prow and a stored face of an LCS crewmember, that person's mustering status is properly updated via a data entry into the Pier Watchman mustering database. Thus, using video data from the camera at the brow, the proposed solution will automatically detect faces and query the mustering section of the database for constant real-time mustering capability of ship personnel.

A portion of the proposed solution was then prototyped in order to confirm its viability through creation of a proof-of-concept system called "Pier Watchman." The Pier Watchman automated physical system consists of a camera that records real-time video data, face detection software that executes on the camera's video image, face recognition software that executes on the camera's video image correlating detected faces with faces stored in a database, and finally, the database of stored facial images. The results from testing performed on the Pier Watchman Proof of Concept System, provided in Chapter V, show that the proposed system solution is viable and that further research and development on a full-scale system is warranted.

To conclude, this thesis provides a concept, ESD, requirements and a functional architecture to a generalized solution for mustering and pier monitoring on LCS ships. This thesis not only addresses the need for an autonomous system, but also uses a Systems Engineering approach to define requirements for the autonomous system. Additionally, a proof-of-concept system was designed and implemented, providing a specific autonomous solution's instantiated physical architecture prototype solution of one specific approach to autonomous mustering and pier monitoring.

# ACKNOWLEDGMENTS

The author wishes to thank Professors Rachel Goshorn, Deborah Goshorn, and Mark Stevens for their guidance during the writing of this thesis.

THIS PAGE INTENTIONALLY LEFT BLANK

xx

# I.    INTRODUCTION

This initial chapter is an introduction that provides a short synopsis of the subjects presented in this thesis.  It first explains the problem that exists, then proposes a system solution, introduces the instantiated proof-of-concept system to a specific solution, and concludes with a thesis outline.

## A.    PROBLEM STATEMENT

One may stipulate that the U.S. Military does not provide adequate Force Protection for its ships, as one recalls the attack on the USS Cole in 2000.  One solution to further enhance Force Protection on Navy ships is to increase the personnel dedicated to Force Protection.  The USS Freedom class of Littoral Combat Ships (LCS) are designed and built, to have minimum crew sizes.  LCS was designed with maximum automation to facilitate this minimum manning concept. The core crew is a compliment of 40 sailors with an additional 35 personnel for the mission package crew (Globalsecurity, 2009).  This minimum crew concept means that while the ship is in port, there are fewer crewmembers to facilitate pier monitoring and maintain pier security.  Understandably, there are also fewer sailors to conduct basic duties, such as the mustering of personnel.  The watch standers and personnel for LCS presently have too many responsibilities to ensure 100% coverage of the Pier area 100% of the time, and they cannot manually maintain a 100% muster of all ship's personnel 100% of the time.  This lack of coverage and situational awareness could make LCS ships vulnerable to terrorist attacks or terrorist monitoring.  Thus, the crews of LCS ships can benefit from the implementation of any technology that relieves the administrative burden on them.  Such a solution is needed in order to enhance the Force Protection capability and reduce administrative burdens.  In order to meet the minimum manning concept that is employed on LCS, the optimal solution would most likely be an automated system that would not require additional personnel to operate.

1

## 1.    Personal Motivation/Experience

I have experienced the difficulty in maintaining both a vigilant watch of the pier area and an accurate muster of ships personnel first hand while serving on multiple different ships during my nearly 17 years in the United States Navy as both an enlisted sailor and officer. Additionally, from January of 2006 until December of 2007, I served as the Production, Test, and Launch Officer for the USS Freedom, (LCS-1), while stationed in Marinette Wisconsin, with Supervisor of Shipbuilding Gulf Coast. My job entailed all aspects of ship construction, test, and working with members of the ships' crew, ensuring that their needs were adequately addressed. At this point in my career, I had been stationed on United States Navy ships for more than seven years. From this experience, I was intimately aware of the duties that ships crew are required to perform. The major difference with LCS-1 in regards to other ships, was that the size of the crew was much smaller than any I had served on; at the same time the ship itself was more complex than the others. This resulted in a ship design that required maximum automation.

The level of engineering that went into all aspects of the ship was very impressive, right down to the external cameras that were utilized to provide 360 degrees of video coverage around the ship. The original purpose of the external cameras was to reduce crew size and watch requirements. All ships are required to maintain a visual watch around the ship (USCG, 2009, 12). Most ships accomplish this by stationing multiple personnel to visually monitor 360 degrees around the ship. My previous ship had three extra people performing this duty: a port, starboard, and aft lookout. However, LCS-1 was able to meet this requirement through utilization of the aforementioned external cameras, thus removing the need for three personnel to stand the lookout watches. The video feeds were displayed on a console so that the personnel on watch on the bridge could easily monitor the images.

While addressing LCS-1 crew concerns, I became aware of the need to simplify all duties that the crew performs in order to make their jobs manageable, while still maintaining the same level of situational awareness and security as any other Navy ship.

2

## B.    SHIP CLASS GENERAL INFORMATION

The USS Freedom (LCS-1) is the lead ship of the Freedom class of Littoral Combat Ships.  An image of the LCS-1, Figure 2, shows the ship underway in August 2008 from Marinette, Wisconsin.  As mentioned earlier, LCS-1 was designed with maximum automation to facilitate a minimum manning concept.  The automation on LCS encompasses systems such as the engineering plant to include automated starting of all main propulsion engines and generators through touch screen interfaces located (Hurley, 2010).  Additionally, the Common Radio Room (CRR) has an integrated and automated external communications system controlled by a single operator that can interface the entire system.  The CRR provides the ability to activate circuits with a single mouse click or schedule circuit activation by time or event, increasing operator efficiency and accuracy while reducing communications watch stander requirements (Lockheed Martin, 2010).  The aforementioned areas of automation are only a few of the automated systems integrated into the LCS platform and are provided as examples of the importance of automation for LCS operability due to the limited crew of seventy-five sailors, forty core crew members and an additional thirty-five personnel for the mission package crew (Global Security, 2009).  To better understand the minimum manning concept, a comparable ship in size would be the Oliver Hazard Perry Class of Frigates (FFG).  FFGs have a crew size of 215 (Navy.mil, 2009).  Both ships have the same requirements for security.

Figure 2. Picture of USS Freedom, LCS-1, Underway from Marinette Wisconsin
(From Scott, 2008)

## C. THE CURRENT MUSTERING PROCESS

The mustering of personnel on United States Navy ships while in port is a vital daily duty that accounts for each member of the crew. This process is generally conducted in the morning by each division on a ship and requires some form of written paperwork to be generated. All mustering paperwork is delivered to a central location where an accurate accounting of all personnel is verified and finally reported to the ship's commanding officer. The mustering process generally provides an accurate muster at the time it is conducted, but this muster is not maintained throughout the workday and is not updated as crewmembers leave and return to the ship. This means that the immediate status of whether a sailor is onboard or not, is not accurately known. Thus, there is an unmet need for constant mustering status of ship personnel.

## D. THE CURRENT FORCE PROTECTION PROCESS

The Department of Defense defines Force Protection as preventive measures taken to mitigate hostile actions against Department of Defense personnel (to include family members), resources, facilities, and critical information (Department of Defense, 2002, 172). Force Protection is a vital duty performed by Navy personnel both while the ship is in port, and underway. The force protection process discussed here is a general procedure, and does not constitute the exact procedure utilized. By describing only a general explanation of the current procedure for force protection, the advantage of the new system will be adequately made known, without providing classified information or compromising the safety of naval vessels.

Ship personnel armed with various weapons perform force protection for LCS class ships while in port. These personnel are responsible for visually monitoring the surrounding pier area. Force protection watches rotate periodically with the average person performing pier monitoring duties between four to six hours at a time. The number of personnel on watch can vary but is generally about six people. The Force Protection Officer (FPO) controls the daily inport force protection of the ship. One person assumes this position for 24 hours and any force protection issues are referred to this person for resolution. However, these people will not be able to observe 100% of the pier area 100% of the time.

## E. SYSTEMS ENGINEERING OVERVIEW

Using a Systems Engineering approach, this thesis proposes a generic solution for one of the problems associated with having a reduced crew size on LCS ships by first introducing a concept, external systems diagram, requirements, and generic functional architecture. Then, an autonomous system that provides real time automatic mustering and pier monitoring capability for enhanced situational awareness that satisfies the requirements from the generic functional architecture is proposed. Finally, a proof-of-concept system to demonstrate the viability of the proposed systems design is designed and built.

This thesis applies the Systems Engineering process to address the capability gap of mustering personnel and situational awareness on LCS and the pier area. Initially, the need for the proposed system is discussed. This is followed by a discussion of the Systems Engineering process applied to the system design of a proposed solution. Through applying the Systems Engineering concepts, conducting a careful review of the system solution concept, and recommendation of the instantiated physical architecture, an apparent technology gap was discovered on LCS ships that could be filled through the utilization of an automated system that performed facial detection, facial recognition, mustering, and area monitoring autonomously. This includes providing the External Systems Diagram (bound system design), and defining system interface requirements. The system architecture for the proposed solution is created and presented following the Systems Engineering "V" approach (as defined in Chapter II). The architectures created and presented for proposed system are as follows: functional architecture hierarchy, functional architecture decomposition, using IDEF0 modeling, and finally, instantiated physical architecture of a specific proposed solution.

To show that a full-scale system is a viable solution to enhancing situational awareness and force protection, a small-scale example, a proof-of-concept system, was designed, implemented, and tested. This thesis presents this implemented proof-of-concept system to demonstrate the functionality of the proposed system solution. This proof-of-concept system, called "Pier Watchman," emulates the existing camera functionality on LCS, without the need to use the exact hardware found on board ship. This is because the software being demonstrated is the software that would be used on any camera on LCS (including for both pier monitoring and automated personnel mustering). Chapter V shows the initial instantiated physical architecture plan for the proposed autonomous approach to the proposed solution proof-of-concept system, which is further described in Chapter VI. Designing, implementing, and testing the proof-of-concept system demonstrates the viability of the larger proposed system solution for LCS.

## F. THESIS OUTLINE

This section presents succinct overviews of each chapter in this thesis. Each chapter in this thesis builds upon the previous chapter through applying the Systems Engineering process.

### 1. Chapter II: Application of Systems Engineering Process

This chapter explains the systems engineering approach that was utilized to design and develop the proposed generalized system architecture and also to design and implement the proposed system Pier Watchman Proof-of-Concept specific solution system. The process of developing this system required a necessary roadmap for architecture design of a proposed system, and design, implementation, and testing of the Pier Watchman Proof-of-Concept System for successful completion. This chapter describes how the Systems Engineering "V" provided the roadmap that allowed for the successful design of the generic architecture and the functional and construction of the Pier Watchman Proof-of-Concept System.

### 2. Chapter III: Design Reference Mission

This chapter discusses the Design Reference Mission (DRM), which provides the operational scenario and the mission that the end system must accomplish. This document is linked back to established Navy requirements and is the basis for development of the system architecture. Overall, this chapter provides the necessary scope to determine how the finished system must work in order to be successful.

### 3. Chapter IV: Generic System Architecture

This chapter provides the generic system External Systems Diagram and Functional Architecture created from the DRM. The generic functional architecture hierarchy and decomposition are provided. Chapter IV then decomposes each level of the Functional Architecture for the proposed solution. The generic architecture provided in this chapter provides the basis for the solution to the identified capability gap.

**4.      Chapter V: Proposed System Solution**

This chapter provides a brief analysis of alternatives for potential approaches to fill the need described in the generic architecture. This chapter then expounds upon one proposed solution and provides procedures that it would utilize. The chapter then discusses how the proposed autonomous approach to the system solution will both enhance pier security and modify the way in which mustering of ship's personnel occurs. Chapter V then discusses a vital portion of this solution, automatic facial recognition, including a description of how a particular algorithm used for facial recognition works, including its benefits and limitations. Additionally, the Pier Watchman Proof-of-Concept System is explained. The need for creating an instantiated physical architecture of a proposed autonomous solution, an actual implementation and demonstration of a proof-of-concept system, how it was created, the components it was assembled from, the issues with its creation, its performance and limitations, and the benefits gained from its creation are all discussed.

**5.      Chapter VI: Summary and Conclusions**

This final chapter provides a summary and conclusion to the thesis. It summarizes the need for the proposed system, the concept of the proposed system, and the benefits of creating this system. Furthermore, it identifies benefits and lessons learned from designing and building a prototype for the proposed autonomous solution, known as, the Pier Watchman Proof-of-Concept System. This chapter concludes with identifying areas for future research.

## II. APPLICATION OF SYSTEMS ENGINEERING PROCESS

This chapter describes the systems engineering approach that was utilized to design and develop a generic system architecture, a proposed system solution, and to both design and implement the instantiated physical architecture of the proposed Pier Watchman Proof-of-Concept System. Additionally, this chapter describes how the Systems Engineering "V" provided the roadmap that allowed for the successful design of a generic system architecture, a proposed solution design, and construction of the Pier Watchman Proof-of-Concept System that met the generic solution design.

### A. SYSTEMS ENGINEERING PROCESS

Systems Engineering can be defined as a multidisciplinary engineering discipline in which decisions and designs are based on their effect on the system as a whole (Maier and Rechtin, 2000). In order to maintain the required engineering discipline, a process must be utilized that details system requirements so that the system that is designed and built meets these requirements. The eventual goal is to produce an actual system that fulfills the requirements of enhancing pier security and real time mustering while not increasing the LCS crew size. The concept, external systems diagram, requirements, and functional architecture for such a system is provided. After a brief analysis of alternatives, a specific solution is proposed and a proof-of-concept system, termed Pier Watchman, is created. The name Pier Watchman is based on its purpose of monitoring the pier area and the fact that it is the application of the graduate system developed by the Naval Postgraduate Systems Engineering Department, Network-Centric Systems Engineering Track and corresponding lab, called "Watchman."

### B. SYSTEMS ENGINEERING V-MODEL

A Systems Engineering Process is a comprehensive, iterative, and recursive problem solving process (Department of Defense, 2001, 31). In the development of the generic architecture, proposed system solution, and implementation of an instantiated physical architecture, the systems engineering V-model was utilized (Department of Defense, 2001, 65). This model can be broken down into distinct phases as displayed in

Figure 3. A new system design should start on the left side of the "V" with the project definition and system concept to establish the system level design requirements. Then continuing down the left side of the "V," item level design requirements are established. This Systems Engineering V-model has predetermined review points along the way, where a detailed review is conducted to ensure the system is ready to move into the next phase. Once the design is completed at the bottom of the "V," then the fabrication, integration, and testing phases can begin, which is shown as moving up the right side of the "V."

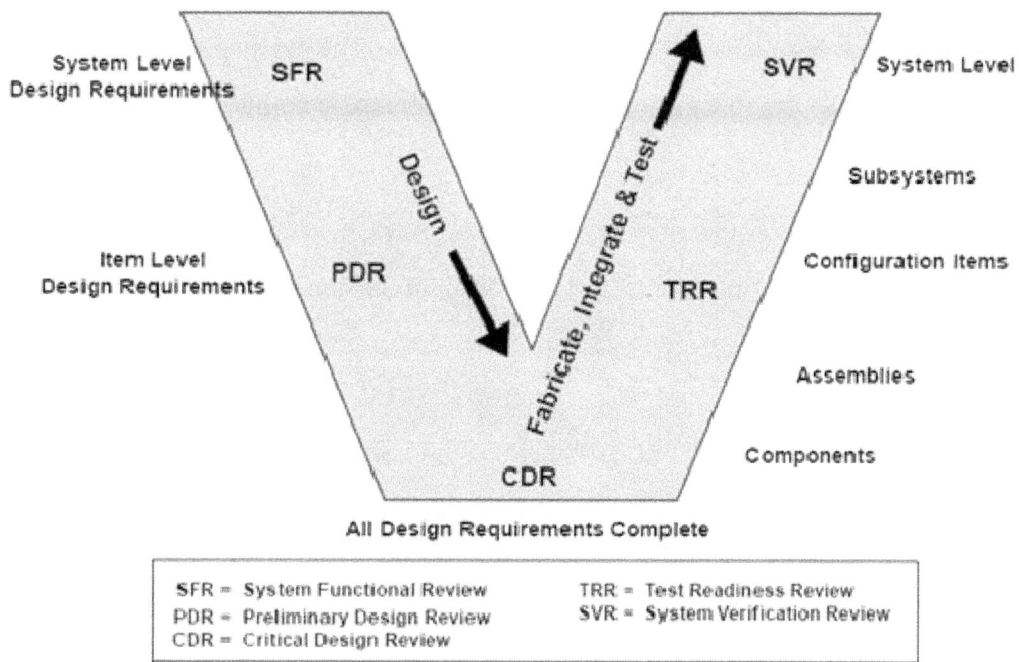

Figure 3.    Systems Engineering V-Model (From Department of Defense, 2001, 65)

## C.    PROBLEM DEFINITION AND SYSTEM CONCEPT

The initial phase of a project starts with defining a problem or identifying a capability gap that needs to be filled. This phase describes what could be built or procured in order to fill the need and can result in the formulation of the idea for a system. This initial phase does not establish that a system will be built; it only states that a system could fill a need and that further evaluation should be conducted.

A need was identified for the USS Freedom class of Littoral Combat Ships (LCS) that the watch standers and personnel for LCS presently have too many responsibilities to ensure 100% coverage of the Pier area 100% of the time and they cannot manually maintain a 100% muster of all ship's personnel 100% of the time. This lack of coverage and situational awareness could make LCS ships vulnerable to terrorist attacks and terrorist monitoring. A system concept was developed and is provided in Chapter IV.

## D. SYSTEM LEVEL DESIGN REQUIREMENTS AND ARCHITECTURE

The requirements and architecture phase is where the generic architecture for system development is created and the system requirements are defined. The architecture provides a top-down view of the system. This phase results in a well-defined system architecture that has clear linkages to requirements. The architecture properly links to the previous phase, so that the system to be built meets the original needs.

In the case of the system solution, a Design Reference Mission (DRM) was developed, which provides all of the necessary information in order to create a scenario in order to perform simulations. The simulations can then be run utilizing different solutions to address the problem defined at the beginning of the DRM. The DRM will be discussed in detail in Chapter III. From the DRM a generic system architecture was created. The generic system architecture consists of the external system diagram, requirements, and functional architecture for the generic system.

### 1. Analysis of Alternatives

The analysis of alternatives (AOA) is a process that looks at the required need, the generic architecture, and identifies potentially viable solutions. Assessments are performed on each possible solution evaluating for effectiveness, achievability, cost, and viability (United States Air Force, 2008). Once an AOA is complete and a solution has been chosen for further development then the item level design can begin.

## E. ITEM LEVEL DESIGN REQUIREMENTS

After one executes an AOA, the next step is to define the proposed alternative's physical architecture through the item level design requirements phase. These detailed specifications provide the bottom-up system design by breaking up the larger system into individual sub-systems and then breaking up the subsystems into components. This

11

thesis selects a particular alternative and provides its instantiated physical architecture. Additionally in this phase, the test and evaluation plans, to include acceptance tests, are developed. The acceptance must ensure that the needs described in the initial phase are satisfied. At the conclusion of this part of the process, all design requirements are complete, the left side of the Systems Engineering "V," and the system is ready to begin fabrication, integration and test phases.

## F. FABRICATE, INTEGRATE, AND TEST

As one moves from the bottom of the "V" and up the right side of the "V," the design that was formulated in the previous sections is turned into a real system. First, individual components are acquired or built and assembled into sub-systems. (Buede, 2000). Then, unit tests are performed on these sub-systems. After the sub-systems have been created and their unit tests have been satisfactorily performed, these sub-systems are ready for integration into the larger system (Buede, 2000).

The systems integration step is where all of the components and sub-systems are assembled and integrated into a complete working system (Blanchard and Fabrycky, 2006). The integration includes debugging of all software and testing of the complete integrated system. The complete system operation is verified when an acceptance test is demonstrated to and approved by the stakeholders. The acceptance test is the same test that was agreed upon earlier with the system's stakeholders, but due to any engineering change orders, the acceptance test may have incurred minor changes during the build cycle. All parties involved must agree upon any changes that have occurred. Upon successful completion of the acceptance test, the system is delivered to the entity that paid for its construction, and a determination for further orders is made. Fabrication and integration is where the majority of the time and work on the system occurs. However, it will only be successful if the earlier design was performed correctly.

For the proposed solution, the actual fabrication, integration, and testing that will be discussed is for a proposed, specific instance of the proposed system's functional architecture. The implemented proof-of-concept system that was designed and assembled in the Network-Centric Systems Engineering (NCSE) lab at NPS was created to provide an instance of the proposed system. The proof-of-concept would accomplish and demonstrate in part the overarching goals that the full proposed system must accomplish as specified in the generic architecture. A detailed description of how the proof-of-concept system was built, is provided in Chapter VI.

To conclude, a Systems Engineering V-model yields an achievable roadmap for system creation. Additionally, the Systems Engineering V-model was utilized for the design of a generic architecture, proposed solution, AOA, and the design and implementation of the Pier Watchman Proof-of-Concept System. The next chapter provides the Design Reference Mission utilized for scenario creation that enables the design of a generic architecture.

THIS PAGE INTENTIONALLY LEFT BLANK

# III.   DESIGN REFERENCE MISSION (DRM)

This chapter discusses the first part of the left side of the Systems Engineering "V" by presenting the Design Reference Mission (DRM) that provides the proposed mission the end system must accomplish.  This DRM document links back to established Navy requirements and is the basis for development of the system architecture.  This chapter provides the necessary scope to determine how the finished proposed system must work in order to be successful.  The DRM provides the basis for the creation of a scenario.  The scenario can then be utilized to simulate how a particular solution would perform in context to the expected environment, while attempting to fill the capability gap or need.

## A.   DESIGN REFERENCE MISSION

The system architecture for the proposed system was based on a Design Reference Mission (DRM) that explains the expectations and requirements the actual system must fulfill.  These expectations and requirements are explained by defining the threat and operational environment.  The DRM seeks to provide a common framework to link systems engineering efforts and help ensure an "apples-to-apples" comparison of analytical results (Skolnick and Wilkins 2000, 209).  The DRM presented here defines the problem in a context that allows for the modeling of a solution.  The object of the DRM is not to provide a solution, but rather allow multiple solutions to be envisioned, as long as they succeed in completing the requirements of the DRM.  The DRM starts with the problem definition and operational need.

### 1.   Problem Definition

As discussed in Chapter I, the watch standers and personnel for LCS presently have too many responsibilities to ensure 100% coverage of the Pier area 100% of the time.  Additionally, the LCS crew cannot maintain a real-time muster status of all ships personnel.  This lack of coverage and situational awareness could make LCS ships vulnerable to terrorist attacks or terrorist monitoring.

15

## 2. Operational Need

A system to enhance Situational Awareness and Pier Security for LCS-1 class ships will need the operational capabilities listed below:

- Provide situational awareness around pier-tied ship at a minimum distance of 200 yards from the ship.
- Provide ability to monitor pier area and alert watch standers of possible threats.
- Provide interface with existing LCS infrastructure (e.g., cameras, power, FPO).
- Provide a real time crew mustering capability.

## 3. Operational Situation (OPSIT) Generation

Operational Situations (OPSITs) are discrete multi-engagement events with specified operational characteristics (Skolnick and Wilkins, 2000, 213). By defining the operating conditions and presenting defined assumptions, a set of operational scenarios can be created. The operational scenarios are described in the next sections starting with the Projected Operating Environment.

## 4. Projected Operating Environment

The Projected Operating Environment (POE) described in this DRM can be utilized in the creation of a scenario. The establishment of scenario criteria allows for the utilization of simulation so that the viability of different system designs can be verified to solve the problem defined earlier. A true representation of system performance can be obtained through simulation by providing a set of environmental conditions that represent a typical operating environment. The next sections of the DRM provide a context from which one can design a system by specifically providing the geography and weather conditions in which the system will be required to operate.

### a.    *Geography*

The location selected for this DRM is the Marinette Marine port in Marinette, Wisconsin, as pictured in Figure 4. Marinette was chosen because the weather conditions for this location encompass most of the weather variations in which the LCS will be expected to operate. Figure 4 shows the LCS located pier side and identified with the arrow. This layout of this port represents the average layout of ports in both the United States and foreign countries.

Figure 4.    Map of Operating Area (From Google Maps, 2009)

### b.    *Weather*

In order to meet the projected operating environment, the solution is expected to operate outdoors in all weather environments. Weather information for the Northeast Wisconsin area is summarized in Figures 5–11.

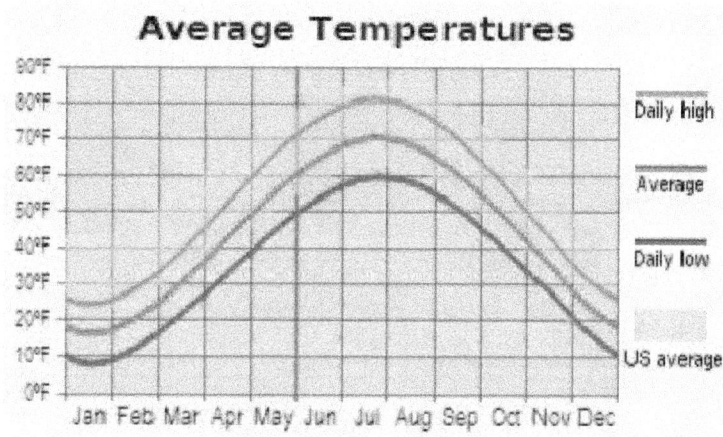

Figure 5.    Average Temperatures (From city–data.com for Marinette, WI)

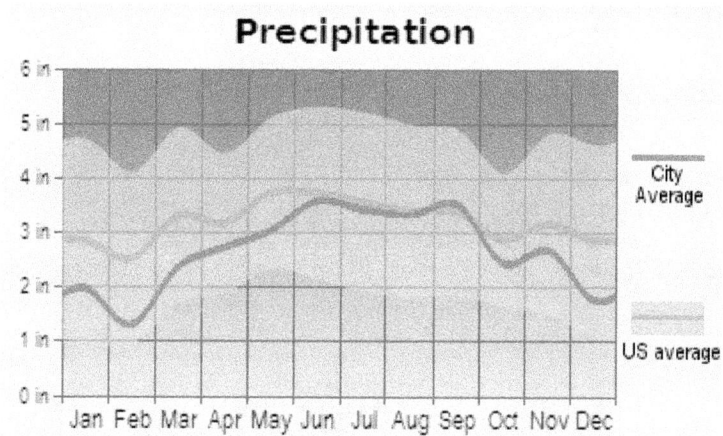

Figure 6.    Precipitation (From city–data.com for Marinette, WI)

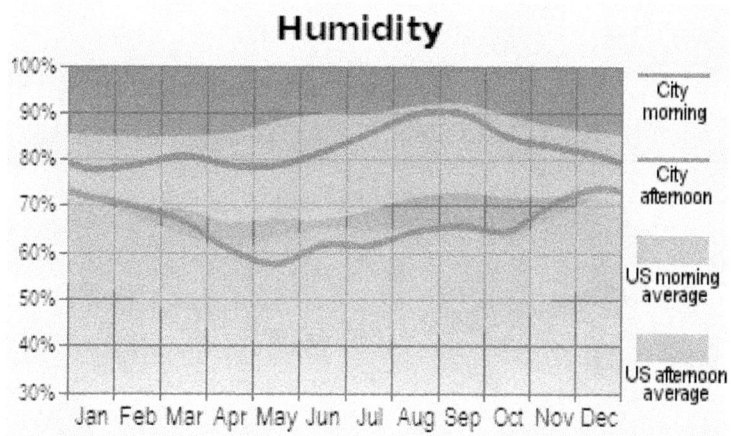

Figure 7.    Humidity (From city–data.com for Marinette, WI)

18

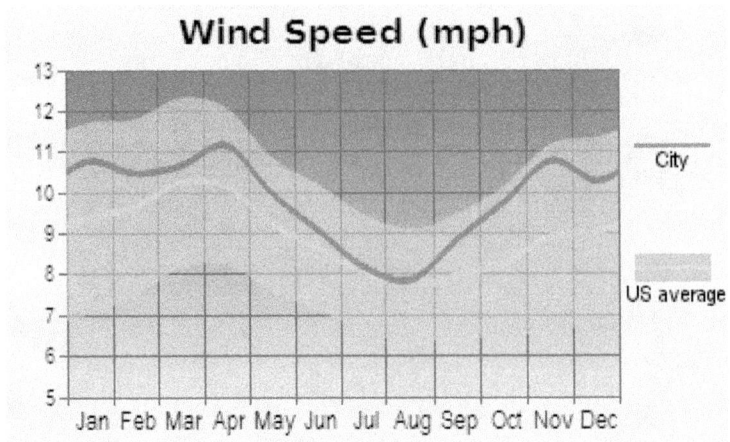

Figure 8.    Wind Speed (From city–data.com for Marinette, WI)

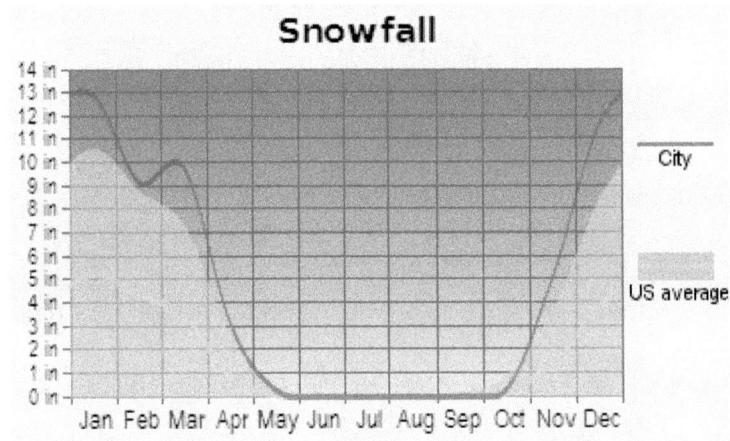

Figure 9.    Snowfall (From city–data.com for Marinette, WI)

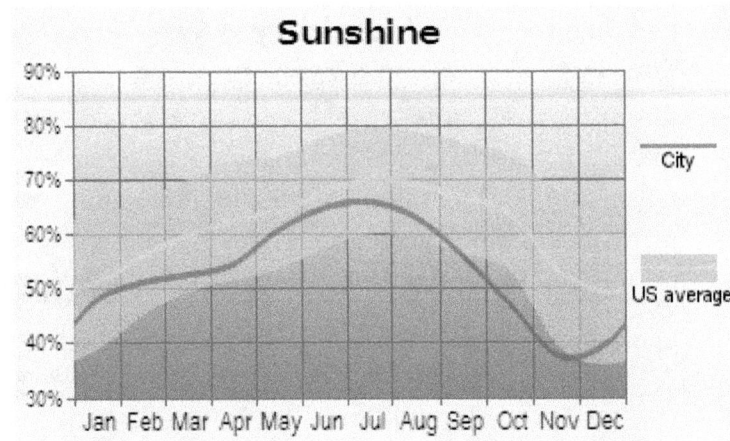

Figure 10.    Sunshine (From city–data.com for Marinette, WI)

19

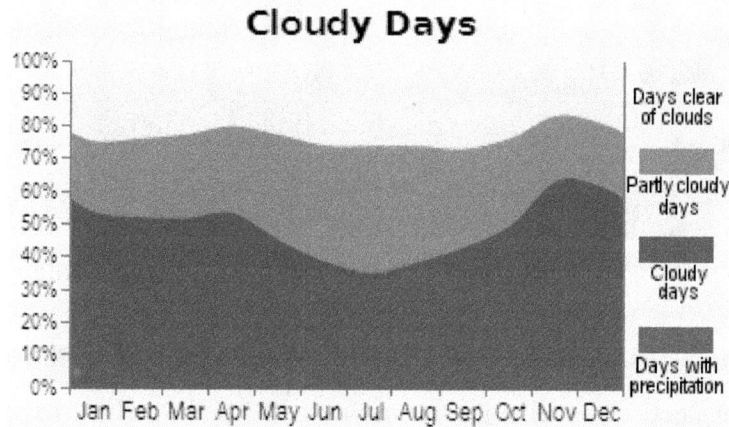

Figure 11.    Cloudy Days (From city–data.com for Marinette, WI)

## 5.    Threat

The threats are an enemy force (e.g., terrorist) that is actively gathering intelligence on the LCS ship in preparation for an asymmetric attack from the pier area in order to damage or destroy the ship and the lack of situational awareness due to unknown crew muster status.

## 6.    Assumed Threat General Conditions

The following information on the general threat conditions provides the basis for creation of the capabilities that the system must have in order to overcome the assumed threats.   The scenario utilized in the development of the system assumes the enemy conducts surveillance on an LCS class ship by personnel that are from a reasonably sophisticated terrorist organization that is non-state sponsored or a suicide bomber capable of a covert land attack.   Such a threat would be recognized when the POIs approach the pier area within the monitoring zone.

The expected threat characterizations can be broken down into a person running, jogging, walking, and standing in the pier area with the probabilities of each as shown in Table 1.  The items in this table assume that all persons are initially outside of 200 yards and proceed at the speeds displayed in Table 1 towards the ship.

| Threat | Speed | Probability | Distance From Ship |
|---|---|---|---|
| Person | Running (15 feet per second) | Low | 200 Yards |
| | Jogging (7 feet per second) | Medium | 200 Yards |
| | Walking (3 feet per second) | High | 200 Yards |
| | Standing (0 feet per second) | High | 200 Yards |

Table 1.     Threat Characterization Table

The next item that is important for system design is the expected number of personnel that need to be identified simultaneously. In order to provide a valid system the determination was made that system must be able to successfully perform personnel identification under the following threat size, attack timing, and coordination:

Threat size (personnel):

- 1

- 3

Attack Timing and Coordination:

- One POI at a time.

- Three POIs all at once in a concentrated location.

- Three POIs surrounding the surveillance area and monitoring simultaneously.

The utilization of a threat size of only one and three persons in this scenario was chosen for an initial requirement with the expectation for future scalability. The system must be able to perform the previous threat detection operations while also constantly maintaining an accurate muster of all personnel on the ship.

### 7.     Metrics

To properly determine if the system can successfully fill the capability gap, a set of key metrics needs to be developed prior to running the simulations. The key metrics that were chosen are listed in Table 2. These metrics were created by first referencing the Naval Tasks (NTA) in the Chairman of the Joint Chiefs of Staff Manual, Universal Joint Task List (UJTL) (current to May 13, 2003) and then by refining the specifics in order to meet the requirements. The metrics chosen here are used within the simulation to map

21

the requirements and functions to the actual system component selection. The simulations of the scenario are also used to validate the functional architecture of the system. The metrics one derives from the simulation are used to study the development of requirements that will map to function and eventually the physical form of the instantiated system solution.

| Metric # | Metric Type | Description of Metric | Supporting Document |
|----------|-------------|----------------------|---------------------|
| M1 | Percent | Of POIs accurately identified. | NTA 2.2 Collect Data and Intelligence |
| M2 | Percent | Of KFPs accurately identified. | NTA 2.2 Collect Data and Intelligence |
| M3 | Seconds | Time required to obtain valid facial image. | NTA 2.2 Collect Data and Intelligence |
| M4 | Seconds | Time required to identify valid facial image. | NTA 2.2 Collect Data and Intelligence |
| M5 | Percent | Of POI alerts judged to be useable by Force Protection Personnel. | NTA 2.4.1 Evaluate Information |

Table 2.    List of Metrics (From UJTL, 2003)

### 8.    Mission Success Requirements

Mission success requirements are based on the functions required of a specific operational activity. All mission requirements must be completed successfully for a successful mission. The activities identified for the success of this DRM are measured in these categories:

- Manage Sensors
- Detect POI
- Detect KFP
- Detect UKP
- Report POI
- Muster Ships Personnel
- Transfer Data
- Provide Appropriate Alerts

22

### 9. Mission Definition

To complete the mission success levels, all operational activities are utilized. Each mission included within a DRM scenario can be decomposed into the individual operational activities necessary to complete the tasks that the DRM scenario requires. The Joint and Naval Capability Terminology List is a compilation of Joint and Navy capabilities areas. The Joint Capability Areas (JCAs) are broken into War fighting Mission Areas (WMA), which include Joint Training, Command & Control, Force Application, Force Protection, Focused Logistics, Battlespace Awareness and Force Management. The Naval capabilities are taken from the Naval Power 21, which is a combination of Sea Power 21 and Expeditionary Maneuver Warfare Capabilities. Naval Power 21 has five pillars, which are Sea Shield, Sea Strike, Sea Basing, Expeditionary Maneuver Warfare, and FORCEnet (ASN RDA, CHENG, 2007).

The mission within Sea Shield that will be focused upon are Force Protection as seen in Table 3. The JCAs that are supported are "Joint Net-Centric Operations" and "Joint Battlespace Awareness." The specific JCAs applicable to this DRM are listed in Table 4. This system supports the FORCEnet Communication and Networks/Infrastructure and Battlespace Awareness/ISR Naval capabilities. The specific FORCEnet capabilities are listed in Table 5.

| Sea Shield | | |
|---|---|---|
| **Mission Capability** | **Definition** | **Mission Sub-Capability** |
| Force Protection | Preventative measures taken to mitigate hostile actions against Department of Defense personnel, resources, facilities, and critical information Force Protection does not include actions to defeat the enemy or protect against accidents, weather, or disease. (JP 1-02) | Protect Against SOF and Terrorist Threats |

Table 3.     Sea Shield from Naval Power 21 (From ASN RDA,CHENG, 2007)

| Tier 1 | Tier 2A | Tier 2B |
|---|---|---|
| Joint Net Centric Operations | Information Transport | Information Transport |
| Joint Battlespace Awareness | Planning and Direction | Conduct Collection Management |
| | Observation and Collection | Radio Frequency |
| | Dissemination and Integration | Enable Smart Push/Pull for Intelligence Products |

Table 4.    Joint Capability Areas (From ASN RDA,CHENG, 2007)

| Mission Capability | Mission Sub-Capability |
|---|---|
| Communication and Networks/Infrastructure | Provide Information Transfer |
| Battlespace Awareness/ISR | Conduct Sensor Management and Information Processing |
| | Detect and ID Targets |
| | Provide Cueing and Target Information |

Table 5.    FORCEnet Mission Capabilities (From ASN RDA,CHENG, 2007)

## 10.    Operational Activities

In any of these situations, the system will respond by completing specific tasks when suspicious activity, a crew member, or a terrorist is positively identified. The Operational Activities that were taken from the Common Operational Activities List (COAL), Version 2 from 2007, because they provide linkage back to standard documents. The Operational Activities identified are listed below.

- Manage sensors and information processing (2.0 ID 459)
- Understand the situation (2.0 ID 950)
- Recognize threats (2.0 ID 951)
- Observe and Collect (2.0 ID 519)
- Task Sensor (2.0 ID 522)
- Control Sensor (2.0 ID 525)
- Collect and Transport Sensor Derived Data (2.0 ID 530)
- Collect Data (2.0 ID 544)

24

- Collect Contact Data (2.0 ID 545)
- Monitor the Area of Interest (AOI) (2.0 ID 612)
- Find Target of Interest (2.0 ID 613)
- Identify/Recognize Target of Interest (2.0 ID 614)

An example of the expectation of the use of the operational activities "Collect Data" represents the collection of all data in the pier area of the ship. This operational activity relates to the data required to be collected in order to identify the people observed in the pier and quarterdeck area. Now that the Operational Activities have been identified, the Operational Tasks necessary to achieve the mission can be identified.

## 11. Operational Tasks

During its missions, the system will be guided by Operational Tasks in performance of the Operational Activities necessary to achieve the Mission Success Requirements. The Operational Tasks Naval Tasks (NTA) for the DRM, from the Navy Tactical Task List (NTTL) 3.0 and the Universal Joint Task List (UJTL) that have been identified are listed below.

- Communicate Information (NTA 5.1.1)
- Conduct Collection Planning and Directing (NTA 2.1.3)
- Collect Target Information (NTA 2.2.1)
- Perform Tactical Reconnaissance (NTA 2.2.3.2)

Once all operational activities have been identified, the functions necessary to achieve the mission are identified and documented.

## 12. Mission Execution

Executing the mission consists of completing certain tasks that can be traced back to their respective operational activities. Two missions relating to this DRM are as follows:

- Identifying a terrorist in within 200 yards of the ship
- Mustering of ships crew as they board and depart the ship

25

## 13.    Operational Concept

The operational concept is defined from both the high-level operational activities and the missions those activities are required to perform.  In order to accomplish this, it is necessary to scope and bound the mission.  Therefore, it is determined that the architecture must consist of only those activities required to perform the data collection and analysis on the personnel within the immediate area of the ship and the ship quarterdeck.  Alerts are then to be issued to the watch standers for any assumed POIs. The Command and Control of the ships alert response are considered external to the system and beyond the scope of its architecture.  Additionally, the transmission of data to any off ship asset is also considered outside the scope of this architecture and thus not modeled here.

In summary, a DRM has been established that provides the need and the context in which the solution must operate.  Additionally, requirements and links back to established Navy requirements have been created.  The DRM provides the basis for development of generic system architecture covered in Chapter IV.

# IV.  GENERIC SYSTEM ARCHITECTURE

The generic system architecture is represented on the top left side of the Systems Engineering "V" (system level design requirements and architecture).  The generic architecture provides a general set of criteria, requirements, and functional decompositions to allow for creation of a solution to the capability gap or need.  This chapter provides the high level operational concept graphic, an external systems diagram, the functional architecture hierarchy, and decomposition diagrams for the generic architecture that allows for the system to successfully address the scenario described in the DRM.

## A.    OPERATIONAL VIEW (OV)

The Operational View (OV) figure is a high-level operational concept graphic that provides a concise pictorial describing the mission the proposed system is to perform (Department of Defense, 2007).  Figure 12 depicts the OV that is based on the DRM. This figure shows the simplified diagram of the operating area from Figure 4 with overlays of the cameras field of views (FOV). Within the camera FOVs the two stars (one red and one blue) represent the locations of two separate persons.  The image of a person (in the FOV with the blue star) correlated as a KFP is displayed in the top left.  The image of a person (in the FOV with the red star) correlated as a POI is displayed in the bottom right.

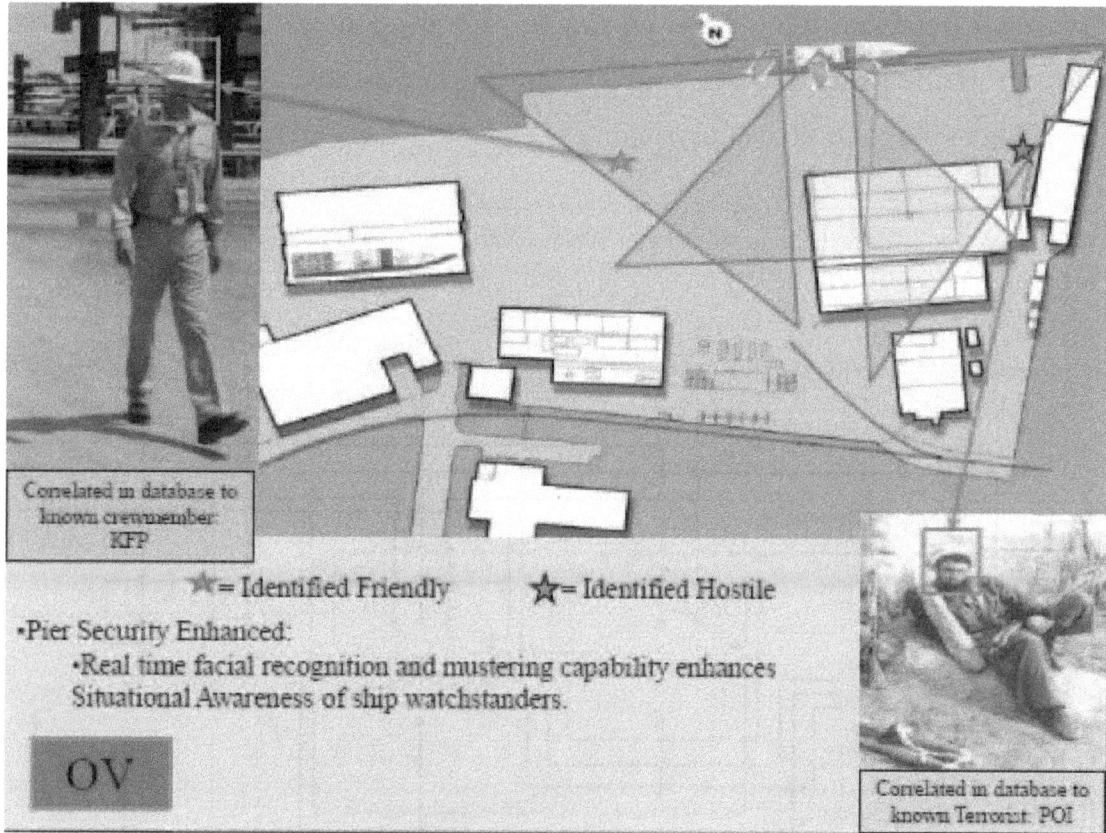

Figure 12.    System Operational View

## B.    EXTERNAL SYSTEMS DIAGRAM (ESD)

The Integrated Definition for Function Modeling (IDEF0) format is utilized in the modeling a system solution.  The following system diagrams are based on this format starting with the external systems diagram.  An external systems diagram (ESD) is defined as the model of the interaction of the system with other (external) systems in the relevant contexts, thus providing a definition of the system's boundary in terms of the system's inputs and outputs (Buede, 2000, 433).  Figure 13 displays the external systems diagram (ESD) created from the DRM and illustrates the top-level function of providing pier monitoring and mustering services.  The ESD is broken down into constraints (represented by arrows going in from the top), inputs (represented by arrows coming in from the left), outputs (represented by arrows exiting on the right), and system top-level functions (represented by arrows coming in from the bottom). Systems are listed at the bottom of the diagram, with arrows going up into a box, representing the top-level function of the corresponding system.

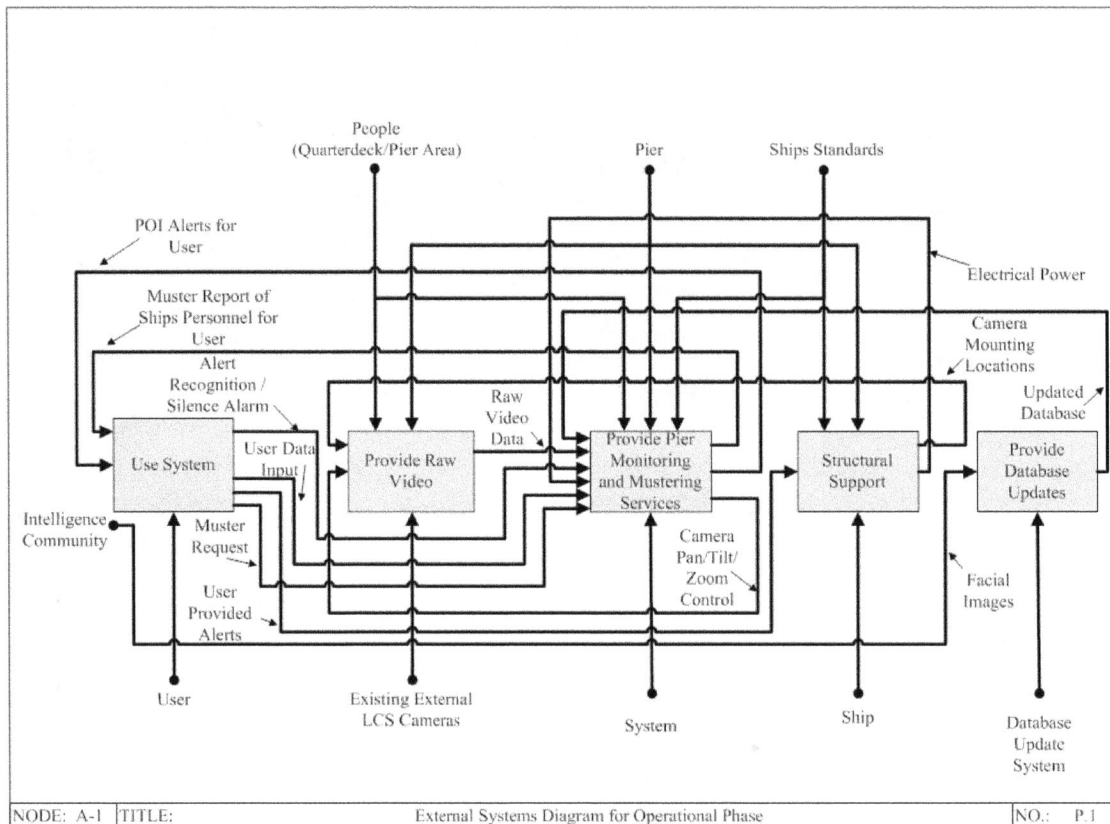

Figure 13.    External Systems Diagram

## C.    REQUIREMENTS

Requirements are established by agreements between all stakeholders of the system. The main stakeholders to establish requirements for a system on LCS were determined to be the end-user, commanders of LCS ships, proposed system contractor, LCS ship contractor, and the program executive officer for the LCS ship program. The stakeholders are to establish requirements based on the concept of operations for the system design. It was decided that due to time constraints the actual stakeholders input would not be solicited, but rather the requirements presented here are based on the DRM, the ESD, determining what is needed so that the system to be built can successfully complete the mission, and personal experience achieved while working with the LCS program. The operational needs listed below come from the DRM:

- Provide situational awareness around pier-tied ship at a minimum distance of 200 yards from the ship.
- Provide ability to monitor pier area and alert watch standers of possible threats.
- Provide interface with existing LCS infrastructure (e.g., cameras, power, FPO).
- Provide a real time crew mustering capability.

The aforementioned operational needs and the External Systems Diagram are translated into high-level requirements, as follows:

C.   Requirements

C.1.0—Input/output requirements

C.1.1—Input requirements

C.1.1.1—The system shall receive raw video data from existing external LCS cameras.

C.1.1.2—The system shall receive a muster request from the user.

C.1.1.3—The system shall receive alert recognition from the user.

C.1.1.4—The system shall receive data from the user.

C.1.1.5—The system shall receive electrical power from the ship.

C.1.2—Output requirements

C.1.2.1—The system shall provide POI alerts to the user.

C.1.2.2—The system shall provide camera pan/tilt/zoom control to the LCS cameras.

C.1.2.3—The system shall provide muster report of ships personnel to user.

C.2.0—External systems requirements

C.2.1—The system shall interface with the user.

C.2.2—The system shall interface with existing external LCS cameras.

C.2.3—The system shall interface with the ship.

C.2.4—The system shall interface with the database update system.

C.3.0—System constraint requirements

C.3.1— The system shall comply with constraints of ships standards.

C.3.2—The system is constrained by obstructions and structures on the pier.

C.3.3— The system is constrained by people on the pier and quarterdeck providing a view to the video cameras of their face.

C.4.0—The system requirements

C.4.1—The system shall provide situational awareness around pier-tied ship at a minimum distance of 200 yards from the ship.

C.4.2—The system shall provide ability to monitor pier area and alert watch standers of possible threats.

C.4.3—The system shall provide interface with existing LCS infrastructure (e.g., cameras, power, FPO).

C.4.3—The system shall provide a real time crew mustering capability.

## D.    GENERIC SYSTEM FUNCTIONAL ARCHITECTURE

The functional architecture of a system contains a hierarchical model of the functions performed by the generic system and a functional architecture decomposition (Buede, 2009).  In order to allow for successful building and implementation of a system that could successfully complete the scenario formulated in the Design Reference Mission, an extensive evaluation was conducted and the resulting functional architecture hierarchy is illustrated in Figure 14.  This functional architecture hierarchy is utilized to ensure the requirements of providing a pier monitoring and mustering capability are met.

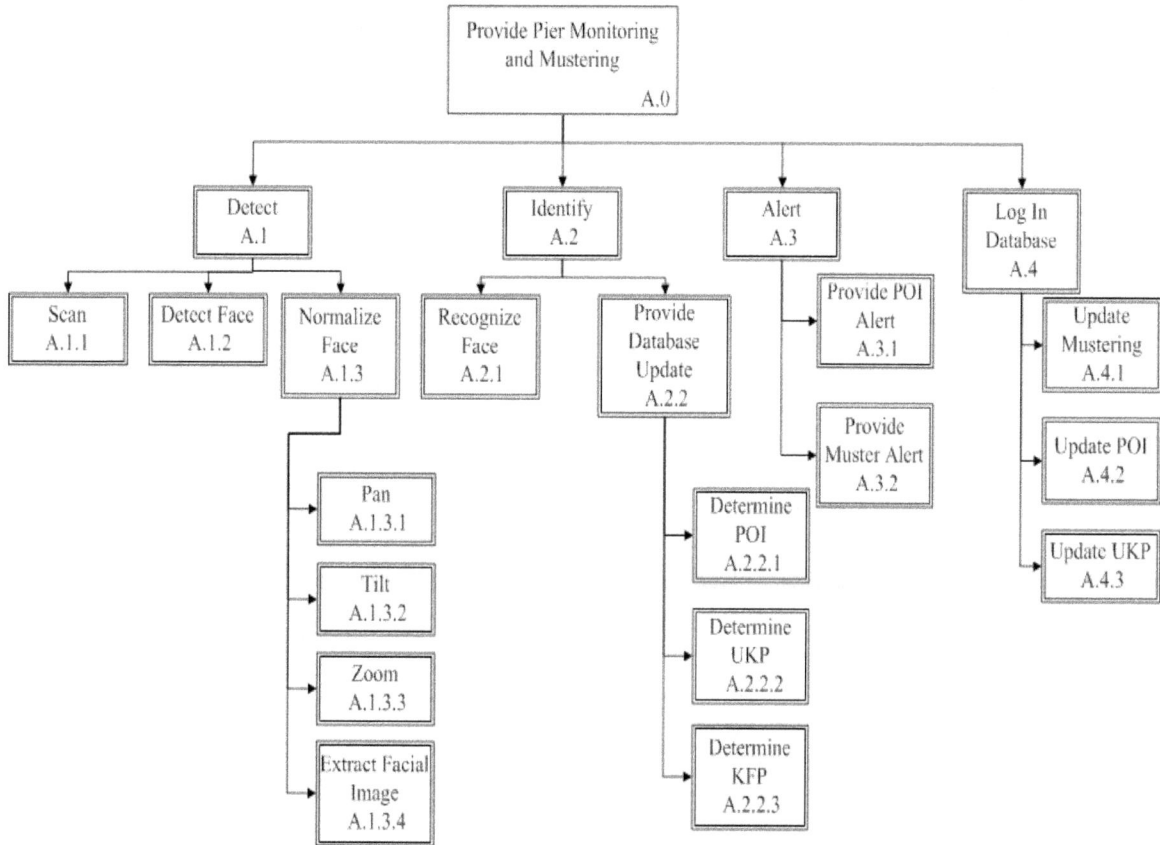

Figure 14.    Generic Functional Architecture Hierarchy

The functional architecture states the following four required functions should be performed in order to accomplish the goal of providing pier monitoring and mustering services:

- Detect
- Identify
- Alert
- Log in Database

Utilizing the IDEF0 modeling process, the functional architecture hierarchy from Figure 14 is decomposed starting at the top function and moving down functions level by level.   This decomposition shows functions at each level with inputs, outputs, and constraints that trace back to the ESD of Figure 14.  The top-level function of providing pier monitoring and mustering services for the generic system is depicted in Figure 15. This IDEF0 decomposition diagram shows that the function performed is inside the block.  The inputs to the function come in from the left, the constraints come in from the top, and the outputs come from the function box and go towards the right side of the diagram.

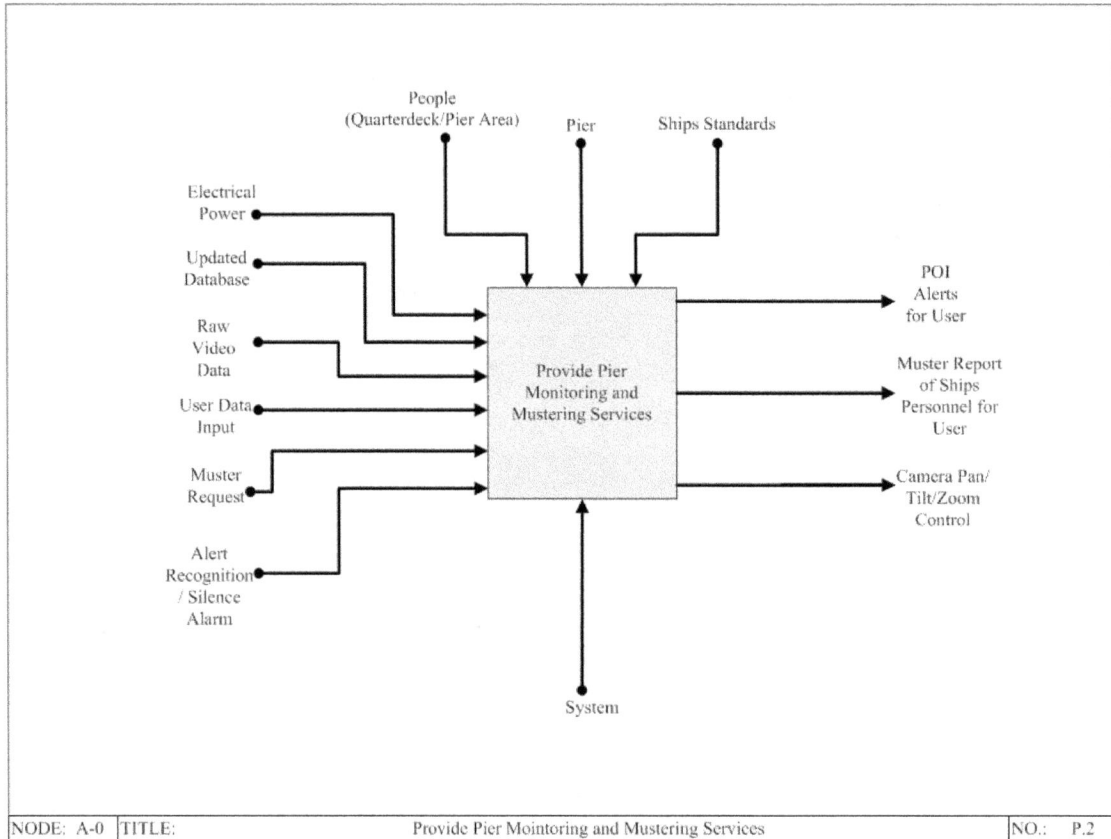

Figure 15.    Top-level Function for the Generic System

The top-level function is then broken down into the first level decomposition provided in Figure 16.  This first level decomposition shows the interactions of the first level from the functional architecture hierarchy individual functions.

33

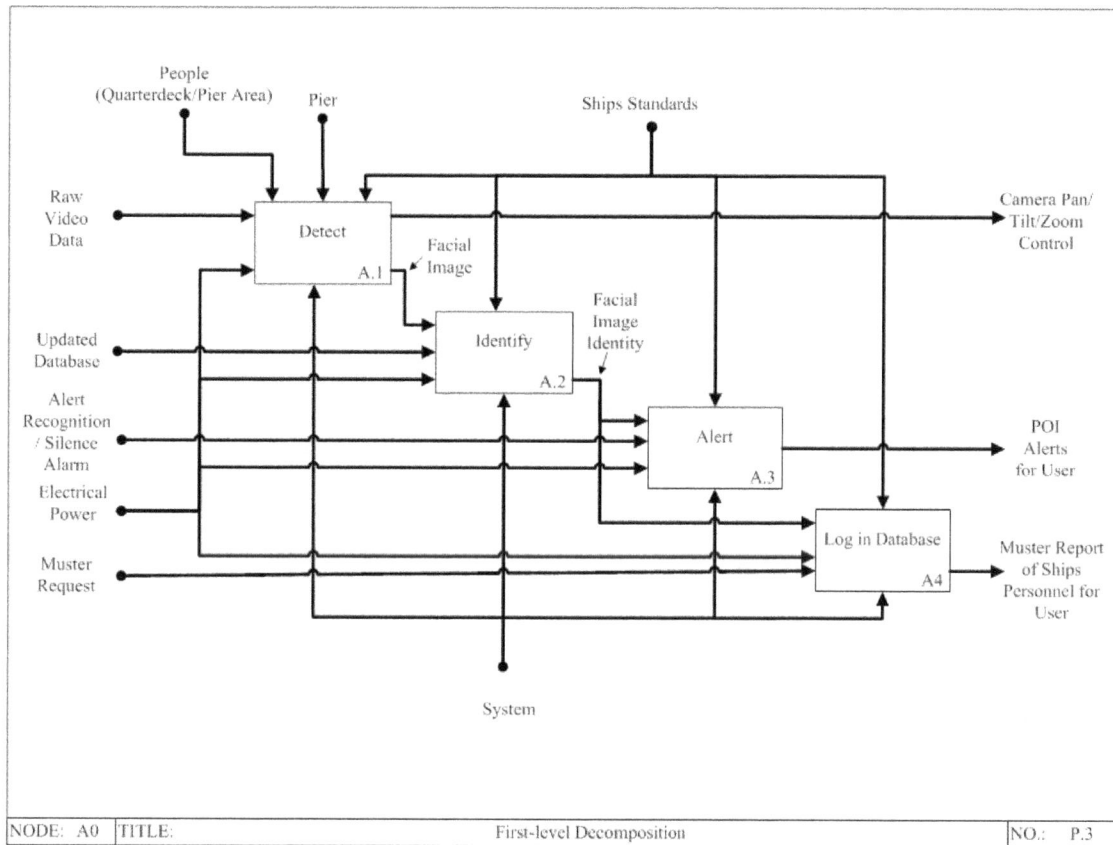

Figure 16. First-level Decomposition of the System Function Provide Pier Monitoring and Mustering Services

Figure 17 provides the decomposition of the Detect Function. This depiction displays how the Detect Function takes the raw video data and scans for an image of a person. It then takes that image of a person and looks for the location of the face. Next, the facial image is processed and normalized with the output being a facial image.

**Note**: In the case of scanning the pier area, there may be more than one person in the camera's field of view. Thus, the scan function includes scanning the camera's video frames for faces, in addition to scanning the pier monitoring area.

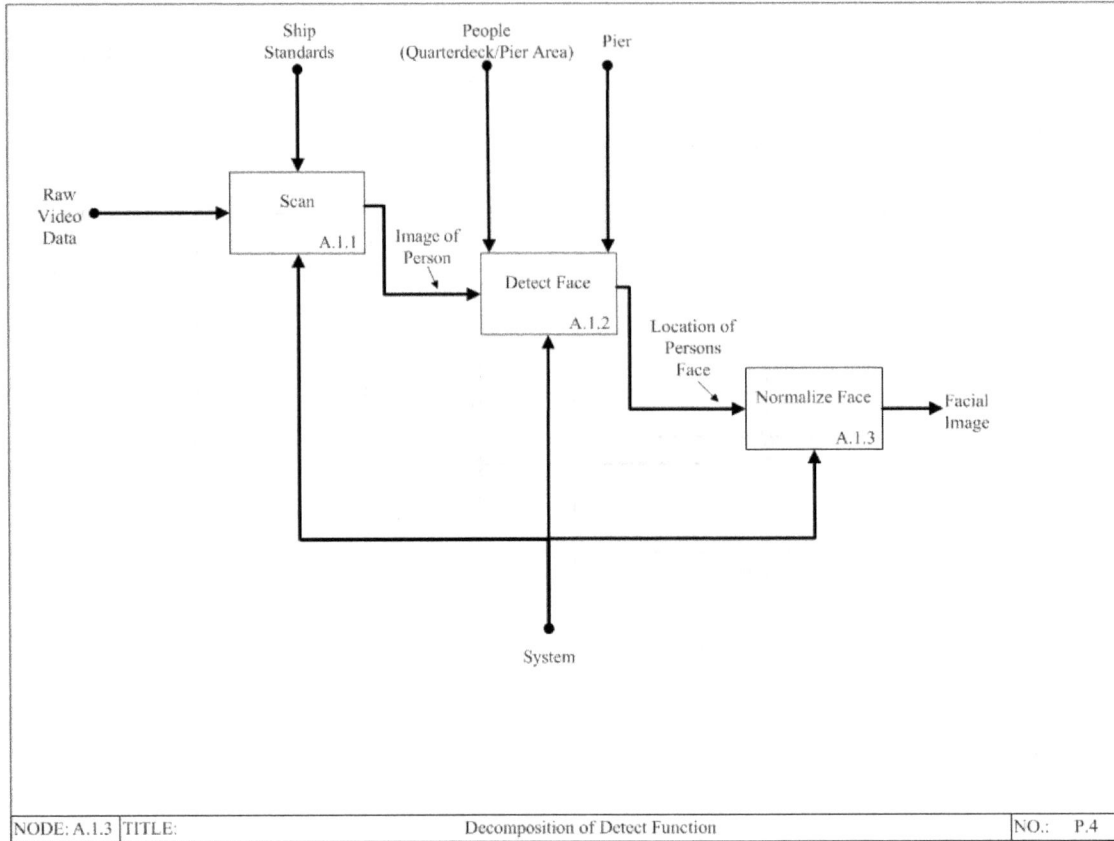

| NODE: A.1.3 | TITLE: | Decomposition of Detect Function | NO.: | P.4 |

Figure 17.    Decomposition of Detect Function

Figure 18 depicts the decomposition of the Normalize Face Function.  This decomposition displays how the Normalize Face Function takes the location of the persons face and creates pan and tilt commands as needed.  Then, once the pan and tilt is complete, the zoom command executes until complete.  The final step is to output the extracted facial image.

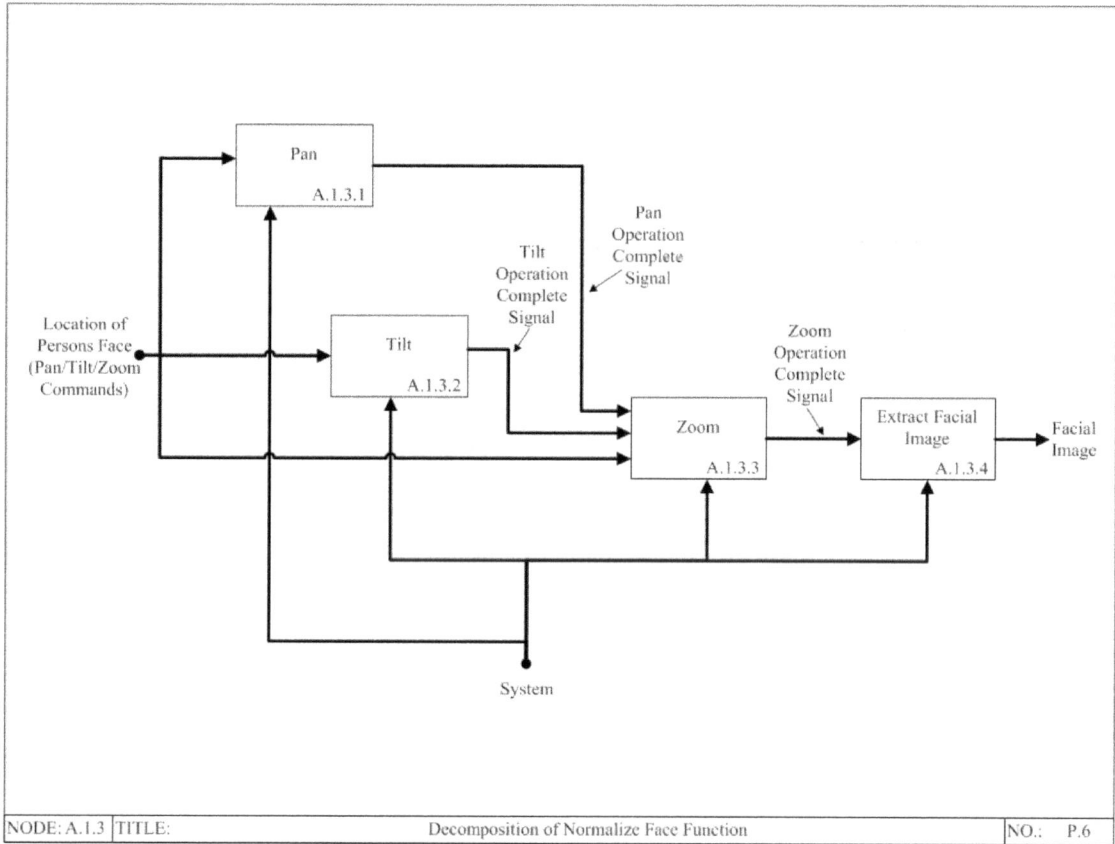

Figure 18.    Decomposition of Normalize Face Function

Figure 19 depicts the decomposition of the Identify Function. This depiction displays how the Identify Function takes the facial image of the person and identifies whether it is a POI, a KFP or a UKP. This function outputs the database classification of the facial image.

36

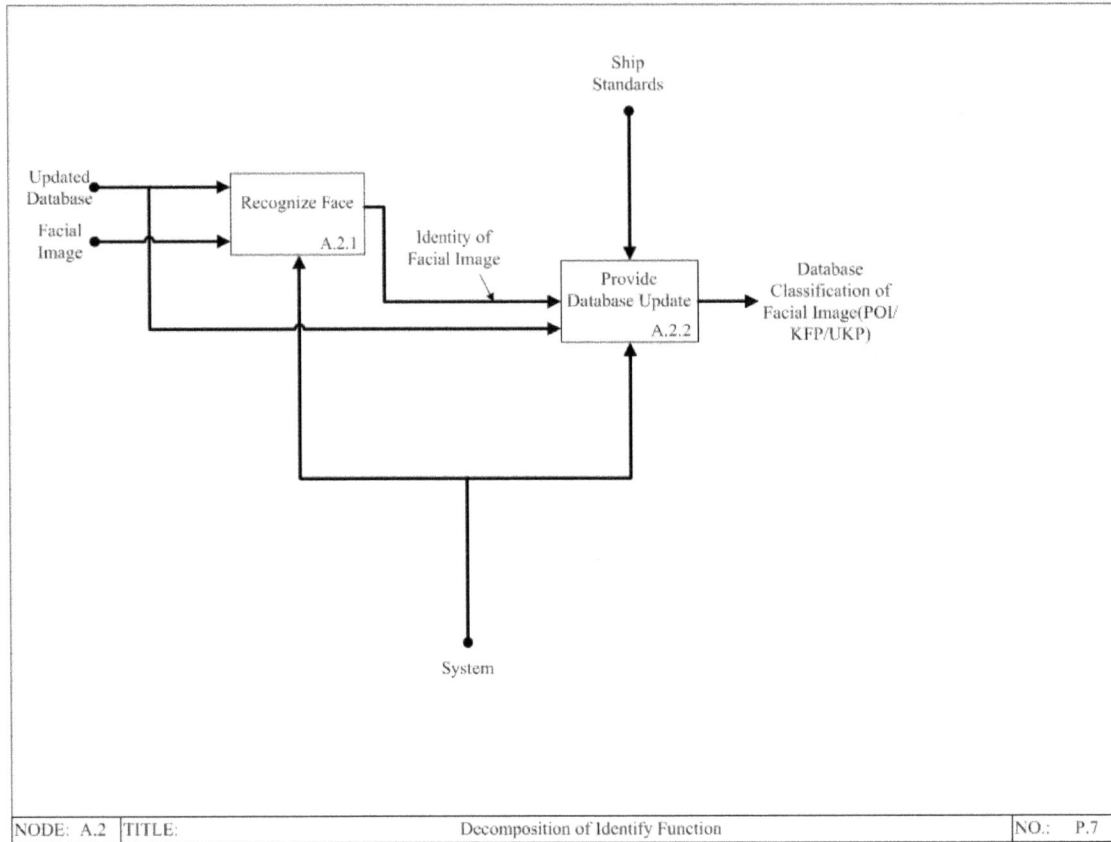

Figure 19.    Decomposition of Identify Function

Figure 20 depicts the decomposition of the Provide Database Update Function. This depiction displays how the Provide Database Update Function takes the identity of the facial image and determines whether it is a POI, KFP, or UKP. The output is the database identity of the person.

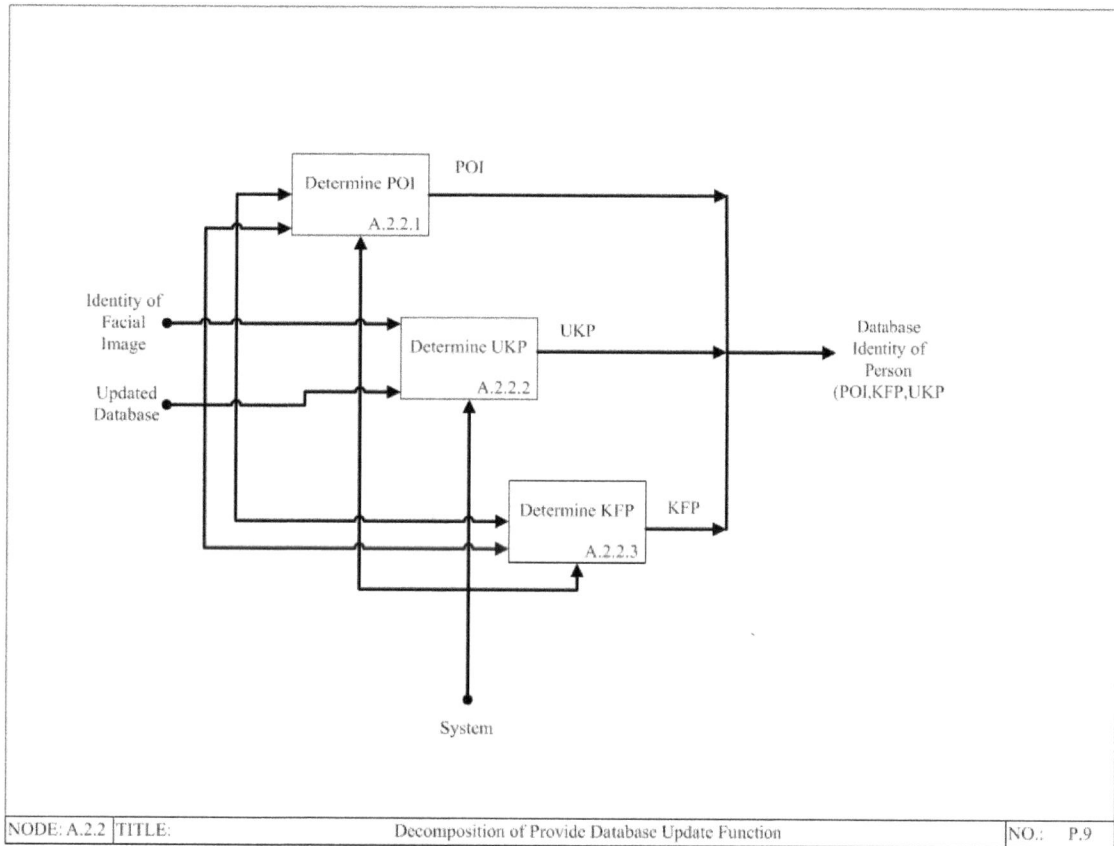

Figure 20.    Decomposition of Provide Database Update Function

Figure 21 depicts the decomposition of the Alert Function. This depiction displays how the Alert Function takes the identified facial image and provides an appropriate alert upon identification of any POIs or KFPs.

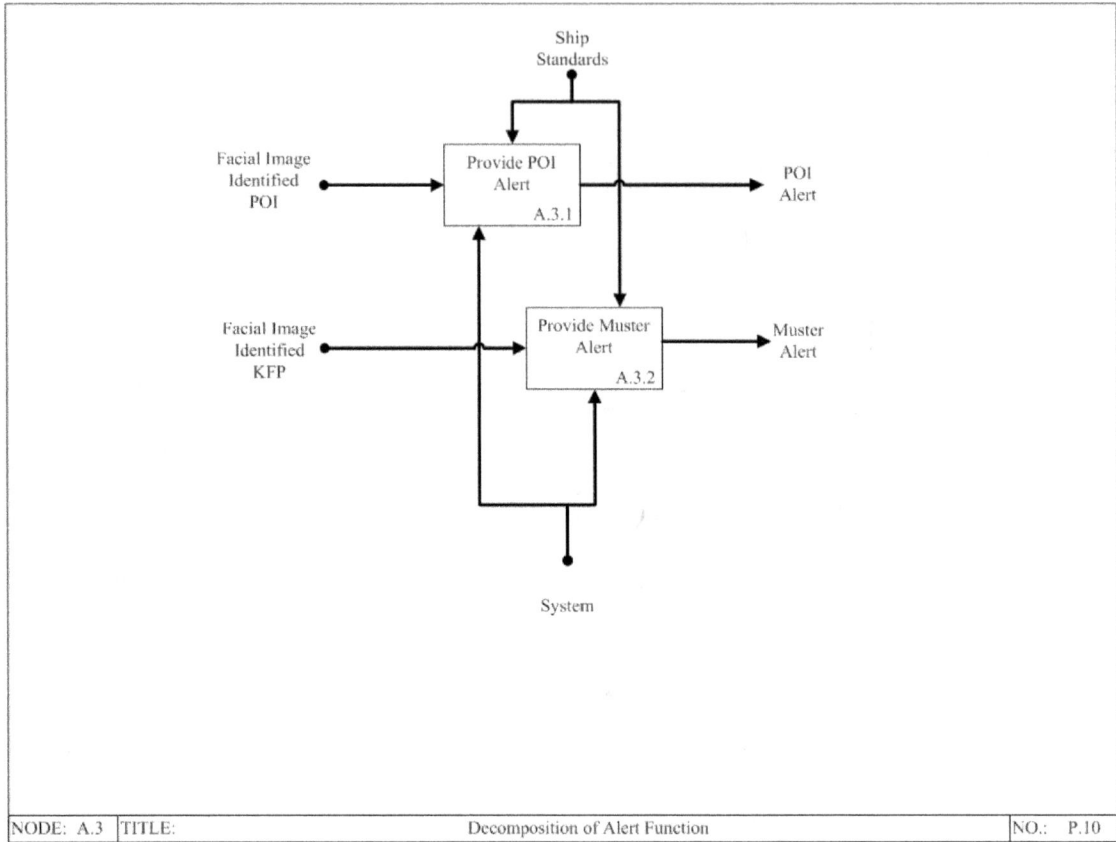

Facial Image Identified POI

Provide POI Alert
A.3.1

Ship Standards

POI Alert

Facial Image Identified KFP

Provide Muster Alert
A.3.2

Muster Alert

System

NODE: A.3 | TITLE: Decomposition of Alert Function | NO.: P.10

Figure 21.    Decomposition of Alert Function

Figure 22 depicts the decomposition of the Log in Database Function. This decomposition displays how the Log in Database Function takes the three different identifications, KFP, POI, and UKP, and updates the appropriate database. The output is a properly maintained and accurate status of each database.

39

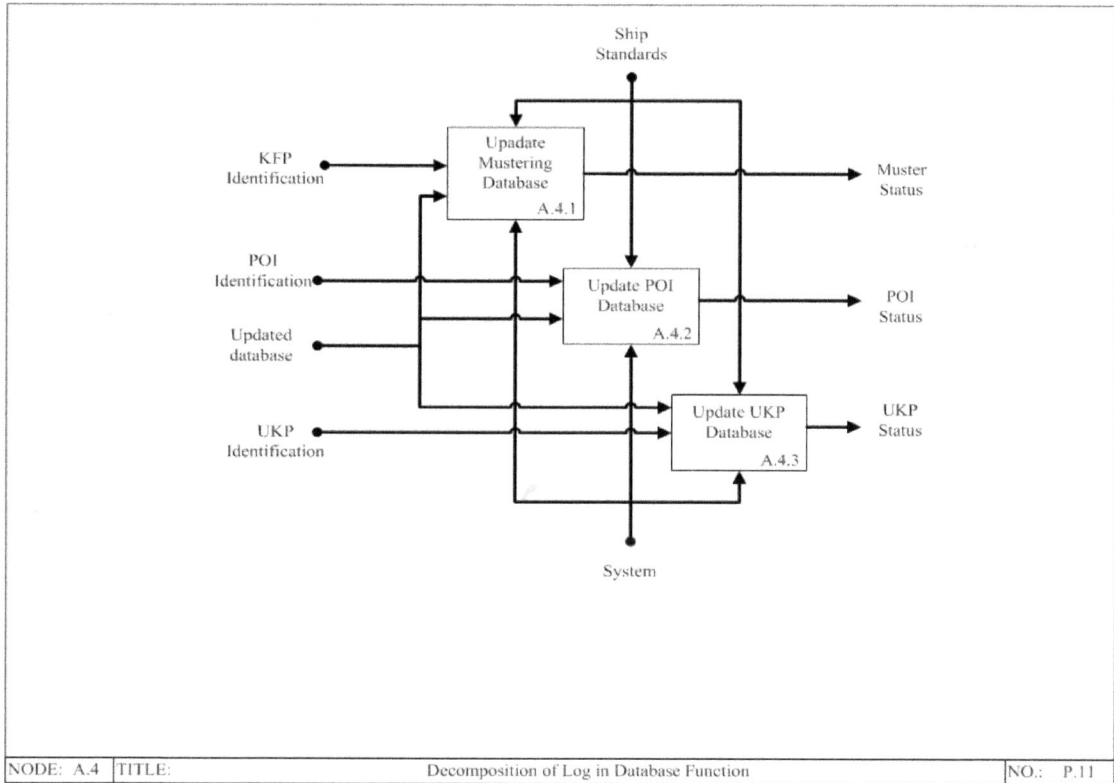

Figure 22. Decomposition of Log in Database Function

In summary, a generic architecture for the development of a system that addresses the capability gap described in the DRM was presented. Initially, a high-level operational view was provided. Using IDEF0 modeling an External Systems Diagram was created and generic requirements were provided. A functional architecture hierarchy and functional architecture decomposition was developed and captured using IDEF0. Chapter V continues the Systems Engineering process by presenting an analysis of alternatives, concept for the proposed solution, a brief explanation of facial recognition theory, the proposed system architecture, a physical architecture, and a proof-of-concept system is demonstrated and validated for viability.

# V.    PROPOSED SYSTEM SOLUTION

The pier security of LCS class ships and the mustering of their personnel are important to the overall security of the ship. This chapter discusses how to further design the system using the Systems Engineering "V" model to meet the operational need. The creation of the generic system architecture was presented in Chapter IV. The next step in applying the Systems Engineering "V" model is to conduct an analysis of alternatives to evaluate potential solutions. From these potential solutions, an alternative is selected as the proposed solution. The proposed solution is further developed in updating the generic functional architecture and requirements. From the updated functional architectures and requirements, an instantiated physical architecture is developed for this proposed solution. Additionally, this chapter provides a brief discussion on the theory behind the proposed solution. Next, the proposed solution is further developed, implemented, and tested through a proof-of-concept system. Finally, lessons learned and conclusions drawn from the Pier Watchman Proof-of-Concept System are discussed.

## A.    ANALYSIS OF ALTERNATIVES

Analysis of Alternatives is a process that looks at the required need, concept, ESD, requirements, and functional architecture to identify potentially viable solutions. Assessments are performed on each possible solution evaluating for effectiveness, achievability, cost, and viability (United States Air Force, 2008).

An extensive list of alternatives could be provided that could fulfill the need established in the DRM and the generic architecture presented in Chapter IV. A potential alternative may include incorporating additional personnel to satisfy all functions including face detection, identification, alerting, and logging in the database. Other alternatives might incorporate alternative biometric sensors for automatic personnel identification, such as fingerprint scanning. Due to time and budget constraints, this thesis will focus on one alternative that utilizes facial recognition technology as the basis for an autonomous mustering and pier monitoring system. By utilizing existing sensors and adding only one more camera, the proposed system concept leverages the existing

LCS systems and infrastructure while not adding additional manning. As discussed in Chapter I, Ship Class General Information Section (Section B), minimal manning and maximum automation is a goal in LCS design. Subsequently, the remainder of the systems engineering process in this thesis focuses on this one proposed alternative.

## B.    PROPOSED SYSTEM CONCEPT

The concept for the proposed solution came out of two experiences of working with LCS-1 and participating in the Artificial Intelligence Systems Engineering courses I and II given during the fall quarter of 2008 and the spring quarter of 2009 at Naval Postgraduate School (NPS) Network-Centric Systems Engineering Track, taught by Professor Rachel Goshorn. During these courses the class designed, built, coded, debugged, tested, integrated, and demonstrated an autonomous mustering and behavior analysis system called "Watchman." This system utilized fixed view cameras, personnel tracking, behavior analysis, and facial recognition software to monitor the second story of the Bullard Hall building at NPS. The system would attempt to capture a facial image as soon as a person climbed the stairs and came onto the second floor. This image would then be autonomously processed and correlated in an attempt to muster the person into the system (Goshorn, 2009).

In support of the AOA, the proposed solution concept came about during construction of the Watchman system. While constructing this system it was determined that a similar network-centric system was both needed and could be easily adapted to the Freedom class of ships. Personal experience provided insight into the fact that the Freedom class of ships already had external cameras similar to those in Watchman, with a pan, tilt, and zoom capability and operated in all weather conditions. Additionally, after a careful review, a decision was made to recommend that the proposed solution for LCS ships be autonomous. To further investigate the feasibility of building and installing an autonomous pier security and mustering system onto the Freedom class of ships, an instantiated physical architecture was developed and demonstrated. The next sections describe the proposed mustering and force protection processes including a brief background of face recognition technology.

## C. THE PROPOSED MUSTERING AND FORCE PROTECTION PROCESSES

Along with providing constant crew status, the utilization of an automated mustering system alleviates some of the administrative burden associated with executing the existing manual system. The proposed system continually monitors and maintains the local LCS mustering databases. The result is that every person coming onto and leaving the ship would be automatically identified and mustered. This provides a quick and accurate muster of who is onboard the ship. The Pier Watchman Proof-of-Concept System demonstrates the functionality and proves that this is feasible. A detailed explanation of its operation is provided in later in this chapter.

The current force protection process, described in Chapter I, needs to be enhanced while the composition and number of watch standers must not increase. The proposed system utilizes an autonomous set of cameras to constantly monitor the pier area. This system will monitor for personnel in the vicinity of the ship. When it identifies a person, it will attempt to perform a digital facial recognition of the person. If a facial image is captured, the system will automatically compare that image with a database of known facial images and look for facial image correlation as seen in Figure 1. If an image is correlated above a prescribed threshold, the system will record the person's name, time, and camera in the database. The image will then be given one of three different designations: Known Friendly Person (KFP), Unknown Person (UKP), and Person of Interest (POI).

The known friendly images will be recorded in the database for future review if needed, but no further action is expected. If the image is correlated to a known person of interest (e.g., terrorist), the system will provide an audible alert to the watch standers so that they can decide on further action. Additionally, all information on the POI will be recorded in its database. The list of POIs will be created and updated for the LCS local database by outside intelligence organizations. All unknown facial images will also be recorded in the UKP database and given a unique alphanumeric identifier so one can reference the facial image without a name. If a person who was previously identified as a UKP is observed, again the pertinent information is recorded under their original database entry.

The system will also monitor all of the UKP persons for further information, such as the length of time that a UKP was monitoring the ship and whether or not he or she was monitoring it on more than one occasion. The goal is to determine whether terrorist groups are monitoring the ship. The proposed system would provide an alert to the watch standers if either a UKP breaches a threshold time (using an established threshold time) for monitoring the ship or a UKP is identified on multiple occasions at pier sites. The watch standers will report this issue to the Force Protection Officer (FPO). The FPO can then review the information and decide on further action.

The proposed procedure for reacting to alerts for POIs or suspicious UKPs will be for the FPO to review the data and determine if it is a possible threat and react accordingly. In the case of UKPs, the FPO will be trying to determine if the image captured is of an authorized individual such as a dockworker or local employee, or confirm if it is someone suspicious. In the case of a POI alert, the FPO will be looking to ensure that the facial image that is captured looks close to the stored POI facial image. Any suspicious UKPs or confirmed POIs will be reported up the chain of command locally and then if required off the ship for resolution. A goal of this thesis is not to set the exact procedure that will be utilized for suspicious UKP or POI identified persons, but instead to propose and establish the viability of a system that can automatically determine that there has been persistent or repeated monitoring of the ship.

One area outside the scope of this thesis is the training required for this proposed system. As with any new system, there will be a certain level of required training for both operation and maintenance of the proposed system. The amount of training required will be based on the exact parameters of the final system. Training should be discussed in detail prior to deployment of the system.

## D.    FACE RECOGNITION THEORY

The proposed automated system relies heavily on the use of facial recognition software. This section will provide a brief explanation of how one particular version of facial recognition software works. This thesis does not prescribe which facial recognition program should be used for a full-scale system; the high-level functionality of any face recognition software is essentially the same (Turk and Pentland, 1991). The selection of a facial recognition program can be made after the decision to move beyond the initial proof-of-concept is made.

Video is composed of several frames (digital images) per second and a facial recognition algorithm can process the digital images (Baxes, 1994). Facial recognition starts with the capturing of digital images with a digital camera. The digital image captures the field-of-view of the camera. A camera's field-of-view is the two-dimensional scene that the camera "sees." The digital image can be stored as matrices in color or in grayscale (Baxes, 1994). If the digital image is stored in color, it is generally stored as three rectangular arrays of pixels (one array for each color channel: red, green, blue), whose pixel values are the intensity level of the specific color channel at that location of the camera field-of-view. The image can also be stored with only one rectangular array, if using grayscale images. In this case, the pixel values are an intensity of the gray value at that pixel value. The number of pixels in an array is dependent on the camera resolution for the camera's field-of-view. Each (x, y) coordinate location on this two-dimensional scene corresponds to a pixel location in the digital image. Each pixel correlates to an actual (x, y) coordinate location of the field-of-view of the camera. (Baxes, 1994). Once the scene is digitized with a digital image, it can be processed for automating intelligence, such as automating facial recognition.

There are numerous algorithms and techniques for face (image) recognition, but in this thesis, and in the Pier Watchman proof-of-concept system, the algorithm utilized is based on the use of an Eigenface (Turk and Pentland, 1991). This is based on the principal that every facial image in a database can be mathematically recreated (approximately) using a linear combination of a small number of Eigenface facial images.

These Eigenfaces do not look like any one person's face, but rather like different skeletons of faces, each capturing a "principal component" that may be present in all faces of the database. This is why each face in the database can be recreated (approximately) by adding or subtracting only these Eigenfaces. Eigenfaces of the database and of the detected face of interest are calculated by performing Principal Component Analysis (PCA) on the images. PCA techniques have the ability to find the principal vectors (or "components") that best represent the distribution of the face within the captured digital image (Turk and Pentland, 1991). Figure 23 shows a typical face before conversion and Figure 24 shows seven Eigenfaces created from that face. The Eigenfaces of this image are correlated with the Eigenfaces of the database. This allows for faster and more robust correlation, then correlating the original facial image of the person of interest with all of the original facial images stored in the database.

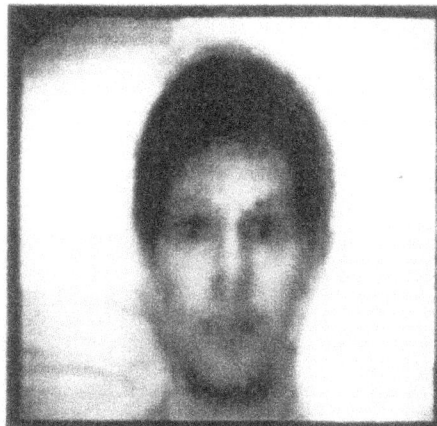

Figure 23.   Typical Face (From Turk and Pentland, 1991, 75)

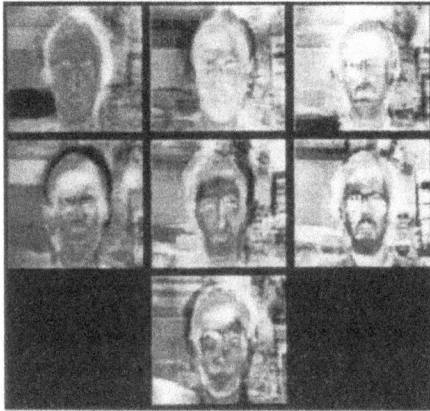

Figure 24.    Seven of the Eigenfaces Calculated from Typical Face in Figure 23 (From Turk and Pentland, 1991, 75)

The University of Maryland (UMD) and Massachusetts Institute of Technology (MIT) Media Laboratory algorithm is an example of facial recognition software. This algorithm utilizes Eigenface transforms, a component of Principal Component Analysis. Figure 25 illustrates a brief explanation of how this process works (Pentland and Tanzeem, 2000, 53). In order to correlate a facial image to a database of facial images, the images must be compiled in the database. Subsequently, the first step explained in Figure 25 is to collect the database of facial images that are then converted into sets of Eigenfaces through PCA. These stored images make up the known images that can be used for correlation. Facial recognition of a person is done by taking their newly captured image, extracting its Eigenfaces, and comparing them to the stored database of Eigenfaces. In the case of the UMD and MIT algorithm, they were looking for at least a similarity of not less than 50% correlation. If the images have a 50% correlation or better, the images would be considered to match and the person would be identified. The correlation threshold is variable and application dependent based on accuracy, tolerance (e.g., false positives, false negatives), and the mission (e.g., could be different for POIs and KFPs).

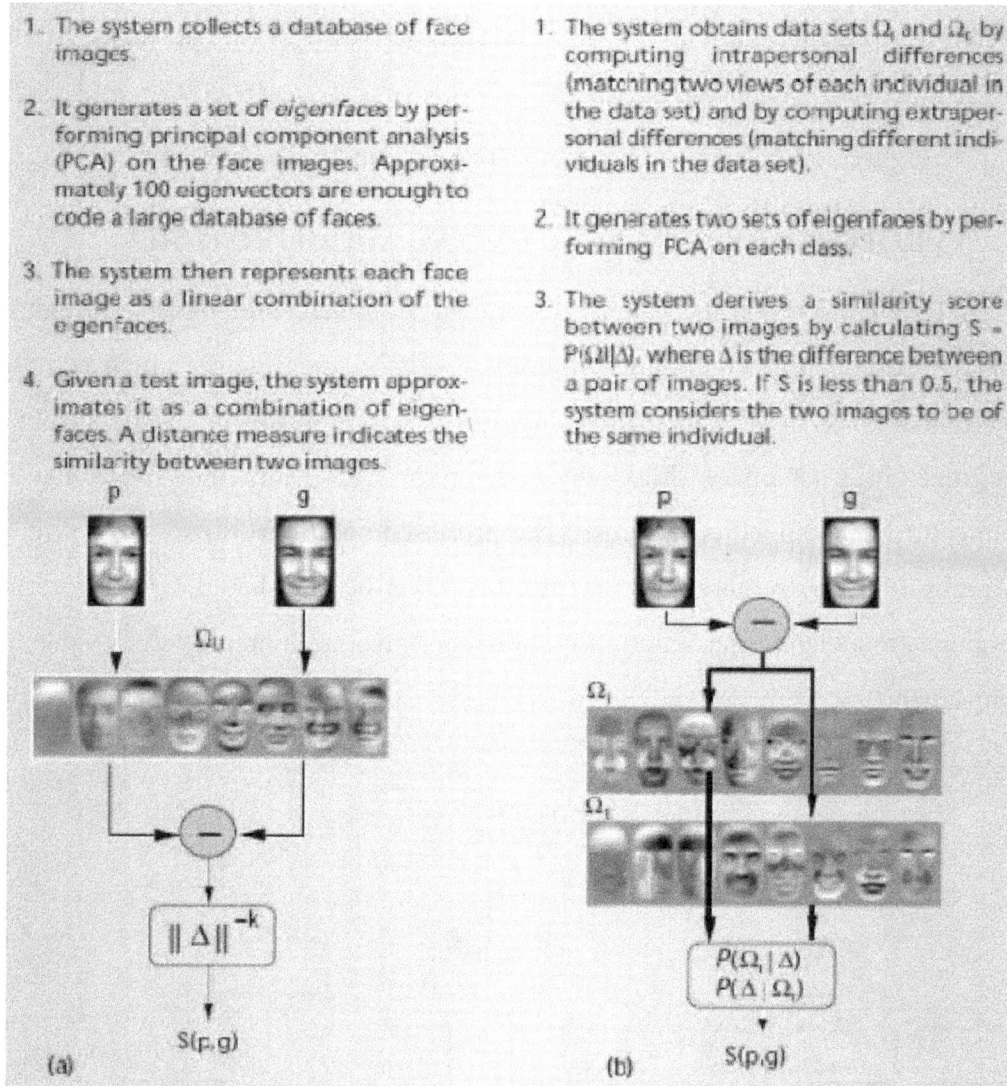

1. The system collects a database of face images.

2. It generates a set of *eigenfaces* by performing principal component analysis (PCA) on the face images. Approximately 100 eigenvectors are enough to code a large database of faces.

3. The system then represents each face image as a linear combination of the eigenfaces.

4. Given a test image, the system approximates it as a combination of eigenfaces. A distance measure indicates the similarity between two images.

1. The system obtains data sets $\Omega_l$ and $\Omega_E$ by computing intrapersonal differences (matching two views of each individual in the data set) and by computing extrapersonal differences (matching different individuals in the data set).

2. It generates two sets of eigenfaces by performing PCA on each class.

3. The system derives a similarity score between two images by calculating $S = P(\Omega_I|\Delta)$, where $\Delta$ is the difference between a pair of images. If S is less than 0.5, the system considers the two images to be of the same individual.

Figure 25.    UMD and MIT Eigenfaces Procedure (From Pentland and Tanzeem, 2000, 53)

## E.    PROPOSED SOLUTION FUNCTIONS

The proposed system follows the functional architecture of the proposed system solution, thus it was designed with the four basic functions described in the generic architecture, to meet the operational need: detect, identify, alert, and log in database. Figure 26 reviews the simplified functional architecture diagram from the generic architecture as applied to the proposed system solution providing the functional workflows for the system.  A proof-of-concept system must be able to perform these functions in order to be successful.

48

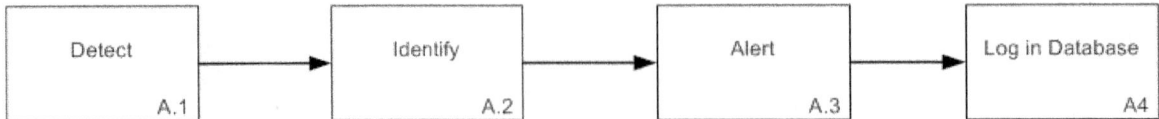

Figure 26.  Proposed Proof-of-Concept Functional Architecture Diagram

## F.  PROPOSED SYSTEM FUNCTIONAL ARCHITECTURE

Expanding upon the generic functional architecture hierarchy and adapting it to proposed solution of an automated solution, results in updating the functional architecture decomposition system components and further decomposition of the detect face and recognize face functions highlighted in Figure 27 and the following functional architecture decomposition figures.  The proposed solution utilizes the entire functional hierarchy with the requirement that the functions be automated.  Therefore, additional functions are added to the generic functional architecture hierarchy due to the automation requirement.

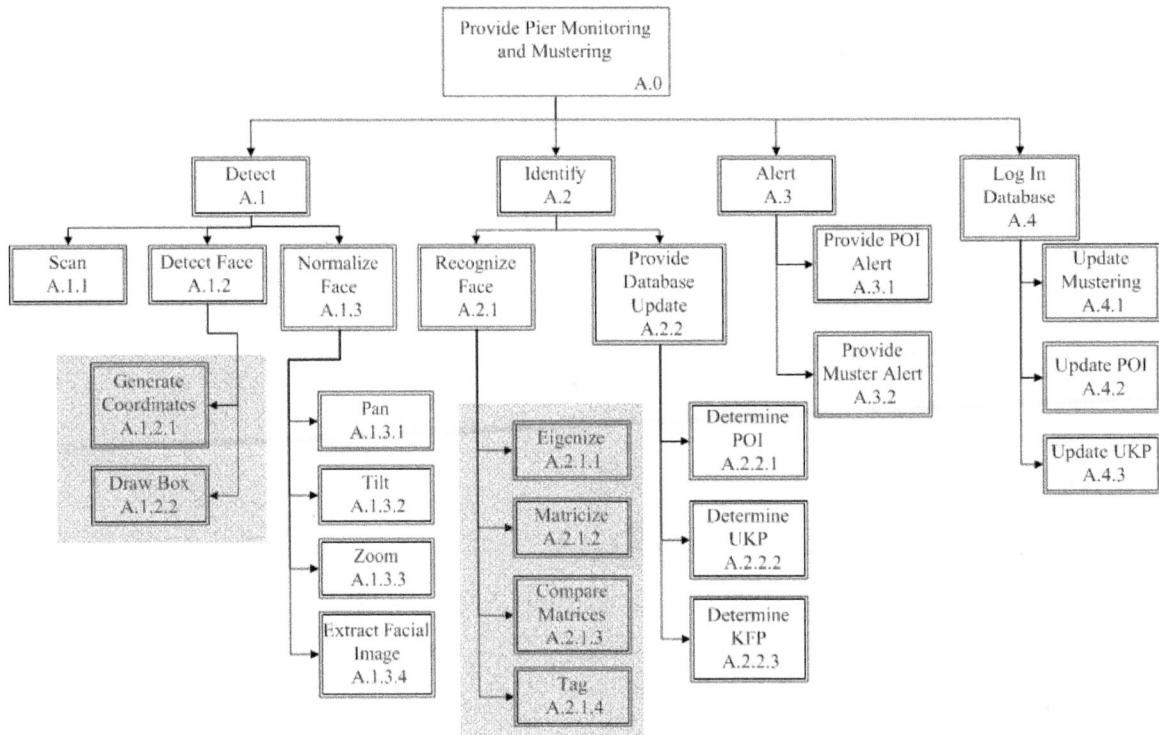

Figure 27.  Functional Architecture Hierarchy for the Proposed System

49

In Figures 28–34 the generic architecture decompositions have been modified to reflect the use of automation (highlighted in each figure). Figures 35–36 are proposed system functional architecture decompositions that further decompose the functions highlighted in Figure 27. The first level decomposition of the proposed solution is provided in Figure 28.

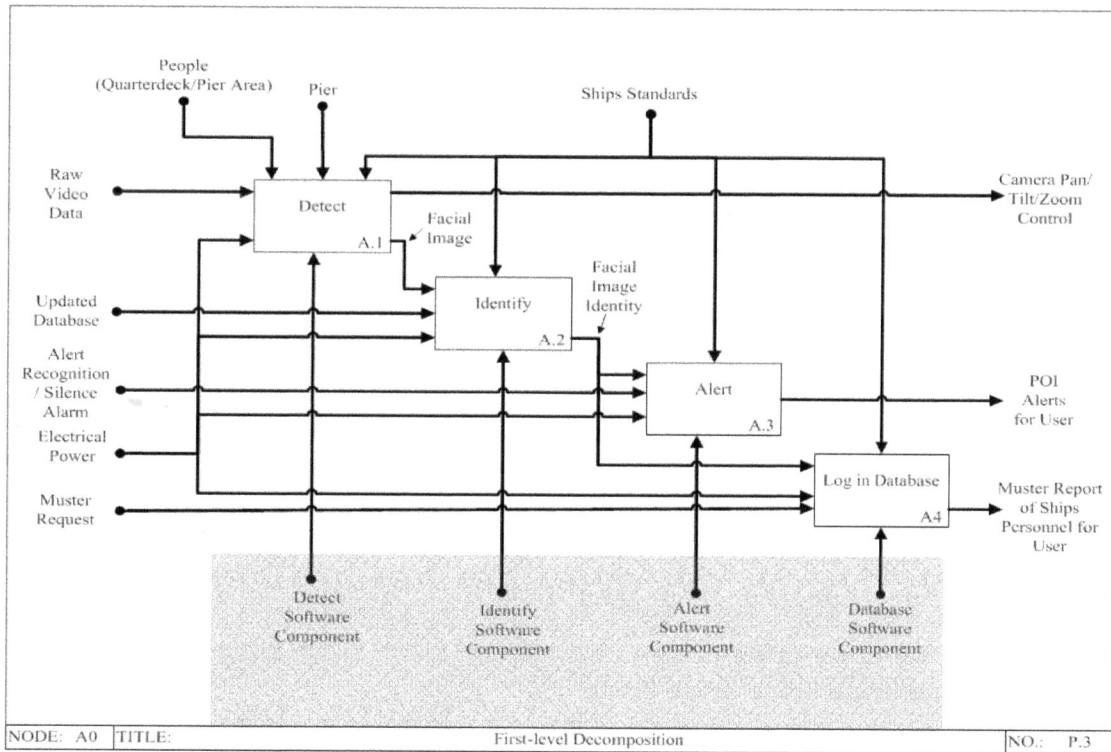

Figure 28. First-level Decomposition of the System Function for the Proposed System

Figure 29 provides the decomposition of the Detect Function for the proposed solution.

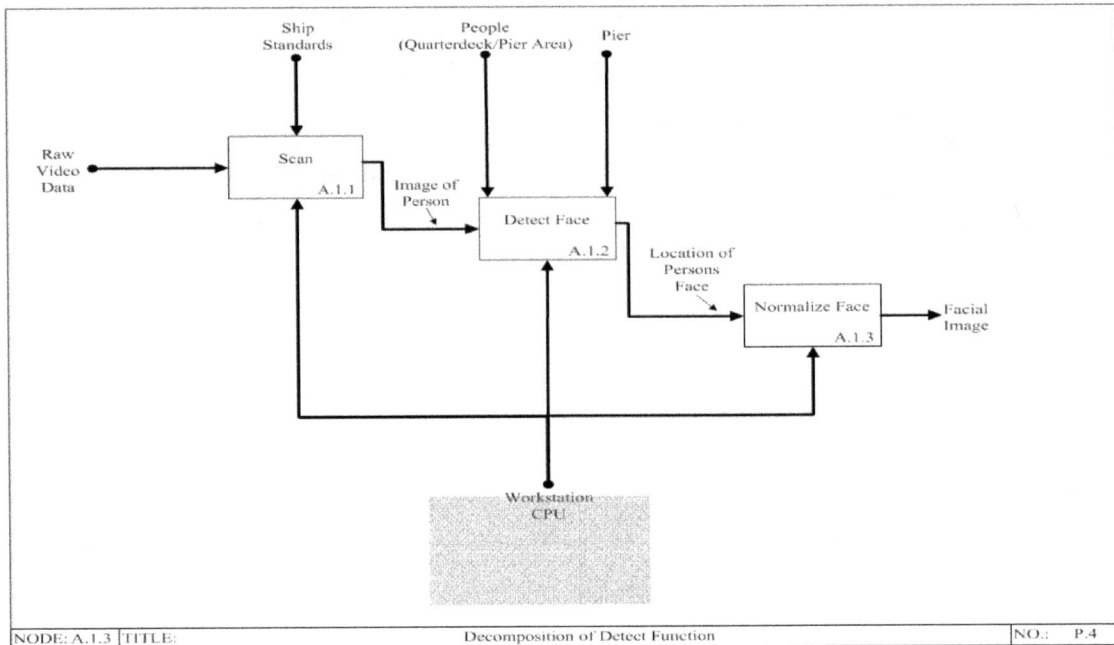

Figure 29.    Decomposition of Detect Function for the Proposed System

Figure 30 provides the decomposition of the Normalize Face Function for the proposed solution.

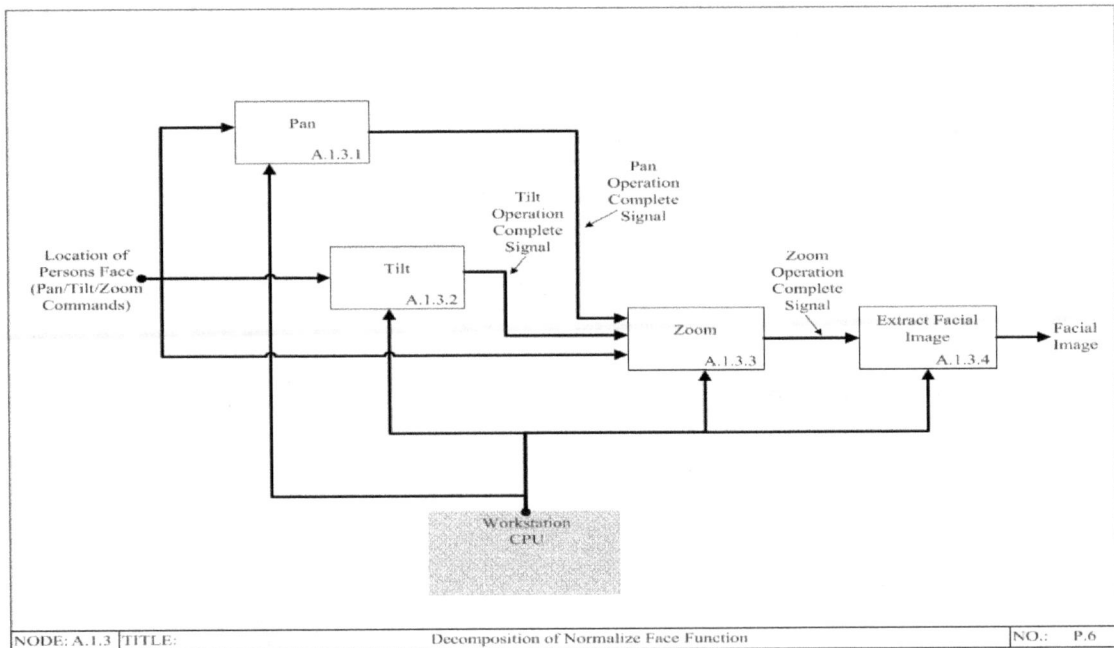

Figure 30.    Decomposition of Normalize Face Function for the Proposed System

Figure 31 provides the decomposition of the Identify Function for the proposed solution.

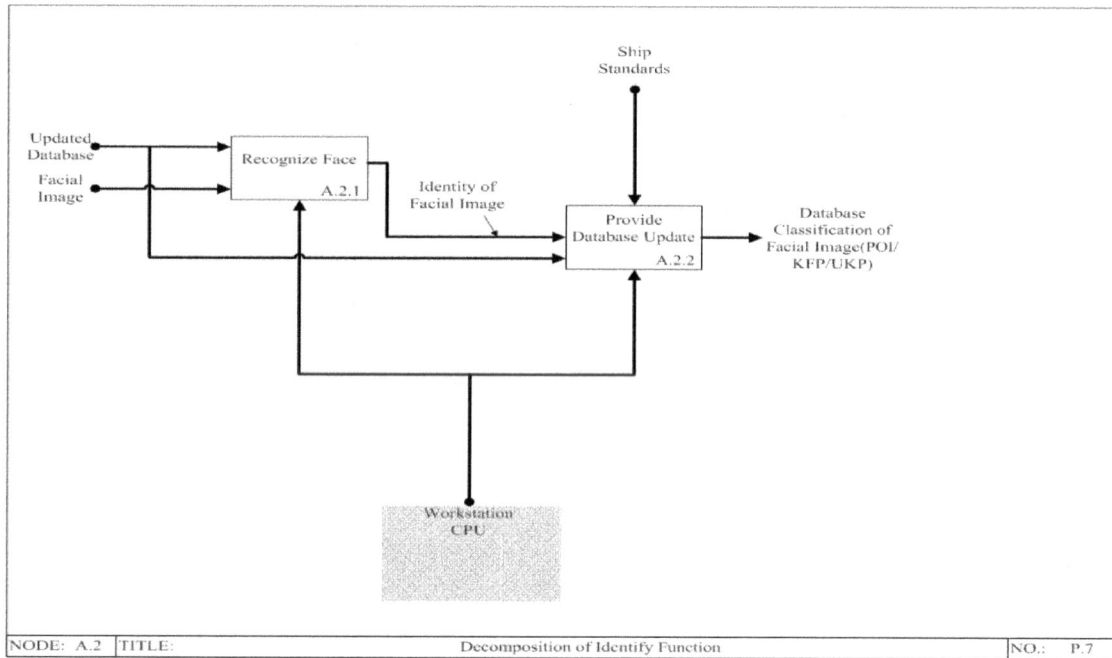

Figure 31.    Decomposition of Identify Function for the Proposed System

Figure 32 provides the decomposition of the Provide Database Update Function for the proposed solution.

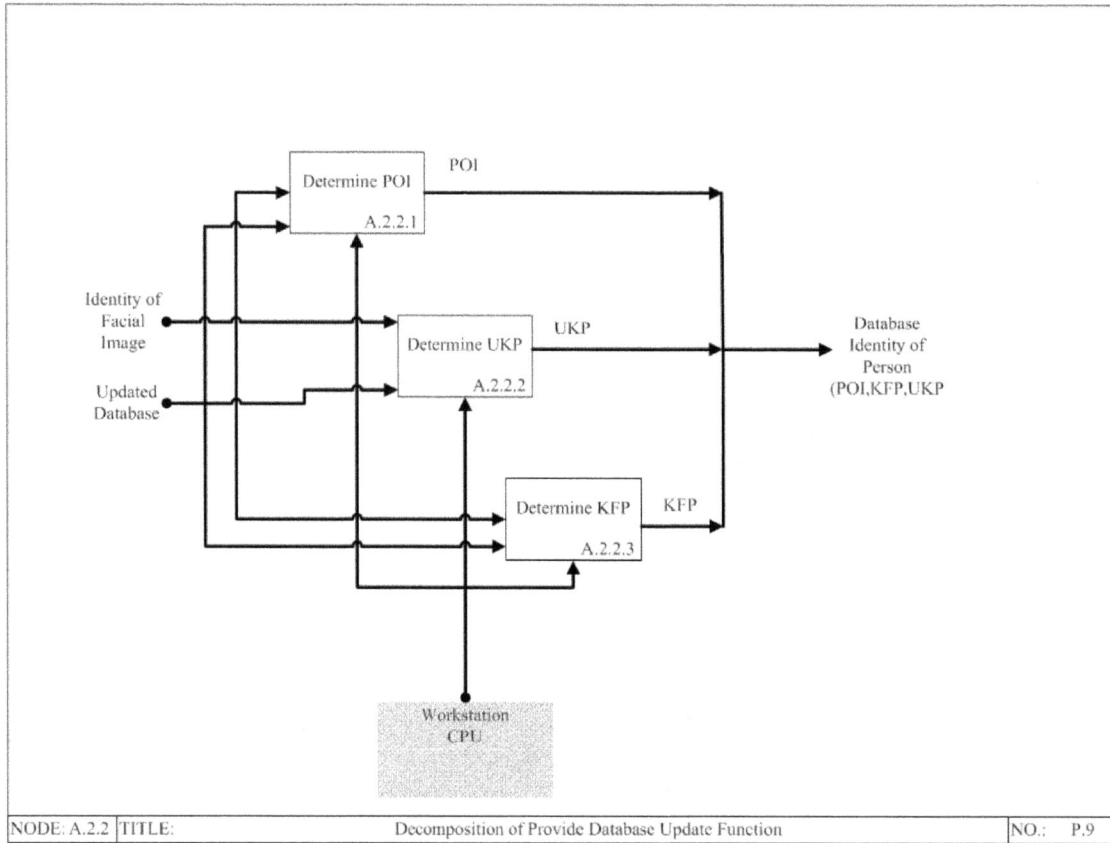

Figure 32.    Decomposition of Provide Database Update Function for the Proposed
System

Figure 33 provides the decomposition of the Detect Function for the proposed
solution.

53

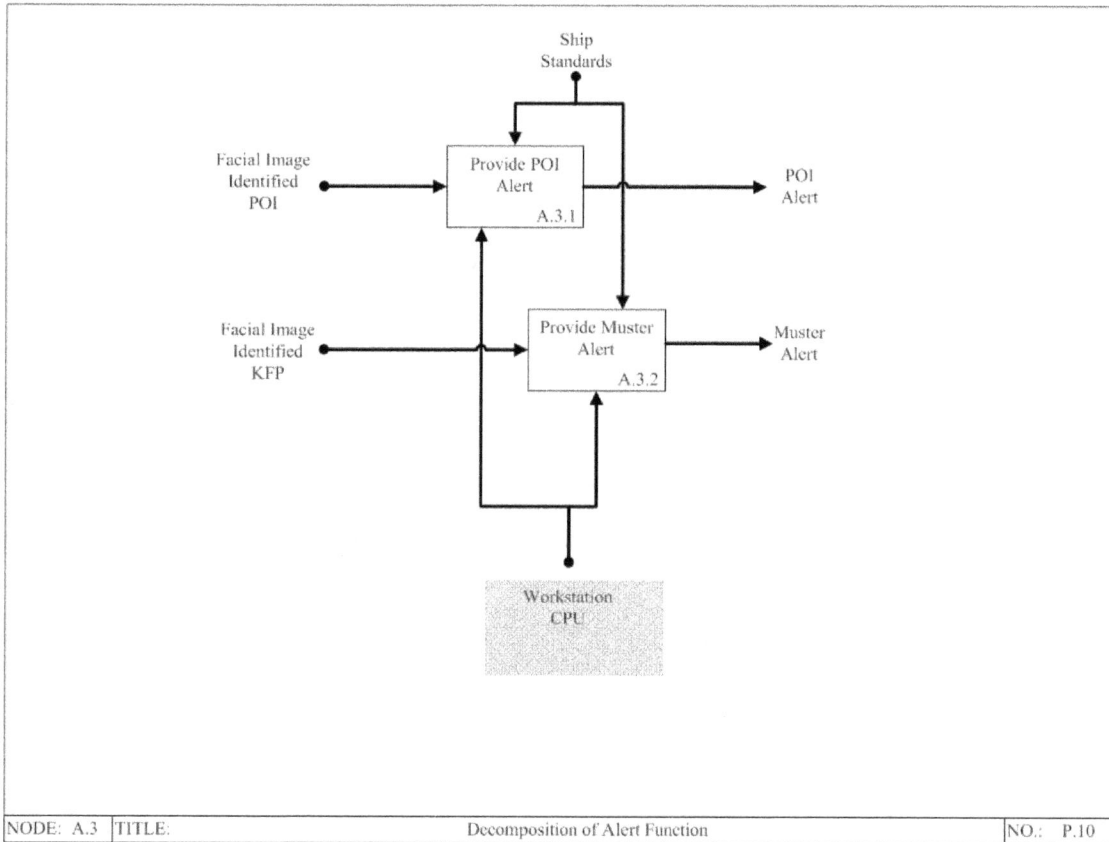

Figure 33.    Decomposition of Alert Function for the Proposed System

Figure 34 provides the decomposition of the Detect Function for the proposed solution.

54

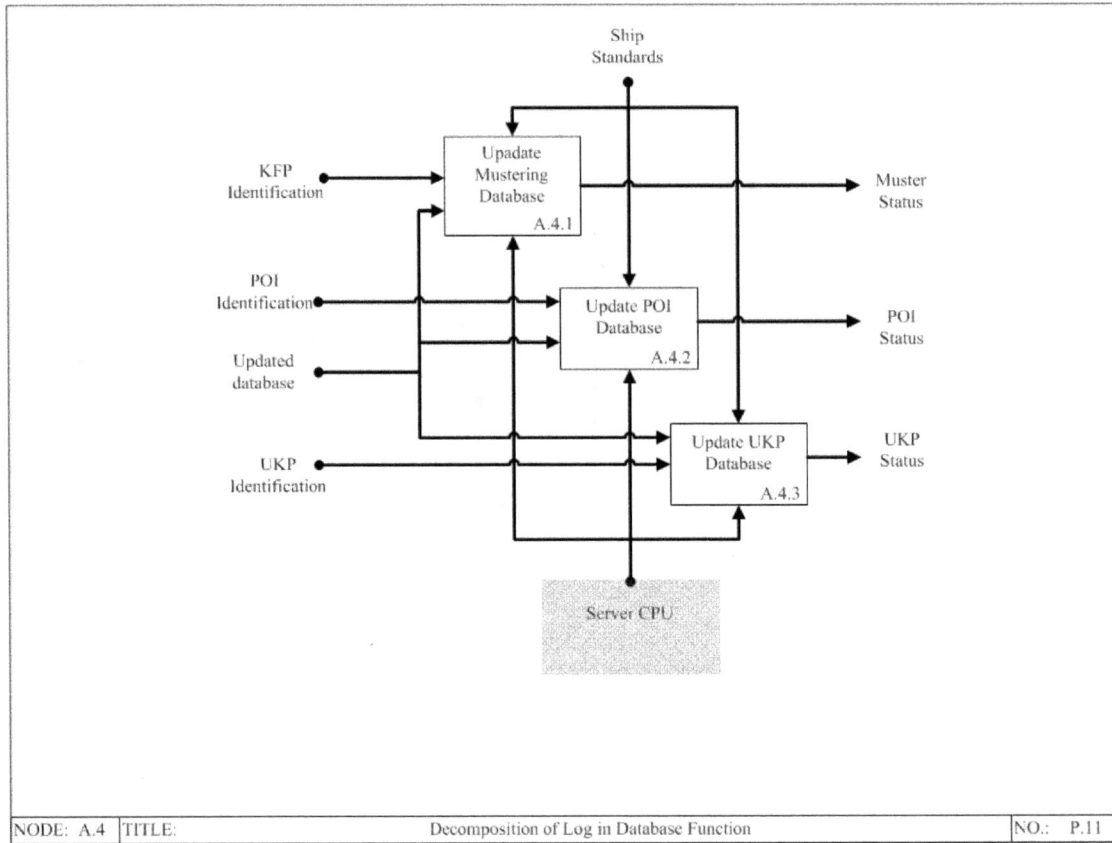

| NODE: A.4 | TITLE: | Decomposition of Log in Database Function | NO.: P.11 |

Figure 34.    Decomposition of Log in Database Function for the Proposed System

Figure 35 depicts the decomposition of the Detect Face Function. This depiction displays how the Detect Face Function takes the image of the person and generates the coordinates for the face within the image of the person. The Detect Face Function then draws a box around the face and outputs the location of the person's facial image.

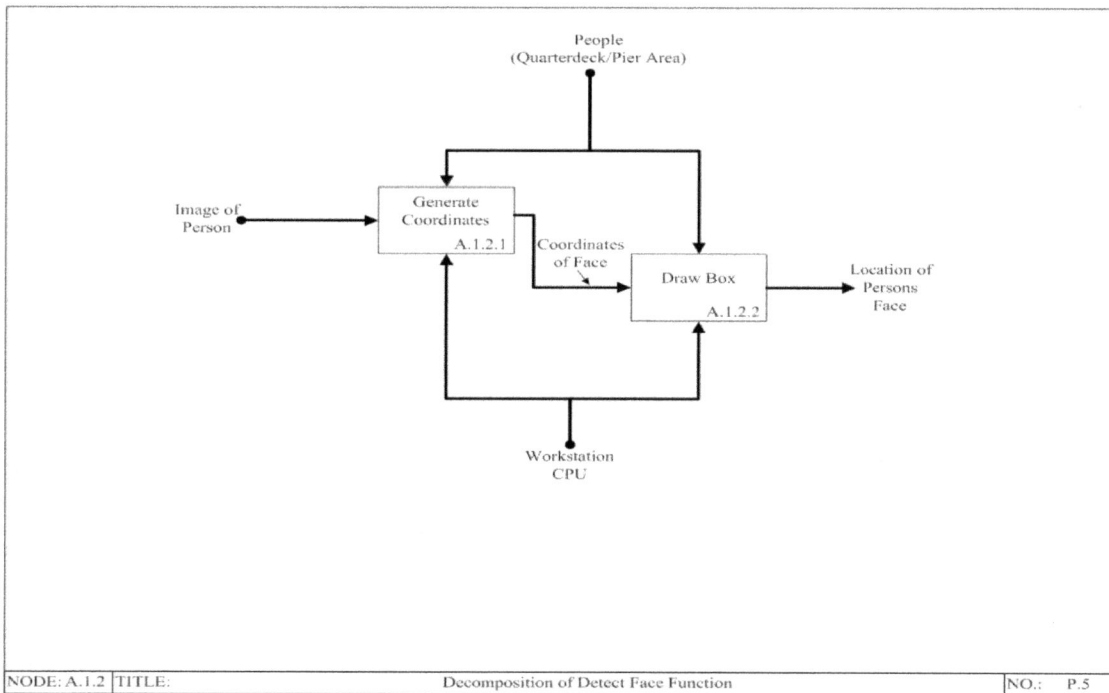

Figure 35. Decomposition of Detect Face Function for the Proposed System

Figure 36 depicts the decomposition of the Recognize Face Function. This depiction displays how the Recognize Face Function takes the facial image and turns it into eigenvectors. These eigenvectors are then put into a matrix so that the current facial image matrix and the matrix of the updated database can be compared to a stored set of matrices (stored in the local database) that correlate to a known facial image. Once a correlation is established, the facial image is tagged with the identity of that facial image.

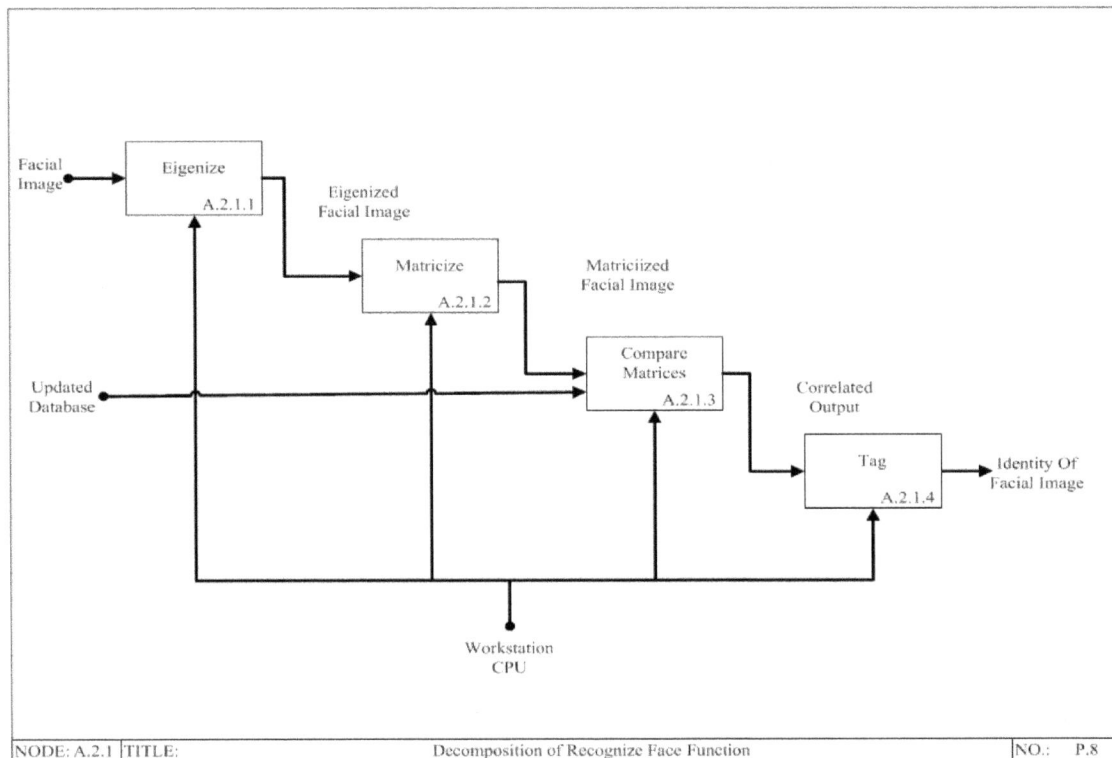

Figure 36.    Decomposition of Recognize Face Function for the Proposed System

The decompositions of each of the expanded functions demonstrate how an automated system could conform to the generic architecture with minimal additions.

## G.    REQUIREMENTS

The requirements established in the generic architecture can be adapted to meet the proposed system solution by adding line items specific to the automation functions. The proposed system requirements are listed below:

G. Requirements

G.1.0—Input/output requirements

G.1.1—Input requirements

G.1.1.1—The system shall receive raw video data from existing external LCS cameras.

G.1.1.2— The system shall receive a muster request from the user.

G.1.1.3— The system shall receive alert recognition from the user.

G.1.1.4—The system shall receive data from the user.

G.1.1.5—The system shall receive electrical power from the ship.

G.1.2—Output requirements

G.1.2.1— The system shall provide POI alerts to the user.

G.1.2.2 — The system shall provide camera pan/tilt/zoom control to the LCS cameras.

G.1.2.3— The system shall provide muster report of ships personnel to user.

G.2.0—External systems requirements

G.2.1—The system shall interface with the user.

G.2.2—The system shall interface with existing external LCS cameras.

G.2.3—The system shall interface with the ship.

G.2.4—The system shall interface with the database update system.

G.3.0—System constraint requirements

G.3.1— The system shall comply with constraints of ships standards.

G.3.2—The system is constrained by obstructions and structures on the pier.

G.3.3— The system is constrained by people on the pier and quarterdeck providing a view to the video cameras of their face.

G.4.0—The system requirements

G.4.1— The system shall provide situational awareness around pier-tied ship at a minimum distance of 200 yards from the ship.

G.4.2— The system shall provide ability to monitor pier area and alert watch standers of possible threats.

G.4.3 — The system shall provide interface with existing LCS infrastructure (e.g., cameras, power, FPO).

G.4.4 — The system shall provide a real time crew mustering capability.

G.4.5— The system shall provide an alert function and, when appropriate, monitor and alert watch standers of possible threats.

G.4.6 — The system shall operate and manage system assets autonomously, including autonomous facial recognition and mustering to minimize human supervision/control/support.

G.4.7 — The system shall process data autonomously to provide a knowledge base for the ship watch standers allowing them to make informed decisions.

G.4.8 — Provide facial recognition accuracy of a minimum of 60% (matches images obtained to correct images in database 60% of the time).

G.4.9 — Provide, at a minimum, enough processing capability to correlate an image to a database of 5,000 images in 5 seconds.

G.4.10 — Provide a networking capability that meets the Ethernet networking standard IEEE 802.3.

G.4.11 — Provide a database that performs the following:

- Maintains a mustering status and provides report.
- Provides alerts for Persons of Interest.
- Has the ability to be updated periodically to add or delete both KFPs and POIs.
- Maintain a UKP list with unique identifiers for each UKP.

## H. APPLICATION OF THE SYSTEMS ENGINEERING PROCESS TO THE PIER WATCHMAN PROOF-OF-CONCEPT SYSTEM

Chapter II discussed the System Engineering "V" that was utilized in designing the Pier Watchman System. The creation of the Pier Watchman Proof-of-Concept System took the design that was created on the left side of the "V" and performed the fabrication, integration, and testing prescribed on the right side of the "V." The intention was to validate a specific, proposed solution design on a small scale, ensuring a particular system would be feasible for large-scale production.

## I.  PURPOSE FOR PROOF-OF-CONCEPT SYSTEM

From a careful review of the proposed system concept, there appeared to be a technology gap in the ability to autonomously provide pier security and mustering. To show that the proposed full-scale system for autonomously performing facial detection, facial recognition, mustering, and area monitoring is a viable solution to enhancing situational awareness and force protection, it was decided that a small-scale prototype system should be designed and implemented. This system needed to emulate the existing set-up for LCS but did not require the use of the exact hardware from LCS.

The Pier Watchman proof-of-concept system was designed and built to be a smart surveillance system that utilizes one camera to perform face recognition. This one camera acts as a prototype for both the existing LCS cameras and the proposed quarterdeck area camera. The system design allows for expandability. The camera used in this system has a pan/tilt/zoom (PTZ) functionality that allows for capturing and processing of images. This video processing is capable of performing blob analysis (object detection), face detection, and face recognition on the captured video and then relaying this data to the server for integration into its high-level analysis.

## J.  PROOF-OF-CONCEPT SYSTEM DESIGN AND IMPLEMENTATION

This section initially reviews the potential components in the functional full-scale proposed system. Then it compares components with the instantiated Pier Watchman Proof-of-Concept System. The components for the full-scale system would consist of the cameras already installed on LCS, the addition of one quarterdeck camera, a database server, workstation computers, and interface with the existing LCS computer network to obtain the images captured by the cameras. All of these components would need to be networked into a cohesive computer network. This network would have dedicated software for each camera's video feed (possibly multiple computers) and one main server to contain and process the facial image databases and alerts.

60

Before fabrication could begin, a suitable camera needed to be selected that could emulate the current cameras on LCS. The external cameras that are presently installed on LCS-1 are Spectra III, outdoor long-range cameras model number PE-SD53CBW-PREO produced by the Pelco Company (Hurley, 2010). The camera chosen to emulate the Spectra III was the Sony SNCRZ30N PTZ. The Sony camera was chosen due to similar functionality to Spectra III and that the Sony camera was previously purchased for the NCSE lab. The Sony camera is not weather proof, but this feature was not vital for the lab-based proof-of-concept system. Table 6 provides the specifications for the existing LCS cameras and the specifications for the camera chosen to emulate them in the Pier Watchman Proof-of-Concept System.

| Option | Camera | Resolution | Zoom | Degrees of Pan | Degrees of Tilt | Indoor/Outdoor |
|--------|--------|-----------|------|---------------|----------------|---------------|
| LCS | Spectra III | 724 X 494 | 23 X | 360 | 94 (+2 to -92) | Yes |
| COTS | Sony | 736 X 480 | 25 X | 340 | 115 | No |

Table 6.    LCS/ Pier Watchman Camera Specification Table (Pelco, 2009) (Sony, 2009)

The plan for the proof-of-concept system was to emulate only one camera with its dedicated computer, the server computer, and all network interfaces needed to integrate these components. Physically, the infrastructure for Pier Watchman proof-of-concept system consisted of the following hardware components with physical connections as per Figure 37:

- 1 Sony Model: SNCRZ30N PTZ camera.
- 1 Dell Latitude Model: D820 laptop computer.
- 1 D-Link DSS-5+ Ethernet switch.
- 1 MAC server.
- Local Area Network (LAN)

## K.    INSTANTIATED PHYSICAL ARCHITECTURE AND NETWORK CONSTRUCTION

The instantiated physical architecture for the proof-of concept system is shown in Figure 37. Figure 37 provides a schematic for how the components are integrated. This includes portraying how the Sony camera captures the raw video and transfers it to the

61

network switch through Category Five (CAT5) network cabling. Then the raw video data routes through the switch to the laptop computer through CAT5 cabling. The raw video data is processed on the Dell laptop for face detection and recognition, and if a face is detected then PTZ commands are sent back to the switch through CAT5 cabling. From the switch, the PTZ commands are sent to the camera through CAT5 cabling. The camera then pan, tilts, and or zooms into the location ordered by the laptop. The camera captures the zoomed in area and this raw video data is sent back to the laptop through the switch as described earlier. Once zoomed in and a valid facial image has been sent to the laptop computer, automatic facial recognition is attempted on the facial image. The laptop assigns an identity to the facial image with a confidence level and then sends it to the switch as a database update through CAT5 cabling. (Note the identity may be tagged "unknown" if a face doesn't fit the facial database.) From the switch, the database update is transferred to the server through CAT5 cabling. Additionally, the server can also pull additional data from the laptop as required through the switch and the associated CAT5 cabling mentioned earlier.

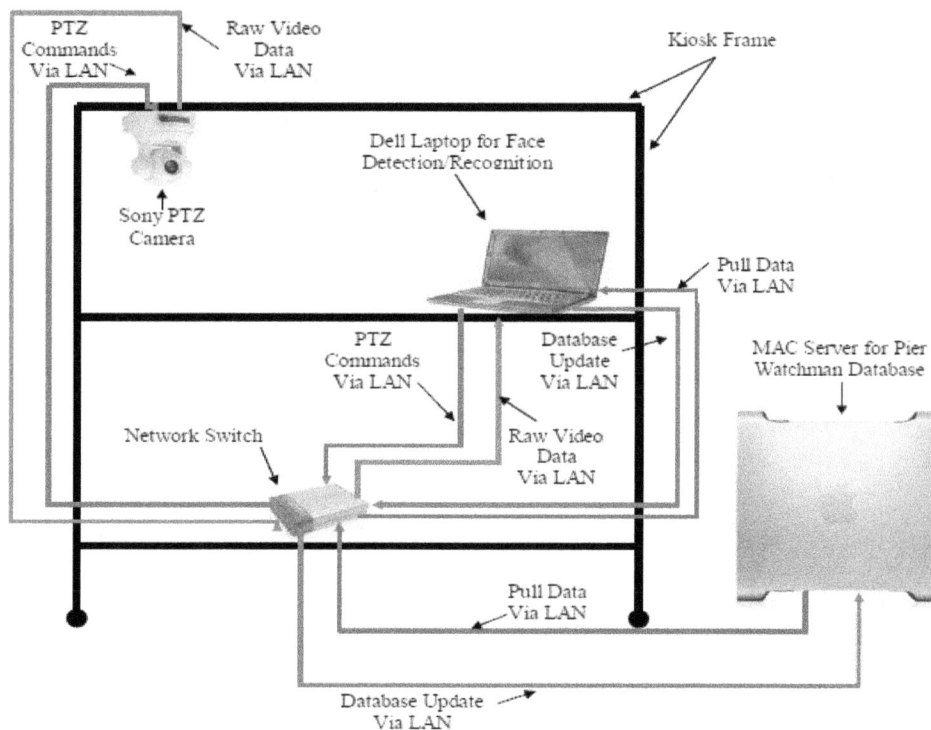

Figure 37.    Instantiated Physical Architecture of Pier Watchman Proof-of-Concept System

62

The Pier Watchman Proof-of-Concept System was networked incrementally to ensure that each component would function properly and was correctly integrated prior to moving to integration of the next component. Initially, the Sony camera and Dell laptop were networked together through the switch. Once the testing for proper operation of both was verified, the server was connected to the switch and its proper operation was verified. The coding of the supporting software was started in conjunction with the completion of this initial setup.

## L.    SOFTWARE UTILIZED

An important aspect of creating the Pier Watchman Proof-of-Concept System was acquiring the necessary software that would be capable of meeting the design requirements. This design required a software capability to perform facial detection, recognition, and file transfer capabilities. Table 7 provides the list of software that the Pier Watchman Proof-of-Concept System utilized and their function.

| Software Name | Function |
|---|---|
| MATLAB | Performed Facial Detection, Recognition |
| Golden FTP Server (Freeware Version) | File Transfer Program to transfer captured Facial image to server for processing. |
| Sony Camera Software | Provides interface and control of Sony camera and its pan tilt zoom capabilities |
| Microsoft Windows XP | Operating System for Dell Laptop |
| Microsoft Access | Database Processing |

Table 7.    Software Utilized in the Fabrication of Pier Watchman Proof-of-Concept System

## M.    PIER WATCHMAN PROGRAM DESIGN LANGUAGE (PDL)

The coding for the Pier Watchman software started utilizing a basic program design language (PDL) syntax that allowed for establishment of a logical structure. PDL allows the programmer to use the English language in an expressive manor while still maintaining the logical structure of a programming language (Pressman, 2010). The initial PDL that was written for Pier Watchman is provided in Appendix A.

## N.    PIER WATCHMAN SOURCE CODE

The aforementioned PDL code was then transferred into actual source code utilizing MathWorks MATLAB software. The source code that was written for Pier Watchman Proof-of-Concept System is provided in Appendix B. Additionally, the instructions for operating the Pier Watchman Proof-of-Concept System are provided as a specific set of startup procedures and are provided in Appendix C.

## O.    SYSTEM OPERATION

Basic functions of the system operation are for the camera and laptop to capture images and perform the facial detection. The facial detection function consists of the computer first localizing a person within the field of view of its associated camera. Then the facial detection algorithm provides pan, tilt, and or zoom commands for the camera to modify the camera's field of view to solely capture what is believed to be the face of the person in question. The camera captures what is assumed to be a facial image and saves it to a file folder. Finally, the assumed facial image is processed by the facial recognition algorithm, looking for a positive match.

For better understanding of the proof-of-concept system, the following figures provide a systematic display of the system in operation. The scenario is that a test subject enters the lab and approaches the proof-of-concept system, taking a seat within ten feet of the camera. Figures 38–41 demonstrate the face detection functions of the proof-of-concept system by displaying temporal snapshots of the camera field of view. Figure 38 is an image captured by the proof-of-concept system that displays the actual field of view of the camera. Figure 39 displays that same field of view with the test subject having entered the room and preparing to sit down. Figure 40 shows the person sitting down. The system prepares to pan, tilt, and zoom into the face. Figure 41 displays the facial image that has been captured by the system.

Figure 38.    Snapshot #1: Initial Field of View of the Proof-of-Concept System

Figure 39.    Snapshot #2: Image of a Person in the Field of View of the Proof-of-Concept System

Figure 40.    Snapshot #3: P/T/Z Preparation of the Proof-of-Concept System

Figure 41.    Snapshot #4: Facial Image Captured

Following face detection the facial recognition algorithm is enacted. Facial recognition consists of comparing the captured image with a database of known images and providing a best match with a percent of correlation, or confidence. If a correlation above an adjustable confidence threshold (e.g., 60%) occurs, the identity of the "matched" individual is provided. Additionally, if the identity is a KFP (e.g., known crewmember), then that person is mustered as present. Alternatively, if the identity displayed is a POI (e.g., terrorist), then the system reacts by providing an appropriate alert. Finally, if the "closest" match to the facial database yields a correlation or confidence level under threshold, then the identity displayed is that of a UKP (e.g., unknown).

To demonstrate the facial recognition feature of the proof-of-concept system, Figures 42 and 43 provide a systematic proof-of-concept of this process. First, Figure 42 displays a subset of facial images from the proof-of-concept database. These images are examples of known persons in the database. They represent only a few of the images that the system would compare against when looking for a match. Figure 43 displays two images: the captured face on the left under "Looking for" and the image it correlates to with its associated confidence level on the right.

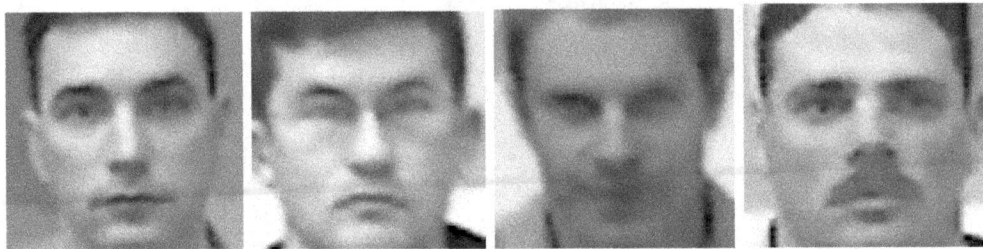

Figure 42.   Facial Images from Known Database

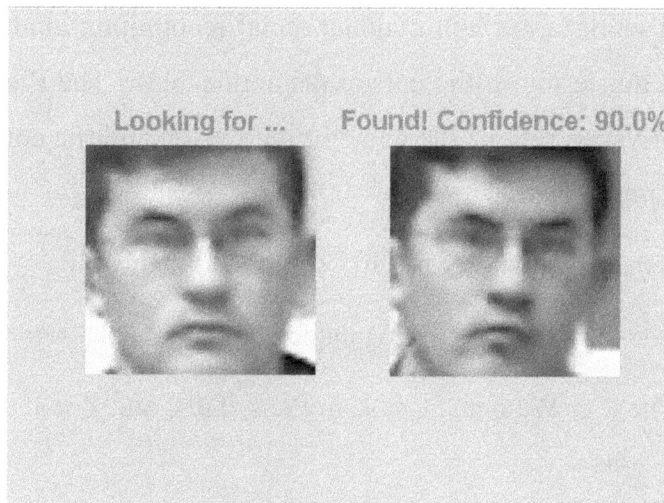

Figure 43.     Correlation of the Facial Image to the Image from the Database

## P.     PROOF-OF-CONCEPT SYSTEM OPERATION AND TESTING

To properly evaluate operation and capability of the proof-of-concept system, an acceptance test was developed.  The acceptance test utilized for the Pier Watchman Proof-of-Concept System subsequently is summarized below.

1. The test will be performed utilizing two separate personnel.  The personnel will have their images entered into the database with one listed as a POI and one as a KFP.  The personnel will then approach the Pier Watchman System one at a time and stand at three locations designated by markers on the floor at distances of five feet, ten feet, and fifteen feet away from the Pier Watchman Proof-of-Concept System.

2. While the test subjects are doing the aforementioned procedures the individual conducting the test will observe the following:

   a.  The camera detects the movement of the person.

   b.  The camera detects the face of the person.

   c.  The camera zooms in to capture a face image.

   d.  A valid picture is obtained.

   e.  The valid picture is properly transferred to the Dell workstation.

3. The Dell workstation will conduct facial recognition, and assignment of POI or KFP and mustering of the person (as applicable). The Pier Watchman Proof-of-Concept System returns the name of the person and the correlation factor that the correct name was selected.

The system will have successfully completed the test if:

- The test subject's face is detected.

- The Pier Watchman System Pans, Tilts, and Zooms in on the test subject's face.

- The face detected is successfully matched to a database record with an accuracy of 60% or greater.

- Each time a KFP is identified, it is accurately mustered.

- Each time a POI is identified, an alarm is indicated.

This acceptance test was completed ten times at each distance on two different subjects (one defined as a POI and one defined as a KFP). Table 8 provides the results from the acceptance testing.

| Test Subject | Distance | | | | | |
| | 5ft | | 10ft | | 15ft | |
| | Sat | Unsat | Sat | Unsat | Sat | Unsat |
| Stubblefield (POI) | 10 | 0 | 8 | 2 | 8 | 2 |
| DeDeaux (KFP) | 9 | 1 | 9 | 1 | 7 | 3 |
| Individual Distance Success Rate | 95% | | 85% | | 75% | |
| Individual Distance Failure Rate | 5% | | 15% | | 25% | |
| Overall Success Rate | 85% | | | | | |

**Note: Each Test Subject carried out 10 tests at each distance of 5ft, 10ft, and 15ft. (Sat=satisfactory, Unsat=unsatisfactory)**

Table 8.    The Pier Watchman Proof-of-Concept Acceptance Test Results

The overall success rate of 85% is higher than the required 60% that was selected for successful completion. However, the original successful completion of 60% was based on automated facial detection, image capturing, and correct facial recognition and not just correctly zooming into the face and capturing the facial image. Due to a communication error between two software programs, the system could not automatically transfer the captured images to the facial recognition program. To accurately test the facial recognition function the facial images captured from the Acceptance test were manually processed through the facial recognition software. This resulted in a 100% success rate in accurately identifying the person, but it was decided to evaluate and judge system effectiveness without these test results until future work could successfully make this feature work without user interaction as originally planned.

## Q.    LESSONS LEARNED WHILE DESIGNING, BUILDING, AND TESTING THE PIER WATCHMAN PROOF-OF-CONCEPT SYSTEM

Before construction began, the design was verified multiple times to ensure that it met the desired goals. To be successful, there needed to be a clear understanding of how each piece interacted with each other. By utilizing the Systems Engineering process and ensuring the design was mature and ready the implementation and programming of the proof-of-concept system went smoothly. Because the initial groundwork was performed thoroughly, the initial proof-of-concept system was constructed, networked, coded, compiled, and tested quickly.

Issues did arise within the code associated with Commercial Off-the-Shelf (COTS) products when attempting to communicate with each other. After some intensive troubleshooting, it was discovered that if a specific start-up procedure, provided in Appendix C, was followed, all components could properly communicate with each other. However, the File Transfer Protocol (FTP) server was unable to send its files across the network to the Dell workstation. The problem was linked to a lack of operability with the freeware version of FTP server that was obtained. This was not seen as a major issue, and a workaround was established that allowed system operability to be evaluated. The workaround was that after the detected facial image was captured, it was manually fed into the facial recognition function. Despite the minor deviation from the original plan, the proof-of-concept system demonstration was deemed successful.

## R.     CONCLUSIONS DRAWN FROM PROOF-OF-CONCEPT SYSTEM

The Pier Watchman Proof-of-Concept System built provides valuable insight into a full-scale proposed automated solution for mustering and pier security for LCS ships. It proved the feasibility and functionality of the systems engineering design. First, the Pier Watchman Proof-of-Concept System proved the ability of the system to detect a person within the camera's field of view and then detect the face of that person. This is vital to the system concept. If the system cannot distinguish both the person and their face, then it will not be able to perform any of the remaining required functions. However, this function was only tested to a limited extent. The test involved only one person at a time at very limited ranges. The full-scale system needs to be able to detect and recognize multiple faces at ranges of at least 200 yards from the ship. An additional challenge will be the detection and recognition of multiple persons at the same time within the same FOV of one camera. This would require the face detection software to send multiple PTZ commands to the camera, and then the camera would have to loop through each command, and the system would execute facial recognition on each face in the loop.

The next function that was tested was the autonomous facial recognition, associated labeling, and processing. The proof-of-concept system was very successful when a valid facial image was captured. It successfully associated the correct label and provided the proper alert 100% of the time. The success rate experienced in this test was well above the required threshold. This high success rate was assumed to be due to the limited database of only twenty images that was utilized for comparison. When the number of database images is expanded to hundreds, and even thousands, the expectation is that the success rate will be lower. In that case, more advanced facial recognition techniques can be applied. The important conclusion from this section of testing was that the facial recognition portion of programming worked successfully. However, the full-scale Pier Watchman System is not required to use the same facial recognition algorithm. In other words, no requirements have been established for the exact facial recognition software that the full-scale Pier Watchman System must use. This allows the developers of the full-scale system to utilize the most current and accurate facial recognition algorithms and software that are available.

In summary, after conducting a brief analysis of alternatives one proposed solution was further investigated. Next, the facial recognition concept utilized for the proposed solution was discussed. Additionally, in order to validate the viability of automatic facial detection and recognition a proof-of-concept system was designed and constructed. The testing of the proof-of-concept system identified risk involved with software compatibility and provided ways to mitigate this risk. The next chapter provides a summary and conclusion of this thesis and some areas that could be further researched.

# VI. SUMMARY AND CONCLUSIONS

## A. SUMMARY

An assessment of current automated mustering and pier security systems identified a critical need for the proposed system solution. Using the Systems Engineering "V" model a formal analysis of the operational need was conducted. Additionally, a DRM was created that established a generic architecture with a high-level operational view, external systems diagram, requirements, and a functional hierarchy and decomposition. An analysis of alternatives led to the selection of a proposed system solution. The proposed solution was further designed and an instantiated physical architecture was created. The proposed solution was verified for viability through construction, integration, demonstration, and acceptance testing of a proof-of-concept system. This thesis applied the entire Systems Engineering "V" model from concept through validation.

## B. CONCLUSION

The results of my research shows that an autonomous system shows great potential to enhance the security and situational awareness of a USS Freedom class of ship while it is pier side anywhere in the world. The proof-of-concept system demonstrated that autonomous facial detection and recognition algorithms are a viable enabling technology to achieve enhanced pier security and a real time mustering capability for LCS ships.

Whether or not the proposed system is further developed depends on the benefits that will be achieved compared to the expected costs and resources required. The first benefit is the reduction of some of the administrative burden of mustering the ship's crew. This benefit is small, but the associated cost is also small. This feature requires one camera that would be located in the quarterdeck area and the database required is merely an add-on feature of the greater database associated with the pier security feature. The mustering capability is also beneficial for knowing which crewmembers are on the ship at any given time. If, for instance, a fire occurs on the ship, the watch standers know immediately who is available onboard to respond. Also, if there is an instance when it is vital that a crewmember be located, the watch standers would immediately know if that crewmember was on the ship.

The greatest benefit of this type of system is the pier security feature that monitors the immediate area around the ship. This feature would provide vital intelligence that can substantially enhance the situational awareness of the watch standers. Through further product development and then deployment of the proposed system, the security of the USS Freedom class of LCS ships could be increased without increasing the ship's crew size.

## C.    AREAS OF FURTHER RESEARCH

There are further areas of research that need to be explored prior to moving forward with developing and installing a full scale proposed system on ships.

First, the facial recognition algorithm that was utilized for the proof-of-concept system is known to be less accurate with large numbers of personnel. Further research and software development needs to be conducted to procure the best facial recognition software possible to utilize in the full-scale system.

Another area for further research is to develop an architecture for off ship reporting and networking configuration. Additionally, this thesis did not discuss how the database for POI images would be created or maintained. Furthermore, the procedures for reporting a confirmed POI were not discussed. The development of a network (or connect to a given network) that could provide real time POI reporting, updating of facial images database, and alert notification to the proper intelligence agency would be another fertile research area.

Finally, research into a behavioral analysis algorithm that could be superimposed onto the proposed system using a detect, identify, predict, and react approach similar to the work done by Goshorn in "Behavior Modeling for Detection, Identification, Prediction, and Reaction (DIPR) in AI Systems Solutions" (Goshorn, 2009) would be

74

warranted. This would give the system the ability to "learn" behaviors and permit the operator to manually input behaviors considered normal. Any behaviors not conforming to normal behavior criteria would then be classified as abnormal. This research should also consider the ability of watch standers to easily update the system by inputting the known abnormal behaviors. With the proposed system, the infrastructure is in place to allow the incorporation of behavior analysis software to predict and prevent terror threats.

THIS PAGE INTENTIONALLY LEFT BLANK

# LIST OF REFERENCES

Baxes, Gregory A.1994. *Digital Image Processing: Principles and Applications*. New York: John Wiley & Sons, Inc.

Blanchard, Benjamin S. and Wolter J. Fabrycky, 2006. *Systems Engineering and Analysis*. Englewood Cliffs, NJ: Prentice-Hall.

Bruce, V. "Understanding Face Recognition," British *Journal of Psychology*, *August* vol 10 (1990).

Buede, D.M.,. 2000.The Engineering Design of Systems: Models and Methods, John Wiley & Sons, Inc., New York.

Chairman of the Joint Chiefs of Staff Manual, May 2003, Universal Joint Task List

City-Data.com. 2009. City-Data Marinette, Wisconsin. Retrieved on January 12, 2010, from http://www.city-data.com/city/Marinette-Wisconsin.html

Department of Defense Systems Management College. January 2001. Instruction 5000.2: Operation of the defense acquisition system.

Department of Defense. Architecture Framework Version 1.5. April 2007.

Department of Defense, Joint Publication 1-02, Department of Defense Dictionary of Military Terms, October 2009.

Forsberg, Kevin and Harold Mooz. July 1995. "Application of the "Vee" to Incremental and Evolutionary Development," Proceedings of the Fifth Annual International Symposium of the National Council on Systems Engineering, St. Louis, Missouri.

Forsberg, Kevin and Harold Mooz. 1992. "The Relationship of Systems Engineering to the Project Cycle," Engineering Management Journal, 4, No. 3, pp. 36–43.

Global Security. 2009. Littoral Combat Ship Design. Retrieved on November 22, 2009, from http://www.globalsecurity.org/military/systems/ship/lcs-design.htm

Google Maps. 2009. Google Maps, Marinette, Wisconsin. Retrieved on 21 February 2009, from http://maps.google.com/maps?hl=en&tab=wl

Goshorn, Rachel. 2009. Theory of Operations Manual for Watchman for Navy Postgraduate School SE4900 course (Artificial Intelligence Systems Engineering courses I and II), Naval Postgraduate School (unpublished).

Goshorn, Rachel, Goshorn, Deborah, Goshorn, J. L. and Goshorn L.A.. 2009. "Abnormal behavior classification and alerting through detection, identification, prediction and reaction (DIPR) system applied to a multi-camera network," submitted to the Workshop on Behavior Monitoring and Interpretation: Moving Objects in a Three Dimensional World.

Hurley, Jeff. 2010. "LCS-1 External Camera Coverage," discussed at the Ship Production Progress Conference (SPPC) for LCS-3, Marincttc, Wisconsin.

John Wiley & Sons, Inc., Hoboken, NJ, 2009. 443.

Joint and Naval Capability Terminology Lists Compiled by Assistant Secretary of the Navy, Research, Development and Acquisition, Chief Systems Engineer (ASN RDA,CHENG), February 2007.

Lockheed Martin. (2010). Communications Center Provides Integrated, Automated Capability. Retrieved on March 7, 2010, from http://www.lmlcsteam.com/?p=922

Maier, Mark W. and Rechtin, Eberhardt. 2000. The Art of Systems Architecting, 2nd Ed., CRC Press LLC.

Navy.mil. 2009. Frigates Fact File. Retrieved on February 16, 2010, from http://www.navy.mil/navydata/fact_display.asp?cid=4200&tid=1300&ct=4

Pelco by Schneider Electric. 2009. Spectra III SE Series Specification Sheet. Retrieved on 09 January 2010, from http://www.global-download.schneider-electric.com/852575770039EC5E/All/BB11624336B35D9085 25763800641B84/$File/c440.pdf

Pentland Alex P. and Choudhury Tanzeem. 2000. Face Recognition for Smart Environments, IEEE Computer, pp. 50–55.

Pressman, Roger. 2010. Software Engineering A Practitioners Approach, 7th ED., McGraw-Hill.

Scott, Jhi, August 2008. LCS-1 Picture, Retrieved February 16, 2010, from http://www.navy.mil/view_single.asp?id=62776

Skolnick, Fred and Wilkins. 2000. Laying the Foundation for Successful Systems Engineering, Johns Hopkins APL Technical Digest, Volume 21, Number 2.

Turk Matthew A. and Pentland Alex P.. 1991. Face Recognition Using Eigenfaces, in Proc. IEEE Conference on Computer Vision and Pattern Recognition., pp. 586–591. Retrieved on September 1, 2009, from http://www.cs.ucsb.edu/~mturk/Papers/mturk-CVPR91.pdf.

Turk Matthew A., Pentland Alex P. 1991. Eigenfaces for Recognition, Journal of Cognitive Neuroscience Volume 3 Number 1, 72–86.

United States Air Force. 2008. Analysis of Alternative (AoA) Handbook: A practical Guide to Analysis of Alternatives. Kirtland AFB, NM: Air Force Materiel Command (AFMC's) Office of Aerospace Studies (OAS).

United States Department of Transportation, United States Coast Guard, Navigation Rules, COMDTINST M16672.2D, October 19, 2009.

THIS PAGE INTENTIONALLY LEFT BLANK

# APPENDIX A     PIER WATCHMAN PROOF-OF-CONCEPT PDL

```
defineGlobals();  // functions defines global variables

syslogin(); // login user and return permissions

setIP(); // get IP addresses

goGui(permissions);  // sets GUI options based on user permissions.

goPW(opt, select);

// Scan using panning algorithm

while runFlag = ! FALSE do; //if user select exit, system shutsdown

while face_detect FALSE do:

            pan(x);

            tilt(y);

            zoom(z);

            if (x, y, z >0) then do;

                    set face_detect TRUE;

            Else;

                    face_detect FALSE;

// Face_recognition Function

normalize();

get_coordinates(a,b);

pan(a);

tilt(b);

determine_zoom_factor();

push_face();
```

```
alert =null;

face_recognition(alert);

while alert =!null do;

        pop(alert,id);

        log(alert,id);

END;
```

# APPENDIX B    PIER WATCHMAN PROOF-OF-CONCEPT CODE

The following pages are the actual code that was written for the Pier Watchman System.  In order to properly run this code it must be utilized operated from the Mathworks MATLAB software with all toolboxes enabled.

```
function timerTest()

clear all;

a = timer;

set(a, 'ExecutionMode', 'FixedRate');

set(a, 'Period', 1.0);

set(a, 'TimerFcn', 'getImage()');

set(a, 'TasksToExecute', 30);

start(a);
```

The 'getImage' function is activated by

```
function getImage()

persistent count;

if size(count) == 0;

    count = 0;

end

% expects all image files to be time stamped in the

% c:\watchman directory

% expects images to be named in the format image09030510063200.jpg

% 09 = year

% 03 = month
```

```
% 05 = day

% 10 = hours

% 06 = minutes

% 32 = seconds

% 00 = hundredths of seconds

imdir = 'c:\Watchman\72\';

name = '.jpg';

prefix = 'image';

timeStamp = clock;

year = mod ( timeStamp(1) , 2000 );

if ( year < 10 )

    yearStr = strcat ( '0' , int2str ( year ) );

else

    yearStr = int2str ( year );

end

month =  timeStamp(2);

if ( month < 10 )

    monthStr = strcat ( '0' , int2str ( month ) );

else

    monthStr = int2str ( month );

end

day = timeStamp(3);

if ( day < 10 )

    dayStr = strcat ( '0' , int2str ( day ) );
```

```
else

    dayStr = int2str ( day );

end


hour = timeStamp(4);

if ( hour < 10 )

    hourStr = strcat ( '0' , int2str ( hour ) );

else

    hourStr = int2str ( hour );

end

sec = timeStamp(6);

min = timeStamp(5);

if (sec < 4)

    sec = sec + 56;

    min = min - 1;

else

    sec = sec - 4;

end

if ( min < 10 )

    minStr = strcat ( '0' , int2str ( min ) );

else

    minStr = int2str ( min );

end

% introduce a delay to allow for differences in time between ftp
```

```matlab
% transfer, the camera's clock, and the system clock used by matlab
if ( sec < 10 )
    secStr = strcat ( '0' , int2str ( sec ) );
else
    secStr = int2str ( sec );
end
% converts current clock to corresponding filename, the trailing '00' is to
% account for hundredths of seconds, which are neglected
timeStr = strcat ( yearStr, monthStr, dayStr, hourStr, minStr, secStr, '00' );
imgname = strcat(imdir, prefix, timeStr, name);
if exist(imgname)
    img = imread(imgname);
    imshow(img);
     gImg = double (rgb2gray(img));
    Face = FaceDetect('haarcascade_frontalface_alt2.xml',gImg);
    if size(Face, 2) > 1
        Rectangle = [Face(1) Face(2); Face(1)+Face(3) Face(2); Face(1)+Face(3)
Face(2)+Face(4); Face(1) Face(2)+Face(4); Face(1) Face(2)];
    else
        Rectangle = [];
    end
    if size(Face, 2) > 1
        isFace = 1;
        count = count+1;
```

```
else
    isFace = 0;
end
figure(1);
imshow (img);
truesize;
if size(Face, 2) > 1
    hold on;
    plot (Rectangle(:,1), Rectangle(:,2), 'g');
    hold off;
end
if (count == 10)
    x = Face(1);

    y = Face(2);
    w = Face(3);
    h = Face(4);
    x = x + 0.5 * w;
    y = y + 0.5 * h;
    if (x <= 320)
        x = -(320-x);
    else
        x = x-320;
    end
```

```
        if (y<=240)

            y = -(240-y);


        else

            y = (y-240);

        end
%       function sonyrz30move(camera, cmd, x, y, height, width)

        sonyrz30move(72, 'zoomin', int2str(x), int2str(y), int2str(h), int2str(w));

    end

end
```

## APPENDIX C   HOW TO DEMONSTRATE THE PIER WATCHMAN PROOF-OF-CONCEPT SYSTEM

1. Turn on the following:

    a. Sony Camera

        i. Ensure Power cord and Network cable are plugged into it.

    b. Dell Laptop #7

    c. D-Link Switch

        i. Ensure it is plugged in and green power light is lit.

    d. Wait Until Dell computer is initialized

2. Start the golden ftp server.

    a. Icon is located in center of desktop on computer. Double Icon

        i. Directory Information C:\ProgramFiles\GoldenFTPServer\GFTP.exe

    b. Wait for program to initialize.

        i. Icon will appear in lower right of startup taskbar menu

3. Start camera 192.168.0.72 in Firefox

    a. Initialize Mozilla Firefox program located on Desktop by double clicking Icon.

        i. Directory Information C:ProgramFiles\Mozilla Firefox\firefox.exe

    b. Wait for program to initialize

    c. Default should be the website: http://192.168.0.72/home/homej.html

        i. If address does not match, type in the above address

4. Put the camera in the home position

    a. Click on Control Icon at the top of the internet window (not the toolbars section)

    b. A menu should pop up.

    c. Use the pull down and select 'home'

        i. Camera should be pointing towards the left side of the Kiosk

5. Initialize the Camera Settings Menu

    a. Click the 'settings' towards the top of the internet window

      b.  Authentication window will pop up.

             i.  Values should already be entered just click 'OK'

            ii.  If values not entered: User Name: watchman  Password: watchman

6.   Set Camera Settings

      a.  Click on System. (located on left of window  just below Basic)

             i.  Under system scroll down to 'Date time setting'

            ii.  Select the first apply button by clicking over apply button. (this synchronizes clocks)

      b.  Click FTP Client (located of left of window under Application section just below Preset Position)

             i.  A window should popup select 'Use FTP client function' then click OK

            ii.  All data should be as follows

           iii.  FTP Server name   192.168.70

           iv.  User name   anonymous

             v.  Password       (blank nothing typed there)

           vi.  Re-type password       (blank nothing typed there)

          vii.  Remote path   Watchman\72

         viii.  Image file name      image

           ix.  Suffix   Date/Time

             x.  Mode   Periodical sending

           xi.  Interval time  00  00  01

          xii.  Available period  always

         xiii.  Schedule no.    1

         xiv.  If the above was all correct click OK

      c.  Note: you should get a popup from the golden ftp server in the bottom of the screen telling you that the incoming connection was started

      d.  Close camera setting window.

      e.  Minimize Firefox window

7.   Load mat lab

a. Select MATLAB R2007a from start menu, all programs, MATLAB, R2007a, MATLAB R2007a

b. Directory 'C:\ProgramFiles\MATLAB\R2007a\bin\matlab.bat"- sd$documents\MATLAB

8. Run 'timerTest'

a. In Mat lab from the top toolbar, select open. (An open window should pop up)

b. Select timer test from Open pop up window

i. Directory: C:\Documents and Settings\R Goshorn\My Documents\MATLAB\timerTest.m

c. Once open click on run from toolbar.

Program is running correctly if a picture appears on screen and then the image is evaluated looking for a face. The camera will then zoom in and look for a face. Demo complete.

THIS PAGE INTENTIONALLY LEFT BLANK

# INITIAL DISTRIBUTION LIST

1. Defense Technical Information Center
   Ft. Belvoir, Virginia

2. Dudley Knox Library
   Naval Postgraduate School
   Monterey, California

3. Program Executive Officer, Information Warfare Systems
   Washington Navy Yard
   Washington, D.C.

# NAVAL
# POSTGRADUATE
# SCHOOL

MONTEREY, CALIFORNIA

# THESIS

EVALUATION OF THE LITTORAL COMBAT SHIP (LCS)
AND SPARTAN SCOUT AS INFORMATION OPERATIONS
(IO) ASSETS

by

Joseph M. Bromley

March 2005

Thesis Advisor:          Michael T. McMaster
Second Reader:           Steven J. Iatrou

Approved for public release: distribution is unlimited

THIS PAGE INTENTIONALLY LEFT BLANK

| REPORT DOCUMENTATION PAGE | | *Form Approved OMB No. 0704-0188* |
|---|---|---|
| | Public reporting burden for this collection of information is estimated to average 1 hour per response, including the time for reviewing instruction, searching existing data sources, gathering and maintaining the data needed, and completing and reviewing the collection of information. Send comments regarding this burden estimate or any other aspect of this collection of information, including suggestions for reducing this burden, to Washington headquarters Services, Directorate for Information Operations and Reports, 1215 Jefferson Davis Highway, Suite 1204, Arlington, VA 22202-4302, and to the Office of Management and Budget, Paperwork Reduction Project (0704-0188) Washington DC 20503. |

| 1. AGENCY USE ONLY (*Leave blank*) | 2. REPORT DATE March 2005 | 3. REPORT TYPE AND DATES COVERED Master's Thesis |
|---|---|---|
| 4. TITLE AND SUBTITLE: Evaluation of the Littoral Combat Ship (LCS) and SPARTAN SCOUT as Information Operations (IO) Assets | | 5. FUNDING NUMBERS |
| 6. AUTHOR(S) Joseph M. Bromley | | |
| 7. PERFORMING ORGANIZATION NAME(S) AND ADDRESS(ES) Naval Postgraduate School Monterey, CA 93943-5000 | | 8. PERFORMING ORGANIZATION REPORT NUMBER |
| 9. SPONSORING /MONITORING AGENCY NAME(S) AND ADDRESS(ES) N/A | | 10. SPONSORING/MONITORING AGENCY REPORT NUMBER |
| 11. SUPPLEMENTARY NOTES   The views expressed in this thesis are those of the author and do not reflect the official policy or position of the Department of Defense or the U.S. Government. | | |
| 12a. DISTRIBUTION / AVAILABILITY STATEMENT Approved for public release; distribution is unlimited | | 12b. DISTRIBUTION CODE |
| 13. ABSTRACT (maximum 200 words) This thesis will address the planned configuration of Lockheed Martin's Flight Zero, Module Spiral Alpha Littoral Combat Ship (LCS) and the ongoing development of the SPARTAN SCOUT, one of the Navy's Unmanned Surface Vessels (USV).  Technology currently available as well as developmental technologies will be recommended for implementation in order to make the LCS and SCOUT assets to Information Operations (IO) objectives.  Specific technology will include Outboard, TARBS, HPM, Loudspeakers, LRAD and Air Magnet.  This thesis will include an evaluation of the current policy for authorizing Information Operations missions, specifically in the areas of Psychological Operations (PSYOP) and Electronic Warfare (EW). | | |

| 14. SUBJECT TERMS  SPARTAN SCOUT, Littoral Combat Ship, Information Operations (IO), PSYOP, Electronic Warfare (EW), Long Rang Acoustic Device (LRAD), COMMANDO SOLO, TARBS. | | | 15. NUMBER OF PAGES 79 |
|---|---|---|---|
| | | | 16. PRICE CODE |

| 17. SECURITY CLASSIFICATION OF REPORT Unclassified | 18. SECURITY CLASSIFICATION OF THIS PAGE Unclassified | 19. SECURITY CLASSIFICATION OF ABSTRACT Unclassified | 20. LIMITATION OF ABSTRACT UL |
|---|---|---|---|

THIS PAGE INTENTIONALLY LEFT BLANK

EVALUATION OF THE LITTORAL COMBAT SHIP (LCS) AND SPARTAN
SCOUT AS INFORMATION OPERATIONS (IO) ASSETS

Joseph M. Bromley
Lieutenant, United States Navy
B.S., Old Dominion University, 1998

Submitted in partial fulfillment of the
requirements for the degree of

MASTER OF SCIENCE IN INFORMATION SYSTEMS AND OPERATIONS

NAVAL POSTGRADUATE SCHOOL
March 2005

Author:        LT Joseph M. Bromley

Approved by:    Michael T. McMaster
                Thesis Advisor

                Steven J. Iatrou
                Second Reader

                Dan C. Boger
                Chairman, Department of Information Sciences

THIS PAGE INTENTIONALLY LEFT BLANK

# ABSTRACT

This thesis will address the planned configuration of Lockheed Martin's Flight Zero, Module Spiral Alpha Littoral Combat Ship (LCS) and the ongoing development of the SPARTAN SCOUT, one of the Navy's Unmanned Surface Vessels (USV). Technology currently available as well as developmental technologies will be recommended for implementation in order to make the LCS and SCOUT assets to Information Operations (IO) objectives. Specific technology will include Outboard, TARBS, HPM, Loudspeakers, LRAD and Air Magnet. This thesis will include an evaluation of the current policy for authorizing Information Operations missions, specifically in Psychological Operations (PSYOP).

THIS PAGE INTENTIONALLY LEFT BLANK

# TABLE OF CONTENTS

THIS PAGE INTENTIONALLY LEFT BLANK

# LIST OF FIGURES

THIS PAGE INTENTIONALLY LEFT BLANK

# LIST OF TABLES

THIS PAGE INTENTIONALLY LEFT BLANK

# ACKNOWLEDGMENTS

I would like to extend my sincere thanks to Professor Mike McMaster for his guidance and encouragement as I worked toward accomplishing the monumental task of researching, editing, and completing this thesis. It was an honor and a privilege to work with him on this project.

I would also like to thank Professor Steve Iatrou for his instruction in the often difficult concepts of Information Operations. He has succeeded in changing the way I think.

Above all, I want to thank my wife, Lisa, for standing by me as I embarked upon the journey of completing my Master of Science degree. Without your love and support, none of this would have ever been possible.

THIS PAGE INTENTIONALLY LEFT BLANK

# I.  INTRODUCTION

Information is the currency of victory on the Battlefield.

General Gordon Sullivan
Former Army Chief of Staff

## A.  AREA OF RESEARCH

This thesis will address the planned configuration of Lockheed Martin's Flight Zero, Module Spiral Alpha Littoral Combat Ship (LCS) and the ongoing development of the SPARTAN SCOUT, one of the Navy's Unmanned Surface Vessels (USV). Technology currently available as well as developmental technologies will be recommended for implementation in order to make the LCS and SCOUT assets to Information Operations (IO) objectives. This thesis will include an evaluation of the current policy for authorizing Information Operations missions, specifically in the areas of Psychological Operations (PSYOP) and Electronic Warfare (EW).

## B.  RESEARCH QUESTIONS

To what degree, if any, can the Littoral Combat Ship (LCS) effectively become an asset to Information Operations? To what degree, if any, does the inclusion of the LCS' employment of the SPARTAN SCOUT (USV) affect the LCS' ability to support IO missions?

In conducting this analysis, this thesis will address the following questions:

1.  How are the LCS and SPARTAN SCOUT currently configured in support of IO missions?

2. Could each be reconfigured in order to support additional IO missions?

3. Should either be reconfigured in order to support IO missions based on cost versus perceived benefits?

4. If the LCS and SPARTAN SCOUT could be used for IO are there existing assets that could provide better IO coverage?

5. If the LCS and SPARTAN SCOUT could be assets to IO objective how would current IO doctrine (i.e. approval process) need to change?

C. DISCUSSION

According to the Joint Information Operations Planning Handbook, "IO involves actions taken to affect adversary information and information systems while defending ones own information and information systems."[1] There is little argument that in recent conflicts there has been more emphasis placed on Information Operations and in turn, Information Warfare. In Operations DESERT SHIELD and DESERT STORM in 1991 the Joint Force Commanders Psychological Operations campaign proved most effective in convincing a very large number of Iraqi solders to surrender without a fight.

As the future of IO is conceptualized on the premise that modern and emerging technologies, particularly information specific advances, will make possible a new level of joint operations capability, it is only appropriate to evaluate the latest class of naval ships and the latest progress in USV development.[2] This point is

---

[1] CJCS. *Joint Information Operations Planning Handbook* (Washington DC: U.S. Government Printing Office, 2002), I-1.

[2] CJCS. *Joint Information Operations Planning Handbook* (Washington DC: U.S. Government Printing Office, 2002), I-7

further illustrated by the Joint IO Planning Handbook which states, "Underlying a variety of technological innovations is information superiority – the capability to collect, process, and disseminate an uninterrupted flow of information while exploiting or denying an adversary's ability to do the same."[3] The LCS is in development with Lockheed Martin's (LM) flight zero scheduled to begin sea trials in December of 2006. The SPARTAN SCOUT is also in development having just completed its Advanced Concept Technology Demonstration (ACTD), under the direction of the Naval Undersea Warfare Center Division, Newport. As both the LCS and SPARTAN SCOUT are in the development phase, a review of currently planned IO configurations and recommendation for future IO module development is entirely appropriate at this time.

This thesis will evaluate whether the LCS could be configured to conduct Information Operations. It will evaluate the complexity of the configuration as compared to the potential IO benefits. This evaluation will suggest whether or not the LCS should become an asset configured to accomplish IO objectives. Following the evaluation of the organic components of the LCS, we will conduct a similar evaluation of adapting the SPARTAN SCOUT to conduct IO missions. If it is determined that the LCS and SPARTAN SCOUT would be viable assets to IO, we will evaluate if there are existing assets that would be able to provide comparable or better IO coverage. If it is determined that either the SCOUT and/or the LCS could and should, be

---

[3] CJCS. *Joint Information Operations Planning Handbook* (Washington DC: U.S. Government Printing Office, 2002), I-10

configured for Information Operations, this thesis will review current IO mission approval doctrine and make suggestions to adapt the process in order to fully take advantage of the quick response capabilities of the LCS and SPARTAN SCOUT.

## D.    BENEFIT OF THE STUDY

This thesis' review of potential IO missions for the LCS and SPARTAN SCOUT could aid in the development of LCS flight one and beyond as well as future development of USVs.

## E.    ROADMAP OF THESIS: A CHAPTER OUTLINE

This thesis is organized in six chapters. Chapter II provides background on the development of both the LCS and the SPARTAN SCOUT.    This chapter will serve as the basis for illustrating the current IO configuration of the LCS and SPARTAN SCOUT.    In addition, this chapter will introduce aspects of each platform that could be used to support IO missions.    These aspects such as speed and maneuverability will be discussed in depth in later chapters.

Chapter III discusses the feasibility and projected benefits of developing an IO module for the LCS.    It will illustrate how currently employed technology could be added to the LCS sea frame to make the LCS a viable IO tool in support of IO missions. In addition, it will illustrate how the inherent aspects of the LCS could be exploited to make the LCS an asset to IO missions. This chapter will also include reasoning as to why the LCS provides unique benefits in support of IO missions that are currently covered by other platforms.

Chapter IV discusses the reconfiguration of SPARTAN SCOUT for IO, much like Chapter III did for the LCS. It will discuss how the inherent aspects of the SPARTAN SCOUT would make it a valuable asset to IO missions.

Chapter V provides background on the current IO doctrine that governs the approval for IO missions, specifically PSYOP. It will illustrate how this current process would not fully take advantage of the response speed that the LCS and SPARTAN SCOUT could provide in rapidly developing IO situations and make recommendations for policy change.

Chapter VI is the conclusion to the thesis. It summarizes the study and provides suggestions for further research.

THIS PAGE INTENTIONALLY LEFT BLANK

## II.  LITTORAL COMBAT SHIP (LCS) AND SPARTAN SCOUT DEVELOPMENT

> Small network combatants have an important role to play in 21st century naval warfare, and the reconfigurable Littoral Combat Ship may make important warfighting contributions as part of the Navy's 21st century "Total Force Battle Network" (TFBN).[4]
>
> Robert O. Work
> Center for Strategic and Budgetary Assessments

### A.  LCS OVERVIEW

The development of the LCS became a program of record in November of 2001 when the Navy announced it would issue a revised Request for Proposal (RFP) for its future surface combatant program.  In this proposal the development of three surface combatants; the DDX, CGX and LCS was authorized.  From its inception, the LCS development process would be like no other Navy or DOD program.  The development would be in spirals and ensure a shift to open architecture.  Spiral development allows for the product to get to the field faster and allows industry the ability to incorporate new technology. The government writes contracts identifying the capabilities needed, but not the end requirement, industry then decides how to meet these capabilities.  With spiral development the Navy program office would maintain a tight feedback loop with its contractors, designing the solution piece by piece.[5]  Also,

---

[4] Robert O. Work, "Naval Transformation and the Littoral Combat Ship" (Center for Strategic and Budgetary, working paper of government LCS design team, 2004). 9.

[5] Joab Jackson, "Pentagon Backs Spiral Development." Washington Technology, 9 June 2003. Database on-line. Available from URL: www.Washingtontechnology.com/news/18_5/cover-stories/20872-1.html.

for the first time a ship would be designed using a modular concept. The design called for the LCS to be divided into core and mission modules. The core would consist of those basic requirements necessary for the ship to operate. For example, the navigation system, the engineering plant, self defense, and command, control, computers, communications, and intelligence (C4I) are all parts of the ship's core.

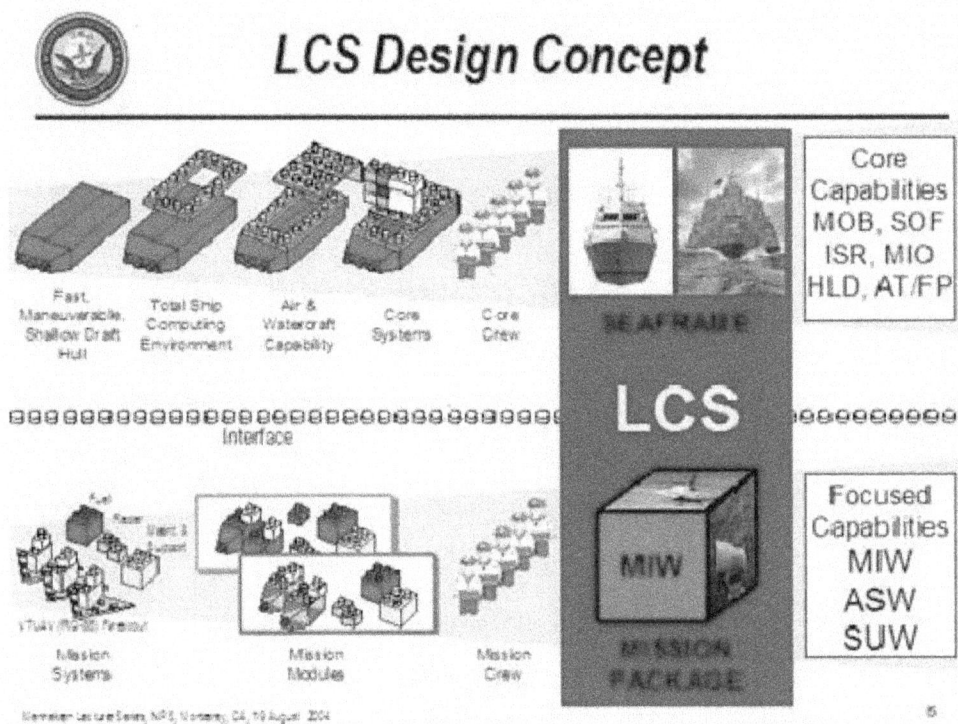

FIGURE 1. LEGO ® CONCEPT OF DESIGN FOR LCS[6]

The mission modules consist of specific equipment necessary to perform very specific missions. The missions for which modules are being developed include, Mine Warfare (MIW), Surface Warfare (SUW), and Undersea Warfare (USW). These modules are being designed with the requirement that

Accessed 3 February 2005.

[6] Jason Pawley, "Littoral Combat Ship: Overview" (Presented at Menneken Lecture Series, Naval Postgraduate School, Monterey, California, 19 August 2004.) 5.

the ship can be completely reconfigured for a different mission within three days. According to Captain Donald Babcock, U.S. Navy, the LCS Naval Sea Systems Command (NAVSEA) Program Manager, the development and employment the LCS is like playing with LEGO's. The core will be standing by to receive additional blocks (modules). Unlike the LEGO's that that are used in figure 1, the actual mission modules will be delivered in standard sized cargo containers. These containers are lowered through a door in the flight deck into the mission module area. The Reconfigurable Mission Systems Interface Control Document (ICD) for the Littoral Combat Ship (LCS) for Detail Design Phase states:

> The LCS platform shall be designed to accommodate multiple reconfigurable modular mission packages to accomplish focused missions via an open and modular design that provides flexibility and ease of upgrade while ensuring rapid and successful installation and integration of the mission packages to the platform. To permit use of a wide range of both present and future mission systems and to permit platform and mission systems to be developed independently, standard interfaces in the form of a standard technical architecture must be used. Industry shall design and build the LCS platform employing an open modular architecture for mission systems based on this standard technical architecture. Separately, mission modules will be developed for the LCS based on this technical architecture.[7]

From this statement comes the next transformational aspect of the LCS development. That is the idea that industry will play a significant role in how this ship is built. The Navy has awarded contracts to Lockheed Martin

---

[7] Naval Sea Systems, "Draft (ICD) Interface Control Document" (working paper of government LCS design team, 13 Sep 2004) 5.

and General Dynamics for each company to produce two LCS'. The ships will be produced by each company completely independent of the other. In order to ensure that industry will drive the development of the LCS, the Navy has produced a document called the Capability Development Document (CDD) for Littoral Combat Ship. This CDD provides the desired performance attributes required for each of the contractors to meet in order to produce a LCS. In order to force each contractor to view cost as an independent variable (CAIV) the navy has assigned a 220 million dollar price tag to development, production, and testing of the LCS.

FIGURE 2. LOCKHEED MARTIN VERSION OF LCS[8]

FIGURE 3. GENERAL DYNAMICS VERSION OF LCS[9]

These performance attributes or requirements are very broad in order to provide industry an incentive to exercise as much initiative as possible.

---

8 LCS homepage, Available from URL: www.peos.crane.navy.mil/lcs/Lockheed.htm. Accessed 4 February 2005.

9 Ibid.

NAVSEA provided the following requirements to Lockheed Martin (LM) and General Dynamics (GD) regarding the LCS communications package, "LCS Flight 0 will have sufficient communications capability to ensure accurate and timely transmission and reception of multi-media information in coordination with naval, joint and combined forces as well as interagency data (shore sites/facilities), including interaction with those units that rely in whole, or in part, upon voice communications."[10] This is a very generic requirement allowing each contractor the ability to determine how to best achieve the requirement. This open minded development procedure is applied to the sea frame or core as well as the mission modules. In addition to rapid module change out, some specific requirements that the Navy has asked both contractors to provide are a shallow draft of less then 20 feet, speed between 40 (threshold) and 50 knots (objective), and have a nominal endurance of 3,500 nautical miles. As a part of the core systems and specific mission modules, the LCS will be equipped with at least one manned helicopter as well as unmanned aerial vehicles (UAVs), unmanned undersea vehicles (UUVs), and manned and unmanned surface vehicles (USVs). The Lockheed Martin version of LCS is developing a stern ramp for launch and recovery of manned and unmanned boats, an extendable rail system for launch and recovery of USVs and a Talon system[11] on the flight deck for recovery of manned and unmanned aerial vehicles.

---

[10] Naval Sea Systems, "Capability Development Document for Littoral Combat Ship" (working paper of government LCS design team, April 2004) 9-2.

[11] The Talon System (also known as in deck light harpoon) is a grid and probe aircraft recovery system that is similar to the system being used for UAV recovery.

B.   LCS COMBAT SYSTEMS

The LCS is being designed with a combat system that provides sufficient self defense capabilities that will allow the LCS to operate independently, or as part of a Expeditionary Strike Group (ESG) or Expeditionary Strike Force (ESF).  Of interest to this thesis, the combat system will include the ability to transmit and receive on HF, VHF, UHF, SHF and SATCOM.  Additionally, the LCS will be equipped with non-secure internet protocol network (NIPRNET), secure internet protocol network (SIPRNET) and joint tactical information distribution system (JTIDS) data connections.  As of September 2004, the LM version of LCS is being configured with minimal Electronic Warfare (EW) capability, that being Electronic Support Measures (ESM), to assist in contact identification.  The LCS will be equipped with an electro-optical infrared scanner designed mainly for use in identifying surface contacts, but will have the ability to assist Naval Surface Fire Support (NSFS) in splash spotting and battle damage assessment (BDA).

C.   SPARTAN SCOUT OVERVIEW

SPARTAN SCOUT meets a need for ship force protection... SPARTAN SCOUT can provide surveillance in a harbor, not only for Navy ships but also U.S. Coast Guard units responsible for port security. It can be modified for mine detection or anti-submarine warfare.

Rear Adm. James Stavridis
Commander of the Enterprise Strike Group[12]

---

[12]  Naval Undersea Warfare Command Public Affairs Officer, "Spartan Deployed on Gettysburg," Navy News Stand, 23 December 2003.  Available from URL: http://www.news.navy.mil/search/display.asp?story_id=10964. Accessed 19 February, 2005.

FIGURE 4. SPARTAN SCOUT TEST BED MODEL[13]

The USV that will be deployed on at least the first
LCS will be the SPARTAN SCOUT. As of September 2004, there
was still debate regarding the future development of USV's
for the Navy.  This debate is between Naval Undersea
Warfare Center who designed the SCOUT and the Office of
Naval Research who in conjunction with the Surface Warfare
Center of NAVSEA is designing a USV called the Unmanned Sea
Surface Vehicle (USSV).  The major difference between the
SCOUT and the USSV is that the USSV will be built as an
unmanned vehicle from the ground up, where as the SCOUT is
simply  a  seven or eleven meter rigid hull inflatable boat

---

[13] Pat Holder, "SPARTAN SCOUT ACTD Unmanned Surface Vessel for
Assured Access and Force Protection" (presentation presented at
Logistics from the Sea Symposium, Washington DC, 4-7 February 2003).

(RHIB) modified for unmanned operations. As the SCOUT will be the USV on the first LCS, it will be the USV considered in this study.

The SCOUT was designed to be an integrated weapon system and a primary force leveler against asymmetric threats, enabling the battleforce commander to match lesser threats with an appropriate, inexpensive response.[14] According to the Advanced Concept Technology Demonstration (ACTD) management plan the SCOUT will be an additional asset to the warfare commander with the capability to conduct critical missions (MIW, ISR/FP, SUW), prepare the water space for sealift operations, and when launched or operated from shore, provide port protection. The management plan goes on to say that the SCOUT has the potential to benefit the warfighter by extending the range of detecting a threat, providing the ability to establish defensive barriers, minimize the risk to personnel and capital assets and serve as a force multiplier or leveler.[15] It is important to note that the management plan does not address the use of SCOUT for Information Operations (IO) missions. The main focus for the SCOUT as with all Naval USV's has been in the mission areas of force protection, MIW and SUW.

The SCOUT, like LCS, will be built with a modular design and in several spirals. The core of the SCOUT will

---

[14] Naval Undersea Warfare Command, "SPARTAN SCOUT ACTD Management Plan Rev 1" (Working paper for SPARTAN SCOUT design team, 14 March 2003) 1.

[15] "SPARTAN SCOUT ACTD Management Plan Rev 1", 6.

be capable of carrying payloads of 3,200 lbs for the seven meter model and approximately 5,000 lbs for the eleven meter model.[16]

FIGURE 5. SPARTAN SCOUT BLOS COMMUNICATIONS[17]

Beginning in fiscal year 2006, the third spiral or version of the SCOUT should be completed and capable of conducting missions such as Intelligence, Surveillance, and Reconnaissance (ISR) and Force Protection (FP) using an Integrated Radar Optical Sighting System (IROSS) coupled with a 7.62mm gattling gun (GAU-17) for moving targets, MIW using an AQS-14 Side Scan Sonar, SUW employing the Hellfire/Javelin Missile for moving targets at sea, and C3 (Command, Control and Communication) extending Beyond the

---

[16] Surface Warfare Magazine, Summer 2004, Vol 29, No 3 Pg 39.

[17] Holder "SPARTAN SCOUT ACTD Unmanned Surface Vessel for Assured Access and Force Protection", 2003.

line of sight capability.[18]  As seen in Figure 5 the SCOUT will have three options in extending it's beyond Line-of-Sight (BLOS) communications out to 100 nautical miles.  It will be cable of relaying communications through manned and unmanned aerial vehicles, manned and unmanned surface vehicles as well as through satellites.

---

[18] "SPARTAN SCOUT ACTD Management Plan Rev 1", 6.

# III. CONFIGURATION OF LCS FOR IO

> Generally, in battle, use the normal force
> (direct approach) to engage; use the
> extraordinary (indirect approach) to win.
>
> Sun Tzu, The Art of War.

## A.    INTRODUCTION

With the first LCS Flight Zero model scheduled for delivery in December of 2006 now is the time to recommend any modifications that could be incorporated into the final design of the sea frame.  In exploring how the LCS' sea frame could be configured to support IO missions, one must first start with systems that are already in existence.

## B.    OUTBOARD AN/SSQ-108

The Classic OUTBOARD (Organizational Unit Tactical Baseline Operational Area Radio Detection) countermeasures exploitation system, AN/SSQ-108(v), could be added to the design of LCS.  OUTBOARD is a U.S. Navy shipboard combat direction finding system that has historically been installed in Guided Missile Destroyers and Cruisers. OUTBOARD provides electronic warfare signals acquisition and direction finding systems with the capability to detect, locate, and identify hostile targets at long-ranges, and input this information into the shipboard tactical data system. With the introduction of the more cost effective LCS (a ship designed to operate closer to shore) adding the OUTBOARD system would be a justifiable modification.  Because LCS will operate closer to shore the ability to intercept signals would be improved over the distantly operating DDG or CG. Because the LCS cost a fraction of what the DDG or CG cost to produce it would free these high priced, high value assets from the OUTBOARD missions for other critical core missions.

C.    AFLOAT PRINT PRODUCTION SYSTEM (APPS)

Another proposed configuration change for the LCS is the development of an IO module. Similar to the other warfare area modules (e.g. MIW, SUW, ASW) the LCS could be configured with the IO module when specifically tasked to conduct IO related missions. This IO module would contain equipment required for leaflet production such as the Afloat Print Production System (APPS) that has been successfully used by USS CONSTELLATION (CV 64) and USS FORT MCHENRY (LSD 43).

In response to the Carrier Battle Group's Information Warfare Commander's (IWC) request the Fleet Information Warfare Command developed and installed the prototype APPS on USS CONSTELLATION prior to her 2003 deployment. This APPS consists of two Risograph duplicators, two Dell laptop computers and one heavy-duty paper cutter. This equipment provides the high speed (120 pages per minute) and high volume (86,000 single color leaflets per hour) required to produce PSYOP leaflets for distribution.[19] These shipboard produced leaflets were distributed via the PDU-5/B bomb dropped from Carrier Airwing aircraft. While the number of personnel that were involved in this evolution is unclear, the results of this exercise displayed that the entire

---

[19] John Solt, "Psychological Operations Go to Sea" FIWC INFOSCOPE Winter 2003, Volume 2, Issue 1. Available from FIWC website at URL: http://www.infoscope.fiwc.navy.smil.mil/vol2_issue2/index.htm. Accessed 12 October, 2004.

process of producing, cutting, rolling, and loading 100,000 leaflets into a PDU-5/B could be accomplished in approximately 12 hours.[20]

D.   COMMANDO SOLO

In addition to the APPS equipment an LCS IO module would include radio and television broadcast equipment much like what is found in the EC-130 COMMAND SOLO aircraft.[21]

FIGURE 6. EXAMPLE OF ACTUAL LEAFLET USED IN AFGHANISTAN.[22]

Translation:  STOP! TURN AWAY NOW!
"The Partnership of Nations has secured the Qandahar Airport to ensure that Humanitarian Aid will reach the people of this area for your own safety please stay away"
HELP US KEEP YOU SAFE

---

[20] Solt, "Psychological Operations Go to Sea".

[21] 193rd Special Operations Wing (ANG), Harrisburg, PA.

[22] Available from the PSYWARRIOR website.
URL:http:// www.psywarrior.com. Accessed 15 February 2005.

Again, with a majority of the LCS missions being conducted in the littorals and closer to shore, these radio and television broadcasts could be tailored and focused to reach a more specific audience. For example, several days prior to a fleet of ships entering a port where security may be an issue the LCS operating in close proximity to the port could broadcast warnings regarding the ships mission and the consequences to an enemy if the ships are attacked. In addition, the LCS leaflet production capability could be used to deliver focused leaflets to this specific port, much like what was done at the Qandahar Airport during Operation ENDURING FREEDOM (Figure 6).

While it is true that COMMANDO SOLO (Figure 7) has been and will continue to be a primary asset that is tasked to deliver focused messages in support of the Joint Force Commanders campaign plan, there are certain unique benefits that a broadcast system onboard the LCS provides the warfare commander.

FIGURE 7. EXTERIOR AND INTERIOR VIEW OF COMMANDO SOLO[23]

---

[23] American Forces Information Services website. Available from: http://www.iwar.org.uk/psyops/resources/afghanistan/commando-solo.htm. Accessed 17 February 2005.

According to a COMMANDO SOLO commander, the EC-130 has been called a 'weapon of mass persuasion'. Equipping the LCS for the mission of PSYOP broadcast would allow focused and localized messages to be delivered over longer time periods. By keeping the broadcast area limited the message being delivered can be tailored to appeal to the target group without the fear of offending other groups. The on-station time is increased when using a broadcast from the LCS as compared to that of COMMANDO SOLO and the LCS does not have the concern of access to ports within a mission radius which may limit COMMANDO SOLO. In addition, it simply makes sense and is cost effective to use the equipment that is already available and that has been operationally validated.

E.   TRANSPORTABLE AM/FM RADIO BROADCAST SYSTEM (TARBS)

In 2003, in addition to the APPS exercise onboard the USS MCHENRY (LSD-43), a test of the newly developed Transportable AM/FM Radio Broadcast System (TARBS) was conducted off the coast of Okinawa. During this test, messages produced by the 4th Psychological Operations Group (POG) where able to be broadcast to target audiences in the littorals.[24] According to Joint Publication 3-53 Doctrine for Joint Psychological Operations:

> TARBS is comprised of an audio transmitter and antenna subsystems capable of operations ashore or afloat. When needed, TARBS will broadcast voice information as directed and authorized by the Joint Force Commander (JFC). PSYOP broadcast information products will be produced for the JFC by the 4th POG (Airborne) or the JPOTF supporting the JFC, and forwarded to the TARBS operators for

---

[24] Solt, "Psychological Operations Go to Sea".

21

final dissemination. The products will be forwarded either electronically to the TARBS laptop computer or by other means as necessary (e.g., cassette and compact disc-read only memory). Once authorized by the JFC, the TARBS operators will conduct both AM and FM broadcasts of this product on designated frequencies.[25]

Joint Publication 3-53 goes on to say, "TARBS ideally will be installed onboard one ship in each amphibious ready group."[26] As the LCS is being designed to assist in reducing the role of the U.S. Navy's aging amphibious fleet it only makes sense that TARBS be included in an LCS IO Module. As TARBS is designated as a portable system divided into three subsystems, mostly contained in a transportable shelter 173 inches long, 86 inches wide, and 84 inches high, with an approximate loaded weight of 9,600 pounds it could easily be configured to fit into the IO module in the LCS.[27]

F.    HIGH POWER MICROWAVE (HPM) AND ELECTROMAGNETIC PULSE (EMP)

In the realm of emerging technology, the addition of the developmental High Power Microwave (HPM) and Electromagnetic Pulse (EMP) weapons would provide the ability for the LCS to be an asset for offensive IO missions. The development of HPM devices is of interest to many different communities, specifically the Department of Defense (DoD), the Department of Energy (DoE), and the Electromagnetic Compatibility (EMC) community. For the DoD interests there are ultra-wide and narrowband applications.

---

[25] CJCS. *Joint Doctrine for Psychological Operations* (Washington DC: U.S. Government Printing Office, 2003), A-4.

[26] Ibid.

[27] Ibid.

Narrowband technology operates in the 1 to 100 GHz range, and the ultra-wideband operates in the 10 MHz to 10 GHz range. The production of narrow and ultra-wideband pulses require different power sources and produce significantly different results. Narrowband pulses are extremely precise and are able to be aimed at a specific target; analogous to a laser. Ultra-wideband pulses provide coverage to large areas; analogous to a flash bulb.[28]

The main application for the ultra-wideband technology that is being developed by the DoD is for active non-lethal denial purposes in crowd control. The DOD is developing narrow band technology for electronic attack purposes. As narrowband is the technology that would provide the LCS with an Electronic Warfare (EW) capability we will focus on it's application. Figure 8 shows a block diagram of how a narrow band pulse is produced. While still under development the inclusion of this HPM equipment in an IO module would allow the LCS to direct an antenna toward a target located miles away and with the precision of a laser conduct an electronic attack. This narrowband weapon is able to penetrate concrete bunkers and would be effective even on equipment that has been shielded from nuclear produced Electromagnetic Pulses (EMP).[29]

---

[28] E. Schamiloglu, "High Powered Microwave Sources and Applications". IEEE MTT-S Digest, (2004): 1000.

[29] Michael Abrams, "The Dawn of the E-bomb", IEEE Spectrum (November 2003): 26.

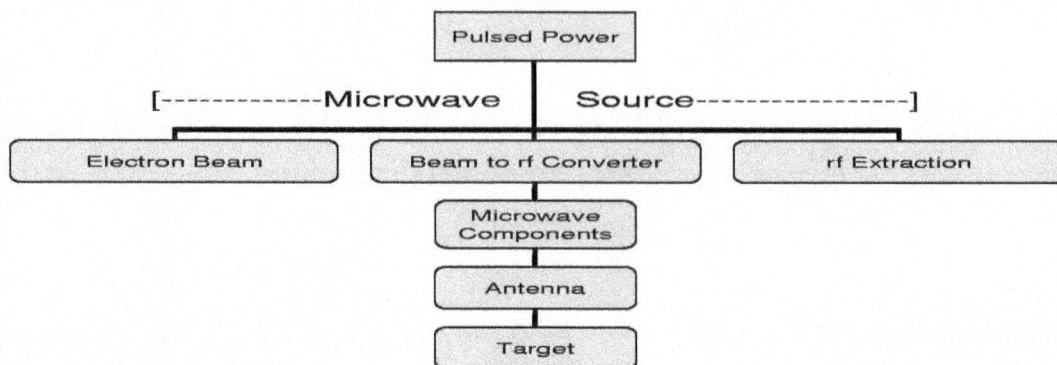

FIGURE 8. HPM NARROWBAND PRODUCTION BLOCK DIAGRAM[30]

Pulsed power is the technology that converts some prime power source (whether the line voltage in the laboratory, jet turbine on an aircraft, or battery pack on an unmanned drone) into a short, properly tailored, high voltage pulse. High voltage capacitors, together with fast switching techniques, are typically used to accomplish this. Once the pulse power portion of the system produces the desirable high voltage waveform, it is applied to an electron gun, also known as an electron beam diode. The electron beam diode produces a high perveance electron beam where space-charged effects dominate the interaction. The relativistic electron beam, once generated, propagates through a radio frequency (rf) interaction region, which converts the beam's kinetic energy into HPM.[31]

Another non-kinetic weapon in development that would provide the LCS the ability to conduct offensive EW missions is the E-bomb. While figures 9 and 10 provide the anatomy of a theoretical E-bomb, there is speculation that the E-bomb was tested in the early days of Operation IRAQI FREEDOM.

---

[30] Schamiloglu, "High Powered Microwave Sources and Applications," 1001.

[31] Ibid., 1002-1003.

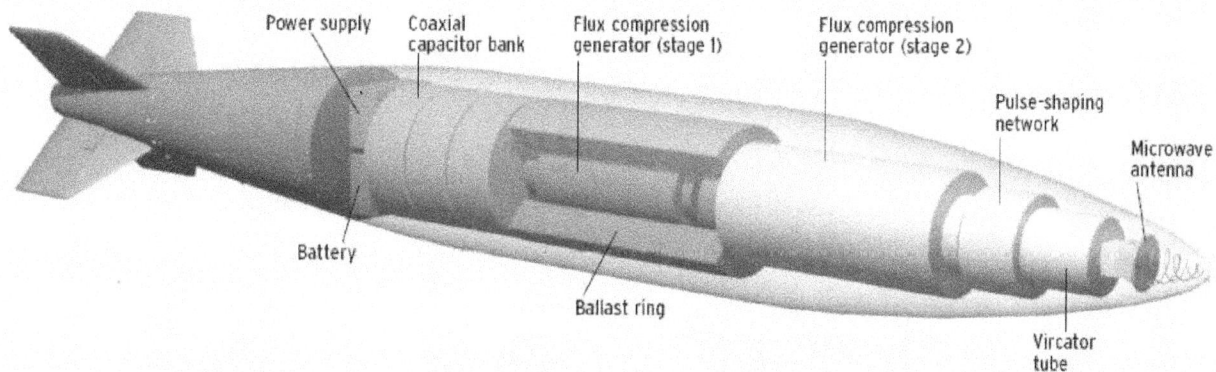

FIGURE 9. DIAGRAM OF AN E-BOMB[32]

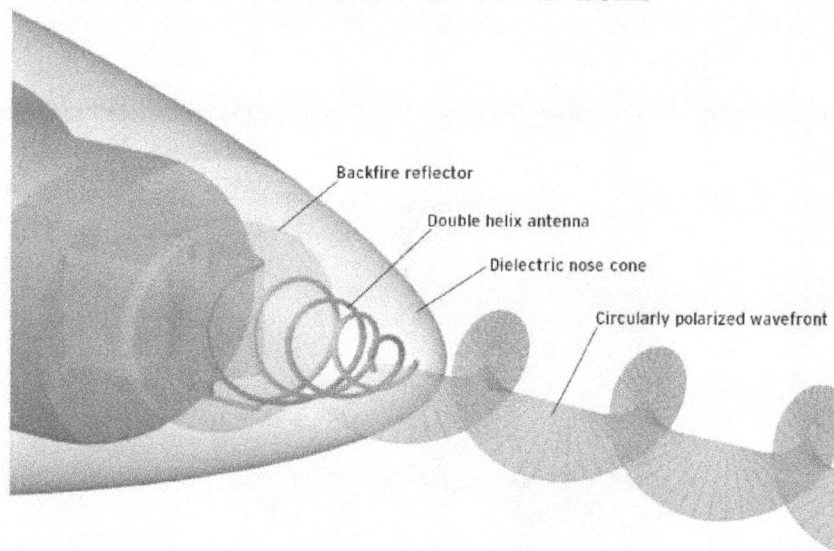

FIGURE 10. DIAGRAM OF E-BOMB NOSE CONE[33]

According to a _Time_ magazine article written by Mark Thompson in January of 2003, the use of microwave weapons would be one of the legacies of the second Gulf War.[34] After seeing footage of a U.S. bomb destroying an Iraqi television studio, Howard Seguine, an expert on emerging weapons technology with Decisive Analytics Corporation said, "I saw the detonation, and then saw the burst-which

---

[32] Abrams, "The Dawn of the E-bomb," 25.

[33] Ibid.

[34] Mark Thompson, "America's Ultra-Secret Weapon". Time, (January 27, 2003. Volume 161 Number 4).

25

wasn't much. If they took the station out with that blast, I strongly suspect that we used Iraq as a proving ground for HPMs."[35] As seen in Figure 11, Dr. Schamilogu[36] is holding a wave guide and antenna capable of producing high power microwaves. This HPM technology exists and should be part of a LCS IO module.

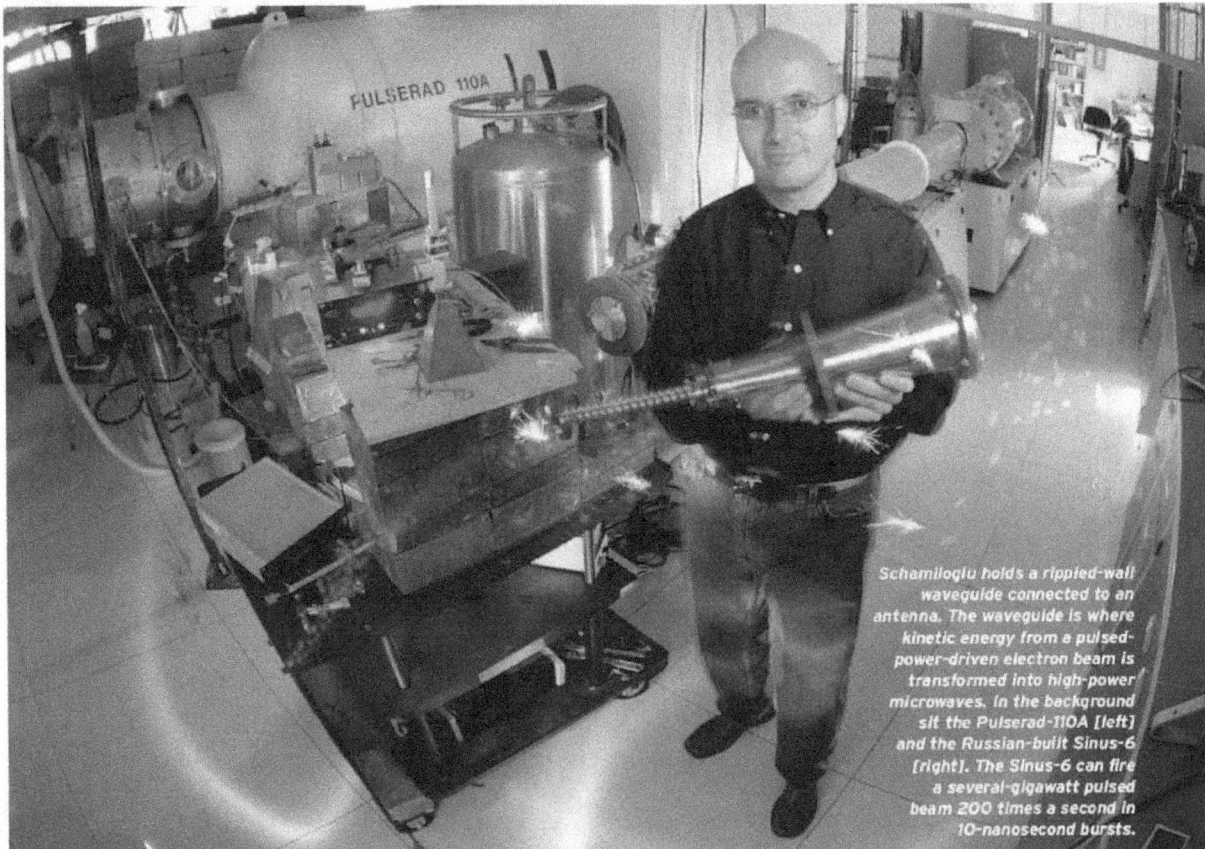

Schamiloglu holds a rippled-wall waveguide connected to an antenna. The waveguide is where kinetic energy from a pulsed-power-driven electron beam is transformed into high-power microwaves. In the background sit the Pulserad-110A [left] and the Russian-built Sinus-6 [right]. The Sinus-6 can fire a several-gigawatt pulsed beam 200 times a second in 10-nanosecond bursts.

FIGURE 11. ACTUAL HIGH POWER MICROWAVE EQUIPMENT[37]

G.    MODULE MANNING

The Goldwater-Nichols Act of 1986 strengthened the concept of joint operations with the DoD. In the 2001 Quadrennial Defense Review Report (QDR) the Secretary of Defense directed that all branches of the Armed Forces

[35] Abrams, "The Dawn of the E-bomb," 26.

[36] Leading Electromagnetic expert from the University of New Mexico.

[37] Abrams, "The Dawn of the E-bomb," 26.

provide a roadmap illustrating how they will become a transformational force. Also included in the 2001 QDR was this direction for joint operations:

> To better meet future warfare challenges, DoD must develop the ability to integrate combat organizations with forces capable of responding rapidly to events that occur with little or no warning. These joint forces must be scalable and task-organized into modular units to allow the combatant commanders to draw on the appropriate forces to deter or defeat an adversary. The forces must be highly networked with joint command and control, and they must be better able to integrate into combined operations than the forces of today.[38]

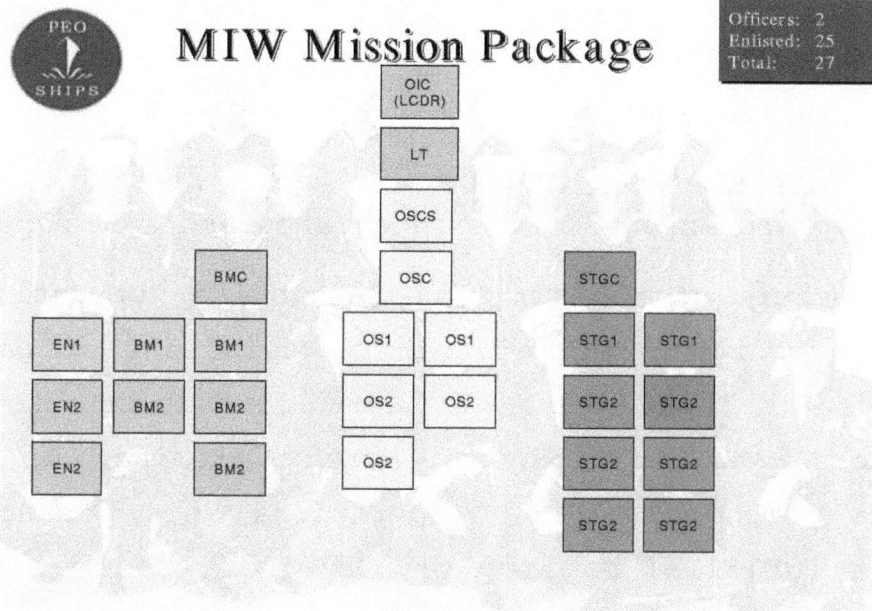

FIGURE 12.    EXAMPLE OF PROPOSED MINE WARFARE MANNING[39]

---

[38] Donald Rumsfeld, *Quadrennial Defense Review.* (Washington DC: Government Printing Office, 2001), 32.

[39] Rob Abbott, *LCS Mission Package Manning Overview.* (Washington DC: PEO Ships, 2005).

Current mission module manning for LCS consists of all naval personnel (Figure 12). As no one branch of the armed forces is the IO authority and in keeping with the Secretary of Defense's direction, the manning for a LCS IO module would optimally consist of members of the Army, Air Force and Navy. Air Force personnel would be provided by the 67th Information Operations Wing (IOW), who for the past ten years have led the charge in executing the next order of battle on the information highways.[40] In addition to Air Force technicians the IO module would include a junior officer to act a liaison with the Information Warfare Flight (IWF) and the Air and Space Operations Center (AOC). According to Air Force IO doctrine, in times of war the IWF becomes the Air Force's key IO expertise whereas the AOC typically is the main organizational structure through which the capabilities of EW operations, net warfare (NW) operations and influence operations planning and execution are integrated and synchronized.[41]

Members of the Army's Psychological Operations Groups (POG), specifically the 4th POG, would make up part of the IO module. According to Army literature, the 4th POG (Airborne) at Fort Bragg, North Carolina, is the only active psychological operations unit, constitutes 26 percent of all U.S. Army psychological operations units.[42] Similar to the Air Force manning, in addition to

[40] Bruce Bingle, "67th IOW Crystallizes Operations" Available from URL: http://aia.lackland.af.mil/homepages/pa/spokesman/jun04/cc.cfm. Accessed 23 February 2005.

[41] Secretary of the Air Force. Information Operations AFDD 2-5 (Washington DC: U.S. Government Printing Office, January 11, 2005), 33.

[42] Herbert L. Altshuler. United States Army Civil Affairs and Psychological Operations Command. Available from URL: http://www.soc.mil/usacapoc/psyopfs.shtml. Accessed 23 February 2005.

technicians a junior officer would act as a liaison to coordinate with The U.S. Army Civil Affairs and Psychological Operations Command (USACAPOC). USACAPOC, headquarter at Fort Bragg, North Carolina, is a subordinate command of U.S. Army Special Operations Command (USASOC).[43]

In addition to a module Officer In Charge (OIC) and technicians, the Navy would provide a junior officer to act as a liaison with the Naval Information Warfare Activity (NIWA). NIWA at Ft Meade is the Navy's principal technical agent to research, assess, develop, and prototype Information Warfare (IW) capabilities.[44] Figure 13 shows the proposed members of the IO module team onboard the LCS that would be in support of the Joint Force Commander (JFC).

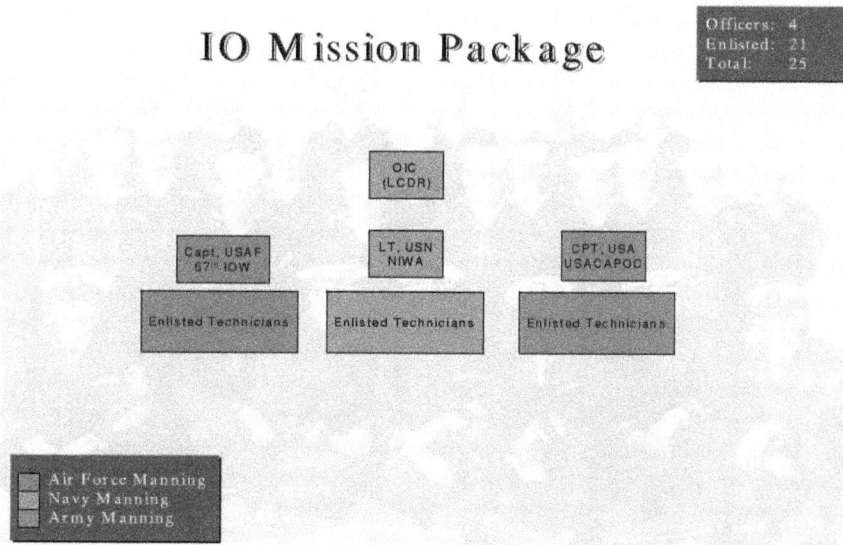

FIGURE 13.        PROPOSED IO MODULE MANNING

---

[43] Herbert L. Altshuler. United States Army Civil Affairs and Psychological Operations Command. Available from URL: http://www.soc.mil/usacapoc/psyopfs.shtml. Accessed 23 February 2005.

[44] Federation of American Scientists website. Available from URL:http://www.fas.org/irp/agency/navsecgru/niwa/. Accessed 23 February 2005.

THIS PAGE INTENTIONALLY LEFT BLANK

# IV. CONFIGURATION OF THE SPARTAN SCOUT FOR IO

> The real target in war is the mind of the enemy command, not the bodies of his troops. If we operate against his troops it is fundamentally for the effect that action will produce on the mind and will of the commander; indeed, the trend of warfare and development of new weapons—promise to give us increased and more direct opportunities of striking at this psychological target.
>
> Captain Sir Basil Liddell Hart
> *Thoughts on War*, 1944

## A. INTRODUCTION

The SPARTAN SCOUT like the LCS, is still under development making now the optimal time to study and recommend configuration changes. In September of 2004 I visited Dr. Ricci and his SPARTAN SCOUT at the Naval Undersea Warfare Center (NUWC) in Newport, Rhode Island. While Dr Ricci assisted his team in the installation of a mock hellfire missile and actual IROSS gun, Dr. Ricci admitted that, "While we've always understood it could be used in Info Ops, we haven't spent a great deal in development of that concept."[45] This chapter will provide recommendations to develop an IO module for SPARTAN SCOUT using existing and developmental technologies.

## B. LOUDSPEAKERS

The first technology to be considered for an IO module for the SPARTAN SCOUT is the 'tried and true' loudspeaker. Loudspeakers have been used by U.S. forces for PSYOP

---

[45] Dr. Vic Ricci, interview by author, Newport, RI. 24 September 2004.

dissemination in every conflict since WWII. They proved to be most effective during Operation JUST CAUSE in Panama where they were credited with reducing casualties on both sides.[46] According to the <u>Final Report to Congress for the Conduct of the Persian Gulf War</u>:

> Loudspeaker teams were used effectively throughout the theater. Each tactical maneuver brigade had loudspeaker PSYOP teams attached. Many of the 66 teams came from the Army Reserve Components. Loudspeaker teams accompanied units into Iraq and Kuwait, broadcasting tapes of prepared surrender messages. Messages were transmitted in Arabic and were developed by cross cultural teams. These messages were similar to those on the leaflets being dropped. Iraqi soldiers were encouraged to surrender, were warned of impending bombing attacks, and told they would be treated humanely and fairly.…
>
> …UH-1Ns used loudspeakers and Arab linguists to convince Iraqi soldiers to surrender along the Kuwait border. The message to the Iraqi soldier was that Saddam Hussein was deliberately endangering their religion and families.…
>
> …Many Enemy Prisoners of War mentioned hearing the loudspeaker broadcasts in their area and surrendered to the Coalition forces because they feared more bombing.[47]

In May of 2000 the Defense Science Board (DSB) Task Force submitted their report on <u>The Creation and Dissemination of All Forms of Information in Support of Psychological Operations in Time of Military Conflict</u>. The DSB is a Federal Advisory Committee established to provide

---

[46] Robert W. Caspers, *Joint Task Force South in Operations Just Cause, An Oral History Interview.* (Washington DC: U.S. Army Center of Military History, 1990), 8.

[47] U.S. Department of Defense, Office of the Secretary of Defense, Final Report to Congress for the Conduct of the Persian Gulf War, April 1992. 192, 623.

independent advice to the Secretary of Defense.[48]   The DSB
Task Force was established due to the limitations exhibited
in military operations in the Balkans, where the *Commando
Solo* (EC 130E) aircraft were unable to effectively
disseminate TV and radio broadcasts.   The DSB recommended
that United States Special Operations Command (USSOCOM)
investigate the creation of small and easily reconfigurable
information-dissemination packages that would be compatible
with multiple platforms, including UAVs and leased
aircraft, for a variety of missions.[49]   The report goes on
to recommend that future tactical PSYOP teams no longer be
loadspeaker teams.   The DSB recommended that PSYOP messages
be routed through wireless networks to unmanned speakers
and that loudspeakers should be mounted on tanks and
dropped in the enemy area.   The goal being to free the
tactical PSYOP units to conduct electronic news and image
gathering in order to produce more effective PSYOP
material.[50]

While the recommendations of the DSB do not
specifically address seaborne application of PSYOP
dissemination it is clear that fitting the SPARTAN SCOUT
with loudspeakers would comply with the overall intentions
of the committee.   Another reason to develop loudspeakers
for the SPARTAN SCOUT is an ongoing effort by the Marine
Corps with respect to loudspeaker systems.

---

[48] Defense Science Board (DSB) Task Force, *The Creation and
Dissemination of All Forms of Information in Support of Psychological
Operations in Time of Military Conflict.* (Washington DC: Government
Printing Office, 2000) i.

[49] Ibid., 4.

[50] Ibid., 10.

C.    LONG RANGE ACOUSTIC DEVICE (LRAD)

In May of 2004, in order to explore non-lethal options for handling force protection, the 24th Marine Expeditionary Unit (MEU) conducted tests on the X-Net, Long Range Acoustic Device (LRAD) and the Vehicle Non-Lethal Munition (VENOM).[51]

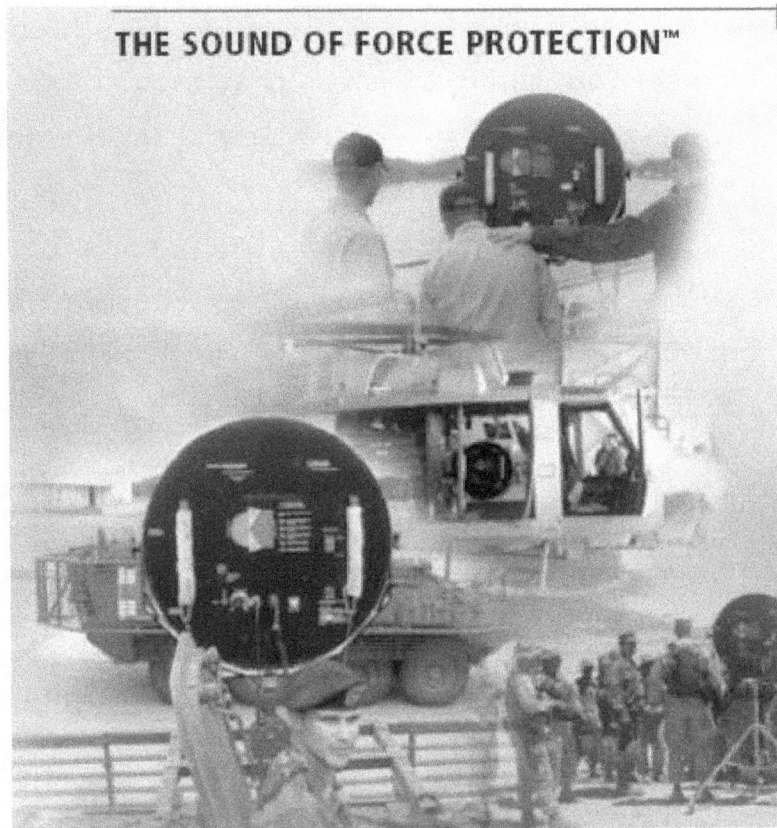

FIGURE 14. EXAMPLES OF LRAD EMPLOYENT[52]

The LRAD is an experimental technology that should be considered for incorporation into an IO module for SPARTAN SCOUT.  The LRAD is disc shaped loudspeaker being developed

---

[51] Sara Beavers, "24 MEU Conducts Non-lethal Training During TRUEX" Marine Link, May 2004. Available from URL: http://www.marines.mil/marinelink/mcn2000.nsf/lookupstoryref/2004525152 639. Accessed 19 February 2005.

[52] American Technology Corporation. "LRAD: The Sound of Force Protection", Available from ATC website. URL:http://www.atcsd.com. Accessed 15 February 2005.

by American Technology Corporation (Figure 14). The LRAD is a 33 inch diameter disc that is capable of clearly delivering a message to a range of more than 500 meters.[53] With it's small, lightweight size, and minimum power requirements (Table 1) not only would the LRAD provide excellent PYSOP dissemination capabilities for the SPARTAN SCOUT, it could also be used in a form of electronic attack (EA).

| LRAD 3300 SERIES TECHNICAL SPECIFICATIONS | |
|---|---|
| WEIGHT : | 45 lbs |
| DIAMETER: | 33" diameter x 5" thickness |
| MAXIMUM SPL TONE: | 146dB sustained, 151dB burst at 1 meter |
| MAXIMUM SPL VOICE: | Less than 120dB sustained, based on individual voice frequencies and harmonic characteristics |
| REGULATED POWER MODE: | Normal operations, tone limited to 120dB at 1 meter |
| DURABILITY: | Thermal conditions have minimal effect on system performance. System meets MIL-STD 810 environmental specifications |
| EMITTER, HARMONIC DISTORTION: | Less than 1% THD at 126dB at 1 meter at 2.5kHz |
| MAXIMUM POWER HANDLING: | 500 watts; 100-240VAC at 50-60Hz, 5 amps at 115VAC |
| NORMAL POWER USAGE (TONE): | 240 watts, 2 amps at 115VAC |
| DIRECTIONALITY: | -20dB at +/- 15° at 2.5kHz |

TABLE 1.    LRAD TECHNICAL SPECIFICATIONS[54]

One of the features of the LRAD is the ability to deliver a sound burst of 150dB at a frequency of 2,100 to 3,100 Hertz.[55] While this sound burst will not completely

---

[53] American Technology Corporation. "LRAD: The Sound of Force Protection".

[54] Ibid.

[55] "US Troops Have Sound Weapon," Washington Times, 7 March 2004. Available from URL: http://www.washingtontimes.com/archive/. Accessed 19 February 2005.

incapacitate an individual it would provide behavior modification. Adding the LRAD to the IO module of the SPARTAN SCOUT would provide the ability for non-lethal EA. The next technology that should be added to the SPARTAN SCOUT IO module would offer a lethal EA capability. Again we look toward a Marine Corps initiative to develop a mobile phased array electronic attack antenna.

D.    COMINT EMITTER SENSING AND ATTACK SYSTEM (CESAS)

In a March 2004 Marine Corps Systems Command (MARCORSYSCOM) message, the Marine Corps delineated what equipment and systems would comprise their C4I needs when a Marine unit embarks a ship. They addressed COMINT Emitter Sensing and Attack System (CESAS), a mobile phased array electronic antenna. According to MARCORSYCOM the CESAS would be a tier three piece of equipment, meaning it would deploy with the MAGTF whenever they embarked a LHD or LHA.

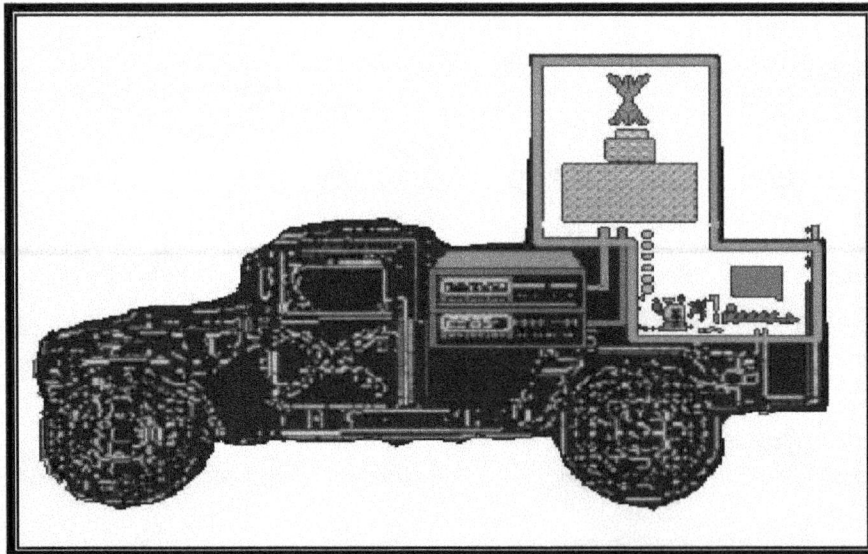

FIGURE 15. OFFICE OF NAVAL RESEARCH CESAS CONCEPTUAL DRAWING[56]

_____

[56]  ONR Future Naval Capabilities website. URL:

CESAS (Figure 15) is a Phased Array Electronic Attack Antenna, operating across a frequency range of 150-2500 MHz, that will enable on-the-move disruption of hostile RF communications by providing a steerable beam of jamming energy while retaining omni-directional receive capability.[57] According to the Office of Naval Research CESAS is a MARCORSYSCOM program that is being developed by BAE Systems Information and Electronic Warfare Department and is in the prototype and testing phase.[58]

As CESAS' development has already been funded and is schedule for final delivery in 2006 it would be cost effective to include this technology in an IO module for SPARTAN SCOUT providing another method for engaging in Electronic Attack (EA). Additionally, as the Marine Corps has identified CESAS as equipment that they will deploy with each time they embark a LHA or LHD and as the LCS with SPARTAN SCOUTs are being designed to assist in reducing the role of the U.S. Navy's aging amphibious fleet, it is logical to include CESAS in an IO module for SPARTAN SCOUT.

E.   AIR MAGNET

Another tool that should be included in the IO module of SPARTAN SCOUT would be an air magnet or similar device used for mapping Wireless Local Area Networks (WLAN). The inclusion of this technology would provide the ability for the SPARTAN SCOUT to assist in Special Information Operations (SIO) missions that may include Computer Network

---

http://www.onr.navy.mil/fncs/explog/litcom/product.asp?productid=65&divisionid=5. Accessed 2 February, 2005.

[57] Ibid

[58] Ibid

Attack (CNA). An Air Magnet as designed is a tool for network administrators to monitor the health of their existing wireless network or for planners to use to develop a wireless network. An additional use for an air magnet is the ability to locate and possibly penetrate existing wireless networks using the 802.11 standard protocol. Once inside the network the operator could conduct surveillance (Figure 16), disrupt, deny, degrade, or destroy information resident in computers and computer networks or the computers and networks themselves[59]. Inclusion of this Commercial Off The Self (COTS) equipment, with minor alteration for military use, in an IO module would be of insignificant cost.

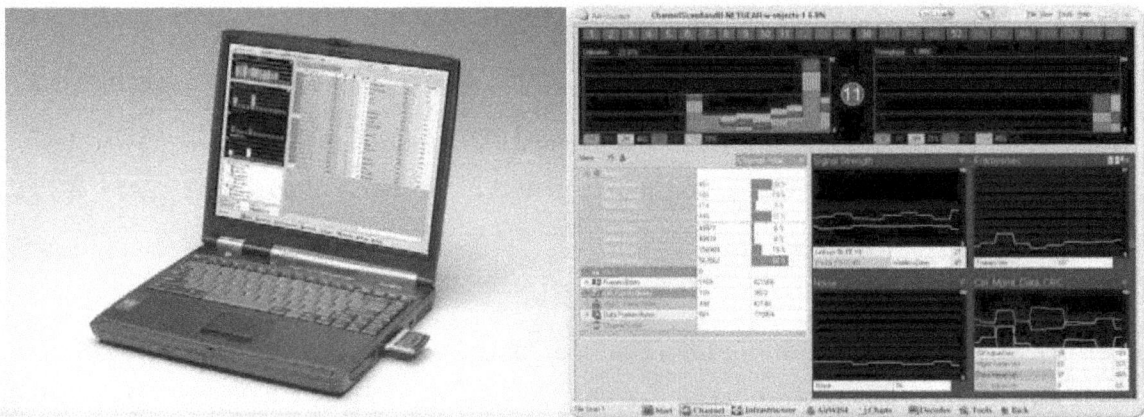

FIGURE 16. EXAMPLE OF AIR MAGNET IN LAPTOP FORM AND SCREEN EXAMPLE OF AIR MAGNET MONITORING WLAN[60]

---

[59] JP 3-13. I-9.

[60] Available from Air Magnet Corporation website. URL: http://www.airmagnet.com/news/image_library.htm. Accessed 15 February 2005.

# V. IO DOCTRINE REVIEW

> The approval chain for PSYOP [psychological operations] should be as short and streamlined as possible to facilitate timely review, approval, production and dissemination. Although coordination of PSYOP with other staff elements and organizations is absolutely critical in maximizing PSYOP effectiveness, the coordination process should not be so cumbersome as to adversely impact dissemination necessary to achieve the intended effect.
>
> CJCSI 3110.05B, Joint Psychological Operations
> Supplement to the Joint Strategic
> Capabilities Plan FY 1998

## A. INTRODUCTION

With the introduction of the LCS and SPARTAN SCOUT there will once again be a divide between technology and doctrine. The current doctrine governing IO mission approval will not allow JFC's the ability to use the LCS and SPARTAN SCOUT to their full potential. Under current IO doctrine the use of the suggested equipment in chapters III and IV would not be able to be utilized in many rapidly developing or changing IO missions in a high paced operational enviornment. To illustrate this limitation created by IO doctrine this chapter will provide a historical account for a technology and doctrine mismatch and an objective and doctrine mismatch. It will discuss how the wrong doctrine in a fast paced information age as we are now in can produce devastating results. This chapter will provide examples of the approval process governed by current joint IO doctrine and current PSYOP doctrine to illustrate the time consuming complexity of the process.

39

B.  CULTURE-BOUND HISTORY

This mismatch between technology and doctrine is not a new phenomenon.  Looking back in history there are many examples as to how outdated doctrine caused significant advances in technology to be disregarded.  In the mid 1800's as the U.S. Navy was beginning to experiment with steam as a prime mover for ships the USS Wampanoag was built.  The Wampanoag was commissioned in 1868, she measured 355 feet on the waterline; her beam was 45.2 feet; she displaced 4200 tons and was able to maintain a speed of almost 18 knots.[61] For her time she was heavily armed, of good size and maintained a speed 3 knots faster then any other ship on the water.  During sea trials she handled well in heavy seas, maneuvered well and according to special observers of the Secretary of the Navy she was steady, efficient and easy.[62]  Despite how revolutionary and well built the Wampanoag was she was cursed by a culture bound by sailing doctrine.

In 1869, one year after commissioning, the Wampanoag found herself under review by a board of naval officers appointed by the Secretary of the Navy to report on all steam vessels in the Navy.[63]  According to the boards findings found in U.S. Document 1411 of the 41st Congress, 2nd session:

> The steam vessel was not a school of seamanship
> for officers or men. Lounging through the watches
> of a steamer, or acting as fireman and coal
> heavers, will not produce in a seaman that

---

[61] Elting E. Morison. Men Machine and Modern Times, The Massachusetts Institute of Technology. Cambridge Mass. 1966. p 98-99.

[62] Ibid., 115.

[63] Ibid., 114.

combination of boldness, strength, and skill which characterized the American sailor of an elder day; and the habitual exercise by an officer, of a command, the execution of which is not under his own eye, is a poor substitute for the school of observation, promptness and command found only on the deck of a sailing vessel.[64]

The board concluded that the Wampanoag was a sad failure, utterly unfit to be retained in the service, and that she was so much of an abortion no amount of changes could be made to improve her.[65] Because the culture of the time was driven by doctrine for sailing vessels the Wampanoag was placed in lay up and some years later sold out of the Navy.

Another example of this technology doctrine mismatch involves the development of the B-10 and B-17 bombers by the U.S. Army Air Corps in the early 1930's. At the time of the B-10 and B-17 development the current doctrine derived from WWI was that bombers would be escorted by fighters for defensive purposes. The problem with the B-10 and B-17 bombers was that their design allowed them to fly faster and further than the available fighters that would provide escort.[66] Because of this culture the fixed perception was that bombers would have fighter escorts and despite prevailing Army Air Corps doctrine that indicated the majority of interceptor attacks could be expected to

---

[64] Morision, Men Machine and Modern Times. 98-99.

[65] Ibid., 115.

[66] Irving B. Holley, Technology and Military Doctrine: Essays on a Challenging Relationship. Air University Press, Maxwell AFB, AL. August 2004. 80-81.

approach within a 30 degree cone aft of the tail, the B-10 and B-17 were designed without tail guns.[67]

Once the B-17 was in production change to the design did not come easy for the bombers. Despite congressional prodding of the Army Air Corps in 1934 after an appropriations committee noticed the Royal Air Force (RAF) had some 200 bombers with nose and tail guns it wasn't until the grim realities of WWII that the B-17 was outfitted with nose and tail guns.[68]

The fact that the LCS is being developed without concern for IO related missions causes fear that it may follow in the foot steps of these historical examples. Like the Wampanoag with a technology and doctrine mismatch the LCS may be discarded. At best if the LCS is developed without planning for supporting IO missions it may be similar to the B-17 where change was difficult to implement.


C.   COLD WAR DOCTRINE

Similar to the historical examples for a mismatch between doctrine and technology the current "war on terror" illustrates a mismatch between doctrine and objectives. Akin to the doctrine mismatch with technology this doctrine mismatch with objectives would limit the use of the LCS and SPARTAN SCOUT if outfitted with IO modules.

In September of 2004, a Defense Science Board Task Force submitted their report on Strategic Communications to

---

[67] Holley, Technology and Military Doctrine: Essays on a Challenging Relationship. 80

[68] Ibid., 81

the Secretary of Defense. According to this report Strategic Communications can be understood to embrace four core instruments: public diplomacy, public affairs, international broadcasting services and information operations.[69] As the task force's definition of 'strategic communications' includes IO, their findings and recommendations effect current and future doctrine that is and will be applied to the LCS and SPARTAN SCOUT IO modules.

According to I.B. Holley, a Duke University History professor and retired Air Force Major General, "The essence of doctrine is that it springs from recorded past experience- the hard-won lessons of the past whether that experience is by one's own forces in actual combat, the recorded participation of foreign forces in combat, or experience derived from extensive peacetime maneuvers and exercises."[70] The DSB task force found that when the U.S. government was faced with a new conflict (the war on terror,) because the Cold War template (doctrine) proved so effective a decade prior to September 11, 2001, without thought or care as to whether these were the best responses, made their decision based on this outdated doctrine.[71] According to the DSB report, the following are reasons we need to move beyond outdated concepts, stale structural models, and institutionally based labels from Cold War doctrine:

---

[69] Defense Science Board (DSB) Task Force, "Strategic Communications." (Washington DC: Government Printing Office, September 2004) 12-13.

[70] Holley, Technology and Military Doctrine: Essays on a Challenging Relationship. 80.

[71] Solt, "Strategic Communications," 34.

The Cold War emphasized dissemination of information to "huddled masses yearning to be free." Today we reflexively compare Muslim "masses" to those oppressed under Soviet rule. This is a strategic mistake. There is no yearning-to-be-liberated-by-the-U.S. ground swell among Muslim societies — *except to be liberated perhaps from what they see as apostate tyrannies that the U.S. so determinedly promotes and defends*.

The Cold War emphasized an enduringly stable propaganda environment. The Cold War was a status quo setting that emphasized routine message-packaging — and whose essential objective was the most efficient enactment of the routine. In contrast the situation in Islam today is highly dynamic, and likely to move decisively in one direction or another. The U.S. urgently needs to think in terms of promoting actual positive change.

The Cold War emphasized an acceptance of authoritarian regimes as long as they were anti-communist. This could be glossed over in our message of freedom and democracy because it was the main adversary only that truly mattered. Today, however, the perception of intimate U.S. support of tyrannies in the Muslim World is perhaps the critical vulnerability in American strategy. It strongly undercuts our message, while strongly promoting that of the enemy.[72]

D.    FAST PACED INFORMATION AGE

Like the dramatic effects the technology doctrine mismatch had on the Wampanoag and B-17 bomber this objective doctrine mismatch has produced dramatic results in the U.S. "War on Terror". The DSB report points out that often the first information to reach an audience (a global audience that is really a galaxy of niche audiences)

---

[72] Solt, "Strategic Communications," 36.

44

frames how an event is perceived and discussed – and thus can shape its ultimate impact.[73] With the speed at which information regarding an event can be broadcast world wide, if the U.S. wants to have a chance in having its facts about the event to be accepted then they must act quickly. The DSB report shows how with technologies such as Arab satellite TV, cell phones, wireless handhelds, videophones, camcorders, digital cameras, miniaturized fly away units used by TV crews in remote locations, high resolution commercial space imaging, blogs, and email the world is becoming more transparent.[74] Countering the speed at which the Arab media is using these technologies to create the frames within which people understand and misunderstand events and U.S. political goals is an area where the U.S. is failing.[75] A June 2004 Zogby[76] poll of Arab opinion shows the audience receptive to the U.S. message is miniscule (Table 2).

---

[73] Solt, "Strategic Communications," 38.

[74] Ibid., 19.

[75] Ibid., 19.

[76] Zogby International has been tracking public opinion since 1984 in North America, Latin America, the Middle East, Asia, and Europe in order to Offer the Best Polling, Market Research, & Information Services Worldwide Based on Accuracy & Detailed Strategic Information.

| Country | June 2004 Favorable/ Unfavorable | April 2002 Favorable/ Unfavorable |
|---|---|---|
| Morocco | 11/88 | 38/61 |
| Saudi Arabia | 4/94 | 12/87 |
| Jordan | 15/78 | 34/61 |
| Lebanon | 20/69 | 26/70 |
| UAE | 14/73 | 11/87 |
| Egypt | 2/98 | 15/76 |

TABLE 2.       RESULTS OF JUNE 2004 ZOGBY POLL
(RESULTS IN PERCENTAGES)[77]

E.    OVERVIEW OF IO PLAN APPROVAL

As in other warfare areas IO has guidance for deliberate and crisis planning. In both types of planning there are several layers of review, deconfliction, and approval. Table 4 illustrates the time consuming steps involved in deliberate planning while Table 3 shows the somewhat abbreviated process for crisis planning.

---

[77] Solt, "Strategic Communications," 44.

| INFORMATION OPERATIONS PLANNING RELATED TO CRISIS ACTION PLANNING | | | |
|---|---|---|---|
| PLANNING PHASE | JOPES | IO CELL PLANNING ACTION | IO PLANNING OUTCOME |
| PHASE I | Situation Development | IO cell identifies planning information requirements as situation develops. | Tasking to gather/obtain required information. |
| PHASE II | Crisis Assessment | IO cell identifies information requirements needed for mission planning. IO cell assists in development of combatant commander's IO planning guidance to support overall operational planning guidance. | IO planning guidance. Initial liaison with units and agencies that may participate in or support IO operations. |
| PHASE III | Course of Action Development | IO cell supports the development of intelligence, operations, and communications staff estimates. | IO portion of staff estimates. |
| PHASE IV | Course of Action Selection | IO cell assists in transforming staff estimates into the Commander's Estimate. IO cell assists in the IO aspect of Combatant Commander's Concept as required. | IO portion of overall plan approved through CJCS. |
| PHASE V | Execution Planning | IO cell develops the complete IO plan and the plans for each of the IO elements in coordination with appropriate staff sections, operational units, and supporting agencies. | Approved offensive and defensive appendices with element tabs, completed supporting plans, and inclusion of IO requirements in TPFDD. |
| PHASE VI | Execution | IO cell monitors IO operations and adapts IO objectives to support changing operational directives. | IO objectives modified as necessary to support changing operational objectives. |
| CJCS = Chairman of the Joint Chiefs of Staff<br>IO = Information Operations<br>TPFDD = Time-Phased Force and Deployment Data | | | |

TABLE 3.    IO CRISIS PLANNING PROCESS[78]

Important to note from both Tables 3 and 4 is the CJCS requirement for approval through the CJCS for IO missions. The inclusion of this step, while necessary, significantly increases the time required to gain approval for an IO plan.

---

[78] JP 3-13., V-7.

| INFORMATION OPERATIONS PLANNING RELATED TO DELIBERATE PLANNING | | | |
|---|---|---|---|
| PLANNING PHASE | JOPES | IO CELL PLANNING ACTION | IO PLANNING OUTCOME |
| PHASE I | Initiation | Notify IO cell members of planning requirements. | N/A |
| PHASE II | Concept Development | | |
| Step 1 | Mission Analysis | IO cell identifies information requirements needed for mission planning. | Tasking to gather/obtain required information. |
| Step 2 | Planning Guidance | IO cell assists in development of combatant commander's IO planning guidance to support overall operational planning guidance. | Combatant commander's planning guidance for IO. |
| Step 3 | Staff Estimates | IO cell supports the development of intelligence, operations, and communications staff estimates. | IO portion of staff estimates. |
| Step 4 | Commander's Estimate | IO cell assists in transforming staff estimates into the Commander's Estimate. | IO portion of Commander's Estimate. |
| Step 5 | Combatant Commander's Concept | IO cell assists in the IO aspect of Combatant Commander's Concept as required. | IO portion of Combatant Commander's Concept. |
| Step 6 | CJCS Concept Review | IO cell assists in the IO aspect of CJCS Concept Review as required. | IO portion of operational concept approved by CJCS. |
| PHASE III | Plan Development | IO cell develops the complete IO plan and the plans for each of the IO elements in coordination with appropriate staff sections, operational units, and supporting agencies. | Draft offensive and defensive IO appendices with element tabs. |
| PHASE IV | Plan Review | IO cell modifies / refines plan as necessary. | Approved offensive and defensive IO appendices. |
| PHASE V | Supporting Plans | Subordinate units and supporting agencies prepare their own IO plans. IO cell coordinates/assists subordinate and supporting IO plan as necessary. Ensure TPFDD supports IO plan. | Completed subordinate and supporting agencies' supporting plans. IO plan supported by TPFDD. |
| CJCS | = | Chairman of the Joint Chiefs of Staff | |
| IO | = | Information Operations | |
| TPFDD | = | Time-Phased Force and Deployment Data | |

TABLE 4.     IO DELIBERATE PLANNING PROCESS[79]

F.   JOINT PSYOP APPROVAL PROCESS

Similar to the Joint IO approval process, the Joint PSYOP approval process is complex and time consuming as well. Figure 17 shows the process for getting a PSYOP

---

[79] JP 3-13. V-8.

48

program approved, while Figure 18 shows all the steps necessary to approve a product for an approved PSYOP program.

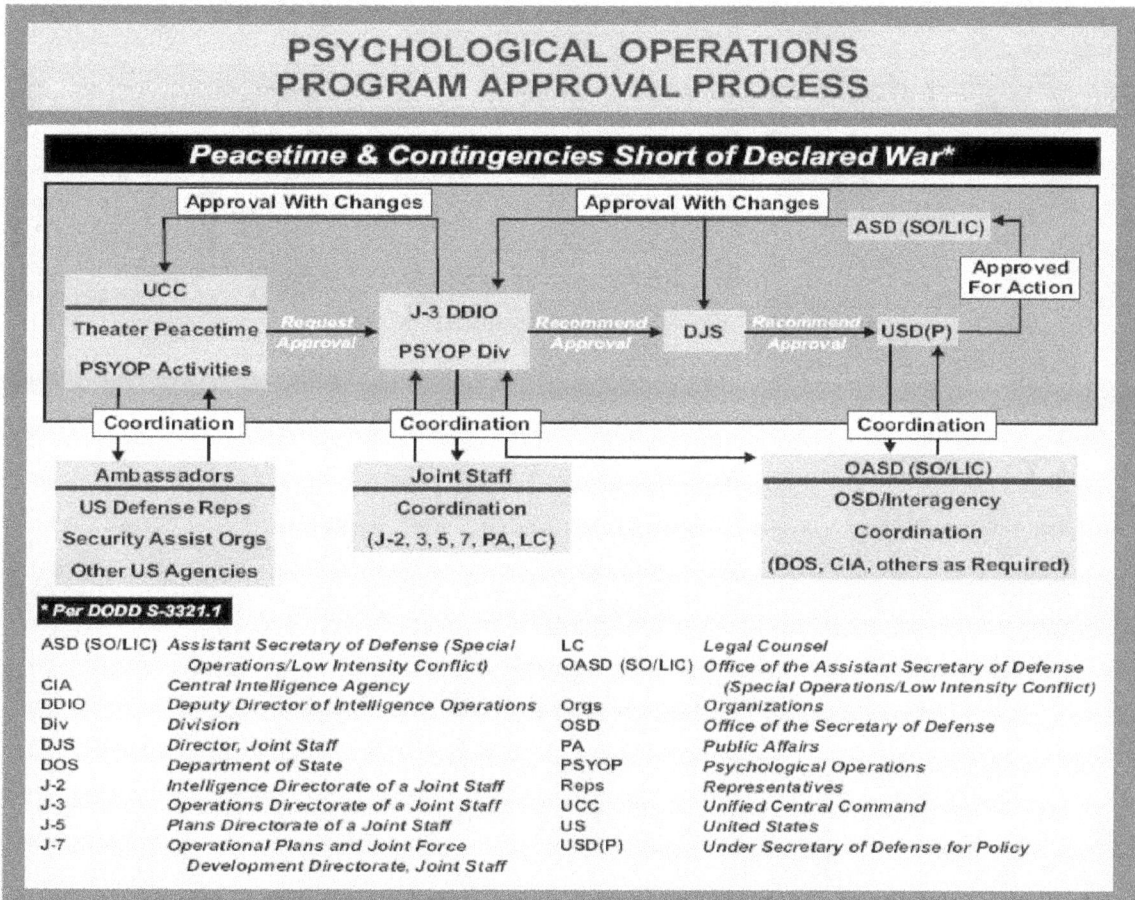

FIGURE 17.    PROCESS TO GAIN APPROVAL FOR A JOINT PSYOP PROGRAM[80]

---

[80] JP3-53., V-4.

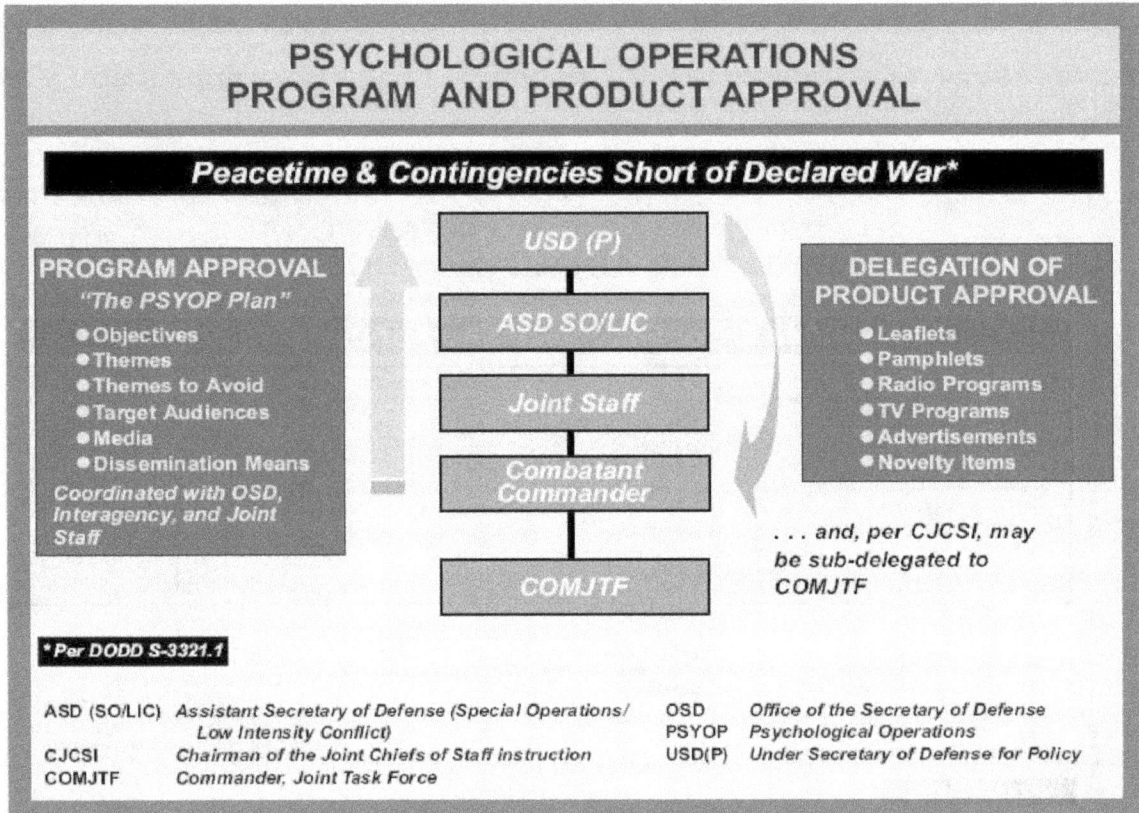

PSYCHOLOGICAL OPERATIONS
PROGRAM AND PRODUCT APPROVAL

**Peacetime & Contingencies Short of Declared War***

PROGRAM APPROVAL
"The PSYOP Plan"
- Objectives
- Themes
- Themes to Avoid
- Target Audiences
- Media
- Dissemination Means

*Coordinated with OSD, Interagency, and Joint Staff*

USD (P)
ASD SO/LIC
Joint Staff
Combatant Commander
COMJTF

DELEGATION OF
PRODUCT APPROVAL
- Leaflets
- Pamphlets
- Radio Programs
- TV Programs
- Advertisements
- Novelty Items

*. . . and, per CJCSI, may be sub-delegated to COMJTF*

*Per DODD S-3321.1*

| | | | |
|---|---|---|---|
| ASD (SO/LIC) | Assistant Secretary of Defense (Special Operations/ Low Intensity Conflict) | OSD | Office of the Secretary of Defense |
| | | PSYOP | Psychological Operations |
| CJCSI | Chairman of the Joint Chiefs of Staff instruction | USD(P) | Under Secretary of Defense for Policy |
| COMJTF | Commander, Joint Task Force | | |

FIGURE 18.     PROCESS TO GAIN APPROVAL FOR PRODUCTS TO BE
PRODUCED FOR AN APPROVED PSYOP PROGRAM[81]

G.    SUGGESTIONS FOR REVISED IO DOCTRINE

While current IO doctrine does include pre-planned and
pre-approved IO missions as part of Operational Plans
(OPLANS), these annexes must be detailed enough to include
pre-approval and possible production of material (leaflets
and taped radio and TV broadcasts) that may be used through
all phases of the conflict.  In addition to having detailed
IO missions and material approved prior to hostilities,
there must be a revision in IO doctrine to allow the
flexibility to make quick adjustments to the overall
mission as unexpected events occur or as the situation

_____

[81] JP 3-53., V-5.

50

changes.  This concept of doctrine providing flexibility is not a revolutionary concept.

In this post September 11, 2001 society there has been several changes made in the military and government agencies where greater authority has been given to commanders in order reduce time consuming approval chains. One such example is that of an "execute order" that the Washington Post wrote about in a February 2005 article "Pentagon Seeking Leeway Overseas: Operations Could Bypass Envoys".  According to the article, the Pentagon is seeking the authority to place Special Forces into countries with out the approval of the countries ambassador, thus reducing the time required to launch counterterrorism missions.[82] The IO community should embrace this concept of reducing the approval process and revise their doctrine so that the U.S. can quickly respond to world events.

---

[82] Ann Scott Tyson and Dana Priest, "Pentagon Seeking Leeway Overseas: Operations Could Bypass Envoys," Washington Post, 24 February 2005, sec. A, p. 1.

THIS PAGE INTENTIONALLY LEFT BLANK

# VI. CONCLUSION

> Master the mechanics and techniques; understand the art and profession; and be smart enough to know when to deviate from it.
>
> GEN Zinni, CENTCOM

## A. TRUE TRANSFORMATION

According to direction in Transformation: A Strategic Approach, the four Military Transformation Pillars identified by the Secretary of Defense include strengthening joint operations, exploiting U.S. intelligence advances, concept development and experimentation, and developing transformational capabilities (Figure 19).

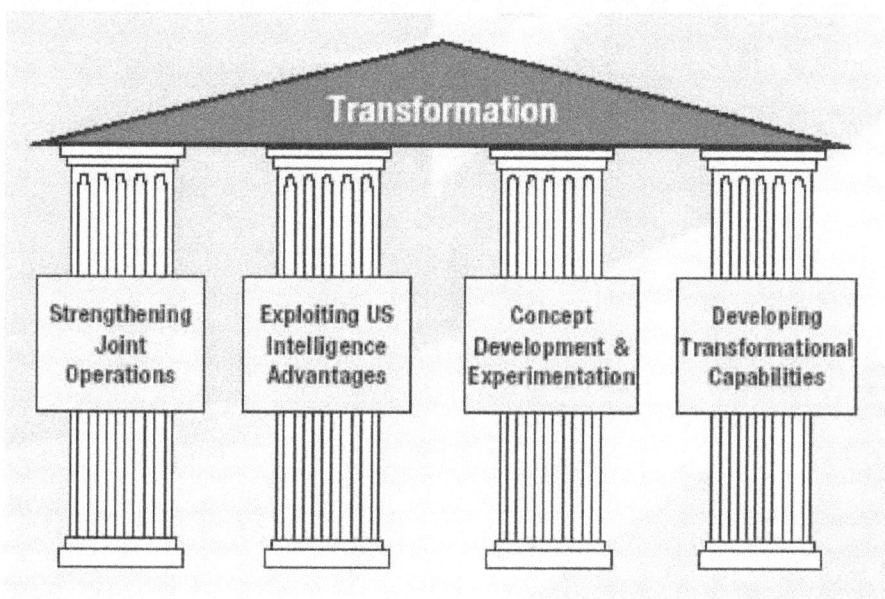

FIGURE 19. FOUR PILLARS OF MILITARY TRANSFORMATION[83]

---

[83] Director, Force Transformation. *Transformation a strategic approach* (Washington DC: U.S. Government Printing Office, 2003), 20.

As mentioned in Chapter II, the concept to produce the LCS that was agreed to by congress was that the LCS would be a transformational platform. While the current configuration does meet the criteria to be classified transformational, as of September 2004, while conducting research for this thesis there had been no attention paid to the use of the LCS in IO missions. The inclusion of an IO module with the joint manning outlined in Chapter III, would provide further justification for continued funding and development of the LCS class. The technology required to develop an IO module is currently being employed in other areas; as such the cost to develop the module would be minimal. As discussed in Chapter III, an IO module on the LCS would provide enormous benefits to the joint force commander and the IO mission as well as providing advantages no other platform currently does.

As of February 2005, there appeared to be progress in the development of IO capabilities for the LCS. There is a draft LCS concept of operations (CONOPS) being circulated that does provide hope for the inclusion of IO in the development of the LCS. This draft CONOPS is being developed through collaboration between the following DoD organizations: Commander Fleet Forces Command, Commander Naval Surface Forces Pacific, Commander Naval Surface Forces Atlantic; Chief of Naval Operations N61, N75, N76, N77, N78; Commander Mine Warfare Command; Commander Undersea Surveillance; Network Warfare Command; Navy Warfare Development Command; Fleet Information Warfare Command; Program Executive Office (PEO) Ships; PEO Littoral and Mine Warfare; PEO (C4I), PEO Integrated Warfare Systems; Naval Sea Systems Command 03 and 06; Naval Air

Systems Command; Naval Special Warfare Command; PMS 501; Surface Warfare Development Group; Fleet Collaborative Team and the Mission Systems and Ship Integration Team.[84] According to this collaborative draft CONOP, "LCS has core and focused mission systems that provide some ISR/IO capability, however, a separate ISR mission package can provide additional ISR capabilities."[85] In section 6.4.4.1 the draft CONOP goes on to say:

> LCS will conduct IO as an inherent mission capability. IO missions appropriate for LCS include Influence Operations, Communications Electronic Attack (EA) and Computer Network Operations. For precursor operations, the ISR/IO mission package is envisioned for use in IPB. The IO mission will take advantage of the capability of LCS networking to perform distributed computing and time critical coordination of assets using core LCS workstations that can be easily configured for the IO mission. LCS is part of the federated process of sensor analysis. Previous ISR sensor data discussion in this section is germane to the IO mission. If analysis or processing of sensor data is not required on LCS, then a SCI facility may not be required.
>
> Influence Operations: As part of the ISR/IO inherent mission capability, LCS may have mobile broadcast capabilities. LCS may also be the conduit for limited-production and robust dissemination of influence products, including the receipt of audio, video and images for turn around into radio broadcasts.
>
> Communications EA: LCS will be able to engage a specified range of non-kinetic targets in the littoral, independently or cooperatively (with other LCS or other platforms). This includes the use of core communications systems and antennas

---

[84] "Collaborative Draft LCS CONOP" (working paper of government LCS design team, August 2004). VIII-IX.

[85] Ibid., 35.

in Electronic Support (ES) and as a time-difference of arrival node for ES, EA and geo-location of emitters. The preferred employment is dual use of LCS communications systems for both connectivity and ES/EA missions; however, a mobile cryptologic sensor package will be available for expanded ES tasking. As an ES/EA node, LCS will be part of a larger Joint targeting process that incorporates integrated kinetic and non-kinetic target engagement. EA tasking may include support for time critical targeting.[86]

It appears that if this draft CONOP does become the official guidance for the LCS, the sea frame will have IO assets as well as IO module. If this draft CONOP is made into doctrine and used for the development the LCS may avoid the ill fate of the Wampanoag and avoid the difficult adjustment process the B-17 had to go through as discussed in Chapter V.

Unlike the LCS, throughout the writing of this thesis SPARTAN SCOUT development and discussions have not addressed the integration of IO tools. However, as mentioned in Chapter II there is competition in USV development within the Navy. Unlike the competition between General Dynamics and Lockheed Martin for the future of LCS where the modules for each companies LCS must be interchangeable, there are no such restrictions between ONR's USSV and NUWC's SPARTAN SCOUT. If NUWC were first to develop an IO module for their SPARTAN SCOUT it would only provide further justification for continued funding and development.

---

[86] "Collaborative Draft LCS CONOP", 37-38.

B.    SUGGESTED FURTHER RESEARCH

If this draft CONOP is accepted as doctrine, it appears the LCS is moving in the right direction with regards to IO. The SPARTAN SCOUT should embrace the development of an IO module out of self preservation. The one area that requires further research is that of doctrine. After September 11, 2001, there have been numerous task forces assigned to conduct reviews over the various U.S. intelligence communities. Several of these task force recommendations have all ready been addressed throughout this thesis. However, one area of further research that should be explored is provided by the DSB taskforce on Strategic Communications. According to the task force:

> We recommend that the Under Secretary of Defense for Policy and the Joint Chiefs of Staff ensure that all military plans and operations have appropriate strategic communication components, ensure collaboration with the Department of State's diplomatic missions and with theater security cooperation plans; and extend U.S. STRATCOM's and U.S. SOCOM's Information Operations responsibilities to include DoD support for public diplomacy. The Department should triple current resources (personnel & funding) available to combatant commanders for DoD support to public diplomacy and reallocate Information Operations funding within U.S. STRATCOM for expanded support for strategic communication programs.[87]

This recommendation to change IO doctrine to include closer collaboration with the Department of State and the support of public diplomacy could further complicate and delay the approval process for IO related materials. A concern with

---

[87] Solt, "Strategic Communications," 9.

this DSB task force recommendation is that the suggestion for collaboration with the Department of State may evolve into a requirement for State Department approval or concurrence for all IO missions. While it is important for the correct message to be conveyed on the battle field as discussed in Chapter V, in order for an influence campaign to be effective in this fast paced global society the U.S. must act fast and ideally be first to get their message out and accepted.

# LIST OF REFERENCES

Abbott, Rob. *LCS Mission Package Manning Overview.* (Washington DC: PEO Ships, 2005).

Abrams, Michael. "The Dawn of the E-bomb", IEEE Spectrum (November 2003)

Air Magnet Website. Available from URL: http://www.airmagnet.com/news/image_library.htm. Accessed 15 February 2005.

Altshuler, Herbert L. United States Army Civil Affairs and Psychological Operations Command. Available from URL: http://www.soc.mil/usacapoc/psyopfs.shtml. Accessed 23 February 2005.

American Forces Information Services website. Available from URL: http://www.iwar.org.uk/psyops/resources/afghanistan/commando-solo.htm. Accessed 17 February 2005.

American Technology Corporation. "LRAD: The Sound of Force Protection", Available from ATC website. URL:http://www.atcsd.com. Accessed 15 February 2005.

Bingle, Bruce. "67th IOW Crystallizes Operations" Available from URL: http://aia.lackland.af.mil/homepages/pa/spokesman/jun04/cc.cfm. Accessed 23 February 2005.

Beavers, Sara. "24 MEU Conducts Non-lethal Training During TRUEX" Marine Link, May 2004. Available from URL: http://www.marines.mil/marinelink/mcn2000.nsf/lookupstoryref/2004525152639. Accessed 19 February 2005.

Caspers, Robert W. *Joint Task Force South in Operations Just Cause, An Oral History Interview.* (Washington DC: U.S. Army Center of Military History, 1990).

Chairman of the Joint Chiefs of Staff. (1998). *Joint Pub 3-13 Joint Doctrine for Information Operations.* Washington DC: U.S. Government Printing Office.

Chairman of the Joint Chiefs of Staff. (2003). *Joint Pub 3-53 Joint Doctrine for Psychological Operations*. Washington DC: U.S. Government Printing Office.

Defense Science Board (2004) Report of the Defense Science Board Task Force on Strategic Communications. (Washington DC: Office of the Under Secretary of Defense for Acquisition, Technology and Logistics).

Defense Service Board. (2000). *Report of the Defense Science Board Task Force on The Creation and Dissemination of All Forms of Information in Support of Psychological Operations (PSYOP) in Time of Military Conflict*. (Washington, D.C.: Office of the Under Secretary of Defense for Acquisition, Technology and Logistics).

Director, Force Transformation. *Transformation a Strategic Approach* (Washington DC: U.S. Government Printing Office, 2003).

Federation of American Scientists website. Available from URL:http://www.fas.org/irp/agency/navsecgru/niwa/. Accessed 23 February 2005.

Holder, Pat. "SPARTAN SCOUT ACTD Unmanned Surface Vessel for Assured Access and Force Protection" (presentation presented at Logistics from the Sea Symposium, Washington DC, 4-7 February 2003).

Holley, Irving B. Technology and Military Doctrine: Essays on a Challenging Relationship. Air University Press, Maxwell AFB, AL. August 2004.

Jackson, Joab. "Pentagon Backs Spiral Development." Washington Technology, 9 June 2003. Database on-line. Available from Washington Technology website at URL:http://www.Washingtontechnology.com/news/18_5/cover-stories/20872-1.html. Accessed 3 February 2005.

"LCS CONOP (Draft)" (working paper of government LCS design team, August 2004).

LCS homepage, Available from: www.peos.crane.navy.mil/lcs/Lockheed.htm. Accessed 4 February 2005.

Morison, Elting E. Men Machine and Modern Times, The Massachusetts Institute of Technology. Cambridge, Massachusetts. 1966.

Naval Sea Systems, "Capability Development Document for Littoral Combat Ship" (working paper of government LCS design team, April 2004).

Naval Sea Systems, "Draft (ICD) Interface Control Document" (working paper of government LCS design team, 13 September 2004).

Naval Undersea Warfare Command Public Affairs Officer, "Spartan Deployed on Gettysburg," Navy News Stand, 23 December 2003. Available from URL: http://www.news.navy.mil/search/display.asp?story_id=10964. Accessed 19 February 2005.

Naval Undersea Warfare Command, "SPARTAN SCOUT ACTD Management Plan Rev 1" (Working paper for SPARTAN SCOUT design team, 14 March 2003).

ONR Future Naval Capabilities website. URL: http://www.onr.navy.mil/fncs/explog/litcom/product.asp?productid=65&divisionid=5. Accessed 2 February 2005.

Pawley, Jason. "Littoral Combat Ship: Overview" (Presented at Menneken Lecture Series, Naval Postgraduate School, Monterey, California, 19 August 2004).

PSYWARRIOR website. URL:http:// www.psywarrior.com. Accessed 15 February 2005.

Ricci, Dr. Vic. interview by author, Newport, RI. 24 September 2004.

Rumsfeld, Donald. *Quadrennial Defense Review*. (Washington DC: Government Printing Office, 2001).

Secretary of the Air Force. Information Operations AFDD 2-5 (Washington DC: U.S. Government Printing Office, January 11, 2005)

Schamiloglu, E. "High Powered Microwave Sources and Applications". IEEE MTT-S Digest, (2004).

Solt, John. "Psychological Operations Go to Sea" FIWC INFOSCOPE Winter 2003, Volume 2, Issue 1.  Available from FIWC website at URL: http://www.infoscope.fiwc.navy.smil.mil/vol2_issue2/index.htm. Accessed 12 October 2004.

Surface Warfare Magazine, Summer 2004, Vol 29, No 3.

Thompson, Mark. "America's Ultra-Secret Weapon". Time, (January 27, 2003. Volume 161 Number 4).

Tyson, Ann Scott and Dana Priest, "Pentagon Seeking Leeway Overseas: Operations Could Bypass Envoys," Washington Post, 24 February 2005, sec. A, p. 1.

U.S. Department of Defense, Office of the Secretary of Defense, Final Report to Congress Conduct of the Persian Gulf War, April 1992.

Washington Times, "U.S. Troops Have Sound Weapon," 7 March 2004.  Available from URL: http://www.washingtontimes.com/archive/.  Accessed 19 February 2005.

Work, Robert O. "Naval Transformation and the Littoral Combat Ship" (Center for Strategic and Budgetary, working paper of government LCS design team, 2004).

# INITIAL DISTRIBUTION LIST

1. Defense Technical Information Center
   Ft. Belvoir, Virginia

2. Dudley Knox Library
   Naval Postgraduate School
   Monterey, California

3. Associate Professor Michael T. McMaster
   Naval War College
   Monterey, California

# NAVAL
# POSTGRADUATE
# SCHOOL

## MONTEREY, CALIFORNIA

# THESIS

LITTORAL COMBAT SHIP (LCS)
MANPOWER REQUIREMENTS ANALYSIS

by

Thaveephone NMN Douangaphaivong

December 2004

Co-Advisors:      Gregory V. Cox
                  William D. Hatch II

Second Reader:    Nita Lewis Miller

THIS PAGE INTENTIONALLY LEFT BLANK

| REPORT DOCUMENTATION PAGE | | *Form Approved OMB No. 0704-0188* |
|---|---|---|

| 1. AGENCY USE ONLY *(Leave blank)* | 2. REPORT DATE<br>December 2004 | 3. REPORT TYPE AND DATES COVERED<br>Master's Thesis |
|---|---|---|
| **4. TITLE AND SUBTITLE:**<br>Littoral Combat Ship (LCS)<br>Manpower Requirements Analysis | | **5. FUNDING NUMBERS** |
| **6. AUTHOR(S)**  Thaveephone NMN Douangaphaivong | | |
| **7. PERFORMING ORGANIZATION NAME(S) AND ADDRESS(ES)**<br>Naval Postgraduate School<br>Monterey, CA  93943-5000 | | **8. PERFORMING ORGANIZATION REPORT NUMBER** |
| **9. SPONSORING /MONITORING AGENCY NAME(S) AND ADDRESS(ES)**<br>OPNAV | | **10. SPONSORING/MONITORING AGENCY REPORT NUMBER** |

**11. SUPPLEMENTARY NOTES:** The views expressed in this thesis are those of the author and do not reflect the official policy or position of the Department of Defense or the U.S. Government.

| 12a. DISTRIBUTION / AVAILABILITY STATEMENT<br>Approved for public release; distribution is unlimited. | 12b. DISTRIBUTION CODE |
|---|---|

**13. ABSTRACT (maximum 200 words)**

 The Littoral Combat Ship's (LCS) minimally manned core crew goal is 15 to 50 manpower requirements and the threshold, for both core and mission-package crews, is 75 to 110. This dramatically smaller crew size will require more than current technologies and past lessons learned from reduced manning initiatives.  Its feasibility depends upon changes in policy and operations, leveraging of future technologies and increased Workload Transfer from sea to shore along with an increased acceptance of risk.

 A manpower requirements analysis yielded a large baseline (~200) requirement to support a notional LCS configuration.  Combining the common systems from the General Dynamics and Lockheed Martin designs with other assumed equipments (i.e. the combined diesel and gas turbine (CODAG) engineering plant) produce the notional LCS configuration used as the manpower requirements basis.  The baseline requirement was reduced through the compounded effect of manpower savings from Smart Ship and OME and suggested paradigm shifts.  A Battle Bill was then created to support the notional LCS during Conditions of Readiness I and III.

 An efficient force deployment regime was adopted to reduce the overall LCS class manpower requirement.  The efficiency gained enables the LCS force to "flex" and satisfy deployment requirements with 25% to 30% fewer manpower requirements over the "one-for-one" crewing concept.  An annual manpower savings of $80M to $110M if each requirement costs $60K.

| 14. SUBJECT TERMS<br><br>Crewing, Human Capital, Littoral Combat Ship, LCS, Manning, Manpower, Minimal Manning, Optimization, Optimal, Manpower, Requirements, Composite Sailor, Technology Leverage, Workload Transfer | | 15. NUMBER OF PAGES 210 |
|---|---|---|
| | | 16. PRICE CODE |

| 17. SECURITY CLASSIFICATION OF REPORT<br>Unclassified | 18. SECURITY CLASSIFICATION OF THIS PAGE<br>Unclassified | 19. SECURITY CLASSIFICATION OF ABSTRACT<br>Unclassified | 20. LIMITATION OF ABSTRACT<br>UL |
|---|---|---|---|

Standard Form 298 (Rev. 2-89)
Prescribed by ANSI Std. 239-18

THIS PAGE INTENTIONALLY LEFT BLANK

## LITTORAL COMBAT SHIP (LCS)
## MANPOWER REQUIREMENTS ANALYSIS

Thaveephone NMN Douangaphaivong
Lieutenant, United States Navy
B.S., United States Naval Academy, 1995

Submitted in partial fulfillment of the
requirements for the degree of

## MASTER OF SCIENCE IN OPERATIONS RESEARCH

from the

## NAVAL POSTGRADUATE SCHOOL
## December 2004

Author:         Thaveephone NMN Douangaphaivong


Approved by:    Gregory V. Cox
                Thesis Advisor


                CDR William D. Hatch II, USN
                Thesis Co-Advisor


                Nita Lewis Miller
                Second Reader


                James N. Eagle II
                Chairman
                Department of Operations Research

THIS PAGE INTENTIONALLY LEFT BLANK

# ABSTRACT

The Littoral Combat Ship's (LCS) minimally manned core crew goal is 15 to 50 manpower requirements and the threshold, for both core and mission-package crews, is 75 to 110. This dramatically smaller crew size will require more than current technologies and past lessons learned from reduced manning initiatives. Its feasibility depends upon changes in policy and operations, leveraging of future technologies and increased Workload Transfer from sea to shore along with an increased acceptance of risk.

A manpower requirements analysis yielded a large baseline (~200) requirement to support a notional LCS configuration. Combining the common systems from the General Dynamics and Lockheed Martin designs with other assumed equipments (i.e. the combined diesel and gas turbine (CODAG) engineering plant) produce the notional LCS configuration used as the manpower requirements basis. The baseline requirement was reduced through the compounded effect of manpower savings from Smart Ship and OME and suggested paradigm shifts. A Battle Bill was then created to support the notional LCS during Conditions of Readiness I and III.

An efficient force deployment regime was adopted to reduce the overall LCS class manpower requirement. The efficiency gained enables the LCS force to "flex" and satisfy deployment requirements with 25% to 30% fewer manpower requirements over the "one-for-one" crewing concept. An annual manpower savings of $80M to $110M if each requirement costs $60K.

THIS PAGE INTENTIONALLY LEFT BLANK

# TABLE OF CONTENTS

# LIST OF FIGURES

THIS PAGE INTENTIONALLY LEFT BLANK

# LIST OF TABLES

THIS PAGE INTENTIONALLY LEFT BLANK

# ACKNOWLEDGMENT

Working on this study has been both challenging and exciting.

I would like to thank all those who have help in this endeavor.  A special thanks to Mr. Charlie Gowen for his expert opinion and assistance.

My deepest appreciation to Dr. Greg Cox, CDR Bill Hatch, USN and Dr. Nita Miller for their expertise, availability, confidence and enthusiastic support.

Your incredible insight, attention to detail and inspirational commitment to excellence were invaluable.

I express my most heartfelt gratitude for my wife, Deborah, and son, Sean, for their loving support.  All of this could not have been possible without their tireless understanding, motivation and patience.

THIS PAGE INTENTIONALLY LEFT BLANK

# EXECUTIVE SUMMARY

The Navy's new LCS, with many novel approaches to ship design and operations, will consist of a hull (or seaframe) that is augmented with either an MIW, ASW, or SUW focused mission module -- with the mission modules rapidly interchangeable to allow the LCS to operate across a broad spectrum of conflict. For operational flexibility, the Navy plans 119 modules to support 56 seaframes.

To keep operating costs low, the LCS (seaframe plus module) is promised to operate with "minimal manning" – originally specified at 75. Questioning the viability of this number, we estimated LCS manning requirements and concluded that if the Navy pursued "business as usual", the crew would be far larger than 75. Past reduced manning initiatives like Smart Ship and Fleet Optimal Manning Experiments will not be enough. A set of "paradigm shifts" were then explored to further reduce the manpower requirements. Each requirement was analyzed for impact from Navy policy, technology leverage and workload management. Even with these new business practices with associated manpower requirement estimates (~45 for seaframe, ~55 for MIW module, ~50 for ASW module, and ~45 for SUW module) the totals sum to about 90-100 manpower requirements, or 15-25 more than the original threshold of 75.

Lastly, because more modules need to be deployable than will actually be deployed – e.g., about 32 deployable for 15 deployed – options for organizing the "module squadron" personnel were considered to avoid potential waste of valuable human capital. Observing that there are many similar systems among the different warfare modules, we analyzed ways to de-link the module personnel from the packaged module systems, so that many of the same personnel could quickly flex from one warfare module to another. This flexible approach has the potential to reduce the Navy-wide module manning by about 25%, when compared to a traditional approach.

# I. INTRODUCTION

The Littoral Combat Ship (LCS) along with the DD(X) and CG(X) is among the first of the 21$^{st}$ century combatant ships to be acquired by the United States Navy. The LCS program is an aggressive acquisition program that started in FY03 with the first Flight 0 ships scheduled for delivery in 2007.

The LCS adopts a unique modular concept for operations in the littorals. The concept begins with a seaframe augmented with a mission package to produce a focused mission LCS in one of the three littoral warfare areas. The seaframe itself has some inherent self-defense capabilities that do not equate to a particular warfare area. To conduct operations in a particular littoral warfare area, the LCS seaframe is complimented with a mission package for either mine warfare (MIW), anti-submarine warfare (ASW), or surface warfare (SUW). The mission package consists of transportable focused mission package (FMP) modules and their pack-up kits (PUK).

Overall, the LCS program plans to acquire 56 seaframes and 119 FMPs, designed to be rapidly changed to allow the LCS to quickly adapt to new missions. If 15 LCS were deployed at a given time, this suggests that about 32 FMPs would be deployable at the same time.

Each FMP module has specific hardware, software and manpower requirements (RQMTS) to conduct operations in a particular littoral warfare area. The modules will include one H-60 series helicopter, unmanned aerial vehicles (UAVs), unmanned surface vehicles (USVs), unmanned underwater vehicles (UUVs) as well as sensors and weapons for these vehicles.  With the sensor and weapon systems onboard, the unmanned vehicles (UVs) will be employed on an unprecedented scale as the littoral combat ship's principal extended sensor and weapon delivery vehicles.

Figure 1 depicts the components of a warfare focused LCS.  For example, the MIW focused LCS is the augmentation of the seaframe with the MIW package.  Note that the warfare package also includes a crew of about 95, if the Navy adopted its legacy approach to manning this module.  When the manning requirements for a package are combined with the manning requirements for the seaframe, the total MIW focused LCS manning would then be approximately 215.  Similar estimates apply to the ASW focused LCS with manning around 210, and the SUW which has about 195.  Overall, the average manning for the warfare focused LCS would be about 207.

Figure 1.    **LCS Modular Approach**

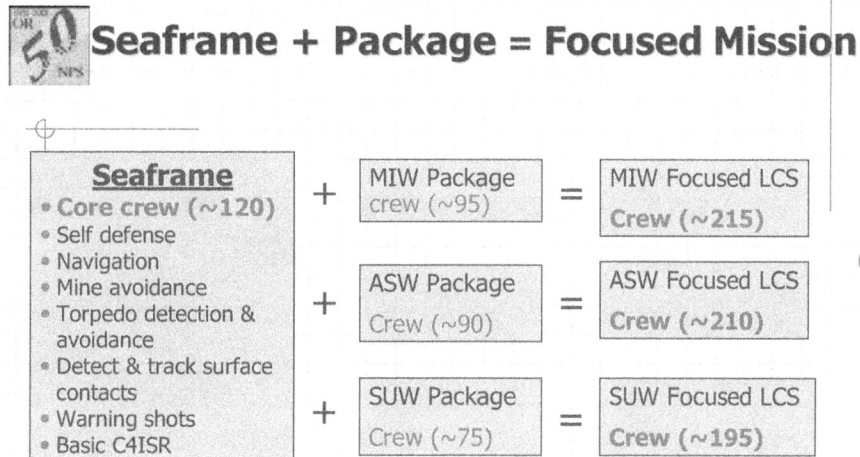

**Seaframe + Package = Focused Mission**

| Seaframe | | MIW Package crew (~95) | | MIW Focused LCS Crew (~215) |
|---|---|---|---|---|
| • Core crew (~120) | + | | = | |
| • Self defense | | | | |
| • Navigation | | ASW Package Crew (~90) | | ASW Focused LCS Crew (~210) |
| • Mine avoidance | + | | = | |
| • Torpedo detection & avoidance | | | | |
| • Detect & track surface contacts | | SUW Package Crew (~75) | | SUW Focused LCS Crew (~195) |
| • Warning shots | + | | = | |
| • Basic C4ISR | | | | |

This level of manning is judged to be too large, and so the LCS program is aggressively pursuing minimally manned seaframes and FMPs – the minimum required to accomplish the mission. To assist in this goal, the crews will be supported by "just-in time training, distance learning, distant support and maintenance." LCS will not have "the wide variety of skills necessary to maintain all shipboard equipment."[Ref 1]

The LCS seaframe crew (called the core crew) is expected to operate the seaframe and installed systems, while the FMP crew (called the mission-package crew) will operate and maintain FMP vehicles, systems, sensors and weapons. Both the core and mission-package crews are to interface with one another through common open system architecture.

> Through Spiral Development, LCS ships will:
> Leverage automation, "smart systems," and human systems integration principles in engineering, damage control, combat systems, ship control, messing, and other ship systems tied into an extensive local area network to optimize and integrate the capabilities of the ship and core crew. [Ref 1: pg 42]

Furthermore, crew knowledge, skills and abilities (KSA) are expected to be refined and enhanced through Human Factors Engineering developments like the "expert agent" used in the mission planning and decision-making process.

THIS PAGE INTENTIONALLY LEFT BLANK

## II. BACKGROUND

Legacy Ship Manpower Documents (SMDs) manpower requirements are determined by, but are not limited to, the following development elements [Ref 5]:

1. Required Operational Capability and Projected Operational Environment (ROC/POE) parameters and analysis,

2. Directed manpower requirements (Master Chief Petty Officer of the Command, Safety, Career Counselor, etc.),

3. Watch stations,

4. Preventive Maintenance,

5. Corrective Maintenance,

6. Facilities Maintenance,

7. Application approved staffing standards (when applicable),

8. On-site workload measurement and analysis,

9. Utility tasking (underway replenishment, flight operations, sea and anchor detail, etc.),

10. Allowances (service diversions, productivity allowance, etc.),

11. Development of officer requirements, and

12. Fleet review of draft documents.

The most critical element in developing manpower documents is the ROC/POE document. The ROC provides a precise definition of the unit's mission statement. The POE is a description of the specific operating environment in which the unit is expected to operate [Ref 5]. The ROC/POE for LCS is still in the development phase, and was not available to support this study. For this reason, part of the thesis research was aimed at deriving a representative ROC/POE.

The Navy's at-sea workload is another key element used in calculating manpower requirements. The workload is computed on a workweek with 168 hours. Of the 168 hours, only 81 hours are available for duty or work. The 81 hours include 70 hours of Productive work, 7 hours of Training and 4 hours of Service Diversion. Table 1 summarizes the workweek hours for at-sea. The workload is different for "shore-based deployable units" [Ref 5].

Table 1.      **Navy Afloat (Wartime) Workweek For Military Personnel (From Ref 4)**

| Category | Hours |
|---|---|
| **Non-Available Time** | |
| Sleep | 56 |
| Messing | 14 |
| Personal Needs | 14 |
| Sunday Free | 3 |
| **Available Time** | |
| Training | 7 |
| Service Diversion | 4 |
| Productive Work | 70 |
| **Total Hours Available Weekly** | **168** |

Unlike the LCS seaframe, the FMP modules will be "shore-based deployable units." The module RQMTS will be defined in the Fleet Manpower Document (FMD) similar to the SMD.

From the manpower perspective, the Navy's most demanding requirements (RQMTS) are at sea during Condition

6

of Readiness I (Battle Readiness) for 24 hours and Condition of Readiness III (wartime/increased tension or forward deployed cruising readiness) for 60 days with opportunity for 8 hours of rest provided per [person] per day [Ref 5].

While in Condition I, the ship must be capable of meeting the following criteria:

1. Able to perform all offensive and defensive functions simultaneously,
2. Able to keep all installed systems manned and operating for maximum effectiveness,
3. Required to accomplish only minimal maintenance - that routinely associated with watch standing and urgent repairs,
4. Perform self-defense measures, and
5. Evolutions such as replenishment, law enforcement or [helicopter] operations are not appropriate unless the evolution stations are co-manned by manpower from other battle stations.

Condition III requires reduced defensive systems and manning to a level sufficient to counter pop-up threats. While in Condition III, the ship must be capable of meeting the following criteria:

1. Able to keep installed systems manned and operating as necessary to conform with prescribed ROCs, and
2. Able to accomplish all normal underway maintenance, support and administrative functions.

All new ship (i.e., LCS seaframe) and aircraft (i.e., RQ-8B Fire Scout VTUAV) acquisitions must be supported by the development of their manpower documents to determine the initial RQMTS. The Program Manager is responsible for developing these documents using the Navy Manpower Requirements System (NMRS) maintained by NAVMAC.

Numerous past studies and experiments have examined the feasibility and effectiveness of reduced manning, although not specifically focused on LCS. One of the studies, the Surface Combatant of the 21st Century (SC-21) Manning Reduction Initiatives [Ref 8], evaluated the potential for minimal manning (95 personnel in that case) and concluded:

1. Reduced manning is feasible if technological advances are realized,
2. Ships lose multi-warfare depth with 95-man crew,
3. Incorporating moderate-risk technology can effect significant manning reductions (45%),
4. We still have unresolved issues (e.g., shore infrastructure),
5. Tradeoffs between minimum manning, quality of life, and mission efficiency must be carefully weighed, and
6. We need an activity to lead/coordinate the manning effort.

However, the bottom line recommendation from that study was to proceed cautiously concluding that a crew of 170 is more achievable than a crew of 95 for the SC-21 family of ships.

Another study, Optimal Manning and Technological Change [Ref 7], evaluated "future trends in naval technology and in civilian labor forces" and concluded:

1. Technological advances will probably require a more skilled, rather than less skilled, workforce,

2. Also, the Navy must use care in automating warfighting because routine peacetime tasks can be automated more easily than inherently chaotic and complex combat evolutions,

3. Skills of the Navy's enlisted force will change markedly as familiar tasks are automated and workload moves from operational units to the infrastructure,

4. Sailors will need new, or different, skills to support collaboration between human and machine, introduction of more COTS technology, and the development of generalists rather than specialists,

5. Damage Control is more difficult to automate because of unpredictable requirements, and

6. Future sailors will understand the general principles in their areas of expertise, will be technically literate, and have strong problem-solving, decision-making, and communication skills.

Reduced manning experiments like the "Smart Ship" program on USS Yorktown (CG-48) and USS Rushmore (LSD-47) and the Fleet Optimal Manning Experiment on USS MILIUS (DDG-69), USS Mobile Bay (CG-51) and USS Boxer (LHD-4) were efforts designed to test Navy culture and technology to reduce the manpower requirements. The Smart Ship experiment successfully introduced seven systems that have the potential to produce significant reductions in manning. However, "technology [alone] did not produce a reasonable return on investment. [T]he technologies were critical to the policy and procedural changes" [Ref 9].

Fleet Manning Experiments (FME) or Optimal Manning Experiments (OME) successfully reduced manning through policy and operational changes with minimal technology installs. The administrative functions were relocated ashore to the Pay and Personnel Ashore (PAPA) detachments. This removed most of the administrative personnel leaving only the minimum to help coordinate ship's force with the PAPA detachment. Regarding optimal manning, VADM LaFleur writes:

> Optimal manning works. We will apply what we learn in these experiments--both to our current force, and to sizing the force of the future--to more efficiently man our ships and reinvest the resultant manpower savings into the type of transformational technologies required for our 21st-century force [Ref 11].

Another attempt to reduce manning involved the Oliver Hazard Perry (FFG-7) class frigates and the Consolidated Maintenance Package (CMP). The FFG-7 was originally designed to operate with minimal manning. The concept was supported by a consolidated maintenance package designed to reduce the ship's maintenance requirements and replace critical parts before at regular intervals regardless of their status. This reduced manning attempt suffered a setback when budget constraints forced CMP workload back onboard and removed the critical parts replacement plan. This setback ultimately increased the FFG's RQMTS which increased berthing requirements and removed crew lounges. The overall effect was a decreased quality of life for those onboard. The failure of the FFG-7 minimal manning project was due to the lack of understanding of the integration of the manpower requirements, acquisition, design capabilities and maintenance process, in short, a failure of human system integration.

DOD transformation efforts and an increasingly squeezed budget have now produced an environment where minimal manning is a necessity, perhaps accelerating its realization. Transformation calls for changes in how the U.S. Navy has been doing business and allocating limited resources. One of the biggest cost drivers for the Navy is the cost of manpower. The Navy can no longer afford to make manpower considerations an afterthought to system design. A less-flexible budget coupled with increasing personnel cost have raised the importance of manpower considerations throughout the system acquisition process. If minimal manning is to be a reality, the U.S. Navy must also change its manpower requirements determination philosophy and emphasize manpower and human factors implications throughout the acquisition process.

> Skilled manpower is an indispensable factor in the successful deployment of new ships, aircraft, equipment, and most other new hardware systems. The human element must be an integral part of system design and logistic support at the earliest acquisition phase. Although there is considerable uncertainty early in the acquisition process, every effort shall be made to use the best available data and techniques in developing manpower estimates. These estimates shall be continuously refined, as the system progresses, to form the basis for operational and maintenance manpower requirements' descriptions, personnel selection and training, training devices and

simulator design, and other planning related to MPT. NAVMAC will review and compare these estimates with current manpower requirements associated with similar existing systems, and for consistency with applicable MPT policies [Ref 5].

# III. PROBLEM AND OBJECTIVE

## A.    PROBLEM

The seaframe and module manpower requirements (RQMTS) for LCS are highly constrained by the crew accommodation threshold.   The LCS critical design parameter for manning is of particular interest.   In the preliminary requirements document, the combined (seaframe plus mission module) RQMTS is limited by the threshold of 75 [Ref 2].

Since the release of the critical design document (CDD) in May 2004, the crew accommodation threshold has been increased to 110, reflecting the difficulty of the manning problem.   This increase added 35 additional bunks, and has eased the constraint for the combined manpower requirements considerably.   However, this relaxed threshold remains much lower than legacy RQMTS, and is still a significant challenge.   Addressing this challenge is the problem at hand.


## B.    OBJECTIVE

This study has two objectives.   The first objective is to determine the aggressiveness of the different approaches to achieve the specified manning levels.   The baseline, or "business as usual", estimates were derived using a methodology similar to the NMRS used to determine new construction RQMTS.   This approach is not as aggressive in looking for ways to reduce the RQMTS or to efficiently manage the personnel.   Because of this, we looked carefully at reduced manning initiatives, as well as to evaluate some "paradigm shifts" that would cause the Navy to significantly change its manning practices.

13

The second objective is to evaluate options for organizing the module personnel. Because there are many more modules than seaframes (119 modules for 56 seaframes, or perhaps 32 deployable modules for 15 deployed seaframes), the assignment of one crew per FMP module would equate to a very large, and very inefficient, LCS force.

Two concepts of mission-package personnel management were evaluated: "pre-packaged" and "flexed". The "pre-packaged" concept is the assignment of one crew per module, much as the Navy assigns personnel to ships. The "flexed" alternative is the collection of all personnel into a single pool, and then organized into generalist and specialist detachments. The module RQMTS are then satisfied with the assignment of the detachments as they are needed.

# IV. ASSUMPTIONS

Because most of the LCS program remains in the development stages, the data required for this analysis is very limited or restricted. Numerous assumptions were therefore made to help frame this manpower requirements analysis.

For both the seaframe and modules, the appropriate manpower requirement is the number needed to support the most demanding notional ROC/POE requirements during Condition I and III for 24-hours and 60 days respectively.

## A.    NOTIONAL LCS SEAFRAME

There are currently two competing shipbuilding teams (General Dynamics and Lockheed Martin), and the actual configuration details for both team's LCS designs are still proprietary. In view of that, this study used information that was publicly available to approximate the two designs, from which a composite "notional" seaframe was developed.

However the information available does not include the engineering plant and other critical items like the aircraft handling and UV launch and recovery systems. Based upon the assumption that LCS is to operate efficiently at both high and low speeds in shallow water, a combined diesel and gas turbine (CODAG) with water jet propulsion was assumed.

Other equipment added includes a common unmanned vehicle launch and recovery system as well as aircraft handling systems on the flight deck. Table 2 summarizes the "notional" seaframe, based upon the available design data.

15

Table 2.    **Notional LCS Seaframe Configuration**

| System | General Dynamics | Lockheed Martin | Notional LCS SeaFrame |
|---|---|---|---|
| Bridge | Integrated Command Center | | Integrated Command Center |
| Combat Management System (CMS) | AMS CMS | | AMS CMS |
| Gun System | Bofors 57mm | Bofors 57mm | 57mm BOFORS |
| CIWS | | | CIWS 1B |
| Low caliber gun | .50 cal (4) | .50 cal (4) | .50 cal (4) |
| Missile System | RAM | RAM | RAM |
| Search RADAR | Sea Giraffe | Air Search RADAR | Search RADAR |
| Air Decoy | SRBOC (6) NULKA(4) | | SRBOC (6) NULKA(4) |
| Torpedo Decoy Launcher | Torpedo Decoy Launcher(2) | | Torpedo Decoy Launcher (2) |
| SONAR | Retractable Mine Sonar | | Retractable Mine Avoidance SONAR |
| MP Propulstion | | | LM2500(2) and Diesel (2) |
| Auxiliary | | | Diesel(2) |
| Propulsor | | | Water Jet |
| RHIB | | | 1 |
| UV Handling System | | | Common SV/USV/UUV L/R Sys |
| Miscellaneous | | | RAST Port |
| | | | UCAR Starboard |

The seaframe's organization was assumed to be similar to the five legacy ships used in this study. The legacy ships are the CG, DDG, FFG, MCM and MHC classes, and were chosen as "proxies" for some of the LCS functions because the seaframe, for the most part, will have the same shipboard organization and regulations. Their systems and RQMTS have proven their effectiveness through countless missions accomplished. Therefore, their configuration will be used as the basis to estimate or approximate the RQMTS for the notional LCS system. Each ship, including the assumed LCS seaframe, is organized into five departments:

1. Executive,

2. Operations,

3. Combat Systems,

4. Engineering, and

5. Supply.

The LCS seaframe Executive Department is akin to legacy executive departments consisting of the commanding and executive officers as well as administrative support. The executive department's administrative functions are greatly supported by the advances of the Pay and Personnel Ashore (PAPA) detachment. The PAPA detachment is a concept that has proven to be a key element of Fleet Manning Experiments like Optimal Manning Experiments (OME). With this detachment ashore, most of the administrative, pay and personnel functions have been transferred off the ship.

The LCS seaframe Operations Department is similar to the operations department of single mission ships like the MCM and MHC ships although the LCS seaframe will be equipped with bigger guns and missiles. It is assumed that the RQMTS from these single-mission ships can be translated into the RQMTS to support the focused-mission LCS. Additionally, the LCS RQMTS will be divided between the seaframe and module. The module will bring onboard additional personnel to support operations in the individual warfare areas.

The LCS seaframe Combat Systems Department is different from legacy Combat Systems Department because the systems themselves are somewhat but not entirely different. See Table 3 for the LCS systems and the closest legacy system. These legacy systems will be used as proxies for the LCS system that is emerging or does not yet exist.

Table 3.     **LCS Seaframe System and Proxy**

| System | Proxy |
|---|---|
| 57mm BOFORS | 5/54 gun |
| CIWS | Actual |
| .50 cal (4) | Actual |
| RAM | Actual |
| Search RADAR | SPS-49 |
| Air Decoy | Actual |
| Torpedo Decoy Launcher | SVTT |
| Mine Avoidance SONAR | SQS-53C |

Therefore, it is assumed that the notional LCS systems the represent, will have the same manpower requirements as the legacy system. For example, the legacy RAM system has manpower requirements of less than one. It is assumed that the RAM system on the notional LCS will also have manpower requirements less than one.

The LCS seaframe Engineering Department with the CODAG design is assumed to be similar to the most demanding legacy gas turbine designs. All legacy gas turbine ships will be potential proxies for the assumed LCS. However, all the legacy engineering plants are of a single configuration (i.e., either gas turbine or diesel main propulsion engines). Therefore, it is further assumed that legacy ships with diesel engineman (EN) RQMTS are a better proxy than those without EN. The auxiliary diesel mechanics are further assumed to be capable of working on main diesel engines after proper training.

The LCS seaframe Supply Department is similar to the legacy Supply Departments using all available advances in technology to allow electronic disbursing and the PAPA detachment supported functions.

## B.    BATTLE BILL

The most demanding manpower requirements are during Conditions I and III for 24-hours and 60 days respectively. The Operational Manning is the requirement driver for supporting these conditions of readiness.

The battle bill delineates the watch stations required to support the different control stations to satisfy the requirements of the Required Operational Capabilities and Projected Operational Environment (ROC/POE) documents. There are eight control stations common to all legacy ships:

1. ship control,

2. communication control,

3. operations control,

4. combat system casualty control,

5. weapons control,

6. engineering control,

7. damage control, and

8. support control.

It is assumed that the LCS will share these common control stations. Additionally, these control stations will be supported with technology similar to the seven core Smart Ship systems (e.g., Integrated Bridge System and Machinery Control System).

The Smart Ship project on USS Yorktown successfully completed numerous demanding assessments, and all concluded that Yorktown "performed consistently well". Yorktown, with the installed Smart Ship technologies, revised policy and procedures and improved maintenance methods, was assessed by NAVMAC and OPTEVFOR. Both concluded that Yorktown was able to satisfy all the ROC/POE requirements [Ref 9].

It is assumed that the favorable assessments and successful completion of a Counter-Narcotics deployment immediately afterwards have rendered the Smart Ship technologies as effective. These systems, along with the revised policy and maintenance procedures, are assumed to be reliable for unrestricted use onboard the LCS seaframe and FMP modules.

OME for USS Milius reduced its RQMTS by changing policy and operational procedures with limited technology installs. The successful completion of OME was determined by the ship's performance throughout the Inter-Deployment and Training Cycle (IDTC) and mission accomplishment during deployment. USS Milius successfully completed all assessments and the deployment immediately following the experiment with the reduced manning.

It is assumed that the success of the USS Milius has paved the way for OME philosophies and methodology for the

LCS.    One  of  the  key  elements  of  OME  was  the  PAPA
detachment  conducting  supporting  a  majority  of  the  ship's
routine  administrative  functions  ashore.    It  is  further
assumed  that  LCS  administrative  functions  will  also  be
supported  by  a  PAPA  detachment.

The  composition  concept  was  also  used  frequently  to
change  the  watch  standing  philosophies  during  the  reduced
manning  experiments.    For  example,  the  DDG  had  two  RQMTS
for  a  NIXIE  Operator  and  a  NIXIE  Repairman  before  the
experiment.    After  OME,  the  DDG  required  only  one  NIXIE
Operator/Repairman.    The  concept  assumes  that  the  workload
for  both  the  NIXIE  Operator  and  Repairman  was  able  to  be
reduced  by  50%.    Table  4  lists  some  of  the  legacy
compositions  from  the  DDG  OME.    The  LCS  composition
concept,  based  upon  the  DDG  NIXIE  RQMTS,  will  also  assume
the  workload  of  two  RQMTS  can  be  reduced  by  50%.    For
example,  the  LCS  EN  who  has  been  trained  to  do  the  GSM
function  will  be  required  to  support  only  50%  of  both  the
EN  and  GSM  workload.

Furthermore,  the  composition  of  the  operator  and
repairman  has  enabled  greater  flexibility  of  operational
personnel.    The  operator  has  the  skills  required  to  adjust
the  system  to  operational  requirements  without  minimal
outside  assistance.    However,  the  system  operator  will  be
the  system  maintainer  while  the  operator  is  not  standing
watch.    The  further  necessitates  the  requirement  to  reduce
the  administrative  workload  for  the  operator/repairman  or
offload  any  additional  responsibilities.

Table 4.     **Legacy Compositions From DDG OME**

**(From Refs 8-9)**

| Legacy Rate Composition From OME | |
|---|---|
| **Before** | **After** |
| Quartermaster | Bridge Specialist |
| Signalman | |
| NIXIE Operator | NIXIE Operator/Repairman |
| NIXIE Repairman | |
| Operator | Operator/Monitor |
| Monitor | |

The Composite Sailor concept is both a policy and operational change item. This concept not only allows the combination of watch stations, it also allows the combination of the rates and functions. For example, a diesel mechanic (engineman or EN rate) who is assigned to the LCS will also be trained to work on gas turbine engines similar to the gas turbine mechanical (GSM) rate. Rates with similar job descriptions onboard the LCS were considered for composition. These rates include, but are not limited to these ratings: BM, CTT, DC, EN, ET, GS, HT, MM, MR, OS, QM, STG and TM. See Appendix O for rate descriptions and Table 5 below for proposed rate combinations.

Table 5.    **Suggested Rate Combination**

| Legacy Rate | LCS Rate |
|---|---|
| BM, EN, MM and QM | BM |
| CTT, ET | ET |
| DC, HT, MR | DC |
| EN, GS | EN/GS |
| OS, QM | OS |
| STG, TM | STG |

The LCS Boatswain's Mate (BM) rate will consist of KSAs from the Engineman (EN), Machinist's Mate (MM) and Quartermaster (QM) rates. Small boat coxswains have traditionally been the BMs. When a small boat is deployed, it is required to have an EN rate onboard. Since BMs are capable of maintaining deck machinery, it is assumed that BMs can also maintain the small boat engines of which they are the coxswain. Similarly, the EN rate should also be able to perform duties as the small boat coxswain. On the bridge, BMs have traditionally stood the watch as the Boatswain's Mate of the watch (BMOW). Today, they are standing watch as the Officer of the Deck (OOD) and Junior Officer of the Deck (JOOD) during Condition III operations. It is assumed that they are now capable of carrying out the duties as the navigator as well when on the bridge, thus removing the requirement for the QM.

Cryptologic Technician, Technical (CTTs) are "advanced [Electronic Technicians (ETs)] who do wiring, circuit testing and repair. They determine performance levels of electronic equipment, install new components, modify existing equipment and test, adjust and repair equipment cooling systems [Ref 6]". Under the assumption that ETs are able to perform these advanced functions, the ETs will replace the CTT RQMTS.

The engineering rates of Damage Controlman (DC), Hull Maintenance Technician (HT) and Machinery Repairman (MR) are very similar. Thus, the LCS DC rate will possess the KSAs from the HT and MR rate. The DC knowledge of damage control can be greatly advanced with the skills of the HT and MR.

In general, The Operations Specialist (OS) rate is responsible for managing secondary charts and performing radar navigation in support of the QM who performs the visual navigation. These two rates are similar, using GPS data to update their positions. The voyage management system (VMS) is capable of updating positions as well as voyage planning using GPS and radar inputs and steering the ship along the planned tracks. Thus, it is assumed the QM rating can be replaced by the VMS and watchstanders in the piloting control stations and supported by the OS in CIC. This also assumes digital charts and permanent electronic recording of ship's movement are acceptable in lieu of hardcopy charts, and the VMS along with the ECDIS are authorized for unrestricted use.

The LCS SONAR Technician (Surface) (STG) rate will possess the KSAs of both the STG and the Torpedoman's Mate (TM). For LCS, the TMs are required for torpedo countermeasures. By extending the ordnance capability to the STG rate, the torpedo countermeasures can be covered by the STG.

### 1. Ship Control

With respect to ship control, it is assumed that the Smart Ship Integrated Bridge System (IBS) and Voyage Management System (VMS) will have matured enough to reduce the LCS piloting control stations to just the OOD and JOOD watches. Both the IBS and VMS systems would be integrated into the notional Integrated Command Centers (ICC).

Furthermore, it is also assumed that the chart coverage provided by the VMS and Electronic Chart Display Information System (ECDIS) will be sufficient to require only minimal paper charts onboard the LCS. If not, the Operations Specialist (OS) is assumed to be capable of preparing and managing the paper charts without the Quartermasters (QM). Operations Specialists (OS) have consistently been the secondary navigation team supporting the Quartermasters (QM). These skills combined with the VMS and IBS can be used to conduct all the LCS seaframe's voyage planning requirements.

The LCS bridge watchstanders will be the primary watchstanders responsible for the safe navigation of the ship. Using the IBS, VMS and ECDIS systems, the Officer-of-the-Deck (OOD) and Junior OOD will be able to receive real-time ship's position and other pertinent navigation data to support their decision-making abilities.

It is assumed that the LCS pilot house will give the bridge watchstanders the ability to see all around the ship. On the bridge with a 360-degree viewing capability, the LCS OOD and JOOD are able to safely navigate and handle the ship without additional lookouts.

These Ship Control assumptions will allow the bridge watch stations to be reduced to just two. The Officer of the Deck (OOD) and the Junior Officer of the Deck (JOOD) is assumed capable of safe ship operations with the IBS, VMS and an all-around viewing capability.

## 2. Operations Control

It is assumed that the LCS seaframe Combat Information Center (CIC) will incorporate the use of multi-modal consoles (MMC) along with an integrated Weapons Control Console (WCC). The MMC is an emerging system that, in the interim, may require the use of legacy sensor and weapon consoles. It is also assumed that the MMC will make available all the sensor inputs (e.g., Search RADAR, EO/IR, SLQ-32, etc.) to the watchstanders.

Decoy controls are assume to be integrated into either the WCC or IBS console. CIC watchstanders will have primary decoy (air, surface and underwater) controls with the secondary controls located in the pilot house's IBS.

Traditional CIC watches required watchstanders to operate stations predominantly dedicated to a single sensor or weapon system. These Operations Control assumptions will consolidate most of the sensor inputs and weapon controls into a few consoles. This will greatly reduce the number of watchstanders down to perhaps only two or three watchstanders using the MMC and WCC.

### 3. Communication Control

It is assumed that the LCS Battle Bill Communication Control stations are similar to legacy Communication Control stations. These watchstanders will maintain communication, tactical and LAN systems.

The communication systems of legacy ships involved the use of many different circuits. Most of these circuits had dedicated handsets which resulted in some difficulty in differentiation. Onboard the LCS, it is assumed that these different circuits are patched into a common system where the executives and watchstanders will be able to access the different circuits with a visual aid to identify the status of the different circuits.

Moreover, the LCS will leverage remote monitoring and sensing systems to reduce the manpower requirements for monitors. The systems are assumed to replace legacy monitoring personnel (i.e., missile launcher monitors) thus allowing the system operators and casualty control personnel the ability to remote monitor all systems and respond as they are needed.

Communications systems are greatly improved through advances in computing technology and commercial off the shelf (COTS) systems. These improvements combined with the Smart Ship fiber optics LAN system, have greatly reduced the need for human monitors to check system performance and security. With the ability to remotely monitor machinery and conditions, a dedicated monitor will not be required. Thus communication systems have the potential to be unmanned.

## 4.   Combat Systems/Electronics Casualty Control

It is assumed that the LCS Battle Bill Combat Systems/Electronics Casualty Control stations are similar to legacy Combat Systems/Electronics Casualty Control stations where the RQMTS respond to combat system casualties as well as electronic system casualties.

However, the assumed LCS will have personnel capable of operating and maintaining their systems. This will greatly reduce the requirement for a separate operator and maintainer. For example, the NIXIE system demonstrated that the requirements for a NIXIE Operator and NIXIE Repairman can be consolidated into a single NIXIE Operator/Maintainer.

## 5.   Weapons Control

The 57MM, RAM, CIWS and decoy controls are assumed integrated into a single Weapons Control Console (WCC) console located in CIC with several back-up consoles located nearby. Additionally, each weapon system will have the local control capability (i.e., CIWS will have an operator at the Local Control Panel).

During Condition I, .50-caliber machine guns on the port and starboard sides will be manned and ready. Each mount will require one operator and one ammo loader. These personnel will also act as decoy loaders in support of the CIC watchstanders who are controlling the decoy launchers. The other two mounts will be augmented by standing down other watchstanders, and the ammo loader will support both mounts on their respective sides.

These assumptions will reduce the requirement for dedicated watch stations and systems. By integrating more than one system into a console, the potential exists to reduce the watch-stander requirements.

The seaframe crew is responsible for the safe launching and recovery of unmanned surface and underwater vehicles. The assumed launch and recovery system is based upon an enlarged variant of the Swedish Visby corvette's UV launch and recovery system. The current U.S. Navy boat launching and recovery systems like the gravity davits found on legacy ships are manpower intensive. The system proposed for LCS is the overhead rail system assisted with electrical winches and controls that spot the UVs to the launch/recovery station and then back its storage station. This system requires only one winch operator assisted by the personnel responsible for the UVs as tenders and assistants. Thus, the boat launching and recovery apparatus onboard LCS may require only one operator.

UAVs will be the responsibility of the aviation detachment personnel. Aviation detachment personnel are responsible for the UAVs spot to the flight deck and then back to the hangar. The seaframe crew will be responsible for the launch and recovery flight operations.

## 6.  Engineering Control

The engineering plant is assumed to be of the combined diesel and gas turbine (CODAG) configuration. The fuel efficiency of the diesel engine at slow speed and the power of the gas turbine engine at high speed make this propulsion system ideal for the LCS. The engineers assigned onboard LCS will not be watchstanders. Their primary function is the maintenance and safe operation of the engineering plant and associated machinery.

Engineers will assist the bridge watchstanders in the start-up and shut-down of engineering systems. Bridge and CIC watchstanders will have the ability to remote start the main engines as well as auxiliary equipment from the bridge or CIC through the Machinery Control System accessible on the fiber optics LAN system. This will allow the bridge and CIC watchstanders to control vital engineering equipments required to safely operate and fight the ship without degradation.

During Condition III steaming, watchstanders are not required in the engineering spaces. All engineers are maintainers during Condition III. The EOOW and their assistant will be the watchstanders during Condition I with a monitor in the main engineroom. This could reduce the LCS engineering watchstanders by 25% to 50% over the legacy engineering watches.

The position of the JP5 Pump Room Operator is not required if it is able to be remotely operated from Central Control Station (CCS). JP5 nozzleman will also have the redundant ability, from CCS, to start and stop the pumps from the flight deck area.

### 7. Damage Control

It is assumed that primary Damage Control Central (DCC) will be located in the Central Control Station (CCS), and secondary DCC will be remotely located on the bridge.

The damage control function relies on the extensive use of the Smart Ship Damage Control System (DCS) and installed shipboard firefighting technology that is available today. For example, the installed AFFF and $CO_2$ systems inside critical spaces such as the main engineering and ordnance spaces.

The Damage Control Officer (DCO) and Damage Control Assistant (DCA) will monitor and control damages from CCS while coordinating damage control efforts with the Engineering Officer of the Watch (EOOW). To facilitate ease of communication and efficiency, the DCO, DCA and the damage control party will be co-located in the same space.

The damage control party will be reduced commensurate with the acceptable risk level and technology leverage. In general, the damage control party will consist of a scene leader, investigators, nozzleman and hoseman. These will be the positions on the Rapid Response Team (RRT).

The damage control philosophy is to engage the RRT to the scene immediately after the casualty. The RRT will estimate the damage and augmentation required. If the damage is beyond their capability, then the decision must be made whether or not to use the automation and installed firefighting system to isolate the damage. This is important especially if the affected space is a critical space. If the damage is too large for the RRT and the decision is made not to use the installed firefighting system, then additional personnel will be required by standing down watch stations that are deemed non essential to the operation at hand.

If the damage is excessively large for the augmented damage control party, then the decision must be made to either continue the operation until it is time to abandon or disengage from the operation.

By changing the Damage Control philosophy, the legacy Damage Controls of 80 personnel can be reduced by 50% to 75%.

### 8. Support Control

LCS seaframe Support Control is assumed to be the same in all respects as the legacy Support Control stations and their functions.

The assumed LCS Supply Department is assumed to use advanced inventory systems like the scanners and commercial inventory management programs. These technologies can reduce the amount of personnel required to locate and issue as well as the time required. Another assumption is that the self-service food line function is capable of reducing the CS requirement by about 25% to 50%.

## C. AVIATION DETACHMENT

The aviation detachment manpower requirement (RQMTS) is based upon the NAVAIR 1.2 LCS Alternative Aviation Support Study for the MH-60R/S and RQ-8B VTUAV system [Ref 21]. Table 6 shows the different NAVAIR manning level estimates and their level of risk.

Table 6.     NAVAIR Manning Option Risk Assessment

(From Ref 21)

| Type | Manning Level | H-60 Flt Hours Achieved | RQ-8B Flt Hours Achieved | Risk to Meeting Flight Scheduled Events |
|---|---|---|---|---|
| MIW | 57 | 98 | 177 | LOW |
| | 44 | 98 | 177 | LOW |
| | 34 | 83 | 177 | MEDIUM |
| | 28 | 42 | 136 | HIGH |
| ASW/SUW | 52 | 110 | 180 | LOW |
| | 40 | 106 | 175 | LOW |
| | 30 | 95 | 175 | MEDIUM |
| | 25 | 50 | 139 | HIGH |
| | 22 | 50 | 139 | HIGH |

It is assumed that the aviation detachment RQMTS will be from the MEDIUM risk category. This means that the MIW module aviation detachment has 34 RQMTS to support 83 manned flight hours and 177 unmanned flight hours. The ASW/SUW modules have 30 RQMTS each and support 95 manned and 175 unmanned flight hours.

Additionally, it is assumed the operators and support elements of the aviation detachment can be organized into the generalist and specialist detachments where:

1. Operator of MH-60R cannot operate MH-60S,

2. Operator of MH-60S cannot operate MH-60R,

3. Operator for MH-60R/S can operate RQ-8B VTUAV. The opposite would not be true,

4. Maintainers of MH-60R can maintain MH-60S and vice versa, and

5. Maintainers of MH-60R/S can maintain RQ-8B and vice versa.

The aviation generalists and specialists are assumed to be independent detachments. This assumption will allow the aviation component to be considered separately in alternative module force structure analysis.

## D.   FOCUSED MISSION PACKAGES

LCS mission packages will include the FMP and its PUK. The FMP modules will consist of the manpower required to operate and maintain the package equipment along with the additional manpower to augment the seaframe crew for messing, administration and medical support [Ref 1].

Figure 2 lists the different modules and their systems. Because a majority of the module systems (i.e., the Advanced Deployable System and the Remote Mine-hunting Vehicle) are emerging systems, the proxy methodology is used to estimate these RQMTS. The module systems are itemized in Table 7 along with the basis for their manning estimates.

Table 7.

Figure 2. **FMP Modules and Systems**

# FMP Modules and Systems

| MIW Modules | QTY |
|---|---|
| USV with | 1 |
| MIW System(s) | |
| VTUAV | 1 set (3 UAVs) |
| COBRA | 2 |
| MH-60S with | 1 |
| OASIS System | 2 |
| ALMDS | 2 |
| AQS-20A | 2 |
| RAMICS | 2 |
| AMNS | 2 |
| AN/WLD-1 RMV | 2 |
| AQS-20A | 2 |
| Periscope Detection | 1 |
| EOD Det | 1 |
| BPAUV (Set) | 1 |
| SCULPIN (set) | 1 |

| ASW Modules | QTY |
|---|---|
| USV with | 2 |
| ASW Systems | 2 |
| VTUAV | 1 set (3 UAVs) |
| MH-60R with | 1 |
| Torpedo | set |
| Sonar | set |
| Sonobuoys | set |
| AN/WLD-1 RMV | 2 |
| with ASW Systems | 2 |
| Periscope Detection | 1 |
| ACES/EER/ IEER/AEER family | 1 |
| Torpedo Countermeasures | 1 |
| ADS | 1 |
| Towed Array | 2 |

| SUW Modules | QTY |
|---|---|
| USV with EO/IR | 2 |
| Gun Package | 1 |
| Missile Package | 1 |
| VTUAV with EO/IR | 1 set (3 UAVs) |
| Rocket/Gun/Missile | set |
| MH-60R with | 1 |
| EO/IR | set |
| Gun/Rockets | set |
| Hellfire | set |
| Netfires | 1 |
| Intermediate Caliber Gun Module | 2 |
| Non-Lethal Weapon | 2 |

ACES – Active Capable Expendable Surveillance
ADS – Advanced Deployable System
ALMDS – Airborne Laser Mine Detection System
AMNS – Airborne Mine Neutralization System
AQS-20A – Minehunting Sonar
BPAUV – Battlespace Preparation Autonomous Underwater Vehicle

COBRA – Coastal Battlefield Reconnaissance & Analysis
EOD Det – Explosives Ordnance Disposal Detachment
OASIS – Organic Airborne & Surface Influence Sweep
RAMICS – Rapid Airborne Mine Clearance System
RMV – Remote Minehunting Vehicle
SCULPIN – Autonomous Bottom Mapping UUV system
USV – Unmanned Surface Vehicle
VTUAV – Vertical Take-off Unmanned Aerial Vehicle

Table 8. **FMP Module System and Proxy**

| System | Proxy |
|---|---|
| USV | RHIB |
| VTUAV | NAVAIR |
| MH-60 R/S | |
| AN/WLD-1 RMV | MNV |
| Periscope Detection | Search Radar |
| EOD Detachment or NSCT | EOD Detachment |
| BPAUV | NIXIE |
| SCULPIN | |
| ACES/EER/IEER/AEER Family | Sonobuoys |
| Torpedo Countermeasure | NIXIE |
| ADS | Sonobuoys |
| Towed Array | TACTAS |
| Intermediate Caliber Gun | 25MM Bushmaster |

35

Module systems and their support personnel are assumed to be independent components of a FMP module. Thus, these systems and personnel can be organized into groups of generalists and specialists. Generalists are non-warfare specific personnel, capable of operating with different module systems or in different warfare areas. They must be able to operate in at least two different warfare areas (e.g., RMV Support personnel can maintain the RMV across the MIW and ASW warfare areas). Specialists are system or mission specific personnel (e.g., mission C4 and MH-60S pilots) who, because of their specialty skill, are limited in system or operational flexibility. They are assigned to one particular system or warfare area. Specialists are assumed to have no more than two main specialties. For example, an engineman (EN) is limited to operating and supporting the diesel and gas turbine engines only.

For module command, control, computers and communications (C4), every FMP will have an Officer-in-charge (OIC) and the administrative and support requirements. The mission C4 may also consist of watchstanders who will help integrate the module systems into the LCS seaframe's architecture and be the standby watchstanders to support the various module systems.

The module generalists and specialists are assumed to be independent detachments. This assumption will allow the individual detachments to be considered in alternative module force structure analysis.

## E.    MAINTENANCE

LCS maintenance will be based upon Condition-based Maintenance (CBM), Engineered Reliability Centered Maintenance (RCM) and the CMP from the FFG. Assume LCS initially utilizes the same maintenance schedule similar to a CONUS-based FFG. Then, the maintenance factor will 1.00 which means LCS will be in the deployment cycle 100% of the time during a 20-month period.

With a shore-based module force and a squadron organization, the LCS has the potential to transfer some of its routine maintenance workload ashore. While in homeport, the LCS can remove failing or suspect equipment and parts and replace them with those already serviced by the supporting shore infrastructure. This will require the shore infrastructure to use some of the LCS force while ashore to perform maintenance that would have been time consuming and non-essential during operations.

Some of the rates assumed to perform routine maintenance work onboard the LCS seaframe include the FC, GM, EM and EN rates. When the workload is transfered ashore, the RQMTS associated with them are also transferred. These RQMTS will be filled by personnel who have just returned from deployment or who are available during the inter-deployment training cycle (IDTC).

These maintenance assumptions have the potential to sustain, and even increase, the reliability of the assumed LCS systems and machinery. Moreover, they have the potential to reduce the manning onboard the seaframe.

THIS PAGE INTENTIONALLY LEFT BLANK

# V. SCOPE AND LIMITATIONS

This study focused on the RQMTS for the LCS seaframe and FMP modules as well as the efficient organization of the module personnel.

Analysis of legacy Ship Manpower Documents (SMD) for the cruisers, destroyers, frigates, mine countermeasure and coastal mine-hunting ships provided the best estimation of the baseline RQMTS for the LCS seaframe and modules. The study showed how the baseline RQMTS can be reduced by compounding the effects of reduced manning initiatives and paradigm shifts. The reduced manning initiatives analyzed in this study were limited to the Smart Ship project on the CG and OME on the DDG. The paradigm shifts are key culture, policy and procedural items taken from past studies and quantifying their effects.

Quantifying the effect of the paradigm shift was a subjective but key element of this analysis. A subject matter expert was used to verify and validate the quantified effects [Ref 22].

The methodology began with the baseline RQMTS and then reduced that RQMTS by compounding the effects from the reduced manning initiatives and paradigm shifts. The methodology was first applied to the seaframe RQMTS, and then was applied to the individual RQMTS. The resulting reduced RQMTS were the minimum RQMTS possible under the assumptions of this thesis.

After compounding all the effects, the resulting reduced module RQMTS were used to explore several personnel management options for the module personnel. The first option was to "pre-package" them, and the second was to "flex" them. The best option led to a more efficient use of the module personnel, and reduced the overall module RQMTS producing even more savings.

Ultimately, the study determined if the LCS minimal manning objective was feasible, and under what level of aggressiveness. It also determined if further savings could be realized by organizing the module personnel more efficiently.

# VI. METHODOLOGY

The baseline RQMTS estimate for the seaframe and modules began with the analysis of the legacy Ship Manpower Documents (SMD) for the Ticonderoga (CG-47), Arleigh Burke (DDG-51), Oliver Hazard Perry (FFG-7), Avenger (MCM-1) and Osprey (MHC-51) classes of ships and their respective configuration. Using these ships as proxies for various functions of LCS, the analysis produced the RQMTS and systems data required for the optimization equations used in this study.

To estimate the baseline RQMTS for the seaframe, the notional LCS systems were itemized similar to the legacy systems data. If the notional system was found as a legacy system, then the minimum associated legacy RQMTS were used as the RQMTS for that particular system. If the system was an emerging system or does not yet exist, then the closest proxy from the legacy system was used to represent the RQMTS for that particular system.

Using a system of optimization equations in EXCEL®, the total seaframe RQMTS were estimated and used as the seaframe baseline RQMTS. The resulting baseline RQMTS was from the "business as usual" approach.

The seaframe baseline RQMTS was then reduced through the compounded effects of the reduced manning initiatives and suggested paradigm shifts. Reduced manning initiatives include the Smart Ship and Optimal Manning Experiments (OME), and paradigm shifts includes Composite Sailor, Technology Leverage and Workload Transfer concepts.

41

The Smart Ship savings realized were based on the analysis of the CG SMD with no Smart Ship (CG (NS)) and with Smart Ship (CG (SS)), and the actual rate and overall savings was applied to the seaframe's baseline RQMTS estimate. Similarly, the DDG OME savings from the DDG without OME (DDG (NO)) and DDG with OME (DDG (OME)) SMDs were analyzed and then applied to the LCS seaframe baseline estimate on the individual rate level. The reduction effects were compounded.

The first paradigm shift was a recommended policy and training procedure change referred to as the Composite Sailor concept. This concept allowed the sailor to gain additional expertise outside their assigned rate, e.g., allowing an engineman trained to work on main diesel engines to also work on main gas turbine engines.

The next paradigm shift was a greater reliance on technology called the Technology Leverage concept. The Smart Ship program successfully introduced several manpower saving technologies like the Integrated Bridge System (IBS), Voyage Management System (VMS), fiber optic Local Area Network (LAN), Damage Control System (DCS), Integrated Condition and Assessment System (ICAS), wireless communication system and the Machinery Control System (MCS). When used to their design capability, these seven core Smart Ship systems promise to further reduce the LCS seaframe RQMTS.

The last paradigm explored the maintenance and workload changes called the Workload Transfer concept where the main theme was to reduce the workload onboard the seaframe and deploying modules. This was similar to the "pit stop" concept used in automotive racing. Through this concept, a greater shift of labor intensive, repetitive and extensive maintenance and workload requirements are performed ashore. The bottom line was removing as much of the workload as possible to allow both the core and mission-package crews to focus upon operational matters with sufficient focus on maintenance of critical combat readiness systems.

The paradigm shift effects were then quantified and reviewed by a manpower technical expert, CDR Charlie Gowen (USN, retired) from AmerInd Inc, who has been determining manpower requirements for both U.S. Navy and U.S. Coast Guard vessels for the past 25 years, and has the qualifications and experience to validate the quantified paradigm shift effects used in this study [Ref 22].

The resulting RQMTS, after applying the effects from the reduced manning initiatives and paradigm shift approaches, was the feasible minimal manning level for the seaframe's core crew.

The last half of the first objective was to estimate the baseline RQMTS for the module. All modular systems were itemized similar to the legacy ships and seaframe. Most of the systems in the modules were either emerging or do not yet have RQMTS determined. If the system was a legacy system, then the minimum associated legacy RQMTS was used as the baseline RQMTS. Otherwise, the proxy method was used to estimate the system's baseline RQMTS. Similar to the seaframe, a system of optimization equation was used in EXCEL® to estimate each warfare module's baseline RQMTS.

Individual module RQMTS were then reduced by applying the paradigm shifts effect. Of the three suggested

43

paradigm shifts, only the Composite Sailor concept provided any significant reduction in the module RQMTS. The other two paradigm shifts appear to have negligible effects. The Technology Leverage concept produced insignificant reductions because most of the module systems were new and emerging technologies. Similarly, the Workload Transfer concept produced very little savings because the modules were shore-based. They were only deployed when needed. Thus, a majority of their maintenance and workload was accomplished ashore while only minimal maintenance and supporting workload went with the module when deployed. Therefore, only the Composite Sailor paradigm shift had the potential to substantially reduce the module RQMTS.

After the module RQMTS have been reduced, the resulting minimum RQMTS were organized into a single "module squadron". Because only a small percentage of the modules acquired actually deploy at a given time, the "pre-packaged" crewing concept lead to inefficient use of valuable human capital. An alternative concept called the "flexed" concept was studied to determine if efficiencies can be gain by deploying the module personnel in detachments as they were needed. The detachments consisted of generalists and specialists. Generalists were personnel capable of supporting more than one specified warfare area, and specialists were limited to supporting a particular warfare area. An organization of these detachments lead to a more efficient employment of the module personnel.

# VII. FORMULATION AND DATA

The core and mission-package crew baselines RQMTS as well as the module "flexed" crewing concept RQMTS were estimated using a system of optimization equations.

## A. FORMULATION

### 1. Indices

$c$   *Class of ship* (*includes LCS / FMPs*)   $c = 0,...,9$

$d$   *Department / Detachment*   $d = 0,...,17$

$s$   *System*   $s = 0,...,22$

A detail listing of the indices can be found in Appendix D.

### 2. Parameters

$X_{c=1,...,5,d=1}$    Executive Department RQMTS of legacy ship classes

$X_{c=1,...,5,d=2}$    Operations Department RQMTS of legacy ship classes

$X_{c=1,...,5,d=4}$    Engineering Department RQMTS of legacy ship classes

$X_{c=1,...,c,d=5}$    Supply Deptment RQMTS ratio of legacy ship classes

$N_{c,s}$    Number of system s on ship class c

$N_{c=6}$    Number of LCS seaframes

$N_{c=7}$    Number of MIW FMP modules

$N_{c=8}$    Number of ASW FMP modules

$N_{c=9}$    Number of SUW FMP modules

### 3. Decision Variable

$X_{c,d,s}$    RQMTS for   ship of class    c

                        department/detachment   d

                        system                 s

### 4.  Objective Function

The first objective was to estimate the LCS seaframe (equation 6) and modules (equation 10) baseline RQMTS. The seaframe RQMTS was calculated using the following series of optimization equations:

$$\min(X_{c=1,\ldots,5,d=1}) \qquad \text{(equation 1)}$$

$$\min(X_{c=4,5,d=2}) \qquad \text{(equation 2)}$$

$$\sum_{s=1}^{8} N_s \min(X_s) \qquad \text{(equation 3)}$$

$$\min(X_{c=1,2,3,d=4}) \qquad \text{(equation 4)}$$

$$\min(X_{c=1,\ldots,5,d=5}) \qquad \text{(equation 5)}$$

$$Seaframe\ RQMTS = \left( \min(Exec_{c=1,\ldots,5}) + \min(Ops_{c=4,5}) + \sum_{s=1}^{8} Q_s \min(X_s) + \min(Eng_{c=1,2,3}) \right) \left( 1 + \min(Supply_{c=1,\ldots,5}) \right)$$

$$\text{(equation 6)}$$

Equations used to estimate the individual module baseline RQMTS are equations 7 (MIW FMP) through 9 (SUW FMP). The total module RQMTS was the sum of three individual equations (equation 10).

$$\sum_{s=10}^{21} N_{c=7,s} X_s \qquad \text{(equation 7)}$$

$$\sum_{s=10}^{21} N_{c=8,s} X_s \qquad \text{(equation 8)}$$

$$\sum_{s=10}^{21} N_{c=9,s} X_s \qquad \text{(equation 9)}$$

$$Total\ module\ RQMTS = \sum_{s=10}^{21} N_{c=7,s} X_s + \sum_{s=10}^{21} N_{c=8,s} X_s + \sum_{s=10}^{21} N_{c=9,s} X_s$$

$$Total\ module\ RQMTS = \sum_{c=7}^{9} \sum_{s=10}^{21} N_{c,s} X_s \qquad \text{(equation 10)}$$

The third and final, objective function was used to
determine the "flexed" module RQMTS:

$$\text{Total "flexed" module RQMTS} = \sum_{d=6}^{17}\sum_{c=7}^{9}\left(G_d N_{c=6} X_d + S_d N_c X_d\right) \qquad \text{(equation 11)}$$

### 5. Constraints

$$X_{c,d,r,s,w} \geq 0 \quad \forall_{c,d,r,s,w}$$

## B.  DATA

The configuration data for legacy platforms were
gathered from unclassified and public sources.

The Ship Manpower Document (SMD) provided ship's
manpower requirements (RQMTS). Section II of the SMD
provided the manpower summary by department, officer and
enlisted. Section III provided the manpower requirements
by billet sequence numbers. The data extracted were the
quantity of each rate required. Section IV was the battle
bill by watchstation numbers. The watchstation numbers
provided the RQMTS to support a particular watchstation
including the systems. Section V provided the functional
workload totals for each division [Refs 6-12].

The data for the aviation detachment RQMTS came from
NAVAIR 1.2 LCS Alternative Aviation Support Study Final
Briefout of 14 June 2004 [Ref 21].

The final data source was the aforementioned subject
matter expert.

THIS PAGE INTENTIONALLY LEFT BLANK

# VIII. ANALYSIS

## A. "BUSINESS AS USUAL" ANALYSIS

The analysis first looked at the RQMTS of legacy ships. The most demanding RQMTS was during Condition I, and these RQMTS were used to estimate the seaframe's baseline RQMTS. The RQMTS for the five legacy platforms were derived from section IV of the respective Ship Manning Document (SMD). Because of the Smart Ship and OME, the study used the SMD for the CG before and after Smart Ship as well as the SMD for the DDG before and after OME. Therefore, there were two variants of the CG and DDG legacy RQMTS. The RQMTS analysis for the legacy ships are summarized in Table 8.

Table 9. **Legacy Manpower Requirements (RQMTS)**
**(From Refs 14-20)**

| Dept | CG(NS) | CG(SS) | DDG | DDG(OME) | FFG | MCM | MHC |
|---|---|---|---|---|---|---|---|
| Executive | 19 | 19 | 15 | 15 | 13 | 5 | 4 |
| Operations | 91 | 92 | 101 | 79 | 73 | 48 | 30 |
| Combat Sys | 104 | 104 | 105 | 95 | 42 | 0 | 0 |
| Engineering | 68 | 54 | 66 | 62 | 46 | 25 | 16 |
| Supply | 57 | 57 | 53 | 45 | 42 | 7 | 5 |
| Total | 339 | 326 | 340 | 296 | 216 | 85 | 55 |

Note: 1) Executive department includes medical
2) Operations department includes deck and navigation

The minimally manned LCS seaframe's baseline RQMTS was calculated based upon the minimum legacy RQMTS for each department or system that has a configuration similar to the notional LCS. Minimum legacy RQMTS for the Executive Department came from the MHC which has a manning of four.

Using the MHC RQMTS directly supports the LCS because both are focused mission ships. The Operations Department for LCS is similar, again, to the MCM and MHC Operations Departments because all are focused mission ships. The minimum RQMTS for the LCS Operations Department came from the MHC which has 30 RQMTS. The LCS Combat Systems Department, however, had more combat systems than the MCM and MHC (i.e., the 57MM gun and the RAM). Therefore, the legacy departmental minimum would not work for the LCS. Rather, a system-specific methodology was used to estimate the total Combat Systems Department RQMTS. Using the proxies, the core LCS combat systems RQMTS are summarized in the right hand section of Table 9 below.

Table 10.    **Combat Systems RQMTS (From Refs 14-20)**

| System | Proxy | CG | CG (SS) | DDG | DDG (OME) | FFG | MCM | MHC | Minimum |
|--------|-------|----|---------|-----|-----------|-----|-----|-----|---------|
| 57mm BOFORS | 5/54 gun | 10 | 10 | 11 | 11 | 6 | 0 | 0 | 6 |
| CIWS | Actual | 5 | 5 | 6 | 6 | 5 | 0 | 0 | 5 |
| .50 cal (4) | Actual | 0 | 0 | 0 | 8 | 8 | 8 | 8 | 8 |
| RAM | Actual | 1 | 1 | 1 | 0 | 0 | 0 | 0 | 1 |
| Search RADAR | SPS-49 | 3 | 3 | 0 | 3 | 3 | 2 | 0 | 2 |
| Air Decoy | Actual | 0 | 0 | 0 | 0 | 1 | 0 | 0 | 1 |
| Torpedo Decoy Launcher | SVTT | 1 | 1 | 2 | 1 | 2 | 0 | 0 | 1 |
| Mine Avoidance SONAR | SQS-53C | 6 | 6 | 7 | 5 | 6 | 7 | 6 | 5 |
| | TOTAL | 26 | 26 | 27 | 34 | 31 | 17 | 14 | 29 |

The LCS Combat System Department has a total of 29 RQMTS which includes the RQMTS for the CIWS 1B gun system which was not a part of the two industry team's LCS designs.

The LCS Engineering Department is both similar and different from its legacy counterparts. The LCS engineering plant was the combined diesel and gas turbine (CODAG) propulsion system. All the legacy ships in this study have a single type of propulsion (i.e., diesel or gas turbine) but not both. The Engineering RQMTS were based upon the most demanding legacy engineering plant which is the gas turbine. Only the CG, DDG and FFG have gas turbines, and the minimum RQMTS comes from the FFG which has 46 RQMTS. Of the 46 RQMTS, there are 10 diesel mechanics to support the auxiliary diesel engines. This thesis assumes that these 10 mechanics can also be trained to support main propulsion diesel engines. Therefore, the LCS Engineering Department has 46 RQMTS.

Lastly, the LCS Supply Department RQMTS was calculated using the minimum ratio instead of the minimum legacy Supply Department RQMTS. The Supply Ratio used was calculated by dividing the number of Supply RQTMS by the total number of Non-Supply RQMTS:

$$Supply\ Ratio = \frac{Supply\ RQMTS}{Total\ Non-Supply\ RQMTS} \qquad \text{(equation 12)}$$

Of the five legacy Supply Ratios, the MHC had the smallest ratio. Using this Supply Ratio, the number of LCS Supply RQMTS was calculated by multiplying it with the total Non-Supply RQMTS onboard the LCS. Therefore, the calculated LCS Supply Department RQMTS was:

$$MHC\ Supply\ Ratio = \frac{5}{50} = 0.10.$$
$$LCS\ Supply\ RQMTS = 0.10*(109) = 10.9 \approx 11\ RQMTS$$

The LCS seaframe baseline RQMTS by department and systems is summarized in Table 10 below.

Table 11.    **LCS Seaframe Baseline RQMTS (business as usual)**

| Department | Crew | Proxy | Core LCS Combat System | Qty | Manning |
|---|---|---|---|---|---|
| | | | 57 mm gun/.50 cal | 1 | 14 |
| Executive[a] | 4 | MHC | RAM | 1 | 1 |
| Operations[b] | 30 | MHC | Search radar | 1 | 2 |
| Combat Systems | 24 + 5[b] = 29 | ← | Surface decoy | 2 | 1 |
| Engineering | 46 | FFG | Air decoy | 3 | |
| Supply | 11 | MHC[a] | Torpedo decoy launcher | 2 | 1 |
| *Total* | *115 + 5[b] = 120* | | Mine avoidance sonar | 1 | 5 |

a. Scaled proportionately to smaller crew size using MHC supply ratio

b. CIWS is not included in current Flight-0 LCS designs. Estimated manning level of 5

The estimated seaframe (without mission module) RQMTS of 115-120 clearly exceeds the threshold of 110 that applies to the composite seaframe and module. Recalling that just the aviation components of the mission modules will require 30-34 personnel, we conclude that this baseline will have to be substantially reduced.

## B.    REDUCED MANNING INITIATIVES

The lessons learned and savings from Smart Ship and OME are the first steps in reducing the LCS seaframe baseline RQMTS. The policies, procedures and technology changes affected every aspect of shipboard routine and organization. The final saving estimates were calculated by analyzing the changes in the rates contained in Section VI (Summary of Manpower Requirements) of the SMD. [Refs 14 to 17]  The effects of Smart Ship and OME on the individual departments are summarized in Table 11.

Table 12.     **Smart Ship and OME Reductions By Department (From Refs 14-17)**

| Department | SmartShip | OME |
|---|---|---|
| Executive | 0.0% | 0.0% |
| Operations | 1.1% | 27.8% |
| Combat Sys | 0.0% | 10.5% |
| Engineering | 25.9% | 6.5% |
| Supply | 0.0% | 17.8% |

However, the overall effects were somewhat sobering. Smart Ship had an overall savings, after analyzing the CG (NS) and CG (SS) SMDs, of 4% while OME overall savings, after analyzing the DDG and DDG (OME) SMDs, was three times that at 12.9%.


### 1.   Smart Ship

For the CG, Smart Ship savings were realized throughout several rates.  The affected rates are summarized in Table 12.

Table 13.     **Smart Ship Effect by Rate (From Refs 14 and 15)**

| Rate | Original | New | Change | Saving Percentage |
|---|---|---|---|---|
| Boatswain's Mate (BM) | 7 | 8 | +1 | -14.3% |
| Damage Controlman (DC) | 10 | 8 | -2 | 20.0% |
| Electrician's Mate (EM) | 6 | 5 | -1 | 16.7% |
| Fireman (FN) | 12 | 9 | -3 | 25.0% |
| Gas Turbine, Electrical (GSE) | 20 | 12 | -8 | 40.0% |

When the effects were applied to the LCS seaframe baseline RQMTS, the 4% Smart Ship savings removed the RQMTS for an EM, DC and three GSs.  The overall LCS manning level of 120 was thus reduced to 115 – not nearly enough of a reduction to accommodate required additional module personnel.

## 2.   Fleet Optimal Manning Experiment (OME)

For the DDG, OME also affected every facet of the ship's organization.  Most reductions were accomplished by policy and procedural changes supported with minimal technology leveraging.  The overall OME savings for the DDG was 12.9%. [Refs 8 and 9]  Compared to the Smart Ship effects, OME definitely had a bigger effect.  Table 13 summarized the effects of OME across the different rates including officers (i.e., 1110, 6120 and 7120).

Table 14.    **Fleet Optimal Manning Experiment Savings by Rate**

**(From Ref 16 and 17)**

| Rate | Original | After OME | Change | Percentage |
|---|---|---|---|---|
| Surface Warfare Officer, Qualified (1110) | 11 | 10 | -1 | -9.1% |
| Surface Warfare Officer, Training (1160) | 5 | 8 | +3 | 37.5% |
| Medical Officer (2100) | 1 | 0 | -1 | -100.0% |
| Limited Duty Officer, Deck (6120) | 1 | 0 | -1 | -100.0% |
| Limited Duty Officer, Surface Engineer (6130) | 1 | 0 | -1 | -100.0% |
| Warrant Officer, Surface Operations Tech (7120) | 0 | 1 | +1 | 100.0% |
| Warrant Officer, Surface Engineer (7130) | 0 | 1 | +1 | 100.0% |
| Command, Master Chief Petty Officer (CMD) | 0 | 1 | +1 | 100.0% |
| Electrician's Mate (EM) | 5 | 7 | +2 | 40.0% |
| Electronic Technician (ET) | 11 | 14 | +3 | 27.3% |
| Fire Controlman (FC) | 39 | 36 | -3 | -7.7% |
| Gunner's Mate (GM) | 17 | 13 | -4 | -23.5% |
| Gas Turbine Tech, Electrical (GSE) | 7 | 6 | -1 | -14.3% |
| Gas Turbine Tech, Mechanical (GSM) | 19 | 14 | -5 | -26.3% |
| Hospital Corpsman (HM) | 2 | 3 | +1 | 50.0% |
| Hull Maintenance Tech (HT) | 4 | 3 | -1 | -25.0% |
| Interior Communications Electrician (IC) | 7 | 4 | -3 | -42.9% |
| Information Systems Tech (IT) | 14 | 12 | -2 | -14.3% |
| Culinary Specialist (CS) | 15 | 11 | -4 | -26.7% |
| Operations Specialist (OS) | 31 | 22 | -9 | -28.1% |
| Quartermaster (QM) | 5 | 6 | +1 | 20.0% |
| Ship's Serviceman (SH) | 7 | 4 | -3 | -42.9% |
| Storekeeper (SK) | 10 | 8 | -2 | -20.0% |
| Signalman (SM) | 6 | 1 | -5 | -83.3% |
| Seaman (SN) | 31 | 26 | -5 | -16.1% |
| SONAR Technician, Surface (STG) | 20 | 17 | -3 | -15.0% |
| Yeoman (YN) | 6 | 2 | -4 | -66.7% |

When the OME effects were compounded with the Smart Ship effects, it reduced the post-Smart Ship LCS seaframe RQMTS from 115 to 96. See Appendix R. OME produced an additional $\frac{115-96}{115} = 16.5\%$ reduction of the baseline RQMTS.

After the compounded savings from Smart Ship and OME were applied to the original seaframe baseline RQMTS, the reduced LCS manning level of 96 would be feasible against the threshold of 110, except that it still left very little room for module personnel. The reduced manning initiative effects are summarized in Figure 3.

Figure 3.     **LCS Seaframe RQMTS Before Paradigm Shift (From Refs 14 - 20)**

**Objective #1: Seaframe RQMTS**

| Department | Proxy | Business as usual | Reduced Manning Initiatives | |
|---|---|---|---|---|
| | | | SmartShip | Optimal Manning |
| Executive | MHC | 4 | 4 | 4 |
| Operations | MHC | 30 | 29 | 23 |
| Combat Systems | System specific | 29 | 29 | 24 |
| Engineering | FFG | 46 | 42 | 36 |
| Supply | MHC | 11 | 11 | 9 |
| Total | - | 120 | 115 | 96 |

Knowing that the modules will require in excess of 30-34 additional personnel, the seaframe RQMTS must be reduced even more. This required some "out of the box" paradigm shifts to further reduce the RQMTS. The paradigm shifts considered were the Composite Sailor, Technology Leverage and Workload Transfer concepts.

## C.     PARADIGM SHIFTS

"[OME] accomplished [the manpower] reductions by combining watch stations underway, by creating and relying on shore detachments to handle routine preventive maintenance and administrative requirements, and by developing and taking advantage of other efficiencies such as self-service laundry and food lines [Ref 9]".

Changes from "business as usual" can accelerate the advances supporting the minimal manning concept. The OME manpower reduction methods can be grouped into three categories of Composite Sailor, Technology Leverage and Workload Transfer. Composite Sailor capitalizes on the watch station combinations and extends that to rates that are similar in function and responsibility. Technology Leverage aggressively uses the Smart Ship technologies to further reduce the RQMTS. Similarly, Workload Transfer builds upon the supporting precepts of the PAPA detachment and ERM. Workload Transfer seeks to reduce the administrative and routine workload onboard the LCS. This concept also supports the Composite Sailor to allow the ship's commanding officer more control of the crew's time.

### 1.   Composite Sailor

The seaframe's post-reduction manning initiatives RQMTS was then analyzed for the effects of the Composite Sailor concept. The Composite Sailor RQMTS reductions are:

> OPS: QM (2)
>
> CS:  GUN/ORD OFF, STG (3)
>
> ENG: MPA, AUXO, EN (4), HT (2), MR
>       and GS (3)

See Appendix R for the detail listing of RQMTS affected by the Composite Sailor concept.

The Composite Sailor reduced the RQMTS from 96 to 78. Part of the reduction includes the GUN/ORD, MPA and

AUXILIARY officer positions. These are assumed covered by the senior FC, GM, GS and EN onboard respectively.

## 2.    Technology Leverage

From the Integrated Bridge System (IBS) to the self-service food lines, technology that supports manpower reductions already exists as evidenced by USS Yorktown's and USS Milius' successful completion of their experiments and the subsequent deployments.

Key technologies used in this study include:

1) Smart Ship technologies

2) Multi-modal consoles (an emerging technology)

3) Automated damage control devices including the automated mechanical and electrical isolation systems as well as the installed firefighting systems such as the CO2, AFFF and HALON firefighting systems.

The remaining RQMTS were analyzed for reductions effects from each of the technologies listed above. The Technology Leverage reductions àre:

OPS: QM, OS (5), BM (2), CTT and IT

CS:  STG (3), FC (4)

ENG: DCA OFF, EN (2), DC (2), GS (2)

SUPPLY: SK (2), CS (2)

## 3.    Workload Transfer (Ship to Shore)

Routine workload or routine maintenance was moved ashore to the shore infrastructure co-located with the LCS module personnel. By conducting the routine items ashore, more time was recapitalized by the crew, saving time and RQMTS onboard the LCS. Some of the routine items included those conducted by the EM, EN, FC, GM, and SK rates. The seaframe crew had the ability to "reach-back" to homeport or other technical supporting sites for assistance, thereby reducing the number of specialties RQMTS onboard the LCS.

Each RQMTS, after the Technology Leverage, was then analyzed for the effects of transferring workload ashore. The Workload Transfer concept reduced the following RQMTS:

CS: GM, FC

ENG: EM, EN

SUPPLY: SK.

## D. CORE CREW ANALYSIS

Figure 4 summarizes the analysis of the seaframe RQMTS as detailed in Appendix R. Table 14 below summarizes the seaframe manning.

Figure 4.     Effects of Paradigm Shifts on LCS Seaframe
Manning

## Effects of paradigm shifts

◆ Analyze for: *Composite Sailor • technology leverage • workload transfer*

| Dept | Business as usual | Reduced Manning Initiatives | | Paradigm Shifts | | |
|---|---|---|---|---|---|---|
| | | SmartShip | Optimal Manning | Composite Sailor | Tech Leverage | Workload transfer |
| Executive | 4 | 4 | 4 | 4 | 4 | 4 |
| Operations | 30 | 29 | 24 | 22 | 12 | 12 |
| Combat Systems | 29 | 29 | 24 | 20 | 13 | 11 |
| Engineering | 46 | 42 | 35 | 23 | 16 | 14 |
| Supply | 11 | 11 | 9 | 9 | 5 | 4 |
| *Total* | *120* | *115* | *96* | *78* | *50* | *45* |

Table 15.     LCS Seaframe Manning (Reduced)

| Department | Crew | | Core LCS Combat System | Qty | Manning |
|---|---|---|---|---|---|
| | | | 57 mm gun/.50 cal | 1 | 2 |
| Executive[a] | 4 | | RAM | 1 | 1 |
| Operations[b] | 12 | | Search radar | 1 | 2 |
| Combat Systems | 9 + 2[b] = 11 | ← | Surface decoy | 2 | 1 |
| Engineering | 14 | | Air decoy | 3 | |
| Supply | 4 | | Torpedo decoy launcher | 2 | 1 |
| *Total* | *43 + 2[b] = 45* | | Mine avoidance sonar | 1 | 2 |

a. Scaled proportionately to smaller crew size using MHC supply ratio

b. CIWS is not included in current Flight-0 LCS designs. Estimated manning level of 2

Of the 45 RQMTS, 15 are Condition III watchstanders, and the remainders are day-workers. Condition III has four watch stations: OOD, JOOD, TAO and ATAO. The watchstanders and recommended positions are summarized in Table 15.

Table 16.    **Seaframe Condition III Watch**

| Watch-stander | Condition III Watch |
|---|---|
| OPS OFF, CSO and CHENG | TAO |
| BM | OOD, JOOD |
| CTT | AIC/ASTAC/ATAO |
| GM | OOD, JOOD |
| OS | TAO, AIC/ASTAC/ATAO |
| STG | AIC/ASTAC/ATAO |

The seaframe RQMTS analysis suggested that a level of 45 RQMTS was possible for the seaframe within the threshold of 110 that must also accommodate a mission package crew.

Next, the analysis determined the individual module RQMTS as well as the total module RQMTS. The modules augment the seaframe with a specific warfare capability. With this added capability comes additional systems and manning. The next section presents the analysis of individual module's systems and their RQMTS.

## E.    MISSION PACKAGE CREW ANALYSIS

The mission package crew was based on the module RQMTS. The RQMTS was calculated using the same methodology as for seaframe. Using the legacy SMD data and an expert opinion, the module's baseline RQMTS (larger total) and reduced RQMTS (smaller total) was estimated and validated. With the exception of the aviation component, most of the module systems were emerging (i.e., SPARTAN, RMV and Periscope Detection). The RQMTS for these emerging systems

61

were estimated using the proxy methodology with legacy
data.   For example, the SPARTAN was a USV based upon the
RHIB seaframe and the RMV was assumed to be similar to the
legacy MNV onboard the MCM and MHC ships.

The module baseline RQMTS were estimated using the
optimization equation 7, 8 and 9.   The first, and perhaps
the biggest, module in the analysis is the mine warfare
(MIW) module.   The module's component systems and estimated
manning are itemized in Figure 5.

Figure 5.      **MIW Module RQMTS**

## MIW Module RQMTS

| System | Baseline RQMTS | Reduced | Comments |
|---|---|---|---|
| USV (1) <br> W/ MIW System(s) | 8 | 3 | 2 Operators/Maintainers <br> 1 – 6 Maintainer |
| VTUAV 1 set (3 UAVs) <br> COBRA (2) | | | NAVAIR/NPS study <br> Equipment Operators part of <br> Air Det |
| MH-60S (1) <br> OASIS Sys (2) <br> ALMDS (2) <br> ALQ-20A (2) <br> RAMICS (2) <br> AMNS (2) | 57 | 34 | |
| AN/WLD-1 RMV (2) <br> ALQ-20A (2) | 10 | 5 | 5 Operators/Maintainers <br> 0 – 5 Maintainer |
| Periscope det (1) | | | Covered by RMV operators |
| EOD Det or NSCT | 8 | 4 | Based on EOD det size |
| BPAUV (1 set) | 2 | 1 | 1 – 2 Operator/Maintainers <br> Covered by RMV operators |
| SCULPIN (1 set) | 2 | 1 | 1 – 2 Operator/Maintainers <br> Covered by RMV operators |
| MIW Mission C4 | 6 | 5 | 5 - 6 OINC & Support |
| Total Personnel | 93 | 53 | |

The baseline sum of the individual MIW systems was 93
RQMTS.   The biggest RQMTS driver was the aviation component
at 57 RQMTS which is over half of the entire module RQMTS.
When this sum of 93 was added to the seaframe RQMTS of 45,
the MIW focused LCS has 138 RQMTS which was more than the

threshold allows. Hence, further reduction must occur. Of the three approaches (Business As Usual, Reduced Manning Initiative and three Paradigm Shifts), only one was applicable here. That was the Composite Sailor paradigm shift.

The Composite Sailor allowed the combination of the Operator and Maintainer RQMTS as well as the suggested rate combinations suggested earlier in Table 5 (Suggested Rate Combination). Table 16 below summarized the suggested rate combinations for the modules.

Table 17.    **Suggested Rate Combination For Modules**

| Legacy Rate | LCS Rate |
|-------------|----------|
| BM, EN, MM | BM |
| EM, TM, STG | STG |
| SK, YN | SK |

Once all the RQMTS were analyzed for the effects of the Composite Sailor, the resulting reduced MIW module had 53 RQMTS. When added to the seaframe's reduced RQMTS, the MIW focused LCS has 98 RQMTS which was within the threshold of 110.

The same methodology was applied to the littoral anti-submarine (ASW) and surface warfare (SUW) modules. The principal differences between these modules and the MIW module are the manned helicopter, which is the MH-60R, and the two USVs. The modules baseline and reduced RQMTS are summarized in Figure 6 and 7.

Figure 6.        ASW Module RQMTS

## ASW Module RQMTS

| System | Baseline RQMTS | Reduced | Comments |
|---|---|---|---|
| USV (2)<br>W/ ASW System(2) | 10 | 5 | 3 Operators/Maintainers<br>2 – 7 Maintainer |
| VTUAV 1 set (3 UAVs)<br>MH-60R<br>Torpedo set<br>Sonar set<br>Sonobuoys set | 52 | 30 | NAVAIR/NPS study<br>Air Crew and Ordnanceman provided by Air Det |
| AN/WLD-1 RMV (2)<br>W/ ASW System(2) | 8 | 5 | 5 Operators/Maintainers<br>0 – 3 Maintainer |
| Periscope detection | | | Covered by RMV operators |
| ACES/EER/IEER/AEER family | 5 | 3 | 3 - 5 Oper/Maint |
| Torpedo Countermeasures | 3 | 1 | 1 - 3 STGs; Assumed covered by Seaframe Torpedo Countermeasures |
| ADS | 5 | 2 | 2 - 5 Operator/Maintainers |
| Towed Array (2) | 0 | | Assumed covered by Seaframe Torpedo Countermeasures |
| ASW Mission C4 | 6 | 5 | 5 - 6 OINC & Support |
| Total Personnel | 89 | 51 | |

Figure 7.        SUW Module RQMTS

## SUW Module RQMTS

| System | Baseline RQMTS | Reduced | Comments |
|---|---|---|---|
| USV w/EO/IR (2)<br>Gun package<br>Missile Package | 10 | 6 | 3 Operators/Maintainers<br>3 – 7 Maintainers<br>Includes 1-2 GMs; assumes seaframe cannot cover this |
| VTUAV w/EO/IR<br>1 set (3 UAVs)<br>Rocket/Gun/Missile set<br>MH-60R<br>EO/IR set<br>Gun/Rockets set<br>Hellfire set | 52 | 30 | NAVAIR/NPS study<br>Air Crew and Ordnanceman provided by Air Det |
| Netfires | | | Covered by mission C4 |
| Intermediate Caliber Gun Module (2) | 4 | | Assume 25mm bushmaster brought onboard |
| Non-Lethal Weapon (2) | 0! | | TBD |
| SUW Mission C4 | 6 | | 6 OINC & Support |
| Total Personnel | 72 | 45 | |

After all the module baselines were reduced, the LCS modules had RQMTS ranging from 45 in the SUW to the large MIW of 53. The maximum RQMTS for a focused mission LCS is 98, and the minimum RQMTS was 90.

## F.    LCS MODULE FORCE ANALYSIS

The Navy plans to procure 56 LCS seaframes, 47 MIW, 34 ASW and 30 SUW FMPs (total of 111 FMPs). The FMPs do not include the 8 FMPs procured during the development phase. It is assumed that these 8 additional FMPs are 3 MIW, 3 ASW and 2 SUW FMPs. When these eight additional FMPs are added with the 111, the sum is 119 FMPs (50 MIW, 37 ASW and 32 SUW). However, not all of the seaframes and FMPs will be deployable at any given time. To assign RQMTS to each FMP, even while not deployed, would be an inefficient use of critical human capital. A better way to assign manpower is by skills vice an entire module. This will allow greater flexibility in manpower assignment and reduce the overall LCS force RQMTS.

Under the "Business As Usual" approach, the LCS force would be a relatively large "pre-packaged" force. "Pre-packaged" means the traditional one-crew one-ship (or in this case, one-module) assignment. The converse is the "flexed" concept where the crew is deployed as needed regardless of the module. Looking ahead to where 56 seaframes and 119 FMP modules are planned, the estimated LCS manpower force size, under the "pre-packaged" approach would be:

$$56 \ seaframes * 45 \ RQMTS = 2520 \ RQMTS$$
$$50 \ MIW \ Modules * 53 \ RQMTS = 2650 \ RQMTS$$
$$37 \ ASW \ Modules * 51 \ RQMTS = 1887 \ RQMTS$$
$$32 \ SUW \ Modules * 45 \ RQMTS = 1440 \ RQMTS$$

$$Total \ LCS \ Force = 2520 + 2650 + 1887 + 1440 = 8497 \ RQMTS$$

8497 RQMTS was a relatively large force size, and this large LCS force size could potentially under-utilize talented human capital. Therefore, more efficient force utilization was assumed under the "flexed" concept.

Lessons learned from Smart Ship and OME include changes in watchstanding philosophies to reduce the workload and, ultimately, reduce manning. Smart Ship's innovative core/flex watchstanding philosophies permitted the ship to meet the spirit of the ROC/POE requirements while improving quality of life and better personnel management. The core/flex watch concept was again used onboard the USS Milius for OME. Similarly, the LCS module force will be organized and "flexed" to meet operational requirements. The module personnel are organized into twelve (12) different detachments of generalists and specialists. Table 17 summarized the different detachments.

Table 18.    **LCS Module Force Flexed Detachments**

| Generalists |
|---|
| **RMV Support** |
| **USV Support** |
| **Air Det Support** |

| Specialists | |
|---|---|
| **FMP Mission C4** | |
| **USV Oper** | |
| **USV Weapons** | |
| **RMV Operator** | |
| **MIW Specialitsts** | |
| | BPAUV |
| | SCULPIN |
| | EOD |
| **ASW Specialist** | |
| ACES/EER/IEER/AEER Family | |
| | Torpedo CM |
| | ADS |
| **SUW Specialist** | |
| **MH-60S & UAV Oper** | |
| **MH-60R & UAV Oper** | |

The detachments were similar to the Smart Ship "flexed" watchstanders who were called upon when they were needed. When the detachments were needed to conduct a particular littoral warfare operation, they were deployed with the modules to the seaframe or theater.

However, the number of deployable modules was much less than 119. Only 25% of the 56 seaframes will be deployable at any given time. Suppose there are 15 deployable seaframe, which is approximately 25% of the 56 seaframes planned, then the number of modules required will also be about 25% of the 119 planned. To properly determine the number of MIW, ASW and SUW modules required, first calculate the ratio of each module against the total modules planned.

$$\text{MIW modules}: \frac{50}{119} = 42\%$$

ASW modules: $\dfrac{37}{119} = 31\%$

SUW modules: $\dfrac{32}{119} = 27\%$

Next, multiply each ratio by the number of deployable seaframes (in this case 15) to determine the number of FMP modules required.

$$\text{MIW modules}: 42\% * 15\ Seaframes = 13.4 \approx 13 \quad MIW\ Modules$$

$$\text{ASW modules}: 31\% * 15\ Seaframes = 9.9 \approx 10 \quad ASW\ Modules$$

$$\text{SUW modules}: 27\% * 15\ Seaframes = 8.6 \approx 9 \quad SUW\ Modules$$

Therefore, 32 modules are required to support 15 deployable seaframes. The "pre-packaged" deployable LCS force for the 15 seaframes and 32 modules would have 2279 RQMTS, of which 1604 would be required for the FMPs.

$$15\ seaframes * 45\ RQMTS = 675\ RQMTS$$
$$13\ MIW\ Modules * 53\ RQMTS = 689\ RQMTS$$
$$10\ ASW\ Modules * 51\ RQMTS = 510\ RQMTS$$
$$9\ SUW\ Modules * 45\ RQMTS = 405\ RQMTS$$

$$Total\ Deployable\ LCS\ Force = 675 + 689 + 510 + 405 = 2279\ RQMTS$$

The "flexed" deployable LCS module force would only consist of module personnel. The seaframe RQMTS must be "pre-packaged" with the seaframe, but the module RQMTS are more flexible because they are shore-based until needed. Ashore, the module force is organized into the 12 detachments seen earlier in Table 17. Appendix V summarizes the "flexed" detachments, supported warfare and the quantity of each rate within the detachment. If a particular rate supports at least two warfare areas, then it is considered a generalist. Otherwise, it is a specialist.

To calculate the total "flexed" RQMTS, the optimization equation 11 was used.

$$\text{Total "flexed" module RQMTS} = \sum_{d=6}^{17}\sum_{c=7}^{9}\left(G_d N_{c=6} X_d + S_d N_c X_d\right) \qquad \text{(equation 11)}$$

For example, to estimate the "flexed" RQMTS for the RMV Support detachments, first determine the number of warfare areas supported. In this case, there are two, the MIW and ASW warfare, which makes it a generalist. Therefore, the "flexed" RQMTS for this detachment is the product of the detachment size and the number of seaframes.

$$\text{RMV Support "flexed" RQMTS} = G_{d=11} N_{c=6} X_{d=11} = 1*15*3 = 45 \quad RQMTS$$

By applying this calculation and methodology to all twelve detachments across the three littoral warfare areas, the 32 total "flexed" modules (13 ASW, 10 MIW, 9 SUW) have 1151 RQMTS, as compared to 1604 RQMTS when "pre-packaged". Table 18 summarized the comparison of the two manpower force structures.

Table 19.   **Deployable Module Force Structure Comparison**

| | With Air Det | W/o Air Det | Air Det |
|---|---|---|---|
| Pre-packaged, total | 1604 | 592 | 1012 |
| Flexed, total | 1151 | 493 | 658 |
| Personnel Saving | 453 | 99 | |
| Reduction | 71.8% | 83.3% | |
| Savings | 28.2% | 16.7% | |
| Cost @ $60K per person ($M) | $      96.2 | $      35.5 | |
| Savings @ $60K personnel cost ($M) | $      69.1 | $      29.6 | |

"Flexed" option has 453 fewer RQMTS than the 1604 "pre-packaged" RQMTS. In the end, the savings is approximately $27.2M per deployment cycle. This estimate used the conservative personnel cost of $60K per RQMT. By multiplying the savings and the deployment rotational factor of 3 to 4, the potential savings range from $80M to $110M.

# IX. SUMMARY

The "business as usual" approach estimated the RQMTS for a focused mission LCS from 195 to 215. Of these numbers, the seaframe has a baseline RQMTS of 120 and the MIW, ASW and SUW modules have 95, 90 and 75 RQMTS respectively. These requirements clearly exceed the LCS total RQMTS of 110.

Applying the lessons learned and savings gained from reduced manning initiatives like Smart Ship and Fleet Optimal Manning Experiments (OME) help, but not enough to meet the targeted manning levels set for LCS. Smart Ship reduced the seaframe baseline RQMTS by 4.2% or from 120 RQMTS to 115; additionally, OME's overall savings of 15.8% reduced that even further to 96. The requirements are within the threshold of 110, but does not include the module RQMTS. More reduction measures are needed to accommodate the module RQMTS.

Additional measures explored were paradigm shifts in policy and operations called the Composite Sailor, Technology Leverage and Workload Transfer concepts. The Composite Sailor reduced the seaframe RQMTS an additional 15.0% down to 78 RQMTS; Technology Leverage yielded the largest reduction at 23.3% reducing the seaframe RQMTS to 50; and Workload Transfer produced the final 4.2% reduction to achieve the minimal manning of 45 RQMTS.

The module baseline RQMTS were reduced using only the paradigm shift Composite Sailor concept. The MIW module RQMTS was reduced by 43% from 93 to 53 RQMTS; the ASW module was reduced by 42.7% from 89 to 51; and the SUW module was reduced by 37.5% from 72 to 45.

Combining the reduced seaframe and module RQMTS, the RQMTS for a focused mission LCS was reduced from the average values of 207 to 95. The reduced seaframe RQMTS was 45 with the MIW, ASW and SUW module RQMTS at 53, 51 and 45 respectively. Therefore, the MIW focused LCS has 98 RQMTS; ASW focused LCS has 96 RQMTS; and SUW focused LCS has 90 RQMTS. These requirements are within the LCS total RQMTS threshold of 110, and the first objective appeared feasible.

Additionally, the study's second objective looked at the LCS force-wide implications of the results from the first objective. The LCS force was expected to have 56 seaframes and 119 FMP modules. The estimated total seaframe RQMTS was 2,520 for the fleet of 56 seaframes. With the estimated module breakout of 50 MIW, 37 ASW and 32 SUW modules, the estimated total module RQMTS was 5977. Therefore, the estimated total LCS force had 8,497 RQMTS.

By de-linking the systems and RQMTS from the different modules, a more efficient way to manage the module personnel is possible. By organizing the module personnel into 12 detachments, the LCS module force could be deployed with greater flexibility and reduced its RQMTS. Using the optimization equations to minimize the module force total RQMTS, the "flexed" concept has proven that it can produce a savings of ~28% over the "pre-packaged" concept for, for example, 15 seaframes with 32 modules. In this example, the LCS module force has 1,604 RQMTS under the "pre-packaged" concept, and it has 1151 RQMTS under the "Flexed" concept. The difference is 453 RQMTS. This means, at a conservative cost of $60K per sailor, the potential saving is ~$27M.   When the rotation factor of 3-4 is considered, the saving is ~$80M to ~$110M per deployment cycle.   By flexing the LCS module force, the Navy can gain, on average, 25% to 30% of its LCS module manpower cost.   This translates into a potential monetary savings of $80M to $110M.

This is one of the ways of "harvesting efficiencies to invest in the Navy of the future [Ref 22]".

THIS PAGE INTENTIONALLY LEFT BLANK

# X. CONCLUSIONS AND RECOMMENDATIONS

## A.    CONCLUSIONS

This thesis supported the minimally manned concept for the LCS seaframe and FMP modules.  The top down manpower analysis used SMDs for legacy ships with "business as usual" approach and yielded a focus mission LCS with an average manning of approximately 207.   This estimate, though large, was used as the RQMTS baseline estimate. When reducing the RQMTS baseline, previous manning reduction initiatives like Smart Ship and OME are not enough.   The Navy can have minimally manned LCS seaframes and FMP modules if, and only if, the suggested paradigm shifts of Composite Sailor, Technology Leverage and Workload Transfer are pursued.   The pursuit could yield an LCS seaframe with 45 RQMTS and the mission-package RQMTS of 45 to 53.   The result is a focused mission LCS that meets the threshold limit.

However, the means to reduce the total RQMTS for a focused mission LCS to 75 or less was not readily identifiable.

Additionally, this study has also demonstrated that a "flexed" concept of module personnel management could potentially yield manpower annual cost savings of 25% to 30% or roughly $80M to $110M over the one-crew per module or "pre-packaged" concept.

## B.    RECOMMENDATIONS

The minimally manned LCS seaframe and modules can be realized if, and only if, the assumed paradigm shifts with the supporting technologies are pursued. The Smart Ship technologies have proven they can advance changes in policy and operations especially in the areas of ship operation, training, maintenance and administrative support.

Recommendation: Pursue the Composite Sailor, Technology Leverage, and Workload Transfer paradigm shifts as well as advancing the technologies assumed in this study. The technologies appear readily available to support the minimal manning concept intended for LCS.

Recommendation: The Composite Sailor paradigm shift requires the synergy of the BM, CTT, DC, EN, ET, GS, HT, MM, MR, OS, QM, STG and TM rates. Examine the KSAs of these rates to determine the Composite Sailor's actual requirements for the BM (combination of BM, EN, MM and QM), ET (combination of CTT and ET), DC (combination of DC, HT and MR), EN/GS and STG/TM rates that have been suggested for the LCS.

Recommendation: Conduct a study to determine the optimal training curriculum for the above rates. A series of schools training time and KSA requirements data will support an optimized training pipeline to train these personnel effectively and efficiently to support the minimal manning concept. Minimal manning onboard LCS will require the ability of this training path to respond to manning shortfalls.

Recommendation: Combine watch-station requirements of Operator and Maintainer into a single Operator/Maintainer requirement to facilitate increased personnel flexibility. This will greatly support flexed organizations like the

Smart Ship Core/Flex watch philosophy as well as the "flexed" module force concept.

Recommendation: Pursue the Integrated Bridge System (IBS) and Voyage Management System (VMS). Increased digital chart coverage could add to the feasibility of the IBS/VMS system. Use the Integrated Bridge System (IBS) along with the Voyage Management System (VMS) more liberally. Supporting this is the recommendation to increase the coverage provided by digital/electronic charts to reduce the time consuming task of chart preparations and management. When combined with other technologies such as bow thrusters, the IBS/VMS could reduce the ship control requirements down to just a few personnel unlike the crowded legacy ship control requirements.

Recommendation: Pursue the Integrated Condition Assessment System (ICAS) and Machinery Control System (MCS) with the improved On-Board Trainer (OBT). Change philosophy to allow ship control and/or operations control personnel to operate and configure ship machinery as required to support operations and changing tactical requirements.

Recommendation: Advance the integrated sensor and communications multi-modal consoles (MMC) and the integrated weapons and decoy Weapons Control Consoles (WCC). The MMC assumes all communication and sensors are integrated into a single station for greater effectiveness. The WCC assumes the control functions of the 57MM, CIWS, RAM, Torpedo Decoy Launcher, Air Decoy Launcher and TACTAS combat systems can be integrated into a single location. These systems can significantly add to the watch station reductions, and manpower reduction, in the Combat Information Center (CIC). More importantly it gives the decision-maker the ability to access all of the ship's assets to make timely and informed decisions.

Recommendation: Pursue a UV launch and recovery system that is similar to an overhead rail system with automated winches and controls operable by only one person. Use Visby Swedish Corvette as a model.

Recommendation: Pursue automation technology. The SONAR can only be supported by two Operator/Maintainers if the log-keeping is automated. Similar to the flight data recorders onboard commercial aircrafts, the log-keeping of the SONAR equipment can be automated. This will allow a more accurate data storage and facilitate data for follow-on analysis. Recommend pursuing this technology.

Recommendation: Operate with unmanned engineering spaces during Condition III steaming. This will leverage the technology to allow the engineers more control of their time. Personnel will only be required for start-ups, shutdowns and condition-based maintenance requirements. The spaces do not have to be manned after start-up and shut-down evolutions. During Condition I, engineering spaces will only require a monitor in the critical engineering spaces (i.e., main engineroom and electrical generation rooms) to respond and stabilize from casualties. Operating in this manner will also permit bridge and CIC watchstanders to operate the engineering plant in direct support of mission readiness without delay.

Recommendation: Operate with reduced Damage Control party requirements and increase reliance on technology/automation. The Rapid Response Team (RRT), or minimum fire party, requires a scene leader, investigators, nozzleman and hoseman. Employ the RRT initially and augment as required.

Primary DCC should be located near machinery controls which is assumed to be in CCS, and secondary should be located near the decision makers either in the pilot house or CIC. In this case, recommend secondary CCS in the pilot house to facilitate greater control and less workload increase in CIC.

Recommendation: Organize the shore infrastructure to support the reduced maintenance onboard the LCS using concepts similar to a "pit stop." Reduce the workload onboard the seaframe. Determine the workload of 45 personnel, and remove the remainder if possible. Conduct as much routine and large maintenance requirements ashore as possible. Both critical and routine spares and parts need to be readily available to sustain the LCS operational availability and reliability.

Recommendation: Assign future LCS personnel to an operational LCS seaframe for indoctrination. With a limited indoctrination period, every LCS sailor must be afforded the opportunity to get familiar with an LCS for a short period of time prior to assignment to either the LCS or the modules. With the largest combined manpower RQMT of 98, a focused LCS can accommodate additional personnel onboard for training and indoctrination with minimal impact on the core crew accommodations. A trainer would be required to manage the training curriculum.

In conclusion, personnel assigned to LCS must be trained and qualified to the fullest extent possible. There is very limited flexibility in the LCS force structure to support gaps beyond a reasonable length of time. If a sailor is unable to fulfill their function onboard LCS, a replacement must be ready and available for immediate relief. Otherwise, mission readiness will quickly become an adverse factor.

# XI. FUTURE STUDY

During the operation of LCS Flight 0 ships, data will be collected on human performance, incidence of human errors and near misses, accidents and mishaps, situations of excessive workload, and habitability/quality-of-life problems. These data will be used in Flight I system design and development to improve human-machine interfaces, and ship and system design for operability, maintainability, supportability, survivability, usability and safety [Ref 1].

## A. FATIGUE STUDY ON LCS FLIGHT "0"

A key element to sustain the minimal manning concept is fully functioning sailor. Personnel effectiveness is highly dependent upon the amount and quality of sleep. Sleep is a force enabler, and a regimented sleeping program to allow optimal sleep will prove vital to enable the crew to perform at the peak effectiveness. For this study, the critical personnel (i.e., bridge and combat information center watchstanders) predicted effectiveness goal was assumed to be 80% with the threshold at 65%.

Table 20.    **Critical Personnel Effectiveness (Hursh FAST & SAFTE model)**

|  | Threshold | Goal |
|---|---|---|
| Personnel Effectiveness Level | 80% | 95% |

On average, to be totally effective, a sailor requires 7-9 hours of moderate to excellent quality sleep. If the sailor is only getting moderate quality sleep, effectiveness will decline. Moderate sleep is defined as that which is almost undisturbed with some tossing and turning. Moderate to excellent sleep will help the sailors sustain, and even regain, their effectiveness. Excellent sleep is defined as undisturbed sleep where all sleep stages, including rapid eye movement (REM), can occur. A regimented sleep program is vital to sustain the sailor's performance, especially in situations of reduced manning.

When a sailor is getting moderate to excellent sleep before getting underway, their average peak effectiveness during waking hours is 95%-99%. Once underway and getting only moderate sleep from 2200-0600, the same individual's average effectiveness drops down to 55%-60%. See Figure 7.

Figure 8.     **Typical Personnel Effectiveness After Underway (From FAST Program)**

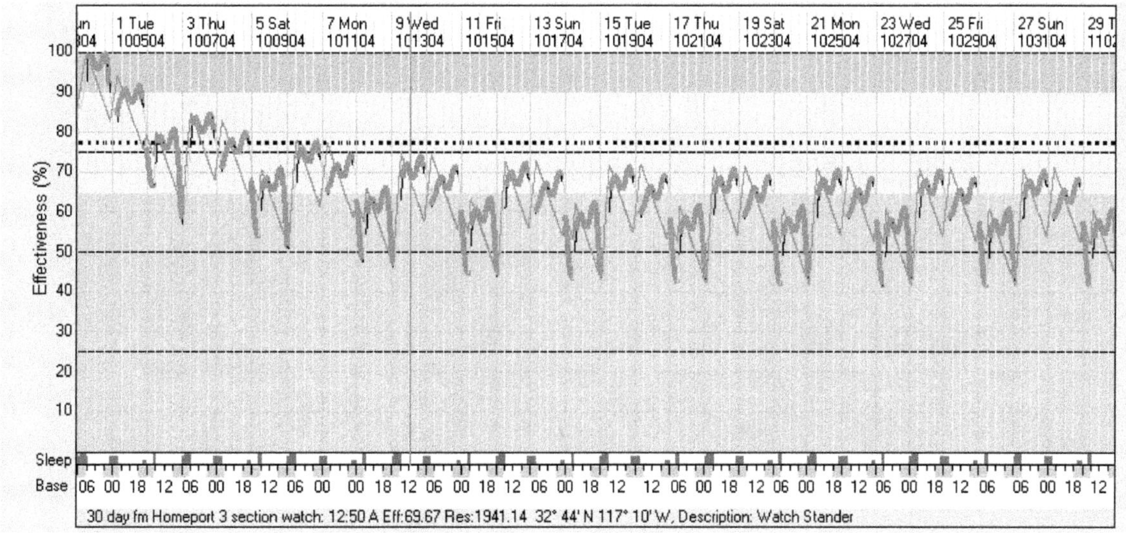

The effectiveness plot reaches the steady state of about 60% after 10 days underway from port. During the steady state, the biggest degradation in effectiveness occurs during the watch hours of midnight-0400 and 2000-2400. During these watches the personal effectiveness level is dangerously low at around 50%.

Overall, this notional daily routine is considered marginal (average effectiveness is 66%) if safe personnel effectiveness level is assumed 65% or above. A regimented sleep program will be required to improve personnel effectiveness to, for example, 75%. This is especially important for minimally manned ships like LCS.

The recommended sleep regiment to obtain 75% personnel effectiveness level is the same from 2200-0600. However, this would require that every sleeping moment be excellent sleep quality. It is also recommended that naps be included into the daily routine from 1200-1300. A 45 to 60 minute nap will improve the original effectiveness from 66% to 70%. Thirty minute naps only improved the original effectiveness by 2%.

Figure 9.          **Personnel Effectiveness After Underway (With Auto Sleep) (From FAST Program)**

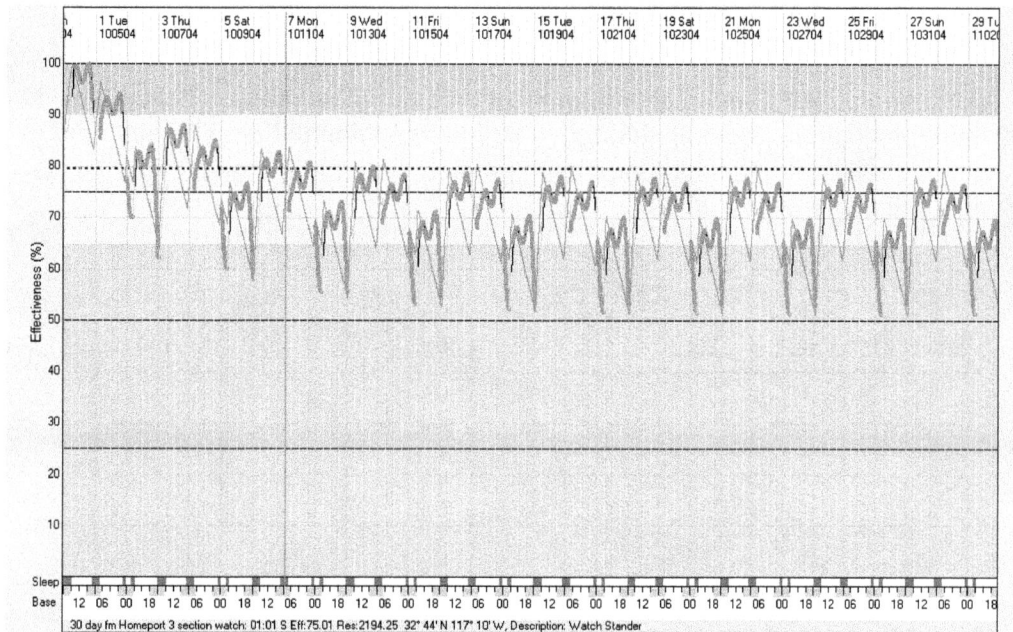

The topic of sleep and fatigue is a growing concern, and the fatigue study has the potential to add value to the understanding crew requirements especially onboard a minimally manned ship like the LCS.


## B.   TASK ANALYSIS ON LCS FLIGHT "0"

One of the key elements used in the current manpower requirements determination process is the workload measured in hours.  The workload data was not available to support this manpower study.   However, workload data can be gathered after the delivery of the two LCS Flight 0 ships.

A future study to gather the workload data, in hours, by conducting on-site data collection would be useful.  The data will then be used to validate manpower estimates from this study and improve the manning requirements for LCS Flight I ships.

84

## C.    LCS MANPOWER COST BENEFIT ANALYSIS

Although this study suggested ways to save manpower costs, the actual cost to pursue the suggested paradigm shifts was not studied. The cost benefit analysis (CBA) of this pursuit would also add to the feasibility of the minimal manning concept as well as predict a more accurate cost savings. The CBA study is expected to produce better (more) savings than the conservative $60K personnel cost used in this study.

THIS PAGE INTENTIONALLY LEFT BLANK

# APPENDIX A. NOTIONAL PROJECTED OPERATIONAL ENVIRONMENT

1.    The LCS XX Class littoral combat ship's mission is to operate offensively in a high density, multi-threat environment as an integral member of a Carrier Strike Group, Surface Action Group or Expeditionary Strike Group. In addition, the LCS XX provides its own limited Air Defense (AD), limited Surface Warfare (SUW), limited Mine Warfare (MIW) and Undersea Warfare (USW) self-defense, and can effectively provide some local subsurface and surface area protection to the Group or Force.

2.    The most demanding operating environment anticipated for the LCS XX Class is forward deployed wartime operations within the littoral battlespace in cooperation with designated joint/allied forces, including operations involving coordination of land and sea-based aviation. These operations are frequently characterized by confined and congested water and air space occupied by friends, adversaries, and neutrals -- making rapid identification and efficient coordination profoundly difficult. In this environment, adversaries can concentrate and layer their defenses.

3.    Peacetime forward operations in littoral areas are also very demanding. In an era characterized by the proliferation of sophisticated weaponry, coupled with the advance of the global war on terrorism, the LCS XX Class can anticipate surprise attack by submarines, coastal missiles, mines, sea-skimming cruise missiles, and theater ballistic missiles, terrorist and other asymmetrical threats. A substantial percentage of operations will be conducted within the highly variable littoral.

4.    LCS XX is capable of performing all assigned primary mission areas simultaneously while maintaining Readiness Condition I, II, III (wartime/forward deployment cruising readiness), IV (peacetime training underway operations) or V (in port training and maintenance).

5.    In an environment in which repair facilities are limited, the ability of the Carrier/ Expeditionary Strike Group and LCS XX Class ship to be self-sufficient is of paramount importance. While operating within a Strike Group, the LCS XX may be called upon, on an infrequent basis, to provide repair assistance to other units. This assistance is provided by existing ship's force personnel,

specifically, by Sailors in billets requiring Journeyman-level skills. Battle Force Intermediate Maintenance Activity (BFIMA) NECs, proficiency-based Journeyman level NECs attained at Fleet Maintenance Activities, are assigned to enhance the capabilities of the Carrier/Expeditionary Strike Group and own unit to be self-sufficient. Specific BFIMA NECs assignments follow:

| RATING | SKILL AREA | NEC |
|--------|-----------|-----|
| BM | Rigger/Weight Tester | BM-0120 |
| EN | Valve Repair Tech | MM-4540 |
| EN | Diesel Engine Repair Tech | EN-4340 |
| GSM | Hydraulics Repair Tech | MM-4541 |
| GSM | Pump Repair Tech | MM-4222 |
| GSM | Gas Turbine Repair Tech | GS-4140 |
| EN | A/C & R Tech | MM-4223 |
| EM | Outside Electrical Repair Tech | EM-4651 |
| IC | Interior Communications Tech | IC-4781 |
| ET | Module Test and Repair (2M) Tech | ET-1591 |

# APPENDIX B. NOTIONAL REQUIRED OPERATIONAL CAPABILITY

1.     The LCS XX Class ship's mission is to operate offensively in a high-density multi-threat environment as an integral member of a Carrier Strike Group, Surface Action Group or Expeditionary Strike Group.     In addition it provides its own limited Air Defense (AD), limited Surface Warfare (SUW) and Undersea Warfare (USW) self-defense and can effectively provide some local area protection to the Force, Group or other military shipping against subsurface and surface threats.  Accordingly, the following primary and secondary warfare mission areas are assigned:

P = Primary        PF = Primary with FMP        S = Secondary

| LCS XX CLASS | | | | | | | | | | | | |
|---|---|---|---|---|---|---|---|---|---|---|---|---|
| AAW | AMW | SUW | ASW | CCC | C$^2$W | FSO | INT | LOG | MIW | MOB | MOS | NCO |
| S | S | PF | PF | P | P | S | S | S | PF | P | P | S |

2.     The LCS XX is not capable of providing facilities for an embarked warfare commander and staff.

3.     Required Operational Capabilities (ROCs) are reported under readiness conditions having major significance in determining the unit's total manpower requirements.  The following summarizes conditions covered:

## Condition I:  Battle Readiness

While in Condition I (Battle Readiness), the ship shall be capable of meeting the following criteria: able to perform all offensive and defensive functions simultaneously; able to keep all installed systems manned and operating for maximum effectiveness; required to accomplish only minimal maintenance - that routinely associated with watch standing and urgent repairs.  For the LCS XX, this condition means self-defense measures are being performed.  Evolutions such as replenishment, law enforcement or helo operations are not appropriate unless the evolution stations are co-manned by personnel from other battle stations.  The maximum expected continuous crew endurance for Condition I is 24 hours.

## Condition II: Modified Battle Readiness

Condition II is Condition I Battle Readiness modified to meet particular imminent threats that are situation-dependent. As such, Condition II is a subset of Condition I that stands up particular Condition I capabilities at the discretion of the task force or group commander, or commanding officer. While in Condition II, the ship shall be capable of meeting the following criteria: able to simultaneously perform those offensive and defensive functions necessary to counter specific imminent, limited threats; able to keep required operational systems continuously manned and operating; able to perform other command and control functions relevant to the threat which are not required to be accomplished simultaneously; able to accomplish urgent underway Planned Maintenance and support functions. The maximum expected continuous duration for Condition II is 10 days, with a minimum of 4 to 6 hours of rest provided per man per day. Since scenarios can't be fixed in advance for all foreseeable combinations of circumstances other than full general quarters, a Condition II column is not portrayed in the table of ROCs.

## Condition III: Wartime/Increased Tension/Forward Deployed Cruising Readiness

Reduced defensive systems are manned to a level sufficient to counter pop-up threats. While in Condition III, the ship shall be capable of meeting the following criteria: able to keep installed systems manned and operating as necessary to conform with prescribed ROCs; able to accomplish all normal underway maintenance, support and administrative functions. To determine manpower requirements, the minimum expected crew endurance for Condition III is 60 days, with opportunity for 8 hours of rest provided per man per day.

## Condition IV: Training Cruising Readiness

While in Condition IV, the ship shall be capable of meeting the following criteria: able to keep installed systems manned and operating only to the extent necessary for safe and effective ship control, propulsion and security; able to accomplish all normal underway maintenance, support and administrative functions. Maximum advantage is taken of training and exercise opportunities. Expected endurance is not constrained by personnel. Ability to immediately change readiness posture to Condition I, II or III is expected.

## Condition V:  In port Readiness

Designated maintenance and training period.  While in Condition V, the ship shall be capable of meeting the following criteria: able to keep installed systems manned and operating to the extent necessary for effective operation as dictated by the existing situation; able to man watch stations as required to provide adequate security; able at all times to meet anticipated in-port emergencies and to perform in-port functions as prescribed by unit ROCs; able to accomplish all required maintenance, support, and administrative functions. Maximum advantage is taken of training and exercise opportunities.  Subject to the foregoing requirements the crew will be provided maximum opportunity for rest, leave and liberty.


4.   ROC symbols are used to specify the desired level of achievement of readiness or other work for or during a particular readiness condition.  Readiness normally applies to watches and/or evolutions, while other work refers to non-watch activity such as performing maintenance or running the galley.

### CAPABILITIES

"F" =      "Full"  The capability is to be fully achieved.  For operational functions (watches), this means that installed equipment or systems will be fully manned to design capability.  For support functions, sufficient manning is provided to ensure effective accomplishment of all included tasks.  The achievement is to be sustained for the duration of the condition unless modified by an "A" or "E."

"L" =      "Limited"  The capability is to be only partially realized.  (Note: "P" for "Partial" is no longer a symbol.).  Even though only limited capability is realized, it is to be sustained for the duration of the condition unless modified by an "A" or "E."  A limiting statement specifying the limitation must support every "L".

### MODIFIERS

"A" =      "Augmentation"  The capability is to be either fully or partially achieved for a **limited time** during the condition.  The capability is achieved by using off-watch or off-duty personnel to achieve the required degree of capability.  This symbol is always associated with an "F" or "L" and establishes a requirement for personnel to be trained, available and on call to augment existing watch stations as required.

"E" =      "Special Team"  The capability is to be either fully or partially achieved for a **limited time** during the condition.  The capability is achieved by using off-watch special teams or details.  This symbol is always associated with an "F" or "L" and denotes a capability that does not require continuous watch manning.  Teams and details as set may either supplement or replace all or part of the existing watch organization.  Man overboard and replenishment details are two examples.

| MODIFIER | CAPABILITY | |
| :---: | :---: | :---: |
| | FULL | LIMITED |
| None | Manned to design capacity for duration of condition | Manned to less than design capacity for duration of condition |
| A | Temporarily manned to design capacity using off-watch personnel | Temporarily manned to less than design capacity using off-watch personnel |
| E | Temporarily manned to design capacity using a special team | Temporarily manned to less than design capacity using a special team |

**Ship's Company and External Personnel Resources.** Normally, using an "A" or an "E" requires no embellishing statement as their meanings are predefined. However, in the case of the FFG as well as other classes that routinely embark external resources, the meaning may not be clear as to whether ship's company or the external resource should provide the augmentation.

This ROC/POE instruction shows:

➢ If the resource is ship's company, no elaboration or statement is provided.
➢ If the resource is external for "F," a Note is added to the ROC stating the resource.
➢ If the resource is external for "L," the resource is added to the capability limiting statement.

# REQUIRED OPERATIONAL CAPABILITIES

| | LCS XXCLASS | I | III | IV | V |
|---|---|---|---|---|---|
| **ANTI-AIR WARFARE (AAW)** | | | | | |
| **AAW 1** | **PROVIDE AIR DEFENSE INDEPENDENTLY OR IN COOPERATION WITH OTHER FORCES.** | | | | |
| AAW 1.2 | Conduct air self-defense using missile, gun, electronic or physical systems (e.g., chaff, flares). NOTE: No missile capabilities. III(L) - Man MK 92 FCS and 76 mm mount (without magazine crew). CIWS operated by WCC Operator. IV, V(L) - Plan and train. | F | L | L | L |
| AAW 1.3 | Coordinate air defense planning and act as AAW Commander (AAWC) for joint/BG/convoy/expeditionary/ amphibious/replenishment operations. NOTE: Functioning as AAWC may limit capabilities in other primary warfare areas. I, III(L) - Capable of functioning as AAWC for a limited duration in emergent situations for a small area/group operations only. IV, V(L) - Plan and train. | L | L | L | L |
| AAW 1.7 | Engage air targets during joint/group operations. NOTE: No missile capabilities. III(L) - Man MK 92 FCS and 76mm mount (without magazine crew). CIWS operated by WCC Operator. IV, V(L) - Plan and train. | F | L | L | L |
| AAW 1.9 | Plan/direct engagement of targets during group operations in cooperation with naval/joint/combined forces. NOTE: Plan/direct engagement of targets of a small area/ group operations may limit capabilities in other primary warfare areas. I, III(L) – Capable of functioning as AAWC for a limited duration in emergent situations for a small area/group operations only. IV, V(L) - Plan and train. | L | L | L | L |

| LCS XXCLASS | | I | III | IV | V |
|---|---|---|---|---|---|
| **AAW 6** | **DETECT, IDENTIFY AND TRACK AIR TARGETS.** | | | | |
| AAW 6.1 | Measure aircraft altitude by fade chart. | F | F | F | L |
| | V(L) - Plan and train. | | | | |
| AAW 6.2 | Recognize by sight friendly and enemy aircraft. | F | L | L | |
| | III, IV(L) – Capability provided by bridge watch team and aft lookout. | | | | |
| AAW 6.3 | Maintain an accurate air plot. | F | F | F | L |
| | V(L) - Plan and train. | | | | |
| AAW 6.4 | Measure aircraft altitude by radar. | F | F | F | |
| AAW 6.5 | Detect, identify and track air targets with radar and/or cooperative sensors. | F | F | F | |
| AAW 6.6 | Acquire and track air targets with Gunfire Control Systems/Missile Fire Control Systems (GFCS/MFCS). | F | F | F/A | L |
| | NOTE: Missile Fire Control System not functional. | | | | |
| | V(L) - Plan and train. | | | | |
| AAW 6.13 | Identify air targets as friendly/non-friendly using transponder interrogation equipment. | F | F | F | L |
| | V(L) – Plan and train. | | | | |
| **AAW 9** | **ENGAGE AIRBORNE THREATS USING SURFACE-TO-AIR ARMAMENT.** | | | | |
| AAW 9.4 | Engage low/medium altitude airborne threats with gunfire. | F | L | L | L |
| | III(L) - Man MK 92 FCS and 76 mm mount (without magazine crew). CIWS operated by WCC Operator. | | | | |
| | IV, V(L) - Plan and train. | | | | |
| AAW 9.5 | Engage airborne threats using installed anti-air weapons. | F | L | L | L |
| | NOTE: No missile capabilities. | | | | |
| | III(L) - Man MK 92 FCS and 76 mm mount (without magazine crew). CIWS operated by WCC Operator. | | | | |
| | IV, V(L) - Plan and train. | | | | |
| AAW 9.6 | Engage airborne threats utilizing soft-kill weapons systems (i.e., chaff/decoys). | F | L | L | L |
| | III(L) – MK 50 DLS not manned. | | | | |
| | IV, V(L) - Plan and train. | | | | |

| LCS XXCLASS | I | III | IV | V |
|---|---|---|---|---|
| AAW 9.7    Engage airborne threats using portable missile systems.<br><br>NOTE: Only when portable missile system detachment embarked.<br><br>IV, V(L) - Plan and train. | F/E | F/E | L | L |
| **AAW 11   REPAIR OWN UNIT'S AAW EQUIPMENT.**<br><br>NOTE: During Condition III and IV, full capability provided by off-watch personnel.<br><br>I(L) - Emergency repairs to equipment critical to ship's mission. All critical Combat System spaces manned with at least one technician in each space. | L | F | F | F |
| **AAW 12   CONDUCT CASUALTY CONTROL PROCEDURES TO MAINTAIN/RESTORE OWN UNIT'S AAW CAPABILITIES.**<br><br>I(L) - Emergency repairs to equipment critical to ship's mission. All critical Combat System spaces manned with at least one technician in each space.<br><br>III, IV(L) - Man Combat System Operational Sequencing System (CSOSS) watch organization with CSOOW/Combat Systems Maintenance Supervisor and Electronics Support Supervisor.<br><br>V(L) - Plan and train. | L | L | L | L |

# AMPHIBIOUS WARFARE (AMW)

| | I | III | IV | V |
|---|---|---|---|---|
| **AMW 12   PROVIDE AIR CONTROL AND COORDINATION OF AIR OPERATIONS IN THE AOA.** | | | | |
| AMW 12.2   Provide coordination of AAW, ASU and ASW air assets for protection of the force in the AOA.<br><br>NOTE: Functioning as AAWC may limit capabilities in other primary warfare areas.<br><br>I, III(L) - Capable of functioning as AAWC for a limited duration in emergent situations for a small area/group operations only.<br><br>IV, V(L) - Plan and train. | L | L/A | L | L |

| LCS XXCLASS | I | III | IV | V |
|---|---|---|---|---|
| AMW 12.3   Control search and rescue (SAR) air operations in the AOA. | L | L/A | L | L |
| NOTE: Functioning as AAWC may limit capabilities in other primary warfare areas. | | | | |
| I, III(L) - Capable of functioning as AAWC for a limited duration in emergent situations for a small area/group operations only. | | | | |
| IV, V(L) - Plan and train. | | | | |
| AMW 12.4   Coordinate air assets in the AOA with Supporting Arms to prevent conflicting actions. | L | L/A | L | L |
| NOTE: Functioning as AAWC may limit capabilities in other primary warfare areas. | | | | |
| I, III(L) - Capable of functioning as AAWC for a limited duration in emergent situations for a small area/group operations only. | | | | |
| IV, V(L) - Plan and train. | | | | |
| **AMW 15   PROVIDE AIR OPERATIONS TO SUPPORT AMPHIBIOUS OPERATIONS** | | | | |
| AMW 15.1   Launch fixed wing and/or rotary wing aircraft. | F/E | F/E | F/E | |
| NOTE: Rotary wing aircraft only. During Condition I, stand down other battle watch stations to man Flight Deck, Rescue Boat Detail, and Crash & Salvage Detail. During Condition III, flight deck operations workload is collected as Own Unit Support (OUS) and only supports logistic helicopter operations. | | | | |
| AMW 15.2   Recover fixed wing and/or rotary wing aircraft. | F/E | F/E | F/E | |
| NOTE: Rotary wing aircraft only. During Condition I, stand down other battle watch stations to man Flight Deck, Rescue Boat Detail, and Crash & Salvage Detail. During Condition III, flight deck operations workload is collected as OUS and only supports logistic helicopter operations. | | | | |
| AMW 15.9   Load/unload ordnance within required aircraft turnaround times. | F/E | F/E | L/E | |
| NOTE: Ship's force not certified for aviation ordnance handling; requires aviation detachment personnel. | | | | |
| IV(L) - Plan and train. | | | | |

| LCS XXCLASS | I | III | IV | V |
|---|---|---|---|---|
| **AMW 20 REPAIR OWN UNIT'S AMW EQUIPMENT.** | L | F | F | F |
| NOTE: During Condition III and IV, full capability provided by off-watch personnel.<br><br>I(L) - Emergency repairs to equipment critical to ship's mission. All critical Combat System spaces manned with at least one technician in each space. | | | | |
| **AMW 43 CONDUCT CASUALTY CONTROL PROCEDURES TO MAINTAIN/RESTORE OWN UNIT'S AMW CAPABILITIES.** | L | L | L | L |
| I(L) - Emergency repairs to equipment critical to ship's mission. All critical Combat System spaces manned with at least one technician in each space.<br><br>III, IV(L) - Man Combat System Operational Sequencing System (CSOSS) watch organization with CSOOW/Combat Systems Maintenance Supervisor and Electronics Support Supervisor.<br><br>V(L) - Plan and train. | | | | |

# ANTISURFACE SHIP WARFARE (ASU)

| | I | III | IV | V |
|---|---|---|---|---|
| **ASU 1 USING ANTISURFACE ARMAMENTS, ENGAGE SURFACE THREATS.** | | | | |
| ASU 1.5 — Engage surface ships with intermediate caliber gunfire (i.e., 3"/75, 76mm).<br><br>III(L) - Man 76 mm mount (without magazine crew).<br><br>IV, V(L) - Plan and train. | F | L | L | L |
| ASU 1.6 — Engage surface ships with minor caliber gunfire (i.e., 25mm, 20mm, .50 cal.)<br><br>NOTE: Requires securing personnel from other battle stations.<br><br>IV, V(L) - Plan and train. | F | F | L | L |
| ASU 1.9 — Engage surface ships with small arms gunfire.<br><br>NOTE: Requires securing personnel from other battle stations.<br><br>IV, V(L) - Plan and train. | F | F | L | L |

| LCS XXCLASS | | I | III | IV | V |
|---|---|---|---|---|---|
| ASU 1.10 | Conduct close-in surface self-defense using crew operated machine guns (i.e., 25mm, 20mm, .50 cal, .30 cal).<br><br>NOTE: Requires securing personnel from other battle stations.<br><br>III(L) – Man self-defense weapons by using off-watch personnel or stand down other non-essential functions.<br><br>IV, V(L) - Plan and train. | F | L/E | L | L |
| ASU 1.11 | Employ self-defense torpedo countermeasures using:<br><br>(a) NIXIE<br>(zz) Other - LEAD/ADC's<br><br>NOTE: Streaming and retrieval of NIXIE performed by standing down other Condition I watch stations or using off-watch personnel during Condition III.<br><br>IV, V(L) - Plan and train. | F | F/A | L | L |
| ASU 1.12 | Plan/direct engagement of surface threats.<br><br>IV, V(L) - Plan and train. | F | F | L | L |
| ASU 1.14 | Direct embarked or non-organic armed helo to engage surface ships.<br><br>IV(L) - Plan and train. | F | F | L | |
| ASU 2 | ENGAGE SURFACE TARGETS IN COOPERATION WITH OTHER FORCES. | | | | |
| ASU 2.1 | Conduct ASU as a member of a multiship CSG, SAG, URG, or amphibious force [e.g., ESG, ARG(MEU)].<br><br>NOTE: Limited to gun and helo capabilities.<br><br>III, IV(L) – Man MK 92 FCS and 76mm Gun Mount (without magazine crew).<br><br>V(L) - Plan and train. | F | L | L | L |
| ASU 2.2 | Conduct ASU to support surface forces.<br><br>NOTE: Limited to gun and helo capabilities.<br><br>III, IV(L) – Man MK 92 FCS and 76mm Gun Mount (without magazine crew).<br><br>V(L) - Plan and train. | F | L | L | L |

| LCS XXCLASS | | | I | III | IV | V |
|---|---|---|---|---|---|---|
| ASU 2.3 | Engage surface targets within assigned antisurface sector.<br><br>NOTE: Limited to gun and helo capabilities.<br><br>III, IV(L) – Man MK 92 FCS and 76mm Gun Mount (without magazine crew).<br><br>V(L) - Plan and train. | | F | L | L | L |
| ASU 2.5 | Plan/direct engagement of surface targets during group operations by surface, subsurface and/or air assets or in coordination with naval/joint/combined forces.<br><br>IV, V(L) - Plan and train. | | F | F | L | L |
| **ASU 3** | **PROVIDE ASU DEFENSE OF A GEOGRAPHICAL AREA (E.G., AOA, BARRIER) INDEPENDENTLY OR IN COOPERATION WITH OTHER FORCES.** | | | | | |
| ASU 3.1 | Provide ASU defense of a geographic area.<br><br>NOTE: Limited to gun and helo capabilities.<br><br>III, IV(L) – Man MK 92 FCS and 76mm Gun Mount (without magazine crew).<br><br>V(L) - Plan and train. | | F | L | L | L |
| **ASU 4** | **DETECT, IDENTIFY, LOCALIZE AND TRACK SURFACE SHIP TARGETS.** | | | | | |
| ASU 4.1 | Detect, localize and track surface contacts with radar.<br><br>V(L) - Plan and train. | | F | F | F | L |
| ASU 4.3 | Detect, localize and track surface contacts with active sonar.<br><br>V(L) - Plan and train. | | F | F | F/A | L |
| ASU 4.4 | Detect, identify, classify and track surface contacts visually.<br><br>III, IV(L) – Capability provided by bridge watch team and aft lookout. | | F | L | L | |
| ASU 4.6 | Detect, identify, classify and track surface contacts by ESM.<br><br>III(L) - ESM Operator only. System operation primarily for Anti-Ship Cruise Missile (ASCM) defense.<br><br>IV, V(L) - Plan and train. | | F | L | L | L |
| ASU 4.7 | Identify surface contacts.<br><br>NOTE: Full capability requires augmentation from off-watch personnel.<br><br>V(L) - Plan and train. | | F | F/A | F/A | L |

| LCS XXCLASS | | I | III | IV | V |
|---|---|---|---|---|---|
| ASU 4.9 | Detect, localize, classify and track surface contacts with tactical towed arrays. | F | F/E | F/E | L |
| | NOTE: TMA requires augmentation from off-watch personnel. | | | | |
| | V(L) - Plan and train. | | | | |
| **ASU 5** | **CONDUCT ACOUSTIC WARFARE (AW) AGAINST SURFACE CONTACTS.** | | | | |
| ASU 5.1 | Employ Acoustic Warfare Support Measures (ACSM) against surface contacts. | F | F | L | L |
| | IV, V(L) - Plan and train. | | | | |
| ASU 5.2 | Employ Acoustic Countermeasures (ACM) against surface contacts. | F | F | L | L |
| | IV, V(L) - Plan and train. | | | | |
| ASU 5.4 | Plan/direct employment of ACSM, ACM and/or Acoustic Counter-countermeasures (ACCM) against surface contacts. | F | F | L | L |
| | IV, V(L) - Plan and train. | | | | |
| **ASU 6** | **DISENGAGE, EVADE AND AVOID SURFACE ATTACK.** | | | | |
| ASU 6.1 | Employ countermeasures. | F | L | L | L |
| | (a)  Surface decoys<br>(b)  Lighting configuration<br>(c)  Hull markings | | | | |
| | III, IV(L) – MK 50 DLS not manned. | | | | |
| | V(L) - Plan and train. | | | | |
| ASU 6.2 | Employ evasion techniques. | F | F | F | L |
| | V(L) - Plan and train. | | | | |
| ASU 6.3 | Employ EMCON procedures. | F | F | F | L |
| | V(L) - Plan and train. | | | | |
| ASU 6.4 | Detect, identify and track surface targets to perform contact avoidance using Electronic Support Measures (ESM) or Radio Direction Finding (RDF/Combat DF/OUTBOARD). | F | L | L | L |
| | III(L) - ESM Operator only.  System operation primarily for ASCM defense. | | | | |
| | IV, V(L) - Plan and train. | | | | |

| | LCS XXCLASS | I | III | IV | V |
|---|---|---|---|---|---|
| **ASU 8** | **PROVIDE AIR OPERATIONS TO SUPPORT SURFACE ATTACKS.** | | | | |
| ASU 8.1 | Launch fixed and/or rotary wing aircraft.<br><br>NOTE: Rotary wing aircraft only. During Condition I, stand down other battle watch stations to man Flight Deck, Rescue Boat Detail, and Crash & Salvage Detail. During Condition III, flight deck operations workload is collected as OUS and only supports logistic helicopter operations. | F/E | F/E | F/E | |
| ASU 8.2 | Recover fixed and/or rotary wing aircraft.<br><br>NOTE: Rotary wing aircraft only. During Condition I, stand down other battle watch stations to man Flight Deck, Rescue Boat Detail, and Crash & Salvage Detail. During Condition III, flight deck operations workload is collected as OUS and only supports logistic helicopter operations. | F/E | F/E | F/E | |
| ASU 8.5 | Provide conventional ordnance within required aircraft turnaround times.<br><br>NOTE: Ship's force not certified for aviation ordnance handling; requires aviation detachment personnel.<br><br>IV(L) - Plan and train. | F/E | F/E | L/E | |
| ASU 8.8 | Control aircraft under all conditions of active jamming.<br><br>IV, V(L) - Plan and train. | F | F | L | L |
| ASU 8.9 | Load/unload ordnance within required aircraft turnaround times.<br><br>NOTE: Ship's force not certified for aviation ordnance handling; requires aviation detachment personnel.<br><br>IV(L) - Plan and train. | F/E | F/E | L/E | |
| ASU 8.10 | Provide air strike control to direct or assist attack aircraft.<br><br>NOTE: Function performed by Antisubmarine Tactical Air Controller (ASTAC) and will require standing down other air control functions.<br><br>IV, V(L) - Plan and train. | F | F | L | L |
| ASU 8.11 | Conduct Precision Radar Controlled Approaches (PRCA) for aircraft under all weather conditions.<br><br>V(L) - Plan and train. | F | F | F/A | L |
| ASU 8.12 | Plan/direct air operations to support surface attacks.<br><br>IV, V(L) - Plan and train. | F | F | L | L |

| LCS XXCLASS | | | I | III | IV | V |
|---|---|---|---|---|---|---|
| ASU 8.13 | Control fixed wing or rotary wing ASU aircraft during coordinated search or attack operations including Over the Horizon Targeting (OTHT). | | F | F | L | L |
| | NOTE: Function performed by ASTAC and will require standing down other air control functions. | | | | | |
| | IV, V(L) - Plan and train. | | | | | |
| ASU 8.14 | Render safe hazardous explosive ordnance during flight operations and ordnance loading/unloading evolutions. | | F/E | F/E | L/E | |
| | NOTE: Ship's force not certified for aviation ordnance handling; requires aviation detachment personnel. | | | | | |
| | IV(L) - Plan and train. | | | | | |
| ASU 8.15 | Provide air strike control to direct or assist naval, combined or joint attack aircraft. | | F | F | L | L |
| | NOTE: Function performed by ASTAC and will require standing down other air control functions. | | | | | |
| | IV, V(L) - Plan and train. | | | | | |
| **ASU 10** | **CONDUCT AIRBORNE OPERATIONS TO SUPPORT SURFACE ATTACK OPERATIONS.** | | | | | |
| ASU 10.5 | Provide OTHT information to support air ASU operations. | | F | F | L | L |
| | IV, V(L) - Plan and train. | | | | | |
| ASU 10.6 | Plan/direct airborne operations to support group or naval/joint/combined ASU operations. | | F | F | L | L |
| | IV, V(L) - Plan and train. | | | | | |
| **ASU 11** | **PERFORM DUTIES OF AIRCRAFT CONTROL UNIT (ACU) FOR AIRCRAFT INVOLVED IN ASU OPERATIONS.** | | | | | |
| ASU 11.1 | Perform aircraft control for aircraft involved in ASU operations. | | F | F | F | L |
| | NOTE: Function performed by ASTAC and will require standing down other air control functions. | | | | | |
| | V(L) - Plan and train. | | | | | |
| **ASU 12** | **SUPPORT/CONDUCT ESCORTING AND INDEPENDENT ASU OPERATIONS.** | | | | | |
| ASU 12.1 | Conduct ASU operations while escorting a convoy and/or URG. | | F | F | L | L |
| | NOTE: Limited to gun and helo capabilities. | | | | | |
| | IV, V(L) - Plan and train. | | | | | |

| LCS XXCLASS | | | I | III | IV | V |
|---|---|---|---|---|---|---|
| ASU 12.2 | Conduct ASU operations while escorting an amphibious force [e.g., ESG, ARG(MEU)].<br><br>NOTE: Limited to gun and helo capabilities.<br><br>IV, V(L) - Plan and train. | | F | F | L | L |
| ASU 12.3 | Conduct independent ASU operations.<br><br>NOTE: Limited to gun and helo capabilities.<br><br>IV, V(L) - Plan and train. | | F | F | L | L |
| ASU 13 | **CONDUCT PREATTACK DECEPTION IN SUPPORT OF ASU OPERATIONS.** | | | | | |
| ASU 13.1 | Perform preattack deception in support of ASU operations.<br><br>IV, V(L) - Plan and train. | | F | F | L | L |
| ASU 14 | **REPAIR OWN UNIT'S ASU EQUIPMENT.**<br><br>NOTE: During Condition III and IV, full capability provided by off-watch personnel.<br><br>I(L) - Emergency repairs to equipment critical to ship's mission. All critical Combat System spaces manned with at least one technician in each space. | | L | F | F | F |
| ASU 17 | **CONDUCT CASUALTY CONTROL PROCEDURES TO MAINTAIN/RESTORE OWN UNIT'S ASU CAPABILITIES.**<br><br>I(L) - Emergency repairs to equipment critical to ship's mission. All critical Combat System spaces manned with at least one technician in each space.<br><br>III, IV(L) - Man CSOSS watch organization with CSOOW/Combat Systems Maintenance Supervisor and Electronics Support Supervisor.<br><br>V(L) - Plan and train. | | L | L | L | L |

# ANTISUBMARINE WARFARE (ASW)

| | | | I | III | IV | V |
|---|---|---|---|---|---|---|
| ASW 1 | **PROVIDE ASW DEFENSE FOR SURFACE FORCES, GROUPS AND UNITS.** | | | | | |
| ASW 1.1 | Defend a convoy (military or mercantile).<br><br>IV, V(L) - Plan and train. | | F | F | L | L |
| ASW 1.2 | Defend a BG or task force.<br><br>IV, V(L) - Plan and train. | | F | F | L | L |

| LCS XXCLASS | | | I | III | IV | V |
|---|---|---|---|---|---|---|
| ASW 1.3 | Defend amphibious forces or an URG. | | F | F | L | L |
| | IV, V(L) - Plan and train. | | | | | |
| ASW 1.5 | Operate in associated support of surface forces. | | F | F | L | L |
| | (a) Picket<br>(b) Choke point patrol<br>(c) Barrier patrol | | | | | |
| | IV, V(L) – Plan and train. | | | | | |
| ASW 1.6 | Operate independently as a Search and Attack Unit (SAU). | | F | F | L | L |
| | IV, V(L) - Plan and train. | | | | | |
| **ASW 2** | **PROVIDE ASW DEFENSE OF A GEOGRAPHIC AREA.** | | | | | |
| ASW 2.1 | Operate as an open ocean or choke point ASW search/barrier unit. | | F | F | L | L |
| | IV, V(L) - Plan and train. | | | | | |
| ASW 2.3 | Operate as an AOA ASW defense barrier unit. | | F | F | L | L |
| | IV, V(L) - Plan and train. | | | | | |
| ASW 2.4 | Defend a group or groups operating in a fixed geographic area (e.g., AOA). | | F | F | L | L |
| | IV, V(L) - Plan and train. | | | | | |
| ASW 2.5 | Sanitize an area of threat submarines in preparation for use by a surface force. | | F | F | L | L |
| | IV, V(L) - Plan and train. | | | | | |
| ASW 2.8 | Operate as a littoral water ASW barrier. | | F | F | L | L |
| | IV, V(L) - Plan and train. | | | | | |
| ASW 2.9 | Conduct shallow water ASW operations (less than 100 fathoms). | | F | F | L | L |
| | IV, V(L) - Plan and train. | | | | | |
| **ASW 3** | **CONDUCT INDEPENDENT ASW OPERATIONS.** | | | | | |
| ASW 3.1 | Support/conduct area search and destroy operations. | | F | F | L | L |
| | IV, V(L) - Plan and train. | | | | | |
| ASW 3.2 | Support/conduct vectored intercept operations. | | F | F | L | L |
| | IV, V(L) - Plan and train. | | | | | |

| LCS XXCLASS | | I | III | IV | V |
|---|---|---|---|---|---|
| **ASW 5** | **PROVIDE FOR AIR OPERATIONS IN SUPPORT OF AIRBORNE ANTISUBMARINE OPERATIONS.** | | | | |
| ASW 5.1 | Launch fixed wing aircraft and/or rotary wing aircraft.<br><br>NOTE: Rotary wing aircraft only. During Condition I, stand down other battle watch stations to man Flight Deck, Rescue Boat Detail, and Crash & Salvage Detail. During Condition III, flight deck operations workload is collected as OUS and only supports logistic helicopter operations. | F/E | F/E | F/E | |
| ASW 5.2 | Recover fixed wing aircraft and/or rotary wing aircraft.<br><br>NOTE: Rotary wing aircraft only. During Condition I, stand down other battle watch stations to man Flight Deck, Rescue Boat Detail, and Crash & Salvage Detail. During Condition III, flight deck operations workload is collected as OUS and only supports logistic helicopter operations. | F/E | F/E | F/E | |
| ASW 5.4 | Provide conventional ordnance within required aircraft turnaround times.<br><br>NOTE: Ship's force not certified for aviation ordnance handling; requires aviation detachment personnel.<br><br>IV(L) - Plan and train. | F/E | F/E | L/E | |
| ASW 5.6 | Conduct operations during all EMCON conditions.<br><br>IV, V(L) - Plan and train. | F | F | L | L |
| ASW 5.7 | Load/unload ordnance within required aircraft turnaround times.<br><br>NOTE: Ship's force not certified for aviation ordnance handling; requires aviation detachment personnel.<br><br>IV(L) - Plan and train. | F/E | F/E | L/E | |
| ASW 5.8 | Control aircraft under all conditions of active jamming.<br><br>V(L) - Plan and train. | F | F | F | L |
| ASW 5.13 | Render safe hazardous explosive ordnance during flight operations and ordnance loading/unloading evolutions<br><br>NOTE: Ship's force not certified for aviation ordnance handling; requires aviation detachment personnel.<br><br>IV(L) - Plan and train. | F/E | F/E | L/E | |
| ASW 5.14 | Conduct PRCA for embarked/controlled fixed wing aircraft or helos under all weather conditions.<br><br>V(L) - Plan and train. | F | F | F/A | L |

| LCS XXCLASS | | I | III | IV | V |
|---|---|---|---|---|---|
| **ASW 6** | **ENGAGE SUBMARINES INDEPENDENTLY OR IN COOPERATION WITH OTHER FORCES.** | | | | |
| ASW 6.1 | Operate as a member of a multiship SAU.<br><br>IV, V(L) - Plan and train. | F | F | L | L |
| ASW 6.2 | Operate as a member of a combined surface and aviation SAU.<br><br>IV, V(L) - Plan and train. | F | F | L | L |
| ASW 6.4 | Detect, localize and track subsurface contacts with active sonar.<br><br>V(L) - Plan and train. | F | F | F | L |
| ASW 6.5 | Detect, localize, classify and track subsurface contacts with passive sonar.<br><br>V(L) - Plan and train. | F | F | F | L |
| ASW 6.6 | Detect, localize and track subsurface contacts with active sonobuoys.<br><br>IV, V(L) - Plan and train. | F | F | L | L |
| ASW 6.7 | Detect, localize, classify and track subsurface contacts with passive sonobuoys.<br><br>IV, V(L) - Plan and train. | F | F | L | L |
| ASW 6.8 | Detect, localize and track subsurface contacts which are at periscope depth visually or with radar.<br><br>III, IV(L) – Visual capability provided by the Bridge watch team and Aft lookout.<br><br>V(L) - Plan and train. | F | L | L | L |
| ASW 6.9 | Detect, localize, classify and track submarines assisted by real time passive acoustic analysis.<br><br>NOTE: TMA requires augmentation from off-watch personnel.<br><br>V(L) - Plan and train. | F | F/E | F/E | L |
| ASW 6.10 | Classify subsurface contacts.<br><br>V(L) - Plan and train. | F | F | F | L |

| LCS XXCLASS | | | I | III | IV | V |
|---|---|---|---|---|---|---|
| ASW 6.12 | Detect, localize, classify and track subsurface contacts with Tactical Towed Arrays. | | F | F/E | F/E | L |
| | NOTE: TMA requires augmentation from off-watch personnel. | | | | | |
| | V(L) - Plan and train. | | | | | |
| ASW 6.14 | Detect, identify, classify and track subsurface contacts that are at periscope depth by ESM. | | F | L | L | L |
| | III(L) - EW Supervisor and ESM Operator positions only. Location and targeting require TMA augmentation. | | | | | |
| | IV(L) - ESM Operator only. | | | | | |
| | V(L) - Plan and train. | | | | | |
| **ASW 7** | **ATTACK SUBMARINES WITH ANTISUBMARINE ARMAMENT.** | | | | | |
| ASW 7.6 | Attack with torpedoes. | | F | F | L | L |
| | NOTE: Full capability for torpedo attack is provided by on-call TM with SVTT loaded and charged. | | | | | |
| | IV, V(L) - plan and train. | | | | | |
| ASW 7.9 | Attack with guns. | | F | L | L | L |
| | III(L) - Man MK 92 FCS and 76mm mount (without gun or magazine crew). | | | | | |
| | IV, V(L) - Plan and train. | | | | | |
| ASW 7.11 | Attack with conventional air-to-surface ordnance. | | L | L | L | L |
| | I, III(L) - Direct armed helo or fixed-wing aircraft. | | | | | |
| | IV, V(L) - Plan and train. | | | | | |
| ASW 7.12 | Plan/direct attack of submarines. | | F | F | L | L |
| | IV, V(L) - Plan and train. | | | | | |
| **ASW 8** | **DISENGAGE, EVADE, AVOID AND DECEIVE SUBMARINES.** | | | | | |
| ASW 8.1 | Employ torpedo countermeasures and evasion techniques including: | | F | F/A | L | L |
| | (a) NIXIE<br>(zz) Other - LEAD/ADC's | | | | | |
| | NOTE: Streaming and retrieval of NIXIE performed by standing down other Condition I watch stations or using off-watch personnel during Condition III. | | | | | |
| | IV, V(L) - Plan and train. | | | | | |

| LCS XXCLASS | | | I | III | IV | V |
|---|---|---|---|---|---|---|
| ASW 8.2 | Employ ACM against submarines. | | F | F | L | L |
| | IV, V(L) - Plan and train. | | | | | |
| ASW 8.3 | Employ ACCM against submarines. | | F | F | L | L |
| | IV, V(L) - Plan and train. | | | | | |
| ASW 8.4 | Conduct deception operations in support of ASW operations. | | F | F | L | L |
| | IV, V(L) - Plan and train. | | | | | |
| **ASW 9** | **REPAIR OWN UNIT'S ASW EQUIPMENT.** | | L | F | F | F |
| | NOTE: During condition III and IV, full capability provided by off-watch personnel. | | | | | |
| | I(L) - Emergency repairs to equipment critical to ship's mission. All critical Combat System spaces manned with at least one technician in each space. | | | | | |
| **ASW 10** | **PERFORM DUTIES OF AIRCRAFT CONTROL UNIT (ACU) FOR AIRCRAFT INVOLVED IN ANTISUBMARINE OPERATIONS (REQUIRES ANTISUBMARINE AIR CONTROLLERS (ASACS)).** | | | | | |
| ASW 10.1 | Control fixed wing and/or rotary wing ASW aircraft in conjunction with coordinated search and/or attack operations. | | F | F | L | L |
| | IV, V(L) - Plan and train. | | | | | |
| ASW 10.2 | Control helicopter screen. | | F | F | L | L |
| | IV, V(L) - Plan and train. | | | | | |
| ASW 10.3 | Provide positive and/or advisory control of ASW aircraft. | | F | F | L | L |
| | IV, V(L) - Plan and train. | | | | | |
| ASW 10.4 | Function as MPA Control Unit (MPACU). | | F | F | L | L |
| | IV, V(L) - Plan and train. | | | | | |
| **ASW 13** | **CONDUCT CASUALTY CONTROL PROCEDURES TO MAINTAIN/RESTORE OWN UNIT'S ASW CAPABILITIES.** | | L | L | L | L |
| | I(L) - Emergency repairs to equipment critical to ship's mission. All critical Combat System spaces manned with at least one technician in each space. | | | | | |
| | III, IV(L) - Man CSOSS watch organization with CSOOW/Combat Systems Maintenance Supervisor and Electronics Support Supervisor. | | | | | |
| | V(L) - Plan and train. | | | | | |

| LCS XXCLASS | I | III | IV | V |
|---|---|---|---|---|
| **COMMAND AND CONTROL AND COMMUNICATIONS (CCC)** | | | | |
| **CCC 2 COORDINATE AND CONTROL THE OPERATIONS OF THE TASK ORGANIZATION OR FUNCTIONAL FORCE TO CARRY OUT ASSIGNED MISSIONS.** | | | | |
| NOTE: Concurrent assignment of multiple Commander functions is not recommended because ship is not configured for embarked staff. | | | | |
| CCC 2.1　Coordinate the reconnaissance of multiple surface, subsurface and/or air contacts.<br><br>V(L) - Plan and train. | F | F | F/A | L |
| CCC 2.2　Function as AAWC for force or sector.<br><br>NOTE: Functioning as AAWC may limit capabilities in other primary warfare areas.<br><br>I, III(L) - Capable of functioning as AAWC for a limited duration in emergent situations for a small area/group operations only.<br><br>IV, V(L) - Plan and train. | L | L | L | L |
| CCC 2.3　Function as ASW commander (ASWC) for force or sector.<br><br>I, III(L) - Can accomplish only for short periods of time if assigned other Command/Coordination responsibilities.<br><br>IV, V(L) - Plan and train. | L | L/A | L | L |
| CCC 2.4　Function as SAU or SAG commander.<br><br>IV, V(L) - Plan and train. | F | F | L | L |
| CCC 2.5　Operate as contact area commander to coordinate multitype search and attack operations.<br><br>IV, V(L) - Plan and train. | F | F | L | L |
| CCC 2.6　Function as force or sector Officer in Tactical Command (OTC)/Composite Warfare Commanders (CWC) (or alternate) to coordinate and control BG/task force operations.<br><br>I, III(L) - Can accomplish only for short periods of time if assigned other Command/Coordination responsibilities.<br><br>IV, V(L) - Plan and train. | L | L/A | L | L |
| CCC 2.8　Function as on-scene commander for a SAR operation.<br><br>V(L) - Plan and train. | F | F/A | F/A | L |

| LCS XXCLASS | | I | III | IV | V |
|---|---|---|---|---|---|
| CCC 2.11 | Control close air support aircraft in support of amphibious operations in coordination with other supporting arms.<br><br>NOTE: Function performed by ASTAC and will require standing down other air control functions.<br><br>IV, V(L) - Plan and train. | F | F | L | L |
| CCC 2.12 | Coordinate and control air SAR operations in the AOA.<br><br>I, III(L) - Back up TACGRU or TACRON.<br><br>IV, V(L) - Plan and train. | L | L | L | L |
| CCC 2.15 | Function as one or more of the following coordinators for force or sector.<br><br>(d) Screen coordinator (SC)<br>(e) Electronic warfare coordinator (EWC)<br>(f) Force air track coordinator<br>(g) Force surface track coordinator (FSTC)<br>(h) Force track coordinator (FTC)<br>(j) Force OTH track coordinator (FOTC)<br>(n) Helicopter element command (HEC)<br><br>I, III, IV(L) - Unable to perform all functions simultaneously.<br><br>V(L) - Plan and train. | L | L/A | L/A | L |
| CCC 2.16 | Assist in the planning of AAW, ASU and ASW for the coordination of air operations in the AOA. | F | F | F | F |
| CCC 2.18 | Function as an Anti-Surface Warfare Commander (ASUWC) for force or sector.<br><br>I, III(L) - Can accomplish only for short periods of time if assigned other Command/Coordination responsibilities.<br><br>IV, V(L) - Plan and train. | L | L/A | L | L |
| **CCC 3** | **PROVIDE OWN UNIT'S COMMAND AND CONTROL FUNCTIONS.** | | | | |
| CCC 3.1 | Maintain a CIC or CDC capable of collecting, processing, displaying, evaluating and disseminating tactical information. | F | F | F | F |
| CCC 3.3 | Provide all personnel services, programs and facilities to safeguard classified material and information. | F | F | F | F |
| CCC 3.4 | Carry out emergency destruction of classified material and equipment rapidly and efficiently.<br><br>III, IV, V(L) - Plan and train. | F | L | L | L |

| LCS XXCLASS | | | I | III | IV | V |
|---|---|---|---|---|---|---|
| CCC 3.5 | Employ Identification Friend or Foe/Selective Identification Feature (IFF/SIF) including secure IFF Mode 4. | | F | F | F | L |
| | V(L) - Plan and train. | | | | | |
| CCC 3.7 | Maintain a CIC or CDC capable of supporting a TAO. | | F | F | F | F |
| **CCC 4** | **MAINTAIN NAVY TACTICAL DATA SYSTEM (NTDS) OR DATA LINK CAPABILITY.** | | | | | |
| CCC 4.3 | Transmit/receive and support Link 11. | | F | F | F | L |
| | V(L) - Plan and train. | | | | | |
| CCC 4.4 | Receive data link information from airborne ASW aircraft. | | F | F | F | L |
| | V(L) - Plan and train. | | | | | |
| CCC 4.5 | Receive and process data link information from Satellite Communication (SATCOM). | | F | F | F | L |
| | V(L) - Plan and train. | | | | | |
| CCC 4.6 | Receive and process data link information from high frequency (HF) systems. | | F | F | F | L |
| | V(L) - Plan and train. | | | | | |
| CCC 4.11 | Receive data link tracks from airborne AAW aircraft. | | F | F | F | L |
| | V(L) - Plan and train. | | | | | |
| CCC 4.12 | Manage, coordinate and direct air assets (airwing, group or joint aircraft) in ASUW/STW using data links. | | F | F | F | L |
| | V(L) - Plan and train. | | | | | |
| CCC 4.13 | Transmit/Receive data via Global Command and Control System - Maritime (GCCS-M). | | F | F | F | L |
| | V(L) - Plan and train. | | | | | |
| **CCC 6** | **PROVIDE COMMUNICATIONS FOR OWN UNIT.** | | | | | |
| CCC 6.1 | Maintain tactical voice communications. | | F | F | F | L/A |
| | V(L) - Communications on harbor common and other voice circuits as directed. | | | | | |
| CCC 6.2 | Maintain visual communications. | | L | L | L | L/A |
| | I(L) - Work one contact and maintain log. | | | | | |
| | III, IV(L) – Initial limited response to visual signal provided by Bridge area watch team. Experienced visual specialist on-call. | | | | | |
| | V(L) - Work one contact for administrative traffic. | | | | | |

| LCS XXCLASS | | I | III | IV | V |
|---|---|---|---|---|---|
| CCC 6.3 | Maintain multichannel cryptographically covered teletype/data receive circuits. | F | F | F | |
| CCC 6.5 | Maintain full duplex cryptographically covered HF teletype/data circuits (simplex for submarines and patrol combatants). | F | F | F | F/A |
| CCC 6.6 | Process messages. | F | F | F | F |
| CCC 6.7 | Maintain underwater communications. | F | F | F | |
| CCC 6.8 | Maintain automatic relay communications. | F | F | F | F/A |
| CCC 6.10 | Maintain voice/teletype/computer data cryptographically covered satellite communication circuits. | F | F | F | F/A |
| CCC 6.11 | Establish and maintain fixed combat communications and relay support for NSW operations. IV, V(L) - Plan and train. | F | F | L | L |
| CCC 6.12 | Maintain internal communications systems. | F | F | F | F |
| CCC 6.13 | Maintain capability for Low Probability of Intercept (LPI) HF communications. | F | F | F | |
| CCC 6.14 | Maintain capability for LPI satellite communications. | F | F | F | |
| CCC 6.15 | Maintain frequency database. | F | F | F | F |
| CCC 6.19 | Maintain tactical, secure voice or data communications. | F | F | F | F/A |
| CCC 6.21 | Provide Officer-in-Tactical Command Information Exchange Subsystem (OTCIXS). | F | F | F | F/A |
| **CCC 9** | **RELAY COMMUNICATIONS.** | | | | |
| CCC 9.1 | Relay visual communications. I(L) - Work one contact and maintain log. III, IV(L) - Initial limited response to visual signal provided by Bridge area watch team. Experienced visual specialist on-call. V(L) - Work one contact for administrative traffic. | L | L | L | L/A |
| CCC 9.2 | Relay acoustic communications. | F | F | | |
| CCC 9.3 | Relay electronic communications. V(L) - Capability limited to single point-to-point circuit. | F | F/A | F/A | L/A |
| **CCC 11** | **CONDUCT ONE OR MORE OF THE FOLLOWING CONTROL FUNCTIONS:** | | | | |
| CCC 11.1 | MPACU. IV, V(L) – Plan and train. | F | F | L | L |

| LCS XXCLASS | | | I | III | IV | V |
|---|---|---|---|---|---|---|
| CCC 11.2 | Air Raid Reporting Control Ship (ARRCS). | | F | F | L | L |
| | IV, V(L) – Plan and train. | | | | | |
| CCC 11.3 | Aircraft Control Unit for AAW, ASW, ASU and/or STW. | | L | L/A | L | L |
| | I, III(L) – Capabilities limited due to reduction of air controllers on board. | | | | | |
| | IV, V(L) – Plan and train. | | | | | |
| CCC 11.4 | Positive Identification Radar Advisory Zone (PIRAZ)/Strike Support Ship. | | F | F | L | L |
| | IV, V(L) – Plan and train. | | | | | |
| CCC 11.5 | NTDS Link 11 Net Control Ship/Station (NCS). | | F | F | L | L |
| | IV, V(L) – Plan and train. | | | | | |
| **CCC 19** | **REPAIR OWN UNIT'S CCC EQUIPMENT.** | | L | F | F | F |
| | NOTE:  During condition III and IV, full capability provided by off-watch personnel. | | | | | |
| | I(L) - Emergency repairs to equipment critical to ship's mission.  All critical Combat System spaces manned with at least one technician in each space. | | | | | |
| **CCC 20** | **CONDUCT CASUALTY CONTROL PROCEDURES TO MAINTAIN/RESTORE OWN UNIT'S CCC CAPABILITIES.** | | L | L | L | L |
| | I(L) - Emergency repairs to equipment critical to ship's mission.  All critical Combat System spaces manned with at least one technician in each space. | | | | | |
| | III, IV(L) - Man CSOSS watch organization with CSOOW/Combat Systems Maintenance Supervisor and Electronics Support Supervisor. | | | | | |
| | V(L) - Plan and train. | | | | | |

# COMMAND AND CONTROL WARFARE ($C^2W$) AND INFORMATION WARFARE (IW)

| | | | | | | |
|---|---|---|---|---|---|---|
| **$C^2W$ 1** | **CONDUCT ELECTRONIC WARFARE SUPPORT (ES) OPERATIONS.** | | | | | |
| $C^2W$ 1.1 | Search for and intercept electromagnetic and directed energy signals and emissions. | | L | L | L | L |
| | I, III, IV(L) - Location and targeting of non-communication emitters requires TMA/plotting team per $C^2W$ 1.4. | | | | | |
| | V(L) - Plan and train. | | | | | |

| | | LCS XXCLASS | I | III | IV | V |
|---|---|---|---|---|---|---|
| | C²W 1.2 | Identify Command and Control (C²) and weapons systems' signals.<br><br>V(L) - Plan and train. | F | F | F | L |
| | C²W 1.3 | Identify threat platforms' communications and weapons signal sources.<br><br>V(L) - Plan and train. | F | F | F | L |
| | C²W 1.4 | Provide location or targeting information of threat weapons/C²/platforms/signal sources.<br><br>I, III, IV(L) - TMA/plotting team personnel required for non-communication emitters only.<br><br>V(L) - Plan and train. | L | L | L | L |
| | C²W 1.5 | Provide timely threat alert for actions involving Electronic Attack (EA), Electronic Protect (EP), EMCON, avoidance, deception and targeting.<br><br>V(L) - Plan and train. | F | F | F | L |
| | C²W 1.6 | Conduct ES for self-defense.<br><br>NOTE: Conduct EP and EA.<br><br>IV, V(L) - Plan and train. | F | F | L | L |
| | C²W 1.8 | Identify and coordinate tactical C²W information requirements and disseminate information derived from ES and other sources to CWC, warfare commanders and naval/combined/joint forces.<br><br>V(L) - Plan and train. | F | F | F | L |
| C²W 2 | **CONDUCT ELECTRONIC ATTACK (EA) OPERATIONS.** | | | | | |
| | C²W 2.2 | Conduct electronic jamming of target acquisition/target tracking/fire control/missile seeker radars.<br><br>IV, V(L) - Plan and train. | F | F | L | L |
| | C²W 2.7 | Conduct electronic deception of target acquisition/target tracking/fire control/missile seeker radars.<br><br>IV, V(L) - Plan and train. | F | F | L | L |
| C²W 3 | **CONDUCT ELECTRONIC PROTECTION (EP) OPERATIONS.** | | | | | |
| | C²W 3.1 | Detect, identify, and protect against electronic jamming of electromagnetically controlled and/or dependent systems.<br><br>IV, V(L) - Plan and train. | F | F | L | L |

| LCS XXCLASS | I | III | IV | V |
|---|:---:|:---:|:---:|:---:|
| C²W 3.2    Detect, identify and protect against electronic deception of electromagnetically controlled and/or dependent systems. | F | F | L | L |
|    IV, V(L) - Plan and train. | | | | |
| **C²W 4    PLAN AND IMPLEMENT OPERATIONS SECURITY (OPSEC) MEASURES.** | | | | |
| C²W 4.1    Implement appropriate/ directed electromagnetic/acoustic EMCON condition. | F | F | F | F |
| C²W 4.2    Transition rapidly from one EMCON condition to another. | F | F | F | F |
| C²W 4.3    Monitor own unit compliance with EMCON condition in effect. | F | F | F | F |
| C²W 4.4    Monitor task group/force compliance with EMCON condition in effect. <br><br> I, III, IV(L) - Non-communication emitters only unless Combat-DF installed. <br><br> V(L) - Plan and train. | L | L | L | L |
| C²W 4.9    Manage electromagnetic/acoustic and/or other emissions to minimize mutual interference among friendly systems. <br><br> V(L) - Plan and train. | F | F | F | L |
| C²W 4.11    Plan, coordinate and control implementation of OPSEC measures. <br><br> V(L) - Plan and train. | F | F | F | L |
| **C²W 14    REPAIR OWN UNIT'S C²W EQUIPMENT.** <br><br> NOTE: During condition III and IV, full capability provided by off-watch personnel. <br><br> I(L) - Emergency repairs to equipment critical to ship's mission. All critical Combat System spaces manned with at least one technician in each space. | L | F | F | F |
| **C²W 16    CONDUCT CASUALTY CONTROL PROCEDURES TO MAINTAIN/RESTORE OWN UNIT'S C²W CAPABILITIES.** <br><br> I(L) - Emergency repairs to equipment critical to ship's mission. All critical Combat System spaces manned with at least one technician in each space. <br><br> III, IV(L) - Man CSOSS watch organization with CSOOW/Combat Systems Maintenance Supervisor and Electronics Support Supervisor. <br><br> V(L) - Plan and train. | L | L | L | L |

| LCS XXCLASS | I | III | IV | V |
|---|---|---|---|---|
| **FLEET SUPPORT OPERATIONS (FSO)** | | | | |
| **FSO 1**    **REPAIR AND OVERHAUL SHIPS, AIRCRAFT AND ASSOCIATED EQUIPMENT.** | | | | |
|     FSO 1.4    Provide inspection, test, calibration and repair services for:<br><br>(k)   Test measurement and diagnostic equipment.<br><br>III, IV, V(L) - Requirement applies to own ship's equipment only. | | L | L | L |
| **FSO 4**    **CONDUCT IN-FLIGHT REFUELING.** | | | | |
|     FSO 4.1    Provide day/night in-flight refueling for helicopters.<br><br>NOTE: Rotary wing aircraft only. During Condition I, stand down other battle watch stations to man Flight Deck, Rescue Boat Detail, and Crash & Salvage Detail. During Condition III, flight deck operations workload is collected as OUS and only supports logistic helicopter operations. | F/E | F/E | F/E | |
| **FSO 6**    **SUPPORT/CONDUCT SEARCH AND RESCUE (SAR) OPERATIONS IN A COMBAT/NONCOMBAT ENVIRONMENT.** | | | | |
|     FSO 6.1    Support/conduct combat/noncombat SAR operations by fixed or rotary wing aircraft. | F | F | F | |
|     FSO 6.2    Conduct combat/noncombat SAR operations by surface ships. | F | F | F | |
|     FSO 6.4    Recover man overboard.<br><br>NOTE: During Condition I, search and recovery requires augmentation by securing other battle stations. During Condition III, search and recovery requires augmentation from off- watch personnel. | F/E | F/E | F/E | F |
|     FSO 6.5    Support/perform planeguard/lifeguard functions.<br><br>NOTE: During Condition I, search and recovery requires augmentation by securing other battle stations. During Condition III, search and recovery requires augmentation from off- watch personnel. | F/E | F/E | F/E | |
|     FSO 6.6    Conduct search and rescue operations (including operations involving submarine disasters/rescues).<br><br>NOTE: During Condition I, search and recovery requires augmentation by securing other battle stations. During Condition III, search and recovery requires augmentation from off- watch personnel. | F/E | F/E | F/E | |
|     FSO 6.7    Conduct general surveillance. | F | F | F | |
|     FSO 6.8    Acquire and display distress data. | F | F | F | |
|     FSO 6.9    Report situation assessment. | F | F | F | |

| LCS XXCLASS | | I | III | IV | V |
|---|---|:---:|:---:|:---:|:---:|
| FSO 6.10 | Coordinate SAR operations. | F | F | F | |
| FSO 6.11 | Conduct multi-unit SAR operations. | F | F | F | |
| **FSO 9** | **PROVIDE MEDICAL CARE TO ASSIGNED AND EMBARKED PERSONNEL.** | | | | |
| FSO 9.1 | Conduct sick call. | | F | F | F |
| FSO 9.4 | Conduct basic ward care. | L | L | L | |
| | I, III, IV(L) - For use in emergency cases where MEDEVAC is not possible or where return to duty can be expected in a short time. | | | | |
| FSO 9.5 | Conduct sanitation and safety inspections. | | F | F | F |
| FSO 9.6 | Conduct occupational health/safety and preventive medicine programs and training using the following personnel:<br><br>(a)  Hospital corpsman | | F | F | F |
| FSO 9.8 | Conduct pharmacy services requiring the following personnel:<br><br>(a)  Hospital corpsman | | F | F | F |
| FSO 9.9 | Conduct associated administrative/maintenance services:<br><br>(a)  Maintain adequate medical supplies for appropriate level health care.<br>(c)  Provide patient/casualty administrative services.<br>(d)  Perform routine medical administrative services. | | F | F | F |
| FSO 9.10 | Conduct on-site emergency medical treatment during hazardous evolutions including flight quarters, underway replenishment/refueling and amphibious assault boat operations. | | F/A | F/A | |
| FSO 9.17 | Identify, equip and maintain suitable spaces to provide medical care. | F | F | F | F |
| FSO 9.19 | Provide medical care, triage and resuscitation commensurate with health care provider credentials using the following personnel:<br><br>(a)  Independent duty corpsman | F | F | F | F |
| **FSO 10** | **PROVIDE FIRST AID ASSISTANCE.** | | | | |
| FSO 10.1 | Identify, equip and maintain appropriate first aid spaces. | F | F | F | F |
| FSO 10.2 | Train assigned and embarked personnel in first aid, self and buddy aid procedures. | | F | F | F |
| FSO 10.3 | Train stretcher-bearers. | | F | F | F |
| **FSO 11** | **PROVIDE TRIAGE OF CASUALTIES /PATIENTS.** | | | | |
| FSO 11.1 | Identify, equip and maintain suitable triage spaces. | F | F | F | F |

| | LCS XXCLASS | I | III | IV | V |
|---|---|---|---|---|---|
| FSO 11.2 | Train assigned and embarked personnel in triage care. | | F | F | F |
| FSO 11.4 | Train designated non-medical personnel to assist in triage management care for CBR contamination casualties. | | F | F | F |
| FSO 11.5 | Train designated non-medical personnel in CBR casualty decontaminated procedures. | | F | F | F |
| FSO 11.7 | Provide medical treatment for chemical, biological radiological casualties.<br><br>I, III, IV, V(L) - Emergency cases where MEDEVAC is not possible or where return to duty can be expected in a short time. | L | L | L | L |
| **FSO 12** | **PROVIDE MEDICAL/SURGICAL TREATMENT FOR CASUALTIES/PATIENTS.** | | | | |
| FSO 12.1 | Identify, equip and maintain suitable resuscitation spaces. | F | F | F | F |
| FSO 12.2 | Train assigned and embarked personnel in resuscitation. | | F | F | F |
| FSO 12.5 | Identify, equip and maintain suitable spaces for emergency minor surgery. | F | F | F | F |
| **FSO 13** | **PROVIDE MEDICAL, SURGICAL, POST-OPERATIVE AND NURSING CARE FOR CASUALTIES/PATIENTS.** | | | | |
| FSO 13.2 | Provide hospital beds:<br><br>(b) Ward<br><br>I, III, IV(L) - For use in emergency cases where MEDEVAC is not possible or where return to duty can be expected in a short time. | L | L | L | |
| FSO 13.7 | Provide surgery by Primary Care Medical Officer.<br><br>I, III, IV, V(L) - Medical Officer is reserve augmentation requirement. Supporting medical equipment and supplies must accompany doctor. Routine medical service during deployment is provided by independent duty corpsman. | L | L | L | L |
| **FSO 20** | **PROVIDE FLEET TRAINING SERVICES.** | | | | |
| FSO 20.1 | Act as target for submarines. | | | F | |
| FSO 20.5 | Act as school ship for gunnery training. | | | F/A | F/A |
| FSO 20.6 | Act as delivery or receiving ship for underway replenishment training. | | | F/E | |
| FSO 20.8 | Recover exercise torpedoes/drones. | | | F/E | |
| FSO 20.67 | Act as school ship for ASW training. | | | F/A | F/A |
| FSO 20.68 | Act as school ship for engineering training. | | | F/A | F/A |

| LCS XXCLASS | I | III | IV | V |
|---|---|---|---|---|
| **FSO 51**   **REPAIR OWN UNIT'S FSO-RELATED EQUIPMENT.** | L | F | F | F |
| NOTE: During condition III and IV, full capability provided by on-call/off-watch personnel. | | | | |
| I(L) - Emergency repairs to equipment critical to ship's mission. All critical Combat System spaces manned with at least one technician in each space. | | | | |
| **FSO 55**   **MAINTAIN READINESS BY PROVIDING FOR TRAINING OF OWN UNITS PERSONNEL.** | | F | F | F |

# INTELLIGENCE (INT)

| LCS XXCLASS | I | III | IV | V |
|---|---|---|---|---|
| **INT 1**   **SUPPORT/CONDUCT INTELLIGENCE COLLECTION.** | | | | |
| INT 1.1   Support/conduct electronic intelligence information collection. | F | F/A | F/A | L |
| V(L) - Plan and train. | | | | |
| INT 1.2   Support/conduct acoustic intelligence information collection. | F | F/A | F/A | L |
| V(L) - Plan and train. | | | | |
| INT 1.3   Support/conduct imagery intelligence information collection. | F | F/A | F/A | L |
| V(L) - Plan and train. | | | | |
| INT 1.5   Support/conduct radar intelligence information collection. | F | F/A | F/A | L |
| V(L) - Plan and train. | | | | |
| INT 1.7   Collect remote sensor information. | F | F/A | F/A | L |
| V(L) - Plan and train. | | | | |
| INT 1.11   Maintain radar scope photography capability. | F | F/A | F/A | L |
| V(L) - Plan and train. | | | | |
| **INT 2**   **PROVIDE INTELLIGENCE.** | | | | |
| INT 2.1   Maintain intelligence summary plots on air, surface and subsurface activities. | F | F/A | F/A | L |
| V(L) - Plan and train. | | | | |
| INT 2.2   Evaluate and disseminate intelligence information. | F | F | F | L |
| V(L) - Plan and train. | | | | |

| | LCS XXCLASS | I | III | IV | V |
|---|---|---|---|---|---|
| INT 2.4 | Establish and maintain access to naval and national intelligence sources. | L | L | L | L |
| | I, III(L) – Only intelligence support is from GCCS-M and message traffic. | | | | |
| | IV, V(L) – Plan and train. | | | | |
| **INT 3** | **CONDUCT SURVEILLANCE AND RECONNAISSANCE.** | | | | |
| INT 3.2 | Conduct overt surveillance and reconnaissance operations. | F | F | F | L |
| | V(L) - Plan and train. | | | | |
| **INT 4** | **CONDUCT OCEAN SURVEILLANCE OPERATIONS AGAINST TARGETS OF INTEREST.** | | | | |
| INT 4.1 | Detect and locate targets of interest. | F | F | F | L |
| | V(L) - Plan and train. | | | | |
| INT 4.2 | Classify and identify targets of interest. | F | F | F | L |
| | V(L) - Plan and train. | | | | |
| INT 4.3 | Track targets of interest. | F | F | F | L |
| | V(L) - Plan and train. | | | | |
| **INT 5** | **PROCESS OCEAN SURVEILLANCE INFORMATION.** | | | | |
| INT 5.1 | Integrate and correlate ocean surveillance information with other source information and intelligence | F | F | F | L |
| | V(L) - Plan and train. | | | | |
| **INT 6** | **CONDUCT SURFACE RECONNAISSANCE.** | | | | |
| INT 6.1 | Conduct surface patrols or barriers. | F | F | F | L |
| | V(L) - Plan and train. | | | | |
| INT 6.3 | Conduct reconnaissance of surface forces. | F | F | F | L |
| | V(L) - Plan and train. | | | | |
| INT 6.7 | Recognize by sight friendly and enemy aircraft, ships, submarines, and potential naval fire support targets which may be encountered in the expected operating areas. | F | L | L | L |
| | III, IV(L) – Capability provided by bridge watch team and aft lookout. | | | | |
| | V(L) - Plan and train. | | | | |

| LCS XXCLASS | I | III | IV | V |
|---|:---:|:---:|:---:|:---:|
| **INT 17**    **REPAIR OWN UNITS INTELLIGENCE-RELATED EQUIPMENT.** | L | F | F | F |
| NOTE:  During condition III and IV, full capability provided by on-call/off-watch personnel. | | | | |
| I(L) - Emergency repairs to equipment critical to ship's mission.  All critical Combat System spaces manned with at least one technician in each space. | | | | |
| **INT 19**    **CONDUCT CASUALTY CONTROL PROCEDURES TO MAINTAIN/RESTORE OWN UNIT'S INT CAPABILITIES.** | L | L | L | L |
| I(L) - Emergency repairs to equipment critical to ship's mission.  All critical Combat System spaces manned with at least one technician in each space. | | | | |
| III, IV(L) - Man CSOSS watch organization with CSOOW/Combat Systems Maintenance Supervisor and Electronics Support Supervisor. | | | | |
| V(L) - Plan and train. | | | | |

## LOGISTICS (LOG)

| | I | III | IV | V |
|---|:---:|:---:|:---:|:---:|
| **LOG 1**    **CONDUCT UNDERWAY REPLENISHMENT.** | | | | |
| LOG 1.12    (U) Replenish other units underway with limited fuel, provisions, munitions, potable and feed water. | | L/E | L/E | L |
| III, IV(L) – Provide fuel to patrol craft (PC) in company after mission-specific contingency astern refueling equipment has been temporarily installed and the crew has been provided with requisite training. | | | | |
| V(L) – Plan and train. | | | | |

| LCS XXCLASS | I | III | IV | V |
|---|:---:|:---:|:---:|:---:|

# MINE WARFARE (MIW)

**MIW 4   CONDUCT MINE COUNTERMEASURES (MCM).**

> Note:  It is intended that the ship remain outside of mined/ suspected waters before and during MCM operations. Below capabilities are intended to 1) permit ROV or Airborne MCM operations from a standoff position when no dedicated MCM assets are available, and 2) to enhance self-defense capability if providing point defense for dedicated MCM assets or if transiting a swept or an unconditional channel.

| | | I | III | IV | V |
|---|---|:---:|:---:|:---:|:---:|
| MIW 4.1 | Detect, classify and plot sea mines. | L | L | L | L |

> NOTE:  Full capability applies only to FFGs equipped with specifically designed MCM systems (not including installed sonar systems).
>
> I, III(L) - For all other FFGs:  Visually or using installed sonar, detect mines for self-defense mine avoidance.
>
> IV, V(L) - Plan and train.

| | | I | III | IV | V |
|---|---|:---:|:---:|:---:|:---:|
| MIW 4.11 | Detect and avoid mines using organic sensors. | L | L | L | L |

> I, III(L) - Visually or using installed sonar, detect mines for self-defense mine avoidance.
>
> IV, V(L) - Plan and train.

**MIW 6   CONDUCT MAGNETIC SILENCING (DEGAUSSING, DEPERMING, ETC.)**

| | | I | III | IV | V |
|---|---|:---:|:---:|:---:|:---:|
| MIW 6.7 | Maintain magnetic signature limits. | F | F | F | F |
| MIW 6.8 | Maintain own unit's degaussing readiness. | F | F | F | F |

| | I | III | IV | V |
|---|:---:|:---:|:---:|:---:|
| **MIW 13   REPAIR OWN UNIT'S MIW EQUIPMENT.** | L | F | F | F |

> NOTE:  During condition III and IV, full capability provided by off-watch personnel.
>
> I(L) - Emergency repairs to equipment critical to ship's mission.  All critical Combat System spaces manned with at least one technician in each space.

# MOBILITY (MOB)

**MOB 1   OPERATE SHIP'S PROPULSION PLANT TO DESIGNED CAPABILITY.**

| | | I | III | IV | V |
|---|---|:---:|:---:|:---:|:---:|
| MOB 1.1 | Operate ship's propulsion plant at full power. | F | F | F | |
| MOB 1.2 | Operate ship's propulsion plant with split plant operations | F | F | F | |

| LCS XXCLASS | | | I | III | IV | V |
|---|---|---|---|---|---|---|
| | MOB 1.5 | Operate at sustained BG/SAG/URG/amphibious force speeds. | F | F | F | |
| | MOB 1.6 | Maintain necessary machinery redundancy to enhance survival in high threat areas. | F | F | F | F |
| | MOB 1.7 | Transit at high speed. | F | F | F | |
| **MOB 3** | **PREVENT AND CONTROL DAMAGE.** | | | | | |
| | MOB 3.1 | Control fire, flooding, electrical, structural, propulsion and hull/airframe casualties. | F | F/E | F/E | F/E |
| | MOB 3.2 | Counter and control chemical, biological and radiological (CBR) contaminants/agents. | F | F/E | F/E | F/E |
| | MOB 3.3 | Maintain security against unfriendly acts. | F | F | F | F |
| | MOB 3.5 | Provide damage control security/surveillance. | F | F | F | F |
| | MOB 3.8 | Provide emergency breathing devices per ship's allowance. | F | F | F | F |
| **MOB 5** | **MANEUVER IN FORMATION.** | | F | F | F | |
| | | NOTE: Capability is supported by Officer of the Deck (OOD)/Junior Officer of the Deck (JOOD) and combined Quartermaster of the Watch (QMOW)/Boatswain's Mate of the Watch (BMOW). | | | | |
| **MOB 6** | **REFUEL IN THE AIR.** | | | | | |
| | MOB 6.3 | Deliver fuel in day/night ship-to-air refueling. | F/E | F/E | F/E | |
| | | NOTE: Rotary wing aircraft only. During Condition I, stand down other battle watch stations to man Flight Deck, Rescue Boat Detail, and Crash & Salvage Detail. During Condition III, flight deck operations workload is collected as OUS and only supports logistic helicopter operations. | | | | |
| **MOB 7** | **PERFORM SEAMANSHIP, AIRMANSHIP AND NAVIGATION TASKS.** | | | | | |
| | MOB 7.1 | Navigate under all conditions of geographic location, weather and visibility. | F | F/E | F/E | |
| | MOB 7.2 | Conduct precision anchoring. | F/E | F/E | F/E | |
| | | NOTE: During Condition I, stand down other battle stations. During Condition III, requires augmentation form off-watch personnel. | | | | |
| | MOB 7.3 | Get underway, moor, anchor and sortie with duty section in a safe manner. | | | | L/E |
| | | V(L) - Deployed, duty section fully capable. Not deployed, recall of personnel is required. | | | | |
| | MOB 7.5 | Utilize programmed evasive steering. | F | F | L | |
| | | IV(L) - Plan and train. | | | | |

| LCS XXCLASS | I | III | IV | V |
|---|---|---|---|---|
| **MOB 7.6**    Abandon/scuttle ship rapidly. | F | L | L | L |
|      III, IV, V(L) - Plan and train. | | | | |
| **MOB 7.7**    Provide life boat/raft capacity in accordance with unit's allowance. | F | F | F | F |
| **MOB 7.8**    Tow or be towed (towing engine not required). | F/E | F/E | F/E | |
|      NOTE: Requires securing personnel from other battle stations in Condition I. | | | | |
| **MOB 7.9**    Operate day and night and under all weather conditions. | F | F | F | |
| **MOB 7.10**    Conduct undetected transits. | F | F | F | |
| **MOB 7.15**    Operate in a chemically contaminated environment. | F | F | F | F |
| **MOB 7.16**    Recover man overboard (shipboard, boat or helicopter). | F/E | F/E | F/E | F |
|      NOTE: During Condition I, search and recovery requires augmentation by securing other battle stations. During Condition III, search and recovery requires augmentation from off-watch·personnel. | | | | |
| **MOB 10**    **REPLENISH AT SEA.** | | | | |
| **MOB 10.1**    Receive vertical replenishment. | | F/E | F/E | |
| **MOB 10.2**    Receive fuel while underway (alongside method). | | F/E | F/E | |
| **MOB 10.3**    Receive munitions and provisions while underway. | | F/E | F/E | |
| **MOB 10.4**    Receive potable and/or feed water while underway. | | F/E | F/E | |
| **MOB 10.5**    Receive COD/VOD aircraft. | | F/E | F/E | |
|      NOTE: VOD aircraft only. | | | | |
| **MOB 10.6**    Receive fuel while underway (astern method). | | F/E | F/E | |
| **MOB 12**    **MAINTAIN THE HEALTH AND WELL-BEING OF THE CREW.** | | | | |
| **MOB 12.1**    Ensure all phases of food service operations are conducted consistent with approved sanitary procedures and standards. | L | F | F | F |
|      I(L) - Battle messing. Requires securing food distribution personnel from Condition I stations at Commanding Officer's discretion. | | | | |
| **MOB 12.2**    Ensure the operation of the potable water system in a manner consistent with approved sanitary procedures and standards. | F | F | F | F |
| **MOB 12.3**    Monitor and/or maintain the environment to ensure the protection of personnel from overexposure to hazardous levels of radiation, temperature, noise, vibration and toxic substances per current instructions. | F | F | F | F |
| **MOB 12.4**    Maintain closed atmosphere within prescribed specifications. | F | F | F | F |

| LCS XXCLASS | | | I | III | IV | V |
|---|---|---|---|---|---|---|
| MOB 12.5 | Monitor the health and well-being of the crew to ensure that habitability is consistent with approved habitability procedures and standards. | | | F | F | F |
| MOB 12.6 | Ensure the operation and maintenance of all phases of shipboard environmental protection systems do not create a health hazard and are consistent with other naval directives pertaining to the prevention of pollution of the environment. | | | F | F | F |
| MOB 12.8 | Provide individual protective clothing and equipment to sufficiently protect shipboard personnel identified being at risk in a CBR-contaminated environment.  III, IV, V(L) - Plan and train. | | F | L | L | L |
| MOB 12.9 | Provide individual protective clothing and equipment to sufficiently protect assigned medical personnel aboard a ship at risk in a CBR-contaminated environment.  III, IV, V(L) - Plan and train. | | F | L | L | L |
| MOB 12.12 | Provide antidotes to ship's company that will counteract the effects caused by a CBR-contaminated environment.  III, IV, V(L) - Plan and train. | | F | L | L | L |
| MOB 12.13 | Train designated medical supervisors and non-medical personnel to detect CBR-contaminated casualties. | | | F | F | F |
| MOB 12.14 | Train designated non-medical personnel to decontaminate CBR casualties. | | | F | F | F |
| MOB 12.15 | Identify, supply and maintain decontamination stations. | | F | F | F | F |
| **MOB 17** | **PERFORM ORGANIZATIONAL LEVEL REPAIRS TO OWN UNIT'S MOB EQUIPMENT.**  I(L) - Emergency repairs to equipment critical to ship's mission. May require standing down selected personnel from their Condition I stations. | | L | F | F | F |
| **MOB 18** | **CONDUCT CASUALTY CONTROL PROCEDURES TO MAINTAIN/RESTORE OWN UNIT'S MOB CAPABILITIES.**  NOTE: During Condition I, emergency repairs to equipment critical to ship's mission. During Condition III and IV, immediate response by existing watchstanders with complete restoration supported by augmentation from off-watch personnel.  V(L) - Plan and train. | | F | F/A | F/A | L |

| LCS XXCLASS | I | III | IV | V |
|---|---|---|---|---|
| **MISSIONS OF STATE (MOS)** | | | | |
| **MOS 1   PERFORM NAVAL DIPLOMATIC PRESENCE OPERATIONS.** | | | | |
| MOS 1.1   Establish a sovereign, mobile sea base in a forward area.<br><br>IV, V(L) - Plan and train. | F | F | L | L |
| MOS 1.2   Conduct force/unit tour for foreign dignitaries. | | F/A | F/A | F/A |
| MOS 1.3   Conduct systems/weapons demonstrations for foreign dignitaries. | | F/E | F/E | F/E |
| MOS 1.4   Conduct foreign port calls. | | | | F |
| MOS 1.5   Conduct force/unit tours for foreign citizens during port calls. | | | | F/A |
| MOS 1.6   Conduct receptions for foreign dignitaries during port calls. | | | | F/A |
| MOS 1.7   Provide volunteers for small project assistance during port calls. | | | | F/A |
| MOS 1.8   Participate in military exercises with allied nations. | | F | F/A | F/A |
| MOS 1.9   Participate in military exercises with nonallied nations. | | F | F/A | F/A |
| MOS 1.10   Participate in or provide participants for foreign/allied commemorative or ceremonial events. | | | F/E | F/E |
| MOS 1.11   Provide lift of opportunity for foreign or national diplomatic material.<br><br>III, IV, V(L) - Small quantities that do not interfere with the regular combat capabilities or logistics load. | | L | L | L |
| **MOS 2   PROVIDE HUMANITARIAN ASSISTANCE.** | | | | |
| MOS 2.1   Deliver relief material.<br><br>III, IV, V(L) - Small quantities that do not interfere with the regular combat capabilities or logistics load. | | L | L | L |
| MOS 2.2   Provide emergency flooding/fire fighting assistance. | | F/E | F/E | F/E |
| MOS 2.4   Provide disaster assistance and evacuation. | | F/E | F/E | F/E |
| MOS 2.5   Clear and repair utilities and facilities damaged by natural disaster, fire, and civil disturbance; decontaminate CBR effects. | | | | F/E |
| MOS 2.9   Plan, direct and coordinate disaster assistance evacuation. | | F/A | F/A | F/A |
| MOS 2.10   Support/provide for the evacuation of noncombatant personnel in areas of civil or international crisis. | | F/A | F/A | F/A |
| MOS 2.11   Support/conduct helicopter/boat evacuation of noncombatant personnel as directed by higher authority from areas of civil or international crisis. | | F/A | F/A | F/A |
| MOS 2.12   Provide for embarkation, identification and processing of evacuees. | | F/A | F/A | F/A |

| LCS XXCLASS | | I | III | IV | V |
|---|---|---|---|---|---|
| MOS 2.13 | Provide care, feeding and berthing of evacuees. | | F/A | F/A | F/A |
| MOS 2.14 | Provide transportation for evacuees to designated safe havens or onward processing centers. | | F/A | F/A | F/A |
| MOS 2.15 | Plan/direct the evacuation of noncombat personnel in areas of civil or international crisis in both a permissive and non-permissive environment (including joint/combined operations). NOTE: During Condition I, stand down other battle stations to man Flight Deck, Rescue Boat Detail and Crash & Salvage Detail. During other Conditions of Readiness, in addition to flight deck crew, boat detail and crash & salvage detail, other off-watch personnel will be required for non-combat personnel processing. | F/E | F/E | F/E | F/E |

**MOS 3 PERFORM PEACEKEEPING**

| | | I | III | IV | V |
|---|---|---|---|---|---|
| MOS 3.2 | Provide logistics support for a joint/allied peacekeeping force. NOTE: During Condition I, stand down other battle stations to man Flight Deck, Rescue Boat Detail and Crash & Salvage Detail. During other Conditions of Readiness, in addition to flight deck crew, boat detail and crash & salvage detail, other off-watch personnel will be required for non-combat personnel processing. | F/E | F/E | F/E | F/E |
| MOS 3.3 | Provide direct participation in a joint/allied peacekeeping force within a foreign country/region. IV, V(L) - Plan and train. | F | F | L | L |

**MOS 4 PERFORM INTERDICTION**

| | | I | III | IV | V |
|---|---|---|---|---|---|
| MOS 4.1 | Conduct naval blockade. IV, V(L) - Plan and train. | F | F/A | L | L |
| MOS 4.2 | Conduct quarantine operations. IV, V(L) - Plan and train. | F | F/A | L | L |
| MOS 4.3 | Enforce sanction enforcement operations. IV, V(L) - Plan and train. | F | F/A | L | L |

| LCS XXCLASS | | | I | III | IV | V |
|---|---|---|---|---|---|---|
| | MOS 4.4 | Conduct Maritime Interception Operations (MIO) and or Visit, Board, Search and Seizure (VBSS) operations with naval/combined /joint forces.<br><br>NOTE: FFG capable of initial MIO/VBSS operations. However, ship unable to maintain sustained operations or security team without support of MIO Detachment.<br><br>I(L) - Requires standing down selected watch stations, unless MIO Detachment is embarked.<br><br>III, IV(L) - Requires supplement from embarked law enforcement personnel/equipment. | L/E | L/E | L/E | |
| MOS 5 | **PROVIDE FOREIGN INTERNAL DEFENSE (FID) ASSISTANCE** | | | | | |
| | MOS 5.4 | Conduct tactical operations in close cooperation with the host nation that focus on neutralizing and destroying the insurgent threat in the maritime environment.<br><br>IV, V(L) - Plan and train. | F | F/A | L | L |
| MOS 8 | **PROVIDE ANTITERRORISM ASSISTANCE** | | | | | |
| | MOS 8.1 | Ensure that the physical security of important persons, facilities and events meets acceptable standards. | | F/A | F/A | F/A |
| | MOS 8.2 | Provide training and advice on how to reduce vulnerability to terrorism and other threats, particularly in the maritime environment. | | F | F | F |
| MOS 10 | **CONDUCT SPECIAL ACTIVITIES AS GOVERNED BY EXECUTIVE ORDER 12333 AND IN ACCORDANCE WITH A PRESIDENTIAL FINDING AND CONGRESSIONAL OVERSIGHT**<br><br>I, III(L) - Provide covering action for Marine or SOC forces.<br><br>IV, V(L) - Plan and train. | | L | L | L | L |
| **NONCOMBAT OPERATIONS (NCO)** | | | | | | |
| NCO 2 | **PROVIDE ADMINISTRATIVE AND SUPPLY SUPPORT FOR OWN UNIT.** | | | | | |
| | NCO 2.1 | Provide supply support services.<br><br>I(L) - Provide emergency supply support only. | L | F | F | F |
| | NCO 2.2 | Provide clerical services. | | F | F | F |
| | NCO 2.3 | Provide disbursing services. | | F | F | F |
| | NCO 2.4 | Provide post office services. | | F | F | F |

| LCS XXCLASS | I | III | IV | V |
|---|---|---|---|---|
| NCO 2.5  Provide messing facilities.<br><br>I(L) - Battle messing requires securing food distribution personnel from Condition I stations at Commanding Officer's discretion. | L | F | F | F |
| NCO 2.6  Provide ships service facilities. | | F | F | F |
| NCO 2.7  Provide inventory and custodial services. | | F | F | F |
| NCO 2.8  Provide personnel for living space maintenance. | | F | F | F |
| NCO 2.9  Provide personnel for area command security. | F | F | F | F |
| NCO 2.11  Provide personnel for fuels support. | F | F | F | F |
| **NCO 3  PROVIDE UPKEEP AND MAINTENANCE OF OWN UNIT.** | | | | |
| NCO 3.1  Provide organizational level preventive maintenance. | | F | F | F |
| NCO 3.2  Provide organizational level corrective maintenance.<br><br>I(L) - Emergency repairs to equipment critical to ship's missions.  May require standing down selected personnel from their Condition I stations. | L | F | F | F |
| NCO 3.3  Provide small arms storage area. | F | F | F | F |
| NCO 3.4  Maintain preservation and cleanliness of topside and internal spaces. | | F | F | F |
| NCO 3.5  Provide for proper storage, handling, use and transfer of hazardous materials. | | F | F | F |
| **NCO 4  PROVIDE CLOSED-CIRCUIT TELEVISION SUPPORT FOR OWN UNIT.** | | F | F | F |
| **NCO 5  CONDUCT METEOROLOGICAL, HYDROGRAPHIC AND/OR OCEANOGRAPHIC COLLECTION OPERATIONS OR SURVEYS.** | | | | |
| NCO 5.1  Collect and disseminate meteorological information. | F | F | F | F |
| NCO 5.2  Collect and disseminate hydrographic information.<br><br>NOTE:  Depth only. | F | F | F | |
| NCO 5.3  Collect and disseminate oceanographic information including bathythermograph operations. | F | F | F | |
| **NCO 7  PROVIDE SPECIAL TECHNICAL RESEARCH.** | | | | |
| NCO 7.1  Serve as a platform for special technical research operations. | | F | F | F |
| NCO 7.2  Conduct special technical research operations.<br><br>III, IV, V(L) - Embarkation of technical support personnel required. | | L | L | L |

| LCS XXCLASS | I | III | IV | V |
|---|---|---|---|---|
| **NCO 8**    **SERVE AS A PLATFORM FOR OPERATIONAL TEST AND EVALUATION OF SYSTEMS, EQUIPMENT, AND TACTICS** | | | | |
| NCO 8.1    Provide technical assistance for installed test and evaluation equipment. | | F | F | F |
| NCO 8.2    Perform the test and evaluation functions set forth in the appropriate test plans.<br><br>III, IV, V(L) - Support projects as required with ship's company as long as primary mission areas are not degraded. | | L/A | L/A | L/A |
| NCO 8.3    Perform the evaluation functions set forth in appropriate TACMEMOS.<br><br>III, IV, V(L) - Support projects as required with ship's company as long as primary mission areas are not degraded. | | L/A | L/A | L/A |
| NCO 8.4    Provide range safety as set forth in appropriate test plans during missile operational tests. | | F | F | |
| **NCO 10**    **PROVIDE EMERGENCY/DISASTER ASSISTANCE.** | | | | |
| NCO 10.1    Provide emergency flooding/fire fighting assistance to another unit.<br><br>I(L) - Requires securing personnel from other battle stations. | L/E | F/E | F/E | F/E |
| NCO 10.4    Provide disaster assistance and evacuation.<br><br>I(L) - Requires securing personnel from other battle stations. | L/A | F/A | F/A | F/A |
| **NCO 11**    **SUPPORT/PROVIDE FOR THE EVACUATION OF NONCOMBATANT PERSONNEL IN AREAS OF CIVIL OR INTERNATIONAL CRISIS.** | | | | |
| NCO 11.1    Support/conduct helicopter/boat evacuation of noncombatant personnel as directed by higher authority from areas of civil or international crisis.<br><br>I(L) - May require securing personnel from other battle stations. | L/E | F/E | F/E | F/E |
| NCO 11.2    Provide for embarkation, identification and processing of evacuees.<br><br>I(L) - May require securing personnel from other battle stations. | L/A | F/A | F/A | F/A |
| NCO 11.3    Provide care, feeding and berthing of evacuees.<br><br>I(L) - May require securing personnel from other battle stations. | L/A | F/A | F/A | F/A |

130

| LCS XXCLASS | I | III | IV | V |
|---|---|---|---|---|
| NCO 11.4   Provide transportation for evacuees to designated safe havens or onward processing centers.<br><br>I(L) - May require securing personnel from other battle stations. | L/A | F | F | |
| **NCO 16   PROVIDE ANTI-TERRORISM/FORCE PROTECTION DEFENSE.** | | | | |
| NCO 16.1   Assimilate and disseminate intelligence on terrorist activities directed at U.S. Navy installations, ships and personnel. | F | F | F | F |
| NCO 16.2   Request and/or provide a threat assessment. | F | F | F | F |
| NCO 16.3   Declare general warnings of possible terrorist activity (THREATCON). | F | F | F | F |
| NCO 16.4   Anticipate and provide defenses against terrorist activities directed at ships, installations, facilities and personnel.<br><br>(a) Include provisions for barriers, access control, surveillance, intruder detection, and electronic security systems.<br>(b) Train and exercise the unit's AT response force to include tactical room/space entry.<br>(c) Implement local FPCON measures.<br>(d) Implement unit terrorist incident response plan.<br>(e) Operate electronic security systems (ESS).<br>(f) Operate duress systems.<br>(g) Train and exercise designated marksman for defense of HVA, boat crews and security personnel. | | F | F | F |
| NCO 16.5   Conduct screening of non-assigned personnel and materials entering the unit or facility using:<br><br>(a) Logical means (validation of identification, documentation, personal recognition, etc.)<br>(b) Physical means (searches, metal detection, explosive detection, etc.) | | F | F | F |
| NCO 16.6   Provide waterside barriers/patrols during port calls and anchorage.<br><br>NOTE: May require rigid-hull inflatable boats (RHIB) and crews. May require augmentation by Mobile Security Detachment (MSD). | | F/E | F/E | F/E |
| NCO 16.7   Determine, maintain and enforce port, harbor and anchorage limited access areas.<br><br>NOTE: May require rigid-hull inflatable boats (RHIB) and crews. May require augmentation by MSD. | | F/E | F/E | F/E |

| LCS XXCLASS | | I | III | IV | V |
|---|---|---|---|---|---|
| NCO 16.8 | Conduct surveillance and interdiction operations of swimmers/swimmer delivery vehicles.<br><br>NOTE: May require rigid-hull inflatable boats (RHIB) and crews. May require augmentation by MSD. | | F/E | F/E | F/E |
| NCO 16.9 | Provide AT information and voluntary training to dependents visiting units in foreign ports/locations. | | | | F |
| NCO 16.10 | Publish/Disseminate anti-terrorism defense instructions that include provisions for appropriate perimeter barriers, access control, surveillance and intruder detection, AT response force including a crisis action team, and evacuation. | | F | F | F |
| NCO 16.11 | Conduct hostage survival and Code of Conduct training. | | F | F | F |
| NCO 16.12 | Direct, conduct and assess unit AT exercises consistent with potential and/or actual threat environment. | | F | F | F |
| **NCO 19** | **CONDUCT MARITIME LAW ENFORCEMENT OPERATIONS.**<br><br>NOTE: For those requirements involving interdiction, visit, board, search and seizure of vessels the FFG is capable of initial operations. However, sustained operations and or maintenance of a security team require embarked law enforcement personnel (i.e., Coast Guard detachment or MIO detachment). | | | | |
| NCO 19.1 | Detect and identify noncombatant vessels. | F | F | F | F |
| NCO 19.2 | Conduct boarding and inspection of noncombatant vessels.<br><br>I(L) - Requires standing down selected watch stations, unless law enforcement detachment is embarked.<br><br>III, IV(L) - Requires supplement from embarked law enforcement personnel/equipment. | L/E | L/E | L/E | |
| NCO 19.3 | Provide assistance to other law enforcement forces.<br><br>I(L) - Requires standing down selected watch stations, unless law enforcement detachment is embarked. | L/E | F/E | F/E | |
| NCO 19.4 | Provide surveillance and protection of maritime resources. | F | F | F | |
| NCO 19.6 | Conduct seizure of noncombatant vessels.<br><br>I(L) - Requires standing down selected watch stations, unless law enforcement detachment is embarked.<br><br>III, IV(L) - Requires supplement from embarked law enforcement personnel/equipment. | L/E | L/E | L/E | |

| LCS XXCLASS | | I | III | IV | V |
|---|---|---|---|---|---|
| NCO 19.9 | Conduct drug traffic suppression and interdiction operations.<br><br>I(L) - Requires standing down selected watch stations, unless law enforcement detachment is embarked.<br><br>III, IV(L) - Requires supplement from embarked law enforcement personnel/equipment. | L/E | L/E | L/E | |
| NCO 19.13 | Support enforcement of fisheries law and treaties.<br><br>I(L) - Requires standing down selected watch stations, unless law enforcement detachment is embarked.<br><br>III, IV(L) - Requires supplement from embarked law enforcement personnel/equipment. | L/E | L/E | L/E | |
| NCO 19.14 | Support enforcement of offshore mining and gas/oil drilling laws.<br><br>I(L) - Requires standing down selected watch stations, unless law enforcement detachment is embarked.<br><br>III, IV(L) - Requires supplement from embarked law enforcement personnel/equipment. | L/E | L/E | L/E | |
| NCO 19.15 | Support drug traffic suppression and interdiction operations.<br><br>I(L) - Requires standing down selected watch stations, unless law enforcement detachment is embarked.<br><br>III, IV(L) - Requires supplement from embarked law enforcement personnel/equipment. | L/E | L/E | L/E | |
| NCO 19.16 | Support illegal entry suppression operations.<br><br>I(L) - Requires standing down selected watch stations, unless law enforcement detachment is embarked.<br><br>III, IV(L) - Requires supplement from embarked law enforcement personnel/equipment. | L/E | L/E | L/E | |
| **NCO 24** | **SUPPORT/CONDUCT ROTARY WING AIRCRAFT OPERATIONS.**<br><br>NOTE: During Condition I, stand down other battle watch stations to man Flight Deck, Rescue Boat Detail and Crash & Salvage Detail. During Condition III, flight deck operations workload is collected as OUS. | | | | |
| NCO 24.1 | Support/conduct day rotary wing aircraft flight operations. | F/E | F/E | F/E | |
| NCO 24.2 | Support/conduct night rotary wing aircraft flight operations. | F/E | F/E | F/E | |
| NCO 24.3 | Support/conduct rotary wing aircraft flight operations during all EMCON conditions. | F/E | F/E | F/E | |

| LCS XXCLASS | | I | III | IV | V |
|---|---|:-:|:-:|:-:|:-:|
| NCO 24.4 | Support/conduct rotary wing aircraft hot and cold refueling operations. | F/E | F/E | F/E | |
| NCO 24.5 | Provide electrical power for rotary wing aircraft starting, testing, etc. | F/E | F/E | F/E | |
| **NCO 25** | **CONDUCT MARINE ENVIRONMENTAL PROTECTION.** | | | | |
| NCO 25.1 | Detect oil or hazardous chemical spill. | F | F | F | F |
| NCO 25.2 | Report spills to proper authority. | F | F | F | F |
| NCO 25.3 | Conduct pollution abatement operations. | | F/E | F/E | F/E |
| **NCO 32** | **CONDUCT COUNTERNARCOTIC AND OTHER LAW ENFORCEMENT SUPPORT OPERATIONS IN CONJUNCTION WITH OTHER FORCES.** | | | | |
| NCO 32.1 | Conduct/support operations with Coast Guard units. | F | F | F | |
| NCO 32.2 | Conduct/support operations with other federal law enforcement agencies. | F | F | F | |
| NCO 32.4 | Conduct operations with other national governments. | F | F | F | |
| **NCO 33** | **SUPPORT/PROVIDE COUNTERNARCOTICS AND OTHER LAW ENFORCEMENT SUPPORT PATROL OF A FIXED GEOGRAPHIC AREA.** | | | | |
| NCO 33.1 | Operate as choke point patrol unit. | F | F | F/A | |
| NCO 33.2 | Operate as an open ocean patrol unit. | F | F | F/A | |
| **NCO 34** | **IN SUPPORT OF COUNTERNARCOTICS AND OTHER LAW ENFORCEMENT OPERATIONS, DETECT AND MONITOR SUSPECT SURFACE CONTACTS.** | | | | |
| NCO 34.1 | Detect and monitor surface contacts with radar. | F | F | F | |
| NCO 34.2 | Detect and monitor surface contacts visually.<br><br>III, IV(L) – Capability provided by bridge watch team and aft lookout. | F | L | L | |
| NCO 34.3 | Detect and monitor surface contacts with infrared equipment.<br><br>III, IV(L) – Capability provided by bridge watch team and aft lookout. | F | L | L | |
| NCO 34.4 | Detect and monitor surface contacts with electronic surveillance methods. | F | F | F | |
| NCO 34.5 | Detect and monitor surface contacts with passive sonar.<br><br>NOTE: TMA requires augmentation from off-watch personnel. | F | F/E | F/E | |
| NCO 34.6 | Detect and monitor surface contacts with active sonar. | F | F | F | |

| LCS XXCLASS | I | III | IV | V |
|---|---|---|---|---|
| NCO 34.7   Detect and monitor surface contacts with surveillance towed arrays. <br><br> NOTE: TMA requires augmentation from off-watch personnel. | F | F/E | F/E | |
| **NCO 36**   **IN SUPPORT OF COUNTERNARCOTICS AND OTHER LAW ENFORCEMENT OPERATIONS, DETECT AND MONITOR SUSPECT AIR CONTACTS.** | | | | |
| NCO 36.1   Detect and monitor air contacts with radar. | F | F | F | |
| NCO 36.2   Detect and monitor air contacts visually. <br><br> III, IV(L) – Capability provided by bridge watch team and aft lookout. | F | L | L | |
| NCO 36.3   Detect and monitor air contacts by electronic surveillance measures. | F | F | F | |
| **NCO 37**   **EMBARK AND SUPPORT LAW ENFORCEMENT DETACHMENTS.** | F | F/A | F/A | F/A |
| **NCO 38**   **RECEIVE, DISPLAY AND MAINTAIN COUNTERNARCOTIC INTELLIGENCE DATA.** | F | F | F | F/A |

THIS PAGE INTENTIONALLY LEFT BLANK

# General Dynamics
## Current Core Mission and Combat System*

### 419 Feet

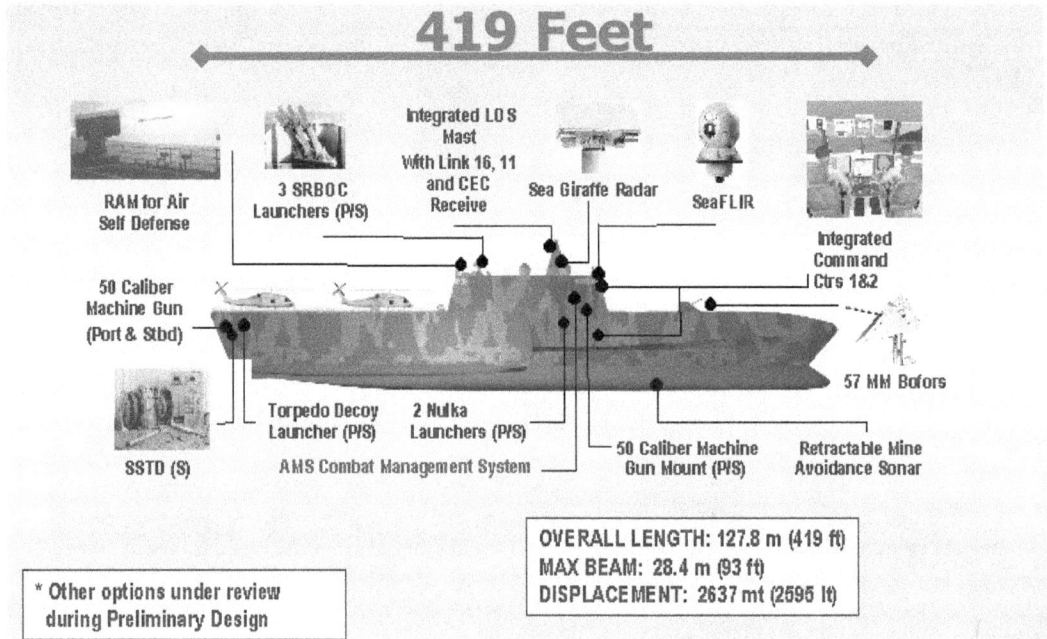

- RAM for Air Self Defense
- 3 SRBOC Launchers (P/S)
- Integrated LOS Mast With Link 16, 11 and CEC Receive
- Sea Giraffe Radar
- SeaFLIR
- Integrated Command Ctrs 1&2
- 50 Caliber Machine Gun (Port & Stbd)
- 57 MM Bofors
- SSTD (S)
- Torpedo Decoy Launcher (P/S)
- 2 Nulka Launchers (P/S)
- AMS Combat Management System
- 50 Caliber Machine Gun Mount (P/S)
- Retractable Mine Avoidance Sonar

OVERALL LENGTH: 127.8 m (419 ft)
MAX BEAM: 28.4 m (93 ft)
DISPLACEMENT: 2637 mt (2595 lt)

* Other options under review during Preliminary Design

34

# Lockheed Martin Seaframe

### 378 Feet

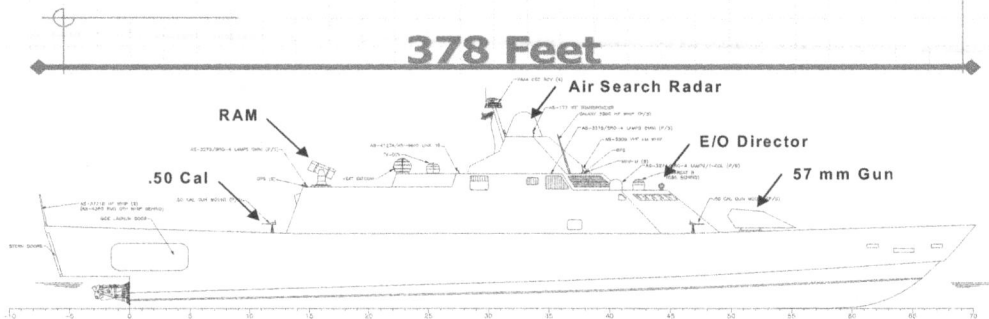

- RAM
- Air Search Radar
- E/O Director
- .50 Cal
- 57 mm Gun

35

137

# APPENDIX D. FORMULATION INDICES

*c   Class of ship*

0 = N/A
1 = CG
2 = DDG
3 = FFG
4 = MCM
5 = MHC
6 = LCS
7 = MIWFMP
8 = ASWFMP
9 = SUWFMP

*d   Department / Detachment*

0 = N/A
1 = Executive
2 = Operations
3 = Combat Systems
4 = Engineering
5 = Supply
6 = FMP/Mission C4
7 = USV Operator
8 = USV Support
9 = USV Weapons
10 = RMV Oper
11 = RMV Support
12 = MIW Specialist
13 = ASW Specialist
14 = SUW Specialist
15 = MH-60R & UAV Operator
16 = MH-60S & UAV Operator
17 = Air Det Composite Support

*s   System*

0 = N/A
1 = Main Gun
2 = CIWS
3 = .50 Cal
4 = RAM
5 = Search RADAR
6 = Air Decoy
7 = Torpedo Decoy Launcher
8 = SONAR
9 = Engineering Plant
10 = FMP C4
11 = Aviation
12 = USV
13 = RMV
14 = BPAUV
15 = SCULPIN
16 = EOD
17 = ACES/EER/IEER/AEER family
18 = Torpedo CounterMeasures
19 = ADS
20 = Towed Array
21 = Intermediate Cal Gun
22 = Non-lethal Weapon Det

THIS PAGE INTENTIONALLY LEFT BLANK

# APPENDIX E. LEGACY SHIP MANPOWER REQUIREMENTS

|  | Rate | CG(NS) | CG(SS) | DDG | DDG(OME) | FFG | MCM | MHC |
|---|---|---|---|---|---|---|---|---|
| **OFFICER** | 1110 | 11 | 11 | 11 | 10 | 9 | 3 | 3 |
|  | 1140 | 0 | 0 | 0 | 0 | 0 | 1 | 1 |
|  | 1160 | 8 | 8 | 5 | 8 | 4 | 1 | 0 |
|  | 1190 | 0 | 0 | 0 | 0 | 0 | 2 | 1 |
|  | 2100 | 1 | 1 | 1 | 0 | 0 | 0 | 0 |
|  | 3100 | 3 | 3 | 2 | 2 | 2 | 1 | 0 |
|  | 4100 | 1 | 1 | 0 | 0 | 0 | 0 | 0 |
|  | 6120 | 1 | 1 | 1 | 0 | 0 | 0 | 0 |
|  | 6130 | 0 | 0 | 1 | 0 | 0 | 0 | 0 |
|  | 6160 | 1 | 1 | 1 | 1 | 0 | 0 | 0 |
|  | 6180 | 1 | 1 | 1 | 1 | 1 | 0 | 0 |
|  | 7120 | 0 | 0 | 0 | 1 | 0 | 0 | 0 |
|  | 7130 | 1 | 1 | 0 | 1 | 1 | 0 | 0 |
|  | 7440 | 1 | 1 | 0 | 0 | 0 | 0 | 0 |
| **ENLISTED** | BM | 7 | 8 | 9 | 9 | 9 | 0 | 0 |
|  | CMD | 1 | 1 | 0 | 1 | 1 | 0 | 0 |
|  | CTA | 1 | 1 | 0 | 0 | 0 | 0 | 0 |
|  | CTM | 2 | 2 | 0 | 0 | 0 | 0 | 0 |
|  | CTO | 2 | 2 | 0 | 0 | 0 | 0 | 0 |
|  | CTR | 6 | 6 | 0 | 0 | 0 | 0 | 0 |
|  | CTT/EW | 7 | 7 | 7 | 7 | 4 | 0 | 0 |
|  | DC | 10 | 8 | 9 | 9 | 6 | 3 | 2 |
|  | DK | 2 | 2 | 2 | 2 | 1 | 0 | 0 |
|  | EM | 6 | 5 | 5 | 7 | 6 | 5 | 3 |
|  | EN | 10 | 10 | 9 | 9 | 10 | 10 | 7 |
|  | ET | 16 | 16 | 11 | 14 | 9 | 4 | 3 |
|  | FC | 43 | 43 | 39 | 36 | 9 | 0 | 0 |
|  | FN | 12 | 9 | 12 | 12 | 4 | 4 | 2 |
|  | GM | 13 | 13 | 17 | 13 | 4 | 0 | 0 |
|  | GS | 1 | 1 | 1 | 1 | 0 | 0 | 0 |
|  | GSE | 6 | 6 | 7 | 6 | 5 | 0 | 0 |
|  | GSM | 20 | 12 | 19 | 14 | 11 | 0 | 0 |
|  | HM | 2 | 2 | 2 | 3 | 2 | 1 | 1 |
|  | HN | 1 | 1 | 0 | 0 | 0 | 0 | 0 |
|  | HT | 3 | 3 | 4 | 3 | 3 | 1 | 0 |
|  | IC | 5 | 5 | 7 | 5 | 3 | 2 | 1 |
|  | IS | 1 | 1 | 1 | 1 | 0 | 0 | 0 |
|  | IT/RM | 12 | 12 | 14 | 12 | 10 | 5 | 4 |
|  | MA | 1 | 1 | 1 | 1 | 1 | 0 | 0 |
|  | MR | 1 | 1 | 1 | 1 | 1 | 0 | 0 |
|  | MS/CS | 14 | 14 | 15 | 11 | 10 | 5 | 3 |
|  | NC | 1 | 1 | 1 | 1 | 1 | 0 | 0 |
|  | OS/MN | 28 | 28 | 31 | 22 | 21 | 20 | 13 |
|  | PC | 1 | 1 | 1 | 1 | 1 | 0 | 0 |
|  | PN | 4 | 4 | 3 | 3 | 2 | 1 | 0 |
|  | PO | 2 | 2 | 2 | 2 | 2 | 0 | 0 |
|  | QM | 7 | 7 | 5 | 6 | 4 | 4 | 2 |
|  | RP | 1 | 1 | 0 | 0 | 0 | 0 | 0 |
|  | SH | 6 | 6 | 7 | 4 | 5 | 0 | 0 |
|  | SK | 11 | 11 | 10 | 8 | 8 | 2 | 2 |
|  | SM | 0 | 0 | 6 | 1 | 1 | 1 | 1 |
|  | SN | 24 | 24 | 31 | 26 | 30 | 12 | 5 |
|  | STG | 16 | 16 | 20 | 17 | 11 | 0 | 0 |
|  | TM | 2 | 2 | 2 | 2 | 2 | 0 | 0 |
|  | YN | 2 | 2 | 6 | 2 | 2 | 1 | 1 |
| TOTAL |  | 339 | 326 | 340 | 296 | 216 | 89 | 55 |

THIS PAGE INTENTIONALLY LEFT BLANK

# APPENDIX F. LEGACY CONDITION I CONTROL STATION SUMMARY

| Control Station (Officer) | CG(NS) | CG(SS) | DDG | DDG(OME) | FFG | MCM | MHC |
|---|---|---|---|---|---|---|---|
| Ship | 4 | 4 | 3 | 4 | 4 | 3 | 2 |
| Operations | 9 | 9 | 6 | 7 | 5 | 1 | 1 |
| Communications | 0 | 0 | 0 | 0 | 0 | 0 | 0 |
| Electronics Casualty | 1 | 1 | 1 | 1 | 0 | 0 | 0 |
| Weapons | 0 | 0 | 0 | 1 | 0 | 1 | 1 |
| ASW/MIW | 2 | 2 | 0 | 1 | 2 | 1 | 0 |
| MIO | 0 | 0 | 0 | 1 | 2 | 0 | 0 |
| Engineering | 2 | 2 | 2 | 2 | 2 | 1 | 1 |
| Damage | 3 | 2 | 3 | 2 | 1 | 1 | 0 |
| Support | 0 | 0 | 0 | 0 | 0 | 0 | 0 |
| Total | 21 | 20 | 15 | 19 | 16 | 8 | 5 |

| Control Station (Enlisted) | CG(NS) | CG(SS) | DDG | DDG(OME) | FFG | MCM | MHC |
|---|---|---|---|---|---|---|---|
| Ship | 22 | 21 | 24 | 21 | 17 | 11 | 8 |
| Operations | 35 | 34 | 27 | 24 | 18 | 4 | 5 |
| Communications | 12 | 12 | 11 | 11 | 10 | 4 | 3 |
| Electronics Casualty | 39 | 39 | 43 | 35 | 13 | 2 | 0 |
| Weapons | 41 | 41 | 37 | 47 | 33 | 4 | 4 |
| ASW/MIW | 34 | 32 | 10 | 29 | 49 | 38 | 20 |
| MIO | 24 | 24 | 0 | 24 | 24 | 0 | 0 |
| Engineering | 57 | 50 | 74 | 53 | 43 | 9 | 3 |
| Damage | 77 | 64 | 80 | 82 | 65 | 41 | 24 |
| Support | 8 | 8 | 8 | 5 | 7 | 3 | 2 |
| Total | 349 | 325 | 314 | 331 | 279 | 116 | 69 |

| Control Station (Total) | CG(NS) | CG(SS) | DDG | DDG(OME) | FFG | MCM | MHC |
|---|---|---|---|---|---|---|---|
| Ship | 26 | 25 | 27 | 25 | 21 | 14 | 10 |
| Operations | 44 | 43 | 33 | 31 | 23 | 5 | 6 |
| Communications | 12 | 12 | 11 | 11 | 10 | 4 | 3 |
| Electronics Casualty | 40 | 40 | 44 | 36 | 13 | 2 | 0 |
| Weapons | 41 | 41 | 37 | 48 | 33 | 5 | 5 |
| ASW/MIW | 36 | 34 | 10 | 30 | 51 | 39 | 20 |
| MIO | 24 | 24 | 0 | 25 | 26 | 0 | 0 |
| Engineering | 59 | 52 | 76 | 55 | 45 | 10 | 4 |
| Damage | 80 | 66 | 83 | 84 | 66 | 42 | 24 |
| Support | 8 | 8 | 8 | 5 | 7 | 3 | 2 |
| Total | 370 | 345 | 329 | 350 | 295 | 124 | 74 |

| Control Station | Min | Max | Range |
|---|---|---|---|
| Ship | 10 | 27 | 17 |
| Operations | 5 | 44 | 39 |
| Communications | 3 | 12 | 9 |
| Electronics Casualty | 0 | 44 | 44 |
| Weapons | 5 | 48 | 43 |
| ASW/MIW | 10 | 51 | 41 |
| MIO | 0 | 26 | 26 |
| Engineering | 4 | 76 | 72 |
| Damage | 24 | 84 | 60 |
| Support | 2 | 8 | 6 |

THIS PAGE INTENTIONALLY LEFT BLANK

# APPENDIX G. LEGACY CONDITION III CONTROL STATION SUMMARY

| Control Station (Officer) | CG(NS) | CG(SS) | DDG | DDG(OME) | FFG | MCM | MHC |
|---|---|---|---|---|---|---|---|
| Ship | 2 | 2 | 2 | 2 | 2 | 1 | 1 |
| Operations | 5 | 5 | 3 | 4 | 1 | 0 | 0 |
| Communications | 0 | 0 | 0 | 0 | 0 | 0 | 0 |
| Electronics Casualty | 0 | 0 | 0 | 0 | 0 | 0 | 0 |
| Weapons | 0 | 0 | 0 | 0 | 0 | 0 | 0 |
| ASW/MIW | 0 | 0 | 0 | 0 | 0 | 0 | 0 |
| MIO | 0 | 0 | 0 | 0 | 0 | 0 | 0 |
| Engineering | 0 | 0 | 0 | 0 | 0 | 0 | 0 |
| Damage | 0 | 0 | 0 | 0 | 0 | 0 | 0 |
| Support | 0 | 0 | 0 | 0 | 0 | 0 | 0 |
| Total | 7 | 7 | 5 | 6 | 3 | 1 | 1 |

| Control Station (Enlisted) | CG(NS) | CG(SS) | DDG | DDG(OME) | FFG | MCM | MHC |
|---|---|---|---|---|---|---|---|
| Ship | 3 | 3 | 10 | 3 | 4 | 3 | 5 |
| Operations | 20 | 20 | 17 | 16 | 9 | 3 | 2 |
| Communications | 4 | 4 | 4 | 4 | 2 | 1 | 1 |
| Electronics Casualty | 3 | 3 | 6 | 6 | 3 | 0 | 0 |
| Weapons | 3 | 3 | 4 | 3 | 0 | 0 | 0 |
| ASW/MIW | 4 | 4 | 5 | 4 | 3 | 0 | 0 |
| MIO | 0 | 0 | 0 | 0 | 0 | 0 | 0 |
| Engineering | 11 | 5 | 7 | 8 | 7 | 5 | 2 |
| Damage | 3 | 2 | 3 | 2 | 1 | 0 | 0 |
| Support | 0 | 0 | 0 | 0 | 0 | 0 | 0 |
| Total | 51 | 44 | 56 | 46 | 29 | 12 | 10 |

| Control Station (Total) | CG(NS) | CG(SS) | DDG | DDG(OME) | FFG | MCM | MHC |
|---|---|---|---|---|---|---|---|
| Ship | 5 | 5 | 12 | 5 | 6 | 4 | 6 |
| Operations | 25 | 25 | 20 | 20 | 10 | 3 | 2 |
| Communications | 4 | 4 | 4 | 4 | 2 | 1 | 1 |
| Electronics Casualty | 3 | 3 | 6 | 6 | 3 | 0 | 0 |
| Weapons | 3 | 3 | 4 | 3 | 0 | 0 | 0 |
| ASW/MIW | 4 | 4 | 5 | 4 | 3 | 0 | 0 |
| MIO | 0 | 0 | 0 | 0 | 0 | 0 | 0 |
| Engineering | 11 | 5 | 7 | 8 | 7 | 5 | 2 |
| Damage | 3 | 2 | 3 | 2 | 1 | 0 | 0 |
| Support | 0 | 0 | 0 | 0 | 0 | 0 | 0 |
| Total | 58 | 51 | 61 | 52 | 32 | 13 | 11 |

| Control Station | Min | Max | Range |
|---|---|---|---|
| Ship | 4 | 12 | 8 |
| Operations | 2 | 25 | 23 |
| Communications | 1 | 4 | 3 |
| Electronics Casualty | 0 | 6 | 6 |
| Weapons | 0 | 4 | 4 |
| ASW/MIW | 0 | 5 | 5 |
| MIO | 0 | 0 | 0 |
| Engineering | 2 | 8 | 6 |
| Damage | 0 | 3 | 3 |
| Support | 0 | 0 | 0 |

THIS PAGE INTENTIONALLY LEFT BLANK

# APPENDIX H. CG (NS) BATTLE BILL REQUIREMENTS

| Control Station | Condition I | | Condition III | | |
|---|---|---|---|---|---|
| **Ship Control** | Officer | Enlisted | Officer | Enlisted | |
| Pilot House | 4 | 13 | 2 | 2 | 1/13 augmented |
| Lookouts | 0 | 3 | 0 | 1 | |
| Steering Aft | 0 | 3 | 0 | 0 | |
| Signal Bridge | 0 | 3 | 0 | 0 | |
| **Operations Control** | | | | | |
| Air Control | 0 | 3 | 0 | 2 | |
| Display and Decision | 7 | 8 | 5 | 4 | |
| Surface/Subsurfaces | 1 | 5 | 0 | 3 | |
| Tactical Information | 0 | 9 | 0 | 7 | |
| CCSS | 1 | 10 | 0 | 4 | |
| **Communications Control** | | | | | |
| Radio Central | 0 | 8 | 0 | 3 | |
| Information Security | 0 | 4 | 0 | 1 | |
| **Electronics Casualty Control** | | | | | |
| Combat Sys Maint Central | 1 | 8 | 0 | 1 | |
| Computer Rm (SPY 1) | 0 | 2 | 0 | 2 | |
| EW Equipment Rm | 0 | 2 | 0 | 0 | |
| SPS 49 Radar Rm | 0 | 3 | 0 | 0 | |
| SPS 55/Mk 99 Mod 4 xmtr Rm | 0 | 2 | 0 | 0 | |
| Aegis Radar Rm 1 | 0 | 2 | 0 | 0 | |
| Aegis Radar Rm 2 | 0 | 2 | 0 | 0 | |
| Aegis Radar Rm 3 | 0 | 3 | 0 | 0 | |
| Aegis Radar Rm 4 | 0 | 2 | 0 | 0 | |
| Aegis Radar Rm 5 | 0 | 3 | 0 | 0 | |
| Radio xmtr Rm | 0 | 4 | 0 | 0 | |
| CIC (SPY 1) | 0 | 2 | 0 | 0 | |
| Sonar Repair (SQQ-89(v)6) | 0 | 2 | 0 | 0 | |
| NIXIE Repair | 0 | 1 | 0 | 0 | |
| Gun Repair | 0 | 1 | 0 | 0 | |
| **Weapons Control** | | | | | |
| MT 51 Loader Drum Rm | 0 | 2 | 0 | 1 | |
| MT 51 Handling Rm | 0 | 8 | 0 | 0 | |
| MT 52 Loader Drum Rm | 0 | 2 | 0 | 0 | |
| MT 52 Handling Rm | 0 | 8 | 0 | 0 | |
| Mk 41 VLS Launcher | 0 | 5 | 0 | 1 | |
| Tomahawk | 0 | 5 | 0 | 1 | |
| CIWS MT 1 | 0 | 5 | 0 | 0 | |
| CIWS MT 2 | 0 | 4 | 0 | 0 | |
| Harpoon Missile Sys | 0 | 2 | 0 | 0 | |
| Total | 14 | 149 | 7 | 33 | |

Note:

| |
|---|
| Augmented by off-watch or standing down other watches |
| Different from CG SS |

| Control Station | Condition I | | Condition III | | |
|---|---|---|---|---|---|
| | Officer | Enlisted | Officer | Enlisted | |
| **ASW Control** | | | | | |
| Sonar Control (SQQ 89(v)6) | 0 | 6 | 0 | 4 | |
| Mk 32 SVTT enclosed | 0 | 2 | 0 | 0 | |
| SQR-19 Control (SQQ 89) | 0 | 1 | 0 | 0 | |
| Helo Control Station | 1 | 0 | 0 | 0 | |
| Flight Deck Control | 0 | 6 | 0 | 0 | 6/6 augmented |
| Ready Life Boat | 0 | 9 | 0 | 0 | 9/9 augmented |
| RAST Control (LAMPS III) | 1 | 0 | 0 | 0 | 1 LAMP OFF |
| Crash and Salvage | 0 | 8 | 0 | 0 | 8/8 augmented |
| AFFF Generator Station | 0 | 1 | 0 | 0 | |
| JP5 Pump Room | 0 | 1 | 0 | 0 | 1/1 augmented |
| **MIO** | | | | | |
| Boarding Team (co-manned) | 0 | 15 | 0 | 0 | |
| Divert Team | 0 | 9 | 0 | 0 | 5/9 augmented |
| **Engineering Control** | | | | | |
| Central Control Station | 1 | 2 | 0 | 5 | |
| ENG Rm Fwd | 0 | 5 | 0 | 2 | |
| ENG Rm Aft | 0 | 5 | 0 | 2 | |
| Aux Machinery Rm 1 | 0 | 4 | 0 | 2 | |
| Aux Machinery Rm 2 | 0 | 1 | 0 | 0 | |
| Generator Rm 3 | 0 | 2 | 0 | 0 | |
| IC and Gyro Rm Fwd | 0 | 2 | 0 | 0 | |
| IC and Gyro Rm Aft | 0 | 2 | 0 | 0 | |
| Converter Rm Aft | 0 | 1 | 0 | 0 | |
| Repair 5 | 1 | 33 | 0 | 0 | |
| **Damage Control** | | | | | |
| Damage Control Central | 1 | 10 | 0 | 2 | |
| Oil Lab | 0 | 1 | 0 | 1 | |
| Repair 2 | 0 | 24 | 0 | 0 | |
| Repair 3 (sec DCC) | 1 | 30 | 0 | 0 | |
| Battle Dressing Station Fwd | 0 | 6 | 0 | 0 | |
| Battle Dressing Station Aft | 1 | 6 | 0 | 0 | |
| **Support Control** | | | | | |
| Battle Messing | 0 | 5 | 0 | 0 | |
| Emergency Issue | 0 | 3 | 0 | 0 | |
| | | | | | |
| Total | 7 | 200 | 0 | 18 | |
| Overall Total | 370 | | 58 | | |

Note:

| |
|---|
| Augmented by off-watch or standing down other watches |
| Different from CG SS |

148

# APPENDIX I. CG (SS) BATTLE BILL REQUIREMENTS

| Control Station | Condition I | | Condition III | | |
|---|---|---|---|---|---|
| | Officer | Enlisted | Officer | Enlisted | |
| **Ship Control** | | | | | |
| Pilot House | 4 | 12 | 2 | 2 | 1/12 augmented |
| Lookouts | 0 | 3 | 0 | 1 | |
| Steering Aft | 0 | 3 | 0 | 0 | |
| Signal Bridge | 0 | 3 | 0 | 0 | |
| **Operations Control** | | | | | |
| Air Control | 0 | 3 | 0 | 2 | |
| Display and Decision | 7 | 8 | 5 | 4 | |
| Surface/Subsurfaces | 1 | 5 | 0 | 3 | |
| Tactical Information | 0 | 8 | 0 | 7 | Less one talker |
| CCSS | 1 | 10 | 0 | 4 | |
| **Communications Control** | | | | | |
| Radio Central | 0 | 8 | 0 | 3 | |
| Information Security | 0 | 4 | 0 | 1 | |
| **Electronics Casualty Control** | | | | | |
| Combat Sys Maint Central | 1 | 8 | 0 | 1 | |
| Computer Rm (SPY 1) | 0 | 2 | 0 | 2 | |
| EW Equipment Rm | 0 | 2 | 0 | 0 | |
| SPS 49 Radar Rm | 0 | 3 | 0 | 0 | |
| SPS 55/Mk 99 Mod 4 xmtr Rm | 0 | 2 | 0 | 0 | |
| Aegis Radar Rm 1 | 0 | 2 | 0 | 0 | |
| Aegis Radar Rm 2 | 0 | 2 | 0 | 0 | |
| Aegis Radar Rm 3 | 0 | 3 | 0 | 0 | |
| Aegis Radar Rm 4 | 0 | 2 | 0 | 0 | |
| Aegis Radar Rm 5 | 0 | 3 | 0 | 0 | |
| Radio xmtr Rm | 0 | 4 | 0 | 0 | |
| CIC (SPY 1) | 0 | 2 | 0 | 0 | |
| Sonar Repair (SQQ-89(v)6) | 0 | 2 | 0 | 0 | |
| NIXIE Repair | 0 | 1 | 0 | 0 | |
| Gun Repair | 0 | 1 | 0 | 0 | |
| **Weapons Control** | | | | | |
| MT 51 Loader Drum Rm | 0 | 2 | 0 | 1 | |
| MT 51 Handling Rm | 0 | 8 | 0 | 0 | |
| MT 52 Loader Drum Rm | 0 | 2 | 0 | 0 | |
| MT 52 Handling Rm | 0 | 8 | 0 | 0 | |
| Mk 41 VLS Launcher | 0 | 5 | 0 | 1 | |
| Tomahawk | 0 | 5 | 0 | 1 | |
| CIWS MT 1 | 0 | 5 | 0 | 0 | |
| CIWS MT 2 | 0 | 4 | 0 | 0 | |
| Harpoon Missile Sys | 0 | 2 | 0 | 0 | |
| Total | 14 | 147 | 7 | 33 | |

Note:

Augmented by off-watch or standing down other watches

Different from CG SS

| Control Station | Condition I | | Condition III | | |
|---|---|---|---|---|---|
| | Officer | Enlisted | Officer | Enlisted | |
| **ASW Control** | | | | | |
| Sonar Control (SQQ 89(v)6) | 0 | 6 | 0 | 4 | |
| Mk 32 SVTT enclosed | 0 | 2 | 0 | 0 | |
| SQR-19 Control (SQQ 89) | 0 | 1 | 0 | 0 | |
| Helo Control Station | 1 | 0 | 0 | 0 | |
| Flight Deck Control | 0 | 6 | 0 | 0 | 6/6 augmented |
| Ready Life Boat | 0 | 9 | 0 | 0 | 9/9 augmented |
| RAST Control (LAMPS III) | 1 | 0 | 0 | 0 | 1 LAMP OFF |
| Crash and Salvage | 0 | 6 | 0 | 0 | 8/8 augmented |
| AFFF Generator Station | 0 | 1 | 0 | 0 | |
| JP5 Pump Room | 0 | 1 | 0 | 0 | 1/1 augmented |
| **MIO** | | | | | |
| Boarding Team (co-manned) | 0 | 15 | 0 | 0 | |
| Divert Team | 0 | 9 | 0 | 0 | 5/9 augmented |
| **Engineering Control** | | | | | |
| Central Control Station | 1 | 1 | 0 | 4 | |
| ENG Rm Fwd | 0 | 3 | 0 | 0 | |
| ENG Rm Aft | 0 | 3 | 0 | 0 | |
| Aux Machinery Rm 1 | 0 | 3 | 0 | 1 | |
| Aux Machinery Rm 2 | 0 | 1 | 0 | 0 | |
| Generator Rm 3 | 0 | 2 | 0 | 0 | |
| IC and Gyro Rm Fwd | 0 | 2 | 0 | 0 | |
| IC and Gyro Rm Aft | 0 | 2 | 0 | 0 | |
| Converter Rm Aft | 0 | 1 | 0 | 0 | |
| Repair 5 | 1 | 32 | 0 | 0 | |
| **Damage Control** | | | | | |
| Damage Control Central | 1 | 4 | 0 | 1 | |
| Oil Lab | 0 | 1 | 0 | 1 | |
| Repair 2 | 0 | 24 | 0 | 0 | |
| Repair 3 (sec DCC) | 0 | 25 | 0 | 0 | |
| Battle Dressing Station Fwd | 0 | 5 | 0 | 0 | |
| Battle Dressing Station Aft | 1 | 5 | 0 | 0 | |
| **Support Control** | | | | | |
| Battle Messing | 0 | 5 | 0 | 0 | |
| Emergency Issue | 0 | 3 | 0 | 0 | |
| | | | | | |
| Total | 6 | 178 | 0 | 11 | |
| Overall Total | 345 | | 11 | | |

Note:

| |
|---|
| Augmented by off-watch or standing down other watches |
| Different from CG SS |

# APPENDIX J. DDG BATTLE BILL REQUIREMENTS

| Control Station | Condition I | | Condition III | |
|---|---|---|---|---|
| **Ship Control** | Officer | Enlisted | Officer | Enlisted |
| Pilot House | 3 | 12 | 2 | 5 |
| Lookouts | 0 | 3 | 0 | 3 |
| Steering Aft | 0 | 3 | 0 | 0 |
| Signal Bridge | 0 | 6 | 0 | 2 |
| **Operations Control** | | | | |
| Air Control | 0 | 3 | 0 | 2 |
| Display and Decision | 6 | 8 | 3 | 7 |
| Tactical Information | 0 | 7 | 0 | 5 |
| Surface Warfare | 0 | 9 | 0 | 3 |
| **Communications Control** | | | | |
| Radio Central | 0 | 8 | 0 | 3 |
| Information Security | 0 | 3 | 0 | 1 |
| **Combat Systems Casualty Control** | | | | |
| Combat Sys Maint Central | 1 | 5 | 0 | 2 |
| CIC | 0 | 1 | 0 | 0 |
| Electronics Workshop #1 | 0 | 3 | 0 | 1 |
| Power Supply/Conversion | 0 | 2 | 0 | 0 |
| Radar Room #1 & #2 | 0 | 8 | 0 | 1 |
| Radar Room #3 | 0 | 2 | 0 | 0 |
| Combat Sys Equipment Rm #1 | 0 | 2 | 0 | 0 |
| Combat Sys Equipment Rm #2 | 0 | 5 | 0 | 2 |
| Combat Sys Equipment Rm #3 | 0 | 3 | 0 | 0 |
| Radio Transmitter Rm | 0 | 3 | 0 | 0 |
| Communication Center | 0 | 1 | 0 | 0 |
| Sonar Equipment Rm #1 | 0 | 2 | 0 | 0 |
| Harpoon Equipment Rm | 0 | 5 | 0 | 0 |
| Gun Repair | 0 | 1 | 0 | 0 |
| **Weapons Control** | | | | |
| MT 51 Loader Drum Rm | 0 | 3 | 0 | 0 |
| MT 51 Handling Rm | 0 | 8 | 0 | 0 |
| CIWS MT 1 | 0 | 6 | 0 | 0 |
| CIWS MT 2 | 0 | 5 | 0 | 0 |
| MK 41 Launcher Station | 0 | 8 | 0 | 2 |
| Tomahawk | 0 | 7 | 0 | 2 |
| Total | 10 | 142 | 5 | 41 |

Note:

Different from DDG(OME)

151

| Control Station | Condition I | | Condition III | |
|---|---|---|---|---|
| **ASW Control** | Officer | Enlisted | Officer | Enlisted |
| Sonar Control (SQQ 89(v)6) | 0 | 7 | 0 | 5 |
| NIXIE | 0 | 2 | 0 | 0 |
| SQR-19 Control (SQQ 89) | 0 | 1 | 0 | 0 |
| **Engineering Control** | | | | |
| Central Control Station | 1 | 3 | 0 | 3 |
| ENG Rm Fwd | 0 | 3 | 0 | 1 |
| ENG Rm Aft | 0 | 4 | 0 | 1 |
| Aux Machinery Rm 1 | 0 | 4 | 0 | 1 |
| Aux Machinery Rm 2 | 0 | 1 | 0 | 0 |
| A/C Machinery and Pump Rm | 0 | 1 | 0 | 0 |
| Generator Rm | 0 | 3 | 0 | 0 |
| IC and Gyro Rm Fwd | 0 | 2 | 0 | 1 |
| IC and Gyro Rm Aft | 0 | 1 | 0 | 0 |
| Repair 5 | 1 | 31 | 0 | 0 |
| Repair 5 Unit A | 0 | 21 | 0 | 0 |
| **Damage Control** | | | | |
| Damage Control Central | 1 | 9 | 0 | 2 |
| Oil Lab | 0 | 1 | 0 | 1 |
| Repair 3 | 0 | 31 | 0 | 0 |
| Repair 2 (sec DCC) | 1 | 35 | 0 | 0 |
| Battle Dressing Station Fwd | 0 | 2 | 0 | 0 |
| Battle Dressing Station Aft | 1 | 2 | 0 | 0 |
| **Support Control** | | | | |
| Battle Messing | 0 | 5 | 0 | 0 |
| Emergency Issue | 0 | 3 | 0 | 0 |

| | | | | |
|---|---|---|---|---|
| Total | 5 | 172 | 0 | 15 |
| Overall Total | 329 | | 61 | |

Note:
Different from DDG(OME)

152

# APPENDIX K. DDG (OME) BATTLE BILL REQUIREMENTS

| Control Station | Condition I | | Condition III | | |
|---|---|---|---|---|---|
| | Officer | Enlisted | Officer | Enlisted | |
| **Ship Control** | | | | | |
| Pilot House | 4 | 10 | 2 | 2 | |
| Lookouts | 0 | 3 | 0 | 1 | |
| Steering Aft | 0 | 3 | 0 | 0 | |
| Signal Bridge | 0 | 5 | 0 | 0 | 2/5 aug |
| **Operations Control** | | | | | |
| Air Control | 0 | 3 | 0 | 2 | |
| Display and Decision | 6 | 8 | 3 | 7 | |
| Tactical Information | 0 | 6 | 0 | 5 | |
| Surface Warfare | 1 | 7 | 1 | 2 | |
| **Communications Control** | | | | | |
| Radio Central | 0 | 7 | 0 | 3 | |
| Information Security | 0 | 4 | 0 | 1 | |
| **Combat Systems Casualty Control** | | | | | |
| Combat Sys Maint Central | 1 | 4 | 0 | 1 | |
| CIC | 0 | 2 | 0 | 0 | |
| Electronics Workshop #1 | 0 | 2 | 0 | 3 | |
| Power Supply/Conversion | 0 | 2 | 0 | 0 | |
| Radar Room #1 & #2 | 0 | 6 | 0 | 0 | |
| Radar Room #3 | 0 | 2 | 0 | 0 | |
| Combat Sys Equipment Rm #1 | 0 | 2 | 0 | 0 | |
| Combat Sys Equipment Rm #2 | 0 | 3 | 0 | 2 | |
| Combat Sys Equipment Rm #3 | 0 | 3 | 0 | 0 | |
| Radio Transmitter Rm | 0 | 2 | 0 | 0 | |
| Communication Center | 0 | 2 | 0 | 0 | |
| Sonar Equipment Rm #1 | 0 | 1 | 0 | 0 | |
| Harpoon Equipment Rm | 0 | 4 | 0 | 0 | |
| **Weapons Control** | | | | | |
| MT 51 Loader Drum Rm | 0 | 3 | 0 | 1 | |
| MT 51 Handling Rm | 0 | 8 | 0 | 0 | |
| CIWS MT 21 | 0 | 6 | 0 | 0 | |
| CIWS MT 22 | 0 | 5 | 0 | 0 | |
| MK 41 Launcher Station | 0 | 4 | 0 | 1 | |
| M 60 Machine Gun #1 | 0 | 2 | 0 | 0 | All aug |
| M 60 Machine Gun #2 | 0 | 2 | 0 | 0 | All aug |
| 25 MM Mount #1 | 0 | 2 | 0 | 0 | All aug |
| 25 MM Mount #2 | 0 | 2 | 0 | 0 | All aug |
| 50 CAL Mount #1 | 0 | 2 | 0 | 0 | All aug |
| 50 CAL Mount #2 | 0 | 2 | 0 | 0 | All aug |
| 50 CAL Mount #3 | 0 | 2 | 0 | 0 | All aug |
| 50 CAL Mount #4 | 0 | 2 | 0 | 0 | All aug |
| Tomahawk | 1 | 5 | 0 | 1 | |
| Total | 13 | 138 | 6 | 32 | |

Note:

Augmented by off-watch or standing down other watches

Different from DDG

| Control Station | Condition I | | Condition III | | |
|---|---|---|---|---|---|
| | Officer | Enlisted | Officer | Enlisted | |
| **ASW Control** | | | | | |
| Sonar Control (SQQ 89(v)6) | 0 | 5 | 0 | 4 | |
| NIXIE | 0 | 1 | 0 | 0 | |
| SQR-19 Control (SQQ 89) | 0 | 1 | 0 | 0 | |
| Helo Control Station | 1 | 0 | 0 | 0 | |
| Flight Deck Control | 0 | 6 | 0 | 0 | All aug |
| JP5 Pump Room | 0 | 1 | 0 | 0 | All aug |
| Crash and Salvage | 0 | 6 | 0 | 0 | All aug |
| Ready Life Boat | 0 | 9 | 0 | 0 | All aug |
| **MIO** | | | | | |
| Boarding Team | 1 | 15 | 0 | 0 | |
| Divert Team | 0 | 9 | 0 | 0 | 5/9 aug |
| **Engineering Control** | | | | | |
| Central Control Station | 1 | 2 | 0 | 4 | |
| ENG Rm Fwd | 0 | 4 | 0 | 1 | |
| ENG Rm Aft | 0 | 4 | 0 | 1 | |
| Aux Machinery Rm 1 | 0 | 3 | 0 | 1 | |
| Aux Machinery Rm 2 | 0 | 1 | 0 | 0 | |
| A/C Machinery and Pump Rm | 0 | 1 | 0 | 0 | |
| Oil Test Lab | 0 | 1 | 0 | 1 | |
| Generator Rm | 0 | 2 | 0 | 0 | |
| IC and Gyro Rm Fwd | 0 | 2 | 0 | 0 | |
| IC and Gyro Rm Aft | 0 | 1 | 0 | 0 | |
| Repair 5 | 1 | 32 | 0 | 0 | |
| **Damage Control** | | | | | |
| Damage Control Central | 1 | 9 | 0 | 2 | |
| Repair 3 | 0 | 25 | 0 | 0 | |
| Repair 2 (sec DCC) | 1 | 30 | 0 | 0 | |
| Battle Dressing Station Fwd | 0 | 6 | 0 | 0 | |
| Battle Dressing Station Main | 0 | 6 | 0 | 0 | |
| Battle Dressing Station Aft | 0 | 6 | 0 | 0 | |
| **Support Control** | | | | | |
| Battle Messing | 0 | 3 | 0 | 0 | |
| Emergency Issue | 0 | 2 | 0 | 0 | |
| | | | | | |
| Total | 6 | 193 | 0 | 14 | |
| Overall Total | 350 | | 52 | | |

Note:

Augmented by off-watch or standing down other watches

Different from DDG(NO)

# APPENDIX L. FFG BATTLE BILL REQUIREMENTS

| Control Station | | With Reserves — Cond. I Officer | With Reserves — Cond. I Enlisted | With Reserves — Cond. III Officer | With Reserves — Cond. III Enlisted | Without Reserves — Cond. I Officer | Without Reserves — Cond. I Enlisted | Without Reserves — Cond. III Officer | Without Reserves — Cond. III Enlisted | CI notes | CIII notes |
|---|---|---|---|---|---|---|---|---|---|---|---|
| Ship Control | Pilot House | 4 | 10 | 2 | 3 | 3 | 7 | 1 | 3 | 4/14 res | 1/2 res |
| | Lookouts | 0 | 2 | 0 | 1 | 0 | 2 | 0 | 1 | | |
| | Steering Aft | 0 | 3 | 0 | 0 | 0 | 3 | 0 | 0 | | |
| | Signal Bridge | 0 | 2 | 0 | 0 | 0 | 1 | 0 | 0 | 1/2 aug res | |
| Operations Control | CIC | 3 | 14 | 1 | 7 | 1 | 9 | 1 | 3 | 7/17 res | 4/7 res |
| | Weapons CIC (MK 92 Mod 6) | 2 | 1 | 0 | 1 | 0 | 1 | 0 | 0 | 2/2 res | 1 res |
| | Electronic Warfare | 0 | 3 | 0 | 1 | 0 | 2 | 0 | 0 | 1/3 res | 1/1 res |
| Communications Control | Radio Central | 0 | 6 | 0 | 2 | 0 | 6 | 0 | 2 | | |
| | Information Security | 0 | 4 | 0 | 0 | 0 | 3 | 0 | 0 | 1/4 res | |
| Combat Systems Casualty Control | Radar/IFF/CIC Equip Rm | 0 | 5 | 0 | 0 | 0 | 4 | 0 | 0 | 1/5 res | |
| | Radio Central | 0 | 2 | 0 | 0 | 0 | 1 | 0 | 0 | 1/2 res | |
| | Combat Sys Maintenance Central | 0 | 2 | 0 | 3 | 0 | 1 | 0 | 0 | 1/2 res | All res |
| | Air Nav/ECM Rm | 0 | 2 | 0 | 0 | 0 | 0 | 0 | 0 | All res | |
| | NIXIE Equipment Rm | 0 | 1 | 0 | 0 | 0 | 0 | 0 | 0 | All res | |
| | MK 92 Mod 6 Equipment Rm | 0 | 1 | 0 | 0 | 0 | 0 | 0 | 0 | | |
| Weapons Control | Gun Control | 0 | 3 | 0 | 0 | 0 | 1 | 0 | 0 | 2/3 res | |
| | 76 MM Magazine | 0 | 3 | 0 | 0 | 0 | 1 | 0 | 0 | 2/3 res | |
| | CIWS MT 1 | 0 | 5 | 0 | 0 | 0 | 2 | 0 | 0 | 3/5 res | |
| | 25 MM Mount #1 | 0 | 2 | 0 | 0 | 0 | 0 | 0 | 0 | All aug | |
| | 25 MM Mount #2 | 0 | 2 | 0 | 0 | 0 | 0 | 0 | 0 | All aug | |
| | 50 CAL Mount #1 | 0 | 2 | 0 | 0 | 0 | 0 | 0 | 0 | All aug | |
| | 50 CAL Mount #2 | 0 | 2 | 0 | 0 | 0 | 0 | 0 | 0 | All aug | |
| | 50 CAL Mount #3 | 0 | 2 | 0 | 0 | 0 | 0 | 0 | 0 | All aug | |
| | 50 CAL Mount #4 | 0 | 2 | 0 | 0 | 0 | 0 | 0 | 0 | All aug | |
| | 50 CAL Mount #5 | 0 | 2 | 0 | 0 | 0 | 0 | 0 | 0 | All aug | |
| | 50 CAL Mount #6 | 0 | 2 | 0 | 0 | 0 | 0 | 0 | 0 | All aug | |
| | M 60 Machine Gun #1 | 0 | 2 | 0 | 0 | 0 | 0 | 0 | 0 | All aug | |
| | M 60 Machine Gun #2 | 0 | 2 | 0 | 0 | 0 | 0 | 0 | 0 | All aug | |
| | 40 MM Grenade Launcher | 0 | 2 | 0 | 0 | 0 | 0 | 0 | 0 | All aug | |
| | Total | 9 | 91 | 3 | 18 | 4 | 44 | 2 | 9 | | |

Note:
Augmented by off-watch or standing down other watches

155

| Control Station | | With Reserves — Condition I Officer | Condition I Enlisted | Condition III Officer | Condition III Enlisted | Without Reserves — Condition I Officer | Condition I Enlisted | Condition III Officer | Condition III Enlisted | CI notes | CIII notes |
|---|---|---|---|---|---|---|---|---|---|---|---|
| **ASW Control** | Sonar Control (SQQ 89(v)9) | 0 | 6 | 0 | 3 | 0 | 3 | 0 | 0 | 3/6 res | All res |
| | SQR-19 Control (SQQ 89) | 0 | 1 | 0 | 0 | 0 | 0 | 0 | 0 | All res | |
| | Sonar Repair (SQQ 89(v)9) | 0 | 2 | 0 | 0 | 0 | 0 | 0 | 0 | All res | |
| | NIXIE | 0 | 1 | 0 | 0 | 0 | 0 | 0 | 0 | All res | |
| | Torpedo Launch Station | 0 | 2 | 0 | 0 | 0 | 0 | 0 | 0 | All res | |
| | Helo Control Station | 1 | 1 | 0 | 0 | 1 | 1 | 0 | 0 | All aug | |
| | Flight Deck Detail | 0 | 8 | 0 | 0 | 0 | 8 | 0 | 0 | All aug | |
| | Ready Life Boat | 0 | 5 | 0 | 0 | 0 | 5 | 0 | 0 | All aug | |
| | Boat davit crew | 1 | 6 | 0 | 0 | 1 | 6 | 0 | 0 | All aug | |
| | RAST Control (LAMPS III) | 0 | 2 | 0 | 0 | 0 | 2 | 0 | 0 | All aug | |
| | Crash and Salvage | 0 | 12 | 0 | 0 | 0 | 12 | 0 | 0 | All aug | |
| | AFFF Generator Station | 0 | 2 | 0 | 0 | 0 | 2 | 0 | 0 | All aug | |
| | JP5 Pump Room | 0 | 1 | 0 | 0 | 0 | 1 | 0 | 1 | All aug | |
| **MIO** | Boarding Team (co-manned) | 1 | 15 | 0 | 0 | 0 | 0 | 0 | 0 | all res, all aug | |
| | Divert Team | 1 | 9 | 0 | 0 | 0 | 0 | 0 | 0 | all res, 5/9 aug | |
| **Engineering Control** | Central Control Station | 1 | 6 | 0 | 7 | 1 | 5 | 0 | 7 | 1/6 res | |
| | ENG Rm | 0 | 2 | 0 | 0 | 0 | 2 | 0 | 0 | | |
| | Aux Machinery Rm 1 | 0 | 2 | 0 | 0 | 0 | 2 | 0 | 0 | | |
| | Aux Machinery Rm 2 | 0 | 4 | 0 | 0 | 0 | 3 | 0 | 0 | 1/4 res | |
| | Aux Machinery Rm 3 | 0 | 2 | 0 | 0 | 0 | 2 | 0 | 0 | | |
| | Switch Gear Rm | 0 | 1 | 0 | 0 | 0 | 1 | 0 | 0 | | |
| | Repair 5 | 1 | 26 | 0 | 0 | 1 | 24 | 0 | 0 | 2/26 res | |
| **Damage Control** | Central Control Station | 1 | 5 | 0 | 1 | 1 | 5 | 0 | 3 | | |
| | Repair 2 (Sec DCC) | 0 | 24 | 0 | 0 | 0 | 23 | 0 | 0 | 1/24 res | |
| | Repair 3 | 0 | 24 | 0 | 0 | 0 | 23 | 0 | 0 | 1/24 res | |
| **Support Control** | Battle Dressing Station Fwd | 0 | 6 | 0 | 0 | 0 | 6 | 0 | 0 | | |
| | Battle Dressing Station Aft | 0 | 6 | 0 | 0 | 0 | 6 | 0 | 0 | | |
| | Battle Messing | 0 | 4 | 0 | 0 | 0 | 2 | 0 | 0 | 2/4 res | |
| | Emergency Issue | 0 | 3 | 0 | 0 | 0 | 2 | 0 | 0 | 1/3 res | |
| | **Total** | 7 | 188 | 0 | 11 | 5 | 146 | 0 | 10 | | |
| | **Overall Total** | 295 | | 32 | | 199 | | 21 | | | All res |

Note:
Augmented by off-watch or standing down other watches

# APPENDIX M. MCM BATTLE BILL REQUIREMENTS

| Control Station | | Condition I | | Condition III | | Condition IM | | Condition IIM | |
|---|---|---|---|---|---|---|---|---|---|
| | | Officer | Enlisted | Officer | Enlisted | Officer | Enlisted | Officer | Enlisted |
| | | | | | | 3/5 aug | | | |
| **Ship Control** | Pilot House | 3 | 8 | 1 | 2 | 2 | 5 | 2 | 7 |
| | Lookouts | 0 | 2 | 0 | 1 | 0 | 5 | 0 | 5 |
| | Signal Bridge | 0 | 1 | 0 | 0 | 0 | 0 | 0 | 0 |
| **Operations Control** | CIC | 1 | 3 | 0 | 3 | 1 | 4 | 1 | 4 |
| **Mine Warfare** | Sonar Control | 0 | 0 | 0 | 0 | 0 | 6 | 0 | 5 |
| | MNV Launch and Recovery | 0 | 0 | 0 | 0 | 0 | 8 | 0 | 1 |
| | Minesweep Launch and Recovery Area | 0 | 0 | 0 | 0 | 1 | 17 | 0 | 0 |
| | Boat Vectoring Crew | 0 | 0 | 0 | 0 | 0 | 0 | 0 | 5 |
| | Boat Handling Detail | 0 | 0 | 0 | 0 | 0 | 7 | 0 | 0 |
| **Communications Control** | Radio Central | 0 | 4 | 0 | 1 | 0 | 2 | 0 | 2 |
| **Electronics Casualty Control** | Electronic Repair | 0 | 2 | 0 | 0 | 0 | 0 | 0 | 0 |
| **Weapons Control** | Gun Control | 1 | 0 | 0 | 0 | 1 | 0 | 1 | 0 |
| | MT 501 | 0 | 2 | 0 | 0 | 0 | 2 | 0 | 2 |
| | MT 502 | 0 | 2 | 0 | 0 | 0 | 0 | 0 | 0 |
| **Engineering Control** | Central Control Station | 1 | 2 | 0 | 4 | 0 | 3 | 0 | 3 |
| | Main Engine Room | 0 | 3 | 0 | 1 | 0 | 0 | 0 | 1 |
| | Aux Machinery Rm | 0 | 2 | 0 | 0 | 0 | 0 | 0 | 0 |
| | IC Room | 0 | 1 | 0 | 0 | 0 | 0 | 0 | 0 |
| | Oil Lab | 0 | 1 | 0 | 0 | 0 | 0 | 0 | 0 |
| **Damage Control** | Damage Control Station | 1 | 1 | 0 | 0 | 0 | 0 | 0 | 0 |
| | Repair 2 | 0 | 19 | 0 | 0 | 0 | 0 | 0 | 0 |
| | Repair 3 | 0 | 19 | 0 | 0 | 0 | 0 | 0 | 0 |
| | Battle Dressing Station | 0 | 2 | 0 | 0 | 0 | 0 | 0 | 0 |
| **Support Control** | Battle Messing | 0 | 2 | 0 | 0 | 0 | 0 | 0 | 2 |
| | Emergency Issue | 0 | 1 | 0 | 0 | 0 | 0 | 0 | 0 |
| **Total** | | 7 | 77 | 1 | 12 | 5 | 59 | 4 | 37 |
| **Overall Total** | | 84 | | 13 | | 64 | | 41 | |

Note:
Augmented by off-watch or standing down other watches

157

THIS PAGE INTENTIONALLY LEFT BLANK

158

# APPENDIX N. MHC BATTLE BILL REQUIREMENTS

| Control Station | | Condition I Officer | Condition I Enlisted | Condition III Officer | Condition III Enlisted | Condition IM Officer | Condition IM Enlisted | Condition IIM Officer | Condition IIM Enlisted |
|---|---|---|---|---|---|---|---|---|---|
| Ship Control | Pilot House | 2 | 6 | 1 | 4 | 2 | 3 | 2 | 4 |
| | Lookouts | 0 | 1 | 0 | 1 | 0 | 5 | 0 | 5 |
| | Signal Bridge | 0 | 1 | 0 | 0 | 0 | 0 | 0 | 0 |
| Operations Control | CIC | 1 | 2 | 0 | 2 | 1 | 5 | 1 | 6 |
| Mine Warfare | Sonar Control | 0 | 0 | 0 | 0 | 0 | 5 | 0 | 3 |
| | MNV Launch and Recovery | 0 | 0 | 0 | 0 | 0 | 8 | 0 | 0 |
| | Boat Vectoring Crew | 0 | 0 | 0 | 0 | 0 | 0 | 0 | 5 |
| | Boat Handling Detail | 0 | 0 | 0 | 0 | 0 | 7 | 0 | 0 |
| Communications Control | Radio Central | 0 | 3 | 0 | 1 | 0 | 2 | 0 | 2 |
| Weapons Control | Gun Control | 1 | 0 | 0 | 0 | 0 | 0 | 0 | 0 |
| | MT 501 | 0 | 2 | 0 | 0 | 0 | 2 | 0 | 2 |
| | MT 502 | 0 | 2 | 0 | 0 | 0 | 0 | 0 | 0 |
| Engineering Control | Central Control Station | 1 | 1 | 1 | 2 | 1 | 2 | 1 | 2 |
| | Main Engine Room | 0 | 1 | 0 | 0 | 0 | 0 | 0 | 0 |
| | Aux Machinery Rm | 0 | 1 | 0 | 0 | 0 | 0 | 0 | 0 |
| Damage Control | Damage Control Station | 0 | 1 | 0 | 0 | 0 | 0 | 0 | 0 |
| | Repair 2 | 0 | 23 | 0 | 0 | 0 | 0 | 0 | 0 |
| Support Control | Battle Messing | 0 | 1 | 0 | 0 | 0 | 1 | 0 | 1 |
| | Main Battle Dressing | 0 | 1 | 0 | 0 | 0 | 0 | 0 | 0 |
| | Total | 5 | 46 | 1 | 10 | 4 | 40 | 4 | 30 |
| | Overall Total | 51 | | 11 | | 44 | | 34 | |

3/5 augmented

Note:
Augmented by off-watch or standing down other watches

159

THIS PAGE INTENTIONALLY LEFT BLANK

# APPENDIX O. NAVY ENLISTED RATE DESCRIPTION

Boatswain's Mate (BMs) train and supervise personnel in all activities relating to marlinspike, deck and boat seamanship, and the maintenance of the ship's external structure and deck equipment. They act as petty officers in charge of small craft and may perform duties as master-at-arms, serve in or take charge of gun crews and damage control parties.

Cryptologic Technicians Technical (CTTs) control the flow of messages and information. Their work depends on technical communications by means other than Morse code and electronic countermeasures.

Electronics Warfare Technician (EWs) operate and maintain electronic equipment used in navigation, target detection and location and for preventing electronic spying by enemies. They interpret incoming electronic signals to determine their source. EWs are advanced electronic technicians who do wiring, circuit testing and repair. They determine performance levels of electronic equipment, install new components, modify existing equipment and test, adjust and repair equipment cooling systems.

The CTT and EW rates have been combined into the CTT rate.

Damage Controlmen (DCs) perform the work necessary for damage control, ship stability, fire-fighting and chemical, biological and radiological (CBR) warfare defense. They instruct personnel in damage control and CBR defense and repair damage-control equipment and systems.

Electrician's Mates (EMs) operate and repair the ship's or station's electrical power plant and electrical equipment. They also maintain and repair power and lighting circuits, distribution switchboards, generators, motors and other electrical equipment.

Enginemen (ENs) keep internal combustion engines, diesel or gasoline in good order. They also maintain refrigeration, air-conditioning, distilling-plant engines and compressors.

Electronics Technicians (ETs) are responsible for electronic equipment used to send and receive messages, detect enemy planes and ships, and determine target distances. They must maintain, repair, calibrate, tune and adjust all electronic equipment used for communications, detection and tracking, recognition and identification, navigation and electronic countermeasures.

Fire Controlmen (FCs) maintain the control mechanism used in weapons systems on combat ships. Complex electronic, electrical and hydraulic equipment is required to ensure the accuracy of Navy guided missile and surface gunfire-control systems. FCs are responsible for the operation, routine care and repair of this equipment, which includes radars, computers, weapons direction equipment, target designation systems, gyroscopes and range finders. It is in the advanced electronics field and requires a six-year enlistment.

Navy Gunner's Mates (GMs) operate, maintain and repair all gunnery equipment, guided-missile launching systems, rocket launchers, guns, gun mounts, turrets, projectors and associated equipment. They make detailed casualty analyses and repairs of electrical, electronic, hydraulic and mechanical systems. They also test and inspect ammunition, missiles and their ordnance components. GMs train and supervise personnel in the handling and stowage of ammunition, missiles and assigned ordnance equipment.

Gas Turbine System Technicians (GSs) operate, repair and maintain gas turbine engines; main propulsion machinery, including gears; shafting and controllable pitch propellers; assigned auxiliary equipment propulsion control systems; electrical and electronic circuitry up to the printed circuit module; and alarm and warning circuitry. They also perform administrative tasks related to gas turbine propulsion system operation and maintenance, (GSE: Electrical) (GSM: Mechanical)

Hull Maintenance Technicians (HTs) are responsible for maintaining ships' hulls, fittings, piping systems and machinery. They install and maintain shipboard and shore based plumbing and piping systems. They also look after a vessel's safety and survival equipment and perform many tasks related to damage control.

Interior Communications Electricians (ICs) operate and repair electronic devices used in the ship's interior communications systems, SITE TV systems, public address systems, electronic megaphones and other announcing equipment. They are also responsible for the gyrocompass systems.

Machinist's Mates (MMs) are responsible for the continuous operation of the many engines, compressors and gears, refrigeration, air-conditioning, gas-operated equipment and other types of machinery afloat and ashore.

They are also responsible for the ship's steam propulsion and auxiliary equipment and the outside (deck) machinery. MMs also may perform duties involving some industrial gases.

Minemen (MNs) test, maintain, repair and overhaul mines and their components. They are responsible for assembling, testing, handling, issuing and delivering mines to the planting agent and for maintaining mine-handling and mine-laying equipment.

Machinery Repairmen (MRs) are skilled machine tool operators. They make replacement parts and repair or overhaul a ship's engine auxiliary equipment, such as evaporators, air compressors and pumps. They repair deck equipment, including winches and hoists, condensers and heat exchange devices. Shipboard MRs frequently operate main propulsion machinery, besides performing machine shop and repair duties.

Operations Specialists (OS) operate radar, navigation and communications equipment in shipboard combat information centers (CICs) or bridges. They detect and track ships, planes and missiles. They also operate and maintain identification friend or foe (IFF) systems, electronic countermeasures (ECM) equipment and radio-telephones.

Quartermasters (QMs) assist the navigator and officer of the deck (OOD), steer the ship, take radar bearings and ranges, make depth soundings and celestial observations, plot courses and command small craft. Additionally, they maintain charts, navigational aids and oceanographic publications and records for the ship's log.

Signalmen (SMs) send and receive various visual messages, handle and route message traffic, operate voice radio and repair visual signaling devices. They also render honors to ships and boats and serve as navigators.

The QM and SM rates have been combined to be called bridge specialists. No acronyms exist to represent this consolidation. The QM rate is still in effect and will be used to fill bridge specialist requirements.

Torpedoman's Mates (TMs) maintain underwater explosive missiles, such as torpedoes and rockets, which are launched from surface ships, submarines and aircraft. They also maintain launching systems for underwater explosives, and are responsible for shipping and storage of torpedoes and rockets.

THIS PAGE INTENTIONALLY LEFT BLANK

# APPENDIX P. SEAFRAME BASELINE BATTLE BILL

| Type of Control | Station ID | BUSINESS AS USUAL Watch station title | CONDITION I Rate |
|---|---|---|---|
| **Ship** | | | |
| | Pilot House | OOD | OFF |
| | | JOOD | OFF |
| | | NAV | OFF |
| | | BMOW | BM |
| | | SCC OPER | SHIP |
| | | Plotter | QM |
| | Lookouts | Lookout | SHIP |
| | Signal Bridge | Signalman/recorder | QM |
| | | recorder | QM |
| **Operations** | | | |
| | Air Control | AIC Supv | OS |
| | | AIC | OS |
| | | ASTAC | OS |
| | Display & Decision | TAO | OFF |
| | | Cbt Sys Coord | FC |
| | | Missile Sys Supv | FC |
| | | CIC Supv | OS |
| | | GCCS-M Adminstrator | OS |
| | | Own Ship display Ctrllr | OS |
| | | Talker | OS |
| | | Talker | OS |
| | | Talker | OS |
| | | Talker | OS |
| | Engagement | Radar Oper | OS |
| | | DRT Oper | OS |
| | | Weps Contrl Officer | OFF |
| | | Weps Console Operator | FC |
| | Tactical Info | Tactical Information Coord | OS |
| | | Radar sys controller | SHIP |
| | | EW Supervisor | CTT |
| | | DCC Operator | CTT |
| **Communications** | | | |
| | Radio Central | Radio Supervisor | IT |
| | | Comm Sys Oper #1 | SHIP |
| | | Comm Sys Oper #2 | SHIP |
| | | Radio Oper | SHIP |
| | | Talker | SHIP |
| | Information Security | Network Security Tech | IT |
| | | System Administrator | IT |
| | | LAN Manager | SHIP |
| | | Tactical Sys Administrator | IT |
| **Electronics Casualty Control** | | | |
| | CS Maint Cntrl | CSOOW | OFF |
| | | CS Maint Supv | FC |
| | | Test & Maint Console Oper | FC |
| | | Talker | SHIP |
| | | Computer Oper | SHIP |
| | | EW Repairman | CTT |
| | Search RADAR | Electronics Repairman | ET |
| | | Electronics Repairman | ET |
| | CIC | Console Repairman | FC |
| | SONAR Repair | Sonar Repairman | STG |
| | NIXIE Repair | Torp Decoy Oper/Repairman | STG |
| | Gun Repair | Gun Repairman | GM |

| Type of Control | Station ID | BUSINESS AS USUAL Watch station title | CONDITION I Rate |
|---|---|---|---|
| **Weapons** | | | |
| | MT 51 Loader Drum Rm | TDT Supv | GM |
| | | EP2 Panel Oper | GM |
| | MT 51 Handling Rm | TDT #1 Oper | SHIP |
| | | POIC/MT Captain | GM |
| | | Ammo Passer | SHIP |
| | | Ammo Passer | SHIP |
| | RAM | RAM Supv | SHIP |
| | CIWS MT 1 | RCP Oper | FC |
| | | LCP Oper | FC |
| | | POIC/Reloader | SHIP |
| | | Ammo Passer | SHIP |
| | | Ammo Passer | SHIP |
| | 50CAL #1 | Gun Oper | SHIP |
| | | Gun Loader | SHIP |
| | 50CAL #2 | Gun Oper | SHIP |
| | | Gun Loader | SHIP |
| | 50CAL #3 | Gun Oper | SHIP |
| | | Gun Loader | SHIP |
| | 50CAL #4 | Gun Oper | SHIP |
| | | Gun Loader | SHIP |
| | SONAR | Sonar Supv/UWS | STG |
| | | SQS-53 Console Oper | STG |
| | | SQS-53 Console Oper | STG |
| | | SQQ-28 Console Oper | STG |
| | | SIMAS Oper/Log Keeper | STG |
| | Torpedo CM | Torp Tube Oper Port | STG |
| | | Torp Tube Oper Stbd | STG |
| | Helo Control Station | HCO | OFF |
| | Flight Deck Control | FD Safety Officer | BM |
| | | LSE | BM |
| | | FD Crewman | SHIP |
| | | FD Crewman | SHIP |
| | | Fuel station Oper | SHIP |
| | | JP5 Nozzleman | SHIP |
| | Ready Life Boat | Coxswain | BM |
| | | Rescue Swimmer | SHIP |
| | | Bow Hook | SHIP |
| | | Boat Engineer | EN |
| | | Boat Deck POIC | BM |
| | | Talker | SHIP |
| | | Davit Oper | SHIP |
| | | Line Handler | SHIP |
| | | Line Handler | SHIP |
| | Aircraft Handling | RAST Oper | OFF |
| | Crash and Salvage | Scene Leader | DC |
| | | Hot Suitman | ENG |
| | | Hot Suitman | ENG |
| | | Hose Team Leader #2 | ENG |
| | | AFFF Nozzleman | ENG |
| | | AFFF Hoseman/plugman | ENG |
| | AFFF Station | AFFF Station Oper | ENG |
| | JP5 Pump Room | Fuel Pump Oper | ENG |

| Type of Control | Station ID | BUSINESS AS USUAL Watch station title | CONDITION I Rate |
|---|---|---|---|
| **Engineering** | | | |
| | CCS | EOOW/Prop/DCO | OFF |
| | | Prop Ctrl Sys Oper | GS |
| | | Elec Plant Ctrl Cons Oper | GS |
| | ENG Rm | Equip Monitor/Oper | GS |
| | Aux Machinery Rm | Aux Oper/Rover | EN |
| | | Equip Monitor/Oper | EN |
| **Damage** | | | |
| | DC Central | DCA | OFF |
| | | Plotter | DC |
| | | Talker | SHIP |
| | Oil Lab | Oil/Water Tester | EN |
| | Repair | Repair Party Leader | DC |
| | | Scene Leader | SHIP |
| | | Team Leader | SHIP |
| | | Plotter | DC |
| | | Investigator/SCBA Man #1 | SHIP |
| | | Investigator/SCBA Man #2 | SHIP |
| | | Nozzleman/SCBA Man #2 | SHIP |
| | | Hoseman/SCBA Man #1 | SHIP |
| | | Hoseman/SCBA Man #2 | SHIP |
| | | Electrical Repair | EM |
| | | IC Repair | IC |
| | | Utilityman | SHIP |
| | | Utilityman | SHIP |
| | | Utilityman | SHIP |
| | | Utilityman | SHIP |
| | | Utilityman | SHIP |
| | | Utilityman | SHIP |
| | | Utilityman | SHIP |
| | | Utilityman | SHIP |
| | | Utilityman | SHIP |
| | | AFFF Station Oper | ENG |
| | Battle Dressing Station | Med Tech | HM |
| | | Talker | SHIP |
| **Support** | | | |
| | Battle Messing | Ships Cook | CS |
| | | Ships Cook | CS |
| | | Ships Cook | CS |
| | Emergency Issue | Stock Ctrl Supv | SK |
| | | Locate/issue clerk | SK |
| | | Locate/issue clerk | SK |

# APPENDIX Q. SEAFRAME BASELINE RQMTS

## LCS SEAFRAME

| Billet Title | Rate |
|---|---|
| **Executive Dept** | |
| COMMANDING OFFICER | OFF |
| EXECUTIVE OFFICER | OFF |
| YEOMAN | YN |
| HOSPITAL CORPSMAN | HM |
| | |
| **Operations Dept** | |
| OPS AFLOAT GEN/SURF SFTY | OFF |
| IT PROFESSIONAL/COMMO | OFF |
| QUARTERMASTER | QM |
| QUARTERMASTER | QM |
| SIGNALMAN | QM |
| OPERATIONS SPECIALIST | OS |
| OPERATIONS SPECIALIST | OS |
| OPERATIONS SPECIALIST | OS |
| OPERATIONS SPECIALIST | OS |
| OPERATIONS SPECIALIST | OS |
| OPERATIONS SPECIALIST | OS |
| OPERATIONS SPECIALIST | OS |
| OPERATIONS SPECIALIST | OS |
| OPERATIONS SPECIALIST | OS |
| OPERATIONS SPECIALIST | OS |
| OPERATIONS SPECIALIST | OS |
| BOATSWAIN'S MATE | BM |
| BOATSWAIN'S MATE | BM |
| BOATSWAIN'S MATE | BM |
| BOATSWAIN'S MATE | BM |
| BOATSWAIN'S MATE | BM |
| ELECTRONICS TECHNICIAN | CTT |
| ELECTRONICS TECHNICIAN | CTT |
| ELECTRONICS TECHNICIAN | CTT |
| INFORMATION SYSTEMS TECHNICIAN | IT |
| INFORMATION SYS TECH | IT |
| INFORMATION SYS TECH | IT |
| INFORMATION SYSTEMS TECHNICIAN | IT |
| | |
| **Combat Systems Dept** | |
| CMBT SYS | OFF |
| GUN/ORD | OFF |
| SHP ELX MTL | OFF |
| ELECTRONICS TECHNICIAN | ET |
| ELECTRONICS TECHNICIAN | ET |
| ELECTRONICS TECHNICIAN (SONAR) | STG |
| ELECTRONICS TECHNICIAN (SONAR) | STG |
| IC ELECTRICIAN | IC |
| IC ELECTRICIAN | IC |
| IC ELECTRICIAN | IC |
| SONAR TECH (SURFACE) | STG |
| SONAR TECH (SURFACE) | STG |
| SONAR TECH (SURFACE) | STG |
| SONAR TECH (SURFACE) | STG |
| SONAR TECH (SURFACE) | STG |
| TORPEDOMAN'S MATE | STG |
| TORPEDOMAN'S MATE | STG |
| GUNNER'S MATE | GM |
| GUNNER'S MATE | GM |
| GUNNER'S MATE | GM |
| GUNNER'S MATE | GM |
| FIRE CONTROLMAN | FC |
| FIRE CONTROLMAN | FC |
| FIRE CONTROLMAN | FC |
| FIRE CONTROLMAN | FC |
| FIRE CONTROLMAN | FC |
| FIRE CONTROLMAN | FC |
| FIRE CONTROLMAN | FC |

## LCS SEAFRAME

| Billet Title | Rate |
|---|---|
| **Engineering Dept** | |
| SHP ENG GASTBN | OFF |
| DC ASST | OFF |
| MPA GASTURBINE | OFF |
| AUX MACH | OFF |
| ELECTRICIAN'S MATE | EM |
| ELECTRICIAN'S MATE | EM |
| ELECTRICIAN'S MATE | EM |
| ELECTRICIAN'S MATE | EM |
| ELECTRICIAN'S MATE | EM |
| ELECTRICIAN'S MATE | EM |
| ENGINEMAN | EN |
| ENGINEMAN | EN |
| ENGINEMAN | EN |
| ENGINEMAN | EN |
| ENGINEMAN | EN |
| ENGINEMAN | EN |
| ENGINEMAN | EN |
| ENGINEMAN | EN |
| ENGINEMAN | EN |
| ENGINEMAN | EN |
| HULL TECHNICIAN | HT |
| HULL TECHNICIAN | HT |
| HULL TECHNICIAN | HT |
| MACHINERY REPAIRMAN | MR |
| DAMAGE CONTROLMAN | DC |
| DAMAGE CONTROLMAN | DC |
| DAMAGE CONTROLMAN | DC |
| DAMAGE CONTROLMAN | DC |
| DAMAGE CONTROLMAN | DC |
| DAMAGE CONTROLMAN | DC |
| GAS TURB SYS TECH MECH | GS |
| GAS TURB SYS TECH MECH | GS |
| GAS TURB SYS TECH MECH | GS |
| GAS TURB SYS TECH MECH | GS |
| GAS TURB SYS TECH MECH | GS |
| GAS TURB SYS TECH MECH | GS |
| GAS TURB SYS TECH MECH | GS |
| GAS TURB SYS TECH MECH | GS |
| GAS TURB SYS TECH MECH | GS |
| GAS TURB SYS TECH MECH | GS |
| GAS TURB SYS TECH ELEC | GS |
| GAS TURB SYS TECH ELEC | GS |
| GAS TURB SYS TECH ELEC | GS |
| GAS TURB SYS TECH ELEC | GS |
| GAS TURB SYS TECH ELEC | GS |
| | |
| **Supply Dept** | |
| STOREKEEPER | SK |
| STOREKEEPER | SK |
| STOREKEEPER | SK |
| STOREKEEPER | SK |
| STOREKEEPER | SK |
| MESS MANAGEMENT SPECIALIST | CS |
| MESS MANAGEMENT SPECIALIST | CS |
| MESS MANAGEMENT SPECIALIST | CS |
| MESS MANAGEMENT SPECIALIST | CS |
| MESS MANAGEMENT SPECIALIST | CS |
| MESS MANAGEMENT SPECIALIST | CS |

THIS PAGE INTENTIONALLY LEFT BLANK

# APPENDIX R. SEAFRAME RQMTS ANALYSIS

## LCS SEAFRAME

| Billet Title | Rate | SmartShip Rate | OME Rate | Composite Sailor Rate | Technology Leverage Rate | Workload Alignment Rate |
|---|---|---|---|---|---|---|
| **Executive Dept** | | | | | | |
| COMMANDING OFFICER | OFF | OFF | OFF | OFF | OFF | OFF |
| EXECUTIVE OFFICER | OFF | OFF | OFF | OFF | OFF | OFF |
| YEOMAN | YN | YN | YN | YN | YN | YN |
| HOSPITAL CORPSMAN | HM | HM | HM | HM | HM | HM |
| **Operations Dept** | | | | | | |
| OPS AFLOAT GEN/SURF SFTY | OFF | OFF | OFF | OFF | OFF | OFF |
| IT PROFESSIONAL/COMMO | OFF | OFF | OFF | OFF | OFF | OFF |
| QUARTERMASTER | QM | QM | QM | | | |
| QUARTERMASTER | QM | QM | QM | QM | | |
| SIGNALMAN | QM | QM | QM | | | |
| OPERATIONS SPECIALIST | OS | OS | OS | OS | OS | OS |
| OPERATIONS SPECIALIST | OS | OS | OS | OS | OS | OS |
| OPERATIONS SPECIALIST | OS | OS | OS | OS | OS | OS |
| OPERATIONS SPECIALIST | OS | OS | OS | OS | | |
| OPERATIONS SPECIALIST | OS | OS | OS | OS | | |
| OPERATIONS SPECIALIST | OS | OS | OS | OS | | |
| OPERATIONS SPECIALIST | OS | OS | OS | OS | | |
| OPERATIONS SPECIALIST | OS | OS | OS | OS | | |
| OPERATIONS SPECIALIST | OS | OS | OS | OS | | |
| OPERATIONS SPECIALIST | OS | OS | OS | OS | | |
| OPERATIONS SPECIALIST | OS | OS | OS | OS | | |
| OPERATIONS SPECIALIST | OS | OS | | | | |
| OPERATIONS SPECIALIST | OS | OS | | | | |
| OPERATIONS SPECIALIST | OS | OS | | | | |
| BOATSWAIN'S MATE | BM | BM | BM | BM | BM | BM |
| BOATSWAIN'S MATE | BM | BM | BM | BM | BM | BM |
| BOATSWAIN'S MATE | BM | BM | BM | BM | BM | BM |
| BOATSWAIN'S MATE | BM | BM | BM | BM | | |
| BOATSWAIN'S MATE | BM | BM | BM | | | |
| ELECTRONICS TECHNICIAN | CTT | CTT | CTT | CTT | CTT | CTT |
| ELECTRONICS TECHNICIAN | CTT | CTT | CTT | CTT | | |
| ELECTRONICS TECHNICIAN | CTT | CTT | CTT | CTT | | |
| INFORMATION SYSTEMS TECHNICIAN | IT | IT | IT | IT | IT | IT |
| INFORMATION SYS TECH | IT | IT | IT | IT | IT | IT |
| INFORMATION SYS TECH | IT | IT | | | | |
| INFORMATION SYSTEMS TECHNICIAN | IT | IT | | | | |
| INFORMATION SYSTEMS TECHNICIAN | IT | IT | | | | |

# LCS SEAFRAME

**Billet Title**

**Combat Systems Dept**

| Billet Title | Rate | SmartShip Rate | OME Rate | Composite Sailor Rate | Technology Leverage Rate | Workload Alignment Rate |
|---|---|---|---|---|---|---|
| CMBT SYS | OFF | OFF | OFF | OFF | OFF | OFF |
| GUN/ORD | OFF | OFF | OFF | | | |
| SHP ELX MTL | OFF | OFF | | | | |
| ELECTRONICS TECHNICIAN | ET | ET | ET | ET | ET | ET |
| ELECTRONICS TECHNICIAN | ET | ET | ET | ET | ET | ET |
| ELECTRONICS TECHNICIAN (SONAR) | STG | STG | STG | STG | STG | STG |
| ELECTRONICS TECHNICIAN (SONAR) | STG | STG | | | | |
| IC ELECTRICIAN | IC | IC | IC | IC | IC | IC |
| IC ELECTRICIAN | IC | IC | IC | IC | IC | IC |
| IC ELECTRICIAN | IC | IC | IC | | | |
| SONAR TECH (SURFACE) | STG | STG | STG | STG | STG | STG |
| SONAR TECH (SURFACE) | STG | STG | STG | STG | | |
| SONAR TECH (SURFACE) | STG | STG | STG | STG | | |
| SONAR TECH (SURFACE) | STG | STG | STG | | | |
| SONAR TECH (SURFACE) | STG | STG | STG | | | |
| SONAR TECH (SURFACE) | STG | STG | STG | | | |
| TORPEDOMAN'S MATE | STG | STG | STG | | | |
| TORPEDOMAN'S MATE | STG | STG | STG | | | |
| GUNNER'S MATE | GM | GM | GM | GM | GM | GM |
| GUNNER'S MATE | GM | GM | GM | GM | GM | GM |
| GUNNER'S MATE | GM | GM | GM | GM | GM | |
| GUNNER'S MATE | GM | GM | GM | | | |
| GUNNER'S MATE | GM | GM | GM | | | |
| FIRE CONTROLMAN | FC | FC | FC | FC | FC | FC |
| FIRE CONTROLMAN | FC | FC | FC | FC | FC | FC |
| FIRE CONTROLMAN | FC | FC | FC | FC | FC | |
| FIRE CONTROLMAN | FC | FC | FC | FC | | |
| FIRE CONTROLMAN | FC | FC | FC | FC | | |
| FIRE CONTROLMAN | FC | FC | FC | FC | | |
| FIRE CONTROLMAN | FC | FC | FC | | | |
| FIRE CONTROLMAN | FC | FC | FC | | | |
| FIRE CONTROLMAN | FC | FC | FC | | | |

## LCS SEAFRAME

| Billet Title | Rate | SmartShip Rate | OME Rate | Composite Sailor Rate | Technology Leverage Rate | Workload Alignment Rate |
|---|---|---|---|---|---|---|
| **Engineering Dept** | | | | | | |
| SHIP ENG GASTBN | OFF | OFF | OFF | OFF | | |
| DC ASST | OFF | OFF | OFF | OFF | OFF | OFF |
| MPA GASTURBINE | OFF | OFF | OFF | | | |
| AUX MACH | OFF | OFF | OFF | | | |
| ELECTRICIAN'S MATE | EM | EM | EM | EM | EM | EM |
| ELECTRICIAN'S MATE | EM | EM | EM | EM | EM | EM |
| ELECTRICIAN'S MATE | EM | EM | EM | EM | EM | |
| ELECTRICIAN'S MATE | EM | EM | EM | | | |
| ELECTRICIAN'S MATE | EM | EM | EM | | | |
| ELECTRICIAN'S MATE | EM | EM | EM | | | |
| ELECTRICIAN'S MATE | EM | EM | | | | |
| ENGINEMAN | EN | EN | EN | EN | EN | EN |
| ENGINEMAN | EN | EN | EN | EN | EN | EN |
| ENGINEMAN | EN | EN | EN | EN | EN | EN |
| ENGINEMAN | EN | EN | EN | EN | EN | |
| ENGINEMAN | EN | EN | EN | EN | | |
| ENGINEMAN | EN | EN | EN | EN | | |
| ENGINEMAN | EN | EN | EN | | | |
| ENGINEMAN | EN | EN | EN | | | |
| ENGINEMAN | EN | EN | EN | | | |
| ENGINEMAN | EN | EN | EN | | | |
| ENGINEMAN | EN | EN | EN | | | |
| HULL TECHNICIAN | HT | HT | HT | | | |
| HULL TECHNICIAN | HT | HT | HT | | | |
| HULL TECHNICIAN | HT | HT | | | | |
| MACHINERY REPAIRMAN | MR | MR | MR | | | |
| DAMAGE CONTROLMAN | DC | DC | DC | DC | DC | DC |
| DAMAGE CONTROLMAN | DC | DC | DC | DC | DC | DC |
| DAMAGE CONTROLMAN | DC | DC | DC | DC | DC | DC |
| DAMAGE CONTROLMAN | DC | DC | DC | DC | DC | |
| DAMAGE CONTROLMAN | DC | DC | DC | | | |
| DAMAGE CONTROLMAN | DC | | | | | |
| GAS TURB SYS TECH MECH | GS | GS | GS | GS | GS | GS |
| GAS TURB SYS TECH MECH | GS | GS | GS | GS | GS | GS |
| GAS TURB SYS TECH MECH | GS | GS | GS | GS | GS | GS |
| GAS TURB SYS TECH MECH | GS | GS | GS | GS | GS | |
| GAS TURB SYS TECH MECH | GS | GS | GS | GS | | |
| GAS TURB SYS TECH MECH | GS | GS | GS | | | |
| GAS TURB SYS TECH MECH | GS | GS | GS | | | |
| GAS TURB SYS TECH MECH | GS | GS | GS | | | |
| GAS TURB SYS TECH MECH | GS | GS | | | | |
| GAS TURB SYS TECH MECH | GS | GS | | | | |
| GAS TURB SYS TECH ELEC | GS | GS | GS | GS | GS | GS |
| GAS TURB SYS TECH ELEC | GS | GS | GS | GS | GS | GS |
| GAS TURB SYS TECH ELEC | GS | GS | GS | GS | | |
| GAS TURB SYS TECH ELEC | GS | GS | GS | | | |
| GAS TURB SYS TECH ELEC | GS | GS | GS | | | |

# LCS SEAFRAME

| Billet Title | Rate | SmartShip Rate | OME Rate | Composite Sailor Rate | Technology Leverage Rate | Workload Alignment Rate |
|---|---|---|---|---|---|---|
| **Supply Dept** | | | | | | |
| STOREKEEPER | SK | SK | SK | SK | | |
| STOREKEEPER | SK | SK | SK | SK | | |
| STOREKEEPER | SK | SK | SK | SK | | |
| STOREKEEPER | SK | SK | SK | SK | SK | SK |
| STOREKEEPER | SK | SK | SK | SK | | |
| MESS MANAGEMENT SPECIALIST | CS | CS | CS | CS | CS | CS |
| MESS MANAGEMENT SPECIALIST | CS | CS | CS | CS | CS | CS |
| MESS MANAGEMENT SPECIALIST | CS | CS | CS | CS | | |
| MESS MANAGEMENT SPECIALIST | CS | CS | CS | CS | | |
| MESS MANAGEMENT SPECIALIST | CS | CS | CS | CS | | |

# APPENDIX S. SEAFRAME REDUCED RQMTS

| Minimal Manning for LCS Seaframe | |
|---|---|
| **Billet Title** | **Rate** |
| **Executive Dept** | |
| COMMANDING OFFICER | OFF |
| EXECUTIVE OFFICER | OFF |
| YEOMAN | YN |
| HOSPITAL CORPSMAN | HM |

| **Operations Dept** | |
|---|---|
| Operations Officer | OFF |
| IT PROFESSIONAL/COMMO | OFF |
| OPERATIONS SPECIALIST | OS |
| OPERATIONS SPECIALIST | OS |
| OPERATIONS SPECIALIST | OS |
| OPERATIONS SPECIALIST | OS |
| BOATSWAIN'S MATE | BM |
| BOATSWAIN'S MATE | BM |
| BOATSWAIN'S MATE | BM |
| ELECTRONICS TECHNICIAN | CTT |
| INFORMATION SYSTEMS TECH | IT |
| INFORMATION SYSTEMS TECH | IT |

| **Combat Systems Dept** | |
|---|---|
| Combat Systems Officer | OFF |
| ELECTRONICS TECHNICIAN | ET |
| ELECTRONICS TECHNICIAN | ET |
| IC ELECTRICIAN | IC |
| IC ELECTRICIAN | IC |
| SONAR OPER/REP | STG |
| SONAR OPER/REP | STG |
| GUN OPER/REPAIRMAN | GM |
| GUN OPER/REPAIRMAN | GM |
| FIRE CONTROLMAN/REP | FC |
| FIRE CONTROLMAN/REP | FC |

| **Engineering Dept** | |
|---|---|
| Chief Engineer | OFF |
| ELECTRICIAN'S MATE | EM |
| ELECTRICIAN'S MATE | EM |
| ENGINEMAN | EN |
| ENGINEMAN | EN |
| ENGINEMAN | EN |
| DAMAGE CONTROLMAN | DC |
| DAMAGE CONTROLMAN | DC |
| DAMAGE CONTROLMAN | DC |
| GAS TURB SYS TECH MECH | GS |
| GAS TURB SYS TECH MECH | GS |
| GAS TURB SYS TECH MECH | GS |
| GAS TURB SYS TECH ELEC | GS |
| GAS TURB SYS TECH ELEC | GS |

| **Supply Dept** | |
|---|---|
| STOREKEEPER | SK |
| STOREKEEPER | SK |
| MESS MANAGEMENT SPECIALIST | CS |
| MESS MANAGEMENT SPECIALIST | CS |

THIS PAGE INTENTIONALLY LEFT BLANK

# APPENDIX T. SEAFRAME REDUCED BATTLE BILL

| Type of Control | REDUX Watch station title | CONDITION I Rate | CONDITION III Rate |
|---|---|---|---|
| **Ship** | OOD | OFF | OFF/BM/GM |
| | JOOD | BM | BM/GM |
| | Secondary DC/Lookout/ | DC | |
| **Operations** | | | |
| | AIC/ASTAC/ATAO | OS | OS/STG/CTT |
| | TAO | OFF | OFF/OS |
| | Radar Oper | OS | |
| | Weps Console oper | FC | |
| | Tact Info Coord | OS | |
| | EW Supv/Repairman | CTT | |
| **Communications** | | | |
| | Comm Sys Oper | IT | |
| | Sys Admin/LAN Manager | OS | |
| | Tactical Sys Admin | IT | |
| **Electronics Casualty Control** | | | |
| | CS Maint Supv | ET | |
| | Electronics Repairman | ET | |
| **Weapons** | | | |
| | MT CAPT/EP2 Panel Oper | GM | GM |
| | Ammo Passer/Gun Rep | FC | FC |
| | MT CAPT/LCP Oper/Gun Rep | GM | GM |
| | Ammo Passer/Gun Rep | BM | BM |
| | Gun Oper | SHIP | SHIP |
| | Gun Loader | SHIP | SHIP |
| | Gun Oper | SHIP | SHIP |
| | Gun Loader | SHIP | SHIP |
| | Gun Oper | SHIP | SHIP |
| | Gun Oper | SHIP | SHIP |
| | Console Oper/SONAR Rep | STG | STG |
| | Console Oper/SONAR Rep | STG | STG |
| | Torp Tube Oper/NIXIE/SQR-19 Winch Oper | BM | BM |
| | HCO/RAST Oper | OFF | OFF |
| | Landing Safety Officer | SHIP | SHIP |
| | FD Crewman | SHIP | SHIP |
| | FD Crewman | SHIP | SHIP |
| | JP5 Nozzleman | SHIP | SHIP |
| | Coxswain/Engineer | SHIP | SHIP |
| | Rescue Swimmer/ Bow Hook | SHIP | SHIP |
| | Boat Deck POIC/Davit Oper | SHIP | SHIP |
| | Line Handler | SHIP | SHIP |
| | Line Handler | SHIP | SHIP |
| | Scene Leader | SHIP | SHIP |
| | Hot Suitman | SHIP | SHIP |
| | Hot Suitman | SHIP | SHIP |
| | Hose Team Leader | SHIP | SHIP |
| | AFFF Nozzleman | SHIP | SHIP |
| | AFFF Hoseman/plugman | SHIP | SHIP |
| **Engineering** | | | |
| | EOOW/Prop/DCO | OFF | EN/GS |
| | Elec Plant Ctrl Cons Oper | GS | GS |
| | Equip Monitor/Oper | EN/GS | EN/GS |
| **Damage** | | | |
| | DCA | DC | DC |
| | Oil/Water Tester | EN/GS | EN/GS |
| | Repair Party Leader | DC | DC |
| | Investigator/SCBA Man #1 | SHIP | SHIP |
| | Investigator/SCBA Man #2 | SHIP | SHIP |
| | Nozzleman/SCBA Man | SHIP | SHIP |
| | Hoseman/SCBA Man | SHIP | SHIP |
| | Hoseman/SCBA Man | SHIP | SHIP |
| | Med Tech | HM | HM |
| **Support** | | | |
| | Ships Cook | CS | |
| | Ships Cook | CS | |
| | Stock Ctrl Supv | SK | |
| | Locate/issue clerk | SK | |

| | | | |
|---|---|---|---|
| **Total** | 59 | 59 | 45 |
| **Augment** | 21 | 21 | 41 |
| **Actual billet** | 38 | 38 | 4 |

THIS PAGE INTENTIONALLY LEFT BLANK

# APPENDIX U. MODULE PRE-PACKAGED RQMTS

| Billet Title | Rate | MIW Normal | MIW Reduced | ASW Normal | ASW Optimized | SUW Normal | SUW Optimized |
|---|---|---|---|---|---|---|---|
| **FMP Executive** | | | | | | | |
| OIC/Analyst | LCDR | 1 | 1 | 1 | 1 | 1 | 1 |
| AOIC/Analyst | LT | 1 | 1 | 1 | 1 | 1 | 1 |
| Yeoman | YN | 1 | | 1 | | 1 | |
| Supply support | SK | 1 | 1 | 1 | 1 | 1 | 1 |
| Comms Support | IT | 1 | 1 | 1 | 1 | 1 | 1 |
| Operations Specialist | MN/OS | 1 | 1 | 1 | 1 | 1 | 1 |
| **USV Detachment** | | | | | | | |
| USV Oper | BM | 3 | 2 | 5 | 3 | 3 | 3 |
| USV Maint | EN | 2 | | 2 | | 2 | |
| USV Maint | EM | 1 | | 1 | | 1 | |
| USV Maint | ET | 2 | 1 | 2 | 2 | 2 | 2 |
| Weapons/Ordnance | GM | | | | | 2 | 1 |
| **RMV Detachment** | | | | | | | |
| RMV Oper | MN | 4 | 3 | 2 | 3 | | |
| RMV Maint | EN | 3 | | 3 | | | |
| RMV Maint | STG | 2 | 2 | 2 | 2 | | |
| RMV Maint | EM | 1 | | 1 | | | |
| **BPAUV Detachment** | | | | | | | |
| BPAUV Oper/Maint | MN | 2 | 1 | | | | |
| **SCULPIN Detachment** | | | | | | | |
| SCULPIN Oper/Main | MN | 2 | 1 | | | | |
| **EOD Detachment** | | | | | | | |
| OIC/Dive Supv | EOD | 1 | 1 | | | | |
| Diver | EOD | 1 | 1 | | | | |
| Diver | EOD | 1 | 1 | | | | |
| Stby Diver | EOD | 1 | 1 | | | | |
| Diver Tender | EOD | 1 | | | | | |
| Diver Tender | EOD | 1 | | | | | |
| Stby Diver Tender | EOD | 1 | | | | | |
| Timekeeper/Recorder | EOD | 1 | | | | | |
| **ACES/EER/IEER/AEER family Det** | | | | | | | |
| Oper/Maint | STG | | | 5 | 3 | | |
| **Torpedo CounterMeasures Det** | | | | | | | |
| Oper/Maint | STG | | | 3 | 1 | | |
| **ADS Det** | | | | | | | |
| Oper/Maint | STG | | | 5 | 2 | | |
| **Towed Array Det** | | | | | | | |
| Oper/Maint | STG | | | | | | |
| **Intermediate Cal Gun Det** | | | | | | | |
| POIC/Det Supv | GM | | | | | 1 | 1 |
| Oper/Maint | GM | | | | | 3 | 3 |
| **Non-lethal Weapon Det** | | | | | | | |
| TBD | TBD | | | | | | |
| **TOTAL** | 32 | 36 | 19 | 37 | 21 | 20 | 15 |
| **Air Det** | | 57 | 34 | 52 | 30 | 52 | 30 |
| **TOTAL w/Air Det** | | 93 | 53 | 89 | 51 | 72 | 45 |

THIS PAGE INTENTIONALLY LEFT BLANK

# APPENDIX V. MODULE FLEXED RQMTS COMPUTATION

| Seaframe | MIW | ASW | SUW | | Total FMP |
|---|---|---|---|---|---|
| 15 | 13 | 10 | 9 | | 32 |

| Billet Title | Rate | MIW Reduced | ASW Reduced | SUW Reduced | Flexed Total |
|---|---|---|---|---|---|
| **FMP Executive** | | | | | |
| OIC/Analyst | LCDR | 1 | 1 | 1 | 32 |
| AOIC/Analyst | LT | 1 | 1 | 1 | 32 |
| Yeoman | YN | 0 | | | 0 |
| Supply support | SK | 1 | | | 15 |
| Comms Support | IT | 1 | | | 15 |
| Operations Specialist | MN/OS | 1 | | 1 | 15 |
| **USV Detachment** | | | | | |
| USV Oper | BM | 1 | 1 | 1 | 32 |
| USV Maint | EN | 1 | | | 15 |
| USV Maint | EM | 1 | | | 15 |
| USV Maint | ET | 1 | | | 15 |
| Weapons/Ordnance | GM | 0 | | 1 | 9 |
| **RMV Detachment** | | | | | |
| RMV Oper | MN | 3 | 3 | 0 | 69 |
| RMV Oper | MN | 0 | | | 0 |
| RMV Maint | EN | 1 | | 0 | 15 |
| RMV Maint | STG | 2 | | 0 | 30 |
| **BPAUV Detachment** | | | | | |
| BPAUV Oper/Maint | MN | 1 | 0 | | 13 |
| **SCULPIN Detachment** | | | | | |
| SCULPIN Oper/Main | MN | 1 | 0 | | 13 |
| **EOD Detachment** | | | | | |
| EOD Detachment | EOD | 4 | 0 | | 52 |
| **ACES/EER/IEER/AEER family Det** | | | | | |
| Oper/Maint | STG | 0 | 3 | 0 | 30 |
| **Torpedo CounterMeasures Det** | | | | | |
| Oper/Maint | STG | 0 | 1 | 0 | 10 |
| **ADS Det** | | | | | |
| Oper/Maint | STG | 0 | 3 | 0 | 30 |
| **Towed Array Det** | | | | | |
| Oper/Maint | STG | 0 | 0 | 0 | 0 |
| **Intermediate Cal Gun Det** | | | | | |
| Oper/Maint | GM | 0 | | 4 | 36 |
| **Non-lethal Weapon Det** | | | | | |
| TBD | | 0 | | | 0 |
| | | | | | |
| Air Det Oper (specialists) | | 16 | 12 | | 388 |
| Air Det Support (generalists) | | 18 | | | 270 |

| | | MIW | ASW | SUW | |
|---|---|---|---|---|---|
| Module TOTAL without air det | | 19 | 21 | 15 | |
| Module TOTAL with air det | | 53 | 51 | 45 | |

THIS PAGE INTENTIONALLY LEFT BLANK

# APPENDIX W. ABBREVIATIONS AND ACRONYMS

| | |
|---|---|
| AFFF | Aqueous Film Forming Foam |
| AIC | Aircraft Intercept Control |
| ASW | Anti-Submarine Warfare |
| BM | Boatswain's Mate |
| BMOW | Boatswain's Mate of the Watch |
| CBM | Condition Based Maintenance |
| CBT | Combat |
| CCS | Central Control Station |
| CG | Cruiser, Guided Missile |
| CG (NS) | Cruiser, Guided Missile (Pre-Smart Ship) |
| CG (SS) | Cruiser, Guided Missile (Post-Smart Ship) |
| CIC | Combat Information Center |
| CIWS | Close-In Weapon System |
| CMP | Consolidated Maintenance Package |
| CO | Commanding Officer |
| CO2 | Carbon Dioxide |
| COMM | Communication |
| CONOPS | Concept of Operations |
| COTS | Commercial off The Shelf |
| CS | Culinary Specialist |
| CS | Combat Systems |
| CSO | Combat Systems Officer |
| CSOOW | Combat Systems Officer of the Watch |
| CTT | Cryptologic Technicians, Technical |
| DC | Damage Controlman |
| DCA | Damage Control Assistant |
| DCC | Damage Control Central |
| DCC | Damage Control Console |
| DCO | Damage Control Officer |
| DCS | Damage Control System |
| DDG | Destroyer, Guided Missile (Pre-FME) |

| | |
|---|---|
| DDG (OME) | Destroyer, Guided Missile (Post-FME) |
| DRT | Dead Reckoning Tracer |
| ECDIS | Electronic Chart Display Information System |
| EM | Electrician's Mate |
| EN | Engineman |
| ENG | Engineering |
| EOOW | Engineering Officer of the Watch |
| ET | Electronics Technician |
| EW | Electronic Warfare Technician (now CTT) |
| EXCEL® | Microsoft Office XP EXCEL® program |
| EXEC | Executive |
| FC | Fire Controlman |
| FFG | Frigate, Guided Missile |
| FME | Fleet Manning Experiment (Refer to OME) |
| FMP | Focused Mission Package |
| GCCS-M | Global Command and Control System - Maritime |
| GM | Gunner's Mate |
| GSE | Gas Turbine System Technician, Electrical |
| GSM | Gas Turbine System Technician, Mechanical |
| HALON | Halogenated Hydrocarbon |
| HCO | Helicopter Control Officer |
| HT | Hull Maintenance Technician |
| IBS | Integrated Bridge System |
| IC | Interior Communications Electrician |
| ICAS | Integrated Condition Assessment System |
| IT | Information Systems Technician |
| JOOD | Junior Officer of the Deck |
| JP5 | Jet Petroleum (Aviation Fuel) |
| LAN | Local Area Network |
| LCP | Local Control Panel |
| LCS | Littoral Combat Ship |
| LSE | Landing Signalman, Enlisted |
| MAINT | Maintenance |

| | |
|---|---|
| MCM | Mine Counter-Measure |
| MCS | Machinery Control System |
| MHC | Mine Hunting, Coastal |
| MIW | Mine Warfare |
| MM | Machinist's Mate |
| MMC | Multi-Modal Consoles |
| MN | Mineman |
| MR | Machinery Repairman |
| MT | Mount |
| NAV | Navigator |
| NAVAIR | Naval Air Systems Command |
| NAVMAC | Navy Manpower Analysis Center |
| NAVSEA | Naval Sea Systems Command |
| NMRS | Navy Manpower Requirement System |
| NO | Non-Optimal Manning Experiment |
| NS | Non-Smart Ship |
| OME | Optimal Manning Experiment (Type of FME) |
| OOD | Officer of the Deck |
| OPER | Operator |
| OPS | Operations |
| OPSO | Operations Officer |
| OS | Operations Specialist |
| PAPA | Personnel and Pay Ashore |
| PMS | Planned Maintenance System |
| POE | Projected Operational Environment |
| POIC | Petty Officer in Charge |
| PUK | Pack-Up Kit |
| QM | Quartermaster or Bridge Specialist |
| RADAR | Radio Direction and Ranging |
| RAM | Rolling Airframe Missile |
| RAST | Recovery Assist, Securing and Traversing |
| RCM | Reliability Centered Maintenance |
| RCP | Remote Control Panel |

| | |
|---|---|
| REP | Repairman |
| RQMTS | Manpower Requirements |
| RMS | Remote Mine-hunting System |
| RMV | Remote Mine-hunting Vehicle |
| ROC | Required Operational Capability |
| SCC | Ship's Control Console |
| SH | Ship's Serviceman |
| SK | Storekeeper |
| SM | Signalman (now QM or Bridge Specialist) |
| SMD | Ship Manpower Document |
| SONAR | Sound Navigation and Ranging |
| SQMD | Squadron Manpower Document |
| SS | 'Smart Ship |
| SUPV | Supervisor |
| SUW | Surface Warfare |
| TAO | Tactical Action Officer |
| TDT | Target Designation System |
| TM | Torpedoman's Mate |
| TORP | Torpedo |
| UAV | Unmanned Aerial Vehicle |
| USV | Unmanned Surface Vehicle |
| UUV | Unmanned Underwater Vehicle |
| UV | Unmanned Vehicle |
| VMS | Voyage Management System |
| VTUAV | Vertical Take-off and Landing Unmanned Aerial Vehicle |
| WCC | Weapons Control Console |
| WEPS | Weapons |
| XO | Executive Officer |

# LIST OF REFERENCES

1.   LCS Concept of Operations (CONOPS), NWDC, 22 January 2004.

2.   LCS Preliminary Design/Interim Requirements Document (PD/IRD), N763F-S03-026, February 2003.

3.   VTUAV Installation Design Requirements (IDR) (Preliminary Draft), DOC NO. 379-6100-051, 30 November 2000.

4.   Clark, Vern, Admiral, USN, *CNO Guidance for 2003*, http://.www.chinfo.navy.mil/navpalib/cno/clark-guidance2003.html, September 2004.

5.   Department of the Navy. *Manual of Navy Total Force Manpower Policies and* Procedures, OPNAVINST 1000.16J, 17 Washington, D.C., June 2002.

6.   http://www.chinfo.navy.mil/navpalib/ratings/navrate.html, April 2004.

7.   Koopman, Martha E. and Heidi L.W. Golding, *Optimal Manning and Technological Change*, Alexandria, VA: Center for Naval Analyses, July 1999.

8.   Gumataotao, Peter A. (CDR, USN) and Donald W. Mennecke (LCDR, USN), SC-21 Manning Reduction Initiatives, Center for Naval Analyses, Alexandria, V.A., May 1997.

9.   Pringle, Cedric E., *Smart Gator: An Analysis of the impact of reduced manning on the mission readiness of U.S. Naval Amphibious Ships*, Master's Thesis, Naval Postgraduate School, Monterey, CA, December 1998.

10.  Walker, Richard G., *Developing acceptance of optimized manning in DD-21: A study of change management*, Master's Thesis, Naval Postgraduate School, Monterey, CA, June 1999.

11.  LaFleur, Timothy W. (VADM, USN), *Change, Innovation, Transformation Today's Surface Force: Ready to Move at Flank Speed into the 21$^{st}$ Century,* http://www.navyleague.org/sea_power/sep_02_41.php, September 2002.

12.  OPNAVINST 3501.145C, Required Operational Capabilities (ROC) and Projected Operational Environment (POE) for FFG-7 (Oliver Hazard Perry) Class Guided Missile Frigates, 10 October 2003.

13.  http://www.globalsecurity.org/military/systems/ship, November 2003.

14.  CG 47 VLS (NS) Class Ship Manpower Document (SMD), NAVMAC, Millington, T.N., 03 November 2003.

15.  CG 47 VLS (SS) Class Ship Manpower Document (SMD), NAVMAC, Millington, T.N., 03 November 2003.

16.  DDG 51 Class (DDG 51 – DDG 67) Ship Manpower Document (SMD), NAVMAC, Millington, TN, 23 February 1998.

17.  DDG 51 Flight I Class (DDG 51 – DDG 71) Ship Manpower Document (SMD), NAVMAC, Millington, TN, 07 August 2003.

18.  FFG 7 Class Ship Manpower Document (SMD), NAVMAC, Millington, T.N., 11 April 2003.

19.  MCM 1 Class Ship Manpower Document (SMD), NAVMAC, Millington, T.N., 11 October 2000.

20.  MHC 51 Class Ship Manpower Document (SMD), NAVMAC, Millington, T.N., 28 September 2000.

21.  Nichols, Frank Captain, USN, NAVAIR 1.2, *LCS Alternative Aviation Support Study Final Briefout* to OPNAV N76, 14 June 2004.


22.  Gowen, Charlie. Consultation with subject matter expert. AmerInd Inc, Naval Postgraduate School, Monterey, C.A., May 2004.


23.  U.S. Navy Diving Manual, SS521-AG-PRO-010.  0910-LP-708-8000, Revision 4 dated 20 January 1999.


24.  OPNAVINST 4700.7J, Maintenance Policy for U.S. Navy Ships


25.  OPNAVINST 4790.4D, Ship's Maintenance and Material Management (3-M) System Policy, 23 Jan 2004


26.  NAVSEAINST 4790.8B, Ship's Maintenance and Material Management (3-M) Manual


27.  OPNAVINST 4790.16, Condition-Based Maintenance (CBM) Policy

THIS PAGE INTENTIONALLY LEFT BLANK

# INITIAL DISTRIBUTION LIST

1. Defense Technical Information Center
   Ft. Belvoir, VA

2. Dudley Knox Library
   Naval Postgraduate School
   Monterey, CA

3. LCDR(sel) Thaveephone NMN Douangaphaivong, USN
   Navy Manpower Analysis Center
   Millington, TN

4. Dr. Gregory V. Cox
   CNA Representative, J7CNA
   Commander Third Fleet
   53690 Tomahawk Drive, Suite 338
   San Diego, CA  92147-5004

5. Dr. Nita Lewis Miller
   Department of Operations Research
   Naval Postgraduate School
   Monterey, CA

6. CDR Bill Hatch, USN
   Naval Postgraduate School
   Monterey, CA

7. Charlie Gowen
   AmerInd, Inc.
   Virginia Beach, VA

8. OPNAV N75
   Pentagon City, VA

9. CAPT Stanley DeGeus, USN
   OPNAV N76
   Pentagon City, VA

10. Dr. James Miller
    OPNAV N76
    Pentagon City, VA

11. CAPT(Sel) Adam Levitt, USN
    OPNAV N81
    Pentagon City, VA

12. Dr. Stuart Dunn
        Center for Naval Analyses
        Alexandria, VA

13. CAPT Perry Bingham, USN
        PERS 412
        Bureau of Naval Personnel
        Navy Personnel Command
        Millington, TN

14. RADM Pearson, USN (Ret)
        Chairman, Mine Warfare
        Naval Postgraduate School
        Monterey, CA

15. CAPT Jeff Kline, USN
        Chairman, Warfare Innovations
        Naval Postgraduate School
        Monterey, CA

16. CAPT Frank Nichols, USN
        NAVAIR 1.2
        Naval Air Systems Command
        Patuxent River, MD

17. CDR Joe Beel, USN
        Naval Air Technical Data and Engineering Services
        Command (NATEC)
        San Diego, CA

18. Michael T. Ribble
        Naval Sea Systems Command
        Washington Navy Yard, DC

19. CAPT Walter J Wright, USN
        Naval Sea Systems Command
        Washington Navy Yard, DC

# NAVAL POSTGRADUATE SCHOOL
## Monterey, California

# THESIS

**LOGISTICAL ANALYSIS OF THE LITTORAL COMBAT SHIP**

by

David D. Rudko

March 2003

| | |
|---|---|
| Thesis Advisor: | David A. Schrady |
| Second Reader: | Kevin J. Maher |

**Approved for public release; distribution is unlimited**

Operational Logistics

| REPORT DOCUMENTATION PAGE | | Form Approved OMB No. 0704-0188 |
|---|---|---|

Public reporting burden for this collection of information is estimated to average 1 hour per response, including the time for reviewing instruction, searching existing data sources, gathering and maintaining the data needed, and completing and reviewing the collection of information. Send comments regarding this burden estimate or any other aspect of this collection of information, including suggestions for reducing this burden, to Washington headquarters Services, Directorate for Information Operations and Reports, 1215 Jefferson Davis Highway, Suite 1204, Arlington, VA 22202-4302, and to the Office of Management and Budget, Paperwork Reduction Project (0704-0188) Washington DC 20503.

| 1. AGENCY USE ONLY *(Leave blank)* | 2. REPORT DATE<br>March 2003 | 3. REPORT TYPE AND DATES COVERED<br>Master's Thesis | |
|---|---|---|---|
| **4. TITLE AND SUBTITLE:**<br>Logistical Analysis of the Littoral Combat Ship | | | **5. FUNDING NUMBERS** |
| **6. AUTHOR(S)** David D. Rudko | | | |
| **7. PERFORMING ORGANIZATION NAME(S) AND ADDRESS(ES)**<br>Naval Postgraduate School<br>Monterey, CA 93943-5000 | | | **8. PERFORMING ORGANIZATION REPORT NUMBER** |
| **9. SPONSORING /MONITORING AGENCY NAME(S) AND ADDRESS(ES)**<br>N/A | | | **10. SPONSORING/MONITORING AGENCY REPORT NUMBER** |

**11. SUPPLEMENTARY NOTES** The views expressed in this thesis are those of the author and do not reflect the official policy or position of the Department of Defense or the U.S. Government.

| 12a. DISTRIBUTION / AVAILABILITY STATEMENT<br>Approved for public release; distribution is unlimited. | 12b. DISTRIBUTION CODE |
|---|---|

**13. ABSTRACT *(maximum 200 words)***

The purpose of the Littoral Combat Ship is to provide the Navy with an affordable, small, multi-mission ship capable of independent, interdependent and integrated operations inside the littorals. The Littoral Combat Ship will be designed to replace high-value Naval assets when conducting high-end missions such as littoral Anti-Submarine Warfare (ASW), Mine Warfare (MIW) and Anti-Surface Warfare (ASuW) as well as perform low-end missions such as Humanitarian Assistance (HA), Non-combatant Evacuation Operations (NEO) and Maritime Intercept Operations (MIO). In order to accomplish these missions and successfully counter the enemy's littoral denial strategy, the Navy has stated the Littoral Combat Ship must incorporate endurance, speed, payload capacity, sea-keeping, shallow-draft and mission reconfigurability into a small ship design. However, constraints in current ship design technology make this desired combination of design characteristics in small ships difficult to realize at any cost. This thesis (1) analyzes the relationship between speed, endurance, and payload to determine the expected displacement of the Littoral Combat Ship, (2) determines the impact of speed, displacement and significant wave height on Littoral Combat Ship fuel consumption and endurance, and (3) analyzes the implication of findings on Littoral Combat Ship logistics.

| 14. SUBJECT TERMS<br>Littoral Combat Ship, speed, range, payload, displacement, significant wave height, fuel consumption, endurance, sea keeping, sea state, crew effectiveness | 15. NUMBER OF PAGES<br>96 |
|---|---|
| | 16. PRICE CODE |

| 17. SECURITY CLASSIFICATION OF REPORT<br>Unclassified | 18. SECURITY CLASSIFICATION OF THIS PAGE<br>Unclassified | 19. SECURITY CLASSIFICATION OF ABSTRACT<br>Unclassified | 20. LIMITATION OF ABSTRACT<br>UL |
|---|---|---|---|

NSN 7540-01-280-5500

Standard Form 298 (Rev. 2-89)
Prescribed by ANSI Std. 239-18

THIS PAGE INTENTIONALLY LEFT BLANK

# LOGISTICAL ANALYSIS OF THE LITTORAL COMBAT SHIP

David D. Rudko
Lieutenant Commander, Supply Corps, United States Naval Reserve
B.S., United States Naval Academy, 1992

Submitted in partial fulfillment of the
requirements for the degree of

## MASTER OF SCIENCE IN OPERATIONS RESEARCH

from the

## NAVAL POSTGRADUATE SCHOOL
**March 2003**

Author:          David D. Rudko

Approved by:     David A. Schrady
                 Thesis Advisor

                 CDR Kevin J. Maher SC, USN
                 Second Reader

                 James N. Eagle
                 Chairman, Department of Operations Research

THIS PAGE INTENTIONALLY LEFT BLANK

# ABSTRACT

The purpose of the Littoral Combat Ship is to provide the Navy with an affordable, small, multi-mission ship capable of independent, interdependent and integrated operations inside the littorals. The Littoral Combat Ship will be designed to replace high-value Naval assets when conducting high-end missions such as littoral Anti-Submarine Warfare (ASW), Mine Warfare (MIW) and Anti-Surface Warfare (ASuW) as well as perform low-end missions such as Humanitarian Assistance (HA), Non-combatant Evacuation Operations (NEO) and Maritime Intercept Operations (MIO). In order to accomplish these missions and successfully counter the enemy's littoral denial strategy, the Navy has stated the Littoral Combat Ship must incorporate endurance, speed, payload capacity, sea-keeping, shallow-draft and mission reconfigurability into a small ship design. However, constraints in current ship design technology make this desired combination of design characteristics in small ships difficult to realize at any cost. This thesis (1) analyzes the relationship between speed, endurance, and payload to determine the expected displacement of the Littoral Combat Ship, (2) determines the impact of speed, displacement and significant wave height on Littoral Combat Ship fuel consumption and endurance, and (3) analyzes the implication of findings on Littoral Combat Ship logistics.

THIS PAGE INTENTIONALLY LEFT BLANK

# TABLE OF CONTENTS

THIS PAGE INTENTIONALLY LEFT BLANK

# LIST OF FIGURES

THIS PAGE INTENTIONALLY LEFT BLANK

# LIST OF TABLES

THIS PAGE INTENTIONALLY LEFT BLANK

# ACKNOWLEDGMENTS

First, I would like to thank my advisor, Professor David Schrady, for his guidance and assistance in the completion of research and thesis development. The many dedicated hours he spent providing direction to ensure the research was accurately represented in the final product is greatly appreciated. In addition, I appreciate his timely turn-around of all submitted material and willingness to assist outside of working hours. I would also like to thank Professor Charles Calvano for his time and dedication to ensuring I had the knowledge and tools necessary to complete the research and model development for this thesis, and my second reader, CDR Kevin Maher, for his insight, thorough attention to detail, and subtle thesis deadline reminders that helped keep me focused and on track.

I would like to thank Dean Hughes and CAPT Jeff Kline for sparking my interest in the Littoral Combat Ship and CAPT James Stewart at Commander, Naval Surface Forces Pacific and CDR Dean Chase and CDR Todd Haeg at the Navy Warfare Development Command for taking the time from their busy schedules to support me with assistance and data as necessary. I would also like to thank the following individuals who provided assistance and direction along with way:

LTCOL Mislick, Naval Postgraduate School

Mr. Bill Stranges, Naval Center for Cost Analysis

Mr. Bob Hiram, Naval Center for Cost Analysis

Dr. Corrado and Dr. Kennel, Naval Surface Warfare Center, Carderock Division

Mr. Jim Heller, Naval Surface Warfare Center, Carderock Division

Ms. Virginia Lustre, Naval Surface Warfare Center, Carderock Division

Mr. Abdul Mondal, NAVSEA Advanced Concepts

I would especially like to thank the faculty and staff at the Naval Postgraduate School. To the staff, especially Lisa Puzon, thank you for all of the assistance you have provided along the way; I could not have done it without you. To the faculty, I cannot thank you enough for providing me with the knowledge necessary to even know where to begin on this thesis. While the numerous exams, projects, and homework assignments made for a long and tiring journey, your dedication to student learning and development is greatly appreciated.

To Jerry, Jana, John, Jordan, Jillian and Jacob (J^6), thank you for not only being such wonderful friends, but also for being my family away from home. I cherish all the fun times we had together during our time in Monterey and look forward to many more wonderful times ahead. And finally, to my family, words cannot express how much I appreciate having you all in my life. Thank you for all the love, support and wonderful things you do.

# EXECUTIVE SUMMARY

According to the United States 2002 Defense Planning Guidance, the Navy must develop the capability to maintain an Aircraft Carrier Operating Area clear of submarine-delivered and floating mines, improve the capability to destroy or evade large numbers of submarines operating in the littorals and develop the capability to destroy large numbers of small anti-ship cruise missile-armed combatants or armed merchant vessels in the littoral areas, without relying on carrier based air. Currently, sensors and weapons in the littoral environment have limited ranges due to environmental conditions and the clutter of maritime traffic. In addition, the proliferation of high-tech weapons and sensors potentially provides the enemy with the tools necessary to exploit the vulnerabilities of our current Naval force when operating inside the littorals. As a result, the Navy's current ability to counter enemy submarines, small craft and mines in the littoral environment is limited. It is for these reasons the Navy has stated the need for the Littoral Combat Ship.

The purpose of the Littoral Combat Ship is to provide the Navy with an affordable, small, multi-mission ship capable of independent, interdependent and integrated operations inside the littorals. In order to accomplish these missions and successfully counter the enemy's littoral denial strategy, the Navy has stated the Littoral Combat Ship must incorporate endurance, speed, payload capacity, sea keeping, shallow-draft, and mission reconfigurability into a small ship design. However, constraints in current ship design technology make this desired combination of design characteristics in small ships difficult and potentially costly, and may compromise supportability and sustainability. This thesis (1) analyzes the relationship between speed, endurance, and payload to determine the expected displacement of the Littoral Combat Ship, (2) determines the impact of speed, displacement and significant wave height on Littoral Combat Ship fuel consumption and endurance, and (3) analyzes the implication of these findings on Littoral Combat Ship logistics. While various hull forms are being considered for the Littoral Combat Ship (including, but not limited to the Surface Effect

Ship, Trimaran, SWATH technology and monohull), the JOINT VENTURE high-speed, wave-piercing catamaran is currently being tested by the military as a surrogate Littoral Combat Ship. As a result, the Littoral Combat Ship modeled in this thesis is based on the JOINT VENTURE seaframe.

The thesis demonstrates that speed, displacement, and significant wave height all result in considerable increases in fuel consumption, and as a result, severely limit Littoral Combat Ship endurance. When operating in a significant wave height of six feet, regardless of the amount of fuel carried, the maximum endurance achieved for a Littoral Combat Ship outfitted with all modular mission packages is less than seven days. Especially noteworthy is that when restricted to a fuel reserve of 50% and a fuel carrying capacity of Day tanks, the maximum achieved endurance is only 4.8 hours when operating at a maximum speed of 48 knots. Refueling, and potentially rearming, will require the Littoral Combat Ship to leave littoral waters and transit to Combat Logistics Force ships operating outside the littorals for replenishment. Given the low endurance of the Littoral Combat Ship, its time on station is seriously compromised. This not only limits the Littoral Combat Ship's ability to conduct independent operations, but restricts interdependent operations as part of a littoral operations force and integrated operations with Carrier and Expeditionary Strike Groups as well.

Significant wave height not only has a considerable negative impact on fuel consumption and endurance, but also has the potential for devastating impact on Littoral Combat Ship operations and crew effectiveness. The anticipated inability of the Littoral Combat Ship to effectively operate in ocean conditions beyond sea state 6 coupled with the real possibility of experiencing sea states 7 and beyond demonstrates the potential for the Littoral Combat Ship to be forced to either delay or abandon assigned missions. With regard to crew effectiveness, of the twenty-two personnel that were given a questionnaire regarding seasickness during joint Navy and Marine Corps testing of the JOINT VENTURE, 70% of those surveyed experienced dizziness, 65% experienced nausea and 30% actually became seasick when operating in sea state 4 and below.

The Littoral Combat Ship can achieve high speeds; however, this can only be accomplished at the expense of range and payload capacity. The requirement for the Littoral Combat Ship to go fast (forty-eight knots) requires a seaframe with heavy propulsion systems. The weight of the seaframe, required shipboard systems (weapons, sensors, command and control, and self-defense) and modular mission packages accounts for 84% of the full displacement, and as a result, substantially limits total fuel carrying capacity. Since initial mission profiles required the high-speed capability at most five percent of the time, the end result is a Littoral Combat Ship that has very little endurance and a high-speed capability it will rarely use. The pursuit for high speed itself demonstrates an inherent bias toward the attribute of speed and the neglect of range and payload requirements. Regardless of which hull form is selected for the Littoral Combat Ship, this thesis demonstrates the price that must be paid for speed as the tradeoffs between speed, endurance, and payload, in general, apply to any ship design.

THIS PAGE INTENTIONALLY LEFT BLANK

# I.    INTRODUCTION

## A.    BACKGROUND

In the late 19th century, the world was introduced to the torpedo boat. These small, swift craft were able to race in close to larger ships, fire their torpedoes and quickly get away without suffering any damage. In 1894, they demonstrated their abilities with overwhelming effectiveness in the Chilean Civil War and Sino-Japanese War. By the mid-1890s, the United States recognized the need for a Naval asset to counter the torpedo boat and in 1902, the first U.S. destroyer, *USS Bainbridge* (DD 1), was commissioned.

During the past century, advances in technology have lead to the creation of a new breed of fast, shallow-draft ships that operate in regions in which our Navy is not designed to operate. Missile Frigates, Corvettes, Fast Patrol Crafts and Fast Attack Missile Boats, all of which are capable of speeds ranging from 30-50+ knots, have become standard equipment in many of the world's Navies. Even though the United States destroyer has evolved into a very capable and survivable Naval asset, its speed is only 30 knots and its draft of approximately 30 feet limit its ability to operate in shallow waters. As a result, the United States is once again faced with developing a ship capable of countering threats with speed, maneuverability and lethality in waters far from our nation's homeland. "Today, the United States is master of the seas. Unless we adapt our Navy for future war fighting in contested, close-in waters, however, we risk our ability to influence events." (Cebrowski and Hughes, 1999). The response to this is Sea Power 21: the new vision to transform the Navy in order to meet the challenges that lie ahead. (Bucchi and Mullen, 2002)

## B.    PROBLEM DEFINITION

The first fundamental concept and core element of Sea Power 21 is Sea Shield. One of the major components of Sea Shield is the concept of forward littoral dominance. According to the United States 2002 Defense Planning Guidance, the Navy must develop the capability to maintain an Aircraft Carrier Operating Area clear of submarine-delivered and floating mines, improve the capability to destroy or evade large numbers of submarines operating in the littorals and develop the capability to destroy large numbers of small anti-ship cruise missile-armed combatants or armed merchant vessels in the littoral areas, without relying on carrier based air. (Navy Warfare Development Command, 2003)

Currently, sensors and weapons in the littoral environment have limited ranges due to environmental conditions and the clutter of maritime traffic. (Bucchi and Mullen, 2002) In addition, the proliferation of high-tech weapons and sensors potentially provides the enemy with the tools necessary to exploit the vulnerabilities of our current Naval force when operating inside the littorals. As a result, the Navy's current ability to counter enemy submarines, small craft and mines in the littoral environment is limited. It is for these reasons the Navy has stated the need for the Littoral Combat Ship.

> The challenge of access and the requirements to perform missions across the operational spectrum – including logistics, medical support, humanitarian assistance in inhospitable areas, non-combatant evacuation operations, force protection, and maritime interception / SLOC patrols – suggest that new capabilities may be needed to rebalance the fleet. The Navy could task the current force structure with these new littoral missions – but there are significant risks and costs associated with using expensive, high-end, power projection platforms against the enemy's fairly inexpensive air, surface, and undersea platforms with their associated combat and information technologies. Current fleet assets are sized for, and tasked with high-end missions and the associated training requirements to prepare for them. Declining force numbers further impair the ability of our capital ships to perform additional access missions. Further, it is unlikely that we would, in the foreseeable future, be able to afford the numbers of multi-mission, high end ships it would take to fill the gaps in needed littoral capabilities. (Navy Warfare Development Command, 2003)

As a result, the Navy has turned toward the development of the Littoral Combat Ship (LCS). The purpose of the Littoral Combat Ship program is to provide the Navy with an affordable, small, multi-mission ship capable of independent, interdependent and integrated operations inside the littorals. In order to accomplish these missions and successfully counter the enemy's littoral denial strategy, the Navy has stated the Littoral Combat Ship must incorporate endurance, speed, payload capacity, sea-keeping, shallow-draft, and mission reconfigurability into a small ship design (Navy Warfare Development

Command, 2003).  However, constraints in current ship design technology make this desired combination of design characteristics in small ships difficult and potentially costly, and may compromise supportability and sustainability.

The Littoral Combat Ship must be able to operate long distances from home while remaining combat effective.  Some of the Littoral Combat Ship logistics requirements, such as fuel, food, stores, provisions and basic supplies, are common to most of the Navy's high-value, blue-water ships.  However, since the Littoral Combat Ship is a modular design, it will also require a suite of modular weapon systems and associated support equipment capable of being configured to successfully achieve its operational tasking.  Currently, there exist a limited number of Combat Logistics Force (CLF) ships that can be utilized for replenishing Navy ships at sea.  Since there is no indication a logistics support ship will be built specifically for the Littoral Combat Ship, the addition of the Littoral Combat Ship fleet is going to place an added strain on the already burdened CLF fleet.  Even though the CLF ships are capable of replenishing basic logistics requirements, they do not possess the capability to support modular reconfiguration.  In addition, to ensure the protection of the CLF ships, they often operate with high-value, blue-water units located outside the littoral environment.  These considerations raise the question of whether or not current replenishment capabilities are sufficient to effectively support sustained Littoral Combat Ship operations inside the littorals.

Through the use of a model developed in Microsoft Office Excel, this thesis (1) analyzes the relationship between speed, endurance, and payload to determine the expected displacement of the Littoral Combat Ship, (2) determines the impact of speed, displacement and significant wave height on Littoral Combat Ship fuel consumption and endurance, and (3) analyzes the implication of these findings on Littoral Combat Ship logistics.

## C.    SMALL SHIP DESIGN CONSIDERATIONS

Ideally, a small warship would be inexpensive and fast, carry a large payload and have high endurance and good sea keeping.  Unfortunately, the current state of technology prevents this combination.  As the offensive and defensive capabilities of a ship increase, so must the size and cost of the ship, therefore, tradeoffs must be considered between speed, endurance, and payload during the design process.

## 1. Definitions

*Size* is physical magnitude, extent or bulk. It is measured as the full displacement of the ship.

*Speed* is the rate of motion. It is achieved through the use of large, powerful engines.

*Endurance* is the ability to sustain a ships mission. It is measured by a ship's range, sea keeping, fuel storage and consumption rate, and ordnance storage and delivery rate.

*Range* is the maximum distance a ship can travel at "best speed" without refueling. It is a combination of fuel capacity, fuel consumption rate and ships speed.

*Sea keeping* is the effect of sea states on crew effectiveness.

*Survivability* is the ability of a ship to avoid and/or withstand an enemy attack. It is a combination of speed, maneuverability, stealth and/or strength of design materials.

*Payload* is the number of weapons systems and their sensors capable of delivering ordnance on target. It is related to speed and endurance by space and weight.

(Kelley, 2002 and Merriam-Webster, 2003)

The United States currently possesses the technology to outfit the Littoral Combat Ship with engines capable of producing ship speeds in excess of 60 knots. However, these engines are large and increase the overall weight and displacement of the ship, thereby increasing fuel consumption and decreasing endurance. Fuel capacity in itself is an opportunity cost; the more space and weight that are dedicated to it, the less that can be allocated to payload. Typically, a modern warship's mission payload makes up ten to fifteen percent of its full displacement; to increase it much beyond this, speed, range or survivability would have to be sacrificed. (Kelley, 2002) Currently, shipboard systems critical to survivability and combat effectiveness, such as the Aegis Combat System, ballistic defense missiles and large guns, cannot fit aboard small ships. "A ship of less

4

than about 4,500 tons displacement would not be able to carry most of the major systems used for critical Navy missions, severely limiting its usefulness." (Kelley, 2002) In order for the Littoral Combat Ship to achieve success as a small, multi-mission ship, these constraints in small ship design must be overcome.

Figure 1 depicts the tradeoffs between ships speed, range, and payload with respect to the projected impact of future technology on ship performance.

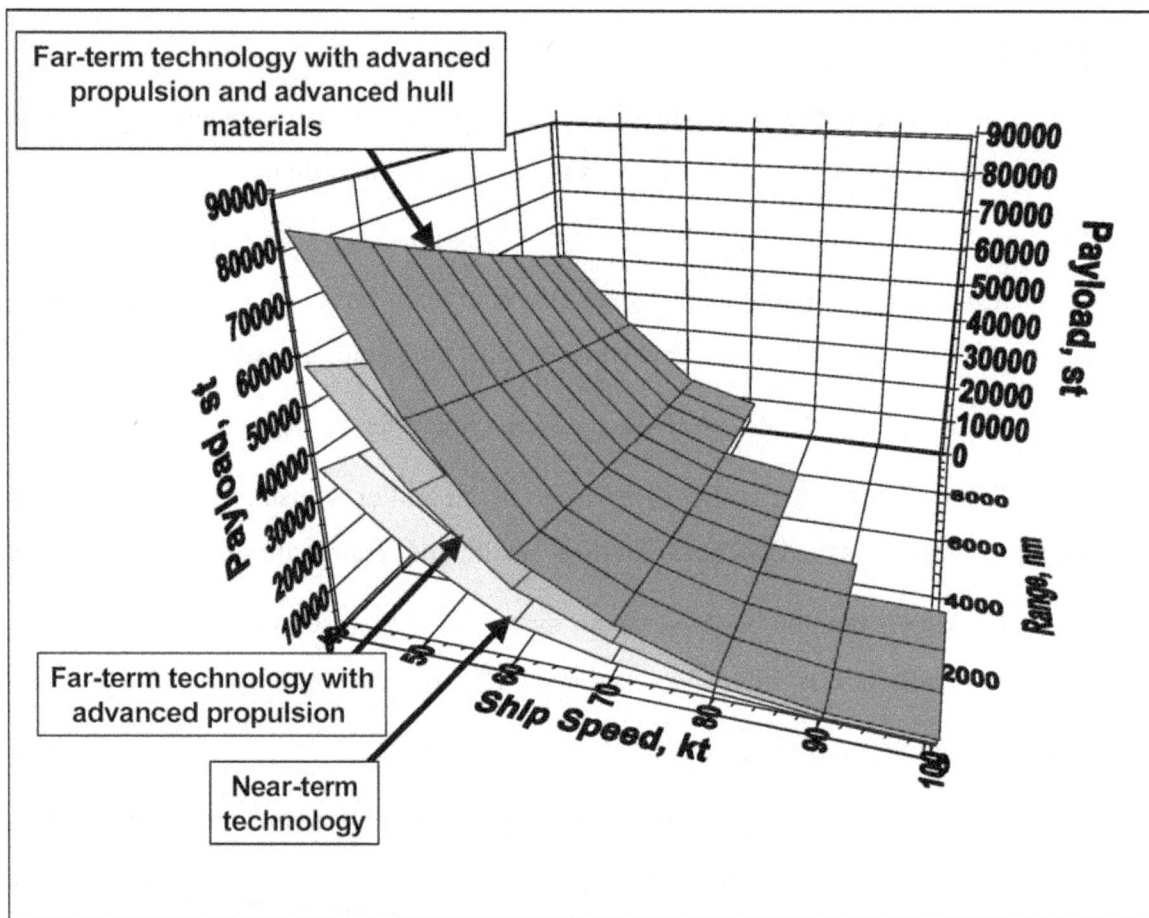

Figure 1.    Predicted Impact of Technology on Ship Performance

It represents the maximum mission performance associated with the technology projections made by the Naval Surface Warfare Center's Carderock Division High-Speed Sealift Innovation Cell project team.  Their work was conducted from May 2000 through August 2001, and the purpose of the project was to define the technology investments required to enable development of the high-speed commercial and military ships needed to provide realistic future mission capabilities. It shows that significant capabilities are scientifically possible using such technology projections in the near-term and the far-term, where the near-term relates to technology that will be available in 5 years and the far-term, 10 years. Full realization of capabilities shown in Figure 1 requires engineering development, particularly in packaging propulsion technology, advanced seaframes, and advanced materials and structures. (Naval Surface Warfare Center, 2002)

## D.   STUDY PLAN

Since the 1960s, the Navy has built three small, high-speed ship classes: patrol gunboats during the 1960s, missile hydrofoils during the 1980s and patrol coastal ships during the 1990s. Chapter II of this thesis considers these three small ship design programs and discusses the reasons for their limited operational usefulness.

In Chapter III, the Littoral Combat Ship concept of operations is discussed and a model is designed to estimate the Littoral Combat Ship displacement. According to a senior Navy official, the Littoral Combat Ship will be a non-traditional seaframe capable of high speeds (Koch, 2002). Currently, the JOINT VENTURE (HSV-X1) high-speed, wave-piercing catamaran is being leased by the Army, in cooperation with the Navy, Marine Corps and Coast Guard, from Australia's Incat International for testing high-speed catamaran capabilities, potential operational impact and technologies. The Joint Venture successfully took part in the Millennium Challenge '02 experiment and performed well in support of Operations Allied Force and Enduring Freedom. (Baumgardner, 2002) As a result, the Joint Venture high-speed, wave-piercing catamaran is utilized in this thesis as the Littoral Combat Ship seaframe to demonstrate the logistical implications of the speed, endurance, and payload tradeoffs with respect to the modular design of the Littoral Combat Ship. The weight and space requirement of each onboard and modular system is determined and added to that of the JOINT VENTURE seaframe. Factors considered for full displacement calculations include the base seaframe; installed weapons systems, command and control systems and sensors; personnel and supply load levels; fuel storage capacity; ordnance load levels and modular systems (embarked manned and unmanned air and sea vehicles). The number and types of systems installed and amount of load-out ordnance varies based on the mission for which the modular ship is configured. Hull design, fuel carrying capacity and supply load levels are derived from the JOINT VENTURE design. Factors considered for endurance calculations include displacement, fuel storage levels, fuel consumption rates, speed and sea state.

In Chapter IV, the impact of speed, displacement and significant wave height on Littoral Combat Ship fuel consumption and endurance is analyzed and the implication of these relationships with regard to Littoral Combat Ship logistics is discussed. An analysis of Littoral Combat Ship off-station time due to required replenishment is conducted by determining the required frequency of replenishments and estimating how far the Littoral Combat Ship will have to transit to the replenishment ship. Littoral Combat Ship replenishment requirements are compared with the current size and replenishment capabilities of the Combat Logistics Force in order to determine the overall impact of the added Littoral Combat Ship requirements.

In Chapter V, a conclusion of the Littoral Combat Ship analysis is provided along with associated recommendations. While this thesis based the design of the Littoral Combat Ship around the JOINT VENTURE hull form, the methodology followed applies to any high-speed ship as the tradeoff between speed, endurance, and payload must be acknowledged during the ship design process.

THIS PAGE INTENTIONALLY LEFT BLANK

## II. USN HISTORY OF HIGH SPEED SHIPS

Throughout history, the United States Navy has invested a considerable amount of time and money in the development of high-speed ships. Since World War Two, three high-speed ship classes have been commissioned and tested in hopes of achieving great military usefulness: the ASHEVILLE class patrol gunboats during the 1960s, the PEGASUS class missile hydrofoils during the 1980s and the CYCLONE class patrol coastal ships during the 1990s. However, each class failed to capitalize on the speed they were designed for and, as a result, failed to achieve the missions for which they were intended. This chapter will provide an overview of these three small ship design programs and discuss the reasons for their limited operational usefulness. Most of the historical information for the ASHEVILLE and PEGASUS class contained in this chapter was obtained from Norman Friedman's book *U.S. Small Combatants, Including Pt-Boats, Subchasers, and the Brown-Water Navy: An Illustrated Design History* (1987).

### A. ASHEVILLE CLASS PATROL GUNBOATS (PG)

In May 1961, the Ship Characteristics Board (SCB) asked for cost and feasibility studies for a small combatant designed primarily for surveillance, blockade, operations against other small crafts in coastal waters, and limited support of troops ashore. Tentative ship design characteristics included a length of 95 to 125 feet, a maximum draft of 8 feet (to allow for coastal operations), a speed of 30 knots, and an endurance of 1,500 nautical miles at 17 knots. A representative from the Long-Range Objectives (LRO) Group, an organization that determines naval requirements based on U.S. national strategy, determined that "in the future, there would be a place for small, relatively inexpensive, lightly manned coastal patrol craft aimed primarily at possible requirements in support of limited wars." (Friedman, 1987) The LRO went on to describe the patrol gunboat as being suitable for destroyer-type missions in waters where destroyers could not go or could not be risked.

In March 1962, Secretary of Defense McNamara specifically called for a navy program of patrol gunboats to deal with Cuban-based covert aggression in South America. Shortly thereafter, fleet commanders were asked for their own patrol gunboat force goals. The Commander-in-Chief Atlantic Fleet (CINCLANTFLT) asked for a total of eight, which were to be used for contingency readiness and cold war operations in the Caribbean, South Atlantic, and Indian Oceans, while the Commander-in-Chief Pacific Fleet (CINCPACFLT) asked for a total of twenty-seven, which were to be used in waters off of South Vietnam, Cambodia, China, and South Korea. Initially, a total of eight ASHEVILLE class patrol gunboats were approved for construction (one per year in fiscal years 1963-1970), however, that figure was later increased for a planned total of twenty-four at a cost of $1 million dollars each.

Design work on a small (length of 95 feet) ship, which began in June 1961, was already running into problems. The Bureau of Ships (BuShips) determined that, keeping within the previous stated ship design limits, they could achieve the desired speed but not the desired range due to the fact that the weight of the powerful diesel engines prevented the ship from carrying the necessary amount of fuel. Additional problems began to surface. Unimpressed with the performance of the 40 mm gun, they turned to the larger, and heavier, 3-inch/.50-caliber gun. With the addition of the new gun, BuShips was now not only unable to obtain the desired range, but also could not achieve the desired speed. As a result, BuShips considered gas turbines as the only method of propulsion that could potentially yield the desired speed, endurance, and payload combinations. In order to accommodate the gas turbine, it was determined the 3-inch/.50-caliber gun had to be moved aft and the length of the ship had to be increased.

As the design process continued, BuShips engineers increasingly struggled with the tradeoffs between speed, payload and range. They quickly realized that in order to achieve the combination they were looking for, they would have to increase the size of the ship. Table 1 contains the first five patrol gunboat design proposals submitted by BuShips. (Friedman, 1987) It includes the ship characteristics for each proposal along with associated costs in both fiscal year 1961 and, for current spending comparison, fiscal year 2003.

|  | Proposal 1 | Proposal 2 | Proposal 3 | Proposal 4 | Proposal 5 |
|---|---|---|---|---|---|
| Length (ft) | 95.0 | 95.0 | 115.0 | 161.0 | 161.0 |
| Beam (ft) | 19.8 | 22.0 | 24.2 | 25.0 | 24.0 |
| Draft (ft) | 6.3 | 6.5 | 8.1 | 7.0 | 7.0 |
| Full Load (tons) [1] | 107.3 | 124.1 | 209.9 | 225.0 | 225.0 |
| Max Speed (kts) [2] | 30 | 28 | 27 | 30 | 30 |
| Endurance (nm / kts) | 1,150 / 12 | 600 / 12 | 1,300 / 17 | 1,700 / 16 | 1,700 / 16 |
| Estimated Cost FY 1961 | $1.00 M | $1.20 M | $1.50 M | $1.70 M | $1.90 M |

Table 1.    Patrol Gunboat Designs, October 1961

Notes:  1.  Includes the following armament:

Forward          Single .50-caliber gun

Aft:                 Twin .50 caliber guns

Amidships:     Two single .50 caliber guns (port and starboard)

3-inch/.50-caliber gun

Two 81 mm mortars at centerline

2.  Maximum speed at 50% fuel level.

As BuShips proposals continued into 1962 none contained the answer senior officials were looking for.  In July, under a great deal of pressure, BuShips finally proposed it's preliminary design, which measured 166.2 feet; however, that proposal was discarded the following month.  As BuShips continued the design process, costs continued to increase.  BuShips was able to design a ship that achieved a range of 1,900 nautical miles at 16 knots; however, the cost to produce this ship rose to $2.7 million ($3.9 million for the lead ship).  The total for the first two ships, $6.6 million, exceeded the $4.1 million that was authorized in the fiscal year 1963 budget, and as a result, officials realized the allocated budget would only be sufficient to purchase the lead ship vice the first two ships of the ASHEVILLE class.

After two years of efforts, speed was still driving the ship design process. The desired speed eventually increased to 40 knots; however, this idea was abandoned after it became clear the ship would not be able to carry the necessary payload at that speed. As a result, the speed requirement was finally dropped to 37 knots. In 1963, the lead ASHEVILLE class ship was finally approved. Table 2 contains the ASHEVILLE class ship specifications (Pike, 2002) and Table 3 contains ASHEVILLE class payload (Donaldson, 2003).

| Length (feet) | Beam (feet) | Draft (feet) | Displacement (long tons) | Maximum Speed (knots) | Range (nm / kts) | Crew |
|---|---|---|---|---|---|---|
| 165 | 24 | 10.5 | 240 | 37 | 2,300 / 13 | 28 |

Table 2.    ASHEVILLE Class Specifications

| Mission Profile | Armament |
|---|---|
| Anti-Surface Warfare | - One 40 millimeter Gun<br>- One 3-inch/.50-caliber Rapid Fire Gun<br>- Two twin .50 caliber Machine Guns<br>- M60 Machine Guns<br>- M79 Grenade Launchers<br>- Two Missile Launchers[1] |
| Anti-Air Warfare | None |
| Anti-Submarine Warfare | None |

Table 3.    ASHEVILLE Class Payload

Note:  1.  Replaced 40 millimeter Gun aboard USS ANTELOPE (PG 86) and USS READY (PG 87) only.

Upon their entrance into the fleet, the ASHEVILLE class ships quickly received a reputation as poor sea-keepers. They would often experience 45 to 65 degree rolls each way in waves up to eight feet and pounding fore-to-aft motion of the ship's bow in up and down angles of 15 to 25 degrees. Resting, sleeping and eating were extremely difficult under these conditions and fatigue overwhelmed even the most seasoned sailors. Crews riding out 10-foot waves for more than 72 hours would become badly fatigued, so maximum ship speeds would generally be reduced from 37 to 20 knots. Logistics was also a limiting factor. The patrol gunboats could spend two weeks at sea without any replenishment if necessary; however, underway time was usually limited to a few days between port visits. Food and fuel could be re-supplied by underway replenishment (UNREP), but the major limiting factor was in the quantity of freshwater that could be made onboard. Even though the gunboat crews were small, the ships evaporators could not keep the crew adequately supplied; a particularly troubling problem. (Donaldson, 2003)

In Vietnam, the ASHEVILLE class became an effective river gunboat; however, it found little use for its high speed. In 1971, the Chief of Naval Operations, Admiral Elmo Zumwalt, directed Project Sixty, a quick look at new ways of using U.S. warships. One of the conclusions was to use the ASHEVILLE class ships to trail Soviet naval formations in the Mediterranean, even though they did not carry enough armament to successfully protect themselves against the Soviet ships. Efforts were undertaken to increase the payload; however, the outcome was a loss of three to four knots in speed. As a result, only four of the seventeen ships built remained in this role. Three ships were moved to the Naval Base at Little Creek, Virginia, three ships were transferred to U.S. allies, and the remaining seven were assigned to gunboat duty patrolling the Marianas trust territory from Guam. By the early 1980s, all of the ASHEVILLE class ships were either decommissioned or transferred to U.S. allies.

The ASHEVILLE class experienced many problems throughout its life cycle. In the design process, the tradeoff between speed, payload and range was a great source of debate and resulted in delayed construction. Each ship cost approximately $5 million, five times greater than the initial $1 million projection, and high maintenance costs made them expensive to operate once commissioned. Additionally, sea keeping problems prevented them from capitalizing on the high speeds for which they were designed. The changes in missions they experienced throughout their service life demonstrated their

13

inability to successfully fulfill the primary mission for which they were designed. Even though the majority of them did end up on gunboat patrol missions based out of Guam, the Navy was already looking at a cheaper and more effective replacement: the PEGASUS class missile hydrofoils.

## B.    PEGASUS CLASS MISSILE HYDROFOILS (PHM)

Once it was determined the ASHEVILLE class ships were too expensive and unable to satisfactorily perform their required missions, the Navy immediately turned their research efforts toward the development of a new small combatant that would replace the expensive patrol gunboats. The goal was to develop a high-speed ship with improved all weather performance, reduced maintenance costs, good sea keeping ability and increased operational availability. By the late 1960s, missile technology provided new hope that a large amount of anti-ship firepower could be generated from aboard a small ship. Due to its projected small size, good sea keeping ability and sustained rough water speed, it was believed these small ships could lie in wait, conduct a quick attack and retreat at high speeds. As a result, they would be able to successfully perform blockades, intercept missions and offshore patrols as necessary.

The missile hydrofoil was initially turned to in the late 1960s as an attractive replacement for the ASHEVILLE class gunboat, particularly in the Mediterranean. The initial concept was to establish a squadron of missile hydrofoils, each carrying a different modular weapons package, capable of functioning collectively as one multi-mission conventional warship. In May 1967, the Naval Ship Systems Command (NavShips) was asked to research a hydrofoil design capable of protecting coastal installations, surface shipping, and amphibious operations against fast-attack boats and conducting covert operations, reconnaissance and surveillance. By November 1968, even though nobody knew how hydrofoils would perform in realistic environments, the Navy was considering a 100-150 ton missile hydrofoil capable of achieving 45 knots sustained in sea state 5. Ship design was focused on high speed, a small crew and reduced life cycle costs; however, the total cost per ship was already estimated at $10.2 million ($18 million for the prototype). Compared to the cost of the ASHEVILLE class ships, this was an increase of more than 100%, however, the Navy believed they would see the savings in operating costs.

In November 1969, operations and technical personnel from eleven North Atlantic Treaty Organization (NATO) nations met to devise a joint fast patrol boat program with the goal of designing a ship that would offer a significant speed advantage over the large Soviet missile ships when operating in rough weather. Admiral Zumwalt made the missile hydrofoil an important element of his Project Sixty program, and in 1970 NavShips received authorization from the Secretary of Defense to continue the design process. At this time, however, NavShips was still far from a prototype as problems were being encountered with regards to the tradeoffs between speed, endurance, and payload. Since the limited size of the ship restricted the weight of the weapon systems to only 18 tons, it was determined that a modular weapons package concept would still be required in order to achieve a foil-borne range of 600 nautical miles and a hull-borne range of 2,000 nautical miles. Table 4 contains proposals for the various missile hydrofoil modular mission payload systems. (Friedman, 1987)

| Modular Weapons Package | Payload |
|---|---|
| Electronic Warfare | Demountable deckhouse with required equipment |
| Anti-Surface Warfare (Coastal) | Sonobuoys and torpedoes, with a high-speed, two-mode sonar to be developed later. |
| Anti-Surface (Gun) Warfare | OTO-Melara 76mm gun, with a lightweight 3-inch/.50-caliber gun as a fallback |
| Anti-Surface (Missile) | 6 Standard or Harpoon missiles in fixed launchers |
| Anti-Air Warfare | 15 Sparrows in fixed launchers |
| Special Operations | Deck-mounted module for 14 SEALS |
| NATO | Undetermined gun plus missile combination |

Table 4.    Proposed Missile Hydrofoil Modular Mission Payload Systems

In mid-1970, the Secretary of Defense decided the United States would lead the NATO fast patrol boat program, and in November the United States formally offered a 142-ton hydrofoil with a maximum speed of 48 knots at sea state 0 and a range of 860 nautical miles foil-borne or 1,500 nautical miles hull-borne. Based on a forty-two ship purchase, the estimated cost was only $3.2 million per ship ($6.9 million for the lead ship). In March 1971, the United States announced that the initial purchase would consist of eight missile hydrofoils with an additional thirty being purchased between fiscal years 1973-1977. The problem was that the modular design was discarded. Therefore, the single hull now had to accommodate a variety of weapons systems. As a result, the ship had to be made larger and in turn, required more fuel and power. By late 1971, the missile hydrofoil grew to a displacement of 160 tons while total armament weight had increased from 18 to 21 tons. Its 40 tons of fuel resulted in a foil-borne range of 750 nautical miles and hull-borne range of 1,500 nautical miles. Since many conventional ships outgrow the future growth margins designed into them, the gradual growth of the missile hydrofoils was a concern since foil-borne operations provided for a relatively small growth margin. As a result, the Navy quickly realized their desire to outfit the missile hydrofoils with the Harpoon Missile System, 76 millimeter anti-destroyer gun and the Sea Sparrow Missile System was going to be a problem.

In order to save time and money, the Navy chose sole-source procurement, and a contract was awarded to Boeing in November 1971. In 1972, letters of intent were received from Italy and Germany; however, all other NATO participants dropped out of the program or reverted to observer status. While the Naval Ship Engineering Center (NAVSEC) completed a feasibility study of a 150-160 ton missile hydrofoil in May 1972, Boeing's design, aimed at both U.S. and German markets, turned out to be much larger. NAVSEC argued that the Boeing proposal, with its relatively short range, large payload and high cost (approximately 25-35 percent more than that of their 160-ton design) was too large for the Navy. In the end, it was the Boeing design, the PEGASUS class missile hydrofoil, which was selected, mainly for its greater growth margins. Table 5 contains PEGASUS class ship specifications (Pike, 2002 and Friedman, 1987) and Table 6 contains PEGASUS class payload. (Pike, 2002)

|  | Length (feet) | Beam (feet) | Draft (feet) | Displacement (long tons) | Maximum Speed (knots) | Range (nm / kts) | Crew |
|---|---|---|---|---|---|---|---|
| **Hull-borne** | 145 | 28 | 23.2[1] | 255 | 12 | 1110 / 10 | 25 |
| **Foil-borne** | 133 | 28 | 8.8 | 255 | 50 | 400 / 50 | 25 |

Table 5.    PEGASUS Class Ship Specifications

Note:  1. With foils extended.  Hull-borne draft with foils retracted is 6.2 feet.

| Mission Profile | Armament |
|---|---|
| Anti-Surface Warfare | - Eight Harpoon Missiles<br>- One 76 millimeter Rapid Fire Gun |
| Anti-Air Warfare | None |
| Anti-Submarine Warfare | None |

Table 6.    PEGASUS Class Payload

By 1974, the PEGASUS class program encountered severe cost overruns and a decision was made to reduce the number of ships in the program from thirty to twenty-five.  The following year brought more funding problems for the PEGASUS class, and a decision was made to further reduce the number of ships in the program to six.  In 1976, construction on the USS HERCULES (PHM-2) was suspended in order to obtain enough money to complete the lead ship, USS PEGASUS (PHM-1).  By 1977, the PEGASUS program incurred such a cost growth ($13.2 million) that the last of the six ships, USS GEMINI (PHM-6), had to be built without armament. (Jenkins, 1995)

As the ships were commissioned in the late 1970s and early 1980s, the Navy made numerous attempts at a trial deployment to the Mediterranean; however, these were prevented by frequent system failures and a long lead-time for repair parts.  Since the PEGASUS class was too small to support itself and mobile logistics support was unavailable, it could not operate in waters far from home.  Just as USS GRAHAM COUNTY (LST 1176) was modified to provide necessary logistics support for the

ASHEVILLE class, USS WOOD COUNTY (LST 1178) was considered essential for logistics support of the PEGASUS class ships if their deployment to the Mediterranean was going to be successful. While the fiscal year 1978 budget provided the necessary funding ($42.8 million) for the conversion, the poor condition of USS WOOD COUNTY's propulsion plant was not taken into consideration. After reviewing the proposal, it was determined the cost of plant replacement plus modification was excessive, and as such, the conversion was cancelled, even though it was previously determined that a logistics support ship was vital for the success of the PEGASUS class. As a result, hopes for a Mediterranean deployment were abandoned and operations beyond the Caribbean were never scheduled. Even though funding was the official basis for cancellation, it seems more likely that the program had lost support and was destined for failure. (Jenkins, 1995)

As with the ASHEVILLE class, it seemed once again the strategic requirements of the United States Navy were not met with the development of the missile hydrofoils. Due to the inability to incorporate a modular weapons capability into the missile hydrofoil design, the squadron concept never came to fruition and the missile hydrofoils limited role was not in keeping with the Navy's emphasis on multi-purpose ships that were more adaptable to the full spectrum of naval operations. On July 30, 1993, the PEGASUS class program came to an end as all six were decommissioned.

## C.    CYCLONE CLASS PATROL COASTAL SHIPS (PC)

In 1990, the Navy awarded a contract to Bollinger Shipyards Incorporated for construction of eight patrol coastal ships. A follow-on contract for five additional ships was awarded in July 1991; in October 1997 Bollinger was awarded a contract to build a fourteenth patrol coastal ship. Construction of the ships was funded by the United States Special Operations Command (USSOCOM), and as such, the ships were assigned to the Naval Special Warfare Command under the cognizance of Special Boat Squadron ONE (Coronado, CA) and Special Boat Squadron TWO (Little Creek, VA). The initial mission of the patrol coastal ships was to conduct Maritime Special Operations, to include maritime interdiction operations, forward presence, escort operations, noncombatant evacuation, foreign internal defense, long-range Special Operations Forces

(SOF) insertion/extraction, tactical swimmer operations, reconnaissance, intelligence collection, operational deception, and SOF support as required. (Matyas, 2003) Table 6 contains CYCLONE class ship specifications and Table 7 contains CYCLONE class payload.

| | Length (feet) | Beam (feet) | Draft (feet) | Displacement (long tons) | Maximum Speed (knots) | Range (nm / kts) | Crew |
|---|---|---|---|---|---|---|---|
| PC 1 - PC 13 | 170 | 25 | 7.9 | 341 | 35 | 2000 | 39 |
| PC 14 | 179 | 25 | 8.5 | 392 | 35 | 2900 | 39 |

Table 7.    CYCLONE Class Ship Specifications

| Mission Profile | Armament |
|---|---|
| Anti-Surface Warfare | - 25mm Machine Guns<br>- Five .50-caliber Machine Guns<br>- Two 40mm automatic grenade launchers<br>- Two M-60 machine guns. |
| Anti-Air Warfare | Stinger Missiles |
| Anti-Submarine Warfare | Sonar transducer retracted within the hull at speeds above 14 knots |

Table 8.    CYCLONE Class Payload

The goal of the CYCLONE class program was to produce ships that provided the Navy with a fast, reliable platform that was able to respond to emergent requirements in a shallow-water environment.  However, the Navy quickly realized they had once again embarked upon another problematic high-speed ship program.  As with the previously discussed high-speed ship designs, the full displacement grew during construction.  The focus on speed during the design process resulted in damaging tradeoffs to range and payload.  Even though the patrol coastal ships are much larger than their predecessors, they only carry about the same payload and their combat systems and ammunition allowance do not compare well with similar ships in most other navies.  Even though they are capable of refueling at sea using astern refueling rigs, they only have a 10-day endurance, which is extremely limited for a ship its size. In order to support the few deployments they made to the Mediterranean, they require a temporarily shore-based Maintenance Support Team that pre-deployed with three 20-foot vans for spare parts and repair work. If these problems weren't bad enough, it was later discovered that they were too large for the close inshore work for which they were intended.

Due to the inability to successfully fulfill the missions for which they were designed, plans to build three additional patrol coastal ships (PC 15 through PC 17) were terminated and the CYCLONE class ships were slated for decommissioning in 2002. However, after the September 11th attacks on New York and Washington, D.C., there appeared to be a need for these ships in providing homeland defense. On November 5, 2001, it was announced that under OPERATION NOBLE EAGLE, five CYCLONE class ships were to be used for U.S. coastal patrol and maritime homeland security operations under the tactical control of the Coast Guard. As a result, they were tailored for maritime homeland security missions and have been employed jointly with the U.S. Coast Guard to assist in protecting U.S. coastlines, ports and waterways against potential terrorist attacks. The lead ship of the class, USS CYCLONE (PC 1), was decommissioned and turned over to the U.S. Coast Guard on February 28, 2000. As of now, no decisions have been made as to the decommissioning dates for the remaining CYCLONE class ships.

## D.    VALUE AND LIMITATION OF SPEED

Throughout Naval history, the development of small combatants in the United States has been driven by two factors: national strategy and technology, particularly the technology of high speed. (Friedman, 1987) While it is clear small ship design should be driven by national strategy, the concept of speed has always been a source of great debate.

> It must be plain to everyone who has ever taken part in any discussion on speed...that those who favour very high speed...are extremely sensitive on those points, and are usually ready to meet even a historical and undisputed statement with a vigorous rejoinder, as though an appeal to history were regarded as a controversion of their opinions. This deserves a good deal of consideration. (The Institution of Naval Architects, 1905)

Those who believe speed is critical to successful Naval operations argue high speed enables ships to arrive in theater faster and increase maneuverability within the assigned operating area. On station, some of the tactical benefits of high speed would seem to include decreased Special Operations Forces insertion and extraction times, increased flexibility in supporting Ship-to-Shore and Ship-to-Objective Maneuver operations, quick attacks against an enemy. and increased ability to evade enemy ships and weapons. Some proponents of speed may refer to war games and computer simulations as proof that speed is, in fact, a tactical advantage when it comes to Naval operations.

> Speed has always been of value in warfare, and daily it is being revalued yet further. If the value of speed is increasing, then those factors, sectors or forces which slow us down must either change or cease to exist. (Cebrowski, 1998)

Others argue high speed is not a tactical advantage. They state history has shown that high speed often appears so attractive that the possibility of obtaining it, even at great expense, seems to alone justify the construction of high-speed, small combatants. Often these proposals for new high-speed ships demonstrated the conflict between an attractive technology and naval requirements and turned out to be nothing more than solutions seeking problems. (Friedman, 1987) The lessons learned from the ASHEVILLE, PEGASUS and CYCLONE classes seem to support this idea.

Whether or not speed is tactically useful may not be the right question to ask. Perhaps, the more appropriate question is whether or not it is possible to overcome the limitations which have, throughout history, prevented previous high-speed ship designs from successfully capitalizing on any value that speed potentially offers. One reason the ASHEVILLE, PEGASUS and CYCLONE classes were all unable to meet the high-speed mission requirements for which they were designed was due to poor sea keeping in rough waters. Figure 2 demonstrates the impact of wave height on speed: as wave height increases, speed significantly decreases. (Lockheed Martin, 2002) While wave height has proven itself to be a major limitation on speed, it is not the only one. The need for the U.S. Navy to operate in potentially hostile waters far from home requires that ships be capable of long range, high endurance, and delivery of ordnance on target when necessary. Considering the small size of these previous high-speed ships and existing

21

constraints in technology, range and payload were always sacrificed in order to achieve high speeds. With endurance rarely exceeding fourteen days, frequent replenishment was necessary if these ships were to remain mission capable. Since the U.S. Navy did not have mobile logistics assets capable of resupplying these ships as often as needed, it made it nearly impossible to support them in their operating areas.

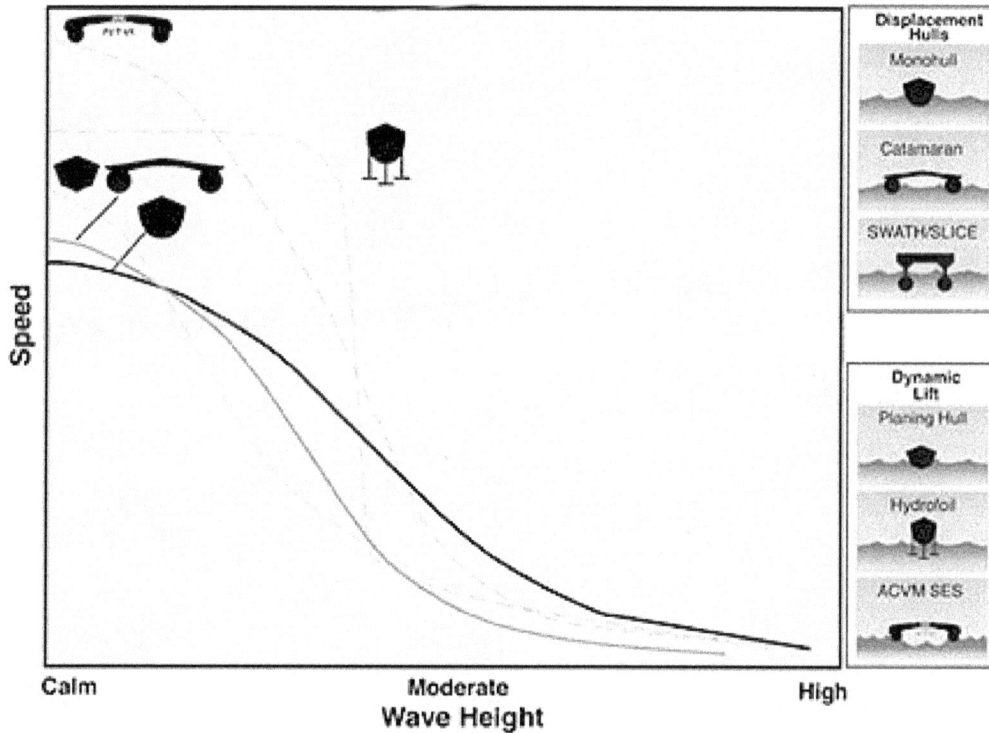

Figure 2.    Impact of Wave Height on Ship Speed

We now stand, according to Sir Reginald Custance, in the position that there is no absolute proof of the value of speed. He is an officer of the largest experience in the handing of fleets, and he tells us that the experiments so far made have not conclusively established one view or the other, and that he considers it is possible to reach a definite conclusion by properly conducted and well arranged, exhaustive experiments. (The Institution of Naval Architects, 1905)

From the ASHEVILLE, PEGASUS and CYCLONE class high-speed ship programs, we have learned there are, in fact, limitations to speed; however, the question regarding the value of speed, relative to the factors one must sacrifice to obtain it, remains. War games and simulation may provide insights into the value of speed; however, the true value of speed will not be determined until the limitations of speed can be eliminated.

THIS PAGE INTENTIONALLY LEFT BLANK

# III. LITTORAL COMBAT SHIP MODEL DEVELOPMENT

The Littoral Combat Ship is scheduled to be a member of the family of future surface combatants in support of the Sea Shield component of Sea Power 21. Its proposed contribution to Sea Shield is through its high-speed capability coupled with its ability to conduct a variety of peacetime and combat missions. In addition, the Littoral Combat Ship is proposed to be an enabler of Sea Basing by providing security for Joint assets and by acting as a logistics element for joint mobility and sustainment. The Littoral Combat Ship is envisioned to be a seaframe, serving much the same purpose as an airframe for a reconfigurable aircraft. It will serve as a platform for modular mission packages that can be changed, modified or removed in a short period of time. Logistics support will be self-contained and possess the capability of supporting additional personnel to augment the core crew as required for modular mission package support and additional tasks such as messing, administration and medical support.

In this chapter, the Littoral Combat Ship concept of operations is discussed, critical design parameters are listed and a model is created to estimate the Littoral Combat Ship size and endurance. Information regarding Littoral Combat Ship operations was obtained from the Naval Warfare Development Command Littoral Combat Ship Concept of Operations. (Navy Warfare Development Command, 2003)

## A.  CONCEPT OF OPERATIONS

The Littoral Combat Ship is designed to accomplish missions inside the littorals in order to support the national strategy tenet of littoral dominance. It will effectively operate throughout the continuum of operations as part of a distributed force. It is networked to off-board systems and to power projecting elements, from Carrier Strike Groups (CSG) and Expeditionary Strike Groups (ESG) to other Service capabilities for influencing events at sea and shore. Effective operations in the littorals are characterized by speed, agility, and integration with off board modular systems, survivability and signature control.

In order to operate effectively, the Littoral Combat Ship must be capable of limited independent operations, interdependent operations as part of a littoral operations force or integrated operations with multi-mission fleet forces such as Carrier and Expeditionary Strike Groups. In the self-deployable mode, a single forward deployed Littoral Combat Ship will be capable of responding rapidly and conducting a wide range of mobility missions such as Special Operations Forces (SOF) support, logistics (LOG), Anti-Terrorism/Force Protection (AT/FP), Maritime Intercept Operations (MIO), Sea Line of Communication (SLOC) patrols, Non-Combatant Evacuation Operations (NEO), Humanitarian Assistance (HA), and Medical Support (MED). The Littoral Combat Ship must be capable of transiting to the assigned operating area without having to rely on valuable and scarce Combat Logistic Force (CLF) ships or an ever-present logistics support ship. A self-deployment range of at least 3,500 nautical miles is desired as it would ensure a quick transfer to and from the theater of operations. In the interdependent operations mode, a number of Littoral Combat Ships would be forward deployed to maintain a continuous presence in critical theaters of operations. They will build the situational awareness in the littorals in anticipation of sanction enforcement, forced entry, information operations, strike operations and land warfare. In the integrated operations mode, several Littoral Combat Ships, with tailored mission configurations, will deploy with a CSG or ESG to provide vanguard scouting, pouncing support, and other tasking as directed.

The two primary mission categories for the Littoral Combat Ship are Focused Missions and Continuing Missions. During Focused Missions, the Littoral Combat Ship will employ reconfigurable modules tailored to specific missions such as littoral Anti-Submarine Warfare, Mine Warfare and Anti-Surface Warfare. As the Littoral Combat Ship will generally operate as part of a distributed force of many Littoral Combat Ships, groups of ships may be discretely configured so that more than one mission is conducted throughout the force. An additional Focused Mission is formalized logistics, which would include inter-theater and intra-theater lift and other joint logistics missions. Table 9 contains the Littoral Combat Ship focused mission profile and associated payload.

| Mission Profile | Armament |
|---|---|
| Anti-Submarine Warfare | - MH-60 R/S Multi-Mission Helicopter<br>- SPARTAN USV |
| Mine Warfare | - MH-60R/S Multi-Mission Helicopter<br>- SPARTAN USV<br>- RMS USV<br>- LMRS UUV |
| Anti-Surface Warfare | - MH-60R/S Multi-Mission Helicopter<br>- AH-58D Army Attack Helicopter [1]<br>- SPARTAN USV |
| Anti-Air Warfare | - AH-58D Army Attack Helicopter |
| Self Defense | - Four .50-caliber M2 Machine Guns<br>- Four M-60 Machine Guns |

Table 9.    Littoral Combat Ship Focus Mission Profile and Payload

Note:   1. The Army AH-58D Warrior aircraft is a version of the Army OH-58D Kiowa Warrior with air-to-air and air-to-surface armament installed.

During Continuing Missions, the Littoral Combat Ship will conduct intelligence, surveillance and reconnaissance (performed by the Fire Scout VT-UAV) or participate in any of the previously listed mobility missions while providing for its own self-defense. The core capabilities of the Littoral Combat Ship (sensing; command, control and communications; processing capability; and modular weapons) will support these continuing missions, which may or may not be conducted in a distributed manner.

The Littoral Combat Ship will contain mission systems and weapons that provide both core self-defense capabilities and the necessary compatibility with off-board sensors and networks. The mission systems will have four components: the host Littoral Combat Ship platform, its organic associated mission systems (installed seaframe systems), its networking capability, and the off-board sensors/vehicles (modular mission packages). Elements of mission modules will be designed to overlap in their applicability, and reconfiguration is anticipated to be a relatively simple and rapid task conducted at sea via Conventional Replenishment (CONREP) or Vertical Replenishment (VERTREP), in port or in a shipyard type environment. Replacement or replenishment modules may be flown in or pre-staged in theater as necessary.

27

## B.    CRITICAL DESIGN PARAMETERS

Table 10 contains the Littoral Combat Ship critical design parameters listed in the Surface Warfare Directorate Ship Systems Division Preliminary Design Interim Requirements Document. (Surface Warfare Directorate, 2003)

| Category | Threshold Level | Objective Level |
|---|---|---|
| Total Price per Ship | Seaframe: $220 M<br>Mission Packages: $180 M | Cost less than threshold |
| Hull Service Life | 20 Years | 30 Years |
| Draft at Full Displacement | 20 feet | 10 feet |
| Sprint Speed at Full Displacement | 40 knots in Sea State 3 [1] | 50 knots in Sea State 3 |
| Range at Sprint Speed [2] | 1,000 nautical miles | 1,500 nautical miles |
| Range at Economical Speed [2] | 3,500 nautical miles, speed greater than 18 knots | 4,300 nautical miles, speed greater than 20 knots |
| Aviation Support | Embark and hangar one MH-60R/S and VT-UAVs | Embark and hangar one MH-60R/S and VT-UAVs |
| Aircraft Launch/Recover | Sea State 4 | Sea State 5 |
| Watercraft Launch/Recover | Sea State 3 within 45 minutes | Sea State 4 within 15 minutes |
| Mission Package Boat Type | 11 Meter RHIB | 40-foot High Speed Boat |
| Time for Mission Package Change-Out to full operational capability | 4 days | 1 day |
| Provisions | 336 hours (14 days) | 504 hours (21 days) |
| Underway Replenishment Modes | CONREP/VERTREP/RAS | CONREP/VERTREP/RAS |
| Mission Package Payload [3] | 177.2 long tons | 206.7 long tons |

| | | |
|---|---|---|
| Core Crew Size | 50 | 15 |
| Accommodations (crew and embarked personnel) | 75 | 75 |
| Operational Availability | 0.85 | 0.95 |

Table 10.    Littoral Combat Ship Critical Design Parameters

Note:   1.  Sea State parameters are defined in Appendix A.

2.  Includes payload for required range.

3.  Includes the weight of fuel required to operate the mission package.

## C.    MODEL DESCRIPTION AND FORMULATION

The purpose of the model is to calculate the estimated size and endurance for the Littoral Combat Ship in order that the logistical implications of speed, endurance, and payload tradeoffs can be studied.    Since the Littoral Combat Ship is still in the conceptual phase, a seaframe suitable for conducting missions listed by the Navy Warfare Development Command (NWDC) in the Littoral Combat Ship Concept of Operations had to be utilized. (Navy Warfare Development Command, 2003)  The lack of logistical analysis for non-traditional hull forms coupled with current military testing of and data availability for the Joint Venture (HSV-X1) high-speed, wave-piercing catamaran resulted in the selection of the Joint Venture as the Littoral Combat Ship surrogate for model development.  The model is developed using Microsoft Office EXCEL.  It is subdivided into seven sections: Seaframe Data, Seaframe Systems, Modular Mission Packages, Ship's Gear Weight, Full Displacement Calculation, Endurance Calculation and Fuel Replenishment Requirement Calculation.  Tables 11 through 13 contain conversion factors used throughout the model.

| Weight Conversion Factors: | |
| --- | --- |
| 1 kilogram (kg) = | 2.2046 pounds |
| 1 long ton (lt) = | 2240 pounds |
| kg to lt conversion factor = | 0.000984 |
| Marginal Growth Factor = | 1.20 |

Table 11.    Weight Conversion Factors

| Storage Area Conversion Factors: | |
| --- | --- |
| 1 square meter (sq m) = | 1.196 sq yards |
| 1 square yard (sq yd) = | 9.000 sq feet |
| sq m to sq ft conversion factor = | 10.764 |
| Marginal Growth Factor = | 1.10 |

Table 12.    Storage Area Conversion Factors

| Full Displacement Calculation Conversion Factors: | |
| --- | --- |
| 1 gallon = | 3.7854 liters |
| 1 ounce = | 0.0078125 gallons |
| 1 pound = | 16 ounces |
| 1 short ton = | 2000 pounds |
| 1 long ton = | 2240 pounds |
| 1 short ton = | 1.12 long tons |
| Crew Member / Embarked Personnel = | 0.15 short ton |
| Ship Growth Margin per Person = | 3 long tons / person |
| Payload Weight Factor = | 15% |

Table 13.    Full Displacement Calculation Conversion Factors

1.    **Seaframe Data**

Ship specifications for the Joint Venture include length, beam, draft, seaframe and maximum displacement, speed, maximum range, and storage area.    Seaframe displacement is defined as the weight of the hull, self-defense machine guns (total of eight), and all installed propulsion systems.    It excludes installed seaframe systems (weapons systems, sensors, command and control systems) and deadweight.    Deadweight is defined as the total weight of the crew, embarked personnel and their effects; fresh water; stores and provisions; fuel; ordnance; modular mission packages; and any additional items of consumable or variable load. Maximum displacement is defined as the maximum weight of the ship, which includes the seaframe and its installed systems and all deadweight. Storage area is defined as the amount of space available for installed seaframe systems and modular mission packages. Military useful storage area was determined based on the Transportability Analysis conducted by the Military Traffic Management Command's Transportation Engineering Agency. (Atwood and Delucia, 2002) Since all seaframe and modular mission package systems listed in the Navy Warfare Development Command Littoral Ship Concept of Operations are of a height less than that of the Joint Venture storage decks, storage areas are calculated in square feet for area vice cubed feet for volume. Table 14 contains JOINT VENTURE ship specifications.

| Length (feet) | Beam (feet) | Draft (feet) | Seaframe Displacement (long tons) | Maximum Displacement (long tons) | Maximum Speed (knots) | Maximum Range (nm / kts) | Crew | Maximum Storage Area (square feet) |
|---|---|---|---|---|---|---|---|---|
| 313.2 | 87.3 | 12.1[1] | 922.3 | 1671.4 | 48 | 2400 / 35 | 30 | 12114[2] |

Table 14.    JOINT VENTURE Ship Specifications

Notes:  1. Maximum draft is 13 feet.
2. Storage area with the Portable Stern Ramp (562 square feet) onboard is 11,552 square feet.

## 2.    Seaframe Systems

The seaframe systems consist of all weapon systems, sensors, and command and control systems that have been used by the Navy as surrogate systems to be permanently installed aboard the Littoral Combat Ship. (Navy Warfare Development Command, 2002) This section contains the number of proposed systems, unit weight and unit area for each system. The total weight and area for each system are calculated and added to determine the total weight and storage area of all seaframe systems. During ship design and construction, growth margins are included to allow for unknowns, inaccuracy of assumptions, and additional unforeseen factors. Allowances, which are excesses of some characteristic beyond known needs, are intentionally built into the ship to be consumed during its life. Figure 3 demonstrates margins and allowances over the life cycle of a ship. (Calvano, 2003) In order to account for these margins and allowances in the model, a marginal growth of 20% for system weight and 10% for system area are added to seaframe system weight and area totals.

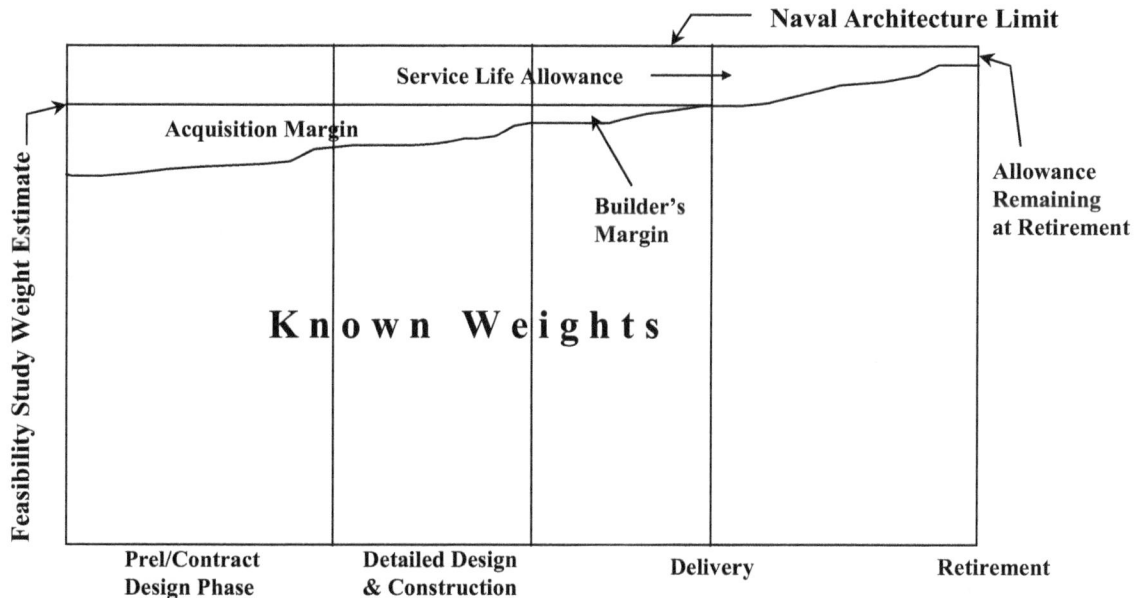

Figure 3.    Margins and Allowances Over Ship Life Cycle

Table 15 contains a list of the proposed Littoral Combat Ship seaframe systems and their associated weight and storage area.

The following formulation is used to determine total weight and space requirements for all seaframe systems:

$$Total\ Weight_{Seaframe\ Systems} = \sum Number\ of\ Systems_i * Unit\ Weight_i$$

$$Total\ Storage\ Area_{Seaframe\ Systems} = \sum Number\ of\ Systems_i * Unit\ Area_i$$

$$\forall i, i \in \{Weapon\ Systems, Sensors, Command\ \&\ Control\ Systems\}$$

| Weapon Systems, Sensors and Command & Control Systems | Number | Total Weight (long tons) | Total Weight including Marginal Growth (long tons) | Total Storage Area (square feet) | Total Storage Area including Marginal Growth (square feet) |
|---|---|---|---|---|---|
| Mk 15 CIWS Block 1B Gun Mount | 1 | 6.47 | 7.8 | 131.3 | 144.5 |
| CIWS Support | 1 | 0.86 | 1.0 | 117.3 | 129.1 |
| Mk 31 RAM Guided Missile System | | | | | |
| Launcher, above deck | 1 | 5.11 | 6.1 | 103.3 | 113.7 |
| RAM, below deck | 1 | 0.89 | 1.1 | 10.8 | 11.8 |
| Mk 53 Mod 4 Decoy Launch System (4 NULKA-SRBOC & 2 SRBOC launchers) | 1 | 10.00 | 12.0 | 158.2 | 174.1 |
| Advanced Surface / Air Search Radar | 1 | 1.00 | 1.2 | 20.0 | 22.0 |
| Electro Optical Sight System | 1 | 1.00 | 1.2 | 20.0 | 22.0 |
| Link 16 (CDLMS & JTIDS) | 1 | 1.60 | 1.9 | 45.2 | 49.7 |
| AN/USG-2(V) Co-operative Engagement Capability (CEC) (Receive Only) | 1 | 1.57 | 1.9 | 58.1 | 63.9 |
| | | TOTAL: | 34.2 | TOTAL: | 730.7 |

Table 15.  Proposed Littoral Combat Ship Seaframe Systems

## 3.  Ship's Gear Weight

Ship's gear consists of items necessary for support of the seaframe.  Table 16 contains a list of ship gear aboard JOINT VENTURE and its associated weight.

| Ship's Gear Item | Number | Unit Weight (long tons) | Total Weight (long tons) |
|---|---|---|---|
| Caterpillar Container: | 1 | 3.6 | 3.6 |
| Incat Container: | 1 | 4.5 | 4.5 |
| Portable Ramp: | 1 | 6.6 | 6.6 |
| ISU-90 W-Locker: | 1 | 2.1 | 2.1 |
| ISU-90 A-Locker: | 1 | 2.1 | 2.1 |
| Oil drums, misc items: | 1 | 8.9 | 8.9 |
| Incat Support Van: | 1 | 2.7 | 2.7 |
| Forklift: | 1 | 6.4 | 6.4 |
| GUV | 1 | 0.6 | 0.6 |
| Generator Set: | 2 | 2.0 | 3.9 |
| RHIB: | 1 | 0.7 | 0.7 |
| | | TOTAL: | 42.2 |

Table 16.  JOINT VENTURE Ship's Gear

The following formulation is used to determine the total weight of all ship's gear items:

$$Total\ Weight_{Ships\ Gear} = \sum Number\ of\ Item_j * Unit\ Weight_j$$
$$\forall j, j \in \{Ship's\ Gear\ Items\ Listed\ in\ Table\ 10\}$$

### 4. Modular Mission Packages

Modular mission packages consist of all manned and unmanned vehicles that are not permanently installed in the seaframe. These systems are designed to support the modular architecture of the Littoral Combat Ship. They provide flexible mission capability to meet different primary, secondary or alternate missions and the future ability to incorporate new technology for given mission functions. This section contains the number of proposed modular mission package systems, unit weight and unit area for each system. The total weight and area for each system are calculated and added to determine the total weight and storage area of all modular mission systems. As previously applied to the seaframe systems, a marginal growth of 20% for system weight and 10% for system area are added to the modular mission package weight and area totals in order to account for modular mission package margins and allowances. Data regarding the five modular mission packages used in the model was obtained from the NWDC Littoral Combat Ship Concept of Operations draft and Surface Warfare Directorate Ship Systems Division Preliminary Design Interim Requirements Document. (Navy Warfare Development Command, 2002 and Surface Warfare Directorate, 2003). They include the MH-60R/S Multi-Mission Helicopter (MMH), AH-58D Warrior Helicopter, Fire Scout Vertical Takeoff-Unmanned Aerial Vehicle (VT-UAV), Remote Mine-hunting System (RMS), Spartan Unmanned Surface Vehicle (USV), and Long-term Mine Reconnaissance System (LMRS). Table 17 contains proposed Littoral Combat Ship modular mission packages, and Table 18 provides the weight and storage area of each modular mission package. The total storage area of all seaframe systems, all modular mission packages, and the onboard ramp is 8,769 square feet, which falls below the maximum storage area of 12,114 square feet listed in Table 14.

34

| MH-60R/S | AH-58D | Fire Scout VT-UAV | RMS | Spartan USV | LMRS |
|---|---|---|---|---|---|
| - Support for 1<br><br>- Payload<br><br>- Fuel | - Support for 2<br><br>- Payload<br><br>- Fuel | - Support for 3<br><br>- Payload<br><br>- Fuel | - Launch, Recovery and Stow System<br><br>- Support for 1<br><br>- Payload<br><br>- Fuel | - Launch, Recovery and Stow System<br><br>- Support for 1<br><br>- Payload<br><br>- Fuel | - Launch, Recovery and Stow System<br><br>- Support for 2<br><br>- Payload<br><br>- No fuel required (battery powered) |

Table 17.    Proposed Littoral Combat Ship Modular Mission Systems

| Modular Mission Package | Number | Total Weight (long tons) | Total Weight including Marginal Growth (long tons) | Total Storage Area (square feet) | Total Storage Area including Marginal Growth (square feet) |
|---|---|---|---|---|---|
| MH-60R/S | 1 | 75.2 | 90.2 | 1551.6 | 1706.8 |
| AH-58D | 2 | 22.0 | 26.4 | 2095.5 | 2305.1 |
| Fire Scout VT-UAV | 3 | 13.5 | 16.2 | 1505.9 | 1656.5 |
| RMS | 1 | 27.6 | 33.1 | 398.3 | 438.1 |
| SPARTAN USV | 1 | 35.8 | 43.0 | 1083.9 | 1192.3 |
| LMRS | 2 | 7.4 | 8.9 | 161.5 | 177.6 |
| | | TOTAL: | 217.8 | TOTAL: | 7476.3 |

Table 18.    Modular Mission Package Weights and Storage Areas

The following formulation is used to determine total weight and space requirements for all modular mission packages:

$$Total\ Weight_{Modular\ Mission\ Packages} = \sum Number\ of\ Modular\ Mission\ Packages_k * Unit\ Weight_k$$

$$Total\ Storage\ Area_{Modular\ Mission\ Packages} = \sum Number\ of\ Modular\ Mission\ Packages_k * Unit\ Area_k$$

$$\forall k, k \in \{MH-60R/S, AH-68D, Firescout\ VT-UAV, RMS, Spartan\ USV, LMRS\}$$

## 5.    Full Displacement Calculation

This portion of the model calculates the full displacement of the proposed Littoral Combat Ship by adding the deadweight to the light displacement. The light displacement is calculated by adding the displacement of the seaframe and all seaframe installed systems. The deadweight is calculated by adding the weight of the crew, embarked personnel and their effects; fresh water; stores and provisions; fuel; lube oil; ship's gear; ordnance; and all modular mission packages installed aboard the seaframe (this varies depending on the assigned mission). The weight of the crew and embarked personnel is calculated by multiplying the total number of crew and embarked personnel by the average weight per person. According to the critical design parameters, there will be between fifteen and fifty crewmembers aboard the Littoral Combat Ship. During the Navy's testing of the JOINT VENTURE, there were a total of thirty-one crewmembers. However, the lessons learned stated the fast pace of JOINT VENTURE testing operations along with duty and watch-standing requirements were too demanding for the current crew size, and as such, recommended a crew size of forty. (Beierl, 2002) Since it appears these added demands were due to the Navy testing a ship that wasn't specifically designed for Littoral Combat Ship operations, it seems reasonable the majority of these problems will be resolved during the actual design process. As a result, a crew size of thirty-five is used as it provides an additional four personnel to compensate for any unforeseen manning requirements. The critical design parameters state the Littoral Combat Ship will be able to provide accommodations for up to seventy-five personnel, which includes personnel to support the various modular mission systems and other passengers as a result of the assigned Littoral Combat Ship mission (examples include Non-Combatant Evacuation Operations, Humanitarian Support and Medical Support). Since the number of personnel required to support all modular mission systems has not been determined, it is assumed to be approximately 25% of the total number of passengers. As a result, 18 personnel are used as the number of embarked personnel in the model full displacement calculation. Adding the number of crewmembers and embarked personnel results in a total of 53 personnel assigned onboard the Littoral Combat Ship. The weight of crew and embarked personnel effects; fresh water; and stores and provisions is calculated by multiplying the total number of crew and embarked personnel by the ship growth margin per person.

The weight of fuel depends on the amount being carried onboard. The JOINT VENTURE has four Day tanks and two Long-Range tanks, for a total carrying capacity of 567,580 liters. Fuel weight is calculated by converting the amount of fuel being carried in liters to tons. Table 19 contains data for the Littoral Combat Ship fuel capacity and weight.

| | Fuel Capacity (liters) | Fuel Weight (pounds) | Fuel Weight (long tons) |
|---|---|---|---|
| 4 Day Tanks: | 174880 | 369588.42 | 164.99 |
| 2 Long-Range Tanks: | 392700 | 829925.50 | 370.50 |
| Combined Tanks: | 567580 | 1199513.92 | 535.50 |

Table 19.     Littoral Combat Ship Fuel Capacity and Associated Weight

The weight of lube oil and ship's gear is obtained from the Transportation Engineering Agency Transportability Analysis. (Atwood and Delucia, 2002)

The amount of ordnance depends on the installed weapon systems and mission profile for which the Littoral Combat Ship is being configured. Typically, the weight of a modern warship's mission payload (consisting of armament and ordnance) makes up ten to fifteen percent of its full displacement. (Kelley, 2002) As a result, the total payload weight is calculated by multiplying the maximum displacement by fifteen percent. Since the ordnance required for modular missions is included in each mission package, the objective level weight for mission module payload, contained in Table 9, is used for the total weight of modular mission packages. The weight of ordnance for seaframe systems is determined by subtracting the weight of all seaframe systems and modular mission packages from the total payload weight.

The following formulation is used to determine the full displacement of the Littoral Combat Ship:

$$Light\ Displacement_{LCS} = Total\ Weight_{Seaframe} + Total\ Weight_{Seaframe\ Systems}$$

$$Weight_{Crew} = Number\ of\ Crew\ Members * Unit\ Weight_{Crew\ Member}$$

$$Weight_{Embarked\ Personnel} = Number\ of\ Embarked\ Personnel * Unit\ Weight_{EmbarkedPersonnel}$$

$$Total\ Number\ of\ Personnel = Number\ of\ Crew\ Members + Number\ of\ Embarked\ Personnel$$

$$Weight_{Effects,\ Stores,\ Provisions} = Total\ Number\ of\ Personnel * Ship\ Growth\ Margin\ Per\ Person$$

$$Weight_{Fuel} = Amount\ of\ Fuel\ Carried\ Onboard * Fuel\ Weight\ Conversion\ Factor$$

$$Weight_{Lube\ Oil} = 0.8929\ long\ tons$$

$$Weight_{Payload} = Maximum\ Displacement * Payload\ Weight\ Factor$$

$$Weight_{Ordnance} = Weight_{Payload} - Weight_{Seaframe\ Systems} - Weight_{Modular\ Mission\ Packages}$$

$$Deadweight_{LCS} = Weight_{Crew} + Weight_{Embarked\ Personnel} + Weight_{Effects,\ Stores,\ Provisions} + Weight_{Fuel} +$$
$$Weight_{Lube\ Oil} + Weight_{Ships\ Gear} + Weight_{Ordnance} + Weight_{Modular\ Mission\ Packages}$$

$$Full\ Displacement_{LCS} = Light\ Displacement_{LCS} + Deadweight_{LCS}$$

## 6. Endurance Calculation

In order to calculate the estimated endurance of the Littoral Combat Ship, a fuel consumption equation is required. Table 20 contains JOINT VENTURE fuel consumption data. (Beierl, 2002)

| Fuel Consumption Rate (liters / hour) | Displacement (long tons) | Ship Speed (knots) | Significant Wave Height (feet) |
|---|---|---|---|
| 1320 | 1500 | 15 | 6 |
| 5940 | 1450 | 33 | 7 |
| 1445 | 1350 | 17 | 7 |
| 5760 | 1300 | 36 | 5 |
| 6800 | 1600 | 34 | 7 |
| 6600 | 1300 | 40 | 3.5 |

Table 20.    JOINT VENTURE Fuel Consumption Data

In order to obtain the required fuel consumption equation, fuel consumption rate is regressed against various combinations of displacement, ship speed and significant wave height raised to the first, second and third powers. Significant wave height is defined as the average of the highest one-third of the waves. (National Oceanic and Atmospheric Administration, 2003) The regression of fuel consumption rate against displacement, ship speed[3] and significant wave height is selected as the preferred regression due to the fact that it is statistically sound and yields the most realistic fuel consumption equation with regard to JOINT VENTURE actual range and endurance data. Since ship power requirements for displacement hulls increase roughly with the cube of speed, this further supports the regression selected for use in the model. (Beierl, 2002) Table 21 contains the fuel consumption rate regression statistics.

| Regression Statistics | |
|---|---|
| Multiple R | 0.998 |
| R Square | 0.996 |
| Adjusted R Square | 0.991 |
| Standard Error | 247.896 |
| Observations | 6 |

ANOVA

| | df | SS | MS | F | Significance F |
|---|---|---|---|---|---|
| Regression | 3 | 32559016.000 | 10853005.333 | 176.608 | 0.006 |
| Residual | 2 | 122904.833 | 61452.417 | | |
| Total | 5 | 32681920.833 | | | |

| | Coefficients | Standard Error | t Stat | P-value | Lower 95% | Upper 95% |
|---|---|---|---|---|---|---|
| Intercept | -7997.867 | 1437.562 | -5.563 | 0.031 | -14183.203 | -1812.531 |
| Displacement | 3.281 | 1.217 | 2.695 | 0.114 | -1.956 | 8.518 |
| Speed^3 | 0.129 | 0.006 | 20.867 | 0.002 | 0.102 | 0.155 |
| Significant Wave Height | 647.403 | 128.246 | 5.048 | 0.037 | 95.605 | 1199.201 |

Table 21.     Fuel Consumption Rate Regression Statistics

The regression demonstrates that increases in displacement, speed and significant wave height result in increases in fuel consumption. This finding is confirmed by the fuel consumption discussion in the Navy's JOINT VENTURE "lessons learned" as it was noted fuel consumption increased dramatically when both displacement and significant wave height increased. (Beierl, 2002) Fuel consumption rates are calculated by adding the intercept coefficient to the sum of the products of the displacement, speed[3], and significant wave height coefficients obtained from the regression and their respective inputs. In reality, the weight of fuel decreases as it is consumed during ship operations.

As a result, full displacement of the ship decreases as well. However, this model uses a constant fuel weight during calculations. The result is a lower bound on endurance since fuel consumption would actually decrease as the ship becomes lighter, thereby, increasing range.

The following formulation is used to estimate Littoral Combat Ship endurance:

$$Fuel\ Consumption\ Rate = -7997.87 + 3.28 * Full\ Displacement +$$
$$0.13 * (Ship\ Speed)^3 + 647.40 * Average\ Wave\ Height$$
$$Endurance = Amount\ of\ Fuel\ Carried\ Onboard\ /\ Fuel\ Consumption\ Rate$$
$$Total\ Fuel\ Consumed = \sum Fuel\ Consumption\ Rate_l * Operating\ Time_l$$
$$\forall l, l \in \{Mission\ Profile\ Speeds\}$$

### 7.  Fuel Replenishment Requirement Calculation

Fuel replenishment requirements depend on the amount of fuel carried onboard, the rate at which it is consumed, and reserve level dictated. On-station speeds and length of time on station both depend upon the mission profile for which the Littoral Combat Ship is assigned. Once a minimum fuel level is reached, the ship must break from assigned operations in order to replenish its fuel before dropping below the pre-determined fuel reserve. For comparison purposes, this thesis uses both 50% and 20% fuel reserves during the analysis. While fuel tanks aboard Navy ships are normally filled to 95% capacity, the analysis in this thesis uses a 100% capacity since future Littoral Combat Ship fuel tank filling capacity is unknown.

The amount of fuel available is determined by multiplying the fuel carrying capacity by the percent of fuel available for assigned operations, which is calculated by subtracting the fuel reserve from 100%. The total amount of fuel consumed is calculated by summing the products of total operating time and fuel consumption rate for each on-station speed as listed in the mission profile. The number of required fuel replenishments is calculated by dividing the total amount of fuel consumed during a specified mission of a set duration by the amount of fuel carried onboard the ship minus the fuel reserve amount. Maximum time on-station is determined by dividing the mission duration by the number of required fuel replenishments. The fuel capacity depends on the mission profile and how much weight has been allocated to fuel with regard to total deadweight capacity; a tradeoff between the amount of fuel (range) and the amount of modular mission packages and ordnance (payload) carried onboard.

The following formulation is used in estimating the number of required fuel replenishments and maximum time on-station for the Littoral Combat Ship:

$$Amount\ of\ Fuel\ Available\ for\ Use = Fuel\ Carrying\ Capacity * (100\% - Fuel\ Reserve)$$

$$Number\ of\ Fuel\ Replenishments\ Required =$$
$$Total\ Amount\ of\ Fuel\ Consumed\ /\ Amount\ of\ Fuel\ Availble\ for\ Use$$

$$Time\ On-Station = Duration\ of\ Mission\ /\ Number\ of\ Fuel\ Replenishments\ Required_{Assigned\ Mission}$$

THIS PAGE INTENTIONALLY LEFT BLANK

# IV.   ANALYSIS

In this chapter, the model developed in the previous chapter is used to study the implications of speed, endurance, and payload tradeoffs through an analysis of the impact of speed, displacement and significant wave height on fuel consumption and endurance. In addition, logistics requirements are identified and a discussion of their impact on Littoral Combat Ship operations is provided.

## A.   FULL DISPLACEMENT ANALYSIS

Table 22 contains the total weight of each modular mission package and its respective percentage of the total modular mission package weight. The total weight of all modular mission packages is listed in bold italics.

| Modular Mission Package | Number of Modular Mission Packages | Total Weight (long tons) | Percent of Total Modular Mission Package Weight |
|---|---|---|---|
| MH-60R/S | 1 | 90.2 | 41.4% |
| AH-58D | 2 | 26.5 | 12.2% |
| Fire Scout VT-UAV | 3 | 16.2 | 7.4% |
| RMS | 1 | 33.1 | 15.2% |
| SPARTAN USV | 1 | 43.0 | 19.8% |
| LMRS | 2 | 8.8 | 4.0% |
| *TOTAL* | | *217.8* [1] | *100%* |

Table 22.   Modular Mission Package Weights and Percentages

Notes: 1. The total modular mission package weight exceeds both the threshold and objective levels in the Littoral Combat Ship critical design parameters listed in Table 9.

Currently, due to the applicability of the MH-60R/S, Fire Scout VT-UAV and SPARTAN USV to the majority of Littoral Combat Ship missions, there is a desire by some Navy officials to permanently embark one of each of these modular mission packages aboard every Littoral Combat Ship. Considering this accounts for 65.23% of the total weight of all modular mission packages, it seems to significantly reduce the benefit of incorporating the modular concept into the Littoral Combat Ship design and further reduces the amount of weight allocated to carrying additional fuel. Due to this information and the desire to obtain upper bounds on fuel consumption and lower bounds on endurance, all modular mission packages are included in the model when calculating full displacement. As such, changes in full displacement are only achieved by varying the amount of fuel carried onboard. Table 23 lists the two Littoral Combat Ship fuel storage profiles that are used for Littoral Combat Ship endurance analysis.

| Weight Component | Displacement at 174,880-liter Carrying Capacity Day Tanks Only (long tons) | Displacement at 281,730-liter Carrying Capacity Day Tanks plus Partial Fill of Long-Range Tanks (long tons) |
|---|---|---|
| Fuel | 165.0 | 265.8 |
| Deadweight (Excluding fuel) | 231.3 | 231.3 |
| Modular Mission Packages | 217.8 | 217.8 |
| Light Displacement | 956.5 | 956.5 |
| Full Displacement | 1570.6 | 1671.4 |

Table 23.    Littoral Combat Ship Fuel Storage Profiles

Table 24 contains the estimated weight of each component of the Littoral Combat Ship and the associated light displacement, deadweight and full displacement (listed in bold italics). It includes configurations with and without all modular mission packages installed and uses the fuel profiles listed in Table 23. Without the modular mission packages (the mode in which the Littoral Combat Ship can be expected to transit), the full displacement is 1352.8 long tons. This leaves 318.6 long tons of deadweight for

44

additional fuel, which is not enough to fill the Long-Range tanks capable of holding a total of 370.5 long tons. With all modular mission packages embarked, only 100.8 long tons of deadweight remain for additional fuel, which again is not enough to fill the two long-range tanks. As a result, even though the full displacement included in the first two profiles falls below the Littoral Combat Ship maximum displacement of 1671.4 long tons, the Littoral Combat Ship is unable to use the maximum fuel carrying capacity (both Day and Long-Range Tanks). The third profile includes a Littoral Combat Ship with all modular mission packages embarked and fuel weight of 265.8 long tons. This results in a fuel level of 281,730 liters and full displacement of 1671.4 long tons.

| Littoral Combat Ship Component | Weight without Modular Mission Packages and Fuel Capacity of 174,880 liters (long tons) | Weight with all Modular Mission Packages and Fuel Capacity of 174,880 liters (long tons) | Weight with all modular Mission Packages Embarked and Fuel Capacity of 281,730 liters (long tons) |
|---|---|---|---|
| Sea frame | 922.3 | 922.3 | 922.3 |
| Onboard Systems | 34.2 | 34.2 | 34.2 |
| *Light Displacement* | *956.5* | *956.5* | *956.5* |
| Number of Crew | 4.7 | 4.7 | 4.7 |
| Number of Embarked Personnel | 2.4 | 2.4 | 2.4 |
| Crew effects, Fresh Water, Stores and Provisions | 142.0 | 142.0 | 142.0 |
| Fuel | 165.0 | 165.0 | 265.8 |
| Lube Oil | 0.9 | 0.9 | 0.9 |
| Ship's Gear | 42.2 | 42.2 | 42.2 |
| Ordnance | 39.2 | 39.2 | 39.2 |
| Modular Mission Packages | 0.0 | 217.8 | 217.8 |
| *Total Deadweight* | *396.3* | *614.1* | *714.9* |
| *Full Displacement* | *1352.8* | *1570.6* | *1671.4* |

Table 24.     Littoral Combat Ship Full Displacement

45

Table 25 demonstrates the impact of fuel weight on the Littoral Combat Ship full displacement both with and without all modular mission systems installed. It shows that when all onboard fuel tanks are filled to maximum capacity, the full displacement of the Littoral Combat Ship exceeds the maximum displacement even when no modular mission packages are embarked. The implication of this is that while the modular design does provide an increase in the amount of fuel that can be carried onboard, the Littoral Combat Ship will be unable to use its maximum fuel carrying capacity regardless of the mission profile because its maximum displacement is only 1671.4 long tons.

| Fuel Tanks | Fuel Storage (liters) | Fuel Weight (long tons) | Full Displacement with Modular Mission Packages (long tons) | Full Displacement without Modular Mission Packages (long tons) |
|---|---|---|---|---|
| Day Tanks | 174880 | 165.0 | 1592.0 | 1352.8 |
| Combined Day and Long-Range Tanks | 567580 | 535.5 | 1962.5 | 1723.3 |

Table 25.     Impact of Fuel Weight on Full Displacement

## B.     FUEL CONSUMPTION AND ENDURANCE ANALYSIS

This section analyzes the impact of speed, displacement and significant wave height on fuel consumption and endurance. Since the model uses a fixed displacement and significant wave height for fuel consumption calculations, the displacement and significant wave height parameters are changed individually in order to determine the impact of that individual parameter on overall fuel consumption and endurance.

### 1. Mission Profiles

In the NWDC Littoral Combat Ship Concept of Operations draft, two potential Littoral Combat Ship mission profiles were originally provided: a 5-day Focused Mission profile and a 21-day Continuous Mission profile. These mission profiles are provided in Table 26 and Table 27 respectively. However, the sprint speed of 55 knots as contained in the Concept of Operations draft was replaced in the model with the JOINT VENTURE maximum speed of 48 knots. Of interesting note is the column containing the percent of time at speed. In the Focused Mission profile, sprint speed is only used 4.17% of the time while in the Continuous Mission profile, sprint speed is used only 0.40% of the time. Since the original Concept of Operations draft, these profiles have been eliminated, although the percent of time when the ships high-speed capability is used argues against the many compromises necessary to achieve this capability.

| Focused Mision Profile | | 5 Days | |
|---|---|---|---|
| Speed (knots) | Op-Time (hours) | Range (nm) | Percent of Time at Speed |
| 10 | 115 | 1150 | 95.83% |
| 48 | 5 | 240 | 4.17% |
| Totals: | 120 | 1390 | |

Table 26.  5-Day Littoral Combat Ship Focused Mission Profile

| Continuous Mission Profile | | 21 Days | |
|---|---|---|---|
| Speed (knots) | Op-Time (hours) | Range (nm) | Percent of Time at Speed |
| 8 | 502 | 4016 | 99.60% |
| 48 | 2 | 96 | 0.40% |
| Totals: | 504 | 4112 | |

Table 27.  21-Day Littoral Combat Ship Continuous Mission Profile

Table 28 lists an alternate 14-day Littoral Combat Ship mission profile that is created for model analysis.

| Analysis Mission Profile | | | | 14 Days | |
|---|---|---|---|---|---|
| Speed (knots) | Op-Time (hours) | Range (nm) | Fuel Consumed (liters) | Percent of Time at Speed | Percent of Total Fuel Consumed |
| 15 | 268 | 4020 | 483507.24 | 79.76% | 51.29% |
| 27 | 34 | 918 | 132677.75 | 10.12% | 14.07% |
| 40 | 34 | 1360 | 326536.83 | 10.12% | 34.64% |
| Totals: | 336 | 6298 | 942,721.82 | | |

Table 28.    14-Day Littoral Combat Ship Analysis Mission Profile

Since the fuel consumption data obtained from the Navy's JOINT VENTURE lessons learned only included a range of speeds from 15 to 40 knots, the selected mission profile speeds are restricted to this range. In addition, the lessons learned stated that speeds between fifteen and seventeen knots obtain the best fuel consumption rates. This information is consistent with the findings of this thesis as Figure 4 demonstrates the impact of speed on range.

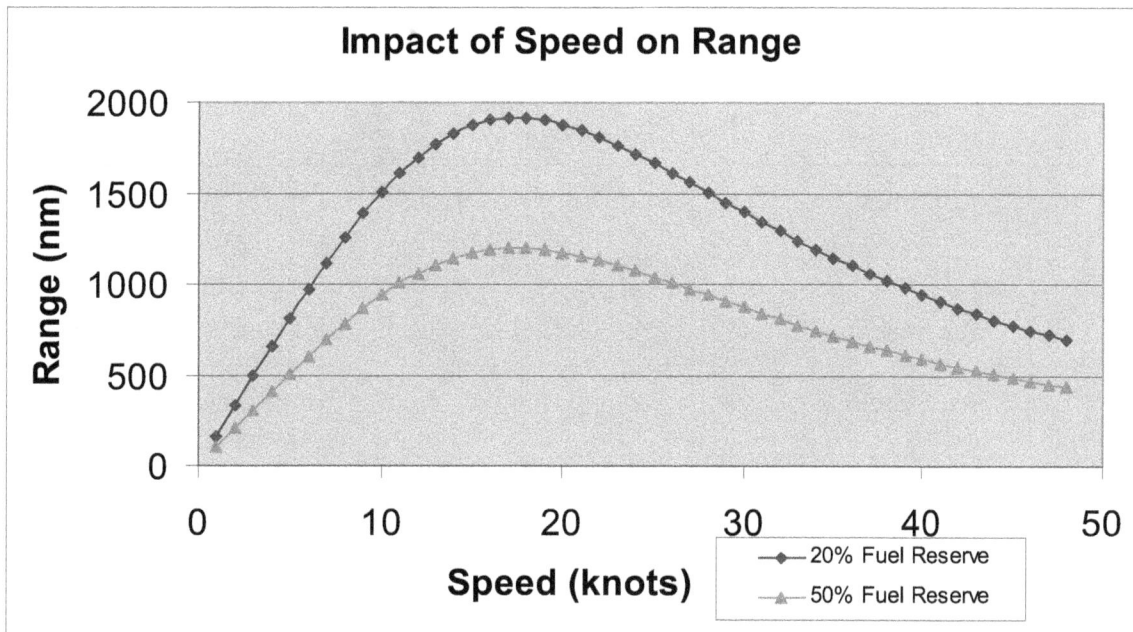

Figure 4.    Impact of Speed on Range at 1671.4 long tons Full Displacement, 6-Foot Significant Wave Height and 281,730 liters Fuel Carrying Capacity

48

As a result, fifteen knots was chosen as the base operating speed as it was estimated the Littoral Combat Ship would operate at these speeds approximately 80% of the time. A moderate speed of twenty-seven knots and a sprint speed of forty knots were estimated operating speeds for approximately 10% of the time each. By comparing the percent of time at and the percent of total fuel consumed for a given speed, one can see the large impact ship speed has on fuel consumption. Even though the Littoral Combat Ship operates at fifteen knots for almost 80% of the time, these operations only account for 51.29% of the fuel consumed while only 10.12% of operating time at forty knots results in 34.64% of total fuel consumed. This is an important finding that is further analyzed later in this chapter.

### 2. Impact of Significant Wave Height

Significant wave height is a limiting environmental condition that was identified by the Navy during JOINT VENTURE operations as having a considerable impact on ship operations with regard to ship speed, fuel consumption and crew. Table 29 contains the Littoral Combat Ship sea state operating requirements as listed in the Littoral Combat Ship Preliminary Design Interim Requirements Document. (Surface Warfare Directorate, 2003)

| Condition | Significant Wave Height (feet) | Requirement |
|---|---|---|
| Sea State 5 | 12.1 | Full capability for all systems |
| Sea State 6 | 18.0 | Continuous efficient operations |
| Sea State 8 and above | 58.1 | Best heading survival without serious damage to mission essential subsystems |

Table 29. Littoral Combat Ship Sea State Operating Requirements

Beyond sea state 5, the Littoral Combat Ship can expect to encounter considerable restrictions to ship operations as significant wave heights exceed twelve feet. Even though probability distributions have been generated to estimate significant wave heights in various regions of the world, actual significant wave heights can vary greatly. Figures 5, 6 and 7 contain global significant wave heights for September 2, 2002, February 24, 2003 and March 1, 2003 respectively. (Colorado Center for Astrodynamics Research, 2003) Looking at Figures 5 and 7, it can be seen that significant wave heights in various regions of the world differ depending on the season (summer versus winter in these figures). However, comparing Figure 6 and Figure 7 demonstrates that significant wave height can also vary considerably from week to week. It is for this reason that significant waves heights can be a severe limiting factor when it comes to Littoral Combat Ship operations. If a Littoral Combat Ship had been assigned to conduct an independent 2-week mission off the east coast of Japan beginning February 24, 2002, it would have been able to conduct operations as wave heights were only approaching sea state 5. However, by March 1, significant wave heights increased to more than 20 feet. As a result, the assigned mission would have been interrupted and the Littoral Combat Ship would likely have been required to find calmer waters in order to protect mission essential systems and reduce the consequences of the increased sea state on crew effectiveness. Even if probability distributions can be used to predict regional significant wave heights with a fair amount of accuracy, military missions cannot always wait for calm waters. The anticipated inability of the Littoral Combat Ship to effectively operate in water conditions beyond sea state 6 demonstrates it may find itself having difficulties operating in the right place at the right time.

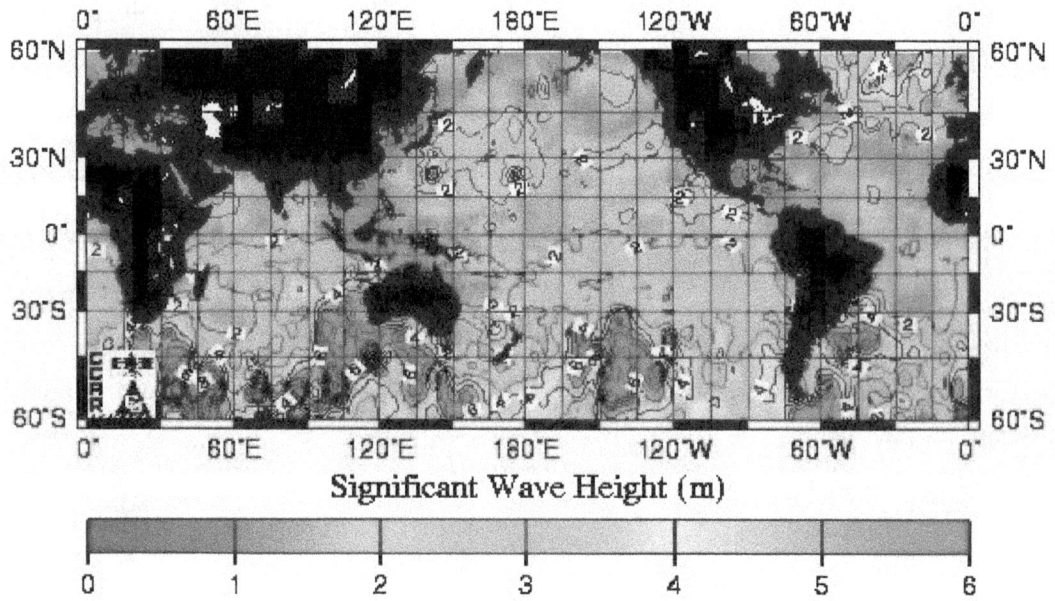

Figure 5.    Global Significant Wave Heights for September 2, 2002

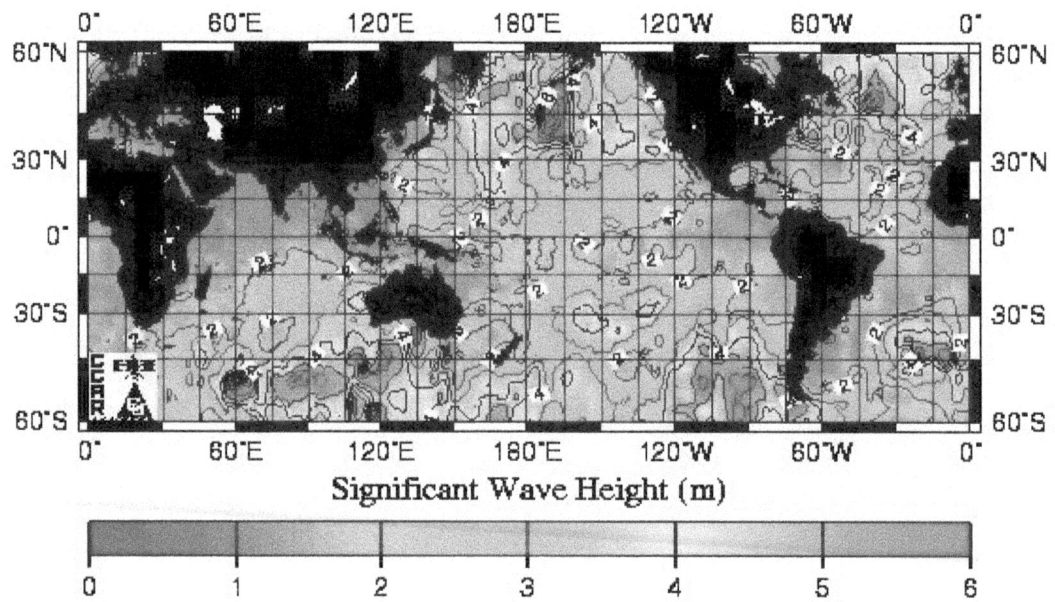

Figure 6.    Global Significant Wave Heights for February 24, 2003

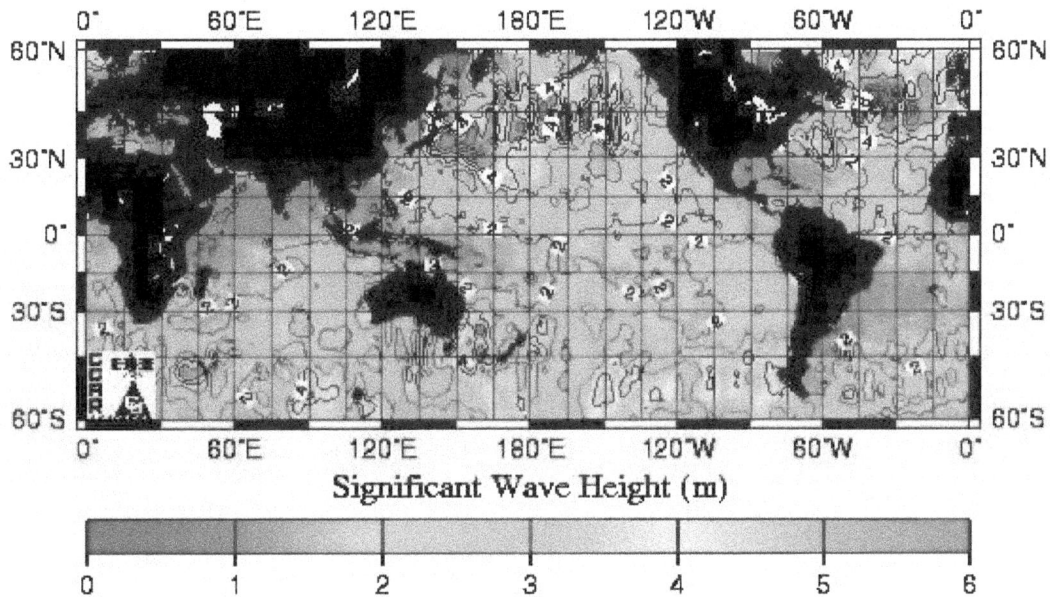

Figure 7. Global Significant Wave Heights for March 1, 2003

In addition to the considerable impact significant wave height has on Littoral Combat Ship operations, it also demonstrates devastating impact on crew effectiveness. Of the twenty-two personnel that were given a questionnaire regarding seasickness during joint Navy and Marine Corps testing of the JOINT VENTURE, 70% of those surveyed experienced dizziness, 65% experienced nausea and 30% actually became seasick. Of those experiencing dizziness, nausea and/or seasickness, 100% of them desired outside visibility and 80% desired weather-deck access in order to ease their symptoms. (Marine Corps Warfighting Laboratory, 2002) While the study did not specify the significant wave height at the time of the survey, it is fair to assume conditions were below sea state 5 since the data range of significant wave height generated during this time for fuel consumption was between 3.5 and 7 feet. Considering the Littoral Combat Ship is expected to operate in wave heights beyond eighteen feet, this is a problem that is certain to have a substantial negative impact on crew effectiveness and endurance.

### 3. Fuel Consumption Analysis

In order to study the impact of speed on fuel consumption, the model is set with a fixed displacement and significant wave height, and fuel consumption rates are calculated for speeds between one and forty-eight knots. A Littoral Combat Ship with a displacement of 1570.6 long tons (includes all modular mission packages and the use of Day tanks only) is used along with a significant wave height of six feet (the average of the significant wave height data used during regression analysis). Figure 8 demonstrates the relationship between speed and fuel consumption in the Littoral Combat Ship: fuel consumption increases with the cube of speed. The relationship produces a fuel consumption curve typical of diesel engines, which is appropriate considering the JOINT VENTURE is equipped with four Caterpillar Marine Propulsion Diesel engines.

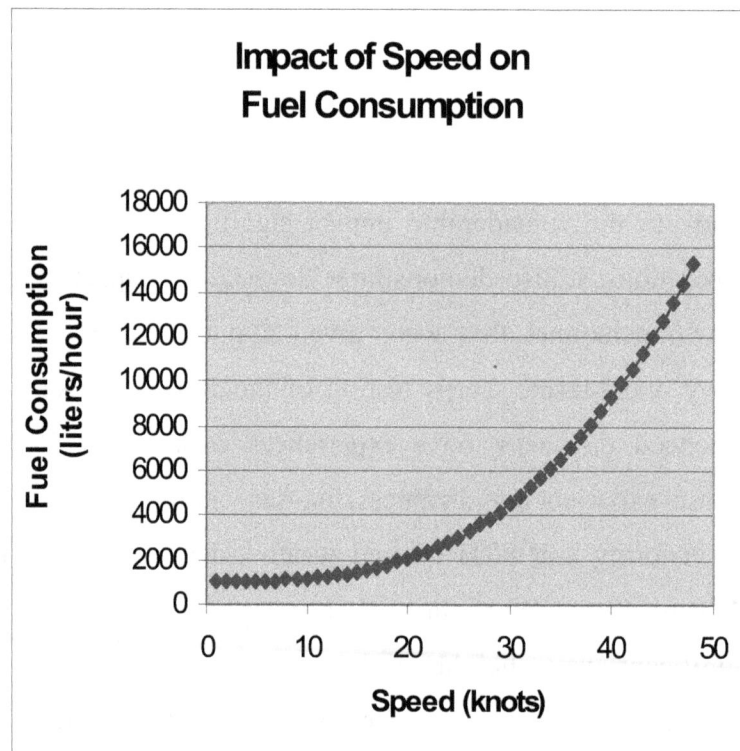

Figure 8.    Impact of Speed on Fuel Consumption at 1570.6 long tons Full Displacement and 6-foot Significant Wave Height

To determine the impact of displacement on fuel consumption, a fixed speed of fifteen knots, fixed significant wave height of six feet and varying full displacements are used. Displacements between 1352.8 and 1671.4 long tons are used since the previous full displacement analysis indicated this was the feasible full displacement range for the Littoral Combat Ship. Figure 9 demonstrates the impact of displacement on fuel consumption for the Littoral Combat Ship at an operating speed of fifteen knots (the analysis mission profile base operating speed). Since displacement is a linear term in the fuel consumption equation, increases in displacement result in the same increase in fuel consumption for any given speed. Figure 9 shows that as the displacement of the Littoral Combat Ship is increased from the minimum feasible displacement (1352.8 long tons) to the maximum displacement (1671.4 long tons), fuel consumption increases by 137.73% (from 758.9 to 1804.1 liters per hour).

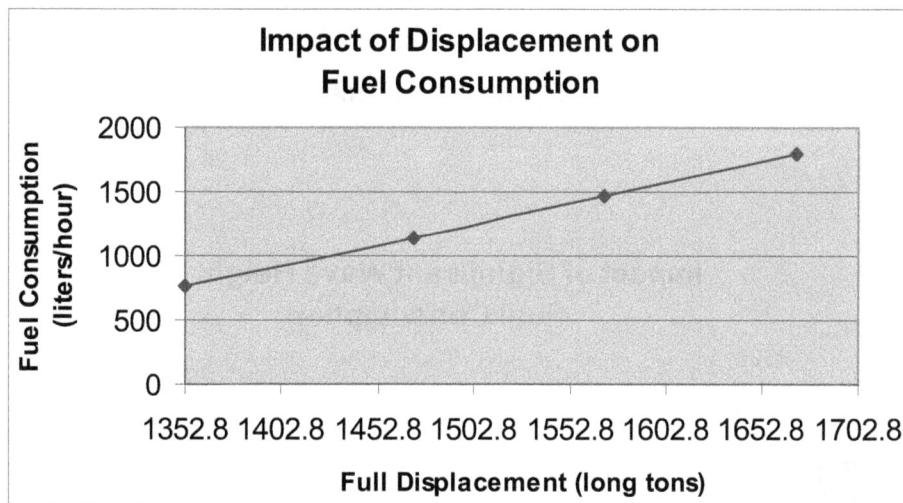

Figure 9.    Impact of Displacement on Fuel Consumption at 15 knots and 6-foot Significant Wave Height

Considering the previous discussion to permanently install one MH-60R/S, one Fire Scout VT-UAV and one SPARTAN USV (which combined has a weight of 118.35 long tons), the minimum feasible displacement of the ship increases by 8.77% (1352.8 to 1471.15 long tons) and fuel consumption increases by 51.16% (758.9 to 1147.2 liters per hour). As a result, at fifteen knots and a significant wave height of six feet, a 1% increase in displacement increases fuel consumption by 5.83%. This finding demonstrates the importance of the modular concept with respect to the Littoral Combat Ship.

Since the significant wave height data utilized in the regression only provides a range between 3.5 and 7 feet, the model could not be used to study the impact of sea states 5 and beyond on Littoral Combat Ship operations. However, the analysis is able to conclude that even when operating in wave heights below sea state 5, significant wave height has a substantial impact on fuel consumption. This is determined using the most economical speed of fifteen knots, fixed displacement of 1671.4 long tons (includes all modular mission packages and the maximum fuel carrying capacity) and varying significant wave heights between 3.5 and 7 feet. Figure 10 demonstrates the impact of significant wave height on fuel consumption at fifteen knots.

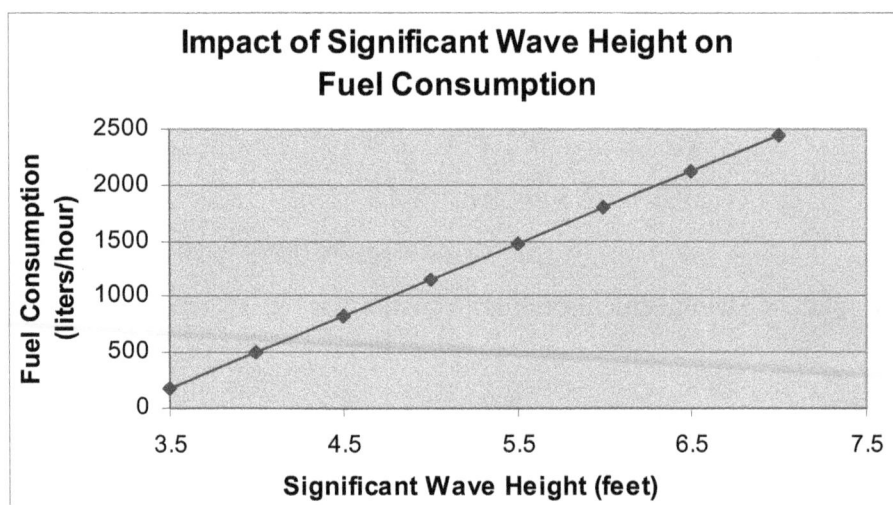

Figure 10.   Impact of Significant Wave Height on Fuel Consumption at 15 knots and 1671.4 long tons Full Displacement

As in the previous case with displacement, since significant wave height is a linear term in the fuel consumption equation, increases in significant wave height result in the same increase in fuel consumption for any given speed. Figure 10 shows that as the significant wave height increases from 3.5 to 7 feet (a 100% increase in significant wave height), fuel consumption increases by 1220.69% (from 185.6 to 2451.53 liters per hour). As a result, at fifteen knots and a full displacement of 1671.4 long tons, a 1% increase in significant wave height increases fuel consumption by 12.2%. This finding demonstrates that even though the Littoral Combat Ship will be able to operate in conditions up to sea state 7, the amount of fuel required during these operations increases quickly as significant wave height increases.

### 4.    Endurance Analysis

The impact of speed on endurance is analyzed by first determining the endurance for a Littoral Combat Ship with all modular mission packages installed (full displacement of 1570.6 long tons) and a minimum fuel storage capacity (use of Day tanks only). Then, the Littoral Combat Ship is modified by increasing the amount of fuel stored until the maximum displacement is attained (increase in full displacement from 1570.6 to 1671.4 long tons). This results in a maximum fuel carrying capacity of 281,730 liters. In both scenarios, significant wave height is held constant at six feet. Figure 11 demonstrates the impact of speed on Littoral Combat Ship endurance.

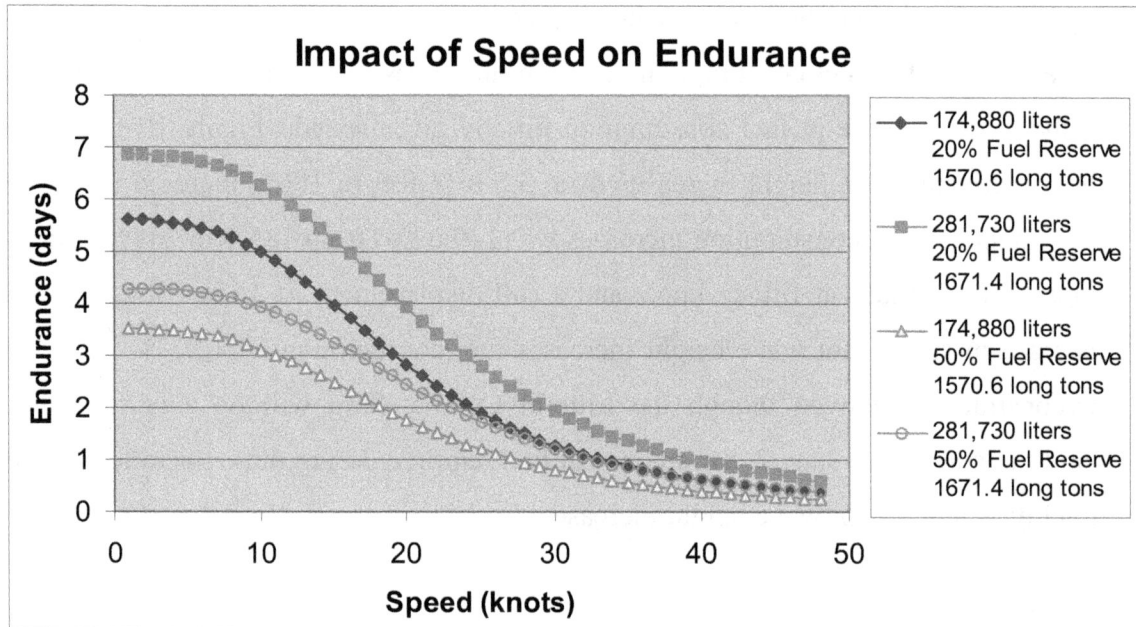

Figure 11.    Impact of Speed on Littoral Combat Ship Endurance at 6-foot Significant Wave Height

Currently, Navy ships utilize a 50% fuel reserve, however, the Navy's JOINT VENTURE lessons learned discusses the penalty paid in fuel economy for carrying excess fuel (this further validates the previous discussion with regard to the relationship between displacement and fuel consumption). As a result, it is recommended that only the fuel required for the mission at hand should be carried unless readiness to meet contingencies dictates otherwise. (Beierl, 2002) Considering this penalty and the use of a 20 percent fuel reserve during JOINT VENTURE maximum range testing, fuel reserve levels of both 20% (top two curves) and 50% (bottom two curves) are used in the analysis. As fuel is consumed, the weight of fuel decreases and as a result, full displacement and fuel consumption decrease as well. By utilizing a 20% vice 50% fuel reserve, the Littoral Combat Ship is able to capitalize on this relationship.

At all speeds, increasing the fuel reserve from 20% to 50% results in a 60% decrease in endurance. However, the same relationship does not hold for increases in fuel carrying capacity. At the base operating speed of fifteen knots, increasing the fuel carrying capacity from 174,880 to 281,730 liters results in an increase of endurance by

31.67%. At a sprint speed of forty knots, the same increase in fuel carrying capacity results in an increase of endurance by 55.57%. This shows that as speed increases, increasing the fuel carrying capacity provides a greater impact on endurance. Figure 11 reveals the two most important findings. *Regardless of the fuel reserve or fuel carrying capacity, the maximum endurance achieved for a Littoral Combat Ship outfitted with all modular mission packages is less than seven days. In addition, when the Littoral Combat Ship is outfitted with all modular mission packages and operated continuously at its maximum speed of forty-eight knots, the maximum achieved endurance is only 14.4 hours. While this endurance is achieved utilizing a 20% fuel reserve and maximum fuel carrying capacity, increasing the fuel reserve to 50% and restricting the fuel carrying capacity to Day tanks results in a maximum endurance of only 4.8 hours.* These findings demonstrate the considerable impact ship speed has on Littoral Combat Ship endurance.

Figure 12 illustrates the impact of displacement on endurance. It is based on the speeds and operating times included in the 14-day mission profile (Table 28) and uses a fixed significant wave height of 6 feet and a maximum fuel carrying capacity. As displacement increases, endurance decreases. However, once again the critical finding is that the maximum obtainable time on-station is only a little more than 5 days (less than 40% of the desired 14-day mission requirement) using a 20% fuel reserve. The implication of this is that the Littoral Combat Ship would require at least two fuel replenishments if it was going to complete the assigned 14-day mission. If the Littoral Combat Ship was required to maintain a 50% fuel reserve, the maximum obtainable endurance would be just over 3 days (less than 25% of the desired 14-day mission requirement), and the Littoral Combat Ship would require at least four fuel replenishments in order to complete its assigned mission.

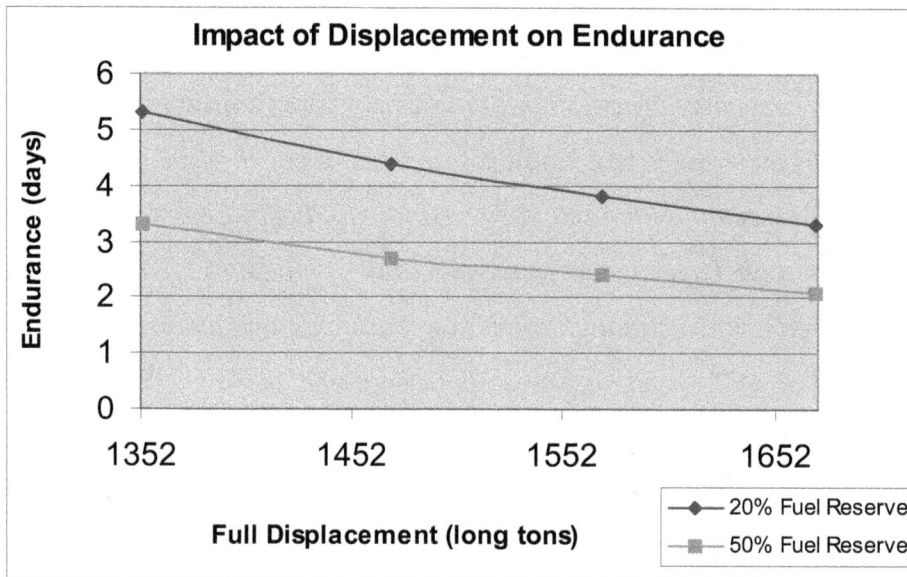

Figure 12. Impact of Displacement on Endurance at a 6-foot Significant Wave Height and
Maximum Fuel Carrying Capacity of 281,730-liters

Figure 13 illustrates the impact of significant wave height on endurance. It is based on the speeds and operating times included in the 14-day mission profile (Table 28) and utilizes a fixed displacement of 1671.4 long tons and a maximum fuel carrying capacity. As with displacement, when significant wave height increases, endurance decreases. With a significant wave height of 3.5 feet and a fuel reserve of 20%, the Littoral Combat Ship is able to achieve an endurance of only eight days and is required to receive one fuel replenishment in order to complete the 14-day mission. By switching to a 50% fuel reserve, the endurance drops to approximately five days, thereby increasing the number of required fuel replenishments to two. As seen earlier with the impact of speed on endurance, as significant wave height increases, the 20% and 50% fuel reserve curves begin to converge. This demonstrates the considerable impact significant wave height has on Littoral Combat Ship endurance.

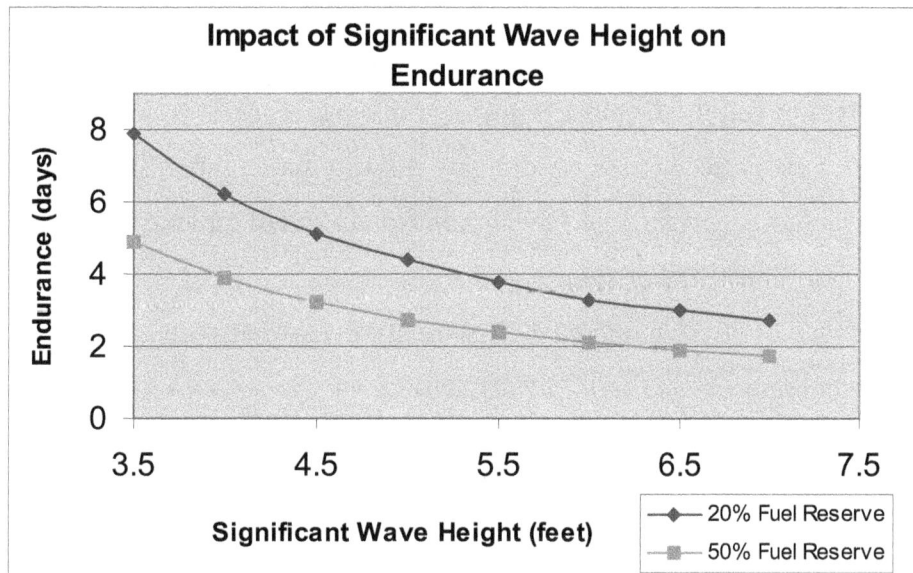

Figure 13.    Impact of Significant Wave Height on Endurance at 1671.4 long tons Full
Displacement and Maximum Fuel Carrying Capacity of 281,730-liters

## C.    IMPLICATION ON LITTORAL COMBAT SHIP LOGISTICS

In order for the Littoral Combat Ship to be an effective asset, it must not only possess the endurance necessary to keep pressure on the enemy without having to disengage often for replenishment, but it must also possess adequate sea keeping characteristics to permit open-ocean transits and extended operations in the world's littorals. Throughout the analysis, it is shown that increases in speed, displacement and significant wave height all result in a considerable increase to fuel consumption and severely limit Littoral Combat Ship endurance. As seen when using the 14-day mission profile, the Littoral Combat Ship requires at least one fuel replenishment in order to complete its assigned two-week mission. In order to receive the required replenishments, the Littoral Combat Ship must transit to a Combat Logistics Force ship off-station. Even though the Navy does not officially define the extent of the littorals by an actual distance from shore, the littorals can be defined as the waterways within 100 miles of the coastline. (Boeing, 2003) Typically, Combat Logistics Force ships operate outside the littorals near high-value, blue water assets. As a result, the Littoral Combat Ship would

60

be required to leave its assigned operating area and transit at least 100 miles to the Combat Logistics Force ship in order to rendezvous for the required refueling at sea. Assuming the Littoral Combat Ship utilizes its base operating speed of fifteen knots during the transit and the Combat Logistics Force ship operates at a safe distance of 150 nautical miles from the shore, it would take the Littoral Combat Ship ten hours to transit each way. Including an estimated two hours for the actual replenishment, total off-station time for the Littoral Combat ship would be 22 hours (6.5% of the total 14-day assigned mission). Table 30 demonstrates the relationship between Littoral Combat Ship replenishment requirements and time off-station.

| Number of Replenishments Required | Total Time Off-Station (days) | Percent of Time Off-Station During 14-Day Mission |
|---|---|---|
| 1 | 0.92 | 6.5% |
| 2 | 1.83 | 13.1% |
| 3 | 2.75 | 19.6% |
| 4 | 3.67 | 26.2% |
| 5 | 4.58 | 32.7% |

Table 30.    Relationship Between Replenishment Requirements and Time Off-Station

Not only does the requirement for replenishments decrease time on-station and availability of the Littoral Combat Ship, it places an increased strain on an already over burdened Combat Logistics Support force. Since the critical design parameters require that the Littoral Combat Ship be able to conduct both conventional and vertical replenishment, the Littoral Combat Ship will rely on the Combat Logistics Force for the necessary logistics support. The deployment of Naval forces in support of OPERATION ENDURING FREEDOM resulted in significant increases in Combat Logistics Force requirements. Increases in Fifth Fleet requirements, which were substantial to begin with, were so dramatic that Seventh Fleet and Third Fleet were both required to provide additional Combat Logistics Force ships in order to satisfy the high demand within the Fifth Fleet operating area. (Haynes, 2002) The situation has become so drastic that some ships have been denied Combat Logistics Force support. As a result, the ships have been forced into port in order to refuel. Not only does this increase costs, it also places an added security risk considering the in-port attack on the USS COLE. Additionally, Combat Logistics Force ships do not receive maintenance while in Fifth Fleet. The negative impact of this has already been demonstrated as the USNS PECOS post-deployment maintenance put her out of service for several months. (Haynes, 2002) The addition of a fleet of Littoral Combat Ships that will potentially require frequent replenishment is only going to make the Combat Logistics Force problem worse.

## D.    ADDITIONAL LOGISTICS CONSIDERATIONS

Even though reconfiguration is not studied in this thesis, modular mission capability, which is the cornerstone of the Littoral Combat Ship design (Katz and Mustin, 2003), has already been identified as the biggest challenge. The critical design parameter for reconfiguration requires that the Littoral Combat Ship must be able to complete reconfiguration within four days and establishes a reconfiguration goal of only one day. This is ambitious considering the capability currently does not exist at sea. While the handling and stowage of modular mission packages in port would not be a problem, completing reconfiguration at sea would be a much greater challenge as it requires good sea keeping. Considering the previous discussion and illustrations regarding the impact of significant wave height on Littoral Combat Ship operations, it is clear the Littoral Combat Ship will not always have the benefit of calm seas to reconfigure modular mission packages when required. Even if reconfiguration is achievable at sea, the logistics required for reconfiguration is complex. Questions such as where will the modular mission packages be stored and how will they be transported and transferred to the Littoral Combat Ship remain unanswered. If for any reason the Littoral Combat Ship is unable to reconfigure for a specific mission while at sea, it would be required to leave its assigned operating area and find a port or shipyard-like environment in which it can be reconfigured. This not only places an additional strain on Littoral Combat Ship logistics but also increases time off-station.

In Chapter I, endurance was defined as the ability to sustain a ship's mission. While for analysis purposes this thesis calculates endurance only using speed and fuel consumption rates, in reality it is also measured by ordnance delivery rates and crew effectiveness. The amount of ordnance consumed depends upon the assigned Littoral Combat Ship mission, the frequency in which ordnance is required to support the mission, and the rate at which it is delivered. While a Littoral Combat Ship conducting a Continuous Mission would most likely have little need for ordnance, one conducting littoral Mine Warfare or Anti-Surface Warfare would, of course, have an ordnance requirement. Just as ship speed, displacement, and significant wave height impacts endurance, the same holds true for ordnance. As the delivery rate of ordnance increases, the need for replenishment increases as well, thereby potentially further reducing Littoral Combat Ship time on-station.

Crew effectiveness has just as much, if not more, impact on endurance as fuel and ordnance. While earlier discussion of dizziness, nausea and seasickness aboard JOINT VENTURE demonstrates the severe negative impact crew effectiveness has on endurance, logistics factors such as fresh water, provisions, stores and laundry also have a major impact on crew effectiveness. While current advances in technology have helped ease the potential negative impact these logistics factors have on crew effectiveness, they cannot be forgotten as they play an important part in crew morale.

The final, and perhaps most important, questions that need to be addressed are where does the Littoral Combat Ship originate from and where does it go back to at the conclusion of its mission. While the Littoral Combat Ship will be required to possess a blue-water transit capability, operations are designed for missions of fixed duration inside the littorals. Discussions of 5-day, 14-day and 21-day mission profiles are provided, however, there has been no indication as to where the Littoral Combat Ship will transit to between missions. While the shallow draft increases the number of ports available for the Littoral Combat Ship to operate out of, they may or may not be friendly. Not only is this an important issue with regard to reconfigurability, it also plays an important role

63

with regard to logistics support and crew effectiveness. While it should be noted that one of the proposed missions of the Littoral Combat Ship is Logistics Support, a Littoral Combat Ship configured for a logistics mission still has the same operating constraints with respect to fuel consumption and endurance as one those studied in this thesis. Without a designated port to base out of, the Littoral Combat Ship endurance problem can only get worse.

# V. CONCLUSIONS AND RECOMMENDATIONS

## A.    CONCLUSIONS

"For the 29-year period ending 1999, almost 60 percent of the missions conducted by ships were mobility related missions." (Navy Warfare Development Command, 2003) These continuous missions, all of which are listed as potential future Littoral Combat Ship requirements, typically require a platform with long endurance, high speed, considerable payload capacity, and excellent sea keeping.   Just as the ASHEVILLE, PEGASUS and CYCLONE class ships were constrained in their operations due to low endurance and limited capability, the output from the Littoral Combat Ship model yields similar problems.

The thesis demonstrates that speed, displacement, and significant wave height all result in considerable increases in fuel consumption, and as a result, severely limit Littoral Combat Ship endurance.  When operating in a significant wave height of six feet, regardless of the amount of fuel carried, the maximum endurance achieved for a Littoral Combat Ship outfitted with all modular mission packages is less than seven days. Especially noteworthy is that when restricted to a fuel reserve of 50% and a fuel carrying capacity of Day tanks, the maximum achieved endurance is only 4.8 hours when operating at a maximum speed of 48 knots.  Refueling, and potentially rearming, will require the Littoral Combat Ship to leave littoral waters and transit to Combat Logistics Force ships operating outside the littorals for replenishment.  Given the low endurance of the Littoral Combat Ship, its time on station is seriously compromised.  This not only limits the Littoral Combat Ship's ability to conduct independent operations, but restricts interdependent operations as part of a littoral operations force and integrated operations with Carrier and Expeditionary Strike Groups as well.

Significant wave height not only has a considerable negative impact on fuel consumption and endurance, but also has the potential for devastating impact on Littoral Combat Ship operations and crew effectiveness.  The anticipated inability of the Littoral Combat Ship to effectively operate in ocean conditions beyond sea state 6 coupled with the real possibility of experiencing sea states 7 and beyond demonstrates the potential for the Littoral Combat Ship to be forced to either delay or abandon assigned missions. With regard to crew effectiveness, of the twenty-two personnel that were given a questionnaire regarding seasickness during joint Navy and Marine Corps testing of the JOINT VENTURE, 70% of those surveyed experienced dizziness, 65% experienced nausea and 30% actually became seasick when operating in sea state 4 and below.

The Littoral Combat Ship can achieve high speeds; however, this can only be accomplished at the expense of range and payload capacity. The requirement for the Littoral Combat Ship to go fast (forty-eight knots) requires a seaframe with heavy propulsion systems. The weight of the seaframe, required shipboard systems (weapons, sensors, command and control, and self-defense) and modular mission packages accounts for 84% of the full displacement, and as a result, substantially limits total fuel carrying capacity. Since initial mission profiles required the high-speed capability at most five percent of the time, the end result is a Littoral Combat Ship that has very little endurance and a high-speed capability it will rarely use. The pursuit for high speed itself demonstrates an inherent bias toward the attribute of speed and the neglect of range and payload requirements. Regardless of which hull form is selected for the Littoral Combat Ship, this thesis demonstrates the price that must be paid for speed as the tradeoffs between speed, endurance, and payload, in general, apply to any ship design.

## B.    RECOMMENDATIONS

As this thesis concludes a Littoral Combat Ship similar in size to the JOINT VENTURE would not have the endurance necessary to effectively operate in the littorals, it would appear the only plausible recommendations would be to either relax the high-speed requirement or increase the size of the Littoral Combat Ship. Recently, Norman Polmar, author of *Ships and Aircraft of the U.S. Fleet*, wrote about the Navy's current Littoral Combat Ship program. Comparing the efforts to the Israeli 1,275-ton Sa'ar V-class corvette and the German 1,690-ton Type 130 corvette (which is currently under construction), he states the Navy will likely opt for a larger and more expensive Littoral Combat Ship. Despite the plans to utilize a modular design, he believes the Navy's desire for larger, multipurpose ships will result in the proposal of a large (frigate size) Littoral Combat Ship. (Polmar, 2002) According to the Navy's latest documentation, he

66

appears to be correct, as the Littoral Combat Ship is no longer being pursued as a small ship, rather one that weighs approximately 3,000 tons. (Stewart, 2003) Whereas the proposed increase in size of the Littoral Combat Ship indicates the Navy has learned something from the previous small, high-speed ship programs, it does not absolve the Navy of the requirement to balance the tradeoffs between speed, endurance, and payload.

THIS PAGE INTENTIONALLY LEFT BLANK

# APPENDIX A: SEA STATE MATRIX

| Sea State | Significant Wave Height (meters) | Significant Wave Height (feet) |
|-----------|----------------------------------|-------------------------------|
| 0 | 0.0 | 0.0 |
| 1 | 0.3 | 1.0 |
| 2 | 0.9 | 3.0 |
| 3 | 1.4 | 4.6 |
| 4 | 2.1 | 6.9 |
| 5 | 3.7 | 12.1 |
| 6 | 5.5 | 18.0 |
| 7 | 12.2 | 40.0 |
| 8 | 17.7 | 58.1 |
| 9 | > 39.0 | > 128.0 |

Note: Data obtained from the Preliminary Design Interim Requirements Document N763F-S03-026, Littoral Combat Ship (LCS) Flight 0 Pre ACAT (Surface Warfare Directorate, 2003)

THIS PAGE INTENTIONALLY LEFT BLANK

# LIST OF REFERENCES

Atwood, J. and Delucia, T., "Joint Venture (HSV-X1) Transportability Analysis of Vessel Loading During Millennium Challenge 2002," Military Traffic Management Command Transportation Engineering Agency, October 29, 2002.

Atwood, J. and Delucia, T., "Joint Venture (HSV-X1) Load Planning and Transportability Analysis," Military Traffic Management Command Transportation Engineering Agency, September 16, 2002.

Baker III, A.D., "Combat fleets," Proceedings, September 2002.

Baumgardner, Neil, "Army Pleased with Performance of Joint Venture High-Speed Catamaran," Defense Daily, August 21, 2002.

Beierl, Philip, Joint Venture (HSV-X1) Officer in Charge, "Lessons Learned Report, Joint Venture (HSV-X1)," March 2002.

Bucchi, Mike and Mullen, Mike, "Sea Shield: Projecting Global Defensive Assurance," Proceedings, November 2002.

Calvano, Charles, "Sea Lance," Total Ship Systems Engineering Publication, November 30, 2000.

Calvano, Charles, "Margins/Allowance over Ship Life Cycle," Total Ship Systems Engineering (TS3002) Presentation, January 2003.

Cebrowski, A.K., "Convocation Speech," Naval War College, August 18, 1998, www.nwc.navy.mil/pres/speeches/conspch98.htm, accessed February 11, 2003.

Cebrowski, A.K. and Hughes, Wayne P. Jr., "Rebalancing the Fleet," Proceedings, November 1999.

Colorado Center for Astrodynamics Research, "Global Near Real-Time Significant Wave Height Data Viewer," www-ccar.colorado.edu/~realtime/global-real-time_waves, accessed March 9, 2003.

Donaldson, Dave, "USS ASHEVILLE PG-84," The ASHEVILLE Class Patrol Gunboat, February 2, 2003, www.gunboatriders.com/theboats/index.html, accessed February 18, 2003.

Friedman, Norman, *U.S. Small Combatants, Including Pt-Boats, Subchasers, and the Brown-Water Navy: An Illustrated Design History*, U.S. Naval Institute, 1987.

Haynes, Jonathan, "Fifth Fleet CLF Requirements," e-mail dated January 31, 2002.

Hughes, Wayne P. Jr., "22 Questions for Streetfighter," Proceedings, February 2000.

Jenkins, George, "Patrol Combatant Missile (Hydrofoil): PHM History 1973-1993," June 13, 1995.

Keeter, Hunter, "Navy Special Warfare Command 'Intrigued' By LCS Concept," Defense Daily, February 11, 2002.

Kelley, Stephen H., "Small Ships and Future Missions," Proceedings, September 2002.

Koch, Andrew, "USN Starts Contest for Littoral Combat Ship," Jane's Defence Weekly, August 28, 2002.

Lockheed Martin, "Hullform Technology," Naval Electronics & Surveillance Systems – Marine Systems. http://ness.external.lmco.com/nessb/hullform/challenge.htm, accessed October 16, 2002.

Marine Corps Warfighting Laboratory, "Battle Griffin 02 Limited Objective Experiment Quicklook Report," Mission Readiness of Personnel Questionnaire, May 6, 2002.

Matyas, Mark, "Information on the New PCs," www.ww2pcsa.org/new.htm, accessed February 20, 2003.

Merriam-Webster Dictionary, "The Language Center," www.m-w.com, accessed October 16, 2002.

National Oceanic and Atmospheric Administration, National Data Buoy Center, "Science Education Pages," www.ndbc.noaa.gov/educate/waves_ans.shtml, accessed March 9, 2003.

Naval Vessel Register, "Definitions," NAVSEA Shipbuilding Support Office Norfolk Naval Shipyard Detachment, www.nvr.navy.mil/def_ld.htm, accessed February 21, 2003.

Navy Surface Warfare Center, Carderock Division, "Total Ship Systems Engineering Directorate Technology Projection Report NSWCCD-20-TR-2002/06," High-Speed Sealift Technology Plan, May 2002.

Navy Warfare Development Command, Littoral Combat Ship Concept of Operations Draft, September 2002.

Navy Warfare Development Command, Littoral Combat Ship Concept of Operations, February 2003.

Pike, John, "Military Systems: Ships," October 2002, http://www.globalsecurity.org, accessed February 20, 2003.

Polmar, Norman, "Small Surface Combatants: Another Try," Proceedings, August 2002.

Public Affairs, "Greyhounds of the Sea," Official United States Navy Website, www.chinfo.navy.mil/navpalib/ships/destroyers/greyhound.html, accessed October 2002.

Stewart, James, "Littoral Combat Ship: Transformation for the Surface Navy," Commander Naval Surface Forces Pacific, Presentation dated February 10, 2003.

Surface Warfare Directorate, Ship Systems Division (N763), "Preliminary Design Interim Requirements Document N763F-S03-026, Littoral Combat Ship (LCS) Flight 0 Pre ACAT," February 2003.

The Catamaran Company, "HSV: One Quick Cat," www.catamaranco.com/details.asp?ID=23, accessed January 28, 2003.

The Institution of Naval Architects, "Discussion on Trafalgar Papers," The Institution of Naval Architects, July 19, 1905, http://home.gci.net/~stall/discus.htm, accessed February 11, 2003.


Walsh, Edward J., "Integrated Combat Systems," Sea Power Magazine, January 2002.


Wolfe, Frank, "CNO, Navy Secretary Interested In Accelerating LCS," Defense Daily, August 15, 2002.

# INITIAL DISTRIBUTION LIST

1.    Defense Technical Information Center
Ft. Belvoir, Virginia

2.    Dudley Knox Library
Naval Postgraduate School
Monterey, California

3.    David A. Schrady, Distinguished Professor
Department of Operations Research
Naval Postgraduate School
Monterey, California

4.    Kevin J. Maher, CDR, SC, USN
Department of Operations Research
Naval Postgraduate School
Monterey, California

5.    Wayne P. Hughes, Jr.
Dean, Graduate School of Operational and Information Sciences
Naval Postgraduate School
Monterey, California

6.    Jeffrey E. Kline, CAPT, USN
Department of Operations Research
Naval Postgraduate School
Monterey, California

7.    Charles N. Calvano
Technical Director, Wayne Meyers Institute
Naval Postgraduate School
Monterey, California

8.    Steven E. Pilnick
Meyer Institute & Department of Operations Research
Naval Postgraduate School
Monterey, California

9.    David H. Olwell
Senior Lecturer of Operations Research
Naval Postgraduate School
Monterey, California

10. James Stewart, CAPT, USN
    Warfare Requirements, N8
    Commander Naval Surface Forces, Pacific
    San Diego, California

11. Dean Chase, CDR, USN
    High Speed Vessel Project Director
    Navy Warfare Development Command
    Newport, Rhode Island

12. Todd Haeg, CDR, USN
    Concepts Development
    Navy Warfare Development Command
    Newport, Rhode Island

13. Doug Noble, LCDR, SC, USN
    Career Development & Training (P31)
    Office of the Naval Supply Corps Personnel
    Millington, Tennessee

14. William M. Kroshl
    Joint Warfare Analysis Department
    Applied Physics Lab
    Laurel, Maryland

9 781608 880898